WORLD LITERATURE CRITICISM

1500 to the Present

WORLD LITERATURE CRITICISM
Advisory Board

———

WORLD LITERATURE CRITICISM

1500 to the Present

*A Selection of
Major Authors from
Gale's Literary
Criticism Series*

García Márquez-Lawrence

JAMES P. DRAPER, Editor

Gale Research Inc. · DETROIT · LONDON

STAFF

James P. Draper, *Editor*

Laurie DiMauro, Tina Grant, Paula Kepos, Jelena Krstović, Daniel G. Marowski, Roger Matuz, James E. Person, Jr., Joann Prosyniuk, David Segal, Joseph C. Tardiff, Bridget Travers, Lawrence Trudeau, Thomas Votteler, Sandra L. Williamson, Robyn V. Young, *Contributing Editors*

Catherine Falk, Grace Jeromski, Michael W. Jones, Andrew M. Kalasky, David Kmenta, Marie Lazzari, Zoran Minderović, Sean René Pollock, Mark Swartz, *Contributing Associate Editors*

Jennifer Brostrom, David J. Engelman, Andrea Gacki, Judith Galens, Christopher Giroux, Ian A. Goodhall, Alan Hedblad, Elizabeth P. Henry, Christopher K. King, Kyung-Sun Lim, Elisabeth Morrison, Kristin Palm, Susan M. Peters, James Poniewozik, Eric Priehs, Bruce Walker, Debra A. Wells, Janet Witalec, Allyson J. Wylie, *Contributing Assistant Editors*

Jeanne A. Gough, *Permissions & Production Manager*

Linda M. Pugliese, *Production Supervisor*
Paul Lewon, Lorna Mabunda, Maureen Puhl, Camille Robinson, Jennifer VanSickle, *Editorial Associates*
Donna Craft, Brandy C. Johnson, Sheila Walencewicz, *Editorial Assistants*

Victoria B. Cariappa, *Research Manager*

Maureen Richards, *Research Supervisor*
Mary Beth McElmeel, Tamara C. Nott, *Editorial Associates*
Andrea B. Ghorai, Daniel J. Jankowski, Julie K. Karmazin, Robert S. Lazich, *Editorial Assistants*

Sandra C. Davis, *Permissions Supervisor* (*Text*)
Maria L. Franklin, Josephine M. Keene, Michele M. Lonoconus, Denise M. Singleton, Kimberly F. Smilay, *Permissions Associates*
Rebecca A. Hartford, Shalice Shah, Nancy K. Sheridan, *Permissions Assistants*

Margaret A. Chamberlain, *Permissions Supervisor* (*Pictures*)
Pamela A. Hayes, *Permissions Associate*
Amy Lynn Emrich, Karla Kulkis, Nancy M. Rattenbury, Keith Reed, *Permissions Assistants*

Mary Beth Trimper, *Production Manager*
Mary Winterhalter, *Production Assistant*

Arthur Chartow, *Art Director*
C. J. Jonik, *Keyliner*
Kathleen A. Hourdakis, Mary Krzewinski, *Graphic Designers*

∞™ This book is printed on acid-free paper that meets the minimum requirements of American National Standard for Information Sciences— Permanence Paper for Printed Library Materials, ANSI Z39.48-1984.

ISBN 0-8103-8361-6 (6-volume set)
A CIP catalogue record for this book is available from the British Library
Printed in the United States of America
Published simultaneously in the United Kingdom
by Gale Research International Limited
(An affiliated company of Gale Research Inc.)

Table of Contents

styles, seeking through artistic expression to order and make meaning of experience, particularly the dark and chaotic aspects of his own life and the world around him

Bernard Malamud 1914-1986
Malamud is one of the most prominent figures in Jewish-American literature. Despite his emphasis on his faith, in such well-known works as *The Natural* and *The Assistant* he stressed human compassion over religious dogma

Thomas Mann 1875-1955
Best known as the author of *Death in Venice* and *The Magic Mountain*, Mann is one of the foremost German novelists of the twentieth century. Though his fiction typically reveals a somber and cerebral fascination with death, his works often display a deep, often humorous sympathy for humanity

Katherine Mansfield 1888-1923
An early practitioner of stream-of-consciousness narration, Mansfield is one of few authors to attain prominence exclusively for short stories. Her works remain among the most widely read in world literature

Christopher Marlowe 1564-1593
Recognized as the first English dramatist to reveal the full potential of blank verse poetry, and as one who made significant advances in the genre of English tragedy through keen examinations of Renaissance morality, Marlowe is the author of such renowned plays as *Doctor Faustus*; *Tamburlaine, Parts I and II*; *The Jew of Malta*; and *Edward II*

Andrew Marvell 1621-1678
One of the last seventeenth-century English metaphysical poets, Marvell is noted for his intellectual, allusive poetry, rich in metaphor and unexpected twists of thought and argument. His best lyric poetry, such as "To His Coy Mistress" and "The Garden," is characterized by ambiguity, complexity, and a thematic irresolution that many critics believe both define his talent and account for his appeal

W. Somerset Maugham 1874-1965
One of the world's most prolific and popular authors, Maugham wrote such novels as *Of Human Bondage* and *Cakes and Ale; or, The Skeleton in the Cupboard*

Guy de Maupassant 1850-1893
Considered one of the finest short story writers of all time and a champion of the realistic approach to writing, Maupassant created a narrative style outstanding in its austere power, simplicity, and vivid sensuousness

Carson McCullers 1917-1967
One of the most enduring authors of the American Southern literary tradition. McCullers is best known for writing *The Heart Is a Lonely Hunter*, *The Ballad of the Sad Café*, and *The Member of the Wedding*

Claude McKay 1889-1948
Jamaican-born American poet McKay was a forerunner of the militant spirit behind the Harlem Renaissance and the civil rights movement, evidenced in his poem "If We Must Die": "If we must die, O let us nobly die. . ./ Like men we'll face the murderous, cowardly pack,/ Pressed to the wall, dying, but fighting back!"

Herman Melville 1819-1891
A major nineteenth-century American literary figure, Melville is best known as the author of *Moby-Dick*, the classic tale of a sea captain's monomaniacal quest to destroy a white whale that he views as the embodiment of all earthly malignity and evil

Arthur Miller 1915-
American dramatist Miller insisted that "the individual is doomed to frustration when once he gains a consciousness of his own identity," a sentiment reflected in two of his most famous works, *Death of a Salesman* and *The Crucible*

Henry Miller 1891-1980
Miller's novel *Tropic of Cancer* has been censured for its bawdy humor, obscene

Introduction

A Comprehensive Information Source
on World Literature

World Literature Criticism, 1500 to the Present (WLC) presents a broad selection of the best criticism of works by major writers of the past five hundred years. Among the authors included in WLC are sixteenth-century Spanish novelist Miguel de Cervantes and English dramatist William Shakespeare; seventeenth-century English poet John Milton and dramatist Aphra Behn; eighteenth-century Anglo-Irish novelist Jonathan Swift, English essayist Samuel Johnson, and French Enlightenment masters Jean-Jacques Rousseau and Voltaire; acclaimed nineteenth-century writers Jane Austen, William Blake, Emily Brontë, Lewis Carroll, Charles Dickens, Fyodor Dostoyevsky, Frederick Douglass, Gustave Flaubert, Edgar Allan Poe, Mary Shelley, Robert Louis Stevenson, William Wordsworth, and Emile Zola; and major twentieth-century authors W. H. Auden, James Baldwin, Albert Camus, Arthur Conan Doyle, Ralph Ellison, F. Scott Fitzgerald, Ernest Hemingway, James Joyce, Franz Kafka, Toni Morrison, Sylvia Plath, J. D. Salinger, Gertrude Stein, John Steinbeck, Virginia Woolf, and Richard Wright. The scope of WLC is wide: more than 225 writers representing dozens of nations, cultures, and time periods.

Coverage

This six-volume set is designed for high school, college, and university students, as well as for the general reader who wants to learn more about literature. WLC was developed in response to strong demand by students, librarians, and other readers for a one-stop, authoritative guide to the whole spectrum of world literature. No other compendium like it exists in the marketplace. About 95% of the entries in WLC were selected from Galo's acclaimed Literary Criticism Series and completely updated for publication here. Typically, the revisions are extensive, ranging from new author introductions to wide changes in the selection of criticism. A few entries—about 5%— were prepared especially for WLC in order to furnish the most comprehensive coverage possible.

Inclusion Criteria

Authors were selected for inclusion in WLC based on the advice of leading experts on world literature as well as on the recommendation of a specially formed advisory panel made up of high school teachers and high school and public librarians from throughout the United States. Additionally, the most recent major curriculum studies were closely examined, notably Arthur N. Applebee, *A Study of Book-Length Works Taught in High School English Courses* (1989); Arthur N. Applebee, *A Study of High School Literature Anthologies* (1991); and Doug Estel, Michele L. Satchwell, and Patricia S. Wright, *Reading Lists for College-Bound Students* (1990). All of these resources were collated and compared to produce a reference product that is strongly curriculum driven. To ensure that WLC will continue to meet the needs of students and general readers alike, an effort was made to identify a group of important new writers in addition to the most studied authors.

Scope

Each author entry in *WLC* presents a historical survey of critical response to the author's works. Typically, early criticism is offered to indicate initial responses, later selections document any rise or decline in literary reputations, and retrospective analyses provide modern views. Every endeavor has been made to include seminal essays on each author's work along with commentary providing current perspectives. Interviews and author statements are also included in many entries. Thus, *WLC* is both timely and comprehensive.

Organization of Author Entries

Information about authors and their works is presented through ten key access points:

- The **Descriptive Table of Contents** guides readers through the range of world literature, offering summary sketches of authors' careers and achievements.

- In each author entry, the **Author Heading** cites the name under which the author most commonly wrote, followed by birth and, where appropriate, death dates. Uncertain birth or death dates are indicated by question marks. Name variations, including full birth names when available, are given in parentheses in the caption below the **Author Portrait**.

- The **Biographical and Critical Introduction** contains background information about the life and works of the author. Emphasis is given to four main areas: 1) biographical details that help reveal the life, character, and personality of the author; 2) overviews of the major literary interests of the author—for example, novel writing, autobiography, poetry, social reform, documentary, etc.; 3) descriptions and summaries of the author's best-known works; and 4) critical commentary about the author's achievement, stature, and importance. The concluding paragraph of the **Biographical and Critical Introduction** directs readers to other Gale series containing information about the author.

- Every *WLC* entry includes an **Author Portrait**. Many entries also contain **Illustrations**—including holographs, title pages of works, letters, or pictures of important people, places, and events in the author's life—that document the author's career.

- The **List of Principal Works** is chronological by date of first book publication and identifies the genre of each work. For non-English-language authors whose works have been translated into English, the title and date of the first English-language edition are given in brackets beneath the foreign-language listing. Unless otherwise indicated, dramas are dated by first performance rather than first publication.

- **Criticism** is arranged chronologically in each author entry to provide a useful perspective on changes in critical evaluation over the years. Most entries contain a detailed, comprehensive study of the author's career as well as book reviews, studies of individual works, and comparative examinations. To ensure timeliness, current views are most often presented, but not to the exclusion of important early pieces. For the purpose of easy identification, the critic's name and the date of the critical work are given at the beginning of each piece of criticism. Unsigned criticism is preceded by the title of the source in which it appeared. Within the criticism, titles of works by the author are printed in boldface type. Publication information (such as publisher names and book prices) and certain numerical references (such as footnotes or page and line references to specific editions of works) have been deleted at the editor's discretion to provide smoother reading of the text.

■ Critical essays are prefaced by **Explanatory Notes** as an additional aid to readers of *WLC*. These notes may provide several types of valuable information, including: 1) the reputation of the critic; 2) the importance of the work of criticism; 3) the commentator's approach to the author's work; 4) the purpose of the criticism; and 5) changes in critical trends regarding the author. In some cases, **Explanatory Notes** cross-reference the work of critics within an entry who agree or disagree with each other.

■ A complete **Bibliographical Citation** of the original essay or book follows each piece of criticism.

■ An annotated list of **Sources for Further Study** appears at the end of each entry and suggests resources for additional study. These lists were specially compiled to meet the needs of high school and college students. Additionally, most of the sources cited are available in typical small and medium-size libraries.

■ Many entries contain a **Major Media Adaptations** section listing important non-print treatments and adaptations of the author's works, including feature films, TV mini-series, and radio broadcasts. This feature was specially conceived for *WLC* to meet strong demand from students for this type of information.

Other Features

WLC contains three distinct indexes to help readers find information quickly and easily:

■ The **Author Index** lists all the authors appearing in *WLC*. To ensure easy access, name variations and changes are fully cross-indexed.

■ The **Nationality Index** lists all authors featured in *WLC* by nationality. For expatriate authors and authors identified with more than one nation, multiple listings are offered.

■ The **Title Index** lists in alphabetical order all individual works by the authors appearing in *WLC*. English-language translations of original foreign-language titles are cross-referenced to the foreign titles so that all references to a work are combined in one listing.

Citing *World Literature Criticism*

When writing papers, students who quote directly from *WLC* may use the following general forms to footnote reprinted criticism. The first example is for material drawn from periodicals, the second for material reprinted from books:

Gary Smith, "Gwendolyn Brooks's 'A Street in Bronzeville,' the Harlem Renaissance and the Mythologies of Black Women," *MELUS*, Vol. 10, No. 3 (Fall 1983), 33-46; excerpted and reprinted in *World Literature Criticism, 1500 to the Present*, ed. James P. Draper (Detroit: Gale Research, 1992), pp. 459-61.

Frederick R. Karl, *American Fictions, 1940/1980: A Comprehensive History and Critical Evaluation* (Harper & Row, 1983); excerpted and reprinted in *World Literature Criticism, 1500 to the Present*, ed. James P. Draper (Detroit: Gale Research, 1992), pp. 541-46.

Acknowledgments

The editor wishes to acknowledge the valuable contributions of the many librarians, authors, and scholars who assisted in the compilation of *WLC* with their responses to telephone and mail inquiries. Special thanks are offered to the members of *WLC*'s advisory board, whose names are listed opposite the title page.

Comments Are Welcome

The editor hopes that readers will find *WLC* to be a useful reference tool and welcomes comments about the work. Send comments and suggestions to: Editor, *World Literature Criticism, 1500 to the Present*, Gale Research Inc., Penobscot Building, Detroit, MI 48226-4094.

WORLD
LITERATURE
CRITICISM

1500 to the Present

Gabriel García Márquez

1928-

(Full name Gabriel José García Márquez; also wrote under pseudonym Septimus) Colombian novelist, short story writer, journalist, critic, and screenwriter.

INTRODUCTION

Nobel laureate García Márquez is included among the group of South American writers who rose to prominence during the 1960s, a period of fruition often referred to as the "boom" of Latin American literature. Like Julio Cortázar and Ernesto Sabato, García Márquez wrote fiction for many years before gaining international recognition. The almost simultaneous publication of major works by these three authors, together with the appearance of skillful first novels by Carlos Fuentes and Mario Vargas Llosa and the newly acknowledged importance of such writers as Jorge Luis Borges and Pablo Neruda, led to recognition of Latin American letters as a potent force in contemporary literature. The enthusiastic critical reception of García Márquez's works is usually attributed to his imaginative blending of history, politics, social realism, and fantasy. He often makes use of techniques of magic realism, embellishing his works with surreal events and fantastic imagery to obscure the distinctions between illusion and reality which, he implies, define human existence.

García Márquez was born in Aracataca, Colombia, where he lived with his grandparents for the first eight years of his life. The storytelling of his grandmother, the long decline of Aracataca, and the myths and superstitions of the townspeople all played major roles in shaping García Márquez's imagination. He enrolled in the University of Bogotá in 1947 to study law, but when civil warfare in Colombia caused the institution to close in 1948, he transferred to the University of Cartagena, simultaneously working as a journalist for the periodical *El universal*. Devoting himself to journalistic and literary endeavors, he discontinued his law studies in 1950 and moved to Barranquilla to work for the daily paper *El heraldo*. At this time he wrote short stories that were published in regional periodicals, and through a circle of local writers he became acquainted with the works of such authors as Franz Kafka, William Faulkner, Virginia Woolf, and James Joyce. García Márquez returned to Bogotá in 1954, serving as a film critic and reporter for *El espectador,* and the next year his novella *La hojarasca* (1955; *Leaf Storm* 1972) was published. During this period he also gained political notoriety for his account in the *Espectador* of the experiences of Luis Alejandro Velasco, a sailor who survived the shipwreck of a Colombian naval vessel in the Caribbean. This series of reports, later published as *Relato de un nánfrago. . . .* (1970; *The Story of a Shipwrecked Sailor,* 1986), exposed the existence of contraband cargo onboard the ship and suggested the general incompetence of the nation's navy. Seeking to avoid governmental retribution, he traveled throughout Europe during 1955, working as a foreign correspondent for the *Espectador.* In 1956, however, the military government of Colombia headed by Gustavo Rojas Pinilla shut down the periodical and García Márquez subsequently settled in Paris.

García Márquez's early short stories were written in the late 1940s and early 1950s and are collected in such retrospective volumes as *Leaf Storm and Other Stories* (1972), *Ojos de perro azul* (1972), *La increíble y triste historia de la cándida Eréndira y de su abuela desalmada* (1972), and *Innocent Eréndira and Other Stories* (1978). Critics generally deem these early stories unsuccessful for their overly self-conscious use of unconventional narrative techniques. In his novella *Leaf Storm* García Márquez introduces Macondo, the fictional setting of several subsequent works based on Aracataca. *Leaf Storm* recounts the story of a colonel and the inhabitants of a small town, dominated by a banana company, who come into conflict over the death of a solitary and unpopular doctor. The story's multiple narrative perspectives contribute to its theme of solitude and reflect the influence of William Faulkner. The recurrence of people and places of Macondo in Márquez's stories and novels has also led commentators to compare the region with that of Yoknapatawpha County in Faulkner's novels.

The collection *Los funerales de la Mamá Grande* (1962; translated in *No One Writes to the Colonel and Other Stories,* 1968) features García Márquez's short fiction written during the early 1960s. Critics frequently commend the stories in this volume for presenting hyperbolic, archetypal characters, such as the deceased village matriarch in the title story (translated as "Big Mama's Funeral"), and for creating a sense of timelessness within Macondo and other unspecified rural locales in Latin America. In *El colonel no tiene quien le escriba* (1961; *No One Writes to the Colonel,* 1968) García Márquez presents a retired military officer who waits unavailingly in a rural village for the mail to arrive with his government pension check. With its depiction of stifling social and political institutions, the novella

has been taken to represent Colombia in general, and in particular the state of the country during *la violencia,* a period of violent social and political crises that culminated during the 1950s.

In his first novel, *La mala hora* (1962; *In Evil Hour,* 1979), García Márquez uses a montage-like narrative style to depict a backwater town torn by political oppression and moral corruption. He won immediate international acclaim and popularity with the publication of *Cien años de soledad* (1967; *One Hundred Years of Solitude,* 1970). This novel, which John Leonard called "a recapitulation of our evolutionary and intellectual experience," chronicles the history of Macondo from its harmonious beginnings under founder José Arcadio Buendía to its increasingly chaotic decline through six generations of descendants. The novel presents Macondo as a microcosm of Colombia and, by extension, of South America and the world. In addition to reflecting the political, social, and economic ills of South America, the novel is replete with fantastic events; for example, a baby is born with a pig's tail. Characterized by nonlinear narration and long, free-flowing sentences, *One Hundred Years of Solitude* is acknowledged as a comic masterpiece for its labyrinthine structure, epic scope, and stylistic complexity. Pablo Neruda called the book "the greatest revelation in the Spanish language since the *Don Quixote* of Cervantes."

García Márquez's next novel, *El otoño del patriarca* (1975; *The Autumn of the Patriarch,* 1975), depicts the evils of despotism as embodied in an unloved dictator, with solitude again emerging as a prominent theme. Described by García Márquez as "a perfect integration of journalism and literature," the novel is a powerful indictment of totalitarianism and a poignant evocation of loneliness. This work is written as a phantasmagorical narrative in which shifting viewpoint and extensive use of hyperbole enhance comedic and horrific effects. Following the publication of *The Autumn of the Patriarch,* García Márquez vowed that he would issue no new fiction until Chile's Pinochet regime was either disbanded or overthrown. Following a six-year hiatus, he published *Crónica de una muerte anunciada* (1981; *Chronicle of a Death Foretold,* 1982), a fictionalized journalistic investigation embellished with stylistic devices typical of his fiction. The story centers upon a murder that occurred twenty-seven years earlier and reportedly involved people with whom García Márquez was acquainted. Presenting eyewitness accounts that ultimately prove unreliable within shifting time sequences and a surreal atmosphere, *Chronicle of a Death Foretold* examines a tragedy that is fostered rather than averted by the inhabitants of a backwater community. Most critics interpreted the novella as a profile of a society trapped in its own myths, either unable to overcome the outmoded customs of its forebears or unable to triumph over fate.

In *El amor en los tiempos del cólera* (1985; *Love in the Time of Cholera*, 1988), García Marquez explores various manifestations of love and examines themes relating to aging, death, and decay. Set in a South American community plagued by recurring civil wars and cholera epidemics from the late nineteenth century to the 1930s, this novel vividly details the emotional states of the three principal characters. The nonlinear narrative delineates poignant events in ordinary life and the history of the region, blending social realism with elements of sentimental literature and soap opera. Conflict arises when Florentino Ariza, a telegraph operator whose interests include music and literature, falls passionately in love with Fermina Daza, the daughter of a wealthy man, and woos her clandestinely through letters and serenades. Disapproving of this teenage romance, Fermina's father takes his daughter on a long, arduous journey. Upon her return, Fermina loses interest in Florentino and eventually marries Dr. Juvenal Urbino, a wealthy and distinguished gentleman whom many critics have likened to the "ideal man" in popular romance fiction. After being rejected, Florentino silently maintains his unrequited affection for Fermina for fifty-one years, nine months, and four days, when they meet again at her husband's wake and he renews his vow of eternal love. Critics generally praised García Márquez's witty epigrams and observations, playful associations between the physical symptoms of cholera and the intense emotions of anger and love, as well as his exploration of the motivation and interpretation of human behavior. In his recent novel, *El general en su laberinto* (1989; *The General in His Labyrinth*, 1990), García Márquez fictionalizes the last days in the life of Simón Bolívar, who led revolutionary armies to oust the Spaniards from the former South American colonies between 1811 to 1824. Despite his dreams of a unified South America, Bolívar sees his hopes for unification destroyed as alliances crumble due to intrigues, secessions, and military coups.

The recipient of the 1982 Nobel Prize for Literature, García Márquez is considered one of the most influential living world authors. Although his recent works have not garnered the near-universal acclaim of his acknowledged masterpiece, *One Hundred Years of Solitude*, his books are eagerly awaited by world audiences and many critics concur with the opinion of Curt Suplee, who asserted that the novel has ensured him "a place in the ranks of twentieth century masters." For his successful fusion of social issues and magic realism, for the universality of the conclusions he draws from the localized fictional setting of Macondo, and for his ongoing interest in stylistic experimentation, García Márquez is credited with helping to reinvigorate the modern novel genre.

(For further information about García Márquez's life and career, see *Contemporary Authors*, Vols. 33-36, rev. ed.; *Contemporary Authors New Revision Series*, Vols. 10, 28; *Contemporary Literary Criticism*, Vols. 2, 3, 8, 10, 15, 27, 47, 55; *Dictionary of Literary Biography Yearbook: 1982*; and *Short Story Criticism*, Vol. 8.)

CRITICAL COMMENTARY

JULIO ORTEGA

(essay date 1969)

[In the essay excerpted below, originally published in Spanish in 1969 in his study *La contemplación y la fiesta*, Ortega examines García Márquez's treatment of time in *One Hundred Years of Solitude*.]

In addition to its obvious quality, part of the great success of *One Hundred Years of Solitude* can be attributed to the fact that it is a lengthy tribute to the reader. This novel demands and obtains the best from each reader, it tests the reader's availability and then assaults and transforms it by transgressing verisimilitude, exciting the imagination, motivating the sensibilities, demanding a sense of humor, and evoking compassion. It also demands that a historical parallel be established with its scheme, with the century of Latin-American events whose vast possibilities of pain and happiness end in death and destruction, that is, in the closing of one period and in the proximity of a different time, because the world and time of this novel are both closed, they have ended. The history of Macondo is another version of the Latin-American past, but it is in the novel itself—between the foundings and the apocalypse—that these births and destructions have their own scheme, motivation, and subtle dialectics.

These relationships between different worlds and times form the central structure of [*One Hundred Years of Solitude*]. This structure includes at least four sequences of worlds and times: (1) the mythical world and time of the founders; (2) the historical world and time ushered in by Aureliano Buendía and his wars; (3) the cyclical time of the old age and death of the initial characters and their world changed by the insertion of

Principal Works

La hojarasca (novella) 1955
  [Leaf Storm, published in Leaf Storm and Other Stories, 1972]

Monólogo de Isabel viendo llover en Macondo (novella); published in journal Mito, 1955; also published as Isabel viendo llover en Macondo, 1967
  [Monologue of Isabel Watching It Rain in Macondo, published in Leaf Storm and Other Stories, 1972]

El colonel no tiene quien le escriba (novella) 1961
  [No One Writes to the Colonel, published in No One Writes to the Colonel and Other Stories, 1968]

*Los funerales de la Mamá Grande (short stories) 1962

La mala hora (novel) 1962
  [In Evil Hour, 1979]

Cien años de soledad (novel) 1967
  [One Hundred Years of Solitude, 1970]

No One Writes to the Colonel and Other Stories (novella and short stories) 1968

La novela en América Latina: diálogo [with Mario Vargas Llosa] (dialogue) 1968

†Relate de un náufrago. . . . (journalism) 1970
  [The Story of a Shipwrecked Sailor, 1986]

‡La increíble y triste historia de la cándida Eréndira y de su abuela desalmada (novella and short stories) 1972

Leaf Storm and Other Stories (short stories) 1972

‡Ojos de perro azul (short stories) 1972

Cuando era feliz e indocumentado (journalism) 1973

El otoño del patriarca (novel) 1975
  [The Autumn of the Patriarch, 1975]

Todos los cuentos de Gabríel García Márquez: 1947-1972 (collected short stories) 1975

Crónicas y reportajes (journalism) 1976

Innocent Eréndira and Other Stories (short stories) 1978

Periodismo militante (journalism) 1978

Crónica de una muerta anunciada (novella) 1981
  [Chronicle of a Death Foretold, 1982]

El amor en los tiempos del cólera (novel) 1985
  [Love in the Time of Cholera, 1988]

Collected Stories (short stories) 1985

El general en su laberinto (novel) 1989
  [The General in His Labyrinth, 1990]

Collected Novellas (novellas) 1990

*The stories in this collection are published together with the novella No One Writes to the Colonel in No One Writes to the Colonel and Other Stories.

†This work was written in 1955.

‡The stories in these collections are published in Innocent Eréndira and Other Stories.

Macondo into a vaster reality; and (4) the deterioration of Macondo, *axis mundi,* by the depleting effect of the exchange of its reality of the external world and time, which is tantamount also to the extinction of the family line, the axis of Macondo. Let us examine these relationships in some detail.

The mythical world and time of Macondo's foundation implies a search for a lost paradise. Hoping to reach the sea, José Arcadio Buendía, patriarch and founder, has undertaken, together with various other families, an exodus through the jungle. (pp. 85-6)

This search, which can be seen as a search for a paradise, is not necessarily equivalent to a religious undertaking. It suggests above all the drive toward the rediscovery of the world, the need to conquer that world through a primordial identity, the dream of reestablishing an original reality. Thus, the journey and the founding are placed in the context of ritual. José Arcadio Buendía decides to leave his village after he kills Prudencio Aguilar to destroy the rumors of Buendía's unconsummated marriage. Already in the motivation of this journey, in this self-imposed expulsion, a ritual begins to form. This episode takes on even greater significance from the fact that Ursula, José Arcadio's wife, is his cousin; they are equivalent to the primordial cou-

ple. For this reason of kinship she tries to insist on not consummating the marriage, horrified by the curse of giving birth to a child with a pig's tail. The sin and punishment of an amorous relationship that is also a blood relationship thus appear at the beginning of this journey. The son is born without the feared pig's tail, but José Arcadio Buendía has killed a man in order to kill a rumor, and his guilty conscience drives him to undertake the journey, to expel himself from the village. The sense of humor with which Gabriel García Márquez relates these incidents and the way he expands them through hyperbole should not prevent our recognizing in them the roots and rituals of an archetypal fantasy: the guilt of love, the expulsion, the search for another world, the pursuit of another innocence. (p. 86)

A dream reveals to José Arcadio Buendía that he has found the site for his city. He sees a city whose walls are mirrors, another emblematic image. Later he comes to believe he has understood the dream when he sees a block of ice for the first time, but these mirrors will also become a mirage in the destruction that occurs at the end of the novel.

In this primordial zone the world is organized archetypically: objects emerge for the first time; José Arcadio Buendía discovers through his own calculations that the world is round; death is still unknown ("The world was so recent that many things lacked names, and in order to indicate them it was necessary to point"); Macondo appears to be an island; and Colonel Aureliano Buendía reports that the region is surrounded by water. This isolated world is sustained by the fantasy of José Arcadio Buendía and by the presence of Melquíades, the magician, a sort of internal author of the work, a hyperbole of the author himself. An unrestrained desire for knowledge leads José Arcadio Buendía to experiment constantly with magnets, magnifying lenses, and maps. This quest is another mythical dream: the need for science, for knowledge. The plague of insomnia is therefore also a parable, inasmuch as it reveals this experience of the world. Realizing "the infinite possibilities of a loss of memory," José Arcadio Buendía marks everything with its name, and "thus they went on living in a reality that was slipping away, momentarily captured by words, but which would escape irremediably when they forgot the values of the written letters." The reality threatened by a loss of memory suggests allegorically that the plague of insomnia will rescue it through knowledge and will make it tangible and alive. The past begins to be constructed starting from this conquest of reality.

José Arcadio Buendía announces the end of the mythical time when he states that "it's Monday" on a Tuesday and continues to affirm this even on Friday. He says: " . . . but suddenly I realized that it's still Monday, like yesterday. Look at the sky, look at the walls, look at the begonias. Today is Monday too." And later: "On Friday, before anyone arose, he watched the appearance of nature again until he did not have the slightest doubt but that it was Monday." From the point of view of the other characters it is in fact not Monday, but in a mythical world time is not linear. Consequently, José Arcadio Buendía is taken for mad and tied to a chestnut tree, where he dies. But actually he does not die. Tied to the tree of life, the enormous patriarch is still the founder, the Father. Melquíades, a sort of serpent who invites his audience to eat of the fruits of science, also dies without dying. He is rejuvenated in the sacred zone of that world, the room of the successive alchemists in which Melquíades has written the history of Macondo and of the Buendías, his prophesies, which are the novel itself. Ursula, the mother, while being perhaps the most pragmatic character in this world, is also an archetypal character. With the exception of her initial march through the swamps, she is the only character who does not experience any transformation apart from that of aging. As the Mother, she is a mirror that reflects the events occurring around her.

After this mythical time, Colonel Aureliano Buendía's wars indicate that Macondo has become part of a more concrete, historical time. Time becomes historical as Macondo's second generation witnesses the expansion of its world. This historical time reveals its political dichotomies and its elements of social injustice in the banana company's transformation of the village through its methods of extortion. Macondo's world is infiltrated by a conflictive, outside world. In the mythical world time was a norm, and the narrator says, "time put everything in its place." In the world transformed by history, on the other hand, time is equivalent to chaos, and the narrator states, "time finally confused everything."

The ludicrous thirty-two armed uprisings instigated and lost by Colonel Aureliano Buendía, the contradictory fortunes of rebellion and politics, and the eventual destruction of Aureliano, who is bewildered by the hidden factors of power, suggest in the novel the madness threatening this history, as well as its deep confusion and its destructive thrust. The thirst for justice becomes in the end, a blind slaughter. Pure rebellion, the total war declared by the Colonel, is thus condemned to the absurd destruction of itself and of the world it jeopardizes. When Aureliano, who has been condemned to death, returns to Macondo, he is startled to see how the town had aged in one year.

As this historical time draws to a close, time becomes a spiral and cyclically recovers the world. In this world the notion of time is governed by the recollections of the characters: old age recalls a bygone time. When Aureliano Segundo asks Ursula if what he has read in the history left by Melquíades is true, "she answered him that it was, that many years ago the gypsies had brought magic lamps and flying mats to Macondo. 'What's happening,' she sighed, 'is that the world is slowly coming to an end and those things don't come here any more.'" (pp. 86-8)

[Cyclical time as] suggested by the repetition of the family line is something akin to a game of mirrors. The kinship ties in this novel are intertwined by the reiterative game of names and by the two personality types: "While the Aurelianos were withdrawn, but with lucid minds, the José Arcadios were impulsive and enterprising, but they were marked with a tragic sign." The only cases impossible to classify are those of José Arcadio Segundo and Aureliano Segundo, identical twins who confuse even the family, but it is precisely through this hyperbolic identity that they reveal the spiral reiteration running through their family history. When José Arcadio Segundo announces that he is setting out for the coast to search for a Spanish galleon that had gone aground many years earlier, Ursula shouts: "I know all of this by heart. It's as if time had turned around and we were back at the beginning." The grandchildren repeat the actions of their grandfather by making another effort to reach the outside world. Aureliano Triste plans to build a railroad and draws a sketch on the table: "Looking at the sketch that

Aureliano Triste drew on the table and that was a direct descendent of the plans with which José Arcadio Buendía had illustrated his project for solar warfare, Ursula confirmed her impression that time was going in a circle."

At the vortex of this spinning time, Ursula can now judge the history of her family; she becomes aware of the full presence of her descendants and understands them for the first time. She realizes Aureliano had fought all his wars out of "pure and sinful pride" and because he was incapable of loving. In the "lucidity of her old age" she discovers that Amaranta was not a hard woman but "the most tender woman who had ever existed." In this time she also realizes "that her clumsiness was not the first victory of decrepitude and darkness but a sentence passed by time. She thought previously, when God did not make the same traps out of the months and years that the Turks used when they measured a yard of percale, things were different." She wants then to allow herself "an instant of rebellion" as a protest for "over a century of conformity." (p. 89)

This cyclical time, like the mythical time before it, brings out the recurring theme of the symbols, of the objects that become archetypes: the Colonel makes little gold fish that he then melts and pounds again into little fish, and Amaranta laboriously weaves her own shroud. This entire time, then, is filled with echoes, it is infiltrated by previous times and worlds. "It's as though the world was going in circles," Ursula says, because time repeats itself.

The death of the characters returns the mythical world to a reality complicated by experience. Death, like love, war, solitude, and the other factors affecting the life of the characters, is also transfigured in this novel through hyperbole. Thus the narrator always transfers us to another reference, to a new possibility of its thematization. In this zone in which the novel turns on itself, the possibilities of death also suggest the allegorical context that suddenly summarizes the life of a character. Raveling and unraveling time through the little gold fish he manufactures, before he dies Colonel Aureliano Buendía hears the shouting of the children and the music of the circus. . . . Aureliano sees in the circus the parable of his own life. As the fanfare ends he recognizes his solitude in the emptiness of the street. He derisively urinates on the tree of life, where the presence of his father can still be felt, and dies leaning against the tree. The flowers that rain from the sky when the founder dies and the thread of blood and gunpowder at José Arcadio's death are also signifiers of these characters. In the shadow of her own death, Amaranta reconstructs the entire presence of her life "in the unbounded comprehension of solitude." Death itself has told her that she will die when she finishes weaving her shroud. Thus, she weaves her complicated life in order to die.

Caught in this spiral of time, the world begins to deteriorate when the family line, which is its axis, goes into a rapid decline. The expectant fullness of the mythical world and the fabulous confusion of the historical world are replaced by a decaying reality, by a decline leading to total destruction. Hinting at this destruction, the narrator announces that the axle had become worn; Macondo is the *axis mundi,* but the line of the Buendías is also an axis, and so is the constructed and reconstructed house, especially Melquíades's room, rooted in its mythical time, where time does not flow and where the grandchildren discover that "it's always March and always Monday."

Macondo ages with the war and is rejuvenated by the banana boom, but its history demands destruction. The shifting realities and the comings and goings of its characters slowly bring about its decay. The flood, which is a parable originated by the exploitation of the banana company, leaves a solitary and lost town from which the young people attempt to flee. Macondo now lives a farcical, insidious past,

> a past whose annihilation had not taken place because it was still in a process of annihilation, consuming itself from within, ending at every moment but never ending its ending. . . . In that Macondo, forgotten even by the birds, where the dust and the heat had become so strong that it was difficult to breathe, secluded by solitude and love and by the solitude of love in a house where it was almost impossible to sleep because of the noise of the red ants, Aureliano and Amaranta Ursula were the only happy beings, and the most happy on the face of the earth.

The last descendants of the line of the Buendías love each other with the courage their ancestors failed to show, but they also bring about the end. They do not realize that they are aunt and nephew, and their child is born with a pig's tail. Amaranta Ursula dies in childbirth, and Aureliano sees his son transformed into "a dry and bloated bag of skin" dragged away by the ants. Then he recalls the epigraph on the parchments left by Melquíades: *"The first of the line is tied to a tree and the last is being eaten by the ants."* Studying the parchments again, he realizes that "Melquíades had not put events in the conventional time, but had concentrated a century of daily episodes in such a way that they coexisted in one instant." Reading the parchments, he discovers in them his own fate, his imminent death. A wind destroys Macondo, "the city of mirrors (or mirages)." In reading the parchments, in reading the novel itself, this character reads himself. The ancient metaphor of the "book of life" thus closes the world and time.

García Márquez has explained that *One Hundred Years of Solitude* is the story of a family trying to avoid the birth of a son with a pig's tail. He has stated that this is the unity of the novel, but aside from being an internal motivation, it would appear that this fear is just another thread in the plot. The unity of the novel, its coherence, is actually found in its structure, in its formulation. The stories of the various characters are interwoven by the author's skillful manipulation of a structure based on temporal discontinuity.

According to García Márquez, this novel was initially developed following a chronological sequence, but he soon realized that it was impossible to write a linear history of Macondo and the Buendías. The key to this structure is found in the sentence that attributes to Melquíades the arrangement of events to coexist in one instant (discontinuous time), rather than in the order of man's conventional, chronological time. The daily episodes of an entire century thus unfold at the same time, because the time of this novel is sustained by the time of reading: the reader constructs the temporality of the novel as he relinquishes his chronological notions of time. Hence the presence of the future in the present time of the narrative, a present time embedded in a weightless past, since the perspective of this writing requires the discourse of the chronicle. The temporal discontinuities, the leaps in time that juggle this century of episodes, are underscored by the profuse use of formulas such as "every year," "many years later," "long hours," "several years," "in a few years," "several centuries later," "for several weeks," and so on, formulas that never clearly state a temporal measurement but that insinuate it by broadening the reverberations of time, insuring a continuity that in fact is essentially temporal. In addition, these formulas evoke the narrative tone of legends and thus introduce a convention of verisimilitude at the very core of the fantasy. In this novel the play of reality and fantasy is never dual; the narrative presence of the temporal compels "fantasy" to be a part of "reality," to be a spontaneous possibility of it.

Fantasy and reality constantly shift back and forth within the only web they form, underscoring the various worlds of the characters. For Ursula, for example, reality is immediate: "The concert of so many different birds became so disturbing that Ursula would plug her ears with beeswax so as not to lose her sense of reality." José Arcadio Beundía, on the other hand, "fascinated by an immediate reality that came to be more fantastic than the vast universe of his imagination," reveals another side of the changing possibilities of reality and fantasy. The men and women that Ursula brings to Macondo carry with them "pure and simple earthly accessories put on sale without any fuss by peddlers of everyday reality," in contrast to the disrupting magic of the gypsies. The plague of insomnia, a fantastic parable, threatens to disintegrate language, on which the characters base their knowledge of reality, and in his dreams José Arcadio Buendía sees himself walking through infinite rooms and "he would find

Prudencio Aguilar in the room of reality. But one night . . . Prudencio Aguilar touched his shoulder in an intermediate room and he stayed there forever, thinking that it was the real room," a parable of his death.

It is more frequent, however, to find the immediate reality being extended in fantasy, which is its echo, its own vision. The mechanism of this extension is hyperbole. Fantastic elements are routinely introduced directly into the narrative. . . . This method of evoking the realm of the fantastic, which is a primary clue to the reading of this novel, is based on humor and on a sense of amazement and of the dramatic, as illustrated by the rain of flowers at José Arcadio Buendía's burial, the ascension of Remedios the Beauty, and many similar episodes. But the fantastic element functions as a reverberation of the referent, especially when an anecdote is distorted by hyperbole. Humor and fantasy are thus provoked in the contrasts, in the intimate oppositions, in the spontaneous exaggerations, and in the use of accumulation and giantism, which García Márquez, a Rabelaisian in the end, prolongs. This hyperbolic mechanism is visible, for example, in all the episodes of amorous initiation. The relations of José Arcadio with Pilar Ternera and the gypsy girl and of Aureliano with a prostitute disclose this mechanism. When he returns to Macondo tattooed from head to foot, José Arcadio, who raffles his virile member among a group of prostitutes, is himself a hyperbole. The same is true of Aureliano Segundo, an outrageous reveler, who fills the house with guests, "invincible worldly carousers," and whose eating contest with The Elephant is typical of this Rabelaisian tone. Aureliano's wars are dramatized by hyperbole, and Amaranta's conduct turns this use of hyperbole inward. The fantastic element is therefore such a clear transparency of reality that García Márquez has not had to resort to objective and accumulate details to represent it. Instead, the hyperbolic mechanism freely sustains the sense of amazement in the chronicle itself. This accounts for the profuse use of adjectives; qualities here are always clearly superlative.

But even the zestfulness of the fantastic element as a prolonging reference eventually feels the drama of cyclical time and of the end time, because on the other side of the hyperbole, at the end of the exaggerated and fervent exercise of fantasy, lies the white circle of solitude and the terror of the curse. The solitude of these one hundred years of events lives in all the protagonists as a condition fixed in the spiral of their history. Solitude is one of the traits of the Buendías, and it is also a precarious form of union: "they took refuge in solitude"; "more than mother and son, they were accomplices in solitude." Melquíades returns from death "because he could not bear the solitude"; Remedios the Beauty matures in solitude; Fernanda is humanized by it; and Aureliano goes astray in the solitude of his immense power. Solitude is also the mirror that recovers a life in the passing instant of a recurring time. In this instant "solitude had selected the memories" for Amaranta, who thinks about Rebeca, unyielding in the intransigence by which she conquered "the privileges of solitude." Colonel Aureliano Buendía also capitulates, reaching "an honorable pact with solitude." Ursula reviews the history of her family from the perspective of solitude as a clairvoyant awareness. The last characters are "secluded by solitude and love and by the solitude of love." In the end we are told that the "races condemned to one hundred years of solitude do not have a second opportunity on earth." Solitude is thus a many-sided condemnation pervading everything from the smallest habits (Ursula looks through the window following "a habit of her solitude") to the most significant moments and even to the summing up of an entire life. In a moment of lucidity in which she sees her life flash before her, Ursula senses her guilt in having lived "over a century of conformity." In the human condition, the novel seems to be saying, conformity condemns us to solitude, to the absence of communion. Conformity reduces existence to the endless daily occurrences in which man is always the object of a world that determines him and in which he succumbs without full consciousness, without being able to fight back.

This conformity and its unchallenged bastion, solitude, are also bound together by an ancient taboo, by an absurd and fanatical curse: the son born with a pig's tail. This fear is spread, above all, by Ursula. It inhibits love and reveals feelings of guilt. Her children are born without the dreaded tail, but Ursula sees the curse in every potential evil. When she discovers the unabashed nakedness of her son José Arcadio, she fears that the curse may have been manifested in this manner, and when Colonel Aureliano Buendía becomes a banal tyrant, she threatens him with death: "It's the same thing I would have done if you had been born with the tail of a pig," she says. However, the curse comes true only for the one couple that freely love each other. The end of the family line betrays the sin at the origin and the guilt in love, part also of the character of this century condemned by its own alienation. Man, who lost paradise and reconquers it by inventing an archetypal world, loses it again in the solitude that transpires in the proximity of punishment and death. The curse of the son born of sin points therefore to a region of explicit guilt and implied rebellion. It reveals the irreversible condemnation of an age, a family line, and a history. These one hundred years of solitude find in the dialectics of several worlds and time the exorcism by which this novel makes them beautiful and terrible and also claims a different time, a time of innocence. (pp. 90-5)

Julio Ortega, "One Hundred Years of Solitude," in his *Poetics of Change: The New Spanish-American Narrative,* translated by Galen D. Greaser and Julio Ortega, University of Texas Press, 1984, pp. 85-95.

MARIO VARGAS LLOSA
(essay date 1971)

[A Peruvian-born novelist, short story writer, journalist, and critic, Vargas Llosa, together with such Central and South American authors as Carlos Fuentes, Julio Cortázar, and García Márquez, was a prominent figure in the Latin American literary "boom" of the 1960s. In the following excerpt, originally published in Spanish in 1971 in his seminal biographical and critical study, *García Márquez: Historia de un deicidio,* he examines narrative technique and the theme of death in García Márquez's early short fiction.]

What is especially surprising in [García Márquez's early stories], in contrast with the later writing, is their intellectualism. Cold and humorless—the first of them written under the devastating influence of Kafka, and the last under the influence (no less devastating) of Faulkner—they reveal a world of extreme sophistication, of mannerisms, of literary tics. The truth of the matter is that García Márquez has not yet come to grips with his literary vocation, for that vocation is in the making. He is already a rebel, to be sure, but not the revolutionary who, on returning to Aracataca with his mother, discovers the collapse of a world that had given him life, and who becomes conscious of a reality which he will dedicate himself thereafter to redeeming (exorcizing) with his pen. He is quite clear on this point: though unsure of the dates, he is able to recall that the trip to Aracataca with his mother took place when all of these stories, with the exception of **"La noche de los alcaravanes" ("The Night of the Curlews"),** had already been written. The new experience strengthened his nascent vocation, opened his eyes to the raw material of his art and transformed the diligent reader and servant of Kafka and Faulkner into a writer who would, in turn, have them serve him in the creation of his own special world.

Although the literary interest of these tales is minimal, they do arouse curiosity as portraits of the emotional and cultural life of the adolescent who, by the end of the forties, far removed from his beloved tropics, was resigning himself to a career in law and discovering—with awe—the great novelists of modern times. Ten short stories appeared that would never be gathered together as a book. Almost invariably they were given enigmatic titles: **"La tercera resignación" ("The Third Resignation"), "Eva está dentro de su** gato" ("Eva inside Her Cat"), "Tubal-Cain forja una estrella" ("Tubal-Cain Forges a Star"), "La otra costilla de la muerte" ("The Other Rib of Death"), "Diálogo del espejo" ("Dialogue in a Mirror"), "Amargura para tres sonámbulos" ("Bitter Sorrow for Three Sleepwalkers"), "Ojos de perro azul" ("Blue-Dog Eyes"), "Nabo" ("Nabo"), "Alguien desordena estas rosas" ("Someone Has Disturbed the Roses") and "La noche de los alcaravanes" ("The Night of the Curlews"). The first five were written in Bogotá between 1947 and the middle months of 1948 and the remainder in Cartagena and Barranquilla.

The dominant theme in almost all of these is death. Sometimes the events of life are narrated from within death; sometimes death is viewed from within life; sometimes there are recurring deaths within death. Most of the stories reach for a setting outside the limits of time and space, within an abstract reality. Throughout, the narrative perspective is subjective and internal: the world of life, or death, is viewed by a consciousness which in narrating narrates itself. Objectivity is lacking even in those stories which spring from an objectively real anecdote, like **"Bitter Sorrow for Three Sleepwalkers"** and **"Nabo."** Apart from these two, all are rooted firmly in an imaginary reality, by degrees which range from the mythic and legendary (**"The Night of the Curlews,"** a tale inspired by a popular superstition) to the truly fantastic. The consistency of this fictional reality is more than anything else psychological: actions, which are few, are dwarfed by bizarre sensations, extraordinary emotions, impossible thoughts. It is what the characters feel or think that is being related; almost never what they do.

An atmosphere of nightmare and neurosis pervades these tales, in which dreams and self-duplications are often important themes. The phenomenon of the double self first appears in **"The Other Rib of Death"** and **"Dialogue in a Mirror"**; here we catch an early glimpse of the great theme of recurring names, personalities and destinies of *One Hundred Years of Solitude.* The last of these stories, however, introduces a concrete element which allows it to be set directly within the "history" of the fictional reality: its curlews belong to a world which is already that of *Leaf Storm.* This may explain why **"The Night of the Curlews"** is the only one of the ten stories "resurrected" by *One Hundred Years of Solitude.* And yet in the previous story, **"Someone Has Disturbed the Roses,"** just as if the subconscious had surfaced to play tricks on the "abstracting" mind of the author, two local elements filter through into the narrative, soon to become established customs of the fictional society as it appears in *Leaf Storm:* little wooden pegs are placed in the eyes of a dead child so that during the wake they will remain "open and unflinching"; "bread and aloe leaves" are hung for good luck at the entrance to a house, as happens in many homes in Macondo.

A pattern which we might term metaphysico-masturbatory is repeated in various of these ten tales: a solitary character tortures himself with thoughts of ontological disintegration, self-duplication and extinction. (pp. 451-52)

"The Third Resignation" pulsates with an agonizing fear of death. In the very first lines, the omniscient narrator draws his reader into an imaginary reality by remarking that the persistent noise which the protagonist hears, "he had heard, for example, at the time of his first death." This fusion of the delirious and fantastic with the routine and trivial, as well as the congealed horror which sprouts droll asides ("He felt handsome wrapped in his shroud; fatally handsome"), are strongly reminiscent of Kafka. A seven-year-old child dies of typhoid, but the doctor manages to "prolong the boy's life even beyond death." In his coffin, the dead boy goes on growing for eighteen years under the loving care of his mother, who examines him each day with a tape measure. At twenty-five years of age he stops growing and suffers "his second death." His body begins to decompose and gives off a foul smell. He realizes that he will now have to be buried and is seized by an infinite dread because, with his conscious mind still alert, he has the impression that he is about to be buried alive. He pictures "life" within the grave, the slow disintegration of his flesh, of his bones, of the wood of his coffin and then how all this dust will rise to the surface, to a new life, as a tree, as a fruit. It will be like living over again. But by then he will probably be so resigned to his condition that he will die anew, this time "from resignation."

The slight narrative thread is lost among the descriptions of the dead character's sensations and the mass of grotesque detail: the living corpse is gradually being eaten away by mice, a maddening noise is torturing his eardrums, the stench of his own decay is offending his sense of smell. The omniscient narrator is so close to his protagonist, so involved in the intimacies of the latter, that the tale often appears a monologue by the dead man. Herein lies one of the few merits of the text: the flawless coherence of the spatial perspective, most unusual in one who has just begun to write. The language is hardly distinctive, but it has a certain flow and is well in keeping with its topic. The vocabulary is dense, disturbing in its impact on the senses, and the syntax tortuous. (p. 453)

"The Other Rib of Death" opens with a surrealistic dream in which anguish and black humor are fused: the protagonist is traveling on a train which crosses a landscape of "still life, sown with unlikely, artificial trees, whose fruits are knives and scissors. . . ." Suddenly, without explanation, he takes a screwdriver and removes from his foot the head of a boil. Through the hole he can make out "the end of a greasy yellow cord." He pulls on the cord and out comes "a long, an immensely long ribbon, which issued forth of its own free will, without causing irritation or pain," at which point he sees his brother, "dressed up like a woman in front of a mirror, trying to extract his left eye with a pair of scissors."

Only the beginning of the tale is so colorful; next there comes a psychic drama aggravated by obsessions with death and with a double self. The narrative viewpoint is that of a character who, at daybreak, finds himself caught between a waking and a sleeping state, and who is assailed by strange sensations, dark terrors and somber visions. Soon after, a more precise and more unnerving experience stands out sharply against the whirl of images: the memory of a twin brother, who died from a tumor on the stomach. Masochistically, the character imagines the tumor, feels it growing within his very being, envisions it devouring muscles, vital organs, dragging him in turn toward his death. Then he is gripped by a terrifying fear of his brother, that "other" self, the double: "They were thus replicas. Two identical brothers, disturbingly repetitive." He begins to feel that the spatial limits separating his dead brother and himself are illusory, that the two share a common identity. He fears that "when putrefaction has taken hold of the dead man's body, he, the one still living, will also start to rot within his animate world." But what if the process were the reverse, with the influence emanating from "the one who had stayed alive"? In that case, perhaps, "both he and his brother would remain intact, achieving a balance between life and death which would ward off putrefaction." Or could it be "that the brother who was buried might remain incorruptible even when the rot of death was spreading through the body of the surviving brother with his fine, blue eyes"? These clammy questions are soon followed by a blissful sensation of peace, and the protagonist, now relaxed, closes his eyes "to await the coming day." (p. 455)

[García Marquez's first five stories are] set within an internal and subjective reality that is best termed abstract: all reference to time and place is eschewed; the language is studiously neutral; in the five stories an identical situation recurs (a solitary character, lying dead or asleep, is plagued by unnatural sensations); in each of them we note the same ambiguity with regard to the type of reality described. Is this an "imaginary" or an "objective" reality? The first of these terms seems more appropriate if the characters are indeed dead, and the second if the resurrections, repeated deaths and reduplications are merely the fantasies of disturbed minds. The rigorous coherence within incoherence which operates among the first five stories begins to weaken with the sixth, and the change is even greater in those that follow: García Márquez has begun to read

Faulkner and the experience will leave a bright imprint on these last tales.

"Bitter Sorrow for Three Sleepwalkers" . . . signals a shift from the internal to the external and from the abstract to the concrete in the treatment of fictional reality. The tale is narrated in the first person plural by the three sleepwalkers of the title, but its subject is a young girl. More than a short story the work is a poetic tableau, an elegy for a girl who, sometime in the past, fell from a second story window into a stone yard and who, instead of dying, remained with "her vital organs in disarray and no longer responsive to her will, as if she were a warm corpse that had not yet begun to stiffen." From that moment on—a long time seems to have elapsed since the accident—she has been a solitary creature, living within a private, hallucinatory world ("She told us once that she had seen a cricket inside the glass of her mirror and that she had gone through the surface of the glass to get it"). But within this world she is gradually—even deliberately—destroying herself. One day she decides to stop moving, to remain seated on the concrete floor, and then she announces: "I shall never smile again." The three narrators, who speak of her with great sorrow and nostalgia (in all probability they are her younger brothers), believe that before long she will tell them: "I shall never see again," "I shall never hear again," and that "of her own free will, she would cut herself off sense by sense, until one day we would find her sitting with her back against the wall, looking as if she had gone to sleep for the first time in her life."

The language is less diffuse than in the earlier texts but it continues to be highly "literary," carefully wrought and reminiscent of certain of the author's (better) readings. The air of mystery and foreboding, of imminent revelation is achieved by means of a Faulknerian syntax, oblique and anticipatory, twisting and turning ("All of this—and even more—we would have believed that afternoon. . . . ," "We could have said that we were doing what we had been doing every day of our lives . . . "), and also by the intrusion—as if some deforming prism had been placed over the narrative material—of the character-narrator, whose sole function in the story is that of a "technical" advisor. (pp. 456-57)

[In **"Nabo"**] we encounter a poetic creature living on the periphery of life: a mute child, unable to walk, who recognizes no one, who is a "dead and solitary girl that liked the phonograph." Of all the writings, this is the one most reminiscent of Faulkner, not only because of its form, but also for its subject matter. It appears to be set in the Deep South, with peasants who live in semi-slavery, estates with horses, aristocratic young ladies and their Black servants, and saxophone players in the public squares. The tale is made up of two parts or dimensions, skilfully drawn together into a single story by two alternating narrators: the omniscient narrator and a plural narrator-character (doubtless the brothers or parents of the child). The two parts of the story take place within different realms of reality—one the reality of external things, the other the fantasy or madness of the protagonist.

The "objective" portion of the story is as follows: Nabo, a young Black, is required to groom the horses on an estate and play the phonograph which keeps the idiot girl amused. The girl discovers—presumably thanks to Nabo—how to move the handle of the phonograph and is one day heard to pronounce the boy's name, "Nabo." The groom is in the habit of visiting the town square on Saturday nights to listen to a black saxophone player who one day gives up playing in the band and disappears forever. Then one morning Nabo is kicked in the head by a horse and remains "disturbed" for the rest of his life. He is bound hand and foot by his master and locked in a room, where food is passed to him from under the door. He lives in this state for fifteen years, like an animal, until one day in a fit of rage he breaks down the door of his cell and runs off—now huge and ferocious—in search of the stable and the horses, which have long since disappeared from the estate. During his escape he smashes mirrors and tears down everything within reach. The girl (now a woman) sees him running by and utters the only word she has ever learned, "Nabo."

The "subjective" portion is this: in the loneliness of his cell, Nabo relives incessantly in his pitiful mind the tragic instant when the horse's hoof shattered his forehead. He has no awareness of the passage of time; his mind revolves obsessively around this single memory. Suddenly, he hears a voice calling to him, urging him to follow. In the shadows he recognizes the saxophone player that he used to listen to in the square. The shadowy figure speaks to him affectionately, urging Nabo to leave with him: "We have been waiting for you in the group." The boy shows little enthusiasm, whereupon the man insists, assuring him that all that has happened was arranged by "them" in order to have him in "the group." But Nabo is not interested and talks about the horses and the comb that he had used to groom their tails. Finally the apparition suggests: "If finding the comb is all that keeps you from joining the group, then go and look for it." It is at this point that Nabo breaks down the door of his prison and escapes, now a "huge and bestial Negro."

This second level or dimension of the story has an ambiguity characteristic of literature involving an imaginary reality. The reader must make up his mind where he stands by eliminating one of the two interpretations possible. The specter of the dead saxophone player who comes and invites Nabo to go with him to the "group" (in other words, to the afterlife, to heaven) could be simply a hallucination occurring in the mind of the protagonist, in which case that part of the story would be taking place on a "subjective" plane within an "objective" reality. But there is another possibility, namely that the dead saxophone player really does appear in Nabo's dark cell as an emissary from the afterlife and that he is, consequently, not a mental vision but a miraculous or fantastic being. If this is indeed the case, then the present portion of the story is occurring within a subjective reality, and the events narrated by this tale are no longer objectively real, but part of an "imaginary" reality.

Also to be noted in "Nabo" are certain motifs which will soon become part of the stock in trade of this fictional reality. One of them is the theme of sequestration. The young girl in "Bitter Sorrow for Three Sleepwalkers" leads a "withdrawn" life, but Nabo even more so, and in his seclusion one may see a precedent for the estrangement of the doctor in *Leaf Storm*. Another motif is that of the girl or woman who is somehow "different," who lives on the periphery of life. The lovely idiot girls of "Bitter Sorrow for Three Sleepwalkers" and "Nabo" are first sketches of characters like Santa Sofía de la Piedad and Remedios the Beauty. What must be emphasized, however, is that with this last tale the author has begun to show a strong interest in telling a story; the technical complexities and careful manipulations of language are now subordinate to this interest, whereas in earlier cases the story seemed a pretext to justify extravagant displays of style. It matters little that the structure, language and even subject matter are still somewhat foreign. The faithful reader is becoming a writer: trading the abstract for the concrete, the psychic for the vital, he is showing an increasing ability to tell a story in a truly *convincing* manner.

In "Someone Has Disturbed the Roses," there appears another cripple, as in "Bitter Sorrow for Three Sleepwalkers" and "Nabo," but with a change of sex (this time it is a boy) and condition (he is dead). As in the first stories, the narrator is also dead: "Since it's Sunday and the rain has now stopped, I think I shall take a bunch of roses to my grave." A very devout woman, who grows and sells flowers, lives all alone in a house, one room of which serves as a chapel. Each Sunday she has the impression that an invisible gust of wind comes and disturbs the roses on the altar. In fact, it is not the wind, but the spirit of a young boy, who died forty years earlier after falling from a ladder—a boy with whom the woman had played when she was a child. The narrator of this story is none other than this spirit-invalid, who, after dying, sat and waited for twenty years in the room now containing the altar for someone to come and occupy the deserted house. One day he sees the woman moving in; even though twenty years have gone by, he is still able to recognize the girl who used to go bird-nesting with him in the stables.

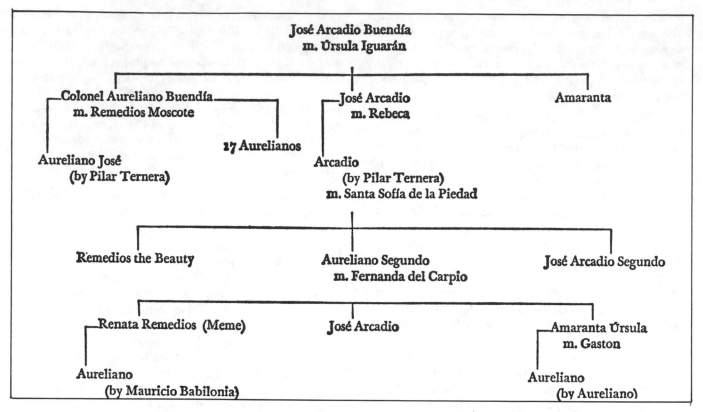

José Arcadio Buendía
m. Úrsula Iguarán

Colonel Aureliano Buendía
m. Remedios Moscote

José Arcadio
m. Rebeca

Amaranta

17 Aurelianos

Aureliano José
(by Pilar Ternera)

Arcadio
(by Pilar Ternera)
m. Santa Sofía de la Piedad

Remedios the Beauty

Aureliano Segundo
m. Fernanda del Carpio

José Arcadio Segundo

Renata Remedios (Meme)

José Arcadio

Amaranta Úrsula
m. Gaston

Aureliano
(by Mauricio Babilonia)

Aureliano
(by Aureliano)

Genealogy of the Buendia family in García Márquez's *One Hundred Years of Solitude.*

From this moment on—another twenty years elapse—he has "lived" with this woman, now in her old age, and has watched her sewing, sleeping and praying. Each Sunday the spirit tries, without success, to take a bunch of roses from the chapel to his grave on the hillside of the town; *he* is that "invisible wind" which disturbs the flowers on the altar.

This is the most successful of the ten stories—the best written and the most skilfully constructed. Despite its magical or fantastic air, it has a number of picturesque details drawn from an objective reality, certain of which will reappear in the Macondo of *Leaf Storm* (the "bread and aloe leaves" at the entrance to the house, the "wooden pegs" in the dead boy's eyes). In addition, the boy-sitting-in-a-chair-waiting is, as we know, the nuclear image of *Leaf Storm;* this is the plight which the narrator-grandchild has to suffer throughout the novel. Little by little, the amorphous reality of the early tales is beginning to take on a recognizable shape. It has begun to move within fixed limits, the same limits that will govern its development, its growth and regrowth in future years. (pp. 457-59)

Mario Vargas Llosa, "A Morbid Prehistory (The Early Stories)," translated by Roger Williams, in *Books Abroad,* Vol. 47, No. 3, Summer, 1973, pp. 451-60.

GEORGE R. MCMURRAY
(essay date 1977)

[In the excerpt below, McMurray provides an overview of García Márquez's career up to the mid-1970s.]

García Márquez's approach to fiction indicates that he has come full circle in at least one respect, namely, in his depiction of subjective states of mind reminiscent of surrealism. Thus, whereas his early short stories are characterized by hermetic morbidity and fantasy, his most recent novel is the most lyrically conceived to date. During the intervening years he has sharpened his literary tools and emerged as a mature, consummate craftsman, the result of extensive reading and experimentation with a wide variety of styles and techniques. The vision of Macondo set forth in *Leaf Storm* reveals possible influences of William Faulkner and Virginia Woolf; Hemingway's aesthetic ideals are brought to mind by **"Tuesday Siesta," "One of These Days,"** and *No One Writes to the Colonel;* other fine pieces such as **"Baltazar's Marvelous Afternoon"** and **"Big Mama's Funeral"** point the way toward the perfect synthesis of realism and fantasy displayed in the internationally acclaimed masterpiece, *One Hundred Years of Solitude;* and the most recent works depict a world in which lyricism and fantasy predominate.

García Márquez's fictional universe consists of three major settings: "the town," Macondo, and a seaside village, or, in the case of *The Autumn of the Patriarch,* a large seaport. Although solitude emerges as his most important theme, "the town" is also the scene of *la violencia.* The other two settings provide the backdrop for the recurring cycle of birth, boom, decay, and death. Time plays an important role in García Márquez's works, the horrors of lineal history serving to convey the failure of man's political, social, and religious institutions. On the other hand, the repetitive patterns and rhythmic momentum generated by mythical time create a mytho-poetic atmosphere that blurs sordid reality and thrusts the reader into a kind of temporal void where the laws of cause and effect tend to become meaningless.

García Márquez displays his mastery of irony and wry humor in *No One Writes to the Colonel,* the protagonist of which emerges as an absurd hero struggling against impossible odds. The subsequent works reveal a trend toward a more Rabelaisian type of humor, with greater emphasis on the absurdities of human existence. These attacks on the tenets of reason are more than likely intended to unveil the other side of reality and in this way question the outmoded conventions that have spawned the disasters of the twentieth century. An antirational outlook on the world is also expressed stylistically through the inordinately long, rambling sentences and jarring shifts in the point of view in **"The Last Voyage of the Ghost Ship"** and **"Blacamán the Good, Vendor of Miracles."** In addition **"The Last Voyage of the Ghost Ship"** presents a schizophrenic view of reality, depending primarily on contrasting images to reflect the protagonist's extreme alienation. The culmination of these tendencies is reached in *The Autumn of the Patriarch,* García Márquez's best portrayal of solitude and most lyrical novel to date.

The fact that many of García Márquez's characters reappear under different circumstances in subsequent works creates the impression that his stories and shorter novels are fragments of a more complete fictional universe. For example, Rebeca Buendía is first introduced in **"Tuesday Siesta"** as the widow who shoots the youth she believes is trying to break into her house. She is next seen as a rather eccentric character in **"One Day after Saturday."** Finally, in *One Hundred Years of Solitude* her entire life unfolds as an integral part of the Genesis-to-Apocalypse chronicle of Macondo. The colonels in *Leaf Storm* and *No One Writes to the Colonel* resemble each other in many respects, leading one to suspect that the protagonist of the second

book is an extension of the portrait begun in the first. The mayor's brief appearance in *No One Writes to the Colonel* is a prelude to his major role in *In Evil Hour.* And the ineffectual Father Angel plays minor roles in *Leaf Storm* and *No One Writes to the Colonel* but emerges as one of the leading figures in *In Evil Hour.*

The widow Montiel appears as the protagonist of ["**Montiel**"], at the end of which she has a mysterious dream about Big Mama. Her connection with Big Mama is clarified in *In Evil Hour* by the fact that she and her husband acquired Big Mama's mansion after the matriarch's death. This relationship between the Montiels and Big Mama constitutes one of the rare discrepancies in García Márquez's works. Big Mama reigned in Macondo, where, we are told, her mansion was dismantled by her heirs moments after her funeral; the Montiels are prominent citizens of "the town."

García Márquez's fiction is also characterized by recurring episodes, details of which are altered in order to avoid monotonous repetition. For example, the extraction of the mayor's abscessed tooth by his enemy, the dentist, occurs in both *In Evil Hour* and **"One of These Days."** In the novel the episode represents a dramatic climax led up to by the mayor's vain efforts to alleviate his unbearable pain and his forced entry into the dentist's office at midnight with his armed guards. In the short story, however, the mayor arrives alone at eight o'clock in the morning threatening to shoot the dentist if he refuses to pull the tooth. Here dramatic tension is generated by the understated tone and the dearth of details, a technique intended to make the reader exercise his imagination. These successful, though widely differing, treatments of the same incident demonstrate García Márquez's skill as a practitioner of both genres of prose fiction.

Solitude resulting from power emerges as one of García Márquez's major themes, culminating with his portrait of the protagonist of *The Autumn of the Patriarch.* This unforgettable character, however, has at least two predecessors representing important stages in the evolution of the theme: the mayor of *In Evil Hour* and Colonel Aureliano Buendía of *One Hundred Years of Solitude.* The mayor stands out as a realistically delineated, though somewhat enigmatic figure, whose agonizing toothache underscores his separation from "the town" he is sent to subdue during *la violencia.* Colonel Aureliano Buendía initiates his military career determined to overthrow the corrupt conservative government and replace it with a just liberal regime. When he retires to the family home in Macondo many years later, he has become a complete cynic due to the futility of his efforts. His final years spent manufacturing gold fishes reflect his solitude as well as the absurdity of his struggles. Unlike the mayor or Colonel Aureliano Buendía, whose solitude can be traced to their roles in civil wars readily identifiable in Colombian history, the patriarch is a schizophrenic personality whose death obsession and greed for power constitute the basis not only for his isolation from other human beings but also for the novel's plot and formal design.

Although García Márquez's male characters have no monopoly on irrational conduct, his female characters are usually stronger, more down to earth, and less likely to be carried away by their emotions, whims, or abstract ideals. Indeed, in several of García Márquez's works the contrast between his male and female characters provides an important source of dramatic tension and irony. The most obvious case in point is José Arcadio Buendía and his wife Ursula of *One Hundred Years of Solitude,* the former emerging as a rudderless dreamer and the latter as the mainstay, who, in spite of her husband's harebrained schemes, manages to hold the clan together for many generations. Similar contrasts between husband-and-wife figures exist in *Leaf Storm, No One Writes to the Colonel,* **"There Are No Thieves in This Town," "Baltazar's Marvelous Afternoon,"** and **"The Sea of Lost Time."** And even in *The Autumn of the Patriarch,* Bendición Alvarado stands out as a pillar of strength for her wavering son, the patriarch, to lean on.

The reader of García Márquez's entire *oeuvre* may be left with the overall impression that today's world is doomed either to imminent annihilation or to entropic stagnation and decay. The fundamental reason for this pessimistic assessment would seem to be man's lost capacity for love, a defect underscored by his overwhelming greed for power and material gain. Nevertheless, ample evidence of eternal virtues is provided by such characters as the impoverished woman in **"Tuesday Siesta,"** whose strength and dignity dominate every episode of the story; the courageous and idealistic colonels in *Leaf Storm* and *No One Writes to the Colonel;* Ursula, the archetype of feminine wisdom and stability in *One Hundred Years of Solitude;* her husband José Arcadio Buendía, who, though flighty and irrational, embodies man's heroic quest for progress and truth in a fathomless universe; their great-grandson Aureliano Segundo and his mistress Petra Cotes, whose sincere love makes them charitable toward others; Esteban, the messenger of hope, beauty, and human solidarity in **"The Handsomest Drowned Man in the World"**; and the generous protagonist of **"Baltazar's Marvelous Afternoon,"** whose creative genius and private world of fabulous dreams represent the antithesis of despair and nihilistic destruction.

As best exemplified by *One Hundred Years of Solitude,* García Márquez's ingenious mixture of realism and fantasy has resulted in the creation of a total fictional universe in which the commonplace takes on an aura of magic and the impossible is made believable. His penetrating insights into the ambiguities of human nature are enhanced by a rich vein of anecdotes and leitmotifs he taps from his private mythology. Though he clearly implies moral indignation against brutality, exploitation, and degradation, he delights his readers with his deft fusion of tragedy and comedy and with his seductive powers of language. García Márquez is presently Latin America's most widely known living novelist. He is, in addition, one of the truly outstanding literary artists of our time. In its totality his work imparts not only the stark reality of an emerging strife-torn continent but, also, through the humanistic and universalizing elements of myth, imagination, and aesthetic perception, a highly original vision of man and his world. (pp. 157-62)

George R. McMurray, in his *Gabriel García Márquez,* Frederick Ungar Publishing Co., 1977, 182 p.

JOSEPH EPSTEIN
(essay date 1983)

[Epstein, editor of the *American Scholar* since 1975, is an influential critic and essayist who has written widely on what he views as the decline of language and literature in the twentieth century. In the following excerpt, he questions whether García Márquez deserves his acknowledged status as a major world author.]

How good is Gabriel García Márquez? "Define your terms," I can hear some wise undergraduate reply. "What do you mean by *is*?" Yet I ask the question in earnest. Over the past weeks I have been reading García Márquez's four novels and three collections of stories—all of his work available in English translation—and I am still not certain how good he is. If I were to be asked how talented, I have a ready answer: pound for pound, as they used to put it in *Ring* magazine, Gabriel García Márquez may be the most talented writer at work in the world today. But talent is one thing; goodness, or greatness, quite another.

Valéry says somewhere that there ought to be a word to describe the literary condition between talent and genius. In writing about García Márquez, most contemporary American literary critics have not searched very hard for that word. Instead they have settled on calling him a genius and knocked off for the day. (pp. 59-60)

In sum, no novelist now writing has a more enviable reputation. His is of course an international, a worldwide reputation—one capped by the Nobel Prize, won in 1982 at the age of fifty-four. The Nobel Prize can sometimes sink a writer, make him seem, even in his lifetime, a bit posthumous. But with García Márquez it appears to have had quite the reverse effect, making him seem more central, more prominent, more of a force. . . .

In Latin America, Gabriel García Márquez has been a household name and face since 1967, when his famous novel *One Hundred Years of Solitude* was first published in Buenos Aires. This novel is said to have sold more than six million copies and to have been translated into more than thirty languages. . . . I thought it quite brilliant and stopped reading it at page 98 (of 383 pages in the paperback edition). A number of intelligent people I know have gone through a similar experience in reading the book. All thought it brilliant, but felt that anywhere from between eighteen to fifty-one years of solitude was sufficient, thank you very much. I shall return to what I think are the reasons for this. (p. 60)

Short of going to Latin American countries on extended visits, how does one find out anything about them? Whom does one trust? New York *Times* reporters capable of prattling on about fifty new poetry workshops in Nicaragua? American novelists—Robert Stone, Joan Didion—who have put in cameo appearances in one or another Latin American country and then returned to write about it? Academic experts, the kernels of whose true information are not easily freed of their ideological husks? Perhaps native writers? On this last count, I have recently read a most charming novel set in Lima, Peru, *Aunt Julia and the Scriptwriter,* by Mario Vargas Llosa, which gives us a portrait of daily life—corrupt, incompetent, sadly provincial though it is—very different from that which Gabriel García Márquez supplies. Whom is one to believe?

So many oddities crop up. How, for example, explain that García Márquez had his famous novel, *One Hundred Years of Solitude,* a book that he has claimed is an argument for change in Latin America, published in Argentina, universally regarded—to hear Jacobo Timerman tell it—as the most repressive of Latin American countries? How for that matter explain the emergence of Latin American literature to a place very near contemporary preeminence? How does one reconcile these various paradoxes, contradictions, confusions? It may be that finally, in reading about Latin America, one has to settle for the virtue which Sir Lewis Namier once said was conferred by sound historical training—a fairly good sense of how things did *not* happen.

Such a sense becomes especially useful in reading a writer like Gabriel García Márquez, who is continually telling us how things did happen. What he is saying is not very new. He speaks of the depredations upon the poor by the rich, upon the pure by the corrupt, upon the indigenous by the colonial—standard stuff, for the most part. But how he says it is new and can be very potent indeed. So much so that Fidel Castro is

supposed to have remarked of him, "García Márquez is the most powerful man in Latin America." (pp. 60-1)

None of this power would exist, of course, if García Márquez were not a considerable artist. Literary artists make us see things, and differently from the way we have ever seen them before; they make us see things *their* way. We agree to this willingly because in the first place they make things interesting, charming, seductive, and in the second place they hold out the promise of telling us important secrets that we would be fools not to want to know. (p. 61)

Sweep and power are readily available to García Márquez; so, too, are what seem like endless lovely touches, such as a man described as "lame in body and sound in conscience." In **"The Handsomest Drowned Man in the World,"** a charming tale about a time when people had hearts capacious enough for the poetic, the way is prepared for a man "to sink easily into the deepest waves, where fish are blind and divers die of nostalgia." The movements of a woman in the story **"There Are No Thieves in *This* Town"** have "the gentle efficiency of people who are used to reality." A man in the story **"One Day After Saturday"** is caught at an instant when "he was aware of his entire weight: the weight of his body, his sins, and his age altogether." García Márquez's stories are studded with such charming bits: a woman with "passionate health," a man with a "mentholated voice," a town "where the goats committed suicide from desolation," another man with "a pair of lukewarm languid hands that always looked as if they'd just been shaved." García Márquez, as Milton Berle used to say of himself, has a million of them.

This fecundity of phrase was not always so readily available to García Márquez. Today his fame is such that his very earliest works are being reprinted and translated—most of them are in the collection *Innocent Eréndira and Other Stories*—and these early stories are dreary in the extreme: dryly abstract, bleak, cut-rate Kafka, without the Kafkaesque edge or the humor. As a novelist, García Márquez seems to have come alive when he began to write about the coastal town he calls Macondo and—the two events seem to have taken place simultaneously—when, by adding the vinegar of politics to his writing, he gave it a certain literary tartness.

García Márquez has claimed William Faulkner as a literary mentor, and the two do have much in common. Each has staked out a territory of his own— Yoknapatawpha County for Faulkner, Macondo and its environs for García Márquez; each deals lengthily with the past and its generations; and finally, each relies on certain prelapsarian myths (Southern grandeur before the American Civil War, Latin American poetic serenity before the advent of modernity and foreign intervention) to bind his work together. There is, though, this decisive difference between the two writers: Faulkner's fiction is almost wholly taken up with the past, while that of García Márquez, as befits a politically minded writer, generally keeps an eye out for the future.

Immersion in the work of such writers provides one of those experiences—perhaps it might be called moral tourism—exclusive to literature. By reading a good deal about a place rendered by a powerful writer, in time one comes to feel one has walked its streets, knows its history and geography, the rhythms of its daily life. Only certain writers can convey this experience through the page: Balzac did it both for Paris and French provincial towns; Faulkner did it; Isaac Bashevis Singer does it for Jewish Poland; and García Márquez does it, too. (pp. 61-2)

Viewed in retrospect, the Macondo stories—they are found in *Leaf Storm and Other Stories* and *No One Writes to the Colonel and Other Stories,* and the town is also the setting for the novel *In Evil Hour*—appear to be an elaborate warm-up for the novel *One Hundred Years of Solitude.* They seem to be sketches, trial runs, dress rehearsals for the big novel ahead. In these stories names will appear in passing—like Colonel Aureliano Buendía, one of the heroes of *One Hundred Years*—almost as if they were coming attractions. Then, working the other way around, incidents occur in *One Hundred Years* that have been the subjects of whole stories in the earlier volumes. To know fully what is going on in García Márquez one has to have read the author in his entirety. In these stories the stages in García Márquez's literary development are on display, rather like specimens inside formaldehyde-filled jars showing progress from zygote to fully formed human. One reads these stories and witnesses his talent growing, his political ardor increasing. In these stories, too, García Márquez shows his taste for that blend of fantasy and hyperbole, exhibited in a context of reality, that is known as magic realism. (p. 62)

"What I like about you," says one character to another in the García Márquez story **"The Incredible and Sad Tale of Innocent Eréndira and Her Heartless Grandmother,"** "is the serious way you make up nonsense." Serious nonsense might stand as a blurb line for *One Hundred Years of Solitude.* E. M. Forster remarked that at a certain age one loses interest in the development of writers and wants to know only about the creation of masterpieces. Certainly *One Hundred Years of Solitude* has everywhere been so acclaimed. The novel is a chronicle of six generations of the Buendía family, founders of the village of Macondo. It recounts such extraordinary happenings as Macondo's insomnia plague, its thirty-two civil wars, banana fever, revolution, strikes, a rain that lasts five years, marriages, intermarriages, madness, and the eventual extinction of the Buendía line with the birth of an infant who has a pig's tail and who is eventually carried off by ants.

"One Hundred Years of Solitude is not a history of Latin America," García Márquez has said, "it is a *metaphor* for Latin America." With that quotation we are already in trouble. What can it mean to say that a novel is a metaphor for a continent?

Before attempting to ascertain what it might mean, tribute must be paid to the sheer brimming brilliance of *One Hundred Years of Solitude.* "Dazzling" does not seem to me in any way an imprecise word to describe the style of this novel, nor "epic" any less imprecise a word to describe its ambitions. Its contents cannot be recapitulated, for in its pages fireworks of one kind or another are always shooting off. Disquisitions on history, memory, time wind in and out of the plot. Yellow flowers fall from the sky marking a man's death; a heart-meltingly beautiful girl ascends to heaven while folding a sheet, a girl whose very smell "kept on torturing men beyond death, right down to the dust of their bones." Everything is grand, poetic, funny, often at once. A man suffers "flatulence that withered the flowers"; a woman has "a generous heart and a magnificent vocation for love." (pp. 62-3)

And yet—why do so many readers seem to bog down in this glittering work? Part of the difficulty seems to me technical, part psychological. *One Hundred Years of Solitude* is peculiarly a novel without pace; it is, for its nearly four-hundred pages, all high notes, service aces, twenty-one-gun salutes. In a novel, such nonstop virtuosity tends to pall. To use a simile to describe a novel that its author describes as a metaphor, reading *One Hundred Years* is like watching a circus artist on the trampoline who does only quadruple back somersaults. At first you are amazed to see him do it; then you are astonished that he can keep it up for so long; then you begin to wonder when he is going to be done, frankly you'd like to see something less spectacular, like a heavy-legged woman on an aged elephant.

Unless, that is, you sense a deeper meaning beneath all this virtuosity. And here it must be said that there has been no shortage of deep readings of *One Hundred Years of Solitude,* a novel which, if critics are to be consulted, has more levels than a ziggurat. There are those who think that the true meaning of the novel is solitude, or, as Alastair Reid puts it, "We all live alone on this earth in our own glass bubbles." There are those who think that the novel is about writing itself. . . . There are those who are fascinated with the book's allusiveness. . . . There are those who believe that the stuff of myth ought not to be looked at too closely. . . . Then there is García Márquez himself, who has given a clear political reading to his own novel, commenting, in an interview, "I did want to give the idea that Latin American history had such an oppressive reality that it had to be changed—at all costs, at any price!" (p. 63)

Along with magic realism, Gabriel García Márquez has given us another new literary-critical label, "political realism," which, in its own way, is itself quite magical.

If *One Hundred Years of Solitude* leaves any doubt about the political intent of García Márquez's mature work, *The Autumn of the Patriarch* wipes that doubt away. When García Márquez says that *One Hundred Years* is a metaphor for Latin America, he is of course putting a political interpretation on his own novel. But *The Autumn of the Patriarch* is neither metaphor nor symbol but a direct representation of a strong political point of view. . . .

The dictator in *The Autumn of the Patriarch* lives for more than two hundred years, his demise, á la Mark Twain, being often reported but much exaggerated. He has been in power—he has been *the* power—longer than anyone can remember, and his is the greatest solitude of all: that of the unloved dictator perpetuating his unearned power. This man, who himself can neither read nor write, is described, examined, and prosecuted with the aid of a novelistic technique as relentlessly modernist as any in contemporary fiction.

The Autumn of the Patriarch is divided into six chapters, but that is the only division in the novel, and the only concession to the reader's convenience. The book has no paragraphs, and while the punctuation mark known as the period may show up from time to time, the novel's sentences are not what one normally thinks of as sentences at all. A sentence might begin from one point of view, and before it is finished include three or four others.

One of the small shocks of this novel is to see the most complex modernist techniques put to the most patent political purposes. Now it must be said that García Márquez did not invent the Latin American dictator. Trujillo, Batista, Perón, Hernández Martinez, Duvalier (dare one add the name Fidel Castro?)—one could put together a pretty fair All Star team, though these boys are bush league compared with what Europe and Asia in this century have been able to produce.

García Márquez's portrait of the dictator in *The Autumn of the Patriarch* is an amalgam of Latin America's dictators, minus . . . Fidel and with a touch or two of Franco added. As a picture of squalor, rot, and bestiality, it is devastating. The devastation is in the details, of which the endlessly inventive García Márquez is never in short supply. (p. 64)

The Autumn of the Patriarch is about more than politics alone—time and the nature of illusion are motifs played upon artfully throughout—but politics give the novel its impetus and are finally its chief subject. These politics are highly selective, predictable, more than a trifle clichéd. Octavio Paz has said that García Márquez, as a political thinker, "repeats slogans." As

a novelist, he can make these slogans vivid, even funny, but they remain slogans. For example, the attacks on the United States in this novel come through the dictator's continuous dealings with a stream of U. S. ambassadors of perfectly Waspish and quite forgettable names—Warren, Thompson, Evans, Wilson—who in the end succeed in swindling him out of the very sea. Americans, the Catholic Church, politicians, all, in the mind and in the novels of Gabriel García Márquez, are swindlers. Liberals or conservatives, it does not matter which, they are crooks, every one of them. Which leaves—doesn't it?—only one solution: revolution.

So talented a writer is García Márquez that he can sustain a longish tale on sheer storytelling power alone, as he does in his most recent book, *Chronicle of a Death Foretold*. It has been said of García Márquez that he combines the two powerful traditions of Latin American writing: the left-wing engagé tradition of the Communist poet Pablo Neruda and the modernist mandarin tradition of Jorge Luis Borges. In this slender novel it is the Borges side that predominates. The book is about a plot on the part of twin brothers who are out to avenge their family's honor against a young man who they mistakenly believe has deflowered their sister, thus causing her husband to return her in shame to her family the morning after the wedding night. (pp. 64-5)

The tale is told with such subtle organization and such complete fluency that García Márquez can insert anything he wishes into it; and indeed the narrator does insert mention of his marriage proposal to his own wife and a brief account of his youthful dalliances with prostitutes. Such is the easy mastery of this novel that the reader is likely to forget that he never does learn who actually did deflower the virgin. *Chronicle of a Death Foretold* is a handsomely written and inconsequential book of a kind that offers ample leeway for deep readings, and one that could have been composed only by a hugely gifted writer. "Intellectuals consider themselves to be the moral conscience of society," García Márquez is quoted as saying in the New York *Times Magazine*, "so their analyses invariably follow moral rather than political channels. In this sense, I think I am the most politicized of them all." Yet, oddly, in García Márquez's fiction morality is rarely an issue; García Márquez himself seems little interested in moral questions, or in the conflicts, gradations, and agonies of moral turmoil. The reason for this, I suspect, is that for him the moral universe is already set—for him, as for so many revolutionary intellectuals, there are the moral grievances of the past, the moral hypocrisies of the present, and, waiting over the horizon, the glories of the future, when moral complexity will be abolished. The moral question is, for García Márquez, ultimately a political question. Outside of his politics, García Márquez's stories and novels have no moral center; they inhabit no moral universe. They are passionate chiefly when they are political; and when they are political, so strong is the nature of their political bias that they are, however dazzling, flawed.

Thus, to return to where I set out, a short answer to my question—how good is Gabriel García Márquez?—is that he is, in the strict sense of the word, marvelous. The pity is that he is not better. (p. 65)

Joseph Epstein, "How Good Is Gabriel García Márquez?" in *Commentary,* Vol. 75, No. 5, May, 1983, pp. 59-65.

SOURCES FOR FURTHER STUDY

Bell-Villada, Gene H. *García Márquez: The Man and His Work.* Chapel Hill: University of North Carolina Press, 1990, 247 p.

Supplements biographical discussion with essays on García Márquez's fiction.

Fau, Margaret Eustella. *Gabriel García Márquez: An Annotated Bibliography, 1947-1979.* Westport, Conn.: Greenwood Press, 1980, 198 p.

Extensive English-language bibliography of primary and secondary sources.

—————, and de Gonzalez, Nelly Sfeir. *Bibliographic Guide to Gabriel García Márquez, 1979-1985.* Westport, Conn.: Greenwood Press, 1986, 181 p.

Continuation of Fau's bibliography, cited above.

Harss, Luis, and Dohmann, Barbara. "Gabriel García Márquez; or, The Lost Chord." *Into the Mainstream: Conversations with Latin-American Writers,* pp. 310-41. New York: Harper & Row, 1967.

Recounts discussion with García Márquez about his childhood, the fictional world of Macondo, his political views, and his major works.

McMurray, George R., ed. *Critical Essays on Gabriel García Márquez.* Boston: G. K. Hall & Co., 1987, 224 p.

Contains several reviews of and essays on García Márquez's short fiction, novellas, and major novels.

Ortega, Julio, ed. *Gabriel García Márquez and the Powers of Fiction.* Austin: University of Texas Press, 1988, 97 p.

Contains discussions of García Márquez's fiction and a translation of his 1982 Nobel Prize lecture.

André Gide

1869-1951

(Full name André Paul Guillaume Gide) French novelist, novella writer, dramatist, diarist, critic, autobiographer, essayist, and poet.

INTRODUCTION

*C*redited with introducing modern experimental techniques to the French novel, Gide is highly esteemed for the autobiographical honesty of his work, which depicts the moral development of a modern intellectual. His work is recognized for its diversity in both form and content, yet critics have also noted that his characters consistently reflect his own moral and philosophical conflicts. For this reason, commentators on Gide's works often attach as much significance to biographical detail as they do to artistic method.

Gide was born in Paris in 1869. His father, a professor of Roman law at the University of Paris, died when Gide was eleven years old. Consequently, Gide was raised by his domineering and highly protective mother, a strict Calvinist whose family background was Norman and Catholic. In later years Gide often attributed his divided nature to this mixed southern Huguenot and Norman Catholic heritage. Gide attended the Ecole Alsacienne and the Lycée Henri IV in Paris, but frequently required private tutoring at home because of his delicate health. As a young man, Gide traveled to the Middle East in an attempt to escape the stifling Calvinist atmosphere of his home. There, the exotic surroundings inspired him to pursue previously denied sensual pleasures; in Algiers, Gide discovered and celebrated his bisexual inclinations for the first time. However, his early religious training continued to influence him, and he became obsessed with resolving the struggle between the puritan and the libertine in his nature. After his return to France, Gide married his cousin Madeleine. Their attachment was deep and unremitting, and Gide described it as "the devotion of my whole life," but the marriage was traumatic for them both. Although Gide expressed an overwhelming spiritual need to share his life with his cousin, and she provided him with a source of stability, her strict Christian values often conflicted with his unconventional life-style which specifically separated love and sexual pleasure. Many of his mature works were inspired by the difficulties that he experienced in this relationship. *La porte étroite* (1909; *Strait Is the Gate*) and *L'immoraliste* (1902; *The Immoralist*), in particular, portray characters who are carried to destructive extremes of behavior by forces within their natures similar to those that Gide perceived in himself and in Madeleine. All of Gide's works are in some way reflections of his emotional struggles, and critics agree that one source of Gide's genius lay in his ability to translate the contradictions and complexities of his nature into art. Two works which effectively delineate the conflict in Gide's personality are *Les cahiers d'André Walter* (1891; *The Notebooks of André Walter*), a poetic treatment of the theme of spiritual love, and *Les nourritures terrestres* (1897; *The Fruits of the Earth*), a lyrical paean to sensuality.

Another important factor in Gide's development as a writer was his concern with social issues. Although Gide occasionally exhibited a conservatism consistent with his privileged position in society, his social conscience was awakened early by his travels to Chad and the Congo in the 1890s. The brutal treatment of natives under Dutch and Belgian rule prompted him to write a controversial attack on the practice of colonialism. In the 1920s he was again embroiled in controversy when *Corydon* (1924), his notorious defense of homosexuality, appeared. Gide turned to communism in the 1930s as did many other intellectuals who saw it as an acceptable compromise to the conflict between the rights of the individual and the need for more equitable social and economic opportunities. However, Gide found a visit to the Soviet Union in 1936 disillusioning. Upon his return he published his negative impressions of the Communist experiment in his *Retour de l'U.R.S.S.* (1936; *Return from the U.S.S.R.*), and was bitterly criticized by many of his former associates. During World War II, when Gide was in his seventies, he once again took a social stand when he left occupied France rather than succumb to pressure from the collaborationist Vichy regime to lend his support to the Nazi cause. Gide died in 1951.

Throughout his literary career Gide adapted his style to suit his subject matter, resulting in an unusually wide variety of works. Such early efforts as *The Notebooks of André Walter* and *The Fruits of the Earth* are rich in metaphor and lyric beauty, as befits works concerned with an impressionable young man's first encounters with life. The poetic prose contained in these books reveals the influence upon Gide of Stéphane Mallarmé and the Symbolists. Gide abandoned Symbolism, however, in favor of a simpler, more classical style when he began experimenting with themes and forms drawn from the Bible and Greek mythology. Gide

also discovered the works of Johann Wolfgang von Goethe, and was influenced by the German writer's classicism. All of these factors played an important part in the development of Gide's mature style. For example, he made use of ancient myth in such works as *Philoctéte, Le Prométhée mal enchainé* (1899; *Prometheus Misbound*), and *Thésée* (1946; *Theseus*), his celebrated study of the problems of the mature artist; while his drama *Saül* and *Numquid et tu . . . ?* (1926), a series of meditations on the New Testament, are both based on biblical materials. Critics have also noted logical and formal similarities between Gide's *récits,* or psychological narratives, such as *Strait Is the Gate* and *La symphonie pastorale* (1919; *The Pastoral Symphony*), and biblical parables. Some believe that his farcical *soties,* such as *Paludes* (1895; *Marshlands*) and *Les Caves du Vatican* (1914; *Lafcadio's Adventures*), are derived from the same source.

Gide's most ambitious and stylistically elaborate achievement was the novel *Les faux monnayeurs* (1925; *The Counterfeiters*), a work that owes a great deal to Gide's reading of Fyodor Dostoevsky. *The Counterfeiters* is an experimental novel, the form of which is derived from patterns in music. In it, Gide attempted to reproduce the unstructured chaos of everyday life through the use of meaningless episodes, conversations, and Dostoevskian interruptions of action at moments of great intensity. Linear chronology is abandoned as several unrelated stories occur simultaneously. The novel's theme, as Justin O'Brien has noted, is entirely Dostoevskian: the demoniacal role of the intelligence and the power of convention to counterfeit life. Although Gide's innovations in *The Counterfeiters* were important to the development of the French novel, he did not continue to pursue that experimental vein. Later works, such as *Oedipe* (1931; *Oedipus*) and *Theseus,* are written in a severely classical style that eschews the inventive audacity of Gide's earlier works.

One of Gide's primary artistic and philosophical concerns was authenticity. He discussed his life in a way that has been called exhibitionistic by some critics, while others discern religious overtones in his "unremitting search for self-correction and self-purification." Alfred Kazin, in discussing the psychology of Gide's highly confessional works, observed that "he would like to be both free and good, and failing both, had compromised by being honest." The much-discussed Gidean notions of "sincerity"—which Germaine Brèe has summarized as signifying the "struggle of human beings with truths compulsively followed"—and *"disponibilité,"* which Gide interpreted as, "following one's inclinations, so long as they lead upward," were products of this lifelong passion for self-awareness. However, Gide's critics are quick to point out that although he used forms conducive to autobiographical honesty, such as first person novels, journals, and personal essays, Gide did not reveal himself completely in his works. There are significant omissions in the *Journals*, and the characters in his fiction, although they are based in part on himself, often distort the image of the artist even as they disclose it. This occurs because Gide's fictional technique was to create a character abstracted from a single aspect of his personality. Thus the nature of his characters often varied widely from work to work. Moreover, Gide was constantly reexamining his assumptions, so it is not uncommon for successive novels to portray contradictory beliefs and situations. Still, Gide's shifting concerns did not reflect indecisiveness, as early critics charged. Rather, they were the external evidence of his continual dialogue with himself.

Although he was well known and respected among his fellow writers, Gide remained unrecognized by the general public until the 1920s, when his involvement as founder and editor of the prestigious *La nouvelle revue française* led to his discovery by a postwar generation of youth who rejected social conventions and embraced both his restless search for spiritual values and his belief that life should be lived to its emotional and intellectual fullest. His influence on the generation of Albert Camus and Jean Genet was significant, and, though he rejected existentialism, he was unarguably one of its forerunners. The importance of his examination of private morality and its effect on society was recognized in 1947 when, after a lifetime of neglect due largely to his public confession of homosexuality, he was awarded the Nobel Prize for literature.

Critics today are divided in their assessment of Gide's novels. While some perceive them as dated and of only minor interest for contemporary readers, others, such as Henri Peyre, maintain that the perfection of Gide's style and the sincerity with which he set out to expose social, religious, artistic, and sexual hypocrisy guarantee the novels a permanent place in twentieth-century literature. There is far more consensus among critics about the value of Gide's voluminous *Journals*. Despite the charges of narcissism that are often raised in discussions of the *Journals*, most critics agree with Philip Toynbee that Gide's "greatest talent was for portraying himself against the carefully delineated background of his time," and that the *Journals* today retain "all the interest for us which can be earned by a patient sincerity, an eager curiosity, and a brilliant pen."

(For further information about Gide's life and works, see *Contemporary Authors*, Vols. 104, 124; *Dictionary of Literary Biography*, Vol. 65: *French Novelists, 1900-1930*; *Major Twentieth-Century Writers*; and *Twentieth-Century Literary Criticism*, Vols. 5, 12, 36.)

CRITICAL COMMENTARY

HERMANN HESSE

(essay date 1933)

[Hesse is considered one of the most important German novelists of the twentieth century. In the excerpt below from a 1933 essay, he provides a brief review of Gide's dialogue, *Corydon*.]

The four dialogues [in **"Corydon"**], beginning with a natural history of love and ending with a kind of metaphysic of love, contain Gide's confession to pederasty and at the same time constitute the most significant contribution to this theme made in our time. They not only vindicate pederasty by freeing it from the character of perversion or crime; they divest the whole theme of that false solemnity and moralism into which it was forced by the middle class and the law. Over and above all this, they become a theory of love in general.

Hermann Hesse, "André Gide: 'Corydon'," in his *My Belief: Essays on Life and Art*, edited by Theodore Ziolkowski, translated by Denver Lindley, Farrar, Straus and Giroux, 1974, p. 336.

RÉGIS MICHAUD

(essay date 1934)

[In the following excerpt, Michaud discusses Gide as moralist and thinker.]

From his *Cahiers d'André Walter* (1891), to his drama *Oedipe* (1932) André Gide's literary career has run uninterrupted for forty years . . . (p. 79)

The *Cahiers d'André Walter*, written at twenty, showed him tortured by contradictions in feeling and thought, between platonic love and the erotic impulse, between mysticism and the critical sense. He called the Bible, Spinoza, poetry and music to his rescue, and he heroically strove to find a new and personal means of

Principal Works

Les cahiers d'André Walter (novel) 1891
    [The Notebooks of André Walter, 1968]
Les poésies d'André Walter (prose poems) 1892
Le traité du Narcisse (essay) 1892
Le voyage d'Urien (novella) 1892
    [Urien's Voyage, 1964]
Paludes (novella) 1895
    [Marshlands published in Marshlands and Prometheus
    Misbound, 1953]
Les nourritures terrestres (prose poems) 1897
    [The Fruits of the Earth, 1949]
Philoctéte (drama) 1899
Le Prométhée mal enchaîné (novella) 1899
    [Prometheus Illbound, 1919; also published as Prome-
    theus Misbound in Marshlands and Prometheus Mis-
    bound, 1953]
Le Roi Candaule (drama) 1901
L'immoraliste (novel) 1902
    [The Immoralist, 1930]
Prétextes (essays) 1903
    [Pretexts, 1959]
Saül (drama) 1903
La porte étroite (novel) 1909
    [Strait Is the Gate, 1924]
Isabelle (novella) 1911
    [Isabelle published in Two Symphonies, 1931]
Les caves du Vatican (novel) 1914
    [The Vatican Swindle, 1925; also published as Lafca-
    dio's Adventures, 1928]
La symphonie pastorale (novella) 1919
    [The Pastoral Symphony published in Two Symphonies,
    1931]
Dostoïevsky (criticism) 1923
    [Dostoevsky, 1925]

Corydon (dialogues) 1924
    [Corydon, 1950]
Les faux monnayeurs (novel) 1925
    [The Counterfeiters, 1927; also published as The Coin-
    ers, 1927]
Si le grain ne meurt (autobiography) 1925
    [If It Die, 1950]
Numquid et tu . . . ? (meditations) 1926
Voyage au Congo (travel essays) 1927
    [Travels in the Congo, 1930]
L'école des femmes (novella) 1929
    [The School for Wives, 1929]
Oedipe (drama) 1931
    [Oedipus published in Two Legends: Oedipus and The-
    seus, 1950]
Retour de l'U.R.S.S. (travel essays) 1936
    [Return from the U.S.S.R., 1937; also published as
    Back from the U.S.S.R., 1937]
Journal, 1889-1939 (journal) 1939
Journal, 1939-1942 (journal) 1946
Thésée (novella) 1946
    [Theseus, 1948]
The Journals of André Gide, 1889-1949. 4 vols. (journals)
    1947-51
Journal, 1942-1949 (journal) 1950
Et nunc manet in te, suivi de journal intime (journal) 1951
    [Madeleine, 1952]
Le journal des faux monnayeurs (journal) 1951
    [Logbook of the Coiners, 1952]
My Theatre (dramas and essays) 1951
Ainsi soit-il; ou, Les jeux sont fait (memoir) 1952
    [So Be It; or, The Chips Are Down, 1959]
The Return of the Prodigal (essays and dramas) 1953

expression. The success of the book did not come up to his expectations, but it brought him into touch with the late Parnassians and the Symbolists, with Herédia and Mallarmé. It marked the beginning of what may be called his Symbolist period, the period of his lyrical treatises from *Le Traité du Narcisse* to *Les Nourritures terrestres.* Gide had found all the fascination of the visible world and was already bent on brooding much over himself. Like Narcissus he went to look at himself in the water of the springs, but the water flowed, and how could he grasp and hold the following phantoms? And which is true, the water or the images in the water?

Gide was already passionately searching for reality through appearances, and reflection was as dear to

him as dreams. He was a poet with a conscience, intent on finding some faith beyond images and words—some faith beyond his books. How pallid, dull and prosaic life was, Gide told half sarcastically, half tragically in *Paludes,* a smart handbook of disillusion. There Tityre did not find any better solace than to fish for worms in the mud while wishing to leave everybody and everything behind. There, as in his other treatises, Gide longed for something new, something unforeseen and gratuitous. To start on a journey somewhere and to stop nowhere! Urien, in *Le Voyage d'Urien,* went on an imaginary journey and reached the polar sea only to wish that he had never been there. The plight of this world was ennui and the only duty was evasion. Anything was better than to live in the dark caves and become blind because of not knowing how to open one's eyes. He had found one of his leit-motifs.

Gide himself, however, did not sail for the Arctic, but in 1893 through southern Italy he left for Algeria, where he spent two years, and we owe to this journey *Les Nourritures terrestres.* This book is Gide's song of songs, a symphony in two movements, an allegro at the beginning and an andante at the end. This hymn to the joy of life ends as a dirge on the vanity of all things. To escape from his scruples he had then come to a capital decision. He would surrender to instinctive life without any reserve and disregard all he had been told to obey. He bathed in cold springs, courted shepherds, loafed in the oases, sang the roundelay of desires, the lure of the desert, and listened to the cynical teachings of Ménalque. He tried, as he declared, to gain his freedom of mind through a thorough exhaustion of all his senses. To cleanse body and soul and be born anew, to find eternity in the bliss of every second, this was the first part of the symphony. Then, alas! came the funeral march and the passionate pilgrim returned empty-handed. Desire was all, provided that it was never fulfilled; traveling was fine if only one stopped nowhere. No thirst could be quenched, no beauty could be grasped, and Gide advised his disciple Nathanael to throw away his song of songs when he had read it. There was nothing to seize and nothing to love; at least one could remain free and ready to start again. Who knows but that wisdom meant giving away all things and above all the desire of possession? Who knows but that self-renunciation was the sum of all wisdom?

Gide dramatized his North African experience in his novel *L'Immoraliste.* . . . , the meaning of which is clearly indicated by the title. In this book he went searching more and more for what he called "the complete possibilities of man," and, as he declared, for the full disposal and employment of oneself through the painstaking exercise of his mind. Could one be daring enough to "turn the page," renounce morals, and be born anew? A man was the only law unto himself. Let him stretch to the utmost all his energies, good and bad, to reach happiness. Culture has killed life; let us revive it through instinct. The story took us to Normandy and to Algeria. Michel, the hero, was married without love to Marceline, and Marceline was an obstacle in his path. Michel was a scholar, but life had become dearer to him than books, and all the dearer as he was threatened with consumption. He would leave all behind, shed the "old man" and exert himself beyond good and evil. Michel answered the call of the wild and lost his moral sense systematically. Health came back to him in the oases, where he consorted with young Arabs. At the advice of his tempter, Ménalque, he shed all his prejudices and his education.

We then see him practising his new ethics on his Normandy estate, where he went so far as to play the poacher at his own expense. He had discovered the dark side of life and went back to Africa to perfect his experience. What would become of poor and devoted Marceline in the company of such a superman? The question was hardly worth debating at this stage, and he let Marceline die in order to better find himself and be happy. But happiness did not come, and at the end of the book Michel had lost all his enthusiasm. Lonely and empty-handed he sent an S.O.S. to his friends in Paris to help him start on a new journey—to what destination we are not told. Would he start again for the sake of starting, as Gide recommended in his treatise on the prodigal son (*Le Retour de l'Enfant prodigue*), or would he learn at last the lesson of self-sacrifice and renunciation as taught in *Philoctéte* and *Le Roi Candaule?* Gide never converted his characters; he left them to their fate and wrote new books.

The leit-motif of renunciation versus self-love was the theme of *La Porte étroite,* where once more Gide staged the conflict of instincts and Christian morals. The story reads as a plea for spiritual versus natural love, for sanctity against passion, until we come to the end of the book to learn from Alissa's journals that pride had been her real motive in refusing Jerôme. She really loved him and would have been his had he been daring enough. Both were victims of their scruples. Their story was the tragedy of timidity and pride parading under the disguise of mysticism and platonic love, the tragedy of hypocrisy. Thus the book shows us Gide already in possession of most of his major themes and already very deft in handling his double-edged tactics. His casuistry could already be summed up in a doctrine of salvation through surrendering to one's instincts. The only true morals taught the integral fulfilment of instinctive desires and the necessity of exploring the worst in man unhampered. No limits nor tabus must be set to personal experience, and only when all his possibilities have been tried can man be put on his road to God.

That Gide insisted on preaching his new morals under the disguise of the gospels shows well what grasp his Puritan education had on him. Even at the time of his most romantic escapades he never parted with his Bible. Long before he wrote his comment on the gospels in *Numquid et tu* and his book on Dostoievsky he had found in the Scriptures a text on which he became very fond of commenting. "He who will save his soul shall lose it" was already quoted in *La Porte étroite* as the A B C of Christianity as interpreted by Gide, and it came back in all his books. In Gide's interpretation it teaches the renunciation not of evil but of good, and especially the doing away with self-respect. It holds sin to be a safer way to perfection than so-called virtue, for virtue is always pride. Sin teaches humility, which is the only approach to God. Let us try our worst instincts, were it only to know that they exist; let us revel in all that is dark and sinister in us, so that at the end of our distress we can find true good and clamor for it. Of all sins hypocrisy is the greatest and all the thoughts in us must be confessed. Let us not shun temptation but rather court it.

Temptation, sin, renunciation, confession, humility—Gide's vocabulary, if not his thoughts, is so far orthodox; and so is the homage he pays to the devil. Evil is no empty word for him; as for Dostoievsky, whom he so much admires, evil is a synonym for the evil one, Satan, in whose existence he confessedly believes and whom he restores to his rights in his last books.

Gide knows well that his moral program runs counter to accepted standards, and this explains the stand he has taken in his later books. *Les Caves du Vatican, Les Faux-Monnayeurs,* are a denunciation of hypocrisy and deceit in a light or a tragic mood. Public morals are a system of tabus meant to forbid man an access to his dark side, a system of conventions intended to hide and disguise man in his own eyes. It puts a premium on duplicity and makes people live a double life as cheaters and counterfeiters. Society has been prospering on the interdiction of what is most personal and original in the individual man or woman. It has made a law of conformity and encouraged every individual to force upon others a false and ready-made portrait of himself. Most personalities are not natural but manufactured, and, as Gide would have us believe, "we live counterfeited." Nobody dares to be himself and there is no prospect of change and progress in what we are. In a world where everybody cheats, an honest man can only be a mountebank. So let us not be duped.

Against social hypocrisy Gide staged his doctrine of "actes gratuits"—of gratuitous and free actions— and he intrusted the defense of his doctrine to one of his most puzzling characters, young and unconventional Lafcadio. Gratuitous actions are the keystone of his ethics and the consistent conclusion of his plea for individual freedom. They set aside causation and motives in conduct and proclaim the right of every man to invent *ex tempore* his actions. They are, to his mind, an efficient weapon to break the moral and social structure and evade what is called responsibility. When he saves a girl from fire or throws an old man out of a train Lafcadio can neither be rewarded nor punished, since he acted without intention. There can be a legal sanction to his acts, according as they are beneficial or harmful to society, but he cannot be judged, since there is nothing to judge. Did not the gospels say, "Judge not, that ye be not judged"? (See his *Souvenirs de la cour d'Assises,* some personal recollections of the criminal courts.) Any act to be pure must be personal, entire and immediate. Forethought and pre-vision forestall innocence. Pride begins when a man reflects too long before he acts and asks himself questions about what he must or can do. Such action is a sin and a challenge to God.

If you cannot act, be content with thinking, and maybe somebody will come to translate your thought into a deed, a poor imitation of what could have been an original masterpiece. Act first and think afterward, as does Lafcadio. Your action then cannot be labeled or pigeonholed, and it does not bind you to any laws and standards. Spontaneity is better than ethics. Gide himself, however, qualified his own theory and felt the flaws in his system when he had Lafcadio contradicted by an opponent and left in a quandary in respect to his own acts at the end of the book.

Les Caves du Vatican was called a "sotie" or light farce by the author. Irony ran on a high key from the beginning to the end of the book. Fantastic as it seemed, Gide had not invented the great Vatican swindle, but had found it in the newspapers. Thenceforth he fondly collected the casual news in the papers— what the French call *faits divers*—especially criminal cases, as a key to the study of human behavior undisguised. He did it especially to write *Les Faux-Monnayeurs,* the central and final episodes of which were found in the newspaper columns. In that book, according to his own confession, he tried to "demonetize beautiful feelings" and dramatize the way social and moral constraints check and stifle our best possibilities. It is a tragedy of appearances, of what is and of what seems to be. So far Gide had not dared to call his stories novels, but *récits.* Now at fifty-five he went systematically into fiction writing, and composed what may be considered the great book of the post-war period, pouring into it, as he said, all he knew of life. The title, as translated into English, tells the true meaning of the book. It takes us among counterfeiters, young and old, in a literal and figurative sense. It is a searching investigation of duplicity, a game where cards have been falsified and where every player cheats himself and others. Some do it unwittingly, others deliberately. It is the book of Gide's sympathies and antipathies, a mirror of his life and of that of his times. He took a cruel revenge on his Puritan boyhood, his parents and educators, and made an excruciating study of delinquent youth. What a Mephistophelian epic, what an assault on conformity, what a lie given to the traditionalists, and what a dissection of the human heart!

Gide's most original trick in the book was to give it to us to read just as it was being thought out and written by the author himself, who was present in the story. Reality, Gide told us, interested him only so far as it was turned into a work of art, and so it was, under our very eyes. Edouard's journal in the book (supplemented by *Le Journal des Faux-Monnayeurs*) was a treatise on the art of fiction written by a novelist eager to conciliate the French tradition and modern and foreign models. Concerning psychology we were told that there were new depths to explore of which French novelists had not been aware, and Edouard's views in this respect were endorsed by a professional psychoanalyst in the novel. Concerning art Edouard took the stand against realism and claimed that fiction must put side by side art and reality. His first duty was to be methodically concrete, but particulars had no value to him unless they were made universal. This was the classical method, than which none was ever more perfect.

This example illustrates very well Gide's favorite method and that inner necessity which forced him always to mix thought with art and fill with comments the margins of his books, an original but not, perhaps, an ideal process. Notes and comments cannot well make up for that perfect fusion of art and life which has been achieved by the great classicists.

Taken all together *The Counterfeiters* is Gide's great work, a sinister and cynical book for those readers who fear to enter the inferno of life, but nevertheless containing some gleams of hope. The devil roams at large in its pages, but there are some guardian angels, and young Bernard, the hero, is not altogether unsympathetic. Gide took up counterfeiting again in his novelettes, *Isabelle, La Symphonie pastorale, L'École des Femmes,* and *Robert.* There, once more, men and women played at blind man's buff and cheated each other more or less knowingly. The blind maid in the Symphony was a transparent symbol of the moral blindness of the minister, her guardian. The *School for Wives* and *Robert* drew two contradictory portraits of a man who forged his identity to the woman he loved.

The critical and personal character of Gide's works must not be overemphasized to the detriment of his positive and more general teachings. We may well conclude from his own confessions in and outside his books that his stories are, to a large extent, his own story and an *apologia pro vita sua,* a record of his evasions. As elusive a personality as his could not be held in a book, but it was there just the same, and critics traced his leit-motifs back to the idiosyncrasies and anomalies which he confessed so candidly in his autobiography. They hinted that perhaps he was a hypocrite himself and used sophistry to hide his abnormalities behind the gospels. Evasion, instability, gratuitous actions and the gospel of sincerity at any cost were the consequence of his personal obsessions and were desperate efforts to cover his morbid propensities.

Yet the value of Gide's books cannot be made to depend only upon his confessions. In the form of exhortations and maxims they are a pathetic plea in favor of a new life. They recommend a free exploration of human resources beyond tabus and barriers. Away with hypocrisy, let us shun happiness and foreclose all our mortgages; let man arise, confess his sins, gird his loins and start on a new journey. Let him live a dangerous life, court risks and adventures and find new gods. Invention is better than imitation and heresy than conformity. Nothing is simple in life; let us like and cultivate our complexities. Who knows but that the impulses we call abnormal, strange and morbid can put us on the way to new discoveries and creations?

"I say that man was made to grow, not to stop," quotes Gide from Browning. Man has not said his last word, and his soul can still expand. Let an author write not to please but to stir and disturb. Let him push his fellow men toward new destinies through the forbidden lands of life.

These formal books, treatises, dramas, farces and novels represent only one phase of Gide's literary activities. They show the point where his secret thoughts came to the surface, but they were fed by many rivulets under ground. He has turned into art only a part of his thoughts. There is a large collection of diaries, letters, notes and essays which must be read to know him fully. Art to him comes only second to thought, and while most writers have put themselves wholly in their books, Gide has kept the best of himself for his marginalia. His influence spread largely through these side issues. It grew slowly at first and unofficially, but little by little he emerged as an intellectual leader. . . . His real triumph came after the war at the age of fifty, and he presided over the brilliant 1920-1930 decade. Then his early books were reprinted and his position could no longer be challenged. He could go undisguised in public and preach or shock as he liked. He did so by publishing his autobiography, *Si le Grain ne meurt,* and *Corydon,* in which he put into practise his doctrine that all thoughts must be confessed.

The young insurgents flocked around his banners and proclaimed him their master. It seemed that he had been twenty-five years in advance of the new generation and that he had drawn its portrait before it was born. Here were the new revoltees with their restlessness, their anarchy and their critical awareness. *The Counterfeiters* was a true epic of the new times. Gide at fifty was still young for liberty, and he hailed the new revolutions, stretched his hand to Dada and renounced all the past. His hour had come, although he knew many contradictions and fell a prey to bitter attacks (at the hands of MM. Henri Massis and Henri Béraud especially). He was not yet at the end of his journey. He had shown the way toward new standards, toward sincerity, integrity, the joys of life and of self-sacrifice. Midway between Nietzsche and Dostoievsky he had announced the advent of a new man. "Sprung out of the unknown," exclaimed Oedipus, "no more past, no more models. Nothing to lean on. All to be created, fatherland, ancestors to be invented and discovered. Nobody to imitate but myself." Oedipus had slain the Sphinx; there were no more sphinxes; the solution of our problems was within ourselves.

Gide so far had paraded as a rugged individualist. His journey to the Congo in 1925 made a Socialist of him after seeing civilization at work. A man could not be happy alone, and everybody must have his fair share of worldly goods and "nourritures terrestres." He came back from Africa with two books purposely written in a prosaic and matter-of-fact way. He had found men among the savages and savages among the civilized white men. . . . Men were the same everywhere and there was no exoticism in Gide's eyes. Pierre Loti's nostalgia was not his; he spent most of his time investigating the conditions in that part of France's colonial empire, and his reports were none too pleasant.. . . . (pp. 80-93)

As a writer Gide has acted as a disintegrating force in French literature. His literary evolution has followed closely his moral evolution. He renounced one by one all literary adornments to reach a sort of asceticism. He left behind all artistic writing as it was practised in his early days. He flirted with Parnasse and with Symbolism and soon renounced them. Herédia and Mallarmé could not be his masters, and as he advanced in life he gave up more and more imagism and lyricism to adhere to the naked truth and the naked style. To music, which was so dear to him, he preferred design. To his mind classicism alone made an art of necessity. Classicism acted, in regard to romanticism, as an instrument of control and sublimation. Romanticism gave the emotions and that inner ardor without which there can be no art, but classicism provided the discipline and the rules. . . . (pp. 93-4)

In regard to his contemporaries none contributed more than he to bringing to a close the nineteenth century tradition and to alienating the new generation from the literary leaders in the first two decades of the new century. This he did through his searching criticism of some of the leaders of the pre-war period, ruining, for instance, Paul Bourget's traditionalism through his attack on family standards, challenging Barrés's position in regard to the "uprooted," dismissing Anatole France as a writer without a conscience and Romain Rolland as a sentimentalist. Call no man your master, but if you need models, follow the example of such men as Stendhal, Baudelaire, Rimbaud, Dostoievsky or Whitman. Writing must put us on our road to life and to freedom, and it must renew itself as everything else. The World War spared nothing; it destroyed cathedrals and factories and upset standards; why should words and the art of writing be spared? How despair of the future when such artists as Proust and Valéry were alive? No limits, no definitions—this, in the last analysis, is Gide's motto. Let it also be a warning to his readers and critics. . . . (pp. 94-5)

Régis Michaud, "The Leadership of André Gide," in his *Modern Thought and Literature in France,* Funk & Wagnalls, 1934, pp. 72-95.

Gide in Biskra, Algeria, during his first visit to Africa in 1893.

GEORGES LEMAITRE

(essay date 1938)

[Lemaitre was an Algerian-born American educator and critic. In the following excerpt, he observes how Gide typically eschews moral conventions in his works.]

The powers of darkness have a favourite lurking place in man's subconscious mind. Gide has a special predilection for hunting them out, not in order to destroy them, but mainly for the sheer interest of discovering them and bringing them to the light. He experiences a strange pleasure in exposing in the most respectable and even most saintly people unsuspected and reprehensible phases of mentality. Quite often these workings of the subconscious mind are hidden, even from the person in whom they occur, behind a sophistry of well-reasoned arguments. For instance, in the *Symphonie Pastorale,* when the pastor, who is passionately in love with young Gertrude, though he is not aware of it, understands that Jacques is about to propose to her, he emphatically disapproves on purely moral grounds, and succeeds in sending away his too obedient son and rival. Almost every man, according to Gide, has a definite ugly strain in him, perhaps limited to subconscious longings, or displaying itself in imagination only—more often finding an outlet in a secret life of shame, carefully concealed from all but his partner in guilt. Gide loves to pry into these most private affairs, not so much, as in the case of Proust, in order to study the intricate psychological mechanism involved but rather because he finds a specific moral—or immoral—interest in the cases themselves. A man whose life is devoid of these complications must, he thinks, have a very poor and empty personality. Has not Goethe said, as Gide remembers only too well, that the power of a man is recognizable by what he has of the Devil in him? Thus Gide is interested particularly in turbid and heavily burdened souls. In *L'Immoraliste* Michel shows a small liking for the good little boys who are his wife's special pets. On a certain occasion, however, he sees one of them steal a pair of scissors and immediately he is greatly attracted to him. Gide presents an insinuating picture of these tendencies in people. He seldom states facts plainly. He merely makes suggestions, awakening suspicions by implications and hints; he stirs the reader's curiosity and often sends the imagination wandering along forbidden paths. So he succeeds in conveying a half-veiled but all the more convincing impression of the hideous festering larvae that are bred at the bottom of man's soul.

Yet love, according to Gide's experiences, appears to be singularly free from these unsavoury elements. He has retained a perfectly pure and almost immaterial conception of love, a legacy of his idealistic education and the youthful enthusiasm of his adolescence. Real love is for him a spiritual longing, which springs up, often at first sight, between two people of noble character. It has its source in the innermost recesses of the human soul—in fact, is part of the very soul and therefore should live and endure as long as the soul itself. Its ethereal nature places it out of the reach of disappointment and decay. Such a pure and exalted sentiment naturally precludes any possibility of defiling relationship; and indeed the very idea of combining ideal love with physical pleasure appears to Gide to be a sort of profanation. Between the two there can be no compromise. Woman as an ideal of moral devotion fills him with respect and admiration. Woman as an object of desire inspires him with loathing and disgust. In the *Faux-Monnayeurs,* young Olivier, speaking of his first experience of physical love, says to a friend: " 'It is disgusting. It is horrible. . . . Afterwards I wanted to spit,

to be sick, to tear my skin off, to kill myself,"—"You are exaggerating!"—"To kill *her.*' " Was this the last remnant of Gide's puritanical abhorrence of the sins of the flesh?—or just the result of his own idiosyncrasy? At any rate the ending of *Le roi Candaule* clearly shows his position. 'That face of yours, so beautiful, Madam, I thought it should remain veiled.'—'Veiled for you, Gyges. Candaule has torn my veil.'—'Well, then, sew it up again.'

Gide does not deny that pleasure is permissible, even right; but it belongs to an entirely different type of experience from love. Just as sensuality would besmirch true love, love would hamper the free play of healthy sensuality. 'I had made up my mind to dissociate pleasure from love; and it even seemed to me that this divorce was desirable, that in this way pleasure was rendered purer, love more perfect, if heart and flesh were not entangled in each other.' A man will attain more harmonious fulfilment of his divergent desires and aspirations by not confining them all to one other person alone; his ideal longings may expend themselves in more or less distant worship of one ideal being, and his earthly passions will best be satisfied by a variety of ephemeral adventure. (pp. 187-89)

Georges Lemaitre, "André Gide," in his *Four French Novelists: Marcel Proust, André Gide, Jean Giraudoux, Paul Morand,* 1938. Reprint by Kennikat Press, 1969, pp. 115-208.

JUSTIN O'BRIEN
(essay date 1951)

[O'Brien is best known for his many studies of modern French literature. In the following excerpt from a 1951 essay, he traces the origin of many of the plot and narrative techniques that Gide used in *Les faux monnayeurs* and earlier works.]

Just what does Gide mean by a *récit?* The word signifies merely a narration and is by no means so exact a designation as *conte* or *nouvelle.* It is vague and not very committal. All his tales have certain elements in common: (1) concentration of action, (2) limitation to two, three, or four characters with almost no incidental figures, (3) a personal form of narration by one of the interested parties, and (4) a directness and simplicity of style. In other words, the tale as Gide conceives it is a narrative of crisis, an active type of fiction, close in form to the famous seventeenth-century novel *La Princesse de Clèves* or even to the French classical tragedy of Racine. It is highly dramatic because of the concentration of action and because of the narration by one of the actors. It is noteworthy that *L'Immoraliste (The Immoralist)* is told entirely by the chief protagonist to a group of friends who may be able to help him. On the very first page he says: "I am going to tell you my life simply, without modesty and without pride, more simply than if I were talking to myself." *La Porte étroite (Strait Is the Gate)* is again a direct narrative made by the principal actor Jérôme, who begins: "Some people might have made a book out of it; but the story I am going to tell is one which it took all my strength to live and over which I spent all my virtue. So I shall set down my recollections quite simply. . . . " But at one point in Jérôme's account he is obliged to describe the most intimate emotions of his beloved, which he could not possibly have known. Hence Gide has him discover her journal after her death and that journal is incorporated verbatim into the novel. *La Symphonie pastorale (The Pastoral Symphony)* is entirely in the form of a journal kept by the principal male character, the Pastor himself. On the very first page the Pastor notes: "I will take advantage of the leisure this enforced confinement affords me to think over the past and to set down how I came to take charge of Gertrude." The use of direct narration and especially of the diary form has obvious advantages and disadvantages. Its appearance in so many of André Gide's works—even in [*Les Faux-Monnayeurs (The Counterfeiters)*] he will have a novelist character commenting on events in his own diary—suggests that the journal is Gide's form *par excellence* and that his imaginative works might almost be considered to be extracted from his own *Journals.* It would be more just to say that the habit of spiritual self-scrutiny contracted during his pious childhood and reinforced by the fairly regular keeping of his own diary has caused him to make his characters indulge in the same practice.

Thus Gide repeatedly risked the dangers of narration in the first person singular. By the time *The Immoralist* appeared Oscar Wilde had already warned Gide never again to use the pronoun "I," but Gide was to flaunt that advice so consistently that in 1921 Marcel Proust had to repeat it to him. It would be hard to imagine, indeed, what his work would be like were it less personal—and one might even say less confessional. Autobiographical elements in *The Immoralist* are so numerous that the author has suffered ever since from the identification of his hero with himself. . . . Yes, Michel was torn from the very heart of his author but this does not mean that Michel is Gide. In one of the most significant letters written by that great letter-writer, whose entire correspondence will doubtless not become known for many years yet, he stated his theory of the creation of a character. It so happens that he related that theory to this particular novel, stating: "That a germ of Michel exists in me goes without saying. . . . How many germs or buds we bear in us which will never flower save in our books! They are 'dormant eyes' as the botanists call them. But if one intentionally suppresses all of them *except one* how it grows! How it en-

larges, immediately monopolizing all the sap! My recipe for creating a hero is quite simple; take one of these buds and put it in a pot all alone, and one soon has a wonderful individual. Advice; choose preferably (if it is true that one *can* choose) the bud that bothers you the most. In this way you get rid of it at the same time. This is probably what Aristotle called katharsis." Others have expressed the same theory, even going so far as to see works of imagination as safety valves preventing the writer from indulging in the excesses which symbolize his characters. Bergson, for instance, remarked that "Shakespeare was not Macbeth nor Hamlet nor Othello but he would have been those various characters if circumstances and the consent of his will had brought to a state of eruption what was but an inner urge."

Gide's theory of katharsis holds of course not only for Michel but also for his other characters. In general, each of the short tales presents a single protagonist who represents the monstrous flowering of one of the buds in the author. Has not Gide said of himself: "I am a creature of dialogue; everything in me is at war and in contradiction"? In *Strait Is the Gate* a very different bud is produced: the heroine Alissa, who is so close in many ways to Mme André Gide that we tend to forget she is a projection of the author. Alissa is the excessively pious young person afraid of life whom Gide might have been had he never transcended his adolescence. . . . By a series of subtle touches, Gide unfolds the obsessive character of Alissa and reveals her motivation. At one point she asks her diary: "Was that sacrifice really consumed in my heart? I am, as it were, humiliated to feel that God no longer exacts it. Can it be that I was not equal to it?" From such a doubt it is but a step to the decision to make the sacrifice anyway, simply to prove that she is capable of it. Commenting on his novel years later, Gide noted that whenever she thought of Jérôme, there welled up in Alissa a sort of unconscious and irresistible burst of heroism. And he adds: "Absolutely useless heroism."

In *The Pastoral Symphony,* still a third bud reaches fruition. Here it is the Pastor with his lamentably good intentions, his sanctimonious hiding behind the Scriptures, and his blind self-deception who reflects a facet of his creator. (pp. 92-5)

[It] was easy for André Gide to put himself in the position of the hero of his *Pastoral Symphony.* Around this figure he constructed a parable of blindness in which the spiritual blindness is so much more dangerous than the physical blindness. Subtly and yet emphatically by repetition Gide established a parallel between Gertrude's actual blindness, her state of innocence, and the Gospels on the one hand, and on the other, lucidity, the state of sin, and the Epistles of St. Paul.

It is important to note a variation of the diary

form in *The Pastoral Symphony.* Obviously the Pastor would not and *could* not have recounted the whole story after the final tragedy. Or if he had, he would inevitably have transferred to its beginning the state of mind with which he witnessed its end. Hence Gide makes him begin to keep his notebook in the middle of Gertrude's evolution, recording at the start events that began two and a half years before. On 10 February he makes his first entry and on 30 May, his last. Meanwhile, on 8 May events catch up with his diary, and from that point on the Pastor is recording the *present* as it unfolds. This skillful technique gives to the tale an extraordinary mounting intensity that could have been achieved in no other way. (p. 95)

Judging his work from the inside, Gide is pleased to emphasize the differences between his *Faux-Monnayeurs* and all the rest of his fiction. In an ironic and unused preface for that novel he declared that he had not classified his earlier works as novels for fear they might be accused of lacking some of the essentials of the *genre,* such as confusion, for instance. In the novel itself he makes his novelist Edouard reflect that his earlier tales resemble those basins in French parks, precise in contour, but in which the captive water is lifeless. "Now," he says, "I want to let it flow according to the slope, at one moment rapid and at another slow, in meanders that I refuse to foresee."

Between *The Pastoral Symphony* and *The Counterfeiters,* Gide gave a series of lectures on Dostoevsky in 1921 and 1922. Rereading the great Russian, he noted certain similarities between Dostoevsky and himself; he found the same type of irresolute, half-formed, contradictory characters to which he has always been drawn himself; he recognized his own familiar themes: the relation of the individual with himself or with God, the demoniacal role of the intelligence, the challenge to conventional ethics and psychology, the value of an audacious deed, the opposition of thought and action and of carnal and emotional love, the influence of convention in counterfeiting us. He became aware that Dostoevsky, too, invariably expresses ideas in relation to individuals, depicts the particular to achieve the general, intentionally interrupts action at its most intense, and creates a painting with a specific source of light rather than a lifeless panorama.

But the break at this point in his career is less abrupt than he implies. In actual fact *The Counterfeiters* covers less ground both spatially and temporally than most of the tales. *The Immoralist* includes scenes in Paris, North Africa, Italy, and Normandy; *Strait Is the Gate* is laid in Rouen, Fongueusemare, Paris, Havre, and Aigues-Vives (near Nîmes); only *The Pastoral Symphony* with its limitation to La Brévine and nearby Neuchâtel rivals the economy of *The Counterfeiters,* which takes us out of Paris only for a brief stay at Saas-Fée in Switzerland. It is equally surprising to note, in view of the novel's complexity, that the action of *The Counterfeiters* is concentrated within a few months, whereas *The Immoralist* records three years, *Strait Is the Gate,* twenty years, and *The Pastoral Symphony,* two years and nine months of life. Furthermore, for all their precise contours, not one of the tales is as balanced in composition as *The Counterfeiters* with its eighteen chapters and 220 pages of the first part exactly paralleling the eighteen chapters and 225 pages of the third part.

The complexity and "confusion" of the novel must be attributable, then, to the number of characters or rather to the number of plots, since the twenty-eight characters are necessitated by the multiple plots. Now, André Gide has noted most loyally in his *Journals* for 1928 that his friend Roger Martin du Gard gave him "the advice to gather together the various plots of *Les Faux-Monnayeurs,* which, had it not been for him, would have formed so many separate 'tales.'" . . . Just now—after noting in passing that even more than the example of Dostoevsky was required to renew Gide's fictional technique—it is more important to emphasize the persistence, nevertheless, of certain elements within that technique.

From June 1919 to June 1925—that is, during the actual writing of *The Counterfeiters*—Gide kept a separate notebook in which to record "inch by inch," as he said in English, the progress of his novel. That fascinating and invaluable [*Le Journal des Faux-Monnayeurs (Journal of "The Counterfeiters")*], which has never been a part of Gide's monumental *Journals,* was first published in French the same year as the novel. . . . In it the author presents the problems encountered in composition, his hesitations and false starts, and the solutions he has found to his difficulties. The novelty of his approach throughout and his little youthful thrill of triumph at each new problem overcome prevent the reader from noticing how many of the apparent technical innovations had already found their place in the earlier tales. For instance, the first entry in *The Journal of "The Counterfeiters"* reads: "For two days I have been wondering whether or not to have my novel related by Lafcadio. Thus it would be a narrative of gradually revealed events in which he would act as an observer, an idler, a perverter." Is this not again the first-person narration of the tales? To be sure, a month later Gide abandoned this plan after writing some pages of Lafcadio's journals; yet in doing so he added: "But I should like to have successive interpreters: for example, Lafcadio's notes would occupy the first book; the second book might consist of Edouard's notebook; the third of an attorney's files, etc." Surely this is the same technique as in *La Porte étroite* where, at a certain point, Jérome's account is broken to admit the diary of the dead Alissa.

In fact, it was not until much later that it occurred

to Gide—possibly as a result of rereading *Tom Jones*—to resort to impersonal narration with frequent interventions of the author. As late as May 1924 he noted: "The poor novelist constructs his characters; he controls them and makes them speak. The true novelist listens to them and watches them function; he eavesdrops on them even before he knows them. It is only according to what he hears them say that he begins to understand *who* they are." . . . "I should like events never to be related directly by the author, but instead exposed (and several times from different vantages) by those actors who will be influenced by those events. In their account of the action I should like the events to appear slightly warped; the reader will take a sort of interest from the mere fact of having to *reconstruct*. The story requires his collaboration in order to take shape properly." But this is already true of the tales. That there are two points of view in *Strait Is the Gate*—thanks to Jérôme's account and Alissa's diary—is obvious. In *The Immoralist*, although there is but one narrator (Michel) who is trying to report himself objectively, he is nevertheless judged by his wife, Marceline, and by his friend, Ménalque, not to mention the Arab youth Moktir; and Michel strives to record those judgments—with the inevitable result that the reader has to re-establish the truth. Likewise in *The Pastoral Symphony* where the lamentable Pastor is judged by his wife, his son, and the blind girl he loves.

After *The Counterfeiters*, when Gide writes *L'Ecole des femmes (The School for Wives)* and its two sequels, *Robert* and *Geneviéve*, he somewhat mechanically presents three views of the same family conflict, one to a volume, much as he had toyed with doing in *The Counterfeiters*.

Perhaps the most generally acknowledged originality of *The Counterfeiters* is that of a novel within the novel. As the author noted in *The Journal of "The Counterfeiters"*: "Properly speaking, the book has no single center for my various efforts to converge upon; those efforts center about two *foci*, as in an ellipse. On one side, the event, the fact, the external *datum;* on the other side, the very effort of the novelist to make a book out of it all. The latter is the main subject," he continued, "the new focus that throws the plot off center and leads it toward the imaginative. In short, I see this notebook in which I am writing the very history of the novel, poured into the book in its entirety and forming its principal interest—for the greater irritation of the reader." With Edouard's journal this is precisely what Gide has done. It was a brilliant idea to set Edouard the novelist at the center of the novel, both an observer and an actor in the events, engaged in grappling with the problems posed by the translation into art of those events. Yet this was far from a new idea with Gide. His very first work, published in 1891, shows a young romantic hero writing the novel we are reading.

And in his *Journals* for 1893, Gide has noted: "I wanted to suggest, in the *Tentative amoureuse,* the influence of the book upon the one who is writing it, and during that very writing. . . . Our acts exercise a retroaction upon us. . . . In a work of art I rather like to find transposed on the scale of the characters, the very subject of that work. Nothing throws a clearer light upon it or more surely establishes the proportions of the whole. (pp. 96-100)

In *The Counterfeiters* this apparent narcissism reaches its height when Gide puts a novelist resembling himself at the center of the novel, engaged in writing a novel to be entitled *The Counterfeiters* and recording and commenting on the action in his diary as it unfolds. Such a device offers the incalculable advantage of narration by indirection, for "a character may well describe himself wonderfully while describing someone else or speaking of someone else—according to the rule that each of us really understands in others only those feelings he is capable of producing himself "—as *Journal of "The Counterfeiters"* points out. Thus it is that the progress of Michel in *The Immoralist*, or of the Pastor in *The Pastoral Symphony*, becomes apparent to us through his wife's attitude toward him *as reported by him himself*. . . . Hence, Gide is stating a principle that has always been his when he says in *Journal of "The Counterfeiters"*: "It is appropriate, in opposition to the manner of Meredith or James, to let the reader get the advantage over me—to go about it in such a way as to allow him to think he is more intelligent, more moral, more perspicacious than the author, and that he is discovering many things in the characters, and many truths in the course of the narrative, in spite of the author and, so to speak, behind the author's back."

Many of us have long admired the ending of *The Counterfeiters* with Edouard's suspensive remark: "I am very curious to know Caloub." And indeed, in his workbook the author notes: "This novel will end sharply, not through exhaustion of the subject, which must give the impression of inexhaustibility, but on the contrary through its expansion and by a sort of blurring of its outline. It must not be neatly rounded off, but rather disperse, disintegrate. . . ." This too is less new than Gide would have us think. Do not the earlier novels likewise blur off, leaving the reader to reflect at length on the situation and emotions of the chief protagonist? Particularly in *The Immoralist* and in *Strait Is the Gate,* when the end is reached, the reader feels better informed—thanks to the technique of indirection—than does the bewildered narrator. Consistently André Gide has allowed the reader the illusion of getting the advantage over him.

It is by no means necessary, or even advisable, to attempt to diminish *The Counterfeiters* in order to build up the earlier tales. That there is a difference is only too apparent. The example of Dostoevsky and the capital advice of Roger Martin du Gard suffice to explain Gide's new orientation in the years 1919 to 1925. But three points must not be forgotten: (1) that as early as 1908 Gide had already sketched a portrait of *Dostoyevsky According to His Correspondence,* (2) that between 1909 and 1914 in the newly formed group of the *Nouvelle Revue Française* the conversation and writings of intimate friends as Jacques Riviére, Roger Martin du Gard, Jean Schlumberger, and Albert Thibaudet had centered about the aesthetics of the novel, and finally (3) that in 1914—directly between *Strait Is the Gate* and *Isabelle* on the one hand and *The Pastoral Symphony* on the other—Gide had brought out *Les Caves du Vatican* (badly titled in one English language edition as *Lafcadio's Adventures*). That thrilling novel—for it is a novel despite the author's timid and misleading classification of it as a *sotie*—has more in common with *The Counterfeiters* than with the tales that precede and follow it. Comprising almost the same multiplicity of plots and contrapuntal composition as the later novel, it is narrated in the third person by a very conscious writer who even indulges in Fieldingesque or Sterne-like apostrophes and asides to disclaim omniscience and responsibility; and it unfolds swiftly with all the complexity and compulsion of a novel of adventure. Furthermore, it comprises a microcosmic novel within the novel, which Julius is writing almost at the dictation of Lafcadio. Clearly it is a tryout of the techniques to be used ten years later in *The Counterfeiters.* Nothing is more natural than that Gide should have begun *The Counterfeiters,* in his first draft, with the journal of Lafcadio, the charming and elusive hero of the earlier novel. His later rejection of Lafcadio reflects his characteristic desire not to take conscious advantage of momentum acquired in an earlier work.

Yet, as we have seen, it was impossible not to benefit from unconscious momentum in the form of the fictional techniques patiently elaborated over the preceding twenty-five years. Some readers will always prefer the concentrated, gemlike tales of Gide's early maturity, whereas others will choose the exasperatingly living, Dostoevskian qualities of *The Counterfeiters.* But, whatever their differences, the men and women who have the good fortune to read those works a century from now will doubtless not hesitate for a moment to recognize the same hand in all of them. (pp. 100-02)

Justin O'Brien, "Gide's Fictional Technique," in his *The French Literary Horizon,* Rutgers University Press, 1967, pp. 91-102.

HERMANN HESSE
(essay date 1951)

[In the following excerpt from a 1951 essay, Hesse discusses the ideological concerns of Gide's work.]

Gide was an author who approached his problems, so similar to mine, in so completely different a fashion, and his noble independence, stubbornness, and constantly renewed self-control of the unwearying truth-seeker continued to please me and in a strange way seem related to me. Principally Gide's development took the course of release from the pious world of faith and religious attitudes; it was the way of one overgifted and much too strictly and morally raised, who can no longer bear the narrowness and knows that the world is waiting for him, but nevertheless is not minded to sacrifice the sensibility of conscience won through that upbringing. Of course, his struggle for freedom is not simply in the intellectual sphere; it has to do with the senses as well, which demand their rights, and from the revolt of the senses against control and tutelage there emerges and grows clear the character of *enfant terrible,* of joy in exposing and stripping bare, in trapping the pious in their piously labeled lusts and depravitites—in short, that element of malice and aggressive love of revenge which without doubt is a part of Gide's character and constitutes for many of his readers his most fascinating and seductive aspect. But important though this motive was in André Gide's life, however much he may have been tempted and seduced into unmasking the righteous and baffling the philistines, there was in this noble spirit something greater, impelling him toward fruition and maturity, than the ability and enjoyment of startling and shocking his readers. He was on the dangerous path of every genius who, after breaking out of a for him unbearable tradition and morality, finds himself dreadfully alone and leaderless in the face of the world and searches on a higher level for a substitute for the lost security, seeks for models or norms that can correct and heal the far too exposed condition of the unfettered individual. So we see him all his life interested in the natural sciences and studying them, and we see him exploring the world of cultures, languages, and literature with a diligence and tenacity that evokes our astonishment and admiration. What he has won in this laborious, lifelong, chivalrous battle is a new kind of freedom, a freedom from dogma and partisanship, but in constant subjection to the service of truth, in constant striving for knowledge. In this he is a true brother to the great Montaigne and to that poet who wrote *Candide.* It has always been difficult to serve the truth as an individual without the protection of a system of faith, of a church, of a community. In serious and exemplary fashion André Gide has pursued this difficult course. (pp. 335-36)

Hermann Hesse, "André Gide," in his *My Belief: Essays on Life and Art,* edited by Theodore Ziolkowski, translated by Denver Lindley, Farrar, Straus and Giroux, 1974, pp. 334-36.

ENID STARKIE

(essay date 1953)

[Starkie was an English literary critic and an authority on twentieth-century French writers. In the following excerpt, she discusses Gide's complex psychological makeup and comments on his role as a moralist who "had aspirations towards spirituality, asceticism and puritanism; but also leanings towards sensuality, self-indulgence and sin."]

In spite of its many contradictions there is one striking characteristic which runs through Gide's work in all its many phases, a deep embedded shining seam; his quality as a moralist, passionately interested in the problem of sin, what it is and where it hides itself, especially in the apparently virtuous and complacent. He describes himself as watching people coming out of Church on a Sunday, and he says that their thoughts are freshly washed and ironed by the sermon they have just heard and put away tidily in their minds, as in a cupboard. 'I would like to rummage in the bottom-drawer', he declares, 'I've got the key'. This bottom-drawer is the hidden part of man's nature. As a young man, when he looked at civilisation, he was appalled by the pressure of outworn codes on the individual personality—the Church, society, political theories—, and he considered that, in his attempt to conform, the individual was obliged to develop an outward personality, a counterfeit personality. Discovery of our unacted desires, emancipation from the counterfeit personality, Gide thought, would bring freedom and fulfilment to the individual. It is the inner personality, beneath the counterfeit one, which he always tried to reach; that inner reality where good and evil overlap as in a marriage of Heaven and Hell. In reaching that inner personality he stirs up its troubled depths, drags up from the thick overlaying mud the hidden motives. This is for him the really fertile soil, the one which, in a state of nature, is overrun by exuberant vegetation and which must be cleared before it can be cultivated. He considered that those who had first studied man's nature did so only where it was most easily accessible and that only very gradually did psychologists come to realise all the hidden possibilities in man. All the troubled, tortured and distressed beings are those who interest Gide because he believes that more can be expected from them, when the subterranean forces have been liberated and subdued, than from the complacent. So he studies cases of disconcerting behaviour, cases of apparent wrongdoing; he observes all the idiosyncrasies, the nervous tics, as signs which reveal the hidden obsessions; he studies all these unconscious gestures as evidence, just as a detective might look for fingerprints, or analyse grains of dust or tufts of hair. Most of the characters in Gide's writings have some maladjustment, or psychological flaw, which drives them to their doom, and often to the destruction of others as well. (p. 9)

Gide was a man who found his own harmony and movement in a duality of polarisation. He needed this perpetual motion to obtain power for creation, just as some writers need to sin to gain the dynamic force of remorse. He had aspirations towards spirituality, asceticism and puritanism; but also leanings towards sensuality, self-indulgence and sin. It was not the contrast and clash between *Spleen* and *Idéal,* which we find in Baudelaire, man's longing for purity and beauty in conflict with his inevitable proclivity towards sin and vice. That was not Gide's problem; his was one of equilibrium and balance. It was necessary for him to find that one point between both poles where he could freely balance, like a see-saw, from one to the other, backwards and forwards, with equal attraction to each, refusing the necessity for blame or remorse when he came down on the side of what is called vice. Yet, at the same time, he desperately needed sanction and approval, and to feel always that he was right. When composing *Corydon* he was not content with merely gaining freedom and immunity for his own instincts, he needed as well the sanction and support of science and history. In the same way, when he had finally accepted atheism, he claimed confirmation for his lack of faith in the Bible itself. This curious twist of his nature was the cause of the accusation of intellectual dishonesty which has so often, unjustly, been made against him. But it came rather from the deep uncertainty in him which no amount of success, no amount of experience, could cure. He needed intellectual sanction to feel that he was right, and to be right was what he wanted more than anything else. But he would not compromise in order to achieve it, and this led him into the contradictory state of desire for martyrdom, which is, in fact, an inverted way of being right. Unable to believe in himself without assurance, he was forced into that vacillation and twisting which are the most characteristic aspect of the Gidian personality. (pp. 56-7)

Although Gide was particularly interested in his own problem as an individual, he was passionately interested as well in the larger problem of individualism in the world today. This brought him many of his readers in all parts of the world, those who seek a remedy to our present discontents. The problem of our time, as Gide sees it—the real crisis of our age—is how to reconcile the inalienable right of the individual to self-development, and the urgent necessity for the diminution of the misery of the masses. In these days of collectivity and massthinking, when security from the womb to the tomb is the goal, there is the danger that the individual may be strangled in the ever-increasing coils of bureaucratic red tape. For Gide there was no contradiction between belief in the individual and belief in the community—he had hoped to find the reconciliation in Communism—but he would not sacrifice the sanctity of each individual human soul, since he believed that only by being truly himself could man be of service or value to others. He had a horror of the slow ruminating of the herd, pedigree or otherwise, chewing over the same cud of ideas. He preferred to wander and be lost rather than follow the well mapped-out paths. He had the pride of the one lost sheep, safe in the knowledge that the Eternal Shepherd will scour the hillsides to look for him, and that there will be more rejoicing in Heaven at his being brought safely back to the fold, than for the ninety-nine which never strayed.

In his sixty years as a writer there had been a constant evolution in Gide's style of the same order as the transformation which occurred in his thought. At first he was a poet, preoccupied with himself, using language to express personal lyric feelings—there are some who regret the disappearance of this personal artist—and eventually he became a moralist with a style of pure and sober classicism. In his early writings he adopted the musical manner of the Symbolists and favoured 'la chanson grise', which gave full freedom to his imagination. By the end of the First World War, however, he had banished all extraneous ornamentation from his style. One need only compare *La Symphonie Pastorale* with the early works to realise the difference. The complete simplicity of the language now matches the dazzling whiteness of the snow. Later his language became still more stripped and bare as he perfected the art of Racine, of expressing most by saying least, a strict form containing and restraining deep emotion.

Although all through his life Gide went out with eager anticipation towards the future, he remained, after he reached maturity, classical and universal in the truest meaning of the expression, and became a repository of the past, to protect it against destruction. European civilization for him, in spite of Christianity, grew from Graeco-Roman roots; and, although he was interested in foreign literatures, reading and absorbing much from such writers as Dostoevsky, Shakespeare, Blake and Nietzsche, he nevertheless felt deep down that it was in French classical culture that it had reached its most perfect flowering.

After an examination of sixty years and eighty odd volumes of Gide's writings the impression remains that he is a moralist, psychologist and stylist rather than a pure novelist or dramatist. Each of his novels is an attitude which he adopts for the sake of argument, of speculation—he tells us so himself—and that makes him less of a novelist than a moralist; less of a novelist than an investigator. He does not concern himself with creating complex characters giving the illusion of life; he is less interested in *men* than in *man,* in the classical sense. 'Man is more interesting than men', he says, 'it is he whom God has made in his own image'. He is less anxious to make an amalgam of contradictions than to isolate some special characteristic. He is a chemist who isolates certain substances to obtain their purest essence. Each of his works is a chemical experiment in purifying some particular quality or vice which he pursues to its logical conclusion.

La Porte Étroite is probably Gide's most perfect and moving book, but his *Journal* is perhaps his most characteristic and original. It is a work unique in French literature—indeed in any literature; a treasure-house of discussion on every artistic and intellectual movement, on every moral problem, of more than sixty years. As a whole it may lack form and unity—indeed how could it be otherwise, with its million words dealing with so many topics and phases of life; but individual passages are amongst his finest writing. He has written few pages of greater beauty, simplicity and poignancy, than his description of the death of the writer Charles-Louis Philippe, and his funeral amongst the simple peasants who were his family. (pp. 57-9)

The tangled skein that is Gide will one day have to be unravelled. There is in everyone, however many the contradictions, one main thread which runs through everything, outlining the individual pattern and making it clear. In Gide it will be found to be a spiritual thread. All through his life, in spite of lapses—even in these lapses—it has been spiritual values that he has always sought, albeit sometimes in the byways. Proust had called his own work, the work of his lifetime, *A la Recherche du Temps Perdu;* Gide might have called his *A la Recherche d'une Ame.* 'All our thoughts which have not God for object', he said, 'are of the realm of death'.

Gide's ultimate fate will be to be considered as a moralist in the great French seventeenth-century tradition—the tradition of La Rochefoucauld and Pascal—whose integrity and nobility of thought, whose purity and harmony of style, give him an immortal place amongst the great masters of French literature. (p. 60)

Enid Starkie, in her *André Gide,* Bowes & Bowes, 1953, 63 p.

ANDRÉ MAUROIS
(essay date 1965)

[Maurois was a French biographer, essayist, and critic. In the following excerpt from his 1965 memoir of Gide, he discusses the moral doctrine of *Les Nourritures Terrestres.*]

Like *Thus Spake Zarathustra, Les Nourritures Terrestres* is a gospel in the root sense of the word—glad tidings. Tidings about the meaning of life addressed to a dearly loved disciple whom Gide calls Nathanaël. The book is composed of Bible verses, hymns, *récits,* songs, rounds, held together on the one hand by the presence of Nathanaël and on the other by the doctrine Gide *seems* to be teaching him. I say *seems* because we shall shortly see that Gide would accept neither the idea of teaching nor that of doctrine.

Besides Nathanaël and the author, there is a third character in *Les Nourritures,* one who reappears in *L'Immoraliste* and who is in Gide's life what Merck was in Goethe's or Mephistopheles in Faust's. This character, whom Gide calls Ménalque, has sometimes been identified with Oscar Wilde, but Gide told me it wasn't Wilde at all. Ménalque is, indeed, no one unless perhaps one aspect of Gide himself, one of the interlocutors in the dialogue of Gide with Gide that comprises his spiritual life.

The core of the book was a *récit* by Ménalque, one not far different from a *récit* Gide might have given after his African rebirth. . . . (pp. 83-4)

This *récit* contains the essence of the "tidings" of *Les Nourritures.* First a negative doctrine: flee families, rules, stability. Gide himself suffered so much from "snug homes" that he harped on its dangers all his life.

Then a positive doctrine: one must seek adventure, excess, fervor; one should loathe the lukewarm, security, all tempered feelings. "Not affection, Nathanaël: love . . ." Meaning not a shallow feeling based on nothing perhaps but tastes in common, but a feeling into which one throws oneself wholly and forgets oneself. Love is dangerous, but that is yet another reason for loving, even if it means risking one's happiness, *especially* if it means losing one's happiness. For happiness makes man less. "Descend to the bottom of the pit if you want to see the stars." Gide insists on this idea that there is no salvation in contented satisfaction with oneself, an idea he shares with both a number of great Christians and with Blake: "Unhappiness exalts, happiness slackens." Gide ends a letter to an *amie* with this curious formula: "Adieu, dear friend, may God ration your happiness!"

It would be a mistake to view the doctrine of *Les Nourritures Terrestres* as the product of a sensualist's egoism. On the contrary, it is a doctrine in which the Self (which is essentially continuity, memory of and submission to the past) fades out and disappears in order that the individual may lose himself, dissolve himself into each perfect moment. The Gide of *Les Nourritures Terrestres* does not renounce the search for the God André Walter was seeking [in *Les Cahiers d'André Walter*], but he seeks him *everywhere,* even in Hell: "May my book teach you to take more interest in yourself than in it, and more in everything else than in yourself !"

There are many objections that might be made to this doctrine. First one might object that this immoralist is at bottom a moralist—that he does teach even though he denies it, that he preaches even though he hates preachers, that he is puritanical in his anti-puritanism, and finally, that the refusal to participate in human society ("snug homes . . . Families, I hate you!") is actually another form of confinement—to the outside.

Gide is too intelligent not to have anticipated this kind of objection. He raises it himself in *Les Faux-Monnayeurs.* In describing Vincent's development, he writes: "For he's a moral creature . . . and the Devil will get the best of him only by providing him with reasons for self-approval. Theory of the totality of the moment, of gratuitous joy . . . On the basis of which the devil wins the day." A subtle analysis of his own case: the beast has found a new way of playing the angel who plays the beast. If the Immoralist weren't a moral being, he would have no need to revolt.

One might further object that this is the doctrine of a convalescent, not a healthy man. . . . But again Gide has taken care to raise this point himself in the very intriguing preface he later added to the book, and to point out further that at the time when he, the artist, wrote *Les Nourritures Terrestres,* he had already, as a man, rejected its message, for he had just got married and, for a time at least, settled down. Moreover, he followed *Les Nourritures* with *Saul,* a play which can only be interpreted as a condemnation of seekers after the moment and sensation. Thus, Gide's wavering course between the angelic pole and the diabolic pole is not all broken by *Les Nourritures Terrestres.*

How should it be when at the end of the book the master himself advises his disciple to leave him. . . . (pp. 85-6)

But why doesn't Gide require of himself the same rejection he so strongly urges on his disciple? And if he has a horror of any and all doctrine, why isn't he horrified by his own? *He is much too much Gide to be Gidean.* He always protested against people's habit of reducing him to a rulebook when he had attempted, contrarily, to create a rulebook for escape. This is Gide's supreme and perilous leap, the leap that makes him impossible to pin down. What others might find to condemn in him, this Proteus condemns in himself.

This brings up an extremely interesting question. Why is this subtle, Protean doctrine which constantly denies itself, why after thirty years is this powerful and dangerous book, still such a source of joy and enthusiasm to so many young men and women? Read Jacques Riviére's letters to Alain Fournier; read in Martin du Gard's *La Belle Saison* the account of the hero's discovery of *Les Nourritures Terrestres;* listen, finally, to some of the young people about you. Many of them intensely admire this book—with an admiration quite beyond the literary. Here is why.

With the discovery of the harshness of life, the magical and sheltered days of childhood are followed, with nearly every adolescent, by a period of rebellion. This is the first adolescent "stage." The second stage is the discovery—*despite* disillusionments and difficulties—of the beauty of life. This discovery ordinarily occurs between eighteen and twenty. It produces most of our young lyric poets.

The special thing about Gide's character, its originality and its force, is that, having been retarded in natural development by reason of the constraints of his upbringing, he went through this second stage when his mind was already relatively mature, the result being that this *retardation enabled him to express the discoveries common to all young people in more perfect form.* In other words, young people are beholden to a retarded and unregenerate adolescent for having so well expressed what they feel. Thus, the necessity, the universality, and the likelihood of endurance of a book like *Les Nourritures Terrestres.* A disciple (as in Wilde's fine story) is someone who seeks himself in the eyes of the master. The young look for and find themselves in Gide.

Readers will find this same lesson in immoralism in *Le Prométhée Mal Enchaîné. . . . Gide calls this book a sotie,* a Middle Ages term used to denote an allegorical satire in dialogue form. Prometheus *thinks* he is chained to the peaks of the Caucasus (just as Gide once was by so many shackles, barriers, battlements, and other scruples). Then he discovers that all that's needed is to *want* to be free, and he goes off with his eagle to Paris where in the hall of the New Moons he gives a lecture explaining that each of us is devoured by his eagle—vice or virtue, duty or passion. One must feed this eagle on love. "Gentlemen, one must love his eagle, love him so he'll become beautiful." The writer's eagle is his work, and he should sacrifice himself to it. (pp. 87-9)

André Maurois, "André Gide," translated by Carl Morse, in *From Proust to Camus: Profiles of Modern French Writers* by André Maurois, translated by Carl Morse and Renaud Bruce, Doubleday & Company, 1966, pp. 71-95.

SOURCES FOR FURTHER STUDY

Ames, Van Meter. *André Gide.* Norfolk, Conn.: New Directions Books, 1947, 302 p.

Literary biography that emphasizes the predominate ideological and moral influences which affected Gide's work throughout his life.

Cordle, Thomas. *André Gide.* New York: Twayne Publishers, 1969, 183 p.

Critical survey of Gide's career.

Ireland, G. W. *André Gide.* New York: Grove Press, 1963, 120 p.

Study that focuses on Gide's creative technique and the development of characters and ideas in various works.

March, Harold. *Gide and the Hound of Heaven.* Philadelphia: University of Pennsylvania Press, 1952, 421 p.

Biography of Gide that thoroughly explores both his influences and his intentions for each of his works.

O'Brien, Justin. *Portrait of André Gide: A Critical Biography.* New York: Alfred A. Knopf, 1953, 390 p.

Critical and biographical study of Gide that draws upon O'Brien's numerous interviews with Gide.

Painter, George D. *André Gide: A Critical and Biographical Study.* London: Arthur Baker, 1951, 192 p.

Critical biography that also contains plot summaries of Gide's works and discusses the similarities of Gide's writings with events in his life.

Allen Ginsberg

1926-

American poet, essayist, and nonfiction writer.

INTRODUCTION

Ginsberg is one of the most celebrated and popular poets in contemporary American literature. A longtime spokesperson for the country's disaffected youth, he was a prominent figure in the counterculture and antiwar movements of the 1960s as well as a leading member of the Beat generation, a literary movement whose members wrote in the language of the urban streets about previously forbidden and unliterary topics. Despite his libertarian beliefs and unconventional literary style, Ginsberg admits that his verse has been influenced by such established poets as William Carlos Williams, William Blake, and Walt Whitman. Fred Moramarco commented that to read and study Ginsberg's canon "is to confront chronologically arranged obituary notices from the anguished soul of America during some of its most troubled days. From very early in his poetic career, Ginsberg has aimed at offering us an omniscient view of the American spirit and a diagnosis of that spirit's ills."

Ginsberg's private life has informed much of the critical discussion of his works. Born in Newark, New Jersey, in 1926, Ginsberg suffered an emotionally troubled childhood that is reflected in many of his poems. His mother, who suffered from various mental illnesses and was periodically institutionalized during Ginsberg's adolescence, was an active member of the Communist Party and other associations of the radical left. In order to balance the parental void left by his mother, Ginsberg's father was a strict disciplinarian. Contributing to Ginsberg's confusion and isolation during these years was his increasing awareness of his homosexuality, which he concealed from both his peers and his parents until he was in his twenties. First introduced to poetry by his father, a high school teacher and poet, Ginsberg furthered his interest through talks with his mentor, William Carlos Williams, who lived in nearby Paterson, where Ginsberg attended high school. Other early literary influences included Lionel Trilling and Mark Van Doren, both of whom taught Ginsberg at Columbia University. Ginsberg also established friendships with writers Jack Kerouac, William S. Burroughs, and Neal Cassady while in college. This group, along with several west coast writers that included Kenneth Rexroth and Lawrence Ferlinghetti, among others, later formed the core of the San Francisco Beat movement.

The title work of *Howl and Other Poems* (1956) established Ginsberg as a leading voice of the Beat movement. His public reading of *Howl* to a spellbound audience in San Francisco in 1955 demonstrated the power of his work as an oral medium and set standards for poetry readings throughout the United States. A reflexive, lyrical lamentation on the moral and social ills of the post-World War II era, the poem is dedicated to Carl Solomon, whom Ginsberg met while undergoing eight months of therapy at the Columbia Psychiatric Institute in 1948. Solomon challenged Ginsberg's academic theories about poetry and strengthened his understanding of contemporary poetry's potential for expressing political resistance. Part I of *Howl* chronicles the despair felt by many individuals during the postwar era. The opening lines are among the most well-known in American poetry: "I saw the best minds of my generation destroyed by madness, starving / hysterical naked, / dragging themselves through the negro streets at dawn looking for an / angry fix. . . . " Evoking a sense of confinement, Ginsberg catalogues the traits of American youths who turned to iconoclastic outlets to cope with social hypocrisy. In Part II, Ginsberg identifies the causes of humanity's discontent. Here, he personifies the origins of social evil—including government bureaucracy, conformity, materialism, and technology—in the character of Moloch, a Semitic god to whom children were sacrificed. In the poem, Moloch is "the heavy judger of men" who destroys the most precious and benevolent qualities of human nature and fills individuals with self-doubt.

In the final section of *Howl*, Ginsberg celebrates his victory over Moloch's control of his emotional and sexual identity. Although Ginsberg acknowledges the influence of many people in the writing of *Howl*, he regards Solomon as his "immediate muse" and in Part III praises his friend's sincerity and self-truth. Through *Howl*'s progression from protest and lamentation to acceptance and vision, Ginsberg chronicles not only the unification of society but of the individual. *Howl*'s raw, honest language and its "Hebraic-Melvillian bardic breath," as Ginsberg once described it, astonished many traditional critics. While many commentators shared the attitude of Walter Sutton, who considered *Howl* "a tirade revealing an animus directed outward against those who do not share the poet's social and sexual orientation," others echoed the opinion of Paul

Zweig, who argued that the poem "almost single-handedly dislocated the traditional poetry of the 1950s."

In 1957 *Howl* became the subject of a landmark obscenity trial. Because of its graphic sexual language, the San Francisco Police Department declared the book obscene and arrested Lawrence Ferlinghetti, the owner of City Lights Books, which published the volume. The ensuing trial attracted national attention as such prominent literary figures as Walter Van Tilberg Clark and Mark Schorer spoke in defense of *Howl*. Schorer testified that "Ginsberg uses the rhythms of ordinary speech and also the diction of ordinary speech. I would say the poem uses necessarily the language of vulgarity." Ferlinghetti was later acquitted of distributing obscene material. Soon after, Ferlinghetti published an article in which he stated: "It is not the poet but what he observes which is revealed as obscene. The great obscene wastes of *Howl* are the sad wastes of the mechanized world, lost among atom bombs and insane nationalisms."

Ginsberg's next volume, *Kaddish and Other Poems: 1958-1960* (1961), delves further into his past. *Kaddish* is an elegy for Ginsberg's mother, who died in a mental hospital in 1956. Based on the Kaddish, a traditional Hebrew prayer for the dead, it poignantly expresses the anger, love, and confusion Ginsberg felt toward his mother while rendering the social and historical milieu which informed his mother's troubled life. Some critics consider *Kaddish* Ginsberg's most important work. John Tytell explained: "[*Kaddish*] testifies to Ginsberg's capacity for involvement with another human in torment, for the acceptance of another's weirdness." *Reality Sandwiches* (1963) collects poems from 1953 to 1960, including such noted verses as "The Green Automobile," "Wales Visitation," "Siesta in Xbalba and Return to the States" and reflects Ginsberg's travels through Africa, Europe, and North and South America during the late 1950s.

Ginsberg admits that much of his poetry, including the second section of *Howl* and *Kaddish*, was written while he was under the influence of amphetamines and hallucinogenic drugs. After a trip to India in 1962, however, during which he was introduced to meditation and yoga, Ginsberg realized the importance of "living in and inhabiting the human form." Upon his return to the United States, Ginsberg began to lecture at college campuses, declaring that yoga and meditation were superior to drugs in raising self-consciousness, although he contended that hallucinogens can prove helpful in writing poetry.

Ginsberg also generated national media attention for his political activism. He helped organize antiwar demonstrations and advocated "flower power," a strategy in which antiwar demonstrators would promote positive values like peace and love to dramatize their opposition to the death and destruction caused by the Vietnam War. In 1968, Ginsberg led demonstrators at the Democratic National Convention in Chicago and later testified for the defense at the "Chicago Seven" conspiracy trial. He was also arrested in 1972 in Miami for demonstrating against President Richard Nixon at the Republican National Convention. These experiences inform much of Ginsberg's work of the 1960s and early 1970s, including *Planet News* (1968), which collects poems that are considered impressionistic collages of that era. Moloch appears again in the guise of the Vietnam War, ecological dangers, racism, and in the disproportion of material prosperity in America. Several pieces in this collection also reveal his personal concern with aging and his anguish over the deaths of Neal Cassady and Jack Kerouac.

The Gates of Wrath: Rhymed Poems, 1948-1952 (1973) collects Ginsberg's earliest verse. These poems and an early letter to William Carlos Williams were misplaced for many years until singer-composer Bob Dylan discovered them in 1968 among his personal papers. Basically an account of Ginsberg's life up to 1952, the poems discuss such topics as unrequited love and the duality of human existence, rendered in traditional rhymes and meters. *The Fall of America: Poems of These States 1965-1971* (1973), Ginsberg's next major work, takes the reader on a mystical cross-country journey, with "stops" to observe the physical and spiritual erosion of the United States. The central piece of the collection, "Poem of These States," is a long sequence intended "to cover like a collage a lone consciousness travelling through these states during the Vietnam War," according to Ginsberg. Dedicated to Walt Whitman and his 1871 book *Democratic Vistas, The Fall of America* won the National Book Award in 1974.

Mind Breaths: Poems 1972-1977 (1978) marks a change of direction in Ginsberg's verse. In an interview, Ginsberg described his previous work as "politically obsessed, ephemeral, too much anger, not enough family, not enough of my personal loves." The poems in *Mind Breaths* are more tranquil, inducing the sense of spiritual meditation and calm suggested in the book's title. Also included is the moving poem "Don't

Grow Old," which commentators described as Ginsberg's Kaddish for his father. Ginsberg returns to political and social issues in *Plutonian Ode* (1982), where he addresses the dangers of nuclear warfare. Here, Ginsberg compares the nuclear age to the reign of Pluto, the Greek god of the underworld. Ginsberg's recent publications include *Collected Poems: 1947-1980* (1984) and *White Shroud: Poems 1980-1985* (1986). Perhaps the most compelling piece in *White Shroud* is the title poem, reminiscent of *Kaddish,* in which Ginsberg relates a dream about his mother living as a bag lady in the Bronx section of New York City. While both volumes received mixed reviews, they signalled a new phase in Ginsberg's career and helped to assimilate his work into mainstream American letters.

Commentators have been sharply divided in their opinions of Ginsberg's work. While some critics have virtually dismissed it, echoing the sentiments of Bruce Bawer who called Ginsberg "the father of a generation of Americans to whom 'culture' is a word most often used immediately following the word 'drug'," others acknowledge Ginsberg's contribution in introducing and legitimizing experimental poetry to a wider audience. Jascha Kessler commented: "The reader of [Ginsberg's] vast collected poetry will spend a lot of time sorting out reactions to Ginsberg's various calls for freedom, and their psycho-mystico-philosophical underpinnings. And it will be a challenging as well as entertaining task too, because the work is never difficult to read as poetry, since it's always rather literary, always polished to the loudspeaking rhetoric of this prophet who was always at the center of his coterie of Beat friends in the 1950's, and has since put himself at the podium of the world."

(For further discussion of Ginsberg's life and career, see *Concise Dictionary of American Literary Biography, 1941-1968; Contemporary Authors,* Vols. 1-4, rev. ed.; *Contemporary Authors New Revision Series,* Vol. 2; *Contemporary Literary Criticism,* Vols. 1, 2, 3, 4, 6, 13, 36, 69; *Dictionary of Literary Biography,* Vols. 5, 16; *Major Twentieth-Century Writers;* and *Poetry Criticism,* Vol. 4.)

CRITICAL COMMENTARY

DIANE MIDDLEBROOK

(essay date 1974)

[In the excerpt below, Middlebrook traces Ginsberg's development as a poet from his earliest verse to *The Fall of America: Poems of These States, 1965-1971* (1973).]

Some of the poems in *The Gates of Wrath* are lovely, and all of them are interesting in retrospect, especially those in which Ginsberg is boldly repetitious: often he writes a good line but knows it's in the wrong poem, so he sets up another poem to give the line a home. We now know that the grownup Allen Ginsberg is a writer of the long free prophetic line associated, in American poetry, with Walt Whitman. So to hear Ginsberg speak initially the language of the English Romantic and metaphysical poets binding themselves to stanzas gives unanticipated delight when he achieves what they were after—as in **"The Voice of Rock"** or **"Stanzas Written at Night in Radio City."** (p. 129)

Still, *The Gates of Wrath* represents in Ginsberg's work the stage of poetic slavery, a period described by Wordsworth in "Immortality": the poet acts "As if his whole vocation / Were endless imitation." . . .

Dependence, in Ginsberg's early poetry, is not merely dependence on older poets, but dependence on a few talismanic words which he often gives the emphasis of rhyme position in a stanza. "Bone," "wrath," and "rose" recur as the mental geometry of this book, the formulae, or sometimes the points of departure, for the visionary art the young Ginsberg treasured. The quality of firmness in these monosyllabic nouns anchors the poems in a consistent metaphysic and a consistently prophetic stance toward the urban locale which thrusts its misery into even the most abstract poems. (p. 130)

A tendency to aphorism strengthens the poems of *The Gates of Wrath* rhetorically. Like the poet of *Poetical Sketches* (Blake's first book), Ginsberg might have gone on to write short lyrics all his life, if an early lyric like this one is indicative of his talent for concision and handling of the line:

I speak of love that comes to mind:
The moon is faithful, although blind;
She moves in thought she cannot speak.
Perfect care has made her bleak.

And, like Blake, Ginsberg appears to have written

these strict poems in order to acquire his poet's licence—the authorization of the untidy consciousness which lies below this stanza-speaker's view of what can be let into the line, and where it should go.

It may be that only poets concerned with the "unconscious program" of the mind's growth into utterance share the Wordsworthian obsessive dread of imitation. . . . But all the modern poets we call Romantic—with the exception of Yeats—share the belief that the growth *up* is growth away from traditional English stanza forms into a verse as free as they can think to make it. Yet free verse too has its impressive fathers. In Allen Ginsberg's case the generative parents are the biblical psalm as rendered in English by the King James translators; Blake; Christopher Smart in "Jubilate Agno"; the majestically enjambed blank verse of Milton, Shelley, and Wordsworth; finally, the poetry of Walt Whitman. Whitman is especially important, because he adds to the ecstatic mode of the long poem in Romantic English verse a tone of righteous democratic American anger as an alternative to meditative affirmation. *The Fall of America* is dedicated to the angry Whitman of *Democratic Vistas* (1871).

Ginsberg profited from all these influences, but by the time of writing the "poems of these states" which make up *The Fall of America,* he has abandoned his early models. Finding one's way to *be* in words is a hard job. "What's to be done with my life, which has lost its idea?" Ginsberg asks in the *Indian Journals.* "I don't even have a good theory of vegetarianism." What to take in, then? Ginsberg's solution is "attention to the actual movie of the mind." "Then you see what a man is, you know what he has in him," Whitman said in "Song of Myself." Ginsberg describes his technique of writing now as a complete abandonment of the sense of structure which dominates *The Gates of Wrath.* (pp. 130-32)

Hence, Allen Ginsberg's mature poems are complicated only by the amount of his personality they contain. In the best of them, as in Whitman, egotism is, movingly, a form of demoting the merely personal. (p. 132)

But Ginsberg is frequently obscure, as Whitman never is. This attribute of his poetry is a direct product of his aesthetic, as he describes it: "If you can actually keep track of your own head movie, then the writing it down is just like a secretarial job, and who gets craft about that? Use dashes instead of semicolons. . . ." A

Principal Works

Howl and Other Poems (poetry) 1956; revised 1971

Siesta in Xbalba and Return to the States (poetry) 1956

Empty Mirror: Early Poems (poetry) 1961

Kaddish and Other Poems, 1958-1960 (poetry) 1961

The Change (poetry) 1963

Reality Sandwiches: 1953-1960 (poetry) 1963

The Yage Letters (correspondence with William Burroughs) 1963

Kral Majales (poetry) 1965

Wichita Vortex Sutra (poetry) 1966

T.V. Baby Poems (poetry) 1967

Airplane Dreams: Compositions from Journals (poetry) 1968

Ankor Wat (poetry) 1968

The Heat Is a Clock (poetry) 1968

Message II (poetry) 1968

Planet News (poetry) 1968

Scrap Leaves, Tasty Scribbles (poetry) 1968

Wales—A Visitation, July 29, 1967 (poetry) 1968

For the Soul of the Planet Is Wakening . . . (poetry) 1970

Indian Journals: March 1962-May 1963; Notebooks, Diary, Blank Pages, Writings (poetry) 1970

The Moments Return: A Poem (poetry) 1970

Notes after an Evening with William Carlos Williams (nonfiction) 1970

Ginsberg's Improvised Poetics (poetry) 1971

Bixby Canyon Ocean Path Word Breeze (poetry) 1972

Iron Horse (poetry) 1972

Kaddish (drama) 1972

New Year Blues (poetry) 1972

Open Head (poetry) 1972

The Fall of America: Poems of These States, 1965-1971 (poetry) 1973

The Gates of Wrath: Rhymed Poems, 1948-1952 (poetry) 1973

The Visions of the Great Rememberer (correspondence) 1974

Allen Verbatim: Lectures of Poetry, Politics, and Consciousness (lectures) 1975

Chicago Trial Testimony (nonfiction) 1975

First Blues: Rags, Ballads, and Harmonium Songs, 1971-1974 (poetry) 1975

Sad Dust Glories: Poems during Work Summer in Woods, 1974 (poetry) 1975

To Eberhart from Ginsberg (correspondence) 1976

Journals: Early Fifties, Early Sixties (journals) 1977

Careless Love: Two Rhymes (poetry) 1978

Mind Breaths: Poems, 1972-1977 (poetry) 1978

Mostly Sitting Haiku (poetry) 1978; revised and expanded 1979

Poems All Over the Place: Mostly Seventies (poetry) 1978

Plutonian Ode (poetry) 1982

Collected Poems, 1947-1980 (poetry) 1984

Howl: Original Draft Facsimile, Transcript and Variant Versions (poetry) 1986

White Shroud: Poems, 1980-1985 (poetry) 1986

---

reader with enough good will can then simply not puzzle over puzzling references (usually from esoteric sources) but simply pass on, since another feature of Ginsberg's sort of writing is amplitude. The obscurity of any one line is merely the obscurity of the mind's momentary distraction into self-delight; in another instant another more accessible metaphor might have occurred as the expressible form of the same perception.

Attending "the movie of the mind" means noticing things rather than mulling them over. Its poetic form becomes the catalogue in long lines, as Ginsberg describes it, "a giant sentence which will include the whole associational mobile." It's not surprising that Ginsberg should have sought out the wisdom of Eastern religions to cultivate this emotional condition, "trapping the archangel of the soul." Writers of English poetry since the 19th century have approached the tantalizing but nearly incomprehensible texts of Eastern wisdom with profitable hopefulness. . . . [Further], comprehending these teaching at all requires enormous effort of the sort we see Ginsberg performing day by

day in the *Indian Journals.* All these writers [Matthew Arnold, Thoreau, Eliot] have enriched the genres they've written in by subsuming Eastern mysticism into their own personal forms of mysticism, demonstrating that the particular is the only source of revelation available to the Eternal.

This is the point of view we find in *The Fall of America,* poems of Ginsberg's return from India to his homeland which reflect a matured view of the application of vision to contemporary reality. In *The Gates of Wrath* Ginsberg was preoccupied with having a visionary perception of reality: in *The Fall* he is interested in using it. (pp. 132-33)

Ginsberg as a poet does not—with one exception—seek to memorialize things in poetry *because* they are worth keeping. When we look at the imagery of reindeer and wolves surviving in the caves at Lascaux and Altamira we know we are beholding objects sacred to their creators. But Ginsberg's picture-making is, by his own acknowledgment, as unselective as possible. Like the TV cameras monitoring the aisles of supermarkets and discount stores, the poems of *The Fall of America* register abundant temporary intersections between objects and the eye as Ginsberg crisscrosses North America. . . . Ginsberg is capable of irony and passionate delight. Nonetheless, after reading only a little of *The Fall,* the reader felt she could put down the book and make her own poem merely by taking a walk. Ginsberg's poetry at its most effective has this influence, the power of awakening a reader to the unfailing sufficiency of his own imagination; and since Ginsberg's idea of poetry is so much like Whitman's, the reader's feeling of not needing the book may very well have been Ginsberg's point in writing it. Still, such an aesthetic does not make for the kind of art Ginsberg ascribes with admiration to bards and prophets, the kind "useful in caves."

I said there was an exception to Ginsberg's genial tendency to include whatever comes along as subject matter in *The Fall of America.* The exception is Ginsberg's obsession with the figure of a young male who appears sometimes in his true identity as Neal Cassady. (pp. 133-34)

Neal Cassady's death in February '68 intrudes violently into Ginsberg's chronological record of "these states 1965-1971." The poems lamenting Cassady are of two types: one elegiac, the other political. The intensity of Ginsberg's grief over the loss of this idealized former lover produces the elegiac poems, which are moving and personal. But because Ginsberg is inescapably a Romantic, thoughts that lie too deep for tears are a mental necessity; he therefore seeks transcendence of the personal by linking Cassady's death thematically to the Vietnam War and the Siege of Chicago, with an effect of surrealism occasionally declining into silliness. . . .

Largely because of his deep feeling for Cassady, Ginsberg's tender lyrical voice is well-represented in *The Fall of America.* But his ambition in this book to speak, like Whitman, from the self-transcendent perspective of a prophet doesn't come off very well. The data remain data, conceptually unmanaged; the mood of outrage seems childishly insufficient as a mode of emotional mastery over the horrors he describes. As in *The Gates of Wrath,* Ginsberg's strength in this latest book is the strength of his belief in the art of poetry itself. Ginsberg remains an imitator, a disciple whose work is always reminding the reader of the 19th-century Romantic masters. As their disciple, however, Ginsberg has no peer: perhaps it is his own form of maturity as a poet. In any case, Ginsberg's whole working life has been an illustration of the capacity of that poetry to revitalize itself in the consciousness of people seeking through every mode of communal effort to find grace, a way to survive with others. (p. 135)

Diane Middlebrook, "Bound Each to Each," in *Parnassus: Poetry in Review,* Vol. 2, No. 2, 1974, pp. 128-35.

JAMES F. MERSMANN
(essay date 1974)

[In the following excerpt from his *Out of the Vietnam Vortex: A Study of Poets and Poetry Against the War* (1974), Mersmann finds in *Empty Mirror: Early Poems* (1961) the genesis of Ginsberg's protest verse.]

Ginsberg is not the best, and surely not the most typical, poet of the [sixties] but the impulses that find exaggerated statement in his life and poetry are found in more muted tones in the writings of nearly every poet at work in this period; and though his poetry and poetic creed may still be at the periphery of general poetic practice, he seems to express the *Zeitgeist,* or that portion of the larger poetic spirit that is peculiar to this moment in history, unique to this time. (p. 31)

If the reader is to appreciate the integrity of Ginsberg's outcry against all forms of spiritual and psychological oppression, he needs first to appreciate how cruel Ginsberg's experience of those forces has been. If Ginsberg's poetic rantings are generally successful and convincing where others fail, it may be largely because he speaks from experience and has earned his right to shout. (p. 32)

Though it is not overtly political, anti-war, or social protest, the little *Empty Mirror* volume demands treatment here because (1) it establishes the autobiographical nature of Ginsberg's poetry and demands from us a different critical approach, (2) it records the origin and source of Ginsberg's rebellion, (3) it demonstrates that his poetry is essentially all "anti-war" poetry, and (4) it points to an important relation between the content and form of his writing. (p. 33)

We must, if we care about humanity and are not entirely caught up in art, objects, abstractions, and arguments, find something interesting in the passions and doubts displayed in such poems. It is true that Ginsberg's poems are not so polished and permanent as to be interesting as finished figurines and sculpture; but they are interesting as flowing amoebas engulfing or fleeing the random particulate experience they encounter, or as naked, shaggy, fibrillating paramecia, shuddering with excitement or revulsion. They offer the soul, brain, guts, and jissum of the man with unique honesty—fully and boisterously in the later work, tentatively and sadly in these early poems. (p. 34)

Apparently written before Ginsberg had his Blakean visions, this poem encapsulates many of the issues with which his entire life and poetic career have been concerned. There is here the painful gap between known spiritual facts and vitally experienced truth; the alienation and separateness; the inadequate and guilt-ridden self-image; the feeling of sordidness; the sensation that all things lack any ultimate significance; and the societally conditioned response. . . . (p. 35)

In many of the poems Ginsberg is simply talking to himself, sorting through things, implicitly or explicitly formulating precepts by which to endure. Occasionally [as in **"The Terms in Which I Think of Reality"**] he achieves an objectivity free of guilty self-laceration and captures his own and modern man's predicament, the predicament against which he later devotes all his energies. (p. 38)

The Empty Mirror is the one volume of Ginsberg's poems that is not "anti-war." It is the volume in which he is busy discovering the enemy. Subsequent poetry is a war against the Moloch not named but experienced in *Empty Mirror*. In *Empty Mirror* he is not on the outside describing and criticizing but on the inside agonizing. (p. 39)

[**"Sakyamuni Coming Out from the Mountain"** represents] a new vista opening for Ginsberg, a new avenue of adjustment, a new stance to take with regard to the "separation" he experiences. The poem . . . shows that he understands and identifies with a "beatness" that need not be guilty, but which is common to spiritual men. It is the opening of a new and alternative reality, the beginning of his *experiences* of the "spiritual facts" he had known were true but didn't feel in *The Empty Mirror*. . . . This poem . . . marks a beginning and is an important milestone along the road toward **"Howl"** and beyond. (p. 41)

The one poem of *The Empty Mirror* [**"Paterson"**] where the verse form points toward the later cataloguing and bardic breath of **"Howl"** is also the one poem that threatens open rebellion against the system; and it is here that Ginsberg first speaks of this contention as war. . . . Implicit here is the assumption that the same dispositional complex or "wrath" that brings physical mutilation on the battlefield is also the source of the psychic scars and existential wounds of competitive American society. (pp. 42-3)

Surprisingly, Ginsberg's special way of juxtaposing war and sex was anticipated at the time of World War I by none other than the surprising Amy Lowell. . . . Like Ginsberg, Amy Lowell senses that war is a "pattern" closely related to other patterns that constrict, stiffen, and stifle life. (p. 49-50)

"Howl" is the moment of breakthrough, the violent externalization of the ulcerous guilt of Ginsberg's discontent. Poetry is act, not object; but the more genuine the act, the more fully shaped is the object that is left behind. . . .

More so than most readers have realized, **"Howl"**

is a vehement anti-war poem. It is anti-war in its specific statements and in its stance towards "control." The poem describes, blames, purges, and transcends the world of relative consciousness, the It-World as described by Martin Buber in his *I and Thou* classic, the world of things, of walls, and doors, and inhibitions, and discriminations. (p. 52)

As Ginsberg draws it, the twentieth century is the dotage of the once vigorous enlightenment of the seventeenth and eighteenth centuries, the prurient and senile old man suffering from the hardened arteries of the intellect. Now that there is little further room for beneficial exploration, the values that were so necessary to man as he pushed back the frontiers of science and the New World have turned to rend their master and suck his soulblood. (p. 58)

It would be wrong to think that Ginsberg is describing only a particular American culture; he is attacking the radix or soul of which our culture is but the body. In that sense Ginsberg is indeed a *radical* poet and thinker. His particular radicalism is not by any means original (it is essentially Christ's battle with the Pharisees, Siddhartha's struggle with Vedic Brahmanas, Tolstoy's struggle with Russian orthodoxy, Lear's struggle with Goneril and Regan), but it is unique in its passion and in its grounding in Ginsberg's own personal suffering. (p. 60-1)

[Surely] with Ginsberg one ought to avoid what Northrop Frye has called the "debauchery of judiciousness." A poet and a poetry that draw inspiration from the battle against Moloch, the heavy judger, may perhaps be granted the boon of our nonjudgment. They deserve attention and description, but are not illuminated by qualitative tags. This poetry purposely seeks to throw away, violate, and make such standards inoperative. It is perhaps formless, but it may be formless as a living amoeba compared to an inanimate clam shell; it is perhaps mixed, but it may be mixed as a rich stew compared to purer but plainer broth. It may be without art, but it is also without artificiality and carries its own natural inscape. (p. 63-4)

As a poet Ginsberg associates language with the deepest spiritual impulses of man. Language that has been made to serve the judgmental rational faculty rather than the imagination and the deeper self will necessarily become as superficial and dangerous as the master it serves. The proliferation and prostitution of language through the mass media has transmogrified the natural magic power of language, words to express the ineffable and the transcendent, into evil black-magic language that denies the ineffable and transcendent and elevates the spiritless untruths of modern politics and culture.

A chief virtue of **"Wichita Vortex Sutra"** is that it makes the reader *experience* the proliferation and abuse of language. Its technique is to notice and reproduce the language that inundates the senses everyday, and in doing so it makes one painfully aware that in every case language is used not to communicate truth but to manipulate the hearer. (p. 71-2)

Ginsberg is not a great poet, but he is a great figure in the history of poetry. We do not win from him many new insights or subtle understandings, but we do take from his poetry a simple intensity and a certain freedom. His poetry has made it easier for others to speak honestly. His unabashed admission of his own insufficiency and anguish have helped make others aware of their own deprivations and insensitivity. Certainly we might have wished for a more tidy apostle of compassion, one who would spare us the unhappy details of his sex life, one who might combine reticence and discrimination with his genuine openness and honesty. . . . But prophets do not come made-to-order. Ginsberg is a flawed but necessary prophet, a man desperately crying in the wilderness for love, searching the world's religions for a sustaining vision, witnessing nakedly to man's timeless spiritual and physical desires. . . . (p. 75)

James F. Mersmann, "Allen Ginsberg: Breaking Out," in his *Out of the Vietnam Vortex: A Study of Poets and Poetry against the War,* University Press of Kansas, 1974, pp. 31-76.

ALLEN GINSBERG WITH KENNETH KOCH

(interview date 1977)

[An American poet, dramatist, nonfiction writer, and novelist, Koch, with Frank O'Hara and John Ashbery, formed what became known as the New York School of Poets, a group of writers whose avantgarde sensibility mirrored that of their contemporaries, the Beats. In the interview excerpted below, Koch and Ginsberg discuss the latter's poetic technique and influences.]

[Kenneth Koch]: *What do you like best about your own poetry?*

[Allen Ginsberg]: Cranky music.

Meaning?

Vowelic melodiousness, adjusted towards speech syncopation.

Vowelic?

Assonance, long mellow mouthings of assonance. Classic example: Moloch Moloch. In **"Howl,"** Moloch whose skyscrapers stand in the long streets—and so on.

You like the music in your poetry more than you like the content. Because your content is so striking and so . . .

My ambition for my content was to be totally personal. So it could rest on fact. I mean the world I knew. But the sound in my throat, that mellow music's part of the world I know. So if I get "hot" poetically, the vowels heat up.

Could you explain getting "hot" in poetry?

I mean inspiration in a literal way, as deep breath flowing out unobstructedly as long vowels, musical.

What brings on this state, if you can say anything about that? I believe some people have the idea about your work that you get poetic inspiration from, or have gotten it from, certain drugs, from certain political experiences, and so on. What's the truth about this?

The vowelic heat comes from single-minded devotional awareness of death. And the preciousness of the human body alive. Drugs have been a side experiment, just to cover those classical possibilities— Baudelaire, Gautier, old Bohemia. Buddhist Vajrayana studies reinforce natural inspiration. Because it's practice of breath awareness.

What helps you most to be in a single-minded devotional state?

Not trying to. It's accident, from resting in ordinary mind. . . .

What would you consider an ideal existence for yourself as a poet?

Retiring from the world, living in a mountain hut, practicing certain special meditation exercises half the day, and composing epics as the sun sets. I did that actually, for 10 days early September in a mountain hut in Southern Colorado. (p. 9)

How long would you have had to stay to feel good about writing?

About a thousand days. There is in Tantric study a specific three-year, three-month solitary retreat doing non-conceptual practices.

What does that do for you as a poet?

It clears the mind of false poetry, let's say. That is to say, self-centered poetry.

You said earlier your ideal in poetry was to be completely personal. Can one be that and not be self-centered?

That's a problem I have, and I'm working on it. I think there is, though. One would still be looking out of one's ego eyes, without attachment. If you sat for three years not doing anything you'd sure wind up that way, if you had a good teacher.

About non-attachment—your poetry seems so admirably attached to the world.

I'd rather use the word "involved."

Could you explain the difference?

Involved means present in the middle of, with complete awareness, and active. *Attached* means neurotically self-centered in the activity. That's the way I'm using those words.

Do you think your poetry may have gotten some of its energy from a conflict between being attached and wishing not to be?

No, I think the biggest energy is probably in the Moloch section of **"Howl"** and the "Hymns to Death" in **"Kaddish"** and the dramatic rants in this new **"Contest of the Bards"** poem. That energy, in the first two cases, comes from total belief in the subject—annihilation of civilization, inevitability of death. In the **"Contest of the Bards"** I found a dramatic form to go all-out into total self-belief through the mouths of characters. They can say anything I want. I don't have to take responsibility.

*Could you say something more about **"Contest of the Bards"**?*

That poem came in a burst of all-night writing. Thirty pages—later to be touched up, unscrambled a little. A few times my attention lapsed and the page got cross-hatched with corrections. But mostly a continuous stream of improvisation. Symmetric and perfect. Like **"Howl," "Kaddish"** and another poem I love, **"September on Jessore Road"** (at the end of *The Fall of America*). Poe said a long poem was impossible because he couldn't conceive of a long poem being written in one sitting. He thought you'd lose the lyric impulse if you worked on it over a period of years—months, years. But I think most poets have found that every few years they're liberated into a composition. That they can accomplish a vast epic in one night. Vast 30, 40 pages. I think most poets have that experience—most big poets. How long did it take Shelley to write "Ode to the West Wind?" Teatime? Before breakfast?

I think he wrote it in a park in Florence in one afternoon or one day.

On the other hand, I write a little bit every other day. I just write when I have a thought. Sometimes I have big thoughts, sometimes little thoughts. The deal is to accept whatever comes. Or work with whatever comes. Leave yourself open.

What do you have to have, or to be, to start with, in order to leave yourself open to produce good poetry?

A little glimpse of death, and the looseness and tolerance that brings.

I think I understand about the glimpse of death, but haven't ambition and passion and the wish for fame and power been at least as important in making you a good poet?

No, I think a glimpse of the death of power, fame and ambition liberated me from rigid interpretation of those stereotypes. Not that they don't exist in my head, but they exist side by side with taxicab noises and the gaps in between sounds. . . .

We were talking before about what you liked about your own poetry. I know the subject sounds a little egomaniacal and odd but,

in fact, what a poet likes about his poetry is what's usually called his taste—or that part of it he uses when he's writing. So what else do you like? You mentioned its music.

The other think I like is that I think it's witty or funny. That is the phrasing itself. (p. 44)

Could you tell me briefly which 20th-century poets have influenced your work?

Most recently, enormously, Charles Reznikoff, for his particular focus on sidewalks, parks and subways of New York. Williams, originally, for a large body of haiku-like concrete particulars in which "things are symbols of themselves." Particularly one poem of Williams lately—"Thursday"—which for me is the intersecting point between Buddhist "mindfullness" and American poetics. Then, further, Kerouac's spontaneous melodiousness (his long-sentence, Melville-like prose paeans to American disillusionment). One line of his particularly, "Trucks driving forward on the highway in a seizure of tarpaulin power." Hart Crane's Shelley-like apostrophes. Their musical structure. Especially "Atlantis." Eliot's nostalgic silent movies—"A crowd flowed over London Bridge, so many." Marsden Hartley's plainness and localism. Creeley's and Olson's mystique of syllables and physiology—that is, the line as an extension of the breath has affected me. In the New York schools, glamorization of the informal.

I thought I noticed in some recent short poems something closer to Gary Snyder than I'd seen before in your poetry.

Gary's always an influence. Towards muscular Chinese. That is to say, sharp specific images rising from actual physical work and familiarity—with woodchopping, Ponderosa pine, Sierra trails, and carpentry. Other influences, particularly toward music, have been the Blues of Richard "Rabbit" Brown (a 20's New Orleans guitar singer) and Dylan's marvelous use of rhyme.

What's the relationship, as you see it, of [**Journals: Early Fifties, Early Sixties**] *to your poetry?*

My poetry's more or less autobiographical. My model was Yeats. . . .

You didn't mention him as an influence.

Well, here we are again. Yeats, in giving a chronological accounting of his changes, from "Responsibilities" through "Crazy Jane." But there is also all this background accounting (which is what is in the [*Journals: Early Fifties, Early Sixties*])—sometimes ephemeral, sometimes traumas central to my life. (p. 46)

Allen Ginsberg and Kenneth Koch, in an interview in *The New York Times Book Review,* October 23, 1977, pp. 9, 44-6.

FRED MORAMARCO
(essay date 1982)

[In the following excerpt, Moramarco surveys Ginsberg's career from *Howl and Other Poems* (1956) to *Plutonian Ode* (1982), concluding that the author's verse follows solidly in the American literary tradition exemplified by Whitman, Thoreau, and Emerson.]

To read Allen Ginsberg's small, nearly square, black and white City Lights paperbacks one after another over a period of a few days—from *Howl and Other Poems* (1956) through *Plutonian Ode* (1982)—is to confront chronologically arranged obituary notices from the anguished soul of America during some of its most troubled days. From very early in his poetic career, Ginsberg has aimed at offering us an omniscient view of the American Spirit and a diagnosis of that spirit's ills. Sometimes that ambition has led him to a megalomania typical of many ambitious young American writers. . . .

But Ginsberg's early desire—to be perceived as a divinely inspired, gifted Dionysian spirit, yoking the poles of the romantic sensibility, the luminous visions of Blake with the Democratic Vistas of Whitman—was largely realized in the poetry he produced during the 1960s and early 1970s which reached probably as large an audience as serious poetry ever has in this country. Ginsberg became a guru to thousands upon thousands of young people who saw in what they perceived as his unrelenting and large-spirited honesty an alternative to the cant and double-speak of establishment America during its most hypocritical (Vietnam-Watergate) years.

Our news of Ginsberg during these years emanated really not from his poetry but rather from a series of important social, political, and literary events in which he participated: Ginsberg and the *Howl* obscenity trial; Ginsberg on the road with Ken Kesey's Merry Pranksters; Ginsberg and the anti-war demonstrations; Ginsberg and the trial of the Chicago Seven; Ginsberg and LSD; Ginsberg and Gay Rights; Ginsberg expressing outrage that Gregory Corso is denied the National Book Award for *Elegiac Feelings American* and winning it himself for *The Fall of America;* Ginsberg and the establishment of the Jack Kerouac School of Disembodied Poetics at the Naropa Institute in Colorado, and Ginsberg and "The Great Naropa Poetry Wars." . . .

Surely no other contemporary poet has lived so closely to the edge of the historical contours of his time;

consequently, Ginsberg's work has always been overshadowed by and overwhelmed by the events of his life. People, including poetry critics, have always been more interested in Ginsberg's actions than in his writing. . . . His detractors will argue that there is not much to *say* about the poetry; that it lacks the subtlety and grace of a John Ashbery, the metaphorical resonance of an Adrienne Rich, the syntactical and linguistic complexity of a John Berryman. Plainly and simply, what you see and what you hear in a Ginsberg poem, is what you get.

But this sort of criticism, it seems to me, misses the center of Ginsberg's primary poetic achievement, which was and is to embody literally several of Ezra Pound's most cherished conceptions of the role of the artist and poet in the twentieth century. Two of the most important of these are his description of artists as the "antennae of the race" and his insistence that a fundamental role of the poet is "to purify the language of the tribe." This dual role, both prophetic and cathartic, has been a part of Ginsberg's poetic strategy from the beginning. Like Frank O'Hara, a writer with whom he is not often associated because of superficial academic distinctions between the beat generation and the New York School, he created new possibilities for a younger generation of poets, providing a framework within which they could verify and articulate their own experience.

The key word there is "experience," for the Pound-Eliot legacy demanded attention not so much to the physical and human environment of an individual's daily life, but rather to the "tradition," to the historical record, and to particular details of poetic craft that can be garnered from that record. In order to "make it new" (Pound's often-repeated adage), a poet had to develop a sense of what poets in the English language had achieved up to the present moment. Working on the forefront of poetic innovation required an ability to subordinate one's individual talent to the dictates of tradition. Ginsberg, shouting his barbaric yawp over the rooftops of the world in *Howl,* began to change that conception and, over the years, consistently validated the primacy of personal experience for contemporary poets. (p. 10)

This emphasis on personal experiences in the poetry itself further directed most readers to look to Ginsberg's life for his poetic sources. The poetry cannot, of course, be separated from that life, but a retrospective look at a handful of his most significant poems shows his work to be firmly grounded in many mainstream literary traditions. In addition to Whitman and Blake, Ginsberg learned much about writing poetry from the English Romantic poets, from Milton and Christopher Smart, from Edgar Allan Poe, and, closer to his own generation, from Pound and William Carlos Williams. He drew on his own Jewish heritage for **"Kaddish,"** the poem many regard as his best, and his travels in the orient and intensive study of Tibetan Buddhism infused his work with yet another layer of allusiveness. I think we can now see both the innovative aspects of Ginsberg's work and its traditional base. On the one hand there is the new freedom he brought to poetry by confronting experience directly, by cleansing and purifying the language of the layers of falsity and indirection that it had accumulated. To write in a "received" language, Ginsberg tacitly proposed—whether of politics, religion, poetry, or whatever field—is to deny the reality of the self's perceptions. On the other hand there is the tradition he garnered from the previous generation—most notably Williams and Pound—whose work similarly reflects both innovative and conservative tendencies. That such a combination of individual talent and tradition should now seem less radical and revolutionary than it did even a short time ago should come as no surprise.

But recent history makes it difficult for us (and certainly for a new generation of students and readers) to resuscitate a society as decorous and with so many suppressed and unarticulated energy centers as the America of the mid-1950s. Blacks sat quietly in the backs of southern buses, gays safely in the closet, women "happy" in the kitchen. It was the best of times—as we see on television's *Happy Days;* it was the worst of times—as we see in Allen Ginsberg's *Howl.* (pp. 10-11)

Looking at the simply literary dimensions of the poem now, apart from the controversy and sensationalism that surrounded its publication and lingered with it for years afterward, one is struck by the sheer aggressiveness of its language, the exotic and esoteric diction through which Ginsberg struggles to make his vision—*what* he saw—palpable, physically tangible. For how does one "see" a mind destroyed by madness? Ginsberg responds by creating images that give the abstraction solidity. He learned early from Ezra Pound to "go in fear of abstractions" and from William Carlos Williams to "make a start out of particulars." The first section of *Howl* embodies both these concepts. Ginsberg offers us a catalog of the particular sorts of madness he saw flourishing in the America of the 1950s. . . .

We might think of the idea expressed . . . [in *Howl*] as an early version of R. D. Laing's by now hackneyed psychological principle: in an insane world, only those thought of as mad have a kind of luminous sanity. This effect is intensified by Ginsberg's associating adjectives with nouns that never knew them before: "unshaven rooms," "ashcan rantings," "hydrogen jukebox," "bop kaballa," "visionary indian angels," "saintly motorcyclists," "wild cooking pederasty," "symbolic ping pong table," "hotrod-Golgotha jail-solitude watch," "naked and endless head."

In these post acid-rock days, when such juxtapo-

sitions have become as common as stone soup, it's hard to recall that the language did not always have this sort of imaginative adaptability. In fact, to a generation whose cultural sensibilities have been shaped by the unrestrained emotional intensity of rock lyrics, by the subversive rhythms of the Rolling Stones and the Kinks and by the social criticism of Bob Dylan, Ginsberg's *Howl* may appear to be a positively conservative document. I played an early recording of *Howl* for my class in contemporary poetry and one student said it sounded to her like the lines had been composed by a computer. Another (a Korean student) said it sounded as if he were running for President. Both these responses, stressing the mechanistic and rhetorical aspects of the poem, would have been impossible until very recently. But in retrospect, one is struck by the attention Ginsberg pays to line length, to repetitive refrains, to balance, to generally formal matters. The "barbaric yawp" seems less barbaric, more clearly tied to highly civilized literary traditions.

The connection between Ginsberg's work and these traditions can be more cogently illustrated in a poem that was written before *Howl* (in 1954 and 1955) but published later in the *Reality Sandwiches* (1963) collection. The long, meditative **"Siesta in Xbalba and Return to the States"** is the centerpiece of that volume, which is based on some of Ginsberg's experiences in Mexico during the first seven months of 1954. The poem is built around the contrast indicated by the title. Lying in a hammock in a small Mexican village, Ginsberg toys with the idea of staying forever, of never returning to his complex, intense, citified life in the States. . . . The feeling here is much like that generated by James Wright's brief but wonderfully evocative lyric, "While Lying in a Hammock on William Duffy's Farm in Pine Island, Minnesota." In both poems the withdrawal from "civilization" and "society" that occurs as the poet lies in the hammock observing the scenery around him is treated ambiguously. Are the months "valuable" *because* he is lying in the hammock, or is he losing "valuable" time by "doing nothing"? Ginsberg's reminiscence of urban life intrudes. . . . The narrator's attention shifts back and forth from the hammock to . . . [a] party in New York, and the experience of straddling the two worlds in his imagination allows him to objectify both of them by stepping outside of himself and observing his participation in both. This is a wonderful moment in the poem—a metamorphosis reminiscent of Ovid via Ezra Pound. . . . (p. 11)

The illumination leads the narrator to speculate on objectifying not only his immediate surroundings and imaginings, but his very relationship to the earth itself. The poem moves outward from the poet's mind to the contours of the landscape around him to the curvature of the earth itself. It is, Ginsberg indicates, a drug-induced vision (prefiguring the LSD-inspired ecological vision of his later poem, **"Wales Visitation"**) but it is also one of the most beautiful descriptions of a natural landscape that occurs in his poetry. . . . The meditation on the landscape around him becomes a meditation on time, death, and eternity as day turns to night in the poem. An image of the rising moon supplants the image of the "Late sun" which began the poem, and Ginsberg's attention is captured by an ancient sculptured figure on the wall. . . . (pp. 11-12)

The poem moves deeper and deeper into the night and early morning hours, and its language, by incorporating Mexican place names, becomes more exotic, dreamlike, apparitional. In a note, Ginsberg tells us that "Xbalba, translatable as Morning Star in Region Obscure, or Hope, and pronounced Chivalva, is the area in Chiapas between the Tobasco border and the Usumascintla River at the edge of the Peten Rain Forest; the boundary of lower Mexico and Guatemala today is thereabouts. The locale was considered a Purgatory or Limbo, the legend is vague, in the (Old) Mayan Empire." The note clarifies certain references in the poem as the reader moves further from the stability of the physical world into the strange, dark limbo of the unknowable. . . . After evoking the names of the pre-Columbian civilizations which flourished in this place, Ginsberg surveys the surviving ruins and notices how they have become intertwined with the natural landscape. Nature's work, and man's, has become one with the passage of time. . . .

A burst of daylight intrudes upon the meditation at this point, and we are made to see time's passage from another perspective. The poem's night has turned into day, and the traditional symbol of morning—of the affirmation and continuity of life—disrupts the narrator's reverie. . . . The disruption is momentary. The narrator closes his eyes (to shut out the present) and returns to ruminating on the ruins of the past. The meditation appears to awaken in him a sense of a personal connection with past civilizations and previous human achievements. He wants to see more of the "ancient continent" before the physical remains of the past are totally obliterated by "the ultimate night / of war."

But his realization of a connection with the past also makes him aware of a specific tradition to which he—as a contemporary American poet—is related, as well as a future to which he has an obligation. In a remarkable passage which embodies imagery from America's greatest literature—Whitman, Melville, Crane (both Stephen and Hart), Pound, and others—Ginsberg appears to *become* the American literary imagination searching for a direction. . . . "Toward what city / will I travel?" Ginsberg asks, "What wild houses do I go to occupy?" The poem's first section ends with the recollection of a mystical experience Ginsberg had in his New York apartment in 1948. At that time Ginsberg believes he heard Blake's voice and saw "the mo-

tionless buildings / of New York rotting / under the tides of Heaven." That recollection evokes a symbolic rendering of Ginsberg's divided muse: is he to be the poet of Moloch or the poet of the inner self ? Does his imagination owe its allegiance to America or to the human spirit? This part of the poem ends with the question unanswered. . . . (p. 12)

The second section of the poem is more easily summarized than the first. There is a "Jump in time" to the future when Ginsberg begins his return to the States, carrying with him some lingering images of his Mexican experience: a busload of blue-hooded nuns, some mummies he saw at Guanajuato, and the memory of a voyeuristic moment as he watched two couples dancing. . . . Looking at death (the mummies) on the one hand and life (the two dancing couples) on the other, Ginsberg identifies what he regards to be the fundamental tragedy of human experience:

> The problem is isolation
> —there in the grave
> or here in oblivion of light.

He feels his solitude deeply, but as he nears the American border he braces himself for the task he sees as his destiny. He is to be Moloch's poet, the heir of Whitman and Pound, the contemporary embodiment of America's poetic soul. . . . [The] concluding lines signal Ginsberg's intention to confront the chaos of contemporary America directly in his poetry—to awaken from the "siesta in Xbalba" and return to the States both in person and in the subject matter of his poetry. The life of the imagination is to be put to work transcribing the world that worships Moloch.

Such a singleness of purpose was not to last long. In 1961, Ginsberg embarked on the S.S. *America* with Peter Orlovsky for a trip to Europe and regions further east. Much of the work in *Planet News* (1968) is an outgrowth of this experience and of a later trip abroad. The poems here do indeed bring news of the planet: from Bombay, Milan, Tokyo, and Calcutta, from Prague, Warsaw, Wales, New York, Washington, and Wichita. It is perhaps the first book of poetry of the "global village," written in the same period that McLuhan coined that suggestive phrase.

A recurrent theme in *Planet News* is what Ginsberg regards as the magical ability of the poet to recapitulate the creation, through the power of language, in every poem he writes. Out of nothing—*ex nihilo*—he creates a vibrant, living world of language over which he has total control. Consequently, the poet can take on earthshaking issues and problems in his work and solve them—exorcize the demons—right there on the page. The creation of poetry is persistently likened to both sexual procreation and theological notions of the creation. . . . This theme reaches its climax in the remarkable verbal conjury of **"Wichita Vortex Sutra,"** where the poet, regardless of his impotence in the world's physical reality, is omnipotent in the realm of language. . . . (pp. 12-13)

The Wichita poem has been exhaustively explicated by a number of critics, but **"Wales Visitation,"** one of Ginsberg's most delicately crafted visionary poems, has not yet had the attention it merits. . . . The sensationalistic LSD associations of this poem—it is dated and placed "July 29, 1967 (LSD)—August 3, 1967 (London)"—have caused some readers to overlook the poem's traditional romanticism. But just as **"Siesta in Xbalba"** is directly related to America's literary past, **"Wales Visitation"** evokes the English Romantic literary tradition more fully than anything else in Ginsberg's work, though his books are punctuated throughout with references to Blake and Shelley.

The poem's first stanza offers us a description of nature as viewed through a window. The linguistic coupling of various discrete natural elements—phrases like "mountain brow," "rivers of wind," "clouds arise / as on a wave"—suggests the interdependence of nature. The fact that our point of view in the poem is situated behind "mullioned glass" proposes a split, a barrier between humankind and nature. Reminiscent of the woman in Whitman's "Song of Myself," who observes twenty-eight young men bathing by the shore from behind the blinds of her window and hence is physically separated from them, though spiritually attuned to them, the narrator of this poem proposes to penetrate the barrier separating humans from nature. The archaic and esoteric language mixed with modern diction ("raine," "Bardic," "Albion," "Visitacione," / "Ecology," "manifest," "lightbulbs") gives the vision expressed in the poem a timelessness. That is, it brings the "continuing timelessness" of ancient nature language very much into the modern world. . . .

[In] the poem's second section, . . . the narrator (who is clearly Ginsberg himself) recalls seeing himself on television in London. The "network of TV pictures flashing bearded your Self " described in this stanza is paralleled later in the poem with "tree-lined canals network through live farmland." We glimpse a modern technological man associated primarily with the city which has separated him from nature—imprisoned him and wounded his spirit—represented in the poem by "London's symmetrical thorned tower." Electronic impulses flash the image of the poet's "Self " throughout London, but the truer "self " remains linked to the English countryside and to the historical tradition of poets of the English language. . . .

The allusion to the English Romantic poets observing nature and writing about it, as well as the images evoking time's passage and death ("cloud's passing through skeleton arches"), reveal the continuity of the poetic act—the human urgency to find words for the ultimate ineffability of nature: "Bard Nameless as

the Vast," Ginsberg writes, "babble to the Vastness!" The landscape description expands to encompass England's entire topography, vibrating with life, breathing, budding, quivering, copulating. The poem's quickening rhythms—clearly imitating the rhythms of sexual intercourse—lead the reader to the climactic moment of enlightenment at the poem's center. This experience is one of feeling a complete oneness with the earth itself—reminiscent of the transcendent moment in the midst of Andrew Marvell's "The Garden," in which the poet feels a sense of the earth's marvelous abundance and falls to the ground in nearly delirious celebration. Ginsberg's visionary moment, magnified by the hallucinogenic properties of LSD, is even more tangibly physical; he observes the fecundity of the earth close up, involving all his senses in an adoration of the earth as the source and sustainer of all life. . . . No longer behind a window observing nature, Ginsberg has become one with it, part of an organic whole that combines an extraordinary delicacy with an overwhelming immensity. The air itself becomes the breath of this whole earth. . . . The secret doctrine of nature has been revealed: whatever is, is right.

Ginsberg's expression of the timelessness and interconnectedness of all life has many antecedents in English literature, from Blake's "world in a grain of sand" to Dylan Thomas's "force that through the green fuse / Drives the flower" and drives the poet's "green age" as well. Its American precursors are Emerson's famous "transparent eyeball" (a less graceful manifestation) and Whitman's very leaves of grass which are "no less than the journey-work of the stars." It appears in some sections of Pound's *Cantos* as well ("Learn of the green world what can be thy place / In scaled invention or true artistry") and Ginsberg's sensibility here appears saturated with all these sources. He finishes the poem as if remembering that he left out someone—William Carlos Williams. . . . (p. 13)

Ginsberg's new sense of human interaction with the physical earth itself leads easily to the vast spaces of the American landscape described throughout the long **"Poem of These States"** which occurs sporadically throughout *The Fall of America* (1972), the collection for which Ginsberg won the National Book Award. The poem was intended, Ginsberg told an interviewer, "to cover like a collage a lone consciousness travelling through these states during the Vietnam War." The war, of course, loomed larger and larger in America's psyche during the years this poem was written (1965-1971) and consequently is an insistently discordant note that punctuates the work from beginning to end. "Discordant," in fact, is a word which only punily suggests the clash of contradictions that typifies the American sensibility of the late 1960s as Ginsberg views it here. Listening to his car radio throughout the poem,

---

Ginsberg on his literary influences:

Christopher Smart, for the long line. Walt Whitman, for an element of the long line. Edward Carpenter, for another element of the long line. Kerouac for spontaneity of mind. Pound for precision and the reconstruction of the entire prosody. Williams for the use of the vernacular. Wordsworth for noting spots of time. Shelley and Hart Crane for mighty breath. Shakespeare for fluidity and liquidity of line. Burroughs for precision in imagery and for the use of *collage* and cut-up. Creeley for control of the breath in a line. Olson for expansion of the breath of the line. Whalen for the randomness of the notation, following the movement of the mind. Lamantia for the introduction of American surrealism. Tzara for the introduction of Dada humor. Breton for the introduction of the litany or the risks of extravagant images. LaForgue for the introduction of conversational style and *collage.*

Ginsberg, in a 1986 interview with Linda Hamalian in *The Literary Review.*

---

he hears the very soul of America in the voices and music emanating from the speaker. . . .

The deep fissures in American consciousness during this time is illustrated even more by the news, the "Radio static from Saigon," or the "California Radio Lady's Voice / Talking about Viet Cong." By paying attention to what is coming over the radio, Ginsberg is able to depict succinctly the late sixties American schizophrenia. News of a "search and destroy" mission in Vietnam is juxtaposed with the lyrics of a rock song from the Kinks. . . .

In contrast to the voice of America's soul emanating from the radio is the voice of Ginsberg himself, a palliative here, a calming influence in a troubled and chaotic time. In *The Fall of America* the Ginsberg presence is a voice of rationality rather than one of excess; he is no longer the "King of the May," the pranksterish persona who dominated *Planet News,* but a bardic figure trying to bring peace to the land. . . . The "money munching war machine" [in the poem **"A Vow"**] is, of course, the Moloch of *Howl* reconstituted and energized by the sacrificial deaths of the young Americans and Vietnamese who died in Vietnam. Ginsberg intends here once again to be Moloch's poet and conscience, purifying its corruptions of language and revealing its life-destructive madness wherever he finds it.

His assumption of this role explains why Ginsberg is one of a surprisingly small number of poets who has incorporated and absorbed modern technology in his poetry. To understand the beast one needs to journey into its belly, and so Ginsberg, progressing with technology, has given us Automobile poems, Airplane

Journal poems, TV Baby poems, and most recently, nuclear poems. At his best, he seems able to merge natural imagery with images of industry and technology with an ease that reflects once again (as **"Wales Visitation"** did) his essentially romantic proclivities, despite the fact that he is at heart thoroughly citified. This is a nature poet who grew up in Paterson. (p. 14)

Mind Breaths, published in 1978, is largely a turning inward toward the "vast empty quiet space" of personal consciousness. It is an elegiac volume, even more so than *The Fall of America,* containing poems on Neruda's death, on the dying and death of his father, on contemplating death's absolute finality. The most significant poem in the book is the long **"Contest of the Bards."** . . . In this poem, an old poet who lives in a stone house by the ocean is visited by a young poet who arrives "naked interrupting his studies & announces his own prophetic dreams to replace the old Bard's boring verities." The poem is a double allegory—of Ginsberg confronting the work of his youth, and of Ginsberg the older poet confronted with the impatience and energy of a new generation of poets.

But apart from the **"Contest of the Bards,"** the poems in *Mind Breaths* generally seem less cohesive and less reflective of specific social issues than most of Ginsberg's other collections. It is easily the most introspective of the City Lights books and it seemed to signal a meditational withdrawal from the social activism of all of Ginsberg's earlier work.

In *Plutonian Ode,* however, the social activist once again emerges, in some ways more strongly than ever, as the book focuses on the ultimate social issue—the issue of whether or not we will continue to exist as human societies and civilizations. The title poem describes the creation of "a new thing under the sun," the artificial element of plutonium, discovered by Dr. Glen Seaborg and others in 1940 and used as the explosive force in nuclear weapons and as a reactor fuel in nuclear power plants. Notice that Ginsberg's poem is called *Plutonian* Ode, not *Plutonium* Ode, and it is clear that he means to connect this demonic discovery with the ancient "Lord of Hades," the god Pluto. Plutonium may be a new thing under the sun, but the destructive impulse in humankind is as old as its history, and the conversion of mass to energy is the very stuff of the universe and precedes even the human presence. . . . (p. 16)

Plutonian Ode is Whitmanic in tone and scope . . . and resonates with exotic, mythical names giving it prophetic, Hebraic and incantatory qualities. But the poem is not at all remote; it is utterly contemporary. In the second of its three sections, Ginsberg sets out to make us more conscious of the presence of a nuclear reality all around us as we go about our daily lives. . . . In contrast to the burgeoning nuclear industry throughout the world, Ginsberg contemplates a "tranquil politic" emanating from a detoxified, denu-clearized world. Section Three of the poem is reminiscent of the famous "Mantra of American language" in **"Wichita Vortex Sutra"** which proclaims the power of language to reverse catastrophic events. Here, Whitman-like, he exhorts "Poets and Orators to come" to carry the anti-nuclear banner across the world. . . . (pp. 16-17)

Not all the poems in *Plutonian Ode* deal specifically with nuclear madness, but the word "plutonium" punctuates the volume like a discordant chord and the artificiality of the element symbolizes the destructive artificiality of contemporary life in many different manifestations. For example, a poem about New Jersey called **"Garden State,"** refers to the separation of individuals from the land they inhabit through layer upon layer of human-made destructiveness. The poem describes New Jersey as it used to be before. . . . Ginsberg's keen sense of place, evident everywhere in his work, laments the progressive alienation of human beings from their natural environments, and in *Plutonian Ode* his concerns seem closer than ever to those of his old friend Gary Snyder. Together they are our "whole earth poets," carrying the tradition of Whitman, Thoreau and Emerson into the latter part of the 20th century.

As we begin to view Ginsberg's work retrospectively, it becomes clearer than ever that his work is far less an aberrant diversion from mainstream American literary traditions as was once widely believed. His work seems now for us in the 1980s a central expression of that tradition, exemplifying the continuity of American poetry as well as its persistent originality. (p. 17)

Fred Moramarco, "Moloch's Poet: A Retrospective Look at Allen Ginsberg's Poetry," in *The American Poetry Review,* Vol. 11, No. 5, September-October, 1982, pp. 10-14, 16-18.

GREGORY STEPHENSON

(essay date 1983)

[In the following excerpt from an essay originally published in *Palantir* in 1983, Stephenson explores the religious and literary traditions that inform "Howl" and views the poem as chronicling the "psychic process" of modern transcendent social consciousness.]

Allen Ginsberg's poem **"Howl"** has been reviled and admired but has received little serious critical attention. Reviewers and critics have generally emphasized the social or political aspects of the poem, its breakthrough use of obscenity and its allusions to homosexuality, or

its long-line, free-verse, open form. For these reasons **"Howl"** is already being relegated to the status of a literary artifact. I want to consider **"Howl"** as essentially a record of psychic process and to indicate its relationship to spiritual and literary traditions and to archetypal patterns.

The concept of transcendence with the inherent problems of how to achieve it and where it leaves us afterward is central to romantic literature. This complex has its antecedents in Orphism, Pythagoreanism, Platonism, heterodox Judaism, Gnosticism, and the mystical tradition. **"Howl"** expresses a contemporary confrontation with the concept of transcendence and examines the personal and social consequences of trying to achieve and return from the state of transcendence.

Transcendence and its attendant problems may be summarized in this way: the poet, for a visionary instant, transcends the realm of the actual into the realm of the ideal, and then, unable to sustain the vision, returns to the realm of the actual. Afterwards the poet feels exiled from the eternal, the numinous, the superconscious. The material world, the realm of the actual, seems empty and desolate. . . . The poet (like Keats' knight-at-arms) starves for heavenly manna. This theme of transcendence is treated in the work of Coleridge, Wordsworth, Keats, Shelley, Nerval, Rimbaud, and many other poets and writers. **"Howl"** describes and resolves the problems, using as a unifying image the archetype of the night-sea journey. (pp. 50-1)

The movement of **"Howl"** (including **"Footnote to Howl"**) is from protest, pain, outrage, attack, and lamentation to acceptance, affirmation, love and vision—from alienation to communion. The poet descends into an underworld of darkness, suffering, and isolation and then ascends into spiritual knowledge, blessedness, achieved vision, and a sense of union with the human community and with God. The poem is unified with and the movement carried forward by recurring images of falling and rising, destruction and regeneration, starvation and nourishment, sleeping and waking, darkness and illumination, blindness and sight, death and resurrection.

In the first section of **"Howl,"** Ginsberg describes the desperation, the suffering, and the persecution of a group of outcasts, including himself, who are seeking transcendent reality. They are "starving" and "looking for an angry fix" in a metaphorical more than a literal sense. Both metaphors suggest the intensity of the quest, the driving need. (William S. Burroughs uses the phrase "final fix" as the object of his quest at the end of his novel *Junkie*.) The metaphor of narcotics is extended by their search for "the ancient heavenly connection." (Connection suggests not only a visionary experience in this context—a link to or a union with the divine—but also refers to the slang term for a source of narcotics in the 1940s and the 1950s.) These seekers are impoverished, alienated, arrested, and driven to suicide both by the hostility of the society in which they pursue their quest and by the desperate nature of the quest itself, by its inherent terrors and dangers.

Ginsberg's "angelheaded" seekers follow a sort of Rimbaudian "derangement of the senses" to arrive at spiritual clarity; they pursue a Blakean "path of excess to the Palace of Wisdom." They "purgatory" themselves in the manner of medieval flagellants with profligate and dissolute living (alcohol, sexual excess, peyote, marijuana, benzedrine). And through these means they achieve occasional epiphanous glimpses: angels on tenement roofs, "lightning in the mind", illuminations, brilliant insights, vibrations of the cosmos, gleamings of "supernatural ecstasy," visions, hallucinations; they are "crowned with flame," tantalized when "the soul illuminated its hair for a second," "crash through their minds," receive "sudden flashes," and make incarnate "gaps in Time & Space"; they trap "the Archangel of the soul" and experience the consciousness of "Pater Omnipotens Aeterna Deus." For such sensualized spirituality and for their frenzied pursuit of ultimate reality, they are outcast, driven mad, suicided (as Artaud says) by society, driven into exile, despised, incarcerated, institutionalized.

Ginsberg has phrased the issue in the first section of the poem as "the difficulties that nuts and poets and visionaries and seekers have. . . . The social disgrace—*dis*grace—attached to certain states of soul. The confrontation with a society . . . which is going in a different direction . . . knowing how to feel human and holy and not like a madman in a world which is rigid and materialistic and all caught up in the immediate necessities. . . . " The anguish of the visionary in exile from ultimate reality and desperately seeking reunion with it is intensified by a society which refuses to recognize the validity of the visionary experience and maintains a monopoly on reality, imposing and enforcing a single, materialist-rationalist view.

A number of the incidents in the first section are autobiographical, alluding to the poet's own experiences, such as his travels, his expulsion from Columbia University, his visions of Blake, his studies of mystical writers and Cézanne's paintings, his time in jail and in the asylum. Some of the more obscure personal allusions, such as "the brilliant Spaniard" in Houston, may be clarified by reading Ginsberg's *Journals.* Other references are to his friends and acquaintances—Herbert Huncke, William S. Burroughs, Neal Cassady, William Cannastra, and others. (pp. 51-3)

Ginsberg presents not only the personal tragedies and persecutions of his generation of seekers but alludes back to an earlier generation with embedded references to Vachel Lindsay "who ate fire in paint hotels" and Hart Crane "who blew and were blown by those

human seraphim, the sailors." And for the poet, the prototype of the persecuted and martyred visionary is his own mother, Naomi Ginsberg, who is twice mentioned in the poem and whose spirit provides much of the impetus for the poem. " 'Howl' is really about my mother, in her last year at Pilgrim State Hospital—acceptance of her later inscribed in *Kaddish* detail."

The personal nature of the references in **"Howl"** do not make it a poem *á clef* or a private communication. Nor is the poem reduced or obscured by its personal allusions. To the contrary, as images, the persons, places, and events alluded to have great suggestive power. They possess a mythic, poetic clarity. . . . For Ginsberg, as for Whitman, the personal communicates the universal. The images are ultimately autonomous and multivalent, engaging our poetic understanding by their very intensity and mystery. (pp. 53-4)

Several lines near the end of the first section (from "who demanded sanity trials" to "animal soup of time—") describe the exploits and sufferings of the dedicatee of the poem, Carl Solomon, the martyr in whom Ginsberg symbolizes his generation of oppressed celestial pilgrims. Ginsberg's statement of spiritual solidarity with Solomon—"ah Carl, while you are not safe I am not safe"—presages the climactic third section of the poem. This compassionate identification with a fellow quester-victim is very similar to the Bodhisattva vow in Buddhism and anticipates the poet's later interest in Buddhist thought.

After a statement on the technique and intention of the poem, the section ends with strong images of ascent and rebirth and with a suggestion that the martyrs are redemptive, sacrificial figures whose sufferings can refine the present and the future.

The second section of the poem continues and expands the image of pagan sacrifice with which the first section concludes. To what merciless, cold, blind idol were the "angelheaded" of section one given in sacrifice?, Ginsberg asks. And he answers, "Moloch!" Moloch (or Molech), god of abominations, to whom children were sacrificed ("passed through the fire to Molech"), the devil deity against whom the Bible warns repeatedly, is the ruling principle of our age. To him all violence, unkindness, alienation, guilt, ignorance, greed, repression, and exploitation are attributable. The poet sees his face and body in buildings, factories, and weapons—as Fritz Lang saw his devouring maw in the furnace of *Metropolis.*

Ginsberg presents a comprehensive nightmare image of contemporary society, an inventory of terrors and afflictions that is as penetrating as Blake's "London." And like Blake in "London," Ginsberg places the source of human woe within human consciousness and perception. Moloch is a condition of the mind, a state of the soul: "Mental Moloch!"; "Moloch whose name is the Mind!" We are born, according to Ginsberg, in a state of "natural ecstasy," but Moloch enters the soul early. (See Blake's "Infant Sorrow.") We can regain that celestial, ecstatic vision of life ("Heaven which exists and is everywhere about us!") by emerging from the belly of Moloch, the monster that has devoured us, who "ate up . . . [our] brains and imagination." We can "wake up in Moloch!"

The remainder of the second section returns to a lament for the visionaries of section one. American society is seen as having consistently ignored, suppressed, and destroyed any manifestation of the miraculous, the ecstatic, the sacred, and the epiphanous.

In the pivotal section two of **"Howl,"** Ginsberg names Moloch as the cause of the destruction of visionary consciousness and describes the manifestations of this antispirit, this malevolent god. Ginsberg also indicates that the Blakean "mind forg'd manacles" of Moloch can be broken and that beatific vision can be regained. In this section the poet has also made clear that transcendence is not merely of concern to poets and mystics but to every member of the social body. Ginsberg has shown the effects of a society without vision. Commercialism, militarism, sexual repression, technocracy, soulless industrialization, inhuman life, and the death of the spirit are the consequences of Mental Moloch.

The third section of the poem reaffirms and develops the sympathetic, affectionate identification of Ginsberg with the man who for him epitomizes the rebellious visionary victim. The section is a celebration of the courage and endurance of Carl Solomon, a final paean to the martyrs of the spirit, and an affirmation of human love.

The piteous and brave cry of Solomon from the Rockland Mental Hospital is the essence of the poem's statement; his is the howl of anguished and desperate conviction. "The soul is innocent and immortal it should never die ungodly in an armed madhouse." The image of the "armed madhouse" is both macrocosmic and microcosmic. Each human soul inhabits the defensive, fearful "armed madhouse" of the ego personality, the social self, and the American nation has also become "an armed madhouse." . . . The psychic armor that confines and isolates the individual ego selves and the nuclear armaments of the nation are mutually reflective; they mirror and create each other. At both levels, the individual and the national, the innocent and the immortal soul is starved, suffocated, murdered.

The imagery of crucifixion ("cross in the void," "fascist national Golgotha") reemphasizes Ginsberg's view of the visionary as sacrificial redeemer. Such images culminate in the poet's hope that Solomon "will split the heavens . . . and resurrect your living human Jesus from the superhuman tomb." I understand this to mean that Solomon will discover the internal messiah, liberate himself from Mental Moloch ("whose ear is a smoking tomb"), and attain spiritual rebirth.

The final images of **"Howl"** are confident and expansive, a projected apocalypse of Moloch, the Great Awakening "out of the coma" of life-in-death. Confinement, repression, alienation, and the dark night of the soul are ended. The "imaginary walls collapse" (walls of egotism, competition, materialism—all the woes and weaknesses engendered by Mental Moloch), and the human spirit emerges in victory, virtue, mercy, and freedom. The "sea-journey" of Solomon and of the human spirit is completed.

"Footnote to Howl," originally a section of **"Howl"** excised by Ginsberg on the advice of Kenneth Rexroth, extends the poet's vision of Blake's phrase "the Eye altering alters all" in "The Mental Traveller." The poem is a rhapsodic, Blakean, Whitmanesque illumination of the realm of the actual, the material world. If we accept and observe attentively, if we see, Ginsberg tells us, then all is reconciled and all is recognized for what it in essence truly is: holy, divine. (pp. 54-6)

The essence of everything, of every being, is holy; only the form may be foul or corrupted; therefore, "holy the visions . . . holy the eyeball." In this way Ginsberg's earlier assertion that "Heaven . . . exists and is everywhere about us" is extended and fulfilled. If we can wake up in Moloch, we can awake out of Moloch.

The acceptance of the body is essential for Ginsberg, for the senses can be a way to illumination. The body is where we must begin. Throughout **"Howl"** sexual repression or disgust with the body or denial of the senses have been seen as forms of Mental Moloch: "Moloch in whom I am a consciousness without a body!"; "where the faculties of the skull no longer admit the worms of the senses." That is why the **"Footnote"** proclaims: "The soul is holy! The skin is holy! The nose is holy! The tongue and cock and hand and asshole holy!" Body and spirit are affirmed and reconciled.

Heracleitus taught that "the way up and the way down are the same way." For Ginsberg, in his night-sea journey, the path of descent described in the first two sections of "Howl" has become the path of ascent, of victory and vision, as presented in section three and in **"Footnote to Howl." "Howl"** records a solstice of the soul, a nadir of darkness, and then a growth again towards light. The poem exemplifies Jack Kerouac's understanding that to be Beat was "the root, the soul of Beatific." (p. 57)

Ginsberg's sense of our common human necessity to redeem light from darkness, to seek vision and to practice virtue, is communicated in verse by the breath-measured, long-line, chant rhythm of **"Howl."** . . .

"Howl" is linked not only to the romantic tradition but also to the preliterary, oral, magic incantations of the universal shamanist tradition.

"Howl" not only invokes and participates in the tradition of vatic poetry but significantly contributes to and furthers that tradition. The poem's considerable achievements, by Ginsberg's use of myth, rhythm, and

prophetic vision, are the resolution of the problems associated with transcendence and the embodiment in verse of a new syncretic mode of spiritual awareness, a new social consciousness. (p. 58)

Gregory Stephenson, "Allen Ginsberg's 'Howl': A Reading," in his *The Daybreak Boys: Essays on the Literature of the Beat Generation,* Southern Illinois University Press, 1990, pp. 50–8.

SOURCES FOR FURTHER STUDY

Breslin, James E. B. "Allen Ginsberg's 'Howl'." In his *From Modern to Contemporary: American Poetry, 1945-1965,* pp. 77-109. Chicago: The University of Chicago Press, 1984.
> Explication of *Howl* with an investigation of the poem's origins.

Hyde, Lewis, ed. *On the Poetry of Allen Ginsberg.* Ann Arbor: The University of Michigan Press, 1984, 462 p.
> Collection of essays and reviews on Ginsberg's works, with selections from Ginsberg's correspondence with critics and writers.

Merrill, Thomas F. *Allen Ginsberg.* Revised edition. Boston: Twayne Publishers, 1988, 161 p.
> Critical overview of Ginsberg's life and career through *Plutonian Ode.* Includes selected bibliography.

Ostriker, Alicia. "Blake, Ginsberg, Madness, and the Prophet as Shaman." In *William Blake and the Moderns,* edited by Robert J. Bertholf and Annette S. Levitt, pp. 111-31. Albany: State University of New York Press, 1982.
> Examines William Blake's influence on Ginsberg's poetry, focusing on the theme of insanity in "Howl," "Kaddish," and *The Fall of America.*

Portugés, Paul. *The Visionary Poetics of Allen Ginsberg.* Santa Barbara, Calif.: Ross-Erikson Publishers, 1978, 181 p.
> Analyzes Ginsberg's verse apropos of his mystical experience in 1948 during which he believes he heard William Blake's voice. Includes conversations with Ginsberg about what he considers essential components of his visionary quest: drugs, mantras, and meditation.

Tytell, John. "Allen Ginsberg and the Messianic Tradition." In his *Naked Angels: The Lives & Literature of the Beat Generation,* pp. 212-57. New York: McGraw-Hill, 1976.
> Analysis of Ginsberg's roots in the work of such authors as Walt Whitman, William Blake, William Carlos Williams, and Jack Kerouac.

Johann Wolfgang von Goethe

1749-1832

(Also Göthe, Göethe) German poet, novelist, dramatist, short fiction writer, essayist, critic, biographer, memoirist, and librettist.

INTRODUCTION

Goethe is considered Germany's greatest writer and a genius of the highest order. He distinguished himself as a scientist, artist, musician, and philosopher, he had successful careers as a theater director and court administrator as well. Excelling in various genres and literary styles, Goethe was a shaping force in the major German literary movements of the late eighteenth and early nineteenth centuries. His first novel, *Die Leiden des jungen Werthers* (1774; *The Sorrows of Young Wether*), epitomizes the *Sturm und Drang,* or Storm and Stress, movement, and his dramas *Iphigenie auf Tauris* (1787; *Iphigenia in Tauris*) and *Torquato Tasso* (1790), as well as the poetry collection *Römische Elegien* (1795; *Goethe's Roman Elegies*), exemplify the neoclassical approach to literature. His drama *Faust* is among the greatest works of nineteenth-century Romanticism. *Faust* is ranked beside the masterpieces of Dante and Shakespeare, thus embodying Goethe's humanistic ideal of a world literature transcending the boundaries of nations and historical periods.

The son of an Imperial Councilor, Goethe was born in Frankfurt am Main into an established bourgeois family. By the age of eight, he had composed an epistolary novel in which the characters correspond in five languages. Against his wishes, Goethe studied law at the university of Leipzig, but devoted most of his time to art, music, science, and literature. His university studies were interrupted by illness, and Goethe spent his convalescense learning about alchemy, astrology, and occult philosophy, subjects which would inform the symbolism of *Faust.* His earliest literary works, including the rococo-styled love poetry of *Buch Annette* (1767), are considered accomplished but not outstanding. A decisive influence on Goethe's early literary work was Johann Gottfried von Herder, whom the poet met in Strasbourg, where he continued his legal studies. Herder taught Goethe to appreciate the elemental emotional power of poetry, directing his attention to Shakespeare, Homer, Ossian, and German folk songs. *Götz von Berlichingen mit dem eisernen Hand* (1773; *Goetz of Berlichingen with the Iron Hand*) exemplifies Goethe's work of this period. Somewhat Shakespearean in its emphasis on action and high emotion, the drama was popular in its time, but modern critics generally consider it superficial.

Having completed his studies, Goethe spent several years in Frankfurt practicing law. During this time he fell in love with Charlotte Buff, a friend's fiancée. These feelings and his reaction to a widely-reported story about a young man who had killed himself over an unhappy love affair inspired *The Sorrows of Young Werther.* An epistolary novel describing the despair and eventual suicide of a young artist in love with a married woman, *Werther* created a sensation throughout Europe and made Goethe famous. Dozens of imitations and satires appeared, and a number of impressionable young readers followed the example of the novel's protagonist. Critics in England and the United States denounced Goethe as immoral for promoting what they saw as perverse emotionalism. However, *Werther* inspired many artists, who embraced Goethe's work as a powerful expression of the spirit of *Sturm und Drang.* One of *Werther*'s admirers was Duke Karl August of Saxe-Weimar-Eisenbach, who invited Goethe to visit him in Weimar. An intended brief stay became a lifelong residence, during which the poet occupied various official positions and served for more than 25 years as director of the ducal theater. Although nourished spiritually by his friendship with Charlotte von Stein, the cultured wife of a court official, Goethe wrote little during his first decade in Weimar. In 1786, restless and discontented, he left for Italy and Greece, where southern landscapes and classical art renewed his creative vigor and brought about a new phase in his development as a writer. *Roman Elegies,* exquisitely sensuous poetry written in classical meter, and *Hermann und Dorothea* (1798; *Herman and Dorothea*), a narrative poem in hexameters, evince Goethe's interest in formal unity and ordered language, contrasting with the emotionally and structurally extravagant works of his *Sturm und Drang* period. The French writer Madame de Staël is among several critics who claim that Goethe's artistic universality stems from his successful integration of northern and southern European literary traditions. The poet himself regarded this period, recounted later in *Italienische Reise* (1816; *Italian Journey*), as a turning point in his career.

Goethe's sojourn in southern Europe also enlivened his interest in science. His *Versuch, die Metamorphose der Pflanzen zu erklären* (1790; *Goethe's Botany: The Metamorphosis of Plants*) expounds the theory that, as Erich Heller explained, "all the single parts which constitute a plant are derived from one original formation." In Goethe's view, metamorphosis from archetypes also operates in the spiritual realm: "Man must be capable of elevating himself to the highest form of reason if he wishes to come in contact with the Divine, which manifests itself in physical as in moral archetypes (*Urphänomene*), concealing itself behind them as they emanate from it." In addition to his work on morphology, Goethe wrote *Beiträge zur Optik* (1791-92), a study of optics, and *Zur Farbenlehre* (1810; *Theory of Colours*), in which he postulated the indivisibility of light; thus opposing the discoveries of the renowned physicist Sir Isaac Newton. Rejected by specialists, Goethe's scientific writings drew praise from thinkers who emphathized with the poet's universalist world view. In the twentieth century, such theorists as Ernest Lehrs and anthroposophist Rudolf Steiner championed Goethe's scientific ideas for their spiritual implications. As Heller stated, "[Goethe's] scientific convictions are mere aspects of that faith which forms the core of his spiritual existence: the faith in a perfect correspondence between the inner nature of man and the structure of external reality, between the soul and the world."

In 1794, Goethe started an artistically and intellectually stimulating friendship with the poet Friedrich Schiller, in whom he found a kindred soul and sympathetic critic. During their ten-year friendship the two poets passionately explored philosophical, scientific, and literary issues. In their correspondence, a virtual intellectual history of their time, they commented on each other's works; Schiller's remarks significantly influenced Goethe's *Bildungsroman, Wilhelm Meisters Lehrjahre* (1795-96; *Wilhelm Meister's Apprenticeship*), as well as *Faust.* Fascinated by the legend of Faust—the scholar who is prepared to endanger his immortal soul to satisfy his tremendous thirst for knowledge—Goethe had been at work on the drama since his student days in Strasbourg. In 1790 he published an incomplete version, *Faust: Ein Fragment.* In 1808, three years after Schiller's death, the complete version of the first part appeared. The subject continued to absorb Goethe throughout his life, and *Faust II* was published posthumously in 1832. Romantic and spirited, the first part is a dazzling reflection of Goethe's youthful mind, while *Faust II,* at once ironic and idealistic, comprises the wealth of his mature intellect. For its poetic power, formal variety and complexity, and philosophical universality, the first part of *Faust* was immediately recognized as a masterpiece of mythic proportions. *Faust II,* however, was not fully analyzed or appreciated until the twentieth century.

During the last decades of life, Goethe took on something of the role of a sage, as writers and artists from Europe and America travelled to Weimar to visit him. Goethe remained active artistically until the end of his life. The massive *Aus meinem Leben: Dichtung und Wahrheit* (1811-33; *The Autobiography of Goethe: Truth and Poetry from My Own Life*) documents the poet's rich intellectual and emotional life, containing ideas and opinions on a wide variety of topics. The novels *Wilhelm Meisters Wanderjahre* and *Die Wahlverwandtschaften* (1809; *Elective Affinities*), innovative in form and modern in the emphasis on the characters' inner life, have been especially acclaimed in the twentieth century. Goethe's later poetry includes some of his greatest accomplishments, from the *West-östlischer Divan* (1819; *Goethe's West-Easterly Divan*), a lyric cycle based on the *Divan* by the Persian poet Hafiz, to the mournful *Marienbader Elegie* (1827). The rich productions of his old age illustrate Goethe's evolution from the impetuous *Sturm und Drang* genius to the wise artist willing to reconcile his mystical idealism with an awareness of human frailty and limitations.

Following his death, Goethe's literary reputation diminished outside of the German-speaking world. Twentieth-century British and American critics have generally acknowledged Goethe's greatness. Benedetto Croce lauded Goethe as a master of lyric expression while questioning the importance of his prose. T. S. Eliot asserted that Goethe is more noteworthy for his genius than for his literary ability. Generally more favorable to Goethe than their American and European colleagues, German critics have viewed their national poet as one of the central figures of world literature. According to Ernst Robert Curtius, Goethe "is the final self-concentration of the western mind in a great individual." As such, Curtius affirmed, Goethe "is something more and something other than a German poet. He is . . . with the spiritual heritage of Europe. He stands in the line of Homer, Sophocles, Plato, Aristotle, Virgil, Dante, and Shakespeare. . . . This consciousness of solidarity through the millenia Shakespeare could not have had, Dante only within the Latin tradition. To Goethe it was given as a legitimation and corroboration of his mission. It is a sign, so to speak, from the 'alphabet of the universal spirit'."

(For further information about Goethe's life and works, see *Dictionary of Literary Biography*, Vol. 94: *German Writers in the Age of Goethe* and *Nineteenth-Century Literature Criticism*, Vols. 4, 22.)

CRITICAL COMMENTARY

JOHANN WOLFGANG VON GOETHE
(poem date 1808)

[In the following elegiac ode, which originally appeared in 1808 as the preface to the first part of *Faust*, Goethe expresses his devotion to his latest work.]

Again you come, you hovering forms! I find you,
As early to my clouded sight you shone!
Shall I attempt, this once, to seize and bind you?
Still o'er my heart is that illusion thrown?
You crowd more near! Then, be the reign assigned
    you,
And sway me from your misty, shadowy zone!
My bosom thrills, with youthful passion shaken,
From magic airs that round your march awaken.

Of joyous days you bring the blissful vision;
The dear, familiar phantoms rise again,
And, like an old and half-extinct tradition,
First love returns, with friendship in his train.
Renewed is pain: with mournful repetition
Life tracks his devious, labyrinthine chain,
And names the good, whose cheating fortune tore
    them

From happy hours, and left me to deplore them.

They hear no longer these succeeding measures,
The souls, to whom my earliest songs I sang:
Dispersed the friendly troop, with all its pleasures,
And still, alas! the echoes first that rang!
I bring the unknown multitude my treasures;
Their very plaudits give my heart a pang,
And those beside, whose joy my song so flattered,
If still they live, wide through the world are scat-
    tered
And grasps me now a long-unwonted yearning
For that serene and solemn spirit-land:
My song, to faint Aeolian murmurs turning,
Sways like a harp-string by the breezes fanned.
I thrill and tremble; tear on tear is burning,
And the stern heart is tenderly unmanned.
What I possess, I see far distant lying;
And what I lost, grows real and undying.

Johann Wolfgang von Goethe, in his dedication to his *Faust: A Tragedy,* translated by Bayard Taylor, 1871. Reprint by Washington Square Press, 1964, p. 1.

Principal Works

Die Laune des Verliebten (drama) 1767

Neue Lieder (poetry) 1769

Die Leiden des jungen Werthers (novel) 1774

[The Sorrows of Werter, 1779; also published as Werter and Charlotte, 1786; and The Sorrows of Young Werther, 1929; and The Sufferings of Young Werther, 1957]

Iphigenie auf Tauris (drama) 1787

[Iphigenia in Tauris, 1793]

Der Triumph der Empfindsamkeit [first publication] (drama) 1787

Faust: Ein Fragment (poetry) 1790

Torquato Tasso (drama) 1790

[Torquato Tasso published in Torquato Tasso: A Dramatic Poem from the German with Other German Poetry, 1827]

Beiträge zur Optik (essay) 1791-92

Reineke Fuchs (poetry) 1794

[History of Renard the Fox, 1840; also published as Reynard the Fox, 1853]

Römische Elegien (poetry) 1795

[Goethe's Roman Elegies, 1876?]

Wilhelm Meisters Lehrjahre (novel) 1795-96

[Wilhelm Meister's Apprenticeship, 1824]

Xenien [with Friedrich Schiller] (poetry) 1797

[Goethe and Schiller's Xenions, 1896]

Faust (drama) 1808

[Faust published in Faust: A Drama by Goethe and Schiller's Song of the Bell, 1823]

Die Wahlverwandtschaften (novel) 1809

[Elective Affinities published in Novels and Tales by Göethe, 1854]

Aus meinen Leben: Dichtung und Wahrheit (autobiography) 1811-22

[Memoirs of Goethe: Written by Himself, 1824; also published as The Autobiography of Goethe: Truth and Poetry from My Own Life, 1848]

Italienische Reise (travel essay) 1816

[Travels in Italy published in Goethe's Travels in Italy Together with His Second Residence in Rome and Fragments on Italy, 1885; also translated as Italian Journey, 1970]

West-östlicher Divan (poetry) 1819

[Goethe's West-Easterly Divan, 1877; also published as West-Eastern Divan, 1914]

Wilhelm Meisters Wanderjahre; oder, Die Entsagenden (novel) 1821; enlarged edition, 1828

[Wilhelm Meister's Travels; or, The Renunciants published in German Romance, 1827; enlarged translation, 1882]

Die Campagne in Frankreich: 1792 (history) 1822

[Campaign in France in the Year 1792, 1849]

Briefwechsel zwischen Schiller und Goethe (letters) 1828

[Correspondence between Schiller and Goethe from 1794 to 1805, 1845]

Novelle (novella) 1828

[Goethe's Novel, 1837; also published as Novella in The Sorrows of Young Werther and Novella, 1972]

Faust II (drama) 1832

[Goethe's Faust: Part II, 1839]

Goethe's Works. 9 vols. (autobiography, drama, poetry, novels, essays, travel essays) 1885

Werke. 14 vols. (poetry, drama, novels, novellas, short stories, autobiography, biography, criticism, essays, history) 1961-64

J.W. GOETHE

(conversation date 1824)

[The following excerpt is from a series of conversations with Goethe held between 1823 and 1832 and transcribed and collected by the interlocutor, Johann Peter Eckermann. Here, the poet shares his thoughts on *Werther*, emphasizing the novel's universal significance.]

The conversation now turned on *Werther*. "That," said Goethe, "is a creation which I, like the pelican, fed with the blood of my own heart. It contains so much from the innermost recesses of my breast that it might easily be spread into a novel of ten such volumes. Besides, I have only read the book once since its appearance, and have taken good care not to read it again. It is a mass of congreve-rockets. I am uncomfortable when I look at it; and I dread lest I should once more experience the peculiar mental state from which it was produced."

I reminded him of his conversation with Napoleon, of which I knew by the sketch amongst his unpublished papers, which I had repeatedly urged him to give more in detail. "Napoleon," said I, "pointed out to you a passage in *Werther*, which, it appeared to him, would not stand a strict examination; and this you allowed. I should much like to know what passage he meant."

"Guess!" said Goethe, with a mysterious smile.

"Now," said I, "I almost think it is where Charlotte sends the pistols to Werther, without saying a word to Albert, and without imparting to him her misgivings and apprehensions. You have given yourself great trouble to find a motive for this silence, but it does not appear to hold good against the urgent necessity where the life of the friend was at stake."

"Your remark," returned Goethe, "is really not bad; but I do not think it right to reveal whether Napoleon meant this passage or another. However, be that as it may, your observation is quite as correct as his."

I asked whether the great effect produced by the appearance of *Werther* were really to be attributed to the period. "I cannot," said I, "reconcile to myself this view, though it is so extensively spread. *Werther* made an epoch because it appeared—not because it appeared at a certain time. There is in every period so much unexpressed sorrow—so much secret discontent and disgust with life, and in single individuals there are so many disagreements with the world—so many conflicts between their natures and civil regulations, that *Werther* would make an epoch even if it appeared today for the first time."

"You are quite right," said Goethe; "it is on that account that the book to this day influences youth of a certain age, as it did formerly. It was scarcely necessary for me to deduce my own youthful dejection from the general influence of my time, and from the reading of a few English authors. Rather was it owing to individual and immediate circumstances which touched me to the quick, and gave me a great deal of trouble, and indeed brought me into that frame of mind which produced *Werther.* I had lived, loved, and suffered much—that was it.

"On considering more closely the much-talked-of *Werther* period, we discover that it belongs, not to the course of universal culture, but to the career of every individual who, with an innate free natural instinct, must accommodate himself to the narrow limits of an antiquated world. Obstructed fortune, restrained activity, unfulfilled wishes, are the calamities not of any particular time but of every individual man; and it would be bad indeed if everybody had not, once in his life, known a time when *Werther* seemed as if it had been written for him alone." (pp. 26-7)

J. W. Goethe, in a conversation with Johann Peter Eckermann on January 2, 1824, in his *Conversations with Eckermann (1823-*

1832), translated by John Oxenford, 1850. Reprint by North Point Press, 1984, pp. 25-7.

THOMAS CARLYLE
(essay date 1832)

[A nineteenth-century Scottish historian and social critic, Carlyle was one of the most influential essayists of his time. His writings include *The History of the French Revolution* (1837) and *Sartor Resartus* (1838). In the excerpt below, he comments on several of Goethe's works, praising the poet as "a man of universal Time."]

In *Goethe's Works,* chronologically arranged, we see this above all things: A mind working itself into clearer and clearer freedom; gaining a more and more perfect dominion of its world. The pestilential fever of Scepticism runs through its stages: but happily it ends and disappears at the last stage, not in death, not in chronic malady (the commonest way), but in clearer, henceforth invulnerable health. *Werter* [is] the voice of the world's despair: passionate uncontroulable is this voice; not yet melodious and supreme,—as nevertheless we at length hear it in the wild apocalyptic *Faust:* like a death-song of departing worlds; no voice of joyful "morning stars singing together" over a Creation; but of red nigh-extinguished midnight stars, in spheral swan-melody, proclaiming: It is ended!

What follows, in the next period, we might, for want of a fitter term, call Pagan or Ethnic in character; meaning thereby an anthropomorphic character, akin to that of old Greece and Rome. *Wilhelm Meister* is of that stamp: warm, hearty, sunny human Endeavour; a free recognition of Life in its depth, variety and majesty; as yet no Divinity recognized there. The famed *Venetian Epigrams* are of the like Old-Ethnic tone: musical, joyfully strong; true, yet not the whole truth, and sometimes in their blunt realism, jarring on the sense. (p. 35)

[In] the third or final period, melodious Reverence becomes triumphant; a deep all-pervading Faith, with mild voice, grave as gay, speaks forth to us in a *Meisters Wanderjahre,* in a *West—Östlicher Divan;* in many a little *Zahme Xenie,* and true-hearted little rhyme, "which," it has been said, "for pregnancy and genial significance, except in the Hebrew Scriptures, you will nowhere match." As here, striking in almost at a venture:

Like as a Star,
That maketh not haste,
That taketh not rest,

Be each one fulfilling
His god-given Hest.

(p. 36)

In such spirit, and with eye that takes in all provinces of human Thought, Feeling and Activity, does the Poet stand forth as the true prophet of his time; victorious over its contradiction, possessor of its wealth; embodying the noblenesses of the past into a new whole, into a new vital nobleness for the present and the future. Antique nobleness in all kinds, yet worn with new clearness; the spirit of it is preserved and again revealed in shape, when the former shape and vesture had become old (as vestures do), and was dead and cast forth; and we mourned as if the spirit too were gone. This, we are aware, is a high saying; applicable to no other man living, or that has lived for some two centuries; ranks Goethe, not only as the highest man of his time, but as a man of universal Time, important for all generations—one of the landmarks in the History of Men. (pp. 37-8)

Of Goethe's spiritual Endowment, looked at on the Intellectual side, we have (as indeed lies in the nature of things, for moral and intellectual are fundamentally one and the same) to pronounce a similar opinion; that it is great among the very greatest. As the first gift of all, may be discerned here utmost Clearness, all-piercing faculty of Vision; whereto, as we ever find it, all other gifts are superadded; nay, properly they are but other forms of the same gift. A nobler power of insight than this of Goethe you in vain look for, since Shakspeare passed away. In fact, there is much every way, here in particular, that these two minds have in common. Shakspeare too does not look *at* a thing, but into it, through it; so that he constructively comprehends it, can take it asunder, and put it together again; the thing melts, as it were, into light under his eye, and anew *creates* itself before him. That is to say, he is a Thinker in the highest of all senses: he is a Poet. For Goethe, as for Shakspeare, the world lies all translucent, all *fusible* (we might call it), encircled with WONDER; the Natural in reality the Supernatural, for to the seer's eyes both become one. What are the *Hamlets* and *Tempests,* the *Fausts* and *Mignons,* but glimpses accorded us into this translucent, wonder-encircled world; revelations of the mystery of all mysteries, Man's Life as it actually is?

Under other secondary aspects, the poetical faculty of the two will still be found cognate. Goethe is full of *figurativeness;* this grand light-giving Intellect, as all such are, is an imaginative one,—and in a quite other sense than most of our unhappy Imaginatives will imagine. Gall the Craniologist declared him to be a born *Volksredner* (popular orator), both by the figure of his brow, and what was still more decisive, because "he could not speak but a figure came." Gall saw what was high as his own nose reached,

"High as the nose doth reach, all clear!
What higher lies, they ask: Is it here?"

A far different figurativeness was this of Goethe than popular oratory has work for. In figures of the popular-oratory kind, Goethe, throughout his Writings at least, is nowise the most copious man known to us, though on a stricter scrutiny we may find him the richest. Of your ready-made, coloured-paper metaphors, such as can be sewed or plastered on the surface, by way of giving an ornamental finish to the rag-web already woven, we speak not; there is not one such to be discovered in all his Works. But even in the use of genuine metaphors, that are not haberdashery ornament, but the genuine new vesture of new thoughts, he yields to lower men (for example, to Jean Paul); that is to say, in fact, he is more master of the *common* language, and can oftener make *it* serve him. Goethe's figurativeness lies in the very centre of his being; manifests itself as the constructing of the inward elements of a thought, as the *vital* embodyment of it: such figures as those of Goethe you will look for through all modern literature, and except here and there in Shakspeare, nowhere find a trace of. Again, it is the same faculty in higher exercise, that enables the poet to construct a Character. Here too Shakspeare and Goethe, unlike innumerable others, are *vital;* their construction begins at the *heart* and flows outward as the life-streams do; fashioning the *surface,* as it were, spontaneously. Those Macbeths and Falstaffs, accordingly, these Fausts and Philinas have a verisimilitude and life that separates them from all other fictions of late ages. All others, in comparison, have more or less the nature of hollow vizards, constructed from without inwards, painted *like,* and deceptively put in motion. Many years ago, on finishing our first perusal *Wilhelm Meister,* with a very mixed sentiment in other respects, we could not but feel that here lay more insight into the elements of human nature, and a more poetically perfect combining of these than in all the other fictious literature of our generation.

Neither, as an additional similarity (for the great is ever like itself) let the majestic Calmness of both be omitted; their perfect tolerance for all men and all things. This too proceeds from the same source, perfect clearness of vision: he who comprehends an object cannot hate it, has already begun to love it. In respect of style, no less than of character, this calmness and graceful smooth-flowing softness is again characteristic of both; though in Goethe the quality is more complete, having been matured by far more assiduous study. Goethe's style is perhaps to be reckoned the most excellent that our modern world, in any language, can exhibit. "Even to a foreigner," says one, "it is full of character and secondary meanings; polished, yet vernacular and cordial, it sounds like the dialect of wise, antique-minded, true-hearted men: in poetry, brief, sharp, simple and expressive: in prose, perhaps still more pleasing; for it is at once concise and full, rich, clear, unpretending and melodious . . . ". (pp. 40-1)

Finally, as Shakspeare is to be considered as the greater nature of the two, on the other hand we must admit him to have been the less cultivated, and much the more careless. What Shakspeare *could* have done we nowhere discover. A careless mortal, open to the Universe and its influences, not caring strenuously to open himself; who, Prometheus-like, will scale Heaven (if it so must be), and is satisfied if he therewith pay the rent of his London Playhouse; who, had the Warwickshire Justice let him hunt deer unmolested, might, for many years more, have lived quiet on the green earth without such aerial journeys: an unparalleled mortal. In the great Goethe, again, we see a man through life at his utmost strain; a man that, as he says himself, "struggled toughly;" laid hold of all things, under all aspects, scientific or poetic; engaged passionately with the deepest interests of man's existence, in the most complex age of man's history. What Shakspeare's thoughts on "God, Nature, Art," would have been, especially had he lived to number four-score years, were curious to know: Goethe's, delivered in many-toned melody, as the apocalypse of our era, are here for us to know. . . .

We can call [Goethe], once more, "a clear and universal man;" we can say that, in his universality, as thinker, as singer, as worker, he lived a life of antique nobleness under these new conditions; and, in so living, is alone in all Europe; the foremost, whom others are to learn from and follow. (p. 42)

Thomas Carlyle, in an originally unsigned essay titled "Goethe's Works," in *The Foreign Quarterly Review,* Vol. X, No. XIX, August, 1832, pp. 1-44.

MARGARET FULLER

(essay date 1841)

[An important intellectual force in the New England Transcendentalist group, Fuller promoted Goethe in the United States. In the following excerpt from an essay that originally appeared in *The Dial* in 1841, she discusses the spiritual depth of Goethe's works, focusing on *Faust* and *Wilhelm Meister's Apprenticeship*.]

Faust contains the great idea of [Goethe's] life, as indeed there is but one great poetic idea possible to man—the progress of a soul through the various forms of existence.

All his other works, whatever their miraculous beauty of execution, are mere chapters to this poem, illustrative of particular points. *Faust,* had it been com-

pleted in the spirit in which it was begun, would have been the *Divina Commedia* of its age.

But nothing can better show the difference of result between a stern and earnest life and one of partial accommodation than a comparison between the "Paradiso" and that of the second part of *Faust.* In both a soul gradually educated and led back to God is received at last not through merit but grace. But oh, the difference between the grandly humble reliance of old Catholicism, and the loophole redemption of modern sagacity! Dante was a *man,* of vehement passions, many prejudices, bitter as much as sweet. . . . [Constantly] retiring to his deepest self, clearsighted to the limitations of man but no less so to the illimitable energy of the soul, the sharpest details in his work convey a larger sense, as his strongest and steadiest flights only direct the eye to heavens yet beyond.

Yet perhaps he had not so hard a battle to wage as this other great poet. The fiercest passions are not so dangerous foes to the soul as the cold skepticism of the understanding. The Jewish demon assailed the man of Uz with physical ills; the Lucifer of the Middle Ages tempted his passions; but the Mephistopheles of the eighteenth century bade the finite strive to compass the infinite, and the intellect attempt to solve all the problems of the soul.

This path Faust had taken: it is that of modern necromancy. Not willing to grow into God by the steady worship of a life, men would enforce his presence by a spell; not willing to learn his existence by the slow processes of their own, they strive to bind it in a word that they may wear it about the neck as a talisman.

Faust, bent upon reaching the center of the universe through the intellect alone, naturally, after a length of trial which has prevented the harmonious unfolding of his nature, falls into despair. He has striven for one object, and that object eludes him. Returning upon himself, he finds large tracts of his nature lying waste and cheerless. He is too noble for apathy, too wise for vulgar content with the animal enjoyments of life. Yet the thirst he has been so many years increasing is not to be borne. Give me, he cries, but a drop of water to cool my burning tongue! Yet in casting himself with a wild recklessness upon the impulses of his nature yet untried, there is a disbelief that anything short of the All can satisfy the immortal spirit. (pp. 252-53)

Faust cannot be content with sensuality, with the charlatanry of ambition, nor with riches. His heart never becomes callous, nor his moral and intellectual perceptions obtuse. He is saved at last.

With the progress of an individual soul is shadowed forth that of the soul of the age; beginning in intellectual skepticism; sinking into license; cheating itself with dreams of perfect bliss, to be at once attained by means no surer than a spurious paper currency; longing itself back from conflict between the spirit and the flesh, induced by Christianity, to the Greek era with its harmonious development of body and mind; striving to re-embody the loved phantom of classical beauty in the heroism of the Middle Ages; flying from the Byronic despair of those who die because they cannot soar without wings, to schemes of practical utility, however narrow—redeemed at last through mercy alone.

The second part of *Faust* is full of meaning, resplendent with beauty; but it is rather an appendix to the first part than a fulfillment of its promise. The world, remembering the powerful stamp of individual feeling, universal indeed in its application but individual in its life, which had conquered all its scruples in the first part, was vexed to find instead of the man Faust, the spirit of the age—discontented with the shadowy manifestation of truths it longed to embrace, and above all disappointed that the author no longer met us face to face, or riveted the ear by his deep tones of grief and resolve.

When the world shall have got rid of the still overpowering influence of the first part, it will be seen that the fundamental idea is never lost sight of in the second. The change is that Goethe, though the same thinker, is no longer the same person.

The continuation of *Faust* in the practical sense of the education of a man is to be found in *Wilhelm Meister.* Here we see the change by strongest contrast. The mainspring of action is no longer the impassioned and noble seeker, but a disciple of circumstance, whose most marked characteristic is a *taste* for virtue and knowledge. Wilhelm certainly prefers these conditions of existence to their opposites, but there is nothing so decided in his character as to prevent his turning a clear eye on every part of that variegated world-scene which the writer wished to place before us.

To see all till he knows all sufficiently to put objects into their relations, then to concentrate his powers and use his knowledge under recognized conditions—such is the progress of man from apprentice to master. (pp. 253-54)

[Far from becoming a Master in the *Wanderjahre*, Wilhelm] has but just become conscious of the higher powers that have ceaselessly been weaving his fate. Far from being as yet a Master, he but now begins to be a Knower. In the *Wanderjahre* we find him gradually learning the duties of citizenship, and hardening into manhood, by applying what he has learned for himself to the education of his child. He converses on equal terms with the wise and beneficent; he is no longer duped and played with for his good, but met directly mind to mind. (pp. 254-55)

The reason for Goethe's choosing so negative a

character as Wilhelm and leading him through scenes of vulgarity and low vice would be obvious enough to a person of any depth of thought, even if he himself had not announced it. He thus obtained room to paint life as it really is, and bring forward those slides in the magic lantern which are always known to exist, though they may not be spoken of to ears polite.

Wilhelm cannot abide in tradition nor do as his fathers did before him, merely for the sake of money or a standing in society. The stage, here an emblem of the ideal life as it gleams before unpracticed eyes, offers, he fancies, opportunity for a life of thought as distinguished from one of routine. Here, no longer the simple citizen but Man, all Men, he will rightly take upon himself the different aspects of life, till, poetwise, he shall have learned them all. (p. 255)

But the ideal must be rooted in the real, else the poet's life degenerates into buffoonery or vice. Wilhelm finds the characters formed by this would-be ideal existence more despicable than those which grew up on the track, dusty and bustling and dull as it had seemed, of common life. He is prepared by disappointment for a higher ambition. (pp. 255-56)

Goethe always represents the highest principle in the feminine form. Woman is the Minerva, man the Mars. As in the *Faust* the purity of Gretchen, resisting the demon always, even after all her faults, is announced to have saved her soul to heaven; and in the second part she appears not only redeemed herself, but by her innocence and forgiving tenderness hallowed to redeem the being who had injured her.

So in the *Meister* these women hover around the narrative, each embodying the spirit of the scene. The frail Philina, graceful though contemptible, represents the degradation incident to an attempt at leading an exclusively poetic life. Mignon—gift divine as ever the muse bestowed on the passionate heart of man, with her soft mysterious inspiration, her pining for perpetual youth—represents the high desire that leads to this mistake, as Aurelia, the desire for excitement; Teresa, practical wisdom, gentle tranquillity, which seem most desirable after the Aurelia glare. (pp. 256-57)

Entering on the *Wanderjahre*, Wilhelm becomes acquainted with another woman who seems the complement of all the former, and represents the idea which is to guide and mold him in the realization of all the past experience. This person, long before we see her, is announced in various ways as a ruling power. (p. 257)

While the apparition of the celestial Macaria seems to announce the ultimate destiny of the soul of man, the practical application of all Wilhelm has thus painfully acquired is not of pure Delphian strain. Goethe draws, as he passes, a dart from the quiver of Phoebus, but ends as Aesculapius or Mercury. Wilhelm at the school of the Three Reverences thinks out what can be done for man in his temporal relations. He learns to practice moderation and even painful renunciation. The book ends, simply indicating what the course of his life will be, by making him perform an act of kindness with good judgment and at the right moment. (p. 258)

The clear perception which was in Goethe's better nature of the beauty of that steadfastness, of that singleness and simple melody of soul, which he too much sacrificed to become the "many-sided One," is shown most distinctly in his two surpassingly beautiful works, the *Elective Affinities* and *Iphigenia.*

Not *Werther,* not the *Nouvelle Héloise,* have been assailed with such a storm of indignation as the first-named of these works on the score of gross immorality. (p. 262)

[It] has always seemed to me that those who need not such helps to their discriminating faculties, but read a work so thoroughly as to apprehend its whole scope and tendency, rather than hear what the author says it means, will regard the *Elective Affinities* as a work especially what is called moral in its outward effect, and religious even to piety in its spirit. The mental aberrations of the consorts from their plighted faith, though in the one case never indulged, and though in the other no veil of sophistry is cast over the weakness of passion, but all that is felt expressed with the openness of one who desires to legitimate what he feels, are punished by terrible griefs and a fatal catastrophe. (pp. 262-63)

There is indeed a sadness, as of an irresistible fatality, brooding over the whole. It seems as if only a ray of angelic truth could have enabled these men to walk wisely in this twilight, at first so soft and alluring, then deepening into blind horror.

But if no such ray came to prevent their earthly errors, it seems to point heavenward in the saintly sweetness of Ottilia. . . .

An unspeakable pathos is felt from the minutest trait of this character, and deepens with every new study of it. Not even in Shakespeare have I so felt the organizing power of genius. Through dead words I find the least gestures of this person stamping themselves on my memory, betraying to the heart the secret of her life which she herself, like all these divine beings, knew not. I feel myself familiarized with all beings of her order. I see not only what she was but what she might have been, and live with her in yet untrodden realms. (p. 263)

I cannot hope to express my sense of the beauty of this book as a work of art. I would not attempt it if I had elsewhere met any testimony to the same. The perfect picture, always before the mind, of the château, the moss hut, the park, the garden, the lake, with its boat and the landing beneath the platan trees; the gradual manner in which both localities and persons grow upon us, more living than life, inasmuch as we are unconsciously kept at our best temperature by the atmosphere of genius, and thereby more delicate in our perceptions than amid our customary fogs; the gentle unfolding of the central thought as a flower in the morning sun; then the conclusion rising like a cloud, first soft and white but darkening as it comes, till with a sudden wind it bursts above our heads; the ease with which we everywhere find points of view all different, yet all bearing on the same circle, for though we feel every hour new worlds, still before our eye lie the same objects, new yet the same, unchangeable yet always changing their aspects as we proceed, till at last we find we ourselves have traversed the circle, and know all we overlooked at first—these things are worthy of our highest admiration.

For myself, I never felt so completely that very thing which genius should always make us feel—that I was in its circle, and could not get out till its spell was done and its last spirit permitted to depart. I was not carried away, instructed, delighted more than by other works, but I was *there,* living there, whether as the platan tree or the architect or any other observing part of the scene. The personages live too intensely to let us live in them; they draw around themselves circles within the circle; we can only see them close, not be themselves. (pp. 263-64)

Iphigenia [is] a work beyond the possibility of negation; a work where a religious meaning not only pierces but enfolds the whole; a work as admirable in art, still higher in significance, more single in expression. (pp. 264-65)

The scenes go on more and more full of breathing beauty. The lovely joy of Iphigenia, the meditative softness with which the religiously educated mind perpetually draws the inference from the most agitating events, impress us more and more. (p. 270)

If it be not possible to enhance the beauty with which such ideal figures as the Iphigenia and the Antigone appeared to the Greek mind, yet Goethe has unfolded a part of the life of this being, unknown elsewhere in the records of literature. The character of the priestess, the full beauty of virgin womanhood, solitary but tender, wise and innocent, sensitive and self-collected, sweet as spring, dignified as becomes the chosen servant of God, each gesture and word of deep and delicate significance—where else is such a picture to be found?

It was not the courtier, nor the man of the world, nor the connoisseur, nor the friend of Mephistopheles, nor Wilhelm the Master, nor Egmont the generous, free liver, that saw Iphigenia in the world of spirits, but Goethe in his first-born glory; Goethe, the poet; Goe-

Goethe as a young man.

the, designed to be the brightest star in a new constellation. Let us not in surveying his works and life abide with him too much in the suburbs and outskirts of himself. Let us enter into his higher tendency, thank him for such angels as Iphigenia, whose simple truth mocks at all his wise *Beschränkungen,* and hope the hour when girl about with many such, he will confess, contrary to his opinion given in his latest days, that it *is* well worth while to live seventy years, if only to find that they are nothing in the sight of God. (p. 272)

Margaret Fuller, "Criticism: Goethe," in *The Writings of Margaret Fuller,* edited by Mason Wade, The Viking Press, 1941, pp. 242-72.

THOMAS MANN
(lecture date 1938)

[One of the greatest literary figures of the twentieth century, Mann explored the conflict between ordinary existence and the spiritual needs of artists. His internationally acclaimed novels include *Buddenbrooks* (1901; *Buddenbrooks*, 1924) and *Der Zauberberg* (1924; *The Magic Mountain*, 1927). In the following excerpt from a 1938 lecture delivered at Princeton University, he offers a searching analysis of *Faust.*]

It is always a pleasure to speak to the young, to beginning students of Goethe's great poem [*Faust*]. For it belongs to their age, it is the conception of one like-minded to them. Originally it was nothing more than the work of a highly gifted student, wherein the author calls faculties and professors over the coals and amuses himself enormously with playing the clever mentor, in diabolic disguise, to the timid freshman newly come up. (p. 19)

[There is a] remarkable phenomenon displayed in *Faust:* the genius of a student youth here usurps the role of humanity itself, and the whole Western world has accepted this valuation and recognized in the symbolism of the Faust-figure its own deepest essence. Much honour is done to youth by this poem and the greatness it achieved. Its uncompromisingness, its spirit of untamed revolt, its scorn of limitations, of peace and quiet, its yearning and heaven-storming soul, are precisely the expression of what age likes to call "youthful immaturity." But, thanks to the power of genius, this immaturity becomes the representative of humanity; youth stands for the human being at large; what was youthful storm and stress becomes ageless and typical.

Of course, in the play it is not a youth but a reverend and learned doctor whom we see at his desk in the dark vault. The filthy brewage of the witches' kitchen is to take thirty years from his age, and he must be a man some thirty years old when he first addresses Gretchen; so at the beginning of the play he would be not less than sixty years old, and as such he is represented on the stage. Yet of this sixty-year-old man Mephistopheles says to God:

Fürwahr, er dient euch auf besonderer Weise.
Nicht irdisch ist des Thoren Trank und Speise.
Ihn treibt die Gährung in die Ferne,
Er ist sich seiner Tollheit halb bewusst;
Von Himmel fordert er die schönsten Sterne
Und von der Erde jede höchste Lust,
Und alle Näh und alle Fern
Befriedigt nicht die tiefbewegte Brust.

Indeed, he serves you in the strangest fashion!
Not earthly food or drink do feed his passion.
His inner ferment drives him far,
Of his own frenzy he is half aware;
From heaven he demands the fairest star,
From earth all bliss supremely rare—
And yet not near nor far
Can he find easement for his anguished breast.

Those are not words that fit a man on the threshold of old age. The poet transplants his youthful urgency into the breast of a man at the same time of life as Goethe's own when he wrote the *Elective Affinities.* His Faust is humanity itself, object at once of the divine

1417

solicitude and of the lust for conquest of the powers of darkness. But the young poet who so facilely sketched this cosmic figure gave it his own traits, his own nature; and thus the youth became a man, the man a youth.

But this particular youth strives for, and achieves, critical detachment even from his own youngness, from his unbounded urge for freedom and the Absolute. Detachment implies irony; and his need of irony just as strongly demands poetic expression as do his other cravings. Irony is his "second soul"; and Goethe makes Faust speak with a sign of the two souls within his breast: the one the lusty hunger for love, the clinging sensuality; the other his longing for the pure and spiritual. The sigh he breathes is half-hypocritical: as well might he lament the duality of irony and enthusiasm, for well he knows that dualism is the soil and the mystery of creative fruitfulness. Enthusiasm—that is fullness with God; and what then is irony? The author of *Faust* is youth enough to see in that urge for the Absolute the divine in man; and in irony the diabolic. But this diabolism of his does not stand on such a bad footing with the divine. The Lord God says of it:

> Ich habe deinesgleichen nie gehasst.
> Von allen Geistern die verneinen
> Ist mir der Schalk am wenigsten zur Last.

> Hatred for your sort I have never felt.
> Of all the spirits that deny
> I find the thorough rascal least offensive.

The diabolism is of an amusing, witty kind, and God has tolerant understanding of it. It is acidulous, unprejudiced worldly sense, unapt for the emotions of the angels but not without sympathy for ordinary human need: "I feel a pity for the pains of men," says Mephisto. It makes superior mock of youthful enthusiasm; it is creative inventiveness and conscious anticipation of maturity and experience, fanaticism and worldly good sense; these are the contradiction, the "two souls" that Goethe likes to project into the dramatic form. Later he will divide himself into Tasso and Antonio; here, on a grander scale, he divides himself into Faust and Mephistopheles. Mephistopheles is the ironic self-corrective to Goethe's youthful titanism.

Mephistopheles is the most vital figure of a devil in all literature; the clearest-cut, the most animated by creative genius. He has not the emotional appeal of Klopstock's and Milton's devils; yet the characterization is so fresh and amusing, so sharply outlined and yet so various, that despite its spirit of ironic self-abrogation it made a permanent conquest of the human imagination for all time. The name Mephistopheles comes from the old Faust-book and the literature of demonology. Has it to do with mephitic? Does it signify sulphurous, pestilential? At any rate, it has the right sound, for the fellow is foul, foul in the grand style, with a sense of humour about his own foulness. He is

the presiding genius of all vermin—rats, mice, frogs, bugs, lice and so on. But his protection of the more repulsive manifestations of creation is really an expression of his nihilism, his denial of creation and of life altogether.

He says so straight out, and his words have become proverbial:

> Ich bin der Geist der stets verneint!
> Und das mit Recht; denn alles was entsteht
> Ist wert, dass es zu Grunde geht;
> Drum besser wär's, dass nichts entstünde.

> I am the spirit that ever denies!
> And rightly so; for all that's born on earth
> Merits destruction from its birth
> And better 'twere it had not seen the light. . . .

The grey-haired poet makes his devil speak just as the audacious youth had made him do, in the selfsame accents. (pp. 20-3)

But Mephistopheles is not only the presiding genius of all the vermin. Above all he is the genius of *fire*, he has reserved to himself that destructive, sterilizing, annihilating element. The red waistcoat and the cock's feather are the outward signs of his infernal nature. It is true that the witch misses in him the other classic attributes, the cloven hoof, the two ravens, which the Christian Devil inherited from the pagan Wotan. But in Mephisto the devil of the myth is tamed down in accordance with the cosmopolitan pose which he humorously finds more appropriate to the times. The cloven hoof is replaced by a slight limp. Wotan's ravens do indeed appear in the second part ("I see my raven pair, what message do they bear?"); but they are as a rule invisible. Mephisto regards himself as a cultural product, and seeks to dissociate himself from the legendary "northern phantom." . . . He completely departs from the role, turns his scepticism upon himself, and quite in the spirit of the Enlightenment regards his own existence as a superstition, or at most as so moderated by enlightenment as to fit the new age. The drollest implications arise, as for instance that scene, in only four verses, wherein Faust and Mephistopheles pass by a crucifix. "Mephisto, why so fast?" says Faust. "And why cast down your eyes before the Cross?" His companion replies:

> Ich weiss es wohl, es ist ein Vorurteil,
> Allein genug, mir ist's einmal zuwider.

> I realize it is a prejudice—
> Anyhow, there it is: I do not like it.

The fear of the crucifix was a mark of the mediaeval Devil. But when Mephisto speaks of prejudice, that is good eighteenth-century, and a proper modernized Satan to match. His enlightenment is not religious, it is not the crucifix that he speaks of as a prejudice, it is his own mediaeval, traditional fear to which he refers, and he excuses it as a weakness and caprice which, despite all his modern culture, he has been unable to overcome. (pp. 23-4)

Thus we see the artist playing with the traditional figure; making it hover in changeful light or even avaunt and void the sight of its own identity. It is even uncertain, for instance, and is deliberately left uncertain, whether this is actually *the* Devil or only *a* devil; only a representative of the infernal powers (*ein Teil von jener Kraft*) or the Evil One himself in person. In the **Prologue in Heaven** he is plainly the Satan of the Book of Job; for why should a lesser one than he ask permission of God to try a human soul? And at the very end, when Faust's immortal soul is in question, he cannot well be other than Satan himself, the thwarted Devil of legend. But in between he functions, so to speak, as a limited liability company; refers to "us" and "folk like us"; says "Bethink thee well, for we shall not forget," and "Did we force ourselves on you, or you on us?" (pp. 24-5)

Mephisto's language is sharply contrasted with the earnest, emotional, passionate key in which Faust speaks. The devil's line is brisk and worldly; it has a careless wit; is eminently critical and contemptuous, spiced with foreign words, altogether diverting. He speaks as it were *en passant;* the result is happy, casual, and most effective. . . . [It is the tone of a] man of the world (and Mephisto is at bottom nothing but a worldling) who shrugs his shoulders over the man with the deep and troubled emotional nature. Faust, in worldly matters, is Mephisto's pupil; he lets himself be led; and in despair over his own striving for the highest things, even strikes a bargain with the devil. Mephisto's relation to Faust is that of the experienced travelling-companion and tutor who knows his way about; he is courier, *maître des plaisirs;* again he is simply the resourceful servant who Lothario-like makes opportunities for his master. He is all these things by turns, with versatility and wit. (pp. 25-6)

But in the end Mephistopheles is the personification of the hatred of light and life; he is primal night and Chaos' son, the emissary of the void—after his own kind he is on a very grand scale. "Thou vile abortion, born of filth and fire!"—thus Faust once rails at him, and it is a splendid description. Something about it, we realize, corresponds to the human intellectual elements which both impress and offend us. The filth, that is the cynicism, the obscene wit, launched by the fires of his infernal will to destruction. The essence of his nature is the profoundest lovelessness. Hatred fairly scintillates in the creature's slanting yellow tiger-eyes. "The bottomless rage that leads thee to destroy," Faust says to him: "thy tig'rish glare, thy all-compelling face. . . ." Here the humorous side fades out, and the

devil emerges in all his specific majesty; not without a certain admiration the poet sees and feels it.

Goethe's own attitude towards evil is not uniform; it hovers between recognition and contempt. He says, in one of the Proverbs:

Ich kann mich nicht bereden lassen:
Macht mir den Teufel nur nicht klein!
Ein Kerl, den alle Menschen hassen,
Der muss was sein.

I still remain quite unconvinced
That it's good sense to paint the devil small:
There must be something in a chap
Who's hated so by all.

But in portraying Mephistopheles as the embodiment of evil, Goethe sometimes injects into the character a trace of self-contempt, a hang-dog note: Mephistopheles will sometimes betray his suspicion that the devil is no great shakes when all is said and done:

Mich darf niemand aufs Gewissen fragen,
Ich schäme mich oft meines Geschlechts;
Sie meinen, wenn Sie Teufel sagen,
So sagen Sie was Rechts.

Let nobody ask me on my oath
Whether I shame me for my kind;
But you, when you speak the words "the devil"—
You've something big in mind.

When you say "the devil," you really are not saying much; in other words, evil is a poor thing after all. The poet could scarcely make the idea more impressive than by putting it in the Evil One's own mouth! And in the Prologue, Mephisto feels flattered by the fact that God condescends to converse with him, the old nihilist:

Es ist gar hübsch von einem grossen Herrn
So menschlich mit dem Teufel selbst zu sprechen!

It's very handsome of so great a lord
To talk with the devil as man to man!

Not for nothing have these two light-hearted lines become so famous. Their humour is complex and subtle. Here is the Divine Absolute, in the role of the Grand Seigneur who is human enough to discuss with the Opposition; and here is the Opposition, flattered by the complaisance and recognizing its own inferiority— truly a cosmic jest, a regular poet's joke, and very characteristic of this particular poet; for when in the presence of opposition and negation, Goethe always thought of himself as the grand seigneur and representative of the government. "If I had had the *misfortune* to be in the Opposition," he once said in conversation. And yet it was precisely Goethe who created, and invested with lyric meaning, the figure of the arch-nihilist, Mephistopheles.

And further: what character in this play—racked,

it is true, by disillusionment, bitterness, yearning, and despair—utters the most crushing, nihilistic words in the whole poem: the great malediction upon life, its joys and its seductions; the great curse upon spirit and sense, fame and possessions, love, hope, faith, endurance. . . . Which character is it? Mephisto? He could never have summoned the pity or pain for such an anathema against life and joy. No, it is the anguished human being, it is Goethe-Faust who utters the frightful words. Here the roles are reversed, and the nihilistic devil becomes the practical and worldly advocate for life against the desperate and rebellious human spirit. . . . The character of Faust in the poem is no simpler, no more uniform, than that of his diabolic mentor. It varies in the same way. Or rather the whole poem in which they play their parts possesses this variability of the Time-Spirit; since the scene, ostensibly, is laid in the sixteenth century, but continually plays over into the eighteenth, the poet's own. Wagner, the famulus, speaks the language of the age of Enlightenment, praises the periods of Gottsched, and feels that science and mankind have made glorious progress. Faust-Goethe, on the contrary, stands for Herder's ideas about the "age of genius." The nature-mysticism of his soliloquies, and the religious feeling he shows to Gretchen—all that is inspired by Swedenborg, Ossian, and Lavater, in particular by the northern mystic, who died in 1772, and whose name Goethe replaced by that of Nostradamus in order to preserve the historical perspective. I spoke of Faust's humanism, the intellectual attitude that makes him fundamentally despise magic as despicable rigmarole, although he surrenders to it, that "through the spirit's mouth and might, mysteries might see the light." As a matter of fact, he remained, as Mephisto's patron, addicted to it up to his old age and made use of it in all his adventures, first with Gretchen, and then in the world, at the Kaiser's court, in battle, in the affair with Helena, whom he wins only by enchantment and illusion. Not till very late does there stir in him the desire "magic from out his path to put away." Yet even so, his attitude towards it from the beginning is highly fastidious—or at least towards its practicants and technicians and their obscene trafficking. He inveighs against the witches' kitchen as a *"Wust von Raserei"* (crazy rubbish). "Why just that old hag?" he asks in disgust. He finds the whole thing as unappetizing as anything he ever saw. Bad taste, offensive—that is his humanistic judgment on the whole of magic art: "frantic stuff, wild goings-on, disgusting humbug"—he knows and despises it already. The blood-pact—vital to Mephisto because after all, in God's name, he really *is* the devil—Faust knows about that too, it is as familiar as repulsive to him; he refers to the pact with contempt, as a piece of tomfoolery. Why must they have such a superstitious flourish as the signature in blood, when after all, in the eternal flux of things, there can be no such thing as a binding promise,

however much a high-minded man would wish to cling to the delusion of truth? Mephisto duly utters his mediaeval patter, just as it stands in the legend:

> Ich will mich hier zu deinem Dienst verbinden
> Auf deinen Wink nicht rasten und nicht ruhn:
> Wenn wir uns drüben wiederfinden,
> Dann sollst Du mir das Gleiche tun.

> Here I bind myself unto your service,
> Ever at your beck and call to be;
> When we find ourselves in the hereafter,
> Then you shall do the same for me.

He speaks of the hereafter as an actuality in the popular mind and his own—in the Prologue, indeed, he stands before God among the heavenly host. But Faust answers him as a humanist and earthbound human spirit, who does not believe in a hereafter, or at least is not interested in one. . . . Neither understands the other—either temporally or morally. The bargain is struck on the basis of two different conceptions: one primitive and diabolic, the other more evolved and with some knowledge of human dignity. . . . [Faust] makes his pact with the devil out of the same high and human aspiration that mind, science, knowledge had been unable to satisfy; with the same absolute and insatiable passion that made him despair of thought he gives himself to pleasure. And all the while he knows but too well that it will be as impotent as knowledge to still his craving for infinity.

> Werd ich beruhigt je mich auf ein Faulbett legen,
> So sei es gleich um mich getan!
> Kannst du mich schmeichelnd je belügen,
> Dass ich mir selbst gefallen mag,
> Kannst du mich wit Genuss betrügen,
> Das sei für mich der letzte Tag!

> If ever on bed of idleness I lay me,
> May I that moment die!
> When thou by flattery canst wile me
> In self-complacency to rest,
> Or e'er with pleasant lusts beguile me—
> Then may that moment be my last!

"Beguile with pleasant lusts." Thus no voluptuary speaks. Rather he who takes up with pleasure as earlier he did with things of the mind, and recognizes but one kind of slavery: inertia and ease. . . . [Faust is] an activist, who seeks not pleasure but life, and binds himself to the devil only so far as a man of intellect does who gives himself to life. The formal bond he despises as pedantic and futile, there being no reason to doubt his complete surrender.

> Nur keine Furcht, dass ich dies Bündnis breche!
> Das Streben meiner ganzen Kraft
> Ist gerade das was ich verspreche.

There needs no fear this promise shall be broken:

The uttermost of all my powers
Is bent to keep what I have spoken.

One asks oneself, indeed, what does actually come of that plumbing of the depths of sense, of the intoxications of life and time, of that furious masculine activity of Faust during his companionship with Mephistopheles. I will not extend the question to the second part of the poem. There it is only after a multitude of involved adventures in magic that Faust engages in any kind of activity that could be called unresting or masculine. As for the first part, we must admit that Goethe has not gone very far towards poetic realization of the depths of sensuality or the life of action, fluctuating between success and failure, to which his hero would devote himself. What does Mephisto do for his hopeful pupil? He takes him to Auerbach's cellar, where the two perform conjuring tricks before bawling philistines just as in the chapbook. Well, at least that is by way of illustration to the lines:

Die schlechteste Gesellschaft lässt dich fühlen
Dass due ein Mensch mit Menschen bist—

Even from the lowest company one borrows
A sense that one's a man like all the rest—

though it is hardly even that, for Faust does not succeed in being hail fellow well met with his brother topers in the cellar. He and the devil behave more like high-born travelling foreigners, very spoilt and capricious at that, and with a smack of the charlatan that would make them suspect to middle-class minds. We hear that they have just got back from Spain; if that is true, what have they been doing there? We do not learn. We are equally puzzled by Faust's remark at the beginning of the Gretchen episode, when he demands that Mephisto deliver the little one straight into his arms:

Hätt ich nur sieben Stunden Ruh,
Brauchte den Teufel nicht dazu
So ein Geschöpfchen zu verführen.

If I had only seven hours free,
I should not need to call the Devil in
To teach that little creature how to sin.

If that is only said in order to excuse him for not being able to seduce the poor child by his own efforts, but needing the powers of hell to help him to do it, then we must deduce that he is occupied indeed—and with what, and how? We remain in the dark. None of the deceased charlatan's famous deeds or misdeeds come into the first part; the Gretchen story stands alone, for nothing stronger had the young poet to give! He magnified it into his own tragedy, he reduced all the rest of the Faustian program to this one exploration of the life of passion. And who would regret the fact? For the result was the loveliest, sincerest, saddest love-story in the German language, perhaps in any language, told in the simplest, most natural, convincing, and moving accents in the world.

We must repeat what has so often been said already: this little Gretchen, the pawnbroker's daughter, as we see her move before our mind's eye, in her grief, her humanness and femininity, her childlike purity, her love and devotion, her vicarious, pitiful fate, is a figure of immortal beauty. We see her in the little German imperial city, a small, idyllic setting, with spinning-wheel and fountain, christening feast and gossiping neighbours. But how the young creature, so simple, yet so warm with life, is lifted out of her lowliness and transfigured by the masculine guilt and remorse! At the end she is nothing less than the spirit of love itself, watching from above over the struggles of the erring one and preparing his welcome and redemption. Like Mignon in Goethe's great novel, she has two of her creator's most marvellous lyrics put in her mouth: *"Meine Ruh ist hin,"* and *"Es war ein König in Thule."* But she is herself a *"Lied,"* a folk-song refined by the most personal art. . . . Such simple, native accents of uncanny fantasy are unknown to Clärchen in *Egmont.* Yet the two are sisters, Clärchen and Gretchen, unmistakably visualized and created by their author to like though varying tragic destinies. One becomes the heroine, the other the martyr of her sex. And just as they are sisters, so their lovers, Faust and Egmont, are brothers, true sons of Goethe both, representing the characteristic Goethian eroticism, a little narcissistic; which finds its peculiar ecstasy in the beguilement of simple innocence, of the little maid of the people by a lordly masculinity stooping down from loftier spheres, and in her utter surrender to her blissful fate. Egmont shows himself to the virtuous Clärchen in Spanish court dress; nothing could be more characteristic of Goethe's own wish-dream world than this scene. In *Faust,* the court dress and the golden fleece are of a metaphysical kind. An elegant, fastidious traveller, from an intellectual sphere unknown to Gretchen's bourgeois simplicity and most impressive; half nobleman, half scholar, Faust appears as from another world. . . . Certainly the Gretchen story is the tragedy of intellect becoming mortally guilty to beauty, with the cynical connivance of the devil. And here, more than anywhere else, does Goethe betray himself a revolutionary, in that he would stir our emotions against the cruelty of human society, which punishes the beauty that falls victim to the beguilement of the superior mind. This once, and never again, Goethe, owing to his own tragic sense of guilt, becomes an accuser and rebel against society. In the prose scene: "Grey day, a field," taken bodily out of the *Urfaust* and put unchanged into the fragment as well as the finished poem, Faust, after the repulsive distractions of the Blocksburg and the Walpurgisnacht dream, learns that Gretchen is in prison and has been handed over to the justice of cruel, unthinking men. Mephistopheles flings at him his cynical "She is not the first."

"Not the first! Oh, horror, horror! How can any human being understand that the writhing death-agony of the first was not enough to atone for the guilt of the rest, in the eyes of the All-Merciful! The agony of this single one pierces me to the heart—and you can stand there and grin at the fate of thousands!"

The scene is written in rough, savage, almost clumsy prose, devoid of irony; it scarcely seems to belong to a poem that otherwise, in all its inward significance, its profound human symbolism, moves with such light-footed creative objectivity. (pp. 26-37)

Gretchen's destruction is almost the ruin of Faust as well. Nowhere else does he, the human being, fall so foul of his companion as here; nowhere does he fling the scorn of his anguished heart so furiously in the grinning face of the demon who mocks at man's double nature: *"Hund! Abscheuliches Untier!"* ("Dog! Detestable monster!")

"Hab' ich doch meine Freude dran!" ("I get my fun out of it too.")

Goethe, in *Faust,* has depicted love as a regular devil's holiday: the "high intuition" whose conclusion and consummation Mephisto indicates with an obscene gesture. . . . For youthful love, the most human thing in the world, wherein the spirit and the body, the natural and the divine, mingle in a way so symbolic and so exemplary for all humanity, is truly the devil's playground, the theatre of his most prized triumphs. There he most easily performs his traditional task of betraying the highest in man to the basest. There truly is his immemorial striving: to seize on that higher part of man, so mingled with his baser self, and in the baser swallow up the higher. And he would triumph, were it not that the Eternal Goodness, with whom in the Prologue the devil is so cringingly conversable, and who sees the highest in the lowest, not, as the devil does, the lowest in the highest, opposes his will to destruction.

The whole Faust-poem is based on the *Prologue in Heaven.* Or rather the Prologue was afterwards shoved underneath the youthful, light-heartedly conceived composition, to prop it up. For it is in the Prologue that the figure of Faust becomes the protagonist and symbol of man, in whom the Eternal Goodness had a share, as he in it. Faust's human trait, which makes him strive after the universally human, is his noble side, the goodness which is at the same time godliness in him. So it comes about that he and the devil, who has no understanding of the painstaking spirit of man, misunderstand each other when they make their pact. When Faust says: "Let us still our glowing passions in the depth of sense," he means something quite different from what the devil thinks; he means even the sensuality with a difference: as something nobler, deeper,

more serious and fervent. . . . The Mephistophelian "world" (the devil is only a worldling) becomes for Faust life, with its tortures and desires; but surrender to it takes on at once a human character; he wishes to live, in the fullest, most human sense, he would be a son of man, would take upon himself and exhaust, as representative and sacrifice, all the joys and sorrows of mankind. . . . [To take this] upon himself, in giving himself to life—nothing else is it that Faust promises the devil. But this "striving to attain man's utmost height," infinite as it always is, and sinful in the sense that it is presumptuous titanism, is after all more allied to God than to the devil; it is generous, upright, and good, and despite all the perils it entails, it never from the first holds out any great hopes to the devil. (pp. 37-40)

A Paralipomenon Faust says to Mephistopheles:

So höre denn, wenn du es niemals hörtest:
Die Menschheit hat ein fein Gehör,
Ein reines Wort erreget schöne Taten.
Der Mensch fühlt sein Bedürfnis nur zu sehr
Und lässt sich gern im Ernste raten.

So hearken now, if thou hast never heard:
The human hearing's very keen,
And glorious deeds can follow one clear word.
Man knows only too sore his human need,
And gladly counsel he will heed. . . .

Nothing could be more Goethian, nothing more Faustian. Its conception of man, its attitude towards the human being, are a part of the Everlasting Goodness; and no differently speaks the Eternal Goodness itself, God the Lord, in the Prologue. . . . For our time, which seems to have fallen a helpless prey to evil and cynicism, how welcome were some kindly greatness, which should know what man needs and instead of offering him mocking sophisms, could give him serious advice in his necessities! A "clear word" and a benevolent, pointing out the better course, seems powerless today; world events pass all such over with brutal disregard. But let us hold fast to the anti-diabolic faith, that mankind has after all a "keen hearing," and that words born of one's own striving may do it good and not perish from its heart. (pp. 40-2)

Thomas Mann, "Goethe's 'Faust'," in his *Essays of Three Decades,* translated by H. T. Lowe-Porter, Alfred A. Knopf, 1947, pp. 3-42.

E. R. CURTIUS

(essay 1949)

[Curtius was a prominent German philologist, literary historian, essayist, and critic. In the following excerpt from a 1949 essay, he describes Goethe as one the great figures of world literature.]

In his essay on granite (1784) Goethe mentions that this rock was forced to "endure some moments of humiliation" when an Italian naturalist advanced the opinion that it had been artificially produced from a fluid mass by the Egyptians. "But this opinion was soon dispelled, and the dignity of the rock was definitively confirmed by the excellent observations of many travellers." In his *Farbenlehre* Goethe says of red: "This color, on account of its high dignity, we have sometimes called purple. . . . " From the "complete determination of the limbs" he derives the "dignity of the most perfect animals." The principal purpose of all sculpture for him is "to represent the dignity of man within the confines of the human form." Latin and Greek are the languages "in which the worth and dignity of the ancient world have been most purely transmitted." But Goethe can also speak of the "natural dignity of the kingdom of Bohemia," "whose nearly square space, enclosed by mountains, does not branch off on any side. . . . A continent in the midst of the continent."

By juxtaposing these sentences one gains a deeper insight into Goethe's intellectual world than is to be obtained from many a scholarly dissertation. Rock, color, animal, man, history, the formation of the earth—everything is apprehended by the same luminous eye; the highest of its kind, in every area, can be designated by the same word. No one did this before Goethe, no one after him. Goethe's gaze comprehends the totality of nature and of spirit; and when he puts his vision into words, he diffuses a stately radiance over the objects of his regard. By being mirrored in Goethe's mind the world participates in an act of transfiguration. It is purified and elevated. To my knowledge, we have no description of Goethe's language. And yet someone with the proper sense for it could build up Goethe's world for us from his language as ancient sarcophagi have been restored splinter by splinter.

While reading about the "dignity" of granite we were already struck by the peculiar sound of the word. To be sure, this sound was still isolated and uncertain. But with each succeeding example a new sound was added harmonically to the original. The result was a full rich chord. But a chord contains a key, and this is also a key to the spirit.

By established rules we may pass from one key to another; from examples of dignity to the concept of the most dignified men.

In his son's album Goethe wrote:

Halte das Bild der Würdigen fest! Wie leuchtende Sterne Teilte sie aus die Natur durch den unendlichen Raum.

[Hold fast the image of dignified men! Like luminous stars nature distributed them throughout infinite space.]

If we try to find sounds which will yield a consonance with this distich, we hit upon "the only fine aperçu that still permits us to take pleasure in history: that the authentic men of all ages herald one another's coming, point toward one another, pave the way for one another." As in infinite space so the dignified men are distributed throughout the duration of time. If we examine older states of mankind, "there come to meet us everywhere out of the dark past capable and excellent men, brave, fair, good, and of splendid stature. Mankind's song of praise, which the Godhead loves to hear, is never silent, and we ourselves feel a divine happiness when we perceive the harmonious effusions distributed throughout all times and regions, sometimes in single voices, single choirs, sometimes as a fugue, sometimes in a magnificent full chorus." This is Goethe's philosophy of history. History is not sanctioned as a whole as it is in Ranke. It exists for the sake of the individual. "The slender thread that moves through the sometimes very extensive fabric of knowledge and science, even in the darkest and most confused ages, is drawn by individuals. These, of the best sort, are born in one century as in another, and always maintain the same attitude toward every century in which they occur. That is, they stand in opposition to the crowd, indeed, in conflict with it." (pp. 73-5)

Truth is for the few. It is that which binds them to one another beyond all the ages. It resembles a golden chain wound through the millennia. The noble souls hand it on to one another. Now it is our turn to seize it:

Das Wahre war schon längst gefunden,
Hat edle Geisterschaft verbunden;
Das alte Wahre, fass es an!

[The truth has long since been discovered, it has united companies of noble spirits; the age-old truth—lay hold of it!]

Scarcely any idea contradicts modern opinion so fundamentally as that the truth was already discovered thousands of years ago. Since Goethe's death dozens, nay, hundreds of new philosophical and poetic revelations have been bestowed on us. In the light of this Goethean principle, how are they to be judged? This question, which could undoubtedly be answered, shall only be glanced at here. The more important matter is to understand the meaning of Goethe's theory of truth. He did not develop it anywhere explicitly; we shall see why not. But he gives us a number of hints. "The main thing," he says to Eckermann (16 December 1828) is to have a soul that loves truth and is receptive to it wherever it may be found. Moreover, the world is now so old and so many important men have lived and thought for thousands of years that there is little new to be discovered or said."

In saying this he was thinking of his theory of colors, which he found prefigured in Plato and Leonardo. But the Eternism of truth (if I may be allowed this abbreviation) is as valid in art as in science. It is not a form of archaism: "The old is not classical because it is old, but because it is strong, fresh, cheerful, and healthy" (to Eckermann, 2 April 1829). But what is valid for art and science must hold even more strongly for the knowledge of divine matters. In this sense the belief in an eternal revelation may be ascribed to Goethe. Were I asked to indicate its contents, I should choose the following text: "Man must be capable of elevating himself to the highest form of reason if he wishes to come in contact with the Divine, which manifests itself in physical as in moral archetypes (*Urphänomene*), concealing itself behind them even as they emanate from it. The Divine, however, is active in living matter, not in dead; it is in the changing and developing, not in what has changed and congealed. That is also why reason, as it tends toward the Divine, deals only with what is vital and developing; but the understanding deals with what has already developed and congealed in order to make use of it" (to Eckermann, 13 February 1829).

I refrain from commenting on this text. Only one maxim, which elucidates it, may be added: "Light and spirit, the former in the physical realm, the latter in the moral, are the highest conceivable indivisible energies." Form as well as content of this utterance deserve attention. It is not an aphorism or a fragment of thought; nor is it a philosophical reflection or scientific thesis. It is a wisdom-saying which recalls those of the pre-Socratics. A prospect is opened upon two of the archetypal phenomena in which, as we heard, the Divine reveals itself. Such sentences are beyond philosophy. The specifically Goethean element is the linking of the physical with the moral, the simultaneous contemplation of God and the world, to use another of Goethe's formulas that stem from Antiquity. What Goethe intuits as the highest truth he does not fit into a system. He "stablishes" it, to use one of his favorite words. He sets it before us in a concise, visionary utterance. (pp. 80-1)

Today, people are asking whether Goethe's view of the world can still be our own. They point out that we are living through a crisis in the very foundations of our culture. Consequently, Goethe is out of date, for reasons that philosophy believes it can specify. I doubt whether philosophy is competent to do so. For philosophy thereby enters areas that are alien to it: history and art. When I examine what modern philosophers say about history, I find in every case that they "construct" (according to the exigencies of their philosophy, of course, and upon an insufficient basis of fact). Their constructions are founded upon borrowings made from outmoded presentations of history. That is why I am not convinced when philosophers call Goethe in question on the grounds of a "diagnosis of the age." Plato, Aristotle, Descartes, Leibniz, Kant made no such diagnoses. Their philosophies were developed out of the subject, not out of the situation. Today, the latter practice seems to be necessary. That would imply a change in the structure of philosophy. At present, however, philosophy resembles a war of all against all. It seems doubtful whether out of this anarchy of first principles a new culture can be evolved.

But of course everyone, philosopher or no, has a perfect right to reject Goethe on some grounds or other. I believe that I have made it abundantly clear that Goethe never pretended to be a teacher for everyone. He wanted to have an effect on a few friends, on kindred souls and spirits. There has never been a unanimous image of Goethe and there cannot be one today. But it may indeed be asked, what the present image of Goethe can be to his friends, as compared with that of previous anniversaries.

On this a few more indications. It is a notable fact that since Goethe our world has brought forth no more classics. Poets like Hugo and Whitman do not fill out the dimensions. The great problematical writers like Dostoevski and Nietzsche do not do so for other reasons. Whether a classic is still possible in a declining civilization is questionable. All our experience speaks against it. In that case Goethe would be the last classic of Europe as Virgil was the last classic of Rome. A classic can never be replaced except by a new classic, who will then be of an entirely different type. We shall not live to see it. The last classic at any given time need not be greater than his predecessors. Shakespeare was not greater than Dante. The great classics can be separated by large expanses of time—between Virgil and Dante there are thirteen hundred years. So long did it take the peoples of northern Europe not only to assimilate the two Mediterranean traditions—the pagan-antique and the Christian—but to be able to express what they had absorbed in their own language. The bond between Virgil and Dante, however, was their share in this historical substance. In the fullness and depth of this substance Shakespeare and Goethe also have their roots.

Dante, Shakespeare, Goethe: these three move close together today. Each of them—and each in his own way—can be viewed as a self-concentration of the western mind in one person. This totalization of tradition in an original creation is successful for the last time in Goethe. But Europe's intellectual foundations were even then being shaken by the first earthquakes. Cracks were beginning to appear in the mass of tradition. Goethe created a universal, positive oeuvre in an era of incipient disintegration. That is why this oeuvre sometimes shows rifts, sometimes too a certain pallor. This may also account for much that is problematical in Goethe's relation to his profession as a writer, a theme which would have to be pursued on a separate occasion. Finally, it may account for his sensitivity toward every sort of opaqueness and obscurity—which, to be sure, he was able to transform by taking the perplexities of the human condition as the subject of his poetry. He felt all these resistances—and not least, "the resistance of the dull world." That at any rate is one of the motives which, as the years advanced, drove him more and more to seek the tiny "company of saints," even if he did not withdraw from external representation. Goethe's esotericism may perhaps be understood as a reaction to the age of the masses, which was then beginning.

But if Goethe is the final self-concentration of the western mind in a great individual, it means that he is something more and something other than a German poet. He is solidary with the spiritual heritage of Europe. He stands in the line of Homer, Sophocles, Plato, Aristotle, Virgil, Dante, and Shakespeare. The consciousness of his place in this series is very much alive in him. His piety toward the "fathers," his alliance with the "dignified men" of old and with the chorus of the spirits of the past, his conviction that there is a realm of the "Masters," with whom he feels he belongs—this most characteristic and remarkable trait of his form of mind acquires its deeper sense only now. This consciousness of solidarity through the millennia Shakespeare could not have had, Dante only within the Latin tradition. To Goethe it was given as a legitimation and corroboration of his mission. It is a sign, so to speak, from the "alphabet of the universal spirit." It is the seal of succession. Was Goethe the last in this line? For those who venerate him as a master that would only increase his importance.

Goethe described himself on occasion as an "epigone poet." "We epigone poets must revere the legacy of our ancestors—Homer, Hesiod, *et al.*—as the authentic canonical books; we bow before these men whom the Holy Spirit has inspired and dare not ask, whence or whither" (to Creuzer, 1817). This attitude can today be the one that a "small number" adopts toward Goethe. (pp. 88-91)

E. R. Curtius, "Fundamental Features of Goethe's World," in his *Essays on European Literature,* translated by Michael Kowal, Princeton University Press, 1973, pp. 73-91.

SOURCES FOR FURTHER STUDY

Croce, Benedetto. *Goethe.* Translated by Emily Anderson. London: Methuen, 1923, 208 p.

> Full-length study that includes chapters on Goethe's intellectual and artistic life as well as analyses of his major poetry and prose works.

Fairley, Barker. *A Study of Goethe.* Oxford: Clarendon, 1947, 280 p.

> A comprehensive modern biography by a noted Goethe scholar.

Heller, Erich. "Goethe and the Idea of Scientific Truth." In his *The Disinherited Mind: Essays in Modern German Literature and Thought*, pp. 3-34. Cambridge, England: Bowes & Bowes, 1952. Reprint. New York: Farrar, Straus and Cudahy, 1957.

> Close study of Goethe's concept of scientific method and inquiry.

Messen, H. J., ed. *Goethe Bicentennial Studies by Members of the Faculty of Indiana University.* Indiana University Publications: Humanities Series, edited by Edward P. Seeber, No. 22. Bloomington: Indiana University, 1950, 325 p.

> Critical and comparative essays on such subjects as Werther and the cult of suicide in France, and the relation between Goethe and Mozart.

Pascal, Roy. *The German Sturm und Drang.* Manchester, England: Manchester University Press, 1953, 347 p.

> Examines the historical, social, and religious background of Germany's *Sturm und Drang* movement, its major proponents, and its position in literary history. Goethe is discussed as a chief exemplar of the movement.

Steiner, Rudolf. *Goethe's Conception of the World.* London: Anthroposophical Publishing Company, 1928, 193 p.

> A thorough examination of Goethe's artistic, philosophical, and scientific views with particular emphasis on the poet's spiritual insights.

Nikolai Gogol

1809-1852

(Full name Nikolai Vasilyevich Gogol; born Gogol-Yanovsky; also transliterated as Nikolay; also Vasilevich, Vasil'yevich, Vasilievich, Vasilyevitch; also Gogol', Gógol; also wrote under pseudonyms V. Alov and Rudy Panko) Russian novelist, dramatist, short story writer, essayist, critic, and poet.

INTRODUCTION

Gogol was an initiator of the Russian Naturalist movement. He began to write when a new literary focus was developing in Russia, one that described the lives of the lower classes of society. Gogol explored contemporary social problems, often in a satiric fashion. His best-known works, the novel *Mërtvye dushi* (1842; *Dead Souls*), the short story "Shinel" (1842; "The Overcoat"), and the drama *Révizor* (1836; *The Inspector General*) are universally praised as masterpieces of Russian Naturalism. Gogol is also acknowledged as a progenitor of the modern short story. His fiction, written in an idiosyncratic style that combines elements of realism, fantasy, comedy, and the grotesque, typically features complex psychological studies of individuals tormented by feelings of impotence, alienation, and frustration. In addition, several of Gogol's stories humorously expose negative aspects of Russian society. Often cited as a major inspiration to such authors as Fyodor Dostoyevsky and Franz Kafka, Gogol's work, while ultimately considered unclassifiable, has elicited a variety of critical interpretations.

Gogol was born into a family of Ukrainian landowners. As a young boy, he attended boarding school, where he developed an interest in literature and drama. After failing both to find employment as an actor and to sell his writing, Gogol used his own money to publish his epic poem *Hans Kuechelgarten* in 1829. When this work received only negative reviews, Gogol collected and burned all remaining copies of the book. Soon after, he obtained a civil service position in St. Petersburg and began writing *Vechera ná khutore bliz Dikanki* (1831; *Evenings on a Farm near Dikanka*), a volume of mostly comic folktales set in his native Ukraine. In these stories, Gogol depicted the world of the Cossack peasantry through an engaging mixture of naturalism and fantasy. Immediately acclaimed as the work of a brilliant young writer, *Evenings on a Farm near Dikanka* brought Gogol to the attention of celebrated poet Alexander Pushkin and noted critic Vissarion Belinsky, who was an early champion of Pushkin and now recognized similar promise in Gogol. Pushkin proved to be Gogol's strongest literary inspiration, and their association from 1831 to 1836 fostered Gogol's most productive period.

Mirgorod (1835), Gogol's next cycle of stories, comprises four tales that encompass a variety of moods and styles. "Starosvetskie pomeshchiki" ("Old-World Landowners") is a light satire of peasant life, while "Taras Bulba," often referred to as the "Cossack *Iliad*," is a serious historical novella that portrays the Cossack-Polish wars of the sixteenth and seventeenth centuries. "Viy," described by Gogol as "a colossal product of folk-imagination," is a tale of supernatural terror reminiscent of Edgar Allan Poe, and "Kak possorilsya Ivan Ivanovich s Ivanom Nikiforovichem" ("The Tale of How Ivan Ivanovich Quarrelled with Ivan Nikiforovich"), considered one of the most humorous stories in Russian letters, details the end of a long friendship due to a trifling argument that culminates in an absurd series of lawsuits.

The three stories in *Arabeski* (1835; *Arabesques,* 1981) rank among Gogol's finest works. Demonstrating a shift from Ukrainian settings to the more cosmopolitan milieu of St. Petersburg, capital of the Russian empire, these pieces form part of what was termed Gogol's Petersburg Tales. These stories reveal the city as nonsensical, depersonalized, and dreamlike. "Nevski Prospekt" ("Nevski Prospect") illustrates the illusory nature of the principal thoroughfare in St. Petersburg through the experiences of two men in pursuit of women whom they believe represent ideal beauty. Their expectations are shattered, however, as one man kills himself when he discovers that his perfect woman is a prostitute and the other receives a beating from the husband of his inamorata. In "Portret" ("Portrait"), Gogol examines conflicts between artistic integrity and financial security, and in "Zapriski sumasshedshago" ("Diary of a Madman"), Gogol's only first-person narrative, he recounts in diary form events that lead to a minor civil servant's delusion that he is the king of Spain. This story has been interpreted as an indictment of the dehumanizing effects of Russian bureaucracy and a comment on the futility of ambition.

In 1836, *The Inspector General* was produced in St. Petersburg. This play, which is often considered the most original and enduring comedy in the history of Russian theater, examines the reactions of the prominent figures of a provincial Russian town to the news that a government inspector will be arriving incognito to assess municipal affairs. An impecunious traveler named Khlestakov, who is mistaken for the expected official, is bribed and fêted, attempts to seduce the mayor's wife and daughter, becomes betrothed to the latter, and departs shortly before the town's residents learn of their mistake and anticipate the arrival of the real government inspector. In this simple plot, constructed within the framework of perverse logic typical of his works, Gogol combined satirical mockery of Russian officialdom with parody of farcical literary conventions and elements of fantasy and satire.

Although the play was an indictment of Russian bureaucracy, it passed the rigid censorship of the time because Czar Nicholas I had read and admired the drama. He ordered all his ministers to attend the premiere and announced, as the final curtain fell: "Everyone has got his due, and I most of all." However, despite the czar's official sanction, the play was violently attacked by a number of influential people who denied that it contained a single honest character. Stung by this criticism, Gogol moved to Italy in 1836, and, except for two brief visits home, remained abroad for twelve years. Most of this time was spent writing *Dead Souls*. Originally planned as a light, picaresque novel, Gogol decided instead to create an epic in several volumes that would depict all elements of Russian life. The liberal Russian critics called *Dead Souls* a true reflection of life, and gave Gogol the title of "supreme realist." Realism, according to Belinsky, required a simple plot, a faithful representation of everyday life, and a humorous exposure of the negative aspects of Russian society. Belinsky saw in *Dead Souls* the embodiment of these ideals, and considered it a plea for Russian writers to fight for civilization, culture, and humankind.

Gogol's final two Petersburg Tales, "Nos" ("The Nose") and "The Overcoat", published as part of *Sochinenya* (1842; *The Works of Nikolay Gogol*), were also written at this time. They are considered among the greatest short stories in world literature. Both pieces exhibit Gogol's subtle intertwining of humor and pathos and, like "Diary of a Madman," focus on the bizarre fate of petty government officials. "The Nose" centers on a vain, ambitious bureaucrat whose nose, apparently severed by his barber, assumes a life of its own and is later encountered dressed in the uniform of a high-ranking Russian officer in the streets of St. Petersburg. Several unsuccessful attempts to regain his nose induce the protagonist's humiliation and loss of self-esteem, until one day he notices it has grown back as mysteriously as it disappeared. While recognized as a satire on Russian bureaucracy and human vanity, some Freudian critics have analyzed "The Nose" as an example of Gogol's castration anxiety. "The Overcoat," deemed by some critics as the greatest short story in the Russian language, has generated much criticism and myriad interpretations. The story revolves around an impoverished clerk, Akaky Akakyvitch, who undergoes extreme deprivation in order to save money for a new overcoat, which he views as essential to his happiness. After Akaky finally acquires the garment, it is stolen. His calls for help go unheeded, and he subsequently catches cold and dies. After his death, however, a ghost resembling Akaky appears and roams the city stealing overcoats. While most readers of Gogol's day construed "The Overcoat" as an example of social realism, believing that the author displayed deep sympathy for his beleaguered hero, later scholars have viewed the story from a psychological perspective, asserting that the overcoat symbolizes a mask that enables Akaky to disguise his spiritual destitution. Others have taken a metaphysical viewpoint, interpreting the ironic loss of the coat and Akaky's futile pleas for help as indicative of humanity's spiritual desolation in an indifferent cosmos. Despite such diverse views, critics have consistently noted the resonant irony and lyrical power with which Gogol invested this story.

Toward the end of his life, Gogol became increasingly convinced that his works should spiritually enrich his readers. *Vybrannye mesta iz perepiski s druzyami* (1847; *Selected Passages of Correspondence with My Friends*), a collection of didactic essays and letters, which many of Gogol's previous admirers condemned as reactionary, reflects this growing religious and moral fanaticism. Following the critical failure of *Selected Passages from Correspondence with My Friends*, Gogol recommenced composition on a second section of his novel *Dead Souls*, a project he had previously abandoned due to a nervous breakdown. By this time, however, Gogol had fallen under the influence of Matthew Konstantinovsky, a maniacal priest who insisted that he burn his manuscript and enter a monastery.

Gogol agonized over the decision but finally complied, convinced that this act would save him from damnation. At Konstantinovsky's insistence, Gogol undertook an ascetic regimen in order to cleanse his soul. He began a fast that weakened his already precarious health and died shortly thereafter. Following his death, a small portion of the second part *Dead Souls* was discovered and published, but critics generally agree that the sequel does not demonstrate the mastery of the first section. Though Gogol's critical appeal waned in his final years, his funeral brought out thousands of mourners. Commenting on the throngs, a passerby asked "Who is this man who has so many relatives at his funeral?" A mourner responded, "This is Nikolai Gogol, and all of Russia is his relative."

Gogol's influence on Russian literature has continued in the twentieth century and is most evident in the poetry of the Russian Symbolists. Such poets as Andrey Bely and Aleksandr Blok cite Gogol's rich prose and "visionary" language as embodiments of supreme fantasy. Yet many critics maintain that Gogol's mixture of realism and satire has proved most influential and remains his greatest achievement. Dostoyevsky acknowledged Russian literature's vast debt to Gogol by stating simply, "We all came out from under Gogol's 'Overcoat'."

(For further information about Gogol's life and works, see *Nineteenth-Century Literature Criticism*, Vols. 5, 15; *Drama Criticism*, Vol. 1; and *Short Story Criticism*, Vol. 4.)

CRITICAL COMMENTARY

C. E. TURNER

(essay date 1868)

[In the following excerpt, Turner labels Gogol a "thoroughly Russian" writer for sensitively and humorously portraying his characters as "living realities" of czarist Russia.]

Admirers of the modern sensational novel, in whose eyes tragedy is inseparably connected with 'ermine-tippets, adultery, and murder' must look upon the tales of Gogol as insipidly commonplace, and exhibiting a sad poverty of imagination. Nothing can exceed their simplicity of plot. In most of them there is an entire absence of intrigue. What is the subject of his **'Old-Fashioned Farmers'?** Two country boors, living in a

dull round of thoughtless content, spend their sixty or seventy years in drinking and eating, eating and drinking; and when they have eaten and drunk their fill, die off. Utterly incapable of the slightest intellectual effort, ignorant of all the higher impulses of nobler aspirations that dignify our nature, unconscious of any pleasure beyond the satisfaction of those instincts which man shares in common with the beast of the field,—what interest can there be in the record of life like theirs? All the emptiness, poverty, and bare nakedness of their existence is exposed; not a single detail in their petty, monotonous career, each to-morrow, the deadening counterpart of yesterday is forgotten or passed over; and yet, such is the power of art, when exercised on even the most trivial of themes, that what in unskilled hands

Principal Works

Hans Kuechelgärten [as V. Alov] (poetry) 1829

Vechera ná khutore bliz Dikanki [as Rudy Panko] (short stories) 1831

[Evenings in Little Russia, 1903; also published as Evenings on a Farm near Dikanka, 1906]

Arabeski (essays and short stories) 1835

[Arabesques, 1981]

Mirgorod (short stories) 1835

[Mirgorod, 1842]

Révizor (drama) 1836

[The Inspector General, 1892; also published as The Government Inspector in The Government Inspector and Other Plays, 1927]

Mёrtvye dushi (novel) 1842

[Tchitchikoff 's Journeys; or, Dead Souls, 1886; also published as Dead Souls, 1915]

Sochinenya. 2 vols. (short stories, dramas, and novel) 1842

[The Works of Nikolay Gogol. 6 vols., 1922-28]

Zhenit'ba; Sovershenno neveroyatnoye sobitye (drama) 1842

[The Marriage: An Utterly Incredible Occurence published in The Modern Theatre, Vol. IV, 1955-60]

Igroki (drama) 1843

[The Gamblers published in The Modern Theatre, Vol. III, 1955-60]

Vybrannye mesta iz perepiski s druzyami (essays and letters) 1847

[Selected Passages from Correspondence with My Friends, 1969]

Letters of Nikolai Gogol (letters) 1967

---

would have sunk into a revolting burlesque, becomes with Gógol the source of truest poetry and kindliest humour.

Combined with, and a natural consequence of this simplicity of plot, we observe in Gógol a rare fidelity of human nature in the delineation of his characters. They are not heroic, gifted with superhuman virtues or superhuman vices. It requires no great genius to sketch incarnations of wild devilry or embodiments of perfection. They are not extraordinary people, still less fancy portraits, but living realities; to many of whom we feel that we could give their true name. It is this which arouses our interest in the humblest and the meanest among them; we perceive that they are no painted puppets put into certain postures at the whim and caprice of the showman, but through every change of circumstance they are allowed to develop themselves naturally, and without the author's controlling intervention. . . . [We] seem to have known them one and all

in real life. Let their story be told however briefly, we feel able to supply some trait in their history which the author has failed to give, relate some additional anecdote about them which the writer has forgotten or passed over.

The next feature in the writings of Gógol of which we would speak is one which, on a first perusal, we are apt to imagine constitutes their sole, or at least chief, recommendation. We refer to their humour. And when we speak of Gógol's humour, we wish the word to be understood in its widest and most comprehensive sense. For though in its source it is one springing from a deep conviction of the vanity of all that is human, it is most varied in its manifestations. At times he will surrender himself to some wild fancy so extravagantly absurd, that no writer less daring than himself would ever have used it to move our laughter, and hold us spell-bound as he describes Vakóola's ride on the devil's back to St. Petersburg [in 'Christmas Eve']. . . . There is in such passages as this an abandonment to the humour of the moment which it is impossible to resist. . . . In general, however, Gógol's humour is quieter and more subdued in its tone. It is this forced absence of passion which gives such strength to Gógol's satire, and makes his irony so biting. By a single word or trifling phrase, which would seem to have fallen accidentally from his pen, he will plant the blow, aimed at the social folly or administrative abuse he is attacking, with a vigour and a certainty that renders it fatal. Thus, in the description of a general's daughter, which he puts into the mouth of a poor *tchinóvnik*, who is infatuated with her beauty, after having made him expatiate on the charms of her person, with what exquisite banter does he sum up the cringing subserviency natural to his position in the one expressive sentence, 'Her very handkerchief breathes the essence of a general's rank!' (pp. 332-34)

In his humour, in his irony, in his language, in his thoughts, in his lyrical outburst of passionate eloquence, and in his pathos, Gógol is thoroughly Russian. And thoroughly Russian, too, are all his personages; and it were difficult to cite one trait in the national character that has not been seized upon by Gógol. His nationality, to use his own words, does not consist 'in describing the saraphan,' but is 'inspired by the very spirit of the people.' And yet, as a true artist, he did not neglect external peculiarities. Nothing can be more remarkable than the pains which he took to render his portraits true to the minutest detail. . . . So true and so outspoken is he, that he was not seldom met with the charge of being unpatriotic: as if, forsooth, patriotism consisted in a blind admiration of whatever is, and an equally blind belief that it therefore must be right. It is a charge which honest writers in every land and in every age have had to bear. 'But,' to quote Gógol's manly reply to such reproaches, 'the accusation is not

founded on any sentiment so pure or so noble as patriotism. It proceeds from those who do not care to remedy
an evil, but are only anxious that none should speak of
the ill they do. A cowardly fear is its sole foundation,
however grandly it may mask itself under the holy
name of patriotism. This mask it is the mission of every
honest writer to tear away, to trample beneath his feet.
Writers have but one sacred duty, and that is to tell the
truth, the whole truth, and nothing but the truth.' (pp.
334-35)

There are a freshness, a simplicity, and a gaiety in
Gógol's descriptions of Little Russian life, which bring
home to us a conviction of their unexaggerated truthfulness, even though we have never visited the country, and are ignorant of its habits, faith, and language.
They are filled with those happy touches which of
themselves reveal the whole character of the people
with a certainty and a precision not to be attained in
pages of ordinary traveller's gossip. (pp. 335-36)

'Tárass Búlba' and 'The Old-Fashioned Farmers' are two companion pictures: the one representing
the complete abnegation of all activity in life; the other,
the heroic energy which knows of no tranquility or
rest. There is something brutal in both these lives: in
the placid contentment, which nothing can ruffle or
disturb so long as the animal instincts are satisfied; and
in the unrestrained abandonment to the fiercest passions, which acknowledge no higher law, admit of no
restraint. And where shall we find the portrait of a savage hero drawn with grander boldness in its colossal
outlines, or with subtler delicacy in its minutest filling
up, than in the first of these stories? (pp. 336-37)

Of Gógol's numerous tales relating to *tchinóvnik*
life, 'The Cloak' strikes us as affording the best example of that knowledge of, and power to describe, the
petty joys and unromantic miseries of homely, commonplace people, which form the most striking characteristics of his genius. It is impossible to read the history of 'Akákia Akakievitch,' and not be touched by the
deep pathos that underlies its very insignificance, and
in the one bright dream, that for a moment gladdened
his dim, narrow existence, recognise the glorious probabilities with which every soul, however thwarted,
however deadened, is originally endowed. (p. 340)

C. E. Turner, in an originally unsigned essay titled "Gógol's
Works," in *The British Quarterly Review,* Vol. XLVII, No. 94,
April 1, 1868, pp. 327-45.

IVAN YERMAKOV
(essay date 1923)

[In the following excerpt from an essay first published in 1923 in his *Ocherki po analizn tvorchestva
N. V. Gogolya,* Yermakov, a leading early twentieth-
century psychoanalyst, draws general conclusions
about Gogol's psyche.]

Gogol's fantastic tale **"The Nose"** occupies a special
position among those works of his which are linked, if
not exactly by the same theme, then by the tormenting
questions he put to himself and endeavored to resolve.
Included in this group are a number of his best stories,
such as **"Viy," "The Tale of How Ivan Ivanovich
Quarrelled with Ivan Nikiforovich," "The Nose,"
"The Overcoat,"** and **"Diary of a Madman."** To be
sure, it is to some extent arbitrary and artificial to lift
just a few stories out of the corpus of Gogol's works,
all of which are organically interconnected; for . . . the
theme of **"The Nose"** had long been in the making, in
stories where the nose itself had not yet been assigned
the role of protagonist. This fact makes it clear that
Golgol did not borrow his theme from elsewhere, as literary historians suppose; he was not simply echoing
certain literary fashions of the beginning of the nineteenth century; rather, he responded to them, interpreted them, and gave them a particular form, out of an
inner need and compulsion to do so. (p. 158)

In his letters and his works of fiction, Gogol betrays an irrepressible need to observe, describe, and
castigate the shortcomings of others and of himself as
well. In neither case is he free, for he is obeying the
command of his unconscious. Gogol torments himself
in order to have the right to torment others.

All of a writer's works are nothing more than a
confession and self-revelation. Gogol—and he speaks
of this specifically in **"An Author's Confession"**—saw
his works as a kind of mirror in which he scrutinized
and studied himself. This, it seems to me, explains his
narrative method, his use of colloquial language and
skaz, [a form of narration in which the speaker's style
is as significant as the story], and his habit of putting
himself into everything he wrote. The clash of two opposing tendencies in the confession—one revealing, the
other concealing—produced a compromise solution to
the task that Gogol set himself, and forced him to resort
to jests, puns, and unfinished utterances. The attempt
to say what cannot be directly expressed in civilized society leads to ambiguity and to witticism. Gogol regarded his works as a confession, an exhibition, for all

to see, of something important and significant. (pp. 159-60)

In the complex and interesting course of Gogol's search for his unique, Gogolian self, there is a natural demarcation of two phases, although they are very intimately interconnected. The first is one of open self-ridicule; the second finds him directing his gaze more deeply into the hidden recesses of his own experiences and seeking out "nastiness" there. **"The Nose"** is one of Gogol's confessions that belongs to this second phase, along with **"Viy," "The Overcoat," "Neysky Prospect,"** and others.

Two sides of Gogol's personality are revealed in the first phase of the development of his work as a satirist: his attempt to depict both comic and terrible things. Here his tendency to try to discredit other people does not go beneath the surface, and his humor is sometimes not of a very high order. He does hit on some very apt names and situations for his characters; but we also constantly find many awkward and rough-cast attempts, such as Dovgochkhun, Pupopuz, Krutoryshchenko, and others.

The second phase is marked by greater care in the selection of such names; the dark and terrible side of life, which was localized in the countryside in the *Dikanka* stories, is now transformed into universal evil, of which every man is the vehicle.

In the first stage, the writer participates in the stories himself, he consistently does the narrating, as if he were retelling old tales and adapting himself to the people he is talking about, putting himself, as it were, on their level. But in the second stage the situation changes. To be sure, Gogol hews to the same narrative method as before. But fundamentally new is his focus on himself, his desire to reveal and identify in himself the same traits he sees in others. In other words, there comes a time in the development of Gogol's work when, preoccupied with self-purification and self-analysis, he gradually shifts to the confessional form until finally, and with complete consistency, he entitles one of his last works **"An Author's Confession."** As this inner development proceeds, Gogol begins to take a different view of his early works, which had made him famous overnight. He does not find in them what is now most important to him: the *spiritual* element, which attracts him and fills his life above anything else. (pp. 160-61)

[Two] opposing and endlessly conflicting tendencies underlay Gogol's art: self-depreciation and self-exaltation. The conflict was explicitly reflected not only in what Gogol wrote, but also in the way he wrote, in the style and the imagery he used. . . .

In his early works Gogol liked to introduce and even elaborate on heroic themes, together with themes drawn from ordinary life. For example, *Taras Bulba,*

"Al-Mamun," "Rome," and others contain epic descriptions and characterizations that might well have been taken from Homer. These two styles—the one intense and epic, the other commonplace—intertwine throughout all his writings, for instance in **"Diary of a Madman,"** in *Dead Souls,* and, as we shall see, in **"The Nose"** as well, even though they are concealed there.

There is something very significant about the ease with which noble and ignoble themes interweave and unfold in tandem. (Gogol's follower, Dostoevsky, brought this tendency to full flower.) Very often such themes develop in unexpected ways; but they grip us, they seem to dull our critical faculties, and we do not notice how outwardly unmotivated and unexpected they are. Among such instances we should include the so-called lyrical digression at the beginning of **"The Overcoat"** and those in *Dead Souls*—the passage in chapter eleven, for example, where the courier gallops by, shouting imprecations and shattering the reverie into which the writer has fallen. (p. 162)

In his art [Gogol] constantly moves between two abysses, falling now into one, now into the other. This is what some critics see as his tendency toward the extreme, the ultimate. These two natures are the masculine and the feminine, the active and the passive, the holy and the sinful, the pregenital and the genital. Laughter and tears, pleasure and pain are expressed simultaneously in Gogol's works; and the coexistence of these two opposing tendencies is intimately linked with his sexual experiences and is marked both by auto-erotism and by fear or bitter repentance for such self-gratification. Active behavior is repressed and directed against the self. (pp. 162-63)

In moving toward the extreme, or the ultimate, Gogol, like many fantasts, consistently starts from reality, from some story he has been told, from anecdotes or incidents current in society. He fixes an inquisitive eye on the world around him as he studies man—his words, his gestures, his expressions, and, above all, his nose, to which he attaches a special and very vital significance. One could compile a whole little anthology from the passages in Gogol's works that mention the nose, so tirelessly does he describe the taking of snuff, nose-blowing, and so on. (p. 163)

We must . . . study **"The Nose"** from the viewpoint of that most unusual work of Gogol's, **"An Author's Confession."** A confession is a serious act. . . . [Gogol] is faced with the equally important task of neither revealing nor concealing anything completely. These two opposing drives give rise to conflicting needs. They very often cross and produce so-called compromise solutions, which end up as puns and double entendres. . . . (p. 191)

Feeling absolutely unrestricted, and burning with

a desire to repent, Gogol sought an opportunity to bare everything that lay in the depths of his soul, and to make a confession as a great sinner. The most blasphemous scenes, the most unforgivable similes, the most cynical images and possibilities pass before his mind's eye; it is his tremendous capacity for self-analysis which allows him to accept them and to regard their exposure as a heroic deed. To discern these conflicting drives within himself, to bring them out for himself and even for all to see, to invite laughter and ridicule and to know that he is "laughing at himself "—this is what makes it possible for Gogol to confess and reveal himself to the ultimate. It is at this ultimate—this realm of our basic, archaic self, this primitive fabric on which the patterns of our life are later embroidered, this dark, unknown, nether-world of the mind into which man is usually so ready to cast everything he finds cumbersome in his conscious life—it is here that the most contradictory drives come into collision and prove to be identical. Here the same word, the same symbol takes on two completely different meanings at the same time. Here religious fervor is blasphemy, things of the greatest value are valueless, good deeds are evil and sinful. Only after he has reached this ultimate, only after he has brought forth the essence of this basic self can a writer free himself from everything accidental and temporary, touch and understand the innermost secrets of the soul, and then forge a truthful and genuine image of man, and thereby a work of art.

But perhaps there is something dubious about this approach. Perhaps **"The Nose"** is simply a joke, a trifle, with none of the serious purposes that we have indicated here. (pp. 191-92)

[The] problem posed in **"The Nose"** is a sexual one. It throws light on the question of the autonomy of man's sexual activity as symbolized by the separate existence of the nose. (The same thing can be seen in the quarrel between the two Ivans.) Sexual activity asserts its rights, which run counter to the urgings of the ego and the norms of society. The thing that cannot be displayed or talked about without shame and embarrassment—"the nose"—itself evokes a feeling of shame and embarrassment if it is not in its proper place, between the two cheeks. The result is an insoluble problem: it is uncomfortable to have a nose but just as uncomfortable not to have one: the two situations are equally discrediting and disgraceful. (p. 192)

In trying as best we can to decipher **"The Nose,"** we must say that two things underlie the story: the fear of castration, which goes along with the repressed wish to possess an enormous sex-organ; and the desire for unlimited erotic pleasures. These desires lead to aggressive acts directed against social life and cultural values, and must be repressed. However, a frivolous individual like Kovalyov is not guided by anything except his own egotistic interests. His activities run counter to the demands of civilized life. They create a feeling of guilt in him which he does not wish to recognize, but which reveals itself to him in the form of an extremely oppressive dream (the dream of castration). But it has been only a dream; on awakening, Kovalyov tries to ignore his painful experiences, and he resumes his interrupted activities. We find him making fun of a military man whose nose is the size of a waistcoat button; he is even buying the ribbon of some order, but it is not known why, since he has not been so honored. In other words, life has once again fallen into its old rut. The mysterious disappearance of the "nose" remains as mysterious as ever to Kovalyov. (p. 194)

Something that could have brought about catharsis, awareness, purification, further growth and development, a turning point in life (an "annunciation"), has been lost beyond recall. The laughter in the story is suffused with tears, the bitter tears of the author: no, man will not become aware of all his vileness, he will not understand what he is really like. Even in the case of a "learned" collegiate assessor such as Kovalyov, the unconscious attempt to reveal his essential inner self in the form of images and actions has passed without leaving a trace.

In keeping with the structural requirements of the humorous story, Gogol is obliged to bring off a happy ending. But somehow, we feel like saying, as he himself does at the end of **"The Two Ivans":** "It's a dreary world, my dear sirs!"

All these surprisingly perceptive discoveries are the result of the same process we observe at work in psychoanalysis: one must be honest and courageous when faced with oneself. Gogol possessed a sufficiency of honesty and therefore succeeded in bringing out a great many things in his own mind and the minds of others, things which need much more extensive elucidation and analysis.

For the present, however, we can draw two conclusions from our analysis of **"The Nose."** First of all, what strikes the reader as being mere chance, "nonsense," a dream yet not quite a dream; what makes Ivan Yakovlevich and Kovalyov constantly test themselves to see whether they are asleep or losing their minds—all this has its own logic and has been skillfully prepared by the author. From here it is only a step to the assertion that sleeping and dreaming are not such nonsense after all. The statement that the nose was found by a near-sighted police officer with a mother-in-law who could not see anything either is fraught with significance. Does it not say that the real meaning of the loss of the nose can be discovered and revealed only when a person is near-sighted, when he can see nothing but his own nose, or, in other words, nothing but a dream?

[Second], Gogol's characters frequently carry on meaningless conversations that would hardly be conceivable for normal people. Evidently they do not understand what they are saying or why. But it is just such utterances which best characterize individuals; in psychoanalysis they are called free associations, and they reveal that area of the mind that contains drives which man cannot understand but which nonetheless determine his actions. (pp. 195-96)

["The Nose"] makes it clear that Gogol grasped the significance of the dream as a phenomenon that threatens us and compels us to give serious thought to ourselves. He discerned the possibility of crisis in Kovalyov's petty and intimidated soul—in his useless running around and in his cynical attitude toward women. He created a tragedy, a tragicomedy, and thereby posed the question: what is more important, the sexual or Kovalyov? Is the sexual subordinate to Kovalyov, or Kovalyov to the sexual? The nose comes off by itself and declares its independence of Kovalyov; so far as it is concerned, Kovalyov is nothing more than a carriage for it to ride in. Kovalyov laughs at himself for being foolish enough to take a dream for reality. He does not notice that it is precisely his predicament in the dream which perhaps does more than anything else to expose the emptiness of his life and the humiliation of being utterly dependent on his own nose. Whenever it seems as if the meaning of these events is about to be revealed, everything is shrouded in fog. Kovalyov is not allowed to see; he does not want to see the person who is to blame for everything: himself.

Gogol says that although such cases are rare, they do happen: this is a subtly ironic commentary on people who do not understand the significance of dreams, and who consider outer reality truer than inner. But

Gogol understands. He takes the fashionable "nosological" theme which intrigued so many writers before him, and does something more with it than simply reshuffle its familiar components. And he is able to make us understand what every person is tormented by, and what must be resolved and grasped so that man can free himself from the power of the dark forces of primitive instinct. He seems to be refusing to give a solution; he leaves the reader baffled; but any attentive eye can see that Gogol knows something about why such dreams occur; and he prods us into "action," into making an effort to see our own dreams in Kovalyov's dream and hearken to the voices that challenge us to evaluate the life and activity of such an individual. (pp. 197-98)

Ivan Yermakov, "The Nose," in *Gogol from the Twentieth Century: Eleven Essays,* edited and translated by Robert A. Maguire, Princeton University Press, 1974, pp. 156-98.

VLADIMIR NABOKOV
(essay date 1944)

[A Russian-born American man of letters, Nabokov is perhaps best known for the novels *Lolita* (1955) and *Pale Fire* (1962). In the following excerpt from his biography *Nikolai Gogol* (1944), he considers Gogol to be a strongly visual writer who excels primarily as a stylist. He concludes that Gogol's work "is a phenomenon of language and not one of ideas."]

Gogol was a strange creature, but genius is always strange; it is only your healthy second-rater who seems to the grateful reader to be a wise old friend, nicely developing the reader's own notions of life. Great literature skirts the irrational. *Hamlet* is the wild dream of a neurotic scholar. Gogol's **"The Overcoat"** is a grotesque and grim nightmare making black holes in the dim pattern of life. The superficial reader of that story will merely see in it the heavy frolics of an extravagant buffoon; the solemn reader will take for granted that Gogol's prime intention was to denounce the horrors of Russian bureaucracy. But neither the person who wants a good laugh, nor the person who craves for books "that make one think" will understand what **"The Overcoat"** is really about. Give me the creative reader; this is a tale for him.

Steady Pushkin, matter-of-fact Tolstoy, restrained Chekhov have all had their moments of irrational insight which simultaneously blurred the sentence and disclosed a secret meaning worth the sudden focal shift. But with Gogol this shifting is the very basis of his art, so that whenever he tried to write in the round hand of literary tradition and to treat rational ideas in a logical way, he lost all trace of talent. When, as in his immortal **"The Overcoat,"** he really let himself go and pottered happily on the brink of his private abyss, he became the greatest artist that Russia has yet produced.

The sudden slanting of the rational plane of life may be accomplished of course in many ways, and every great writer has his own method. With Gogol it was a combination of two movements: a jerk and a glide. Imagine a trap-door that opens under your feet with absurd suddenness, and a lyrical gust that sweeps you up and then lets you fall with a bump into the next traphole. The absurd was Gogol's favorite muse—but when I say "the absurd," I do not mean the quaint or the comic. The absurd has as many shades and degrees as the tragic has, and moreover, in Gogol's case, it borders upon the latter. It would be wrong to assert that Gogol placed his characters in absurd situations. You cannot place a man in an absurd situation if the whole world he lives in is absurd; you cannot do this if you mean by "absurd" something provoking a chuckle or a shrug. But if you mean the pathetic, the human condition, if you mean all such things that in less weird worlds are linked up with the loftiest aspirations, the deepest sufferings, the strongest passions—then of course the necessary breach is there, and a pathetic human, lost in the midst of Gogol's nightmarish, irresponsible world would be "absurd," by a kind of secondary contrast.

On the lid of the tailor's snuff-box there was "the portrait of a General; I do not know what general because the tailor's thumb had made a hole in the general's face and a square of paper had been gummed over the hole." Thus with the absurdity of Akaky Akakyevich Bashmachkin. We did not expect that, amid the whirling masks, one mask would turn out to be a real face, or at least the place where that face ought to be. The essence of mankind is irrationally derived from the chaos of fakes which form Gogol's world. Akaky Akakyevich, the hero of **"The Overcoat,"** is absurd *because* he is pathetic, *because* he is human and *because* he has been engendered by those very forces which seem to be in such contrast to him.

He is not merely human and pathetic. He is something more, just as the background is not mere burlesque. Somewhere behind the obvious contrast there is a subtle genetic link. His being discloses the same quiver and shimmer as does the dream world to which he belongs. The allusions to something else behind the crudely painted screens, are so artistically combined with the superficial texture of the narration that civic-minded Russians have missed them completely. But a creative reading of Gogol's story reveals that here and there in the most innocent descriptive passage, this or that word, sometimes a mere adverb or a preposition, for instance the word "even" or "almost," is inserted in such a way as to make the harmless sentence explode in a wild display of nightmare fireworks; or else the passage that had started in a rambling colloquial manner all of a sudden leaves the tracks and swerves into the irrational where it really belongs; or again, quite as suddenly, a door bursts open and a mighty wave of foaming poetry rushes in only to dissolve in bathos, or to turn into its own parody, or to be checked by the sentence breaking and reverting to a conjuror's patter, that patter which is such a feature of Gogol's style. It gives one the sensation of something ludicrous and at the same time stellar, lurking constantly around the corner—and one likes to recall that the difference between the comic side of things, and their cosmic side, depends upon one sibilant.

So what is that queer world, glimpses of which we keep catching through the gaps of the harmless looking sentences? It is in a way the *real* one but it looks wildly absurd to us, accustomed as we are to the stage setting that screens it. It is from these glimpses that the main character of **"The Overcoat,"** the meek little clerk, is formed, so that he embodies the spirit of that secret but real world which breaks through Gogol's style. He is, that meek little clerk, a ghost, a visitor from some tragic depths who by chance happened to assume the disguise of a petty official. Russian progressive critics sensed in him the image of the underdog and the whole story impressed them as a social protest. But it is something much more than that. The gaps and black holes in the texture of Gogol's style imply flaws in the texture of life itself. Something is very wrong and all men are mild lunatics engaged in pursuits that seem to them very important while an absurdly logical force keeps them at their futile jobs—this is the real "message" of the story. In this world of utter futility, of futile humility and futile domination, the highest degree that passion, desire, creative urge can attain is a new cloak which both tailors and customers adore on their knees. I am not speaking of the moral point or the moral lesson. There can be no moral lesson in such a world because there are no pupils and no teachers: this world *is* and it excludes everything that might destroy it, so that any improvement, any struggle, any moral purpose or endeavor, are as utterly impossible as changing the course of a star. It is Gogol's world and as such wholly different from Tolstoy's world, or Pushkin's, or Chekhov's or my own. But after reading Gogol one's eyes may become gogolized and one is apt to see bits of his world in the most unexpected places. I have visited many countries, and something like Akaky Akakyevich's overcoat has been the passionate dream of this or that chance acquaintance who never had heard about Gogol.

The plot of **"The Overcoat"** is very simple. A poor little clerk makes a great decision and orders a new overcoat. The coat while in the making becomes the dream of his life. On the very first night that he wears it he is robbed of it on a dark street. He dies of grief and his ghost haunts the city. This is all in the way of plot, but of course the *real* plot (as always with Gogol) lies in the style, in the inner structure of this transcendental anecdote. In order to appreciate it at its true worth one must perform a kind of mental somersault so as to get rid of conventional values in literature and follow the author along the dream road of his superhuman imagination. Gogol's world is somewhat related to such conceptions of modern physics as the "Concertina Universe" or the "Explosion Universe"; it is far removed from the comfortably revolving clockwork worlds of the last century. There is a curvature in literary style as there is curvature in space,—but few are the Russian readers who do care to plunge into Gogol's magic chaos head first, with no restraint or regret. The Russian who thinks Turgenev was a great writer, and bases his notion of Pushkin upon Chaïkovsky's vile libretti, will merely paddle into the gentlest wavelets of Gogol's mysterious sea and limit his reaction to an enjoyment of what he takes to be whimsical humor and colorful quips. But the diver, the seeker for black pearls, the man who prefers the monsters of the deep to the sunshades on the beach, will find in **"The Overcoat"** shadows linking our state of existence to those other states and modes which we dimly apprehend in our rare moments of irrational perception. The prose of Pushkin is three-dimensional; that of Gogol is four-dimensional, at least. He may be compared to his contemporary, the mathematician Lobachevsky, who blasted Euclid and discovered a century ago many of the theories which Einstein later developed. If parallel lines do not meet it is not because meet they cannot, but because they have other things to do. Gogol's art as disclosed in **"The Overcoat"** suggests that parallel lines not only may meet, but that they can wriggle and get most extravagantly entangled, just as two pillars reflected in water indulge in the most wobbly contortions if the necessary ripple is there. Gogol's genius is exactly that ripple— two and two make five, if not the square root of five, and it all happens quite naturally in Gogol's world, where neither rational mathematics nor indeed any of our pseudophysical agreements with ourselves can be seriously said to exist.

The clothing process indulged in by Akaky Akakyevich, the making and the putting on of the cloak, is really his *disrobing* and his gradual reversion to the stark nakedness of his own ghost. From the very beginning of the story he is in training for his supernaturally high jump—and such harmless looking details as his tiptoeing in the streets to spare his shoes or his not quite knowing whether he is in the middle of the street or in the middle of the sentence, these details gradually dissolve the clerk Akaky Akakyevich so that towards the end of the story his ghost seems to be the most tangible, the most real part of his being. The account of his

A montage of the cast of the 1909 Moscow Art Theater production of *The Inspector General.*

ghost haunting the streets of St. Petersburg in search of the cloak of which he had been robbed and finally appropriating that of a high official who had refused to help him in his misfortune—this account, which to the unsophisticated may look like an ordinary ghost story, is transformed towards the end into something for which I can find no precise epithet. It is both an apotheosis and a *dégringolade.* Here it is:

The Important Person almost died of fright. In his office and generally in the presence of subordinates he was a man of strong character, and whoever glanced at his manly appearance and shape used to imagine his kind of temper with something of a shudder; at the present moment however he (as happens in the case of many people of prodigiously powerful appearance) experienced such terror that, not without reason, he *even* expected to have a fit of some sort. He *even* threw off his cloak of his own accord and then exhorted the coachman in a wild voice to take him home and drive like mad. Upon hearing tones which were generally used at critical moments and were *even* [notice the recurrent use of this word] accompanied by something far more effective, the coachman thought it wiser to draw his head in; he lashed at the horses, and the carriage sped like an arrow. Six minutes later, or a little more, [according to Gogol's special timepiece] the Important Person was already at the porch of his house. Pale, frightened and cloakless, instead of arriving at Caroline

Ivanovna's [a woman he kept] he had thus come home; he staggered to his bedroom and spent an exceedingly troubled night, so that next morning, at breakfast, his daughter said to him straightaway: 'You are quite pale today, papa.' But papa kept silent and [now comes the parody of a Bible parable!] he told none of what had befallen him, nor where he had been, nor whither he had wished to go. The whole occurrence made a very strong impression on him [here begins the downhill slide, that spectacular bathos which Gogol uses for his particular needs]. Much more seldom *even* did he address to his subordinates the words 'How dare you?—Do you know to whom you are speaking?'—or at least if he did talk that way it was not till he had first listened to what they had to tell. But still more remarkable was the fact that from that time on the ghostly clerk quite ceased to appear: evidently the Important Person's overcoat fitted him well; at least no more did one hear of overcoats being snatched from people's shoulders. However, many active and vigilant persons refused to be appeased and kept asserting that in remote parts of the city the ghostly clerk still showed himself. And indeed a suburban policeman saw with his own eyes [the downward slide from the moralistic note to the grotesque is now a tumble] a ghost appear from behind a house. But being by nature somewhat of a weakling (so that once, an ordinary full-grown young pig which had rushed out of some private house knocked him off his feet to the great merriment of a group of cab drivers from whom he demanded, and obtained, as a penalty for this derision, ten coppers from each to buy himself snuff), he did not venture to stop the ghost but just kept on walking behind it in the darkness, until the ghost suddenly turned, stopped and inquired: 'What d'you want, you?'—and showed a fist of a size rarely met with *even* among the living. 'Nothing,' answered the sentinel and proceeded to go back at once. That ghost, however, was a much taller one and had a huge moustache. It was heading apparently towards Obukhov Bridge and presently disappeared completely in the darkness of the night.

The torrent of "irrelevant" details (such as the bland assumption that "full-grown young pigs" commonly occur in private houses) produces such a hypnotic effect that one almost fails to realize one simple thing (and that is the beauty of the final stroke). A piece of most important information, the main structural idea of the story is here deliberately masked by Gogol (because all reality is a mask). The man taken for Akaky Akakyevich's cloakless ghost is actually the man who stole his cloak. But Akaky Akakyevich's ghost existed solely on the strength of his lacking a cloak, whereas now the policeman, lapsing into the queerest paradox of the story, mistakes for this ghost just the very person who was its antithesis, the man who had stolen the cloak. Thus the story describes a full circle: a vicious circle as all circles are, despite their posing as apples, or planets, or human faces.

So to sum up: the story goes this way: mumble, mumble, lyrical wave, mumble, lyrical wave, mumble, lyrical wave, mumble, fantastic climax, mumble, mumble, and back into the chaos from which they all had derived. At this superhigh level of art, literature is of course not concerned with pitying the underdog or cursing the upperdog. It appeals to that secret depth of the human soul where the shadows of other worlds pass like the shadows of nameless and soundless ships. (pp. 140-49)

Vladimir Nabokov, in his *Nikolai Gogol,* 1944. Reprint by New Directions Books, 1961, 172 p.

VSEVOLOD SETCHKAREV
(essay date 1953)

[In the following excerpt from a work originally published in German in 1953, Setchkarev offers an in-depth analysis of Gogol's major works.]

Gogol deals with a problem [in **"The Portrait,"** from the collection *Arabesques*] that was to torment him all his life: evil is capable of infecting even artistic inspiration. Through this means it does the greatest harm, for they are indeed the best who engage in the arts or take pleasure in them. How great, therefore, is the responsibility of the artist, how he must control his actions! Nature, which has passed through an artistic consciousness and thus resulted in the work of art, is raised to a higher sphere of universal validity; but there is a limit beyond which art leaves its proper domain. The highest mastery of art gives the artist the means to go beyond this limit, to advance beyond art to the ultimate, to the first causes of Nature, into that reality which is the basis of all reality that is perceptible to the senses. The artist who reaches this stratosphere of art "steals something that cannot be produced by human action; he tears from life something living which animates the original." And this original reality, which is perceived by the artistic imagination, when strained to the utmost and propelled by a blow from without, it flies off its axis, is truly terrible. It is revealed to him "who thirsts for this reality, when in his desire to comprehend beautiful Man, he opens him up with his scalpel and catches sight of the repulsive Man within."

Thus, basically the same theme as in the Dikanka tales is present here: beneath the surface of the beautiful world the chaos of evil bubbles, and according to God's decree the world is to end after it has been tempted by Satan. The older the world, the stronger the power of the devil. "Wonder, my son, at the terrible power of Satan," says the old monk, "he will permeate everything: our works, our thoughts, yes, even the inspiration of the artist. Countless will be the victims of this hellish spirit who lives on earth invisible and shapeless." And is there any escape? "No" is the unspoken answer, for according to God's laws, so it is to be; the reprieve gained by the pious artist in years of renunciation is only a rare exception, attained through the intercession of the Mother of God. But the world is drifting helplessly toward its destruction—no sanctity is capable of saving it. But Gogol is less concerned here with the religious problem, for which reason he carelessly leaves the question open. It is the problem of the essence of art that excites him, and nowhere do we perceive so clearly his struggle to find a definition of that irrational effect produced on men by a great work of art as in this tale. The description of the good picture that causes the radical change in Chertkov is an example of these efforts. The "inexpressibly expressible" is the formula he comes upon. He is aware of the difficulty of the creative process; he knows how much work is involved in producing the apparently simple in art, for "everything unforced and light for the poet and painter is attained only forcibly and is the fruit of great exertions." Only one who dedicates himself to pure art will be able to achieve something great. The artist must serve art alone; if he lives only for his work, it can happen that in a mystical experience, knowledge of the coherence of the world within the divine order is revealed to him—but only if he does not strive for this knowledge, but rather serves art alone and dedicates himself to his work.

It is not hard to see that Gogol is here following the romantic conception of art. (pp. 125-27)

Gogol built up his material with great stylistic skill. ["**The Portrait**"] consists of two parts, which are not apparently connected with each other, but stand next to one another like two unrelated tales, yet in both of them, the mysterious picture is the center point; the first only becomes comprehensible after a reading of the second as an episode explaining the fatal effect of the picture. The author's tone is serious, and only at times are there flashes of satiric light (e.g., the policeman, the distinguished lady and her daughter) or traces of Gogol's humorous stylistic devices (e.g., "slight disagreements" used to designate absolute contradictions in the chatter of the lady . . .). In the second part, which is narrated by the "buyer," any attempt to have the language sound like that which is really spoken is given up, so that the scattered apostrophes produce a jarring effect. Several uncertainties in expression, false pathos ("He threw himself on his knees and was completely transformed into prayer"), and superfluous sentimentalities, especially in the religious scenes, prove that Gogol was not entirely successful here with the serious, solemn style which he later worked so hard to perfect. (pp. 127-28)

[In "**Nevsky Prospect**,"] Gogol simultaneously combines two different literary genres: the gruesome naturalistic *feuilleton* of late French romanticism with its strongly sentimental tendency and an anecdote recounted in the style of a farce. (pp. 128-29)

A description of the main street in St. Petersburg, Nevsky Prospect, constitutes both the beginning and the end of the whole work. Both adventures begin on this street. In the introduction the changing appearance of this avenue according to the time of day is described in an apparently admiring, positive tone—but in reality, a fair of human vanity and stupidity is passing by. As soon as the sun sets, the action of both stories immediately begins; at the end of both stories we again find ourselves in the twilight on Nevsky Prospect, just as the street lamps are being lit. And now the author shows his cards:

Everything is deceit, everything is a dream, nothing is what it seems! . . . It lies at all times, this Nevsky Prospect, but most of all when night presses against it like a condensed mass and outlines the white and straw-colored walls of the houses, when the whole city turns into thunder and glitter, myriads of carriages swarm the bridges, the outriders shout and hop up and down on their horses, and when the demon himself lights the lamps only to show everything differently from the way it really is.

We have again come to Gogol's theme: the devil is lying in wait for Man, and there is no escape from him. The painter who thinks he sees the ideal of womanhood when he takes the beautiful exterior for the mirror of the soul is in reality meeting a whore. His dream, which he seeks to prolong by means of opium and which is turning into real life for him, cannot save him in the long run. Our life involves a contradiction between the ideal and reality, but the imagination does not have the power to deliver Man—a conception which essentially distinguishes Gogol from his literary model at this time, E.T.A. Hoffmann. The stupid, unimaginative, crude, run-of-the-mill Lieutenant Pirogov lives more happily than anyone, as he forgets his righteous anger with some pastry and a mazurka, and on the next day is ready to go out on a new adventure of the same sort. The two dull-witted beauties who are the heroines of the two stories are also happy. (Gogol inserts a charming observation on the beauty of married people at this point.) But what terrible happiness it is! It is the happiness of the enslaved beast, for the devil already has power over such a man. Incapable of any higher impulse, his soul is paralyzed, and he will fittingly join the crowd on the streets which conceal its gaping inner emptiness beneath a brilliant appearance and vain splendor. It is again noteworthy that at this time Gogol does not speak a word about God or religiosity. His conception of the world is one-sidedly pessimistic: Evil rules. In art and in love a glimpse of salvation is granted Man; it is shining somewhere as something lofty and noble in which Man feels the need to believe. But Satan holds his deceiving prism in front of everything so that Man cannot see the truth. And what is truth? . . . Man stands in the world uncertain and alone—will he find in himself something to hold on to? Thus the Nevsky Prospect becomes a symbol of the world. . . . (pp. 129-30)

[In **"The Diary of a Madman,"** Gogol again] interweaves naturalism and the fantastic in an aesthetically convincing manner. The development of the mental disturbance into delusions of grandeur as a consequence of an inferiority complex resulting from an unhappy love affair is described with realistic detail and considerable empathy. However, the hero writes his memoirs himself, and, in addition, in the madhouse—a complete impossibility. The letters of the dogs are represented as really existing and their contents are so *normal* (in contrast with the memoirs themselves), that in spite of the precision and detail of the description, one constantly feels oneself in a fantastic and unreal atmosphere. The fact that the comedy of events and ideas has a bitter aftertaste is quite understandable in view of the subject chosen. . . . (p. 133)

It would be wrong to try to see in this tale a social bias on Gogol's part. He is concerned with something higher; as the King of Spain is assuring the object of his affections of his favor, he suddenly breaks off to cry out: "Oh, she's a perfidious creature—Woman! I just now realized what Woman is. Up till now, no one had yet recognized with whom she is in love: I am the first to discover it: Woman is in love with the devil. Yes, no joking. The physicists write a lot of nonsense that she is this and that—she loves no one but the devil." Woman is the devil's tool—with Gogol, this old theme of Russian ascetic literature takes on a profound significance. Passion for earthly things is the snare of the devil, who thus changes the world into a dead-end of absurdity; and whoever succumbs to him can assert with doctrinaire gravity that the moon is usually manufactured in Hamburg and that noses inhabit it, that every cock bears a Spain under its tailfeathers and that China and Spain are one and the same country.

In Poprishchin's eyes the gruesome, extremely matter-of-fact treatment of the mentally ill in the madhouse acquires another aspect; he interprets it in his own way and ascribes a new meaning to reality. Is this not what we do in this devil-directed world? Where is the fixed point by which truth and illusion can be distinguished? Even when complete nonsense is related, the style of a factual report is brilliantly maintained. Only when the hero thinks of his beloved is it interspersed with stereotyped interjections which are intended to strengthen the artistic unity of the work as a whole. (p. 134)

Nowhere does Gogol so clearly reveal the vanity

of the world as in this story. All sense of reality is abolished; and absolute nothingness rises up in its stead. All of Man's ambitious striving, which, according to Poprishchin, is caused by a worm as tiny as a pinhead in a pimple under the tongue, is senseless and causes him to consider things important which are only illusions produced by the devil. But at this time Gogol saw only the negative side; at this time he was not consciously aware of the positive side, which allows the kingdom of God's grace to appear behind the dissolved world. (p. 135)

[In **"Taras Bulba"** there] is no plot in the strict sense of the word. It is a description of cossack life and some cossack campaigns in which Gogol does not tie himself down chronologically (first he speaks of the fifteenth century, then of the sixteenth; at the same time, however, many details suggest that the action takes place in the first half of the seventeenth century) and also does not present any concrete events but merely generalizes and typifies the period of the Ukrainian War of Liberation against Poland (sixteenth to seventeenth centuries), its events and personalities. The whole work suffers from this use of types. Even the heroes, the cossack colonel Taras Bulba and his sons Ostap and Andriy, are abstractions which come alive only in a few episodes. On the one hand, Gogol would like to render a faithful picture "of that rough, cruel time . . . ;" on the other hand, however, he wants to patriotically glorify (as is customary in the epic), and the results are idealized beasts whose deeds one reads of with a feeling of embarrassment because they lack inner truth. . . . The battle descriptions are veritable orgies of horror: an *Iliad* faithfully transposed into modern times, but without its human breath. The idea of creating a Ukrainian epic caused Gogol to turn to Homer, but he makes use only of Homer's technique of describing battles—naming of the individual names of otherwise unknown heroes along with a short biography and an account of their character and physical appearance before the description of their death, precise statement of the horrible kinds of wounds, and very detailed comparisons expressed in tensely rhythmic speech. (pp. 141-42)

Taras Bulba's character has no unity. He does not reach even the level of the stereotype of the brave warrior with the golden heart and the rough exterior for which Gogol strove; this is made impossible by his deviousness and the inhumanities which can supposedly be excused by casual references to "that cruel time," but which are not at all appropriate for the picture of a hero who is intended to be altogether admirable. His son Ostap is also a cold abstraction of heroic blamelessness. The love story involves the youngest son, Andriy, with the beautiful Polish girl, of whom Gogol can say only that "her breast, neck, and shoulders were enclosed within those sublime limits which are appointed to fully developed beauty."

Their love dialogues, moreover, strike one as only embarrassing declamations. Andriy's betrayal is not motivated from within; and even less motivated is his passivity when about to be murdered by his father. Undoubtedly one can again see in this story Gogol's old theme of the destructive power of diabolical beauty which causes one to forget all other values. (p. 142)

Serious pathos is not Gogol's forte. He immediately becomes rhetorical and hollow. It is interesting to observe how his normal style breaks through in many places (e.g., in the comparison of the captured Andriy with the misbehaving schoolboy, which is absolutely unsuitable under the circumstances, or in the enumeration of the many Pysarenkos among the cossacks). At once the tone tightens and becomes natural. Gogol also succeeds in nature descriptions which, however unreal, possess an astonishing glow. (pp. 142-43)

While in **"Taras Bulba"** Gogol does not succeed in organically uniting the heterogenous stylistic elements, in the third tale of the [*Migorod*] cycle, **"Viy,"** he is much more successful. (pp. 143-44)

Basically, Gogol continues here the style employed in [*Evenings on a Farm near Dikanka*], but the realistic element is strengthened and the fantastic intensified to the point of uncanniness until it approaches the limits of possibility. (p. 144)

The feverish atmosphere that was so successfully maintained in **"The Portrait"** is conveyed here with even greater tension. Gogol achieves his effect by eliminating intermediary stages from the descriptions of motion, showing only completed states (hence the effective use of perfective verbs) and suggesting, as it were, the intervening sinking into unconsciousness. (p. 145)

[In **"The Story of How Ivan Ivanovich and Ivan Nikoforovich Quarrelled"** it] becomes more and more clear how unimportant the construction of a plot is for Gogol. A little anecdote is all that he needs to produce a work of art that touches all the depths of the human soul through the manner in which it is told. . . . Gogol brings into play all his humorous technical devices and thus glosses over the disturbing gravity of the plot. The catastrophe occurs in the moment of greatest peace; in the midst of harmless comedy a radical change takes place which acts like a clap of thunder and which brings a sharp change in tone along with it. The vantage point from which the author was describing the action shifts with great suddenness. The tale begun in a cheerfully ironic conversational tone ends up in hopeless pessimism. "It's tedious in this world, my friends!" This now famous concluding sentence sounds like a last judgment, like the final product of a philosophical conception of the world, precisely because it stands at the end of such a lively, such a tremendously amusing story. And this liveliness, this amusing quality—they are but a senseless confusion of human desires and strivings that appear so important and so colorful when one participates in them oneself, but seen from the outside they turn into an irrelevant grayness.

The unity of the narrative tone is brilliantly maintained. The subtitle reads: "One of the unpublished true events related by the beekeeper Red-haired [Rudy] Panko." This enables the author to ramble on with apparent freedom, to act as if he presupposes extensive knowledge of the background on the part of the reader so that only an allusion, a name suffices to make him aware of what is going on. Since in reality this is not the case, this procedure increases suspense as well as comedy.

The first chapter is devoted to the description of the two heroes of the tale. Every paragraph begins with the declaration that they are fine men, but the proofs which follow are very strange. . . . (pp. 148-49)

[This is true also of the comparison of the two Ivans, in which their] human qualities will allegedly become especially clear. At first all goes well: one is like this, the other like that; one does this, the other that; but hardly has Gogol lulled the suspicions of the reader by means of the stylistic consistency of the comparison, when we suddenly read: "Ivan Ivanovich is of a somewhat timid nature. Ivan Nikiforovich, on the other hand, has wide breeches with such wide pleats that if they were inflated, one could comfortably store the whole farm with granaries and building in them."

The irrelevance of these people and their characteristics becomes strikingly clear by means of this stylistic illogicality. And yet after the pages of comparison, the two heroes—the lean, pretentious Ivan Ivanovich and the fat, crude Ivan Nikiforovich—stand before us as if alive. "However, in spite of a few dissimilarities, both Ivan Ivanovich as well as Ivan Nikiforovich are excellent men." Thus Gogol concludes the chapter in which, in a laudatory style, he has proven the exact opposite. In its composition, it reflects the absurdity of the world it describes.

The quarrel between the two described in the second chapter is simply the logical consequence of the conglomeration of human qualities governed by irrationality. (p. 150)

The increasing improbability reaches its climax in the theft of Ivan Nikiforovich's petition by Ivan Ivanovich's pig. This is a parody on the retardation at all costs customary in literature and a demonstration of the freedom of the author, who is able to narrate a complete impossibility in such a way that it appears completely conceivable. The episode sounds even a bit sinister: the brown pig was offered by Ivan Ivanovich in exchange for the rifle and was indignantly refused by

Ivan Nikiforovich for completely nonsensical reasons . . .—and this same pig now steals the petition. "When they informed Ivan Nikiforovich of this, he said nothing and merely asked whether it was by any chance the brown one?" From this passage we become aware of the fact that the surface of the world is again cracking up and that strange things are trying to come out. But this time Gogol bypasses the subject. Ivan Nikiforovich's new, second petition so far surpasses the parody in the first two that, in the chaos of quasi-official formulations, all sense is lost. (It is amusing to compare the ways in which some translators have tried to insert their own meanings into these *intentionally meaningless sentences*. (pp. 151-52)

[*The Marriage*] signifies a decisive break with the usual traditions of [the comedy]. Apart from a few unimportant attempts at original treatment, the comedy plot as such had become firmly established in world literature: in spite of certain complications, two lovers find their way into the harbor of marriage. . . . Love is parodied in *The Marriage*. It is surrounded with such a swarm of banalities and clichés that it produces a simply ridiculous effect. In none of the persons involved is love the driving force of his actions; it is either greed for money or convention and convenience, or perhaps sensual attraction (Podkolesin, Zhevakin), in which there is no concern for the person of the girl. (pp. 174-75)

There are above all two problems dealt with in the . . . Christian social structure and Christian art. They are closely related, for in the divinely ruled social structure demanded by Gogol, art can play only a very definite role—it submits to the hierarchy of a divine state as a servant of God, who inspires it; the artist is a priest who creates his works of art for the glory of God and preaches God's law in them. The testament, which opens the book, states: "I am a writer, and the duty of the writer is not only to provide a pleasant occupation for mind and taste; he will be held responsible if no benefit to the soul is disseminated by his works and if he leaves nothing for the edification of men."

The poet is called by God; he feels his calling within him, and it does not permit him to follow other, perhaps more lucrative professions. But this selection by God also involves obligations: "The poet must be just as blameless in the field of the word as everyone else in his own field." . . . (pp. 233-34)

Gogol wrote his *Correspondence* in a definite style, which he surely and consistently maintained and which is entirely appropriate for the positive, idyllic utopia that results. It is the combination of the unctuous calmness of the sermon with the simple tone of an idyll, of plain colloquial speech between man and man with cleverly calculated, elevated climaxes. It is not the language of one searching, nor the speech of a fanatic who wants to force his opinion on others—fanaticism

and humility generally are not easily united, and Gogol consistently calls the fanatic a cancerous sore on society—but the wise tone, one that is beyond all doubt, of a person firmly convinced, who does not need to take great pains to make clear what is evident. Antitheses, exclamations, and imaginary dialogues are far more rare than repetitions, intentional assonances, polysyndeta, and archaisms; a rich vocabulary, slightly archaic in sentence structure, is handled with great skill. (pp. 242-43)

One can only make vague conjectures concerning the contents of the missing part [of the second part of *Dead Souls*]. Gogol was never a master at constructing a plot, so that the whole work probably possessed a mosaiclike character. (p. 255)

In comparison with the first part, the tone of the narrator is much more serious. This gravity appears to have increased more and more towards the end. Only on a few occasions does the comedy peek through, surprisingly enough. The scandal in connection with the will, for example, expands and spreads over the whole province: "In another part of the province the Old Believers were stirring. Someone circulated among them the rumor that the Antichrist had been born, who would not even leave the dead any peace as he went around buying up some sort of dead souls. They did penance and they sinned, and under the pretext of catching the Antichrist, they did in some non-Antichrists." This is genuine Gogol, but one clearly feels that he is forcibly restraining himself. The writer is a preacher: jokes are out of place in matters of great concern. Gogol succeeded in doing violence to his talent, but only with great difficulty; what could the burnt completed version have been like?

Looking back on Gogol's work we recognize in him a poet who succeeded in finding the only form suitable for *his* statement about the world. It is filled with a profound pessimism in regard to human nature, which, due to the influence of evil powers, is incapable of recalling its real essence, which inclines toward the good. Man is the battleground of good and evil principles, and evil is victorious in most men by means of petty trifles. Instead of recognizing himself in all and instead of bringing about an earthly paradise through love towards his actual, flesh-and-blood neighbor, everyone considers himself the center of the world, indulges in his petty passions, and does not think of the great whole. In the face of this attitude, there is place only for a knowing irony that sees the pettiness of that which deems itself great, portrays it, and smiles at it resignedly. The smaller the motives and results of human actions, the clearer the true nature of this world, which could indeed be so good. Gogol portrays these trifles with such a deep inner truth that one feels touched by the Immediacy of it; he knows how to make his reader feel the essence of the real, even in what is most unreal.

A wealth of inner human life moves on an extremely narrow foundation of external events, which nevertheless fascinate in spite of their triviality. "The task of the writer of novels," says Schopenhauer, "is not to relate great events, but to make little ones interesting." Gogol performed this task in perfect fashion. (pp. 255-56)

Vsevolod Setchkarev, in his *Gogol: His Life and Works,* translated by Robert Kramer, New York University Press, 1965, 266 p.

FRANK O'CONNOR

(essay date 1956)

[In the following excerpt, O'Connor argues that Gogol's caricatures flesh out the characteristics of the average Russian and are reflections of Gogol's own personality and outlook on life.]

[Gogol was] an intensely subjective writer. Though he gradually gained control over his own fantasy in the same way as Balzac did, it always remained there, intact and unmodified by observation and analysis. Like Goldsmith, he always writes of himself.

> Having taken some bad feature or other of my own, I persecuted it under a different name and in a different character, endeavouring to make it appear before my eyes as my deadly enemy—an enemy who had inflicted a terrible injury on me; I persecuted it with malice, with irony, with anything I could get hold of. Had anyone seen those monsters which came from my pen at the beginning, he would have shivered with fear.

It is this which makes him such a wonderful chronicler of Tsarist Russia. Fantasy is the folk art of every autocracy. Where decisions are arbitrary and the secret manipulations of a single official can bring about the downfall of any individual, people live in fear of the unknown. In such an atmosphere anything is possible. Gogol's clerk Khlestyakov can paralyze the administration of a whole area with fear. So, in *Dead Souls,* when the problem arises as to who Chichikov is, it is suggested that he may be a shadowy captain who lost an arm and leg in the Napoleonic wars, and when someone points out that Chichikov has two of both, the postmaster explains that "mechanical devices had been much perfected in England." He may even be Napoleon. Three years before, a prophet had appeared, "wearing bast shoes and an unlined sheepskin coat, and smelling terribly of stale fish; and he had announced that Napoleon was Antichrist and was kept on a stone chain behind six walls and seven seas, but that afterwards he would break his chains and master the whole world. The prophet was very properly jailed for this

prediction, but nevertheless he had done his job and set the merchants in a flutter."

Under such a rule, authority itself takes on the quality of fantasy. (pp. 103-05)

But what are we really dealing with in these brilliant scenes? Is it autocracy or a psychological state? For all this time Gogol himself is driven on by a sense of undistributed guilt which sends him flying from place to place in the attempt to escape it. . . . [Between] Gogol's Tsar and Gogol's God there is very little difference; if anything, the heavenly Tsar is a little more capricious than the earthly one. He was able to master the personal fantasy by turning it into literature, but even the literary exercise is never with him more than a temporary expedient, nor is it ever free of the pangs of conscience in which it originated.

Our problem, then, is to decide whether Chichikov is no more than the amusing rogue of picaresque comedy (in which case the idea of his redemption is pretentious and absurd and Gogol was really insane when he attempted it) or whether he is something different, something out of the nineteenth century, a modern Everyman in whom we are expected to see an aspect of ourselves. The former view turns Chichikov into a flat character and makes the significance of the book depend upon the wonderful caricatures of men and women whom he meets on his travels; a series of disjointed episodes, disconnected not only from their sequel, but also from one another.

The second view is, I am quite sure, the correct one. It is the meaning behind the repeated statements that Chichikov was neither too young nor too old; too handsome nor too ugly; too stout nor too thin; too distinguished nor too humble. He is, in fact, the average sensual man, and before the first part of the novel was complete, Gogol no longer attempted to conceal this meaning from himself or his readers. "And if any one of you is full of Christian humility in the solitude of his heart rather than for all the world to hear, in moments of communion with himself he will ponder this weighty question in the depths of his soul: 'Is there not a trace of Chichikov in me too?' "

Chichikov is not really a rogue. He is merely Everyman playing his eternal part. His vision is consistently a snug middle-class one of wife and children, and he is particularly devoted to the children, whom—like Gogol himself—he has failed to beget. His life is really a distressful one, for though he is a clever man and even a conscientious one in a world of thieves and liars, his own little theft, his own little falsehood is forever being exposed. When we meet him, he has already lost two tidy little fortunes—one acquired in the Treasury, another in the Customs. He will also lose the fortune he acquires through his brilliant deal in dead souls. It is a foregone conclusion because essentially he is a decent man, a man whose heart can rise to the inspiration of a good landowner or a saintly merchant. Yet he cannot save himself from falling into petty acts of knavery which the real knaves exploit against him. Nothing, in fact, can settle Chichikov's problem but salvation. Hence, in principle and in spite of the critics, Gogol is right.

It is only by realizing this that we can realize the difference between Gogol's caricatures and those of Dickens and Balzac. In all of them the caricatures are produced by the addition to the realistic imagination of Jane Austen and Stendhal of the romantic imagination of Mrs. Radcliffe and Monk Lewis. All of them tend to let their characters turn into monsters. But whereas the monsters of Dickens and Balzac represent little more than passions run wild, Gogol's represent, as well as a fantasist could see it, life itself, his own life, above all, Russian life. For no more than Turgenev can Gogol resist identifying himself with his native land.

It is this which gives his caricatures such extraordinary richness compared with the puppets of Dickens and the monsters of Balzac. Gogol has an amazing power of generalizing from slight aspects of his own character in order to form the impression of a type, almost of a community. (pp. 105-07)

Pursued by guilt like Goldsmith, Gogol was haunted by some vision of childhood and home which, in the final analysis, was a vision of his mother and an Eden to which he could never return. "And as the hare whom hounds and horn pursue pants to the place from which at first he flew," when he felt the necessity for representing the redemption of Chichikov, it was to this vision of childhood innocence he returned, only to flounder in ill-digested chauvinism and religiosity. He had turned his magnificent intelligence on the passions in himself; he had not turned it on his own ideals; and when he tries to represent these, they turn out to be a life without French, without pianos, dancing or fashionable clothes—"a simple and sober life," as one of the characters describes it. Gogol's intelligence is purely negative; when he turns it on the enemies of his ideal, like the mad Colonel Koshkaryov, who has learned organization and method abroad, the fun is as good as ever; it is only when he has to depict the alternative to Koshkaryov that Gogol collapses into his chaos of negations; no lawns, no factories, no busts of Shakespeare, no porticoes, no back scratchers, no tea, no views, no . . . no . . . no . . .

Perhaps, after all, the man who sobbed after the destruction of his masterpiece was not haunted so much by the fear of hell as by the fear of his own negations. (pp. 109-10)

Frank O'Connor, "Gogol's Shoe," in his *The Mirror in the Roadway: A Study of the Modern Novel,* Alfred A. Knopf, 1956, pp. 97-110.

SOURCES FOR FURTHER STUDY

Driessen, F. C. *Gogol as a Short-Story Writer: A Study of His Technique of Composition.* Translated by Ian F. Finlay. The Hague: Mouton & Co., 1965, 243 p.

> A critical guide to Gogol's stories, including detailed plot summaries and listings of all major themes.

Ehre, Milton. Introduction to *The Theater of Nikolay Gogol: Plays and Selected Writings,* by Nikolai Gogol, edited by Milton Ehre, translated by Milton Ehre and Fruma Gottschalk, pp. ix-xxvi. Chicago: University of Chicago Press, 1980.

> Discusses Gogol's career as a dramatist and the place of his works in the Russian theater.

Erlich, Victor. *Gogol.* New Haven and London: Yale University Press, 1969, 230 p.

> A valuable general study of Gogol's life and works, designed to provide a complete survey for the English-speaking reader.

Lavrin, Janko. *Gogol.* London and New York: George Routledge & Sons, 1925, 263 p.

> Biographical and critical appreciation of Gogol's life and works. Lavrin states that his objective is "to introduce to English readers a great and complex foreign author in as simple terms as possible."

Magarshack, David. *Gogol: A Life.* London: Faber and Faber, 1957, 329 p.

> A biographical study which emphasizes Gogol's artistic development. Magarshack includes a number of reminiscences by Gogol's contemporaries.

Rowe, William Woodin. *Through Gogol's Looking Glass: Reverse Vision, False Focus, and Precarious Logic.* New York: New York University Press, 1976, 201 p.

> An examination of Gogol's creative process. Rowe emphasizes the world of vision and perception in Gogol's writings.

William Golding

1911-1991

(Full name William Gerald Golding) English novelist and essayist.

INTRODUCTION

*T*he winner of the 1983 Nobel Prize in literature, Golding is among the most popular and influential British authors to have emerged after World War II. Golding's reputation rests primarily upon his acclaimed first novel *Lord of the Flies* (1954), which he described as "an attempt to trace the defects of society back to the defects of human nature." A moral allegory as well as an adventure tale in the tradition of Daniel Defoe's *Robinson Crusoe* (1719), R. M. Ballantyne's *The Coral Island* (1857), and Richard Hughes's *A High Wind in Jamaica* (1929), *Lord of the Flies* focuses upon a group of British schoolboys marooned on a tropical island. After having organized themselves upon democratic principles, their society degenerates into primeval barbarism. While often the subject of diverse psychological, sociological, and religious interpretations, *Lord of the Flies* is consistently regarded as an incisive and disturbing portrayal of the fragility of civilization.

Golding was born in St. Columb Minor in Cornwall, England. He enrolled in Brasenose College, Oxford, in 1930, initially intending to obtain a degree in the sciences. After several years of study, however, he decided to devote himself to the study of English literature. He published a volume of poetry, *Poems,* in 1934 to scant critical notice; he himself later repudiated the work. Receiving a degree in English in 1935, he worked in various theaters in London, and in 1939 he moved to Salisbury, where he was employed as a schoolteacher. He served five years in the Royal Navy during World War II, an experience that likely helped shape his interest in the theme of barbarism and evil within humanity. Following the war Golding continued to teach and to write fiction. In 1954, his first novel, *Lord of the Flies,* was published to much critical acclaim in England. He continued to write novels, as well as essays, lectures, and novellas, throughout the next three decades. Most of these works, however, were overshadowed by the popular and critical success of *Lord of the Flies.*

Golding's *Lord of the Flies* presents a central theme of his oeuvre: the conflict between the forces of light and dark within the human soul. Although the novel did not gain popularity in the United States until several years after its original publication, it has now become a modern classic, studied in most high schools and colleges. Set sometime in the near future, *Lord of the Flies* is about a group of schoolboys abandoned on a desert island during a global war. They attempt to establish a government among themselves, but without the restraints of civilization they quickly revert to savagery. Similar in background and characters to Ballantyne's *The Coral Island, Lord of the Flies* totally reverses Ballantyne's concept of the purity and innocence of youth and humanity's ability to remain civilized under the worst conditions.

While none of Golding's subsequent works achieved the critical success of *Lord of the Flies,* he continued to produce novels that elicit widespread critical interpretation. Within the thematic context of exploring the depths of human depravity, the settings of Golding's works range from the prehistoric age, as in *The Inheritors,* (1955), to the Middle Ages, as in *The Spire* (1964), to contemporary English society. This wide variety of settings, tones, and structures presents dilemmas to critics attempting to categorize them. Nevertheless, certain stylistic devices are characteristic of his work. One of these, the use of a sudden shift of perspective, has been so dramatically employed by Golding that it both enchants and infuriates critics and

readers alike. For example, *Pincher Martin* (1956) is the story of Christopher Martin, a naval officer who is stranded on a rock in the middle of the ocean after his ship has been torpedoed. The entire book relates Martin's struggles to remain alive against all odds. The reader learns in the last few pages that Martin's death occurred on the second page—a fact that transforms the novel from a struggle for earthly survival into a struggle for eternal salvation.

Golding's novels are often termed fables or myths. They are laden with symbols (usually of a spiritual or religious nature) so imbued with meaning that they can be interpreted on many different levels. *The Spire,* for example, is perhaps his most polished allegorical novel, equating the erecting of a cathedral spire with the protagonist's conflict between his religious faith and the temptations to which he is exposed. *Darkness Visible* (1979) continues to illuminate the universal confrontation of Good and Evil; Golding was awarded the James Tait Black Memorial Prize for this novel in 1980. Throughout the 1980s Golding's novels, essays, and the travel journal *An Egyptian Journal* (1985) have received general praise from commentators. *Lord of the Flies,* however, remains central to Golding's popularity and his international reputation as a major contemporary author.

(For further information about Golding's life and works, see *Contemporary Authors,* Vols. 7-8; *Contemporary Authors New Revision Series,* Vols. 13, 33; *Contemporary Literary Criticism,* Vols. 1, 2, 3, 8, 10, 17, 27, 58; *Dictionary of Literary Biography,* Vols. 15, 100; and *Major 20th-Century Writers.*)

CRITICAL COMMENTARY

V. S. PRITCHETT
(essay date 1958)

[Pritchett, an English author, is highly acclaimed for his short stories and for what commentators consider judicious, reliable, and insightful literary criticism. In his essays and reviews, he approaches literature from the viewpoint of an informed but not overly scholarly reader, stressing his own experience and sense of literary art rather than following a codified critical doctrine derived from a system of psychological or philosophical theory. In the following excerpt from a 1958 *New Statesman* essay, he offers an

overview of *Lord of the Flies, The Inheritors,* and *Pincher Martin.*]

The essence of the novelist's art—especially the English novelist's—is the quotidian. From the moment Crusoe domesticates and diaries his desert island, the novel reflects the confidence the individual derives from the society he lives in. The risks of romance are gone; he is safe in the realists's nest: Selkirk was lonely, but Crusoe is the least lonely man in the world. This confidence has lasted in our tradition. But when we look up from our books into the life around us today, we wonder how the prosaic observer in realistic fiction can be so certain of himself. The quotidian art goes on describ-

Principal Works

Poems (poetry) 1934

Lord of the Flies (novel) 1954

The Inheritors (novel) 1955

Pincher Martin (novel) 1956; also published as The Two Deaths of Christopher Martin, 1957

The Brass Butterfly: A Play in Three Acts (drama) 1958

Free Fall (novel) 1959

The Spire (novel) 1964

The Hot Gates, and Other Occasional Pieces (essays) 1965

The Pyramid (novel) 1967

The Scorpion God (novellas) 1971

Darkness Visible (novel) 1979

Rites of Passage (novel) 1980

A Moving Target (essays) 1982

The Paper Men (novel) 1984

An Egyptian Journal (travel journal) 1985

Close Quarters (novel) 1987

Fire Down Below (novel) 1989

ing and describing and, as far as externals are concerned, we cannot complain that the modern realist fails to describe the features of a changing, violent or collapsing society. But he is the spectator, in some lucky way insured and untouched; rarely does the novelist find the point at which we are involved or committed; rarely does he touch the quick, so that for once the modern alibi—'it is beyond the power of the imagination to grasp. etc., etc.'—does not work. The imagination will never grasp until it is awakened; and facts will not awaken it. They merely strengthen opinion; and there is nothing so apt to shut us off from the world as the correct opinion about it. The imagination can be awakened only by the imagination, by the artist who has the power to break us down until the point of secret complicity is reached. It was this point which the writer of romance, undeterred by the day's events, and lost in his world of dramatic wishes, once knew how to reach.

Mr William Golding is an artist of this kind. His three books, *Lord of the Flies* (1954), *The Inheritors* (1955) and *Pincher Martin* (1956), are romance in the austere sense of the term. They take the leap from the probable to the possible. *Lord of the Flies* has a strong pedigree: island literature from Crusoe to *Coral Island, Orphan Island* and *High Wind in Jamaica*. All romance breaks with the realistic novelist's certainties and exposes the characters to transcendent and testing dangers. But Golding does more than break; he bashes, by the power of his overwhelming sense of the detail of the physical world. He is the most original of our con-

temporaries. Many writers have been concerned, as a matter of argument, with what is rhetorically called 'the dilemma of modern man', and have given us, as it were, lantern slide lectures on the anarchy of a poisoned future; they are really essayists sitting in comfort. Golding, on the contrary, scarcely uses an argument or issues a warning. He simply shakes us until we feel in our bones the perennial agony of our species. By their nature, his subjects—prep school boys on a desert island in a world war, the calvary of a sailor who gave the right order but whose half-conscious body is being washed about the gullies of an Atlantic rock, the conflicts of a handful of Neanderthalers—could easily become the pasteboard jigsaw of allegory, pleasing our taste for satire and ingenuity; but the pressure of feeling drives allegory out of the foreground of his stories. He is a writer of intense visual gift, with an overpowering sense of nature and an extraordinary perception of man as a physical being in a physical world, torn between a primitive inheritance and the glimmer of an evolving mind. A dramatic writer and familiar with the strong emotions that go with the instinct of self-preservation—blind love for his kind, hatred, fear and elation—he is without hysteria. He is not cooking up freakish and exotic incident; he is not making large proclamations about man against nature, God, destiny and so on; he is seriously and in precise, individual instances gripped—as if against his will—by the sight of the slow and agonising accretion of a mind and a civilised will in one or two men, struggling against their tendency to slip back, through passion or folly, and lose their skills in panic. And there is pity for the pain they feel.

Pain is the essence of Mr Golding's subject. In *The Inheritors* it is the obscure pain of a baffled and dying group of ape men who see themselves supplanted by the more skilful new being called Man. The ape man experiences the pain of the grunt, of trying to communicate from one poor mind to another—'I have a picture. Can you see my picture?'—and also the pain of trying to distinguish, for a moment, what is inside from what is outside himself. From his tree he sees Man who is not afraid of water, as he is, who gets drunk on honey, who has invented love play; he sees with a kind of grieving as an animal might grieve. In *Pincher Martin,* the tale of a modern sailor whose broken body is washed about the Atlantic rock, who eats limpets, is poisoned by his store of food and who eventually goes mad and dies, the pain is in the fight against physical hurt and loss of consciousness, in the struggle to put his educated will against his terrors. It is also in the Job-like protest against a defeat which wrongs everything he had believed in. In *Lord of the Flies*—the first and, I think, the best of these books—a group of schoolboys reenact the *Coral Island* story and the pain is in the struggle between the boys who revert, through fear, to the primitive and turn into savage hunters, and those who are trying vainly to preserve foresight and order. In the end, the boys are rescued, but not before they have lived through the modern political nightmare.

Mr Golding's sensibility to pain is the spring of his imagination and if, in all three stories, the heroes are smashed up, he is by no means a morbid or sadistic writer. The chest of the creature, running in terror from its enemies, scorches, the calves cramp, the skin tears, the body has to endure what animal panic lets it in for. Pain is simply the whole condition of man; it is the sign that he is awake and struggling with his nature, and especially with the terror which so suddenly scatters the mind. *Lord of the Flies* contains one episode of great horror. The rotting body of a dead parachutist is blown across the island in the night, almost stepping on the trees and the beaches, until it is taken out to sea. The sight is the final and clinching argument to the very young boys that a devouring Beast has really been among them; and one might conclude that this is a decisive symbol of human defeat and the meaninglessness of the struggle. The idea is irrelevant. Mr Golding's imagination is heroic. Against the flies that buzz round the dangling scarecrow must be put the elation of the adventure, the love of natural life, the curiosity of the eye, that run through the writing. And the compassion.

It is natural to compare *Lord of the Flies* with *Coral Island*—and then with *High Wind in Jamaica.* In *Coral Island* we see the safe community. A century without war and with a settled sense of the human personality has produced it. In Richard Hughes's book, we saw the first sign of disintegration: the psychologists have discovered that children are not small fanciful adults, but are a cut-off, savage race. In *Lord of the Flies* we understand that the children are not cut-off; anthropology, the science of how people live together, not separately, reflects the concern of the modern world which has seen its communities destroyed. The children in *Lord of the Flies* simply re-enact the adult, communal drama and by their easy access to the primitive, show how adult communities can break up. Of course, Mr Golding's improbable romances remain improbable; they are narrow and possible. The modern romancer has the uncluttered chance of going straight to the alienation of the individual and to the personal solitude that is one of the forgotten subjects. In our world, which is so closely organised, we are hardly aware of what we are privately up to. We use large words like calamity, disaster, racial suicide, devastation; they are meaningless to us until an artist appears who is gifted enough to identify himself with a precise body being washed up against a precise collection of rocks, a precise being sniffing the night air for his enemy or feeling the full force of a particular blow. Until then, we are muffled in our alibi: 'the imagination cannot grasp.'

Lord of the Flies is the most accomplished of Mr

Golding's novels. Its portraits of the shipwrecked boys and its understanding of them are touching and delightful and he is master of a rich range of scene and action. In this book his spirit and his serenity are classical. *Pincher Martin* is more chock-a-block, but it has fine descriptions of the roaring, sucking, deafening sea scene on the rock which we know stone by stone. He is a modern writer here in that his eyes are pressed close to the object, so that each thing is enormously magnified. We see how much a man is enclosed by his own eyes. The important quality of all Golding's descriptions is that they are descriptions of movement and continuous change and are marked by brilliant epithets. (One remembers: 'three prudish anemones'.) There is this picture of the swimming sailor, almost at the rock: . . .

But this book succeeds less when it takes us into the sailor's chaotic recollections of his life. It contains some flashes back to scenes of jealousy and rivalry which are hard to grasp. It may be that Golding's sense of theatre—often strong in writers of romance—has overcome him here. (He is the author of a witty satirical play, *The Brass Butterfly,* which is excellent reading.) But in making us feel in the current of the modern world, instead of being stranded and deadened by it; in providing us with secret parables; in unveiling important parts of the contemporary anguish and making them heroic, knowable and imaginable, he is unique. (pp. 46-50)

V. S. Pritchett, "Pain and William Golding," in *William Golding Novels, 1954-67: A Casebook,* edited by Norman Page, Macmillan Publishers Ltd., 1985, pp. 46-50.

JAMES R. BAKER
(essay date 1963)

[Baker, an American critic, coedited a critical edition of *Lord of the Flies* (1964) and wrote *William Golding: A Critical Study* (1965). The following essay first appeared in *Arizona Quarterly* in 1963. Here, Baker discusses *Lord of the Flies*, particularly examining Golding's use of the ancient Greek myth of Dionysus in the novel.]

Lord of the Flies offers a variation upon the ever-popular tale of island adventure, and it holds all of the excitements common to that long tradition. Golding's castaways are faced with the usual struggle for survival, the terrors of isolation, and a desperate but finally successful effort to signal a passing ship which will return them to the civilized world they have lost. This time, however, the story is told against the background of atomic war. A plane carrying some English boys away from the center of conflict is shot down by the enemy and the youths are left without adult company on an unpopulated Pacific island. The environment in which they find themselves actually presents no serious challenge: the island is a paradise of flowers and fruit, fresh water flows from the mountain, and the climate is gentle. In spite of these unusual natural advantages, the children fail miserably, and the adventure ends in a reversal of their (and the reader's) expectations. Within a short time the rule of reason is overthrown and the survivors regress to savagery.

During the first days on the island there is little forewarning of this eventual collapse of order. The boys (aged six to twelve) are delighted with the prospect of some real fun before the adults come to fetch them. With innocent enthusiasm they recall the storybook romances they have read and now expect to experience in reality. Among these is *The Coral Island,* Robert Michael Ballantyne's heavily moralistic idyl of castaway boys, written in 1857, yet still, in our atomic age, a popular adolescent classic in England. In Ballantyne's story everything comes off in exemplary style. For Ralph, Jack, and Peterkin (his charming young imperialists) mastery of the natural environment is an elementary exercise in Anglo-Saxon ingenuity. The fierce pirates who invade the island are defeated by sheer moral force, and the tribe of cannibalistic savages is easily converted and reformed by the example of Christian conduct afforded them. *The Coral Island* is again mentioned by the naval officer who comes to rescue Golding's boys from the nightmare island they have created, and so the adventure of these modern *enfants terribles* is ironically juxtaposed with the spectacular success of the Victorian darlings.

The effect is to hold before us two radically different pictures of human nature and society. Ballantyne, no less than Golding, is a fabulist who asks us to believe that the evolution of affairs on his coral island models or reflects the adult world—a world in which men are unfailingly reasonable, cooperative, loving and lovable. We are hardly prepared to accept such optimistic exaggerations, but Ballantyne's tale suggests essentially the same flattering image of civilized man found in so many familiar island fables. In choosing to parody and invert this romantic image, Golding posits a reality the literary tradition has generally denied.

The character of this reality is to be seen in the final episode of *Lord of the Flies.* When the British cruiser appears offshore, the boy Ralph is the one remaining advocate of reason; but he has no more status than the wild pigs of the forest and is being hunted down for the kill. Shocked by their filth, their disorder, and the revelation that there have been real casualties, the officer, with appropriate fatherly indignation, expresses his disappointment in this "pack of British boys." There is no real basis for his surprise, for life on the island has only imitated the larger tragedy in which the adults of the outside world attempted to govern themselves reasonably but ended in the same game of hunt and kill. Thus, according to Golding, the aim of his narrative is "to trace the defects of society back to the defects of human nature"; the moral illustrated is that "the shape of society must depend on the ethical nature of the individual and not on any political system however apparently logical or respectable." And, since the lost children are the inheritors of the same defects of nature which doomed their fathers, the tragedy on the island is bound to repeat the actual pattern of human history.

The central fact in that pattern is one which we, like the fatuous naval officer, are virtually incapable of perceiving: first, because it is one that constitutes an affront to our ego; second, because it controverts the carefully and elaborately rationalized record of history which sustains the pride of "rational" man. The reality is that regardless of the intelligence we possess—an intelligence which drives us in a tireless effort to impose an order upon our affairs—we are defeated with monotonous regularity by our own irrationality. "History," said Joyce's Dedalus, "is a nightmare from which I am trying to awake." But we do not awake. Though we constantly make a heroic attempt to rise to a level ethically superior to nature, and to our own nature, again and again we suffer a fall, brought low by some outburst of madness because of the limiting defects inherent in our species.

If there is any literary precedent for the image of man contained in Golding's fable, it is obviously not to be discovered within the framework of a tradition that embraces *Robinson Crusoe* and *Swiss Family Robinson* and that includes also the island episodes in Conrad's novels where we see the self-defeating skepticism of a Heyst or a Decoud serving only to demonstrate the value of illusions. All of these novels offer some version of the rationalist orthodoxy we so readily accept, even though the text may not be so boldly simple as Ballantyne's fable for innocent Victorians.

Quite removed from this tradition (which Golding mocks in nearly everything he has written) is the directly acknowledged influence of classical Greek literature. Within this designation, though Golding's critics have ignored it, is the acknowledged admiration for Euripides. Among the plays of Euripides it is *The Bacchae* that Golding, like his Mamillius of *The Brass Butterfly,* obviously knows by heart. The tragedy is a bitter allegory on the degeneration of society, and it contains a basic parable which informs much of Golding's work. It is clearly pertinent in *Lord of the Flies,* for here the point of view is similar to that of Euripides after he was driven into exile from Athens. Before his departure the tragedian brought down upon himself the mockery and disfavor of a mediocre regime like the one which later condemned Socrates. *The Bacchae,* however, is more than an expression of disillusionment with a failing democracy. Its aim is precisely what Golding has declared to be his own: "to trace the defects of society back to the defects of human nature," and so to account for the failure of rational man who invariably undertakes the blind ritual-hunt in which he seeks to kill the threatening "beast" within his own being.

The Bacchae is based on a legend of Dionysus wherein the god (a son of Zeus and the mortal Semele, daughter of Cadmus) descends upon Thebes in great wrath, determined to take revenge upon the young king, Pentheus, who has denied him recognition and prohibited his worship. Dionysus wins the daughters of Cadmus as his devotees; and, through his power of enchantment, he decrees that Agave, mother of Pentheus, shall lead the group in frenzied celebrations. Pentheus bluntly opposes the god and tries by every means to preserve order against the rising tide of madness in his kingdom. The folly of his proud resistance is shown in the total defeat of all his efforts: the bacchantes trample on his rules and edicts; in wild marches through the land they wreck everything in their path. Thus prepared for his vengeance, Dionysus casts a spell over Pentheus. With his judgment weakened and his identity obscured by dressing as a woman, the humiliated prince sets out to spy upon the orgies. In the excitement of their rituals the bacchantes live in a world of illusion, and all that falls within their sight undergoes a metamorphosis which brings it into accord with the natural images of their worship. When Pentheus is seen, he is taken for a lion. Led by Agave, the blind victims of the god tear the king limb from limb. The final punishment of those who denied the god of nature is to render them conscious of their awful crimes and to cast them out from their homeland as guilt-stricken exiles and wanderers upon the earth.

For most modern readers the chief obstacle in the way of proper understanding of *The Bacchae,* and therefore of Golding's use of it, is the popular notion that Dionysus is nothing more than a charming god of wine. This image descends from

> the Alexandrines, and above all the Romans—with their tidy functionalism and their cheerful obtuseness in all matters of the spirit—who departmentalized Dionysus as "jolly Bacchus" . . . with his riotous crew of nymphs and satyrs. As such he was taken over from the Romans by Renaissance painters and poets; and it was they in turn who shaped the image in which the modern world pictures him.

In reality the god was more important and "much more dangerous": he was "the principle of animal life . . . the hunted and the hunter—the unrestrained potency which man envies in the beasts and seeks to assimilate." Thus the intention and chief effect of the baccha-

nal is "to liberate the instinctive life in man from the bondage imposed upon it by reason and social custom. . . ." In his tragedy Euripides also suggests "a further effect, a merging of the individual consciousness in a group consciousness" so that the participant is "at one not only with the Master of Life but his fellow-worshippers . . . and with the life of the earth."

Dionysus was worshiped in various animal incarnations (snake, bull, lion, boar), whatever form was appropriate to place; and all of these incarnations were symbolic of the impulses he evoked in his worshipers. In *The Bacchae* a leader of the bacchanal summons him with the incantation, "O God, Beast, Mystery, come!" Agave's attack upon the "lion" (her own son) conforms to the codes of Dionysic ritual; like other gods, this one is slain and devoured, his devotees sustained by his flesh and blood. The terrible error of the bacchantes is a punishment brought upon the proud Greeks by the lord of beasts: "To resist Dionysus is to repress the elemental in one's own nature; the punishment is the sudden collapse of the inward dykes when the elemental breaks through perforce and civilization vanishes."

This same lesson in humility is meted out to the schoolboys of *Lord of the Flies.* In their innocent pride they attempt to impose a rational order or pattern upon the vital chaos of their own nature, and so they commit the error and "sin" of Pentheus, the "man of many sorrows." The penalties (as in the play) are bloodshed, guilt, utter defeat of reason. Finally, they stand before the officer, "A semicircle of little boys, their bodies streaked with colored clay, sharp sticks in their hands. . . . " Facing that purblind commander (with his revolver and peaked cap), Ralph cries "for the end of innocence, the darkness of man's heart"; and the tribe of vicious hunters joins him in spontaneous choral lament. But even Ralph could not trace the arc of their descent, could not explain why it's no go, why things are as they are. For in the course of events he was at times among the hunters, one of them; and he grieves in part for the appalling ambiguities he has discovered in his own being. In this moment of "tragic knowledge" he remembers those strange interims of blindness and despair when a "shutter" clicked down over his mind and left him at the mercy of his own dark heart. In Ralph's experience, then, the essence of the fable is spelled out: he suffers the dialectic we must all endure, and his failure to resolve it as we would wish demonstrates the limitations which have always plagued our species.

In the first hours on the island Ralph sports untroubled in the twilight of childhood and innocence, but after he sounds the conch he must confront the forces he has summoned to the granite platform beside the sunny lagoon. During that first assembly he seems to arbitrate with the grace of a young god (his natural bearing is dignified, princely); and, for the time being, a balance is maintained. The difficulties begin with the dream revelation of the child distinguished by the birthmark. The boy tells of a snakelike monster prowling the woods by night, and at this moment the seed of fear is planted. Out of it will grow the mythic beast destined to become lord of the island. There is a plague of haunting dreams, and these constitute the first symptoms of the irrational fear which is "mankind's essential illness."

In the chapter entitled "Beast from Water" the parliamentary debate becomes a blatant allegory in which each spokesman caricatures the position he defends. Piggy (the voice of reason) leads with the statement that "life is scientific," and adds the usual utopian promises ("when the war's over they'll be traveling to Mars and back"); and his assurance that such things will come to pass if only we control the senseless conflicts which impede our progress. He is met with laughter and jeers (the crude multitude), and at this juncture a little one interrupts to declare that the beast (ubiquitous evil) comes out of the sea. Maurice interjects to voice the doubt which curses them all: "I don't believe in the beast of course. As Piggy says, life's scientific, but we don't know, do we? Not certainly. . . ." Then Simon (the inarticulate seer) rises to utter the truth in garbled, ineffective phrases: there *is* a beast, but "it's only us." As always, his saving words are misunderstood, and the prophet shrinks away in confusion. Amid the speculation that Simon means some kind of ghost, there is a silent show of hands for ghosts as Piggy breaks in with angry rhetorical questions: "What are we? Humans? Or animals? Or Savages?" Taking his cue, Jack (savagery *in excelsis*) leaps to his feet and leads all but the "three blind mice" (Ralph, Piggy, and Simon) into a mad jig of release down the darkening beach. The parliamentarians naïvely contrast their failure with the supposed efficiency of adults; and Ralph, in despair, asks for a sign from that ruined world.

In "Beast from Air" the sign, a dead man in a parachute, is sent down from the grownups, and the collapse of order foreshadowed in the allegorical parliament comes on with surprising speed. Ralph himself looks into the face of the enthroned tyrant on the mountain, and from that moment his young intelligence is crippled by fear. He confirms the reality of the beast, insuring Jack's spectacular rise to absolute power. Yet the ease with which Jack establishes his Dionysian regime is hardly unaccountable. From its very first appearance, the black-caped choir, vaguely evil in its military *esprit*, emerged ominously from a mirage and marched down upon the minority forces assembled on the platform. Except for Simon, pressed into service and out of step with the common rhythm, the choir is composed of servitors bound by the rituals and the mysteries of group consciousness. They share in that communion, and there is no real "conversion" or trans-

fer of allegiance from good to evil when the chorus, ostensibly Christian, becomes the tribe of hunters. The god they serve inhabits their own being. If they turn with relief from the burdens and responsibilities of the platform, it is because they cannot transcend the limitations of their own nature. Even the parliamentary pool of intelligence must fail in the attempt to explain all that manifests itself in our turbulent hearts, and the assertion that life is ordered, "scientific," often appears mere bravado. It embodies the sin of pride and, inevitably, it evokes the great god which the rational man would like to deny.

It is Simon who witnesses his coming and hears his words of wrath. In the thick undergrowth of the forest the boy discovers a refuge from the war of words. His shelter of leaves is a place of contemplation, a sequestered temple scented and lighted by the white flowers of the night-blooming candle-nut tree. There, in secret, he meditates on the lucid but somehow oversimple logic of Piggy and Ralph and on the venal emotion of Jack's challenges to their authority. There, in the infernal glare of the afternoon sun, he sees the killing of the sow by the hunters and the erection of the pig's head on the sharpened stick. These acts signify not only the final release from the blood taboo but also obeisance to the mystery and god who has come to be lord of the island world. In the hours of one powerfully symbolic afternoon, Simon sees the perennial fall which is the central reality of our history: the defeat of reason and the release of Dionysian madness in souls wounded by fear.

Awed by the hideousness of the dripping head—an image of the hunters' own nature—the apprentice bacchantes suddenly run away; but Simon's gaze is "held by that ancient, inescapable recognition"—an incarnation of the beast or devil born again and again out of the human heart. Before he loses consciousness, the epileptic visionary "hears" the truth which is inaccessible to the illusion-bound rationalist and to the unconscious or irrational man alike. " 'Fancy thinking the Beast was something you could hunt and kill!' said the head. For a moment or two the forest and all the other dimly appreciated places echoed with the parody of laughter. 'You knew, didn't you? I'm part of you? Close, close, close! I'm the reason why it's no go? Why things are as they are?' " When Simon recovers from this trauma of revelation, he finds on the mountaintop that the "beast" is only a man. Like the pig itself, the dead man in the chute is fly-blown, corrupt; he is an obscene image of the evil that has triumphed in the adult world as well. Tenderly the boy releases the lines so that the body can descend to earth, but the fallen man does not descend. After Simon's death, when the truth is once more lost, the figure rises, moves over the terrified tribe on the beach, and finally out to sea—a tyrannous ghost (history itself) which haunts and curses every social order.

In his martyrdom Simon meets the fate of all saints. The truth he brings would set us free from the repetitious nightmare of history, but we are, by nature, incapable of perceiving the truth. Demented by fears our intelligence cannot control, we are "at once heroic and sick," ingenious and ingenuous at the same time. Inevitably we gather in tribal union and communion to hunt the molesting "beast," and always the intolerable frustration of the hunt ends as it must: within the enchanted circle formed by the searchers the beast materializes in the only form he can possibly assume, the very image of his creator. And once he is visible, projected (once the hunted has become the hunter), the circle closes in an agony of relief. Simon, the saintly one, is blessed and cursed by those unique intuitions which threaten the ritual of the tribe. In whatever culture he appears, the saint is doomed by his insights. There is a vital, if obvious, irony to be observed in the fact that the lost children of Golding's fable are of Christian heritage; but, when they blindly kill their savior, they reenact not only an ancient tragedy but a universal one because it has its true source in the defects of the species.

The beast, too, is as old as his maker and has assumed many names, though of course his character must remain quite consistent. The particular beast who speaks to Simon is much like his namesake, Beelzebub. A prince of demons of Assyrian or Hebrew descent, but later appropriated by Christians, he is a lord of flies, an idol for unclean beings. He is what all devils are: merely an embodiment of the lusts and cruelties which possess his worshipers and of peculiar power among the Philistines, the unenlightened, fearful herd. He shares some kinship with Dionysus, for his powers and effects are much the same. In *The Bacchae* Dionysus is shown "as the source of ecstasies and disasters, as the enemy of intellect and the defense of man against his isolation, as a power that can make him feel like a god while acting like a beast. . . ." As such, he is "a god whom all can recognize."

Nor is it difficult to recognize the island on which Golding's innocents are set down as a natural paradise, an uncorrupted Eden offering all the lush abundance of the primal earth. But it is lost with the first rumors of the "snake-thing," because he is the ancient, inescapable presence who insures a repetition of the fall. If this fall from grace is indeed the "perennial myth" that Golding explores in all his work, it does not seem that he has found in Genesis a metaphor capable of illuminating the full range of his theme. In *The Bacchae* Golding the classicist found another version of the fall of man, and it is clearly more useful to him than its Biblical counterpart. For one thing, it makes it possible to avoid the comparatively narrow moral implications

most of us are inclined to read into the warfare between Satan (unqualifiedly evil) and God (unqualifiedly good). Satan is a fallen angel seeking vengeance on the godhead, and we therefore think of him as an autonomous entity, as a force in his own right and as prince of his own domain. Dionysus, on the other hand, is a son of God (Zeus) and thus a manifestation of one aspect of the godhead or mystery with whom man seeks communion or, perverse in his rational pride, denies at his own peril. To resist Dionysus is to resist nature itself, and this attempt to transcend the laws of creation brings down upon us the punishment of the god. Further, the ritual hunt of *The Bacchae* provides something else not found in the Biblical account of the fall. The hunt on Golding's island emerges spontaneously out of childish play, but it comes to serve as a key to the psychology underlying adult conflicts and, of course, as an effective symbol for the bloody game we have played throughout our history. This is not to say that Biblical metaphor is unimportant in *Lord of the Flies,* or in the later works, but that it forms only a part of the larger mythic frame in which Golding sees the nature and destiny of man.

Unfortunately, the critics have concentrated all too much on Golding's debts to Christian sources, with the result that he is now popularly regarded as a rigid Christian moralist. This is a false image. The emphasis of the critics has obscured Golding's fundamental realism and made it difficult to recognize that he satirizes both the Christian and the rationalist point of view. In *Lord of the Flies,* for example, the much discussed last chapter offers none of the traditional comforts of Christian orthodoxy. A fable, by virtue of its far-reaching suggestions, touches upon a dimension that most fiction does not—the dimension of prophecy. With the appearance of the naval officer, it is no longer possible to accept the evolution of the island society as an isolated failure. The events we have witnessed constitute a picture of realities which obtain in the world at large. There, too, a legendary beast has emerged from the dark wood, come from the sea, or fallen from the sky; and men have gathered for the communion of the hunt.

In retrospect, the entire fable suggests a grim parallel with the prophecies of the Biblical Apocalypse. According to that vision, the weary repetition of human failure is assured by the birth of new devils for each generation of men. The first demon, who fathers all the others, falls from the heavens; the second is summoned from the sea to make war upon the saints and overcome them; the third, emerging from the earth itself, induces man to make and worship an image of the beast. It also ordains that this image shall speak and cause those who do not worship the beast to be killed. Each devil in turn lords over the earth for an era, and then the long nightmare of history is broken by the second coming and the divine millennium. In *Lord of the Flies* (note some of the chapter titles) we see much the same sequence, but it occurs in a highly accelerated evolution. The parallel ends, however, with the irony of Golding's climactic revelation. The childish hope of rescue perishes as the beast-man comes to the shore, for he bears in his nature the bitter promise that things will remain as they are—and as they have been since his first appearance ages and ages ago.

The rebirth of evil is made certain by the fatal defects inherent in human nature, and the haunted island we occupy must always be a fortress on which enchanted hunters pursue the beast. There is no rescue. The making of history and the making of myth are finally the selfsame process—an old one in which the soul makes its own place, its own reality.

In spite of its rich and varied metaphor *Lord of the Flies* is not a bookish fable, and Golding has warned that he will concede little or nothing to *The Golden Bough*. There are grave dangers in ignoring this disclaimer. To do so is to ignore the experimental sources of Golding's art and to obscure its contemporary relevance. During the period of World War II, he witnessed at firsthand the expenditure of human ingenuity in the old ritual of war. As the illusions of his earlier rationalism and humanism fell away, new images emerged; and, as for Simon, a picture of "a human at once heroic and sick" formed in his mind. When the war ended, Golding was ready to write (as he had not been before), and it was only natural to find in the tradition he knew the metaphors which could define the continuity of the soul's ancient flaws. In one sense, the "fable" was already written. Golding had but to trace over the words upon the scroll and so collaborate with history. (pp. 22-30)

James R. Baker, "Why It's No Go," in *Critical Essays on William Golding,* edited by James Baker, G. K. Hall & Co., 1988, pp. 22-31.

SAMUEL HYNES

(essay date 1968)

[Hynes is an American scholar and critic. In the following excerpt from a 1968 essay, he probes thematic conflicts in *Lord of the Flies*.]

Golding has founded *Lord of the Flies* on a number of more or less current conventions. First of all, he has used the science-fiction convention of setting his action in the future, thus substituting the eventually probable for the immediately actual, and protecting his fable from literalistic judgments of details or of credibility. A planeload of boys has been evacuated from an En-

gland engaged in some future war fought against "the reds"; after their departure an atomic bomb has fallen on England, and civilization is in ruins. The plane flies south and east, stopping at Gibraltar and Addis Ababa; still farther east—over the Indian Ocean, or perhaps the Pacific, the plane is attacked by an enemy aircraft, the "passenger tube" containing the boys is jettisoned, and the rest of the plane crashes in flames. The boys land unharmed on a desert island.

At this point, a second literary convention enters. The desert island tale shares certain literary qualities with science fiction. Both offer a "what-would-happen-if " situation, in which real experience is simplified in order that certain values and problems may be regarded in isolation. Both tend to simplify human moral issues by externalizing good and evil; both offer occasions for Utopian fantasies. Golding's most immediate source is R. M. Ballantyne's *Coral Island,* a Victorian boys' book of South Sea adventure, but Ballantyne didn't invent the island dream; that dream began when man first felt the pressures of his civilization enough to think that a life without civilization might be a life without problems.

The relation of Golding's novel to Ballantyne's is nevertheless important enough to pause over. In *Coral Island,* three English boys called Ralph, Jack, and Peterkin are shipwrecked on a tropical island, meet pirates and cannibals, and conquer all adversities with English fortitude and Christian virtue. We may say that *Coral Island* is a clumsy moral tale, in which good is defined as being English and Christian and jolly, and especially an English Christian *boy,* and in which evil is unchristian, savage, and adult. The three boys are rational, self-reliant, inventive, and virtuous—in short, they are like no boys that anyone has ever known.

Golding regards *Coral Island* morality as unrealistic, and therefore not truly moral, and he has used it ironically in his own novel, as a foil for his own version of man's moral nature. In an interview Golding described his use of Ballantyne's book in this way:

> What I'm saying to myself is "don't be such a fool, you remember when you were a boy, a small boy, how you lived on that island with Ralph and Jack and Peterkin.". . . . I said to myself finally, "Now you are grown up, you are adult; it's taken you a long time to become adult, but now you've got there you can see that people are not like that; they would not behave like that if they were God-fearing English gentlemen, and they went to an island like that." There savagery would not be found in natives on an island. As like as not they would find savages who were kindly and uncomplicated and that the devil would rise out of the intellectual complications of the three white men on the island itself.

One might say that *Lord of the Flies* is a refutation of *Coral Island,* and that Golding sets about to show us that the devil rises, not out of pirates and cannibals and such alien creatures, but out of the darkness of man's heart. The *Coral Island* attitude exists in the novel—Jack sounds very like Ballantyne's Jack when he says: "After all, we're not savages. We're English; and the English are best at everything." And the naval commander who rescues the boys at the end of the book speaks in the same vein: "I should have thought that a pack of British boys—you're all British aren't you?—would have been able to put up a better show than that—I mean—" But Jack and the commander are wrong; the pack of British boys are in fact cruel and murderous savages who reduce the island to a burning wreckage and destroy the dream of innocence.

The fable of the novel is a fairly simple one. The boys first set out to create a rational society modeled on what "grown-ups" would do. They establish a government and laws, they provide for food and shelter, and they light a signal fire. But this rational society begins to break down almost at once, under two instinctual pressures—fear and blood lust. The dark unknown that surrounds the children gradually assumes a monstrous identity, and becomes "the beast," to be feared and propitiated; and hunting for food becomes killing. The hunters break away from the society, and create their own primitive, savage, orgiastic tribal society. They kill two of the three rational boys, and are hunting down the third when the adult world intervenes.

This fable, as sketched, is susceptible of several interpretations, and Golding's critics have found it coherent on a number of levels, according to their own preoccupations. Freudians have found in the novel a conscious dramatization of psychological theory: "denied the sustaining and repressing authority of parents, church and state, [the children] form a new culture the development of which reflects that of genuine primitive society, evolving its gods and demons (its myths), its rituals and taboos (its social norms)." The political-minded have been able to read it as "the modern political nightmare," in which rational democracy is destroyed by irrational authoritarianism ("I hope," said V. S. Pritchett, "this book is being read in Germany"). The social-minded have found in it a social allegory, in which life, without civilized restraints, becomes nasty, brutish, and short. And the religious have simply said, in a complacent tone, "Original Sin, of course."

It is, of course, entirely possible that Golding has managed to construct a fable that does express all these ideas of evil, and that what we are dealing with is not alternative interpretations, but simply levels of meaning. The idea of Original Sin, for example, does have political, social, and psychological implications; if it is true that man is inherently prone to evil, then certain conclusions about the structure of his relations to other men would seem to follow. The idea of Original Sin seems, indeed, to be one of the "great commonplaces,"

one of those ideas which are so central to man's conception of himself that they turn up, in one form or another, in almost any systematic account of human nature. It describes one of perhaps two possible accounts of the nature of human behavior (*Coral Island* assumes the other one).

Since the novel is symbolic, the best approach would seem to be to examine first the "meaning" of each of the major characters, and then to proceed to consider the significance of their interactions. Ralph—in *Coral Island* the first-person narrator—here provides the most consistent point of view, because he most nearly speaks for us, rational, fallible humankind; Ralph is the man who accepts responsibility that he is not particularly fitted for because he sees that the alternative to responsibility is savagery and moral chaos. He tries to establish and preserve an orderly, rational society; he takes as his totem the conch, making it the symbol of rational, orderly discussion.

Ralph's antagonist is Jack, who represents "the brilliant world of hunting, tactics, fierce exhilaration, skill," as Ralph represents "the world of longing and baffled common-sense." Between them there is an "indefinable connection"; like Cain and Abel, they are antithetical, but intimately linked together—man-the-destroyer confronting man-the-preserver. Jack is the hunter, the boy who becomes a beast of prey (and who uses *kill* as an intransitive verb, an act which is for him an end in itself). He is also the dictator, the authoritarian man-of-power who enters the scene like a drill sergeant, who despises assemblies and the conch, and who becomes in the end an absolute ruler of his tribe. He devises the painted mask of the hunter, behind which a boy may hide, "liberated from shame and self-consciousness," and by painting the boys he turns them into an anonymous mob of murderous savages, "a demented but partly secure society." Jack is the first of the bigger boys to accept "the beast" as possible, and the one who offers the propitiatory sacrifice to it; he is the High Priest of Beelzebub, the Lord of the Flies.

Associated with each of these antagonists is a follower who represents in a more nearly allegorical form the principal value of his leader. Piggy, Ralph's "true, wise friend," is a scientific-minded rationalist, who models his behavior on what he thinks grownups would do, and scorns the other children for "acting like a crowd of kids." He can think better than Ralph, and in a society in which thought was enough he would be supremely valuable; but on the island he is ineffectual; he is incapable of action, and is a physical coward. His totem is his spectacles, and with them he is the fire-bringer; but when Jack first breaks one lens and then steals the other, Piggy becomes blind and helpless, a bag of fat. His trust in the power and wisdom of grownups is itself a sign of his inadequacy; for if the novel makes one point clearly, it is that adults have no special wisdom, and are engaged in a larger scale, but equally destructive, version of the savage game that the hunters play. (When Ralph wishes that the outer world might "send us something grown-up . . . a sign or something," the adult world obliges with the dead parachutist, an image of terror that destroys Ralph's rational society.)

Beside or slightly behind Jack stands Roger, around whom clings "the hangman's horror." Roger's lust is the lust for power over living things, the power to destroy life. In the beginning he is restrained by "the taboo of the old life . . . the protection of parents and school and policemen and the law." Jack and the paint of savagery liberate Roger from these taboos, and "with a sense of delirious abandonment" he rolls the rock down the cliff, killing Piggy, his opposite.

One character, the most difficult to treat, remains. Simon, the shy visionary, perceptive but inarticulate, occupies a central position in the symbolic scheme of the book. It is Simon who first stammers that perhaps the beast is "only us," who sees the beast in terms of "mankind's essential illness," and who goes alone to confront *both* beasts, the grinning pig's head and the rotting airman, because, as he says, "What else is there to do?" Golding has described Simon as a saint, "someone who voluntarily embraces this beast, goes . . . and tries to get rid of him and goes to give the good news to the ordinary bestial man on the beach, and gets killed for it." He would appear to be, then, at least in Golding's intentions, the embodiment of moral understanding. If this is so, those symbolic scenes in which he appears will be crucial to an understanding of the novel. (pp. 15-19)

[One] . . . distinction between Golding's novels and allegory is that the novels are meaning-in-action, general truth given narrative or dramatic form by the creative imagination. In considering the meaning of *Lord of the Flies,* one cannot therefore stop at an examination of character—meaning must emerge from character-in-action. In the narrative action certain scenes stand out as crucial, and most of these announce their importance by being overtly symbolic. There is, for example, a series of scenes in which Jack's hunters evolve a ritual dance. On the first occasion, in Chapter 4, a child *pretends* to be the pig, and the hunters *pretend* to beat him. A chapter later the dance has become crueler, "and littluns that had had enough were staggering away, howling." After the next hunt Robert, acting the pig in the dance, squeals with real pain, and the hunters cry "Kill him! Kill him!" After the dance the boys discuss ways of improving the ritual: " 'You want a real pig,' said Robert, still caressing his rump, 'because you've got to kill him.' "

" 'Use a littlun,' said Jack, and everybody laughed." In the final ritual dance, the sacrificial function is acknowledged; the boys' chant is no longer "Kill the pig," but "Kill the *beast!* " and when Simon crawls from the forest, the boys fulfill their ritual sacrifice, and by killing a human being, make themselves beasts ("there were no words, and no movements but the tearing of teeth and claws"). Ironically, they have killed the one person who could have saved them from bestiality, for Simon has seen the figure on the mountaintop, and knows that the beast is "harmless and horrible."

Simon's lonely, voluntary quest for the beast is certainly the symbolic core of the book. The meaning of the book depends on the meaning of the beast, and it is that meaning that Simon sets out to determine. His first act is to withdraw to a place of contemplation, a sunlit space in the midst of the forest. It is to the same place that Jack and his hunters bring the pig's head, and leave it impaled on a stick as a sacrifice to the beast they fear. When they have gone, Simon holds hallucinatory conversation with the Lord of the Flies, Beelzebub, the Lord of Filth and Dung. The head, "with the infinite cynicism of adult life," assures Simon that "everything was a bad business," and advises him to run away, back to the other children, and to abandon his quest. "I'm part of you," it tells him (in words that echo Simon's own "maybe it's only us"), "I'm the reason why it's no go." Simon, apparently epileptic, falls in a fit. But when he wakes, he turns upward, toward the top of the mountain, where the truth lies. He finds the airman, rotting and fly-blown, and tenderly frees the figure from the wind's indignity. Then he sets off, weak and staggering, to tell the other boys that the beast is human, and is murdered by them.

How are we to interpret this sequence? We may say, first of all, that the beast symbolizes the source of evil in human life. Either it is something terrifying and external, which cannot be understood but must simply be lived with (this is Jack's version), or it is a part of man's nature, "only us," in which case it may be understood, and perhaps controlled by reason and rule. Simon understands that man must seek out the meaning of evil ("what else is there to do?"). By seeking, he comes to know it, "harmless and horrible." Thus far the moral point seems orthodox enough. But when he tries to tell his understanding to others, they take *him* for the beast, and destroy him in terror. Another common idea, though a more somber one—men fear the bearers of truth, and will destroy them. This has both political and psychological implications. A "demented but partly secure society" (read: Nazi Germany, or any authoritarian nation) will resist and attempt to destroy anyone who offers to substitute reason and responsible individual action for the irresponsible, unreasoning, *secure* action of the mass. And in psychological terms, the members of a "demented society" may create an irrational, external evil, and in its name commit deeds that as rational men they could not tolerate (the history of modern persecutions offers examples enough); such a society *has* to destroy the man who says, "The evil is in yourselves."

At this point, I should like to return to the argument that this novel is a symbolic form but not an allegory. One aspect of this distinction is that Golding has written a book that has a dense and often poetic verbal texture, in which metaphor and image work as they do in poetry, and enrich and modify the bare significances of the moral form. Golding's treatment of Simon's death is a particularly good case in point. At this instant, a storm breaks, the wind fills the parachute on the mountain, and the figure, freed by Simon, floats and falls toward the beach, scattering the boys in terror before passing out to sea. The storm ends, stars appear, the tide rises. Stars above and phosphorescent sea below fill the scene with brightness and quiet.

> Along the shoreward edge of the shallows the advancing clearness was full of strange, moonbeam-bodied creatures with fiery eyes. Here and there a larger pebble clung to its own air and was covered with a coat of pearls. The tide swelled in over the rain-pitted sand and smoothed everything with a layer of silver. Now it touched the first of the stains that seeped from the broken body and the creatures made a moving patch of light as they gathered at the edge. The water rose farther and dressed Simon's coarse hair with brightness. The line of his cheek silvered and the turn of his shoulder became sculptured marble. The strange attendant creatures, with their fiery eyes and trailing vapors, busied themselves round his head. The body lifted a fraction of an inch from the sand and a bubble of air escaped from the mouth with a wet plop. Then it turned gently in the water.

> Somewhere over the darkened curve of the world the sun and moon were pulling, and the film of water on the earth planet was held, bulging slightly on one side while the solid core turned. The great wave of the tide moved farther along the island and the water lifted. Softly, surrounded by a fringe of inquisitive bright creatures, itself a silver shape beneath the steadfast constellations, Simon's dead body moved out toward the open sea.

This is Golding's rhetoric at its richest, but it works. The imagery of light and value—*moonbeam, pearls, silver, brightness, marble*—effect a transfiguration, by which the dead child is made worthy, his death an elevation. In terms of allegory, this sort of metaphorical weighting would perhaps be imprecise and deceptive; in terms of a symbolic novel, it seems to me a legitimate application of a skillful writer's art.

In discussing the actions of *Lord of the Flies* I have again and again slipped from talking about boys to describing the characters as men, or simply as human beings. It is true that as the action rises to its crises—to the *agon* of Chapter 5, Simon's confrontation with the beast, the murders, the final hunt—we cease to respond to the story as a story about children, and see them simply as *people,* engaged in desperate, destructive actions. Consequently, Golding can achieve a highly dramatic effect at the end of the book by bringing our eyes down, with Ralph's, to a beach-level view of an adult, and then swinging round, to show us Ralph from the adult's point of view. The result is an irony that makes two points. First, we see with sudden clarity that these murderous savages were civilized children; the point is not, I take it, that children are more horrid than we thought (though they are), but rather that the human propensity for evil knows no limits, not even limits of age, and that there is no Age of Innocence (Ralph weeps for the end of innocence, but when did it exist, except as an illusion made of his own ignorance?). Second, there is the adult, large, efficient, confident—the "grown-up" that the children have wished for all along. But his words show at once that he is a large, stupid *Coral Island* mentality in a peaked cap, entirely blind to the moral realities of the situation. He may save Ralph's life, but he will not understand. And once he has gathered up the castaways, he will return to his ship, and the grown-up business of hunting men (just as the boys have been hunting Ralph). "And who," asks Golding, "will rescue the adult and his cruiser?"

To return briefly to the question of levels of interpretation: it seems clear that *Lord of the Flies* should be read as a moral novel embodying a conception of human depravity which is compatible with, but not limited to, the Christian doctrine of Original Sin. To call the novel religious is to suggest that its values are more developed, and more affirmative, than in fact they are; Golding makes no reference to Grace, or to Divinity, but only to the darkness of men's hearts, and to the God of Dung and Filth who rules there. Simon is perhaps a saint, and sainthood is a valuable human condition, but there is no sign in the novel that Simon's sainthood has touched any soul but his own. The novel tells us a good deal about evil; but about salvation it is silent. (pp. 19-21)

Samuel Hynes, "William Golding's 'Lord of the Flies'," in *Critical Essays on William Golding,* edited by James Baker, G. K. Hall & Co., 1988, 13-21.

JAMES GINDIN

(essay date 1988)

[An American critic and educator, Gindin has written extensively on modern English fiction and is the author of the 1988 critical study *William Golding.* In the following excerpt from this work, he analyzes Golding's major works in relation to his essays, interviews, and lectures.]

Although his statements are sometimes arch or cryptic, Golding's own essays and the interviews he has given are generally the best sources for the genesis and development of his ideas. In 1970, he acknowledged that he had, in his fiction, always been an 'ideas man' rather than a 'character man', although he hoped that he might some day combine the two. He saw the concentration on 'ideas', like that in Aldous Huxley's fiction, as a 'basic defect'. Citing Angus Wilson's *The Middle Age of Mrs. Eliot* as an example of the opposite kind of fiction, he stated that he admired such fiction that could create 'fully realized, rounded, whole, believable' characters. In more recent accounts, as in a 1977 lecture on his first visit to Egypt in 1976, Golding has tended to see the concentration on ideas or things at the expense of character as an accusation, which may or may not be true, that others level at his work. In this particular instance, he resolved to include character sketches in his journal.

Golding's interest in Egypt and archaeology began in childhood. As he explains in **'Egypt from My Inside',** an essay first published in *The Hot Gates* and reprinted in *A Moving Target,* when he wanted, at the age of seven, to write a play about ancient Egypt, he decided to learn hieroglyphics so that his characters might speak in their appropriate language. He persisted with the symbols although the play never got very far. He also reports that, whenever his mother took him to London, he 'nagged and bullied' to visit the Egyptian mummies and papyri in the British Museum. On one occasion, Golding stood transfixed before a showcase. The curator, noticing him, asked if he would like to assist and led him to a part of the Museum closed to the public to see a huge sarcophagus and help unwrap a shrouded mummy. Golding's enthusiasm for Egyptian artifacts slightly antedated the exhibition of the relics from the recently unearthed tomb of Tutankhamen that so excited London in 1922, but there is little doubt that both Golding's interest and that of the large public were imaginative responses to a whole series of archaeological discoveries in the first quarter of the twentieth century. Golding's fascination with ancient Egyptian relics continued, even though he was unable to visit the actual land for more than half a century. Inevitably, the visit was something of a disappointment. Planning to tour Egypt by car, with his wife, he was understandably distracted by the difficulties in finding hotels, the unreliability of arrangements, the dirt of travel and accommodations, the suffering from constant diarrhoea, and the 'swarm' of people. Crowds and discomfort impeded his appreciation of the Great Pyramid. Only when he and his wife joined some American tourists more knowledgeable about contemporary Egypt did he see more of the tombs and antiquities around Cairo.

Something of Golding's removal from people is apparent in his description of these tourists. Although grateful for their knowledge and friendship, he concludes his account of the episode, in the essay entitled **'Egypt from My Outside',** with a flatly chilling emphasis on the fact that 'I don't suppose we shall ever see each other again'. Later, through these friends and others, Golding and his wife stayed at a large archaeological encampment in Luxor, run by the British and the Americans. There, with frequent guides and minimal comfort assured, he was able to explore the pyramids and other antiquities, to live within the Egyptian 'Mystery' of his imagination. His second trip, piloting the boat down the Nile in 1984, was more efficiently prepared. Even so, he found it difficult not to be distracted or appalled by the Egyptian dirt, sloth, helplessness and random violence. In trying to conclude *An Egyptian Journal,* to match the ancient with the contemporary or the imaginative with the physical reality, as well as to satisfy his commission by 'having an opinion on everything', Golding can only summarise by appealing to 'strange and nonsensical complexity' and hope that the reader can share something of the 'irritations and excitements of our absurd journey'.

Egypt as a specific locus is less significant for Golding than what it represents as excavating a buried past. Growing up in Marlborough, reading about Egyptian legends and the discoveries of tombs, cycling

Golding in 1955.

around Wiltshire and visiting Stonehenge, Old Sarum, and various forts and burial mounds, Golding's imagination was always archaeological. In a 1966 essay called **'Wiltshire'**, he discusses the combination of the survivals of the prehistoric, the Roman, the Celtic, the legendary (the grave of Merlin is said to be in the grounds of a Wiltshire school), the early Christian, the Saxon and the Norman. He concludes: 'This is antiquity on a time scale to compete with Egypt.' He is also fascinated by the flowers of Wiltshire, the botanical variety, but has little interest in the touristy, manufactured medieval festivals or revivals of Morris dancing. Constructions propel Golding's imagination almost as strongly as do excavations, and the cathedral at Salisbury is an important landmark in Golding's consciousness. In an interview, Golding, asked about what research he had done in preparation for writing *The Spire,* replied that he had not needed particular research, for 'if you have lived for half a century or more in the south of England and you are naturally curious about a great many things, one of the things you're curious about is churches'. He goes on to demonstrate more than ordinary curiosity, talking of the distribution of constructive forces like an engineer and the suggestions of design like a historically sensitive architect. He has firm historical opinions as well, as in claiming that the Normans, in building their churches, 'always overplayed their hand': 'They weren't taking any risks; everything was gorillalike'. In contrast, the later medieval builders combined technical knowledge with high imagination to create something like the spire of Salisbury Cathedral. In an essay in *A Moving Target,* originally written for *Holiday* magazine in 1965, called **'An Affection for Cathedrals'**, Golding first brings up his respect for the 'diver' who, early in the twentieth century, worked daily in the slime beneath Winchester Cathedral to underpin the walls and shore up the shaky foundations. He then contrasts this with Salisbury, with the spire, equally shaky in construction, but able to 'pull' the surrounding landscape. The spire is the nobler structure, as if all rivers and roads gather toward it as it draws the community and the landscape into an image that transcends itself. Golding recalls that, during the seventeenth-century civil war, zealots smashed the faces depicted in the Salisbury stained glass and that, at these and other times, vandals have smashed or broken off the stone noses of sculpted figures. But the spire is beyond such random and personal desecration, both as symbol and as a miracle of engineering.

Golding's sensitivity to place is by no means limited to the archaeological or to his geographical origins. Other pieces published in *A Moving Target,* for example, crystallise historical and social impressions of various other locales. **'Through the Dutch Waterways'** effectively describes the 'wide light' and 'soft' sky visible on one of Golding's boat trips with his family. Canals lead to a 'huddle' of houses 'with a golden crown hanging over them'; the bridges that control squat traffic so calmly are structures of 'delicate elegance'. The light and sky, the 'defined luminosities', combine with the 'mudpats' of islands and the engineering marvels of the canals to create what Golding sees as a 'poetry of order'. Another piece called **'Delphi'** connects the harsh and remote landscape with the oracles and Gods of ancient Greece. Ancient Greece, in fact, is frequently central to Golding's imagination. He studied Greek while in the Navy during the war, initially, he has stated, to help pass the dull hours on watch. Although most of the Greek literature he has taught has been Greek in English translation, Greek myths and symbols infuse his novels. The essay from *The Hot Gates* that gives the collection its title describes his visit to the mountains of Thessaly and the Pass of Thermopylae, where Golding, climbing the cliffs, recalls his sense of peril: 'I stayed there, clinging to a rock . . . I was clinging to Greece herself '. The locus and the connection recall the principal metaphor of *Pincher Martin,* a novel which can also be read as a suggestive and expanded retelling of the Aeschylean version of Prometheus chained to a rock by the Gods as punishment for his *hubris.*

Sometimes, Golding's use of Greece is referential and mythical, a saturation in the culture that gives him material for the creation of his own metaphorical statements about the human condition (and he has, at moments, thought of his work as attempts to create myths for contemporary man). At other times, however, the idea of Greece functions as a significant contrast to the idea of Egypt in Golding's imagination. Golding establishes a polarity of historical and cultural influence, contrasting the rationalism and light associated with the Greek tradition with the mystery and the darkness, swaddled in a mummy-like unknown that he has always connected with the Egyptian tradition and its appeal. In **'Egypt from My Inside'**, after giving the facts of his early attraction to Egyptian artifacts, he talks of his fascination with mystery as a child, regarding the fascination as something quite different from trying rationally to work out the puzzle. He saw his attraction to the artifacts as an attraction to darkness, to mystery with no solution. In retrospect, he can see what has persisted from childhood as feeling himself linked to the Egyptian's 'unreason, spiritual pragmatism and capacity for ambiguous and even contradictory belief '. In *An Egyptian Journal,* he conveys the polarity in more referential literary terms. He begins the book by explaining his sixty-year attachment to ancient Egypt as an attraction to its 'immobility' amidst change. This is the quality visible in the fiction of Rider Haggard, full of adventure, contradiction and mystery. The rational and puzzle-solving is represented by the Sherlock Holmes fiction. As a child, and still (although he realises that the fiction bears little resemblance to reality), Golding preferred Rider Haggard.

The polarity between the rational and the imaginative or mysterious is always visible in all Golding's work, a consistency that balances the variety of the location of experience in particular different places. The locations, the places, are the tangible moments of particular intensity, while the polarity itself, the constant opposition of the rationally understandable and the mysterious in human experience, is the nature of all human experience. In ways, the polarity reflects Golding's early consciousness of experience, and can be connected to both his desire to separate himself from the father he regarded as 'incarnate omniscience' and his switch at Oxford from doing sciences to doing literature. But Golding also sees the polarity as universal, as a permanent quality that justifies its compressed elaborations in the novels. Although he always values most the side more difficult to apprehend, the mysterious or imaginative, the dark side, he never oversimplifies the issue, never, for example, abandons his interest in and respect for engineering, as, even in the midst of his rebellion and self-definition, he never lost his considerable respect and affection for his father. Yet within the fictional dramatisations of varieties of the polarity, varieties that reveal his constantly interesting and imaginative mind, he does see the two sides of experience as identifiably separate, as pressures that pull the human being in different directions and comprise a constant source of human pain.

As he has indicated in interviews, Golding thinks we live constantly in 'two worlds', one physical and the other spiritual, and that the experience of the 'two worlds' is basically emblematic of our nature. As he explained in his defence of the title for *Free Fall*, he thinks the 'model intellectual' is 'literally in this state of free fall' both in terms of theology and in terms of science. The theology underlines man's suspension between the base 'physical' and the elevated 'spiritual', the science reflects man floating in a universe in which 'gravity has *gone*'. For Golding, who most often uses the conventional religious terms, 'physical' and 'spiritual', to identify the polarity, the 'physical' is equated with the rational. He sees the rational view of experience as denying the irrational, the mysterious, or the 'spiritual'. Yet, for Golding, the 'spiritual' is always felt, always there. And the polarity leads, in Golding's perspective, to the constant 'dissociation of thought and feeling'. Golding has often said that he has no solution to the dissociation, no 'bridge' between the worlds of thought and feeling. And he has always been interested in the thought of people he regards as seers, like Rudolf Steiner, whose cosmology attempts to combine the scientific and the religious. While Golding has not, at least publicly, committed himself to any particular theoretical 'bridge', he has repeatedly expressed his faith that some sort of 'bridge' between the two separate worlds exists. The compressed metaphors of Golding's fictions are most frequently attempts to synthesise the constant problem or to suggest a plausible 'bridge'.

Seeing human experience in terms of a basic polarity, of physical and spiritual worlds or of thought and feeling, is a frequent corollary of a religious perspective. The polarity between the physical and the spiritual, for example, dominates various forms of religious Puritanism, a theology in which the various claims of the physical being must be suppressed or denied in order to ensure the claims of the spiritual for salvation. Puritanism postulates an inverse relationship between the two, as if the human being has a finite amount of energy and spending less in one world will guarantee a richer expenditure in the other. For most Puritans, sex represents the threat of physical waste, the profligate expenditure that will leave little energy for the possibility of spiritual salvation. Golding's version of the two worlds, however, is different from this. Sexuality is not always stigmatised as simply physical—in fact, at times, sexuality becomes a tangible means for exploring a world of richer and more rewarding imagination. As he has often said in interviews, Golding thinks sex is sinful only when it is exploitive. His fiction is full of graphic descriptions of waste, of the functions of excretion. Many of the novels, like *Lord of the Flies, The Spire* and *The Pyramid* connect excretion with the limitations of rationalism or dwell on it as an example of the loathsome inferiority of the being immersed in the sole realm of the physical. Mud, slime, faeces, waste of all sorts are points of focus in Golding's fictional landscapes, which often seem to resemble a massive lavatory. As in Swift's similar fiction, the excremental also suggests ugliness, moral failure, depravity and inadequacy. In the words of the critics Bernard S. Oldsey and Stanley Weintraub, Golding's Swiftian 'obsession' illustrates his 'dung-heap-and-rose principle of beauty'. His two worlds are morally and aesthetically far apart, and 'bridges' are difficult to build. In Golding's more recent literal accounts of experience, as in recording his trips to Egypt, he emphasises mud and excretion almost as much as he does in his fiction, commenting frequently on the barely operative lavatories on the boat, the Nile as sewer, and the rarely achieved ideal of a bath in fresh water. Here, however, instead of representing the rational, the excretory and the physical are irrational, connected with the bad engineering of all those unfinished bridges across the Nile. Despite his constant use of polarities to represent the pains and problems of human experience, Golding never allows a falsifying and abstract consistency to distort the complexity of experience he visualises and presents.

Golding's polarities are not illustrations of particular doctrine or attitude; rather, they are shaped carefully to reflect the complicated nature of the human being. In his fiction, he uses his knowledge of the ancient Greeks, of engineering, of English literature, of Egyptian civilisation, and of a whole chain of ideas about human sin and goodness implicit within the Western Christian tradition, to condense his sense of the human condition into essence. Unlike most of his contemporaries writing in the 1950s, Amis, Wain, Wilson and Lessing, Golding was not primarily interested in issues of society or class, issues about the relationships between people all of whom he depicted and accepted as fallible. In the works of others, human beings lived, temporised, sorted themselves out by choice in equivocal relationships that were seen as partial or comic, as if no absolute or universal statement could ever be made about the nature of man. In contrast, Golding saw man as finally and inherently wicked. As he has said when interviewed, 'The basic point my generation discovered about man was that there was more evil in him that could be accounted for simply by social pressures.' Although over the last twenty-five years Golding has come to deal with issues of society and class, has extended the forms and the concerns of his fiction, his sense of an inexpungeable evil or darkness in man remains. His most copious recent social novel is called *Darkness Visible,* and, like most of his others, it compresses a great deal of human material into a metaphor for human evil and bestiality.

The concentration on darkness is also necessarily a concentration on light. Golding never attenuates his seriousness or his drama by any complacent satisfaction in the darkness of the human condition. In seeing the human being as 'morally diseased', as he said in **'The Hot Gates'**, Golding has tried to use his fiction to suggest possible counterweights to the human condition. If man is evil and is not socially perfectible, not perfectible by any of the measures taken by or the illusions of the conscious and rational society, Golding often suggests, at the fringes of his fiction, what 'light' might mean in contrast to the prevailing human 'darkness'. His work is, as he sees it, constantly moral, concerned with which 'light' might locate the 'darkness', what consciousness might put human experience in a more serious, profound and accurate perspective. His early novels have been defined frequently enough as fables (a complicated definition that applies in some instances more than in others and that requires examination in the terms of specific novels), and Golding has sometimes accepted the definition in so far, as he said in his essay called **'Fable'** in *The Hot Gates,* as it carries the recognition that 'The fabulist is a moralist', one who, either implicitly or explicitly, didactically propounds a 'lesson' or instruction about the human condition. At other times, Golding has been more hesitant about accepting the term 'fable' for his work. As he said in a well-known interview with Frank Kermode on the

BBC in 1959, he would regard it as a 'tremendous compliment' were someone to substitute the word 'myth' for 'fable' in describing his work because 'myth is a much profounder and more significant thing than a fable . . . something which comes out from the roots of things in the ancient sense of being the key to existence, the whole meaning of life.' Golding never claims to have achieved such significance, only to have attempted it and to have suggested its possible moral components. Some early Golding critics, like Samuel Hynes, ducked the issue of definition involved in distinguishing 'fable' from 'myth' and referred more simply and safely to Golding's 'moral models'. The 'models' are necessary in that the fiction gives the morality coherent form.

Golding's moral didacticism, like the tightness of his fictional forms, has eased somewhat over the last two decades. In a 1980 talk called **'Belief and Creativity'**, published in *A Moving Target,* Golding has asserted that *Lord of the Flies* yields perhaps too easily 'to explication, to instruction, to the trephining of the pupil's skull by the teacher and the insertion into the pupil's brain by the teacher of what the pupil ought to think about it.' Although he has become less didactic since, he thinks 'in general terms I would still assent to the philosophical or theological implications about the nature of man and the universe presented in the book.' Golding asserts that all his novels attempt to deal with the essential human condition, with 'man at an extremity, man tested like a building material, taken into the laboratory and used to destruction; man isolated, man obsessed, man drowning in a literal sea or in the sea of his own ignorance.' Convinced that the writer must describe the indescribable, the mystery of the human essence, Golding sees his statements about the human being as fundamentally religious. Yet he follows no particular religious doctrine, is in fact sceptical of all doctrines and systems, just as he finds, in their systems and in the images those systems create, Marx, Darwin and Freud 'the three most crashing bores of the Western world'. Golding is always likely to be dismissive of other's icons, of any concept that replaces the size and scale of what he thinks of as God. He believes in a God that is beyond the triviality of man, not a God as 'confident authority' or system, but God as a principle of universal creation. Modern life, and particularly the theorists like Marx, Darwin and Freud, has glorified man and consequently ignored or reduced the concept of God: 'We have diminished the world of God and man in a universe ablaze with all the glories that contradict that diminution.' The polarities or dichotomies within which man struggles or strangles himself are all signs of human incapacity and ignorance, for 'Truth is single'. The divisions, the complexities, and the polarities of human experience are multiple evidence of human triviality and pettiness, of human distance from God.

Golding is, however, a believer and a writer with a unique and interesting mind, not a systematic theologian or a preacher. He thinks that lyric poetry, in its possible crystallisations of essence through metaphor, is likely to reflect something closer to religious belief or truth than is narrative prose. Yet the novelist also tries to approach religious truth, 'a kind of diver' searching the mud and depths of experience 'looking for a theme'. In his talks and essays, in which the primary subject is most likely to be his writing, his religious impulses embedded within and only hesitantly emerging from accounts of the writing, he is usually deferential about the role of the writer. In more recent essays, he has been even less likely than he was earlier to accept for himself definitions of forms like 'fable' or 'myth'. In **'A Moving Target'**, as in some other recent essays, he regards himself as a teller of stories, calling the novel a 'story which is in part a fiction'. He wonders to what extent stories really have 'themes' of any importance and questions what value such themes might have. In retrospect, he thinks that *Lord of the Flies* 'has either no theme or all theme', and, after giving an account of both the personal and the generational circumstances of its genesis, concludes that he now sees its theme, found through the novel, as 'grief, sheer grief, grief, grief, grief '. In contrast, *The Inheritors* was written to the intellectual specification of a theme already thought through. Subsequent novels, in their variety, have illustrated other versions of the relationship between 'story' and 'theme' or meaning. And Golding is honestly searching and unprogrammatic in trying to account for the various ways in which meaning or that singular truth behind or beneath experience may or may not emerge from the stories he wants to tell.

Golding is also the writer in developing a good deal of his self-definition through the literature of others, illustrating the fact that literature more than abstract ideas serves as the knowable source for his perspectives. He often goes back to his initial love for poetry. In a 1981 essay called **'My First Book'**, after citing the irony that his slim volume of thirty-four pages of poetry, remaindered in 1934, was worth $4000 in the United States in 1981, he talks of all the attention given to reciting poetry at the dame school he attended when he was a child. The recitations gave him an interest in 'interior stance', in simple lyrics, and in the vocative like 'Oh!' and 'Ah!' This helped him to feel poetry as something closer to singular truth, to the emotions of what simply transcends, a kind of poetry far from intellectualised, intricately complex and dichotomous 'aber-

rations like metaphysical poetry'. He thinks of his poetry as having no concern with social issues, no interest in progressive reform or in the values of social amelioration with which he was brought up. Rather, he calls his poetry 'conservative and anarchist, in so far as it can be described in social terms at all'. As a poet, however, his closest identification is with the poetry of Tennyson, which he has always loved although he knew, even as a young man, that it was very much out of fashion. Although Golding grants that Tennyson's poetry, like his own, 'lacked intellectual mobility', he found, in some of Tennyson's lyrics, the singular voice, the 'interior stance' and the purity of evocative sound that he thought closest to the human expression of truth.

In a less pure and singular manner, Golding also defines something of himself as writer through the fiction of others. In a 1977 talk called **'Rough Magic'**, he described some of the fictional practices and conventions that had influenced him. He used a passage from *Wuthering Heights,* one of wild emotion generated from slight and unconvincing detail, the 'splashes of blood' when Heathcliff dashes his head against a tree, to illustrate what Golding calls 'badly written, implausible, ridiculous'. More positively, he uses Dickens, the pithy compression of Jane Austen in sentences in which the carefully controlled irony might be seen as going in several different directions, and the tentative although 'extraordinary strength' of Henry James's narration. Golding also appreciates the natural rhythms and 'sheer daring' in John Steinbeck's prose—an interesting identification in the light of some subsequent exterior identifications when Golding won his Nobel Prize and numbers of critics complained that, like Steinbeck, he did not deserve it. Sometimes, Golding's quotations from others seem eccentric or out of context—he never follows any version of a standard or canonical apprehension of English literature. He wrenches T. S. Eliot's statement that mankind cannot bear too much reality into an elitist scorn for the common man, a distortion that Golding can then, too simply, define himself against. Yet he also does appreciate some of Eliot's verse, and uses him as an example of a writer who can sometimes create a 'higher language', a form of language that both creates and achieves significant mystery. For Golding, in both poetry and prose, art inheres in the language and the form that elicits the mysterious, the truth so singular and simple in itself yet so difficult for man to find, to know, or to express. (pp. 8-19)

James Gindin, in his *William Golding,* Macmillian Publishers Ltd., 1988, 124 p.

SOURCES FOR FURTHER STUDY

Baker, James R., and Ziegler, Arthur P., Jr., eds. *"Lord of the Flies": A Casebook.* New York: Putnam, 1964, 291 p.

> Reprints the text of *Lord of the Flies* and provides extensive notes and critical commentary on the novel.

Biles, Jack I. *Talk: Conversations with William Golding.* New York: Harcourt Brace Jovanovich, 1970, 112 p.

> Includes interviews with Golding in which he discusses his literary aesthetics and philosophy.

Crompton, Don. *A View from the Spire: William Golding's Later Novels.* London: Basil Blackwell, 1985, 199 p.

> Studies Golding's novels *The Spire, The Pyramid, Darkness Visible, Rites of Passage,* and *The Paper Men,* as well as the novellas collected in *The Scorpion God.*

Kinkead-Weekes, Mark, and Gregor, Ian. *William Golding: A Critical Study.* New York: Brace & World, 1967, 257 p.

> Major study of Golding's first five novels, particularly *Lord of the Flies* and *The Inheritors.*

Redpath, Philip. *William Golding: A Structural Reading of His Fiction.* London: Vision Press, 1986, 222 p.

> Addresses Golding's novels published through the mid-1980s, offering "a structural reading that not only explores the structures of [Golding's] novels, but also explores the implications of these structures for the reader and for meaning generally."

Tiger, Virginia. *William Golding: The Dark Fields of Discovery.* London: Calder & Boyars, 1974, 244 p.

> Critical study of Golding's early literary career. Includes a substantial secondary bibliography.

Oliver Goldsmith

1728?–1774

Anglo-Irish novelist, dramatist, poet, essayist, journalist, critic, biographer, and translator.

INTRODUCTION

*O*ne of the most important writers of the Augustan age, Goldsmith made notable contributions to nearly every literary form that was in vogue during the mid-eighteenth century. His only novel, *The Vicar of Wakefield* (1766), for example, is a pioneering work that has captivated readers and aroused critical discussion for more than two hundred years. Although most often interpreted today as a parody of the popular sentimental novel of the time, Goldsmith's satiric touches were so subtle that the novel has been read for generations as a gentle, pastoral, moral tale—the very thing that modern critics believe he was satirizing. His most important play, *She Stoops to Conquer* (1773), was also popular from its first performance and remains one of a very few plays from its time that is still performed. It has been credited with ushering in a new era of robust comedy to an eighteenth-century theater overwhelmed by sentimentalism. Goldsmith's principal fame during his lifetime was as the author of two long narrative poems, *The Traveller* (1764) and *The Deserted Village* (1770), both of which exerted a profound influence on descriptive landscape poetry for a century after they were written.

Goldsmith was the fifth child born to the Reverend Charles Goldsmith and his wife. The family was poor, but not in serious financial straits during his youth. His parents had planned for a university education for their son, but his older sister's marriage necessitated a large dowry and left no money for tuition. As a result, Goldsmith entered Dublin's Trinity College in 1745 as a sizar. The sizar system enabled indigent students to attend college for a nominal fee in exchange for maintenance work on school property. They were often pressed into more menial labor, however, and were generally scorned by wealthier students. Biographers theorize that Goldsmith had looked forward to college as an opportunity to distinguish himself; however, profoundly disappointed with the uncongeniality of his situation at Trinity, Goldsmith neglected his studies and was frequently reprimanded for infractions of college regulations. The most serious of these was his participation in a riot, during which several people were killed, that grew out of a protest at another student's arrest. Although he left college briefly, he eventually returned and took a Bachelor of Arts degree in 1749.

Goldsmith spent the next several years idly. Casting about for a profession, he prepared halfheartedly for holy orders but reportedly was rejected as a candidate after appearing for an interview with a bishop wearing tight red trousers. He also studied medicine for a short time in Edinburgh, Scotland, before embarking on a walking tour of the Continent in 1753; his wanderings provided the inspiration for several later works, including *The Traveller* and the adventures of George Primrose in *The Vicar of Wakefield*. After three years of travel, he arrived in London early in 1756, penniless and without an acquaintance in the city. During the next several years, he held a variety of poorly paying jobs. However, an important opportunity was provided by Ralph Griffiths, the publisher and owner of the *Monthly Review*, who commissioned book reviews for his publication from Goldsmith. This arrangement introduced Goldsmith to professional magazine writing, a vocation which would eventually provide most of his income. After his association with Griffiths ended, he obtained a proofreading job with the novelist and printer Samuel Richardson and continued to contribute essays as well as book and theater reviews to a number of journals. From October through November of 1759 Goldsmith wrote the entire contents of a new magazine, *The Bee*, commissioned by the bookseller John Wilkes (or Wilkie). Goldsmith furnished *The Bee* with miscellaneous essays, short pieces of fiction, and book and play reviews for its eight-issue run. One such essay by Goldsmith praising the works of Samuel Johnson and Tobias Smollett came to Smollett's attention, and he invited Goldsmith to contribute to his *Critical Review* and to a forthcoming publication, the *British Magazine;* another magazine publisher, John Newbery, also solicited contributions to his *Publick Ledger*. Goldsmith's first book, *An Enquiry into the Present State of Polite Learning in Europe,* appeared in 1759. This long essay on European culture and literature was published anonymously; however, members of London's literary scene were easily able to learn the writer's identity, and Goldsmith's reputation as an author began to grow.

In the *Publick Ledger* in 1760, Goldsmith began his most famous series of periodical essays, the "Chinese Letters." Purporting to be a succession of letters from a Chinese philosopher visiting London, the essays—often humorous and witty, sometimes introspective and philosophical—provided thinly veiled social satire on the customs, manners, and morals of Londoners for more than a year and a half. The ninety-eight "Letters," with four additional essays, were published in 1762 as *The Citizen of the World; or, Letters from a Chinese Philosopher Residing in London to His Friends in the East,* the first book to appear under Goldsmith's name. He was becoming increasingly prominent in London literary society, a position that was reinforced through his association with a coterie of well-known intellectuals led by Samuel Johnson who called themselves The Club (later the Literary Club), a group that included the painter Sir Joshua Reynolds, writers James Boswell, Edmund Burke, and Thomas Percy, and actor and theater manager David Garrick. The success of *The Citizen of the World* assured Goldsmith a readership that welcomed his subsequent works, but his own financial improvidence required that he spend much of his time at anonymous literary hackwork. Periodical essays, translations, and popularized versions of existing works could be quickly written and sold, providing him a precarious hand-to-mouth existence. Boswell's account of the sale of *The Vicar of Wakefield* indicates that Goldsmith's masterpieces were often hastily sold to the first publisher who offered any cash advance. Throughout the remainder of his literary career in London, his life followed a pattern of ever-mounting debts, paid with the income from his hack writing, with occasional intervals spent on the few but notable literary works on which his reputation rests.

Goldsmith's most important literary works were in many respects inspired by his dislike of contemporary literary sensibilities. In the eighteenth century, English literature had turned increasingly toward sentimentalism as a reaction against what was perceived to be the immorality of Restoration-period literature. In the service of the sentimental ideal, authors composed morally instructive works based on the premise that human nature was essentially good and that humankind was potentially perfectible. In drama, this trend took the form of the sentimental comedy—so termed because of formulaic and often implausible happy endings. The didactic purpose of a sentimental work often superseded such purely artistic elements as characterization or plot. In his critical works Goldsmith had noted and deplored the absence of humor in contemporary sentimental literature, especially in drama. In his "Essay on the Theatre; or, A Comparison between Laughing and Sentimental Comedy," published in the *Westminster Magazine* in January 1773, Goldsmith expressed his preference for the "laughing" over the sentimental comedy, and a widespread modern critical assumption is that he intended his own light and humorous plays to stand as a corrective to the popular sentimental comedies. When Goldsmith's first play, *The Good Natured Man* (1768), was staged by George Coleman at the Covent Garden Theatre, the Drury Lane Theatre debuted Hugh Kelly's sentimental comedy *False Delicacy* on the same night, giving the appearance of a competition, not just between the two plays and playwrights, but between the two types of comedy as well.

Goldsmith's reputation as a dramatist rests primarily on his second play, *She Stoops to Conquer.* It was a popular success and remains one of the few plays of the period, with Richard Brinsley Sheridan's *The Rivals* and William Congreve's *The School for Scandal,* that is still staged today. The play contains Goldsmith's characteristic weaknesses as well as his strengths: the plot is preposterous, depending on a series of highly unlikely misunderstandings, and many of the minor characters are archetypes. However, several of the central characters, particularly Kate Hardcastle and Tony Lumpkin, are considered masterpieces of comic theater. Good-humored and containing no ulterior instruction, the play is still a viable theatrical work, a straightforward, robust "comedy of continuous incident," in Oscar James Campbell's words, that "opened the door" to a new type of lively, unsentimental, and, above all, funny, comedy.

Goldsmith is probably best known to twentieth-century readers as the author of *The Vicar of Wakefield.* This novel chronicles the history of Charles Primrose—the vicar—and his family. The Primroses suffer a reversal of their modest fortunes and a series of shattering blows to the unity of their family, until all difficulties are suddenly resolved in an improbable but wholly predictable happy ending. Critics have commonly called the plot of *The Vicar of Wakefield* unrealistic and the characters unbelievable but note that these flaws do not seem to detract from the story's charm and appeal. Early critics considered the work an example of the fashionable sentimental novel, noting that it shared with this didactic literary form a tendency to demonstrate the superiority of the simple Christian virtues of the middle class over the sophistication and worldliness of the wealthy. Most modern critics, however, remembering Goldsmith's lifelong aversion to sentimental literature, maintain that the novel's seemingly sentimental touches are actually meant to be satiric thrusts at the conventions of sentimental literature. Much critical discussion focuses on the character of the vicar. Goldsmith brought a new dimension to the eighteenth-century novel by having a central character—Primrose—function both as a figure within the action of the novel and as the sole narrator, without the intervention of an omniscient third-person narrative voice. The reader is told no more than the vicar himself knows; however, the vicar's lack of insight provides a source of irony and increases the humor for the reader, who is aware of distinctions that are lost on the credulous vicar.

Goldsmith was most widely known as a poet during his lifetime. Written in the heroic couplet form popularized by Alexander Pope, Goldsmith's narrative poems *The Traveller* and *The Deserted Village* are noted for their descriptive, pastoral content. They have often received biographical interpretations because their themes—international wandering in search of happiness and a concern with the gradual disappearance of agrarianism—seemed to be drawn from Goldsmith's own experiences. Twentieth-century critics have for the most part abandoned attempts to link Goldsmith's life with his poetic works. They focus instead on a political interpretation of the two long narrative poems, finding that both reflect Goldsmith's conservative Tory dismay at the changes that were taking place in England's social and economic life with the waning of agrarianism and the gradual migration of rural populations to the cities. Goldsmith's light verse is generally regarded as an entertaining, highly personal expression of his wit and good humor. *Retaliation* (1774), in particular, which was written in response to a disparaging rhymed couplet "epitaph" composed by David Garrick about Goldsmith, is considered a minor comic verse masterpiece. In *Retaliation,* Goldsmith provides humorous eulogies for Garrick, Johnson, and other Literary Club members.

Goldsmith has retained great popularity with readers and theatergoers. Unable to reconcile their varied interpretations of *The Vicar of Wakefield,* readers have been interested in the work for more than two hundred years, and it has become a standard text in the study of the English novel. Similarly, although literary commentators continue to debate Goldsmith's intent in writing *She Stoops to Conquer,* audiences unconcerned with possible shades of authorial intent continue to enjoy the play as an entertaining theatrical comedy. While some modern critics reexamine Goldsmith's life in an attempt to create an accurate portrait free of the sentimentalizing of earlier biographical efforts, far more readers and critics concur with Ricardo Quintana, who stated: "It is time that we concerned ourselves less with his ugly face, his awkward social presence, and more with the actual nature of his achievement as a writer."

(For further information about Goldsmith's life and works, see *Dictionary of Literary Biography, Vol. 39: British Novelists, 1660-1800; Literature Criticism from 1400-1800,* Vol. 2; and *Something about the Author,* Vol. 26.)

CRITICAL COMMENTARY

JAMES BOSWELL AND SAMUEL JOHNSON
(conversation date 1773)

[Boswell, an eighteenth-century Scottish biographer, diarist, essayist, poet, and critic, is best known for his 1791 biography of Samuel Johnson; Johnson was a remarkably versatile and talented English lexicographer, essayist, and literary critic. In the following excerpt from Boswell's *Life of Johnson*, Boswell recounts conversations he had with Johnson in 1773 about Goldsmith's intellect and writing ability.]

[Dr. Johnson] owned that he thought Hawkesworth was one of his imitators, but he did not think Goldsmith was. Goldsmith, he said, had great merit. BOSWELL. 'But, Sir, he is much indebted to you for his getting so high in the publick estimation.' JOHNSON. 'Why, Sir, he has perhaps got *sooner* to it by his intimacy with me.'

Goldsmith, though his vanity often excited him to occasional competition, had a very high regard for Johnson, which he at this time expressed in the strongest manner in the Dedication of his comedy, entitled, *She Stoops to Conquer.* (p. 486)

[Goldsmith] was often very fortunate in his witty contests, even when he entered the lists with Johnson himself. Sir Joshua Reynolds was in company with them one day, when Goldsmith said, that he thought he could write a good fable, mentioned the simplicity which that kind of composition requires, and observed, that in most fables the animals introduced seldom talk in character. 'For instance, (said he,) the fable of the little fishes, who saw birds fly over their heads, and envying them, petitioned Jupiter to be changed into birds. The skill (continued he,) consists in making them talk like little fishes.' While he indulged himself in this fanciful reverie, he observed Johnson shaking his sides, and laughing. Upon which he smartly proceeded, 'Why, Dr. Johnson, this is not so easy as you seem to think; for if you were to make little fishes talk, they would talk like WHALES.' (p. 497)

Dr. Goldsmith's new play, *She Stoops to Conquer,* being mentioned; JOHNSON. 'I know of no comedy for many years that has so much exhilarated an audience, that has answered so much the great end of comedy—making an audience merry.' (p. 498)

Goldsmith being mentioned; JOHNSON. 'It is amazing how little Goldsmith knows. He seldom comes where he is not more ignorant than any one else.' SIR JOSHUA REYNOLDS. 'Yet there is no man whose company is more liked.' JOHNSON. 'To be sure, Sir. When people find a man of the most distinguished abilities as a writer, their inferiour while he is with them, it must be highly gratifying to them. What Goldsmith comically says of himself is very true,—he always gets the better when he argues alone; meaning, that he is master of a subject in his study, and can write well upon it; but when he comes into company, grows confused, and unable to talk. Take him as a poet, his *Traveller* is a very fine performance; ay, and so is his *Deserted Village,* were it not sometimes too much the echo of his *Traveller.* Whether, indeed, we take him as a poet,—as a comick writer,—or as an historian, he stands in the first class.' BOSWELL. 'An historian! My dear Sir, you surely will not rank his compilation of the Roman History with the works of other historians of this age?'' JOHNSON. 'Why, who are before him?' BOSWELL. 'Hume,—Robertson,—Lord Lyttelton.' JOHNSON (his antipathy to the Scotch beginning to rise). 'I have not read Hume; but, doubtless, Goldsmith's *History* is better than the *verbiage* of Robertson, or the foppery of Dalrymple.' BOSWELL. 'Will you not admit the superiority of Robertson, in whose *History* we find such penetration—such painting?' JOHNSON. 'Sir, you must consider how that penetration and that painting are employed. It is not history, it is imagination. He who describes what he never saw, draws from fancy. Robertson paints minds as Sir Joshua paints faces in a history-piece: he imagines an heroic countenance. You must look upon Robertson's work as romance, and try it by that standard. History it is not. Besides, Sir, it is the great excellence of a writer to put into his book as much as his book will hold. Goldsmith has done this in his *History.* Now Robertson might have put twice as much into his book. Robertson is like a man who has packed gold in wool: the wool takes up more room than the gold. No, Sir; I always thought Robertson would be crushed by his own weight,—would be buried under his own ornaments. Goldsmith tells you shortly all you want to know: Robertson detains you a great deal too long. No man will read Robertson's cumbrous detail a second time; but Goldsmith's plain narrative will please again and again. . . . Goldsmith's abridgement is better than that of Lucius Florus or Eutropius; and I will venture to say, that if you compare him with Vertot, in the same places of the Roman History, you will find that he excels Vertot. Sir, he has the art of compiling, and

Principal Works

An Enquiry into the Present State of Polite Learning in Europe (essay) 1759

The Citizen of the World; or, Letters from a Chinese Philosopher Residing in London to His Friends in the East. 2 vols. (essays) 1762

The Life of Richard Nash, Esq. (biography) 1762

The Traveller (poetry) 1764

The Vicar of Wakefield (novel) 1766

The Good Natured Man (drama) 1768

The Deserted Village (poetry) 1770

She Stoops to Conquer; or, The Mistakes of a Night (drama) 1773

Retaliation (poetry) 1774

New Essays by Oliver Goldsmith (essays) 1927

Collected Works. 5 vols. (essays, dramas, poetry, and novel) 1966

of saying every thing he has to say in a pleasing manner. He is now writing a Natural History and will make it as entertaining as a Persian Tale.' (pp. 500-01)

James Boswell, in a conversation with Samuel Johnson in 1773, in his *Boswell's Life of Johnson: 1709-1776, Vol. I,* Oxford University Press, 1933, pp. 486-501.

JAMES BOSWELL

(essay date 1791)

[In the following excerpt from his 1791 biography of Samuel Johnson, Boswell briefly summarizes then-prevailing views about Goldsmith's career and character.]

As Dr. Oliver Goldsmith will frequently appear in this narrative, I shall endeavour to make my readers in some degree acquainted with his singular character. He was a native of Ireland, and a contemporary with Mr. Burke at Trinity College, Dublin, but did not then give much promise of future celebrity. He, however, observed to Mr. Malone, that 'though he made no great figure in mathematicks, which was a study in much repute there, he could turn an Ode of Horace into English better than any of them.' He afterwards studied physick at Edinburgh, and upon the Continent; and I have been informed, was enabled to pursue his travels on foot, partly by demanding at Universities to enter the lists as a disputant, by which, according to the custom of many of them, he was entitled to the premium of a

crown, when luckily for him his challenge was not accepted; so that, as I once observed to Dr. Johnson, he *disputed* his passage through Europe. He then came to England, and was employed successively in the capacities of an usher to an academy, a corrector of the press, a reviewer, and a writer for a news-paper. He had sagacity enough to cultivate assiduously the acquaintance of Johnson, and his faculties were gradually enlarged by the contemplation of such a model. To me and many others it appeared that he studiously copied the manner of Johnson, though, indeed, upon a smaller scale.

At this time I think he had published nothing with his name, though it was pretty generally known that *one Dr. Goldsmith* was the authour of *An Enquiry into the present State of polite Learning in Europe,* and of *The Citizen of the World,* a series of letters supposed to be written from London by a Chinese. No man had the art of displaying with more advantage as a writer, whatever literary acquisitions he made. *'Nihil quod tetigit non ornavit.'* His mind resembled a fertile, but thin soil. There was a quick, but not a strong vegetation, of whatever chanced to be thrown upon it. No deep root could be struck. The oak of the forest did not grow there; but the elegant shrubbery and the fragrant parterre appeared in gay succession. It has been generally circulated and believed that he was a mere fool in conversation; but, in truth, this has been greatly exaggerated. He had, no doubt, a more than common share of that hurry of ideas which we often find in his countrymen, and which sometimes produces a laughable confusion in expressing them. He was very much what the French call *un étourdi,* and from vanity and an eager desire of being conspicuous wherever he was, he frequently talked carelessly without knowledge of the subject, or even without thought. His person was short, his countenance coarse and vulgar, his deportment that of a scholar awkwardly affecting the easy gentleman. Those who were in any way distinguished, excited envy in him to so ridiculous an excess, that the instances of it are hardly credible. When accompanying two beautiful young ladies with their mother on a tour in France, he was seriously angry that more attention was paid to them than to him; and once at the exhibition of the *Fantoccini* in London, when those who sat next him observed with what dexterity a puppet was made to toss a pike, he could not bear that it should have such praise, and exclaimed with some warmth, 'Pshaw! I can do it better myself.'

He, I am afraid, had no settled system of any sort, so that his conduct must not be strictly scrutinised; but his affections were social and generous, and when he had money he gave it away very liberally. His desire of imaginary consequence predominated over his attention to truth. When he began to rise into notice, he said he had a brother who was Dean of Durham, a fiction so easily detected, that it is wonderful how he should have been so inconsiderate as to hazard it. He boasted to me at this time of the power of his pen in commanding money, which I believe was true in a certain degree, though in the instance he gave he was by no means correct. He told me that he had sold a novel for four hundred pounds. This was his *Vicar of Wakefield.* But Johnson informed me, that he had made the bargain for Goldsmith, and the price was sixty pounds. 'And, Sir, (said he,) a sufficient price too, when it was sold; for then the fame of Goldsmith had not been elevated, as it afterwards was, by his *Traveller;* and the bookseller had such faint hopes of profit by his bargain, that he kept the manuscript by him a long time, and did not publish it till after *The Traveller* had appeared. Then, to be sure, it was accidentally worth more money.'

Mrs. Piozzi and Sir John Hawkins have strangely misstated the history of Goldsmith's situation and Johnson's friendly interference, when this novel was sold. I shall give it authentically from Johnson's own exact narration:—'I received one morning a message from poor Goldsmith that he was in great distress, and as it was not in his power to come to me, begging that I would come to him as soon as possible. I sent him a guinea, and promised to come to him directly. I accordingly went as soon as I was drest, and found that his landlady had arrested him for his rent, at which he was in a violent passion. I perceived that he had already changed my guinea, and had got a bottle of Madeira and a glass before him. I put the cork into the bottle, desired he would be calm, and began to talk to him of the means by which he might be extricated. He then told me that he had a novel ready for the press, which he produced to me. I looked into it, and saw its merit; told the landlady I should soon return, and having gone to a bookseller, sold it for sixty pounds. I brought Goldsmith the money, and he discharged his rent, not without rating his landlady in a high tone for having used him so ill.' (pp. 275-78)

Goldsmith . . . was one of the brightest ornaments of the Johnsonian school. Goldsmith's respectful attachment to Johnson was then at its height; for his own literary reputation had not yet distinguished him so much as to excite a vain desire of competition with his great Master. He had increased my admiration of the goodness of Johnson's heart, by incidental remarks in the course of conversation, such as, when I mentioned Mr. Levet, whom he entertained under his roof, 'He is poor and honest, which is recommendation enough to Johnson;' and when I wondered that he was very kind to a man of whom I had heard a very bad character, 'He is now become miserable, and that insures the protection of Johnson.' (p. 278)

James Boswell, in an extract from "Life of Samuel Johnson (Sept. 18, 1709-March, 1776)," in his *Boswell's Life of Johnson: 1709-1776, Vol. 1,* Oxford University Press, 1933, pp. 275-79.

JOHANN WOLFGANG VON GOETHE
(essay date 1811)

[Goethe was a shaping force in the major literary movements of the late eighteenth and early nineteenth centuries in Germany. His first novel, *The Sorrows of Young Werther* (1774), epitomizes the Sturm und Drang ("Storm and Stress") movement; his dramas *Iphigenia in Tauris* (1787) and *Torquato Tasso* (1790), and the poetry collection *Roman Elegies* (1795), exemplify the neoclassical approach to literature, which he helped inaugurate with Friedrich von Schiller; and his drama *Faust (I,* 1808; *II,* 1832) is ranked beside the masterpieces of Dante and William Shakespeare. In the following excerpt from his 1811 autobiography, he commends *The Vicar of Wakefield* as one of the best novels ever written, calling it a highly moral tale that avoids cant and pedantry through a saving touch of irony.]

How far I must have been behindhand in modern literature, may be gathered from the mode of life which I led at Frankfort, and from the studies to which I had devoted myself; nor could my residence in Strasburg have furthered me in this respect. Now [Johannes Gottfried von] Herder came, and together with his great knowledge brought many other aids, and the later publications besides. Among these he announced to us *The Vicar of Wakefield* as an excellent work, with the German translation of which he would make us acquainted by reading it aloud to us himself. (pp. 367-68).

A Protestant country clergyman is, perhaps, the most beautiful subject for a modern idyl; he appears, like Melchizedek, as priest and king in one person. To the most innocent situation which can be imagined on earth, to that of a husbandman, he is, for the most part, united by similarity of occupation, as well as by equality in family relationships; he is a father, a master of a family, an agriculturalist, and thus perfectly a member of the community. On this pure, beautiful, earthly foundation, rests his higher calling; to him is it given to guide men through life, to take care of their spiritual education, to bless them at all the leading epochs of their existence, to instruct, to strengthen, to console them, and, if consolation is not sufficient for the present, to call up and guarantee the hope of a happier future. Imagine such a man, with pure human sentiments, strong enough not to deviate from them under any circumstances, and by this already elevated above the multitude, of whom one cannot expect purity and firmness; give him the learning necessary for his office, as well as a cheerful, equable activity, which is even passionate, as it neglects no moment to do good,—and you will have him well endowed. But at the same time add the necessary limitation, so that he must not only pause in a small circle, but may also perchance pass over to a smaller; grant him good-nature, placability, resolution, and everything else praiseworthy that springs from a decided character, and over all this a cheerful spirit of compliance, and a smiling toleration of his own failings and those of others,—then you will have put together pretty well the image of our excellent Wakefield.

The delineation of this character on his course of life through joys and sorrows, the ever-increasing interest of the story, by the combination of the entirely natural with the strange and the singular, make this novel one of the best which has ever been written; besides this, it has the great advantage that it is quite moral, nay, in a pure sense, Christian—represents the reward of a good will and perseverance in the right, strengthens an unconditional confidence in God, and attests the final triumph of good over evil; and all this without a trace of cant or pedantry. The author was preserved from both of these by an elevation of mind that shows itself throughout in the form of irony, by which this little work must appear to us as wise as it is amiable. The author, Dr. Goldsmith, has without question great insight into the moral world, into its strength and its infirmities; but at the same time he can thankfully acknowledge that he is an Englishman, and reckon highly the advantages which his country and his nation afford him. The family, with the delineation of which he occupies himself, stands upon one of the last steps of citizen comfort, and yet comes in contact with the highest; its narrow circle, which becomes still more contracted, touches upon the great world through the natural and civil course of things; this little skiff floats on the agitated waves of English life, and in weal or woe it has to expect injury or help from the vast fleet which sails around it. (pp. 368-69)

Johann Wolfgang von Goethe, "Strasbourg (continued)— Herder—Tour in Alsace and Lorraine—Frederika," in his *The Autobiography of Goethe: Truth and Poetry, from My Own Life, Vol. I,* translated by John Oxenford, revised edition, George Bell and Sons, 1881, pp. 342-87.

W. D. HOWELLS

(essay date 1895)

[Howells was the chief progenitor of American Realism and one of the most influential American literary critics of the late nineteenth century. In the following excerpt, he reminisces about the pleasure of first reading Goldsmith.]

When I began to have literary likings of my own, and to love certain books above others, the first authors of my heart were Goldsmith, Cervantes, and Irving. In the sharply foreshortened perspective of the past I seem to have read them all at once, but I am aware of an order of time in the pleasure they gave me, and I know that Goldsmith came first. He came so early that I cannot tell when or how I began to read him, but it must have been before I was ten years old. . . . I do not know in the least how Goldsmith's [*The Grecian History, from the Earliest State to the Death of Alexander the Great*] came into my hands, though I fancy it must have been procured for me because of a taste which I showed for that kind of reading, and I can imagine no greater luck for a small boy in a small town of Southwestern Ohio well-nigh fifty years ago. (pp. 10-11)

Goldsmith's history of Rome came to me much later, but quite as immemorably, and after I had formed a preference for the Greek Republics, which I dare say was not mistaken. (p. 11)

I do not think I yet felt the beauty of the literature which made them all live in my fancy, that I conceived of Goldsmith as an artist using for my rapture the finest of the arts; and yet I had been taught to see the loveliness of poetry, and was already trying to make it on my own poor account. I tried to make verses like those I listened to when my father read Moore and Scott to my mother, but I heard them with no such happiness as I read my beloved histories, though I never thought then of attempting to write like Goldsmith. I accepted his beautiful work as ignorantly as I did my other blessings. I was concerned in getting at the Greeks and Romans, and I did not know through what nimble air and by what lovely ways I was led to them. Some retrospective perception of this came long afterward when I read his essays, and after I knew all of his poetry, and later yet when I read the *Vicar of Wakefield;* but for the present my eyes were holden, as the eyes of a boy mostly are in the world of art. (pp. 12-13)

Before I speak . . . of the beneficent humorist who next had my boyish heart after Goldsmith, let me acquit myself in full of my debt to that not unequal or unkindred spirit. I have said it was long after I had read those histories, full of his inalienable charm, mere potboilers as they were, and far beneath his more willing efforts, that I came to know his poetry. My father must have read the *Deserted Village* to us, and told us something of the author's pathetic life, for I cannot remember when I first knew of "sweet Auburn," or had the light of the poet's own troubled day upon the "loveliest village of the plain." *The Vicar of Wakefield* must have come into my life after that poem and before *The Traveler.* It was when I would have said that I knew all Goldsmith. We often give ourselves credit for knowledge in this way without having any tangible assets; and my reading has always been very desultory. I should like to say here that the reading of any one who reads to much purpose is always very desultory, but perhaps I had better not say so, but merely state the fact in my case, and own that I never read any one author quite through without wandering from him to others. When I first read the *Vicar of Wakefield,* (for I have since read it several times, and hope yet to read it many times,) I found its persons and incidents familiar, and so I suppose I must have heard it read. It is still for me one of the most modern novels: that is to say, one of the best. It is unmistakably good up to a certain point, and then unmistakably bad, but with always good enough in it to be forever imperishable. Kindness and gentleness are never out of fashion; it is these in Goldsmith which make him our contemporary, and it is worth the while of any young person presently intending deathless renown to take a little thought of them. They are the source of all refinement, and I do not believe that the best art in any kind exists without them. . . . As to Goldsmith, I do not think that a man of harsh and arrogant nature, of worldly and selfish soul, could ever have written his style, and I do think that, in far greater measure than criticism has recognized, his spiritual quality, his essential friendliness, expressed itself in the literary beauty that wins the heart as well as takes the fancy in his work.

I should have my reservations and my animadversions if it came to close criticism of his work, but I am glad that he was the first author I loved, and that even before I knew I loved him I was his devoted reader. I was not consciously his admirer till I began to read, when I was fourteen, a little volume of his essays, made up, I dare say, from the *Citizen of the World* and other unsuccessful ventures of his. It contained the papers on Beau Tibbs, among others, and I tried to write sketches and studies of life in their manner. (pp. 15-18)

I have never greatly loved an author without wishing to write like him. I have now no reluctance to confess that, and I do not see why I should not say that it was a long time before I found it best to be as like myself as I could, even when I did not think so well of myself as of some others. I hope I shall always be able and willing to learn something from the masters of literature and still be myself. . . . I think it hardly less fortunate that Cervantes was one of my early passions, though I sat at his feet with no more sense of his mastery than I had of Goldsmith's. (pp. 18-19)

W. D. Howells, "Goldsmith," in his *My Literary Passions,* Harper & Brothers Publishers, 1895, pp. 10-19.

VIRGINIA WOOLF
(essay date 1934)

[Woolf was an English novelist, essayist, and literary critic. In the following excerpt from a 1934 essay, she notes Goldsmith's qualities as an essayist, novelist, and dramatist.]

The [literary] patron is always changing, and for the most part imperceptibly. But one such change in the middle of the eighteenth century took place in the full light of day, and has been recorded for us with his usual vivacity by Oliver Goldsmith, who was himself one of its victims:—

When the great Somers was at the helm . . . patronage was fashionable among our nobility. . . . I have heard an old poet of that glorious age say, that a dinner with his lordship had procured him invitations for the whole week following; that an airing in his patron's chariot has supplied him with a citizen's coach on every future occasion. . . .

But this link . . . now seems entirely broken.

(pp. 3-4)

In the old days, he said, the patron was a man of taste and breeding, who could be trusted to see "that all who deserved fame were in a capacity of attaining it." Now in the mid-eighteenth century young men of brains were thrown to the mercy of the booksellers. Penny-a-lining came into fashion. Men of originality and spirit became docile drudges, voluminous hacks. They stuffed out their pages with platitudes. They "write through volumes while they do not think through a page." Solemnity and pomposity became the rule. "On my conscience I believe we have all forgot to laugh in these days." The new public fed greedily upon vast hunks of knowledge. They demanded huge encyclopaedias, soulless compilations, which were "carried on by different writers, cemented into one body, and concurring in the same design by the mediation of the booksellers." All this was much to the disgust of a man who wrote clearly, shortly and outspokenly by nature; who held that "Were angels to write books, they never would write folios"; who felt himself among the angels but knew that the age of the angels was over. (pp. 4-5)

Goldsmith did his share of the work manfully, as a glance at the list of his works shows. But he was to find that the change from the Earl to the bookseller was not without its advantages. A new public had come into existence with new demands. Everybody was turning reader. The writer, if he had ceased to dine with the nobility, had become the friend and instructor of a vast congregation of ordinary men and women. They demanded essays as well as encyclopaedias. They allowed their writers a freedom which the old aristocracy had never permitted. As Goldsmith said, the writer could now "refuse invitations to dinner"; he "could wear just such clothes as men generally wear" and "he can bravely assert the dignity of independence." Goldsmith by temper and training was peculiarly fitted to take advantage of the new state of things. He was a man of lively intelligence and outspoken good sense. He had the born writer's gift of being in touch with the thing itself and not with the outer husks of words. There was something shrewd and objective in his temper which fitted him admirably to preach little sermons and wing little satires. If he had little education and no learning, he had a large and varied stock of experience to draw on. He had knocked about the world. He had seen Leyden and Paris and Padua as a foot traveller sees famous cities. But his travels, far from plunging him into reverie or giving him a passion for the solitudes and sublimities of nature, had served to make him relish human society better and had proved how slight are the differences between man and man. He preferred to call himself a Citizen of the World rather than an Englishman. "We are now become so much Englishmen, Frenchmen, Dutchmen, Spaniards or Germans that we are no longer . . . members of that grand society which comprehends the whole of human kind." He insisted that we should pool our discoveries and learn from each other.

It is this detached attitude and width of view that give Goldsmith his peculiar flavour as an essayist. Other writers pack their pages fuller and bring us into closer touch with themselves. Goldsmith, on the other hand, keeps just on the edge of the crowd so that we can hear what the common people are saying and note their humours. That is why his essays, even the early ones, in *The Bee,* make such good reading. That is why it is just and fitting that *The Bee* and *The Citizen of the World* should be reprinted again today. . . . The Citizen is still a most vivacious companion as he takes his walk from Charing Cross to Ludgate Hill. The streets are lit up for the Battle of Minden, and he pokes fun at the parochial patriotism of the English. . . . He peeps into St. Paul's and marvels at the curious lack of reverence shown by the English at their worship. He reflects that rags "which might be valued at half a string of copper money in China" yet needed a fleet and an army to win them. He marvels that the French and English are at war simply because people like their muffs edged with fur and must therefore kill each other and seize a country "belonging to people who were in possession from time immemorial." Shrewdly and sarcastically he casts his eye, as he saunters on, upon the odd habits and sights that the English are so used to that they no longer see them. Indeed he could scarcely

have chosen a method better calculated to make the new public aware of itself or one better suited to the nature of his own genius. If Goldsmith stood still he could be as flat, though not as solemn, as any of the folio makers who were his aversion. Here, however, he must keep moving; he must pass rapidly under review all kinds of men and customs and speak his mind on them. And here his novelist's gift stood him in good stead. If he thinks he thinks in the round. An idea at once dresses itself up in flesh and blood and becomes a human being. Beau Tibbs comes to life: Vauxhall Gardens is bustling with people: the writer's garret is before us with its broken windows and the spider's web in the corner. He has a perpetual instinct to make concrete, to bring into being.

Perhaps it was the novelist's gift that made him a little impatient with essay writing. The shortness of the essay made people think it superficial. "I could have made them more metaphysical had I thought fit," he replied. But it is doubtful if he was prevented by circumstances from any depth of speculation. The real trouble was that Beau Tibbs and Vauxhall Gardens asked to be given a longer lease of life, but the end of the column was reached; down came the shears, and a new subject must be broached next week. The natural outlet, as Goldsmith found, was the novel. In those freer pages he had room to give his characters space to walk round and display themselves. Yet *The Vicar of Wakefield* keeps some of the characteristics that distinguish the more static art of the essayist. The characters are not quite free to go their own ways; they must come back at the tug of the string to illustrate the moral. This necessity is the stranger to us because good and bad are no longer so positively white and black; the art of the moralist is out of fashion in fiction. But Goldsmith not only believed in blackness and whiteness: he believed—perhaps one belief depends upon the other— that goodness will be rewarded, and vice punished. It is a doctrine, it may strike us when we read *The Vicar of Wakefield,* which imposes some restrictions on the novelist. There is no need of the mixed, of the twisted, of the profound. Lightly tinted, broadly shaded with here a foible, there a peccadillo, the characters of the Primroses are like those tropical fish who seem to have only backbones but no other organs to darken the transparency of their flesh. Our sympathies are not put upon the rack. Daughters may be seduced, houses burnt, and good men sent to prison, yet since the world is a perfectly balanced place, let it lurch as it likes, it is bound to settle into equilibrium in the long run. The most hardened of sinners—here Goldsmith stops characteristically to point out the evils of the prison system—will take to cutting tobacco stoppers if given the chance and thus enter the straight path of virtue again. Such assumptions stopped certain avenues of thought and imagination. But the limitation had its advantages;

he could give all his mind to the story. All is clear, related, and uncrowded. He knew precisely what to leave out. Thus, once we begin to read we read on, not to reach the end, but to enjoy the present moment. We cannot dismember this small complete world. It hems us in, it surrounds us. We ask nothing better than to sit in the sun on the hawthorn bank and sing "Barbara Allen," or Johnny Armstrong's last good night. Shades of violence and wrong can scarcely trespass here. But the scene is saved from insipidity by Goldsmith's tart eighteenth-century humour. One advantage of having a settled code of morals is that you know exactly what to laugh at. (pp. 5-9)

[When] we turn from Goldsmith's novel to Goldsmith's plays his characters seem to gain vigour and identity by standing before us in the round. They can say everything they have to say without the intervention of the novelist. This may be taken, if we choose, as proof that they have nothing of extreme subtlety to say. Yet Goldsmith did himself a wrong when he followed the old habit of labelling his people with names—Croker, Lofty, Richlands—which seem to allow them but one quality apiece. His observation, trained in the finer discriminations of fiction, worked much more cunningly than the names suggest. Bodies and hearts are attached to these signboard faces; wit of the true spontaneous sort bubbles from their lips. He stood, of course, at the very point where comedy can flourish, as remote from the tragic violence of the Elizabethans as from the minute maze of modern psychology. The "humours" of the Elizabethan stage had fined themselves into characters. Convention and conviction and an unquestioned standard of values seem to support the large, airy world of his invention. Nothing could be more amusing than *She Stoops to Conquer*—one might even go so far as to say that amusement of so pure a quality will never come our way again. It demands too rare a combination of conditions. Nothing is too far fetched or fantastical to dry up the life blood in the characters themselves; we taste the double pleasure of a comic situation in which living people are the actors. It may be true that the amusement is not of the highest order. We have not gained a deeper understanding of human oddity and frailty when we have laughed to tears over the predicament of a good lady who has been driven round her house for two hours in the darkness. To mistake a private house for an inn is not a disaster that reveals the hidden depths or the highest dignity of human nature. But these are questions that fade out in the enjoyment of reading—an enjoyment which is much more composite than the simple word amusement can cover. When a thing is perfect of its kind we cannot stop, under the spell, to pick our flower to pieces. There is a unity about it which forbids us to dismember it.

Yet even so, in the midst of this harmony and completeness we hear now and again another note. "But they are dead, and their sorrows are over." "Life at its greatest and best is but a froward child, that must be humoured and coaxed a little till it falls asleep, and then all the care is over." "No sounds were heard but of the shrilling cock, and the deep-mouthed watch-dog at hollow distance." A poet seems hidden on the other side of the page anxious to concentrate its good-humoured urbanity into a phrase or two of deeper meaning. And Goldsmith was a true poet, even though he could not afford to entertain the muse for long. (pp. 9-11)

Virginia Woolf, "Oliver Goldsmith," in her *"The Captain's Death Bed" and Other Essays,* Harcourt Brace Jovanovich, Inc., 1950, pp. 3-14.

GEORGE ORWELL
(essay date 1944)

[Orwell, an English novelist and essayist, wrote one of the best-known novels of the twentieth century: *1984* (1949). In the following excerpt from a 1944 essay, he discusses the social and political views expressed in *The Vicar of Wakefield*, commending especially Goldsmith's meticulously constructed plot and lucid prose.]

The Vicar of Wakefield . . . is essentially a period piece, and its charm is about equalled by its absurdity. It is impossible to be moved by its story, which has none of the psychological realism that can be found in some eighteenth-century novels—for instance, *Amelia*. Its characters are sticks and its plot is somewhat less probable than those of the serial stories in *Peg's Paper*. But it remains extremely readable, and it has never been quite out of print in the 177 years since its first appearance. Like a Japanese woodcut, it is something perfectly executed after its own fashion, and at this date there is an historical interest in the remoteness of the standards of conduct which it is trying to uphold.

The Vicar of Wakefield is intended as a "moral tale", a sermon in fiction form. Its theme is the familiar one, preached without much success by hundreds of writers from Horace to Thackeray, of the vanity of worldly ambitions and the pleasures of the simple life. Its hero, Dr Primrose (he tells his own story in the first person), is a clergyman in what used to be called "easy circumstances", who temporarily loses his fortune and has to remove to another parish, where he supports himself by farming his own land. Here a whole series of disasters fall upon the family, traceable in every case to their having ambitions "above their station" and trying to associate with the nobility instead of with the neighbouring farmers. The eldest daughter is seduced by a heartless rascal, the farm-house is burnt to the ground, the eldest son is arrested for manslaughter, Primrose himself is thrown into a debtors' prison, and various other calamities happen. In the end, of course, everything is put right in an outrageously improbable way, one detail after another clicking into place like the teeth of a zip-fastener. Primrose's fortune is restored, the seemingly seduced daughter turns out to be an "honest woman" after all, the suitor of the second daughter, who has been posing as a poor man in order to try her affections, is discovered to be a wealthy nobleman, and so on and so forth. Virtue is rewarded and vice punished with relentless thoroughness. But the confusion in Goldsmith's mind between simple goodness and financial prudence gives the book, at this date, a strange moral atmosphere.

The main incidents are the various marriages, and the cold-blooded eighteenth-century attitude towards marriage is indicated on the first page when Dr Primrose remarks (Goldsmith probably does not intend this ironically): "I had scarcely taken orders a year, before I began to think seriously of matrimony, and chose my wife, as she did her wedding gown, not for a fine glossy surface, but such qualities as would wear well." But quite apart from this notion of choosing a wife as one might choose a length of cloth, there is the fact that getting married is inextricably mixed up with the idea of making a good financial bargain. A thumping dowry or a secure settlement is the first consideration, and the most passionate love match is promptly called off if the expected cash is not forthcoming. But together with this mercenary outlook there goes a superstitious regard for the sanctity of marriage which makes the most dramatic episode in the book ridiculous and even slightly disgusting.

Olivia is seduced by a Mr Thornhill, a wealthy young squire who has dazzled the Primrose family with his fashionable clothes and London manners. He is represented as a complete scoundrel, the "betrayer", as it was called, of innumerable women, and with every possible vice, even including physical cowardice. To entrap Olivia he uses the favourite eighteenth-century device of a false marriage. A marriage license is forged, somebody impersonates a priest, and the girl can then be "ruined" under the delusion that she is married. . . . Having been deceived in this manner, Olivia is now finished for life. She herself is made to express the current outlook by singing the justly famous lyric which Goldsmith throws into the tale:

> When lovely woman stoops to folly,
> And finds too late that men betray,
> What charm can soothe her melancholy?
> What art can wash her guilt away?
> The only art her guilt to cover,
> To hide her shame from every eye,

> To give repentance to her lover,
> And wring his bosom, is—to die.

Olivia indeed ought to die, and does actually begin to die—of sheer grief, after the manner of novel heroines. But here comes the *dénouement,* the great stroke of fortune that puts everything right. It turns out that Olivia was *not* seduced; she was legally married! Mr Thornhill has been in the habit of "marrying" women with a false priest and a false licence, but on this occasion a confederate of his, for purposes of his own, has deceived him by bringing a genuine licence and a real priest in holy orders. So the marriage was valid after all! And at this glorious news "a burst of pleasure seemed to fill the whole apartment. . . . Happiness was expanded upon every face, and even Olivia's cheeks seemed flushed with pleasure. To be thus restored to reputation and fortune at once was a rapture sufficient to stop the progress of decay and restore former health and vivacity."

When Olivia was believed to have "lost her virtue" she had lost all reason for living, but when it is discovered that she is tied for life to a worthless scoundrel all is well. Goldsmith does not make the ending quite so ridiculous as he might, for it is explained that Olivia continues to live apart from her husband. But she has the all-important wedding-ring, and a comfortable settlement into the bargain. Thornhill's rich uncle punishes him by depriving him of his fortune and bestowing part of it on Olivia. We are never indeed allowed quite to forget the connection between cash and virtue. Olivia sees herself "restored to reputation *and fortune at once*", while Thornhill sees "a gulf of infamy *and want*" opening before him.

Except for a scene or two in the debtors' prison and a few minor adventures at horse fairs and on muddy country roads, there is no realistic detail in *The Vicar of Wakefield.* The dialogue is quite exceptionally improbable. But the main theme—the hollowness of fashionable life and the superiority of country pleasures and family affection—is not so false as the absurd incidents which are meant to illustrate it make it appear. In inveighing against social ambition, against absentee landlords, against fine clothes, gambling, duelling, cosmetics and urban raffishness generally, Goldsmith is attacking a real tendency of his time, which Swift and Fielding had also denounced after their own fashion.

A phenomenon he is very much aware of is the growth of a new moneyed class with no sense of responsibility. Thanks to the expansion of foreign trade and wealth accumulated in the capital, the aristocracy were ceasing to be rustics. England was becoming more and more of an oligarchy, and the life of the countryside was broken up by the enclosure of the common lands and the magnetic pull of London. The peasants were proletarianised, the petty gentry were corrupted. Goldsmith himself described the process in the often-quoted lines from **"The Deserted Village"**:

Ill fares the land, to hastening ills a prey,
Where wealth accumulates and men decay;
Princes and lords may flourish or may fade,
A breath can make them, as a breath has made;
But a bold peasantry, their country's pride,
When once destroyed, can never be supplied.

Thornhill stands for the new kind of rich man, the Whig aristocrat; the Primroses, who make their own gooseberry wine and even in the days of their wealth have hardly been ten miles from home, stand for the old type of yeoman farmer or small landlord.

In praising country life, Goldsmith was probably praising something that he did not know much about. His descriptions of country scenes have an unreal, idyllic atmosphere, and the Primroses are not shown as doing much work on their farm. More often they are sitting under some shady tree, reciting ballads and listening to the blackbirds—pastimes that a practical farmer would seldom have time for. Nor do we hear much of Dr Primrose's ministrations as a clergyman: indeed, he only seems to remember at intervals that he is in orders. But the general moral of the book is clear enough, and thrust rather irrelevantly into one chapter there is a long political discourse against oligarchy and the accumulation of capital. Goldsmith's conclusion—no doubt it was a common Tory theory at the time—is that the only defence against oligarchy is a strong monarchy. Dr Primrose's son George, returning from travels in Europe, is made to come to the same conclusion: "I found that monarchy was the best government for the poor to live in, and commonwealths for the rich." Dictatorship is defended on the same grounds in our own day, and it is an instance of the way in which the same political ideas come up again and again in slightly different forms that George continues: "I found that riches in general were in every country another name for freedom; and that no man is so fond of liberty himself as not to be desirous of subjecting the will of some individuals in society to his own."

But though there is some serious social criticism buried under its artificialities, it is not there that the enduring charm of *The Vicar of Wakefield* lies. The charm is in its manner—in the story, which for all its absurdity is beautifully put together, in the simple and yet elegant language, in the poems that are thrown in here and there, and in certain minor incidents, such as the well-known story of Moses and the green spectacles. Most people who read at all have read this book once, and it repays a second reading. It is one of those books which you can enjoy in one way as a child and in another as an adult, and which do not seem any the worse because you are frequently inclined to laugh in the wrong places. (pp. 269-73)

George Orwell, "Review of 'The Vicar of Wakefield' by Oliver Goldsmith," in his *The Collected Essays, Journalism and Letters of George Orwell: As I Please, 1943-1945, Vol. III,* edited by Sonia Orwell and Ian Angus, Harcourt Brace Jovanovich, 1968, pp. 268-73.

RICARDO QUINTANA
(essay date 1967)

[Quintana has written extensively on the works of Jonathan Swift, as well as other studies of seventeenth- and eighteenth-century prose, poetry, and drama. In the following excerpt from his 1967 critical biography of Goldsmith, he provides an overview of Goldsmith's literary career.]

The earliest stage of Goldsmith's career as a writer defines itself readily enough. It begins with his first review in the April, 1757, number of the *Monthly Review* and includes the other reviews of that year (those in the five ensuing issues of [*Monthly Review*'s publisher-owner Ralph] Griffiths' periodical from May through September); a translation from the French entitled *The Memoirs of a Protestant,* brought out by Griffiths in February, 1758; the **"Memoirs of M. de Voltaire,"** finished by the close of 1758 though for some reason withheld until its appearance in monthly installments in the *Lady's Magazine* in the course of 1761; and *An Enquiry into the Present State of Polite Learning in Europe,* published by the Dodsley brothers on April 2, 1759. This body of work stands more or less by itself. . . . Though only the *Enquiry* can be said to be of intrinsic importance—it is really one of Goldsmith's major works, having an acknowledged place among the notable books of the period dealing with similar matters—both it and the earlier items in the *Monthly Review* deserve careful reading because of what they tell us about Goldsmith's intellectual equipment at the outset of his career. *The Memoirs of a Protestant* is of only secondary importance; the **"Memoirs of M. de Voltaire"** is significant mainly for showing how great Goldsmith's admiration for Voltaire was, and because it is the earliest and a rather crude example of the kind of popular biographical sketch or profile of which he was later on to become a master. (pp. 17-18)

[Goldsmith] was always planning ahead. . . . Even his frankly second-rate works—the later potboilers in the way of history, biography, and natural science—were not executed on the spur of the moment but were given a good deal of thought well in advance of composition. In the case of the major works the planning was of a much subtler and more imaginative kind, *The Traveller* growing organically out of the *Enquiry, The Vicar of Wakefield* out of the **"Chinese Let-**

ters," and the plays out of the comic presentations in the essays and fiction that preceded. (pp. 19-20)

The *Enquiry* deserves to rank as Goldsmith's first major work. It is not difficult to understand, however, why its true importance has not always been recognized even by his better-informed critics, for it is a youthful performance exhibiting in several places an only too obtrusive immaturity of thought and presentation and occasionally of style. Furthermore, the eighteenth-century intellectual context in which it stands can easily be overlooked if one regards the work less as an enquiry than as a protest—Goldsmith's protest, voiced on the eve of his anticipated departure for India, against the prevailing conditions of authorship in London. The note of protest is clear enough, but it is by no means dominant. The *Enquiry* is a highly intellectual work which orders and gives emphatic meaning to a whole group of ideas—ideas then in the air, ideas encountered by Goldsmith during his student days in Ireland and later in Edinburgh and on the continent, and more recently brought directly to his attention by the books he had had access to as one of Griffiths's reviewers. By the 1750s a whole new area of investigation had defined itself in European thought and was attracting some of the best minds of the age. Here questions of aesthetics, as in Burke's *Enquiry,* converged with broader questions concerning the history and sociological implications of what was then termed "taste." Goldsmith, when he came to write his own *Enquiry,* was well up in his subject. He was conversant with other men's views, and he went on to fashion a surprisingly comprehensive statement—one might almost call it a system—of his own. . . . It is Goldsmith's manifesto in defense of what is known to us today as Western civilization. Johnson's repeated statements to the effect that Goldsmith knew nothing, that he had no settled notions upon any subject, are here effectively refuted. That he did not again engage in systematic philosophic discourse—though, as we shall see, *The Citizen of the World* contains a most subtle statement but a curiously masked one—can be attributed to some extent to his reluctance to bore his readers with what might have seemed tiresome speculations to them, but chiefly to his ultimate concern as a poet—he seems always to have thought of himself as a poet, even in his role of prose writer—with supervening aspects of human experience grasped at the imaginative and emotional levels. (pp. 29-30)

If there are individual essays that are possibly better than anything in *The Citizen of the World,* the latter, taken as a whole, unquestionably deserves first place. In its way it is superb. There is no other essay serial quite like it. Here for the first time Goldsmith had the opportunity to give free rein to his inventive capacities, and the result is to be seen in the brilliant variety of the materials making up the work. The London scene

has rarely been portrayed with richer comic effect, though from time to time the comedy yields to harsher satire. There is the framed story, preposterous enough to please both the naive and the sophisticated reader. There are amusing characters—Lien Chi Altangi, the Chinese visitor in London and master of ceremonies; the Man in Black; the pawnbroker's widow; Beau Tibbs and his wife. There are commentaries, serious and otherwise, on literary topics. There are disquisitions on philosophic matters and problems of civilization. And running through it all, giving to it a peculiar kind of imaginative unity, is Goldsmith's irony—an irony of contrasting values, of multiple viewpoints. Irony is, in fact, central to this entire series of letters, and it is from an ironic point of view that Goldsmith is here examining those broad questions of civilization previously taken up in the *Enquiry.*

The *Public Ledger,* a daily newspaper owned by the publisher John Newbery, made its initial appearance on January 12, 1760. Goldsmith's first two **"Chinese Letters"** appeared in the issue of January 24. Newbery, we are told, desired to add a dash of humor to his paper and entered into an agreement with Goldsmith, who for £100 a year was to supply two **"Chinese Letters"** a week. Once the series got under way it proved to be highly popular and was accordingly featured by the editors. It ran through 1760 and well into 1761, coming to an end on August 14 of the latter year. There had been in all one hundred and nineteen of the **"Letters."** These, with the addition of four **"Letters"** not in the original series, were brought out in a collected edition of two volumes on May 1, 1762, under the title of *The Citizen of the World.* (pp. 63-4)

It was a genre—this of the pseudo-letter or series of letters purportedly containing an Oriental traveler's observations on European customs—which was now well-established. . . . Montesquieu's *Persian Letters* [was] the recognized masterpiece of this kind. . . . (p. 65)

Goldsmith must have entered upon his new journalistic venture in the highest of spirits. He was now a thoroughly practiced hand at the essay, adept in his touch and tonal command. The scheme he was committed to was something that had been taking shape in his imagination over a long period, gradually exciting his enthusiasm and bringing his invention into full play. And the public was ready for just such a comic diversion. In short, few literary projects were ever launched under more favorable auspices than these **"Chinese Letters"** commissioned by John Newbery.

The thing that might have deterred another writer proved no difficulty at all for Goldsmith. His Chinese who talked like an Englishman was not to be too palpably a fraud. He would, of course, not be Chinese—that was part of the joke. (pp. 66-7)

Portrait of Goldsmith by Joshua Reynolds.

It may be, as has sometimes been suggested, that the readers of the *Public Ledger* began by accepting the **"Chinese Letters"** as the genuine correspondence of a real Chinese visitor. If they did—though this is difficult to believe—they must have realized their error before very long, and they certainly took the deception with good grace, for they continued to read Goldsmith's column with zest. The fame of Lien Altangi, some of which was now rubbing off onto his creator, began to spread. The **"Letters"** were widely discussed; they were soon being reprinted in other publications, and parodies were appearing. They were regarded as a novelty, however, and by the time the collected edition appeared in 1762 public interest had begun to fall off. *The Citizen of the World* enjoyed no spectacular sale. (p. 68)

[No one] can miss the exhilarating comedy in Lien Chi Altangi's accounts of the strange and astonishing things he meets as he diligently pursues his travels about London, taking note of places and events, people, and such venerable institutions as English funerals and visitation dinners. Irony plays steadily over all these descriptions, but it is delicately controlled. Goldsmith makes sure that humor, not sharp wit, prevails, even when the role of Lien Chi is altered and he is turned into a downright satirist, taking aim at critics, sham doctors, booksellers, pretenders to knowledge, religious enthusiasts, the fear of mad dogs, and—how

strange coming from a Chinese—even chinoiserie as it flourishes among the more sophisticated of the English.

There are a few individual essays, exceptional in quality and able to stand more or less by themselves, which have found their way into most anthologies of eighteenth-century prose and for that reason are better known. One is **"A City Night-Piece"** (Letter CXVII), taken from the *Bee.* Another . . . is **"On the distresses of the poor, exemplified in the life of a private centinel"** (Letter CXIX), that had originally appeared in the *British Magazine.* The first is a descriptive piece, a mood piece we might call it, giving an image of the city as it was in Goldsmith's time, with an affective power like that experienced in our dreams. **"On the distresses of the poor"** is one of the memorable bits of sociological writing to appear in this period. How strongly developed Goldsmith's consciousness of social conditions and social problems was when he departed from Ireland it is impossible to say, but it is apparent that by the time of his arrival in London he was viewing European culture from a sociological point of view similar to that established by Voltaire and his fellows. He had a sense of the forces making for cultural differences and social change, and along with this a profound hatred of social injustices. . . . Goldsmith unquestionably articulated the awakening conscience of the average Englishman. But his vision was sharper and broader than many of his contemporaries. . . . **"On the distresses of the poor,"** with its account of the disabled soldier forced to beg at the town's end, warrants close reading. Swift used statistics with devastating irony in pieces like the *Modest Proposal* and the *Drapier's Letters.* Goldsmith chose to work in quite a different manner. There are no statistics, there is no irony. Instead, there is what we accept as a kind of realism, but as in the case of the **"City Night-Piece"** it is a realism made unforgettable by reason of a strongly affective quality. There is no sentimentalism here, but there *is* sentiment—emotionalism consciously aroused and controlled with an express purpose in view.

But it is the characters we are introduced to which are probably the best-known thing about the **"Letters"**: the Man in Black and his lady, the pawnbroker's widow; Mr. Fudge, the bookseller; shabby Beau Tibbs and his enduring wife. As Austin Dobson pointed out many years ago, Goldsmith was here disclosing for the first time his true gift for character delineation, in which respect he can be seen as the forerunner of Dickens, though there was no direct influence. It is, however, the Goldsmith legend which has really fixed the usual response to someone like the Man in Black. According to the legend the best things in Goldsmith's work come directly out of his own life and are for that reason so heartwarming. (pp. 69-71)

The **"Letters"** reflect Goldsmith's sound journalistic sense. A newspaper column of this sort, appearing regularly, is most successful when it proceeds in much the same fashion day after day but manages to be always different, providing as it were variety within a familiar, expected setting. Thus, though our friend Lien Chi Altangi is always, or almost always, with us, and we are in London most of the time, observing its life through his eyes, nothing is static. London affords an endless succession of new scenes, people of widely different appearances and behavior cross our line of vision, and the letters Lien Chi receives from abroad bring us news of strange events in exotic places.

Reasons of sound journalism, however, do not fully account for the variety of material and subjects, which is far greater than necessary. The scenes of every-day social life predominate, it is true, but how much else there is! Memorable events of the period are noted. . . . Satiric commentary sometimes supervenes. There are episodes involving characters like the Man in Black and Beau Tibbs. The framed story of Hingpo and Zelis is gradually unwound. We are given a number of short narrative pieces. The wanderer motif—Lien Chi, like others, has left home behind him—appears and then recedes. There is literary and theatrical criticism. It is only natural, too, that as a citizen of the world Lien Chi should from time to time enter into discussions with his friends about various aspects and problems of civilization. And so luxury is defended, democracy, oligarchy, and despotism are compared, the influence of climate and soil is investigated, beauty and utility are analyzed, and the question whether the arts and sciences are more useful or harmful to mankind is taken up. Goldsmith's imaginative resourcefulness in finding themes and supporting material is great.

If the entire series of "**Letters**" is vitalized by this rich diversity, it is also in a manner unified, for we see that the ultimate effect is something which has been carefully gauged. But there is another factor which also serves—perhaps more obviously—to give a shape to the work as a whole. This is the masterly control of tone. With Goldsmith tone is not everything, to be sure, but it is probably the most important single constituent in his art. No prose writer of the century commanded a wider register of tonal values—indeed, the variations of voice are in his case sometimes so extreme as to result in wholly different styles of prose. (pp. 72-3)

Irony may be said to be the key element in the "**Letters,**" constituting a distinctive environment enfolding the entire series. It is irony, however, of more than one sort, irony which operates at different levels. At its simplest and most apparent it is the comic doubleness which we are kept constantly aware of throughout Lien Chi's adventures—the comic doubleness which results when what is familiar is presented from a surprising angle of perception. London has two appearances, our London and Lien Chi's. And who is to say which is the right one? (p. 75)

With the appearance of *The Traveller* late in 1764 Goldsmith all at once came into his own as a poet. The critics were for the most part unhesitating in their praise. . . . (p. 116)

Goldsmith seems always to have thought of himself as a poet whether he was writing verse or prose, but to his readers he had hitherto been a prose man. That he was likewise a poet of unmistakable stature, came as a gratifying surprise. . . . *The Deserted Village,* coming six years later, left no room for doubt in the minds of his contemporaries as to his preeminence among the poets of the time. And on the strength of the two long poems and *Retaliation,* the latter published fifteen days after his death, we can still almost agree. Today Johnson the poet seems nearly as great, and Christopher Smart, who never enjoyed much of a reputation among the Georgians, probably greater. But we fully recognize the validity of Goldsmith's poetry, and this despite the fact that *The Traveller* and *The Deserted Village* represent modes of poetic expression which are no longer ours.

It is to be borne in mind, however, that Goldsmith is not solely a poet of three poems. By the end of 1764, when *The Traveller* came out, a number of his poems had already appeared in print—in the *Enquiry,* the *Bee, The Citizen of the World,* and several periodicals—and the three poems in *The Vicar of Wakefield,* of which one is the imperishable song "**When lovely woman stoops to folly,**" had presumably been written by this time. Several verse compositions for the theater—a prologue, epilogues, and a song—appeared before his death. On the other hand, many of his short poems and some of his longer ones were not published during his lifetime. Knowing as we now do the exact extent of his work in the medium of verse, we do not associate him exclusively with *The Traveller, The Deserted Village,* and *Retaliation,* as in the absence of any collected edition his contemporaries naturally did during his lifetime. His scope in poetry was somewhat broader than was then generally recognized. But even so, after taking into account all the verse which has now been established as his, we return to those pieces on which his reputation as a poet once rested. Their superiority to everything else is unquestionable. (pp. 116-17)

Goldsmith was not a prolific poet. His entire verse production . . . consists of no more than thirty-five items, many of which are short compositions, some of them only trifles. There are the pieces—mostly epilogues—written for the theater. The majority of the shorter poems belong to the period of the prose essays and were placed by Goldsmith in the *Enquiry,* the *Bee* and subsequent essays, and *The Citizen of the World. Edwin and Angelina,* printed separately and also given in *The Vicar of Wakefield,* is Goldsmith's only literary ballad. Two of the longer compositions are unhappily distinguished by what to us is their patent inferiority: the oratorio entitled *The Captivity,* and the *Threnodia Augustalis.* A readily recognizable group comprises four of the happiest things he ever wrote. These are all social poems, varying in idiom and pace from the colloquialism of the two verse letters sent to Sir George Baker and Mrs. Bunbury, from the amusing comedies of *The Haunch of Venison, a Poetical Epistle to Lord Clare,* to the memorable wit of *Retaliation.* Finally, in a class by themselves, are the two great poems, *The Traveller* and *The Deserted Village.* (p. 126)

For eighteenth-century readers *The Traveller* combined something surprisingly new and something pleasingly familiar, and this fact doubtless explains much of the enthusiasm with which it was greeted. What was new was the voice, the distinctive manner. On the other hand it was a prospect poem, and this kind or type was well established, going back to *Cooper's Hill* in the previous century. . . . *The Traveller* is prospect poetry literally and figuratively; it is a series of verse *characters,* by means of which the different national cultures of the west are compared; it is a patriotic poem, though the patriotism is of a different order from the uncritical nationalism of Addison's [*Letter from Italy to Lord Halifax*]; it is an estimate of contemporary conditions, condemning much but finding consolation in the thought that nature and reason afford mankind a moral mean between deplorable extremities.

The letter of dedication, though perhaps an afterthought, is to be seen as an integral part of the composition, a kind of overture announcing the motifs which are to appear in the poem. The dedication to a brother, an obscure clergyman, and not to some distinguished patron, was in itself an act of defiance and suggestive of one of the central themes of the poem, i.e., the overwhelming importance of the middle ranks of society. The personal terms of the letter serve to establish the poem itself as direct personal expression: the "I" who is speaking in the verses is, we naturally assume, the writer who addresses his brother, and in consequence the entire piece is interiorized, the prospects and the meditations to which they give rise all taking on a subjective quality. The resentment of the new fashions in poetry—blank verse, Pindaric odes, and partisan satire—betoken a wider resentment extending to aspects of national life. The last paragraph is a direct statement of the theme that gives the poem its structure: there are contrasts between different societies; every society, examined by itself, reveals contrasting features; wherever antithetical extremes exist, there is also a point of natural equilibrium.

The poem is carefully proportioned. The first section of 104 lines—the Traveller far from home; the Alpine prospect; his emotional and intellectual reactions—is balanced by the closing section—England

considered—of 122 lines. The mid-section, with its surveys of Italy, Switzerland, France, and Holland, is about twice as long, having 212 lines. It is a discursive poem, presenting a series of ideas developing out of one another in an orderly, if not always strictly logical, fashion. Readers of the time responded eagerly to this kind of poetry. And for them it *was* poetry. It was not necessary, they said, that all the ideas be acceptable so long as the statement given them was effective. It was art enhanced by being intellectualized, and though Goldsmith as we know was fully, passionately committed to the social and political views enunciated in both *The Traveller* and *The Deserted Village,* he was ready to acknowledge that the statements he was making acquired, from the fact that they were made in terms of poetry, an aesthetic value. But he did not sense the intellectual and artistic aspects as a bifurcation. The two were really one, and we can see in the symmetrical form of *The Traveller* an outward, artistic expression of the poem's intellectuality.

But it is in more subtle ways that *The Traveller* achieves a harmony of art and ideational statement. The language of the poem is constantly shifting between a rather formal style and a simple idiom of direct, personal utterance. The former is the language traditional to neoclassical ethic poetry; it generalizes, it makes discreet use of poetic diction and gradus epithets, and the syntax encouraged by the couplet form orders through parallelism, antithesis, and balance the statements being made. It is public speech, rhetorically directed. The contrasting language is singularly plain and limpid, with nothing of the ceremonial about it; it conveys the poet's emotions and invites us to share in them. On the one hand, through intellectual discourse, the apprehension of moral contrasts. On the other, the deep emotional response to the ambiguities in all human experience.

In the way that *The Traveller* may be described as a kind of prospect poem, *The Deserted Village* may be said to be a kind of pastoral. It conforms, at least, to that definition of a pastoral which Johnson had given in the *Rambler* (No. 37): "a poem in which any action or passion is represented by its effects upon a country life." (pp. 129-32)

To Goldsmith, the depopulation of modern villages as a result of enclosure had long been a matter of deep concern. He had taken up the question in his essay **"The Revolution in Low Life."** . . . And it could not have been long afterward that he was fashioning for his *Traveller* that prospect of England which discloses, as counterpoise to Freedom's blessings, the opulence which leads stern depopulation in her train. . . . (p. 133)

In *The Traveller* Goldsmith had spoken out loud and clear against the growing materialism of the time, denouncing the upper-middle class—the rich men who ruled the laws which ground the poor—in the manner of some public-spirited citizen outraged to see one class endangering the welfare of the whole nation. Such a manner is by no means entirely absent from *The Deserted Village,* though it is easy to overlook those passages in which the style is that of public speech. As a matter of fact, were we to think of the entire poem as in effect an oration against the injustice of enclosure we should not be far out. The surprising fact is that Goldsmith's historical pastoral is rhetorical throughout. That is, it has been devised with great artfulness to win our attention and thereafter to appeal both to our reason and emotions. It is not a *cri de coeur* in the way that so many have assumed it to be. In certain passages we have entirely impersonal public speech, and at these points the couplets become pointed, assertive. The dominant tone is, of course, something quite different, for the greater part of the poem is personal in accent and highly emotional. But here the poet's purpose is not to find self-expression but rather, in the manner and according to the principles of rhetoric, to sway his audience. The poet's experience becomes ours; his feelings, his passions are communicated to us; it is we who become personally engaged. Much of *The Deserted Village* is argument by pathos. Comedy has been dismissed. This is more in the nature of denunciatory satire. . . . (pp. 135-36)

Sentimentalism is under attack in both of his plays, though in *The Good Natur'd Man,* as we shall see, a highly sophisticated form of irony is employed, for at least part of the time the satire is delivered in terms of characters, situations, and spoken sentiments which are for all the world like those of the sentimental drama which is being ridiculed. The two comedies turn on quite traditional plots, involving, in each case, two pairs of lovers who find happiness when the complications keeping them apart are at length resolved. There are humorous characters in both, and both are distinguished by a naturalism of atmosphere and voice which can easily be mistaken for the typical naturalism which then prevailed on the comic stage. It is to be observed, however, that in one very important respect Goldsmith kept clear of standard practice: he never allowed the comic distance between characters and audience to disappear.

But despite this element of conformity Goldsmith's playwriting was the culminating phase of his development as a comic writer. The anti-benevolence theme, which underlies all of *The Good Natur'd Man,* had been present in his mind from the first, as the early essays show. There had been humorous characters of rare appeal in *The Citizen of the World* and the *Vicar.* He had used the romantic plot, with its delightful absurdities, more than once. His comic vision and his ironic technique had, however, been shifting over the years. Scenic comedy, based upon ironic differences in

points of view, had begun in *The Citizen of the World* to evolve into those ironies of opinion which make us aware of the natural forces acting as mediating influences. In *The Vicar,* comedy of the domestic scene and the portrait of the Vicar himself with his amusing shortcomings and his essential nobility had led, by way of the ambiguities of the romantic plot, to the voyage theme—our passage from home into the world, our ultimate enlightenment, and the things then recognized. In taking up dramatic writing Goldsmith had no intention of merely manipulating the shallow formulas of the then-popular comedy. Playwriting was a challenge to one who, though now a seasoned literary workman, had never before used the dramatic form. He was forced to shift his stance, to find new terms for the comic interpretation of experience. Fortunately, drama was by its very nature a medium which enabled him to organize his creative energies more tellingly than had any of the forms of writing he had been using in the past. New devices, new ironies, new insights—these are the important things about *The Good Natur'd Man* and *She Stoops to Conquer.* Here Georgian comedy acquired a depth to be found nowhere else, save—some might insist—in the best of Sheridan. (pp. 143-44)

A wide diversity of opinion marks the criticism which has appeared since the eighteenth century. Many commentators have found *The Good Natur'd Man* a badly constructed play without any dramatically controlling center, its only significance the fact that the author of *She Stoops to Conquer* wrote it. A few have pronounced it admirable despite faulty stagecraft. A whole line of critics have said that despite Goldsmith's declared views it must really be considered a sentimental comedy. Only in the course of the last thirty years or so has there emerged an entirely different interpretation of the play. Today, few who read it against its full Georgian background are likely to miss its satiric intent and its characteristic Goldsmithian irony. It is not a great play—dramatically it is much too ingenious, and the plot is overly complicated—but it is true comedy and a fitting prelude to *She Stoops to Conquer.* (p. 147)

The Good Natur'd Man had taught him most of the things he needed to learn about dramatic craftsmanship. In his second comedy he was able to maneuver with ease and assurance, and this freedom gave him greater comic scope. *She Stoops to Conquer* is a triumph of effective dramatic art. Its construction, its voice are flawless, and underneath the almost farcical exterior there is deep, quiet wisdom. His unexpected death only a year later put a lamentably untimely end to his already brilliant career as a playwright. Had he lived somewhat longer it is reasonable to suppose that he would have lifted Georgian comedy to a still higher level, comparable perhaps to what is attained in the novels of Jane Austen. (p. 152)

Though the full comic import of *She Stoops to Conquer* does not lie entirely at the surface, there is nothing in it, as there is in *The Good Natur'd Man,* to perplex or mislead an audience. One cannot properly enjoy the earlier play unless one sees through it and grasps the irony which is governing much of it. In this sense there is nothing in *She Stoops to Conquer* to be seen through. If it means more than we are immediately aware of, its fuller meanings are not contradictory to the readily apparent ones but are rather subtilizations of the obvious. The farcical elements of the play—all the bustle, the deceptions, the errors, the successive *contretemps*—are the outward evidences of that vital energy which great comedy seeks to release in us. The amusing ironies which arise when the characters act in ignorance of some or all of the immediate circumstances and are suddenly enlightened—these betoken the ironies which we ourselves experience in the course of discovering who and what we truly are.

Again Goldsmith was content to use the going formulas, and as a result *She Stoops to Conquer* is completely Georgian. There is no verbal wit here; the conversation is easy and natural, or seems to be. Tone and setting are natural. The plot is a typical one, involving the affairs of two youthful couples. There are several humor characters: Mr. and Mrs. Hardcastle, Young Marlow, and perhaps Tony Lumpkin. Sentimentalism is effectively but not too obtrusively ridiculed in the alehouse scene, in the "sober sentimental interview" between Kate and Young Marlow in the second act, and best of all in those scenes which find Marlow, as a result of his as-yet split personality, suffering genteel embarrassment in the presence of women who are ladies and then displaying self-assured aggressiveness toward those who are only barmaids. The action, turning largely on deceptions and errors, was complicated enough to satisfy theatergoers of the period, who were used to this sort of thing. Mrs. Hardcastle practices several deceits, Constance Neville must pretend affection for Tony Lumpkin, and Hastings is forced to conceal the fact that he is Constance's suitor. The two central deceptions, which together serve as the backbone of the comedy, are Tony's misrepresentation of the Hardcastle house as an inn, and Kate's unmasked masquerade as a barmaid. All of these lead to ironic situations that are sometimes broadly farcical, sometimes—when human nature is displayed rather than accidental confusions—genuinely comic.

Yet all the contrivances of the plot and the artificialities by which the story is carried along do not spoil the naturalism of this, one of the few great comedies of the later eighteenth-century theater. The naturalism of which we speak occurs at different levels. The naturalism of the language has been mentioned. The Hardcastle home, its grounds, the surrounding countryside, and the people living in the neighborhood are present in a most realistic way. There is psychological naturalism, and although we do not identify ourselves with the characters on the stage—as we do, or are supposed to do in sentimental comedy—they are in no way strangers to us. Always, Goldsmith's naturalism is an expression in one way or another of that belief which underlies his comic intuition. For him, Nature is the central force. It is both accuser and healer. It brings home to us the follies we commit in our blindness; and in enlightening us, in rectifying our vision, it restores within us our life-sustaining energies. *She Stoops to Conquer* proceeds through much of the action as a comedy of deceptions. It ends as a comedy of discovery. Marlow discovers his own identity, which lies between two unnatural extremes, and simultaneously he recognizes the true Kate, who is health and sanity personified. (pp. 156-58)

Ricardo Quintana, in his *Oliver Goldsmith: A Georgian Study,* The Macmillan Company, 1967, 213 p.

SOURCES FOR FURTHER STUDY

Ginger, John. *The Notable Man: The Life and Times of Oliver Goldsmith.* London: Hamish Hamilton, 1977, 408 p.

Biography that uses many contemporary sources, including letters, periodicals, and biographies, to present Goldsmith's milieu and his contemporaries' opinions of him.

Hopkins, Robert H. *The True Genius of Oliver Goldsmith.* Baltimore: Johns Hopkins Press, 1969, 241 p.

Controversial critical examination treating all of Goldsmith's major works as satires.

Kirk, Clara M. *Oliver Goldsmith.* New York: Twayne, 1967, 202 p.

Biographical and critical overview of Goldsmith's life and career, focusing on the major works.

Wardle, Ralph. *Oliver Goldsmith.* Lawrence: University of Kansas Press, 1957, 330 p.

Comprehensive biography, utilizing many contemporary sources.

Wibberley, Leonard. *The Good-Natured Man: A Portrait of Oliver Goldsmith.* New York: William Morrow, 1979, 255 p.

Sympathetic biography based on contemporary accounts of Goldsmith's life.

Woods, Samuel H., Jr. *Oliver Goldsmith: A Reference Guide.* Boston: G. K. Hall, 1982, 208 p.

Chronologically arranged annotated bibliography of Goldsmith criticism from 1759 through 1978.

Maxim Gorky

1868-1936

(Also transliterated as Maksim; also Gorki, Gorkii, and Gor'ky; pseudonym of Aleksei Maksimovich Peshkov; also transliterated as Alexey, Alexei, and Aleksey; also Maximovich and Mikhaylovich; also Pyeshkov) Russian novelist, dramatist, short story writer, essayist, autobiographer, diarist, and poet.

INTRODUCTION

Gorky is recognized as one of the earliest and foremost exponents of socialist realism in literature. His brutal yet romantic portraits of Russian life and his sympathetic depictions of the working class had an inspirational effect on the oppressed people of his native land. From 1910 until his death, Gorky was considered Russia's greatest living writer. Gorky the tramp, the rebel, is as much a legend as the strong, individual characters presented in his stories. His hero was a new type in the history of Russian literature—a figure drawn from the masses of a growing industrialized society; his most famous novel, *Mat'* (1907; *Mother*), was the first in that country to portray the factory worker as a force destined to overthrow the existing order.

Gorky was orphaned at the age of ten and raised by his maternal grandparents. He was often treated harshly by his grandfather, and it was from his grandmother that Gorky received what little kindness he experienced as a child. During his thirteenth year, Gorky ran away from Nizhniy Novgorod, the city of his birth (now called Gorky), and lived a precarious existence as a tramp and vagrant, wandering from one job to another. Frequently beaten by his employers, nearly always hungry and ill-clothed, Gorky came to know the seamy side of Russian life as few writers before him. At the age of nineteen, he attempted suicide by shooting himself in the chest. The event became a turning point in Gorky's life; his outlook changed from one of despair to one of hope. Within a few years he began publishing stories in the provincial press. Written under the pseudonym Maxim Gorky (Maxim the Bitter), these stories stressed the strength and individualism of the Russian peasant. When they were collected and published in *Ocherki i rasskazy*, (1898-99), Gorky gained recognition throughout Russia. His second volume of stories,

Rasskazy (1900-10), along with the production of his controversial play *Na dne* (1902; *The Lower Depths*), assured his success and brought him acclaim in western Europe and the United States. Gorky's fame in the West coincided with increasing suspicion from the Russian authorities, who considered the author a source of the country's growing political unrest. In 1901 he was briefly jailed for publishing the revolutionary poem "Pesnya o burevestnike" ("Song of the Stormy Petrel") in a Marxist review. Three years later, he established the Znanie publishing firm to provide a forum for socially conscious writers. The friendship and advice of Nikolai Lenin strengthened Gorky's growing political radicalism. He was very active during the revolution of 1905, and after its failure he was forced to flee abroad. He was allowed to return home in 1913, and again he resumed his revolutionary activities. During the 1917 Revolution and the ensuing years of political chaos, Gorky saved the lives of several intellectuals by interceding on their behalf with the communist regime. He left Russia one last time and settled on the island of Capri for health reasons. In 1928 he returned to a national celebration of his literary, cultural, and moral contributions to the socialist cause, which took place on his sixtieth birthday. His death several years later, allegedly by poisoning, is still enveloped in mystery.

Gorky's work can be divided into three distinct groups. The first comprises his short stories, which many critics consider superior to his novels. In a highly romantic manner, these stories portray the subjugation of Russian peasants and vagrants. Many of these tales, such as "Makar Chudra" and "Chelkash," are based on actual peasant legends and allegories. In them Gorky championed the wisdom and self-reliance of his vagabonds over the brutality of the decadent bourgeoisie. One of the most accomplished of these stories is "Dvádtssat' shest' i odná" ("Twenty-Six Men and a Girl"), a tale in which Gorky described the sweatshop conditions in a provincial bakery. The second group consists of Gorky's autobiographical works, notably the trilogy *Detstvo* (1928; *My Childhood*), *V liudiakh* (1916; *In the World*), and *Moi universitety* (1923; *My Universities*), and his reminiscences of Tolstoy, *Vospominaniya o Lve Nikolaieviche Tolstom'* (1919; *Reminiscences of Leo Nicolayevitch Tolstoi*). The trilogy is considered one of the finest autobiographies in the Russian language. The work reveals Gorky as an acute observer of detail with a particular talent for describing people. The third group, by far the largest, consists of a number of novels and plays which are not as artistically successful as his short stories and autobiography. Gorky's first novel, *Foma Gordeyev* (1900; *Foma Gordeiev*), illustrates his characteristic admiration for the hard-working, honest individual. He contrasts the rising capitalist Ignat Gordeyev with his feeble, intellectual son Foma, a "seeker after the meaning of life," as are many of Gorky's other characters. The novel was the first of many in which the author portrayed the rise of Russian Capitalism. Of all Gorky's novels, *Mother* is perhaps the least artistic, though it is interesting from a historical perspective as his only long work devoted to the Bolshevik movement. Among the twelve plays Gorky wrote between 1901 and 1913, only one, *The Lower Depths,* deals with the "dregs of society." Though the play has most of the structural faults of his other dramas, primarily one-dimensional characters and a didactic tone, it is still regarded as one of the greatest proletarian dramas of the twentieth century. Gorky's other plays, including *Meshchane* (1902; *The Smug Citizens*), *Varvary* (1906; *The Barbarians*), and *Yegor Bulychyov i drugiye* (1932; *Yegor Bulichov and Others*), focus either on the intelligentsia or on the struggle between capitalist and socialist forces in pre-Soviet Russia.

Despite his success and importance as a socialist writer, most modern critics agree that Gorky deserves little of the idolatrous attention that he has received. They argue that his work suffers from an overly dramatic quality, a coarse, careless style, and an externally imposed structure which results in fiction motivated by ideology rather than by artistry. Many critics suggest that his failure to develop his characters and his tendency to lapse into irrelevant discussions about the meaning of life greatly damage the seriousness of his subjects. However, it is in his short stories and, especially, in his autobiography that Gorky fully realized his artistic powers. In these works he managed to curb his ideology and focus on those talents for which he has been consistently lauded: realistic description and the ability to portray the brutality of his environment. It is for these that Gorky has been called by Stefan Zweig, one of "the few genuine marvels of our present world."

While critical regard for his work fluctuates, Gorky himself has passed into history not only as a remarkable personality, but also as the precursor of socialist realism and, therefore, an important stimulus in twentieth-century Russian literature. With Vladimir Mayakovsky and Aleksandr Blok, he was one of the few Russian writers who played an equally important part in his country both before and after the Bolshevik Revolution. Although Gorky was an intellectual, and thus distanced from the common people who overthrew the Czarists and Mensheviks, he used his influence and talent after October 1917 to prevent the revolution from consuming itself in a savage blood-frenzy. As Janko Lavrin has noted, "It was here that his personality and his work served as a bridge between the creative values of the old intelligentsia culture and the culture of the risen masses, anxious to build up a new world."

(For further information about Gorky's life and works, see *Contemporary Authors,* Vol. 105 and *Twentieth-Century Literary Criticism,* Vol. 8.)

CRITICAL COMMENTARY

ANTON TCHEKHOV
(letter date 1898)

[Tchekhov (also transliterated "Chekhov") is the most significant Russian author of the literary generation that succeeded Leo Tolstoy and Fyodor Dostoevsky. In the following excerpt from a letter he wrote to Gorky on 3 December 1898, he praises Gorky as an important new talent while objecting to his unrestrained writing style.]

You ask what my opinion is about your stories. My opinion? Yours is an unmistakable talent, and a real, great talent. For instance, in your story **"In the Steppe"** it is expressed with extraordinary power, and I was even seized with envy that it was not I who wrote it. You are an artist, a wise man; you feel superbly, you are plastic; that is, when you describe a thing you see it and touch it with your hands. That is real art. There you have my opinion, and I am very glad to be able to express it to you. I repeat, I am very glad, and if we came to know each other and talk for an hour or two you would be convinced how highly I value you, and what hopes I build on your talent.

Shall I speak now of defects? But that is not so easy. To speak of the defects of a talent is like speaking of the defects of a great tree growing in the orchard; the chief consideration is not the tree itself, but the taste of the man who is looking at the tree. Is not that so?

I shall begin by saying that, in my opinion, you do not use sufficient restraint. You are like a spectator in the theatre who expresses his rapture so unreservedly that he prevents both himself and others from listening. Particularly is this lack of restraint felt in the descriptions of Nature with which you interrupt your dialogues; when one reads those descriptions one wishes they were more compact, shorter, put, say, into two or three lines. The frequent mention of tenderness, whispering, velvetiness, and so on, gives to these descriptions a certain character of rhetoric and monotony—and they chill the reader, almost tire him. Lack of restraint is felt also in the descriptions of women (**"Malva," "On the Rafts"**) and in the love scenes. It is not vigour, nor breadth of touch, but plain unreserve. Then there is a frequent use of words unsuitable in stories of your type. "Accompaniment," "disc," "harmony"—such words mar. You talk often about waves. In your descriptions of educated people there is a feeling of strain, and, as it were, wariness; that is not because you have not sufficiently observed educated people;

you know them, but you do not know precisely from what side to approach them. (pp. 261-62)

Anton Tchekhov, in a letter to Maxim Gorki on December 3, 1898, in *The Life and Letters of Anton Tchekhov,* edited and translated by S. S. Koteliansky and Philip Tomlinson, George H. Doran Company, 1925, pp. 261-62.

ANTON TCHEKHOV
(letter date 1899)

[In the following excerpt from a letter written to Gorky on 3 January 1899, Tchekhov offers further criticism concerning Gorky's prose style.]

Apparently you haven't quite understood me. I did not write to you of the crudeness but of the unfitness of foreign, not genuinely Russian, or rarely used words. With other writers such words as, for instance, "fatalistically" pass unnoticed, but your things are musical, harmonious, so that any crude little touch screams at the top of its voice. Of course, this is a matter of taste, and perhaps this is a sign of excessive irritability in me, or of the conservatism of a man who long ago adopted definite habits. In descriptions I can put up with "collegiate councillor" and "captain of the second rank," but "flirt" and "champion" (when they are used in descriptions) arouse my disgust.

Are you a self-taught man? In your stories you are a complete artist, and a cultured one in the truest sense. Least of all is crudeness characteristic of you; are are wise, and your feelings are subtle and elegant. Your best things are **"In the Steppe"** and **"On the Rafts"**—did I write to you about that? These are superb things, models; one sees in them an artist who has passed through a very good school. I do not think I am mistaken. The only defect is lack of restraint, lack of grace. When a man spends the fewest number of movements on a certain definite action, that is grace. In your expenditure there is felt excess.

The descriptions of nature are artistic; you are a real landscape painter. But the frequent personification (anthropomorphism)—the sea breathes, the sky gazes, the steppe caresses, Nature whispers, speaks, mourns, and so on—such personifications make the descriptions somewhat monotonous, at times sugary, at times

Principal Works

Ocherki i rasskazy. 3 vols. (short stories) 1898-99

Foma Gordeyev (novel) 1900
  [Foma Gordeiev, 1901]

Rasskazy. 9 vols. (short stories) 1900-10

Orlóff and His Wife (short stories) 1901

Meshchane (drama) 1902
  [The Smug Citizens, 1906; also published as The Petty
  Bourgeois, 1972]

Na dne (drama) 1902
  [The Lower Depths, 1912]

Dachniki (drama) 1904
  [Summer Folk, 1905]

Creatures that Once Were Men (short stories) 1905

Varvary (drama) 1906
  [The Barbarians published in Seven Plays of Maxim
  Gorky, 1945]

Mat' (novel) 1907
  [Mother, 1907]

Ispoved (novel) 1908
  [A Confession, 1910]

Chelkash, and Other Stories (short stories) 1915

V liudiakh (autobiography) 1916
  *[In the World, 1917; also published as My Apprentice-
  ship, 1952]

Vospominaniya o Lve Nikolaieviche Tolstom' (memoirs)
  1919
  [Reminiscences of Leo Nicolayevitch Tolstoi, 1920]

Moi universitety (autobiography) 1923
  *[My University Days, 1923; also published as My Uni-
  versities, 1952]

Zametki iz dnevnika. Vospominaniya (diary) 1924
  [Fragments from My Diary, 1924]

Delo Artamonovykh (novel) 1925
  [The Artamonov Business, 1948]

Zhizn' Klima Samgina. 4 vols. (novel) 1927-36
  [Published in four volumes: Bystander, 1930; The Mag-
  net, 1931; Other Fires, 1933; The Specter, 1938]

Detstvo (autobiography) 1928
  *[My Childhood, 1915]

Dvádtsat' shest' i odná (short stories) 1928
  [Twenty-Six Men and a Girl, 1902]

Sobranie sochinenii. 4 vols. (short stories, novels, dramas,
  essays, and poems) 1928-30

Yegor Bulychyov i drugiye (drama) 1932
  [Yegor Bulichov and Others published in The Last Plays
  of Maxim Gorki, 1937]

Zhizn' Matveya Kozhemyakina (novel) 1933

The Last Plays of Maxim Gorky (dramas) 1937

Seven Plays of Maxim Gorky (dramas) 1945

Orphan Paul (novel) 1946

Reminiscences (autobiography) 1946

*These works were published as Autobiography of Maxim
  Gorky in 1949.

vague. Colour and expressiveness in descriptions of Nature are attained only by simplicity, by such simple phrases as "the sun set," "it became dark," "it began to rain," and so on—and that simplicity is inherent in you to a high degree, rare to anyone among the novelists. . . . (pp. 262-63)

Anton Tchekhov, in a letter to Maxim Gorki on January 3, 1899, in *The Life and Letters of Anton Tchekhov,* edited and translated by S. S. Koteliansky and Philip Tomlinson, George H. Doran Company, 1925, pp. 262-63.

MAX BEERBOHM
(essay date 1903)

[Although he lived until 1956, Beerbohm is chiefly associated with the fin de siècle period in English literature, especially with its lighter phases of witty sophistication and mannered elegance. In the follow-

ing 1903 review of *The Lower Depths,* he dismisses the play as a disjointed portrait of unsavory characters.]

I am all for relaxing the girths of modern drama. The modern technique is much too tight, in my opinion. . . . [Any sign] of a movement towards looser form is always sped very heartily by me. But looseness of form is one thing, formlessness is another. Such devices as prologues, and epilogues, and scenes of mere conversation, are all quite defensible, quite commendable. But the line must be drawn somewhere, and drawn a long way before we come down to *The Lower Depths* of Gorki. There must be some kind of artistic unity—unity either of story or of idea. There must be a story, though it need not be stuck to like grim death; or there must be, with similar reservation, an idea. Gorki has neither asset. At any rate he does nothing with either asset. Enough that he gives us, honestly and fearlessly, "a slice of life"? Enough, certainly, if he did anything of the kind. But he doesn't. *The Lower Depths* is no "slice." It is chunks, hunks, shreds and gobbets, clawed off anyhow, chucked at us anyhow. "No thank you" is the only possible reception for such work. We are not at all squeamish. But we demand of the playwright who deals with ugly things, just as we demand of the playwright who deals with pretty things, something more than the sight of his subject-matter. . . . Aesthetic pain or pleasure depends not at all on the artist's material: it does depend, entirely, on the artist. A convenient proof of this law may be made through comparison of *The Lower Depths* with another foreign play, "The Good Hope," which the Stage Society produced in its past season. [Herman] Heijermans, its author, had taken a not less ghastly theme than Gorki's. Fisher-folk doomed to starve or to sacrifice their lives for the enrichment of an unscrupulous shipowner are not less ghastly a theme than are drink-sodden wastrels in a "night refuge." But Heijermans had an idea, and this idea he expressed, very beautifully, through a coherent story. He evoked, through art, a sense of pity and awe; and so he sent us away happy, despite our very real indignation that in real life such things should be. I would willingly subscribe something to any "fund for the amelioration of the condition of Dutch fishermen." But, also, I cherish the memory of a delightful afternoon. On the other hand, no "fund for the amelioration of the condition of wastrels in Moscow" would extract from me a brass farthing. I am not interested in them. I may become so, in the future. I shall become so, if some Russian artist arise and handle well the theme which Gorki has botched. If ever I meet Gorki, who is said to be an impressive person in real life, or if ever I read one of his books, which are said to be impressive, I shall be awakened doubtless, to a quick sympathy with Russian wastrels. But Gorki on the stage is merely a bore, and a disgusting bore. I dare say the characters in *The Lower Depths* are closely observed from life. But so are the figures in the lower depths of Madame Tussaud's quaint establishment. I defy you to leave the Chamber of Horrors a wiser and a better man, or a man conscious of an aesthetic impression. Where there is no meaning, no unity, nothing but bald and unseemly horror, you must needs be merely disgusted and anxious to change the subject. It is just possible, as I have hinted, that Gorki may have meant to express some sort of an idea. Let us credit him with having meant to express a very noble idea. But that idea is not enubilable from the muzzy maunderings of the wastrels. They maunder muzzily on, these wastrels, just as they would in real life; but no ray is cast from without on their darkness. There is an old man, who appears suddenly, and in whom we dimly descry a "raisonneur." But he disappears, not less suddenly, leaving behind him no lesson except a vague sentimental optimism. This lack of any underlying idea would not matter if there were any narrative unity. An artist has the right to tell a story without any criticism of its meaning. The story itself produces that artistic unity which, if there is no story, can be produced only by an underlying

idea. But Gorki as story-teller is not less far to seek than Gorki as thinker. Two or three clumsy little bits of a story are wedged in here and there. But they have nothing to do with the play. (pp. 302-04)

Gorki's work is to dramaturgy as snap-shot photographs are to the art of painting; and a proscenium (literally a gold frame) deserves something better than the misuse of being made to nullify such value as such work may have. (p. 305)

Max Beerbohm, "The Lower Depths," in his *Around Theatres*, revised edition, Rupert Hart-Davis, 1953, pp. 302-05.

PRINCE D. S. MIRSKY
(essay date 1926)

[Mirsky was a Russian prince who fled his country after the Bolshevik Revolution and settled in London. While in England, he wrote two important histories of Russian literature, *Contemporary Russian Literature* (1926) and *A History of Russian Literature* (1927). In 1932, having reconciled himself to the Soviet regime, he returned to the USSR. He continued to write literary criticism, but his work eventually ran afoul of Soviet censors and he was exiled to Siberia. He disappeared in 1937. In the following excerpt from *Contemporary Russian Literature*, he provides an overview of Gorky's career.]

The greatest name in the realistic revival is Maxim Gorky's. Next to Tolstoy he is to-day the only Russian author of the modern period who has a really world-wide reputation and one which is not, like Chekhov's, confined to the *intelligentsias* of the various countries of the world. Gorky's career has been truly wonderful; risen from the lowest depths of the provincial proletariate, he was not thirty when he became the most popular writer and the most discussed man in Russia. After a period of dazzling celebrity during which he was currently placed by the side of Tolstoy, and unquestionably above Chekhov, his fame suffered an eclipse, and he was almost forgotten by the Russian educated classes. But his fame survived abroad and among the lower classes at home, and after 1917 his universal reputation and his connexion with the new rulers of Russia made him the obvious champion of Russian literature. However, this new position was due to his personal rather than to his literary merits, and though in the general opinion of competent people Gorky's last books (beginning with *Childhood* . . .) are superior to his early stories, his literary popularity is to-day quite out of proportion to what it was a quarter of a century ago. And those works by which he is most likely to survive as a classic will never have known the joy and wonder of immediate success. (pp. 106-07)

In all Gorky's early work his Realism is strongly modified by Romanticism, and it was this Romanticism that made for his success in Russia, although it was his Realism that carried it over the frontier. To the Russian reader the novelty of his early stories consisted in their bracing and dare-devil youthfulness; to the foreign public it was the ruthless crudeness with which he described his nether world. Hence the enormous difference between Russian and foreign appreciations of the early Gorky—it comes from a difference of background. Russians saw him against the gloom and depression of Chekhov and the other novelists of the eighties; foreigners, against a screen of conventional and reticent Realism of Victorian times. His very first stories are purely romantic. Such are his first published story, *Makar Chudra, The Old Woman Izergil* . . . and his early poetry. . . . (p. 112)

This Romanticism is very theatrical and tawdry, but it was genuinely infectious and did more to endear Gorky to the Chekhov-fed Russian reader than all the rest of his work. It crystallized in a philosophy which is expressed most crudely and simply in the very early parable of *The Siskin Who Lied and the Truth-loving Woodpecker,* and which may be formulated as a preference of a lie that elevates the soul to a depressing and ignoble truth.

By 1895 Gorky abandons the conventional stock-in-trade of his early gipsy and robber stories and develops a manner which combines realistic form and romantic inspiration. His first story, published in the "big" press, *Chelkash* . . . , is also one of the best. His subject is the contrast between the gay, cynical, and careless smuggler Chelkash and the lad he employs to help him in his dangerous business, a typical peasant, timid and greedy. The story is well constructed, and though the romantic glamour round Chelkash is anything but "realistic," his figure is drawn with convincing vividness. Other stories of the same kind are *Malva* . . . , who is a female Chelkash, and *My Fellow-Traveller* . . . , which from the point of view of character-drawing is perhaps the best of the lot; that primitive immoralist, the Georgian Prince Sharko, with whom the narrator makes on foot the long journey from Odessa to Tiflis, is a truly wonderful creation, which deserves to stand by the side of the best of his recent character sketches. There is not an ounce of idealization in Sharko, though it is quite obvious that the author's "artistic sympathy" is entirely on his side. One of the features of the early Gorky which won him most admirers was his way of "describing nature." A typical instance of this manner is the beginning of *Malva*, with the famous opening paragraph consisting of the two words, *"More smeyalos"* (The sea was laughing). But it must be confessed that the brightness of these descriptions has greatly faded and fails to-day to take us by storm. About 1897 Realism begins to outweigh Romanticism, and in *Ex-People (Byvshii lyudi* . . . ; in the English version, *Creatures That Once Were Men,* an arbitrary mistranslation) Realism is dominant, and the heroic gestures of Captain Kuvalda fail to relieve the drab gloom of the setting. In this story and in all other stories of these years, a feature appears which was to be the undoing of Gorky: an immoderate love for "philosophical" conversations. As long as he kept free from it, he gave proof of a great power of construction, a power which is rare in Russian writers, and which gives some of his early stories a solidness and cohesion almost comparable to Chekhov's. But he had not Chekhov's sense of artistic economy, and though in such stories as *Her Lover* (in Russian, *Boles* . . .) and *To Kill Time* (untranslated) the skeleton is firm and strong, the actual texture of the story has not that inevitableness which is the hall-mark of Chekhov. Besides (and in this respect Chekhov was not better), Gorky's Russia is "neutral," the words are mere signs and have no individual life. If it were not for certain catchwords, they might have been a translation from any language. The only one of Gorky's early stories which makes one forget all his shortcomings (except the mediocrity of his style) is that which may be considered as closing the period, *Twenty-six Men and a Girl*. . . . The story is cruelly realistic. But it is traversed by such a powerful current of poetry, by such a convincing faith in beauty and freedom and in the essential nobility of man, and at the same time it is told with such precision and necessity, that it can hardly be refused the name of a masterpiece. It places Gorky, the young Gorky, among the true classics of our literature. But *Twenty-six Men and a Girl* is alone in its supreme beauty—and it is the last of Gorky's early good work: for fourteen years he was to be a wanderer in tedious and fruitless mazes. (pp. 112-114)

[Gorky's autobiographical works] have, up to the present, formed the contents of five volumes: the three volumes of the autobiographical series [*Childhood, Among Strangers,* and *My Universities*] . . . , a volume of *Recollections* (of Tolstoy, Korolenko, Chekhov, Andreev, etc); and *Notes from a Diary.* . . . In these works Gorky has abandoned the form of fiction and all (apparent) literary invention; he has also hidden himself and given up taking any part in his characters' "quest for truth." He is a realist, a great realist finally freed from all the scales of romance, tendency, or dogma. He has finally become an objective writer. This makes his autobiographical series one of the strangest autobiographies ever written. It is about everyone except himself. His person is only the pretext round which to gather a wonderful gallery of portraits. Gorky's most salient feature in these books is his wonderful visual convincingness. The man seems to be all eyes, and the reader sees, as if they were painted, the wonderfully live and vivid figures of the characters. We can never forget such figures as those of the old Kashirins, his grandfather and grandmother; or of the good Bishop Chrysanthus; or of that strange heathen and barbaric orgy of the inhabitants of the little station *(My Universities)*. The series invariably produces an impression of hopeless gloom and pessimism on the foreign, and even on the older Russian, reader, but we who have been trained to a less conventional and reticent realism than George Eliot's, fail to share that feeling. Gorky is not a pessimist, and if he is, his pessimism has nothing to do with his representation of Russian life, but rather with the chaotic state of his philosophical views, which he has never succeeded in making serve his optimism, in spite of all his efforts in that direction. As it is, Gorky's autobiographical series represents the world as ugly but not unrelieved—the redeeming points, which may and must save humanity, are enlightenment, beauty, and sympathy. The other two boks reveal Gorky as an even greater writer than does this autobiography. The English-speaking public has appreciated the wonderful *Recollections of Tolstoy* (which appeared in the *London Mercury* soon after their first publication), and in speaking of Tolstoy I have mentioned them as the most worthwhile pages ever written about that great man. And this in spite of the fact Gorky is most certainly nothing like Tolstoy's intellectual equal. It is his eyes that see through, rather than his mind that understands. The wonderful thing is that he saw and noted down things other people were incapable of seeing, or, if they saw, powerless to record. Gorky's image of Tolstoy is rather destructive than constructive: it sacrifices the unity of legend to the complexity of life. It deals a death-blow to the hagiographical image of "St. Leo." Equally remarkable are his *Recollections of Andreev,* which contain one of his best chapters—the one which describes the heavy and joyless drunkenness of the younger writer. *Notes from a Diary* is a book of characters. Nowhere more than here does Gorky reveal his artist's love for his country, which is after all to him the best country in the world in spite of all his Internationalism, of all his scientific dreams, and of all the dirty things he has seen in her. "Russia is a wonderful country, where even fools are original," is the burden of the book. It is a collection of portraits, striking characters, and of glimpses of strange minds. Originality is the keynote. Some of the characters are those of very eminent men: two fragments are devoted to Alexander Blok. Memorable Portraits are drawn of the well-known Old-Believer millionaire Bugrov, who himself used to cultivate Gorky as an original; and of Anna Schmidt, the mystical correspondent of Vladimir Soloviev. Other interesting chapters are those on the morbid attraction exercised on human beings by fires; and the uncanny things people sometimes do when they are alone and don't expect to be over-

looked. With the exception of *Recollections of Tolstoy,* this last book is perhaps the best Gorky ever wrote. Other stories have appeared in periodicals signed by him which partly continue the manner of *Notes from a Diary,* partly seem to indicate a return to more conventional and constructed forms of fiction. This seems dangerous, but Gorky has so often deceived us by his developments that this time our misgivings may again be deceived.

Gorky's last books have met with universal and immediate appreciation. And yet he has not become a living literary influence. His books are read as freshly discovered classics, not as novelties. In spite of his great personal part in the literature of to-day (innumerable young writers look up to him as their sponsor in the literary world), his work is profoundly unlike all the work of the younger generation; first of all, for his complete lack of interest in style, and, secondly, for his very unmodern interest in human psychology. The retrospective character of all his recent work seems to emphasize the impression that it belongs to a world that is no more ours. (pp. 118-20)

Prince D. S. Mirsky, "Gorky," in his *Contemporary Russian Literature: 1881-1925,* Alfred A. Knopf, Inc., 1926, pp. 106-20.

LEON TROTSKY
(essay date 1936)

[Considered the principal strategist of the Bolshevik Revolution, Trotsky was also a brilliant and influential political theorist who contributed thousands of essays, letters, and political tracts to the literature of Marxism. Described by Alfred Kazin as "the most brilliant, the most high-minded, the most cultivated of the Russian Communists," he was also a highly regarded historian, biographer, and literary critic. As the foremost critic of Soviet dictator Josef Stalin, Trotsky became a figure of violent international controversy: vilified by Marxists who considered his opposition to Stalin counterrevolutionary, he was conversely held as a symbol of revolutionary purity by those who were disillusioned with the growing totalitarian nature of the Soviet Union. The passions engendered by the public image of Trotsky have tended to obscure his contributions to political and cultural thought—contributions that place him among the seminal thinkers of the twentieth century. In the following excerpt from a 1936 essay, Trotsky admires Gorky's dedication to the proletariat yet asserts that the didacticism of his works prevents their being considered as great literature.]

Gorky died when there was nothing more for him to say. This makes quite bearable the decease of a great writer who has left a deep mark on the development of the Russian intelligentsia and the Russian working class during the last forty years.

Gorky started his literary career as a tramp poet. This was his best period as an artist. From the lower depths, Gorky carried to the Russian intelligentsia the spirit of daring, the romantic bravery of people who had nothing to lose. The Russian intelligentsia was preparing to break the chains of czarism. It needed daring. It passed on its spirit to the masses.

In the events of the revolution, however, there was no place for a real live tramp, excepting as a participant in robbery and pogroms. By December 1905 the Russian proletariat and the radical intelligentsia that was bearing Gorky on its shoulders met—in opposition. Gorky did the honest thing. It was, in its way, a heroic effort. He turned his face to the proletariat. The important product of this about-face was *Mother.* A wider vista opened to the writer, and he now dug deeper. But neither literary schooling nor political training could replace the splendid spontaneity of his first creative period. A tendency to cool reasoning made its appearance in the ambitious tramp. The artist began to resort to didacticism. During the years of reaction, Gorky shared himself out almost evenly between the working class, which had then abandoned the open political arena, and his old enemy-friend, the Russian intelligentsia, who had now taken unto themselves a new enthusiasm—religion. Together with the late [Anatoli] Lunacharsky, Gorky paid his tribute to the vogue of mysticism. As a monument to his spiritual capitulation, we have his weak novel *Confession.* (pp. 217-18)

The last period of his life was undoubtedly the period of his decline. But even this decline was a natural part of his life's orbit. His tendency to didacticism received now its great opportunity. He became the tireless teacher of young writers, even schoolboys. He did not always teach the right thing but he did it with sincere insistence and open generosity that more than made up for his too inclusive friendship with the bureaucracy. (p. 219)

The Soviet press is now piling over the writer's still warm form mountains of unrestrained praise. They call him no less than a "genius." They describe him as the "greatest genius." Gorky would have most likely frowned at this kind of praise. But the press serving bureaucratic mediocrity has its criteria. If Stalin, [Lazar] Kaganovich and [Anastas] Mikoyan have been raised to the rank of genius in their lifetime, one naturally cannot refuse Gorky the epithet upon his death. Gorky will enter the history of Russian literature as an unquestionably clear and convincing example of great literary talent, not touched, however, by the breath of genius. (p. 220)

Leon Trotsky, "Maxim Gorky," in his *Leon Trotsky On Literature*

and Art, edited by Paul N. Siegel, Pathfinder Press, 1970, pp. 217-20.

GEORG LUKÁCS
(essay date 1950)

[Lukács, a Hungarian literary critic and philosopher, is acknowledged as one of the leading proponents of Marxist thought. He wrote primarily about the nineteenth-century Realists—Balzac and Tolstoy—and their twentieth-century counterparts, including Gorky. In such major works as *Studies in European Realism* (1950) and *The Historical Novel* (1955), he explicated his belief that "unless art can be made creatively consonant with history and human needs, it will always offer a counterworld of escape and marvelous waste." In the following excerpt, he examines Gorky's autobiographical works.]

In Gorki's life-work as in that of many other great modern narrators—one need think only of Rousseau, Goethe or Tolstoy—the autobiographical element plays a very important part. Those great narrators who summed up the essential traits of their epoch in mighty works of literature, had themselves experienced in their own lives the emergence and maturing of the problems of the age. This process of digesting the historical content of an epoch is itself most characteristic for the epoch. (p. 221)

Gorki's own autobiographical writings, [*My Childhood, My Apprenticeship,* and *My Universities*], follow the tradition of the old classical autobiographies. One might even say that their distinctive characteristic, their *leitmotiv,* is precisely their extraordinary objectivity. This objectivity does not mean that the tone of the narration is impartial. The *tone* of Goethe's autobiographical writings is far more objective than Gorki's. The objectivity consists rather in the content of his autobiography, in the attitude to life expressed in it; it contains very little subjective, personal material.

Gorki shows us his development indirectly, through the circumstances, events, and personal contacts which have influenced it. Only at certain critical points does he sum up his subjective experience of the world as raising his personality to a higher level. But even this is not always a directly subjective summary; the reader is often made to see for himself Gorki's own evolution under the influence of objectively depicted events. (pp. 221-22)

This objectivity is the most subjective, most personal trait of Gorki's autobiography, for it is here that his profound ties with the life of the working masses, which is the basis of his implacable, militant humanism, finds expression. In the first pages of [*My Child-hood*] he already reveals these ties very plainly. He says that the story of his childhood appears to him like a "sombre fairy-tale" which he must nevertheless truthfully tell, despite all the horrors it contains. (p. 222)

Only a passionate acceptance of the world such as it is, with all its inexhaustible multiplicity and incessant change, only a passionate desire to learn from the world; only love of reality, even though there are many abominations in it against which one has to struggle and which one hates—a love which is not hopeless because in the same reality one can see a road leading to human goodness—faith in life, and in its movement, through human endeavour towards something better, in spite of all the stupidity and evil manifested every day—only passionate receptivity, provides a foundation for a practical activity of the right kind.

This is optimism without illusions and Gorki possessed it. (p. 224)

Real types can be created only by writers who have an opportunity to make many well-founded comparisons between individuals, comparisons which are based on rich practical experience and which are such as to reveal the social and personal causes of affinities between individuals. The richer the life of the writer, the greater will be the depth from which he can bring up such affinities; the wider the compass embracing the unity of the personal and social elements in the type presented, the more genuine and the more interesting will the character be.

Gorki's autobiography shows us how a rich and eventful life developed in the young Gorki this faculty of creating types by comparing superficially quite different types. In this education of a great writer literature itself, of course, played a very important part. The young Gorki, still in his formation period, already saw that the great vocation of classical literature lay in teaching men to see and express themselves. From the outset Gorki always linked literature with life in his reading. As he read Balzac's *Eugenie Grandet,* he was not only delighted with the magnificent simplicity of the presentation—he immediately compared the old moneylender Grandet with his own grandfather. (pp. 225-26)

Gorki's autobiography shows us how a great poet of our time was born, how a child developed into a mirror of the world. Gorki's objective style emphasizes this character of the book. It shows Maxim Gorki as an important participant in the human comedy of pre-revolutionary Russia and it shows us life as the true teacher of every great poet. Gorki introduces us to this great teacher who formed him and shows us how it was done, how he, Gorki, was taught by life itself to be a man, a fighter and a poet. (p. 226)

Georg Lukács, "The Human Comedy of Pre-Revolutionary Russia," in his *Studies in European Realism: A Sociological Survey of the Writings of Balzac, Stendhal, Zola, Tolstoy, Gorki and Others,* translated by Edith Bone, Hillway Publishing Co., 1950, pp. 206-41.

MARC SLONIM
(essay date 1953)

[Slonim was a Russian-born American critic who wrote extensively on Russian literature. In the following excerpt, he traces the development of Gorky's literary career.]

When young Gorky passed from [the] romantic gypsies, Promethean Dankos, and heroic falcons [of his early tales] to more ordinary folk, he endowed his new heroes and heroines—tramps and prostitutes—with the same pride, strength, and love of freedom he had celebrated in his first legends. Chelkash (in the story of the same name), a wharf rat and a drunkard, despises the weakness and the bourgeois dreams of the peasant lad Gavrila, with whom he has temporarily joined forces; he has utter contempt for money and squanders it right and left whenever he manages to get any; he is ready to commit crime and robbery, since he accepts the laws of the human jungle: the merciless struggle for existence and the survival of the fittest. Malva, a Carmen of the Black Sea, maintains freedom in all her love affairs and always acts as an independent, strong-willed creature. In general, the strong men and women who maintain their individuality are Gorky's favorite heroes and heroines. He respects strength of character wherever he finds it—and this explains the note of admiration with which in his later works he portrayed not only rebels and revolutionaries but also those extremely predatory representatives of capitalism of whom he could hardly approve according to his political convictions. Silan Petrov, the boss in **"On the Rafts,"** one of Gorky's early stories, an old slave driver who is tireless in work and in love-making, is the prototype of Ilya Artamonov in the novel *The Artamonov Business* and is akin to old Bulychev in the play *Egor Bulychev and Others.* Vitality, pulsing life, the manifestation of primitive impulses—both moral and physical—appealed to Gorky, and in his first period he was the poet of what has come to be known as rugged individualism.

This was one of the reasons for the immediate success of his romantic and somewhat Nietzschean stories. Their impressionistic style was hardly a novelty in the late 'nineties, when various deviations from classical realism were prevalent. Their spirit, however, was something unexpected and novel, and it delighted readers who had become tired of the drab and bleak literary palette. The newcomer's picturesque brigands, romantic tramps, and legendary gypsies—all these magnificent specimens of manhood who vociferously proclaimed 'Life is narrow but my heart is wide'—created a startling eruption amid the depressing atmosphere of the period. (p. 133)

Unlike the Populists, who did pastels of the patience and saintliness of the traditional peasantry, Gorky portrayed the denizens of the slums, of the ports and lodging houses, as turbulent, violent, and seething with conscious and instinctive protest against the inhuman conditions in which they were compelled to exist. Yet poverty, crime, and despair could not kill the sparks of love and creativeness within them.

Still, it was not solely this affirmation of common humanity that made Gorky so popular. When Gorky was highly praised for having shown these qualities in his heroes, Tolstoy shrugged his shoulders and made a caustic remark: 'I knew long before Gorky that tramps have souls.' Much more significant was the refusal of his hoboes to be passive or to become resigned to their fate. They were wrathful, forceful human beings, ready to challenge the very order of things that turned them into thieves, drunkards, and derelicts. They symbolized the revolt of the downtrodden individual against the political and social machine that continued to exploit and crush them. This was the true message readers received from Gorky's stories and it found a response amid the general mood of the turn of the century, with its awakening of the masses and the increasing political activities of educated society.

The romantic tendency and the spirit of protest in Gorky's short stories between 1894 and 1898 ran parallel to the trend of critical realism: he concentrated more and more on the depiction of poverty, ignorance, and the sufferings of the lower classes. The directness and

Gorky and Anton Chekhov (left) at Yalta in 1900.

even the brutality of these pictures led some critics to speak of Gorky's naturalism. If this term is applied as it was in connection with Zola, it becomes quite obvious that Gorky never aimed at the documentary objectivity of the French school: his tales always have warm lyrical overtones that are definitely lacking in the novels of the French master. Gorky painted the dregs of humanity with the passion and compassion of a romantic and a revolutionary. Certain defects of these works are due precisely to their emotional overflow: the pity, indignation, or anger of the author is all too vocal, and he uses almost melodramatic devices to score direct hits on the sympathy of his readers. Two *leitmotifs* are predominant in Gorky's work: realistic and crude representation of misery and violence, and a dream of humaneness and beauty that emphasizes the dreariness of reality, yet also builds up a sense of revolt. (pp. 134-35)

Although often marred by sentimentality [Gorky's] tales fitted into that great category of works about the 'wronged and the humiliated' which played such a prominent part in Russian letters. They revealed the same concern for the underdog, the same love for the 'little man' which has been so often considered the most characteristic trait of nineteenth-century Russian novelists. Their difference lay in that besides compassion and humanitarian sentimentalism Gorky displayed in his sketches other significant features. His realism was harsh, crude, pitiless; easy tears and sentimental situations did not hide the feelings of hatred and rebellion, which were completely lacking in Gogol, and were sublimated into preachments of Christian slave-morality in Dostoevsky. Although in many instances—particularly in his morbid interest in human suffering—Gorky has been linked to the latter, he is as far from the spirit of Christian quietism as was another writer who had influenced him—Saltykov-Shchedrin.

For Gorky evil is not a metaphysical problem as it is for the author of *The Brothers Karamazov,* or a result of the discrepancy between the truth of religion and the wrongs of civilization, as it is for Tolstoy: it is mainly a question of the ways of life, of its faulty organization, of material conditions and social wrongs. Man's sufferings are, for Gorky, caused by political despotism, class division, and social injustice. There is nothing vague about his criticism: like his predecessors of the 'forties and the 'sixties he is strongly attached to the earth. He was often reproached for his lack of depth, for his avoidance of the fundamental issues of human nature. But Gorky believed that the so-called metaphysical or philosophical approach to life which disregards the particular for imaginary generalities is hypocritical and obnoxious. A truthful and fearless observer, he scarcely saw anything beyond the concreteness of life as it is actually lived. Almost from the beginning of his literary career he evinced this tendency toward realism. He concentrated on the sordid details, primarily those of a physical nature: hunger, drunkenness, pain, filth, the lack of all physical essentials. With the exception of Dostoevsky, there is no other Russian writer of the nineteenth century who dealt as much as Gorky did with physical violence and murder. Whatever the psychological explanation may be in terms of Gorky's personality, it would be next to impossible to detect any grin of sadistic pleasure in his gruesome descriptions of wives mangled by their husbands, of vagabonds beaten up by police. . . . He had become aware of physical violence as a main feature of Russian life, and its exposé remained one of his principal objectives; he denounced it not only as an Asiatic heritage, a survival of the Tartar yoke, but also as a result of ignorance and oppression: the cruelty of the common people was bred by their misery and was a release as well as a compensation for their slavery. (pp. 135-36)

Most of the sketches and tales he wrote between 1892 and 1895 are weak and imitative, yet even in these attempts of the young writer, as well as in his more successful and occasionally brilliant stories of later years (1895-8 are the best of this period), there is a core of constant elements. The themes of violence, brutality, and despair appear even in *Paul the Unfortunate* (*Orphan Paul* in the English version), his first novel, which he refused—quite wisely—to include in his collected works, but the revision of which he began toward the end of his life. (p. 136)

In Gorky's early writings [the] theme of man's inhumanity to man runs parallel to two other powerful themes: humanity amid beastliness and man's yearning for liberation. The bakers in **"Twenty-six Men and a Girl,"** one of Gorky's best stories, lead the joyless existence of slaves, but they idealize Tania, a girl who personifies for them beauty and love. But when she fails to live up to this exalted idealization and succumbs to a soldier, they compensate for their frustration by vile oaths and atrocious behavior against their fallen idol. All of Gorky's unhappy heroes are forever seeking true love and freedom. (p. 137)

Gorky's artistry during the first period (1882-1902) was uneven. The tales that made him famous then have lost most of their charm for the reader of today. They are certainly colorful, dramatic, and vigorous, and already show that power of characterization which later was Gorky's principal asset as a writer. Their defects, however, are also patent: their primitive construction, a sentimentality so naïve as to border on bad taste, picturesque language, and lusty details lapsing into rhetoric and bathos. And the author is over-exuberant and high-pitched, using too many words of indignation and wrath or of tenderness and sympathy. He is, in general, inclined toward exaggeration and employs only blacks and whites. His philosophy is too obvious and his desire to put over a message and to con-

vince the reader makes him obtrusive and didactic. The dramatic element is the dynamic force within his plots, yet he lacks the sense of structure. This is particularly evident in his first novels, such as *Three of Them*—an almost formless sequence of incidents, of isolated scenes and repulsive details; despite the intensity and rich texture of the narrative, it never acquires an organic unity.

The same may be said of *Foma Gordeyev* . . . , a novel that marked an important milestone in Gorky's literary development. It represents the Masters of Life, the rising capitalist class—a subject that fascinated Gorky and to which he was to return in later works. (p. 139)

The story of [Foma's] downfall is unfolded in a series of scenes, and although the main characters are masterfully drawn, with that abundance of vivid details so typical of Gorky's style, the novel leaves the impression that the author lacks control of his material—that he is, in fact, somewhat overwhelmed by it.

The looseness of construction is compensated for, however, by forceful descriptions of provincial life, and particularly by the 'national flavor' of the Volga merchants. This makes Gorky akin to the Regionalists and the Writers of the Soil. In general, Gorky's whole manner—his broad canvasses, colorful bold strokes, folkloristic reminiscences, popular expressions, and heroes who have not severed their ties with ancient customs and traditions—puts him close to . . . the Populists. What made him different from writers with Slavophile overtones, however, was his decidedly Western and socialist orientation. He wanted to change the life he portrayed in his tales and novels, and he was convinced he had to contribute to that end not only by his writings but by direct activity as well. (pp. 139-40)

The period after the *Lower Depths* (from 1902 on) . . . culminated in *Mother,* the novel in which Gorky attempted to portray the revolutionary, the New Hero of his time. He had already outlined this type in some of his plays. . . . As material for *Mother,* Gorky utilized the strike and the political demonstrations that actually had taken place in 1902 in the industrial town of Sormovo, and the workman Peter Zalomov and his mother served as prototypes for the hero and his mother. . . . The aesthetic drawbacks of this work are obvious. Some of the minor characters are well drawn, but Paul and his comrades, as well as Nilovna herself, are done as smudged romantic stencils. The whole canvas utilizes but two colors: unrelieved black for officers, policemen, and other representatives of the ruling classes, and a poetic pastel pink for their opponents. The revolutionaries are so idealized that they become as sweet and unreal as angels in children's picture books. They all talk a great deal, as if they were reciting propaganda leaflets, and even Nilovna makes a speech after her arrest—a scene of brutality and martyrdom bringing the novel to a close. The rhetorical eloquence throughout makes the book's message too shrill and often distorts the contours of characters. From the first pages the reader can easily guess what is coming next, and the story follows an obvious pattern, with no surprises. The characters, except for Nilovna, are static and uniform, and the manner of description is two-dimensional and never conveys any feeling of depth. But the most exasperating thing about *Mother* is that while Russian revolutionaries have very often been men and women of extraordinary moral rectitude who lived and died like saints, when Gorky tried to portray them that way, the result was flat and false. The similarity of his heroes to actual persons has nothing to do with their artistic reality: they do not ring true and are not aesthetically convincing. (pp. 140-41)

The new period in Gorky's literary development, immediately following the publication of *Mother*, produced his most mature works. Between the thwarted Revolution of 1905 and the triumphant Revolution of 1917 he maintained all the good qualities of his early work and succeeded in overcoming many of his defects. While the intelligentsia fell prey to morbid disillusionment and escapism, Gorky continued to profess his faith in the inner goodness of man and kept his socialistic convictions, which were for him a logical corollary of his humaneness and his hatred of the iniquities and inequalities of Russian life. *Confession* and *Summer* . . . were strongly optimistic. Matthew, the hero of *Confession,* is a God-seeker, one of those Russian peasants who wandered through the country in search of true faith; he finally comes to the conclusion that humanity is God and that people, as a collective force, may truly work miracles. Egor Trofimov, the leading character in *Summer,* who was at one time a military clerk, propagandizes revolution among the peasants with a thoroughly Gorkian feeling of the saintliness of the cause, and the book ends on a symbolic, almost religious, note.

While *Confession* reflected the interest Russian intellectuals displayed after 1905 in religious problems, *Summer* was more in the traditional socialistic vein; both novels, however, were not without Populist overtones. They also had a strong folkloristic flavor—as a matter of fact, in his Italian exile Gorky spent a great deal of time studying folklore. Both novels are supposedly stories told by men whose style maintains all the inflections and peculiarities of popular idiom. Stylization, rhythmic divisions of sentences, inversions, and Biblical images prevail in *Confession* and make it highly lyrical and a trifle artificial. *Summer* is written in a simpler vein, although its hero also uses idiomatic expressions and occasionally talks like a village preacher. These two transitional works bear the stigmata of sentimentalism and of splashed primary colors, but they do reveal Gorky's intensified concern with his crafts-

manship. In the years to come he retained his new manner of using folkloristic devices and poetic language, but with more discernment and a greater sense of proportion. In general, he became more sensitive to formal problems and consciously bridled his natural inclinations toward a profusion of language and a plethora of detail. He turned deliberately to realistic descriptions of Old Russia, and his later novels, drawn from his personal experience, remain his highest achievements. (pp. 142-43)

Marc Slonim, "Gorky," in his *Modern Russian Literature: From Chekhov to the Present,* Oxford University Press, 1953, pp. 125-52.

F. M. BORRAS
(essay date 1967)

[In the following excerpt from his critical study *Maxim Gorky: The Writer*, Borras outlines the thematic evolution of Gorky's works.]

[Gorky's first attempt at a novel, *Paul the Wretched*], is the story of the life of an orphan, Pavel Gibly, from his birth to his imprisonment for the murder of the prostitute Natalya Krivtsova with whom he is in love. (p. 95)

This early work establishes the pattern for almost all of Gorky's subsequent attempts to write a novel. This pattern is the story of a man's life from his birth either to his death or to the occurrence of a catastrophe which brings about the destruction of his inner life. There is an obvious resemblance between the pattern of such works and that of Gorky's own autobiography, with the striking difference that Alexei Peshkov survives the trials and vicissitudes of his youth and early manhood and emerges triumphantly as Maxim Gorky the eminent writer. . . .

[Gorky's second novel, *Foma Gordeev*], follows the general pattern of the earlier novel, tracing the story of the hero's life from birth to an emotional crisis in early manhood which destroys his inner world. In each case this crisis is the culminating point of the hero's conflict with his surroundings which begins in youth and gains in intensity until it erupts, in Gibly's case, in the murder of his mistress, and in Gordeev's in an impassioned speech of moral condemnation of his fellow-merchants. (p. 96)

[In his short stories **"On a Raft"** and **"A Fit of the Blues"**] Gorky depicts the merchants Silan Petrov and Tikhon Pavlovich within the limits of a single incident which reveals how they think and act in a specific set of circumstances. In Ignat Gordeev, Foma's father, he draws a finished portrait of the type of boisterous, dynamic businessman of whom Petrov and Pavlovich were preliminary sketches. Ignat is the most sympathetic character in the whole of Gorky's early work, a true son of the writer's native region, the middle Volga, vital, creative, generous, and resolute. Gorky invests his hero with all the affection and admiration which he felt for men like him in real life, men whose commercial achievement delighted and flattered his regional compatriots. (p. 97)

Foma Gordeev is a failure as a novel because in it Gorky reduced a theme of great national significance—the conflict of historical forces in a large provincial town on the eve of a great revolution—to the story of one young hooligan's feud with his elders. Although within the confines of a short story Gorky at his best could develop a dramatic situation with great skill, within the longer framework of a novel he could not manage the interrelationships of a group of characters or conduct the unfolding of a series of events. Perhaps the best critical comment upon the artistic defects of *Foma Gordeev* was Gorky's own, made in a letter to the publisher, S. P. Doravatovsky, while he was still writing it: 'Much in it is superfluous and I do not know what to do with the essential and indispensable.' (pp. 103-04)

Gorky's next novel after *Foma Gordeev* was *The Three of Them*. . . . The hero of *The Three of Them*, Ilya Lunyev, is a boy who grows up among the filth and brutality of an urban slum, conceives a dream of middle-class respectability as the peak of human happiness, and achieves his dream through successful commercial activity, only to perceive that the social sphere to which he had so fervently aspired is morally corrupt. (pp. 104-05)

The 'three' of the title of this novel are Lunyev and his two boyhood friends, Yakov Filimonov and Pavel Grachev, the sons respectively of a publican and a blacksmith. The childhood and youth of these two boys is one long tale of suffering and misfortune, and at the end of the novel Filimonov is dying of consumption and Grachev is ill with venereal disease. Calamity after calamity overtakes them while Lunyev is growing ever more prosperous. The bitter contrast between Lunyev's well-being and the wretchedness of his old friends causes him great anguish and intensifies the discontent which he already feels with his material success through his growing disillusionment with middle-class morality. His spiritual drama, which is the theme of the novel, is made up of the inner conflict which arises in him through the interaction of these two factors. (pp. 105-06)

The resemblance of the plot of this novel to that of *Crime and Punishment* attracted the attention of the critics from the time of its publication. . . . Lunyev and Raskolnikov are similar in that they both commit murder for reasons unconnected with theft and steal during the carrying out of the murder, as it were to rationalize it. Both thereafter feel keener remorse for the theft than for the murder. With Lunyev the money becomes an object of irony because it enables him to achieve the *bourgeois* happiness he wants but comes to despise. This irony increases the agony of his inner crisis and makes him stamp and spit on Poluetakov's grave. Although not an irreligious man (he feels the falsity of his commercial ambitions most intensely in church) he is little troubled by the fact of being a murderer. . . . Lunyev, unlike Raskolnikov, remains convinced to the end that his reason for murdering another human being was a good one, but finds himself in an insoluble dilemma because the workings of his social (not his Christian) conscience make him incapable of enjoying the fruits of his crime, whereas his fellow-merchants live happily on the proceeds of every kind of crime, including murder. (pp. 106-07)

[The] message of Gorky's early stories was directed against the generally bewildered and passive mood of the Russian intelligentsia during the 'eighties, even though by the time he began his career that mood was passing. After 1905 he again planned to use his talent to combat the new predominant mood of political depression, which was more intense than that of twenty years before because it followed a period of almost manic elation. Thus he wrote of his purpose in writing *Mother*—'to sustain the failing spirit of opposition to the dark and threatening forces in life'.

In pursuit of his goal Gorky presents a group of Social Democrat revolutionaries engaged in stimulating peasants and workers to revolt during the years immediately preceding 1905; their confidence in the rightness of their cause and its ultimate triumph, their mutual devotion, their indifference to personal interests contrast sharply with the pessimism, militant individualism, and sensual self-indulgence which Gorky saw as the basic vices of Russian society when the novel was written. (p. 109)

Gorky's attempt in *Mother* to reconcile in the figure of Pelageya Nilovna his socialist convictions with the religious aspirations he acquired in childhood from his grandmother and never completely lost was a reflection of the religious preoccupations widespread among the Russian intelligentsia after the failure of the revolution of 1905. Many Russian thinkers at this time, convinced of the impossibility of realizing the kingdom of God on earth, turned their attention to the seemingly more tractable problem of assuring their personal immortality in heaven. Gorky, however, from his Italian exile, kept his eyes firmly fixed upon the evils of this world, as exemplified in Russian reality, and sought in religious thinking stimulus to revive and sustain the revolutionary cause at home. . . . Rejecting traditional concepts of God which seemed to him either to sanction repression or to encourage resignation, he began to look for a new faith which would further the cause of the Russian revolution while still exalting Christian notions of freedom and justice. This new quest, which involved a search for suitable men and women to put the faith into practice, replaced after 1905 his earlier attempts to find a strong, individualistic hero. He has left an artistic record of his spiritual seeking during these years in the short novel *Confession*. . . . (pp. 112-13)

Confession is the account of the disillusionment of Matvei, an orphan boy, with traditional Christianity and his subsequent wandering through Russia in search of a new image of God. In describing this boy's physical vagabondage in quest of a spiritual ideal, Gorky is externalizing his own inner seeking. (p. 113)

In each of Gorky's novels so far examined, except *Mother*, the author has based his narrative upon the life story of a single young man. In each case this man's spiritual seeking, which constitutes the theme of the novel, is conditioned by his childhood experiences. . . . In each of these novels the hero's life story is followed up to his middle twenties, that is, approximately to the age at which Gorky closes his own autobiography. Each one of them is short. In *The Life of Matvei Kozhemyakin* . . . Gorky writes a very long novel in which he recounts the life of his hero from birth to his death at the age of about fifty-five. As in earlier works, he begins by relating the formation of a boy's outlook and personality under the influence of his surroundings; Matvei Kozhemyakin grows up in the small provincial town of Okurov, the son of Saveli Kozhemyakin, a self-made merchant in the style of Ignat Gordeev. In this novel, however, it is not Gorky's purpose to describe the inner conflicts of a merchant's son who does not wish to follow a commercial career. His attention is focused rather upon the town of Okurov, the manners and customs of which are the decisive influence upon the formation of his hero's personality. (pp. 115-16)

This novel is the story of a struggle between the forces of light, represented by Mansurova and Vasilev, and the forces of darkness, embodied in the life of Okurov, for the possession of a man's soul. The final result of this struggle is the total defeat of the forces of light—not only do Mansurova and Vasilev fail to change Kozhemyakin, but Mansurova's short sojourn in Okurov adversely affects her sense of revolutionary purpose. . . . The defeat of Gorky's radical thinkers in this novel by the medieval atmosphere of Russian provincial life (the Russian people's Asiatic inheritance, insisted the writer) is as complete as the rout of his rebellious hobos by the nineteenth-century forces of law and order in his early stories. Like Dostoevsky, Gorky seeks God but shows the Devil as the stronger. (p. 117)

Like *Foma Gordeev* and *The Life of Matvei Kozhemyakin* [*The Artomonov Business*] depicts,

against the mid-century background of ever-quickening commercial activity, the meteoric rise of a business founded by an ex-serf in a stagnant Russian provincial town. Whereas, however, the first of these novels is concerned with the inner life of the central character and the second with the intimate connexion between life in the town and the development of the hero's personality, the basic theme of the later novel, as the title makes clear, is the fate of the business itself. . . . Although the fate of the business (and with it that of Russian capitalism in general) is the basic theme of the novel, Gorky, always predominantly concerned with people, is more interested in the influence which its management exerts upon each member of the family than in the political and economic processes which result in its destruction. Because of the interweaving of the historical theme with personal destinies and the distribution of the narrative interest among three generations instead of its concentration upon one person, Gorky in this work could more justly claim to have written a true novel than in either of the other two. (p. 118)

The theme of *The Artomonov Business* is based upon the ideas Gorky had expressed many years earlier in the articles **"The Destruction of Personality"** and **"Notes on the petty bourgeois mentality"**, and in the novel *Confession*. Gorky wishes us to compare, to their detriment, each succeeding member of the family with [the ex-serf] Ilya and to show how each generation, moving further away from the people, diminishes correspondingly in spiritual stature. This progressive estrangement is expressed in the deterioration of relations between the family and their workers. Ilya behaves very simply with them, attends their weddings and christenings, and they regard him as a peasant like themselves only more favoured by fortune. Pyotr is sullen and tyrannical with them because they represent the business cares which have spoilt his life. Alexei, half-nobleman, calls them rogues and ne'er-do-wells and scolds them. Yakov despises the workers, but he is terrified by the ever-growing proletarian movement. Miron understands that they are not concerned merely with obtaining reforms and attempts to win their cooperation by establishing for them libraries and sporting clubs, 'feeding wolves with carrots', as he puts it. Young Ilya, the Marxist, regards them, of course, in a different light from his relatives; in him, the best member of the third generation, old Ilya's oneness with the Russian people is restored, but whereas the commercial path chosen by the latter begins the alienation of the family from their own social class, his grandson's political activity reunites them, at least until the revolution. Gorky presents the short heyday of Russian capitalism as an aberration in the history of the nation.

Gorky wrote his last novel, *The Life of Klim Samgin*, during the years 1925 to 1936. His purpose in this work was to draw an epic picture of the ideological conflicts among the Russian intelligentsia from the mid eighteen-seventies to the revolution of 1917, and to fit into this picture a condemnatory portrait of his central character, Klim Samgin, a liberal intellectual. This was a most promising subject for a major novel, and Gorky's work, if successful, would have been a significant contribution to world literature; unfortunately it is an abject failure. (pp. 125-26)

Gorky's long novel was foredoomed to failure when he decided to place at its centre such a footling nonentity as Samgin; the length of the work springs not from the significance of its subject but from the fact that the author enjoys venting his hatred on his puppet hero through four considerable volumes. The reader quickly tires of this protracted persecution. In a book of this length one would have expected Gorky to exploit his exceptional gifts of characterization and to compensate to some degree for the insignificance of his central character with a striking gallery of minor figures. Even in this realm, however, he fails utterly. As so often happened with him when he was dealing with members of the intelligentsia, he presents the great body of Samgin's innumerable acquaintances not as people but as vehicles for the expression of political, religious, and aesthetic opinions current during the decades covered by the action of the novel. In striving to impart ideological significance to all their personal relationships he destroys their reality as human beings. (p. 128)

F. M. Borras, in his *Maxim Gorky the Writer: An Interpretation,* Oxford at the Clarendon Press, 1967, 195 p.

BORIS BYALIK

(essay date 1968)

[In the excerpt below, Byalik characterizes *The Life of Klim Samgin* as the culmination of Gorky's artistic aspirations.]

Gorky's manuscripts show the tremendous amount of work he put into *The Life of Klim Samgin:* almost the whole of his life as an artist was a prelude to the writing of the novel, and he continued his quest even after he began to write it. In the early version, the historical background of his story was still of relatively small importance, and the composition was entirely subordinate to the "history of a hollow soul." Gorky subsequently filled out the historical background, now and again subordinating the composition to it, and saying in many more of his letters that the whole was a "historical chronicle." Eventually he evolved the main princi-

ple behind the architectonics of the novel placing in juxtaposition "the history of a hollow soul"—the story of the "disintegration of the personality" of Klim Samgin and his like—and the logic of history, a chronicle of 40 years of life in Russia. (p. 148)

The Life of Klim Samgin is not just a summing up; it is a fresh, comprehensive and cogent picture of the historical tendencies which produced men like Samgin. He is a type on a par with the greatest in world literature. In fact, the name of this character has become a common noun for it is now used to designate a typical phenomenon of bourgeois reality of the imperialist epoch, an epoch of wars and revolutions smashing the old world and the pillars of its ideology. "Samginism" is the bankruptcy of individualism as a weapon of self-defence of the bourgeoisie and bourgeois intellectuals. It signifies the inefficacy of the philistine "spiritual make-up." (pp. 148-49)

In order to show the real class content of Samginism, Gorky surrounded Samgin with hundreds of characters who are in constant touch with him. Some put in only a fleeting appearance and depart after delivering themselves of one or two pithy statements. Others are seen again and again, each time in a different aspect, corresponding to the changing historical scene. Then there are Samgin's more or less constant companions. This numerous and varied host is the vehicle of diverse principles, beliefs and ideas—political, philosophical, aesthetic and so on. These ideas and their exponents help to shape Samgin's mind, either by subordinating him, or by repelling him and thus inducing him to defend himself. (p. 149)

The numerous characters of the novel may be variously grouped, depending on how they interact with Klim Samgin. Some of them are his doubles, revealing this or that of his traits and helping to show his true essence. There are the *agent provocateur* Nikonova, a woman with whom Samgin finds himself most at ease, and the informer Mitrofanov, whose "sober" views of life Samgin appreciates.

The characteristic thing is that he is apt to find his mental kin among those who have made a profession out of treachery.

A few other characters may be classified as Samgin's doubles only with substantial reservations. Their temperaments and fortunes are in no sense like Samgin's, but they happen to have tripped up on the same thing—the individualistic approach to life.

A special place belongs to the capitalists portrayed in the novel. They are the masters of the life in which Samgin hopes to find a quiet niche for himself, they are the fathers of the ideas that constitute the chief diet of his brain. Some of them give full and open vent to bourgeois principles, and while they are a motley crowd, they are in a way epitomized by Varavka, one of the "pioneers" of capitalist progress in Russia. Some of them have a tendency to "break out" of their proper *milieu,* like the highly complex Lyutov, who commits suicide, and the merchant woman Marina Zotova, who has a very prominent part to play in Samgin's life. Hers is a curious role, for she stands somewhere midway between Varavka (Samgin calls her "a petticoat Varavka") and Lyutov (the "redundant man" of the bourgeoisie whom Samgin thinks she somehow resembles). She matches the former in the frenzy of her money-grubbing, and the latter in the keenness of her perception that "this little old world of ours is going to pieces."

Apart from the numerous characters emphasizing Samgin's various traits or shedding light on the sources of his ideas and moods, there is an important gallery of characters whose presence spells the doom of Samginism and the whole of the old world. But let me say at this point that on the whole the characters in the novel should not be viewed only in connection with Samgin, an approach that would have been adequate had it been nothing but an exposé of Samginism, which it definitely is not. (pp. 149-50)

The Life of Klim Samgin is both a social and psychological novel showing the formation of Samgin's character, and a chronicle recording a number of historical facts and personalities. But both definitions fall short, because the novel and the chronicle are parts of a larger whole which could well be called an epopee.

The historical chronicle in *The Life of Klim Samgin* is merely the foundation on which is erected a broader, more generalized and truly epic portrayal of the destinies of the various classes in the people's revolution which unfolds under the leadership of the Communist Party. Samgin is repeatedly made to witness popular demonstrations and to admit that on each successive occasion the people are stronger, more united and more determined. (pp. 150-51)

What makes *The Life of Klim Samgin* so complex and original is the fact that it shows reality almost as Samgin sees it. Almost, but not quite, because it was not Gorky's task to show life through Samgin's dark glasses, but to discard and break them. As in old Russian fairy-tales, where the hero is resurrected by first being sprinkled with the "water of death" and then with the "water of life," so in the novel, the reader is first plunged into the dull deadening bog of philistine thinking, and then led out into the bright world of progressive ideas, with reliable protection against the influence of Samginism. (p. 151)

[In a letter to Romain Rolland] Gorky said he linked up Samgin with literary characters like Stendhal's Julien Sorel, Goethe's Werther, [Alfred de] Musset's "son of the age," and [Paul] Bourget's "disciple." Hints of this link-up are given in the novel itself, as in the description of Marina Zotova's library, with its many novels about the "young man of the 19th century."

What then was behind the idea of comparing Samgin and these young men? It was that their attitude to life, once historically warranted, had lost its rationale in the new conditions. In making his comparison between the "redundant people" and Samgin, Gorky was in fact saying: anyone who took the attitude of the "young man of the 19th century" in this new epoch, the epoch of proletarian revolutions and great socialist transformations, would inevitably develop into a Samgin. Thus, Gorky's concept of the "history of a young man" as reflected in his novel, *The Life of Klim Samgin,* was of momentous importance, for it was shot through with his desire to safeguard readers, notably young people, from the venom of individualism, and to show man's great responsibility and great joy of living in the epoch when the people shape their own life.

The novel makes quite clear the tremendous possibilities which the art of socialist realism opens up for the artist. Gorky's novel also helps to see the connections running between this art and the best artistic traditions of the past, as well as its innovating character, which enables it to portray reality in its revolutionary development, as the triumphant shaping of history by the masses.

Two main themes run right through the whole of Gorky's writing: the resurrection of the human soul, and the disintegration of the personality. The former is most strikingly embodied in Gorky's *Mother,* and the latter in *The Life of Klim Samgin,* which shows the terrible emptiness in store for anyone who sets his ego against the people and tries to use it as a hideout in face of the inexorable march of history. (pp. 151-52)

Gorky's great epopee is not one of those books which provide recreation. Not at all. It is one of those works which demand of the reader an effort of all his intellectual powers, which augment with the reading of each page of this outstanding book. The reader is shown a whole new world, depicted with an incomparable knowledge of life and unsurpassed skill, as hundreds of human lives are unfolded in a complex and instructive panorama, and as the writer's sage and fearless thought illumines the past with the light of the future. (p. 152)

Boris Byalik, "A Great Epopee," in *Soviet Literature,* No. 3, 1968, pp. 147-52.

RUFUS W. MATHEWSON, JR.

(essay date 1975)

[In the following excerpt, Mathewson discusses thematic and stylistic aspects of Gorky's *Mother*.]

Mother contains two formulas often found in later Soviet fiction: the conversion of the innocent, the ignorant, or the misled to a richer life of participation in the forward movement of society; and the more important pattern of emblematic political heroism in the face of terrible obstacles. The first theme is embodied in the figure of the mother, whose life is transformed by affiliation with the revolutionary movement, and the second in the grim figure of her son, Pavel. Actually the two themes are interwoven, with Pavel acting as the principal agent in restoring his mother to a life of dignity and purpose. This relationship also illustrates the kind of inspiriting effect the image of Pavel is intended to have on the sympathetic reader.

Pavel's inspirational value derives from the moral qualities he displays and the kind of purposeful activity in which he displays them. When courage, endurance, strength of will are exercised in certain kinds of tactically "correct" political behavior, during the May Day parade, for example, it is always a calculated effect he aims for. His later defiance of the Tsarist court reflects a public, not a private, emotion in the sense that it is not a personal defense, but an occasion to instruct the masses in the workings of the hateful system. Pavel acts on this, and on all other occasions, out of two supplementary kinds of knowledge that make up class consciousness: the abstract generalizations about society learned from his precious books, plus the documentation of working-class misery which is daily before his eyes. Thus equipped with emotion and knowledge, Pavel goes forth to permanent battle with the status quo.

This, at least, is the way we are asked to read the novel. It may be read quite differently, however. The novel's conflict is posed between moral absolutes and the writer's attitude toward the conflict is not that of an observer but of a partisan who is, himself, engaged in the bitter class warfare. In this rigid opposition there is no opportunity for the emblematic good man to move in the area between good and evil, or to be involved with, tempted by, or overcome from within by evil. He may reproach himself for lacking the endurance he needs to carry out the tasks history has set for him. He may search his soul to find the courage he needs. He may examine the reasons which brought him

to his exposed position. But he will not question the position itself. Evil is tangible and external, and all man's resources are needed to combat it. Since, according to the formula in *Mother,* the good man is the most distant from evil, he cannot yield to it without forfeiting his position in the novel's moral hierarchy. Pavel's revolutionary colleague, the Ukrainian, Andrei Nakhodka, asks a question which is vital for the revolutionary and suggests at the same time a fruitful approach for the writer to the tensions of revolutionary activity. After he has confessed to the murder of a police spy, he asks, in effect, what crimes he will commit in the name of the revolution, what violations of his private moral code are permissible (or bearable) for the dedicated man. But Nakhodka is too weak, too susceptible. He is a good-hearted follower, but not the leader Pavel is. In Pavel's eyes such questions have a certain validity, but they do not really concern *him,* and can always be resolved in the terms of his political-moral absolutes.

But the ease with which he does resolve them seriously challenges his adequacy as a literary portrait. He is, among other things, a fanatical moralizer and prophet. It may be argued that these qualities have been forced on him by the stringencies of his situation, or that they are inevitable costs of his kind of life. In any case they are there—we know because Gorky, perhaps unwittingly, shows them to us—to be accounted for, overcome, or read into any final assessment of his human worth. At the very least they are barriers to awareness, if not to action. By failing to record his hero's limitations fully Gorky has provided grounds for seriously questioning his human and literary judgment in this matter. (pp. 167-69)

When Nakhodka, whose humane awareness is in inverse proportion to his political effectiveness, reproaches [Pavel] for his harshness, and for acting the hero in front of his helpless mother, Gorky the writer has brought to light a legitimate conflict of values. Pavel's pomposity, rigidity, and fixity of purpose, with their suggestions of sublimation and megalomania, are predictable consequences of his personality and of his way of life, as given. But Gorky the propagandist betrays his persuasive insight, a few moments later, by extracting a quick apology from Pavel. For the rest of the novel the insight is forgotten. Gorky's uncritical approval of Pavel is unmistakable as the latter grows into the most effective political leader in the area. Finally, when Pavel rises to speak at his trial, "A party man, I recognize only the court of my party and will not speak here in my defense," he has become in his own eyes the selfless incarnation of the public cause, without doubts, hesitations, or concern for personal loss, and Gorky, having surrendered his control over the character, can only agree.

The matter of tension between private and public

life appears constantly, but it is resolved with one exception in favor of the latter. Sacrifice and suffering are often mentioned but seldom shown, and never explored to any depth. (pp. 169-70)

Only once does raw human experience force its way through the web of political rationalization. Nakhodka's anguish at his casual blow which turned out to be an act of murder bespeaks real inner conflict. He knows the conventional terms in which the crime can be justified, and he recites them with an air of conviction. . . . (p. 170)

The crime which is justifiable in public terms is nevertheless unacceptable to Nakhodka's moral sensibility. It is the most terrible and destructive act of self-renunciation the revolutionary can be asked to carry out, even though he believes, as he does it, that it is in the name of the time when "free men will walk on the earth" and "life will be one great service to man." . . .

Despite the congealed rhetoric, this is intelligible moral utterance, exposing grounds for the deepest division between the individual and his cause, including permanent banishment from the Utopia to come. One need not agree with his definition of the dilemma to see in this the germ of genuine tragic conflict, the real drama of the revolution's honorable casualties. Gorky does not develop it further. Pavel, who, with his mother, remains in the center of the stage, understands and sympathizes: "Andrei won't forgive himself soon," he says, "if he'll forgive himself at all." But he reduces it again to the comforting blacks and whites of the political morality which Andrei has for a moment seen through. . . . (p. 171)

The hardheaded visionaries of *Mother* . . . have their minds fixed firmly on the emergent future. They are struggling to forward a trend which, they are convinced, is both inevitable and infinitely preferable to the unbearable present. Gorky makes no attempt to hide his own partisanship in this contest. Completely identified with his protagonists, he is as committed as they are to the overthrow of life as it is, in the name of a compelling vision of life as it should be. But the question again arises: how can the conflict between future and present be dramatized within the confines of the realistic novel? Apart from the many "utopian" speculations in the novel, the desirability of the future can be suggested only indirectly, through the intensity of the characters' dedication to it. Otherwise the affirmative case must be set forth in declamatory assertions by the hero or his lieutenants. In spite of the endless, florid talk about the better world their personal struggle brings closer, what these men are fighting against is always more vividly realized than what they are fighting for. Their anger is thus better motivated than their invincible optimism. In a novel of repeated tactical defeats this assurance is communicated only by defiant speeches.

The source of their optimism is a political truth founded upon abstractions. That the historical force championed by Pavel and his comrades is somehow benign is an assumption outside the novel which may or may not be accepted by the reader. Gorky's abandonment of a more traditional novelist's vantage for overt political commitment, therefore, prejudices any claims the novel may have to universal interest. The novel of open political partisanship can be acceptable only to like-minded readers. The only possibility of reaching a more indifferent audience rests in the acceptability or credibility of the human material—above all, of the hero—in the novel. And we have seen, I think, that the partisan blight has effectively neutralized his (or their) appeal.

The general difficulties we have indicated—involvement with the future, motivation by doctrine, and this writer's close identification with his heroes and with their cause—have one marked effect on the texture of the novel: it is shaped, down to the smallest technical details, by the spirit of political evangelism. It is not only that the climax of the novel is declamatory (Pavel's speech before the court), or that all the characters' actions and utterances are shaped by political considerations. The dialogue often resembles a verbal exchange of newspaper editorials, written in the turgid rhetoric which also disfigures Gorky's pamphleteering. The expository passages, the dramatic passages, the physical descriptions of the characters and of nature are likewise permeated with evangelism. As the mother goes down under the strangling fingers of the police spy at the novel's end she shouts a slogan, "You will not drown the truth in seas of blood." When Pavel has overcome her doubts about the essential justice of Nakhodka's act of homicide, "The mother arose agitated, full of a desire to fuse her heart into the heart of her son, into one burning, flaming torch." Class virtue manifests itself in the bodies, postures, faces, above all in the eyes of the characters. The eyes of the class enemy are muddy, bleared, or shifty, but, in the midst of his courtroom speech, "Pavel smiled, and the generous fire of his blue eyes blazed forth more brilliantly." At times Gorky comes very close to self-parody: "You'd better put on something; it's cold," one character remarks; and the other answers, "There's a fire inside of me." This is not simply bad writing but a striking example of the fusion of form and content. At the heart of the matter is Gorky's total partisanship. Under its influence all literary and human truth—even the truth of the physical universe—becomes subordinated to a single dogmatic view of political truth. (pp. 172-74)

Gorky knew that his approach to literature implied important departures from classical realism. In his letter to Chekhov about the need for "the heroic," Gorky exposed some of the thinking that underlay this demand:

So there you go, doing away with realism. And I am extremely glad. So be it! And to hell with it! . . . Everyone wants things that are exciting and brilliant so that it won't be like life, you see, but superior to life, better, more beautiful. Present-day literature must definitely begin to color life and as soon as it does this, life itself will acquire color. That is to say, people will live faster, more brilliantly.

The "realism" that must give way to the "heroic" was neutral, he felt, hopeless, and rooted in the present, in life as it is; the "heroic" that was to replace it was not escapist, but functional, in that it was to quicken and change men's lives and set them in motion toward an unspecified vision of life as it should be. On the single occasion when this general feeling was translated into political myth-making, he invested the "color" and the promise in Pavel and the other Bolsheviks. This lapse has been seized upon and made the theoretical basis of "socialist romanticism," the ingredient of socialist realism which directs the writer not to a general heightening of experience as Gorky originally intended, but to the celebration of the emergent future exactly as it is defined in the Party program and in the five-year plans. This is the obligatory step beyond the present, beyond reality, beyond realism, and beyond the empirical truth that the figure of the Soviet hero must express. Pavel Vlasov is valued as an *ideological* portrait, made up of hope, doctrine, and tendency as much as he is of flesh and blood. Thus the grounds for doubting his human validity are built into the very basis of the theory he stands on. (pp. 175-76)

Rufus W. Mathewson, Jr., "Lenin and Gorky: The Turning Point," in his *The Positive Hero in Russian Literature*, second edition, Stanford University Press, 1975, pp. 156-76.

SOURCES FOR FURTHER STUDY

Gourfinkel, Nina. *Gorky.* Westport, Conn.: Greenwood Press, 1975, 192 p.

A detailed biographical and critical account of Gorky's career. Gourfinkel supplements her study with extracts from his writings.

Hare, Richard. *Maxim Gorky: Romantic Realist and Conservative Revolutionary.* Westport, Conn.: Greenwood Press, 1978, 156 p.

Presents an illuminating account of Gorky's life and work, including numerous personal reminiscences of some of Gorky's contemporaries and letters Gorky wrote while living in the United States.

Levin, Dan. *Stormy Petrel: The Life and Work of Maxim Gorky.* New York: Appleton-Century, 1965, 332 p.

Comments on Gorky's work in relation to his life.

Olgin, Moissaye J. *Maxim Gorky: Writer and Revolutionist.* New York: International Publishers, 1933, 64 p.

Evaluates Gorky's work while focusing on his revolutionary activities.

Troyant, Henri. *Gorky.* Translated by Lowell Bair. New York: Crown Publishers, 1989, 216 p.

Biography of Gorky.

Wolfe, Bertram D. *The Bridge and the Abyss: The Troubled Friendship of Maxim Gorky and V. I. Lenin.* New York: Frederick A. Praeger, 1967, 180 p.

Wolfe reevaluates Gorky's character and work by examining "the peculiar ambivalence of his troubled and frequently stormy friendship with Lenin."

Günter Grass

1927-

(Full name Günter Wilhelm Grass; has also written under pseudonym Artur Knoff) German novelist, essayist, poet, dramatist, nonfiction writer, editor, and scriptwriter.

INTRODUCTION

Among the most significant and controversial authors to emerge in Germany after World War II, Grass established his reputation with the novels *Die Blechtrommel* (1959; *The Tin Drum*), *Katz und Maus* (1961; *Cat and Mouse*), and *Hundejahre* (1963; *Dog Years*), collectively known as *The Danzig Trilogy.* These works graphically capture the reactions of German citizens to the rise of Nazism, the horrors of war, and the guilt that has lingered in the aftermath of Adolf Hitler's regime. Influenced by Surrealism, German Expressionism, and such disparate authors as Bertolt Brecht, Herman Melville, and Alfred Döblin, Grass combines naturalistic detail with fantastical images and events. His exuberant prose style and blend of diverse stylistic techniques, through which he makes extensive use of black humor, satire, and wordplay, have prompted comparisons to the work of James Joyce, Laurence Sterne, and François Rabelais.

Grass's imagination and artistic sensibilities derive largely from his childhood experiences. Some critics have suggested that his fiction often centers on perversions of youth as a result of his own Nazi indoctrination and the advent of war during his adolescence. Grass was a member of the Hitler Youth in his native Danzig. Drafted as a Luftwaffe auxiliary in World War II, he was wounded and captured during the German defense of Berlin in 1945. Following the war, Grass studied painting and sculpture at the Düsseldorf Academy of Art. He later joined "Gruppe 47," a prestigious association of German writers formed after World War II. This group published much of Grass's early poetry in the literary journal *Akzente* and awarded him the prestigious annual "Gruppe 47" prize in 1958 for his first novel, *The Tin Drum*, which forms the first part of *The Danzig Trilogy.*

The Danzig Trilogy, which is considered Grass's

most distinguished achievement, depicts the effects of nazism on everyday life in Danzig by examining such themes as loss of innocence, individual responsibility, and national guilt arising from Germany's wartime atrocities. George Steiner reflected critical opinion when he remarked of *The Danzig Trilogy:* "It is not Grass's enormous success that matters most. . . . It is the power of that bawling voice to drown the siren-song of smooth oblivion, to make the Germans—as no writer did before—face up to their monstrous past." As the first book of *The Danzig Trilogy, The Tin Drum* earned Grass international acclaim and popularity. The protagonist of this novel is Oskar Matzerath, a precocious dwarf who had willfully stunted his physical growth at an early age to protect himself from the chaos and destruction of his era. Oskar is portrayed as a wild, erratic, and adaptive personality who vividly recounts the traumas of Hitler's rule while playing a tin drum from his cell in a mental institution in the late 1950s. Rich in allusions to mythology and the New Testament, *The Tin Drum* combines fantasy with realism and prose with poetry to produce what Anthony Burgess proclaimed "a big, bawdy, sprawling triumph."

Cat and Mouse, the second book of *The Danzig Trilogy,* relates the story of Joachim Mahlke, an alienated Danzig youth whose oversized adam's apple, or "mouse," leads him to seek social acceptance through athletics and, later, the Nazi military. Despite his heroic accomplishments, Joachim remains an outcast at the novel's conclusion. While some reviewers considered this work's allegorical and symbolic content obtrusive, others praised Grass's sensitive rendering of Mahlke's guilt and self-torment. In *Dog Years,* the final book of *The Danzig Trilogy,* Grass employs the disparate perspectives of three narrators to describe the forces in German society between 1917 and 1957 that led to the emergence and subsequent fall of nazism. Central to this novel is the relationship between Walter Matern and his half-Jewish friend, Eduard Amsel. Juxtaposing Matern's childhood defense of Amsel from a gang of ruffians with his vicious beating of Amsel after Matern has become a Nazi stormtrooper, *Dog Years* returns the focus of the trilogy to postwar Germany, where Matern, now vengeful and guilt-ridden, stalks the German countryside, infecting the wives and daughters of his former Nazi peers with venereal disease. This work also examines how the German language became defiled by fascist rhetoric.

Grass's later novels have been less popular with readers than the books of *The Danzig Trilogy* and are sometimes faulted for failing to assimilate ideological digressions within their fictional narratives. Often addressed to Germany's younger generation, these works explore the futility of simplistic solutions to contemporary conflicts. In *Örtlich betäubt* (1969; *Local Anaesthetic*), Grass discourses on the Berlin student up-

risings of the 1960s. The central scene of this novel is a confrontation between a teacher and an admired student who threatens to publicly burn his pet dachshund to protest the use of napalm in the Vietnam War. *Aus dem Tagebuch einer Schnecke* (1972; *From the Diary of a Snail*) combines fiction and autobiography with a factual analysis of snails, which Grass characterizes as apt symbols of slow but persistent democratic change. Written in the form of a diary, this book also records Grass's involvement with the Social Democratic campaign during the 1969 West German elections. *Der Butt* (1977; *The Flounder*) spans several historical periods and blends scatological humor with ideological discussions to address the divergent roles of men and women throughout civilization. This novel derives from the fairy tale "The Fisherman and His Wife," in which a magical flounder rescinds wishes granted to a fisherman after his wife insists that she be designated as God. In Grass's work, a group of feminists attempts to put the magical flounder on trial for its past conspiracies with men. Criticism of *The Flounder* ranged from charges of misogyny to praise from those who considered the text an endorsement of feminism. John Simon called the book both "the first major satirical feminist novel" and "the first major satirical anti-feminist novel. For in it Grass scrupulously makes both men and women equally ridiculous in their more fanatical isms."

Grass's next novel, *Das Treffen in Telgte* (1979; *The Meeting at Telgte*), set during the final days of the Thirty Days War, describes the fictitious gathering of twenty seventeenth-century German writers who seek to reconstruct their homeland through a purified language and literature. Their intentions closely parallel those of Grass and other members of "Gruppe 47." *Kopfgeburten; oder, Die Deutschen sterben aus* (1980; *Headbirths; or, The Germans Are Dying Out*) is a blend of travelogue and fiction inspired by Grass's travels through Asia in 1979 and by his negative reaction to West Germany's 1980 elections. In this book, Grass deliberates on such topics as the reuniting of East and West Germany, the declining birth rate of the West German populace, and the emergence of neo-Nazi organizations. Grass also imagines the creation of a film in which a young couple debate whether or not to raise a child in an unstable world. John Leonard described *Headbirths* as "part fiction, part travelogue, part screenplay, and part political pamphlet . . . , a wise, sad, witty mess." The narrator of Grass's novel *Die Rättin* (1986; *The Rat*) is troubled by apocalyptic dreams in which a talking rodent, known as she-rat, sardonically documents the history of political and ecological ignorance that has led to humanity's demise. While some reviewers faulted the book's exhaustive length and esoteric allusions, Eugene Kennedy deemed *The Rat* "a disturbing modern-day book of Revelations written in dream language by an artist who draws easily on the enormous resources of his unconscious to render a bleak and not-so-bleak vision of what is really at stake in the world."

In addition to fiction, Grass has written poetry, dramas, and essays. Although English-speaking critics generally consider his poetry of lesser significance than his prose works, Grass's verse is well-regarded in Europe. The tone of his poems has shifted from ebullience and playfulness in such early volumes as *Die Vorzüge der Windhühner* (1956) and *Gleisdreieck* (1960) to a more restrained examination of moral and political issues in *Ausgefragt* (1967). *Gesammelte Gedichte* (1971; *Collected Poems*) and *In the Egg and Other Poems* (1977) include representative verse from various periods in Grass's career. Several of Grass's plays have been linked with the Theater of the Absurd for their startling imagery, black comedy, and bleak view of society and existence. These dramas, which employ diverse theatrical techniques to create what Martin Esslin called "poetic metaphors . . . for the stage," are considered powerful statements but have achieved only modest popular success. Grass's plays include *Hochwasser* (1957), *Noch zehn Minuten bis Buffalo* (1957), *Onkel, Onkel* (1965), and *Die Plebejer proben den Aufstand: Ein deutsches Trauerspiel* (1966; *The Plebeians Rehearse the Uprising; A German Tragedy*). Grass's essays on political topics are collected in *Über das Selbstverständliche: Politische Schriften* (1969). *On Writing and Politics, 1967-1983* (1985) features Grass's previously published articles on literature and contemporary German society. Grass has also worked as an editor with Heinrich Böll and Carola Stern on *L-80*, a German literary journal.

Regarded as one of the most important and provocative contemporary authors, Grass is renowned for novels that expose what he views as the madness of modern civilization. Through his passionate social and political commitment—reflected in all facets of his work and derived from his youthful experiences with the Nazi regime—Grass hopes to liberate readers from the trauma of the past and provide a saner course of action for humankind. By imaginatively combining elements of fantasy, satire, the grotesque, and black humor, Grass has rejuvenated postwar German letters and secured an esteemed position among world authors.

(For further information about Grass's life and works, see *Contemporary Authors*, Vols. 13-16; *Contemporary Authors New Revision Series*, Vol. 20; *Contemporary Literary Criticism*, Vols. 1, 2, 4, 6, 11, 15, 22, 32, 49; *Dictionary of Literary Biography*, Vol. 75: *Contemporary German Fiction Writers*; and *Major Twentieth-Century Writers*.)

CRITICAL COMMENTARY

HENRY HATFIELD

(essay date 1967)

[Hatfield is an American educator, critic, and editor who has written several books on German literature, including *Crisis and Continuity in Modern German Fiction: Ten Essays* (1969). In the following excerpt from an essay that first appeared in 1967, he discusses Grass's use of satire and symbolism in *The Tin Drum, Cat and Mouse,* and *Dog Years.*]

The Tin Drum has been called a picaresque novel, a *Bildungsroman,* and sheer pornography. In a famous account of modern German literature, Grass's style is described as "naturalistic . . . with an alloy of surrealist gags," and as "the attempt at a 'black' literature in Germany." I should like to approach his novels primarily as satires and to begin by considering *The Tin Drum* from the points of view of folklore, myth, and above all of literature. Certainly it is a work of linguistic art. . . . (pp. 129-30)

Basically the grotesque gnome Oskar Matzerath is an artist, and as such, mainly a satirist. People cannot resist the magic rhythms of his drum: he has the impact of a bizarre Orpheus; his spell is more powerful, though less sinister, than that of the magician Cipolla in Thomas Mann's *Mario and the Magician*. Further, his own voice has telekinetic power. . . . Thus Oskar cannot only enrapture the masses; he can destroy and sabotage, and often does. Sometimes he acts out of sheer mischief: he often indulges in satire for satire's sake. Yet in his major performances he destroys, or at least ridicules, the meretricious and corrupt. (p. 131)

Oskar's far-reaching voice makes one think of Apollo; and it should be no surprise that the dwarf combines, in his own scurrilous way, Apollonian and Dionysiac aspects. Needless to say, Grass's use of mythological allusions is not highfalutin. Neither is it obvious, but it is there. For one thing, a writer so steeped in Joyce's work and obviously familiar with

Principal Works

Die Vorzuege der Windhuenhner (poetry, prose) 1956

Die Blechtrommel (novel) 1959
  [The Tin Drum, 1962]

Gleisdreieck (poetry) 1960

Katz und Maus (novella) 1961
  [Cat and Mouse, 1963]

Hundejahre (novel) 1963
  [Dog Years, 1965]

Die Plebejer proben den Aufstand: Ein deutsches Trauerspiel (play) 1966
  [The Plebeians Rehearse the Uprising: A German Tragedy, 1967]

Ausgefragt (poetry) 1967

*Four Plays (plays) 1967

Oertlich betaeubt (novel) 1969
  [Local Anesthetic, 1970]

Aus dem Tagebuch einer Schnecke (novel) 1972
  [From the Diary of a Snail, 1973]

Der Butt (novel) 1977
  [The Flounder, 1978]

In the Egg and Other Poems (poetry) 1978

Das Treffen in Telgte (novel) 1978
  [The Meeting at Telgte, 1981]

Kopfgeburten; oder Die Deutschen sterben aus (novel) 1980
  [Headbirths; or, The Germans Are Dying Out, 1982]

On Writing and Politics: 1967-1983 (essays) 1985

Die Raettin (novel) 1986
  [The Rat, 1987]

*Includes "The Flood," "Onkel, Onkel," "Only Ten Minutes to Buffalo," and "The Wicked Cooks."

Mann's would not be likely to eschew the employment of myth completely. (p. 132)

A destroyer of shams, conventions, or anything else that annoys him, Oskar Matzerath is pretty clearly a miniature Apollo. As we know from the *Iliad,* Apollo, when angry, is formidable indeed: he slaughters his victims from afar. . . . Similarly, Oskar directs the music of his drum or his piercing voice against anyone who has incurred his anger or disapproval—whether a relative, a schoolteacher, or a particularly unpleasant Nazi. Only images of Jesus and the Dove prove invulnerable, but Oskar is annoyed, rather than religiously moved, by this circumstance.

His greatest feat, however, is a Dionysiac one. He refused to join the spectators in front of a grandstand where the Nazis are about to stage a political demonstration, for his friend Bebra has told him that "people

like us"—artists, that is—belong *on* the grandstand, not in front of it. But typically, he approaches it from behind—seeing its seamy side, so to speak—and then takes advantage of his tiny stature to slip underneath the stand, drum and all. Here he deliberately sabotages the celebration by striking up "The Beautiful Blue Danube" from his hiding place. There is loud laughter; many of the spectators join in. The color blue suffuses the whole place, Grass tells us; the nationalistic songs of the brown shirts are driven away. When the Nazi leaders (Grass uses their actual names) approach the speakers' stand, Oskar strikes up even bluer music, a Charleston, "Jimmy the Tiger." All the spectators begin to dance; the occasion is ruined, from the Nazi point of view; but the squads of SA and SS men sent to look for socialist or communist saboteurs never suspect that a whistling three-year-old child is the culprit.

Since Oskar's drum is apparently only a toy, few people take it seriously: he is an artist among Philistines. (pp. 132-33)

Whatever his vices, Oskar . . . is basically concerned with finding and expressing the truth. We recall that, at the age of three, he deliberately arranged the accident which made him a dwarf for life—or so he claims. Better to remain an outsider, a grotesque cripple, than to grow into a Philistine or a Nazi. In fact, there is a hint that Oskar's eventual hospitalization corresponds to his own preference: he would rather retreat into a metaphorical hermit's cell than be involved in the teeming but to him boring activity of the Federal Republic. . . . (p. 134)

To turn to *The Tin Drum* as a verbal work of art: one may best characterize it, I believe, as baroque. This long, rich book is full of the violent contrasts, the extreme tensions which we generally ascribe to that style. . . . While there are scenes and images of great beauty—like the evocation of the January night in the chapter "Show Windows"—the language inevitably tends toward the grotesque. Of course Oskar's presence alone would account for that; his love affairs are particularly bizarre. Grass is addicted to picturing eels in a remarkably repulsive way, and his descriptions of vomit are almost literally emetic. His sense of death and underlying evil resembles that of the seventeenth century or the late Middle Ages. At the very end of the book, a sinister black cook is evoked; she seems to symbolize guilt and may remind us of the black spider in Jeremias Gotthelf's novella of that name. For all his sense of comedy and wit, Oskar is whistling—or rather drumming—in the dark. (pp. 135-36)

Although *The Tin Drum* is basically a satirical novel, it has another, in a sense tragic, aspect. There is much concern with guilt, with Oskar's loss of innocence, and with related themes. When he changes from a dwarf into a small hunchback, he realizes, perhaps even exaggerates, his responsibility for the deaths of his mother, of Jan Bronski, and of his putative father, Matzerath. . . . At the end of the novel, Oskar is no longer primarily the satiric genius and rogue, but a man heavily burdened by his past.

In its title, *Cat and Mouse* (1961), Grass's novella recalls the cat-and-mouse situation typical of Kleist's dramas: the protagonist, like the Prince of Homburg, Alcmene, or the Marquise of O———, is cruelly played with by a stronger power (or person), though he may eventually fight his way to salvation. Further, a central symbol of the novella is the Adam's apple of the protagonist, Joachim Mahlke, which happens to be exceptionally prominent. . . . I believe that the interwoven, and typically Kleistian, motifs of cat and mouse and Adam's apple provide the key to Grass's story. In the first paragraph of *Cat and Mouse* one of his schoolfellows encourages a young cat to leap at Mahlke's twitching Adam's apple while he lies resting, apparently asleep, and the characteristic motifs recur consistently.

To turn to the action of the novella: it too is set at the time of the Second World War. Joachim Mahlke is an unusual youth, extremely brave, ambitious to a fault, and rather grotesque in appearance. He is tall and very thin, with an embarrassingly large Adam's apple. (There is said to be a belief among German schoolboys that this protuberance is an index to the sexual powers of its possessor. Although the actually highly sexed Mahlke is the most chaste of his group, the familiar association of apple, sin, and sex is clearly established.) In any case, his Adam's apple stamps the protagonist as a marked man. (pp. 138-39)

Grass has "distanced" the story by making a personal defeat, not some Nazi crime, the occasion of Mahlke's defection. It is nevertheless, I believe, a moral parable. Joachim Mahlke is a person of quite exceptional will power and courage. He also has more than his share of the "old Adam," but generally he keeps it in check: normally, he is downright ascetic. Here of course his devotion to the Virgin is relevant. His greatest strength—and weakness—is his extraordinarily competitive spirit. . . . Typically, the appeal to competition is responsible for his only indulgence in one of the less attractive forms of adolescent sexual play. An obscure sense of rivalry also leads him to steal the officer's decoration; characteristically, he confesses the theft voluntarily. Clear now about his own motives, he can win a cross of his own. In his eagerness to blot out his disgrace by appearing at his old school, he is abnormally sensitive: the director's refusal amounts to the end of his career. Fate or the era is playing a cat-and-mouse game with him.

Symbolically seen, the Knight's Cross represents to Mahlke a talisman, in fact a sort of "antiapple," which makes the embarrassing "apple" or "mouse" on his own throat irrelevant. When, however, he realizes that the way of life represented by that decoration is false, he throws it—and presumably his life—away. By so doing he saves his soul—to use an expression which Grass might find old-fashioned. Mahlke is the most admirable person in Grass's fiction, and the narrator . . . is impelled by a persistent guilt complex to write about his friend. We have no way of knowing whether the mouse Mahlke would have survived in a time when the cats were less cruel and vicious. (pp. 140-41)

Equally ambitious and almost equally long, *Dog Years* is darker in tone than *The Tin Drum.* It treats the same period, and most of its action takes place in the same areas: the territory of the Free City and the Rhineland. In fact, Oskar and his drum are mentioned several times. Its overall structure is more complex: there are three sections, each with its own narrator.

The other side of the coin is that *Dog Years* is less sharply focused than its predecessor. For one thing, the dog, or rather the succession of dogs, is not as potent a centralizing symbol as is Oskar with his drum—and with all respect for dogs, one must say that the dwarf is much more interesting than they. The second novel is harsher and less distanced than *The Tin Drum.* At times, the satire is heavy-handed, as in the account of the rumors circulated about Hitler's dog Prince after the Führer's inglorious demise. Yet *Dog Years* is a rewarding, many-faceted, and important book. (p. 142)

The plot of *Dog Years* is basically simple: we read of boys growing up in and around Danzig, of the impact of Hitlerism and of the war, and of the postwar period. Perhaps the most interesting figure is Walter Matern, who protects his gifted, half-Jewish friend Eddie Amsel from bullies, but later betrays him. After the war, Matern, filled with guilt and anger, takes grotesque revenge on all the former Nazis he can reach. Amazingly enough, Eddie Amsel survives; his nickname in the third part is Gold Mouth: Nazi bullies, including his ambivalent friend Matern, have knocked all his teeth out.

The most striking aspect of the book is Grass's phenomenal virtuosity of style. Adroitly rotating his narrators, and repeatedly shifting the time of the narrative from around 1960 to the days before the war and back again, Grass revels in parody, puns, and other Joycean devices. (p. 143)

Usually exuberant, sometimes excessively wordy, Grass's style can be concentrated and nervous. At times, to avoid banality, he breaks off a sentence before its end, leaving the reader to infer the rest. . . . Grass is indeed a man of many devices, and often his verbal arabesques and baroque flourishes obscure the narrative line.

Often fantastic though he is, Grass includes realistic, even naturalistic touches. To recreate the atmosphere of the Danzig region, he brings in local history, mythology, and superstitions. Frequently he has recourse to dialect. He names actual persons and firms. . . . (p. 145)

Yet, as in *The Tin Drum,* it is the major symbols which really take us to the heart of the matter. The first important one arises from Eddie Amsel's hobby of constructing grotesque scarecrows. . . . Although Amsel's creations do actually frighten away the birds, they are essentially artistic renderings of his own experiences: he portrays in them people he has met and even records in scarecrow form an incident in which his schoolmates, already anti-Semitic, beat him cruelly. Surrealistic though these unusual mobiles are, they are based on nature: he feels that they are part of nature. Amsel's most important constructs, however, are images of SA men. . . . While the ordinary, obedient Germans appear as dogs, the Nazis are scarecrows, monsters. Amsel also plans to build a giant, phoenix-like bird which will always burn and give off sparks but never be consumed—a symbol of the creative artist, and perhaps of his own survival.

As the strength of the Nazi movement increases, in the second part of the story, so does the number of swastika flags along the Danzig waterfront. Eventually the war breaks out. The dog motif becomes more important: nasty little Tulla, so called after a mythical figure . . . repeatedly sets the dog Harras on an inoffensive piano teacher. Prince, the puppy Harras has sired, is trained by the Danzig police and then presented to the Führer. For her part, Tulla, shocked by a swimming accident, regresses for a time into sheer animality: she spends a week in Harras' kennel, sleeping there and sharing his rations. Dog years indeed! (pp. 146-47)

The symbol of the prophetic meal worms—they live in a bag of flour belonging to Matern's father—is of a farcical sort. These worms can foretell the future, so leading industrialists and intellectuals make pilgrimages to the house of old miller Matern, who becomes more and more prosperous as the "economic miracle" continues. Finally the East Germans kidnap the remarkable little animals. All this may seem—or be—excessively farfetched, but I believe that Grass is satirizing a vein of superstition which still persists in Germany. (p. 147)

The most successful symbol . . . is the magic spectacles which play a decisive role in the radio program. . . . These eyeglasses, produced in great quantity by the mineowner Brauxel—as Eddie Amsel now calls himself—enable young people to see exactly what their elders did in the Nazi years. Thus when the ten-year-old Walli sees Matern through the spectacles he has just bought her, she screams and runs away—and Matern is by no means the worst of his generation. Such eyeglasses are indeed easily available in Germany today—in accounts of the trials of Eichmann and other

criminals, in movies, in dramas like *The Diary of Anne Frank* and *The Deputy,* and of course in innumerable books. The chasm between the generations could hardly be wider and deeper. It is a bitter but inevitable situation. (pp. 147-48)

Henry Hatfield, "The Artist as Satirist: Günter Grass," in his *Crisis and Continuity in Modern German Fiction: Ten Essays,* Cornell University Press, 1969, pp. 128-49.

MICHAEL HAMBURGER
(essay date 1970)

[Hamburger is a German-born English poet, translator, and critic. An accomplished lyric poet in his own right, he has been praised for his translations of several German poets previously unfamiliar to English readers, including Grass. He has also written extensively on modern German literature. In the following excerpt from an essay first published in 1970, he assesses Grass's poetry, emphasizing its combination of playfulness and moralizing.]

When I ask myself what makes Günter Grass so outstanding a phenomenon as a poet, the first answer that occurs to me is: the circumstance that he is so many other things as well, an outstanding novelist, playwright, draughtsman, politician and cook. In an age of specialists such diversity of interest and accomplishment could well be suspect, as indeed it is to some of Günter Grass's critics. Yet the more one looks at Grass's diverse activities the more clearly one sees that they all spring from the same source and centre; also, that the unfashionable diversity is inseparable from his achievement in each of and other, fields, because the whole man moves together, within the area of his dominant tensions and concerns. I am far from wanting to claim that this area, in Günter Grass's case, is unlimited: but it is strikingly and decisively larger than that of most other poets in our time, and that is one reason why Günter Grass's poetry is so difficult to place in terms of literary history, trends and genres.

In the early nineteen-fifties, when Grass was writing the poems collected in his first book, *Die Vorzüge der Windhühner,* Gottfried Benn was still advocating what he called 'absolute poetry', 'words assembled in a fascinating way' and not subject to moral or social criteria. On the other hand, and on the other side, Bertolt Brecht was still advocating a kind of poetry to be judged by its moral and social usefulness. Benn's emphasis was on self-expression, the enacting of inner states; Brecht's on the rendering of external and communal realities. If we ask ourselves to which of these sides Günter Grass belonged as a poet—and almost all the better poetry written by German writers of Grass's generation follows a line of development that can be traced back to that crucial divergence—we come up against one aspect of Grass's capacity to embrace and balance extreme opposites. Shortly after the publication of *Die Vorzüge der Windhühner* Grass wrote three short prose pieces which appeared in the periodical *Akzente* under the title 'Der Inhalt als Widerstand' ('Content as Resistance'), in which imagination and reality, fantasy and observation, are treated not as alternatives but as the generators of a necessary tension. The middle piece, a brief dramatic account of a walk taken by two poets, Pempelfort and Krudewil, presents the extreme alternatives. Pempelfort is in the habit of stuffing himself with indigestible food before going to bed, to induce nightmares and genitive metaphors which he can jot down between fits of sleep; the quoted specimens of his poems place him in the line of development which includes German Expressionism and the Surrealism that was rediscovered by German poets after the war. Krudewil, on the other hand, wants to 'knit a new Muse', who is 'grey, mistrustful and totally dreamless, a meticulous housewife'. This homely and matter-of-fact Muse points to the practice of Brecht, who drew on dreams not for metaphors or images, but moralities. Grass's treatment of these two characters is good-humouredly and humorously impartial. Those who misunderstand Grass's moderation, and moderation generally, as either indifference or weakness, when it is the strength of those who don't lose their heads in a crisis, could regard this piece as an early instance of Grass's equivocation; but Grass would not have bothered to write the dialogue if he had not been deeply involved in the issues which it raises.

Before turning to Grass's poems I want to touch on one other prose piece, published nearly ten years later in the same periodical, when Grass had become a celebrated writer and a controversial public figure. It is the lecture 'Vom mangelnden Selbstvertrauen der schreibenden Hofnarren unter Berücksichtigung nicht vorhandener Höfe' ('On the Lack of Self-confidence among Writing Court Fools in View of Non-existent Courts'). . . . Grass came out in favour of a position half-way between what the radicals understood by commitment—the subordination of art to political and social programmes—and the essential demand of art itself for free play of the imagination, the freedom which Grass identifies with that of the court fool or jester. If a writer is worried about the state of affairs in his country and elsewhere, Grass argues—and there can be no doubt at all that Grass himself cares about it passionately—the best way to do something about it is the way of political action proper—the kind of action which Grass himself has undertaken on behalf of the political party which he supports. (pp. 134-36)

Grass is not only an anti-specialist but an anti-ideologist. Even his theoretical pronouncements are nourished and sustained by his awareness of complexity, an awareness which he owes to first-hand experience. In his imaginative works, including his poems, the mixture has not remained constant. Just as in his prose fiction there has been a gradual shift away from subjective fantasy to observed realities, a shift parallelled in his plays, it is the first book of poems that shows Grass at his most exuberantly and uninhibitedly clownish. This is not to say that these early poems lack normal or metaphysical seriousness, but that the element of free play in them is more pronounced and more idiosyncratic than in the later poems, in which the clown has to defend his privilege of freedom, a special freedom begrudged to him by the moralist and the politician.

It has become something of a commonplace in Grass criticism to note that his imagination and invention are most prolific where he is closest to childhood experience, by which I mean both his own, as evoked in the more or less autobiographical sections of *Die Blechtrommel* and *Katz und Maus* or in the more or less autobiographical poem 'Kleckerburg', and childish modes of feeling, seeing and behaving. Almost without exception, the poems in Grass's first book owe their vigour and peculiarity to this mode of feeling, seeing, and behaving. These early poems enact primitive gestures and processes without regard for the distinctions which adult rationality imposes on the objects of perception. They have their being in a world without divisions or distinctions, full of magical substitutions and transformations. To speak of surrealism in connection with those early poems tells us little about them, because they are as realistic as they are fantastic, with a realism that seems fantastic only because it is true to the polymorphous vision of childhood. As far as literary influences are concerned, Grass's early poems are far less closely related to the work of any Surrealist poet than to that of a Dadaist, Jean (or Hans) Arp, whose eye and ear had the same mischievous innocence, giving a grotesque twist to everyday objects and banal phrases. In his later, post-Dadaist work, Arp also adapted his unanchored images and metaphors to increasingly moral and social preoccupations, not to mention the metaphysical ones which, much like Grass, he had always combined with his comic zest.

Most of the poems in *Die Vorzüge der Windhühner* deal in unanchored images, like the 'eleventh finger' which cannot be tied down to any particular plane of meaning or symbolism, but owes its genesis and function to a complex of largely personal associations. Such unanchored and floating images were also carried over into Grass's prose, especially in *Die Blechtrommel*, and some of them had such obsessional power over Grass's imagination that they recur with variations in his poems, prose narratives, plays and drawings. . . .

The substitution practised by Grass in these poems also includes drastic synaesthesia, as in the many poems connected with music, orchestras, musical instruments. Sounds are freely transposed into visual impressions and vice versa, as in **'Die Schule der Tenöre' ('The School for Tenors').** (pp. 136-37)

I shall not attempt a lengthy interpretation of this poem which would amount to a translation of it into the terms of adult rationality—terms irrelevant to the poem, in any case. In my context it is enough to point out that its subject—or content, to link up with Grass's early contribution to poetics—is little more than a sequence of kinetic gestures, derived in the first place from a personal response to the singing of tenors, but proceeding by a series of free substitutions and transpositions. These substitutions and transpositions observe no distinctions between one order of experience and another, between aural and visual phenomena, between what is physically plausible and what is not. As in surrealist writing, metaphor is autonomous; but, though one thing in the poem leads to another by associations that are astonishingly fluid, the poem is held together by an organization different from automatic writing in that the initial phenomenon is never quite left behind. (p. 140)

But for the wit and the more ingenious allusions in poems like **'The School for Tenors'** they would belong to a realm of clown's and child's play which is amoral and asocial. Yet even in **'The School for Tenors'** satirical implications arise from references to historical phenomena like seaside resorts, shrapnel and, above all, to audiences in an opera house. The very short, almost epigrammatic pieces in the same collection present Grass the moralist looking over the shoulder of the clown and child, not least incisively in **'Familiär' ('Family Matters'),** which has the additional irony of judging the adult world from a child's point of view—a device most characteristic of the man who was to write *The Tin Drum,* as well as later poems like **'Advent'.** (p. 141)

Very few of Grass's later poems are as exuberantly playful as most of those in his first collection; but just as the moralist was not wholly absent from the early poems, the clowning fantast and the polymorphous sensualist keep popping up in later poems seemingly dominated by political and social satire. The creative tension permits, and indeed demands, a good deal of movement in one direction; but it does not break.

In Grass's next collection, *Gleisdreieck,* it is the poems that touch on divided Berlin which give the clearest indication of how fantasy interlocks with minute observation in Grass's work. The elaborate documentation that preceded the writing of *The Tin Drum* is one instance of a development that can also be traced in the poems and the drawings, from the high degree of abstraction in the drawings done for *Die Vorzüge der*

Windhühner to the grotesque magnification of realistic detail in the drawings done for *Gleisdreieck,* and on to the meticulous verisimilitude of the clenched hand reproduced on the cover of the third collection, *Ausgefragt.* (pp. 141-42)

The underlying seriousness of Grass's clowning—as of all good clowning—is even more evident in *Gleisdreieck* than in the earlier collection. Without any loss of comic zest or invention Grass can now write existential parables like **'Im Ei' ('In the Egg')** or **'Saturn',** poems that take the greater risk of being open to interpretation in terms other than those of pure zany fantasy. One outstanding poem in *Gleisdreieck* has proved utterly untranslatable, because its effect depends on quadruple rhymes and on corresponding permutations of meaning for which only the vaguest equivalents can be found in another language. Grass himself has a special liking for this poem, the sinister nursery rhyme **'Kinderlied',** perhaps because it represents the most direct and the most drastic fusion in all his poetry of innocence and experience. This artistic fusion results from the confrontation of the freedom most precious to Grass, the freedom of child's play which is also the court jester's prerogative, with its polar opposite, the repression of individuality imposed by totalitarian political régimes. (pp. 142-43)

No other poem by Grass has the same combination of simplicity and intricacy, extreme economy of means and extreme wealth of implication. Apart from the taut syntactic structure and the rhyme scheme, the poem is untranslatable because no single word in English has the familiar and horrible connotations of a German word like 'angezeigt'—reported to the police or other official authority as being ideologically suspect—or 'abgeworben'—the bureaucratic counterpart to being excommunicated, blackballed, expelled, deprived of civil rights, ceasing to exist as a member of a corporative and collective order that has become omnipotent. (pp. 143-44)

It is characteristic of the state of West German literature in the late sixties that Günter Grass's third collection of poems, *Ausgefragt,* gave rise to political controversies rather than to literary ones; and the collection does contain a relatively high proportion of poems that respond directly—perhaps too directly in some cases—to political and topical issues. Some of them, like **'In Ohnmacht gefallen' ('Powerless, with a Guitar'),** were bound to be read as provocations or correctives aimed at the radical left. . . . (p. 144)

Compared with Grass's earlier poems this one gives little scope for playfulness. An almost Brechtian literalness and austerity seem to contradict Grass's resolve to keep the court fool separate from the politically committed citizen. Yet I think it would be wrong to read this poem primarily as a polemic against the radicals. The gravity of its manner suggests that Grass is quarrelling more with himself than with others, that he is rendering a painful experience of his own. The old exuberance re-asserts itself elsewhere in the same collection, even in thematically related poems like 'Der Dampfkessel-Effekt' ('The Steam Boiler Effect') which *are* primarily polemical. . . . Perhaps the happiest poem of all in *Ausgefragt*—happiest in two senses of the word—is 'Advent', since it blends social satire with the freedom and zest which—in Grass's work—appertain to the world of childhood. (pp. 145-46)

Whatever Günter Grass may do next—and he is the most unpredictable of artists—his third book of poems points to a widening awareness; and this means that he is unlikely to take his realism and literalness beyond a certain point. His involvement in the practical business of politics has imposed a very perceptible strain on him, but his essentially unpuritanical temper has ensured that the creative tension between innocence and experience, spontaneity and self-discipline is always maintained. Another way of putting it is that, unlike the ideologists and radicals, Grass does not want to carry politics over into private life or into those artistic processes which have to do with personality. If *Ausgefragt* is dominated by public concerns, it also contains this short poem, 'Falsche Schönheit' ('Wrong Beauty'): . . .

> This quiet
> life,
>   I mean the period from yesterday to Monday morning,
>   is fun again:
> I laugh at the dish of parsnips,
> our guinea pig pinkly reminds me,
> cheerfulness threatens to flood my table,
> and an idea,
>   an idea of sorts,
>   rises without yeast;
>   and I'm happy
>   because it is wrong and beautiful.

Ideas that make one happy because they are 'wrong and beautiful' have no place in the austere post-Brechtian verse written by so many West and East German poets in the nineteen-sixties. When he wants to be, Grass can be as realistic as they are; but the court jester's freedom includes the right to be fantastic, playful and grotesque.

Grass's insistence on this freedom has a special importance against the background of a general crisis in West German literature, precipitated by its increasing politicization. While East German poets like Wolf Biermann and Reiner Kunze have been defending the individual against encroachments on his privacy on the part of an all-powerful collective, or of an all-powerful bureaucracy that claims to represent the collective, many West German writers have done their best to deprive themselves of such personal liberty as they

enjoy. . . . Those who have followed critical opinion in West Germany over the years will be familiar with statements about what can no longer be written: love poems, because love is a form of bourgeois self-indulgence; nature poems, because we live in a technological age; confessional poems, or poems of personal experience, because they are poems of personal experience; moon poems, because, as Peter Rühmkorf suggested well before the first moon landing, cosmonauts are better qualified to deal with the moon than poets. Needless to say, all those kinds of poems have continued to be written, even if they have been written in new ways. (pp. 147-49)

Günter Grass, in any case, has not worried too much about what can and cannot be written, according to the latest theoretical appraisal of the state of civilization. He has written what he was impelled to write, with a prodigal energy which—even in poems—has involved the risk of error, of tactlessness, of 'wrong beauty', of bad taste. It remains to be seen whether Günter Grass can maintain his energy and spontaneity as a poet not only in the teeth of the ideological constrictors, to whom he has made no concessions, but also as he moves farther and farther away from childhood and the peculiar imaginative sources of his art. Since there is a limit to the fruitful tension between the politician and the clown, or between any kind of arduous practical involvement and the state of openness which poetry demands, it is my hope that conditions in Germany will soon make it unnecessary for Grass to assume responsibilities that ought to be borne by persons without his unique talents as a writer and artist. The tension, as I have tried to show, was there from the first, even when the clown seemed to have it all his way, and the moralist in Grass had not yet involved him in party politics. There is no reason why it should cease if my hope is fulfilled, since in poets practical experience is transmuted into awareness, and innocence is never lost, but renews itself within the awareness. (p. 149)

Michael Hamburger, "Moralist and Jester: The Poetry of Günter Grass," in his *Art As Second Nature: Occasional Pieces, 1950-74,* Carcanet New Press, 1975, pp. 134-49.

NORRIS W. YATES
(essay date 1971)

[In the excerpt below, Yates analyzes political content in Grass's novels.]

Satire . . . , especially in the grotesque mode, prevails in Grass's treatment of the more blatantly political subject matter in [*The Tin Drum*]. But Grass is protean in his use of other materials and devices. Closely related to the author's views on Hitlerism is his emphasis on history: Through historical summary, anecdote, place legends, superstitious lore, allegory, myth, and symbolism, Grass tries to convey the reality of living through a certain continuity of events in historical space and time—"great" events which in their totality are no more but no less real than the mishaps and the fortunes of the individuals in the historical continuum. (pp. 220-21)

Making the characters a part of history forces Grass to raise, at least indirectly, the question of whether they have free will or are moved by social and political currents beyond their control and in consequence bear no moral responsibility for their actions. In *The Tin Drum*, unlike his stance in *Dog Years* and in *The Plebeians Rehearse the Uprising*, Grass evades giving a clear-cut answer to the question by presenting the entire narrative as the artistic recreation of a possibly disordered and certainly immature mind. In a novel which, regardless of the elaborate pose of objectivity, is one long *j'accuse*, this evasion is a moral inconsistency and possibly an artistic flaw. However, two arguments may be advanced in defense of this evasion. First, Oskar has been called a moral monster; he is not one, but he may be schizoid, as is implied by the frequent shifts in viewpoint between the first and third person, and throughout most of the book he is definitely a child who, when he reaches thirty, is still far from being full-grown, physically and mentally. (pp. 221-22)

Second, despite his concern with history, Grass presents history as meaningful only in its effect on individuals. In one of his essays he criticizes Hegel's theory of history as a "fatal guide," and in his fiction he is indifferent to any alleged laws or principles of historical development that might lighten the individual's load of responsibility. This indifference is consistent with his general distrust of systematic ideologies.

This distrust is part of his artistic as well as his political credo. He felt no obligation to present positive alternatives to the situation of Oskar and his society. In suggesting that involvement is better than withdrawal, Grass scarcely goes beyond Camus's *The Stranger*. (p. 222)

The theme of involvement and withdrawal likewise dominates *Cat and Mouse*, a novella in which, as in *The Tin Drum*, the problem involves religious belief as well as psychological growing up. But the political element is always present, though often submerged. Again Grass has constructed his tale in the form of a reminiscence written long afterward by a major character, a framework that allows the author to present all judgments as provisional. (p. 223)

[The] overtly political content of *Dog Years* is greater than in his two previous novels. As a whole, the work still lies within the tradition of the realistic, panoramic novel, but the political and religious allegory tends to dehumanize the characters; their voices tend to merge into the single voice of the author. Moreover, much of the social and political satire is aimed at language and ideas rather than at actions—for example, the many parodies of Martin Heidegger. In an author less brilliant at re-creating scenes with vivid, sensuous detail, the increase in allegory and parody might be a gain; in Grass it is a net loss.

This tendency to talk and allegorize more and to re-create less may have developed because Grass's increasingly political orientation drew him into a task beyond even his powers, nothing less than awakening the consciousness and conscience of the entire German people by offering a cross-sectional history of the German middle class before, during, and after the war. (p. 224)

Grass seems to imply that one ingredient of the new Germany is art perverted by technology and industry, which, thus perverted, helps to create a grotesque, materialistic caricature of what a society should be. The social and political satire of the postwar leaders who base their policies on the predictions of the mealworms is specific and relatively good-natured; the satirical allegory of the scarecrow mine is far-reaching, savage, and much more radical than anything Grass has said in his nonliterary speeches and writings.

Since the 1965 campaign, Grass's art has come progressively closer to undiluted political discussion—with results not altogether pleasing. *The Plebeians Rehearse the Uprising* (1966) had a promising theme: a theatrical producer and playwright (inspired by, but not a portrait of, Bertolt Brecht) who refuses to support the East German workers' uprising in 1953 partly because it is badly planned and partly because it is not good theater. However, like Brecht's weaker plays, *The Plebeians* bogs down in long-winded discussion, and it was coolly received by reviewers and audiences. *Davor (Therefore)*, which opened in West Berlin early in 1969, is reportedly little more than a series of interconnected dialogues, largely on political and philosophical themes. (p. 225)

Though the juxtapositions of episodes and dental conversations [in *Local Anesthetic*] are often comic in their incongruity, the speech and narrative lack the baroque richness and excitement of Grass's prose in *The Tin Drum* or even in parts of *Dog Years*. Moreover, *Local Anesthetic* lacks the multidimensionality of his earlier fiction: *The Tin Drum* was a religious and a picaresque novel as well as a political novel and a *Bildungsroman*. Finally, as reviewers of *Local Anesthetic* have noted, Grass is here too often content to state his views in discussion rather than to embody them in description, action, or characterization. (p. 226)

The content, or substance, of Grass's work has always included ideas consonant with his belief in practical reform rather than in doctrinaire programs of either the left or the right. One commits a logical fallacy in saying that Grass's increasing preoccupation with the role of the artist as militant citizen has led him to overstress political themes in his work with the enthusiasm of the doctrinaire liberal and to impose the form of political discussion on his raw material quite arbitrarily rather than making a genuine attempt to overcome its "resistance"—that is, doing full justice to the complexities, nuances, and grotesque elements latent in that material and which he actualized so effectively in *The Tin Drum.* But whatever the causes of this doctrinaire imposition, the effect has been a debilitation of his art. (p. 227)

Norris W. Yates, "Günter Grass," in *The Politics of Twentieth-Century Novelists,* edited by George Panichas, Hawthorn, 1971, pp. 215-28.

KEITH MILES

(essay date 1975)

[In the following excerpt from his *Günter Grass* (1975), Miles provides an overview of Grass's novels, plays, and poetry.]

Günter Grass is the most consistently interesting and disturbing writer at work in Europe today. With his prodigious talents, unmistakable voice, alarming energy, wayward genius and sheer physical presence, he has made himself a tremendous force in modern European literature. He has faults, naturally: as befits a great writer, he sometimes has great faults. But—as he himself might say—this much is certain: for the German novel he has once more gained an international audience. (p. 11)

The facts of Grass's life have been repeatedly recorded in his fiction. In the Danzig Trilogy—*The Tin Drum, Cat and Mouse* and *Dog Years*—the suburb of Langfuhr is presented to us with such ferocious devotion and in such meticulous detail that we almost feel we could find our way around the area like residents. (p. 12)

Yet Grass is not an autobiographical writer in the sense that O'Neill is in *Long Day's Journey into Night* or Joyce is in *A Portrait of the Artist as a Young Man.* Grass begins with familiar events and places, but then transforms his own experience into highly artistic fiction. What may start out in the realm of fact can quickly and deftly be developed in terms of allegory or fantasy or legend or fairy-tale. Grass's emphasis on his personal

history is not merely a case of providing a firm, recognisable basis from which his novels can take flight. It has two other functions. In the first place, that personal history is offered as a set of credentials—"I, too, born almost late enough, am held to be free from guilt. Only if I wanted to forget, if you were unwilling to learn how it slowly happened, only then might words of one syllable catch up with us: words like guilt and shame; they, too, resolute snails, impossible to stop." . . . Grass wants to hide nothing. (pp. 12-13)

[Grass] is obsessed with the historical process itself. The present is an extension of the past and quite inseparable from it. Furthermore past and present can co-exist. . . . Grass's preoccupation with the importance of history and antecedent informs his whole creative approach. In the Grass universe, everybody has a pedigree. (p. 13)

[There is a bold arrogance in the theme of *The Tin Drum* (1962)]: an investigation of a whole, sensitive period of German history, a forbidden area as far as many of Grass's countrymen were concerned. Grass is not the only author to reconstruct the story of the nation from the last days of the Weimar Republic through the horrors of National Socialism and on to the war. Heinrich Böll in *Billiards at Half-Past Nine* (1959) deals with the same subject matter. Böll, the realist, the committed moralist, the radically Christian observer of the human condition, gives us a work of subtlety, irony and compelling craftsmanship. It appeals to the mind, and occasionally to the heart. *The Tin Drum,* on the other hand, assaults the intellect, the soul and the emotions, makes impossible demands on the reader, leaves him exhausted. *Billiards at Half-Past Nine* confirms our prejudices against Nazi Germany with skill and humour and is oddly reassuring; *The Tin Drum* explores the darkness beyond our worst suspicions and is constantly unnerving. Böll contrives something approaching a happy ending. Grass's ending spreads unease. (p. 22)

[A] feature of Grass's first novel which places it apart from, and above, any competitors is the quality of its language. The vitality, thrust and range of Grass's language is stunning. He writes freely and convincingly in a bewildering variety of modes—a dialect, schoolboy slang, biblical parody, officialese, idiom, literary allusion, fairy-tale, dramatic dialogue, prose-poetry—and yet manages to blend them into a single, coherent mode. Here is no Thomas Mann, writing graceful, detached prose, which is marked by its linguistic refinement. Grass has an immense gusto for words themselves and uses every device in the language, sometimes out of sheer enjoyment. Yet he never permits himself to be completely overwhelmed by his love of language. (pp. 22-3)

Grass the poet wears a variety of hats; he takes on the roles of lyric poet, educationist, jester, moralist, realist, surrealist, traditionalist, experimentalist. His poems can evoke the light-heartedness and delicacy of a Paul Klee or the nightmarishness and abrasiveness of a Georg Heym. They can be playful celebrations of innocence or grim reflections of experience. They can reproduce the exterior world or exist in a realm of their own. . . . [Grass is able] to wear all the hats at the same time, to fuse the disparate personalities into one. The artist does not vanish when the political activist speaks: the jester does not disappear in the presence of the moralist. It is the characteristic feature of Grass's poetry that it finds a way to make each cap, separately and simultaneously, fit. (pp. 25-6)

What is being established [in *The Railroad Track Triangle* (1960), a volume of poetry,] is the autonomy of the object, the supremacy of the thing. It is a concept which is fundamental to all of Grass's work and which accounts, in his poetry, for the proliferation of such objects as beds, doorbells, hats, mirrors, chairs, tables, cigarettes, scissors, spoons, forks, musical instruments and so on. Grass objectivises everything, even language itself. . . . (p. 31)

His third volume of poetry, *Questioned* [1967], is no essay in didacticism. The illustrations may have taken on a more savagely realistic shape, the number of poems which relate to political issues may be considerably higher than in the two previous collections, and the title-poem itself may be unequivocally about the modern German; but the volume is still pre-eminently the work of a remarkable lyric talent. (p. 33)

Grass the poet is indistinguishable from Grass the dramatist. The same principles inform his approach, the same bewildering variety of hats is worn. In a much-quoted discussion in 1961, Grass explained that poetry, plays and prose were, for him, all built upon dialogue. The transition from the lyric to the stage play was thus smooth and natural: Grass wrote poems in dialogue form and elaborated upon them. This process is at its clearest in the plays *Flood* and *The Wicked Cooks*, which have their origin in poems from the first and second collections respectively. It accounts for the strengths and the weaknesses of Grass's earliest dramas. (p. 35)

Rocking Back and Forth [Grass's first play] is an ingenious, inventive play, propelled by a simple idea. It has wit, satire and surrealistic values which recall the poems. Its shortcomings are equally obvious. It is too theoretical, too discursive, too pointlessly obscure. (p. 37)

The autonomy of objects is stressed even more forcefully in Grass's next play, *Onkel, Onkel* (1956). Like its predecessor, this four-act play reveals genuine anarchic talent which specialises in the grotesque. (p. 40)

Grass breaks all the rules of playwriting in order to argue [in *Only Ten Minutes to Buffalo* (1957)] that the rules must be broken and scrapped and ignored if art is to make any meaningful progress. In its precision, invention, concentrated imagery, sureness of control and uninhibited fun, *Only Ten Minutes to Buffalo* is the most effective and appealing of Grass's early plays.

The Wicked Cooks (1957) is an altogether more ambitious play, and one which is prefigured in the poem, **"Chefs and Spoons"**. Grass's obsession with cooks and with cooking is proverbial. Metaphors from the kitchen have eaten hungrily into his poetry, prose and drama. *The Wicked Cooks* is a scarifying but irrepressible allegory in five acts. (p. 44)

There is no surer guide through the undergrowth of Grass's first novel than that which he himself provides in his title. For *The Tin Drum* is primarily about just that. It is not a study of Oskar Matzerath and his problems: it is a novel about the tin drum and its relationship to Oskar. Throughout, the drum stands central. It is the key symbol, the mainspring of the narrative, and the controlling influence on the imagery and style of the work. . . . [The] drum is at once an organic part of Oskar, and something quite separate which has to be strapped on to him; a gaping red wound, and a proudly-held weapon: a source of vulnerability and a perfect protection. The drumsticks, too, are both organic and separate: monstrous growths or bone-like sticks held by the embryo hands. The duality is even more pronounced in the figure of Oskar. He is at once simple and complex, child and adult. The pointed hat and the apparel suggest a dwarf, but the face is that of a baby. Malevolence competes with innocence, protest with pathos, freakishness with normality. The novel starts here, with this striking demonstration of realism at one with surrealism. Imagine the drawing without the drum, and one realises how much it contributes. (p. 56)

The Tin Drum is, at bottom, a hymn to individuality, and Grass counters the flatness and sameness of Nazi Germany by introducing a host of highly individualised characters. He indicates the enormous loss which takes place in human terms, when any organisation imposes uniformity from above. (p. 73)

Objects dominate [*The Tin Drum*]. They control, influence, symbolise or in other ways reflect the behaviour of its characters. The tin drum itself is pivotal and the importance of other objects is affirmed in the table of contents. Very few of the chapter headings contain the names of the figures who people the novel. For the most part, it is a case of wide skirts, light bulbs, photograph albums, windows, schedules, rostrums, card houses, ring fingers, walls, preserving jars, scrap metal, clothes cupboards, tombstones, firestones and fibre rugs. These objects are joined in the story itself by many others of equal significance. They are representational details of that environment which Oskar first assesses, then rebels against, then reconciles himself to, then reexamines critically, then flees from. And in the course of it all, the drum does take him and us towards a measure of light and of truth. (pp. 81-2)

The book has the defects of its virtues. Linguistic brilliance sometimes distracts from a serious point that is being made; the sheer number of characters sometimes diffuses the interest; the surrealistic flights are sometimes counter-productive; and the astonishing range of choice which is offered to the reader in the way of ideas and symbols and insights is occasionally too great to be assimilated. . . . But these are minor reservations and dwindle into impertinence when we consider the strengths of *The Tin Drum*—its intelligence, its assurance, its wit, its vigour, its uninhibitedness, its invention, its tirelessness, its delineation of character, its bravery, its poetry, its profusion, its universality, its narrative magic. (pp. 82-3)

The appearance of *Cat and Mouse* (1961) confounded the many critics who had declared, on the evidence of *The Tin Drum*, that Grass's prose talent suffered from the common German maladies of complexity and prolixity. Beside its predecessor, *Cat and Mouse* looks taut, frugal and disconcertingly lucid. . . . It has a precision and severity which is in the best traditions of the German *novelle*, and is executed with a consummate artistry. (p. 84)

[The] title and the design on the book-jacket are integral parts of the work. The cat who sprawls across both sides of the cover is no fireside decoration. It is an act of criticism upon the book, selecting and displaying all the salient features of the text. The cat looks solid and self-assured, at once a contented, domesticated animal and a creature of fierce independence. It wears its ribbon and medal as if they have been awarded by competition judges, and yet is aware how provocative it is being in mocking Germany's most revered military honour. (p. 85)

The family likenesses are evident from the start. Like *The Tin Drum*, the *novelle* is set in Danzig, explores the world of adolescence, and tells its story retrospectively. . . . The potentialities of protest are not neglected, and the role of the clown is once more filled. The protagonist is acquainted with impotence. These similarities have been trimmed to fit into the smaller scope of the *novelle*. Action is limited to wartime Danzig for the most part, and the work gains from this sharper focus; the weakest parts of *The Tin Drum* are those which are set outside Danzig and after the war. The world of adolescence is the entire world of *Cat and Mouse*, and its population is strictly limited so that its central figure, Joachim Mahlke, can be observed without distraction. (p. 86)

Cat and Mouse is outstanding for many things— the firmness of its control, the deftness of its comic touches, the cunning of its imagination, the clarity of its argument, the relevance and integrity of its themes. (p. 107)

The content of *Dog Years* (1963) is prefigured in the title and in the design on the book-jacket. Once again Grass has provided a front cover which is both starting point and destination, and invitation to read on and a warning of what we shall find. . . . At the heart of the novel is the fable of the shepherd dog who was presented to Hitler by the party leadership of the Danzig District. (p. 108)

The dog is a symbol of totalitarianism; it is thus appropriate that Prinz's conception should take place under police supervision. It stands for National Socialism and its gratuitous violence. At the same time it represents a nation's misplaced, dog-like faith in its master. It is an embodiment of evil and its comprehensive blackness sets it alongside Oskar's Black Witch and Mahlke's cat. (p. 109)

The prose itself is deliberately chopped, checked and interrupted in a way that makes it quite unlike some of the mellifluous flights in *The Tin Drum* or some of the poetic felicities in *Cat and Mouse*. Sentences are short, barked, repetitious and entirely in keeping with the subject-matter. . . .

Viewed in its totality, the prose seems rich and matted, while the most vivid patterning on the carpet is provided by the imagery. The purpose of *Dog Years* is clearer and bolder than that of *The Tin Drum*, and it is assisted in the pursuit of that purpose by its more precise imagery. (p. 119)

[The] novel with which it must finally be compared is *The Tin Drum*. Is it a greater or lesser work? The answer must surely be that *Dog Years* marks an advance. Its wit is keener, its comprehension is deeper, its scope is larger, its construction is more subtle and delicate, its themes are presented in a more challenging way, its satire is more caustic, its imagery more controlled, its effect more disturbing. *Dog Years* finds a better balance between its artistic needs and their method of treatment. *The Tin Drum* profited from the central presence of Oskar, whose drum years were the staple of the novel. But when Oskar's drumming lost its power for a time in the post-war period, the novel, too, lost some of its impetus. There is no loss of impetus in *Dog Years*. . . . By rejecting the concept of omniscience, *Dog Years* gets closer to reality. Its three narrators can qualify and refine and adjust and restate. Paradoxically, this splitting-up leads to a more unified picture of reality than is the case in *The Tin Drum*. (pp. 140-41)

[The] third novel in the Danzig trilogy is a finer work because it attempts, and succeeds in, more difficult aims. It brings politics into the realm of art and does not become either documentary or hortatory. It can take its deserved place beside that greatest ideological novel, Dostoevsky's *The Possessed*. The essential concern of the Russian master and the German novelist alike is the politics of salvation. The ruling obsession is with the redemptive powers of confession of past crimes. (p. 141)

The Plebeians Rehearse the Uprising [1967] is a study of the possibilities of peaceful coexistence between a man's political attitudes and his artistic abilities. The conclusions which it reaches are anything but reassuring. (p. 147)

The basic premise which gives the play its title and scope is an authentic *coup de théâtre*. For the first time in his dramatic work, Grass has found a form which is a generous host to content instead of one which is a shoulder against the door. There are no Absurdist fantasies here, no lyrical flights across the skies of the image and metaphor. To select is to begin. And to select an idea as brilliant and fecund as that which underlies *The Plebeians Rehearse the Uprising* is to begin with considerable advantages. At a stroke, before the play has even started, the title has connected Shakespeare, Brecht and Grass. Shakespeare's play [*Coriolanus*], within Brecht's rehearsal method, within Grass's play. The

distancing effect of the narrative approach to *Dog Years* has found its counterpart on the stage. Each character acts out his story, but each is audience to the other's performance. Once again, Grass is able to argue, reply, simplify, embroider, and shift perspective at will. It is an important freedom because it gives the play much of its tension, and allows Grass to dwell on the interplay between reality and illusion with a Pirandellian relish. At a linguistic level, it enables him to point up the contrasts between Shakespearean verse, a Brechtian idiom (subtly recreated by means of borrowings from Brecht's works), the East Berlin dialect of the workers, the officialese of Kozanka, and the more characteristically Grassian moments, such as the fine speech which closes Act Three—"Benighted children, worshipping a dove". The clever juxtaposing of these different modes enriches the text, adds variety, permits great use of bathos, assists the mobility of the changing perspective, and helps to underline both the universality and particularity of the event which is at the centre of the play. (p. 151)

Self-inflicted pain is the essence of [the novel *Local Anaesthetic* (1968)]. It is the common ground on which author, characters and readers meet. For in sub-

Grass addressing the German Writers' Union.

ordinating himself so completely to his compositional aims, Grass has had to make several painful artistic sacrifices; in pursuing their individual courses, his characters are the creators of their own discomfort; and in pressing on through the novel's deliberate and sharp pin-pricks, the reader is like a dentist's patient, enduring pain in the cause of improvement. (p. 172)

First impressions suggest that the Danzig trilogy is a long way off. *Local Anaesthetic* has no Danzig setting, no acutely observed adolescent world, no journey across a nation's history, no wealth of episode, no superabundance of character, no value-free moral sphere, no acres of vitalistic prose, no playfulness and irreverence, no sudden, exhilarating descents into the Brauxel mine of Grass's surrealistic imagination. Seneca has replaced Rabelais: the whole tone of things has changed. (p. 173)

Narrative approach, too, segregates *Local Anaesthetic* from its predecessors. Starusch's first-person narration is no return to the exuberant style of Oskar's memoirs. For all his ubiquitousness, mental and physical, the tin drummer did adhere to a definite chronological scheme. Starusch does not do this. In his mind, past and present are locked in such a desperate embrace that they are virtually indistinguishable. He insists that historical awareness is all. But he does not view history as a process of organic growth that is generated by cause and effect. He sees it as the unending and oscillating interplay between past, present and future. While this idea of the simultaneity of time is not new in Grass's work, the intensity with which it is taken up is unparalleled. It determines the whole structure of the novel, sabotaging coherence and exploding any possibility of conventional linear story-telling. In each of the books in the Danzig trilogy, a figure of action declines into impotence. . . . In *Local Anaesthetic,* there is no such movement from energy to inaction. Because of Starusch's treatment of time, they coexist. He does not need to trace the line from action to impotence; he continuously exemplifies it. (p. 174)

Local Anaesthetic predicated a new relationship between author and reader. . . . To get its argument across Grass needed to induce a different state of mind in his reader. He does this in a most individual and daring way. Having put Starusch and, by extension, society at large, into the dentist's chair, the author does precisely the same to the reader. Whoever opens the novel will find himself surrounded by oppressive evidence of modern scientific and technical advance— clipped phrases, hygienic metaphors, neat functional imagery, white-coated control, laundered situations, and almost complete freedom from the element of chance. (p. 194)

From the Diary of a Snail [1973] is a celebration of the art of collecting. Stories, ideas, people, images, observations, definitions, fears, hopes, illusions, statis-

tics, arguments, insights, memories and doubts are gathered together, arranged and re-arranged into intricate patterns. . . . Politics, autobiography and fiction are treated as related—often interchangeable—species. Election speeches, family conversations and cellared snails are collected with equal passion. The book is, in every sense, a collector's piece. (pp. 199-200)

From the Diary of a Snail reveals an even greater politicisation of Grass's art than its predecessor did. Like the slug which Lisbeth Stomma finds in a cemetery, the book resists classification. It is not a political novel like *Local Anaesthetic:* it is a work which calls in question all the assumptions made about the dividing lines between literature and politics and autobiography. It is a re-examination of the purpose and of the possibilities of the novel. Where *Local Anaesthetic* dispensed with the artist in its title, its successor restores artist alongside political symbol; and, unlike Starusch, the diarist never allows the reader to forget that he is primarily an artist. The contents of the diary are directed at the author's children and, by extension, at the whole of the younger generation in Germany. (pp. 200-01)

The snail stands central. It is author, main character, writing method and political philosophy. . . . In commending the virtues of the snail, Grass clearly has in mind the attributes of both snail and slug (the German word 'Schnecke' in the title means both). The snail suggests deliberation, self-sufficiency, protection; the slug denotes sensitivity, defenceless nakedness, the sluggish. In mythology both gasteropods were thought to possess curative powers. Both are resoundingly unspectacular in their life-styles. (p. 202)

The tin drummer has come a long way. He began by revelling in his freedom and individuality and artistic power. The absurd presumption that he was the father of Maria's child prompted the firstlings of parental duty in him. Now, dog and snail years later, he has become an exemplary father. To convert his children to the religion of doubt, he has told them the story of the Jews, and justified the nature of the telling in the process. His art has matured with his outlook. *From the Diary of a Snail* extends the conventional boundaries of the novel. It disposes of the complaint that politics and literature do not blend by making the author, in whom the didactic and the artistic self-evidently unite, central. It goes a stage beyond *Local Anaesthetics* in this respect, and is a testimony to the health and versatility of Grass's talent. It moves, it debates, it excites, it teases, it is artful in its artistry. Like Dürer, it communicates mood and message with graphic suddenness. The reader is left . . . 'with fewer and fewer certitudes'. One can ask no more of a book. (p. 223)

Keith Miles, in his *Günter Grass,* Barnes & Noble, 1975, 227 p.

H. WAYNE SCHOW
(essay date 1978)

[In the excerpt below, Schow views Grass's conception of protagonist-narrator Oskar Matzerath as the catalyst for the diverse fictional modes he employs in *The Tin Drum*.]

[*The Tin Drum* has] an epic range in its temporal and cultural matter [and] a largeness of vision which, in its own way, comprehends the tragicomic implications of personal existence and historical development. (p. 5)

In confronting the structural variety and ambiguous richness of *The Tin Drum,* we find that they . . . derive from an extraordinary cornerstone—the functional complexity of the protagonist-narrator, Oskar Matzerath, whose creation is an achievement of imaginative and technical brilliance. As a result of Oskar's bizarre stance and strange capabilities, Grass manages to combine features of the most disparate novelistic forms as well as provide multiple perspectives on his social and historical materials.

Grass's most obvious departure from convention was to make Oskar a dwarf and a highly unusual one at that. (p. 6)

Though *The Tin Drum* is not a historical novel in the strictest sense, it is firmly embedded in a recent, particularized (and for these reasons highly convincing) historical matrix. Oskar's family history through three generations unfolds between 1899 and 1945 in the highly charged political and cultural tensions of Danzig and from 1945 to 1953 amid the post-war contradictions of West Germany. . . . Such "placing" inclines us to regard him (with certain reservations) primarily as a real person in an immediately real world and, therefore, capable of being influenced by that world. Thus, even though Oskar outrages us frequently, we have some encouragement to sympathize and identify humanly with him. (Perhaps he is so upsetting to us at times, because he seems potentially "one of us". . . .) (pp. 7-8)

[But Oskar's characterization is not] wholly consistent with the limitations implicit in the surface realism of the novel. Grass has endowed him with several powers of a kind ordinarily encountered only in fantasy, including precocious adult awareness from birth, and the ability to arrest arbitrarily his normal physical growth at the age of three and to commence it again, ostensibly by choice, some years later. (p. 8)

[These capabilities make Oskar] doubly an outsider. Not merely is he a freakish "exceptional child" freed from conforming to conventional patterns of development; almost as if by virtue of his supernatural awareness, unique abilities, and shrewd willfulness he stands above adults in the normal world, marching to his own drumming, exploiting the climate of license in which he moves.

This relationship to society suggests in some obvious ways the stance of the picaresque hero, as critics have frequently noted. Like the Spanish picaro, Oskar stands socially, morally, and to an often surprising extent, emotionally removed from the events around him. He makes his way through the world largely on his own terms, confident in his ability to manipulate and survive. Where the picaro moves up and down the social-class structure, usually in the role of a resourceful servant, Oskar by virtue of his small size and seeming insignificance enjoys considerable mobility and can turn up in the most improbable places. As an observer he enjoys an additional advantage: people around him assume unthinkingly that his arrested growth extends to his mental development as well, an impression he deliberately cultivates. Accordingly, no one pays any serious attention to him, and he comes and goes freely, witness to the most private acts of family, neighbors, and even public figures.

Characteristically, picaresque fiction lends itself to satire because the picaro's mobility provides a wide range of material for satiric attack and an appropriately detached viewpoint. If in *The Tin Drum* Grass is an eclectic novelist incorporating a surprising number of fictional modes, he is not least of all a satirist. His targets range from the quixotism of Polish patriotism to the morally bankrupt aestheticism of the Nazis; from the petty pleasures of the *petite bourgeoisie* between the wars to the indulgence of post-war Germans in excesses of guilt; from the shallowness of post-war German materialism to the special lunacies of modern art. For all such subjects, Oskar is a remarkably effective satiristic medium, an advantageously placed reflector of what is outside himself. (pp. 8-9)

Grass himself acknowledged that his novel was indebted to the form of the picaresque novel, in the same breath observing that it was similarly descended from the *Bildungsroman*. . . . To see how Grass has spanned these genres is to grasp in part Oskar's psychological complexity. (p. 9)

From his early years . . . Oskar has been searching for self-understanding in the way of a *Bildungsroman* protagonist. He is involved in a quest for identity which has intensified to the point of crisis as he lies in the mental institution writing his autobiography. Unquestionably, writing his story is his attempt to clarify and resolve that crisis. (p. 11)

One of the most persistent means by which Grass discloses Oskar's identity-quest—thereby emphasizing the inward focus characteristic of *Bildungs*-fiction—is the series of symbolic polarities in relation to which Oskar compulsively attempts to project and understand himself. . . . Grass's protagonist returns repeatedly to the opposition of Dionysus-Apollo—especially as exemplified in Rasputin and Goethe, those heroes of his idiosyncratic early education and figures of his own ambivalence ("my two souls," he calls them, echoing Faust). . . . Similarly, Oskar persistently sees himself in relation to both Jesus and Satan. In the former comparison he seeks a bit desperately to realize a transcendental identity and mission, seeing himself as the offspring of a holy triangle (however comically ironic). . . . [Disappointed] in his pleas for a miracle to build faith on, he responds with a psychologically predictable perversity, blasphemes Christ by setting himself up as the sacrilegious Jesus of the teenage-hoodlum Dusters. . . . (pp. 11-12)

[Women] are used to clarify symbolically the protagonist's spiritual struggle. Oskar's mother epitomizes certain paradoxes which lame Oskar in his quest for self-identity. . . . As Oskar's education in life continues, the contradictions of the feminine increasingly contribute to his spiritual and psychological ambivalence, in particular the tension between woman as spiritual ideal and woman as destructive force. (p. 12)

[Oskar's] conscious decision to grow . . . [is] a metaphor for acceptance of personal and social responsibility in the *Bildungsroman* sense. His physical growth is appropriately a painful ordeal (he becomes eventually an undersized hunchback rather than a dwarf), symbolizing the difficult and half-fearful reluctance he experiences now that he can (and must) pursue his identity independent of the deceased parental generation. . . .

Oskar's inconclusive posture at the end of his narrative can hardly be called a triumph. His reluctance to leave the psychological shelter of the mental institution and face the challenges of the world outside is the obverse of the conventional pattern of development in the *Bildungsroman*. (p. 13)

Oskar's failures are not entirely due to his own shortcoming. If he is morally and psychically lamed, as symbolized by his grotesque hump, he is so (Grass seems to imply) because that is the inevitable effect of a barbaric and bored world on one of Oskar's sensibilities. Oskar cannot escape the moral imperative to accept human responsibility. . . . His difficulty to find some adequate basis and direction as he is impelled from within to come to terms with his life. Quite clearly to Oskar's credit, he ultimately finds the life of materialistic superficiality in post-war Germany ("the bourgeois smug" he had denoted prophetically in a satiric poem during the war) attractive to neither of the two souls in him. . . . [His] retreat to the mental institution and ambivalence about leaving suggest that such ex-

ploitation is out of harmony with the humanly significant direction his growth is seeking. . . . Grass surrounds his protagonist with a corrupting cultural environment, implying that in such a world the traditionally positive outcome of the *Bildungsroman* is no longer possible. (p. 14)

Viewing Oskar with some sympathy is not meant to oversimplify his character nor to deny that at times he is offensively amoral and spiritually impotent. Emphasizing the intensity of his human involvement should correct a view which sees him as exclusively responsible for such failures, regarding him as primarily a picaro, primarily as picaro, more an influence than influenced. . . . [Grass managed to make Oskar so convincingly complex] by making him a dwarf and exploiting the natural and symbolic ambiguity of that position, by making him an uneven participant in the life around him by virtue of his limitations and relative disinclinations, but by allowing him some partial emergence from his purely dwarfish, ahuman position. . . .

As if this were not enough, Oskar is given a drum on his third birthday. . . . On the psychological level . . . the drum can be seen as a crutch for Oskar's insecurities: "for without my drum I am always exposed and helpless," he says. . . . Clearly, reliance on the drum implies a stance inimical to normal adjustment, an aesthetic detachment opposed to social conformity. If the drum signifies an idiosyncratic limitation in Oskar, it is also paradoxically the symbol and means of his superiority, for his virtuoso mastery of it clearly marks him as an artist.

Through Oskar as drummer (. . . and *litterateur*, since he has created an extraordinary autobiography), Grass explores . . . the unique, lonely, demanding, powerful, and at times dehumanizing role of the artist. . . . Grass's inquiry seems to epitomize in Oskar several artistic stances simultaneously, including some which are ostensibly contradictory. What kind of artist is Oskar? In one simple way he is a drummer whose art is romantic self-expression, a means of celebrating his triumphs, of venting his sorrows. (pp. 15-16)

In another romantic perspective, Oskar is a drummer whose art mystically clarifies reality and truth. His drum is a medium of both memory and imagination through which he is able to reconstruct the past. . . . (p. 16)

The ramifications of Oskar's art do not end with these imaginative forays and mystical revelations, for the possession of such unusual powers presents opportunities for manipulation, whether for good or ill, and Oskar quickly discovers these exploitive possibilities. In his provocative exploration of these multiple tensions, Grass raises the central questions of the artist's relations to life and society, including the moral implications of his position. (pp. 16-17)

In Grass's treatment Oskar's stance as artist repeatedly yields ambiguity and paradox. (p. 17)

The implications of Oskar's artistic ambiguity are "both/and" rather than "either/or." Oskar's art can express the conscience of grieving humanity, as in the lyrical concluding chapter to Book One when he is contrasted with the artist-musician, Meyn, who sells out to the Nazis; but it is (in the perversity of its pied-piper musical magic) an analogue of Hitler's aesthetic entrancement of the German people. . . .

In this sphere Grass's criticism of modern culture and of German culture, in particular, is relevant. While the artist may attempt to influence his age, his stance is at least as likely to be influenced by the culture in which he lives. Historically, as in the later nineteenth century, aestheticism wins adherents among the sensitive in proportion to the disillusioning conditions and values prevailing in a culture or an age. Oskar is not alone in being driven into the arms of aestheticism. (p. 18)

In his loosely rambling but probing analysis of the uses of art and the implications of the artist's role, Grass does not provide a single view or simple answers but rather paradox after paradox. The ambiguities central to Oskar's developmental problem reflect the challenges, anguish, and failures experienced by twentieth-century German artists and intellectuals and, finally, have their universal applications. Oskar's psychological and situational flexibility, more than anything else, allows Grass so many explorative opportunities.

The hero as detached picaro, the hero as involved apprentice to life, the hero as artist, the hero as existential man; the novel as social history, the novel as satire, the novel as philosophical inquiry, the novel as psychological study, the novel as tragicomedy, the novel as realism *and* the novel as symbolic imagination; offensive yet satisfying, amoral yet profoundly moral, pessimistic yet paradoxically affirmative: what a remarkable combination to be found in a single work, what a complex vision. And Oskar unifies it all. (p. 19)

H. Wayne Schow, "Functional Complexity of Grass's Oskar," in *Critique: Studies in Modern Fiction*, Vol. XIX, No. 3, 1978, pp. 5-20.

SOURCES FOR FURTHER STUDY

Cunliffe, W. Gordon. *Günter Grass*. New York: Twayne Publishers, 1969, 146 p.

> Biographical and critical study of Grass's career through 1967.

Forster, Leonard. "Gunter Grass since the Danzig Trilogy." *University of Toronto Quarterly* XLVII, No. 1 (Fall 1977): 56-73.

> Examines similarities and differences in Grass's Danzig Trilogy with the novels written after it.

Lawson, Richard H. *Günter Grass*. New York: Frederick Ungar Publishing Co., 1985, 176.

> Favorable critical study of Grass's work through *Headbirths; or, The Germans Are Dying Out*. Includes bibliography.

Mason, Ann L. *The Skeptical Muse: A Study of Günter Grass' Conception of the Artist*. Bern: Herbert Lang, 1974, 138 p.

> Views Grass's parodistic use of the artist in his work as a subversion of German literary tradition.

O'Neill, Patrick, ed. *Critical Essays on Günter Grass*. Boston: G. K. Hall, 1987, 230 p.

> Collection of reviews and essays on Grass's major works by such critics as George Steiner, Stanley Edgar Hyman, and J. P. Stern.

Stern, J. P. "Gunter Grass's Uniqueness." *London Review of Books* 3, No. 2 (5-18 February 1981): 11-14.

> Assesses Grass's position in the context of postwar German literature, stressing the importance of place in his fiction.

Thomas Gray

1716-1771

English poet and essayist.

INTRODUCTION

*G*ray was one of the most influential English poets of the mid-eighteenth century. Although his poetic canon is small—throughout his lifetime he wrote around one thousand lines of verse—Gray was a major transitional figure between the sensibility and classical perfection of the Augustans and the emotional reverberation of the Romantics. While the influence of the Augustans is manifested in Gray's concentration on complicated metrical schemes and intellectual ideals, he was in fact a precursor to the Romantic movement because of his sensitive and empathetic portrayal of the common man. Nowhere is this more evident than in his "Elegy Written in a Country Churchyard" (1751), Gray's most famous work and one of the most beloved poems in English literature. While Gray wrote a number of odes, among them "Ode on a Distant Prospect of Eton College" (1747) and "Ode on the Spring" (1748), it is the language of the "Elegy" that has infused modern colloquial speech more than any other piece of English literature that contains so few consecutive lines. Alfred, Lord Tennyson recapitulates the "Elegy's" universal appeal by declaring it contains "divine truisms that make us weep."

Born in London, Gray was the son of a milliner and her husband, a respected scrivener. Although the family was fairly prosperous, Gray's father was a morose and violent man who at times abused his wife unmercifully. There is uncertainty as to whether Gray's parents separated, but it is well documented that it was arranged for Gray to attend Eton College when he was eight years old so that he could be properly educated. A studious and solitary boy, Gray formed intimate friendships with only three other students: Thomas Ashton, Horace Walpole, and Richard West. They proclaimed themselves the "Quadruple Alliance" and were given to precocious conversation on life and literature. West and Walpole figured significantly in Gray's literary development and later in his poetic career, which blossomed during Gray's four years at Cambridge. While at Cambridge, Gray attracted attention as an accomplished writer of Latin verse, though he left in 1738 without taking a degree. Shortly thereafter, Gray joined Walpole on an extended tour of Europe, but in 1741 they quarreled violently, the cause of their differences still a matter of speculation, and the two parted company until their reconciliation in 1745.

After returning to England alone, Gray postponed his reinstatement to Cambridge for two years, spending the interval with his mother, now a widow, at the house she had recently taken in rustic Stoke Poges, Buckinghamshire. Here, in 1742, Gray composed his first major poem, "Ode on the Spring," which he sent to Richard West—unknowingly on the very day of the latter's unexpected death at age twenty-six. Gray's bereavement only served to enhance his creative activity; his level of production at this time was so intense that it was seldom to be repeated during his lifetime. During the next three months Gray wrote "Ode on a Distant Prospect of Eton College," "Hymn to Adversity" (1753), and "Sonnet on the Death of Mr. Richard West" (1775). Gray also turned from Latin to English as his primary poetic medium at this time. He worked intermittently on "Elegy Written in a Country Churchyard," which was not published until 1751, though it is speculated that Gray began this poem as early as 1742, when he was still living in Stoke Poges in close proximity of the inspirational "ivy-covered spires" of the local church.

Gray returned to Cambridge and settled into the life of a university scholar after being awarded a Bachelor of Civil Law degree in 1743. He resided at the college for the better part of his life, but was never a fellow and never took part in tutoring, lecturing or other academic duties. He occasionally spent time away from Cambridge, either visiting his mother in Stoke Poges, studying at the newly opened British Museum, or journeying to the Lake District and Scotland. Throughout his life Gray quietly pursued his studies, taking advantage of the intellectual amenities of the university setting. Classical literature, medieval history, painting, architecture, Celtic and Norse mythology, and botany were only a few of his interests. "Perhaps he was the most learned man in Europe," wrote Gray's contemporary, William J. Temple. Scarcely anything remains to attest to his profound and varied scholarship, apart from a vast accumulation of notes and letters, but Gray enjoyed his academic pursuits immensely, finding great pleasure in knowledge and discovery despite the lack of any developed work or critical recognition. Of the importance of his studies, Gray wrote, "To be employed is to be happy," and "to find oneself in business is the great art of life." It was during this time of intense per-

sonal scholarship that Gray was elected Regius Professor of Modern History at Cambridge, an office he held until his death in 1771.

"Gray wrote at the very beginning of a certain literary epoch of which we, perhaps, stand at the very end," wrote G. K. Chesterton in 1932. "He represented that softening of the Classic which slowly turned into the Romantic." Gray's "Elegy Written in a Country Churchyard" represents more than any other work during Gray's time the elements of the intuitive, the emotional, and the metaphysical which, when introduced, were in direct opposition to the established tenets of English neo-classical literature. From the onset, Gray's technical accomplishments were impressive, but what set him apart from his contemporaries were his evocative descriptions of the sights around him and his ability to spark a catharsis of mood and feeling in his readers. Some critics have suggested that while Gray's earliest poems, among them "Ode on the Spring" and "Hymn to Adversity," are intensely personal and represent an impassioned response to life and death, his later poems are emotionally distant in comparison. This development, critics suggest, may have been due in part to Gray's precarious position as a bridge between two conflicting poetic movements. As Matthew Arnold stated, "Gray, a born poet, fell upon the age of prose. . . . [With] the qualities of mind and soul of a genuine poet, [he] was isolated in his century."

Despite Gray's sometimes antithetical poetic voice, his "Elegy Written in a Country Churchyard" is still considered a classic in English poetry. In this poem, Gray gave expression to the thoughts that were buried deep in the English consciousness of the eighteenth century—thoughts about history and tradition, the Anglican religion, and the tranquility of English landscapes and village life. Even Samuel Johnson, Gray's harshest critic, found the "Elegy" rich "with images which find a mirrour in every mind, and with sentiments to which every bosom returns an echo." While this poem brought Gray immediate critical and popular acclaim and was frequently reprinted throughout his lifetime, it was almost published in a disreputable magazine without Gray's sanction. If it had not been for Walpole's intervention, the initial publication of the "Elegy" may have been radically modified, lessening the impact of the poem. Controversy also surrounds the last four stanzas of this work, the portion commonly called "The Epitaph." When first published, critics were discontented with its lack of harmony in comparison to the rest of the poem, but Gray, in due course, made some significant alterations. While various commentators have speculated on the purpose and origin of these last four stanzas, the process of the "Elegy's" composition will always remain uncertain.

The success of the "Elegy" focused critical attention on Gray for the rest of his life, leading to close scrutiny of his subsequent works. "The Progress of Poesy" and "The Bard" were his efforts to imitate the stanzaic structure of the Greek poet Pindar. In the first ode, Gray set himself to glorify the poet's calling; and he did so with an exhaltation and allusiveness that render many of the passages difficult. "The Bard," the second in Gray's *Odes* (1757), portrays a traditional episode during the final subjugation of Wales by English forces. Although Gray demonstrated that he was widely versed in English history, these odes, on the whole, were not well received and he was accused of being obscure in his attempt to write not for the world but for his fellow poets. While the *Odes* were widely read and discussed, they were not understood or appreciated by the general readership or highly respected by literary authorities. In the midst of this critical controversy, with some critics praising the significance of the *Odes* and others freely parodying them, documentation shows that Gray was unconcerned with public displeasure. In a letter written to his friend, the Reverend James Brown, Gray justified his concentration on classical allusion and imagery: "The odes in question . . . were meant to be vocal to the intelligent alone."

From the time of his first publication to the present day, Gray's poetry has had as many admirers as detractors. Although scholars continue to praise the "Elegy" as a brilliant piece of verse, they also puzzle over the inconsistancies in theme and approach that marbled the rest of Gray's poetic output. Yet it is almost unanimous among critics that in the "Elegy" Gray broke new ground in concepts and attitudes by tapping into the pulse of the common man with great insight and passion. To the neo-classicists, Gray's statement that "any fool may write a most valuable book by chance, if he will only tell us what he heard and saw with veracity" would appear impetuous and incognizant, but it is the very veracity in Gray's work that has established his place in literary history as the author of one of the most exquisite poems in English literature.

(For further information about Gray's life and works, see *Literature Criticism from 1400 to 1800,* Vol. 4 and *Poetry Criticism,* Vol. 2.)

CRITICAL COMMENTARY

SAMUEL JOHNSON

(essay date 1781)

[Johnson was an English poet, essayist, and critic whose moralistic criticism strongly influenced eighteenth-century taste. In the following excerpt from a 1781 essay, he disparages the language and thought of Gray's poetry but reserves unqualified praise for the "Elegy."]

Gray's poetry is now to be considered, and I hope not to be looked on as an enemy to his name if I confess that I contemplate it with less pleasure than his life.

His **"Ode on Spring"** has something poetical, both in the language and the thought; but the language is too luxuriant, and the thoughts have nothing new. There has of late arisen a practice of giving to adjectives, derived from substantives, the termination of participles, such as the *cultured* plain, the *daisied* bank; but I was sorry to see, in the lines of a scholar like Gray, 'the *honied* Spring.' The morality is natural, but too stale; the conclusion is pretty.

The poem ["**Ode on the Death of a Favourite Cat**"] was doubtless by its author considered as a trifle, but it is not a happy trifle. In the first stanza 'the azure flowers that blow' shew resolutely a rhyme is some-

times made when it cannot easily be found. Selima, the Cat, is called a nymph, with some violence both to language and sense; but there is good use made of it when it is done; for of the two lines,

What female heart can gold despise?
What cat's averse to fish?

The first relates merely to the nymph, and the second only to the cat. The sixth stanza contains a melancholy truth, that 'a favourite has no friend,' but the last ends in a pointed sentence of no relation to the purpose; if what glistered had been 'gold,' the cat would not have gone into the water; and, if she had, would not less have been drowned.

The **"Prospect of Eton College"** suggests nothing to Gray which every beholder does not equally think and feel. His supplication to father Thames, to tell him who drives the hoop or tosses the ball, is useless and puerile. Father Thames has no better means of knowing than himself. His epithet 'buxom health' is not elegant; he seems not to understand the word. Gray thought his language more poetical as it was more remote from common use: finding in Dryden 'honey redolent of Spring,' an expression that reaches the utmost limits of our language, Gray drove it a little more beyond com-

Principal Works

Ode on a Distant Prospect of Eton College (poetry) 1747

*"Ode on the Death of a Favourite Cat, Drowned in a Tub of Gold Fishes" (poetry) 1748

*"Ode on Spring" (poetry) 1748

An Elegy Wrote in A Country Church Yard (poetry) 1751; also published as Elegy Written in a Country Churchyard, 1834.

Designs by Mr. R. Bentley for Six Poems by Mr. T. Gray (poetry) 1753

†Odes (poetry) 1757

Poems by Mr. Gray (poetry) 1768

Ode Performed in the Senate-House at Cambridge July 1, 1769, at the Installation of His Grace Augustus Henry Fitzroy, Duke of Grafton, Chancellor of the University (poetry) 1769

On Lord Holland's Seat near Margate, Kent (poetry) 1769

The Poems of Mr. Gray (poetry) 1775

‡"Sonnet on the Death of Mr. Richard West" (poetry) 1775

The Works of Thomas Gray; Containing His Poems, and Correspondence with Several Eminent Literary Characters (poetry and letters) 1807

The Letters of Thomas Gray, Including the Correspondence of Gray and Mason 3 vols. (letters) 1900-1912

Essays and Criticism (essays) 1911

Ode on the Pleasure Arising from Vicissitude, Left Unfinished by Mr. Gray, and Since Completed 2 vols. (poetry) 1933

The Selected Letters of Thomas Gray (letters) 1952

*Both poems were first published in A Collection of Poems by Several Hands, 1748.

†This volume contains what are commonly called Gray's Pindaric odes: "The Bard" and "The Progress of Poesy."

‡Published in the journal Universal Magazine, 1775.

---

mon apprehension, by making 'gales' to be 'redolent of joy and youth.'

Of the **"Ode on Adversity"** the hint was at first taken from 'O Diva, gratum quae regis Antium'; but Gray has excelled his original by the variety of his sentiments and by their moral application. Of this piece, at once poetical and rational, I will not by slight objections violate the dignity.

My process has now brought me to the 'Wonderful Wonder of Wonders,' the two Sister Odes ["**The Progress of Poetry"** and **"The Bard"**]; by which, though either vulgar ignorance or common sense at first universally rejected them, many have been since persuaded to think themselves delighted. I am one of those that are willing to be pleased, and therefore would gladly find the meaning of the first stanza of **"The Progress of Poetry."**

Gray seems in his rapture to confound the images of 'spreading sound' and 'running water.' A 'stream of musick' may be allowed; but where does Musick, however 'smooth and strong,' after having visited the 'verdant vales,' 'rowl down the steep amain,' so as that 'rocks and nodding groves rebellow to the roar'? If this be said of Musick, it is nonsense; if it be said of Water, it is nothing to the purpose.

The second stanza, exhibiting Mars's car and Jove's eagle, is unworthy of further notice. Criticism disdains to chase a schoolboy to his common-places.

To the third it may likewise be objected that it is drawn from Mythology, though such as may be more easily assimilated to real life. 'Idalia's velvet-green' has something of cant. An epithet or metaphor drawn from Nature ennobles Art; an epithet or metaphor drawn from Art degrades Nature. Gray is too fond of words arbitrarily compounded. 'Many-twinkling' was formerly censured as not analogical; we may say *many-spotted,* but scarcely *many-spotting.* This stanza, however, has something pleasing.

Of the second ternary of stanzas the first endeavours to tell something, and would have told it had it not been crossed by Hyperion; the second describes well enough the universal prevalence of poetry, but I am afraid that the conclusion will not rise from the premises. The caverns of the North and the plains of Chili are not the residences of 'Glory' and 'generous Shame.' But that Poetry and Virtue go always together is an opinion so pleasing that I can forgive him who resolves to think it true.

The third stanza sounds big with Delphi, and Egean, and Ilissus, and Meander, and 'hallowed fountain' and 'solemn sound'; but in all Gray's odes there is a kind of cumbrous splendour which we wish away. His position is at last false: in the time of Dante and Petrarch, from whom he derives our first school of poetry, Italy was overrun by 'tyrant power' and 'coward vice'; nor was our state much better when we first borrowed the Italian arts.

Of the third ternary the first gives a mythological birth of Shakespeare. What is said of that mighty genius is true; but it is not said happily: the real effects of this poetical power are put out of sight by the pomp of machinery. Where truth is sufficient to fill the mind, fiction is worse than useless; the counterfeit debases the genuine.

His account of Milton's blindness, if we suppose it caused by study in the formation of his poem, a supposition surely allowable, is poetically true, and happily imagined. But the 'car' of Dryden, with his 'two coursers,' has nothing in it peculiar; it is a car in which any other rider may be placed.

"The Bard" appears at the first view to be, as Algarotti and others have remarked, an imitation of the prophecy of Nereus. Algarotti thinks it superior to its original, and, if preference depends only on the imagery and animation of the two poems, his judgement is right. There is in **"The Bard"** more force, more thought, and more variety. But to copy is less than to invent, and the copy has been unhappily produced at a wrong time. The fiction of Horace was to the Romans credible; but its revival disgusts us with apparent and unconquerable falsehood. (pp. 433-38)

To select a singular event, and swell it to a giant's bulk by fabulous appendages of spectres and predictions, has little difficulty, for he that forsakes the probable may always find the marvellous. And it has little use: we are affected only as we believe; we are improved only as we find something to be imitated or declined. I do not see that **"The Bard"** promotes any truth, moral or political.

His stanzas are too long, especially his epodes; the ode is finished before the ear has learned its measures, and consequently before it can receive pleasure from their consonance and recurrence.

Of the first stanza the abrupt beginning has been celebrated; but technical beauties can give praise only to the inventor. It is in the power of any man to rush abruptly upon his subject, that has read the ballad of *Johnny Armstrong,*

Is there ever a man in all Scotland—

The initial resemblances, or alliterations, 'ruin,' 'ruthless,' 'helm nor hauberk,' are below the grandeur of a poem that endeavours at sublimity.

In the second stanza the Bard is well described; but in the third we have the puerilities of obsolete mythology. When we are told that Cadwallo 'hush'd the stormy main,' and that Modred 'made huge Plinlimmon bow his cloud-top'd head,' attention recoils from the repetition of a tale that, even when it was first heard, was heard with scorn.

The 'weaving' of the 'winding sheet' he borrowed, as he owns, from the northern Bards; but their texture, however, was very properly the work of female powers, as the art of spinning the thread of life in another mythology. Theft is always dangerous; Gray has made weavers of his slaughtered bards by a fiction outrageous and incongruous. They are then called upon to 'Weave the warp, and weave the woof,' perhaps with no great propriety; for it is by crossing the woof with the warp that men weave the web or piece; and the first line was dearly bought by the admission of its wretched correspondent, 'Give ample room and verge enough.' He has, however, no other line as bad.

The third stanza of the second ternary is commended, I think, beyond its merit. The personification is indistinct. Thirst and Hunger are not alike, and their features, to make the imagery perfect, should have been discriminated. We are told, in the same stanza, how 'towers' are 'fed.' But I will no longer look for particular faults; yet let it be observed that the ode might have been concluded with an action of better example: but suicide is always to be had without expence of thought.

These odes are marked by glittering accumulations of ungraceful ornaments: they strike, rather than please; the images are magnified by affectation; the language is laboured into harshness. The mind of the writer seems to work with unnatural violence. 'Double, double, toil and trouble.' He has a kind of strutting dignity, and is tall by walking on tiptoe. His art and his struggle are too visible, and there is too little appearance of ease and nature.

To say that he has no beauties would be unjust: a man like him, of great learning and great industry, could not but produce something valuable. When he pleases least, it can only be said that a good design was ill directed.

His translations of Northern and Welsh Poetry deserve praise: the imagery is preserved, perhaps often improved; but the language is unlike the language of other poets.

In the character of his **"Elegy"** I rejoice to concur with the common reader; for by the common sense of readers uncorrupted with literary prejudices, after all the refinements of subtility and the dogmatism of learning, must be finally decided all claim to poetical honours. The **"Church-yard"** abounds with images which find a mirrour in every mind, and with sentiments to which every bosom returns an echo. The four stanzas beginning 'Yet even these bones' are to me original: I have never seen the notions in any other place; yet he that reads them here persuades himself that he has always felt them. Had Gray written often thus it had been vain to blame, and useless to praise him. (pp. 438-42)

Samuel Johnson, "Gray," in his *Lives of the English Poets, Vol. III,* edited by George Birkbeck Hill, 1905. Reprint by Octagon Books, Inc., 1967, 421-43.

MATTHEW ARNOLD
(essay date 1880)

[A nineteenth-century English poet and critic, Arnold wrote widely on social and literary issues. In the following excerpt from an essay first published in 1880, he addresses the brevity and unevenness of Gray's poetic canon, using as a refrain James Brown's statement that Gray "never spoke out."]

He never spoke out. In these four words is contained the whole history of Gray, both as a man and as a poet. The words fell naturally, and as it were by chance, from their writer's pen; but let us dwell upon them, and press into their meaning, for in following it we shall come to understand Gray.

He was in his fifty-fifth year when he died, and he lived in ease and leisure, yet a few pages hold all his poetry; *he never spoke out* in poetry. Still, the reputation which he has achieved by his few pages is extremely high. True, Johnson speaks of him with coldness and disparagement. Gray disliked Johnson, and refused to make his acquaintance; one might fancy that Johnson wrote with some irritation from this cause. But Johnson was not by nature fitted to do justice to Gray and to his poetry; this by itself is a sufficient explanation of the deficiencies of his criticism of Gray. We may add a further explanation of them which is supplied by Mr. Cole's papers. 'When Johnson was publishing his *Life of Gray,'* says Mr. Cole, 'I gave him several anecdotes, *but he was very anxious as soon as possible to get to the end of his labours.'* Johnson was not naturally in sympathy with Gray, whose life he had to write, and when he wrote it he was in a hurry besides. He did Gray injustice, but even Johnson's authority failed to make injustice, in this case, prevail. Lord Macaulay calls the *Life of Gray* the worst of Johnson's *Lives,* and it had found many censurers before Macaulay. Gray's poetical reputation grew and flourished in spite of it. (pp. 70-1)

The immense vogue of Pope and of his style of versification had at first prevented the frank reception of Gray by the readers of poetry. The **"Elegy"** pleased; it could not but please: but Gray's poetry, on the whole, astonished his contemporaries at first more than it pleased them; it was so unfamiliar, so unlike the sort of poetry in vogue. It made its way, however, after his death, with the public as well as with the few; and Gray's second biographer, Mitford, remarks that 'the works which were either neglected or ridiculed by their contemporaries have now raised Gray and Collins to the rank of our two greatest lyric poets.' Their reputation was established, at any rate, and stood extremely high, even if they were not popularly read. Johnson's disparagement of Gray was called 'petulant,' and severely blamed. Beattie, at the end of the eighteenth century, writing to Sir William Forbes, says: 'Of all the English poets of this age Mr. Gray is most admired, and I think with justice.' Cowper writes: 'I have been reading Gray's works, and think him the only poet since Shakespeare entitled to the character of sublime. Perhaps you will remember that I once had a different opinion of him. I was prejudiced.' Adam Smith says: 'Gray joins to the sublimity of Milton the elegance and harmony of Pope; and nothing is wanting to render him, perhaps, the first poet in the English language, but to have written a little more.' And, to come nearer to our own times, Sir James Mackintosh speaks of Gray thus: 'Of all English poets he was the most finished artist. He attained the highest degree of splendour of which poetical style seemed to be capable.'

In a poet of such magnitude, how shall we explain his scantiness of production? Shall we explain it by saying that to make of Gray a poet of this magnitude is absurd; that his genius and resources were small, and that his production, therefore, was small also, but that the popularity of a single piece, the **"Elegy,"**—a popularity due in great measure to the subject,—created for Gray a reputation to which he has really no right? He himself was not deceived by the favour shown to the **"Elegy."** 'Gray told me with a good deal of acrimony,' writes Dr. Gregory, 'that the **"Elegy"** owed its popularity entirely to the subject, and that the public would have received it as well if it had been written in prose.' This is too much to say; the **"Elegy"** is a beautiful poem, and in admiring it the public showed a true feeling for poetry. But it is true that the **"Elegy"** owed much of its success to its subject and that it has received a too unmeasured and unbounded praise.

Gray himself, however, maintained that the **"Elegy"** was not his best work in poetry, and he was right. High as is the praise due to the **"Elegy"**, it is yet true that in other productions of Gray he exhibits poetical qualities even higher than those exhibited in the **"Elegy"**. He deserves, therefore, his extremely high reputation as a poet, although his critics and the public may not always have praised him with perfect judgment. We are brought back, then, to the question: How, in a poet so really considerable, are we to explain his scantiness of production? (pp. 71-4)

The reason, the indubitable reason as I cannot but think it, I have already given elsewhere. Gray, a born poet, fell upon an age of prose. He fell upon an age whose task was such as to call forth in general men's powers of understanding, wit and cleverness, rather than their deepest powers of mind and soul. As regards literary production, the task of the eighteenth century in England was not the poetic interpretation of the world, its task was to create a plain, clear, straightforward, efficient prose. Poetry obeyed the bent of mind requisite for the due fulfilment of this task of the century. It was intellectual, argumentative, ingenious; not seeing things in their truth and beauty, not interpretative. Gray, with the qualities of mind and soul of a genuine poet, was isolated in his century. Maintaining and fortifying them by lofty studies, he yet could not fully educe and enjoy them; the want of a genial atmosphere, the failure of sympathy in his contemporaries, were too great. . . . Coming when he did, and endowed as he was, he was a man born out of date, a man whose full spiritual flowering was impossible. The same thing is to be said of his great contemporary, Butler, the author of the *Analogy.* In the sphere of religion, which touches that of poetry, Butler was impelled by the endowment of his nature to strive for a profound and adequate conception of religious things, which was not pursued by his contemporaries, and which at that time, and in that atmosphere of mind, was not fully attainable. Hence, in Butler too, a dissatisfaction, a weariness, as in Gray; 'great labour and weariness, great disappointment, pain and even vexation of mind.' A sort of spiritual east wind was at that time blowing; neither Butler nor Gray could flower. They *never spoke out.* (pp. 91-4)

Gray's production was scanty, and scanty, as we have seen, it could not but be. Even what he produced is not always pure in diction, true in evolution. Still, with whatever drawbacks, he is alone, or almost alone (for Collins has something of the like merit) in his age. Gray said himself that 'the style he aimed at was extreme conciseness of expression, yet pure, perspicuous, and musical.' Compared, not with the work of the great masters of the golden ages of poetry, but with the poetry of his own contemporaries in general, Gray's may be said to have reached, in style, the excellence at which he aimed; while the evolution also of such a piece as his **"Progress of Poesy"** must be accounted not less noble and sound than its style. (pp. 98-9)

Matthew Arnold, "Thomas Gray," in his *Essays in Criticism, second series,* The Macmillan Company, 1924, pp. 69-99.

JAMES RUSSELL LOWELL

(essay date 1886)

[Lowell, an American poet and essayist, is noted for his satirical and critical writings, especially *A Fable for Critics* (1848). In the following excerpt from an 1886 essay, he assesses Gray's stylistic strengths and creative limitations.]

[Gray] is especially interesting as an artist in words and phrases, a literary type far less common among writers of English, than it is in France or Italy, where perhaps the traditions of Latin culture were never wholly lost, or, even if they were, continued to be operative by inheritance through the form they had impressed upon the mind. Born in 1716, he died in his 55th year, leaving behind him hardly fourteen hundred verses. Dante was one year older, Shakespeare, three years younger when he died. It seems a slender monument, yet it has endured and is likely to endure, so close-grained is the material and so perfect the workmanship. When so many have written too much, we shall the more readily pardon the rare man who has written too little or just enough.

The incidents of Gray's life are few and unimportant. Educated at Eton and diseducated, as he seemed to think, at Cambridge, in his twenty-third year he was invited by Horace Walpole to be his companion in a journey to Italy. At the end of two years they quarrelled, and Gray returned to England. (p. 14)

Gray was a conscientious traveller, as the notes he has left behind him prove. One of these, on the Borghese Gallery at Rome, is so characteristic as to be worth citing: "Several (Madonnas) of Rafael, Titian, Andrea del Sarto, etc., but in none of them all that heavenly grace and beauty that Guido gave, and that Carlo Maratt has so well imitated in subjects of this nature." This points to an admission which those who admire Gray, as I do, are forced to make, sooner or later, that there was a tint of effeminacy in his nature. That he should have admired Norse poetry, Ossian, and the Scottish ballads is not inconsistent with this, but may be explained by what is called the attraction of opposites, which means merely that we are wont to overvalue qualities or aptitudes which we feel to be wanting in ourselves. Moreover these anti-classical yearnings of Gray began after he had ceased producing, and it was not unnatural that he should admire men who did without thinking what he could not do by taking thought. Elegance, sweetness, pathos, or even majesty he could achieve, but never that force which vibrates in every verse of larger-moulded men.

Bonstetten tells us that "every sensation in Gray was passionate," but I very much doubt whether he was capable of that sustained passion of the mind which is fed by a prevailing imagination acting on the consciousness of great powers. That was something he could never feel, though he knew what it meant by his observation of others, and longed to feel it. In him imagination was passive; it could divine and select, but not create. Bonstetten, after seeing the best society in Europe on equal terms, also tells us that Gray was the most finished gentleman he had ever seen. . . . We cannot help feeling in the poetry of Gray that it too is finished, perhaps I should rather say limited, as the greatest things never are, as it is one of their merits that they never can be. They suggest more than they bestow, and enlarge our apprehension beyond their own boundaries. Gray shuts us in his own contentment like a cathedral close or college quadrangle. He is all the more interesting, perhaps, that he was a true child of his century, in which decorum was religion. He could not, as Dryden calls it in his generous way, give his soul a loose, although he would. He is of the eagle brood, but unfledged. His eye shares the aether which shall never be cloven by his wing.

But it is one of the school-boy blunders in criticism to deny one kind of perfection because it is not another. Gray, more than any of our poets, has shown what a depth of sentiment, how much pleasurable emotion, mere words are capable of stirring through the magic of association, and of artful arrangement in conjunction with agreeable and familiar images. For Gray is pictorial in the highest sense of the term, much more than imaginative. Some passages in his letters give us a hint that he might have been. For example, he asks his friend Stonehewer, in 1760, "Did you never observe (*while rocking winds are piping loud*) that pause as the gust is re-collecting itself?" But in his verse there is none of that intuitive phrase where the imagination at a touch precipitates thought, feeling, and image in an imperishable crystal. (pp. 15-17)

Gray's great claim to the rank he holds is derived from his almost unrivalled skill as an artist, in words and sounds; as an artist, too, who knew how to compose his thoughts and images with a thorough knowledge of perspective. This explains why he is so easy to remember; why, though he wrote so little, so much of what he wrote is familiar on men's tongues. There are certain plants that have seeds with hooks by which they cling to any passing animal and impress his legs into the service of their locomotion and distribution. Gray's phrases have the same gift of hooking themselves into the memory, and it was due to the exquisite artifice of their construction. His **"Elegy,"** certainly not through any originality of thought, but far more through originality of sound, has charmed all ears from the day it was published; and the measure in which it is written, though borrowed by Gray of Dryden, by Dryden of Davenant, by Davenant of Davies, and by him of Raleigh, is ever since associated with that poem as if by some exclusive right of property. Perhaps the great charm of the **"Elegy"** is to be found in its embodying that pensively stingless pessimism which comes with the first gray hair; that vague sympathy with ourselves, which is so much cheaper than sympathy with others; that placid melancholy which satisfies the general appetite for an emotion which titillates rather than wounds.

The **"Progress of Poesy"** and **"The Bard"** made their way more slowly, though the judgment of the elect (the δυvαrol ["powerful lords"] to whom Gray proudly appealed) placed them at the head of English lyric poetry. By the majority they were looked on as divine in the sense that they were past all understanding. (pp. 31-2)

Goldsmith preferred **"The Bard"** to the **"Progress of Poesy"**. We seem to see him willing to praise and yet afraid to like. He is possessed by the true spirit of his age. For my part I think I see as much influence of the Italian "Canzone" as of Pindar in these odes. Nor would they be better for being more like Pindar. Ought not a thing once thoroughly well done to be left conscientiously alone? And was it not Gray's object that these odes should have something of the same inspiring effect on English-speaking men as those others on Greek-speaking men? To give the same lift to the fancy and feeling? Goldsmith unconsciously gave them the right praise when he said they had "caught the spirit" of the elder poet. I remember hearing Emerson say some thirty years ago, that he valued Gray chiefly as a comment on Pindar. (p. 33)

Wordsworth is justified in saying that [Gray] helped himself from everybody and everywhere—and yet he made such admirable use of what he stole (if theft there was) that we should as soon think of finding fault with a man for pillaging the dictionary. He mixed himself with whatever he took—an incalculable increment. In the editions of his poems, the thin line of text stands at the top of the page like cream, and below it is the skim-milk drawn from many milky mothers of the herd out of which it has risen. But the thing to be considered is that, no matter where the material came from, the result is Gray's own. Whether original or not, he knew how to make a poem, a very rare knowledge among men. The thought in Gray is neither uncommon nor profound, and you may call it beatified commonplace if you choose. I shall not contradict you. I have lived long enough to know that there is a vast deal of commonplace in the world of no particular use to anybody, and am thankful to the man who has the divine gift to idealize it for me. Nor am I offended with this odor of the library that hangs about Gray, for it recalls none but delightful associations. It was in the very best literature that Gray was steeped, and I am glad that both he and we should profit by it. If he appropriated a fine phrase wherever he found it, it was by right of eminent domain, for surely he was one of the masters of language. His praise is that what he touched was idealized, and kindled with some virtue that was not there before, but came from him. (pp. 39-40)

Any slave of the mine may find the rough gem, but it is the cutting and polishing that reveal its heart of fire; it is the setting that makes of it a jewel to hang at the ear of Time. If Gray cull his words and phrases here, there, and everywhere, it is he who charges them with the imaginative or picturesque touch which only he could give and which makes them magnetic. For example, in these two verses of **"The Bard"**:—

> Amazement in his van with Flight combined,
> And Sorrow's faded form and Solitude behind!

The suggestion (we are informed by the notes) came from Cowper and Oldham, and the amazement *combined* with flight sticks fast in prose. But the personification of Sorrow and the fine generalization of Solitude in the last verse which gives an imaginative reach to the whole passage are Gray's own. The owners of what Gray "conveyed" would have found it hard to identify their property and prove title to it after it had once suffered the Gray-change by steeping in his mind and memory. (pp. 40-1)

The commonplace is unhappily within reach of us all, and unhappily, too, they are rare who can give it novelty and even invest it with a kind of grandeur as Gray knew how to do. If his poetry be a mosaic, the design is always his own. He, if any, had certainly "the last and greatest art," the art to please. Shall we call everything mediocre that is not great? Shall we deny ourselves to the charm of sentiment because we prefer the electric shudder that imagination gives us? Even were Gray's claims to being a great poet rejected, he can never be classed with the many, so great and uniform are the efficacy of his phrase and the music to which he sets it. This unique distinction, at least, may be claimed for him without dispute, that he is the one English poet who has written less and pleased more than any other. Above all it is as a teacher of the art of writing that he is to be valued. If there be any well of English undefiled, it is to be found in him and his master, Dryden. They are still standards of what may be called classical English, neither archaic nor modern, and as far removed from pedantry as from vulgarity. (p. 42)

James Russell Lowell, "Gray," in his *Latest Literary Essays and Addresses of James Russell Lowell,* edited by C. E. Norton, Houghton Mifflin Company, 1920, pp. 1-42.

LORD DAVID CECIL
(lecture date 1945)

[Cecil was an English educator and critic who wrote biographical and critical studies of such writers as Jane Austen, Max Beerbohm, Charles Lamb, and Thomas Hardy. In the following excerpt from his 1945 Warton Lecture, he provides a thematic and formalistic analysis of Gray's poetry.]

[Gray was] a typical eighteenth-century scholar-artist with a peculiarly intense response to the imaginative appeal of the past and whose pervading temper was a sober melancholy. His memorable poems—for some are mere craftsman's exercises—are the characteristic expression of such a man. They divide themselves into two or three categories, in accordance with the different aspects of his complex nature. His three long odes are inspired by the historical and aesthetic strain in him. That on the Installation of the Duke of Grafton as Chancellor of Cambridge was, it is true, originally designed as an occasional piece. But in it Gray takes advantage of the occasion to show us in what particular way Cambridge did appeal to his own imagination. As might be expected, this is historical. For him the groves and courts of the University are haunted by the ghosts of its founders, Margaret of Anjou, Edward III, Henry VI, and Henry VIII; and of the great spirits, Milton and Newton, who had studied there. **"The Bard"** gives Gray's historical imagination greater scope. The last of the Druids prophesies to Edward I the misfortunes that are to overtake his line: in a sort of murky magnificence, names and events heavy with romantic and historic associations pass in pageant before us. **"The Progress of Poesy"** is less historical, more aesthetic. Though in the second part Gray traces the development of poetic art from Greece to Rome and from Rome to England, this historical motive is made subsidiary to an exposition of what the author considers to be the place of poetry in human life. Like Keats's "Ode on a Grecian Urn," the **"Progress of Poesy"** is a meditation about the fundamental significance of art. Not at all the same sort of meditation though. The difference between the Augustan and Romantic attitude to life could not appear more vividly than in the difference between these two poems. There is nothing mystical about Gray's view, no transcendental vision of art as an expression of ultimate spiritual reality, where Truth is the same as Beauty and Beauty the same as Truth. No—poetry to Gray, as to any other sensible eighteenth-century gentleman, was just a pleasure: and the poet so far from being the priest of a mystery was a purveyor of pleasure—"above the great, but," he is careful to point out, "far below the good." But poetry was useful and even educative: a necessary part of the good life, soothing the passions, civilizing the heart and manners, celebrating beauty and virtue, and, above all, providing an alleviation to the inevitable ills of the human lot.

The second category of Gray's poems deals with his personal relation to life: his impressions of experience and the conclusions he drew from them. In one poem, indeed—the sonnet on the death of his friend West—he draws no conclusion: the poem is a simple sigh of lamentation. But, in all the other expressions of this phase of his work, sentiment leads to reflection and reflection to a moral. The Eton College Ode shows Gray surveying the scenes of his youth and observing the unthinking happiness of childhood through the eyes of a disillusioned maturity. With a sad irony he draws his conclusion:

Where ignorance is bliss, 'tis folly to be wise.

The **"Ode on the Spring"** is inspired by the spectacle of a fine day in early spring, with the buds hastening to open and the insects busily humming. How like the activities of the world of men! says Gray, and hardly more ephemeral. But once more irony steps in—Who is he to condemn? It is true he has chosen to be spectator rather than actor: but he is no wiser than the actors and perhaps enjoys himself less. The unfinished **"Ode on Vicissitude"** points yet another moral. Though life is a chequer-work of good and ill, sad and happy, we ought not to repine: perhaps without the sadness we should enjoy the intervals of happiness less than we do. The Adversity Ode is sterner in tone. Adversity is a trial sent by God to school us to virtue, if we are strong enough to profit by it. Finally there is the **"Elegy."** Here the sight of the graveyard stirs the poet to meditate on the life of man in relation to its inevitable end. Death, he perceives, dwarfs human differences. There is not much to choose between the great and the humble, once they are in the grave. It may be that there never was; it may be that in the obscure graveyard lie persons who but for untoward circumstances would have been as famous as Milton and Hampden. The thought, however, does not sadden him; if circumstances prevented them achieving great fame, circumstances also saved them from committing great crimes. Yet there is a special pathos in these obscure tombs; the crude inscriptions on the clumsy monuments are so poignant a reminder of the vain longing of all men, however humble, to be loved and to be remembered. This brings Gray round to himself. How does he expect to be remembered? Not as a happy man: he has been sad, obscure, misunderstood. Yet, he reminds himself with his customary balance, there have been alleviations. He has known friendship, loved learning, and attained, in part at least, to virtue. Soberly, but with faith, he resigns himself to the judgement of his God.

This group of poems is all concerned with the same thing, the relation of a sensitive contemplative spirit to the thronging, mysterious, tragic, transient world into which he finds himself thrown. For all their formality of phrase, they are consistently and intensely personal.

There remains the brief and brilliant category of Gray's satirical and humorous verse—**"The Long Story," "The Ode on a Cat," "Hymn to Ignorance,"** and the **"Impromptu on Lord Holland's House."** Now and again in these poems, more particularly in **"The Long Story,"** Gray the historian shows his hand; while they all display his scholarly sense of finish. Mainly, however, they reveal Gray the man of the world—Gray the admirer of Pope and the friend of Walpole. In the best eighteenth-century manner he uses his taste and his learning to add wit and grace to the amenities of social life. But they are none the less characteristic for that. As much as pindaric or elegy they contribute essential features to our mental portrait of their author.

Gray's mode of expression is as typical of him as is his choice of themes. His style is pre-eminently an academic style, studied, traditional, highly finished. . . . His choice of forms, too, is a scholar's choice. Sedulously he goes to the best authors for models. He writes the Pindaric Ode—making a more careful attempt than his predecessors had, exactly to follow Pindar—the Horatian Ode, the classical sonnet, and the orthodox elegy, leading up to its final formal epitaph. His diction is a consciously poetic affair; an artificial diction, deliberately created to be an appropriate vehicle for lofty poetry. "The language of the age," he stated as an axiom, "is never the language of poetry." Certainly his own language was not that of his age—or of any other, for that matter. It is an elaborate compound of the language of those authors whom he most admired: Horace and Virgil, Pope and Dryden, above all, Milton—the youthful Milton who wrote "L'Allegro" and "Lycidas." For Milton, as the greatest English Master of the artificial style, appealed peculiarly to Gray. Sometimes the influence of one of these poets predominates, sometimes of another, according to which Gray thinks is the best in the kind of verse he is attempting. He follows Pope in satire, Dryden in declamation, Milton in elegiac and picturesque passages. It was from Milton, incidentally, he learnt the evocative power of proper names. . . . Nor does he just imitate other authors. He openly quotes them. The Pindaric Odes especially are whispering galleries, murmurous with echoes of dead poets' voices—Shakespeare's, Spenser's, Cowley's. Sometimes he will lift a whole passage; the image of Jove's eagle in the second stanza of **"The Progress of Poesy"** is transplanted from Pindar's First Pythian. Sometimes he will adapt a phrase: "ruddy drops that warm my heart" in **"The Bard"** is a modification of the "ruddy drops that visit my sad heart" in *Julius Caesar.* Once again, Gray curiously reminds us of a modern author. This device of imbedding other people's phrases in his verse anticipates Mr. T. S. Eliot. Gray's purpose, however, is very different. The quoted phrase is not there to point an ironical contrast as with Mr. Eliot; rather it is inserted to stir the reader's imagination by the literary associations which it evokes. Conscious, as Gray is, of poetry developing in historic process, he wishes to enhance the effect of his own lines by setting astir in the mind memories of those great poets of whom he feels himself the heir.

The trouble about such devices is that they limit the scope of the poem's appeal. Gray's pindarics, like Mr. Eliot's "Waste Land," can be fully appreciated only by highly educated readers. Indeed, Gray's education was not altogether an advantage to him as a writer. At times his poetry is so clogged with learning as to be obscure. **"The Bard"** and **"The Progress of Poesy"** are crowded with allusions that need notes to explain them. While we are painstakingly looking at the notes, our emotional response to the poem grows chilly. In his effort to concentrate his allusion into one polished, pregnant phrase, Gray tends to leave out the facts necessary to make it immediately intelligible:

The bristled Boar in infant-gore
Wallows beneath the thorny shade.

To Gray fresh from the libraries of Cambridge this may have seemed lucid enough. But how can the common reader be expected to realize straight away that it refers to Richard III's death at the battle of Bosworth? Like some poets of our own time, Gray seems at moments to forget the difference between a poem and a conundrum.

It is another defect of Gray's academic method—and, it may be added, of his academic temperament—that it involved a certain lack of imaginative heat. Scholars are seldom fiery spirits: Gray's poems are, compared with those of Burns let us say, a touch tepid. This tepidness shows itself in his personifications. Gray is very fond of personifications:

Warm Charity, the gen'ral Friend,
With Justice to herself severe,
And Pity, dropping soft the sadly-pleasing tear.

These personifications are clear and sensible enough. Charity—were she a person—might reasonably be expected to be a friendly one; and Pity to shed tears. But somehow the effect is lifeless. We feel that—having decided to personify these virtues—Gray deliberately, and with the help of his intellect, gets to work to make suitable puppets in which to incarnate them. On the other hand when Keats speaks of

Joy, whose hand is ever at his lips
Bidding adieu;

the impression we get is that Joy spontaneously embodied itself in a living figure, which flashed unbidden, and as in a vision, before the poet's mental eye.

Indeed Gray's head is stronger than his fancy or his passions. Always we are aware in his work of the conscious intellect, planning and pruning: seldom does his inspiration take wing to sweep him up into that empyrean where feeling and thought are one. The words clothe the idea beautifully and aptly and in a garment that could only have been devised by a person of the most refined taste and the highest culture. But they clothe it, they do not embody it. For that absolute union of thought and word which is the mark of the very highest poetry of all, we look to Gray in vain. He had not that intensity of inspiration; and, anyway, education had developed his critical spirit too strongly for

him to be able completely to let himself go. His poetry, in fact, illustrates perfectly the characteristic limitations of the academic spirit.

But it also reveals, in the highest degree, its characteristic merits. Always it is disciplined by his intellect and refined by his taste. The matter is rational; Gray never talks nonsense; each poem is logically designed, with a beginning, a middle, and an end. Every line and every phrase has its contribution to make to the general effect; so that the whole gives one that particular satisfaction that comes from seeing a problem completely resolved. Even the best lines—and this is a typical beauty of conscious art—are better in their context than when they are lifted from it. Moreover, though Gray fails to achieve the highest triumphs of expression, he maintains a consistently high level of style—better than some greater men do. No doubt it is a style that takes getting used to: artificial styles always do. We must accustom ourselves to the tropes and the antitheses, the abstractions, classical allusions and grandiose periphrases which are his habitual mode of utterance. They are as much a part of it as the garlands and trophies which ornament a piece of baroque architecture; for Gray lived in the baroque period and shared its taste. A poem like **"The Progress of Poesy"** is like nothing so much as some big decorative painting of the period in which, posed gracefully on an amber-coloured cloud, allegorical figures representing the arts and the passions offer ceremonious homage to the goddesses of Poetry or Beauty:

Slow melting strains their Queen's approach declare:
Where'er she turns the Graces homage pay.
With arms sublime, that float upon the air,
In gliding state she wins her easy way:
O'er her warm cheek, and rising bosom, move
The bloom of young Desire, and purple light of
    Love.

Does not that recall some radiant, florid ceiling painted by Tiepolo?

And it is executed with a similar virtuosity. Gray attempts the most complex and difficult metres. His work is thickly embroidered with image and epigram. But the images and epigrams are appropriate. Every cadence is both musical in itself and an apt echo of the sense. . . . [It is in the] Pindaric Odes that Gray's virtuosity appears most conspicuously. They are not, however, his most successful works. For in them he is dealing with subject-matter which does reveal his limitations. This is especially true of **"The Bard."** Here Gray tries to write dramatically; he addresses us in the person of a medieval druid about to commit suicide. Such a role does not suit him. Gray was excited by reading about druids; but he was not at all like a druid himself. Nor had he the kind of imagination convincingly to impersonate one. He tried very hard—"I felt myself the Bard," he said—but, alas, the result of all his efforts was only a stagey, if stylish, example of eighteenth-century rhetoric, elaborately decked up with the ornaments of a Strawberry Hill Mock-Gothic. In **"The Progress of Poesy"** Gray wisely refrains from any attempt at impersonation and the result is far more successful. Indeed, in its way, the poem is a triumph. But a triumph of style rather than substance. The pleasure we get from the work is that given by watching a mastercraftsman magnificently displaying his skill in an exercise on a given conventional theme.

No—Gray writes best when he does not try a lofty flight of imagination but, with his feet planted firmly on the earth, comments lightly or gravely on the world he himself knew. Here, once more, he is typical of his period. Eighteenth-century writers are, most of them, not so much concerned with the inward and spiritual as with the social and moral aspects of existence— less with man the solitary soul in relation to the ideal and the visionary, than with man the social animal in relation to the people and the age in which he finds himself. For all he lived a life of retirement, Gray is no exception to his contemporaries. The region of romance and art in which he liked to take refuge was to him a place of pleasant distraction, not the home of a deeper spiritual life, as it was for Blake, for instance. Even when in the **"Ode on the Spring"** he contrasts his own inactive existence with that of his fellows, his eye is on them; his interest is to see how his life relates to theirs. And the thoughts stirred in him by his contemplations here, as also in his Eton ode, are of the straightforward kind which they could understand. So might any thoughtful person feel on a spring day, or when revisiting their old school. What Johnson said of **"The Elegy in a Country Churchyard"** is equally true of Gray's other elegiac pieces. "They abound with sentiments to which every bosom returns an echo." Indeed Gray's relative lack of originality made him peculiarly able to speak for the common run of mankind. But he spoke for them in words they could not have found for themselves. Poetry, says Pope, should be "what oft was thought but ne'er so well expressed." This is not true of all poetry. But it is true of Gray's. The fact that he was an exquisite artist made it possible for him to express the commonplace with an eloquence and a nobility that turn it into immortal poetry. Moreover, his vision is deepened and enriched by his historic sense. His

The country churchyard in Stoke Poges. Gray's tomb is seen close to the church, between the two large windows.

meditations in the churchyard acquire a monumental quality, because they seem to refer to it at any time during its immemorial history: his reflections on his Eton schooldays gain universality from the fact that he perceives his own sojourn there as only an episode in the School's life, and his personal emotions about it as the recurrent emotion of generations of Etonians.

These reflective poems, too, are more moving than the Pindaric Odes. No wonder: they were the product of the deepest emotional crisis of his life. The Pindarics were written in his tranquil middle age; these other poems, all except the **"Elegy,"** in the later months of 1742; and the **"Elegy,"** composed a few years later, is a final comment on the same phase of his experience. Two events produced this phase. Gray's prospects were very dark; poverty was forcing him back to take up life at Cambridge at a moment when he felt a strong reaction against it: and the pair of friends who were his chief source of happiness were during this time lost to him. He quarrelled with Walpole, and West died. Under the combined stress of these misfortunes his emotional agitation rose to a pitch which found vent in an unprecedented outburst of poetic activity. Even when inspired by such an impulse, the result is not exactly passionate: but it is heartfelt. The sentiment it expresses has its birth in the very foundations of the poet's nature; it is distilled from the experience of a lifetime. . . . Is not [the sonnet on the death of West] poignant? Once more, you will remark, its effect is intensified by what I can only call Gray's commonplaceness. It is interesting in this connexion to compare it with a more famous lamentation over the dead, with "Lycidas." Poetically, of course, it is of a lower order. Gray had nothing like Milton's imaginative and verbal genius. All the same, and just because Gray was not so original a genius, his poem does something that Milton's does not. It expresses exactly what the average person does feel when someone he loves dies.

Nor does its eighteenth-century formality weaken its emotional force. On the contrary, it makes it seem more authentic. Personal feelings of this kind always present peculiar difficulties to a poet; for it is so hard to express them without sentimentality, so hard for the poet not to seem as if he was calculatedly exploiting his private emotions in order to bring tears to the eyes of his readers. The more colloquial and informal the language he uses, the more likely this is to happen. Gray's formality acts as a filter of good-mannered reticence through which his private grief comes to us, purged of any taint of sentimentality or exhibitionism, and with a pathos that seems all the more genuine because it is unemphasized:

I fruitless mourn to him, that cannot hear,
And weep the more because I weep in vain.

In lines like these, as in the more famous **"Elegy,"**

the two dominant strains in Gray serve each to strengthen the effect of the other. The fastidious artist and the eighteenth-century gentleman combine to produce something that is in its way both perfect and profound.

Equally perfect and from similar causes is Gray's lighter verse. Light verse rarely attains classical quality. Either it is so conversational and careless as to be vulgar; or, if the author tries to dignify it by a more stately style, he only succeeds in being pedantically facetious. The writer of light verse walks a narrow path between the abysses of donnish jocularity, on the one hand, and music-hall slanginess, on the other. Gray's curiously compounded nature enabled him to keep to this path unerringly. He is never pedantic, he jests with the elegant ease of a man of fashion. But the solid foundation of scholarly taste, which underlies everything he writes, gives his most frivolous improvisation distinction. Nor do those characteristics of his style which sometimes impede our appreciation of his other work trouble us here. In light verse it does not matter if we are aware of the intellectual process at work. It is right in comedy that the head should rule the heart and fancy. As for Gray's baroque conventionalities of phrase, these, when introduced, as it were, with a smile, enhance his wit by a delightful ironical stylishness:

The hapless Nymph with wonder saw:
A whisker first and then a claw,
With many an ardent wish,
She stretch'd in vain to reach the prize.
What female heart can gold despise?
What Cat's averse to fish?

"The Cat," says Dr. Johnson caustically, "is called a nymph, with some violence both to language and sense." Perhaps she is. Nevertheless—and one can dare to say so aloud now Dr. Johnson is no longer with us— the effect is charming.

Gray has two masterpieces in this lighter vein; these lines on the Cat [**"Ode on the Death of a Favourite Cat"**], and those on the artificial ruins put up by Lord Holland at Kingsgate [**"On Lord Holland's Seat near Margate, Kent"**]. The poem on the Cat is the more exquisite, in its own brief way as enchanting a mixture of wit and prettiness as "The Rape of the Lock" itself. But the bitter brilliance of the other shows that, had he chosen, Gray could equally have rivalled Pope as a satirist in the grand manner. . . . (pp. 49-59)

Horace Walpole said that "humour was Gray's natural and original turn, that he never wrote anything easily but things of Humour." In view of these poems, it is hard to disagree with him. Nowhere else does Gray's virtuosity seem so effortless; nowhere else does he write with the same spontaneity and gusto. For once Gray seems to be sailing with the wind behind him the whole way. Of all his work, his light verse appears the most inspired. (pp. 59-60)

Lord David Cecil, "The Poetry of Thomas Gray," in *Proceedings of the British Academy,* Vol. XXXI, 1945, pp. 43-60.

WALLACE JACKSON
(essay date 1986)

[Jackson is an authority on eighteenth-century English literature. In the following excerpt, he refutes the common critical assessment that Gray's poetry is dominated by two antithetical voices.]

What may we learn from what has been written about Thomas Gray's poetry and how may we escape from the perspective it has imposed upon us? On the face of it even the most influential and insightful criticism seems strangely repetitive, as though bound to a model that forces antithesis, variations on a theme. Gray was unhappily separated from his age or from the deeper sources of his power; his voice was divided against itself and he lost the essential imaginative integrity of his own being. From the publication in 1757 of the notorious Pindarics, **"The Progress of Poesy"** and **"The Bard,"** criticism has spoken its uneasiness. Here was a man who was to be the first poet of the age, yet who dwindled into fastidious protest against publication and into infrequent creativity. The initial charge has always remained foremost. Why did the poet who wrote the **"Elegy"** write two such unaffecting and coldly remote works as those? What, then, had happened to the man who imagined the **"Elegy,"** that poem abounding "with sentiments to which every bosom returns an echo"? Insofar as Johnson's brief, even perfunctory, life of Gray takes up the issue of his poetry, it does so in terms of explicit opposition. The **"Elegy,"** in a brief and well-remembered concluding paragraph, is established as the delight of the "common reader," even as the Pindarics are antithetically rejected as his despair. W. P. Jones's modern survey of the contemporary reception of the odes confirms the judgment: they were "unintelligible, or at least unacceptable, to the average reader." (p. 361)

Gray is either or seems to be oddly flawed, divided against himself; such a view requires then confirmation or correction. If division is present in the poetry, it is so as a symptom of his relation to an uncongenial age, or the result of his own unfulfilled sexuality, and is manifested in a language dominated by two antithetical voices, which may be resolved into some sort of unity through various critical strategies. Even should it turn out to be the case that Gray was obsessed with conflicts ("life's incessant and intolerable presentation of opposites") not "capable of poetic resolution," it yet remains true that in many of his poems "form and content are triumphantly interfused, the subject is frequently the universal plight of mankind, the statement peculiarly personal." This accolade accompanies a marriage, a restoration of equilibrium with which the scene closes upon Thomas Gray, now the conquerer of his own dualisms and at peace with himself. (pp. 363-64)

Yet who and where are the redemptive voices and will they speak to me? In the **"Ode on Vicissitude,"** "Yesterday . . . Mute was the music of the air." Today ("Now the golden Morn aloft . . . wooes the tardy spring, / Till April starts, and calls around"), voice is the invoked "presence" in the ode. Awakened it compels other voices ("The birds his [April's] presence greet: / But chief the sky-lark warbles high / His trembling thrilling ecstasy"). To invoke voice is also to invoke the memory of its absence ("Mute"), as well as its capacity to accuse, indict, and speak the unspecified guilt, as in the **"Ode to Adversity"** ("With thundering voice and threatening mien"). From the beginning, in Gray's canon, there is a special alertness to what is voiced. The implied ironic deflationary speakers at the close of the **"Ode on the Spring"** impugn the youth who repudiates pleasure: "Methinks I hear in accents low / The sportive kind reply: / Poor moralist! and what are thou? / A solitary fly!" Antithetical voice is almost always a creation of (a projection of, and thereby an ambivalence within) primary voice. In the **"Elegy,"** "some hoary-headed swain may say." In **"A Long Story"** an unidentified voice impatiently interrupts the narrative ("Your history wither are you spinning? / Can you do nothing but describe?"). Subsequently the poet in the poem speaks his own apologia and is forgiven his propensity to scribble by the Viscountess who invites him to dinner. **"A Long Story"** is an intentional fragment; the mock self-justificatory mode determining its progress is obviously affiliated with other less playful modes of apology. Far more solemnly, for example, the **"Elegy"** offers its own excuse for the poet ("Large was his bounty and his soul sincere"), as does of course **"The Progress of Poesy,"** locating Gray himself as the end and goal of Poesy's enforced pilgrimage. In the **"Descent of Odin"** the hero makes his way to the underworld, awakening the "prophetic maid," and requiring that she foretell the future, the death of Hoder by Odin's son. Odin conjures the maid with "runic rhyme," the "thrilling verse that wakes the dead." The journey to voice in the **"Descent"** is only a variation of the related journey in the **"Elegy,"** for the churchyard is yet a place of speaking ("Ev'n from the tomb the voice of Nature cries"), but equally a place where the power of voice is mocked and denied: "Can Honour's voice provoke the silent dust, / Or Flattery soothe the dull cold ear of Death?" Yet to what purpose is speaking if voice is betrayed by time? The question catches up the vocal chorus of Gray's many voices and underscores the entire quest that comprises the paratactically narrated myth of journey within the canon. There is always the tendency to dismiss transmitted (voiced) knowledge ("Ah tell them they are men!") in the melancholic pessimist, concluding the Eton ode: "Yet ah! why should they know their fate?" The power to become self-creative, to find the way back to originary voice, is rejected in the inevitable enactments or remembrances of suffering, the "groan" that at the close of the Eton ode displaces voice or substitutes for it. Or there is the most famous occasion where voicelessness is justified as another example of the law, Nature's edict, the result of which is the diminished and paradoxical thing, "Some mute inglorious Milton." Every common reader intuits the churchyard as the center of Gray's imagination, the place where he pauses in the midst of passage to insist that the vast negative absolute of death renders voice impotent:

> The breezy call of incense-breathing morn,
> The swallow's twittering from the straw-built shed,
> The cock's shrill clarion or the echoing horn,
> No more shall ruse them from their lowly bed.

All the authority that elegy enables him to summon is marshalled against the power of voice, as though the vanity of voice and the deep humanity of it are barely audible antagonists among the tombs.

Understood in this way, the **"Elegy"** is an extended meditation on what voice can or cannot accomplish. The legacy passed from generation to generation, from poet to "kindred spirit," is the commemorative word itself, and the self is contextualized ("Their name, their years, spelt by the unlettered muse") within other texts ("And many a holy text around she strews, / That teach the rustic moralist to die"). The **"Elegy"** is surely Gray's most subversive poem, restricting and limiting the power of voice while universalizing the need to speak. All the dead are predecessor voices. The poet's way is, literally and figuratively, toward those forebears, precursors who had voices, even if not those of Pindar or Shakespeare, Dryden or Milton. The kindred spirit is there to receive the legacy of voice, to make of it what he will or can, for the inheritance is the common fate of those who are and are not poets.

"He spoke," begins the penultimate line of **"The Bard."** The entire poem has been a prophetic speaking, the authoritative summoning for Edward of futurity, and the Bard's voice is confirmed as oracular utterance. Such speaking affirms both the truth and cost of voice. What curious kindredness haunts the relation between the poet of the **"Elegy"** and the seer of **"The Bard"**? Each poem leads to the death of voice, as though its exercise compels its cessation. The **"Elegy"** chronicles village legend, "village Hampdens," "guiltless Crom-

wells." **"The Bard"** writes unborn history. Taken together, the speaking in each poem seems to comprehend opposed modes of human activity, as though the **"Elegy"** is an alternative text to **"The Bard,"** and **"The Bard"** a soliloquy within the high heroic pageant of historical drama. Is this the way Gray would make his epic, constitute the polarities of his vision by antithetical addresses which define the range and scope of his poetic speaking? His own version of knowledge enormous becomes, then, a received and cumulative wisdom derived from various distant envisionings, the recovery in the **"Elegy"** of precedent lives, the revelation in **"The Bard"** of futurity.

Yet there runs through all of this the self-conscious mockery implicit in the plaint of the drowning Selima [in **"Ode on the Death of a Favourite Cat"**]: "Eight times emerging from the flood / She mewed to every watery god, / Some speedy aid to send." It may be just one more case of voice unheard, prayer unanswered. Are Selima's mewings a parody of poetic invocation, a self-deflationary response to the particular poetic act that characterizes the poet Gray?

On the other hand, the recovery of voice is widely recognized as the special archaeology of poets in the middle and later years of the Eighteenth Century. It is the one certain and shared enterprise, of which Chattertonian and Macphersonian ventriloquism is merely one phrase, oracularity (as in **"The Bard"**) another. Blake's Piper and Bard, the various dissonantal voices of *Innocence* and *Experience*, define—not to say satirize—the problematics of voice itself. What Blake brings to the subject is pluralistic and dialogical. Voice is composed in opposition to other voices, reconstituted in the interplay between contrasting voices. The relation becomes choral and choric, itself a commentary on, or critique of, the adequacy of voice. Gray's disillusioned speaker of the [**"Ode on a Distant Prospect of Eton College"**] is thus in retrospect a voice of Experience; the rationalizing philosopher of mutability in the **"Ode on Vicissitude"** another such spokesman for restraint and limitation, the optimism of a mechanical view of temporality. Blake's *Songs,* so regarded, are satires of authoritative voice, the numen or nominated power that presides over the multiple voices that make up the *Songs of Innocence and of Experience*. The daemonology of mid-eighteenth-century verse modulates between the invocation of the poetical character and, say, the hobgoblin spookiness of Collins's ode on highland superstitions. In Gray the range is from Selima's desperate and forlorn speaking, to inattentive feline gods, to the spectral Medusan presence of Adversity, the strong figure and voice of harsh universal law.

The range includes the journey to graveyard voices, the distant way taken to precursor poets, even the attentive listening to Margaret, Countess of Richmond and Derby, mother of Henry VII, as she leans, like a Blakean Piper "From her golden cloud" and speaks her welcome to the Duke of Grafton, newly installed as Chancellor of Cambridge and the occasion for Gray's late **"Ode for Music."** Such summoning and listening may have a relation to the *tradition.* There must be a difference between widely assimilated poetic influence, as in Pope's poetry, wherein voice is allusively deployed, and the petitioning of voice that so amply fills Gray's pages. More so than Pope, Gray reflects the poet's uncertain claim to voice; his own poetry is vocal to a few or, in its alternative churchyard mode, voice is a " 'Muttering [of] wayward fancies,' " an incoherence presumably vocal to none.

    "A Long Story" reproduces a similar poetic mumble ("Yet something he was heard to mutter, / How in the park beneath an old-tree / . . . 'He once or twice had penned a sonnet' ") and loses "500 stanzas" after the Viscountess condescends to " 'Speak to a commoner and poet!' " In one way or another voice is private or, as in **"A Long Story,"** simply lost. The distant way is thus not only back to an originary voice, but outward to an audience that may be, as the reception of the two Pindaric odes so fully demonstrated, largely baffled by the voices they hear. To be so isolated between voice and audience seems the familiar fate of mid-eighteenth-century poets. In Gray the problem is especially acute, and unlike Chatterton or Macpherson he does not choose a voice that assumes particular priority. He becomes instead a petitioner of voices, the ode itself, as Paul Fry observes, finding its motive in invocation, "a purposeful calling in rather than a calling out." "The poet who can prolong presence . . . has 'taken on,' strictly speaking, the identity he has striven for." "I felt myself the Bard," said Gray.

    The taking on of a strong identity correlates to the escape from a weak one. These self-identifications may be, as Northrop Frye long ago remarked, either manic or bizarre, but they require pilgrimages, journeys to voice, and they arise from the initial malady of displaced voice from which all mid-century speaking seems to suffer. Thus the *journey to,* the immediate function of *way* in Gray's poems, is explicable in terms of the necessity to find the voice that is always to be appropriated or always abandoned: "He spoke, and headlong from the mountain's height / Deep in the roaring tide he plunged to endless night." The self merges with inchoate sound (the mighty sound of waters, the very source of voice), enters the endless night of bardic or churchyard death. These poems are all elegies for the poets who speak them, memorials of heroic or contemplative speaking, acknowledgments of the fate of voice. (pp. 366-70)

    I want to propose now that many of Gray's poems may be comprehended under the head of progress pieces. The historical and geographical movements delineated in the eighteenth-century progress poem blend in his work with the movement of spiritual autobiography, and the "public" and "private" ways of progress are enacted before the reader as separate and yet merged actions in which man and men participate. **"The Progress of Poesy"** ends with Thomas Gray. Historical movement is traced by the man writing the poem to the same man who is now the immediate goal of history, the agent upon whom it closes. Thomas Gray, man and poet, is derived from history; there is no other way of explaining or accounting for him. He originates in the distant logic of Poesy's westward movement, and the vast aggregation of events, the momentous causes of Poesy's flight, lead to him. This is not simply an occasion for the egotistical sublime; it is an apologia for the self derived from a myth of progress, a figuration of journey, however much Johnson may find the logic of Poesy's course merely a pleasing fiction. Behind the poet Gray are not only Dryden and Milton, Shakespeare and Pindar. There are also Venus and Cybele, Jove and Hyperion. They are as much "ministers of human fate" as are Misfortune, Anger, Shame, et al. of the [**"Ode on a Distant Prospect of Eton College"**]. They are all creatures and creations of the mind mindful of time, forms of history's making by which the imagination marks human progress. They may even be the forms out of which history is constituted. Such phantoms and realities ground human identity in various knowable objectifications, renderings of the self 's sense of itself and of the myths it creates and inhabits so as to further know itself. To the imagination Venus is only an alternative figure to Love, an alternative to allegoresis. Gray keeps grounding the self in what it knows. The Bard's projected history is only another variation of this kind of perception, dependent upon our knowledge of the veracity of his historical prophecy. What does Edward I know of those future persons? Who to him could be the " 'She-wolf of France' " or " 'The bristled Boar' "? As she-wolf and boar such entities are the figurations of an historical identity that is not literal, a transformation of fact into figure, of history into metaphor. Gray figures, then, the forms inhabiting time; it is his version of plenitude.

    The self knowing itself knows history, which means that it knows the stages of its real and imagined progress (they are ultimately the same). It means also that it knows what can only be called metahistory, the personifications that arise from the mind's sense of its location in time. It means also that it knows the myths in which it is inevitably captured, contextualized. Such ways of knowing comprise the textuality of Gray's poems, an allusive and referential structure, densely layered, in which the self, public and private, always and simultaneously exists. The progress poem offered Gray just this sort of generic openness, a *kind* that could "explain" or dramatize historical change but could equally incorporate what was, strictly speaking, beyond or outside the province of history (as are, for example, the agents of prosopopoeia). Miner refers to Dryden's *The Hind and the Panther,* remarking: " . . . it can best be described as a historical structure infused and controlled by typological elements suggestive both of matters beyond history and of areas in which history is not the proper mode of regarding human experience." History as public myth is only limitedly "the proper mode."

Prosopopoeia and myth are public and private in different ways, expressive of the self 's sense of its own daemons and its own gods, and also of what is general, collective, and the common property of a civilization. The **"Elegy"** elegizes everyone and no one. It is the only major poem of its kind in English precipitated by no death. Lives, like poesy, move westward, though occasioned by no political or moral motive, but only by the fact of mortality itself. In his early discussion of the progress piece in the Eighteenth Century, R. H. Griffith speaks of "the conception of history [that] passes from that of a pageant of independent, unconnected scenes to that of a pageant dominated by a principle of continuity, of cause and effect, with each scene alternating its role as effect and cause." Something of this sort is apparent in **"The Bard"** and **"The Progress of Poesy,"** but something less logically formal, less causally sequential, is equally evident in other of Gray's poems. Origin, meaning cause, is hid, though not uncommonly invoked by the poet. "With what song, Goddess," asks Gray of Nature in **"De Principiis Cogitandi,"** "shall I speak of you, the dearest offspring of Heaven, and of your origin?" The poem is itself another occasion of progress, dominated by metaphors of movement and motion: "Moreover, on every side, wherever the field of awareness extends, the companions of diverse pleasures, an idle crowd, are borne along, and the forms of pain, terrible to behold, which darken every doorway."

Characters as various as the poet of the **"Elegy"** and Milton of the **"Ode for Music"** roam across the landscape at the same time of day and with presumably the same companions. " 'Oft have we seen him at the peep of dawn / 'Brushing with hasty steps the dews away / 'To meet the sun upon the upland lawn.' " Milton is comparably self-described: " 'Oft at the blush of dawn / 'I trod your level lawn, / 'Oft wooed the gleam of Cynthia silver-bright / 'In cloisters dim, far from the haunts of Folly, / 'With Freedom by my side, and soft-eyed Melancholy.' " The poet and Milton are similar figures in transit; that they are not going anywhere in particular does not matter. Excursion is a mere synecdoche, a notation of journey.

"I felt myself the Bard," said Gray of himself during the writing of that poem. Yet he is also the musing, melancholic poet of the **"Elegy,"** the prosopopoeically companioned, otherwise solitary, Milton. Such self-similitudes are the recurrent investitures of the self

(public and private), alternative and yet like forms of identity, fictions of the self in incompleted narratives, forms of passage. The audacious Milton of **"The Progress of Poesy"** is yet another solitary voyager: "He passed the flaming bounds of place and time." In **"Luna Habitabilis"** Gray's muse tells "of the first colonist emigrating to the moon. . . . As once Columbus sailed across the watery plains of an unknown sea to see the lands of Zephyr, new realms." (pp. 372-74)

Should we now look to those familiar antitheses that have comprised the canonical interpretation of Gray and recompose them within the textuality of progress itself ? The journey is historical and biographical, cultural and individual. Such an engagement with time seeks its own structuration, seeks, one might argue, to escape the local and personal, yet to inform the general and public with the "I" that is a part (even when unspecified) of all the imagined journeys on which Gray's personae are embarked. It is useless to call such adventures "pre-romantic," yet they no more belong to those "psychological self-identifications," manic and bizarre, on which Frye long ago founded his notion of "Sensibility." The tradition here is almost as old as Wordsworth's hills. It is found in the journeying soul of Chaucer's pilgrims and Bunyan's Pilgrim. Gray brings it up to date, by which I mean he finds alternative poetic forms for it in elegy and fills those with the mind's consciousness of its own being as historical and individual entity, derived from the flow of time and to be returned to that movement.

His poetry is one of various resurrections, of voice but also of vanished ages, of village dead, of childhood, all of which occur as an effort to assume mastery over what has suffered closure and now requires revisiting and assimilation into the meditative self. In the **"Hymn to Ignorance"** the "sacred age" of Ignorance is petitioned mockingly to return again and "bring the buried ages back to view." In the **"Hymn"** and in the **"Eton College Ode"** childhood and the darkness of ignorance are equivalent moments in the history of consciousness. They exist as compatible events of origin, distant stages in the history of the race and of the self, and the occasion of summoning them is predicated, ironically or not, on the assumption that they have something to say. Ignorance is a "soft salutary power!" that the poet "adore[s]." "Oh say, successful," he implores, "dost thou still oppose / Thy leaden aegis 'gainst our ancient foes?" But: "Oh say—she hears me not." In the Eton ode, Father Thames is summoned: "Say, Father Thames, for thou hast seen," but he does not speak. What voice there is exists as the insinuation of futurity, another muffled prophetic speaking, which the children of Eton hear: a "voice in every wind." The quasi-autobiographical locales, Eton and Cambridge, suggest on Gray's part a return to origin, a desire to solicit sources that remain partially or wholly mute.

To write in this way is to belong to an age, to the greater rising awareness of the self as historical and individual presence that concentrates our focus on Gray as poet and historian. To see him in this way raises legitimate questions about the scope of a vision he clearly does not control in the usual sense of writing it out, seeing it through. But it does indicate something of what he sees and what is to be seen in his poetry, the turn to what Fredric Bogel rightly calls "the literary order of time itself" in the second half of the Eighteenth Century. Gray's place in this "turn" is in the ef-fort to create a figure for time's progress and man's location within it, while simultaneously evoking those voices that have sounded throughout it, disputing or rationalizing the logic and law of its judgments. This is the large-scale subject Gray largely evaded, leaving in its place the fragments, those surviving notations that are his poems and tell us much of what he did perceive and what he could not. (pp. 375-76)

Wallace Jackson, "Thomas Gray: Drowning in Human Voices," in *Criticism,* Vol. XXVIII, No. 4, Fall, 1986, p. 361-77.

SOURCES FOR FURTHER STUDY

Downey, James, and Jones, Ben. *Fearful Joy: Papers from the Thomas Gray Bicentenary Conference at Carleton University.* Montreal and London: McGill-Queen's University Press, 1974, 266 p.

> Fifteen essays on various aspects of Gray's works. The essayists include Ian Jack, Alistair MacDonald, and Arthur Johnston.

Gosse, Edmund. *Gray.* 1882. Reprint. London: Macmillan and Co., 1934, 231 p.

> A detailed critical biography that seeks to separate Gray's life and work from the distortions and adulatory appraisals of the poet's admirers.

Hazlitt, William. "On Swift, Young, Gray, Collins, etc." In his *Lectures on the English Poets,* pp. 160-89. New York: Oxford University Press, 1924.

> Favorable overview of Gray's poetic canon.

Hudson, William Henry. *Gray & His Poetry.* London: George G. Harrap & Co., 1920, 111 p.

> An introductory critical biography.

Jones, William Powell. *Thomas Gray, Scholar: The True Tragedy of an Eighteenth-Century Gentleman.* Cambridge: Harvard University Press, 1937, 191 p.

> Critical study of Gray's scholarly interests. Jones examines the poet's reading in the classics, his study of travel writings and natural history, and his delving into the sources of English poetry.

Ketton-Cremer, R. W. *Thomas Gray: A Biography.* Cambridge: Cambridge University Press, 1955, 310 p.

> Detailed biography. Includes quotations from Gray's correspondence and several portraits of Gray and his contemporaries.

Graham Greene

1904-1991

(Full name Graham Henry Greene) English novelist, short story writer, dramatist, travel writer, memoirist, journalist, critic, essayist, screenwriter, editor, biographer, poet, and author of books for children.

INTRODUCTION

*G*reene's stature as a major author is matched by the great popularity of his novels. His protagonists typically struggle from the darkness of human suffering toward the light of redemption. This redemption is usually preceded by an instance of *felix culpa*—the "fortunate fall" that strips the characters of human pride and piety, enabling them to perceive God's grace. While these novels reflect Greene's Roman Catholic faith, heretical actions abound. In Greene's most famous novel, *The Power and the Glory* (1940), for example, the protagonist is a "whiskey priest" who marries, fathers a child, and doubts the existence of God. Greene's novels often take place in foreign and exotic settings—a composite geographical frontier named "Greeneland" by critics. Like W. H. Auden, with whom his work is often compared, Greene employed these landscapes allegorically to convey the undeveloped nature of modern humanity's faith. Greene's prose also resembles Auden's poetry, especially in its extensive catalogues of features and inanimate objects that symbolically convey the true essence of a person or location. The popularity of Greene's novels, some critics observe, results from a terse style that immediately engages the reader in the book's action. Greene's prose style also resembles modern film, containing descriptive passages that recall such cinematic techniques as camera movement, jump edits, and dissolves. The use of film modes reflects Greene's experience as a film critic and as an adaptor of many of his books for the screen.

Greene's father was headmaster of England's Berkhamstead School, which Greene attended as a youth. Greene's mother claimed the writer Robert Louis Stevenson as a relative. While a student of modern history at Oxford's Balliol College, Greene published a volume of poems, *Babbling April* (1925), that was dismissed by critics as derivative. The following year, he converted to the Roman Catholic Church in preparation for his marriage to Vivien Dayrell-Browning in 1927. Greene worked first as a literary journalist and then as subeditor of the London *Times,* a position he resigned after publication of his first novel, *The Man Within* (1929). During World War II, Greene worked several months with the Ministry of Information and later served with the British Foreign Office in Sierra Leone and Nigeria, experiences that inform his spy thrillers and adventure stories. Afterwards, world travel became an integral part of Greene's life. His impressions and experiences during these trips, recorded in his nonfiction, contributed to the authenticity of detail and setting in his novels. His journey to Mexico in 1938, for example, is documented in *The Lawless Roads: A Mexican Journey* (1939), from which many passages appear verbatim in *The Power and the Glory.* His trips to Africa resulted in the travel books *Journey without Maps* (1936) and *In Search of a Character: Two African Journals* (1961) and the novels *The Heart of the Matter* (1948) and *A Burnt-Out Case* (1961).

While Greene himself claimed to write two kinds of novels, Catholic ones and what he termed "entertainments," critics discern similar elements in all his fiction: the struggle between faith and doubt; the despair and alienation of modern humanity; and protagonists who are forced to engage in events that reveal their true character. Greene's epigraph for *The Lawless Roads,* taken from the nineteenth-century theologian Cardinal John Henry Newman—"Either there is no Creator, or this living society of men is in a true sense discarded from His presence . . . *if* there be a God, *since* there is a God, the human race is implicated in some terrible aboriginal calamity"—is seen by critics to exemplify Greene's thematic concerns. Samuel Hynes noted: "Newman was describing sinful, fallen man in terms of Christian doctrine, but his vision of humankind—fearful, defeated, and alone—might just as well be described in the contemporary language of alienation and anxiety. And the same is true of Greene's characters; they may be lapsed Catholics, or whiskey priests, but their situations are metaphors for the human condition, and in this fundamental sense Greene's novels are relentlessly contemporary."

Greene portrayed his male protagonists as cognizant of their pronounced character weaknesses. This recognition precludes any hypocrisy or self-delusion the men might possess and allows them to perceive both the frailty and beauty of humankind. The whiskey priest in *The Power and the Glory,* for example, regards himself as a coward and mortal sinner. In a pivotal scene of the novel, however, the priest, unrecognized as a man of religion, is jailed overnight for drunkenness in a Mexican province that has outlawed Catholicism and executes priests an burns religious artifacts. He

allows his identity to be known by his fellow prisoners who, despite their criminal nature, refuse to turn him in to the authorities for a ransom. To the sounds of a couple copulating in a dark corner of the cell, the priest is harangued by a pious woman whose rigid faith will not allow her to acknowledge any good in a whiskey priest, the physical act of love between a man and a woman, or the criminals in the cell. He rejects the pious woman's views and derives from the experience the faith in humanity that precipitates his martyrdom. Similarly, Major Scobie, the protagonist of *The Heart of the Matter,* commits the sin of pity—an act of pride that leads to adultery, smuggling, and murder. Scobie commits the mortal sin of suicide, an act Greene depicted as a final act of redemption. Greene's other Catholic novels, *Brighton Rock* (1938), *The End of the Affair* (1951), and *A Burnt-Out Case,* also examine the state of humankind after the Fall as well as other Catholic themes.

Greene's "entertainments" include comedies, spy fiction, and thrillers that take place in foreign countries. *The Confidential Agent* (1939) is often seen as the model for all modern thrillers. In a review of *The Ministry of Fear* (1943), W. H. Auden wrote: "[Greene's] thrillers are projected into outer melodramatic action of the struggles which go on unendingly in every mind and heart. . . . Just as Balzac came back again to avarice and Stendahl to ambition, so, in book after book, Graham Greene analyses the vice of pity, that corrupt parody of love and compassion which is so insidious and deadly for sensitive natures." *The Quiet American* (1955) is set in South Vietnam and anticipates U.S. involvement in the Vietnam conflict. The novel's protagonist, Alden Pyle, who is ignorant of Oriental culture, is depicted as a symbol of American arrogance. *Our Man in Havana* (1958) is set in Cuba during the Battista regime shortly before Fidel Castro's revolution. The novel satirizes the British Secret Service working in Cuba and the corruption of the reigning Cuban government. *Travels with My Aunt* (1969) details the adventures of an eccentric older woman introducing her conventional nephew to marijuana and other aspects of the counterculture. *The Human Factor* (1978) concerns a British double agent who attempts to aid black South Africans by leaking information to the Soviet Union. The publication of *The Tenth Man* (1985) was hailed as a significant literary event. Originally written as a screenplay in 1944—the period many critics agree was Greene's most fruitful—the manuscript was shelved and forgotten until its discovery in 1983. Like many of Greene's novels, *The Tenth Man* examines a wealthy French lawyer's conscience after a single act of cowardice—trading his family heritage to another man willing to die in the lawyer's place—and contains the moral dilemmas present in Greene's best works.

Critical response to Greene's novels has been favorable with several exceptions. Some critics fault Greene's prose style for not developing beyond straightforward journalism and abjuring the experimental modes of twentieth-century literature. Other critics argue that Greene's characters are little more than two-dimensional vehicles that convey Greene's Catholic ideology. Most commentators, however, would agree with Richard Hoggart's assessment: "In Greene's novels we do not 'explore experience'; we meet Graham Greene. We enter continual reservations about what is being done to experience, but we find the novels up to a point arresting because they are forceful, melodramatic presentations of an obsessed and imaginative personality." When he died in 1991, Greene was eulogized widely as a major novelist of the twentieth century.

(For further information about Greene's life and works, see *Contemporary Authors*, Vols. 13-16, rev. ed.; *Contemporary Authors*, Vol. 133, *Contemporary Authors New Revision Series*, Vol. 35, *Contemporary Literary Criticism*, Vols. 1, 2, 6, 9, 14, 18, 27, 37; *Dictionary of Literary Biography*, Vols. 13, 15, 77, 100; *Dictionary of Literary Biography Yearbook: 1985;* and *Something about the Author*, Vol. 20.)

CRITICAL COMMENTARY

EVELYN WAUGH
(essay date 1948)

[From the publication in 1928 of his novel *Decline and Fall* until his death in 1966, Waugh was England's leading satirical novelist. He is best known today for the novel *Brideshead Revisited* (1945), which examines the lives of the members of a wealthy Roman Catholic family. In the essay excerpted below, *"Felix Culpa?,"* he praises Greene's adept handling of predominently Catholic themes.]

Of Mr. Graham Greene alone among contemporary writers one can say without affectation that his breaking silence with a new serious novel is a literary "event." It is eight years since the publication of *The Power and the Glory*. During that time he has remained inconspicuous and his reputation has grown huge. . . .

Mr. Greene has long shown an absorbing curiosity in the [existence of Hell]. In *Brighton Rock* he ingeniously gave life to a theological abstraction. We are often told: "The Church does not teach that any man is damned. We only know that Hell exists for those who deserve it. Perhaps it is now empty and will remain so for all eternity." . . . Mr. Greene challenged the soft modern mood by creating a completely damnable youth. Pinkie of *Brighton Rock* is the ideal examinee for entry to Hell. He gets a pure alpha on every paper. His story is a brilliant and appalling imaginative achievement but falls short of the real hell-fire sermon by its very completeness. We leave our seats edified but smug. However vile we are, we are better than Pinkie. The warning of the preacher was that one unrepented slip obliterated the accumulated merits of a lifetime's struggle to be good. *Brighton Rock* might be taken to mean that one has to be as wicked as Pinkie before one runs into serious danger.

Mr. Greene's latest book, *The Heart of the Matter*, should be read as the complement of *Brighton Rock*. It poses a vastly more subtle problem. Its hero speaks of the Church as "knowing all the answers," but his life and death comprise a problem to which the answer is in the mind of God alone, the reconciliation of perfect justice with perfect mercy. It is a book which only a Catholic could write and only a Catholic can understand. I mean that only a Catholic can understand the nature of the problem. (p. 322)

Mr. Greene divides his fiction into "Novels" and "Entertainments." Superficially there is no great difference between the two categories. There is no Ruth Draper switch from comic to pathetic. "Novels" and "Entertainments" are both written in the same grim style, both deal mainly with charmless characters, both have a structure of sound, exciting plot. You cannot tell from the skeleton whether the man was baptized or not. And that is the difference; the "Novels" have been baptized, held deep under in the waters of life. (pp. 322-23)

[Mr. Greene's style of writing is] not a specifically literary style at all. The words are functional, devoid of sensuous attraction, of ancestry and of independent life. Literary stylists regard language as intrinsically precious and its proper use as a worthy and pleasant task. A polyglot could read Mr. Greene, lay him aside, retain a sharp memory of all he said and yet, I think, entirely forget what tongue he was using. The words are simply mathematical signs for his thought. Moreover, no relation is established between writer and reader. The reader has not had a conversation with a third party such as he enjoys with Sterne or Thackeray.

Principal Works

Babbling April (poetry) 1925

The Man Within (novel) 1929

The Name of Action (novel) 1930

Rumour at Nightfall (novel) 1931

Stamboul Train (novel) 1932

It's a Battlefield (novel) 1934

England Made Me (novel) 1935

The Basement Room and Other Stories (short stories) 1935

A Gun for Sale: An Entertainment (novel) 1936

Journey without Maps (travel) 1936

Brighton Rock (novel) 1938

The Confidential Agent (novel) 1939

The Lawless Roads (travel essay) 1939

Twenty-Four Short Stories (short stories) 1939

The Power and the Glory (novel) 1940

The Ministry of Fear: An Entertainment (novel) 1943

Nineteen Stories (short stories) 1947

The Heart of the Matter (novel) 1948

The Third Man and The Fallen Idol (novels) 1950

The End of the Affair (novel) 1951

The Living Room (drama) 1953

Loser Takes All (novel) 1955

The Quiet American (novel) 1955

The Potting Shed (drama) 1957

Our Man in Havana: An Entertainment (novel) 1958

The Complaisant Lover: A Comedy (drama) 1959

A Burnt-Out Case (novel) 1961

In Search of a Character: Two African Journals (travel essays and autobiography) 1961

The Comedians (novel) 1963

May We Borrow Your Husband? and Other Comedies of the Sexual Life (short stories) 1967

Travels with My Aunt: A Novel (novel) 1969

A Sort of Life (autobiography) 1971

The Honorary Consul (novel) 1973

The Return of A. J. Raffles: An Edwardian Comedy in Three Acts Based Somewhat Loosely on E. W. Hornung's Characters in "The Amateur Cracksman" (drama) 1975

The Human Factor (novel) 1978

Doctor Fisher of Geneva, or the Bomb Party (novel) 1980

Monsignior Quixote (novel) 1982

The Tenth Man (novel) 1985

Nor is there within the structure of the story an observer through whom the events are recorded and the emotions transmitted. It is as though, out of an infinite length of film, sequences had been cut which, assembled, comprise an experience which is the reader's alone, without any correspondence to the experience of the protagonists. The writer has become director and producer. Indeed, the affinity to the film is everywhere apparent. It is the camera's eye which moves from the hotel balcony to the street below, picks out the policeman, follows him to his office, moves about the room from the handcuffs on the wall to the broken rosary in the drawer, recording significant detail. It is the modern way of telling a story. . . .

Mr. Greene is a story-teller of genius. Born in another age, he would still be spinning yarns. His particular habits are accidental. The plot of *The Heart of the Matter* might well have been used by M. Simenon or Mr. Somerset Maugham. (p. 323)

[Mr. Greene] makes of his material a precise and plausible drama. His technical mastery has never been better manifested than in his statement of the scene—the sweat and infection, the ill-built town which is beautiful for a few minutes at sundown, the brothel where all men are equal, the vultures, the priest who, when he laughed "swung his great empty-sounding bell to and fro, Ho ho, ho, like a leper proclaiming his

misery," the snobbery of the second-class public schools, the law which all can evade, the ever-present haunting underworld of gossip, spying, bribery, violence and betrayal. There are incidents of the highest imaginative power—Scobie at the bedside of a dying child, improvising his tale of the Bantus. It is so well done that one forgets the doer. The characters are real people whose moral and spiritual predicament is our own because they are part of our personal experience.

As I have suggested above, Scobie is the complement of Pinkie. Both believe in damnation and believe themselves damned. Both die in mortal sin as defined by moral theologians. The conclusion of the book is the reflection that no one knows the secrets of the human heart or the nature of God's mercy. It is improper to speculate on another's damnation. Nevertheless the reader is haunted by the question: Is Scobie damned? One does not really worry very much about whether Becky Sharp or Fagin is damned. It is the central question of *The Heart of the Matter*. I believe that Mr. Greene thinks him a saint. Perhaps I am wrong in this, but in any case Mr. Greene's opinion on that matter is of no more value than the reader's. Scobie is not Mr. Greene's creature, devised to illustrate a thesis. He is a man of independent soul. Can one separate his moral from his spiritual state? Both are complex and ambiguous. (p. 324)

Mr. Greene has put a quotation from Péguy at the beginning of the book *"Le pécheur est au coeur même de chrétienté . . . Nul n'est aussi compétent que le pécheur en matière de chrétienté. Nul, si ce n'est le saint,"* and it seems to me probable that it was in his mind to illustrate the *"Nouveau Théologien"* from which it is taken, just as in *Brighton Rock* he illustrates the Penny Catechism. The theme of that remarkable essay is that Christianity is a city to which a bad citizen belongs and the good stranger does not. . . . If Péguy is saying anything at all, he is saying something very startling and something which people seem to find increasingly important. Mr. Greene has removed the argument from Péguy's mumbled version and re-stated it in brilliantly plain human terms; and it is there, at the heart of the matter, that the literary critic must resign his judgment to the theologian. (p. 325)

Evelyn Waugh, "Felix Culpa?," in *The Commonweal,* Vol. XLVIII, No. 14, July 16, 1948, pp. 322-25.

GEORGE ORWELL
(essay date 1948)

[An English novelist and essayist, Orwell is admired for essays that combine observation and reminiscence with literary and social criticism. In the following excerpt from an essay that originally appeared in *The New Yorker* in 1948, he finds fault with Greene's *The Heart of the Matter,* pointing out that Greene's Roman Catholic characters, no matter how base, expound doctrines that they cannot realistically understand.]

A fairly large proportion of the distinguished novels of the last few decades have been written by Catholics and have even been describable as Catholic novels. One reason for this is that the conflict not only between this world and the next world but between sanctity and goodness is a fruitful theme of which the ordinary, unbelieving writer cannot make use. Graham Greene used it once successfully, in *The Power and the Glory,* and once, with very much more doubtful success, in *Brighton Rock.* His latest book, *The Heart of the Matter,* is, to put it as politely as possible, not one of his best, and gives the impression of having been mechanically constructed, the familiar conflict being set out like an algebraic equation, with no attempt at psychological probability.

Here is the outline of the story: The time is 1942 and the place is a West African British colony, unnamed but probably the Gold Coast. A certain Major Scobie, Deputy Commissioner of Police and a Catholic convert, finds a letter bearing a German address hidden in the cabin of the captain of a Portuguese ship. The letter turns out to be a private one and completely harmless, but it is, of course, Scobie's duty to hand it over to higher authority. However, the pity he feels for the Portuguese captain is too much for him, and he destroys the letter and says nothing about it. Scobie, it is explained to us, is a man of almost excessive conscientiousness. He does not drink, take bribes, keep Negro mistresses, or indulge in bureaucratic intrigue, and he is, in fact, disliked on all sides because of his uprightness, like Aristides the Just. His leniency toward the Portuguese captain is his first lapse. After it, his life becomes a sort of fable on the theme of "Oh, what a tangled web we weave", and in every single instance it is the goodness of his heart that leads him astray. Actuated at the start by pity, he has a love affair with a girl who has been rescued from a torpedoed ship. He continues with the affair largely out of a sense of duty, since the girl will go to pieces morally if abandoned; he also lies about her to his wife, so as to spare her the pangs of jealousy. Since he intends to persist in his adultery, he does not go to confession, and in order to lull his wife's suspicions he tells her that he has gone. This involves him in the truly fearful act of taking the Sacrament while in a state of mortal sin. By this time, there are other complications, all caused in the same manner, and Scobie finally decides that the only way out is through the unforgivable sin of suicide. Nobody else must be allowed to suffer through his death; it will be so arranged as to look like an accident. As it happens, he bungles one detail, and the fact that he has committed suicide becomes known. The book ends with a Catholic priest's hinting, with doubtful orthodoxy, that Scobie is perhaps not damned. Scobie, however, had not entertained any such hope. White all through, with a stiff upper lip, he had gone to what he believed to be certain damnation out of pure gentlemanliness.

I have not parodied the plot of the book. Even when dressed up in realistic details, it is just as ridiculous as I have indicated. The thing most obviously wrong with it is that Scobie's motives, assuming one could believe in them, do not adequately explain his actions. Another question that comes up is: Why should this novel have its setting in West Africa? Except that one of the characters is a Syrian trader, the whole thing might as well be happening in a London suburb. The Africans exist only as an occasionally mentioned background, and the thing that would actually be in Scobie's mind the whole time—the hostility between black and white, and the struggle against the local nationalist movement—is not mentioned at all. Indeed, although we are shown his thoughts in considerable detail, he seldom appears to think about his work, and then only of trivial aspects of it, and never about the war, although the date is 1942. All he is interested in is his own progress toward damnation. The improbability of this shows up against the colonial setting, but it is an improbability that is present in *Brighton Rock* as well, and that is bound to result from foisting theological preoccupations upon simple people anywhere.

The central idea of the book is that it is better, spiritually higher, to be an erring Catholic than a virtuous pagan. Graham Greene would probably subscribe to the statement of Maritain, made apropos of Léon Bloy, that "there is but one sadness—not to be a saint." A saying of Péguy's is quoted on the title page of the book to the effect that the sinner is "at the very heart of Christianity" and knows more of Christianity than anyone else does, except the saint. All such sayings contain, or can be made to contain, the fairly sinister suggestion that ordinary human decency is of no value and that any one sin is no worse than any other sin. In addition, it is impossible not to feel a sort of snobbishness in Mr. Greene's attitude, both here and in his other books written from an explicitly Catholic standpoint. He appears to share the idea, which has been floating around ever since Baudelaire, that there is something rather *distingué* in being damned; Hell is a sort of high-class night club, entry to which is reserved for Catholics only, since the others, the non-Catholics, are too ignorant to be held guilty, like the beasts that perish. We are carefully informed that Catholics are no better than anybody else; they even, perhaps, have a tendency to be worse, since their temptations are greater. In modern Catholic novels, in both France and England, it is, indeed, the fashion to include bad priests, or at least inadequate priests, as a change from Father Brown. (I imagine that one major objective of young English Catholic writers is not to resemble Chesterton.) But all the while—drunken, lecherous, criminal, or damned outright—the Catholics retain their superiority since they alone know the meaning of good and evil. Incidentally, it is assumed in *The Heart of the Matter,* and in most of Mr Greene's other books, that no one outside the Catholic Church has the most elementary knowledge of Christian doctrine.

This cult of the sanctified sinner seems to me to be frivolous, and underneath it there probably lies a weakening of belief, for when people really believed in Hell, they were not so fond of striking graceful attitudes on its brink. More to the point, by trying to clothe theological speculations in flesh and blood, it produces psychological absurdities. In *The Power and the Glory,* the struggle between this-worldly and other-worldly values is convincing because it is not occurring inside one person. On the one side, there is the priest, a poor creature in some ways but made heroic by his belief in his own thaumaturgic powers; on the other side, there is the lieutenant, representing human justice and material progress, and also a heroic figure after his fashion. They can respect each other, perhaps, but not understand each other. The priest, at any rate, is not credited with any very complex thoughts. In *Brighton Rock,* on the other hand, the central situation is incredible, since it presupposes that the most brutishly stupid person can, merely by having been brought up a Catholic, be capable of great intellectual subtlety. Pinkie, the race-course gangster, is a species of satanist, while his still more limited girl friend understands and even states the difference between the categories "right and wrong" and "good and evil." In, for example, Mauriac's *Thérèse* sequence, the spiritual conflict does not outrage probability, because it is not pretended that Thérèse is a normal person. She is a chosen spirit, pursuing her salvation over a long period and by a difficult route, like a patient stretched out on the psychiatrist's sofa. To take an opposite instance, Evelyn Waugh's *Brideshead Revisited,* in spite of improbabilities, which are traceable partly to the book's being written in the first person, succeeds because the situation is itself a normal one. The Catholic characters bump up against problems they would meet with in real life; they do not suddenly move on to a different intellectual plane as soon as their religious beliefs are involved. Scobie is incredible because the two halves of him do not fit together. If he were capable of getting into the kind of mess that is described, he would have got into it years earlier. If he really felt that adultery was mortal sin, he would stop committing it; if he persisted in it, his sense of sin would weaken. If he believed in Hell, he would not risk going there merely to spare the feelings of a couple of neurotic women. And one might add that if he were the kind of man we are told he is—that is, a man whose chief characteristic is a horror of causing pain—he would not be an officer in a colonial police force.

There are other improbabilities, some of which arise out of Mr Greene's method of handling a love affair. Every novelist has his own conventions, and, just as in an E. M. Forster novel there is a strong tendency for the characters to die suddenly without sufficient cause, so in a Graham Greene novel there is a tendency for people to go to bed together almost at sight and with no apparent pleasure to either party. Often this is credible enough, but in *The Heart of the Matter* its effect is to weaken a motive that, for the purposes of the story, ought to be a very strong one. Again, there is the usual, perhaps unavoidable, mistake of making everyone too highbrow. It is not only that Major Scobie is a theologian. His wife, who is represented as an almost complete fool, reads poetry, while the detective who is sent by the Field Security Corps to spy on Scobie even writes poetry. Here one is up against the fact that it is not easy for most modern writers to imagine the mental processes of anyone who is not a writer.

It seems a pity, when one remembers how admirably he has written of Africa elsewhere, that Mr Greene should have made just this book out of his wartime African experiences. The fact that the book is set in Africa while the action takes place almost entirely inside a tiny white community gives it an air of triviality. However, one must not carp too much. It is pleasant to see Mr Greene starting up again after so long a silence, and in post-war England it is a remarkable feat for a novelist to write a novel at all. At any rate, Mr Greene has not been permanently demoralised by the habits acquired during the war, like so many others. But one may hope that his next book will have a different theme, or, if not, that he will at least remember that a perception of the vanity of earthly things, though it may be enough to get one into Heaven, is not sufficient equipment for the writing of a novel. (pp. 439-43)

George Orwell, "Review of 'The Heart of the Matter' by Graham Greene," in his *The Collected Essays, Journalism and Letters of George Orwell: In Front of Your Nose, 1945-1950, Vol. IV,* edited by Sonia Orwell and Ian Angus, Harcourt Brace Jovanovich, 1968, pp. 439-43.

GRAHAM GREEN WITH MARTIN SHUTTLEWORTH AND SIMON RAVEN

(interview date 1953)

[The interview excerpted below originally appeared in *The Paris Review* in 1953. Here, Greene discusses the writing process and his belief that he is not a "Catholic writer" but, instead, a "writer who happens to be Catholic."]

[Shuttleworth and Raven]: *Shall we begin by working backwards from your latest production, your play* **The Living Room.** *It has not been seen in America yet so you will excuse us if we go into it in some detail.*

[Greene]: Have you seen this play yourselves?

No, a percipient girl saw it for us—she went down to Portsmouth and came back with a review, a synopsis and a great admiration for it.

I am glad; it's my first play. I've been a film man to date and I was rather afraid that I had written it in such filmic terms that it might not have succeeded as a play.

She enjoyed it well enough. She felt that you had conveyed the tense, haunted atmosphere of a house in which a family was decaying because of its ill-conceived gentility and religion; that you had made a drama out of the situation of the girl who was lost in the desert between the unhappiness, truth and family that lay in the background and the lover and mirage of happiness that lay in the foreground. Her main criticism, and this perhaps has something to do with what you were saying just now about the difference be-

tween film and theatrical technique, was that you had made the drama depend too much on dialogue and not enough on action.

There I disagree. I obeyed the unities. I confined myself to one set and I made my characters act, one upon the other. What other sort of action can you have? I get fed up with all this nonsense of ringing people up and lighting cigarettes and answering the doorbell that passes for action in so many modern plays. No, what I meant about filmic terms was that I was so used to the dissolve that I had forgotten about the curtain and so used to the camera, which is only turned on when it is wanted, that I had forgotten that actors and actresses are on the stage all the time and I had left out many functional lines. Still most of that has been put right now.

Then the criticism, if it stands, means that the dialogue fell short in some other way; perhaps it was too closely related to the dialogue of your novels which doesn't often carry the burden of the action.

I think that is nearer the mark: I tried to fuse everything and put it into the dialogue but I did not quite succeed. (With a smile) I will next time.

The particular thing which impressed this critic of ours was your attitude towards the girl's suicide. This is what she writes: "The central point of much of Greene's writing has been suicide, in Catholic doctrine the most deadly sin. But in this play at least his interpretation of it is not a doctrinal one. We are left quite definitely feeling that her soul is saved, if anyone's is, and the message of the play, for it does not pretend not to have a message, is not mere Catholic propaganda but of far wider appeal. It is a plea to believe in a God who Father Browne, the girl's confessor, admits may not exist, but belief can only do good not ill and without it we cannot help ourselves . . . the girl's suicide will probable be the only answer visible to most people but Father Browne's own unshaken faith, his calm acceptance of her death, implies that there is another, but that the struggle for it must be unceasing."

Yes I would say that that is roughly true but the message is still Catholic.

How do you make that out?

The church is compassionate you know . . .

Sorry to interrupt you but could we ask a correlative question now to save going back later?

Go ahead.

Scobie in **The Heart of the Matter** *committed suicide too. Was it your purpose when you wrote* **The Living Room** *to show a similar predicament and to show that suicide in certain circumstances can almost amount to an act of redemption?*

Steady, steady. Let's put it this way. I write about situations that are common, universal might be more correct, in which my characters are involved and from which only faith can redeem them, though often the actual manner of the redemption is not immediately clear. They sin, but there is no limit to God's mercy and because this is important, there is a difference between not confessing in fact and the complacent and the pious may not realize it.

In this sense Scobie, Rose (the girl in **The Living Room**), *the boy Pinkie in* **Brighton Rock** *and the whiskey priest of* **The Power and the Glory** *are all redeemed?*

Yes, though redemption is not the exact word. We must be careful of our language. They have all understood in the end. This is perhaps the religious sense.

So we have touched the nerve of the theme, the theme that gives, as you have said somewhere yourself, to a shelf of novels the unity of a system?

Yes, or rather it explains the unity of a group of my novels which is now, I think, finished.

Which group?

Brighton Rock, The Power and the Glory, The Heart of the Matter, and *The End of the Affair.* My next novel will not deal explicitly with Catholic themes at all.

So the New Statesman *gibe that* **The End of the Affair** *is the last novel which a layman will be able to read is about to be disproved?*

Yes, I think so, as far as one can tell oneself. I think that I know what the next novel is about but one never really knows, of course, until it's finished.

Was that so of the earlier books?

The very earliest ones particularly . . .

Yes, what about them? How did you find their subjects? Their historical romanticism is so different from what came later, even from the Entertainments.

How does one find one's subjects?—gradually I suppose. My first three—*The Man Within, The Name of Action, Rumour at Nightfall*—as far as one is influenced by anybody and I don't think that one is consciously influenced, were influenced by Stevenson and Conrad and they are what they are because at the time those were the subjects that I wanted to write about. The Entertainments (*Stamboul Train,* written a year after *Rumour at Nightfall* is the first of them; then *Gun for Sale, The Confidential Agent, The Ministry of Fear,* and *The Third Man* and *The Fallen Idol*) are distinct from the novels because as the name implies they do not carry a message (horrible word).

They show traces though of the same obsession; they are written from the same point of view . . .

Yes, I wrote them. They are not all that different.

There is a great break between **Rumour at Nightfall** *and* **England Made Me** *(our favorite novel of yours). What caused the historical novelist to turn into the contemporary one?*

I have a particularly soft spot for *England Made Me,* too. The book came about when I began *Stamboul Train.* I had to write a pot-boiler, a modern adventure story, and I suddenly discovered that I liked the form, that the writing came easily, that I was beginning to

find my world. In *England Made Me* I let myself go in it for the first time.

You had begun to read James and Mauriac?

Yes, I had begun to change. I had found that what I wanted to express, my fixations if you like, could best be expressed in the melodramatic, the contemporary and later the Catholic novel.

What influence has Mauriac had over you?

Again very little I think.

But you told Kenneth Allott, who quotes it in his book about you, that Mauriac had a distinct influence.

Did I? That is the sort of thing that one says under pressure. I read Thérèse in 1930 and was turned up inside but, as I have said, I don't think that he had any influence on me unless it was an unconscious one. Our Catholicism is very different: I don't see the resemblance that people talk about.

Where do the differences in your Catholicism lie?

Mauriac's sinners sin against God whereas mine, however hard they try, can never quite manage to . . . *(His voice fell.)*

Then Mauriac is almost a Manichee whereas you. . . . (The telephone rang and when, after a brief conversation, Greene came back to his long low seat between the electric fires and topped up the glasses, the conversation was not resumed, for the point, we thought, if not implied, was difficult for him to discuss.)

Can we now discuss this fresh period that you mentioned just now?

We can but I don't think that you'll find out much, for it has not begun yet. All that I can tell you is that I do know that my next novel is to be about an entirely different set of people with entirely different roots.

Perhaps then it would be more profitable to talk about the roots of your previous sets of characters? If we leave the historical romantic novels and the Entertainments out of it for the moment and concentrate on the contemporary ones it is obvious that there is a relationship between the characters which is a product in part of your absorption with failure, pursuit and poverty, and in part with interest in a particular type of person.

I agree with you, of course, when you say that there is a relationship between, let us say, Anthony Farrant in *England Made Me* and Pinkie, or Scobie, even—but they are not the same sort of person even if they are the expressions of what critics are pleased to call my fixations. I don't know exactly where they came from but I think that I have now got rid of them.

Ah, now, these fixations—they are what really matter, aren't they? We don't quite understand why you consider that it is so important for a novelist to be dominated in this way.

Because if he is not he has to rely on his talent, and talent, even of a very high order, cannot sustain an achievement, whereas a ruling passion gives, as I have said, to a shelf of novels the unity of a system.

Mr. Greene, if a novelist did not have this ruling passion, might it be possible to fabricate it?

How do you mean?

Well, put it this way and I hope we won't seem to be impertinent: the contrast between the Nelson Places and the Mexicos of the novels and this flat in St. James's is marked. Urbanity, not tragedy, seems to reign in this room. Do you find, in your own life, that it is difficult to live at the high pitch of perception that you require of your characters?

Well this is rather difficult to answer. Could you perhaps qualify the question a bit?

You made Scobie say in **The Heart of the Matter:** *Point me out the happy man and I will show you either egotism, selfishness, evil or else an absolute ignorance. What worries us is that you yourself seem to be so much happier than we had expected. Perhaps we are being rather naive but the seventy-four miniature whiskey bottles, the expression on your face, so different from the fixed set look of your photograph, the whole atmosphere, seem to be the products of something much more positive than that very limited optimum of happiness that you described in* **The Power and the Glory** *in this passage: the world is all much of a piece: it is engaged everywhere in the same subterranean struggle . . . there is no peace anywhere where there is life; but there are quiet and active sectors of the line.*

(*With a smile*) Oh yes, I see what troubles you. I think that you have misjudged me and my consistency. This flat, my way of life—these are simply my hole in the ground.

A moderately comfortable hole.

Shall we leave it at that?

Of course. There are just one or two other questions on a similar tack: many of your most memorable characters, Raven for instance, are from low life. Have you ever had any experience of low life?

No, very little.

What did you know about poverty?

I have never known it. I was "short," yes, in the sense that I had to be careful for the first eight years of my adult life but I have never been any closer.

Then you don't draw your characters from life?

No, one never knows enough about characters in real life to put them into novels. One gets started and then, suddenly, one can not remember what toothpaste they use: what are their views on interior decoration, and one is stuck utterly. No, major characters emerge: minor ones may be photographed.

Well now, how do you work? Do you work at regular hours?

I used to; now I set myself a number of words.

How many?

Five hundred, stepped up to seven fifty as the book gets on. I re-read the same day, again the next morning and again and again until the passage has got too far behind to matter to the bit that I am writing. Correct in type, final correction in proof.

Do you correct much?

Not over-much.

Did you always want to be a writer?

No, I wanted to be a businessman and all sorts of other things; I wanted to prove to myself that I could do something else.

Then the thing that you could always do was write?

Yes, I suppose it was.

What happened to your business career?

Initially it lasted for a fortnight. They were a firm, I remember, of tobacco merchants. I was to go up to Leeds to learn the business and then go abroad. I couldn't stand my companion. He was an insufferable bore. We would play double noughts and crosses and he always won. What finally got me was when he said: "We'll be able to play this on the way out, won't we?" I resigned immediately.

Then you became a journalist?

Yes, for the same reason—that I wanted to prove I could do something else.

But after **The Man Within** *you gave it up?*

Then I became a professional author.

So that is what you meant when you said "I am an author who is a Catholic?"

Indeed it is. I don't believe that anyone had ever realized that I was a Catholic until 1938 when I began to review for *The Tablet* and, for fun, or rather to give system to a series of reviews of unrelated books, I started to review from a Catholic standpoint. If it had not been for that . . .

But surely a person would have to be very obtuse who reads any novel from **Brighton Rock** *onwards and does not realize it?*

Some people still manage to. In fact, a Dutch priest wrote to me the other day, discussing *The Power and the Glory,* and concluded his letter: "Well I suppose that even if you aren't a Catholic, you are not too hostile to us."

Oh well, internal criticism.

All the same you see what I mean.

Yes, you are "a writer who is a Catholic," we seem to have cleared up that, but there are still a few gaps to be filled before we can know why you are a writer. Do you remember that you once said on the wireless that when you were fourteen or so and read Marjorie Bowen's Viper of Milan *you immediately began to scribble imitation after imitation: from that moment I began to write. All the other possible futures slid away . . .*

Yes, that was so, I am very grateful to Marjorie Bowen. In that talk I was engaged on a little mild bait-ing of the intellectuals. Pritchett had said that Turgenev had influenced him most; somebody else, somebody else. I chose Marjorie Bowen because as I have told you, I don't think that the books that one reads as an adult influence one as a writer. For example, of the many many books on the art of the novel, only Percy Lubbock's *The Craft of Fiction* has interested me at all. But books such as Marjorie Bowen's read at a young age do influence one considerably. It is a very fine book you know. I re-read it again recently.

We haven't read it but from your description in the broadcast . . . it seems that the book has many features in common with your writing as well as with your philosophy. You said that The Viper of Milan *gave you your pattern of life: that religion later might explain it to me in other terms, but the pattern was already there—perfect evil walking the world where perfect good can never walk again, and only the pendulum ensures that after all in the end justice is done. That explains a great deal about your philosophy and it seems that the heightened colors and the violence of the Renaissance, as it is depicted by Miss Bowen and also as it is shown in the plays of Webster, also have their counterpart in your writing. As Edwin Muir has said of you: "Everything is shown up in a harsh light and casts fantastic colors."*

Yes, there is a lot to that. It is true, to a certain extent, about the earlier books but I don't think that it does justice to the later ones, for melodrama is one of my working tools and it enables me to obtain effects that would be unobtainable otherwise, but on the other hand I am not deliberately melodramatic; don't get too annoyed if I say that I write in the way that I do because I am what I am.

Do you ever need the stimulus of drink to write?

No, on the contrary, I can only write when I am absolutely sober.

Do you find collaboration easy, in particular collaboration with directors and producers?

Well, I have been exceptionally lucky both with Carol Reed and recently with Peter Glanvill. I like film work, even the impersonality of it. I have managed to retain a certain amount of control over my own stories so I have not suffered as badly as some people seem to have; all the same, film-making can be a distressing business for, when all is said and done, a writer's part in making a film is relatively small.

Did it take you long to learn?

I learnt a lot on some not very good films before the war so I was into my stride by the time that **The Fallen Idol** and **The Third Man** came along.

Do you see much of your fellow authors?

Not much, they are not one's material. A few of them are very dear friends of mine but for a writer to spend much of his time in the company of authors is, you know, a form of masturbation.

What was the nature of your friendship with Norman Douglas?

We were so different that we could be friends. He was very tolerant in his last years and if he thought me odd he never said so.

Is there, in fact, any relationship between his paganism and your Catholicism?

Not really, but his work, for which I have the very greatest admiration, was so remote from mine that I was able to enjoy it completely; to me it was like a great block of stone, which not being a sculptor myself, I had no temptation to tamper with, yet could admire wholeheartedly for its beauty and strength.

Yes, of course, there couldn't be any real connection between your writing and his—or between yours and Mauriac's. For as you have said, your sinners can never sin against God no matter how hard they try but . . .

(The telephone rang. Mr. Greene smiled in a faint deprecatory way as if to signify he'd said all he wished to say, picked up the instrument and spoke into it.) (pp. 157-67)

Graham Greene, Martin Shuttleworth and Simon Raven, in an interview in *Graham Greene: A Collection of Critical Essays,* edited by Samuel Hynes, Prentice-Hall, Inc., 1973, pp. 154-67.

MORTON DAUWEN ZABEL
(essay 1957)

[Zabel, an American poet and critic, edited *Poetry* magazine. The essay excerpted below first appeared in his *Craft and Character (1957)*, a collection of his literary essays. Here, he argues that Greene, along with W. H. Auden, shows in his writings the influence of the turbulent social and political changes of the twentieth century.]

Again [in *The Ministry of Fear*] we enter the familiar spectre of our age—years of fear and mounting premonition in the 1930s, war and its disasters in the forties, its aftermath of treachery and anarchy still around us in the fifties: no matter what the decade, Greene's evocation of it through fourteen novels (of which *The Ministry of Fear* may be taken as typical of those he calls "entertainments") invariably brings with it an effect that he has made classic of its time and that has justly won him the title "the Auden of the modern thriller." Here once more is the haunted England of the Twentieth Century, the European nightmare of corruption and doom, a *Blick ins Chaos.* . . . (pp. 30-1)

The fustian stage-sets of Oppenheim, Bram Stoker, and Edgar Wallace are gone with their earlier innocent day. We are in a world whose fabulous realities have materialized appallingly out of contemporary legend and prophecy—the portentous journalism of Tabouis, Sheean, Thompson, Gunther, and the apotheosis of the foreign correspondent; the films of Lang, Murnau, Renoir, and Hitchcock; the Gothic fables of Ambler, Hammett, and Simenon; the putsches, pogroms, marches, and mobilizations that have mounted to catastrophe in the present moment of our lives. Its synthetic thrills and anarchic savagery are ruses of melodrama no longer. Guilt pervades all life. All of us are trying to discover how we entered the nightmare, by what treachery we were betrayed to the storm of history. (p. 31)

Greene, dealing in a "whole barbarism" equaling or surpassing anything in history, has undertaken to redeem that dilapidation from the stupefying mechanism and inconsequence to which modern terrorism has reduced it. Arthur Calder Marshall has rightly said, in an article in *Horizon,* that "few living English novelists derive more material from the daily newspaper than Graham Greene." His *mise-en-scène* includes the Nazi underground and fifth column (*The Confidential Agent, The Ministry of Fear*), Communist politics riddled by schisms and betrayals (*It's a Battlefield*), Kruger and his international swindles (*England Made Me*), Zaharoff and the alliance between munitions-making and *Machtpolitik* (*This Gun for Hire*), the English racetrack gang warfare (*Brighton Rock*), the Mexican church suppression (*The Power and the Glory*), wartime in the Gold Coast (*The Heart of the Matter*), in London (*The End of the Affair*), and in Indochina (*The Quiet American*); while his *Orient Express* is the same train we've traveled on all the way from *Shanghai Express* to *Night Train* and *The Lady Vanishes.* But where once—in James, Conrad, Dostoevsky, in Dickens, Defoe and the Elizabethans—it was society, state, kingdom, world, or the universe itself that supplied the presiding order of law and justice, it is now the isolated, betrayed, but finally indestructible integrity of the individual life that must furnish that measure. Humanity, having contrived a world of mindless and psychotic brutality, reverts for survival to the test of the single man. Marked, hunted, or condemned, he may work for evil or for good, but it is his passion for a moral identity of his own that provides the nexus of values in a world that has reverted to anarchy. His lineage is familiar—Raskolnikov, Stavrogin, Kirilov; Conrad's Jim, Razumov, and Heyst; Mann's Felix Krull and Gide's Lafcadio; Hesse's Steppenwolf and Demian, and, more immediately, Kafka's K. He appears in almost every Greene novel—as hero or victim in Drover, Dr. Czinner, the nameless D., and Major Scobie; as pariah or renegade in Raven, Farrant, Rowe, and the whisky priest of *The Power and the Glory;* as the incarnation of pure malevolence in Pinkie, the boy gangster of *Brighton Rock.*

The plot that involves him is fairly consistent.

Brighton Rock may be taken as showing it in archetype. Its conflict rests on a basic dualism of forces, saved from the prevalent danger of becoming an inflexible mechanism by Greene's skill in suggestion and insight, yet radical in its antithesis of elements. Pinkie is a believing Catholic. He knows Hell as a reality and accepts his damnation. *Corruptio optimi pessima* is the last faith left him to live or die by. Ida Arnold, the full-blown, life-loving tart whose casual lover the gang has killed, sets out to track him down: "unregenerate, a specimen of the 'natural man,' coarsely amiable, bestially kind, the most dangerous enemy to religion." She pursues him with ruthless and convinced intention, corners him, sees him killed. The boy is sped to his damnation and Ida triumphs ("God doesn't mind a bit of human nature. . . . I know the difference between Right and Wrong.") The hostility is crucial. It figures in all of Greene's mature books—Mather the detective against Raven the assassin in *This Gun for Hire;* the Inspector against Drover in *It's a Battlefield;* the Communist police lieutenant, accompanied by the *mestizo* who acts as nemesis, against the hunted, shameless, renegade priest in *The Power and the Glory,* trailing his desecrated sanctity through the hovels and jungles of the Mexican state yet persisting in his office of grace and so embracing the doom that pursues him. It reappears in the hunting down of Major Scobie by the agent Wilson in *The Heart of the Matter,* and it counts in the tragic passion of Bendrix for Sarah Miles in *The End of the Affair.* A critic in *The New Statesman* once put the case concisely: "Mr. Greene is a Catholic, and his novel *Brighton Rock* betrays a misanthropic, almost Jansenist, contempt for the virtues that do not spring from grace."

It is this grace that operates as the principle which makes palpable its necessary enemy, Evil. And it is the evil that materializes out of vice, crime, nightmare, and moral stupefaction in Greene's books that brings him into a notable company. The same evil is made to work behind the dramatic mystery and psychic confusion in *The Turn of the Screw* and beneath the squalid violence in Conrad's *The Secret Agent,* that parent classic in this field of fiction which, appearing in 1907, established the kind of novel that Greene and his generation have carried to such exorbitant lengths. To define and objectify the evil, to extricate it from the relativity of values and abstractions—arbitrary justice, impersonal humanitarianism and pity, right and wrong, good and bad is the ultimate motive of Greene's work. . . .

Greene has pointed to another definition of his subject in one of the epigraphs he prefixed to his book on Mexico in 1939—a passage, too long to quote here in full, from [Cardinal John Henry] Newman: . . .

[Either] there is no Creator, or this living society of men is in a true sense discarded from His presence . . . *if* there be a God, *since* there is a God, the human race is implicated in some terrible aboriginal calamity.

The drama and present issue of that calamity are what make the continuous theme of Greene's fiction in its development over the past quarter-century.

II

Greene's beginnings in the novel were in a vein of romantic Stevensonian adventure in *The Man Within,* but he emphasized even there, in a title taken from Thomas Browne, the dualism of the moral personality ("There's another man within me that's angry with me," a derivation from Paul's "law in my members" in the Epistle to the Romans). He next applied the motif to the situation of moral anarchy in modern politics and society and began to adopt for the purpose the devices of intrigue and mystery as the modern thriller had developed them (*The Name of Action, Rumour at Nightfall, Orient Express*). These tales, at first crude and exaggerated in contrivance (Greene has dropped the first two of the last named from his collected edition), soon advanced into his characteristic kind of expertness, and all of them implied a dissatisfaction with the current tendencies in English fiction. This became explicit in his reviews of the modern novelists. Henry James, possibly Conrad, were the last masters of the English novel to preserve its powers in anything like their full tragic and moral potentialities. (pp. 33-7)

Greene, whatever his sense of human and moral complexity or his sophisticated insight into the riddled situation of his time, early decided to address himself to a primitive order of fiction. But since the social and political conditions of the age had likewise reverted to primitive forms of violence, brutality, and anarchy he found his purpose matched in the events of the historic moment. For that moment the thriller was an obvious and logical imaginative medium, and Greene proceeded to raise it to a skill and artistry few other writers of the period, and none in English, had arrived at. His novels between 1930 and 1945 record the crisis and confusions of those years with an effect of atmosphere and moral desperation perfectly appropriate to the time. If their expert contrivance often seems to descend to sleight of hand; if the surrealism of their action and settings can result in efflorescences of sheer conjuring; if the mechanics of the thriller—chases, coincidences, strokes of accident, and exploding surprises—can at times collapse into a kind of demented catastrophe, these were not too remotely at odds with the possibilities of modern terrorism, police action, international intrigue and violence. His superiority to the convention in which he worked was clear; if at times it ran uncomfortably close to the jigsaw-puzzle manipulation which entertainers like Ambler, Hammett, and Raymond Chandler had made so readable and finally so trivial, there was always working in it a poetry of desperation and an in-

stinct for the rudiments of moral conflict that lifted it to allegoric validity. It was apparently at such validity that Greene was aiming in these books. "What strikes the attention most in this closed Fagin universe," he has said in writing on *Oliver Twist,* "are the different levels of unreality"; and of Mauriac's novels he has said that "One is never tempted to consider in detail M. Mauriac's plots. Who can describe six months afterwards the order of events, say in *Ce Qui Était Perdu?*. . . . We are saved or damned by our thoughts, not by our actions."

In fiction of this kind, action itself becomes less real or representative than symbolic. Disbelief is suspended in acceptance of the typical or the potential; incredulity yields to imaginative recognition; and since the events of modern politics and militarism had already wrenched the contemporary imagination out of most of its accepted habits and disciplines, Greene's plots found the thriller fully conditioned to his purpose. If a writer like David Cecil could say, to the charge that John Webster's plays are "extravagant, irrational, and melodramatic," that "the battle of heaven and hell cannot be convincingly conveyed in a mode of humdrum everyday realism" and that "the wild and bloody conventions of Elizabethan melodrama provided a most appropriate vehicle for conveying his hell-haunted vision of human existence," a similar defense could be argued for Greene's melodrama—the more so because the battle of heaven and hell and the hell-haunted vision had become part of the European and contemporary experience.

Moreover, in tales of this kind (to which the adjective "operatic," used by Lionel Trilling to describe certain features in the novels of Forster, applies) character itself tends to reduce to primary or symbolic terms. The tests of average consistency or psychological realism are not of the first importance. A more radical appeal acts to suspend them. The novel refers to something more than the principles of temperament; the "humors" become not only moral but philosophic. At times, in books like *It's a Battlefield* and *England Made Me,* Greene worked in terms of Freudian or abnormal character types and so brought his characters into an uncomfortable but effective relation with his melodrama. At others—*This Gun for Hire* and *The Confidential Agent*—the psychic pathology submitted openly and conveniently to the claims of political violence and so left the story to rest at the level of the historical or political parable (hence "an entertainment"). In *Brighton Rock* the fable became explicitly religious; in *The Power and the Glory* it perhaps became "metaphysical" as well. The last-named novel is certainly one of Greene's finest achievements, possibly his masterpiece. In it the action and milieu are not only invested with a really convincing quality of legend. The fable itself, and the truth it evokes, are believably enacted by the two central characters—the priest with his inescapable vocation, the police lieutenant with his—in a way that is not pressed to exaggerate or simplify their primitive and symbolic functions in the drama. The book is sustained from first to last by a unity of atmosphere that harmonizes its setting, characters, moral values, and historic reference into a logical consistency of effect, and the result is one of the most haunting legends of our time.

Greene's ambition was not, however, content to rest with this kind of result. His more serious books had already aimed at being more than fables or parables. He had before him the examples of Mauriac and Faulkner, both of whom he has acknowledged as major influences in his work. *It's a Battlefield, Brighton Rock,* and *The Power and the Glory* pointed the way to a fiction of full-bodied and realistic substance, and in *The Heart of the Matter* in 1947 he undertook to write a complete and consistent novel. (His "entertainments" since that time have been frankly written for film production—*The Third Man* and *Loser Takes All*.) This brought him squarely up against the problem of reconciling his religious and didactic premises to the realistic and empirical principles of the novel form; of harmonizing an orthodoxy of belief (however personal or inquisitive) with what George Orwell once called "the most anarchical of all forms of literature." (pp. 39-41)

Greene's plots from the first showed a tendency to enforce absolutes of moral judgment—a kind of theological *vis inertiae*—which resulted in the humors to which his characters tended to reduce. The "sanctified sinner" who appears in most of Greene's books is the most prominent of these. The type has become a feature of modern religious literature. Baudelaire, Rimbaud, and Bloy (*Une Femme pauvre*) seem to have combined to give it its characteristic stamp and utility in literary mysticism, and since their day it has become a virtual cliché of religious drama and symbolism. The idea has been put bluntly by its critics: "vice is defined as the manure in which salvation flowers." Orwell made a critical issue of it when he reviewed Greene's *The Heart of the Matter* [see essay by Orwell dated 1948]. It was not only the frivolity of the cult he found suspect: its suggestion "that there is something rather *distingué* in being damned" and its hint of a "weakening of belief " ("when people really believed in Hell, they were not so fond of striking graceful attitudes on its brink"). It was also its results in dramatic artistry: "by trying to clothe theological speculations in flesh and blood, it produces psychological absurdities." The cases of both Pinkie in *Brighton Rock* and Scobie in *The Heart of the Matter* were taken as showing its liabilities for a novelist: that of Pinkie by presupposing "that the most brutally stupid person can, merely by having been brought up a Catholic, be capable of great intellectual subtlety"; that of Scobie "because the two halves of him do not fit together." ("If he were capable of getting into the kind of mess that is described, he would have got into it earlier. If he really felt that adultery is mortal sin, he would stop committing it; if he persisted in it, his sense of sin would weaken. If he believed in Hell, he would not risk going there merely to spare the feelings of a couple of neurotic women.")

In other words, the arguments which such characters enact tend to become increasingly "loaded" as they advance toward explicit theological conclusions. And the fiction that embodies such arguments soon runs into the difficulty which all tendentious or didactic fiction sooner or later encounters. It no longer "argues" the problems and complexities of character in terms of psychological and moral forces; it states, decides, and solves them in terms of preestablished and dictated premises. Grace is always held in reserve as a principle of salvation, a principle which soon becomes too arbitrary and convenient to find justification in conduct or purpose. It descends like a Christianized *deus ex machina* to redeem its vessels when they have driven themselves into the impasse or sacrilege that would, on moral grounds alone, be sufficient to damn them. Greene of course shirks nothing in presenting his men and women as psychically complex and morally confounded. But as he advances out of parable into realism, out of the tale of violence into the drama of credible human personalities, he still keeps an ace up his sleeve, and grace is called upon to do the work that normally would be assigned to moral logic and nemesis. "O God," says Scobie after he has taken communion in a state of mortal sin and is beginning to plan his suicide, "I am the only guilty one because I've known the answers all the time." This admission of his damnation is also his plea for salvation ("I think," says the priest afterward to his widow, "from what I saw of him, that he really loved God"); and what it implies is the kind of presumption or arrogance that has become a feature of recent religious fiction: namely, that neither conduct nor morals are of final importance to the believer. *Corruptio optimi pessima:* it is not only a case of the corruption of the best being the worst. It is by their capacity for corruption or damnation that the best—the believers—qualify for redemption. "The others don't count."

What accompanies this premise in Greene's later novels is likely to take a form which, whatever its theological tenability, can be as repugnant (intentionally repugnant no doubt) to normal religious feeling as it is to aesthetic judgment. "O God, I offer up my damnation to you. Take it. Use it for them," Scobie murmurs at the communion rail; and when, presently, he contemplates future repetitions of his sacrilege, he has "a sudden picture before his eyes of a bleeding face, of eyes closed by the continuous shower of blows: the punch-drunk head of God reeling sideways." On such passages it is difficult not to agree with the critic who acts in revulsion: "a stern theological dogma [is] grossly degraded into melodrama, to an extent which allows even a nonbeliever to speak of blasphemy. . . . It is intolerable. Whether we accept the dogma or not, it is intolerable that it should be expressed in such luridly anthropomorphic terms as these . . . a hotting-up of religious belief for fictional purposes, a vulgarization of the faith" [Philip Toynbee, *The Observer* (London), December 4, 1955]. Greene has made a repeated point of indicting pity as a sin of presumption. Rowe, Scobie, and Bendrix are all made to suffer the consequences of assuming a divine prerogative. It is, however, hard to believe that a similar presumption does not underlie the special pleading that accompanies Scobie's catastrophe. "A priest only knows the unimportant things," says Father Rank to Mrs. Scobie. "Unimportant?" "Oh, I mean the sins," he replies impatiently. "A man doesn't come to us and confess his virtues." To reasoning as conveniently circular as this no practical moral appeal is possible.

The Heart of the Matter is Greene's most ambitious book thus far but in spite of its advance beyond the schematic pattern of its predecessors it is not finally his most convincing one. Its excessive manipulation keeps it from being that. *The End of the Affair* in 1951 showed an important development. It was Greene's first novel to put aside entirely the devices of intrigue, mystery, and criminal motivation. Its scene is modern London, its drama is intimately personal, and though the action takes place in wartime, war does not figure in the events except accidentally. Its plot shows a radical simplicity, and its characters, if tormented to the point of abnormality, remain recognizable as people of credible moral responsibility. (pp. 43-5)

The tale is closely and powerfully developed, and its three principal characters are perhaps the most subtly drawn and intimately created of any in Greene's gallery. It is true that here again, especially in the final section of the book, they assume a disembodied abstraction of conduct which recalls the cases of Pinkie and Scobie, and the introduction of the miracle, shrewdly handled though it is, risks the dissolution of the entire conflict in an arbitrary conclusion. The symbolic effect that might make such an event convincing is weakened by the realistic basis on which the drama is built; it ends as the later, more schematized novels of Mauriac do, in an unprepared shift from realism to didacticism, an arbitrary change of moral (and consequently of dramatic) premises which has the effect of detaching the characters from their established logic as personalities and forcing them to serve a function outside themselves. The result is an effect of metaphysical contrivance which it would take the powers of a Dostoevsky to justify. But if Greene here resorts to an artificiality of argument that has weakened a share of

Mauriac's later work, he also invites in this novel a comparison with Mauriac's psychic and moral insight. By applying himself to an intimate human conflict and laying aside the melodramatic historical framework of his earlier work, he achieves a substance that brings him to a point of renewal and fresh departure in his fiction.

He remains significant, however, because of what he has done to recreate and reassert the moral necessity in his characters, and to project its reality, by symbolic means, into the human and social crisis of his time. He has used guilt and horror for what they have signified in every age, Elizabethan, Gothic, Romantic, or Victorian—as a mode of exploring the fears, evasions, and panic that confuse men or betray the dignity of reason to violence and brutality, but which must always, whatever the historic situation in which they appear, be faced, recognized, and mastered if salvation is to escape the curse of self-deception. The identity Greene's heroes seek is that of a conscience that shirks none of the deception or confusion in their natures. If the "destructive element" of moral anarchy threatens them, it is their passion for a moral identity of their own that redeems them. It is by that passion that they give his work, to quote one of its most acute critics—whatever "its intellectual dishonesty, its ellipses of approximation and selective omissions, as well as its fragmentation of character"—its "sense of history." The drama he presents, "with its evasions and its apologia, is part of our climate of fear and guilt, where it is hard for a man of goodwill, lacking good actions, to see straight or to speak plain. The personal tragedy is in the womb of the general one, and pity is their common bloodstream" [from Donat O'Donnell, *Maria Cross: Imaginative Patterns in a Group of Modern Catholic Writers* (1952)].

It is because he dramatizes the hostile forces of anarchy and conscience, of the moral nonentity with which nature or history threatens man and the absolute tests of moral selfhood, that Greene has brought about one of the most challenging combinations of historical allegory and spiritual argument that have appeared in the present dubious phase of English fiction. His style and imagery can be as melodramatic as his action, but he has made of them an instrument for probing the temper and tragedy of the age, the perversions that have come near to wrecking it, and the stricken weathers of its soul. It still remains for him to get beyond its confusions, negative appeals, and perverse standards—not to mention the tricky arguments by which these are too often condemned in his books and which are too much left to do the work of the honest imagination—to become a fully responsible novelist in his English generation. This is a role to which his acute sense of history and his remarkable gifts in moral drama have assigned him. His skill already puts him in the descent of the modern masters—James, Conrad, Joyce—in whom

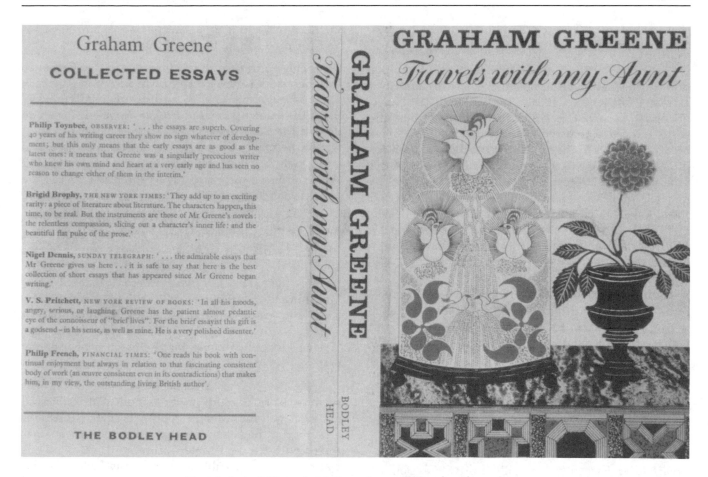

Dust jacket of Greene's 1969 comic novel, *Travels with my Aunt.*

judgment and imagination achieved their richest combination, as well as in the company of the few living novelists—Mauriac, Malraux, Hemingway, Faulkner—in whom their standard survives. He is one of the few contemporary English talents who insist on being referred to that standard and who give evidence that it means to persist. (pp. 46-8)

Morton Dauwen Zabel, "The Best and the Worst," in *Graham Greene: A Collection of Critical Essays,* edited by Samuel Hynes, Prentice-Hall, Inc., 1973, pp. 30-48.

RICHARD JONES

(essay 1969)

[In the essay excerpted below, Jones finds Greene to be a "superb entertainer."]

After more than 50 years before the reading public, Graham Greene has become an institution, the living proof that a contemporary novelist can tackle important subjects and still enjoy immense popularity. As a result, a new work by him is a major event in the international publishing season. (p. 338)

It is difficult to pin down unerringly the source of Greene's popularity. His appeal cuts across several classes of reader, and the link is probably his readability. For Greene, the novel still tells a story, and all his considerable craftsmanship is directed towards this end. He is uninterested in technical innovation, although he has been open to the influence of many different fashions from English historical romance and spy thriller to the French Catholic moralists—with glances at Conrad, Hemingway, and even Faulkner and the existentialists. Accents and passages can reflect these influences, but nothing deflects Greene from the main business of holding the reader's attention. To do this, he resorts to the tricks of the cinema—swift juxtaposition of scene, character, and tone—and is often, because of this, slick and ambiguous in his effects. . . . [What] makes Greene stand out is that from 1938, the year of **Brighton Rock,** he has used popular forms to explore his own very special obsessions, such as the operation of divine grace, man's moral responsibility to himself and other people, and the nature of love and disloyalty. The serious reader likes to recognize in these obsessions the proof of Greene's seriousness and claim to greatness. They respect his obsessions, even though the vocabulary of Greene's Catholicism and of his mysterious brand of radicalism is not shared.

Anyone writing about Greene has to face up at once to the Catholicism, not in order to argue with it, as many Orthodox Catholics have done. . . . Nor to dismiss it, as some free-thinkers tend to . . . , but rather to recognize that a Catholic novelist like Greene brings restraints to the novel that the Anglo-Saxon tradition is not used to. George Orwell's statement that "the novel is a Protestant art form, requiring the free play of mind" never seems truer than at the end of those novels in which Greene has drawn most heavily on his beliefs, such as *The Power and the Glory* and *The Heart of the Matter.* The reader is left as uneasy by the locked gears of the novel's progress as by the rigid optimism of Soviet socialist realist fiction. . . . Greene may be right to claim "not to be a writer of Catholic novels, but a writer who in four or five books took characters with Catholic ideas for his novels," but the influence is there; it is the religious sense that Greene himself believes was lost to the English novel with the death of Henry James. . . . [His] sounding the religious note has been of the utmost value in reminding an increasingly agnostic century that man has existed on another level of being. This leads to the most interesting aspect of Greene's work: that despite the special nature of his obsessions few readers feel that they are being preached at. Each novel is really a private exploration of the possibilities of certain lines of conduct which Greene later shares with his public. . . . [There] is much that is ideologically dubious in Greene's work, but for the general public this matters less than the simple fact that Greene is a superb entertainer. . . .

[In] considering the mass of his work, a line of demarcation wavers through it. On the one side are the novels that operate in what might be called a free market, and they include *Our Man in Havana, Travels with my Aunt,* and most of the early work. The other side of the line are the works that are the products of a closed market, where Greene's obsessions distort the values. By this rough and ready classification, *The Human Factor,* because it lacks either Catholic or left-wing dialectic, ought to belong to the free market, but in fact it belongs to the second. What we see operating, in place of Greene's acquired ideologies, is his native passion, not far removed from Thomas Hardy's, for plotting the destruction of small men and the half-baked hopes that inspire them. The fact that Greene is on the small man's side for most of the novel does not soften the inexorable way he so shapes events that his hero ends up cornered by actions of his own devising. In some respects, the novel is a throwback to the ones Greene wrote in the thirties, a spy thriller set against important political events. . . . Fascism was the accepted evil of many of the 1930's novels; apartheid is the one that dominates *The Human Factor.* In publishing his novel at this time, Greene once again shows his flair for producing a topical document. (pp. 338-41)

The South African situation dominates the novel, but the reader is never taken there except in flashback and conversation. The "beautiful, doomed country" plays the same role in *The Human Factor* as Paraguay does in *The Honorary Consul.* It is the place of injustice, where the main characters cannot, may not, live, and it is also their private climate. Greene's version of South Africa offers no surprises; it is accepted as a police state and, as such, fair game for subversion and harassment.

In establishing Castle as the non-political, non-religious, non-ideological man of good will, Greene had to give him qualities of heart, even of passion. He tries hard, but the result, perhaps from lack of practice, is little more than banal. Greene lavishes much detail on establishing the Castles' mousy life with Sarah's child by a black professor—accepted as Castle's—and a dog; but after years of writing about the horrors of marriage, Greene can only fumble for the essence of a happy match. . . . (p. 343)

At the end of this unconvincing story, Greene seems to be saying: this is where foolish affections and gratitude get you. Men of good will beware. Castle is a traitor, but he is a traitor that the reader has sympathized with for the simple reason that there is no one else in the novel capable of rousing any feeling. In this respect, Greene has produced a variation on an old theme. Otherwise, Castle as a hero is a washout, a soft-centered bumbler. His activities have been, on the whole, trifling, and he lacks the ability of the true ideologic spy, to claim that he is in some way "on the side of history." Why should Greene have given us such an old softie as hero? Was he trying to produce the anti-spy novel hero or to show us that the man without a real ideology is nothing and that it hardly matters what becomes of him since his actions are devoid of any real significance? (p. 345)

It is easy to accept that Greene is moved by poverty, exploitation, and corrupt dictatorships—the classic ills of the Third World—but does he classify as a political animal? It is hard to say "yes" on the strength of *The Human Factor!* It is not that anyone expects Greene to fill a novel with half-baked propaganda, but we are entitled to expect from him a greater resonance. Everything Castle does lacks common sense and gravity, and this failure in the central character exposes the defects in the framework of the novel.

What comes as a surprise is the realization that despite the sleaziness of many of Greene's settings and his capacity for converting any given place into a landscape in Greeneland, Greene is not a realistic writer. What is important for him is the poetic idea. In *Brighton Rock* he had the idea of the good-natured, rather beery woman become avenging angel; in *A Burnt-Out*

Case, Greene was moved by the notion of a great man at the end of his moral rope, as it were, burying himself alive among lepers in steamy central Africa; in *The End of the Affair* he worked out the battle between the loves of this world and the love of God. The reader recognizes the poet's insights, but he expects the novelist's working out. This demands that the writer pay frequent tribute to the great god Probability, the one who presides over the fiction writer's desk. Nearly all of Greene's books are flawed by the schism between the poet's dream and the novelist's realization. (pp. 346-47)

[*The Human Factor*] sets up the great poetic idea of a love that wipes out traditional loyalties and then unsuccessfully tries to support it with a novel that is neither genuine thriller nor comedy of errors. Suspense is missing except at the end, and the exploration of character is minimal. Nowhere is this more evident than in the character of Sarah. She and Castle are an archetypal Greene pair, the elderly man and the young woman available for bed and domestic service. Greene's women are the least contemporary aspect of the novels. In book after book the reader is faced with the same subjugated type, incapable of sharing the battle of ideas. Nothing is less convincing than the scene in *The Human Factor* after Castle has confessed to his wife that he has been a double-agent. Given the hard, even pitiless, rhetoric of some female political activists at this time, Sarah is an Aunty Tomasina.

There are so many things off key in *The Human Factor* that it is difficult to know where to begin. The Castle household is wrong; the setting in Berkhamsted is not right; the handling of the details of the child's education is clumsy; the impact of such a strangely assorted couple in a conservative community is misjudged. Then, London is inaccurately placed. In some cases the mistakes are nugatory: errors that could have been put right by careful editing. In the end, so perfunctory is Greene's English setting that one wonders why he bothered, after so many years living abroad, to return home for a fictional enterprise.

Greene's absence from England had appeared to be an important factor in his youthfulness as a writer. . . . Greene has made the world his province and has found exotic settings and themes which excited him in places as diverse as Africa, Southeast Asia, Haiti, and Spanish America. Greene has made himself a true man of the world, in the best sense, and has been an eyewitness for a generation of readers for whom he has made concrete the great bugbear of our time, the reality of political power that ignores the will of the people and refuses to be restrained by any moral consideration.

In *The Human Factor* there is no electricity between Greene's eye and the landscape. Southeast England is too well-known to be exciting, and to see Greene trying at one or two points in the book to create an uneasy nighttime London—a city that goes to bed about eleven o'clock—is to see that there are certain tricks he has grown used to employing that do not work on the home scene. Greene is really quite limited in his atmospheric effects, and the reader of his novels must often be struck by how much a cliché the sudden storm has become . . . although realizing that it makes highly effective cinema. This is fine in Mexico, West Africa, or Vietnam, but the English, grown stoic in their oceanic climate, do not recognize rain as the stuff of melodrama. (pp. 347-49)

Richard Jones, "The Improbable Spy," in *The Virginia Quarterly Review,* Vol. 55, No. 2, Spring, 1979, pp. 338-49.

GENE KELLOGG
(essay date 1970)

[In the following excerpt, Kellogg discusses the theme of responsibility in Greene's novels.]

Greene is such a complex artist that before one can even hope to know what he was attempting to do one must look at his origins. James, Conrad, and Mauriac were the chief writers who influenced him. Most obvious is his connection with Mauriac and through him with the whole carefully developed, highly self-aware French critical Catholic tradition. . . . The fate of souls which will be saved or lost is the strongest source of drama in Greene's stories. Though his handling of it derives from the French tradition, nevertheless, as with all debts Greene owes, he changes the gift he receives and develops it in his own way. . . . (pp. 111-12)

Greene understood the accumulated encrustations of popular misconceptions among Catholics about Catholic orthodoxy. He worked to eliminate them, and in Newman's sense "develop" the fullest possible true meaning. Greene believes the biblical teaching, greater love hath no man than that he lay down his life for his friend, but he also believes that there should be added as a logical corollary the principle that man must be ready to lay down not only his temporal but his eternal life. . . . Greene . . . makes [this theme] specially his own and develops his own variation. Like all his dramatic themes, its central element is the search for the highest measure of love, a search that leads into a paradox, yet again the drama is one whose power depends on evoking and enlarging for modern times a timeless teaching. Whoever shall seek to lose his soul in Greene's superbly generous way shall save it, as Rose does in *Brighton Rock.* (pp. 112-13)

Volumes could be written about his achievements

in developing the novel. . . . As in James, all the component personalities combine to create the whole personality as it finally develops. But compared to Greene, James seems to write in slow motion. Greene shifts from one person to another, one place to the next, one action to consequent action with a rapidity that can only be called cinematographic. The effect is as if Greene were swinging the boom of a huge camera. The changes come the more swiftly because for plots Greene uses the patterns of the modern thriller, with intrigue, betrayal, mystery, suspense, surprise, and particularly the chase as main elements. (p. 114)

Greene's books were a symptom of Catholic thinking that was increasing in depth, but inevitably his work collided with the pious rigidity inherited from the nineteenth century. Nevertheless his widely read fiction exerted a strong influence. The "open Church" of the 1960s, with its acceptance of all "men of good will" had in its background the puzzled, slowly comprehending, worldwide Catholic audience on which Greene's themes were working in the 1940s and 1950s. These were the decades when the separatism that had dominated the nineteenth century was surrendering to the older recognition that had begun with such men as Campion and continued with such men as Newman: that there was good in all people. Greene's work was a sign of the accelerated convergence between the Catholic and the non-Catholic worlds. (p. 127)

When one bears in mind Greene's lifelong development of the theme of God's mercy, and when one looks back on his fiction with today's larger view of Catholic orthodoxy that does away with such mistaken encrustations as the notion of some sort of automatic damnation for suicides, one remembers Pinkie's verse about the stirrup and the ground [in *Brighton Rock*], and one feels sure that what Scobie found [in *The Heart of the Matter*] was indeed mercy, a compassion and a responsibility infinitely greater than his own. As in all Greene's novels, the measure of the protagonist before God is his love. And the measure of God is the same, except that God's love in its illimitable vastness is immeasurable. Here again we see that Greene's best work goes back to forms that are very old, and far more complex than dramas in which the good suffer and the evil prosper, as in the early *Orient Express* and *England Made Me.* (p. 131)

After Greene produced his finest novel, *The Heart of the Matter,* his strength seemed somehow impaired. A study of the works that followed gives one the impression that whatever he experienced while developing the character of Scobie must have exhausted him. From the time of his first novels Greene's theme had been responsibility. In 1932, in his earliest widely read entertainment, *Orient Express,* the antifascist Dr. Czinner was a protagonist who dedicated his life to the political liberation of his fellowmen. In 1935, in the depths of the financial crisis that shook the world, Greene examined the theme on its economic side and portrayed the amoral financier, Krogh, a type of creature who, Greene felt, had by his irresponsibility brought about the sufferings of the countless millions of starving and unemployed. Later Greene examined figures of heroic responsibility, and created the child-woman, Rose, in *Brighton Rock* and the whiskey priest in *The Power and the Glory.*

But after *The Power and the Glory* in 1940, Greene apparently began to reassess his major theme. The reassessment must have been painful, for responsibility had been not only Greene's answer to life as he saw it in the 1930s but it was the answer of the whole intellectual world of that era. The feeling was that irresponsibility had brought on all of the world's crises from depression to impending war. (p. 133)

The Power and the Glory had been particularly moving in its treatment of the theme of responsibility because the protagonist was a priest and the book traced the theme to its deepest roots, which lay in the Christian origins of Western civilization and Christ's commandment of love from man to man. *The Power and the Glory* is written by an artist who is carried by surging self-confidence in the rightness of his evolved beliefs, and who feels his command of his talent reaching a peak. When one puts down *The Power and the Glory,* however, and picks up *The Heart of the Matter,* one is immediately aware of a change in spirit. *The Heart of the Matter* moves deliberately—painfully. It is one of those works in which one can almost sense the sweat on the author's pen. The brilliant cinematographic flashing from scene to scene is gone, the plot unfolds with terrible slowness, a crescendo of inexorability. (p. 134)

Where did Scobie go "wrong"; what was the nature of Greene's painful and astounding reassessment of the theme that had lain at the heart of his own beliefs and of the Western world's convictions since the 1930s? Greene's Scobie is shown as "corrupted" by the force of his pity. (pp. 134-35)

Thus in his portrait of Scobie Greene reversed his great theme. Love of man for his fellow beings is the second commandment; the first and greatest is love for God "with all thy heart, with all thy soul, with all thy mind." An ineradicable part of this love of God must be trust, and Scobie does not trust. Greene's theme now is that a man should indeed help and serve his fellow beings, but there are limits beyond which he cannot go, and times when trust in God must replace his own efforts. Scobie's lack of trust is self-destructive, and his ultimate suicide is inevitable.

In *Brighton Rock, The Power and the Glory,* and *The Heart of the Matter* Greene had been like an embodied spirit of compassion, contemplating more and more deeply in each book the nature of man's fate in a fallen world. It would seem that the ordeal of writing *The Heart of the Matter* may have driven him spiritually into dryness, and, intellectually, he may have said, if not all, at least the utmost he had to say. The later Greene is like his own Querry in *A Burnt-Out Case.* Only one book, *The End of the Affair,* whose craftsmanship was such that it evoked the warm sponsorship in America of William Faulkner, can even remotely be compared to the major novels; and the theme of *The End of the Affair* is significant: it is love and loyalty to God over love and loyalty to man; it is trust in God's own "responsibility" and a placing of final trust in the goodness of creation when one reaches the place beyond which one's own effort cannot prevail.

Looking back after fifteen years, one realizes that the steady deepening of Greene's achievements ended in mid-century, at the time of the reassessment of his great theme. Afterwards he turned increasingly to the mode of fiction that had always enabled Catholic writers to express their vision and yet maintain the detachment that is the artist's protection against pain. Satire is prominent in the skillful entertainment, *The Third Man* in 1950; it provides the framework of *The Quiet American* in 1955; and it is almost the entire substance of *The Comedians* ten years later. (pp. 135-36)

Gene Kellogg, "Graham Greene," in his *The Vital Tradition: The Catholic Novel in a Period of Convergence,* Loyola University Press, 1970, pp. 111-36.

JOHN SPURLING

(essay date 1983)

[In the following excerpt, Spurling describes what he views as nineteenth-century qualities of Greene's fiction.]

[Jorge Luis Borges, Anthony Powell, Vladimir Nabokov, Samuel Beckett, and Graham Greene] are all writers born around the turn of the century, all romantics with sheltered childhoods who have had to face up to the twentieth-century failure of the Victorian world-order and the questioning of its values in both public and private terms. Borges and Powell, by their different techniques for neutralizing themselves, have evolved into classicists; Nabokov, driven out of his own country by the revolution, turned Russia into a fairy-tale landscape for ever out of reach and therefore for ever potent as a romantic standard by which to judge his characters' and the world's inadequacy; Beckett, like Greene a rebel against the world that sheltered him and a voluntary exile, retreated into the cave of himself.

Only Greene has tried to retain the romantic forms of the old world—including the romantic protagonist and the romantic self within the protagonist—and to use them as the direct expression of a reality which conflicts with the original content of the forms. If it is a bold solution, it is also rather naïve. If it makes things easy for the conservative reader and plays a part in Greene's enormous popularity, it raises increasing problems of credibility as the novels get older and are more objectively analysed.

Romanticism and reality will seem to square with one another only as long as the particular brand of romanticism is shared by the author and his or her public. Once that becomes suspect, or even ludicrous, the work loses its current value and drops away into the past, to be remembered, if at all, only as a forerunner, a historical phenomenon, a book for children or the basis for adaptations to another medium. Some of the work of Buchan, Hope and Haggard, for example—Greene's second-division masters—will survive in this way, in spite of the new embarrassingly 'period' attitudes it enshrines. Clearly Greene's rather too schematic reaction against those attitudes—his substitution in the make-up of his protagonists of weakness, corruption, disloyalty and uncertainty for the strength, integrity, loyalty and self-confidence that characterize Buchan's and Haggard's imperialist heroes—will date in its turn, though for the present it is still sufficiently widely shared by readers and imitated by younger writers to appear normal and therefore realistic. The question is how much will remain when the attitudes have lost their savour. Three things, I suggest, which are perhaps only three aspects of the same thing, guarantee Greene's staying-power.

The first is that behind the attitudes—the authorial *pensées,* the preaching of Javitt and others, the forced similes—Greene does explore real pain and unhappiness and not always solely in his protagonists. The pain is felt through his protagonists, but it is often drawn off the subsidiary characters, the protagonists acting as a kind of central conduit for whatever *Angst* or suffering is around, much in the way that a priest does or is supposed to do. In this sense, one can say that Greene's fiction has a genuine religious dimension, not to be confused with that melodramatic backdrop of good and evil which he used as a way of raising the stakes and laying on the colours.

I am not certain whether Greene himself is fully conscious of this active core in his work—if he were, I suspect he would have formulated it more obviously into a *pensée* or a sermon—but it accounts not only for the powerful effect some of his books have had on those in need of spiritual comfort but also for the ordinary reader's feeling that, for all the mud that can be thrown at the rhetorical style, the over-controlled plots, the morality-play characters and the artificial theology, these are not negligible fictions. Why does the whisky priest in *The Power and the Glory* turn back into danger and sacrifice his life in order to hear a criminal's confession, why is it so appalling that Scobie can't make his confession, why does Fowler in *The Quiet American* wish that there was someone to whom he could say he was sorry for causing Pyle's death? These are not just Catholic quibbles. Even the irreligious Brown wonders whether the happiest moment he and his mistress ever knew was not the time when they trusted each other with mutual self-revelations instead of caresses.

The act of confession, in itself and regardless of its ritual orthodoxy—the sharing of one's pain with someone else—is a movement towards 'the city called Peace of Mind', just as the schoolboy Greene was pulled back from despair by his visit to the psychoanalyst. Yet Scobie and Castle can approach that city only by complete withdrawal into themselves. The tension set up between these two incompatible kinds of happiness—or at least temporary alleviations of unhappiness—is at the heart of *The Heart of the Matter*, as of all Greene's best work. Indeed, it is there in most of his work in some form; only that in the novels which are most likely to outlast the decay of their overt attitudes—*The Heart of the Matter, The Power and the Glory, The Quiet American, The Comedians*—it is tauter and more deeply lodged in the story.

The second thing that makes Greene more than a temporary phenomenon is, paradoxically, what is most contemporary about him: his settings and situations. In spite of its distortions, Greeneland is real. No European writer since Conrad has put the hot, poor and foully governed places of the earth on paper as vividly as Greene. This is not to say that he has described them as they are, from the point of view of God or even of their inhabitants, but as they appeared and smelt and felt and tasted to the European visitor in the middle decades of the twentieth century. Nor are these simply heightened descriptions—or a good travel writer or journalist might have done them as well—but, like Conrad's, they are moral landscapes, characterizations of what is there and of whom it is experienced by. In other words, they contain to a remarkable degree the history and politics of both parties to the encounter. The political part of Greene's plots is fairly standard and even banal—inevitably so, since tyrants, spies, corruption and oppression are hardly newer than human society—but, just as the spiritual element is to be found not in his well-publicized Catholic backdrop but buried deep in his protagonists, so the true political element is intrinsic to his settings and forms a kind of parallel to the spiritual element, for it too involves the tension between apartness and collusion.

The European is safe and in control of himself so long as he keeps the place at arm's length, but the place offers him—and surely it's the reason he came there—loss of control, a temporary unburdening, the opportunity to give and receive. Scobie gives way and then regains control, Querry holds on to himself and then gives way, Brown's is a long process of slipping into collusion with the place, Fowler thrashes to and fro. And of course the fact that, since the days of Conrad, the Europeans have resigned their empires to the United States makes collusion easier for Greene's characters than it was for Conrad's, whose apartness was supported and indeed demanded by a whole society and its patriarchal ethos. From Scobie, who still inhabits a largely Conradian tropic, to Brown and Plarr in their especially squalid pockets of the new American hegemony, Greeneland documents and mythologizes this transitional phase of history, providing the equivalent to Dickens's early industrial London, say, or Chekhov's pre-revolutionary Russia. In so far as the subsidiary characters in Greene's novels have an existence independent of the protagonists, it is as emanations of their political landscapes. To read Greene's novels is to be haunted ever afterwards by places and times with human features or humans who are half made up of places and times. The dentist and the half-caste in *The Power and the Glory* are the ghosts of pre-war Mexico; the two young guards in the roadside watchtower in *The Quiet American* are Vietnam in the last days of the French; Rycker and Deo Gratias in *A Burnt-Out Case* are the Congo when it was still Belgian, and so on.

The third thing takes us back to the *pensée*. . . . In a generation or two, if it doesn't already, this kind of detachable sentiment, which can be put into the mouth of any protagonist, will sound as quaint as some of Richard Hannay's sentiments. But in that the protagonists' self-examinations, however slickly expressed, reflect those of a man who could never forgive or forget the process of growing up, they will continue to have meaning: not just for students of the particular author Graham Greene, but for any reader trapped in that narrow but sometimes lifelong defile leading from dependence and immaturity to responsibility for one's own actions and the happiness of others. It is one of the central themes of literature, especially of English literature, and although it may have been handled with broader sympathy and deeper understanding by the greatest writers—including Greene's own first-division masters, James and Conrad—it has never been done with more intimate passion than by Greene. (pp. 71-5)

John Spurling, in his *Graham Greene*, Methuen, 1983, 80 p.

SOURCES FOR FURTHER STUDY

Allott, Kenneth and Farris, Miriam. *The Art of Graham Greene*. New York: Russell & Russell, Inc., 1963, 253 p.

> Traces the stages of development of Greene's novels and features an extensive discussion of Greene's examination of pity.

Atkins, John Alfred. *Graham Greene*. London: John Calder (Publishers) Ltd., 1957, 240 p.

> Examines literary, biographical, and cultural influences on Greene's novels, poems, and plays.

Hynes, Samuel, ed. *Graham Greene: A Collection of Critical Essays*. New Jersey: Prentice-Hall, Inc., 1973, 183 p.

> Fourteen essays on Greene's works by such critics as R. W. B. Lewis, W. H. Auden, George Orwell, and Evelyn Waugh and two interviews with Greene.

Lodge, David. *Graham Greene*. New York & London: Columbia University Press, 1966, 48 p.

> A concise examination of the recurring themes in Greene's novels.

Sherry, Norman. *The Life of Graham Greene, Volume One: 1904-1939*. New York: Viking Penguin, a Division of Penguin Books USA Inc., 1989, 783 p.

> Chronicles Greene's life from birth to the events leading up to the writing of *The Power and the Glory*.

Smith, Grahame. *The Achievement of Graham Greene*. New Jersey: Barnes & Noble, 1986, 228 p.

> Presents a respected account of Greene's "fertile and complex novelistic career," and posits that Greene's Catholicism distinguishes his novels from those of other liberal writers of the twentieth century.

Thomas Hardy

1840-1928

English novelist, poet, short story writer, dramatist, and essayist.

INTRODUCTION

*H*ardy is considered one of the greatest novelists in English literature. In works that resemble those of earlier Victorian novelists in technique, Hardy daringly violated literary traditions of his age, realistically examining love relationships and sexuality and presenting some of the earliest psychological studies of individual characters in English fiction. Hardy depicted human existence as tragic, largely determined by powers beyond the individual's command—in particular, by external societal pressures and by internal compulsions of character. His forthright treatment of hitherto taboo subject matter and his essentially pessimistic worldview engendered controversy during his lifetime and continues to be an issue of critical contention.

Hardy was born and raised in the region of Dorsetshire, which influenced his fiction and poetry as the basis for the Wessex countryside, one of the most extensive and minutely developed fictional settings in world literature. Hardy originally sought recognition as a poet but turned to prose as a more ready means of literary success. His unpublished first novel, *The Poor Man and the Lady*, was rejected for being overly satirical by George Meredith, author of several important novels and a reader for the publishing firm of Chapman and Hall. Meredith advised Hardy to incorporate such popular fictional devices into his work as lively plot twists and melodrama. In 1871 Hardy wrote *Desperate Remedies*, a novel that defined many of the fundamental characteristics of his emerging style. Because he considered strict realism insufficient to hold reader attention, Hardy wrote novels with artificially elaborate plots, extensive use of coincidence, and the frequently oppressive mood of Gothic melodrama. Hardy's first important novel to display the definitive strengths of his narrative art was *Far from the Madding Crowd*, published in 1874. His depiction of Bathsheba Everdene in this novel demonstrates Hardy's ability to create a vivid and believable psychological portrait of a female protagonist—a skill many critics believe is best exemplified in his later creation of the eponymous heroine of *Tess of the d'Urbervilles* (1891).

Over the next twenty-one years, Hardy wrote a number of novels considered among the finest in the English language, including *The Return of the Native* (1878), in which the powers that control human existence are dramatically symbolized in the natural forces that sweep across Egdon Heath, and *The Mayor of Casterbridge* (1886), which presents Hardy's belief that "character is fate." Heralded as a turning point in Hardy's career, primarily for the skill with which he presented a male protagonist, *The Mayor of Casterbridge* is further acclaimed as a pivotal work in the development of the English novel, demonstrating that the genre could present a significant psychological history and still serve as an important social document.

With the publication in 1891 of *Tess of the d'Urbervilles,* Hardy came under attack from critics who charged that his exploration of the conflict between Victorian social convention and the forces of human love and sexuality was immoral, anti-Christian, and unduly pessimistic. Hardy had always been sensitive to critical censure, and when he incurred further harsh disapproval for his unidealized portrayal of marriage and human relationships in his next novel, *Jude the Obscure,* his response was to cease writing fiction and to devote himself to poetry, which he had composed intermittently throughout his career.

Much of Hardy's poetry constitutes a sermon on pessimistic themes. Although faulted for their unusual structure and their emphasis on abstract ideas, these poems are often praised for their lyric power and their unique blend of traditional and experimental forms. While Hardy is considered a major poet by some, critics generally agree that his novels are a more consistently

impressive body of work. Hardy's last major work, *The Dynasts: A Drama of the Napoleonic Wars* (1904-08), is an epic historical drama of the Napoleonic wars written in verse which summarizes his philosophy on the forces that influence human existence.

Between 1874 and 1900, in addition to writing novels and poetry, Hardy published short fiction in various English and American periodicals. Most of these pieces were later reprinted in Hardy's short story collections, including *Wessex Tales* (1888), *A Group of Noble Dames* (1891), and *Life's Little Ironies* (1895). In his short stories, Hardy frequently depicted grotesque situations in the lives of rural characters and made extensive use of irony to demonstrate the lack of control his protagonists hold over their own lives. While his reputation as a seminal figure in the development of the nineteenth-century novel overshadows his achievement in short fiction, several of Hardy's tales, including "The Three Strangers" and "The Distracted Preacher," continue to be read by students and scholars as exemplary works of late Victorian literature.

Criticism of Hardy has encompassed diverse interpretations. Early critics viewed Hardy as a consummate realist, while later evaluations by such critics as Albert J. Guerard suggest that he may be recognized as a predecessor of anti-realist trends in twentieth-century fiction. For the integrity of his moral and philosophical views and for the imaginative achievement in creating the world of Wessex, he continues to receive undiminished acclaim from critics, scholars, and the reading public.

(For further information about Hardy's life and works, see *Contemporary Authors,* Vols. 104, 123; *Dictionary of Literary Biography,* Vols. 18, 19; *Short Story Criticism,* Vol. 2; *Something about the Author,* Vol. 25; and *Twentieth-Century Literary Criticism,* Vols. 4, 10, 18, 32.)

CRITICAL COMMENTARY

VIRGINIA WOOLF

(essay date 1928)

[An English novelist, essayist, and critic, Woolf is one of the most prominent literary figures of the twentieth century. She is renowned as an innovator of the novel form, in particular for her contributions to the development of stream-of-consciousness narrative. Her critical essays, which cover nearly the

entire range of English literature, contain some of her finest prose and are commended for their insight. In the following 1928 essay, she discusses Hardy's development as a novelist and pronounces him a novelist of genius.]

When we say that the death of Thomas Hardy leaves English fiction without a leader, we mean that there is no other writer whose supremacy would be generally

Principal Works

Desperate Remedies (novel) 1871

Under the Greenwood Tree (novel) 1872

Far from the Madding Crowd (novel) 1874

The Return of the Native (novel) 1878

The Mayor of Casterbridge: The Life and Death of a Man of Character (novel) 1886

Wessex Tales: Strange, Lively, and Commonplace (short stories) 1888

A Group of Noble Dames (short stories) 1891

Tess of the d'Urbervilles: A Pure Woman Faithfully Presented (novel) 1891

Life's Little Ironies (short stories) 1894

Jude the Obscure (novel) 1895

The Wessex Novels. 18 vols. 1895-1913

Wessex Poems, and Other Verses (poetry) 1898

Poems of the Past and Present (poetry) 1901

The Dynasts: A Drama of the Napoleonic Wars. 3 vols. [first publication] (drama) 1904-08

The Works of Thomas Hardy in Prose and Verse, with Prefaces and Notes. 24 vols. (novels, short stories, and poetry) 1912-31

Satires of Circumstance, Lyrics and Reveries (poetry) 1914

The Complete Poems (poetry) 1976

The Personal Notebooks of Thomas Hardy (notebooks) 1978

1871 he was a man of thirty-one; he had written a novel, *Desperate Remedies,* but he was by no means an assured craftsman. He 'was feeling his way to a method', he said himself; as if he were conscious that he possessed all sorts of gifts, yet did not know their nature, or how to use them to advantage. To read that first novel is to share in the perplexity of its author. The imagination of the writer is powerful and sardonic; he is book-learned in a home-made way; he can create characters but he cannot control them; he is obviously hampered by the difficulties of his technique and, what is more singular, he is driven by some sense that human beings are the sport of forces outside themselves, to make use of an extreme and even melodramatic use of coincidence. He is already possessed of the conviction that a novel is not a toy, nor an argument; it is a means of giving truthful if harsh and violent impressions of the lives of men and women. But perhaps the most remarkable quality in the book is the sound of a waterfall that echoes and booms through its pages. It is the first manifestation of the power that was to assume such vast proportions in the later books. He already proves himself a minute and skilled observer of Nature; the rain, he knows, falls differently as it falls upon roots or arable; he knows that the wind sounds differently as it passes through the branches of different trees. But he is aware in a larger sense of Nature as a force; he feels in it a spirit that can sympathize or mock or remain the indifferent spectator of human fortunes. Already that sense was his; and the crude story of Miss Aldclyffe and Cytherea is memorable because it is watched by the eyes of the gods, and worked out in the presence of Nature.

accepted, none to whom it seems so fitting and natural to pay homage. Nobody of course claimed it less. The unworldly and simple old man would have been painfully embarrassed by the rhetoric that flourishes on such occasions as this. Yet it is no less than the truth to say that while he lived there was one novelist at all events who made the art of fiction seem an honourable calling; while Hardy lived there was no excuse for thinking meanly of the art he practised. Nor was this solely the result of his peculiar genius. Something of it sprang from his character in its modesty and integrity, from his life, lived simply down in Dorsetshire without self-seeking or self-advertisement. For both reasons, because of his genius and because of the dignity with which his gift was used, it was impossible not to honour him as an artist and to feel respect and affection for the man. But it is of the work that we must speak, of the novels that were written so long ago that they seem as detached from the fiction of the moment as Hardy himself was remote from the stir of the present and its littleness.

We have to go back more than a generation if we are to trace the career of Hardy as a novelist. In the year

That he was a poet should have been obvious; that he was a novelist might still have been held uncertain. But the year after, when *Under the Greenwood Tree* appeared, it was clear that much of the effort of 'feeling for a method' had been overcome. Something of the stubborn originality of the earlier book was lost. The second is accomplished, charming, idyllic compared with the first. The writer, it seems, may well develop into one of our English landscape painters, whose pictures are all of cottage gardens and old peasant women, who lingers to collect and preserve from oblivion the old-fashioned ways and words which are rapidly falling into disuse. And yet what kindly lover of antiquity, what naturalist with a microscope in his pocket, what scholar solicitous for the changing shapes of language, ever heard the cry of a small bird killed in the next wood by an owl with such intensity? The cry 'passed into the silence without mingling with it'. Again we hear, very far away, like the sound of a gun out at sea on a calm summer's morning, a strange and ominous echo. But as we read these early books there is a sense of waste. There is a feeling that Hardy's genius was obstinate and perverse; first one gift would have its way with him and then another. They would not consent to run together easily in harness. Such indeed was likely to be the fate of a writer who was at once poet and realist, a faithful son of field and down, yet tormented by the doubts and despondencies bred of book-learning; a lover of old ways and plain countrymen, yet doomed to see the faith and flesh of his forefathers turn to thin and spectral transparencies before his eyes.

To this contradiction Nature had added another element likely to disorder a symmetrical development. Some writers are born conscious of everything; others are unconscious of many things. Some, like Henry James and Flaubert, are able not merely to make the best use of the spoil their gifts bring in, but control their genius in the act of creation; they are aware of all the possibilities of every situation, and are never taken by surprise. The unconscious writers, on the other hand, like Dickens and Scott, seem suddenly and without their own consent to be lifted up and swept onwards. The wave sinks and they cannot say what has happened or why. Among them—it is the source of his strength and of his weakness—we must place Hardy. His own word, 'moments of vision', exactly describes those passages of astonishing beauty and force which are to be found in every book that he wrote. With a sudden quickening of power which we cannot foretell, nor he, it seems, control, a single scene breaks off from the rest. We see, as if it existed alone and for all time, the wagon with Fanny's dead body inside travelling along the road under the dripping trees; we see the bloated sheep struggling among the clover; we see Troy flashing his sword round Bathsheba where she stands motionless, cutting the lock off her head and spitting the caterpillar on her breast. Vivid to the eye, but not to the eye alone, for every sense participates, such scenes dawn upon us and their splendour remains. But the power goes as it comes. The moment of vision is succeeded by long stretches of plain daylight, nor can we believe that any craft or skill could have caught the wild power and turned it to a better use. The novels therefore are full of inequalities; they are lumpish and dull and inexpressive; but they are never arid; there is always about them a little blur of unconsciousness, that halo of freshness and margin of the unexpressed which often produce the most profound sense of satisfaction. It is as if Hardy himself were not quite aware of what he did, as if his consciousness held more than he could produce, and he left it for his readers to make out his full meaning and to supplement it from their own experience.

For these reasons Hardy's genius was uncertain in development, uneven in accomplishment, but, when the moment came, magnificent in achievement. The moment came, completely and fully, in *Far from the Madding Crowd*. The subject was right; the method was right; the poet and the countryman, the sensual man, the sombre reflective man, the man of learning, all enlisted to produce a book which, however fashions may chop and change, must hold its place among the great English novels. There is, in the first place, that sense of the physical world which Hardy more than any novelist can bring before us; the sense that the little prospect of man's existence is ringed by a landscape which, while it exists apart, yet confers a deep and solemn beauty upon his drama. The dark downland, marked by the barrows of the dead and the huts of shepherds, rises against the sky, smooth as a wave of the sea, but solid and eternal; rolling away to the infinite distance, but sheltering in its folds quiet villages whose smoke rises in frail columns by day, whose lamps burn in the immense darkness by night. Gabriel Oak tending his sheep up there on the back of the world is the eternal shepherd; the stars are ancient beacons; and for ages he has watched beside his sheep.

But down in the valley the earth is full of warmth and life; the farms are busy, the barns stored, the fields loud with the lowing of cattle and the bleating of sheep. Nature is prolific, splendid, and lustful; not yet malignant and still the Great Mother of labouring men. And now for the first time Hardy gives full play to his humour, where it is freest and most rich, upon the lips of country men. Jan Coggan and Henry Fray and Joseph Poorgrass gather in the malthouse when the day's work is over and give vent to that half-shrewd, half-poetic humour which has been brewing in their brains and finding expression over their beer since the pilgrims tramped the Pilgrims' Way; which Shakespeare and Scott and George Eliot all loved to overhear, but none loved better or heard with greater understanding than Hardy. But it is not the part of the peasants in the Wessex novels to stand out as individuals. They compose a pool of common wisdom, of common humour, a fund of perpetual life. They comment upon the actions of the hero and heroine, but while Troy or Oak or Fanny or Bathsheba come in and out and pass away, Jan Coggan and Henry Fray and Joseph Poorgrass remain. They drink by night and they plough the fields by day. They are eternal. We meet them over and over again in the novels, and they always have something typical about them, more of the character that marks a race than of the features which belong to an individual. The peasants are the great sanctuary of sanity, the country the last stronghold of happiness. When they disappear, there is no hope for the race.

With Oak and Troy and Bathsheba and Fanny Robin we come to the men and women of the novels at their full stature. In every book three or four figures predominate, and stand up like lightning conductors to attract the force of the elements. Oak and Troy and Bathsheba; Eustacia, Wildeve, and Venn; Henchard, Lucetta, and Farfrae; Jude, Sue Bridehead, and Phillotson. There is even a certain likeness between the different groups. They live as individuals and they differ as individuals; but they also live as types and have a likeness as types. Bathsheba is Bathsheba, but she is woman and sister to Eustacia and Lucetta and Sue; Gabriel is Gabriel Oak, but he is man and brother to Henchard, Venn, and Jude. However lovable and charming Bathsheba may be, still she is weak; however stubborn and ill-guided Henchard may be, still he is strong. This is a fundamental part of Hardy's vision; the staple of many of his books. The woman is the weaker and the fleshlier, and she clings to the stronger and obscures his vision. How freely, nevertheless, in his greater books life is poured over the unalterable framework! When Bathsheba sits in the wagon among her plants, smiling at her own loveliness in the little looking-glass, we may know, and it is proof of Hardy's power that we do know, how severely she will suffer and cause others to suffer before the end. But the moment has all the bloom and beauty of life. And so it is, time and time again. His characters, both men and women, were creatures to him of an infinite attraction. For the women he shows a more tender solicitude than for the men, and in them, perhaps, he takes a keener interest. Vain might their beauty be and terrible their fate, but while the glow of life is in them their step is free, their laughter sweet, and theirs is the power to sink into the breast of Nature and become part of her silence and solemnity, or to rise and put on them the movement of the clouds and the wildness of the flowering woodlands. The men who suffer, not like the women through dependence upon other human beings, but through conflict with fate, enlist our sterner sympathies. For such a man as Gabriel Oak we need have no passing fears. Honour him we must, though it is not granted us to love him quite so freely. He is firmly set upon his feet and can give as shrewd a blow, to men at least, as any he is likely to receive. He has a prevision of what is to be expected that springs from character rather than from education. He is stable in his temperament, steadfast in his affections, and capable of open-eyed endurance without flinching. But he, too, is no puppet. He is a homely, humdrum fellow on ordinary occasions. He can walk the street without making people turn to stare at him. In short, nobody can deny Hardy's power—the true novelist's power—to make us believe that his characters are fellow-beings driven by their own passions and idiosyncrasies, while they have—and this is the poet's gift—something symbolical about them which is common to us all.

And it is when we are considering Hardy's power of creating men and women that we become most conscious of the profound differences that distinguish him from his peers. We look back at a number of these characters and ask ourselves what it is that we remember them for. We recall their passions. We remember how

deeply they have loved each other and often with what tragic results. We remember the faithful love of Oak for Bathsheba; the tumultuous but fleeting passions of men like Wildeve, Troy, and Fitzpiers; we remember the filial love of Clym for his mother, the jealous paternal passion of Henchard for Elizabeth Jane. But we do not remember how they have loved. We do not remember how they talked and changed and got to know each other, finely, gradually, from step to step and from stage to stage. Their relationship is not composed of those intellectual apprehensions and subtleties of perception which seem so slight yet are so profound. In all the books love is one of the great facts that mould human life. But it is a catastrophe; it happens suddenly and overwhelmingly, and there is little to be said about it. The talk between the lovers when it is not passionate is practical or philosophic, as though the discharge of their daily duties left them with more desire to question life and its purpose than to investigate each other's sensibilities. Even if it were in their power to analyse their emotions, life is too stirring to give them time. They need all their strength to deal with the downright blows, the freakish ingenuity, the gradually increasing malignity of fate. They have none to spend upon the subtleties and delicacies of the human comedy.

Thus there comes a time when we can say with certainty that we shall not find in Hardy some of the qualities that have given us most delight in the works of other novelists. He has not the perfection of Jane Austen, or the wit of Meredith, or the range of Thackeray, or Tolstoy's amazing intellectual power. There is in the work of the great classical writers a finality of effect which places certain of their scenes, apart from the story, beyond the reach of change. We do not ask what bearing they have upon the narrative, nor do we make use of them to interpret problems which lie on the outskirts of the scene. A laugh, a blush, half a dozen words of dialogue, and it is enough; the source of our delight is perennial. But Hardy has none of this concentration and completeness. His light does not fall directly upon the human heart. It passes over it and out on to the darkness of the heath and upon the trees swaying in the storm. When we look back into the room the group by the fireside is dispersed. Each man or woman is battling with the storm, alone, revealing himself most when he is least under the observation of other human beings. We do not know them as we know Pierre or Natasha or Becky Sharp. We do not know them in and out and all round as they are revealed to the casual caller, to the Government official, to the great lady, to the general on the battlefield. We do not know the complication and involvement and turmoil of their thoughts. Geographically, too, they remain fixed to the same stretch of the English countryside. It is seldom, and always with unhappy results, that Hardy leaves the yeoman or farmer to describe the class above theirs in the social scale. In the drawing-room and clubroom and ballroom, where people of leisure and education come together, where comedy is bred and shades of character revealed, he is awkward and ill at ease. But the opposite is equally true. If we do not know his men and women in their relations to each other, we know them in their relations to time, death, and fate. If we do not see them in quick agitation against the lights and crowds of cities, we see them against the earth, the storm, and the seasons. We know their attitude towards some of the most tremendous problems that can confront mankind. They take on a more than mortal size in memory. We see them, not in detail but enlarged and dignified. We see Tess reading the baptismal service in her nightgown 'with an impress of dignity that was almost regal'. We see Marty South, 'like a being who had rejected with indifference the attribute of sex for the loftier quality of abstract humanism', laying the flowers on Winterbourne's grave. Their speech has a Biblical dignity and poetry. They have a force in them which cannot be defined, a force of love or of hate, a force which in the men is the cause of rebellion against life, and in the women implies an illimitable capacity for suffering, and it is this which dominates the character and makes it unnecessary that we should see the finer features that lie hid. This is the tragic power; and, if we are to place Hardy among his fellows, we must call him the greatest tragic writer among English novelists.

But let us, as we approach the danger-zone of Hardy's philosophy, be on our guard. Nothing is more necessary, in reading an imaginative writer, than to keep at the right distance above his page. Nothing is easier, especially with a writer of marked idiosyncrasy, than to fasten on opinions, convict him of a creed, tether him to a consistent point of view. Nor was Hardy any exception to the rule that the mind which is most capable of receiving impressions is very often the least capable of drawing conclusions. It is for the reader, steeped in the impression, to supply the comment. It is his part to know when to put aside the writer's conscious intention in favour of some deeper intention of which perhaps he may be unconscious. Hardy himself was aware of this. A novel 'is an impression, not an argument', he has warned us, and, again

Unadjusted impressions have their value, and the road to a true philosophy of life seems to lie in humbly recording diverse readings of its phenomena as they are forced upon us by chance and change.

Certainly it is true to say of him that, at his greatest, he gives us impressions; at his weakest, arguments. In *The Woodlanders, The Return of the Native, Far from the Madding Crowd,* and above all, in *The Mayor of Casterbridge,* we have Hardy's impression of life as it came to him without conscious ordering. Let him once begin to tamper with his direct intuitions and his

power is gone. 'Did you say the stars were worlds, Tess?' asks little Abraham as they drive to market with their beehives. Tess replies that they are like 'the apples on our stubbard-tree, most of them splendid and sound—a few blighted'. 'Which do we live on—a splendid or a blighted one?' 'A blighted one,' she replies, or rather the mournful thinker who has assumed her mask speaks for her. The words protrude, cold and raw, like the springs of a machine where we had seen only flesh and blood. We are crudely jolted out of that mood of sympathy which is renewed a moment later when the little cart is run down and we have a concrete instance of the ironical methods which rule our planet.

That is the reason why *Jude the Obscure* is the most painful of all Hardy's books, and the only one against which we can fairly bring the charge of pessimism. In *Jude the Obscure* argument is allowed to dominate impression, with the result that though the misery of the book is overwhelming it is not tragic. As calamity succeeds calamity we feel that the case against society is not being argued fairly or with profound understanding of the facts. Here is nothing of that width and force and knowledge of mankind which, when Tolstoy criticizes society, makes his indictment formidable. Here we have revealed to us the petty cruelty of men, not the large injustice of the gods. It is only necessary to compare *Jude the Obscure* with *The Mayor of Casterbridge* to see where Hardy's true power lay. Jude carries on his miserable contest against the deans of colleges and the conventions of sophisticated society. Henchard is pitted, not against another man, but against something outside himself which is opposed to men of his ambition and power. No human being wishes him ill. Even Farfrae and Newson and Elizabeth Jane whom he has wronged all come to pity him, and even to admire his strength of character. He is standing up to fate, and in backing the old Mayor whose ruin has been largely his own fault, Hardy makes us feel that we are backing human nature in an unequal contest. There is no pessimism here. Throughout the book we are aware of the sublimity of the issue, and yet it is presented to us in the most concrete form. From the opening scene in which Henchard sells his wife to the sailor at the fair to his death on Egdon Heath the vigour of the story is superb, its humour rich and racy, its movement large-limbed and free. The skimmity ride, the fight between Farfrae and Henchard in the loft, Mrs. Cuxsom's speech upon the death of Mrs. Henchard, the talk of the ruffians at Peter's Finger with Nature present in the background or mysteriously dominating the foreground, are among the glories of English fiction. Brief and scanty, it may be, is the measure of happiness allowed to each, but so long as the struggle is, as Henchard's was, with the decrees of fate and not with the laws of man, so long as it is in the open air and calls for activity of the body rather than of the brain, there is greatness in the contest, there is pride and pleasure in it, and the death of the broken corn merchant in his cottage on Egdon Heath is comparable to the death of Ajax, lord of Salamis. The true tragic emotion is ours.

Before such power as this we are made to feel that the ordinary tests which we apply to fiction are futile enough. Do we insist that a great novelist shall be a master of melodious prose? Hardy was no such thing. He feels his way by dint of sagacity and uncompromising sincerity to the phrase he wants, and it is often of unforgettable pungency. Failing it, he will make do with any homely or clumsy or old-fashioned turn of speech, now of the utmost angularity, now of a bookish elaboration. No style in literature, save Scott's, is so difficult to analyse; it is on the face of it so bad, yet it achieves its aim so unmistakably. As well might one attempt to rationalize the charm of a muddy country road, or of a plain field of roots in winter. And then, like Dorsetshire itself, out of these very elements of stiffness and angularity his prose will put on greatness; will roll with a Latin sonority; will shape itself in a massive and monumental symmetry like that of his own bare downs. Then again, do we require that a novelist shall observe the probabilities, and keep close to reality? To find anything approaching the violence and convolution of Hardy's plots one must go back to the Elizabethan drama. Yet we accept his story completely as we read it; more than that, it becomes obvious that his violence and his melodrama, when they are not due to a curious peasant-like love of the monstrous for its own sake, are part of that wild spirit of poetry which saw with intense irony and grimness that no reading of life can possibly outdo the strangeness of life itself, no symbol of caprice and unreason be too extreme to represent the astonishing circumstances of our existence.

But as we consider the great structure of the Wessex Novels it seems irrelevant to fasten on little points—this character, that scene, this phrase of deep and poetic beauty. It is something larger that Hardy has bequeathed to us. The Wessex Novels are not one book, but many. They cover an immense stretch; inevitably they are full of imperfections—some are failures, and others exhibit only the wrong side of their maker's genius. But undoubtedly, when we have submitted ourselves fully to them, when we come to take stock of our impression of the whole, the effect is commanding and satisfactory. We have been freed from the cramp and pettiness imposed by life. Our imaginations have been stretched and heightened; our humour has been made to laugh out; we have drunk deep of the beauty of the earth. Also we have been made to enter the shade of a sorrowful and brooding spirit which, even in its saddest mood, bore itself with a grave uprightness and never, even when most moved to anger, lost its deep compassion for the sufferings of men and women. Thus it is no mere transcript of life at a certain

time and place that Hardy has given us. It is a vision of the world and of man's lot as they revealed themselves to a powerful imagination, a profound and poetic genius, a gentle and humane soul. (pp. 256-66)

Virginia Woolf, "The Novels of Thomas Hardy," in her *Collected Essays, Volume I,* Harcourt Brace Jovanovich, 1932, pp. 256-66

ALBERT J. GUERARD
(essay date 1949)

[Guerard, an American novelist and critic, has written extensively on Joseph Conrad and Thomas Hardy. In the following excerpt from his *Thomas Hardy: The Novels and Stories*, he praises the characterization of Michael Henchard and the nearly perfect structure of *The Mayor of Casterbridge*.]

Hardy's men, prior to *The Mayor of Casterbridge,* are inadequate as human beings and even more inadequate as fictional creations. Hardy's great gift for conveying living personality reveals itself rather in his portraits of rustics and of women. It is perhaps significant that the women in particular are seen as objects—fascinating, incomprehensible, strange. (pp. 121-22)

None of Hardy's women are unalive, and very few of them are wholly uninteresting; even the innocent ingénues are capable of occasional violent flare-ups. . . . More importantly, Hardy's six greatest women characters differ radically among themselves: Elfride, nervous and evasive; Bathsheba, curiously masculine and feminine; the wild, proud, and unreconciled Eustacia; the tender and "pure" Tess; the tormented yet funloving Sue; and Arabella, the female animal. Against these six major characters and a host of convincing minor ones, Hardy offers only two men of more than average interest and vitality: Michael Henchard and Jude Fawley.

Henchard, who is Hardy's Lord Jim, stands at the very summit of his creator's achievement; his only tragic hero and one of the greatest tragic heroes in all fiction. He takes his place at once with certain towering and possessed figures of Melville, Hawthorne, and Dostoevsky: a man of character obsessed by guilt and so committed to his own destruction. He anticipates not merely Lord Jim and the Razumov of *Under Western Eyes* but also the Michel of André Gide's *L'Immoraliste.* Fifty years before Karl Menninger, Hardy recognized— as Shakespeare did three centuries before him—that the guilty not merely flagellate themselves but also thrust themselves in the way of bad luck; *create* what appear to be unlucky accidents. Henchard's decline in

Casterbridge was no more fortuitous than Lord Jim's in Patusan. These two "men of character" pursued strikingly similar destinies: forceful, conscientious, and proud, alike outcasts thanks to the unaccountable flarings of a moment's fear and anger, dedicating their lives to an impossible rehabilitation and a distant ideal of honor. They are isolated and obsessed by guilt even in their fate years of power and prestige; they are determined to bear yet face down the past. Both are men of character in a strangely double sense. They want to atone for the past through self-punishment; yet they resist, humanly, merely compulsive self-punishment. In the end both are paralyzed by "chance" reminders from the past (Brown and the furmity-woman)—reminders which, in fact, they had never ceased to carry about with them. They achieve death in solitude, each having one dull-witted uncomprehending native who remains faithful to the last. Of the two Henchard, whose will was a final self-condemnation, may have shown more courage than Lord Jim, who turned to his executioners and to the world with a last look of proud defiance. Henchard was a "man of character"; Lord Jim was "one of us."

There was nothing in Hardy's earlier novels to suggest that he would some day produce such a figure; there is no series of links and experiments leading from Springrove or Manston to Henchard. Gabriel Oak, Diggory Venn, and many others seem to act perversely against their own interest, but this is owing to meditative impotence and a lack of normal aggressiveness. They are spectators rather than actors against themselves. Unlike them Henchard is a man of great force and destructive energy, which he turns outward occasionally but inward far more often. He has thus nothing in common with the irresponsible Wildeve, but a great deal in common with both Jude and Sue. There is little justification for the critic who sums up Henchard's tragic flaws as temper and addiction to drink; these were symptoms of the self-destructive impulse rather than its causes. Hardy himself was explicit enough:

> Thereupon promptly came to the surface that idiosyncrasy of Henchard's which had ruled his courses from the beginning, and had mainly made him what he was. Instead of thinking that a union between his cherished stepdaughter and the energetic thriving Donald was a thing to be desired for her good and his own, he hated the very possibility.

> Among the many hindrances to such a pleading, not the least was this, that he did not sufficiently value himself to lessen his sufferings by strenuous appeal or elaborate argument.

> He had not expressed to her any regrets or excuses for what he had done in the past; but it was a part

of his nature to extenuate nothing and live on as one of his own worst accusers.

Henchard is simply incapable of acting consistently in his own interest. Captain Ahab, traveling the wide seas in pursuit of his own destruction, supposes cosmic hostilities in a whale. And so Henchard, earthbound in Casterbridge, comes at last to think "some sinister intelligence bent on punishing him." Had someone roasted a wax image of him? Was some power working against him? Unaware that the power was wholly inward, he "looked out at the night as at a fiend."

Thus Hardy, who had seldom troubled himself with crime and punishment, at last explored the great nineteenth-century myth of the isolated, damned, and self-destructive individualist—the more impressively because his Lara, Vautrin, Tito Melema, and Ahab was an ordinary Wessex farmer-merchant. The particular myth was conceived in terms as grand as the Wessex environment would allow—beginning with no less than the angry, drunken, and impulsive sale of a wife on the fairgrounds of Weydon Priors, to which Henchard would return a quarter of a century later in full circle. The tendency to paranoia and self-flagellation must have had its origin, like that of Sue Bridehead, in some part of an undisclosed childhood. At the very beginning Henchard has already the "instinct of a perverse character"; he drinks too much and thinks he has ruined his chances by marrying at eighteen. It is the crime of selling his wife which concentrates his energies, however; which both makes his character and destroys it. (Here too he is exactly like Lord Jim, who might have remained, in innocence, a fairly ordinary sea captain and trader.) Henchard looks in vain for his wife; swears an oath not to drink for twenty years; becomes mayor of Casterbridge, though equipped with little more than energy—becomes a man of character. When Susan finally reappears, he stolidly and conscientiously marries her; when Lucetta reappears, he acts honorably, though long tempted to revenge himself on Farfrae through her; when the furmity-woman reappears, he publicly acknowledges his guilt. He is fair in his savage fashion, and fights Farfrae with one hand tied behind his back. Ruined, he is the most conscientious of bankrupts.

The Mayor of Casterbridge is a novel of temperament in action, in minute action even; its distinction derives from a severe concentration on the self-destructive aspects of that temperament. The obligation to punish and degrade the self is at times fairly conscious. Thus Henchard marries Susan not merely to make amends to her and to provide Elizabeth-Jane with a home, but also "to castigate himself with the thorns which these restitutory acts brought in their train; among them the lowering of his dignity in public opinion by marrying so comparatively humble a woman."

He licks his wounds by demanding that the journeyman sing the terrible One Hundred and Ninth Psalm; he goes to work for Farfrae wearing the rusty silk hat of his former dignity; he humbles himself unnecessarily before Lucetta; he lingers on the second stone bridge where the failures and drifters of the town gather. But Hardy recognized, intuitively at least, that the guilty may also punish themselves unconsciously and cause their own "bad luck." The man who repeatedly cuts and burns himself is no mere victim of absurd mischance; he is compelled to cut and burn himself, though he may not understand his compulsion. Freud has documented the hidden psychology of errors; Menninger the motives of chronic failures and of those who suffer repeated "accidents." Psychologists have proved that the unfortunate are more often than not the guilty, who must pay daily hostages to their fear.

Henchard is such a man, for whom everything "goes wrong" once he has begun to struggle with his guilt. So his elaborate public entertainment fails dismally while Farfrae's modest one succeeds. Rain does not fall at the beck of the accusing conscience, but Henchard's party is ruined by more than rain. "A man must be headstrong stunpoll to think folk would go up to that bleak place today." Later he gambles on disastrous rains to drive up the price of corn and is confirmed in his prophecy by the mysterious Mr. Fall; he buys enormous quantities of corn and is ruined by the blazing August weather. But the adverse force was his own lack of Wessex prudence. "He was reminded of what he had well known before, that a man might gamble upon the square green areas of fields as readily as upon those of a card-room . . . 'For you can never be sure of weather till 'tis past.' " Henchard's subconscious self-destructiveness shows itself far less equivocally at the time of the Royal Progress. He has a "passing fancy" to join in welcoming the royal visitor, though no longer a member of the town council. But what might have appeared a last conscious effort to reassert his dignity was in fact a half-conscious effort to degrade himself before the collected townfolk in the most humiliating way. "He was not only a journeyman, unable to appear as he formerly had appeared, but he disdained to appear as well as he might. Everybody else, from the Mayor to the washerwoman, shone in new vesture according to means; but Henchard had doggedly retained the fretted and weather-beaten garments of bygone years." And he was drunk. When he resumed drinking after twenty years, a short time before this, he had committed himself to focal suicide and certain self-punishment. Character is fate; and Newson and the furmity-woman, those symbolic reminders, were part of his character and fate. Henchard would have destroyed himself even had they not returned. As a man of character he was morally obligated to do so. Yet he was also obligated to resist mere compulsive self-destructiveness. Here too, in fighting his suicidal destiny, he was a man of character.

Thus grandly and minutely conceived, Henchard might yet have remained as wooden as Farmer Boldwood. But he is very nearly the most personalized of Hardy's men: a voice and an unforgettable massive presence, with his twitching mouth and distant gaze, his "vehement" gloominess, his severe friendliness, and his businesslike bluntness even when proposing marriage. No doubt it is as a well-meaning man isolated by guilt that he makes his strongest appeal to our sympathy. Loneliness as well as guilt prompts him to hire Farfrae impulsively and to pour out his confession at once. And guilt as well as loneliness attaches him to Elizabeth-Jane: "He had liked the look of her face as she answered him from the stairs. There had been affection in it, and above all things what he desired now was affection from anything that was good and pure." Finally, though his history is highly selective, we have the impression that we know Henchard's life in its every significant detail. The measure of the characterization's success is our unquestioning acceptance in its context of Henchard's stylized and symbolic will. It does not seem to us a gratuitous or merely ornamental offering of Hardy's pessimism, as a few of Jude Fawley's philosophical speeches do. Michael Henchard's excommunication of self is a reasoned one, for his life has actually so added up:

> That Elizabeth-Jane Farfrae be not told of my
> death, or made to grieve on account of me.
>   & that I be not bury'd in consecrated ground.
>   & that no sexton be asked to toll the bell.
>   & that nobody is wished to see my dead body.
>   & that no murners walk behind me at my funeral.
>   & that no flours be planted on my grave.
>   & and that no man remember me.
> To this I put my name.

"Let the day perish wherein I was born, and the night in which it was said, There is a manchild conceived"— Jude Fawley might have signed Henchard's will.

Jude is not, however, a tragic hero—if only because he is a "modern." Henchard's will is a final condemnation of self and of the "old mankind"; it is an achievement of the self-knowledge which tragedy compels. Jude's dying words are instead a condemnation of the cosmos in its dark and at last recognized absurdity. Not Jude but the cosmos is to blame. There are certain obvious links between the two characters: the common sensitiveness to music, the imprudent early marriages, the addiction to drink, the need to punish and degrade the self publicly. But the significant link occurs in the final paragraph of *The Mayor of Casterbridge;* in Elizabeth-Jane's observation "that neither she nor any human being deserved less than was given." The observation is pathetic and of course pessimistic in the commoner sense of that word. But it is not tragic, as all but the last pages of the novel are tragic. For the tragic attitude lays the blame not on the stars but on ourselves; it sees fate in character; its pessimism is grounded in the insufficiency of the human endowment; it insists, with Conrad's Marlow, that "nobody is good enough." (pp. 146-52)

Hardy was a great popular novelist and not a great deliberate artist. The rare popular novelist who also deserves our esteem is perhaps the most difficult one to account for and to analyze. We add up his distinguishable virtues patiently, only to arrive at an absurdly small sum. Dissatisfied with this sum, we posit still other virtues. This is what most of Hardy's critics have done. Starting from a wholly justified liking for the novels, they have gone on to discern the qualities which they assume a great novelist must show: profound thought, high unremitting seriousness of purpose, insight into social problems, exceptional psychological understanding, perfection of structure and style, realism and poetry. But we must look elsewhere than to Hardy for such qualities as these; we must look, for instance, to Conrad at his best. Hardy revealed repeatedly an initial sluggishness of mind, most often perhaps in his tendency to schematize and oversimplify dilemmas. His frank purpose through most of his career was to write books which would sell easily. Although he showed an aesthetic understanding of agricultural Dorset, he showed, prior to *Jude the Obscure,* little understanding of the moral and social condition of the late nineteenth century. His power to dramatize the personality and temperament of women was indeed extraordinary, but he presents fewer interesting men than almost any important novelist. And with the two exceptions of *The Mayor of Casterbridge* and *Under the Greenwood Tree,* his novels are radically imperfect in structure. His style conveys temperament but is abnormally relaxed and diffuse. And for realism and poetry his poems, not his novels, invite us.

His final and unmistakable appeal therefore rests on much less austere grounds than these: on the popular storytelling of a singularly uninhibited imagination, on an occasional mastery of atmosphere in relation to character, on a variety of manner and mood frankly modeled on Shakespeare's, on a fine purity of temperament—and, above all, on an incorrigible sympathy for all who are lonely and all who long for happiness. He understood the plight of ordinary, simple, and well-meaning persons, subjected to the extraordinary, complex, and seemingly malign circumstances of life. He could find a saving grace in all failure, while Conrad found evil in all success and behind every act of benevolence. Even the heroes of Conrad are subjected to pitiless analysis; the unworthy are looked upon with cold disdain. But which of Hardy's villains is irrevocably damned? And which . . . does not benefit at least briefly from this universal sympathy? Hardy's dark vi-

sion of the world compelled him, in compensatory fairness, to a certainly excessive charity. Good and evil seemed irrelevant in such an indifferent universe; he wanted people to be happy. He was not concerned with damnation and salvation—as Dostoevsky and Melville and the very greatest writers have been, as Conrad and Gide were to be.

The literary historian and the modern novelist alike can benefit from a study of Hardy's anti-realism and occasional symbolist experiments; they can discover in Hardy ways of escaping inanimate drabness. But it would be absurd to read into Hardy's anti-realism any profound metaphysical intentions, or into his symbolist experiments the complex aesthetic intentions of Conrad. For Hardy did not take his craft seriously in the way that James, Conrad, Proust, and Gide were to take it seriously; he did not conceive of fiction as a high art, at least not until very late; he rested on his poems all claims to uncompromising greatness. Was he finally persuaded by his admirers that novels too could be great works of art? In the end he did write, and seemingly with full consciousness of what he was doing, three very great novels: *Tess of the D'Urbervilles, The Mayor of Casterbridge,* and *Jude the Obscure.* But only two of these explore at all the great theme of nineteenth- and twentieth-century fiction: the myth of the morally isolated individualist lost in a world he never made; who searches for freedom, though bereft of faith, and who wills his own destruction. It would require Conrad, once thought a popular storyteller and historian of simple hearts, to explore the destructive element exhaustively. There will never be too many such exploring pessimists; there will never be too many Conrads. But in our darkening world there is also much to say for Hardy's purity of mind and antique simplicity of art. There may also be something to say for his charity. Less austere and less ambitious than Conrad, Hardy confined himself to our unregenerate longing for happiness and our common destiny of suffering. (pp. 157-59)

Albert J. Guerard, in his *Thomas Hardy: The Novels and Stories,* Cambridge, Mass.: Harvard University Press, 1949, 177 p.

IRVING HOWE

(essay date 1966)

[A longtime editor of the leftist magazine *Dissent* and a regular contributor to the *New Republic*, Howe is one of America's most highly respected literary critics and social historians. In the excerpt below from his book-length study of Hardy, he gives an appreciative overview of Hardy's short fiction, naming

"The Fiddler of the Reels" "one of the great, if bare-ly known, stories in the English language." This chapter was originally published in the *Hudson Review* in 1966.]

That Hardy's stories are little read is not a scandal, it is merely a pity. Most of his stories, serviceable products for magazines, are not worth salvaging; seven or eight are very fine; and one, **"The Fiddler of the Reels,"** can be called great. To write a history of modern fiction or modern poetry without seriously considering Hardy would be unthinkable. To omit his name from a study of the modern short story would be plausible. I would only add to this usual judgment that the best of Hardy's stories can still yield a distinct pleasure.

They have little to do with the main line of the modern short story. Hardy cannot be said to have anticipated such masters as Chekhov, Joyce and Hemingway in the short story even to the limited extent that as a novelist he anticipated D. H. Lawrence. There is little in Hardy's stories of Chekhov's psychological plasticity, even less of the impressionistic economy of the *Dubliners,* and nothing whatever of the tight-lipped stylization we associate with Hemingway. As if to sharpen the contrast, Hardy's short fictions might be described as tales, since that is to put them in a mellower light and relate them to a more easy-paced and amiable mode of narrative than we can usually find in the modern short story.

Hardy's manuscript draft of the title page of *Tess of the D'Urbervilles.*

The bulk of his stories were composed during the 1880s and 1890s, the period of Hardy's most prolific and accomplished work as a novelist. He seems to have regarded the writing of stories as mere journeyman's work by which to earn a living, and to have dashed them off with the casualness of purpose and desire to please a large audience which he claimed to be characteristic—though we have reason to be skeptical—of the way he wrote his novels. Yet anyone who has become familiar with the timbre of Hardy's voice, both in an early work like *Under the Greenwood Tree* and a late one like *Tess of the D'Urbervilles,* could not fail immediately to recognize a tale like **"The Withered Arm"** or **"The Three Strangers"** as uniquely his. Like most short fictions composed by novelists, Hardy's are fragments chipped off his larger work, or developments of major themes in modest scope, or exercises at sketching the figures and locale of his more ambitious books.

If once you have fallen under the spell of the kind of writer who creates his own fictional world and keeps turning to it in book after book—as Faulkner does with Yoknapatawpha, or Balzac with Paris, or Hardy with Wessex—even his minor stories will hold a lively interest. For in them loose narrative ends may be tied together, bits of information casting light on the novels casually provided, and an imaginary place we have come to know once again exhibited. And exhibited more quietly, more reassuringly than in the full-scale narratives. The reader who has suffered vicariously the blows and disasters of Hardy's major novels may find a special charm in turning to **"A Few Crusted Characters,"** an utterly winning survey of Wessex conduct and idiosyncrasy, free from the darkness of spirit that hovers over Hardy's novels and buoyant with the delight of coming back to a familiar world of youth. Does the pleasure in reading a great novelist's minor work rest on a childlike desire for "just a little more"—another glance at Wessex, its places, customs and people? Perhaps so. But which writer would not be delighted to command precisely this "naive" response from his audience?

Now, what crucially distinguishes the stories from the novels is that in the former there is hardly a trace of the "modern" Hardy, the writer who created Jude Fawley and kept fretting himself over "Crass Casualty" and "Immanent Will." You could barely know from these stories that Hardy had ever been captivated by the theories of Herbert Spencer, John Stuart Mill and Thomas Huxley; you could never suppose he would keep struggling with the pessimistic visions of von Hartmann and Schopenhauer. In the stories Hardy allows himself to feel more pleasure for the ordinary course of life than he does in the major novels, and perhaps more pleasure than, strictly speaking, his philosophy allows. He relaxes into nostalgia and anecdote; the pastoral impulse flows with a purity he could seldom preserve in his more ambitious novels. There is little in these stories of that thwarted, painful and exhausting struggle with the dilemmas of estrangement which distinguishes *Jude the Obscure;* but then neither are there the cumbered prose, the tiresome philosophizing and the inert submission before intellectual fashion that mar even the best of his novels.

In atmosphere, though not narrative tone, Hardy's stories recall the pastoral fiction of George Eliot. Perhaps the greatest success of this kind among Hardy's shorter pieces is the string of anecdotes, set-pieces and miniature portraits called **"A Few Crusted Characters."** Most of his critics, eager for philosophical big game, have ignored this work, but to me it seems a minor masterpiece full of that good humor and acceptance of common life which one associates, if not with the English countryside itself, then with a certain tradition in writing about it. . . . Except for a sketch of obsessional vengeance, the whole thing is light and untroubled, certainly untroubled by those philosophic notions that burden Hardy's major work. The story-in-the-round structure is familiar enough, but Hardy's ease in rendering country manners and byplays of humor is a rare thing, possible only to a great writer relaxing with a small effort. Such mild sketching of English country life—whether by Hardy, George Eliot or Mrs. Gaskell—is not much admired in our theoretic age, but in the long run it may require more literary tact to enjoy fiction of this kind than to play with the symbols of *Moby-Dick.* (pp. 75-8)

In the country world of Wessex, what may seem to us extraordinary is looked upon, with a credulous fatalism, as quite ordinary. It is here to be expected that a woman wronged, as in **"The Withered Arm,"** will cast a spell upon her fortunate rival and cause her to suffer physical waste. Read with the expectations of conventional realism, this story groans with improbability, yet as often happens in Hardy, it can be valued as a curious mixture of traditional folk belief and modern hypothesis, assumptions drawn from before and after the Enlightenment. (p. 80)

In some of his stories, the grotesque and demonic are entirely absent, and what claims our attention is a familiar landscape faithfully drawn, solidly sketched figures in their appropriate place, a setting of work, pleasure and trouble. In **"The Distracted Preacher"** the stress is comic, a sly thrust at Victorian convention in the person of the Reverend Stockdale, who meets an attractive young widow in a coastal town where, to his dismay but her profit, she is cheerfully engaged in smuggling. The story not only permits Hardy to skim a favorite theme—the overflow of youthful energy past the perimeters of moralism—but also to indulge in zestful descriptions of the smugglers teasing and tricking customs men. Hardy controls the scene expertly, and except for a concluding lapse into virtue, presum-

ably forced upon him by the needs of magazine publication, he makes no excessive demands upon this material. He does not hover and ruminate, squeeze and prod, as even in his best novels he is inclined to do. He accepts, records, enjoys.

In other stories a similar grasp of local detail is used to support some of Hardy's usual concerns: betrayal, dismay, moral confusion, crossed fates. **"The Waiting Supper"** is a fine tale about the interplay of personal vanity and social ambition: two lovers are separated through class prejudice, the girl marries a man of higher status only to suffer quick desertion, and years later her spurned lover, now wealthy, returns to woo her. But how different from, how much less exalted and more sadly probable than *Wuthering Heights*! For the reunited lovers do not know whether the missing husband is still alive; and only late, too late, as they drift into old age, neither quite together nor quite apart, do they learn that the husband is indeed dead. The aging lover continues to propose marriage at intervals, but time has grayed their passion: "Occasionally he ventured to urge her to reconsider the case, though he spoke not with the fervour of earlier years."

The writing in these stories is happiest when Hardy is most at ease in his country world. Then the prose is pure and unstrained; there is no grasping after unearned intensities; the very rhythms suggest psychic comfort. Rarely approaching the sublimity that Hardy can now and again reach in his novels, the best of his stories are also free of the turgidity to which the novels frequently succumb. (pp. 80-1)

There remains **"The Fiddler of the Reels,"** one of the great, if barely known, stories in the English language. Wessex is the familiar locale, and equally familiar are the disruption and excitement that follow upon a stranger's arrival. But this time Hardy strikes into depths of obsession that he never approaches in his other short fictions. (p. 82)

It is a country tale, but told with severity and sophistication. The rhythms speed up, the language swells, a note of tentative abandon is struck. Not even in the quiet of Wessex can there be assurance that a life will not be disordered or exalted by some intruding power, some obsession bearing possibilities of the unknown. Mop himself is kept at a distance, ominous but unexplained: a demon-lover of country taverns, for whom music and sexuality flow together and the lure of abandon speeds through the scrape of a bow. (pp. 82-3)

Irving Howe, in his *Thomas Hardy,* The Macmillan Company, 1967, 206 p.

F. B. PINION
(essay date 1990)

[Pinion is an English editor and critic who has written extensively on nineteenth- and twentieth-century English literature. He has contributed to the *Thomas Hardy Annual* and was editor of the *Thomas Hardy Society Review* from 1975 to 1984. In the following excerpt, he discusses the varying degrees of success with which Hardy informed scenes from his works of fiction with his philosophy of life.]

All great art is moral in its implications; it is, as Matthew Arnold said, 'a criticism of life', since it reflects its creator's values. To some degree or other, it will rouse sympathy, approval, ridicule, or condemnation; it will appeal to a sense of misfortune or injustice, of social rightness and proportion, promoting those higher, disinterested, humanitarian perceptions without which no propaganda or philosophy can be wise or perennially convincing. Through comic satire and tragedy Jane Austen and Shakespeare make us realize human absurdity and error, evil and injustice, more intensely and agreeably than any writer who sacrifices art to overt writing for any cause or for the assertion of his own point of view. Thomas Hardy had a ready gift of humour, but *The Hand of Ethelberta* and the general course of his fiction suggest very strongly that the writing of comic satire appealed to him less than the writing of tragedy. Adverting in his General Preface of 1912 to 'what has been called the present writer's philosophy of life', he writes: 'Some natures become vocal at tragedy, some are made vocal by comedy, and it seems to me that to whichever of these aspects of life a writer's instinct for expression the more readily responds, to that he should allow it to respond.' The bias of his genius is best indicated in his **'Candour in English Fiction'**:

All really true literature directly or indirectly sounds as its refrain the words in the *Agamemnon:* 'Chant Aelinon, Aelinon! but may the good prevail.'

The present essay seeks to exemplify ways in which Hardy, to use George Eliot's expression, sought to 'incarnate' ideas, indicating points of view through artistic presentations of life, either pictorially or through human action. At its most successful, the informing idea does not modify the functioning of the scene or action in itself. It cannot spoil the effect on the reader whose imaginative range is limited to narrative and spectacle, and it cannot but deepen, intensify, and enlarge the vision of more intellectually imaginative readers. The crucial question for the novelist is how to dissolve philosophical import in scenes and images which play a necessary or significant part in the main action of his story.

The philosophy which informs the scenes selected to illustrate Hardy's varying degrees of success in 'aesthetic'modes of presentation may appear to be an impression of life appropriate to a character at a particular time or in a given situation, or it may be that of the author contemplating the circumstances in which a character is involved. The implicit philosophy may extend further, giving the author's view, as far as it is definable, of the ultimate cause of things, and particularly of those chances (as they seem) which determine, for better or worse, so much in the course of people's lives. Since Hardy's philosophy was conditioned by the scientific discovery of his age (geological, cosmic, and Darwinian), it may be externalized fictionally in natural scenes with a scientific emphasis. Lives may be presented with reference to the infinite dimensions of space and time. The lovers of *Two on a Tower* are 'infinitesimal' against 'the stupendous background of the stellar universe', yet, as Hardy says in his preface, the smaller of the 'contrasting magnitudes' is the greater to us 'as men' or readers. This is usually taken for granted, since each of us is the centre of his own universe. Hardy's ambivalence is often found in reverse, the relative insignificance of human individuals in times of stress being shown with reference to insect life.

It is not unlikely that Hardy associated a sensationally climactic scene in Wilkie Collins' *Basil* with the high cliffs of Cornwall which he saw for the first time in 1870, for it was from a steep shelving rock on a high Cornish promontory that the villain Mannion, in pursuit of the hero, fell to his death in waves at an unfathomable depth below, after a frantic struggle to secure his hold. Such a threat to Knight in *A Pair of Blue Eyes* is the occasion for a passage which brings home to the reader the insignificance of man in geological time. The heroine's resourcefulness in rescuing Knight by a rope discreetly contrived from her underwear was authorially calculated to give Grundyan readers a *frisson* rather than a thrill. If Hardy had forgotten the circumstances of Mannion's death, as seems very unlikely, they were probably recalled by Leslie Stephen's 'A Bad Five Minutes in the Alps', which appeared in the November

1872 number of *Fraser's Magazine.* Resemblances between this and Hardy's *tour de force* are not very significant; they are far outweighed by striking differences between imaginative, excitingly dramatized narrative and the rather tedious philosophizing of an essay which is so abstract, methodical, and prolonged within a fictional framework ending in anticlimax that the concept as a whole fails to carry conviction.

Suspended on a slope of rock above the Cliff without a Name, with only a tuft of vegetation saving him from certain death, Knight finds himself, by 'one of those familiar conjunctions of things wherewith the inanimate world baits the mind of man when he pauses in moments of suspense', face to face with an imbedded fossil with eyes which seem to regard him; it is a trilobite. 'Separated by millions of years in their lives, Knight and this underling' seem 'to have met in their place of death'. We are asked to believe that, being a geologist, Knight by force of habit, even at this 'dreadful juncture', had time to consider 'the varied scenes that had had their day between this creature's epoch and his own':

> Time closed up like a fan before him. He saw himself at once extremity of the years, face to face with the beginning and all the intermediate centuries simultaneously. Fierce men, clothed in the hides of beasts, and carrying, for defence and attack, huge clubs and pointed spears, rose from the rock, like the phantoms before the doomed Macbeth. They lived in hollows, woods, and mud huts—perhaps in caves of the neighbouring rocks. Behind them stood an earlier band. No man was there. Huge elephantine forms, the mastodon, the hippopotamus, the tapir, antelopes of monstrous size, the megatherium, and the myledon—all, for the moment, in juxtaposition. Further back, and overlapped by these, were perched huge-billed birds and swinish creatures as large as horses. . . .

Hardy's technique works, but it does not present an integration of action and idea, such as obtains in some of the most imaginative forms of fusing philosophy and fiction. The events, external and internal, are linked but appositional or sequential. His intention is clear, and his viewpoint is so striking and final that we rarely pause to consider the probability, in the circumstances, of such concentration on prehistoric life even for 'less than half a minute'. The possibility must have seemed indubitable to Hardy after reading in Stephen's essay 'It is often said that persons in similar situations have seen their whole past existence pass rapidly before them.'

The sequential mode of presenting fiction philosophically is found in the Darwinian example which follows from *The Return of the Native.* Mrs Yeobright makes her way across Egdon Heath in torrid sunshine, hoping for reconciliation with Eustacia. Circumstances combine in an extraordinary manner to make her believe that Eustacia has deliberately kept the door closed against her, and she begins her return journey depressed, exhausted, and without refreshment. She is found too late, suffering fatally from toxaemia after being stung by an adder. On her outward journey, the air had been 'pulsating silently, and oppressing the earth with lassitude':

> Occasionally she came to a spot where independent worlds of ephemerons were passing their time in mad carousal, some in the air, some on the hot ground and vegetation, some in the tepid and stringy water of a nearly dried pool. All the shallower ponds had decreased to a vaporous mud amid which the maggoty shapes of innumerable obscure creatures could be indistinctly seen, heaving and wallowing with enjoyment.

The author hints at his descriptive purpose by telling us that Mrs Yeobright, 'being a woman not disinclined to philosophize', sometimes sat down under her umbrella 'to rest and to watch their happiness'. She then asks her way, and is told to follow a furze-cutter. It is her son Clym, and he appears in the distance 'not more distinguishable from the scene around him than the green caterpillar from the leaf it feeds on'. As he stops to cut brambles for tying his furze into bundles, he seems to be 'of no more account in life than an insect'. So, briefly, idea is fused with image, and humanity is scaled down to a level of significance in the natural order which makes Mrs Yeobright rather like the ephemerons she has observed. Nature is indifferent: conditions which are life-giving to one species are life-denying to another.

To Mrs Yeobright, on her return journey, the sun appears 'like some merciless incendiary, brand in hand, waiting to consume her'. Then 'all visible animation' disappears from the landscape, though husky notes of male grasshoppers indicate that 'amid the prostration of the larger animal species' there is 'an unseen insect world' which is vigorously active. Mrs Yeobright sits on a 'perfumed mat' of shepherd's thyme. She has reached a state of passivity. Her last thoughts are dictated by what catches her eye; a bustling colony of ants in front of her reminds her that such activity as theirs had been in progress for years at the same spot. A heron then flies towards the sun, and she wishes she could enjoy its freedom and a happy release from earth. 'Had the track of her next thought been marked by a streak in the air, like the path of a meteor, it would have shown a direction contrary to the heron's, and have descended to the eastward upon the roof of Clym's house.' In this way, after re-emphasizing the relative insignificance of the mortal lot in the context of creation, the scene closes with one of those 'contrasting magnitudes', the undying love of a mother for her son.

Mrs Yeobright's fatal journey is the main subject

of 'The Closed Door', the fourth book of *The Return of the Native.* This section opens with the gorgeousness of Egdon in the happy first weeks of Clym and Eustacia's marriage, when the July sun 'fired its crimson heather to scarlet'. The heath harmonizes with moods. Its significant mood for Hardy is set in the opening chapter of the novel; for him 'the great and particular glory of the Egdon waste' began when the shades of the heath fraternized with the growing darkness of night.

> Only in summer days of highest feather did its mood touch the level of gaiety. Intensity was more usually reached by way of the solemn than by way of the brilliant, and such a sort of intensity was often arrived at during winter darkness, tempests, and mists. Then Egdon was aroused to reciprocity; for the storm was its lover, and the wind its friend.

Before summoning up resolution to call, Mrs Yeobright sits beneath a clump of fir trees on the knoll near Clym and Eustacia's home, and for a few minutes dismisses 'thoughts of her own stormbroken and exhausted state' to contemplate that of the trees, 'splintered, lopped, and distorted by the fierce weather that there held them at its mercy whenever it prevailed'. In the opening paragraph of 'The Closed Door' we find that the flowering period of the heath is the second of three seasons, representing morning, noon, and eve, which create a cycle of superficial changes. Egdon's deeper reality can be felt most when it assumes 'the dark hue of the winter period, representing night'. Only then can 'its true tale' be fully understood; the gaiety of life and all its milder seasons are superficial.

The Egdon scene of the opening chapter, in November as twilight darkens, almost foreshadows the scene in **'The Darkling Thrush'**, when, at the end of the day, at the end of the last year of the century, the poet gazes on a sombre scene which seems devitalized and dispirited, until suddenly the joyous note of a frail, windberuffled thrust startles him into the thought that his philosophy of life may be wrong, and that the happy bird, instinctively in touch with nature, may be wiser than he. The *Leitmotiv* struck in the opening chords of **'A Face on which Time makes but Little Impression'** is darker in tone than Hardy's philosophical retrospect in **'He Never expected Much'**, where he confirms that the world has faithfully maintained the limited promise it made in his childhood:

> 'I do not promise overmuch,
>   Child; overmuch;
> Just neutral-tinted haps and such',
>   You said to minds like mine.
> Wise warning for your credit's sake!
> Which I for one failed not to take,
> And hence could stem such strain and ache
>   As each year might assign.

Yet the thought is similar: the 'strain and ache' are im-

aged in the trees which suffer on a heath loved by the storm; and 'to minds like mine' recalls the affinity of the heath's sombreness with 'the more thinking among mankind', but not with 'our race when it was young'.

Egdon Heath therefore is associated with 'the ache of modernism', as Hardy defined it in *Tess of the d'Urbervilles.* It was the product of Darwinism and the loss of faith consequent on the clash between science and superannuated Christian theology. Hardy lost his faith in Providence about 1865, and concluded, as he expresses it in 'Hap', that Crass Casualty or blind insensitive Chance obstructs 'the sun and rain' (which bring life and hope), and 'dicing Time for gladness casts a moan'. (The maimed trees under which Mrs Yeobright sits keep up a perpetual moan.) The defects of natural law, especially in heredity, made Hardy feel with Keats that 'but to think is to be full of sorrow / And leaden-eyed despairs'. In Walter Pater's essay on Winckelmann a contrast is drawn between the serenity attained by the Greeks (which Hardy had in mind when he wrote of the time when 'our race' was young) and the fever and fret of modernity. The fever and fret are depicted in Clym Yeobright: his beauty would 'in no long time be ruthlessly overrun by its parasite, thought'; 'he already showed that thought is a disease of the flesh, and indirectly bore evidence that ideal physical beauty is incompatible with emotional development and a full recognition of the coil of things'. To this Hardy adds, in a more general vein,

> What the Greeks only suspected we know well; what their Aeschylus imagined our nursery children feel. That old fashioned revelling in the general situation grows less and less possible as we uncover the defects of natural laws, and see the quandary that man is in by their operation.

The conflict between 'the ache of modernism' and the desire to return to pagan joyousness is centred in Clym and Eustacia.

In his essay Pater insists that pagan worship survives in various forms of ritual, and instances the kindling of fire and the dance as 'the anodyne' administered by 'the religious principle' to 'the law which makes life sombre for the vast majority of mankind'. Here we can see the probable germ for Hardy's creative ideas at the opening of *The Return of the Native.* The heath is the sombre face of life for the more thinking, if not the majority, of mankind; the fire ritual owes far more, as Hardy makes abundantly clear, to paganism than to the Gunpowder Plot; it is accompanied by rustic dancing; and the whole scene marks 'a spontaneous, Promethean rebelliousness against the fiat that [winter] shall bring foul times, cold darkness, misery and death. Black chaos comes, and the fettered gods of the earth say, Let there be light.' Egdon is Eustacia's Hades; she sees in marriage to Clym the means of escaping to a life of gaiety in Paris. Unfortunately Clym has more serious aims; he wishes to enlighten his fellow-men, but he is a blind Prometheus who brings unhappiness to his mother and Eustacia, and fails to realize that the means of enjoying life are, for the majority, more prized than enlightenment.

As seen at the opening of the novel, therefore, Egdon Heath is 'a place perfectly accordant with man's nature—neither ghastly, hateful, nor ugly; neither commonplace, unmeaning, nor tame; but, like man, slighted and enduring'. Its immensity and mystery had not changed through the ages. Its 'sombre stretch of rounds and hollows seemed to rise and meet the evening gloom in pure sympathy'; its lonely face suggested 'tragical possibilities'. 'The most thorough-going ascetic' (such as Clym) 'could feel that he had a natural right to wander on Egdon'; it reflected his view of life. The scene and its immediate sequel, with their implications, succeed in making such an imaginative appeal that Egdon becomes the supreme entity of the novel, its overtones being intensified in the funereal darkness of its catastrophe. Hardy's highly charged overture was nevertheless daringly experimental. Few can assimilate all its connotations at first reading, yet it sets the tone most appropriate to the theme and tragic narrative of the novel, and leads most impressively by slow artistic gradations to Rainbarrow, 'the pole and axis of this heathery world', and to the focal point which crowns it, the mysterious distant figure of Eustacia, whose first audible notes, 'a lengthened sighing', harmonize with those 'plaintive November winds' which form 'the linguistic peculiarity of the heath'.

The potential advantages of using a scene as a correlative for reflecting a philosophy of life may be better realized perhaps by comparing Hardy's initial presentation of Egdon Heath with his concluding remarks on Elizabeth-Jane's impressions of life in what may be called the postscript of *The Mayor of Casterbridge*. The latter must gain by being read with heartfelt knowledge of what the heroine has suffered, yet its effect is weakened by increasing ambivalence, the author disengaging himself and stepping (as it were) outside the novel to make extraneous comments, as the transfer of 'brief transit through a sorry world' to the preface of his next novel, *The Woodlanders*, confirms.

Natural images such as storm (or wind and rain) and frost are used by Hardy as symbols of mischance or suffering. Frost is employed symbolically at length in *Desperate Remedies* but never more intensively than in *Tess of the d'Urbervilles*, where he reaches his highest level more often and more sustainedly than in any other novel; at such times the poet, philosopher, and novelist are often working in imaginative unison. The incidental thought-image of 'wailing gnats' in the setting which depicts the heroine's dilemma in *Desperate Remedies* becomes a miniature poem in *Tess*. The love of Angel and Tess is more ethereal than earthy. She does not wish to marry him; her desire is for 'a perpetual betrothal' in which everything remains unchanged, summer and autumn, and Angel is always courting her. In such a mood she walks with him in the meadows; looking towards the sun, they see 'a glistening ripple of gossamer webs . . . like the track of moonlight on the sea. Gnats, knowing nothing of their brief glorification', wander 'across the shimmer of this pathway, irradiated' as if they bear fire within them, then pass out of its line, and are 'quite extinct'. The 'quite' underlines her one life, 'the single opportunity of existence ever vouchsafed to Tess by an unsympathetic First Cause— her all; her every and only chance'. The poem-picture is proleptic: so compounded does Tess's initial misfortune become that her life is cut short before it can reach its prime.

Taken in conjunction with one of Hardy's poems, a scene in *Tess* suggests that he had at first hoped to develop it symbolically to promote his philosophy of a First Cause which was not only unsympathetic but blind and unheeding. In **'The Lacking Sense', 'Doom and She'**, and **'The Sleep-Worker'** this indifference is transferred to Nature or the Great Mother, who, as the agent or medium of the Prime Mover, is presented as blind and asleep, working Darwinistically by mindless rote. The birds of **'The Bullfinches'**, which follows, discuss 'queenly Nature's ways':

> All we creatures, nigh and far
>   (Said they there), the Mother's are;
> Yet she never shows endeavour
>   To protect from warrings wild
>   Bird or beast she calls her child.
> Busy in her handsome house
>   Known as Space, she falls a-drowse;
> Yet, in seeming, works on dreaming,
>   While beneath her groping hands
>   Fiends make havoc in her bands.

Alec d'Urberville is presented as Satan or the Archfiend. One of Tess's duties is to teach his mother's bullfinches to sing by whistling to them; she does this in her employer's bedroom. Mrs d'Urberville, who sleeps in a large four-post bedstead, is old and blind.

> Once while Tess was at the window where the cages were ranged, giving her lesson as usual, she thought she heard a rustling behind the bed. The old lady was not present, and turning round the girl had an impression that the toes of a pair of boots were visible below the fringe of the curtains.

Hardy, who regarded mankind as birds caged in by Necessity or the force of circumstances, makes it clear that Alec had been there in ambush.

Bearing a child after her rape, Tess is regarded as a fallen woman. When she recovers from her ignominy and shame, she has at last been mastered by that 'irresistible, universal, automatic tendency to find sweet pleasure somewhere, which pervades all life, from the meanest to the highest'; it is 'the "appetite for joy" which pervades all creation'. On 'a thyme-scented, bird-hatching morning in May', as she walks towards the Valley of the Great Dairies, and sees the Froom waters as 'clear as the pure River of Life shown to the Evangelist', her hopes mingle with the sunshine; she hears 'a pleasant voice in every breeze' and detects joy in every bird's note. Soon she herself begins to sing, but finds nothing adequate to express her feelings, except, ironically, the Benedicite (a pagan 'Fetichistic utterance in a Monotheistic setting', Hardy thought), until the words 'O ye Children of Men, bless ye the Lord, praise Him, and magnify Him for ever' make her stop short with the reflection that perhaps she does not 'quite know the Lord as yet'. (Though apparently mild, these are ambivalent words, conveying Tess's unsophisticated thought and a weight of authorial irony.) When she reaches the valley, she stands still, not knowing her direction, and appears 'like a fly on a billiard-table of indefinite length, and of no more consequence to the surroundings than that fly'. Here we have the first phrases of a motif which is last heard in the final paragraph of the novel, where the words 'the President of the Immortals, in Aeschylean phrase, had ended his sport with Tess' echo a comment in *King Lear* (to which Hardy draws attention in his 1892 preface): 'As flies to wanton boys are we to the gods; They kill us for their sport.'

The motif recurs when Tess is seen on the cold uplands of Flintcomb-Ash, after she has been deserted by Angel Clare. Season and setting are a deliberate contrast to those at Talbothays Dairy in the days of love and happiness. The scene in which Tess and Marian 'grub up' swedes has a drab monotony which communicates the extinction of hope:

> the whole field was in colour a desolate drab; it was a complexion without features, as if a face, from chin to brow, should be only an expanse of skin. The sky wore, in another colour, the same likeness; a white vacuity of countenance with the lineaments gone. So these two upper and nether visages confronted each other all day long, the white face looking down on the brown face, and the brown face looking up at the white face, without anything standing between them but the two girls crawling over the surface of the former like flies.

'So the two forces were at work as everywhere, the inherent will to enjoy, and the circumstantial will against enjoyment', Hardy adds.

The human being can choose, but the more deprived a person is the less freedom of choice he or she enjoys; such choice adds to the whole network of cause and effect, which continues endlessly, as it has done from the beginning. Pater presents this 'web' of universal law, 'penetrating us with a network . . . yet bearing in it the central forces of the world', at the end of his essay on Winckelmann; and Hardy refers to it in *The Woodlanders* when he states that the lonely courses of Winterborne and Marty South were 'part of the pattern in the great web of human doings then weaving in both hemispheres'. Logically, proceeding from antecedent to antecedent, the human mind can posit a First Cause or Prime Mover, and scientific philosophers at the time of Hardy's early intellectual development were particularly prone to think in terms of such an ultimate abstraction. To regard its neutrality (its indifference to human suffering, for example) as 'unsympathetic' or cruel is a form of subjective personification which is exceptional in Hardy's fiction; it is comparable to the Aeschylean impression that the President of the Immortals took delight in mortal woe. For a long period Hardy believed that 'the Cause of Things' is 'neither moral nor immoral, but *un* moral'; ultimately he reached the wise conclusion that the Scheme of Things (including the Cause) is incomprehensible.

Chance is the principal determining factor in Tess's brief life, which is directed by hereditary traits, her feckless parents, and (above all) by two such extreme types as Alec d'Urberville and Angel Clare. Yet she is a pure woman, who does no wrong intentionally, and who is the essence of Christian charity (one of the virtues of which is long-suffering). That events over which she has no control lead her first to dishonour, then to abandonment after marriage, then to a *de facto* marriage with someone she instinctively dislikes (though he has been kind to her and her family), finally to his murder and her early death, constitutes, on the face of it, a highly sensational series of events; in masterly hands, it becomes a tragic indictment of a world which is outwardly Christian. Just before presenting Tess's rape, the author asks where was the Providence of 'her simple faith'; it is the question one should ask at the end of the novel.

There is one scene in which action reflects Hardy's philosophy without comment, and it is his most successful achievement of that kind. This is the account of the wheat-threshing at Flintcomb-Ash. Tess is given the most exhausting task by Groby, the farmer who persecutes her; she has to unbind the sheaves for the 'feeder' of the thresher, and she has no respite, for Groby, having to pay by the hour for the threshing-machinery, is set on using it to the maximum capacity. By the third break during the day, she can hardly walk from the shaking of the machine. When she hears of Alec's arrival, she decides to avoid him by staying on the rick for her dinner; though he is a preacher, and she is officially married, he cannot resist her, and joins her on the stack. When he refers to Angel, who has abandoned her, as 'that mule you call husband', her d'Urberville temper gets the better of her, and she smites him across the cheek with one of her leather gloves, drawing blood. 'Turning up her eyes to him with the hopeless defiance of the sparrow's gaze before its captor twists its neck', she cries, 'Whip me, crush me; you need not mind those people under the rick! I shall not cry out. Once victim, always victim—that's the law!' The zest for life which had caused her to rally and set out for the Valley of the Great Dairies is almost exhausted; later, after her father's death, and the eviction of her family from their home, when it seems that Angel will never return, she becomes Alec's mistress in recompense for his continued kindness to them. This, combined with Angel's 'Too late, beloved' return, reduces her to a frenzy which unhinges her mind and impels her to the murder of Alec, for which she is hanged. A hint of this is probably intended in the anticipated twisting of the sparrow's neck.

The crisis on the wheat stack is the most dramatic pointer to the final exhaustion of, first, Tess's patience when Angel's return makes her think that she has been tricked into spiritual degradation by fate, and, secondly, that renewed will to live after the initial victimization from which all her subsequent suffering springs. This process of exhaustion has its correlative in the gradual wearing-down of Tess's physical energy on the thresher, the 'red tyrant' that has to be served. It is driven by a sooty and grimy engine, the man in charge of which looks equally unpropitious, as if he had come from Tophet. The engine is 'the *primum mobile* of this little world', the world of Tess's suffering. It connotes the Primum Mobile or Prime Mover which had been hypostatized in the pre-Copernican era as the source of life and movement in the universe which it surrounded, this being imagined as a series of concentric revolving spheres, the stars on the outer, earth and man at the centre, as if mankind were the supreme creation in the eyes of God. Hardy, who loved the Church of England, especially its music and architecture, and had at one time hoped to be a country curate, with enough leisure to write poetry, had lost his faith in Christian theology. The Darwinian internecine struggle for existence in nature, and the tragic lot of people, individually or internationally, confirmed his belief that the Cause of Things is blind or indifferent, and that life goes on automatically (he twice uses this term with reference to Tess's rally) or by rote. The threshing-scene illustrates a philosophy of the Ultimate which Hardy presented on a large scale in *The Dynasts:*

> Thus does the Great Foresightless mechanize
> In blank entrancement now as evermore. . . .

Nowhere in Hardy are the particular and the universal, the picture and the philosophy, more synoptically and dramatically fused. The scene provides a splendid example of how (in the words of Pater's essay on Winckelmann) 'the imaginative intellect' of one nineteenth-century artist could command 'that width, variety,' and 'delicacy of resources' which enable it 'to deal with the conditions of modern life'. (pp. 81-93)

F. B. Pinion, in his *Hardy the Writer: Surveys and Assessments,* The Macmillan Press Ltd., 1990, 361 p.

SOURCES FOR FURTHER STUDY

Brady, Kristin. *The Short Stories of Thomas Hardy.* New York: St. Martin's Press, 1982, 235 p.

> Examines Hardy's short fiction to arrive at an understanding of his conception of the short story as a literary form.

Butler, Lance St. John, ed. *Alternative Hardy.* London: Macmillan, 1989, 229 p.

> Collects critical essays on Hardy by Jean Jacques Lecercle, Christine Brooke-Rose, Patricia Ingham, Howard Jacobson, Michael Rabiger, J. Hillis Miller, Jagdish Chandra Dave, Henre Quéré and Janie Sénéchal, and the editor.

Cox, R. G., ed. *Thomas Hardy: The Critical Heritage.* London: Routledge & Kegan Paul, 1970, 473 p.

> Collects important early reviews of Hardy's literary works. The editor supplies an introductory overview of Hardy's critical reputation.

Millgate, Michael. *Thomas Hardy: A Biography.* New York: Random House, 1982, 637 p.

> Noncritical biography. Millgate presents a comprehensive account of Hardy's life, drawing on diaries, notebooks, correspondence, and local records inaccessible to previous biographers.

Pinion, F. B. *A Hardy Companion: A Guide to the Works of Thomas Hardy and Their Background.* London: Macmillan, 1968, 555 p.

> Survey of Hardy's work and its major influences, with biographical background.

Taylor, Dennis. *Hardy's Poetry, 1860-1928.* New York: Columbia University Press, 1981, 204 p.

> Examines Hardy's development as a poet through an investigation of characteristic patterns and themes in his verse.

Bret Harte

1836?-1902

(Full name Francis Brett Harte) American short story writer, novelist, poet, and dramatist.

INTRODUCTION

*A*t the height of his career, Harte was one of the best-known American writers of the nineteenth century. In such classic short stories as "The Luck of Roaring Camp," "The Outcasts of Poker Flat," and "Tennessee's Partner," he nostalgically portrayed the mining camps and ethnic groups of California during the gold rush of 1849. Although Harte's fiction received less recognition later in his career, elements of his work—especially its regional flavor and his creation of such stock characters as the seedy prospector, the cynical gambler, and the frontier prostitute—greatly influenced his contemporaries and later writers of popular Westerns.

Harte was born in Albany, New York, to a schoolteacher and his wife. An unhealthy child, he was tutored at home, where he read such authors as Charles Dickens, Edgar Allan Poe, and Washington Irving. When Harte was nine years old his father died, and his family moved to New York City. When Harte was eighteen his mother remarried, and the family moved to San Francisco; shortly thereafter Harte left home. Over the next decade he held several jobs, most significantly that of apprentice printer for the journal *Northern Californian*, where he was eventually given editorial responsibilities. After his marriage in 1862, Harte supplemented his journalist's income by serving as a government clerk at the San Francisco mint. In 1865 Harte became editor of the *Californian*, where he commissioned Mark Twain, who was then a relatively unknown author, to write a weekly story for the journal. Regarding Harte's editorial influence, Twain later remarked that it was Harte who "trimmed and schooled me patiently until he changed me from an awkward utterer of coarse grotesqueness to a writer of paragraphs and chapters." Harte became editor of the *Overland Monthly* in 1868, and during his tenure with the journal his poem

"Plain Language from Truthful James" (also called "Heathen Chinee"), as well as such stories as "The Luck of the Roaring Camp," appeared in its pages and inspired what his biographer George Stewart termed a "literary epidemic" of imitations. Afterward Harte received offers of editorial positions from across the country. In 1871 he signed a one-year contract for $10,000 with the *Atlantic Monthly,* which gave the magazine exclusive rights to a minimum of twelve stories and poems and made Harte the highest paid American writer of the time. However, he was careless about fulfilling his contract, and it was not renewed. In need of a new source of income, he went on a lecture tour from 1872 to 1875, but the proceeds barely covered his expenses and the demands of creditors became an increasing problem. In a further attempt to recover his financial solvency, Harte collaborated with Twain on a stage adaptation of "Heathen Chinee," entitled *Ah Sin.* Performed in 1877, the drama was a failure. Later that year, Harte called on contacts in political circles who helped him obtain a consulate in Crefeld, Germany, and, two years later, in Glasgow, Scotland. He remained a prolific writer for the last twenty-two years of his life, publishing a volume of short stories almost yearly. Supported by a wealthy patron named Mrs. Van de Velde, Harte moved to London in 1885 and became a favorite in literary and social circles. He died in London in 1902.

In his stories Harte offered a sentimental depiction of the goldrush era of 1849, finding favor with the reading public through sensationalistic fiction that featured grotesque or idealized characters and a strong appeal to sentiment, qualities which earned him the title "Dickens among the pines." Just as Charles Dickens had created larger-than-life characters who became standard representations of English personalities, Harte invented such standard frontier types as the seedy prospector Kentuck, the hard-bitten gambler Jack Hamlin, and the dance-hall girl—characters whose outward churlishness is essential to Harte's most familiar plot formula: to expose the "heart of gold" beneath a coarse or depraved exterior. Thus, the callous miners in "The Luck of Roaring Camp" become the sensitive and self-sacrificing guardians of a child born to a prostitute, and the cynical Jack Hamlin reveals a concern for others in "An Heiress of Red Dog" and "Mr. Jack Hamlin's Meditation." Reversing the formula, Harte portrayed corruption disguised as innocence in *M'liss,* a novella in which a pubescent schoolgirl becomes a seductress, and juxtaposed outward respectability with underlying viciousness in "Heathen Chinee," a ballad relating how two Anglo-Saxon Americans scheme to cheat, but are instead outwitted by, a Chinese immigrant. Perhaps the most outstanding example of the typical Harte story is "Tennessee's Partner." Presenting an idealized view of friendship between two miners, the story contrasts the uncouth and untutored appearance of Tennessee's partner with his extremely virtuous magnanimity toward Tennessee. Not only does the partner forgive Tennessee for seducing his wife, but he also tries to save Tennessee from execution during a trial for robbery. Loyalty is further celebrated by the story's sentimental ending, in which the two men are pictured embracing after death as they meet at heaven's gate. Although Harte occasionally experimented with different characters and settings, his stories of American frontier life in the mid-nineteenth century are considered his most typical and important works.

Early in his career, Harte received virtually undisputed acclaim as a short story writer, with critics offering similar praise for his skill as a humorist. After 1880, however, reviewers began to criticize Harte's fiction for its reliance on coincidence and melodramatic prose. Mark Twain, whose talent Harte had discovered and fostered, was one of the earliest and most outspoken detractors of Harte's fiction. Applying the criteria of realism, with its demand for a faithful rendering of details, Twain noted grave flaws in Harte's work, including inaccurate representations of frontier vernacular, faulty observation, and subservience of fact to sentiment. Despite such criticism, commentators have noted that Twain was indebted to Harte; as Twain scholar Margaret Duckett suggests, the technique in "Heathen Chinee" of employing a naive narrator to reveal information and attitudes of which he is unaware influenced Twain's method in *Adventures of Huckleberry Finn.* Other critics concurred with Twain's judgments, emphasizing the maudlin emotional responses Harte solicited in even his best stories. In spite of the decline of his critical standing in the United States, Harte continued to please audiences abroad and became especially popular in England, where his fiction was favorably compared with that of Dickens. Nevertheless by 1943, when Cleanth Brooks and Robert Penn Warren wrote a derisive appraisal of "Tennessee's Partner," the view of Harte as a Victorian sentimentalist was widely held.

In the last three decades, however, some critics have begun to reassess the strengths and modernity of Harte's fiction. J. R. Boggan, for instance, contends that the sentimentality of the narrator of "The Luck of Roaring Camp" is intended to be ironic rather than sincere. Others note that Harte's influence as a preeminent regionalist writer and creator of standard American character types helped further the evolution of an American literature independent of European tradition. In describing Harte's influence, Granville Hicks wrote: "Harte, though he may not have been in any strict sense the founder of American regionalism, was the first writer to gain popularity after the Civil War by the exploitation of sectional peculiarities, and there is little doubt that his example directly inspired many of the writers of the seventies, eighties, and nineties." For this achievement Harte remains an important figure in the development of American literature.

(For further information about Harte's life and works, see *Contemporary Authors*, Vol. 104; *Dictionary of Literary Biography*, Vol. 12; *Something about the Author*, Vol. 26; and *Twentieth-Century Literary Criticism*, Vols. 1, 25.

CRITICAL COMMENTARY

FRED LEWIS PATTEE

(essay date 1923)

[Pattee was an American literary historian, critic, poet, and novelist. In the following excerpt, he delineates Harte's contribution to the short story genre.]

Harte did perhaps six distinctive things for the short-story form. First, he threw over his stories, especially over his early masterpieces, a peculiar atmosphere of locality, one that to the readers of his day was startlingly new. He did for California what Dickens had done for London: he romanticized it; he gave it a mythology with a background perfectly in keeping. His methods of securing his localizing effect were unusual. Seemingly he made little of his setting: one may glance through one of his tales and be surprised to find only here and there a sentence touching upon landscape or surroundings, and yet one carries away from it local coloring as the dominating impression. Never does Harte, in notable contrast with many of his disciples, describe the landscape setting simply because it is unusual or unique. Always it is introduced as background, as scenery for his little theater, and, like all scenery, it is painted splashingly with swift impressionistic strokes. The tragedy of **"The Outcasts of Poker Flat"** is played before this drop curtain:

> The spot was singularly wild and impressive. A wooded amphitheatre surrounded on three sides by precipitous cliffs of naked granite, sloped gently toward the crest of another precipice that overlooked the valley. . . .

It is like directions to a scene painter. (p. 234)

The second element emphasized by Harte was a saving dash of the new Western humor. In **"Tennessee's Partner"** he has recorded that in the gulches and the bar-rooms of early California "all sentiment was modified by a strong sense of humor." The statement is illuminating: without this peculiar quality in his work, which often is an atmosphere rather than a quotable entity, Harte would have been as sentimentally extreme as Dickens, his master. The funeral scene in **"Tennessee's Partner"** would have been mere gush. (p. 235)

The third characteristic was his startling use of paradox and antithesis. The world he presents is topsy-turvy. Of the dwellers in Roaring Camp he notes that

> The greatest scamp had a Raphael face, with a profusion of blonde hair; Oakhurst, a gambler, had the melancholy air and intellectual abstraction of a Hamlet; the coolest and most courageous man was scarcely over five feet in height, with a soft voice and an embarrassed, timid manner. . . . The strongest man had but three fingers on his right hand; the best shot had but one eye.

This became a mannerism with Harte. His heroes are men whom the world usually brands as villains. **"A Passage in the Life of Mr. John Oakhurst"** illustrates his method perfectly. (p. 236)

His fourth characteristic concerns his methods of characterization. He peopled his stories with highly individualized types, with picturesque extremes in an abnormal social régime. They are not photographs, they are not actual individuals, they are composites made up by fusing the unique qualities of many actual men or women into a single personality. Yuba Bill is the dream of a romancer who has known or has read about many California stage drivers. Colonel Starbottle is redolent of the make-up box: he changes from story to story. He is a gargoyle, and yet for all that he is alive, for Harte had learned from his master, Dickens, that art of creating what in reality is a realm of Munchausen, and then, miracle of miracles, of actually breathing into it the breath of life.

The fifth distinctive element in his work is a splashy type of impressionism. His treatment of background we have noted: he painted with broad strokes and strong colors, and he applied the method to his characters. Usually he works with extremes, with in-

Principal Works

Condensed Novels, and Other Papers (parodies) 1867; enlarged edition, 1871

The Lost Galleon, and Other Tales (poetry) 1867

The Luck of Roaring Camp, and Other Sketches (short stories) 1870; enlarged edition, 1871

Poems (poetry) 1871

Stories of the Sierras, and Other Sketches (short stories) 1872

M'liss (short story) 1873

Mrs. Scaggs's Husbands, and Other Sketches (short stories) 1873

Idylls of the Foothills (short stories) 1874

Tales of the Argonauts, and Other Sketches (short stories) 1875

Gabriel Conroy (novel) 1876

Ah Sin (drama) [first publication] 1877

Thankful Blossom, and Other Tales (short stories) 1877

The Twins of Table Mountains, and Other Stories (short stories) 1879

In the Carquinez Woods (short story) 1883

California Stories (short stories) 1884

On the Frontier (short stories) 1884

Maruja (short story) 1885

The Crusade of the Excelsior (novella) 1887

Cressy (short story) 1889

A Sappho of Green Springs, and Other Stories (short stories) 1891

Colonel Starbottle's Client, and Some Other People (short stories) 1892

A Protegee of Jack Hamlin's, and Other Stories (short stories) 1894

Barker's Luck, and Other Stories (short stories) 1896

The Writings of Bret Harte. 20 vols. (short stories, novel, and poetry) 1896-1914

Three Partners; or, The Big Strike on Heavy Tree Hill (short stories) 1897

Tales of Trail and Town (short stories) 1898

Mr. Jack Hamlin's Meditation, and Other Stories (short stories) 1899

Trent's Trust, and Other Stories (short stories) 1903

---

carnated peculiarities, sharply emphasized. From him it was that Kipling learned the secret of the colorful impressionistic epithet, of the telling comparison, the single adjective that flashes a vivid picture. Harte describes a certain squaw as "a berry-eyed old woman with the complexion of dried salmon." Her daughter he describes as having also "berry eyes, and a face that seemed made of a moist laugh." Another character he pictures as "a stout, middle-aged woman of ungirt waist and beshawled head and shoulders."

Finally, like James and Aldrich, who were contemporaneous workers, he emphasized the technique of his art. He, too, had found Poe by way of France, he, too, was a conscious workman who knew the rules. Like Poe, too, he brought to the short story the training of the experienced magazine editor, and it was a training that kept him so long upon short, single-issue effects that he grew powerless to work effectively with the longer units. . . . He was brilliant in short dashes, but he had not the patience to hold himself to a long and leisurely plot and to slow character development. There were other reasons for his failure: Harte lacked moral basis; he was superficial; he was theatric. He was temperamental, too, like Irving, and worked by impulse. Moreover, he dealt with materials impossible to be prolongated to novel length. If one is to make John Oakhurst or Mother Shipton heroic, one must deal with episodes: must make impressionistic sketches of vivid moments: to go farther would be to relate mere

picaresque miscellany. It was only within narrow limits with single situations and highly colored materials that he could work at all effectively or artistically. (pp. 238-39)

Unquestionably the influence of Harte upon the American short story has been greater than that exerted by any other American author, always excepting Irving. His influence was far greater than the quality of his work entitled him to exert. He was peculiarly fortunate: everything for a time conspired to give him the center of the stage. The imagination of the whole world had been fired by the California gold era and the field had been untouched by romancers: his material was timely to the moment. Dickens had just visited America and the fame of him and his work had penetrated every household; then had come the news of his death, and enormous space had been given to him in all the journals of the world and new editions had crowded upon one another, until everyone had his Dickens:— the reading public had been educated to appreciate the type of work that Harte was to give them. Moreover, he came at the moment when better art was demanded, when the feminized fiction of the mid-century was no longer satisfying the majority of the readers, and he gave them his work in a form that seemed to them to be peculiarly adequate. In him may be found all the elements that had characterized the popular fiction of the earlier period, and yet his fresh, wild materials, his new Western humor, and his peculiarly effective technique made him appear like the inspired creator of a new *genre*.

Great as has been his influence, however, he can never be a permanently commanding figure in American fiction. He lacked sincerity. (pp. 239-40)

In all of his work there is no experience, no genuine feeling, no sympathy of comprehension; it is the theater and not life. Moreover, the moral perspective of it is wrong. Men do not at will put on a new suit of morals as they put on a new suit of clothes. Ruled by emotion and not by principle, by the desire to create wonder and sensation in his reader rather than to interpret for him life, he tells not the truth, and the ultimate basis of all great fiction, be it long or be it short, is the Truth. (p. 241)

Fred Lewis Pattee, "Bret Harte," in his *The Development of the American Short Story: An Historical Survey*, Harper & Brothers Publishers, 1923, pp. 220-41.

GRANVILLE HICKS
(essay date 1935)

[Hicks was an American literary critic whose famous study *The Great Tradition: An Interpretation of American Literature Since the Civil War* (1933; revised edition, 1935) established him as the foremost advocate of Marxist critical thought in Depression-era America. After 1939, he sharply denounced communist ideology, which he called a "hopelessly narrow way of judging literature," and in his later years adopted a less ideological posture in critical matters. In the following excerpt, he contends that Harte's career established a pattern for later American regional writers.]

California was waiting for Bret Harte, who, as editor of the newly founded *Overland Monthly*, announced in 1868 that it was the duty of the magazine to print material pertaining to its own state, and then, in illustration of his theory, published **"The Luck of Roaring Camp."** This young man, thirty-two years old when the story appeared, had taught school, worked in a drug store, and set type. He had also served a brief term as Wells Fargo express messenger and perhaps had done some mining. But his background was academic and his aims were literary, and the decade before the appearance of **"The Luck of Roaring Camp"** had been chiefly devoted to writing. He had written sketches, burlesque novels, and an occasional story for the *Golden Era* and the *Californian*, edited a collection of state verse, and published a volume of prose and one of poetry. He had been given a comfortable sinecure as secretary of the California mint, and his choice as editor of the *Overland*

Monthly indicated public recognition of his talents. Already he had outstripped his friends and colleagues—Charles Warren Stoddard, Mark Twain, Charles Henry Webb, and the rest—and when the amazing popularity of **"Plain Language from Truthful James"** followed in 1870 the success of **"The Luck of Roaring Camp,"** he was a national figure.

Harte had, he later said, a "very early, half-boyish but very enthusiastic belief " in the possibility of "a peculiarly characteristic Western American literature." Whatever that phrase may have meant to him, many of his sketches of Californian scenery and his adaptations of Spanish legend obviously owed more to his reading of Washington Irving than to any immersion in the life of the frontiersman. And it is clear that the same appreciation of the picturesque determined the themes of his short stories. If one examines the tales collected in the volume called *The Luck of Roaring Camp,* one notices not only the use of an amusing and perhaps inaccurate dialect, the reliance on bizarre details, and the emphasis on eccentricities of character; one notices also that the theme of each is the emergence of fine qualities in some character whose rough exterior gives no promise of such virtues. The very basis, then, of his stories is the picturesque contrast between superficial uncouthness and inner nobility, and he was far more interested in stating this contrast dramatically than he was in analyzing the true character of the pioneer.

Moreover, the California of the gold miners was being rapidly transformed, at the time he wrote his stories, into the California of the business men, and this change may have had something to do with his admiration for the miners. We know that he had once regarded these men as vulgar and unworthy of literary attention, and we know that his subsequent respect for them accompanied the growth of a bitter hatred for the money-grubbing spirit. As a boy he had worshipped the heroes of Froissart's *Chronicles,* Dumas' romances, the sea-stories of Marryat, and the *Leatherstocking Tales* of Cooper; and his own character, in its impulsiveness and even irresponsibility, was closer to the hearty good nature of the first settlers than it was to the well-mannered ruthlessness of the entrepreneurs. And this antipathy alone would have prevented him from following, in his fiction, the development of California from the pioneering to the commercial stage.

There were, then, two obstacles to the growth of the realistic elements in his stories, and when he added a third by leaving for the East he was forever committed to the romantic, sentimental tale of the mining camps. He went East both because he dreamt of living a free, idealistic life among men of literary aims and because he wanted to escape from the commercialism of his San Francisco contemporaries. He discovered that Boston had changed, just as California was changing, and the tranquil life of its men of letters did not blind him to the power of the new Boston, the city of factories and brokers' offices and struggling immigrants. Longfellow still seemed to him the embodiment of quiet nobility, and he venerated him accordingly; but the younger men of letters he distrusted. Having to make a living, he continued to write stories, tried his hand at plays, wrote one novel, and suffered on the lecture platform. Seven years passed, and at last, unhappy and poor, he accepted, from a government that he hated for its subservience to commercial interests, a minor post in Germany. Thence, in 1880, he went to Glasgow, and when he lost his post there five years later, he settled in London. America he never revisited.

Reading carefully the letters Harte wrote to his wife during those long years abroad, one detects the tragic note. Though he seems to have found life in London pleasanter than life elsewhere, and though he appreciated the prestige he enjoyed there and the larger income he was able to earn, he found much to distress him in his adopted home, and his affection for the United States grew with absence. As for his own work, it was cheap and he knew it. His writing was pure drudgery. "You," he wrote his wife, "cannot possibly hate pen and ink as I do who live in it and by it perpetually." "Sick or not," he said, "in spirits or out of spirits, I must work, and I do not see any rest ahead." So he went on, grinding out story after story about the golden hearts of profane miners and quick-shooting gamblers. Yet sometimes, in a story such as **"A Protégée of Jack Hamlin's"** or **"Colonel Starbottle's Client,"** a little of the old vigor returned, as if memory suddenly woke in him and he found himself back in frontier California. The life there, it must have seemed to him, was after all the best he had known, and he may not have been wholly sorry that popular demand forbade him to desert his one great theme.

Bret Harte's literary career ended, to all intents, when he left California in 1871, and it is possible that even his early work has been too highly esteemed. He has been called a stylist of distinction, a master of the short story, and a penetrating student of human nature. Yet it is easy to find flaws in his style, to expose the superficiality of his characterization, and to list many short story writers more dextrous than he. Even his own claim, that he founded a peculiarly western literature, will not bear scrutiny, for he owed much to picturesque writers of other regions, and he portrayed only so much of California life as happened to fit his formula. Yet it is impossible to deny that there is power in his early work, and that something of the frontier does live in these romantic tales. Harte did not found a peculiarly western literature, but he did make a beginning. And then, with the beginning scarcely made, he turned his back on the West and on the hope of literary growth. What he had written, out of a real desire

to express the spirit of the region he knew, was, he discovered, merely entertainment for his readers. He accepted—harassed, one must admit, by personal difficulties and financial troubles—the rôle of entertainer, and as an entertainer survived for thirty years his death as an artist.

Harte, though he may not have been in any strict sense the founder of American regionalism, was the first writer to gain popularity after the Civil War by the exploitation of sectional peculiarities, and there is little doubt that his example directly inspired many of the writers of the seventies, eighties, and nineties. It is, therefore, striking that the pattern of his life should be the pattern, to a great extent, of the regional movement in American literature. Writer after writer began with a sincere desire not merely to portray the life of a particular section but to express its spirit; writer after writer ended as a mere entertainer, providing formularized amusement for an appreciative nation. Individual careers varied, but the fundamental pattern scarcely changed: the writer did not grow with his section. The region that appeared in his books was always the region as he had known it when he began writing, or even when he was a child. Often he left the region, and thus freed himself to live with memories of what it had been. In any case nostalgia and often sentimentality filled his tales. Again and again the tragedy of Bret Harte in London repeated itself. (pp. 34-8)

Granville Hicks, "A Banjo on My Knee," in his *The Great Tradition: An Interpretation of American Literature Since the Civil War,* revised edition, Macmillan Publishing Company, 1935, pp. 32-67.

WALLACE STEGNER

(essay date 1969)

[Stegner is an American novelist, short story writer, educator, and critic. In the following excerpt, he assesses the strengths and weaknesses of Harte's fiction.]

The consensus on Harte [at the time of this essay] is approximately what it was at the time of his death: that he was a skillful but not profound writer who made a lucky strike in subject matter and for a few heady months enjoyed a fabulous popularity; that once the artifice, narrowness, and shallowness of his work began to be perceived, he fell out of public favor; and that through the last twenty-four years of his life, while he lived abroad, he went on tiredly repeating himself in potboiler after potboiler, turning over his own tailings in a pathetic attempt to recapture what had first made him.

That estimate is not true in all its details or in all its implications, but it is broadly true. Harte *was* lucky, he *was* limited, he *did* swiftly lose his popularity in America, he *did* go on repeating himself. Of the scores of stories that he wrote during his years in Germany, Scotland, and England, all but a small handful return to the picturesque gulches of the Sierra foothills from which, in one blazing strike, he had extracted the nugget of his reputation. Now, no critic takes him very seriously; he is read principally by children and students. And yet he cannot be dismissed. More than a hundred years after his first sketches and poems began to appear in *The Golden Era* in the late 1850's, he remains embedded in the American literary tradition, and it looks as if he will stay. It is worth trying to discover what is keeping him there.

Whatever virtues he had, they were not the virtues of realism. His observation of Gold Rush country, character, and society was neither very accurate nor very penetrating; neither was much of it firsthand. (pp. 223-24)

His geography sounds authentic, but when one attempts to pin it down to locality it swims and fades into the outlines of Never-Never Land. Harte had no such personal familiarity with the Sierra as his contemporaries Clarence King and John Muir had, and no such scientific accuracy of observation. (p. 225)

He did not have, as the great fiction writers have, the faculty of realizing real characters on the page in terms more vivid than reality. His practice was to select occupations and turn them into types; and though individual models were sometimes present, as in the case of the gambler-duelist prototype of Jack Hamlin, the gamblers, schoolmarms, stage drivers, and miners of the stories are usually predictable. (pp. 225-26)

Unlike Mark Twain's human swarm, Harte's characters do not strike us with their lifelikeness. They are self-consistent, they have clear outlines and logical coherence, and they speak a lingo that sounds suitably rough and crude. Yet they look *made,* and they are.

These are, in fact, early forms of some of our most venerable literary stereotypes. Since Harte it has been next to impossible for a writer to present a western gambler who has not some of the self-contained poise, readiness, and chivalry of Jack Hamlin and John Oakhurst. Even Stephen Crane, in his superb short story "The Blue Hotel," succumbed to the pattern that Harte had laid down. Since Harte showed the world how, every horse-opera stage driver has driven with the picturesque recklessness and profanity of Yuba Bill. The schoolmarms of our movie and television westerns owe about as much to Harte's Miss Mary, in **"The Idyl of Red Gulch,"** as to Molly Wood in Owen Wister's *The Virginian*—and it should be noted, in Harte's favor,

that **"The Idyl of Red Gulch"** came thirty-two years before *The Virginian.*

Harte's geography seems vague because he did not know the real geography of the Sierra well, and didn't feel that he needed to. His characters seem made because they *were* made, according to a formula learned from Dickens: the trick of bundling together apparently incompatible qualities to produce a striking paradox. (pp. 226-27)

Harte's popularity . . . was always greatest in direct proportion to the reader's distance from and ignorance of the mines. By a happy chance of lagging factual reports, his stories reached Eastern readers when they were still titillated by rumor but unsatisfied in detail. As in the Currier and Ives prints about the buffalo plains, art passed for fact until fact overtook it, whereupon it began to lose its currency even as art. Then, after his popularity had dwindled on the Eastern seaboard, Harte found still another audience, even more remote from the Mother Lode, in England, and that audience stuck loyally with him until his death and after. In a way, it was the worst thing that could have happened to him, for it helped keep him from becoming anything more than the writer he already was. (p. 228)

Bret Harte represented two very common American literary phenomena. For one thing he was victimized, as many of our writers have been, by the boom-and-bust freakishness of public favor. For another, he was that American type, the local writer whom fame has drawn away from the local, and who now has a choice between developing new themes and a literary manner more suitable for a sophisticated audience, or repeating from exile, with increasing thinness and unreality, the localism he has left behind.

The very perfection of Harte's little world of the local picturesque made it all but impossible for him to break out of it. Mark Twain, who had never been so typed or so limited, was freed by the variety of his own life and by the vitality with which he welcomed new experience; he escaped into travel literature, into history, into causes, into his rich nostalgia for boyhood and the river. But Harte was imprisoned in his own creation. Pressed for money as he always was, he dared not vary locale or tone. (p. 230)

And so, from necessity, timidity, incapacity, or whatever, Harte made hardly a gesture toward discovering new sources of stories. He did now and then turn to poetry, but "only as a change to my monotonous romances. Perhaps it is very *little change,* for my poetry, I fear, is coming from the same spring as my prose, only the tap is nearer the fountain—and filtered." (p. 231)

[In] the *Letters* there is a more personal Bret Harte, one who makes us realize almost with a shock how little Harte's personality shows in the stories. There he is as scrupulously aloof and "indifferent," as "refined out of existence," as the most rigorous dramatic ideal could ask. His characters, whatever else they are, are never made in Harte's image, but are themselves, creations, clean of any taint of their creator. Like the perfect little world of picturesque localism and romantic paradox that they inhabit, they eventually controlled their creator as much as he controlled them; they were a thing he hid behind.

Reading the *Letters,* one wishes that Harte had let himself be revealed more: he is himself more interesting than his gallery of types. For one thing, the letters give evidence that if he had chosen to, he might have become a lively, biased, and outrageous travel reporter in the jingoist tradition of Mark Twain. (p. 232)

Admitting that there is in them little honest observation of people or of nature, no real character, no accurate picture of a society however fleeting, no true ear for the lingo, no symbolic depth, no valid commentary upon the human condition, no inadvertent self-revelation, and no real weight of mind, there is still something. There is humor—pervasive, unprudish, often still fresh and natural. There is good prose, and this is nearly unfailing. He was master of a flexible instrument, and if his language was rather more literary than native, if he leaned toward the King's English and never made of his dialect much more than a sort of decoration, he can hardly be blamed. Of all his contemporaries, only Mark Twain managed to make the vernacular do everything a true literary language has to do. Harte's prose was sometimes inflated and self-conscious, but more often it was markedly clean and direct. He was capable of a notable economy, passages and sometimes whole stories of a striking nervous compactness in which character, situation, and realized place come off the page instantly visual. Try the opening of **"A Protégée of Jack Hamlin's,"** a story written as late as 1893.

Economy and a formal precision were part of both his temperament and his training. In *Condensed Novels,* a series of parodies written during the sixties, he had learned to boil whole novelists down to a few pages of essence. But it was his adaptation of the short story to Californian materials that created something like a revolution. His example emancipated writers in every region, confirming them in their subject matter and confirming them in their preference for the short story form. So great was Harte's influence upon the whole local color school that in 1894 he modestly felt compelled to deny, in an article for *Cornhill,* that he had invented the short story itself. Invent it he did not, but no historian of the short story can overlook his shaping influence upon it or his enormous influence in popularizing it through the expanding magazines. (pp. 234-35)

Wallace Stegner, "Three Samples: The West Synthetic, Bret Harte," in his *The Sound of Mountain Water,* Doubleday, 1969, pp. 223-36.

DONALD E. GLOVER
(essay date 1973)

[In the following excerpt, Glover argues that Harte experimented in his later work with new themes, more realistic treatment of setting and character, and greater emotional restraint.]

Harte's career conveniently falls into two major periods: the brief, glittering success of 1868-1872, and the long exile in England from 1880 to his death in 1902. These periods reveal the basic dichotomy and paradox which control his art and the critical response to his work as a whole. The majority of critics suggest that the important period in Harte's life and work ends with the production of **"The Outcasts of Poker Flat"** in 1869. His later career is tantalizing for the mystery surrounding his twenty year separation from his wife and his relationship with Mme. Van de Velde, but the scores of short stories that constitute his later works are traditionally thought of as sad and negligible repetitions of an earlier style and themes.

However, it was after 1878 that Harte won at least partial acceptance of his own image, the image of a Victorian man of taste who happened to have been "out West." This image led him on an Easterly course from the crude response in San Francisco to the brief plaudits of New York, and finally to acceptance in London— Mecca for American writers of that day. Harte was an expatriate more by necessity than by real inclination or choice, but like all artistic expatriates, he was looking for an audience which would appreciate his writing and flatter his artist's ego. In England, he met Hardy and George Eliot. He was the frequent guest of the Duke of Northampton; Sullivan asked for a libretto; the Prince of Wales requested an introduction. Harte even had the temerity to criticize Henry James, whom he had just met, for being "un-American."

Met Henry James, Jr. the American novelist, who is creating quite a reputation here. He looks, acts, and thinks like an Englishman, I am sorry to say, excellent as his style is. I wish he had more of an American flavor.

Public and private interest was such that Harte was asked to lecture at Oxford and to present the "Response" to the Royal Academy Toast to Literature; magazines deluged his agent with requests for stories.

Feeling successful in Europe, for the first time Harte stopped writing about California, choosing German (**"The Legend of Saamstadt"**) and later Scottish locales (the **"St. Kentigern"** stories narrated by an urbane consul) drawn from his experiences in Crefeld and Glasgow. More secure financially, and approved by his audience as something more than a local phenomenon, he wrote what he wanted: a disastrous series of plays (*The Luck of Roaring Camp* and *Thankful Blossom,* both in 1882) adapted from earlier successful stories. Here we see a paradox in his career. Although contemporary criticism in England showed that Harte was fully appreciated for his skill as a technician and wit, the English reader clearly wanted only local color stories dealing with the romantic Gold Rush era. The irony of Harte's dilemma now becomes apparent. The conflict is no longer between his own view of himself as artist and an unappreciative audience, but between his desire to escape the old materials and his English reader's insistence that he continue with stereotyped California materials. By 1890, the strain shows through in a letter to Mrs. Florence Henniker, daughter of Lord Houghton and Harte's literary protégé.

> You are quite right; I have been "working hard" lately, but I fear that the "numbness at the back of the head" will be reserved for my readers. My writing lately has *revealed* to me *hitherto* unknown depths of weariness and stupidity! (Harte's italics)

He tried to escape the boredom by writing more plays (unsuccessful); by experimenting with various themes, such as racial prejudice and the social outcast; and by completing the libretto for an opera, *The Lord of Fontenelle,* which was set to music by Emanuel Moōr, but left unperformed. Harte frequently escaped from London to the country estates of friends like James Anthony Froude or Geraldine Webb and even made one trip to Switzerland. But sheer financial necessity forced him to write for the only audience who would pay—the very sort of story which he undoubtedly wrote best and which American critics now thought him incapable of writing because of his distance from the source of inspiration.

What then of the later work, by far the bulk of his creative output? A study of these stories uncovers several factors that help put the total work in critical perspective. First, Harte continued to follow the pattern established in the early work: use of local color materials (now German, Scottish, English, and Californian), humor-tempering sentiment, melodramatic endings, simple characters and plot lines. Second, the development of his later writing was dictated by the reaction of his audience. During the period 1882-1885, he wrote for both American and English readers. By the late 1880's, he had turned, through financial necessity, almost entirely to an English public. The late stories clearly reflect the reactions of his readers and their effect on any innovations in technique and theme which he attempted. Third, between 1882 and 1902, Harte experimented with many other story types using appro-

priately developed styles. He returned to the theme of social criticism, especially attacking prejudice against minority groups in stories presented with increasing realism; he attempted international stories along the lines of James and Howells; he used a new, urbane tone with the consular narrator of the St. Kentigern stories. Each experiment met opposition from his readers and their continued demand for the favorite California Gold Rush story. Finally, forced by his financial dependence on a receptive audience, Harte adjusted his style and technique to produce highly colored, melodramatic stories combining humour, sentiment, and pathos with a strong dash of not always factually accurate local color.

The process of adapting his style to the demands of an English audience was a slow one for Harte, and one he frequently rebelled against, but it was this adaptation which brought into being a quite different kind of western story from that which he had produced in America in the 1870's. By observing selected works from the later period, we can recognize the process of change and its end product.

"In the Carquinez Woods" (1882) best serves as the example of Harte's indecision about his audience and his treatment of materials as he began adjusting to new demands from an English audience. The English magazine reader was, like his American counterpart ten years earlier, receptive to the glamour of the Golden West, but as Boynton points out, "So far as it [the reading public] was English, it had a pretty vague notion of the veracity of his replicas of the early California sketches."

As his first work commissioned by a major magazine in two years, **"In the Carquinez Woods"** represents an active return to magazine writing after the failure of the dramatic adaptation of **"The Luck of Roaring Camp,"** a production on which Harte had mistakenly placed high expectations. Critical reception of **"In the Carquinez Woods"** was mixed; most critics praised scene depiction and plotting, while the *Spectator* disliked its lack of moral force. The *Spectator* review, however, notes the appeal of "novel scene" and "novel states of society," personified by the hero, the half-breed Indian botanist Low, and the half-breed Mexican gypsy, Teresa.

The plot of this romance is incredible. L'eau Dormant, popularly known as Low Dorman, lives in a hollowed-out redwood tree. He saves the runaway Teresa from jail by stabbing her lover. They set up housekeeping in the tree. Low's ex-sweetheart, Nellie Wynn, frivolous daughter of the bigoted local minister, plays with the affections of Teresa's former lover, Sheriff Dunn—who in turn is Low's unknown father. In the *dénouement* of this intricate plot, a cataclysmic forest fire conveniently burns Low and Teresa to death.

Unlike the earlier stories, **"Carquinez Woods"**

was conceived on a grand scale, appearing in four weighty installments. Long sections are devoted to developing the grandeur of the local setting, which critics are quick to point out is inaccurately portrayed as a redwood forest rather than the grassy plain it is in fact. These "slips" give presumed further evidence of Harte's fading memory. The description, however, clearly shows Harte manipulating his memories and materials for an effect to be produced on an audience unfamiliar with the actual geography of California.

The characters and plot, as well as setting of **"Carquinez Woods"** are intensified. Such characters are uncommon even in the context of **"The Outcasts of Poker Flat"** or **"The Luck,"** where local color figures are set against an indigenous background. In England, removed from the demands for local realism, Harte places his highly exaggerated characters before a vivid backdrop. The major characters are least credible; at times they are noble savages living in a pastoral setting. But they swiftly become merely savages living in a tree. As sensational personalities, however, they were eminently successful with English readers.

Although this story touches on the theme of social ostracism, one which appears throughout Harte's work and perhaps relates to his own father's position as the unrecognized son of a wealthy Jew, social inequality here is hidden by a sensational overlay of sentimental love and intrigue. It is quite unlike Harte's harsh and stark treatment of the same theme in **"Three Vagabonds of Trinidad"** (1900).

"Maruja" (1885) marks Harte's commitment to a new audience. Although he had used California-Mexican and Spanish materials earlier, he had never used these materials extensively, nor used a woman of aristocratic Spanish background as the heroine in such an extended plot. The intricacy and length of the plot required certain changes in Harte's technique.

He arouses interest by using a legendary curse, a picturesque heroine (based on Majendra Atherton, a woman known by the Hartes), a down-trodden hero, and an insane villain. The sensationalism of plot, with its dramatic encounters between father and abandoned son, its violent deaths, and its passionate love scenes, contributes to what the *Athenaeum* called a "quite new picture of old Spanish life." Harte manages to use the unwieldy materials well, combining them into fast-moving melodrama. The characters, however, remain stiff and inconsistent, Maruja, for example, shifting abruptly from heartless coquette to tender lover. There is less wrenching of coincidence for effect, although the chance meeting of West and his son strains credibility.

"Maruja" shows Harte moving a step away from the simple tales of the early seventies, from the integrated local color of setting, character, and action, toward the more artificial, albeit more dramatic, presen-

THE

LUCK OF ROARING CAMP,

AND

OTHER SKETCHES.

BY

FRANCIS BRET HARTE.

BOSTON:
FIELDS, OSGOOD, & CO.
1870.

Title page of *The Luck of Roaring Camp.*

tation of picturesque characters in a heightened California setting. Characters are more important and more fully developed, as seen in a comparison of Maruja and Teresa. Serial publication helped to enforce more rigid control of plot and suspense than in earlier, shorter works, and **"Maruja"** moves rapidly and smoothly to its conclusion with all the plot elements integrated.

Comparing Harte stories of the early seventies and mid-eighties, one sees that the tone of the early work, bordering on broad farce and sentimental melodrama, becomes more sophisticated as Harte's lovers move into polite society. Gone are the rude, grizzled miners and tawdry, golden-hearted prostitutes. A tone of refinement pervades all dialogue indicating both Harte's desire to meet his audience on their own level and his awareness of the success of the stories of his countrymen, Howells and James.

By 1889, with American criticism of his catering to English taste on the rise, Harte began, on commission, the first story in a trilogy: **"A Waif of the Plains"** (1889), **"Susy"** (1893), and **"Clarence"** (1895). This trilogy marks the high point of his later career. These three stories reveal a new sense of realism, a controlled use of coincidence and sentiment, and a fully developed grasp of effective dramatic scenes.

The major reviews of **"A Waif"** repeat the trans-Atlantic critical dichotomy. The *Nation* commented that the later work showed "aimless incompleteness." Strachey of the *Spectator* captured the essence of Harte's appeal to the typical English reader.

> In none of his previous work . . . has Bret Harte exhibited more powerfully his rare faculty of bringing a scene vividly before us, or more skillfully his delicate appreciation of character in old and young alike.

Taking his traditional outcast orphan as central figure, Harte convincingly depicts Clarence Brant as a sensitive and independent boy rejected by those on whom he has an honest claim. His youthful enthusiasm and discouragement, however reminiscent of Oliver Twist, are handled with more realism. The setting gives ample local color material; yet, Harte shows restraint by depicting only scenes integral to plot movement. Local setting is carefully used for dramatic and realistic effect, as in the children's early sighting of an Indian for the first time, and later in a child's realistic view of the bloody bodies of savagely massacred whites. There is less coincidental and sensational matter, and greater realism in descriptions of death without the usual pathos and sentimentality. There are faults with the inconsistent characters and incomplete ending, but clearly Harte has developed the technical skill of narration well beyond the level of **"The Luck."**

"Susy" added sub-themes of squatter's rights, problems of Spanish land grants, and Mexican superstitions, and **"Clarence"** incorporated the Civil War as background effectively. Taken together, they indicate that Harte was equipped to meet the demands of novel writing as he had not been in 1875. More interesting, however, is the new realistic treatment of setting and character, the interest in new themes, and the new emotional restraint which diminishes his usual sentimentality.

Harte attempted to return to Scottish material in **"The Heir of the McHulishes"** (1893), and **"A Rose of Glenbogie"** (1894). Once again, the critics rejected his bid for a new subject matter. And, compared with other stories of this period which have an American setting, the Scottish stories do seem flat and artificial. Harte's talent was for action and natural description, not for recording social dialogue. His works are invariably dullest when two characters are placed face to face in a drawing room and required to talk. His style is most effective where it deals with dramatic episodes, characters in action, the humor of situation or event, and broad, sweeping melodrama; all of which Hollywood took from his stories into the silent Western movie and then into our era via television.

Although Harte continued to use the themes of social injustice and racial prejudice, and experimented with combinations of old and new material, only two stories during the last nine years of his career, **"An Ingénue of the Sierras"** (1893), and **"Dick Boyle's Business Card"** (1899), stand out as signifciant in this discussion. In **"Ingénue,"** Harte resurrected Yuba Bill, the irrepressible stage driver of the early stories. The dialect and humor are perfect as the plot moves to a surprise ending of O. Henry smoothness. There are no improbable actions forced upon the reader, who enjoys Bill's silent consternation as he slowly realizes that the ingénue he has been duped into helping is in fact a "she-devil." Harte united character with plot using local color only as a necessary background. Unlike his earlier successes, there is no hint of sentimentality; humor and irony remain the central focus.

"Dick Boyle's Business Card" stands at the end of Harte's career as evidence of the considerable achievement of his mature style. A traveling salesman rides with an Army Commandant's daughter, who is secretly conveying needed arms to a nearby fort. Indians attack while the soon-to-be lovers fall behind the wagon in conversation, and the hero kills an Indian and of course wins the lady. The story succeeds because Harte keeps tight rein on the emotional element. The narrative shifts deftly from the lovers to the Indian attack. The characters and situations are credible. Harte infuses the story with realism and humor and escapes the usual sentimental clichés of his earlier love stories.

We are left with essentially two views of Harte's later writing. One suggests that, " . . . he lived quietly in London, an over-worked hack, scraping the bottom of the California barrel to turn his thousand words a day. . . . " The other states,

> California was all the subject he ever needed rather than the only subject he could think of, and the limitations of his accomplishment are rather those of his art than of the opportunities of his material. . . . His range was small, his heights and depths neither lofty nor profound, his mind not richly stocked with intellectual goods. But he has not been surpassed in what he did best. This is enough to guarantee his permanent place in American letters.

I prefer the second view. It avoids the pitfalls of the "native writer-spontaneous creation" trap and does justice to Harte fairly on his own ground. Early critics overestimated Harte as a literary artist who displayed great originality, sensitivity, and descriptive genius in his early stories, and whose later years were a tragic descent into despair, penury, and hackwork.

Perhaps his English readers assessed him more nearly at his real level. For them, he was not primarily a nationalistic writer; he was a *raconteur*. His fame rested neither on his personality nor on his anticipated novel. In England, free from the constricting demands for accurate local description, he allowed his inclination to bend realistic local color for the purpose of excellent story telling. (pp. 143-51)

Donald E. Glover, "A Reconsideration of Bret Harte's Later Work," in *Western American Literature,* Vol. VIII, No. 3, Fall, 1973, pp. 143-51.

PATRICK D. MORROW
(essay date 1979)

[Morrow is an American educator and critic. Regarding his writings, he commented: "I consider myself primarily a critic—of life, culture, human relationships, and art. To me the primary function of criticism is explication and not attack. My ideal critic strives to make clear what is obscure, not to pass moral judgements from on high. I strive for the personal voice and vision that the shared experience of reader and writer under these terms makes all concerned better able to understand life and cope with it." In the following excerpt, he discusses Harte's literary criticism, distinguishing the ideas and attitudes expressed in his critical writings from those expressed in his fiction.]

Harte's fiction is at least known, if not always well respected, through a handful of perennially anthologized pieces, but his literary criticism is virtually unrecognized. No standard work on American literary criticism even mentions Harte as a critic, and only two aspects of his critical career are at all widely known. Anthologies and handbooks frequently note that Harte was the editor of and book reviewer for the *Overland Monthly* (1868-1871). And, Harte is commonly chided for being one more Victorian too stuffy to appreciate the "barbaric yawp" of Walt Whitman. In 1870, editor Harte rejected Whitman's "Passage to India" as "a poem too long and too abstract," interestingly a view that Roy Harvey Pearce also holds in his highly acclaimed modern study, *The Continuity of American Poetry.*

In addition to numerous reviews, essays and prefaces, Harte wrote critical commentary in letters to a variety of people. He also wrote parodies of topical poems, *Condensed Novels,* and literary advice to aspiring novelists. Harte's parodies and *Condensed Novels,* satiric burlesques of popular writers including Poe, Longfellow, Hugo, Cooper, Dickens, and Reade, were such careful distortions of the originals that they constituted a dimension of literary criticism. An anonymous critic in the *North American Review* of April, 1866, considered Harte "a parodist of such genius that he seems a mirror into which novelists may look and be warned."

There are two diverse explanations that may account for the neglect of this body of literary criticism. First, *all* of Bret Harte's writings have been obscured because a dual stream of literary criticism has developed around him. Criticism of Harte is characterized by a pair of mutually antagonistic types—the amateur enthusiasts and the moral elitists. Both types of critics reduce Harte to mere caricature. The amateur enthusiast simply enjoys sentimentality, which Harte's writings contain in bountiful amounts. Dramatic chronicler of the Mother Lode, Harte moves the amateur enthusiast's powerful feelings to overflowing, for such a person sees Harte's local color as a kind of nationalism of region, making him a Booster with a gift for words. It is hard to take the amateur enthusiast very seriously though, because he wilts when faced with factual knowledge and rational observation. Actually, Harte was much more an Eastern Dude than a Western Rotarian. Previous to his *Overland* stories, Harte's references to miners, the Gold Rush, California in general, and even the sainted San Francisco in particular had been almost totally abusive. He had frequently lambasted the area for its earthquakes and foggy climate, and the people for their barbaric cultural depravity. Harte's experience in, and enthusiasm for the Gold Country was—to be generous—of a limited sort, as his **"How I Went to the Mines"** vividly and hilariously shows. If Harte came to write glowingly of California from being converted to new beliefs, then this should be considered a literary change, not the enthusiastic voice of experience. The amateur enthusiast may tell us much about his own interest in high-pitched drama and tourism, but he gives little insight concerning the complex writer that was Francis Bret Harte.

Conversely, elitist literary critics with ethical and financial investments in editing and explicating "The Great Works" could hardly have conjured anything better than Bret Harte, prototype of the minor author. His writing is usually devoid of paradox, ambiguity, and stylistic complexities, while filled with sentimentality and stereotyped characters, orchestrated in what Mark Twain intimated was a "mincing" style. Worse, Harte wrote volume upon volume for the frank purpose of making money, a veritable strip-mining of his long-gone fame and milieu. Where is that well-wrought novel of personal agony, the fiction of rage and outrage, however suppressed, or the testimony of a labyrinthine vision that would render him at least some redeeming moral value? Nowhere to be found. No wonder Bret Harte is often dismissed as "merely of historical interest" or "of secondary importance." Besides idolizing great writers, moral critics frequently attack "inferior" writers, and in making such clear distinctions they aim to establish *themselves* among the elite. Harte is a set-up for ready-made moral judgments in terms of his life (the money, women, and drinking scandals) and his writing (who *could* seriously rank Harte above Hawthorne, Faulkner, Melville, James, or even Howells?). Perhaps the most devastating single blow to Harte's reputation came with long-time friend Mark Twain's vicious, prolonged, and largely unsubstantiated personal and literary attacks, culminating in the posthumous volume *Mark Twain in Eruption.* So to the moral elitists, sometimes led by self-righteous Twainians, Harte is not worthy of serious study, and anyone who thinks he is, is suspect. Both the elitists and the enthusiasts have a deep commitment to their cause, and Harte serves as unwitting grist.

In addition, much of Harte's criticism—his "other side"—has been scattered, sometimes not even readily identifiable, in obscure California newspapers, defunct magazines, or rare books. Harte never gathered his critical theories, or ways of reading literature into a definitive essay; nor did he make an effort to collect his own criticism. Unlike such contemporaries as William Dean Howells or E. P. Whipple, Harte for most of his life was not an armchair critic, operating as the literary voice of an influential magazine. The expository criticism Harte wrote was typically occasional: book reviews, prefaces, essays on topical figures, or close readings of authors specifically contracted by journals. Harte established no new school in literary theory. While we can associate "beauty" with Poe, "realism" with Howells, "romance" with the early James, and "veritism" with Garland, no such term can be associated with Harte. "Local color," "satire," and "humor" describe Harte's fiction, but his criticism was not written from the vantage point (or precipice) of defending or demanding some particular critical ideal. Schooled in the tradition of journalism and little magazines, Harte was a practical critic. He searched for incompetence and affectation, and stressed a just analysis above judgment by taste.

Harte always thought of himself as a creative writer rather than a literary critic. Yet in letters spanning almost the length of his adult life, he demonstrated a penchant to estimate and evaluate literature, although he typically seemed embarrassed, even apologetic, for this "fault." A Harte letter in 1869 to William Dean Howells concluded a discussion of the latter's fiction by saying: "But what I meant to say before I fell into this attitude of criticism. . . ." Twenty-four years later, Harte wrote a long letter of critical comment to Mrs. Mary Boyd about novels, romances, and "real" characters, and then ended the letter with a highly self-conscious paragraph: "That's all! Please, Ma'am, may I go out and play now? I am very busy today and am dining out, or I should try to tell you all of this by word of mouth."

His contemporaries considered Harte not only a fine writer but a fine critic, and several important authors turned to him for help with their own writings. Ambrose Bierce, Henry George, Joaquin Miller, Pren-

tice Mulford, Artemus Ward, Charles Warren Stoddard, Orpheus C. Kerr, and especially Mark Twain gathered around Harte for literary advice. According to Margaret Duckett, "The lively young writers on 'San Francisco's Literary Frontier' . . . acknowledged Harte as their leader and recognized in him an uncompromising critic of his own work as well as of the work of his companions." (pp. 7-10)

A writer most grateful for help from Harte was Mark Twain. Mark Twain once stated that Bret Harte "trimmed and trained and schooled me patiently until he changed me from an awkward utterer of coarse grotesquenesses to a writer of paragraphs and chapters that have found a certain favor in the eyes of even some of the very decentest people in the land." Sydney J. Krause in *Mark Twain as Critic,* a book which scrupulously avoided overpraising Harte, felt that: "This was the highest tribute Twain paid Harte. In fact, on the matter of help, Twain paid no one as high a tribute, not even Howells. . . . " Harte's criticism also led to friction with Mark Twain. In a letter of November 26, 1870, Mark Twain explained to Charles Webb how Mark and Bret were now "off." But this same letter also mentioned Harte's part in helping to shape the enormous text of the "Quaker City Letters" into *The Innocents Abroad:*

> Harte read all the MS of the "Innocents" & told me what passages, paragraphs & chapters to leave out—& I followed orders strictly. It was a kind thing for Harte to do, & I think I appreciated it. He praised the book so highly that I wanted him to review it *early* for the *Overland,* & help the sale out there.

Besides acting as a strong influence on a number of important writers with whom he came in contact, Harte also in a sense "discovered" Mark Twain, the most important one. Harte's widely-read column in the *Springfield Republican* (1866) singled out Mark Twain's comic brilliance and brought "the Washoe Giant" to the Eastern readers' attention. With frequent mention of Mark Twain and his work in essays, lectures, and reviews, Harte helped establish him as the most important American humorist. Paul Fatout in *Mark Twain on the Lecture Circuit* stated that Harte recognized Mark Twain's greatness "a generation before many critics discovered that Mark Twain was more thoroughly American than Lowell or any other."

In his own time Harte gained considerable recognition as a critic for his reviews in the *Overland Monthly.* Many Eastern journals, including *Putnam's, Knickerbocker, The North American Review,* and even the *Atlantic,* praised the *Overland's* "Current Literature" section for its independent literary judgment and it became known to many as the most worthwhile part of the magazine. Harte's criticism continued to be in some demand throughout the rest of his life. In 1874 he prepared a lecture on **"American Humor"** and in 1882 wrote a long "Preface" to his first collected works. During the later English years he was asked to write critical pieces for publication by such magazines as the *New Review* and *Cornhill.* Although his popularity as a fiction writer far eclipsed his reputation as a critic, Harte continued to write criticism and to act as a literary advisor to several aspiring writers, particularly Mrs. Florence Henniker. In these later years, Harte became an important apologist for popular fiction and drama, writing on Dumas, Anthony Hope, Kipling, and others.

To understand Harte's literary criticism we must first understand something of his fiction, for the two are both interrelated and opposed in some important ways. In Harte's heyday of popularity, the early 1870's, many readers regarded his fiction as a whole new and strange world. Actually, Harte's strange new world was often nothing more than a new set and stage to dramatize the values of his East Coast reading public. Today, most critics believe that Bret Harte's fiction declined in quality as the author got older and farther removed in time and space from California. But this may be a misreading of Harte's work. In "A Reconsideration of Bret Harte's Later Work," Donald E. Glover makes the fascinating assertion, backed by illuminating analysis, that Harte's later stories are *qualitatively* very similar to his earlier ones [see excerpt dated 1973]. If this is true, Harte may not have been writing increasingly inferior art, but creating the same product for a changing audience, one that became increasingly less sophisticated. This could explain why in the 1870's Harte was publishing in the *Atlantic, Lippincott's,* and a handful of the most respected literary journals, but why in 1895 he was for the most part publishing in such slick and conservative illustrateds as *Weekly Graphic, Windsor Magazine, The Strand,* and *Cosmopolitan.* The sophisticated *literati* had moved on to new forms and ideas. Over a thirty-year period Harte's successful, essentially unchanged literary product increasingly appealed to those who wanted familiarity instead of discovery. It is perhaps not coincidental that in the last decade or so of his life Harte published numerous stories in magazines intended for children or adolescent girls.

At this point we need to make some distinctions between high or serious literature and formula fiction, realizing that these two exist on a continuum and are not two separate and mutually exclusive forms. Serious literature is usually considered to be the development and statement of a brilliant individual's consciousness delivered into artistry through great skill with words and mastery of form. Serious literature gives us a philosophical sense of the world, articulates new possibilities and perspectives, and often makes moral statements showing us the difference between good and evil, the genuine and the spurious. Typically, great writers tend to change, to mature and develop; witness

Mark Twain, James and Faulkner. Formula writers tend to repeat the successful performance of a product; witness, to go outside literature, the portraits of Sir Joshua Reynolds or Lawrence Welk's homogenized arrangements of any song his orchestra plays. Formula literature reinforces an audience's values and expectations, often with the skillful manipulation of cliche, stereotype, convention and predictable plot. By means of formula art an audience can find both a justification of its covert and overt values and a dramatization of wishfulfillment. Formula literature often restates old myths in new ways, creating a product that shows how people feel about issues and values at a given time. For example, Peter Bogdanovich took Larry McMurtry's scathing but unpopular anti-small-town novel, *The Last Picture Show,* and turned it into a black and white film of bittersweet 1950's nostalgia that helped articulate a rising national feeling. Most of Harte's stories work in a similar way: They dramatize an audience's feelings and values far more than they show an artist's "world picture" and personal vision. The literary critic, then, must try to uncover in a formula work the why and how of its success. Questions about a formula work's "quality" are secondary, since by definition its audience is convinced that it is "good entertainment."

With this distinction between formula and serious literature in mind, let us examine one of Harte's most famous stories, **"The Luck of Roaring Camp."** **"The Luck"** forms the prototype for Harte's most famous fiction. This story has been attacked, like many of Harte's tales, for being facile, filled with slick language, overdrawn in sentiment, and riddled with cliches. Roy R. Male delivers a typical critical judgment:

> Harte's tone is uneven, insecure, and facile. . . . The reader is apparently intended to take the smooth rhetoric of these comments [about Cherokee Sal] seriously, but after the author's earlier flippancy he cannot. The same is true of the idyllic passages in which Nature sympathizes with the infant. . . . This is what John Ruskin called the pathetic fallacy in a rather slick and sentimental form. Harte strains for effect, as he does again in the ending, with its cliche about the drowning man and its pale euphemisms concerning death.

These statements contain much truth; and, Male is perceptive enough to see the story as an essentially mythic one about a mysterious stranger. But he, following Brooks and Warren in *Understanding Fiction* [see Sources for Further Study] as well as others, measures Harte's fiction against the standard of high art and serious literature, making failure and dismissal inevitable. Justifications of the story as a piece of sophisticated literature have proved to be less convincing than arguments attacking the story. For example, J. R. Boggan sees in this story a narrator of "ironic voice that tells us the story and intrudes to comment freely if somewhat ambiguously on the happenings in Roaring Camp . . . " [See Sources for Further Study]. But there is no indication that Harte saw in the story any ambiguity or irony. On the contrary, there is every indication that he took the sentiment of **"The Luck of Roaring Camp"** most seriously. In a letter dated August 29, 1879, Harte wrote to his wife, Anna: "Do you remember the day you lay sick in San Jose and I read you the story of 'The Luck' and took heart and comfort from your tears over it, and courage to go on and *demand* that it should be put in the magazine (the *Overland*)?"

I am inclined to follow Allen B. Brown who views the story as a Christian parable of redemption. Seeing **"The Luck"** as a "parable" instead of a "short story" explains the lack of realism (except for touches of detail), psychological motivation, and organization around a central conflict. Parables are designed to illustrate truths, reinforce an audience's expectations, or reaffirm an audience's ideal values. They are not typically well-wrought statements from an artistic consciousness. Read as parable, much formula literature may be seen not as "escapist," but as a disguised intensification of typical experience. *Gone With the Wind* has been convincingly interpreted as an uplifting parable about the Great Depression. Similarly, *The Exorcist* and *Jaws* have been interpreted as achieving vast popularity through their veiled commentary on Richard Nixon's Presidential administration. Bret Harte recognized his debt to the parable form in the "Preface" to his first *Collected Works.* There Harte related that he "will, without claiming to be a religious man or a moralist, but simply as an artist, reverently and humbly conform to the rules laid down by a Great Poet who created the parable of the 'Prodigal Son' and the 'Good Samaritan'. . . . But Allen Brown, I believe, mistakes the motif for the message. To me, the **"Luck"** parable, although outfitted with Christian trappings, primarily illustrates the triumph of Victorian civilization over the anarchistic wilderness.

Using a mixture of picturesque and realistic details within a Romantic setting, this particular parable depicts the ultimate nobility of all (white) men, especially in times of crisis. The story is mythic, not realistic, and presents the age-old convention of a Mysterious Stranger as a rescue figure. The characters are carefully stereotyped into external villains and internal saints. Roaring Camp is an outpost, a "city of refugees," and clearly these lawless types need to be saved—regenerated—repatriated to civilization. Cherokee Sal, of course, must succumb to the conventions of nineteenth-century melodrama, but it is a shocker that in 1868 a woman of such "low vartue" would even be "on-stage" for so long. Her role as perverse madonna, who brings forth in miracle and mystery the faithgiving Tommy Luck, flouts decorum and propriety; but in a striking way she reaffirms Harte's keystone belief

that potentially everyone has some good. Complete with creche and adoring bucolics (the miners), Tommy is born as "the pines stopped moaning, the river ceased to rush, and the fire to crackle. It seemed as if Nature had stopped to listen too." Of course this is a cliche bedecked in purple prose—but consider the audience. They want a reconfirmation that their cultural beliefs hold validity. The Luck is sent to redeem men fallen from a worthy civilization, and Harte concentrates not on developing the title figure, but on portraying his effect on other characters.

James Folsom in *The American Western Novel* indignantly berates Harte for turning the story into an "Eastern." Indeed, Folsom is correct. After the Luck arrives, Roaring Camp goes Middle Class. Stumpy turns from a profane miner into a devoted house-husband, lovingly cooing at the infant and calling him "the d—n little cuss." According to Harte, the Luck makes the camp regenerate by returning to civilized ways, as the miners take on parental roles, tidy up sleazy cabins, hold a christening, build new living quarters, and "produce stricter habits of personal cleanliness." Somewhat as in *Snow White and the Seven Dwarfs,* hard work and lyrical adoration create a chosen community during a halcyon summer. The luck is with them; gold claims yield enormous profits, and the "town fathers" want to move in "respectable families in the fall." Says the area's mail carrier: "They've a street up there in Roaring that would lay over any street in Red Dog. They've got vines and flowers round their houses, and they wash themselves twice a day. But they're mighty rough on strangers, and they worship an Ingin baby." . . . These strangers have not reached that "highly civilized" plateau of "Roaring's" denizens who regard the white settlement of the area as an ideal goal, symbolized by the baby. How could anyone ask for a tale that more beautifully renders the myth of Manifest Destiny recovered?

One serious problem with the mysterious stranger story, as Roy R. Male notes in *Types of Short Fiction,* is what to do with the stranger once his function is completed. If he lingers, he may move to the position of protagonist, and the story becomes something else, in the case of **"The Luck of Roaring Camp"** possibly a *bildungsroman.* Such a complication would also change the parable into a more involved piece of fiction. Male, and probably most contemporary readers, considers the story's ending ineptly comic bathos. But to the Victorian audience, with its very different values and expectations, the ending was tinged with high pathos. What Harte regarded as sentiment (deep, valid feelings), we would likely regard as sentimental (gratuitous, sham feeling). Like his mother, Tommy is killed by a literary convention, a flood, which also drowns several miners, including Stumpy and Kentuck. These men receive some redemption in that they died better men than they were before The Luck's arrival. But Harte's real pitch is for repatriation, and is made to the audience. The story should regenerate *us* by providing renewed purpose, optimism, faith, belief in human potential, and if we are Victorian enough, a good cry. Serious literature produces a theme, but parables and Western Union—with luck—deliver messages.

Similarly, **"Tennessee's Partner"** should not be dismissed as merely a mawkish story of implausible events and psychologically invalid characters cohabiting in a world of melodramatic conventions. **"Tennessee's Partner"** is a parable about the power of brotherly love. Harte treats the subject with high pathos and obscures some of the issues the story raises by plating them with his golden rhetoric. He tends to substitute dramatic effect for character development. The brotherly love theme fascinated Harte, and among his other treatments of the partner relationship are **"Barker's Luck," "In the Tules,"** and **"Uncle Jim and Uncle Billy."** The custom of partnership was firmly rooted in mining camp folkways, as contemporary journals and historical studies have shown. Like so many of Harte's tales, **"Tennessee's Partner"** has a realistic basis carefully crafted into a romantic scenario that portrays man's goodness.

Numerous other Bret Harte stories follow this parable formula. **"The Outcasts of Poker Flat"** shows that in a crisis, there is good in even the worst people. This tale has a fair sampling of Harte's famous colorful and picturesque characters, including the slick gambler, the whore with a heart of gold, the ingenue, and "the innocent." **"Outcasts"** has little to do with realistic conventions such as character motivation. Rather, the tale describes the conversion of several characters from evil to good when they are isolated by a blizzard in the High Sierras. **"Brown of Calaveras"** is a parable that demonstrates the nobility of duty over desire. This tale marks the first appearance of Jack Hamlin, whose masculine objectivity and laconic stoicism Harte used in some twenty other works. **"How Santa Claus Came to Simpson's Bar"** is a parable with the theme of "never give up." The town's miners, a rough but chivalrous bunch, contrive to rescue a deprived boy from having a solitary and disillusioning Christmas. On the edge of despair, the boy is emotionally resurrected by Dick Bullen, who, after a torturous mountain ride to a faraway town, returns with a present. Harte's use of parables spanned his career, and they may be found in his children's stories, and even in his few fictional works with settings other than California.

By writing formula stories, however innovatively, Harte frequently boxed himself into the role of satisfying an audience's demand for very predictable and superficial conventions. With overuse, these conventions have become hallmarks of familiar cliches—the happy ending, the sentimental tryst, the gentleman

gambler, the melodramatic incident, the amazing coincidence, and, of course, the whore with a heart of gold. Despite his use of realistic detail, Bret Harte was seldom what *we* would call a truly realistic artist; that is, someone who perceives, with a shock of recognition for the reader, an in-depth view of the calamities, conflicts, incoherencies, and particular characteristics of a people and their area. Rather, Harte saw California in mythic and archetypal terms and wrote parables which showed the Eastern reading public that picturesque Western scenes really were a part of universal experience and truth. (It is an axiom that the farther away from California's shores an audience is, the more likely they will respond favorably to Harte's mythic view of the West.)

It would be wrong, of course, to say that Harte merely wrote simple parables. In addition to literary criticism, his stories sometimes contained social criticism and complex statements about the human condition. Margaret Duckett has noted Harte's concern with race relations. She regards **"Three Vagabonds of Trinidad"** (1900) as a story which condemns the idea of Manifest Destiny, an historical concept which Harte celebrated some thirty years before in **"The Luck of Roaring Camp."** Professor Duckett in an article on Harte's novella, *The Crusade of the Excelsior,* points to Harte's historical perspective in the story to show that he attacks social and racial injustice. The story protests militarism and exploitation, through the Church and government, of the gentle, pastoral Mexicans. The parable has some ironic twists in its obvious moral, "honesty is the best policy," for the individuals who follow this moral in *Crusade* have their rights curtailed by a Church desperately trying to maintain orthodoxy. Another Harte story, **"The Right Eye of the Commander,"** also explores moral and social issues. Harte occasionally ranged far beyond the parable framework in stories about men-women relationships, as Jeffrey F. Thomas's article "Bret Harte and the Power of Sex" so clearly demonstrates. (pp. 12-20)

However much Harte emphasized the formula parable or masked his true meanings, a definite schism is apparent between Harte the critical thinker and Harte the story writer, profitably producing for a philistine audience. In several stories Harte expresses not only his characteristic liberal and humanitarian beliefs, but criticism against social practices, criticism directed *at* his audience. Furthermore, Harte's stories contain virtually no direct autobiographical incidents. Perhaps this omission was simply Victorian diffidence, but as numerous letters and the recollections of others reveal, Harte led a far more interesting life than most people. Like his idol, Longfellow, Harte may have found his experiences at odds with his ideals, and chose to portray a vision of man's humanity to man in the hope that with enough good examples, this ideal would become truth.

Whatever the case, readers should notice in Bret Harte's fiction the consistent use of a third person narrator, not merely to establish a sense of distance, or as author intrusion, but as authorial control. Harte's narrators manipulate and withhold information to the point of condescension. At his most extreme, Harte's narrators separate themselves so much from their story that a distinct archness divides action, reader and narrator. Harte's narrator not only tells a story but interprets it—giving his version, obscuring or emphasizing material, analyzing the scene, characters and audience with a penetrating sophistication.

Occasionally, Harte places directly in the story some literary analysis, as happens in **"Who Was My Quiet Friend?"** where a madman quotes his favorite author, Charles Dickens. Or, in **"A Ward of the Golden Gate,"** Harte portrays a humorously strained version of *Uncle Tom's Cabin.* He even delves into self-satire in **"Jinny,"** a story on the order of **"The Luck of Roaring Camp"** except the birth of a mule substitutes for the birth of a child. More frequently Harte can be seen in the role of author as director, manipulating character and scene in the third person. . . . Sometimes Harte's narrator moves to the first person, as in **"The Man on the Beach."** "Whether this arose from a fear of reciprocal inquiry and interest, or from the profound indifference before referred to, I cannot say." But even here, the narrator is not the action's central figure. Other stories, such as **"Maruja,"** contain footnotes, Harte stressing here the validity of his factual data, the reliability of his narrator, sometimes disguised as a sensitive, "literary" country editor. Other stories, **"The Heritage of Dedlow Marsh"** or **"A First Family of Tasajara,"** for example, reveal subtle, covert narrative manipulation.

The narrator's high diction too stresses the distance between himself and the story. Harte sees the function of the narrator and literary-cultural critic as one, a joining of roles sometimes further emphasized by the narrator's comments about literature. The use of a narrator who assumes the *persona* of a literary critic suggests Harte's commitment to this perspective. My purpose here has been to suggest *types* of narrative hold, not list numerous examples, although this would be easy enough to do as anyone who has read much Harte fiction knows very well. In all his writings, Harte is at his best and most comfortable posing as the concerned and witty man of taste evaluating these unusual manifestations of American culture, instructing his audience as to their meaning and value.

The weaknesses of Bret Harte's short stories point to some strengths in his literary criticism. Harte's stories are typically schematic rather than visionary, with a strong sense of authorial control or narrative hold. This, taken with his use of high diction and dense metaphors frequently obscures or hides meaning. But in his criticism, the narrator as detached man of taste becomes the voice of an objective, logical critic, an explicator with a talent for insightful, imaginative phrases. As a critic, Harte had more freedom than in his role of formula fiction writer; he could analyze much more objectively and to his own taste instead of catering to the demands of an audience and being bound by formulaic conventions. . . . [Critic] Harte roundly condemned sentimentality, a lack of realism, and weak characterization, all faults of his own fiction. Unlike his typical fiction, Harte's criticism is full of inquiry and experimentation. (pp. 21-3)

Patrick D. Morrow, in his *Bret Harte: Literary Critic,* Bowling Green State University Popular Press, 1979, 193 p.

SOURCES FOR FURTHER STUDY

Barnett, Linda D. "Bret Harte: An Annotated Bibliography of Secondary Comment." *American Literary Realism* 5, No. 3-4 (Summer-Fall 1972): 189-484.

> Comprehensive annotated bibliography of writings about Harte.

Boggan, J. R. "The Regeneration of 'Roaring Camp'." *Nineteenth-Century Fiction* 22, No. 3 (December 1967): 271-80.

> Questions the standard Christian reading of "The Luck of Roaring Camp," finding its use of Christian symbolism essentially ironic.

Brooks, Cleanth, and Warren, Robert Penn. "Tennessee's Partner." In their *Understanding Fiction*, pp. 205-20. New York: Appleton-Century-Crofts, 1943.

> Discusses "Tennessee's Partner," finding Harte's portrayal both unconvincing and sentimental.

Duckett, Margaret. "The Question of Influence." In her *Mark Twain and Bret Harte*, pp. 312-32. Norman: University of Oklahoma Press, 1964.

> Traces the influence of Harte's fiction on the writings of Mark Twain and later American authors.

Quinn, Arthur Hobson. "Bret Harte and the Fiction of Moral Contrast." In his *American Fiction: An Historical and Critical Survey*, pp. 232-242. New York: Appleton-Century-Crofts, 1936.

> Praises Harte's artistry as a fiction writer, particularly his sympathetic portrayal of disreputable characters.

Quinn states that Harte "remains a world artist not merely because of his depiction of the gold rush of California, but because he discovered that other, richer vein, the sympathy which even the most puritanical feel for the sinner who leads them vicariously into the paths of adventure which they have shunned, but of which they love to read in the pages of fiction."

Stewart, George R. *Bret Harte: Argonaut and Exile.* Port Washington, New York: Kennikat Press, 1935, 385 p.
Considered the definitive account of Harte's life.

Nathaniel Hawthorne

1804-1864

American novelist, short story writer, and essayist.

INTRODUCTION

*H*awthorne is considered one of the greatest American fiction writers. His novel *The Scarlet Letter* (1850), with its balanced structure, polished prose style, and skillful use of symbols, is acknowledged as a classic of American literature, and several of his short stories are ranked as masterpieces of the genre. Hawthorne's works reflect his dark vision of human nature, frequently portraying Puritanism as an expression of humanity's potential for cruelty, obsession, and intolerance. His literary style—particularly his use of symbolism and his fascination with the macabre—exerted a marked influence upon the development of short fiction in the United States during the nineteenth century. Along with Edgar Allan Poe, Hawthorne is regarded as one of the principal architects of the modern American short story.

Biographers view Hawthorne's preoccupation with Puritanism as an outgrowth of his background. Born in Salem, Massachusetts, he was descended from a line of staunch Puritans that included William Hathorne (Hawthorne himself added the "w" to the family name), an ardent defender of the faith who participated in the persecution of Quakers during the seventeenth century, and his son John Hathorne, a presiding judge at the infamous Salem witch trials. This melancholy heritage was augmented by the premature death of Hawthorne's father, which left the four-year-old Nathaniel in the care of his grief-stricken and reclusive mother. Spending much time alone during his childhood, Hawthorne developed an intensely introspective nature and eventually came to believe that the misfortunes of his immediate family were the result of divine retribution for the sins of his ancestors.

An avid reader with a taste for John Bunyan and Edmund Spenser, Hawthorne began to write while attending Bowdoin College, where he met Franklin

Pierce and Henry Wadsworth Longfellow. After graduation, Hawthorne returned to his mother's home in Salem where he passed a twelve-year literary apprenticeship, occasionally publishing unsigned tales in journals but more often than not destroying his work. He published a novel, *Fanshawe: A Tale* (1828), but later withdrew it from circulation and burned every available copy. Many of Hawthorne's early pieces appeared in *The Token,* an annual anthology published by Samuel Goodrich, during the early 1830s. Goodrich played a major role in the development of the young author's career, naming him editor of the *American Magazine of Useful and Entertaining Knowledge* in 1836 and arranging for the publication of his first collection of short stories, *Twice-Told Tales* (1837), one year later. *Twice-Told Tales* contains historical sketches and stories displaying the dark themes and skillful technique that would characterize his later work. According to Poe, who was greatly impressed by these early stories, the collection made of Hawthorne "*the* example, *par excellence,* in this country, of the privately-admired and publicly-unappreciated man of genius." Although lavishly praised by critics, the volume sold poorly, and an enlarged edition issued in 1842 fared no better. This pattern of critical appreciation and public neglect continued throughout Hawthorne's literary career, and he was forced to occupy a series of minor governmental posts in order to supplement the meager income from his writings.

Soon after the publication of *Twice-Told Tales,* Hawthorne became engaged to Sophia Peabody, a neighbor who had admired his work. Hoping to find a permanent home for himself and Sophia, Hawthorne joined Brook Farm in 1841. An experimental utopian community outside of Boston, Brook Farm was intended to be an agricultural cooperative that would provide its members—through the principle of shared labor—with a living while allowing them leisure for artistic and literary pursuits. The community was founded by the literary critic and social reformer George Ripley, and various prominent authors expressed interest in the scheme, including Margaret Fuller, Ralph Waldo Emerson, Theodore Parker, and Orestes Brownson. Hawthorne's enthusiasm for the venture quickly wore off, however. He left after six months, convinced that intellectual endeavor was incompatible with hard physical exertion. Although his literary efforts at Brook Farm proved a failure, Hawthorne kept careful records of his time there in his journals and letters; these later bore fruit in the plot, physical settings, and characters of *The Blithedale Romance* (1852).

In July of 1842, Hawthorne married Sophia, and the couple moved into a large house in Concord, Massachusetts, known locally as the "Old Manse." There Hawthorne wrote many of the pieces included in his next collection of stories and sketches, *Mosses from an Old Manse* (1846). Critics agree, however, that Hawthorne's most fruitful period of short story production had already ended by this time. Although two of his most highly regarded works, "Young Goodman Brown" and "Roger Malvin's Burial," first appeared in *Mosses from an Old Manse,* they had been written more than a decade earlier.

From 1839 to 1840, Hawthorne was employed as a salt and coal measurer in the Boston Custom House; he later held the position of Surveyor in the Salem Custom House from 1846 to 1849. His abrupt dismissal from that post, when Zachary Taylor's administration came to power, left Hawthorne poor and embittered, though free to devote himself fully to writing.

Troubled about money and saddened by the recent death of his mother, Hawthorne began a novel that he had brooded over for years. *The Scarlet Letter,* considered by many to be a culmination of the best characteristics of his earlier tales, brought Hawthorne recognition and some financial security, despite the resentment of his Salem neighbors, who took the sardonic "Custom House" introduction to the book as a criticism of their community. Critics have long acknowledged *The Scarlet Letter* as Hawthorne's greatest achievement and as a seminal work in American literature. His perceptive portrayal of the novel's protagonists set the standard for psychological realism for generations of writers. Through his depiction of the consequences of Hester Prynne and Arthur Dimmesdale's adulterous union, Hawthorne explored the historical, social, theological, and emotional ramifications of sin, concealment, and guilt. Scholars characterize his handling of the pair's defiance of the Puritan community's laws of behavior as one of literature's most powerful treatments of the theme of the individual versus society. In addition, many praise the novel's intricate structure and evocative symbolism.

The Hawthornes, with their son and two daughters, moved to Lenox where they befriended Herman Melville, who dedicated his novel *Moby Dick* to Hawthorne. In the next several years, Hawthorne wrote *The House of the Seven Gables* (1851), set in contemporary New England and treating the theme of ancestral sin. *The Blithedale Romance,* also written at this time and based on Hawthorne's experience at Brook Farm, dealt explicitly with the vanity of human pride.

In 1852, Hawthorne wrote a campaign biography for Franklin Pierce who later appointed him consul to Liverpool. Hawthorne spent three years in England and two in Italy, where he wrote *The Marble Faun; or, The Romance of Monte Beni* (1860), the last of his novels. *The Marble Faun* addresses Hawthorne's common theme of the effects of sin and guilt on the human psyche. Unique among his novels in its European setting, *The Marble Faun*—which Hawthorne called "my own moonshiny Romance"—evokes the splendor of

Rome's historical and legendary past, its artistic treasures, and the blended grandeur and squalor of life there in the mid-nineteenth century. Although the book received generally good reviews, its structure, language and symbolism, which in Hawthorne's other work had been subtle and natural, appeared to some critics to be stilted and poorly integrated.

The last years of Hawthorne's life were marked by declining health and creativity. He continued to write and to struggle with the themes of ancestral sin and mortality, but was unable to translate his thoughts into fiction. The works which occupied his last years, published posthumously, are mere fragments which show little of Hawthorne's former power. He is nonetheless considered among the greatest American authors. By projecting profound moral concerns on a distinctly American background, Hawthorne sought to interpret the spiritual history of a nation. Today, as strongly as in his own time, the comment made about him by Emily Dickinson applies: he "appalls, entices."

(For further information about Hawthorne's life and works, see *Concise Dictionary of American Literary Biography, 1640-1865; Dictionary of Literary Biography*, Vol. 1 *The American Renaissance in New England; Nineteenth-Century Literature Criticism*, Vols. 2, 10, 17, 25; *Short Story Criticism*, Vol. 3; and *Yesterday's Authors of Books for Children*, Vol. 2.)

CRITICAL COMMENTARY

E. P. WHIPPLE

(essay date 1860)

[Whipple was a prominent American critic and biographer. In the following excerpt, he discusses the progression of Hawthorne's literary tone and style.]

The style [of Hawthorne's early books], while it had a purity, sweetness, and grace which satisfied the most fastidious and exacting taste, had, at the same time, more than the simplicity and clearness of an ordinary school-book. But though the subjects and the style were thus popular, there was something in the shaping and informing spirit which failed to awaken interest, or awakened interest without exciting delight. Misanthropy, when it has its source in passion,—when it is fierce, bitter, fiery, and scornful,— . . . this is always popular; but a misanthropy which springs from insight,—a misanthropy which is lounging, languid, sad, and depressing,— . . . this is a misanthropy which can expect no wide recognition; and it would be vain to deny that traces of this kind of misanthropy are to be found in Hawthorne's earlier, and are not altogether absent from his later works. He had spiritual insight, but it did not penetrate to the sources of spiritual joy; and his deepest glimpses of truth were calculated rather to sadden than to inspire. A blandly cynical distrust of human nature was the result of his most piercing glances into the human soul. He had humor, and sometimes humor of a delicious kind; but this sunshine of the soul was but sunshine breaking through or lighting up a sombre and ominous cloud. There was also observable in his earlier stories a lack of vigor, as if the power of his nature had been impaired by the very process which gave depth and excursiveness to his mental vision. . . . As psychological portraits of morbid natures, his delineations of character might have given a purely intellectual satisfaction; but there was audible, to the delicate ear, a faint and muffled growl of personal discontent, which showed they were not mere exercises of penetrating imaginative analysis, but had in them the morbid vitality of a despondent mood.

Yet, after admitting these peculiarities, nobody who is now drawn to the **"Twice-Told Tales,"** from his interest in the later romances of Hawthorne, can fail to wonder a little at the limited number of readers they attracted on their original publication. For many of these stories are at once a representation of early New-England life and a criticism on it. They have much of the deepest truth of history in them. . . . In the **"Prophetic Pictures," "Fancy's Show-Box," "The Great Carbuncle," "The Haunted Mind,"** and **"Edward Fane's Rose-Bud,"** there are flashes of moral insight, which light up, for the moment, the darkest recesses of the individual mind; and few sermons reach to the depth of thought and sentiment from which these seemingly airy sketches draw their sombre life. . . . Interspersed with serious histories and moralities like these, are others which embody the sweet and playful, though still thoughtful and slightly saturnine action of Hawthorne's mind,—like **"The Seven Vagabonds," "Snow-Flakes," "The Lily's Quest," "Mr. Higgenbotham's Catastrophe."** . . .(pp. 615-16)

The **"Mosses from an Old Manse"** are intellectually and artistically an advance from the **"Twice-Told Tales."** . . . In description, narration, allegory, humor, reason, fancy, subtilty, inventiveness, they exceed the best productions of Addison; but they want Addison's

Principal Works

Fanshawe: A Tale (novel) 1828

Twice-Told Tales (sketches and short stories) 1837

Twice-Told Tales (second series) (sketches and short stories) 1842

Mosses from an Old Manse (sketches and short stories) 1846

The Scarlet Letter (novel) 1850

The House of the Seven Gables (novel) 1851

The Snow Image and Other Tales (short stories) 1851

The Blithedale Romance (novel) 1852

Life of Franklin Pierce (biography) 1852

A Wonder-Book for Girls and Boys (short stories) 1852

Tanglewood Tales for Girls and Boys: Being a Second Wonder-Book (short stories) 1853

The Marble Faun: or, The Romance of Monte Beni (novel) 1860; published In England as Transformation: or, The Romance of Monte Beni, 1860

Our Old Home: A Series of Sketches (essays) 1863

Passages from the American Note-Books of Nathaniel Hawthorne (journal) 1868

Passages from the English Note-Books of Nathaniel Hawthorne (journal) 1870

Passages from the French and Italian Note-Books of Nathaniel Hawthorne (journal) 1872

Septimius Felton; or, The Elixir of Life (unfinished novel) 1872

The Dolliver Romance and Other Pieces (unfinished novel) 1876

Doctor Grimshawe's Secret (unfinished novel) 1883

---

sensuous contentment and sweet and kindly spirit. . . . The defect of the serious stories is, that character is introduced, not as thinking, but as the illustration of thought. The persons are ghostly, with a sad lack of flesh and blood. They are phantasmal symbols of a reflective and imaginative analysis of human passions and aspirations. The dialogue, especially, is bookish, as though the personages knew their speech was to be printed, and were careful of the collocation and rhythm of their words. The author throughout is evidently more interested in his large, wide, deep, indolently serene, and lazily sure and critical view of the conflict of ideas and passions, than he is with the individuals who embody them. He shows moral insight without moral earnestness. He cannot contract his mind to the patient delineation of a moral individual, but attempts to use individuals in order to express the last results of patient moral perception. Young Goodman Brown and Roger Malvin are not persons; they are the mere, loose, personal expression of subtle thinking. **"The Celestial Railroad," "The Procession of Life," "Earth's Holo-**caust," **"The Bosom Serpent,"** indicate thought of a character equally deep, delicate, and comprehensive, but the characters are ghosts of men rather than substantial individualities. . . . [In **"The Scarlet Letter,"** Hawthorne] first made his genius efficient by penetrating it with passion. This book forced itself into attention by its inherent power. . . . (p. 617)

Two characteristics of Hawthorne's genius stand plainly out, in the conduct and characterization of the romance of **"The Scarlet Letter,"** which were less obviously prominent in his previous works. The first relates to his subordination of external incidents to inward events. . . . Hawthorne relies almost entirely for the interest of his story on what is felt and done within the minds of his characters. Even his most picturesque descriptions and narratives are only one-tenth matter to nine-tenths spirit. The results that follow from one external act of folly or crime are to him enough for an Iliad of woes. (p. 618)

The second characteristic of his genius is connected with the first. With his insight of individual souls he combines a far deeper insight of the spiritual laws which govern the strangest aberrations of individual souls. But it seems to us that his mental eye, keen-sighted and far-sighted as it is, overlooks the merciful modifications of the austere code whose pitiless action it so clearly discerns. In his long and patient brooding over the spiritual phenomena of Puritan life, it is apparent, to the least critical observer, that he has imbibed a deep personal antipathy to the Puritanic ideal of character; but it is no less apparent that his intellect and imagination have been strangely fascinated by the Puritanic idea of justice. . . . Throughout **"The Scarlet Letter"** we seem to be following the guidance of an author who is personally good-natured, but intellectually and morally relentless.

"The House of the Seven Gables," . . . while it has less concentration of passion and tension of mind than **"The Scarlet Letter,"** includes a wider range of observation, reflection, and character; and the morality, dreadful as fate, which hung like a black cloud over the personages of the previous story, is exhibited in more relief. Although the book has no imaginative creation equal to little Pearl, it still contains numerous examples of characterization at once delicate and deep. . . . The whole representation, masterly as it is, considered as an effort of intellectual and imaginative power, would still be morally bleak, were it not for the sunshine and warmth radiated from the character of Phoebe. In this delightful creation Hawthorne for once gives himself up to homely human nature, and has succeeded in delineating a New-England girl, cheerful, blooming, practical, affectionate, efficient, full of innocence and happiness. . . . (pp. 618–19)

[In **"The House of the Seven Gables"**] there is also more humor than in any of his other works. It peeps out, even in the most serious passages, in a kind of demure rebellion against the fanaticism of his remorseless intelligence. In the description of the Pyncheon poultry, which we think unexcelled by anything in Dickens for quaintly fanciful humor, the author seems to indulge in a sort of parody on his own doctrine of the hereditary transmission of family qualities. (p. 619)

[It] is necessary to say a few words on the seeming separation of Hawthorne's genius from his will. He has none of that ability which enabled Scott and enables Dickens to force their powers into action, and to make what was begun in drudgery soon assume the character of inspiration. Hawthorne cannot thus use his genius; his genius always uses him. This is so true, that he often succeeds better in what calls forth his personal antipathies than in what calls forth his personal sympathies. His life of General Pierce, for instance, is altogether destitute of life; yet in writing it he must have exerted himself to the utmost, as his object was to urge the claims of an old and dear friend to the Presidency of the Republic. The style, of course, is excellent, as it is impossible for Hawthorne to write bad English, but the genius of the man has deserted him. General Pierce, whom he loves, he draws so feebly, that one doubts, while reading the biography, if such a man exists. . . . (pp. 619-20)

[In **"The Wonder-Book"** and **"Tanglewood Tales"**] Hawthorne's genius distinctly appears, and appears in its most lovable, though not in its deepest form. These delicious stories, founded on the mythology of Greece, were written for children, but they delight men and women as well. . . .

[**"The Blithedale Romance"**] is far from being so pleasing a performance as **"Tanglewood Tales,"** yet it very much better illustrates the operation, indicates the quality, and expresses the power, of the author's genius. His great books appear not so much created by him as through him. They have the character of revelations,—he, the instrument, being often troubled with the burden they impose on his mind. His profoundest glances into individual souls are like the marvels of clairvoyance. It would seem, that, in the production of such a work as **"The Blithedale Romance,"** his mind had hit accidentally, as it were, on an idea or fact mysteriously related to some morbid sentiment in the inmost core of his nature, and connecting itself with numerous scattered observations of human life, lying unrelated in his imagination. . . . On the depth and intensity of the mental mood, the force of the fascination it exerts over him, and the length of time it holds him captive, depend the solidity and substance of the individual characterizations. In this way Miles Coverdale, Hollingsworth, Westervelt, Zenobia, and Priscilla become real persons to the mind which has called them into being. He knows every secret and watches every motion of their souls, yet is, in a measure, independent of them, and pretends to no authority by which he can alter the destiny which consigns them to misery or happiness. They drift to their doom by the same law by which they drifted across the path of his vision. (p. 620)

"The Marble Faun" [his current book], which must, on the whole, be considered the greatest of his works, proves that his genius has widened and deepened in [the interval since **"The Blithedale Romance"** was published]. . . . The most obvious excellence of the work is the vivid truthfulness of its descriptions of Italian life, manners, and scenery; and, considered merely as a record of a tour in Italy, it is of great interest and attractiveness. The opinions on Art, and the special criticisms on the masterpieces of architecture, sculpture, and painting, also possess a value of their own. The story might have been told, and the characters fully represented, in one-third of the space devoted to them, yet description and narration are so artfully combined that each assists to give interest to the other. . . .

[Hawthorne writes] the sweetest, simplest, and clearest English that ever has been made the vehicle of equal depth, variety, and subtilty of thought and emotion. His mind is reflected in his style as a face is reflected in a mirror; and the latter does not give back its image with less appearance of effort than the former. His excellence consists not so much in using common words as in making common words express uncommon things. (p. 621)

In regard to the characterization and plot of **"The Marble Faun,"** there is room for widely varying opinions. Hilda, Miriam, and Donatello will be generally received as superior in power and depth to any of Hawthorne's previous creations of character; Donatello, especially, must be considered one of the most original and exquisite conceptions in the whole range of romance; but the story in which they appear will seem to many an unsolved puzzle, and even the tolerant and interpretative "gentle reader" will be troubled with the unsatisfactory conclusion. It is justifiable for a romancer to sting the curiosity of his readers with a mystery, only on the implied obligation to explain it at last; but this story begins in mystery only to end in mist. . . . The central idea of the story, the necessity of sin to convert such a creature as Donatello into a moral being, is also not happily illustrated in the leading event. When Donatello kills the wretch who malignantly dogs the steps of Miriam, all readers think that Donatello committed no sin at all; and the reason is, that Hawthorne has deprived the persecutor of Miriam of all human attributes, made him an allegorical representation of one of the most fiendish forms of unmixed evil, so that we welcome his destruction with something of the same feeling with which, in following the allegory of Spenser or Bunyan, we rejoice in the hero's victory over the Blatant Beast or Giant Despair. Conceding, however, that Donatello's act was murder, and not "justifiable homicide," we are still not sure that the author's conception of his nature and of the change caused in his nature by that act, are carried out with a felicity corresponding to the original conception.

In the first [section], and in the early part of the second, the author's hold on his design is comparatively firm, but it somewhat relaxes as he proceeds, and in the end it seems almost to escape from his grasp. Few can be satisfied with the concluding chapters, for the reason that nothing is really concluded. (pp. 621-22)

In intellect and imagination, in the faculty of discerning spirits and detecting laws, we doubt if any living novelist is [Hawthorne's] equal; but his genius, in its creative action, has been heretofore attracted to the dark rather than the bright side of the interior life of humanity, and the geniality which evidently is in him has rarely found adequate expression. In the many works which he may still be expected to write, it is to be hoped that his mind will lose some of its sadness of tone without losing any of its subtilty and depth. . . . (p. 622)

E. P. Whipple, in an originally unsigned essay titled "Nathaniel Hawthorne," in *The Atlantic Monthly,* Vol. V, No. XXXI, May, 1860, pp. 614-22.

ARTHUR SYMONS

(essay date 1904)

[Symons was a British poet and critic. In the excerpt below, he critiques Hawthorne's depiction of the soul.]

With Tolstoi, [Hawthorne] is the only novelist of the soul, and he is haunted by what is obscure, dangerous, and on the confines of good and evil; by what is abnormal, indeed, if we are to accept human nature as a thing set within responsible limits, and conscious of social relations. . . . [Finding] the soul, in its essence, so intangible, so mistlike, so unfamiliar with the earth, he lays hold on what to him is the one great reality, sin, in order that he may find out something definite about the soul, in its most active, its most interesting, manifestations. (p. 52)

All Hawthorne's stories are those of persons whom some crime, or misunderstood virtue, or misfortune, has set by themselves, or in a worse companionship of solitude. Hester Prynne "stood apart from moral interests, yet close beside them, like a ghost that revisits the familiar fireside, and can no longer make itself seen or felt." The link between Hester and Arthur Dimmesdale, between Miriam and Donatello, was "the

iron link of mutual crime, which neither he nor she could break. Like all other sins, it brought along with it its obligations." Note how curious the obsession by which Hawthorne can express the force of the moral law, the soul's bond with itself, only through the consequences of the breaking of that law! And note, also, with how perfect a sympathy he can render the sensation itself, what is exultant, liberating, in a strong sin, not yet become one's companion and accuser. "For, guilt has its rapture, too. The foremost result of a broken law is ever an ecstatic sense of freedom." (pp. 53-4)

[Hawthorne] is interested only in those beings, of exceptional temperament or destiny, who are alone in the world; and yet what he represents is the necessity and the awfulness, not the pride or the choice, of isolation. . . . His men and women are no egoists, to whom isolation is a delight; they suffer from it, they try in vain to come out of the shadow and sit down with the rest of the world in the sunshine. Something ghostly in their blood sets them wandering among shadows, but they long to be merely human, they would come back if they could, and their tragedy is to find some invisible and impenetrable door shut against them. (p. 55)

[Hawthorne's attitude was] that of a sensitive but morbidly clear-sighted friend, or of a physician, affectionately observant of the disease which he cannot cure. It was his sympathy with the soul that made him so watchful of its uneasy moods, its strange adventures, especially those which remove it furthest from the daylight and perhaps nearest to its true nature and proper abode. (pp. 55-6)

To Hawthorne it was the wonder and the mystery which gave its meaning to life, and to paint life without them was like painting nature without atmosphere. Only, in his endeavour to evoke this atmosphere, he did not always remember that, if it had any meaning at all, it was itself a deeper reality. And so his weakness is seen in a persistent desire to give an air of miracle to ordinary things, which gain nothing by becoming improbable; as in the sentence which describes Hester's return to her cottage, at the end of **"The Scarlet Letter"**: "In all these years it had never once been unlocked; but either she unlocked it, or the decaying wood and iron yielded to her hand, or she glided shadowlike through these impediments—and, at all events, went in." His books are full of this futile buzzing of fancy; and it is not only in the matter of style that he too often substitutes fancy for imagination.

Hawthorne never quite fully realised the distinction between symbol and allegory, or was never long able to resist the allegorising temptation. Many of his shorter stories are frankly allegories, and are among the best of their kind, such as **"Young Goodman Brown,"** or **"The Minister's Black Veil."** But, in all his work, there is an attempt to write two meanings at once, to turn what should be a great spiritual reality into a literal and barren figure of speech. He must always broider a visible badge on every personage: Hester's "A," Miss Hepzibah's scowl, the birthmark, the furry ears of the Faun. In all this there is charm, surprise, ingenuity; but is it quite imagination, which is truth, and not a decoration rather than a symbol? He passes, indeed, continually from one to the other, and is now crude and childish, as in the prattle about the Faun's furry ears, and now subtly creative, as in the figure of the child Pearl, who is in the true sense a living symbol. . . . He has used the belief in witchcraft with admirable effect, the dim mystery which clings about haunted houses, the fantastic gambols of the soul itself, under what seem like the devil's own promptings. But he must direct his imps as if they were marionettes, and, as he lets us see the wires jerking, is often at the pains to destroy his own illusion. (pp. 56-7)

[Hawthorne] is at home in all those cloudy tracts of the soul's regions in which most other novelists go astray; he finds his way there, not by sight, but by feeling, like the blind. He responds to every sensation of the soul; morbidly, as people say: that is, with a consciousness of how little anything else matters.

Yet is there not some astringent quality lacking in Hawthorne, the masculine counterpart of what was sensitively feminine in him? . . . No one has ever rendered subtler sensations with a more delicate precision. . . . Yet there is much in his sentiment and in his reflection which is the more feminine part of sensitiveness, and which is no more than a diluted and prettily coloured commonplace. That geniality of reflection, of which we find so much in **"The House of the Seven Gables,"** is really a lack of intellectual backbone, a way of disguising any too austere truth from his sensibilities. The two chapters, in that often beautiful and delightful book, written around Judge Pyncheon, as he sits dead in his chair, show how lamentable a gap existed in the intellectual taste of Hawthorne. (pp. 57-8)

His style, at its best so delicately woven, so subdued and harmonious in colour, has gone threadbare in patches; something in its gentlemanly ease has become old-fashioned, has become genteel. There are moments when he reminds us of Charles Lamb, but in Lamb nothing has faded, or at most a few too insistent pleasantries: the salt in the style has preserved it. There is no salt in the style of Hawthorne. Read that charming preface to the **"Mosses from an Old Manse,"** so full of country quiet, with a music in it like the gentle, monotonous murmur of a country stream. Well, at every few pages the amateur peeps out, anxiously trying to knit together his straying substance with a kind of arch simplicity. In the stories, there is rarely a narrative which has not drifted somewhere a little out of his control; and of the novels, only **"The Scarlet Letter"** has any sort of firmness of texture; and we have only to set it beside a really well-constructed novel, beside "Ma-

dame Bovary," for instance, to see how loosely, after all, it is woven. . . . [Hawthorne seems incapable of looking at things] without thinking of something else, some fancy or moral, which he must fit into the frame or the cube, or else draped around it, in the form of a veil meant for ornament. Yet, in all this, and sometimes by a felicity in some actual weakness, turned, like a woman's, into a fragile and pathetic grace, there is a continual weaving of intricate mental cobwebs, and an actual creation of that dim and luminous atmosphere in which they are best seen. And, in the end, all that is finest in Hawthorne seems to unite in the creation of atmosphere. (pp. 59-60)

Something unsubstantial, evasive, but also something intellectually dissatisfied, always inquiring, in his mind, set Hawthorne spinning [his] arabesques of the soul, in which the fantastic element may be taken as a note of interrogation. Seeing always "a grim identity between gay things and sorrowful ones," he sets a masquerade before us, telling us many of the secrets hidden behind the black velvet, but letting us see no more than the glimmer of eyes, and the silent or ambiguous lips.

Hawthorne's romances are not exactly (he never wished them to be) novels, but they are very nearly poems. And they are made, for the most part, out of material which seems to lend itself singularly ill to poetic treatment. In the preface to **"Transformation"** he says: "No author, without a trial, can be conscious of the difficulty of writing a romance about a country where there is no shadow, no antiquity, no mystery, no picturesque and gloomy wrong." Yet this shadow, this antiquity, this mystery, this picturesque and gloomy wrong, is what he has found or created in America. . . . [Each of his novels] is not so much a narrative which advances, as a canvas which is covered; or, in his own figure, a tapestry "into which are woven some airy and unsubstantial threads, intermixed with others twisted out of the commonest stuff of human existence." A Puritan in fancy dress, he himself passes silently through the masquerade, as it startles some quiet street in New England. Where what is fantastic in Poe remains geometrical, in Hawthorne it is always, for good and evil, moral. It decorates, sometimes plays pranks with, a fixed belief, a fundamental religious seriousness; and has thus at least an immovable centre to whirl from. And, where fancy passes into imagination, and a world, not quite what seems to us the real world, grows up about us with a new, mental kind of reality, it is as if that arrangement or transposition of actual things with which poetry begins had taken place already. I do not know any novelist who has brought into prose fiction so much of the atmosphere of poetry, with so much of the actual art of composition of the poet. It is a kind of poetry singularly pure, delicate, and subtle, and, at its best, it has an almost incalculable fascination, and some not quite realised, but insensibly compelling, white magic. (pp. 60-2)

Arthur Symons, "Nathaniel Hawthorne," in his *Studies in Prose and Verse*, E. P. Dutton & Co., 1904, pp. 52-62.

W. C. BROWNELL
(essay date 1909)

[Brownell was an American critic and biographer. In the excerpt below, he discusses Hawthorne's "unconquerable reserve" and its incidence in allegory, characterization, and setting in his works.]

[Hawthorne's works] are thoroughly original, quite without literary derivation upon which much of our literature leans with such deferential complacence. Even the theme of many of them—the romance of Puritan New England—was Hawthorne's discovery. They are works of pure literature and therefore in a field where competition is not numerous. They altogether eschew the ordinary, the literal, and they have the element of spiritual distinction, which still further narrows their eminence and gives them still greater relief. Withal they are extremely characteristic, extremely personal. They represent, only and all, their author and no one but their author. . . . (pp. 63-4)

A recluse in life, [Hawthorne] overflows to the reader. He does not tell very much, but apparently he tells everything. His confidences are not ample. Nothing is ample in his writings but the plethora of detail and the fulness of fancies. But he has no reticences. If he communicates little, he has nothing to conceal. (p. 66)

[Hawthorne thought his status of recluse] the most material fact about both him and his work, as is plain from his calling his reserve "unconquerable." So that it is impossible to share his uncertainty as to whether the tameness of his touches proceeds from this reserve or from lack of power. The answer clearly is: both. And to go a step further, and as I say to the root of the matter, his unconquerable reserve proceeds in all probability from his lack of power—at least of anything like sustained, unintermittent power that can be relied upon and evoked at will by its possessor.

Power at all events is precisely the element most conspicuously lacking in the normal working of this imagination. . . . Repeatedly he seems to be on the point of exhibiting power, of moving us, that is to say; but, except, I think, in **"The Scarlet Letter,"** he never quite does so. His unconquerable reserve steps in and turns him aside. He never crosses the line, never makes the attempt. He is too fastidious to attempt vigor and

fail. . . . [Hawthorne] follows his temperamental bent with tranquil docility instead of compelling it to serve him in the construction of some fabric of importance. The latter business demands energy and effort. And if he made so little effort it is undoubtedly because he had so little energy. His genius was a reflective one. . . . Reality repelled him. What attracted him was mirage. Mirage is his specific aim, the explicit goal of his art—which thus becomes inevitably rather artistry than art. His practice is sustained by his theory. Speaking of a scene mirrored in a river he exclaims, "Which, after all, was the most real—the picture or the original?—the objects palpable to our grosser senses, or their apotheosis in the stream beneath? Surely the disembodied images stand in closer relation to the soul." . . . [Hawthorne preferred] the vague and the undefined in nature itself as nearer to the soul. Nearer to the soul of the poet it may be, not to that of the artist. The most idealizing artist can count on enough vagueness of his own—whether it handicap his effort or illumine his result in dealing with his material. And it is not near to the soul of the poet endowed with the architectonic faculty—the poet in the Greek sense, the maker. It is the congenial content of contemplation indeterminate and undirected. (pp. 69-71)

In general, one imagines [Hawthorne] did not have to set fancy resolutely to work, but merely to give it free play. The result was amazingly productive. How many **"Mosses"** and **"Twice-Told Tales"** are there? Certainly a prodigious number when one considers the narrowness of their range and their extraordinary variety within it. Their quality is singularly even, I think. Some of them—a few—are better than others, but mainly in more successfully illustrating their common quality. What this is Hawthorne himself sufficiently indicates in saying, "Instead of passion there is sentiment; and even in what purport to be pictures of actual life we have allegory." (p. 72)

Sentiment replaces passion, it is true. But the sentiment is pale for sentiment. It is sentiment insufficiently *senti*. Allegory, it is true, replaces reality, but the allegory itself is insufficiently real. The tales are not merely in a less effective, less robust, less substantial category than that which includes passion and actual life, but within their own category they are—most of them—unaccented and inconclusive. They are too faint in color and too frail in construction quite to merit the inference of Hawthorne's pretty deprecation. . . . There is not a shiver in them. Their tone is lukewarm and their temper Laodicean. Witchery is precisely the quality they suggest but do not possess. Their atmosphere is not that of the clear brown twilight in which familiar objects are poetized, but that of the gray day in which they acquire monotone. The twilight and moonlight, so often figuratively ascribed to Hawthorne's genius, are in fact a superstition. There is nothing eerie or elfin about his genius. He is too much the master of it and directs it with a too voluntary control. . . . There is no greater sanity to be met with in literature than Hawthorne's. The wholesome constitution of his mind is inveterate and presides with unintermittent constancy in his prose. Now caprice, conducted by reason, infallibly incurs the peril of insipidity, and it is not to be denied that many of the tales settle comfortably into the category of the prosaic. (pp. 73-4)

[Hawthorne's tales] won and have kept their classic position, it is not to be doubted, because of their originality, their refinement, and their elevation. There is certainly nothing else like them; their taste is perfect; and, in general, they deal with some phase of the soul, some aspect or quality or transaction of the spiritual life. . . . [Their] informing purpose lies quite outside the material world and its sublunary phenomena. No small portion of their originality consists, indeed, in the association of their refinement and elevation with what we can now see is their mediocrity. Elsewhere in the world of fiction mediocrity is associated with anything but fineness of fibre and spirituality. The novelty of the combination in Hawthorne's case was disconcerting, and it is small wonder that for a time at least . . . the importance of the **"Twice-Told Tales"** and the **"Mosses"** was argued from their distinction. Finally, some of them—too few assuredly—are good stories.

The rest are sterilized by the evil eye of Allegory. . . . [Allegory] is art only when its representation is as imaginatively real as its meaning. The mass of allegory—allegory strictly devoted to exposition and dependent upon exegesis, allegory explicitly so called—is only incidentally art at all.

Hawthorne's is of this order. His subject is always something other than its substance. Everything means something else. Dealing with the outer world solely for the sake of the inner, he is careless of its character and often loses its significance in mere suggestiveness. His meaning is the burden of his story, not the automatic moral complement of its vivid and actual reality. (pp. 74-7)

[Hawthorne's] faculty of discovering morals on which tales could be framed is prodigious. . . . It is, as one may say, a by-product of the Puritan preoccupation. He did not find sermons in stones. He had the sermons already; his task was to find the stones to fit them. And these his fancy furnished him with a fertility paralleling his use for them. But his interest in shaping these was concentrated on their illustrative and not on their real qualities. Instead of realizing vividly and presenting concretely the elements of his allegory, he contented himself with their plausibility as symbols. (pp. 78-9)

[Hawthorne] was, in fact, allegory-mad. Allegory

was his obsession. Consequently, he not only fails to handle the form in the minimizing manner of the masters, but often fails in effectiveness on the lower plane where the moral occupies the foreground. **"The Birthmark"** is an instance. Nothing could be finer than the moral of this tale. . . . But it is a moral even more obscurely brought out than it is fantastically symbolized. In the same way, the moral of **"Rappacini's Daughter,"** distinctly the richest and warmest of Hawthorne's productions, is still less effectively enforced. It is quite lost sight of in the development of the narrative, which is given an importance altogether disproportionate to the moral, and which yet is altogether dependent upon the moral for significance—sustained as it is, and attractive, as it might have been, had it been taken as a fairy tale frankly from the first. . . .

[The] tales in which he leaves [allegory] alone altogether or at all events does not lean upon it, are the best, I think. His excellent faculty is released for freer play in such tales as **"The Gentle Boy,"** in which if he is less original, he is more human, and takes his place and holds his own in the lists of literature—instead of standing apart in the brown twilight and indulging his fancy in framing insubstantial fictions for the illustration of moral truths. . . . (p. 81)

[The] real misfortune of Hawthorne—and ours—was the misconception of his talent, resulting in this cultivation of his fancy to the neglect of his imagination. (p. 82)

I do not suppose anything could have been made of **"Septimius Felton, or the Elixir of Life"** in any case, except under the happiest circumstances and with the nicest art. But it is a capital instance of what Hawthorne's fancy can do with a theme of some suggestiveness in the way of emptying it of all significance. . . . [Its] profound and sombre power resides in its appalling reality. *This* is what a draught of the Elixir of Life would produce if the puerile decoction over which Septimius Felton labors through so many wearisome pages had crowned his hopes—this, and not the insipid experiences foreshadowed in the vaporings of his infatuated fancy.

But **"Septimius Felton"** is a posthumous production and one of Hawthorne's failures. Consider a work of far more serious ambition if not in all respects of more representative character—**"The Marble Faun."** There is the same *kind* of ineffectiveness and for the same reason, the frivolity of fancy. The theme of **"The Marble Faun,"** the irretrievableness of evil conjoined with its curious transforming power—the theme in short of that profoundly imaginative masterpiece, the myth of the Fall of Man—is rather stated than exemplified in the story, overlaid as this is with its reticulation of fantastic unreality. Its elaboration, its art, tends to enfeeble its conception; its substance extenuates its subject. . . . Probably its admirers considered that the treatment poetized the moral. That is clearly the author's intention. But a truth is not poetized by being devitalized. . . . The lack of construction, of orderly evolution, in the book is an obvious misfortune and shows very clearly Hawthorne's artistic weakness, whatever his poetic force. But its essential defect is its lack of the sense of reality, to secure which is the function of the imagination, and through which alone the truth of the fundamental conception can flower into effective exposition. (pp. 85-7)

[However Hawthorne's] divorce from reality and consecration to the fanciful may have succeeded in giving him a unique position and demonstrating his originality . . . there is one vital respect, at all events, in which he almost drops out of the novelist's category. . . . [A Hawthorne character] has not enough features for an individual and he has not enough representative traits for a type. His creator evokes him in pseudo-Frankenstein fashion for some purpose, symbolical, allegorical, or otherwise illustrative, and has no concern for his character, apart from this function of it, either for its typical value or its individual interest. . . . Consequently his dramas have the air of being conducted by marionettes. This is less important in the short stories, of course. It may be said that of such a character as the minister in **"The Black Veil"** the reader needs to be told nothing, that his character is easily inferred and, anyhow, is not the point, that the point is his wearing the veil and thereby presenting a rueful picture illustrative of our uncleansed condition from secret faults. In that case the idea is enough, and a hortatory paragraph would have sufficed for it. And in any case it is easy to see how immensely the idea would have gained in effectiveness, in cogency, if the minister had been characterized into reality. . . . (pp. 89-91)

[Hawthorne's] characters, indeed, are not creations, but expedients. Roger Chillingworth is an expedient—and as such the only flaw in **"The Scarlet Letter,"** whose impressive theme absorbed its author out of abstractions, . . . except in the case of Chillingworth, to create the only real people of his imaginary world. In creating Dimmesdale and Hester—and I am quite sure Pearl, also—Nature herself, as Arnold says of Wordsworth, "seems to take the pen out of his hand and write for him." (pp. 91-2)

[Hawthorne's novels elude reality] not only in their personages but in their picture of life in general. **"The Scarlet Letter"** itself is the postlude of a passion. Just so much of the general Salem scene as is necessary for the setting of the extremely concentrated drama is presented and no more. Nowhere else is the scene treated otherwise than atmospherically, so to speak. It does not constitute a medium or even background, but penumbra. The social picture does not exist. The quiet Salem streets of **"The House of the Seven Gables,"** the community life of Blithedale, the village houses and hillocks and gossip and happenings of **"Septimius Felton,"** though the War of Independence is in progress and Concord fight is actually an incident, contribute color, not substance, to the story. (p. 93)

The incompleteness of Hawthorne's characters, the inadequacy of his social picture, the lack of romantic richness in his work, have, to be sure, been attributed largely to the romantic poverty of his material—his environment. (p. 95)

[One] may well doubt if Ibsen . . . would ever have suggested Shakespeare, even to the order of appreciation to which he does suggest Shakespeare, if he had had to deal with a world remotely approaching Shakespeare's in richness of material. But as to Hawthorne there is no possible question. His environment furnished him material exactly, exquisitely, suited to his genius. His subject was the soul, and for the enactment of the dramas of the soul Salem was as apt a stage as Thebes. . . . **"The Scarlet Letter"** is so exclusively a drama of the soul as to be measurably independent of an elaborate setting in a social picture. But if Hawthorne's other works were as well placed, as firmly established, as deeply rooted in their environment, they would be works of very different value. That they are not is not the fault of their *milieu*, but of their author. (p. 97)

Hawthorne's style, doubtless less original than his substance, is nevertheless indubitably his own. . . . It is, to begin with, difficult to define, and its lack of positive qualities quite exactly parallels the insubstantiality of its subject-matter. Only by a miracle, one reflects, could subject-matter of much vital importance be thus habited—so plainly, placidly, unpretendingly presented, though in such an exceptional instance as **"The Scarlet Letter"** the latent intensity of the theme is doubtless set off by the sobriety of its garb, to which also it gives a deepened tone. But the harmonious, rather than contrasting, services of such a style as Hawthorne's in general, could be useful only for the direct expression of something bordering on informing insipidity. It is above all a neat style. It wears no gewgaws of rhetoric and owes little or nothing to the figures of speech. . . . Nothing shows more clearly the dilettante character of Hawthorne's exercise of his fancy than this neatness, which is never discomposed by fervor or thrown into disarray by heat.

It is in fact the antithesis of heat, and the absence of heat in Hawthorne's genius appears nowhere so markedly as in his style. His writings from beginning to end do not contain an ardent, or even a fervent passage. They are as empty of exaltation as of exhilaration. (pp. 123-25)

[Hawthorne] writes as the scribes, and lacks the conviction, the assurance of his vocation, the authentic literary and artistic commission for exclamation or utterance with any fire or particular fervor. It is simply extraordinary that so voluminous a writer should care so little for writing as an art of effective expression, should practise it so exclusively as an exercise—as mere record and statement. (p. 126)

[But Hawthorne's style] has the great merit of ease, conjoined with exactness. One without the other is not uncommon, but the combination is rare. The kind of care that goes with deliberateness he undoubtedly took, though he certainly took none that demanded strenuous and scrupulous effort, or his result would have been more distinguished instead of being purely satisfactory. . . . [Hawthorne's] style has in some degree the classic note. . . . And though often as familiar in tone as it is simple in diction its smoothness never lacks dignity and often attains grace. Why has it not in greater degree the truly classic note? Why is it that after all—perfectly adapted as it is to the expression of its substance, to the purpose of its author—it lacks quality and physiognomy? Or at all events why is its quality not more marked, more salient? Because it *is* such an adequate medium for its content, for the expression of a nature without enthusiasm, a mind unenriched by acquisition and an imagination that is in general the prey of fancy rather than the servant of the will. Hawthorne should have taken himself more seriously at the outset—in his formative period—and less so in the maturity of powers whose development would have produced far more important results than those achieved by their leisurely exercise in tranquil neglect of their evolution. (pp. 129-30)

W. C. Brownell, "Hawthorne," in his *American Prose Masters,* Charles Scribner's Sons, 1909, pp. 63-130.

FREDERIC I. CARPENTER

(essay date 1944)

[In the following excerpt from his study of *The Scarlet Letter*, Carpenter analyzes three different critical approaches to the novel—the traditional, the romantic, and the transcendental—and the concept of sin inherent in each interpretation.]

From the first *The Scarlet Letter* has been considered a classic. It has appealed not only to the critics but to the reading public as well. . . .

But in modern times *The Scarlet Letter* has come to seem less than perfect. Other novels, like [Leo Tolstoy's] *Anna Karenina,* have treated the same problem with a richer humanity and a greater realism. If the book remains a classic, it is of a minor order. Indeed, it now seems not quite perfect even of its own kind. Its

logic is ambiguous, and its conclusion moralistic. The ambiguity is interesting, of course, and the moralizing slight, but the imperfection persists.

In one sense the very imperfection of *The Scarlet Letter* makes it classic: its ambiguity illustrates a fundamental confusion in modern thought. To the question "Was the action symbolized by the scarlet letter wholly sinful?" it suggests a variety of answers: "Yes," reply the traditional moralists; "Hester Prynne broke the Commandments." But the romantic enthusiasts answer: "No; Hester merely acted according to the deepest of human instincts." And the transcendental idealists reply: "In part; Hester truly sinned against the morality which her lover believed in, but did not sin against her own morality, because she believed in a 'higher law.' To her own self, Hester Prynne remained true." (p. 173)

The traditional answer remains clear, but the romantic and the idealistic have usually been confused. Perhaps the imperfection of the novel arises from Hawthorne's own confusion between his heroine's transcendental morality and mere immorality. Explicitly, he condemned Hester Prynne as immoral; but implicitly, he glorified her as courageously idealistic. And this confusion between romantic immorality and transcendental idealism has been typical of the genteel tradition in America.

According to the traditional moralists, Hester Prynne was truly a sinful woman. Although she sinned less than her hypocritical lover and her vengeful husband, she nevertheless sinned; and, from her sin, death and tragedy resulted. At the end of the novel, Hawthorne himself positively affirmed this interpretation:

Earlier in life, Hester had vainly imagined that she herself might be the destined prophetess, but had long since recognized the impossibility that any mission of divine and mysterious truth should be confided to a woman stained with sin.

And so the traditional critics have been well justified. *The Scarlet Letter* explicitly approves the tragic punishment of Hester's sin and explicitly declares the impossibility of salvation for the sinner.

But for the traditionalists there are many kinds and degrees of sin, and *The Scarlet Letter,* like Dante's *Inferno,* describes more than one. According to the orthodox, Hester Prynne belongs with the romantic lovers of the *Inferno,* in the highest circle of Hell. For Hester sinned only through passion, but her lover through passion and concealment, and her husband through "violating, in cold blood, the sanctity of the human heart." Therefore, Hester's sin was the least, and her punishment the lightest.

But Hester sinned, and, according to traditional Puritanism, this act shut her off forever from paradise.

Indeed, this archetypal sin and its consequent tragedy have been taken to symbolize the eternal failure of the American dream. Hester suggests "the awakening of the mind to 'moral gloom' after its childish dreams of natural bliss are dissipated." Thus her lover, standing upon the scaffold, exclaimed: "Is this not better than we dreamed of in the forest?" And Hawthorne repeated that Hester recognized the eternal justice of her own damnation. The romantic dream of natural freedom has seemed empty to the traditionalists, because sin and its punishment are eternal and immutable. (pp. 173-74)

[All] the traditionalists agree that Hester's action was wholly sinful. That Hester herself never admitted this accusation and that Hester is never represented as acting blindly in a fit of passion and that Hester never repented of her "sin" are facts which the traditionalists overlook. Moreover, they forget that Hawthorne's condemnation of Hester's sin is never verified by Hester's own words. But of this more later.

Meanwhile, other faults in Hester's character are admitted by the traditional and the liberal alike. Even if she did not do what she believed to be evil, Hester nevertheless did tempt her lover to do what he believed to be evil and thus caused his death. And because she wished to protect her lover, she consented to a life of deception and concealment which she herself knew to be false. But for the traditional moralists neither her temptation of her lover nor her deception of him was a cardinal sin. Only her act of passion was.

Therefore Hester's passion was the fatal flaw which caused the tragedy. Either because of some womanly weakness which made her unable to resist evil, or because of some pride which made her oppose her own will to the eternal law, she did evil. Her sin was certain, the law she broke was immutable, and the human tragedy was inevitable—according to the traditional moralists.

But, according to the romantic enthusiasts, The Scarlet Letter points a very difficult moral. The followers of Rousseau have said that Hester did not sin at all; or that, if she did, she transformed her sin into a virtue. Did not Hawthorne himself describe the radiance of the scarlet letter, shining upon her breast like a symbol of victory? "The tendency of her fate had been to set her free. The scarlet letter was her passport into regions where other women dared not tread." Hester—if we discount Hawthorne's moralistic conclusion—never repented of her "sin" of passion, because she never recognized it as such.

In absolute contrast to the traditionalists, the romantics have described The Scarlet Letter as a masterpiece of "Hawthorne's immorality." Not only Hester but even the Puritan minister becomes "an amoralist and a Nietzschean." "In truth," wrote Hawthorne, "nothing short of a total change of dynasty and moral code in that interior kingdom was adequate to account for the impulses now communicated to the . . . minister." But Hester alone became perfectly immoral, for "the world's law was no law for her mind." She alone dared renounce utterly the dead forms of tradition and dared follow the natural laws of her own instinctive nature to the end. (pp. 174-75)

Therefore, according to the romantics, the tragedy of The Scarlet Letter does not result from any tragic flaw in the heroine, for she is romantically without sin. It results, rather, from the intrinsic evil of society. Because the moral law imposes tyrannical restraints upon the natural instincts of man, human happiness is impossible in civilization. The Scarlet Letter, therefore, becomes the tragedy of perfection, in which the ideal woman is doomed to defeat by an inflexible moral tradition. Because Hester Prynne was so perfectly loyal and loving that she would never abandon her lover, she was condemned by the Puritans. Not human frailty, therefore, or any tragic imperfection of character, but only the inevitable forces of social determinism caused the disaster described by The Scarlet Letter—according to the romantic enthusiasts.

Between the orthodox belief that Hester Prynne sinned utterly and the opposite romantic belief that she did not sin at all, the transcendental idealists seek to mediate. Because they deny the authority of the traditional morality, these idealists have sometimes seemed merely romantic. But because they seek to describe a new moral law, they have also seemed moralistic. The confusion of answers to the question of evil suggested by The Scarlet Letter arises, in part, from a failure to understand the transcendental ideal.

With the romantics, the transcendentalists agree that Hester did wisely to "give all to love." But they insist that Hester's love was neither blindly passionate nor purposeless. "What we did," Hester exclaims to her lover, "had a consecration of its own." To the transcendental, her love was not sinful because it was not disloyal to her evil husband (whom she had never loved) or to the traditional morality (in which she had never believed). Rather her love was purposefully aimed at a permanent union with her lover—witness the fact that it had already endured through seven years of separation and disgrace. Hester did well to "obey her heart," because she felt no conflict between her heart and her head. She was neither romantically immoral nor blindly rebellious against society and its laws.

This element of conscious purpose distinguishes the transcendental Hester Prynne from other, merely romantic heroines. Because she did not deny "the moral law" but went beyond it to a "higher law," Hester transcended both romance and tradition. As if to emphasize this fact, Hawthorne himself declared that she "assumed a freedom of speculation which our forefathers, had they known it, would have held to be a deadlier crime than that stigmatized by the scarlet letter." Unlike her lover, she had explicitly been led "beyond the scope of generally received laws." She had consciously wished to become "the prophetess" of a more liberal morality.

According to the transcendentalists, therefore, Hester's "sin" was not that she broke the Commandments—for, in the sight of God, she had never truly been married. Nor was Hester the blameless victim of society, as the romantics believed. She had sinned in that she had deceived her lover concerning the identity of her husband. . . . Not traditional morality, but transcendental truth, governed the conscience of Hester Prynne. But she had a conscience, and she had sinned against it.

Indeed, Hester Prynne had "sinned," exactly *because* she put romantic "love" ahead of ideal "truth." She had done evil in allowing the "good" of her lover to outweigh the higher law. She had sacrificed her own integrity by giving absolutely everything to her loved one. . . . True love is a higher law than merely traditional morality, but, even at best, human love is "daemonic." The highest law of "celestial love" is the law of divine truth.

According to the transcendental idealists, Hester Prynne sinned in that she did not go beyond human love. In seeking to protect her lover by deception, she sinned both against her own "integrity" and against God. If she had told the whole truth in the beginning, she would have been blameless. But she lacked this perfect self-reliance.

Nevertheless, tragedy would have resulted even if Hester Prynne had been transcendentally perfect. For the transcendental ideal implies tragedy. Traditionally, tragedy results from the individual imperfection of some hero. Romantically, it results from the evil of society. But, ideally, it results from a conflict of moral standards or values. The tragedy of *The Scarlet Letter* resulted from the conflict of the orthodox morality of the minister with the transcendental morality of the heroine. For Arthur Dimmesdale, unlike Hester Prynne, did sin blindly through passion, committing an act which he felt to be wrong. And because he sinned against his own morality, he felt himself unable to grasp the freedom which Hester urged. If, on the contrary, he had conscientiously been able to flee with her to a new life on the western frontier, there would have been no tragedy. . . . To those who have never believed in it, the American dream of freedom has always seemed utopian and impossible of realization. Tragedy results from this conflict of moralities and this unbelief.

According to the orthodox, Hester Prynne sinned through blind passion, and her sin caused the tragedy. According to the romantic, Hester Prynne heroically "gave all to love," and tragedy resulted from the evil of society. According to the transcendentalists, Hester Prynne sinned through deception, but tragedy resulted from the conflict of her dream of freedom with the traditional creed of her lover. Dramatically, each of these interpretations is possible: *The Scarlet Letter* is rich in suggestion. But Hawthorne the moralist sought to destroy this richness.

The Scarlet Letter achieves greatness in its dramatic, objective presentation of conflicting moralities in action: each character seems at once symbolic, yet real. But this dramatic perfection is flawed by the author's moralistic, subjective criticism of Hester Prynne. And this contradiction results from Hawthorne's apparent confusion between the romantic and the transcendental moralities. While the characters of the novel objectively act out the tragic conflict between the traditional morality and the transcendental dream, Hawthorne subjectively damns the transcendental for being romantically immoral.

Most obviously, Hawthorne imposed a moralistic **"Conclusion"** upon the drama which his characters had acted. But the artistic and moral falsity of this does not lie in its didacticism or in the personal intrusion of the author, for these were the literary conventions of the age. Rather it lies in the contradiction between the author's moralistic comments and the earlier words and actions of his characters. Having created living protagonists, Hawthorne sought to impose his own will and judgment upon them from the outside. Thus he described Hester as admitting her "sin" of passion and as renouncing her "selfish ends" and as seeking to "expiate" her crime. But Hester herself had never admitted to any sin other than deception and had never acted "selfishly" and had worn her scarlet letter triumphantly, rather than penitently. In his **"Conclusion,"** therefore, Hawthorne did violence to the living character whom he had created.

His artificial and moralistic criticism is concentrated in the **"Conclusion."** But it also appears in other chapters of the novel. (pp. 175-78)

[The] scene between Hester and her lover in the forest also suggests the root of Hawthorne's confusion. To the traditional moralists, the "forest," or "wilderness," or "uncivilized Nature" was the symbolic abode of evil—the very negation of moral law. But to the romantics, wild nature had become the very symbol of freedom. In this scene, Hawthorne explicitly condemned Hester for her wildness—for "breathing the wild, free atmosphere of an unredeemed, unchristianized, lawless region." And again he damned her "sympathy" with "that wild, heathen Nature of the forest, never subjugated by human law, nor illumined by higher truth." Clearly he hated moral romanticism. And this hatred would have been harmless, if his heroine had merely been romantic, or immoral.

But Hester Prynne, as revealed in speech and in action, was not romantic but transcendental. And Hawthorne failed utterly to distinguish, in his moralistic criticism, between the romantic and the transcendental. (p. 178)

Having allowed his imagination to create an idealistic heroine, he did not allow his conscious mind to justify—or even to describe fairly—her ideal morality. Rather, he damned the transcendental character whom he had created, for being romantic and immoral. But the words and deeds by means of which he had created her contradicted his own moralistic criticisms.

In the last analysis, the greatness of *The Scarlet Letter* lies in the character of Hester Prynne. Because she dared to trust herself and to believe in the possibility of a new morality in the new world, she achieved spiritual greatness in spite of her own human weakness, in spite of the prejudices of her Puritan society, and, finally, in spite of the prejudices of her creator himself. For the human weakness which made her deceive her lover in order to protect him makes her seem only the more real. The calm steadfastness with which she endures the ostracism of society makes her heroic. And the clear purpose which she follows, despite the denigrations of Hawthorne, makes her almost ideal.

Hester, almost in spite of Hawthorne, envisions the transcendental ideal of positive freedom, instead of the romantic ideal of mere escape. . . .

Hester Prynne embodies the authentic American dream of a new life in the wilderness of the new world, and of self-reliant action to realize that ideal. In the Puritan age in which he lived, and in Hawthorne's own nineteenth century, this ideal was actually being realized in practice. Even in our modern society with its more liberal laws, Hester Prynne might hope to live happily with her lover, after winning divorce from her cruel and vengeful husband. But in every century her tragedy would still be the same. It would result from her own deception and from the conflicting moral belief of her lover. But it would not result from her own sense of guilt or shame.

In *The Scarlet Letter* alone among his novels, Hawthorne succeeded in realizing a character embodying the authentic American dream of freedom and independence in the new world. But he succeeded in realizing this ideal emotionally rather than intellectually. And, having completed the novel, he wondered at his work: "I think I have never overcome my adamant in any other instance," he said. Perhaps he added the moralistic **"Conclusion"** and the various criticisms of Hester, in order to placate his conscience. In any case, he never permitted himself such freedom—or such greatness—again. (p. 179)

Frederic I. Carpenter, "Scarlet A Minus," in *College English,* Vol. 5, No. 4, January, 1944, pp. 173-80.

JAMES G. JANSSEN
(essay date 1976)

[In the following excerpt, Janssen examines how Hawthorne used fictional techniques to achieve his didactic aims.]

In one of Hawthorne's minor sketches, the narrator tells the child he is about to take on a sight-seeing walk through the streets, "but if I moralize as we go, do not listen to me. . . . " Unlike little Annie, readers of Hawthorne's short stories and sketches have not found this very appropriate advice, for if there is one demonstrable thing about Hawthorne it is that he does indeed mean meanings, and that his works are presentations of moral confrontations of one sort or another. In speaking of his "blasted allegories," he seems surely to have been describing a haunted moral consciousness more than he was apologizing for inclusion of that acute moral awareness in his work. His lamenting of an allegorical imagination and the wish that he could have written books with more sunshine in them should be taken with no more seriousness than one does his ambiguous remarks about a Puritan background, claimed as it is rejected.

In reading the short works, one discovers at least three different categories based on the way in which the meaning or moral is expressed specifically with regard to its directness and accuracy, either by Hawthorne or some character or narrator invented for that particular purpose.

In a great many of his short stories—and these among the best—Hawthorne, like the narrator of **"The Antique Ring,"** is happily unable to "separate the idea from the symbol in which it manifests itself." There is no authorial voice present to announce a moral at the beginning or the conclusion of great works like **"My Kinsman, Major Molineux,"** **"Roger Malvin's Burial,"** **"Rappaccini's Daughter,"** and **"Young Goodman Brown,"** to name only a few which fall into this first category. Their enduring quality is in part their presentation of complex moral and psychological dilemmas without the detraction of instant explication within the text.

Another group of short works involves a characteristic if less fortunate approach in that the meaning or significance is explicitly stated at the beginning or the end (or both) and seems to be the "right" reading, the one most of us would have arrived at without such pushing. Examples here would include **"The Threefold Destiny,"** **"John Inglefield's Thanksgiving,"** **"Sun-**

day at Home," "The Old Apple Dealer," and "Egotism; or, the Bosom Serpent." The obviousness of Hawthorne's assertions of moral significance in these works ranges from the observation made in **"The Birthmark"** that the marriage of a perfection-seeking scientist to a flawed wife "was attended with truly remarkable consequences and a deeply impressive moral," to the directive addressed to the reader of **"Earth's Holocaust"** that "the illumination of the bonfire [indiscriminately destroying civilization] might reveal some profundity of moral truth heretofore hidden in mist or darkness."

But although involving fewer works, it is a third category that is especially interesting for what it says about Hawthorne's attitude toward moralizing in fiction. Within this group are works in which the moral is expressed with ironic playfulness, sometimes offered as an afterthought or a hastily discharged duty, other times stated in what are at best puzzling, inadequate, and even misleading terms.

One of the most remarkable statements in this connection appears at the beginning of **"Wakefield,"** a story of a husband who whimsically absents himself from his wife for twenty years. After announcing his source ("some old magazine or newspaper"), Hawthorne suggests that such a mind provoking subject repays the study he intends to give it. "If the reader choose, let him to his own meditation; or if he prefers to ramble with me through the twenty years of Wakefield's vagary, I bid him welcome; trusting that there will be a pervading spirit and a moral, *even should we fail to find them,* done up neatly, and condensed into the final sentence" (emphasis mine).

Hawthorne's cavalier attitude toward the moral is provocative. What good is the moral if we fail to find it, and how does it get there if its author is indifferent to it? True, his comment that "thought has always its efficacy and every striking incident its moral" would seem to imply, in its Emersonian point of view, that all things have meaning beyond themselves, regardless of our artistic design and perception. But a better explanation of his initial toying with the idea of a moral is that it is a surfacing of Hawthorne's never long submerged playful spirit—a spirit that causes him to undercut what he recognized as a generally allegorical turn in his work. By treating the matter with some degree of lightness at the beginning, he disarms the critic who expects only another typically nineteenth century dramatization of bare truth—in this case, the notion that isolation is destructive. What is gained is the absence of condescension: a reader cannot feel lectured to if his guide announces with such tenuity the possibility of a moral at the beginning.

In a somewhat similar fashion the narrator of **"Night Sketches,"** after several pages in which he catalogs scenes from a rainy night, arrives at "a moral, wherewith, *for lack of a more appropriate one,*" he can conclude his sketch, it being that "we, night wanderers through a stormy and dismal world, if we bear the lamp of Faith, enkindled at a celestial fire, it will surely lead us home to that heaven whence its radiance was borrowed" (emphasis mine.) In addition to the casual admittance of its questionable appropriateness (there has been nothing up to that point to make us think heavenly thoughts), even the inflated rhetoric of the moral seems at first glance out of place in a sketch featuring one of Hawthorne's typical artist-narrators, attempting with some degree of wry and sober observation to attune himself to the sights and sounds of nighttime humanity. Upon closer observation, however, the casual and inaccurately expressed moral is seen to be appropriate for this Oberon-type onlooker in life who, caught up in the web of his poetic phrasings and rhetoric, cannot resist the impulse to moralize his way out of the sketch, albeit irrelevantly. It appears, then, that Hawthorne's ironic employment of an enthusiastic though "wrong" moral is consistent with the overall tone of the sketch more than it is indicative of a distaste for moralizing.

Sometimes indeed Hawthorne does not seem to treat the moral as a fictional requirement into which he can put little enthusiasm. He exemplifies this in **"The Antique Ring"** where Edward Caryl, a would-be author, has just finished reciting a tale he has composed to accompany the engagement ring he gives to Clara Pemberton. The story he writes is one of misplaced confidence and treacherous intrigue, involving the long history of the ring from the time it is given to Essex by Elizabeth, to its appearance in a collection box in a New England church centuries later. Asked by Clara for a satisfying moral, Edward first replies—as noted earlier—that he is unable to separate symbol from idea, but then as though to acquit himself of an authorial obligation (as well as to please his lover), he quickly makes up a patently obvious set of allegorical equivalents ("the Gem to be the human heart, and the Evil Spirit to be Falsehood . . . " etc.) and concludes without much heart, "I beseech you to let this suffice." It does; for Clara, typical of a large segment of Hawthorne's reading public, requires nothing profounder than the generalities of nineteenth century impressionistic criticism with which Edward's audience had greeted his story in the first place: " 'Very pretty!—Beautiful!—How original!—How sweetly written!—What nature!—What imagination!—What power!—What pathos!—What exquisite humor!' " The entire story has become a parable of the role of the writer, Hawthorne, pressured by an audience he wishes to please and for whom he must draw out the moral design in a way which is occasionally awkward for him, as for example in his **"Procession of Life,"** where a piously hopeful moral is loosely attached to a work cataloging some of life's crueller ironies.

In suggesting that Hawthorne's wry sense of humor is sometimes responsible for his ironic employment of the moral—either in treating the matter lightly or inaccurately or in passing off its message as mere duty—it would be very easy to assert too much. Surely if one looks over the canon of Hawthorne's short works, numbering well over one hundred, it becomes difficult to take seriously his various comments, for example in the preface to *The House of the Seven Gables,* that he does not wish, like some, "to impale the story with its moral as with an iron rod." While there seems little doubt that he was aware, as he states in that preface, that works instruct best "through a far more subtile process than the ostensible one," knowing the ease with which he acknowledges the potential misuse of the convention at the same time that he typically risks it, few readers will be able to agree with those who hold that Hawthorne normally found onerous the inclusion of a moral in his work. As Professor Turner has observed [in his *Nathaniel Hawthorne: An Introduction and Interpretation* (1963)], "it came natural for Hawthorne to search out moral implications, and in the main he offered in good faith the moral statement he supposed his readers would welcome." As has been observed in the preceding paragraphs, several examples of a statement not offered in such "good faith" are traceable to an enthusiasm for the ironic mode, coupled with a willingness to adopt a supportive attitude, especially with regard to self-conscious narrative voices who apologize for what they continue to do. But in several cases there is a less clear-cut reason for the misstated moral.

Although the concern in this study is with the short works, the point might be raised more effectively by thinking for a moment of *The Scarlet Letter.* Near the conclusion of that work we are told that "among many morals" possible, the one we are to take with us is " 'Be true! Be true! Show freely to the world, if not your worst, yet some trait whereby the worst may be inferred!' " Even though this moral is singled out for Dimmesdale, a sensitive reading of the novel would leave few satisfied that such an aphoristic sentiment does justice to a complex symbolic work and a character within it whose psychological turmoil can hardly be reduced to something as simplistic as "tell the truth about yourself and all will be well."

Typical of those shorter works in which the moral supplied seems equally misdirected is **"Fancy's Show Box,"** a tale which seems fairly obvious upon casual reading. Its slender narrative involves one Mr. Smith, visited by personifications of Fancy, Memory and Guilt, each contributing to vivify for him some recollection of past intentions or incomplete acts of questionable morality (e.g., a sinful thought about a young girl; a lawsuit proposed but dropped; a bottle thrown at, but missing, the head of a young friend). In each case a picture of the thought or deed is presented as accomplished fact.

The idea seems clear enough, its obviousness causing us in fact to recall Hawthorne's self-accusation in the preface to the 1851 edition of *Twice-Told Tales* that "in what purport to be pictures of actual life, we have [only] allegory." But near the conclusion of the piece, we are suddenly presented with a lengthy defense of Mr. Smith, compellingly argued in terms of artistic creation. The schemes of a man who does not manage to do what he feels tempted to do are like the schemes of an artist's unexecuted plots, so that Mr. Smith is no more guilty of these mental crimes than a man is an artist before he gives actuality to what are only seed ideas for a work. Furthermore, most men "over-estimate their capacity for evil," and anyway, there are few times when man's deeds can truly be said to be of "settled and firm resolve, either for good or evil." But just when he seems to be exonerating Mr. Smith by means of a formal cause/efficient cause distinction, a shorter, final paragraph announces that the "said and awful truth" demonstrated in all of this is that "man must not disclaim his brotherhood, even with the guiltiest, since, though his hand be clean, his heart has surely been polluted by the flitting phantoms of iniquity."

Lest it be thought that it is only in the obscure works that the oblique moral is found, one of the best examples, the last to be treated here, is also one of Hawthorne's most highly regarded stories, **"The Prophetic Pictures,"** a work whose plot must be recalled in some detail so as to appreciate the outrageously simplistic moral which Hawthorne draws from it.

A young couple about to be married engages a renowned artist to do their portraits. When they come to approve the finished canvases, they are surprised to find the expressions there: Elinor's is one of grief and terror, Walter's one of unnatural vividness. As he prepared the portraits, the painter also made a sketch which he shows only to Elinor. Years later he visits the couple in order to see his prized work, arriving in time to see enacted what he had foreshadowed on each face and drawn specifically in his sketch: Walter in the act of drawing a knife against his wife. When the artist separates them and reminds Elinor that he tried to warn her of this in the sketch, she replies only that she loved Walter. Hawthorne draws from this the moral that even if we were able to foresee our futures, most of us would go about the business of life undeterred by prophetic pictures.

Such a plot summary is deceiving, for it implies that the story is primarily about Walter and Elinor and the relative importance of knowledge and fate in determining future events. But surely most readers would catalog **"The Prophetic Pictures"** with those works concerned with the problem of the artist, and would see within the creator of the pictures most of the forces surrounding Hawthorne's artists generally: divinely creative genius on the one hand, and arrogant manipulation of individuals on the other; perceptivity and insight, along with a suggestion of "dark" knowledge that goes beyond what finite man should attempt; responsiveness to the individual as artist's model, but indifference to him in terms of humanitarian regard and love.

Even in terms of quantitative measurement, the story is given over to a depiction of the artist's character, and specifically to the question of whether he is merely the observer and recorder of human appearances or a causal factor in the playing out of the human drama. "A strange thought darted into [the painter's] mind. Was not his own the form in which that destiny had embodied itself, and he was a chief agent of the coming evil which he had foreshadowed?" Throughout the story Hawthorne suggests that in the painter's extensive learning and reputation there is something that is both impressive and frightening. When he recommends the artist's erudition and reputation, Elinor asks Walter if he is speaking of "a painter or a wizard." Stepping back from the "foolish fancies" of the mob at the same time that he asserts them as viable, Hawthorne reminds us that the artist's skill is such that his work seems a "presumptuous mockery of the Creator." No less damning than his reputation for prescience among the old woman of Boston, however, is the extent to which he, like others of Hawthorne's men of "engrossing purpose," has isolated himself from mankind. "Though gentle in manner and upright in intent and action, he did not possess kindly feelings; his heart was cold; no living creature could be brought near enough to keep him warm." Nothing sums this up better than the mistake the painter makes when, in calling at the home of Walter and Elinor on the fatal day, he asks for an audience with the portraits rather than with the couple.

The evidence is so familiar, the character type so much a Hawthorne staple as to need no further recollection. What does remain, however, is the gnawing question of the significance of Hawthorne's extracting from all of this an inaccurate moral which makes no mention of what the story has been about. In a tale clearly questioning aspects of the Romantic theory of the artist, are we really being invited to think only about our willingness to let destiny unfold despite warnings of disaster? And, most significantly, what is the aesthetic effect of this and other episodes of Hawthorne's studied obtuseness in not being able to find the true moral, especially in view of his general practice in doing so?

Any suggestion must, of course, remain tentative, for Hawthorne does not have much to say about his inaccurately drawn morals. But several things do seem clear, among them that he is certainly aware of what he is about in works like **"Fancy's Show Box"** and **"The Prophetic Pictures,"** nor does it seem likely that the exceptions to the rule discussed in this study prove that Hawthorne is primarily nervous about moralizing in fiction. Quite the contrary, in fact; for in the works discussed in the preceding pages, his apparent reluctance to moralize accurately does not discourage the reader but in fact challenges him to pursue meanings of the sort we have come to associate with Hawthorne (**"Wakefield,"** after all, turns out to be one of the most morally assertive of his tales). What seems more reasonable is that the inaccurately stated moral legitimatizes the entire idea of moralizing through the kind of indirection, subtlety and suggestion one expects from a writer who, unlike the artist of **"The Prophetic Pictures,"** is not so presumptuous as to circumscribe in every case the precise boundaries of meaning.

The justification for the misleading moral in **"The Prophetic Pictures"** seems to be not primarily a comic pose (as it was in **"Wakefield"** and **"Night Sketches"**), nor a sportively ironic handling of the whole idea of moralizing (**"The Antique Ring"**), but rather an attempt to open up the field of the moral by means of a tantalizing misstatement of it, thereby goading the reader into doing better for himself. The device is not unlike Hawthorne's more familiar employment of suggestive alternatives, validating readings beyond those he himself is willing to assert, a bit like the instructor who misreads by way of challenging his students. In a way then, even when he seems to take a holiday from moralizing, Hawthorne willingly risks what he warned against in the preface to *The House of the Seven Gables:* treating the moral like a pin to be stuck through a butterfly. Rather than rendering the story lifeless, "in an ungainly and unnatural attitude," however, Hawthorne's use of the obviously inaccurate moral in certain of his works allows the butterfly to remain unimpaled and yet arrested, the better to be understood and appreciated. (pp. 269-75)

James G. Janssen, "Impaled Butterflies and the Misleading Moral in Hawthorne's Short Works," in *The Nathaniel Hawthorne Journal,* 1976, pp. 269-75.

SOURCES FOR FURTHER STUDY

Crews, Frederick. *The Sins of the Fathers: Hawthorne's Psychological Themes.* New York: Oxford University Press, 1966, 279 p.

> Seminal study of psychological dimensions of Hawthorne's fiction.

Fogle, Richard Harter. *Hawthorne's Fiction: The Light and the Dark.* Rev. ed. Norman: University of Oklahoma Press, 1964, 239 p.

> Examines the imagery of the stories and novels, especially the "light and dark" patterns associated with some of Hawthorne's principal characters.

Lathrop, George Parsons. *A Study of Hawthorne.* 1876. Reprint. New York: AMS Press, 1969. 350 p.

> An overview of Hawthorne's life and career, written by his son-in-law.

Pearce, Roy Harvey, ed. *Hawthorne Centenary Essays.* Columbus: Ohio State University Press, 1964, 480 p.

> Essays on Hawthorne's art, philosophy, and critical heritage by Harry Levin, R. W. B. Lewis, Lionel Trilling, and other distinguished critics.

Van Doren, Mark. *Nathaniel Hawthorne.* New York: Viking, 1949. 279 p.

> Critical biography.

Waggoner, Hyatt H. *Hawthorne: A Critical Study.* Cambridge, Mass.: The Belknap Press of Harvard University Press, 1963. 278 p.

> Critical survey of Hawthorne's works.

H. D.

1886-1961

(Full name Hilda Doolittle) American poet, novelist, dramatist, and editor.

INTRODUCTION

H. D. is often called "the perfect Imagist," and her early free verse poetry is credited with inspiring Ezra Pound's formulation of Imagism. H. D.'s later poetry transcended the principles of Imagist verse to include mythology, occult and religious themes, psychoanalytic concepts, and symbolism. Her work retains interest for its role in establishing the tenets of Imagism and because much of it reflects H. D.'s association with some prominent figures in English and American intellectual life in the early twentieth century, including Pound, Richard Aldington, D. H. Lawrence, and Sigmund Freud.

Doolittle was born in Bethlehem, Pennsylvania, and for two years attended Bryn Mawr College, where the poet Marianne Moore was also a student. In the early 1900s H. D., Moore, Pound, and William Carlos Williams were friends, studying and writing together. H. D. and Pound were briefly engaged, but her family forbade the marriage, and some biographers theorize that she traveled to England in 1911 to rejoin him. From London Pound arranged for the publication of several of H. D.'s poems in Harriet Monroe's *Poetry* magazine in January 1913; submitted under the name "H. D., Imagiste," the poems "Hermes of the Ways," "Priapus," and "Epigram" embodied Pound's concept of Imagism, which includes the use of concrete, sensual images, common speech, concision, a wide range of subject matter, and the creation of new rhythms, intended to produce, according to the Imagist credo, "poetry that is hard and clear, never blurred nor indefinite." H. D.'s participation in the social and intellectual life of literary London included association with D. H. Lawrence, May Sinclair, W. B. Yeats, and Aldington, whom she married in 1913. Together Aldington and H. D. edited the *Egoist,* a literary forum for Imagist writers, and both were major contributors to *Some Imagist Poets:*

An Anthology, a collection of Imagist poetry edited by Pound and published in 1915. When Pound abandoned Imagism following the publication of this volume, H. D. and Aldington, in conjunction with Amy Lowell, led and further developed the movement: they were instrumental, for example, in arranging for the publication of three succeeding Imagist anthologies. H. D.'s first volume of poems, *Sea Garden,* was published in 1916.

Following a series of stressful events, including Aldington's absence while in military service during World War I, the deaths of H. D.'s brother and father, and the miscarriage of her first pregnancy, she and Aldington separated in 1918. For many years thereafter she lived with the novelist Winifred Ellerman. They traveled extensively after the birth of H. D.'s daughter in 1919, eventually settling in Switzerland. Two subsequent volumes of poetry, *Hymen* (1921) and *Heliodora and Other Poems* (1924), established H. D. as one of the most important free verse writers in English. After her first three volumes of poetry were gathered as *Collected Poems* in 1925, she began to experiment more widely with different genres and techniques. In ensuing works of poetry, she expanded the technical innovations of Imagist verse, and ultimately departed altogether from the tenets of Imagism. She also wrote drama and fiction, including two experimental works, *Palimpsest* (1926) and *Hedylus* (1928), which are nominally considered novels, although they defy easy categorization and are primarily commended for their poetic prose. Critics have acknowledged the complexities of these prose works; Babette Deutsch, for example, termed *Palimpsest* a book "for poets and patient intellectuals." In 1933 and 1934 H. D. underwent psychoanalysis with Sigmund Freud, and in 1956 published her recollections of the experience in *Tribute to Freud,* characterized by her biographer Vincent Quinn as essentially "a self-portrait brought into focus by her confrontation with Freud." H. D. returned to England during the Second World War and subsequently wrote her "war trilogy," comprising *The Walls Do Not Fall* (1944), *Tribute to the Angels* (1945), and *The Flowering of the Rod* (1946), works inspired by the realities of living in war-torn London that make greater use of religious imagery than her previous poetry. After the war she returned to Switzerland, where she wrote her third major work of fiction, *Bid Me to Live* (1960), a semiautobiographical account of her life in London in the 1920s. H. D.'s last major poetic work, *Helen in Egypt* (1961),

is a book-length mixture of poetry and prose in three parts that retells the Helen of Troy legend. In 1960 she became the first woman to receive the Award of Merit Medal from the American Academy of Arts and Letters. She died in 1961.

H. D. is best remembered as an exemplar of Imagism, the first important movement in twentieth-century poetry and a precursor of literary Modernism, and thus remains of primary interest as an important influence on modern poetry. Examination of her own career reveals that H. D. continued to experiment with different poetic techniques after writing the works that established the essential principles of Imagism. Poetry written after the publication of the *Collected Poems,* for example, employs increasingly complex rhymes and rhythms. H. D. ultimately moved away from the predominantly visual imagery characteristic of Imagist verse, instead relying increasingly on phonetic and rhythmic effects to recreate moods and objects. Many commentators contend that the works that follow the *Collected Poems* are her best, although a few maintain that she broadened her range at the expense of the clarity and conciseness that had been her trademark as the quintessential Imagist poet. Still, her technical achievements, her poignant portrayals of her personal struggles, and the beauty of her work have all earned a significant amount of praise. As C. H. Sisson pointed out, the prospective reader of H. D. might be a little surprised to find that "H. D. offers more than the formal virtues which are usually allowed to her work, and that . . . work abundantly repays the not very strenuous labor of reading it."

To many, H. D. will be remembered as "a poets' poet." "To be 'a poets' poet,' " wrote Horace Gregory, "has few tangible rewards, for this means that the poet who holds that title must often wait upon the future for true recognition. For the time being, however, H. D.'s achievement has been measured in comparison with the "major poets of the twentieth century," as Hyatt H. Waggoner asserted, and "the notes she made in her journey, in her poems, compose one of the really distinguished bodies of work of this century."

(For further information about H. D.'s life and works, see *Contemporary Authors,* Vols. 97-100; *Contemporary Literary Criticism,* Vols. 3, 8, 14, and 31; and *Dictionary of Literary Biography,* Vol. 4: *American Writers in Paris, 1920-1939.*)

CRITICAL COMMENTARY

HARRIET MONROE
(essay date 1925)

[Monroe was the founder and editor of *Poetry* magazine, the first periodical devoted exclusively to poetry and poetry criticism. In the following excerpt, she notes some essential qualities of H. D.'s poetry.]

The amazing thing about H. D.'s poetry is the wildness of it—that trait strikes me as I read her whole record in the *Collected Poems*. . . . She is as wild as deer on the mountain, as hepaticas under the wet mulsh of spring, as a dryad racing nude through the wood. . . . She is, in a sense, one of the most civilized, most ultra-refined, of poets; and yet never was a poet more unaware of civilization, more independent of its thralls. She doesn't talk about nature, doesn't praise or patronize or condescend to it; but she is, quite unconsciously, a lithe, hard, bright-winged spirit of nature to whom humanity is but an incident.

Thus she carries English poetry back to the Greeks more instinctively than any other poet who has ever written in our language. Studying Greek poetry, she finds herself at home there, and quite simply expresses the kinship in her art. (p. 268)

It would be an interesting speculation to consider how much H. D. owes to the pioneers whom all Americans descend from more or less. The pioneers took a shut-in race out of doors, exposed it to nature's harsh activities, and thus restored a certain lost fibre to its very blood and bones. H. D., eastern born and bred as she was, has inherited from them rather than from the barons and earls of England's past. And her poetry is more akin to that of our aborigines than it is to the Elizabethans or Victorians, or any of the classicists or romanticists between them. . . .

Her technique, like her spiritual motive, is lithe and nude. The free-verse forms she chooses are not even clothing, so innocent are they of any trace of artificiality; they are as much a part of her spirit, they complete it as essentially, as harmoniously, as the skin which encloses and outlines the flesh of a human body.

One may follow her flight from worldliness in all her poems, but perhaps it is most explicit in two of them. *Sheltered Garden* is a protest—observe that even her protests are uttered out-of-doors. . . . (p. 269)

There is a bold and trained athleticism in such poetry. . . . H. D.'s art has not the unstudied spontaneity of folk-lore, often so beautiful in its naiveté; it is

shaped by an artist, carefully wrought to an effect of seeming improvisation. Its lines are simple in their strict firmness, but their simplicity is the result, not of instinct alone, but of right instinct sternly educated and disciplined. The keen rhythms of her poems respond with lyric magic to a spirit ever accepting nature's rhythms, a spirit growing with the grass, circling with the sun, racing with the wind, resting with the rocks on the slow beating-out of seasons.

In a certain sense she is inhuman, or perhaps superhuman. Her art is above and beyond little individual loves and hates; these, if they appear at all, merely serve to emphasize passions more ascetic in their indestructible hardihood. One feels that she has lived through and left behind the fierce surge of emotion which drowns so many souls. . . . Indeed, her intercourse is with gods. Her poetry is familiar with them, like that of the Greeks, and she claims them under their familiar Hellenic names as the natural companions of her spirit.

Perhaps, in the last analysis, the much abused word mystic should be invoked to describe the supersensuous significance of her poetry. Her real subject is the experience and aspiration of the human soul—the flowers and trees she writes about, the rocks and winds and mountains, are symbols of the soul's adventures, of a soul which discards and transcends and sublimates the daily events and emotions of ordinary life. (pp. 271-73)

There is in this poet's work a cool hardness—indeed, the parallel is with sculpture in bronze or marble. *Hymen* carves a marble frieze, stained with clear colors in the old Greek or Chinese fashion. . . . The mood, and the April-of-life freshness of it, are sustained by an art singularly serene and sure.

The later poems, *Heliodora* and the rest, are further testimonies to this poet's quality, enriching her fame though scarcely advancing it. She has rarely done a lovelier thing than *Fragment Thirty-six*, her variations on a Sapphic theme. And we may reasonably hope that her work is not yet half done, for her firm and practiced art is no mere passing impulse of youthful talent.

H. D. has been called "the most imagistic of the Imagists." When some of her poems first appeared in the fourth number of *Poetry* (January, 1913), following Richard Aldington's beautiful *Charicos* in the second, it was evident that a new spirit was in the air, a spirit de-

Principal Works

Sea Garden (poetry) 1916

Hymen (poetry) 1921

Heliodora and Other Poems (poetry) 1924

Collected Poems of H. D. (poetry) 1925

Palimpsest (novel) 1926

Hedylus (novel) 1928

Red Roses for Bronze (poetry) 1931

The Walls Do Not Fall (poetry) 1944

Tribute to the Angels (poetry) 1945

The Flowering of the Rod (poetry) 1946

Tribute to Freud (memoir) 1956

Selected Poems of H. D. (poetry) 1957

Bid Me to Live (novel) 1960

Helen in Egypt (poetry and prose) 1961

* End to Torment (memoir) 1979

HERmione (memoir) 1981

*This work includes "Hilda's Book," a collection of poems by Ezra Pound.

manding for the art precision, economy of word and phrase, rhythm personal and not metronomic or derived, and direct presentation of the image, stripped of superfluous ornament. Her own stern instinct had been verified and strengthened by Ezra Pound's harsh discipline, and reticence had saved her from exposing immature work to the world. Thus there are no juvenilia in her record—she was a finished product when she began. (pp. 274-75)

Harriet Monroe, "H. D.," in *Poetry*, Vol. XXVI, No. 5, August, 1925, pp. 268-75.

STANLEY KUNITZ

(essay date 1947)

[In the following excerpt from an essay that originally appeared in *Poetry* in 1947, Kunitz discusses structure, presentation, use of legend and myth, and linguistic techniques and innovations in *The Flowering of the Rod*, the final volume of H. D.'s war trilogy.]

The publication of *The Flowering of the Rod* brings to a close H. D.'s war trilogy. . . . "War trilogy" (the publisher's phrase) requires some qualification. It is true that the poem, which will be considered here *in toto*, begins amid the ruins of London, in the flaming terror of the Blitz, but it is equally true that it ends in an ox-stall in Bethlehem. The war was the occasion, it is not the subject-matter of the poem. Neither is "trilogy" wholly satisfactory, since it implies more of temporal continuity and progressive narrative line than the three parts possess. The relation between the parts seems to me more that of a triptych than of a trilogy, each book being a compositional unit, though conceptually and emotionally enriched by association with its companion units; each composition, furthermore, embodying a dream of vision. This formal arrangement is particularly suited to H. D., whose art has unmistakable affinities with the pictorial.

Pursuing the triptych analogy, we find the second book, *Tribute to the Angels* (1945), falling naturally into place as the central composition; in the background "a half-burnt-out apple-tree blossoming," in the foreground the luminous figure of the Lady, who carries, under her drift of veils, a book.

> her book is our book; written
> or unwritten, its pages will reveal

> a tale of a Fisherman,
> a tale of a jar or jars.

The left side-panel, titled *The Walls Do Not Fall* (1944), shows the ruins of bombed-out London. They have an Egyptian desolation, like the ruins of the Temple of Luxor. The ascendant Dream-figure is Amen, not as the local deity of Thebes, ram-headed god of life and reproduction, nor even in his greater manifestation as Amen-Ra, when he joined with the sun-god to become a supreme divinity incorporating the other gods into his members, but the Amen of Revelation . . . with the face and bearing of the Christos. . . . The background figure recording the scene is Thoth (to the Greeks, Hermes Trismegistus), scribe of the gods, in whose ibis-head magic and art married and flourished.

The interior of an Arab merchant's booth is represented in the foreground of the right side-panel *The Flowering of the Rod.* Half-turned towards the door stands a woman, frail and slender, wearing no bracelet or other ornament, with her scarf slipping from her head, revealing the light on her hair. ("I am Mary of Magdala, / I am Mary, a great tower; / through my will and my power, / Mary shall be myrrh.") The noble merchant with the alabaster jar is Kaspar, youngest and wisest of the Three Wise Men, transfixed in the moment of recognition, of prophetic vision, before he will present her with the jar containing "the myrrh or the spikenard, very costly." In the background he is seen again, making his earlier gift, also a jar, to the other Mary of the manger.

Much has been omitted in this simplified presentation, but enough has been given at least to suggest the materials of the poem and its psychological extensions out of the modern world into pre-history, religion, legend, and myth. "This search for historical parallels, / research into psychic affinities, / has been done to death before, / will be done again," writes H. D. in a self-critical passage. No hint of staleness or weariness, however, blemishes the page. On the contrary, the poem radiates a kind of spiritual enthusiasm. (The composition-period for two of the books is given: a fortnight apiece.) What H. D. is seeking for, what she has obviously found, is a faith: faith that "there was One / in the beginning, Creator, / Fosterer, Begetter, the Same-forever / in the papyrus-swamp, / in the Judaean meadow"; faith that even to the bitter, flawed Mary is given the gift of grace, the Genius of the jar; faith in the survival of values, however the world shakes; faith in the blossoming, the resurrection, of the half-dead tree. (pp. 204-06)

The modulations and variety of effects that H. D. achieves within [a] limited pattern are a tribute to her technical resourcefulness and to her almost infallible ear. Her primary reliance, orally, is on the breath-unit; aurally, on assonance, with an occasional admixture . . . of slant or imperfect rhyme. . . .

Like Yeats, though with a different set of disciplines, founded on her Imagist beginnings, H. D. has learned how to contain the short line, to keep it from spilling over into the margins. For straight narrative or exposition she usually employs a longer, more casual line that approaches prose without becoming, in context, fuzzy or spineless. . . . (p. 207)

The lyric passages have, at once, purity and tension, delicacy and strength, seeming to rejoice in the uncorrupted innocence of the worshiping eye. . . . (p. 208)

One of H. D.'s innovations is a form of word-play that might be called associational semantics. "I know, I feel," she writes, "the meanings that words hide." She sees them as "anagrams, cryptograms, / little boxes, conditioned / to hatch butterflies." To a large extent her poem develops spontaneously out of her quest for the ultimate distillations of meaning sealed in the jars of language. ("Though the jars were sealed, / the fragrance got out somehow.") . . . Most of [the word-play] passages impress me as being too self-conscious, too "literary," in the bad sense, though I recognize their catalytic function.

Although the significant fusion, the mutation into a new kind of experience, a new large meaning, does not take place in the body of the poem, it would be wrong to say that this ingenious, admirably sustained, and moving work fails because it does not achieve monumentality. H. D.'s is not a monumental art. Her poem remains as precise as it is ambitious. It is like the vision seen by the Mage on the occasion of his meeting with Mary of Magdala:

and though it was all on a very grand scale
yet it was small and intimate.

(pp. 208-09)

Stanley Kunitz, "H. D.'s War Trilogy," in his *A Kind of Order, A Kind of Folly,* Atlantic-Little Brown, 1975, pp. 204-09.

HORACE GREGORY
(essay date 1958)

[Gregory, an American poet and critic, cowrote, with Marya Zaturenska, the important study *American Poetry 1900-1940*. In the following excerpt, he discusses H. D.'s association with the Imagist movement and the development of her unique lyric voice.]

The following notes on the poems of H. D. are written to pay tribute to an American poet whose writings have yet to receive full measure of critical attention in the United States. . . .

Today, and in view of her later poems, it seems somewhat strange that most people still associate her writings only with the cause of "free verse" and "imagism," "the School of Images," that Ezra Pound in 1912 so cheerfully announced held the future "in their keeping." In 1956 H. D. remarked, "One writes the kind of poetry one likes. Other people put labels on it. Imagism was something that was important for poets learning their craft early in this century. But after learning his craft, the poet will find his true direction." Although she learned much from Pound, who included her among *Les Imagistes,* H. D.'s lyric gift, even in her early poems, soon found its own voice, its own themes and measures—all of which were clearly unlike those of her contemporaries. This individual voice is evident throughout her *Selected Poems.*

The kind of poetry the early H. D. liked and wrote was of a classic purity of diction and imagery. No poet since Walter Savage Landor in his "Ianthe" and "Rose Aylmer" moved more surely in the direction of classic lyricism than did H. D. This is not to say that H. D. emulated or imitated Landor, but her economies of statement, her precise choice of rhythms and colors, her sense of the dramatic incident revealed in lyric forms brought her closer to the best of Landor than any American poet of her times.

H. D.'s choice of Greek themes and incidents had been inspired by epigrams from the Greek Anthology, lines of Meleager on Heliodora, the epigram of Plato which recited a prayer offered up to Aphrodite. Through these inspirations and others of their kind

H. D. wrote her own lyrics on Lais, on Heliodora, on Helen of Troy, on Penelope at Ithaca. These were re-creations in modern verse of enduring passions and situations—"the showing-forth" of the timeless moment in situations that are as true today as they were three thousand years ago. (p. 82)

[The] majority of H. D.'s critics have been so preoccupied by the presence of her imagery that several of her better known poems seem to have been unheard. The way toward a renewed understanding of her poems is not to strain the eyes, but to hear the poems clearly.

So much then for the early sources of H. D.'s inspiration and her particular revival of pure melody in English verse. What of the content of her poems? (pp. 82-3)

During the years of World War II which H. D. spent in London, she wrote a trilogy of poems, *The Walls Do Not Fall, Tribute to the Angels, The Flowering of the Rod,* all in celebration of the spirit in time of war. . . .

It should be remembered that the trilogy of H. D.'s devotional poems had been written at least ten years before the present decade of poets has turned to a revaluation of religious verse. H. D. in her perceptions of timelessness, and in her search for the "real," has always seemed to be writing in advance of her times. In that respect the present generation might well regard her as "a poets' poet."

To be "a poets' poet" has few tangible rewards, for this means that the poet who holds that title must often wait upon the future for true recognition. Yet the poems of H. D. have acquired a life, a being of their own; at this date one need not argue that they should be read. Of contemporary poets H. D. is among the few whose writings are likely to endure. (p. 83)

Horace Gregory, "A Poet's Poet," in *The Commonweal,* Vol. LXVIII, No. 3, April 18, 1958, pp. 82-3.

KATHRYN GIBBS GIBBONS
(essay date 1962)

[In the following excerpt, Gibbons offers an assessment of H. D.'s poetic achievement.]

Perhaps this is a time not so much for an evaluation of H. D.'s art as it is an appropriate time to acquaint ourselves with just what H. D.'s art is. (p. 152)

The most common adverse criticism of H. D.'s early poetry was that it made no social protest and that it was not journalism. . . . Keeping the elements of style for which she was praised early, H. D. has developed a poetic structure that is clearly unique and yet one could say that it is in the tradition of the best meditative lyricists (Herbert, Donne, Dickinson), and of the best elegists (Milton, Wordsworth, Whitman). For H. D. writes directly to the hugest problem of our time, that of life against destruction. Her answer may not be new in all its facets, but the elaboration is poignant. (pp. 154-55)

[A close examination of] *The Walls Do Not Fall* reveals the simultaneous complexity and simplicity of the answer to the problem which exists between man's intellectual seeking for spiritual reality and the historical fact of the destruction of civilizations. Internal evidence proves that the impact of destruction from a particular war does not occasion the whole poem. For other civilizations, particularly the Egyptian, are cited, and other gods than Christian are invoked. This poem's answer is that a spiritual regeneration has arisen from the destruction of previous cultures and can survive any possible destruction of our own. A spiritual reality has survived for man through both the written word, that tells of past cultures, and through the recurrent manifestation of the Logos, the Word born as man. Through enchantment, the poem states, rather than through sentiment, that spiritual reality may be ours. In the poem there is an affirmation of faith that through enchantment with the idea of regeneration, which is in the mystery of the Logos, a man may find the spiritual reality he seeks and turn from destruction.

"Enchantment" is the word that is the philosopher's stone to our understanding of the poem. Enchantment is both the attitude of the poet in the poem and the resulting effect of the poem upon the reader, i.e., the tone. "Magic" is a synonym for enchantment which is reminiscent of the Persian Magi, those mighty prophets and interpreters of dreams of whom three were said to have found their way to Bethlehem; whereby the poet declares that she has found a new master over love. . . . There is enchantment, in the sense of delight to a high degree, in the poet's attitude toward the words themselves. This is particularly true because of the etymological feeling H. D. has for words. . . . In this poem the historical sensitivity toward words, together with the selection of kinds of words—words which are as distant in space from each other as a star is from sea coral, as distant in time as is Osiris from a Moravian in Pennsylvania—combine the far away and long ago, the minute and the immense with a perilous immediacy, and the spell is cast. "Enchantment" is from the Old French verb *enchanter* that means to sing against. The poem itself is a long lyric, singing against destruction—an incantation in which the words are so accurately chosen that the spell is upon us. . . . Words in H. D.'s poetry have an emotional effect as well as an intellectual content. (pp. 155-57)

There is also in *The Walls Do Not Fall* a respect for passion and a conquering of passion by reason's limits—or by the poet's classic sensitivity. (p. 157)

H. D.'s images are not all visual or even kinesthetic. Sound is intricate in her poetry, sound is repeated, and, as we can hear, the repetition of sound adds to the effect of enchantment. As Horace Gregory suggests, "The way toward a renewed understanding of her poems is not to strain the eyes, but to hear the poems clearly." Any selection from H. D.'s poetry would bear examination for this effect; that is what one would expect of a poet who in the words of her own epitaph was following "intricate song's lost measure." (p. 158)

H. D. wrote, after the death of Freud, a book that is a free verse poem in the best elegiac tradition, titled *Tribute to Freud.* . . . To indicate something of the elegiac structure of the book, I refer you to the 4th section of it in which H. D. explains that she wanted to send gardenias to "the Professor" but could not find them. By her request, a friend sent orchids to him instead. . . . The flower motif, the theme of the death of the young Dutch flier, the excursion into the dimension of death or immortality, the dreams and the visions, the ruined cities and the broken idols, the affirmation—these are all indicative of the elegiac structure of the book. The poetic prose form was not new in *Tribute to Freud,* although it startled some uninitiated readers of H. D. She had been developing it at least since her early novel *Palimpsest* in 1926.

Among other books she has written there is *By Avon River* in which lyric prose and elegiac structure are again employed. After the lyric prose section that enlarges a myth about Shakespeare, H. D. has written a metrical poem, *Good Frend* (*sic*). In this poem she imagines herself the Claribel of *The Tempest.* . . . (pp. 159-60)

H. D.'s last book, *Helen in Egypt,* is a long psychological meditative lyric which represents the height of her art. It is actually a series of lyrics with transitional and introductory prose passages, the whole containing a clear narrative that carries the enchanted reader quickly from the first to the final line. It is the culmination of long years of poetic experimentation and refinement. As we would have expected, the writing does not lack depth or intricacy in its examination of the relation of the personal problem of guilt to the social problem of war. . . .

We who believe in the enchantment that language contains may find in H. D.'s songs of affirmation something that is significant, not only for our small and important literary circles, but for our young scholars we may find something more in poetry of this day than a protest, an irritation, or a lost world. (p. 160)

Kathryn Gibbs Gibbons, "The Art of H. D.," in *The Mississippi Quarterly,* Vol. 15, No. 4, Fall, 1962, pp. 152-60.

DENISE LEVERTOV
(essay date 1962)

[Levertov is an American poet and critic. In the following excerpt from an essay first published in *Poetry* in 1962, she examines H. D.'s development from her early to her mature poetry.]

Like so many others, I was for years familiar only with a handful of H. D.'s early poems, **"Peartree," "Orchard," "Heat," "Oread."** Beautiful though they were, they did not lead me to look further, at the time. Perhaps it was that being such absolutes of their kind they seemed final, the end of some road not mine; and I was looking for doors, ways in, tunnels through.

When I came, late, to her later work, not searching but by inevitable chance, what I found was precisely doors, ways in, tunnels through. One of these later poems, **"The Moon in Your Hands,"** says:

If you take the moon in your hands
and turn it round
(heavy slightly tarnished platter)
you're there;

This was to find not a finality but a beginning. The poem ends with that sense of beginning. . . . In **"Sagesse"** the photograph of an owl—a White Faced Scops Owl from Sierra Leone, which is reproduced along with the poem—starts a train of thought and feeling which leads poet and reader far back into childhood, by way of word origins and word-sound associations, and back again to a present more resonant, more full of possibilities and subtle awareness, because of that journey. The interpenetration of past and present, of mundane reality and intangible reality, is typical of H. D. For me this poem (written in 1957) was an introduction to the world of the Trilogy—*The Walls Do Not Fall* (1944), *Tribute to the Angels* (1945), *The Flowering of the Rod* (1946). (pp. 244-45)

What was it I discovered, face to face at last with the great poetry of H. D.'s maturity? What was—is—the core of the experience? I think this is it: that the icily passionate precision of the earlier work, the "Greek" vision, had not been an *end,* a closed achievement, but a preparation: so that all the strength built up, poem by poem, as if in the bones, in the remorseless clear light of that world . . . was *there,* there to carry darkness and mystery and the questions behind questions when she came to that darkness and those questions. She showed a way to penetrate mystery; which means, not to flood darkness with light so that darkness is destroyed, but to *enter into* darkness, mystery, so that it is experienced. And by *darkness* I don't mean *evil;* not evil but the Other Side, the Hiddenness before which man must shed his arrogance; Sea out of which the first creeping thing and Aphrodite emerge. . . . (pp. 245-46)

The "style"—or since style too often means *manner,* I would rather say the *mode,* the means—is invisible: or no, not invisible but transparent, something one both sees and sees through, like hand-blown glass of the palest smoke-color or the palest water-green. And in this transparent mode H. D. spoke of essentials. It is a simplicity not of reduction but of having gone further, further out of the circle of known light, further in toward an unknown center. Whoever wishes a particular example, let him read part VI of *The Walls Do Not Fall.* . . . (pp. 246-47)

After I had begun to know the later poems I returned to the *Collected Poems* of 1925 and saw them anew. . . . The poems I had thought of as shadowless were full of shadows, planes, movement: correspondences with what was to come. But I, and perhaps others of my generation, could come to realize this only through a knowledge of the afterwork. (p. 247)

There is no poet from whom one can learn more about precision; about the music, the play of sound, that arises miraculously out of fidelity to the truth of experience; about the possibility of the disappearance, in the crucible, of *manner.* . . .

Her last book, *Helen in Egypt* . . . is (like *Bid Me to Live* in its different form) a world which one may enter if one will; a life-experience that gives rise to changes in the reader, small at first, but who knows how far-reaching. The alternations, in *Helen,* of prose and poetry are not alternations of flatness and intensity but of contrasted tone, as in a Bach cantata the vocal parts are varied by the sinfonias, and each illumines and complements the other. *Bid Me to Live* and *Helen in Egypt* are neither of them works to be idly dipped into: one must go inside and live in them, live them through.

Indeed this is true of all her work: the more one reads it, the more it yields. It is poetry both "pure" and "engaged"; attaining its purity—that is, its unassailable identity as word-music, the music of word-sounds and the rhythmic structure built of them—through its very engagement, its concern with matters of the greatest importance to everyone: the life of the soul, the interplay of psychic and material life. (p. 248)

Denise Levertov, "H. D.: An Appreciation," in her *The Poet in the World,* New Directions, 1973, pp. 244-48.

BABETTE DEUTSCH
(essay date 1963)

[Deutsch was an American poet, novelist, and critic. In the following excerpt, she discusses ways that H. D.'s post-World War II poetry both resembles and diverges from her earlier work.]

Until the horrors of the second world war broke in upon her, [H. D.'s] subjects were limited to the toll demanded by a rigorous art, the agony of physical passion, a seascape or an orchard as these laid upon the beholder the burden of natural beauty. The narrowness that makes for intensity gives to some of her poems a feverish quality not to be found in the most ardent of Sappho's fragments. Un-Greek, too, is her care for the minute detail, the sharpness with which she outlines flower and fruit, the "cyclamen-purple, clyclamen-red" of the last grapes, the crisp line of a shadow at evening, the hot color of a petal, the texture of cliff grass. She did not fully exploit her limited vocabulary and her work displayed no glint of ironic wit. But her sensitiveness to tone-color is unquestionable. (p. 106)

H. D.'s rhythms are almost the rhythms of speech, but speech at its most passionate, restrained by the very emotion with which it is charged. She has the classical scholar's sense of quantity. The lines are short, often monosyllabic, yet slowed for emphasis. Rhyme is used sparingly and not always effectively, but only in the longer poems and the verse dramas are the insistent repetitions felt as a flaw. Elsewhere, the frequent spondees, the recurrence of certain phrases, the parallelism of others, produce an effect of symmetry. (pp. 106-07)

The poems with which H. D. emerged from a silence of nearly two decades point up her early work alike by their resemblance to and their departures from it. As before, she relies largely on the short, heavily loaded line, on incantatory phrasing, on pure luminous color. But the old altars were veritably shattered by fire from heaven. The poet left ancient Greece for the rubble-strewn London of the Blitz. The sense of miracle felt by the survivors is symbolized by the flowering of a charred tree in the city. The compelling passages are those which, in a few bare words, present desolation. . . . (p. 107)

Babette Deutsch, "The Earthly and the Definite," in her *Poetry in Our Time: A Critical Survey of Poetry in the English-Speaking World, 1900-1960,* revised edition, Doubleday & Company, Inc., 1963, pp. 85-128.

C. H. SISSON
(essay date 1975)

[Sisson is an English poet, novelist, and critic. In the following excerpt, he examines H. D.'s poetic development beyond her adherence to Imagism.]

H. D. is one of the most elusive writers of the century, and she has in fact eluded many readers who might find pleasure in her work. Her work is scattered among a score of volumes, most of them slight. There is no *Collected Poems;* the volume so named dates from 1925 and most of her best work was done after that. The work itself is elusive, and the reader might easily wonder, when he has run some slim volume to earth, whether he has really caught anything. In fact he has, if he can hold it. It is tenuous but not absolutely a ghost. A living spirit, running like quicksilver among sparse verses. (p. 85)

There was no doubt a great awareness, among the more teachable in Pound's circle, of the web of interrelationship in Renaissance literature, Italian, French and English, and of their dependence on Greek and Latin originals. . . . This background is to be remembered in considering the work of H. D. People say 'Imagist' and they say 'Greek' when her name is mentioned. They should think also of the Renaissance—Pater's as well as Spenser's—and recall that T. E. Hulme, who was killed in 1917, had made a case for thinking that the significant work of the twentieth century would turn its back on that period. It is not to the anti-humanistic art which Hulme saw or foresaw that H. D.'s work belongs. Nor does it belong to that movement of taste which has put Donne so near the centre of our understanding of the seventeenth century and displaced the more pastoral Elizabethans, including Spenser himself. (pp. 85-6)

However harmless, or even useful, when it was first applied, the [Imagist] label has certainly served to obscure the nature of H. D.'s development. There is, even in [the] early verses, a psychological as well as an objective element. The rapidity of movement answers to a breathless apprehension of the external world. . . .

H. D.'s early work is well illustrated—and readily accessible—in Peter Jones's Penguin, *Imagist Poetry.* It is evidence of the high degree of training of which her temperament made her capable. A person so fastidious as she was was no doubt glad of a formula which relieved her of the necessity of saying more than she had

to say, and invited her to efface herself before appearances. (p. 86)

[*Bid Me to Live*] is certainly unusual in its kind. There is none of the fluttering and showing off of *The Waves*—if Virginia Woolf's book is to be included as another uncharacteristic member of the *genre.* There is none of the special pleading inseparable from D. H. Lawrence's recordings. Most of the book shows a quiet, almost withdrawn, observation. H. D. carries her fastidiousness into the midst of the most personal observation. There are many—all too many—books of reminiscences by women who have slept with or otherwise known writers of notoriety enough to make the reminiscences publishable. They are usually horrible, less for what they record than for the lack of perception they betray. It needs more talent to venture into a book than into a bed. One peculiarity of the H. D. book, which indeed makes it unique, is that the observer is herself a woman of original, and not merely reflected, literary talent. Her observation may be partial but it is veridical. (p. 87)

On a small scale, much of the work in *Hymen* has considerable formal merit. There is the imagist trick, learned long before. There is also what is perhaps best described as a sort of rhetoric, elegant enough, but which leaves the reader in the end with a sense of emptiness. (p. 88)

Pound talked of 'Hellenic hardness' in connection with H. D.'s work. There is certainly a persistent use of Greek sources, and of Greek allusions. . . . Behind this there was no doubt a good deal of work. . . . [The] impression left by much of H. D.'s earlier work is, after all, of a certain emptiness, as if not much was found in all this fumbling among Greek deities and Greek islands. The elegance of manner is often striking, and it is no small thing. But the twentieth century is not a happy time for a writer who has formal gifts but has to seek his material. So many conventions have become unusable. H. D.'s notes on Elizabethan and seventeenth-century poets, in the prose part of *By Avon River,* indicate where her sympathies lie. Her taste, sure in its way, veers from the more energetic poetry to the more formal celebration of beauty and death. There is, in her own work of this period, a lack of intellectual content. (pp. 88-9)

There is a marked development in depth in the later poems, in particular the (second) wartime sequence of *The Walls Do Not Fall, Tribute to Angels,* and *The Flowering of the Rod* and the poems in *Hermetic Definition.* The long poem *Helen in Egypt* (1961), has its place in H. D.'s *oeuvre* but is less satisfactory, truth to tell, partly on account of its length. There is a surging to and fro over the legend of Helen—that she was in Egypt and that only an illusion appeared on the walls of Troy. That the confusions of H. D.'s own past are as much in her mind as the fate of Helen could not be in doubt for anyone who has read her work at all extensively. There are passages between Helen and Achilles which are certainly not free of allusion to the personal history recorded in *Bid Me to Live.* The successful long poem is an extreme rarity, and one can say of H. D.'s attempt that it is creditably near to a style in which a long poem *could* be written in the twentieth century—the long poem conceived not as having, on an impossible scale, the quickening of the lyric but the combination of sobriety and movement which carries us on in Drayton or in Golding. But H. D.'s poem, as a whole, has not quite these qualities. The impression is often of a mulling over of old worries—and old Greeks—and the sense of direction is not sustained.

The change in the character of H. D.'s later work, as compared with the earlier, may be related to her exploration of those distresses which took her to Vienna as a patient of Freud in 1933-4. . . . H. D.'s interest in Greece took her back to Egypt and muddling among the pattern of ancient mysteries, so obscurely known as to allow more room for fantasy than Christian theology, with its vulgar links with rationalism and the crudities of social structure. H. D. carried her interest in magic and ancient mumbo-jumbo into the world of her analyst. . . . [*Tribute to Freud*] is a masterpiece of its kind, accurate and inconclusive, the work of an observer immensely gifted and profoundly trained to record her impressions. It is a little classic in its own right, however one may rate the contribution it can offer to the understanding of H. D.'s verse.

The verse of the later period is continuously concerned with interpretation of experience by the dark help afforded by ancient cults. There is, however, much of a more overt and accessible character. (pp. 89-90)

The poems in *Hermetic Definition* take up a number of themes. . . . But the life of these poems—what makes them unique, perhaps—is the delineation, with the precision her long training allowed her, of the reflections of an old woman, still thinking of love, still with her habitual lack of restraint as to what needs to be said, and complete restraint as to what does not. (pp. 90-1)

Where does one place H. D.? It is perhaps imprudent to try to place her firmly in relation to her contemporaries. Her preoccupations, as well as the superficial severity of her verse, have kept her out of the main flow of interest. The Greek carapace may seem forbidding. But it should not be. In her essence H. D. is a slight, extremely feminine figure, whose battles are all inward, and who scarcely sought to link her thought with the public preoccupations of the age. She lived obscurely with the illusion—which is not entirely an illusion—that if the artist gets on with his art all will be well. For her this was not a personal thing, but a thing which took her, through and beyond current social necessities—as she saw it—to the permanent concerns

embodied in the ancient religions, including our own. The connections she established were exploratory, not dogmatic. The point for the prospective reader is merely that H. D. offers far more than the formal virtues which are usually allowed to her work, and that that work abundantly repays the not very strenuous labour of reading it. (p. 91)

C. H. Sisson, "H. D.," in *Poetry Nation*, No. 4, 1975, pp. 85-91.

RACHEL BLAU DUPLESSIS
(essay date 1979)

[In the following excerpt, DuPlessis discerns a pattern of exploration of male-female relationships in H. D.'s life and work.]

In her life's work, H. D. returned constantly to a pattern of personal relations that she found perplexing and felt to be damaging to herself and other women: thralldom to males in romantic and spiritual love. In her later writing, she invented a number of strategies to transform this culturally mandated and seductive pattern of male-female relations. Romantic thralldom is a feature of many literary plots because of conventions surrounding love and marriage, quest and vocation, hero and heroine. These conventions could be termed "Scripts" for both literary plots and personal relations. In order to transform these psychocultural scripts, H. D. had to invent in her works patterns for male-female relationships less damaging than, but . . . as satisfying as those she and other women had experienced.

Romantic thralldom is an all-encompassing, totally defining love between unequals. . . . Viewed from a critical, feminist perspective, the sense of completion or transformation that often accompanies thralldom in love has the high price of obliteration and paralysis, for the entranced self is entirely defined by another. (pp. 178-79)

Female thralldom occurs with startling, even dismal frequency throughout H. D.'s published and unpublished works. In particular, H. D. was vulnerable to the power of what she termed the "héros fatal," a man whom she saw as her spiritual similar, an artist, a healer, a psychic. Again and again this figure that she conspired to create betrayed her; again and again she was reduced to fragments from which her identity had once more to be painfully reconstructed. She states, for instance, that one famous "Héros"—D. H. Lawrence—"conditioned me to deception, loss, destruction," and that another, "Lord Howell," "was the perfected Image" of this former lover. Though H. D. lived for many years as the companion of Winifred Bryher, her work returned obsessively to the "héros" figure and to the damage she suffered in her relations with him. Whatever personal and sexual arrangements she made could not obliterate the culturally reinforced plot of thralldom. She had to remake this psychocultural pattern in her writing in order fully to break with it.

The impact of sexual subordination on H. D. as woman and artist can be seen in two autobiographical novel-memoirs written about her early adulthood: the unpublished *Her* (c. 1927), an ungainly but interesting work which justifies H. D.'s decision not to marry Pound, and the more serious and desperate *Bid Me to Live* (1960), a *roman à clef* about the London Bohemian set during the First World War. In tandem, these works describe the situation of a woman of artistic leanings and achievements within a male-dominated society in the early part of this century. In every role in which she is cast, the woman is unsatisfied and tormented: as courtesan, as deceived wife, as muse, as consort. She is prevented from claiming the end to that torment: equality. (pp. 179-80)

[*Her*] concerns a classic dilemma for woman: the necessity to choose between being a muse for another and being an artist oneself. . . . The heroine's authentic identity, indicated in the image of a tree which recurs throughout the novel, and . . . in the contrast between austere Greek and sensual Roman pantheons, is mirrored and intensified by Her's relationship with Fayne. Fayne represents self-love, self-identification, and a twinship between spiritual sisters. Through Fayne, Her makes contact with herself and her vision. Instead of being George's muse, she takes Fayne as her inspiration.

The name "Her" has a particular meaning bound up with the image of Fayne. Whenever H. D. writes "Her realizes" or "Her says," she is using the wrong form of the pronoun in subject place; and every time this ungrammatical usage occurs, one is jarred into a recognition of the situation of generic woman. Though "Her" is the object form, the very ungainly quality of the name used as the subject of a verb ("Her does," "Her realizes") suggests that we are in the presence of some resistant, stubborn matter which will not be captured. The contradictory features of this striking nickname are brought into focus and then resolved as Her strokes Fayne's forehead with "healing hands" and says, "I will not have her hurt. I will not have Her hurt. She is Her. I am Her. Her is Fayne. Fayne is Her. I will not let them hurt HER." By identifying with another wounded woman, the heroine perceives her own hurt and her own capacity for self-protection. The heroine must love herself through another woman as a sign of selfhood. However, the novel does not deal directly with the alternative loves which are so clearly delineated within it. In any case, thralldom to males has been only temporarily rejected. *Her* is a first skirmish in the almost endless battle of H. D.'s psychic life.

At the end of her life, H. D. returned to this formative World War I period in her novel *Bid Me to Live*. The title epigram, from Herrick, wittily presents the life of the emotions as a playful religion of love:

> Bid me to live, and I will live
>   Thy Protestant to be:
> Or bid me love, and I will give
>   A loving heart to thee. . . .

The poem refers to the time in a relationship when adoration is mutual and commands are not burdensome. The novel explores the attempt by Julia and Rafe Ashton to sustain such a "blithe arrangement." But equal comradeship and romantic love appear to be contradictory states. The circumstances faced by the couple—the war, the birth of a dead child—make it difficult, even impossible, to sustain equality and interdependence. She becomes vulnerable, neurasthenic, needy; he is bluff, willful, callous. They fall into stereotypic behavior, their needs at cross-purposes. Therefore the woman in *Bid Me to Live* feels completely inadequate—a sexual failure and a professional anomaly within the group of male artists that surrounds her. (pp. 180-82)

In Julia's encounters with Rico and Rafe, we confront the unedifying spectacle of male poets compelling a female poet to curtail her ambition, to dissolve the complete world she strove for, to concentrate on the item, not on the *oeuvre*. . . . *Bid Me to Live* shows male poets limiting the shape and force of a woman's material by using sexual and personal acceptance as a weapon. Julia's response reveals the internalization and acceptance of these demands, which diminished her ambition and limited or negated her power. The issue is larger than the relationship of these three writers. The encounter raises the question whether male writers, in complicity with prescribed roles for women, have helped create poetesses where there could have been poets. This is the issue underlying the censorship with which H. D. grappled. The stakes were poetic achievement itself. Thralldom to male power had to be attacked; yet it was the most difficult thing to attack. For the pain of thralldom seemed to fire H. D.'s creativity even as it undercut the conditions necessary for her fullest, uncensored flowering.

While resistance is one solution to thralldom, H. D. also tries to articulate a creative and psychic power transcending the claims of romantic love. (pp. 185-86)

H. D. was trying to construct some perspective that avoided the constant subordination of the woman to the man in normal sexual and cultural life. In her view, men and women are equals in the spiritual realm, not seeking the distinctions of fixed sex roles, but rather a mutual suffusion of insight and wisdom. (p. 187)

H. D.'s profound psychic damage from sexual and spiritual thralldom continued to torment her. The kinds of rejections she suffered were coupled in her mind with the First World War as linked aspects of that destructive force which shattered the possibility of a cultural life. Yet the themes of the first war recurred to be resolved during World War II, which H. D. spent, by choice, in the London of the Blitz. In her inner patterning of these events, the first war was death, and the second was rebirth. The long-awaited consummation of her poetic force did occur; the evidence can be seen in the brilliance of *Trilogy,* for its symbols of resurrection, its vision of a new city, and its invention of the role of Mary Magdalene constitute the materials of a psychic and cultural reconstruction. At the same time, however, H. D. returned to the forms of sexual polarization and entrapment represented by the thralldom of women to men. (p. 188)

The strategy of outright resistance and confrontation of male by female forces is not paramount in H. D.'s poetry. The transposition of conflicts to a spiritual area beyond conflict . . . sometimes makes H. D. lose contact with her materials. I surmise that these exits from the script of thralldom do not wholly succeed for H. D., although the transposition of conflicts into a spiritual area of unification remains an important end in her writing. The first option represents conflict and defiance, the second represents sheer resolution, unity by the suppression of conflict. Only in the final solution to romantic thralldom—what I term the sufficient family—do both conflict and resolution exist in a complex and nuanced balance, with a full account both of the engendering conflict and of the transpositions that create resolution. This solution, paramount in *Helen in Egypt,* builds a new structure of relationships to substitute for thralldom. (pp. 189-90)

H. D. wrote this poem in the aftermath of strong spiritual and psychic attraction to men on whom she had depended for some kind of self-justification. She suffered rejection; her response is the poem. But although the poem was provoked by rejection, within it the pattern of thralldom is broken: the same needs are met by different relationships, and nurturance and vision are achieved without sexual or spiritual damage from men.

Helen in Egypt is engaged with one particular literary "order of reality," a prominent myth of Western culture. H. D. has not precisely displaced the *Iliad* or the story of the war following an abduction; that tale is taken for granted as the plot that precedes this new alignment of characters and actions. But criticism of the epic realm is present, if indirect. Before the poem begins, H. D. has replaced the sexually centered woman and her bellicose lover with two liminal figures, waver-

Hilda Doolittle.

ing between worlds of fragmentation and wholeness: Achilles, the vulnerable "New Mortal," and an incubating psyche, still in chrysalis but nonetheless fully winged (Helen-Thetis). H. D. chooses her characters not because of their capacity for sensual love or savage war but because of their visionary ability to crystallize the dissolved or latent meanings hidden in the former story. The characters act as catalyzing precipitants of nonepic material already "dissolved" in culture. By postulating that another shape to traditional stories occurs necessarily, H. D. mutes the critique she is making. In her view, stories are not created but recovered; they are not new-made but really old. *Helen in Egypt* is the archeological site where those recovered stories are found. . . . H. D., like other women writers, had difficulty establishing an authority sufficient to remake a culturally sanctioned story. So the story is "the same"—the old legend—when she felt her own authority most weakly, and "different"—the "flame of thoughts"—when she could plumb the depths of her desire for critique and transformation. (pp. 191-93)

The form of *Helen in Egypt* also dramatizes the question of the poet's authority to remake this story, and that question becomes part of the strain of remaking it. There are prose passages preceding every poem which summarize the contents of that section. This is helpful, because the material is difficult and obscure. But the prose also has the effect of making the events seem more elusive, challenging both their place in time and their reality. Sometimes the prose passages make a statement implying that something has happened, while the poetry which comes later poses the same fact as a question. After having read the two statements, the reader is unsure whether or not something has occurred. While generally the prose and poetry are simple retellings of the same events, at other points a degree of difference is emphasized: the event is first present, then absent or obscured.

The poem concerns the parallel quests of Helen and Achilles which are not journeys to each other, but quests for access to the unifying mother. Helen's quest is emphasized, but both have found Thetis at the end; this is what finally unites them. (p. 193)

[All] the males in *Helen in Egypt*—Achilles, Paris, and Theseus (the figure of Freud)—have begun to form a postheroic personality, and all give Helen permission to make her quest, which must include understanding herself as a post-romantic woman. The granting of permission by all three males is a female fantasy, based on extraordinary need for male approval and fear of male judgment. All the male characters know of and approve of her desire for reintegration within Thetis, the mother: all instruct her in one way or another to "call on Thetis." . . . Yet they want different Helens. She must avoid the polarized roles which the two lovers give her while at the same time retaining their approval. . . . [Her] multiple identities indicate her own lack of inner integration. This dilemma is solved when she transcends these opposites through the healing mediation of Theseus in Part II, who "reparents" her, acting as both mother and father and healing the divisions found in the traditional nuclear family. She becomes Helen-Thetis in Part III, uniting Troy and Greece and uniting her own torn consciousness in love and death.

Making Achilles and Helen into fellow questers is the first move in H. D.'s strategy for breaking the script of romantic thralldom. The lover and woman are imagined as brother-sister questers, so that totally spiritual, not sexual, forces define the relationship. The quests of Helen and Achilles are finally not journeys toward love for each other, but a single quest to identify the source: the mother. Further, Helen avoids a replay of the drama of sexual thralldom by asking Paris, too, to join her on a brother-sister quest. Paris then emerges as Helen's child by Achilles; for the lover, displaced from dominance in the plot of thralldom, can return in the role of a child. (pp. 195-96)

The "child-mother, yourself " is a way of moving beyond both war and romantic love, beyond the strains of the heroic and romantic scripts. Helen is both the Great Mother, avatar of Thetis, and the baby in her mother's arms. "Helen in Hellas forever" is the climactic, reverberating phrase which suggests an ongoing exchange of force in the closed circuit of mother-child-mother. . . . This closure solves for H. D. the needs and themes of her major work—the needs for undamaging nurturance and undamaging powers. Helen is the complete family represented by the petals of the nenuphar, but most particularly she is "the child in the father, / the child in the mother," the child-mother herself. . . .

By this set of solutions, H. D. was attempting to end her submission to male power, constructing from available male and female roles, especially from parent and child roles, some set of relationships that would be less emotionally damaging to her as a woman than those she had actually experienced with men. To do this she creates a female quest whose final answer is the central revelation of mother and child, flanked by father and brother; "the thousand-petalled lily" contains and presents all the relations of the sufficient family. . . . (p. 201)

Through the superficially bizarre connections among her characters, H. D. constructed an answer to thralldom to male power, inventing relationships that would make specific kinds of transformations of that damaging script. In the hieroglyph of the sufficient family, a strict division of sexual roles is often retained, but female insight is approved of and assisted as if it were a valued cultural and personal resource. Under the system of romantic thralldom, love, care, and nurturing come with a very high price: sexual bitterness and despair. But in the system of the sufficient family, the father or mother figure, and more rarely the brother, give care and nurturing to the female character without exacting the debilitating price which the male lover always seemed to extort.

Further, in the system of thralldom which H. D. experienced, male power always stood first, and female power was unequal to it. This meant that a man expected a woman to be subsumed under him and to experience a loss of identity, as in *Her,* while the woman at once desired to be equal and experienced guilt about that desire. Certainly it is an old story. Within the sufficient family, rather than being subsumed in an unequal power relation, the woman has two special sources of force—in biological creation (as the mother through the child) and in self-creation, as the child through herself as mother—on the psyche quest.

While the sufficient family composed of brother-sister questers, reparenting fathers and mothers, and the psyche madonna is not the product of any social or political analysis, this family could nonetheless be taken as an accurate postulation of all the relationships that would have to be transformed in order for a new kind of male-female sexual and spiritual relation to exist; that is, in order to end romantic thralldom. Some sense of the enormity of the task of cultural reconstruction is revealed by the immense changes that H. D. makes in her poetic family. Since psychocultural patterns are learned within the family, it must surely be recast in order to change our images of women, culture, and society. (pp. 202-03)

Rachel Blau DuPlessis, "Romantic Thralldom in H. D.," in *Contemporary Literature,* Vol. 20, No. 2, Spring, 1979, pp. 178-203.

SUSAN STANFORD FRIEDMAN

(essay date 1981)

[In the following excerpt, Friedman discusses H. D.'s role in the Imagist movement, her development of a Modernist perspective in her post-World War I poetry, and the impact of her psychoanalysis with Sigmund Freud.]

Hilda Doolittle's emergence on the pages of *Poetry* magazine in 1913 as "H. D., Imagiste" heralded the beginnings of a writer whose canon spans half a century and the genres of poetry, fiction, memoir, essay, drama, and translation. This achievement was firmly rooted in H. D.'s central participation in the imagist movement, a short-lived moment in literary history, but one whose experiments changed the course of modern poetry with its concept of the "image" and its advocacy of vers libre. (p. 1)

Sea Garden, published in 1916, was the poet's culmination of her early apprenticeship in London, and it won for her the reputation of being the best of the imagist poets. Her poems avoided the vague moralizing and sentimental mythologizing that the imagists deplored in much of the "cosmic" poetry of the late nineteenth century. They were crisp, precise, and absolutely without excess. The imagist emphasis on hard, classical lines, however, did not mean that the poems were without emotion. Most imagist poems rely heavily on precisely delineated objects from nature to embody subjective experience. But as poems like **"Heat"** and **"Oread"** demonstrate vividly, H. D.'s imagist poetry was not a form of nature poetry adapted to the modern world. The essence of the imagist task was to locate the "image" that incarnated an "intellectual and emotional complex in an instant of time"—or, to use T. S. Eliot's later term, the "objective correlative" of subjective experience. In *Sea Garden,* H. D. fulfilled that task by rendering intense passions and perceptions in images that originated in her visits to Cornwall and her American childhood. . . . The mythological personae that appear in many of her poems did not represent an escapist attempt to return to ancient Greece, but rather

served as personal metaphors or masks that allowed her to distance intense emotion sufficiently for artistic expression.

H. D.'s ability to fulfill the aesthetic demands of imagist doctrine has been well recognized. Less frequently understood, her contribution to the major shift in modern poetry was organizational as well as aesthetic. She, along with Amy Lowell, helped to insure the continuation of the imagist community after Pound's efforts to retain sole editorial power split the original group in 1915. As editor of *The Egoist* from 1915-1917, H. D. encouraged poets to write and helped them find an audience during the difficult war years. But H. D.'s efforts to keep alive the poetic visions of her soldier-husband, Richard Aldington, and the other members of their artistic community were doomed by the violence and meaninglessness of the First World War. (pp. 2-3)

Bid Me to Live (A Madrigal), her roman à clef, tells the story of the intersecting personal and cultural catastrophes that ended her "specialized" success. Aldington's affair with Dorothy Yorke and the dissolution of her marriage, the deaths of her brother and father, the loss of D. H. Lawrence's friendship, and her own grave illness during the last stage of her pregnancy merged with the general destruction of war to break apart the relatively secure world of imagist compatriots. The war did more than strain personal relationships, however. It produced the historical conditions that made the intensely aesthetic world of imagism inadequate and gave enormous impetus to the growth of modernism. The hysteria of mindless patriotism and the omnipresence of death in a trench war for inches and feet of blasted territory created the necessity for a different kind of art, one that could record the fragmentation of culture and begin the quest for new meanings. (p. 3)

The dissolution of symbolic systems unveiled as grand illusions impelled a literature centered on quest, art whose forms and themes were consistent with the search for new patterns of meaning. The bitter events of history forced H. D. and her writing companions to emerge from the limited perfection of imagism. With its emphasis on the poem as the instantaneous visual incarnation of an "emotional and intellectual complex," imagism could not explain the violence of war and the fragmentation of belief systems. . . . Imagism had begun as a philosophy of art, but it evolved into a craft that could be incorporated into the larger explorations of modernist literature. H. D.'s reflections in an interview with the *New Haven Register* in 1956 are a perceptive commentary on the significance of imagism in the development of modern poetry. She emphasized to the reporter that "the term [imagist] cannot be applied to describe her work since World War I." . . . H. D. described "her early work as 'a little sapling,' which in the intervening years, 'has grown down into the depths and upwards in many directions.' " (pp. 3-4)

In the postwar years, artists went beyond the earlier imagist breakthrough and turned increasingly to the archetypes of quest in mythological and literary traditions for models of search. . . . H. D.'s development from imagist to epic art places her squarely in the center of this modernist mainstream. Her work shares with [such writers as Ezra Pound, T. S. Eliot, William Carlos Williams, James Joyce, W. B. Yeats, and Hart Crane] the fundamental spirit of quest given shape by myth and mythic consciousness, by religious vision or experience, and by a new synthesis of fragmented traditions.

H. D. did not, however, find the direction that led to her mature art with the immediacy of compatriots like Pound and Williams. While *The Cantos* and *Paterson* began to take shape in the twenties, H. D.'s route to a modernist perspective and aesthetic was more indirect and included considerable experimentations with a variety of genres and even art forms as she attempted to find her "true direction." (pp. 4-5)

H. D.'s artistic efforts during the twenties were extensive although the results were uneven and often left in draft form. . . . H. D. experimented with her own technique of interior monologue in her two published novels, *Palimpsest* (1926) and *Hedylus* (1928) and a number of shorter prose works like **"Moose Island"** and **"Narthex."** All of them prose masks for her own life, primarily her marriage to Aldington, these autobiographical fictions disturbed many of the readers who had admired "H. D., Imagiste." Her "specialized" success as an imagist created narrow expectations for her new work that inhibited her desire to expand into new forms and subjects. . . . In actuality, her desire to develop a new "H. D." involved fiction to a greater extent than her critics imagined. She left in manuscript form three thinly disguised autobiographical novels. . . . (p. 6)

Interest in fiction did not lead H. D. to abandon poetry, however. In *Hymen* (1922) and *Heliodora* (1924) she expanded the imagist gems of *Sea Garden* into more diffuse, exploratory correlatives for emotion. Her *Collected Poems* (1924) presented an overview of the poetic achievement begun in 1913, and, at the end of the decade, she brought out *Red Roses for Bronze* (1931). Her work on translations from Greek lyrics and verse drama in *Hippolytus Temporizes* (1927) as a source of influence on her own poetry paralleled the pattern of Pound's work. By the end of the twenties, H. D. did not appear to be in search of her "true direction." She had worked enormously hard at a variety of manuscripts. . . . Some two decades of writing and publication had established H. D. in the public domain of literature. But this achievement reached an aesthetic dead end in the thirties. With the rise of fascism and

the imminence of a second catastrophic war, H. D. wrote far less regularly and published little in any genre. She did translate and publish Euripides' *Ion* with her own commentary (1937), work that Pearson said was very important to her later development. She did write a few short stories and a group of nine loosely connected poems, apparently intended for a small volume called *The Dead Priestess Speaks.* But none of the short stories were published, and only parts of a few poems appeared in little magazines such as *Life and Letters Today.* The unfinished volume, with its multiple drafts and various tables of contents, testifies that H. D. seemed to have lost that certain sense of direction, that sure inner knowledge of "WHO H. D. is" or should be. (pp. 6-7)

The violence of war jolted H. D. out of a decade of relative latency. . . . The Second World War functioned for her much as the First World War had for writers like Pound. Her sense of destiny as poet-prophet in the modernist apocalypse was certain and took on various forms of quest in *The Gift, Tribute to Freud,* and most importantly in her epic, *Trilogy,* composed of three volumes published as she wrote them: *The Walls Do Not Fall* (1944), *Tribute to the Angels* (1945), and *The Flowering of the Rod* (1946). In the *Trilogy,* which can serve as both primer and profound expression of the modernist spirit, H. D. sought to discover or create through the "Word" some ordering pattern that could redeem the surrounding ruin. . . . The *Trilogy* is a record of quest, a search deep within the unconscious and throughout many mythological traditions for the knowledge of unity beneath division and destruction. In short, H. D. began to write the kind of "cosmic poetry" the imagists had sworn to abandon. . . . Her "rebirth" as a revitalized poet during the war gave her a sense of her "true direction" that led her with steady inspiration to produce the mature work written in the late forties and fifties: *By Avon River* (1949); *Helen in Egypt* (1961); *Winter Love* (1973); *Sagesse* (1973); *End to Torment* (1979); and *Hermetic Definition* (1973).

Cosmic quest did not, however, lead H. D. to abandon imagist craft. Her later work bears a strong resemblance to imagist technique in the continued clarity and simplicity of her poetic line and the precise shape of her images. She continued to anchor the poem in the concrete world with images of flowers, rocks, insects, birds, and the seashore. The continuities between her imagist and epic work recall the way Pound's "superpositions" survived as small units within *The Cantos.* Similarly, the intensely personal emotion masked by mythological personae in poems like *Helen in Egypt* and *Winter Love* was present in her imagist lyric. Conversely, the seeds of later growth existed in the nearly animistic apprehension of nature in her imagist poetry. . . . But her growth "into the depths and upwards" fundamentally transformed the function of both myth and subjective experience in her poetry. In the *Trilogy* and in all the poetry she wrote thereafter, the personal and mythological are made to serve the needs of a religious and philosophical quest to explore basic humanistic questions about women and men, life and death, love and hate, destruction and renewal, war and peace, time and eternity.

With the benefit of hindsight made possible by the explosion of H. D.'s writing in the early forties, it is clear that the extensive experimentation of the twenties and the relative latency of the thirties were a sort of "incubation" period out of which the new H. D. emerged. Why did it take her twenty years to develop her own modernist voice when her writing companions of the First World War made the shift so much earlier? What, in fact, were the conditions of H. D.'s gradual metamorphosis? The clues to her development lie in her own images of self-exploration in *Tribute to Freud.*

Although this memoir revolves structurally around Freud, it reveals the framework of her search in the thirties for a regenerated and redirected artistic identity. As she had done even in her earliest imagist poetry, H. D. identified herself with a figure from mythological tradition to stimulate the unfolding reflections of memory and myth. For her persona, she chose Psyche, the mortal woman whose search for Eros has frequently been interpreted as the soul's quest for divine immortality. The name "Psyche" comes for the Greek word for "soul," often portrayed in Greek art as a butterfly that leaves the body at death. (pp. 7-9)

H. D. wove together these fragments of myth and imagery to create her own "legend" of metamorphosis, as she called it. . . . The First World War and its subsequent personal and cultural consequences had constituted a kind of death for H. D., a descent to the underworld from which she had to emerge in a process of spiritual rebirth that was decades in the making. Repeatedly, she used imagery based on the life cycle of the butterfly to describe the journey of her soul from death to life. . . . After a period of living death, the soul begins its emergence as butterfly. In her autobiographical novel *Her,* H. D. recalled such a period in her life. Hermione is her persona, and "Her" is her nickname as she images her emergence from breakdown in the correlative of the butterfly leaving the cocoon. . . . (p. 9)

In the *Trilogy,* H. D. announced the rebirth of Psyche, the butterfly who emerges from the cocoon of near-death. (p. 10)

Psyche's "gestation" was gradual, unlike the transformations that produced *The Cantos, Paterson,* and *The Waste Land* in the twenties. *Tribute to Freud* once again points to a possible explanation for this. A pervasive undercurrent in the book is the theme of her "dif-

ference": her recognition of, desire for, and pride in multiple forms of "difference." What set H. D. apart most profoundly, however, was her status as a woman writing in a predominantly male literary tradition. . . . Even as a woman in the male circle of imagists and artists in London, H. D. was alone. Sappho's influence on imagists no doubt helped to validate H. D.'s leadership role in the development of the modern lyric. But as historical forces fostered a poetry of quest that borrowed from epic and heroic tradition, H. D. became even more of an anomaly. Few women poets have ventured into the masculine domain of quest literature. . . .

Archetypes of questors in both literary and mythological tradition are overwhelmingly male: figures like Perseus, Hercules, Jason, Theseus, Lancelot, Percival, and Beowulf overshadow the travels and trials of Demeter, Isis, and Psyche. Indeed, cultural definitions of the heroic presume masculinity while the complementary assumptions about the nature of the heroine frequently presuppose feminine passivity and helplessness. Patriarchal tradition held out little encouragement for H. D. to develop a woman-centered epic in which woman was the seeker and doer instead of the angelic or evil object of male quest. From this perspective, it is not so amazing that H. D.'s growth was more gradual than that of her fellow modernists. Rather, it is extraordinary that she ultimately managed to defy the dominant tradition entirely by creating woman heroes whose search for meaning bears so little resemblance to the stereotyped female figures in the quest poetry written by men. . . . H. D.'s woman-identified questors spun a different web of meanings, ones that resurrected the life-giving female symbols and values which J. J. Bachofen had identified with the goddesses of ancient matriarchies.

The roots of H. D.'s emergence from the cocoon of the thirties lay in two sources of inspiration that seem antithetical, but which she experienced as parallel forms of spiritual quest. Broadly defined, those inveterate foes science and religion took her "down into the depths and upwards in many directions," to quote from her own definition of growth. Her experience with psychoanalysis, highlighted by her sessions with Freud in 1933 and 1934, led her down into the depths of unconscious memory and dream. As modern "Door-Keeper" of the human psyche, Freud appeared to her like the Egyptian god Thoth, the "infinitely old symbol, weighing the soul, Psyche, in the Balance." . . . Psychoanalysis took H. D. inward in a way that systematized and expanded on her early fascination for intense, subjective experience. In the unconscious decoded with Freud's help, H. D. found the wellsprings of inspiration. At the same time, this journey inward taught her to relate the personal to the universal. (pp. 10-11)

Esoteric tradition, including the many shapes of the occult, contained the "tribal myths" that reproduced her personal dreams on a cultural level. Complementing the impact of psychoanalysis, syncretist religious traditions led her out of her moment in history, took her through many cultures and eras, and revealed universal patterns underlying the shape-shifting forms of all experience. . . . With Freud's help in decoding her dreams and visions, H. D. found the spiritual and philosophical underpinnings of a chaotic and violent world.

With the war as her catalyst, H. D. wove the science and religion of the psyche together to produce an art that was both deeply personal and broadly based in religious traditions that are the legacy of time. The impact of Freud and of esoteric religion was enormous, both personally and aesthetically. Both influences permeate her mature work and form the context in which it can be most fully comprehended.

To research the parallels in H. D.'s work with psychoanalytic or occult tradition, however, would result in a superficial understanding of their significance for her development. . . . Whether or not we accept Harold Bloom's hypothesis that the anxiety of influence reenacts the Oedipal family romance, the process of influence must surely be recognized as fluid and personal, dialectical and never static. It operates as a creative collaboration in which the artist interacts with her or his sources and ultimately transforms them to serve the requirement of individual vision. This dynamic quality in the process of influence is clearly delineated in H. D.'s case, particularly in her interactions with Freud. Their relationship was a complex emotional and intellectual dialogue in which their disagreements did as much as their agreements to focus Psyche's quest. Especially because she left a record of that dialogue, their collaboration serves as a virtual paradigm of working influence. Because Freud's impact on twentieth-century art has been so enormous, H. D.'s creative transformation of his theories can serve as a superbly outlined case study of his influence on literary artists.

The interplay of their creative minds, however, points to the paradoxical nature of Freud's influence on H. D. and other modern artists. She described Freud as the "guardian of all beginnings," but she also reminded herself repeatedly that "the Professor was not always right." . . . . His impact on H. D. and other artists was dependent upon their ability to revise fundamental assumptions in his work. . . . [Freud] celebrated reason over passion and belief, and looked forward to a future when the infantile consolations of religion would be re-

placed by the rational power of "logos." . . . In contrast, H. D. and others influenced by Freud were disillusioned with the limited truths of rationalism and the destructive horrors of technological progress. They celebrated intuition, the vision of dreams, and the "primitive" myths still living in the human psyche and recorded in tradition.

On another level, H. D.'s very survival as a woman artist required her to confront Freud's misogyny if she were to continue in the traditionally male roles of questor and poet. . . . His theories of psychosexual development became "scientific" arguments for the inferiority of women and therefore rationalizations for inequality. H. D. sought inspiration from one of the greatest legitimizers of patriarchy. Her success as a woman depended upon conflict.

Mutual warmth and respect characterized their relationship, as both their letters and *Tribute to Freud* attest. But in another sense, their sessions together represent a prototypical confrontation between the polarities that permeate the modern world: man against woman, science versus religion, fact versus faith, objective versus subjective reality, reason versus intuition, the rational versus the irrational. H. D. and Freud dramatically personified the intellectual opposition of the age. Their "argument," played out in his office at Berggasse 19 and in the pages of H. D.'s memoir, is a microcosm of vital twentieth-century debate.

H. D.'s response to the confrontation was fundamentally dialectical. To serve the needs of spiritual quest, she developed aspects of Freud's thought until they became antithetical to his own perspectives. Freud, she wrote, was "midwife to the soul." . . . But, once reborn, Psyche emerged with a voice distinctly her own. Once having clarified the poles of opposition, her search for synthesis led to a transcendence of their differences in a vision that incorporated the whole. This transformation of Freudian theory simultaneously served as the basis of her mature art and as a brilliant reevaluation of Freud's significance for the twentieth century. Long before theorists like Norman O. Brown and Herbert Marcuse reinterpreted Freud's thought, H. D. reflected on the man who survived in her memories and in his books until she found the artist within the scientist, a prophet within the apostate, and the woman within the man. (pp. 11-14)

Susan Stanford Friedman, in her *Psyche Reborn: The Emergence of H. D.*, Indiana University Press, 1981, 332 p.

SOURCES FOR FURTHER STUDY

Gubar, Susan. "The Echoing Spell of H. D.'s 'Trilogy'." *Contemporary Literature* 19, No. 2 (Spring 1978): 196-218.

> Close critical examination of *The Walls Do Not Fall, Tribute to the Angels,* and *The Flowering of the Rod,* calling the trilogy "one of H. D.'s most coherent and ambitious poetic narratives" and maintaining that the work contains hidden or encoded revisions of male myths from a female perspective.

Moore, Harry T. "The Faces Are Familiar." *The New York Times Book Review* (1 May 1960): 4.

> Review of *Bid Me to Live* that focuses on the novel's autobiographical basis.

Quinn, Vincent. *Hilda Doolittle.* New York: Twayne Publishers, 1967, 160 p.

> Provides an overview of H. D.'s career, focusing on her principal works. Includes primary and secondary bibliographies.

Robinson, Janice S. *H. D.: The Life and Work of an American Poet.* Boston: Houghton Mifflin Co., 1982, 490 p.

> Biographical and critical study.

Waggoner, Hyatt H. "Science and Poetry: Imagism." In his *American Poets: From the Puritans to the Present*, pp. 331-53. Rev. ed. Baton Rouge: Louisiana State University Press, 1984.

> Includes discussion of H. D. in a chapter devoted to Imagist poetry.

Watts, Emily Stipes. "1900-1945: A Rose Is a Rose with Thorns," in her *The Poetry of American Women from 1632 to 1945*, pp. 149-76. Austin: University of Texas Press, 1977.

> Examines H. D.'s role as one of the formulators of Imagism, her use of mythology in her poetry, and her anticipation of literary Modernism in her work, concluding that "H. D.'s verse represents the very earliest expression of those tendencies by which we identify poetry as Modern."

Joseph Heller

1923-

American novelist, playwright, scriptwriter, and short story writer.

INTRODUCTION

Heller is a popular and respected writer whose first and best-known novel, *Catch-22* (1961), is considered a classic of the post-World War II era. Presenting human existence as absurd and fragmented, this irreverent, witty novel satirizes capitalism and the military bureaucracy. Heller's tragicomic vision of modern life, found in all of his novels, focuses on the erosion of humanistic values and highlights the ways in which language obscures and confuses reality. In addition, Heller's use of anachronism reflects the disordered nature of contemporary existence. His protagonists are antiheroes who search for meaning in their lives and struggle to avoid being overwhelmed by such institutions as the military, big business, government, and religion. *Catch-22* is most often interpreted as an antiwar protest novel that foreshadowed the widespread resistance to the Vietnam War that erupted in the late 1960s. While Heller's later novels have received mixed reviews, *Catch-22* continues to be highly regarded as a trenchant satire of the big business of modern warfare.

Heller was born in Brooklyn, New York, to first generation Russian-Jewish immigrants. His father, a bakery-truck driver, died after a bungled operation when Heller was only five years old. Many critics believe that Heller developed the sardonic, wisecracking humor that has marked his writing style while growing up in the Coney Island section of Brooklyn. After graduating from high school in 1941, he worked briefly in an insurance office, an experience he later drew upon for the novel *Something Happened* (1974). In 1942, Heller enlisted in the Army Air Corps. Two years later he was sent to Corsica, where he flew sixty combat missions as a wing bombardier, earning an Air Medal and a Presidential Unit Citation. It is generally agreed that Heller's war years in the Mediterranean theater had only a minimal impact on his conception of *Catch-22.* Discharged from the military in 1945, Heller married Shirley Held and began his college education. He obtained a B. A. in English from New York University, an M. A. from Columbia University, and attended Oxford University as a Fulbright Scholar for a year before becoming an English instructor at Pennsylvania State University. Two years later Heller began working as an advertising copywriter, securing positions at such magazines as *Time, Look,* and *McCall's* from 1952 to 1961. The office settings of these companies also yielded material for *Something Happened.* During this time Heller was also writing short stories and scripts for film and television as well as working on *Catch-22.* Although his stories easily found publication, Heller considered them insubstantial and derivative of Ernest Hemingway's works. After the phenomenal success of *Catch-22,* Heller quit his job at *McCall's* and concentrated exclusively on writing fiction and plays. In December of 1981, he contracted Guillain-Barré syndrome, a rare type of polyneuritis that afflicts the peripheral nervous system. Heller chronicled his medical problems and difficult recovery in *No Laughing Matter* (1986) with Speed Vogel, a friend who helped him during his illness.

Catch-22 concerns a World War II bombardier named Yossarian who believes his foolish, ambitious, mean-spirited commanding officers are more dangerous than the enemy. In order to avoid flying more missions, Yossarian retreats to a hospital with a mysterious liver complaint, sabotages his plane, and tries to get himself declared insane. Variously defined throughout the novel, "Catch-22" refers to the ways in which bureaucracies control the people who work for them. The term first appears when Yossarian asks to be declared insane. In this instance, Catch-22 demands that anyone who is insane must be excused from flying missions. The "catch" is that one must ask to be excused; anyone who does so is showing "rational fear in the face of clear and present danger," is therefore sane, and must continue to fly. In its final, most ominous form, Catch-22 declares "they have the right to do anything we can't stop them from doing." Although most critics identify Yossarian as a coward and an antihero, they also sympathize with his urgent need to protect himself from this brutal universal law. Some critics have questioned the moral status of Yossarian's actions, noting in particular that he seems to be motivated merely by self-preservation, and that the enemy he refuses to fight is led by Adolf Hitler. Others, however, contend that while *Catch-22* is ostensibly a war novel, World War II and the Air Force base where most of the novel's action takes place function primarily as a microcosm that demonstrates the disintegration of language and human value in a bureaucratic state.

Heller embodies his satire of capitalism in the character of Milo Minderbinder, whose obsessive pursuit of profits causes many deaths and much suffering among his fellow soldiers. Originally a mess hall officer, Milo organizes a powerful black market syndicate capable of cornering the Egyptian cotton market and bombing the American base on Pianosa for the Germans. On the surface Milo's adventures form a straightforward, optimistic success story that some commentators have likened to the Horatio Alger tales popular at the turn of the twentieth century. The narrative line that follows Yossarian, on the other hand, is characterized by his confused, frustrated, and frightened psychological state. The juxtaposition of these two narrative threads provides a disjointed, almost schizophrenic structure that reasserts the absurd logic depicted in *Catch-22.*

Structurally, *Catch-22* is episodic and repetitive. The majority of the narrative is composed of a series of cyclical flashbacks of increasing detail and ominousness. The most important recurring incident is the death of a serviceman named Snowden that occurs before the opening of the story but is referred to and recounted periodically throughout the novel. In the penultimate chapter, Yossarian relives the full horror and comprehends the significance of this senseless death as it reflects the human condition and his own situation. This narrative method led many critics, particularly early reviewers, to condemn Heller's novel as formless. Norman Mailer's oft-repeated jibe: "One could take out a hundred pages anywhere from the middle of *Catch-22,* and not even the author could be certain they were gone" has been refuted by Heller himself, and has inspired other critics to carefully trace the chronology of ever-darkening events that provide the loose structure of this novel.

Heller poignantly and consistently satirizes language, particularly the system of euphemisms and oxymorons that passes for official speech in the United States Armed Forces. In the world of *Catch-22* metaphorical language has a dangerously literal power. The death of Doc Daneeka is an example: when the plane that Doc is falsely reported to be on crashes and no one sees him parachute to safety, he is presumed dead and his living presence is insufficient to convince anyone that he is really alive. Similarly, when Yossarian rips up his girlfriend's address in rage, she disappears, never to be seen again. Marcus K. Billson III summarized this technique: "The world of [*Catch-22*] projects the horrific, yet all too real, power of language to divest itself from any necessity of reference, to function as an independent, totally autonomous medium with its own perfect system and logic. That such a language pretends to mirror anything but itself is a commonplace delusion Heller satirizes throughout the novel. Yet, civilization is informed by this very pretense, and Heller shows how man is tragically and comically tricked and manipulated by such an absurdity."

Heller's second novel, *Something Happened,* centers on Bob Slocum, a middle-aged businessman who has a large, successful company but who feels emotionally empty. Narrating in a monotone, Slocum attempts to find the source of his malaise and his belief that modern American bourgeois life has lost meaning, by probing into his past and exploring his relationships with his wife, children, and co-workers. Although critics consider Slocum a generally dislikable character, he ultimately achieves sympathy because he has so thoroughly assimilated the values of his business that he has lost his own identity. Many commentators have viewed Slocum as an Everyman, a moral cipher who exemplifies the age's declining spirit. While initial reviews of *Something Happened* were mixed, more recent criticism has often deemed this novel superior to and more sophisticated than *Catch-22,* particularly citing Heller's shift from exaggeration to suggestion. In his critical biography *Joseph Heller,* Robert Merrill described *Something Happened* as "the most convincing study we have of what it is like to participate in the struggle that is postwar America."

Good as Gold (1979) marks Heller's first fictional use of his Jewish heritage and childhood experiences in Coney Island. The protagonist of this novel, Bruce Gold, is an unfulfilled college professor who is writing a book about "the Jewish experience," but he also harbors political ambitions. Offered a high government position after giving a positive review of a book written by the president, Gold accepts, leaves his wife and children, and finds himself immersed in a farcical bureaucracy in which officials speak in a confusing, contradictory language. In this novel, Heller harshly satirizes former Secretary of State Henry Kissinger, a Jew who has essentially forsaken his Jewishness. As a result, the author draws an analogy between the themes of political powerlust and corruption with Jewish identity. Similarly, Gold's motives for entering politics are strictly self-aggrandizing, as he seeks financial, sexual, and social rewards. When his older brother dies, however, Gold realizes the importance of his Jewish heritage and family, and decides to leave Washington. Throughout the novel, Heller alternates the narrative between scenes of Gold's large, garrulous Jewish family and the mostly gentile milieu of Washington, employing realism to depict the former and parody to portray the latter. Heller's next novel, *God Knows* (1984), is a retelling of the biblical story of King David, the psalmist of the Old Testament. A memoir in the form of a monologue by David, the text abounds with anachronistic speech, combining the Bible's lyricism with a Jewish-American dialect reminiscent of the comic routines of such humorists as Lenny Bruce, Mel Brooks, and Woody Allen.

In an attempt to determine the origin of his despondency near the end of his life, David ruminates on the widespread loss of faith and sense of community, the uses of art, and the seeming absence of God. In *Picture This* (1988), Heller utilizes Rembrandt's painting "Aristotle Contemplating the Bust of Homer" to draw parallels between ancient Greece, seventeenth-century Holland, and contemporary America. Moving backward and forward among these eras, this novel meditates on art, money, injustice, the folly of war, and the failures of democracy. Critics questioned whether *Picture This* should be considered a novel, a work of history, or a political tract.

Heller's first play, *We Bombed in New Haven* (1967), concerns a group of actors who believe they are portraying an Air Force squadron in an unspecified modern war. The action alternates between scenes where the players act out their parts in the "script" and scenes where they converse among themselves out of "character," expressing dissatisfaction with their roles. This distancing technique, which recalls the work of Bertolt Brecht and Luigi Pirandello, alerts the audience to the play's artificiality. As in *Catch-22,* this drama exposes what Heller perceives as the illogic and moral bankruptcy of the United States military. Many critics have also interpreted *We Bombed in New Haven* as a protest against America's participation in the Vietnam War. Heller has also adapted *Catch-22* for the stage, but critics generally consider this work inferior to the novel.

While Heller's place in twentieth-century letters is assured with *Catch-22,* he is also highly regarded for his other works, which present a comic vision of modern society with serious moral implications. A major theme throughout his writing is the conflict that occurs when individuals interact with such powerful institutions as corporations, the military, and the federal government. Heller's novels have displayed increasing pessimism over the inability of individuals to reverse society's slide toward corruption and degeneration. He renders the chaos and absurdity of contemporary existence through disjointed chronology, anachronistic and oxymoronic language, and repetition of events. In all his work, Heller emphasizes that it is necessary to identify and take responsibility for our social and personal evils and to make beneficial changes in our behavior.

(For further information about Heller's life and works, see *Contemporary Authors,* Vols. 5-8; *Contemporary Authors New Revision Series,* Vol. 8; *Contemporary Authors Bibliographical Series,* Vol. 1; *Contemporary Literary Criticism,* Vols. 1, 3, 5, 8, 11, 36, 63; *Dictionary of Literary Biography,* Vols. 2, 28; and *Dictionary of Literary Biography Yearbook: 1980.*)

CRITICAL COMMENTARY

VICTOR J. MILNE

(essay date 1970)

[In the following excerpt, Milne analyzes Heller's use of the mock-epic form in *Catch-22* to illustrate the conflict between Christianity's "universal benevolence" and capitalism's competitive ethos.]

Most recent studies of *Catch-22* share the assumptions that the novel presents the world as absurd and chaotic, and that Yossarian's desertion reflects the currently widespread sentiment in favor of dropping out of a mad society. Thus Yossarian has been variously presented as an idealistic "puer eternis" who "refuses the traditional journey of learning in manhood" [according to Sanford Pinsker], and as the traditional comic rogue-figure who "never tries to change the society that he scorns." Although most critics are agreed on these points, their evaluative judgments run through the whole spectrum from laudatory to condemnatory, and the majority of them register some uneasiness about the moral perspective which they impute to Heller. (p. 50)

The intention of the present study is to substitute for these opinions a new and more positive interpretation of Heller's ethical and metaphysical perspective, and in so doing to justify the formal peculiarities of the novel as appropriate to the author's vision. At the root of the dissatisfaction with *Catch-22* lies a failure to recognize its epic inspiration, which not only explains its digressive structure but also constitutes the vehicle for Heller's moral vision. *Catch-22* uses the mock-epic form to dramatize a clash between two opposing moralities. The one ethic, exemplified by Yossarian, is a Christian ethic of universal benevolence, which, as the symbolic importance of Sweden suggests, expresses itself economically in terms of socialism and politically in terms of non-repressive government. The conflicting outlook, which will be referred to as the competitive ethic, is associated with capitalism, false patriotism, and the heroic code of the true epic and is exemplified by Colonel Cathcart and the other villains. The conflict between the two codes inevitably raises a second question: how is the man of good will to succeed or even survive in dealing with the unscrupulous adherents of the competitive ethic? Yossarian's desertion, seen in the context of the symbolism of the novel and the explicitly theological language of the last chapter, attempts to answer that question. The answer is a religious one, which is in harmony with classical Protes-

tant doctrine, and which is most readily explicated in terms of the ethical teaching of a great modern theologian—Dietrich Bonhoeffer.

The parody of the epic is most apparent in the plot of *Catch-22*, which offers notable parallels to the *Iliad*. When Yossarian refuses to fly any more missions and marches "backward with his gun on his hip," Colonel Korn inquires, "Who does he think he is—Achilles?" Although this seems to be the only occasion in the novel on which explicit reference is made to the *Iliad*, it is sufficient to remind the reader that Yossarian's situation is identical with that of Achilles. Let us review briefly the relevant facts about the *Iliad*. The "argument" of the epic is not the fall of Troy but the wrath of Achilles, and the main plot is concerned with the efforts of the Greeks to bring Achilles back into battle, just as the main plot of *Catch-22* is concerned with the pressures put on Yossarian to fly more combat missions. The *Iliad* begins *in medias res* with the bitter quarrel between Achilles and Agamemnon, in which Achilles berates his commander for much the same flaws that are most prominent in Colonel Cathcart—acquisitiveness and cowardice. Achilles retires to his quarters to sulk, his friend Patroclus voluntarily goes into battle, and his death precipitates Achilles' reconciliation with Agamemnon, his return to battle, and consequently his death.

If *Catch-22* is carefully examined, it will be found to present a close parallel to these events. The novel opens *in medias res* at the point where Yossarian has "made up his mind to spend the rest of the war in the hospital." Nately serves as the Patroclus-figure, and since the novel provides a mirror-image of the values of the epic—that is, everything is seen in reverse, Nately's death precipitates Yossarian's firm resolve to fly no more combat missions. Paradoxically, this results in a reconciliation between Yossarian and Cathcart when Yossarian accepts the "odious" deal whereby he is to be sent home transformed into a hero for purposes of public relations. (A minor parallel is that both commanders are incompetent blusterers and must rely on their shrewd subordinates—Ulysses and Korn—to win over the recalcitrant warriors.) Yet the novel cannot end at this point, and the crisis of decision is repeated in Chapter Forty-One where Nately's place is taken by all of Yossarian's dead pals, and Yossarian tells Danby that he intends to break the odious deal.

From the foregoing account, Heller's novel is ob-

Principal Works

Catch-22 (novel) 1961

We Bombed in New Haven (drama) 1967

Catch-22: A Dramatization (drama) 1973

Something Happened (novel) 1974

Good as Gold (novel) 1979

God Knows (novel) 1984

No Laughing Matter [with Speed Vogel] (prose) 1986

Picture This (novel) 1988

---

viously far from a detailed reworking of an ancient legend. Inevitably, in accommodating the plot of the *Iliad* to a modern military situation, Heller has made considerable changes. . . . The only important change is dictated by Heller's need to make the plot of the *Iliad* serve his own moral vision. There must be two crises of decision in order to present Yossarian's flight to Sweden as an act of heroism and responsibility rather than of cowardice. Yossarian is free to choose the odious deal but does not, and Heller clearly indicates that his decision is motivated largely by loyalty to his dead friends: "Goddammit, Danby. I've got friends who were killed in this war. I can't make a deal now." The morally responsible nature of Yossarian's desertion is further underscored by Yossarian's allusion to a well-known biblical paradox when he tells Danby that the odious deal is not a way to save himself but a way to lose himself.

As well as parodying the plot of the *Iliad,* Heller makes use of some of the generic devices of the epic form. A characteristic feature is the digressive amplitude of the narrative, which confers the liberty of developing minor characters far more fully than their roles in the plot require. Several critics have been troubled by this violation of the strictest canons of structural unity in *Catch-22.* Yet the digressions make an essential contribution to the texture of the novel and the epic. In the *Iliad* an undertone of universal pathos is built up by the accumulated effect of the structurally irrelevant descriptions of the heroes' homelands and of the ways in which they came to join the Achaian host, and the end result is that the epic achieves cosmic significance. Heller, too, uses digressions to give his work a universal frame of reference so that war is treated not so much as a problem in its own right but rather as a symbol of the plight of modern western civilization, and this he accomplishes with a fine blend of pathos and comedy, appropriate to his mock-epic form, as, for example, in the digression on Major Major's upbringing and his induction into the army. (pp. 51-4)

George Steiner holds that the *Iliad* is the prototype of all tragedy, and he affirms that the essence of tragedy is doubt about the rationality and justice of the uni-

verse, an assertion "that the forces which shape or destroy our lives lie outside the governance of reason." The *Iliad* taken as a whole may be said to pose this root question of theodicy and to hint at a despairing answer, but none of the characters in the epic ever engages in such radical questioning. In this respect Yossarian goes beyond Achilles to become Job: "Good God, how much reverence can you have for a Supreme Being who finds it necessary to include such phenomena as phlegm and tooth decay in His divine system of creation." The question of the justice of the universe runs like a black thread through the novel, sometimes hyperbolically bitter as above, sometimes unrelievedly tragic, and sometimes transmuted into comedy as when one of the hospital patients observes: "There just doesn't seem to be any logic to this system of rewards and punishment. . . . Who can explain malaria as a consequence of fornication?" In *Catch-22* the tragic questioning of God's ways to men is prompted above all by the war, by the pointless extinction of one human life after another:

> Kraft was a skinny harmless kid from Pennsylvania who wanted only to be liked, and was destined to be disappointed in even so humble and degrading an ambition. Instead of being liked, he was dead. . . . He had lived innocuously for a little while and then had gone down in flame over Ferrara on the seventh day, while God was resting. . . .

Homer's tragedy is intensified because the Olympian gods provide "a comic background to the tragedy below." For example, Ares' complaint to Zeus when he is lightly wounded by Diomedes is comically outrageous in its insignificance following a battle in which scores of warriors stoically accepted death. In *Catch-22* the equivalent comedy is provided by the upper echelons of the military, who are safe from the dangers of combat, and who at all times act as though they had no share in mortality. Just as the gods urge whole armies into battle and doom certain men to death, all the while quarrelling jealously among themselves, so the headquarters staff in *Catch-22,* in the midst of their scramble for status, deliver pep talks and issue the orders that doom men like Nately to an unnecessary death. (pp. 54-5)

One other illuminating parallel between these two literary universes may be developed. Although all the other gods tremble at the words of Zeus almost as much as Colonel Cathcart does at the frown of General Dreedle, neither Zeus nor the Gods as a whole are supreme in the universe. They themselves must submit to the decrees of the *Moirai,* the impersonal fates that rule the cosmos. In the same way, Dreedle, Peckem, Cathcart, Korn and the rest do not really run the microcosm of Pianosa but merely ratify the decrees of Milo Minderbinder and ex-Pfc Wintergreen. As Colonel Korn explains in a moment of self-revelation, he and the other non-combatant officers are all helpless victims of the competitive ethic: "Everyone teaches us to aspire to higher things, a general is higher than a colonel, and a colonel is higher than a lieutenant-colonel. So we're both aspiring." The competitive ethic is the law decreed by omnipotent capitalism, personified in Milo Minderbinder, who, as his very name indicates, has the power to shackle thought and decent human feelings, and who, Heller makes plain, is to be conceived of as the supreme deity of this insane world: "Milo was the corn god, the rain god and the rice god in backward regions where such crude gods were still worshipped, and deep inside the jungles of Africa, he intimated with becoming modesty, large graven images of his mustached face could be found overlooking primitive stone altars red with human blood." Of course, from a Christian point of view the pagan gods are no more than devils, and Milo, whose "argosies . . . filled the air," does indeed represent the prince of the powers of the air. As we shall soon see, he is elsewhere unmistakably identified with Satan.

Heller, then, uses the mock-epic form to reject the pre-Christian (and sub-Christian) values of the military-economic complex, whose competitive ethic is another manifestation of the ancient heroic code. Yossarian, a twentieth-century man with a Christian attitude to the sanctity of human life, finds himself—up to the last chapter—plunged into the indifferent pre-Christian universe of the primary epic. . . . Whereas the warriors of the *Iliad* submit stoically to sudden death, Yossarian resolves "to live forever or die in the attempt." Whereas they chiefly prize fame won in battle, Yossarian answers with a negative Colonel Korn's question: "Don't you want to earn more unit citations and more oak leaf clusters for your air medal?" Yossarian categorically rejects the heroic code in his talk, but the definitive disavowal of these outworn values comes in the act of desertion. Thus above all else, the conflict between the competitive ethic and the humanistic Christian ethic determines the literary form of the novel as a "Bologniad," as a mock-epic embellished with comedy and horror, in which a modern Achilles says "baloney" to the demands of a corrupt society with its iniquitous heroic code requiring the sacrifice of human lives.

For the very reason that Yossarian opposes himself to the competitive ethic and its attendant heroic code we cannot view him as the traditional rogue figure who delights us by his impudent, self-centered indifference to conventional morality. Although he is concerned with his personal safety, he wants to save his life in both senses of the phrase. We have observed that Heller makes every effort to show that the desertion is a responsible, moral act; to this we must now add that he is not inconsistent in drawing attention to the moral perplexities involved in Yossarian's choice. . . . [Yos-

sarian] is faced with a choice between two incompatible relative goods—a patriotism that is justifiable because his country is engaged in a just war and a rebellion against an inhumane system of exploitation, whereby Cathcart and Korn enjoy their meaningless triumphs of egotism at the expense of men's lives. The opposition between the two goods means that each good has an evil inseparably annexed to it. Rebellion against the American system of exploitation involves abandonment of the struggle against the inhumanity of the Nazi state; support of the American war effort entails supporting the evil system and being disloyal to the friends who have suffered under it. Although Heller leaves no doubt that the American system, which gives so much scope to the petty oppressors, is still a lesser evil than the frank tyranny of the Nazis, we are made to feel in the course of the novel that Yossarian must take a stand against the exploitation that confronts him. (pp. 55-8)

If Heller had implied that the question of an Allied victory in World War II was morally neutral, we should have despised such a shallow view of human affairs, and the lack of dramatic tension in Yossarian's choice would have rendered the novel boring. . . . Although the novel needs no defence beyond a demonstration that Heller has dealt faithfully with the moral complexities of his hero's situation, the recognition of the paradox inevitably does prompt the question whether there is a resolution within the novel. There is some evidence of such a resolution, and to understand it we must examine the theological background of the novel—particularly, the concept of guilt. (pp. 58-9)

From a theological viewpoint the novel presents exploitation and submission to exploitation as the two great sins. Exploitation, however, need not involve the imposition of physical hardships; it is better defined in Erich Fromm's phrase as "the reification of man." Thus Milo, viewing the men only as a market to be manipulated, exploits them fully as much in providing broiled Maine lobster as in trying to introduce chocolate-coated cotton to the menu. It is in this sense—the denial of humanity—that Milo, or capitalism, requires human sacrifice. The political system, as much as the market place, encourages the process of reification, and it is particularly noticeable in the idealists, Clevinger and Danby. Even though their actions are externally indistinguishable from those of men who have responsibly decided to serve a cause, they have, in fact, reified themselves in accepting the notion that their value resides only in their utility as cogs in the war-machine. The soldier in white, who functions only as part of a pipeline between two glass jars, and of whom life can be predicated only on the basis of a thermometer reading, is the perfect symbol of the reification of man. Yossarian, then, in insisting upon the unique value of his individual life, constitutes a focal point of resistance to exploitation. Milo and Colonel Korn both recognize his importance and treat him as the bellwether whom the rest of the flock will follow. If Yossarian will allow himself to be used in any way, even in accepting the odious deal, none of the others will refuse to fly combat missions.

In stripping off his clothes Yossarian is trying to deny his complicity in the evils of the world. However, in the chapter entitled "The Eternal City"—let us note in passing that Rome is the "Babylon" of the Book of Revelation, the epitome of the worldly lust for pomp and power—Yossarian acknowledges the guilt that he shares with the rest of humanity: . . .

> Yossarian thought he knew why Nately's whore held him responsible for Nately's death and wanted to kill him. Why the hell shouldn't she? It was a man's world, and she and everyone younger had every right to blame him and everyone older for every unnatural tragedy that befell them; just as she, even in her grief, was to blame for every man-made misery that landed on her kid sister, and on all other children behind her. Someone had to do something sometime. Every victim was a culprit, every culprit a victim, and someone had to stand up sometime to try to break the lousy chain of inherited habit that was imperiling them all.

In this passage there is (in addition to a modern redefinition of original sin) a significant explanation for the puzzling attacks of Nately's whore: hers is the role of an accuser, almost a comic equivalent of the Eumenides. Interestingly enough, she succeeds only once in stabbing Yossarian, immediately after he commits his one unequivocally loathsome action in agreeing to the odious deal. Her attack is obviously the incident which jolts Yossarian into rejecting the deal: "Goddammit, Danby. I've got friends who were killed in this war. I can't make a deal now. Getting stabbed by that bitch was the best thing that ever happened to me." Thus Nately's whore is to be viewed in the latter part of the novel as an allegorical projection of Yossarian's own conscience, which will not let him come to terms with any form of exploitation.

At this point the moral dilemma of the novel is posed in its acutest form. If Yossarian were to accept the deal, he would be guilty towards his friends, who have been exploited by Milo and Cathcart. If he were to desert he would be guilty towards his country and the just cause in which it is engaged. If he were neither to accept the deal nor to desert, he would face a court-martial on trumped-up charges. A superficial application of Christian ethics would suggest that Yossarian could escape guilt by staying to face the false accusation. However, Yossarian's suffering could have no redemptive value for the other victims since, as Danby points out, all without exception will believe the

charges. Yossarian's situation raises in a peculiarly acute form the question of passive suffering as against active resistance. By offering himself as a victim, by trying to keep his conscience spotless, Yossarian would really be helping the powerful exploiters of humanity. In other words, excessive scrupulosity can be dangerous, for it can too easily reconcile hope for social justice with a passive submission to the bluff of the authorities that "Catch-22" says "they have a right to do anything we can't stop them from doing." Thus Yossarian's decision to desert enacts Heller's ethical judgment that an individual has no right to submit to injustice when his action will help to maintain an unjust system, for the desertion is a positive moral act calculated to discomfort the exploiters, whereas facing the court-martial would represent a paralysis of the will, a desire to maintain purity of conscience at the cost of inaction.

To understand the problem more clearly and Heller's resolution of it, we must examine two subordinate characters, Chaplain Tappman and Major Major. So far as *Catch-22* can be allegorized, we may say that these two represent the Christian virtues as popularly conceived and in particular the disabling "virtue" of excessive scrupulosity. They are both men of good will, and they both submit patiently to all the indignities thrust upon them. Major Major, especially, is characterized by his adherence to the Decalogue and the moral teachings of Christ:

> He turned the other cheek on every occasion and always did unto others exactly as he would have had others do unto him. When he gave to charity, his left hand never knew what his right hand was doing. He never once took the name of the Lord his God in vain, committed adultery or coveted his neighbour's ass. In fact, he loved his neighbour and never even bore false witness against him.

The result of such characteristics is that Major Major and the chaplain are both exiled from human society and become ineffectual hermits unable to influence the world for good or evil. This is the price exacted by excessive concern with purity of conscience; one can avoid evil but cannot do good: "The chaplain was a sincerely helpful man who was never able to help anyone . . .". In fact, the chaplain has become so paralyzed by his undeniable virtues that at the end of the novel Yossarian must urge him: "For once in your life, succeed at something." (pp. 59-62)

Catch-22 has seemed inconsistent to a number of critics because the theological substructure of the novel is in full accord with the paradoxical insights of classical Protestant thought. On the one hand, Protestant doctrine recognizes the sinfulness of all human endeavour, and on the other hand, it refuses to be seduced into ignoring the imperfect world of becoming in favour of the perfect world of being. On the contrary,

Protestant theology insists on activism even though sin inevitably results; the principle is enshrined in Luther's startling maxim, *pecca fortiter*—sin resolutely. The same notion is expounded more thoroughly in a modern Protestant classic, Dietrich Bonhoeffer's *Letters and Papers from Prison,* a work which may be profitably read in conjunction with *Catch-22* as it also comes out of World War II and shows a remarkable affinity in temper to Heller's novel. (pp. 63-4)

It would be impossible to summarize Bonhoeffer's complex doctrine of responsibility which forms the core of his ethical thought. Basically, we may say that responsibility involves an acceptance of the need to relate all moral action to the concrete situation of mingled good and evil, and thus it is opposed to a Kantian affirmation of abstract ethical demands which are to be practised universally without regard to the concrete situation. Yossarian recognizes that he must make his choice in the real situation which offers only relative good and relative evil. Any choice will involve sinning against some abstract ethical principle. And according to Bonhoeffer's doctrine a choice such as Yossarian's is justified by God even if the greater evil is unintentionally chosen, for "if any man attempts to escape guilt in responsibility, he detaches himself from the ultimate reality of human existence" and "sets his own personal innocence above his responsibility for men." Yossarian, then, is the responsible man, in Bonhoeffer's sense, while Clevinger and Danby in their arguments with Yossarian show themselves to be Kantians who cannot understand his reluctance to affirm that an ethical abstraction must be honoured at all times and at all places and under all conditions.

Our theological perspective can be completed only by a consideration of the God of *Catch-22*, the true God who stands in opposition to Milo Minderbinder's demonic claims. One persistent motif in the narrative is the chaplain's progressive loss of faith in God. Like Yossarian the chaplain is led by the spectacle of meaningless death to question the justice of the universe, and after his failure to dissuade Colonel Cathcart from raising the required number of missions, he is ready to disbelieve "in the wisdom and justice of an immortal, omnipotent, omniscient, humane, universal, anthropomorphic, English-speaking, Anglo-Saxon, pro-American God." Why should he believe in such a God? This God has based his reputation on his abilities as a benevolent stage-magician who will always intervene on behalf of a right-thinking, humane Anglo-Saxon, but "there were no miracles; prayers went unanswered, and misfortune tramped with equal brutality on the virtuous and the corrupt." The chaplain's "atheism" may be regarded as an essential preliminary condition of true faith; he must reject the anthropomorphic idol invented to ratify the pretensions and prejudices of a particular culture if he is ever to believe in the mysterious Biblical God who impartially distributes temporal blessings and misfortunes. (pp. 64-5)

[The] chaplain never wholly loses faith in God but only in the man-made idol, and when the time comes, he is given a new revelation. The chaplain has rejected the stage-miracles of religious tradition, but he discovers that there is a different kind of miracle. When news of Orr's safe arrival in Sweden reaches Pianosa, he exclaims: "It's a miracle, I tell you! A miracle! I believe in God again." Orr's escape has a quite obvious religious significance, for seen in a theological context, his crash-landing in the Adriatic is a symbolic baptism and the sudden news of his safety gives the whole episode the quality of resurrection following death—a miraculous reversal of the seemingly irrevocable catastrophe.

Orr is an important figure but remains enigmatic up to the last chapter of the novel. To Yossarian he seems a comic figure, a sucker, the prototypal victim of all the forms of exploitation that Yossarian himself protests against. To him Orr is "a freakish, likeable dwarf with . . . a thousand valuable skills that would keep him in a low income group all his life," and he is convinced that Orr needs to be shielded "against animosity and deceit, against people with ambition and the embittered snobbery of the big shot's wife, against the squalid, corrupting indignities of the profit motive and the friendly neighbourhood butcher with inferior meat." Yossarian is wrong, of course, because, though seeing the qualities that lie behind Orr's apparent innocence, he does not understand their value. Orr is self-reliant ("a thousand valuable skills"), patient, enduring ("oblivious to fatigue"), and adaptable ("not afraid . . . of foods like scrod or tripe"). Above all, Orr is a doer rather than a contemplative like the chaplain, and he is admirably equipped to survive. The imagery identifies Orr closely with the natural world—he is "a gnome," "a dwarf," "as oblivious to fatigue as the stump of a tree" and has "an uncanny knowledge of wildlife." He may be seen as a mischievous and resilient earth-spirit like Puck or as the true embodiment of the seemingly naive but really shrewd and self-reliant archetypal Yankee farmer, of whom Major Major's father is a ludicrous parody. In any case, Orr is the personification of the qualities of intelligence and endurance which make possible the survival of humanity under the worst conditions of oppression and exploitation. While the chaplain engages in futile efforts to reason with Colonel Cathcart, while Yossarian carries on a futile and dangerous revolt, Orr quietly practises the skills that will ensure his survival. Only after Orr has acted can Yossarian grasp the possibility of escape that was and still is open to him, and then he realizes that he must imitate Orr in being "as wise as serpents and harmless as doves." . . . (pp. 65-7)

Throughout the novel, Yossarian, for all the verbal energy displayed in his revolt, has been paralyzed by his moral quandary. In the Snowden episode he was an impotent good Samaritan, and in the chapter, "The Eternal City," he was a Pharisee walking past terrible spectacles of human misery and not daring to aid the victims; only now, with the example of Orr before him, can he perform a positive moral action. The forgiveness of sins promised in baptism has important consequences not only on the eternal level but also on the temporal level in that the consciousness of divine forgiveness can break the neurotic paralysis of the will induced by the fear of sinning. Thus the baptismal symbolism of Orr's escape indicates that Orr's qualities, including his all too human shrewdness, are forgiven, sanctified, and employed in a miracle that has redemptive value for Yossarian and the chaplain. Yossarian then realizes that he must follow Orr—even though it involves him in the sin of withdrawing his resistance to Nazism—because it will help no one if he is put in prison on false charges. The moral effects of Yossarian's action are admittedly almost insignificant; he may be able to help Nately's whore's kid sister, and he will be able to embarrass Cathcart and Korn. Yet this is the only morally valid possibility for Yossarian and he must not shrink from it either to accept the odious deal or to help the exploiters by submitting to martyrdom. However, Heller makes clear that Orr's course of action is not necessarily the proper one for everyone. The chaplain, though similarly freed from his moral paralysis by Orr, does not face the same dangers as Yossarian; while endorsing Yossarian's decision to flee, he realizes that he can and ought to continue the struggle on Pianosa: "If Orr could row to Sweden, then I can triumph over Colonel Cathcart and Colonel Korn, if only I persevere."

This is the God of *Catch-22.* He does not help out men with stage-tricks, but to the man who is willing to act for the sake of righteousness He promises that evil will not ultimately prevail against good. From this theological perspective we can see an explanation for a problem that has troubled several critics—the discontinuity of the last chapter with the rest of the novel. The reason is that nature and grace are discontinuous, as are human wisdom and faith. In the last chapter of the novel Yossarian and the chaplain discard their vision of the pagan universe of the epic for the Christian faith in a God of salvation: "There is hope, after all . . . Even Clevinger might be alive somewhere in that cloud of his, hiding inside until it's safe to come out."

Just as important as the promise that justice shall prevail is the promise of forgiveness for the sins committed in a sincere pursuit of righteousness. And that is how the novel ends. Yossarian sins in acting morally. He decides as a free and responsible man to resist the exploitation of himself and others in the only way left open to him—by fleeing from it even though the very

exploiters do have a valid claim on his conscience. Danby points out the sinful quality of the action and warns Yossarian: "Your conscience will never let you rest." To which Yossarian replies: "God bless it. . . . I wouldn't want to live without strong misgivings." In symbolic terms the last paragraph of the novel reinforces the theme of forgiveness for responsible action with the appearance of Nately's whore, the embodiment of Yossarian's accusing conscience:

> Yossarian jumped. Nately's whore was hiding just outside the door. The knife came down, missing him by inches, and he took off.

Yossarian can sin in his pursuit of the kingdom of heaven because he is *simul iustus et peccator.* (pp. 67-9)

Victor J. Milne, "Heller's 'Bologniad': A Theological Perspective on 'Catch-22'," in *Critique: Studies in Modern Fiction,* Vol. XII, No. 2, 1970, pp. 50-69.

JEAN E. KENNARD
(essay date 1971)

[In the excerpt below, Kennard examines how Heller's experimental narrative techniques impinge upon one of his themes in *Catch-22:* the absurdity of the human condition.]

Heller's vision of the horrifying absurdity of service life in World War II is, as the constant references in [*Catch-22*] to its wider implications indicate, merely an illustration of the absurdity of the human condition itself. *Catch-22* reflects a view of the world which is basically that of Jean-Paul Sartre and the early Albert Camus. The world has no meaning but is simply there; man is a creature who seeks meaning. The relationship between man and his world is therefore absurd; human action having no intrinsic value is ultimately futile; human beings have no innate characteristics. Reason and language, man's tools for discovering the meaning of his existence and describing his world, are useless. When a man discovers these facts about his condition he has an experience of the absurd, an experience which Sartre calls "nausea." But there are innumerable contemporary novels which are fundamentally Existentialist. What is interesting about *Catch-22* is that the experimental techniques Heller employs have a direct relation to Existentialist ideas; they are an attempt to "dramatize" his view of the human condition rather than merely describe it. (pp. 75-6)

The question of authority is central to the novel. God certainly no longer runs the organization, though

He lingers on in certain distorted images some characters still have of Him. (p. 76)

Duty is now owed to such vague abstractions as patriotism and free enterprise, which have become exactly the tyrannous absolute values that Camus talks of in *L'Homme révolté.* The old man in the brothel in Rome exposes patriotism as illogical: "Surely so many countries can't all be worth dying for". . . . Capitalism and free enterprise lead Milo to bomb his own unit and he excuses his action with the old slogan that what is good for money-making interests is good for the country. "Incentive" and "private industry" are "goods" and their evil results cannot change anyone's attitude towards them.

Such assertive values as patriotism, then, are merely words, words which have become divorced from meaning. Heller's awareness of the separation of word and idea, which Sartre talks of, is apparent in several places in the novel. General Peckem who "laid great, fastidious stress on small matters of taste and style" . . . has lost all sense of what words *mean* and writes his directives in a manner which combines impeccable grammar and trite adjectives. Language no longer communicates but serves to confuse things further. When Yossarian makes a game of censoring letters, declaring one day "death to all modifiers," the next declaring a "war on articles" and finally blacking out everything except "a", "an", and "the", he finds that it creates "more dramatic interlinear tensions . . . and in just about every case . . . a message far more universal". . . . (pp. 76-7)

Catch-22 is, of course, Heller's illustration of the irrational nature of the world. Any attempt to argue logically and reasonably ends in a paradox; one reaches that point where thought reaches its confines, which Camus talks of. . . .

Catch-22 is composed of rules which apparently operate to make it impossible for a man to find a reasonable escape from them. They do not exactly contradict each other, but are continually inadequate to the occasion and always disregard the individual human life. They are intended to impose order upon chaos, but life so exceeds these rules that they only serve in the end to create more chaos. One of the clearest examples of this is the firemen who leave the blaze they are attempting to control at the hospital in order to obey the rule that they must always be on the field when the planes land. . . .

Since the rules do not work, anything may happen. There is no reasonable justice. (p. 77)

Heller with packaged manuscript of *Catch-22.*

In a world where philosophical ideas, traditional morality and reason itself are apparently useless, all man has to hold on to is his own physical body. The value which Heller supports throughout the novel is that of human existence, the individual human life. . . . There is no talk of love or even of close friendship in the book; the pleasures of life are purely physical—food, liquor, sex—just as the only real horror is physical pain and ultimately death. "In an absurd universe," writes Frederick Karl, "the individual has the right to seek survival; . . . one's own substance is infinitely more precious than any cause."

The view of the world in *Catch-22*, then, is the same view as that presented by Sartre and Camus, and the aware individual in this world comes to very much the same realizations about it as do Roquentin and Mathieu in Sartre's novels. He realizes that there is no ultimate reason for doing one thing rather than another. . . . (p. 78)

The aware individual realizes, too, that there is "no way of really knowing anything." . . . [We] learn that there are always two widely divergent official reports for every event that takes place.

When everything is questionable, it is a small step to questioning one's own identity. . . . Names, uniforms, marks of identification are all a man has in Heller's world to assure him of his own identity.

Yossarian and the chaplain, probably the two most aware characters in the novel, both have experiences of the absurd very similar to those of Roquentin in Sartre's *La Nausée*. The chaplain experiences "terrifying, sudden moments when objects, concepts and even people that the chaplain had lived with all his life inexplicably took on an unfamiliar and irregular aspect that he had never seen before and made them seem totally strange." . . . Yossarian's experiences also have the effect of alienating him from his environment, but are less concerned with the strangeness of objects than with their profusion and gratuitousness. (pp. 78-9)

Heller, like Sartre and Camus, is not however totally pessimistic. Valid action is possible for the individual; there is even the suggestion of a sane universe which Sweden may represent. The hope of Sweden is perhaps a false note in the novel, but it is important to remember that it is only a possibility, a state of mind rather than a real place. Although Orr has, at least reportedly, reached Sweden, ironically by pretending to be "crazy," Yossarian at the end of the novel does not really expect to get further than Rome.

In a discussion of the techniques which Heller has employed to convey his view of the world it would be easy to ignore the obvious. *Catch-22* is a very funny book. It would be easy to ignore this because, in spite of the laughter it evokes, the overall impression is as much of horror as of humor. The laughter evoked is not of the kind that unites us warmly in sympathy with the human race as we enjoy its foibles, but rather that which serves to alienate us by exposing the bitter ironies of existence. Nevertheless I believe that humor is a way of understanding the techniques of the novel. Laughter, as Bergson suggests, is caused by incongruity, by a frustrating of our expectations of a certain result, and it is a failure to fulfill certain of the reader's expectations which is the link underlying the so-called absurd techniques of the novel. (p. 79)

[When] the reader is confronted with the juxtaposition in one sentence of references to several unrelated events about which he so far knows nothing, we cannot say that it is not like life. Actually it is; we often overhear conversations which are meaningless to us because we do not understand to whom or to what they refer. Yet we are surprised to find it in a novel. In this instance, obviously, it is our expectations about the nature of the novel, not about life, which are not being fulfilled. This is, I think, the key to defining the absurd techniques. In some way each of them plays against and frustrates the reader's expectations of a novel, the illusions, one could say, that he has about the nature of the novel. . . .

It is obvious that the narrative technique of *Catch-22* does not fulfill the expectation of the reader for a continuous line of action in which one episode is related to the next, at the very least chronologically, and in which events are life-size and probable. Situations which are initially familiar enough to the reader may be gradually exaggerated to the point of absurdity. (p. 80)

The futility of all human action is suggested by Heller in the number of times events or conversations are repeated so that the reader, like Yossarian, eventually has the feeling that he has "been through this exact conversation before." . . .

The narrative technique serves to confuse the reader about time and to destroy any certainty he may have about what has taken place, thus creating in him the same doubts about reality that Yossarian experiences and that Sartre and Camus speak of. Heller employs three basic methods of disrupting the expected chronological flow of the action. The first is a simple one. He often makes a statement about an event which has taken place and deliberately omits the clarification which the statement requires. Therefore many of the major events in the novel are referred to two or three times, sometimes in increasing detail, before the full account is given. . . .

The second device creates confusion in the mind of the reader by presenting him with two apparently contradictory statements about the same event before providing a clarification. (p. 81)

The third method is an extension of the second:

contradictory accounts are given of an event and no solution is provided. The reader is left uncertain of the truth and in some instances asked to believe the incredible. . . .

As well as confusing the reader about the time or exact nature of the events in the novel, Heller also frequently shocks him by adopting attitudes to objects or situations opposite to the expected ones. By introducing these unexpected attitudes in a very casual way, he not only challenges the traditional value system but suggests through his tone that nothing unusual is being said, thus doubling the shock effect. . . .

Heller's methods of characterization, like his narrative techniques and his use of tone, depend upon a frustration of the reader's expectations. (p. 82)

There are two possible ways . . . of failing to fulfill a reader's expectations about character in a novel: one is to change the character's identity, provide multiple personalities for the same name, or one name for various figures, and thus disturb the reader's whole conception of identity, as do John Barth and Samuel Beckett; the other is to provide caricatures, figures who are no more than puppets and in whom the reader is not expected to believe. Heller occasionally appears to experiment with the first method, as, for example, in the scene where Yossarian pretends to be a dying officer whose parents fail to recognize him, or where Yossarian and Dunbar discover they can change identities by changing hospital beds. But although in these scenes the characters experience doubts about their identities, the reader is always quite clear about the identity of the character and no real confusion is created.

Most of the characters in *Catch-22* are, however, caricatures, cardboard figures who are distinguished for the reader by their particular obsessions. Each lives with an illusory view of the world which isolates him and makes the results of his actions very different from his expectations. Each is, in his way, the unaware individual who, as Camus illustrates in *Le Mythe de Sisyphe*, believes that he can operate in the world as he imagines it and that his actions will achieve their purpose. (p. 83)

Most of these characters are introduced to us in deceptively explanatory paragraphs which appear to sum up their personalities in a few adjectives, but which really provide the reader with irreconcilably opposite traits. . . . Gradually the characters become increasingly absurd as the personality traits of each are seen to be one, an obsession. It is believable that one of Milo's moral principles was that "it was never a sin to charge as much as the traffic could bear," . . . but by the time his activities have taken over Europe and North Africa in one vast syndicate and he has bombed his own men, he has become little more than a personification of greed. Scheisskopf's enjoyment of parades may be initially credible but his childish delight in calling off parades that have never been scheduled is not. These characters may have names, parents, heredity, professions and faces, but we cannot very long sustain the illusion that they are "real" human beings.

The most important device a novelist has to suggest an irrational world is, of course, the treatment of reason itself. Reasoning, in *Catch-22,* invariably ends up in some variation of Catch-22; apparent logic is used to destroy sense. The reader is led into following an argument which progresses logically, but which arrives at an absurd conclusion. (pp. 83-4)

Sentence structure is used throughout *Catch-22* to add to the reader's confusion about characters and events and contributes to the impression of an irrational world. The novel is full of complex sentences in which the individual clauses and phrases are not related to each other or are related at a tangent. . . . (p. 84)

Frederick Karl describes Yossarian as "the man who acts in good faith to use Sartre's often-repeated phrase," and claims that all Yossarian "can hope to know is that he is superior to any universal force (man-made or otherwise), and all he can hope to recognize is that the universal or collective force can never comprehend the individual." He goes on to call Yossarian's final decision "a moral act of responsibility," "reflective, conscious and indeed free," while the other characters are not free, he considers, because they are unaware. This is all true; it is obvious that Yossarian is a man of whom Sartre would approve, but it does not go far enough. Certainly awareness is a prerequisite to the right action as Heller sees it. It is proved useless to be simply good like the chaplain or merely innocent like Nately, unable to detach himself from his father's values. And certainly Yossarian acts in freedom, but in the name of what? I do not think that it is only in the name of his own individual life, although this is his starting point. What most critics have overlooked is that Yossarian changes, is the one character who learns from his experience in the novel.

At the beginning of *Catch-22* Yossarian attempts to exercise his reason to escape from the situation he is in. "Everywhere he looked was a nut, and it was all a sensible young gentleman like himself could do to maintain his perspective against so much madness." . . . He soon learns, however, that everyone considers everyone else "a nut" and that when he attempts to argue logically against flying more missions he comes up against Catch-22. He realizes that to use reason in the face of the irrational is futile and that the way out of Catch-22 is simply to rebel, in Camus' sense, to take a stand, to say "no." He refuses to fly any more missions. This is, of course, the way the problems of Catch-22 have been solved earlier in the novel: the young officers solve the problem of the "dead man" in Yossarian's tent simply by throwing out his possessions; Major de Coverley solves the "great loyalty oath" Catch, which is preventing the men from getting their meals, simply by saying " 'Give everybody eat'." . . .

Until the final episode in the book, Yossarian is the great supporter of individual right. . . . "That men would die was a matter of necessity; which men would die, though, was a matter of circumstance and Yossarian was willing to be a victim of anything but circumstance." . . . Yossarian indeed realizes, as Karl suggests, "that one must not be asked to give his life unless everybody is willing to give his," but by the end of the novel he has come to realize the logical extension of this concept, that, if what is true for one must be applied to all, then one cannot attempt to save one's own life at the expense of others. One cannot give tacit acceptance to other people's deaths, without giving everyone the same right over oneself. (pp. 85-6)

Yossarian is given the chance to save his own life if he lies about Colonels Cathcart and Korn to their superior officers. He will, in accepting the offer, probably act as an incentive to his fellow officers to fly more missions in which many of them may be killed. He is given a chance, in Camus' terms, to join forces with the pestilences. After accepting the offer he is stabbed by Nately's whore and realizes perhaps that by joining those who are willing to kill, he has given everyone the right to kill him. If one rebels, one must rebel in the name of a value which transcends oneself, human life is the value for which Yossarian rebels and runs off to Rome, but it is not merely his own individual existence. (p. 86)

If we look back at the novel in the light of what Yossarian's decision reveals, we can see that Heller has presented us with a series of character studies of selfish men and has shown how their actions for their own gain have involved death for others. They are all like Major Major's father, "a long-limbed farmer, a God-fearing, freedom-loving, rugged individualist who held that federal aid to anyone but farmers was creeping socialism." . . . Milo, another "rugged individualist," bombs his own men; Colonel Cathcart, aiming at impressing the Generals to obtain promotion, keeps raising the number of missions his men must fly. To claim as Karl does, that these characters "are not really evil in any sinister way" but just "men on the make" is inaccurate. The "man on the make" is evil to Heller, since he gains at the expense of others and asks them to do what he is not willing to do himself.

The last ten pages or so of the novel may be sentimentally handled, as critics have suggested, but they present the key to a full understanding of what Heller is saying. In an irrational and gratuitous world the aware individual has to rebel, but his rebellion must be a free act and in the name of a value which can be applied to all men and does not limit their freedom.

The style of *Catch-22*, like the narrative tech-

nique, the tone and the methods of characterization, serves to frustrate the reader's expectations. . . . The reader expects to be drawn into the world of a novel, then, but *Catch-22*, while initially providing him with familiar human situations, ends by rejecting him. The novel itself becomes an object which provides the reader with the experience of the absurd, just as the trees provide it for Roquentin in Sartre's *La Nausée*. After attempting to relate his preconceptions about novels, his "illusions" about the form, to this novel, the reader is finally stripped of them. *Catch-22* simultaneously shows man's illusory view of the world, employs techniques to suggest the irrational nature of the world and is itself an object against which the truth of its statements may be tested. (pp. 86-7)

Jean E. Kennard, "Joseph Heller: At War with Absurdity," in *Mosaic: A Journal for the Comparative Study of Literature and New Views of the English and American Novel,* Vol. IV, No. 3, Spring, 1971, pp. 75-87.

JOHN W. ALDRIDGE
(essay date 1974)

[An American educator, critic, editor, and novelist, Aldridge is the author of such respected critical studies as *After the Lost Generation* (1951), *Time to Murder and Create: The Contemporary Novel in Crisis* (1966), and *The American Novel and the Way We Live Now* (1983). In the following excerpt, he praises *Something Happened* for its caustically candid portrayal of contemporary American life.]

[There] is evidence everywhere in [*Something Happened*] that Heller's originality is of the order that depends on the constant reexamination of imaginative premises and the deepening exploration of more and more complex areas of consciousness. Its driving impulse is self-renewal rather than self-imitation, and the terms of its expression are those wholly appropriate to the new work, hence derivative of nothing antecedent to that work. There can be no doubt that the author of *Catch-22* wrote *Something Happened.* Tonal and stylistic continuities between the two books are numerous and unmistakable. But Heller has objectified his now greatly darkened vision of life through very different and much more complicated materials. He has discovered and possessed new territories of his imagination, and he has produced a major work of fiction, one that is as distinctive of its kind as *Catch-22* but more ambitious and profound, an abrasively brilliant commentary on American life that must surely be recognized as the most important novel to appear in this country in at least a decade.

The size of Heller's achievement is perhaps best demonstrated by his success in coming to terms with what is unquestionably the most difficult problem facing the American novelist today: how to give dramatic life and, above all, dramatic concreteness to individual experience at a time in our cultural history when the most urgent awareness is of the *un*dramatic nature of individual experience, and when the typifying obsession stemming from that awareness is with abstract states of consciousness—shifting and largely morbid psychological moods, anxieties arising out of a pervasive sense of the running out and running down of vital energies, entropic processes in society and within the self, the collapse of moral and social structures that once helped to give purpose and continuity to the individual life and provided the novelist with readily dramatizable materials. (p. 18)

[The] characteristic personal dilemma of our time is one in which the individual suffers, not from a conflict with oppressive social forces, but from the apparent absence of social forces that may effectively be engaged in conflict. This afflicts him with a helpless sense that society at large has no relation to him personally. . . . His mental state is shaped by chronic feelings of loss divorced from an understanding of what precisely has been lost. Hence, his response to the world is not heroic combativeness—since he cannot identify the enemy—but aggressive paranoia—since in a society seemingly governed by no principle of sanity or coherence literally anything can happen and probably will, and literally anyone may suddenly and for no reason *become* the enemy. The only reality is the constant likelihood of disaster, for nothing can reliably be known or relied upon, and the behavior of people, when they share no common moral assumptions and have no reason to be kind to one another, is altogether unpredict-

able. "A man was shot today in the park," says Heller. "Nobody knows why." "No one's in charge." The separation of action from motive, event from cause, creates anarchy in the public world and anomie in the individual. (p. 19)

To humanize a dehumanized condition in a novel would seem to be achievement enough. But to humanize a condition in which dehumanization is not merely the primary fact of life but the primary subject of consciousness is a nearly miraculous artistic feat.

Heller accomplishes this by making brilliant use of the technique of psychological realism. His theme is social and psychological entropy, and his material is the flow of impressions and memories through the mind of his protagonist, a middle-aged corporation executive named Bob Slocum, whose obsession is with the gathering evidence of the entropic processes at work within himself and his society. Slocum's consciousness is the very center of the drama and, in fact, constitutes the drama. The objective reality of the life he experiences is of small importance when compared with his subjective view of it. Hence, it is perfectly proper that the social context in which and upon which the action of his consciousness is played out should be rendered only marginally. His family, friends, business associates, and mistresses are finally realized in his perception of them, and it is his perception of them that creates their most significant reality. Like Dostoevski's Underground Man—and the whole of the novel is Dostoevskian in its compulsiveness and pathological morbidity—Slocum is a man raging in a vacuum, and the character of his raging identifies him as belonging squarely in the anti-heroic tradition.

In presenting such a portrait of Slocum's consciousness, Heller was faced with yet another technical difficulty: how to dramatize a condition of acute psychic disturbance, which may well be the most common and *normal* condition of our time, without making it seem actual mental derangement and thus untrustworthy as the locus of the novel's point of view. He also had to cope with the problem that it is of the essence of Slocum's exacerbated vision of reality that there should be so little objective justification for it. (pp. 19-20)

Heller has confronted, with an authenticity few writers possess, some of the most unpleasant truths about our situation at this time, and he has dramatized a crisis that is manifest in far more ominous ways than in shortages of fuel and natural resources, a failing economy, and the spoliation of our physical environment. In so doing, he has created a darkened, demonic, perhaps partly hallucinated fictive portrait of contemporary America, but one that has at the same time a disquieting verisimilitude. We hear from everywhere that we have fallen away from some large conception we once had of ourselves, a conception that gave meaning to the past and promise to the future and made the present endurable. Something happened. Heller does not attempt to tell us what. Like most major artists, he is an adversary force, offering no comfort whatever and recognizing no obligation except to honor his subversive vision of the truth. (p. 21)

John W. Aldridge, "Vision of Man Raging in a Vacuum," in *Saturday Review/World,* Vol. 2, No. 3, October 19, 1974, pp. 18-21.

JEFFREY WALSH
(essay date 1982)

[In the excerpt below, Walsh discusses Heller's concept of the "catch" and his use of satire in *Catch-22.*]

Catch-22 (1961) has probably contributed more than any other work to the literary apprehension of war during the last two decades. The interpenetration between literary form and the movements of history is clearly shown in the commercial success of Heller's labyrinthine novel: the symbolisation of war as a labyrinth has now become firmly established in the way that earlier myths had been (the First World War metaphor of the soldier's farewell to arms was a previous example of equally potent symbolism); such images act as primary vehicles for our consciousness of men at arms. It is hardly an exaggeration to say that the idea of an all-pervasive catch has become the most widely accepted image of battle Pentagon-style, its structures and forms. Heller's invention of a catch which simultaneously determines, reflects and distorts the attitudes of various ranks of soldiers to the deadness of military institutionalism symbolises most effectively the nature of hegemonic relations. The intellectual genesis of the catch is difficult to identify, although one can take pleasure in drawing analogies with the processes of formal logic or such complex constructs as those inspired by generative grammar. The catch, of course, coerces, yet in a barely perceived manner which relies upon intellectual beauty and coherence:

> Yossarian saw it clearly in all its spinning reasonableness. There was an elliptical precision about its perfect pairs of parts that was graceful and shocking, like good modern art, and at times Yossarian wasn't quite sure that he saw it at all, just the way he was never quite sure about good modern art.

The catch obliquely implies the reification of military procedures in its formal autonomy; its uses, as the novel reveals, are exploitative. Through its mystique and *Gestalt*-like powers the catch may be drawn upon

in a variety of ways to instil loyalty and obedience to the military creed. It may provide legitimation for raising the number of bombing missions or justify the arrest of persons thought to be opposed to the bureaucratic hierarchy. The metaphor of a catch works structurally and imaginatively to symbolise in microcosm the seemingly willing mass subjection of soldiers to the interests of the industrial-military complex. Colonel Korn's educational sessions supply an example of the infallible theory in operation: only men who never ask questions are admitted, and then the sessions are discontinued on the grounds that it was neither possible nor necessary to educate people who never questioned anything.

Taken at this level *Catch-22* embodies a satire upon system building, a hypostastisation directed at grammarians, logicians and positivists in a neo-Swiftian mode. Tony Tanner has drawn attention to the abiding concern of American writers with conspiracy theories, their fear that the simple 'unpatterned' life, inward-directed (and analogous with the mythical past of the virginal continent) becomes impossible to achieve in a world where individual identity is increasingly obfuscated (as the extended wordplay upon the names of characters in Heller's masterpiece suggests); spontaneous conduct grows more and more difficult. Tanner emphasises the role of behaviourism and the linguistic sciences in convincing Americans that freedom of action is more and more constricted:

> American writers dread . . . all conditioning forces to the point of paranoia which is detectable not only in the subject matter of many novels but also in their narrative devices. Narrative lines are full of hidden persuaders, hidden dimensions, plots, secret organisation, evil systems, all kinds of conspiracies against spontaneity of consciousness, even cosmic take over. The possible nightmare of being totally controlled by unseen agencies and powers is never far away in contemporary American fiction. The unease revealed in such novels is related to a worried apprehension on the part of the author that his own consciousness may be predetermined and channelled by the language he has been born into.

Given that the long tradition (from Ortega Y Gasset to Marcuse) of predicting the growth of dehumanisation has authentic roots, the artist is increasingly likely to create literary modes which permit him to portray a social world of an indeterminate and anxious character, and one inimical to the individual's rational understanding. Heller's fictional work displays these features, and his formal procedures such as the devices of satiric distortion, allegory, parody and burlesque contribute to the formation of a vision of breakdown. His novel exploits the departure from literal truth in order to arrive at a representation of the monolithic power of modern institutions, in this case conveyed through the metaphor of the army's hierarchy. Such bewilderment experienced by the reader throughout the novel seems warranted if *Catch-22* is read in this way as a new kind of satire, one whose elaborate fabrications communicate a profound national *Angst*. One example should make this clear, the way individual generals are as helpless as their men, which is shown in their oversensitivity to the media; their wish to be presented in a favourable light indicates that they are as much victims of 'the system' as the combat airmen trying to escape from flying more bombing missions. The image communicated throughout the novel is of men lost in psychological corridors.

If one accepts such an interpretation of the novel, *Catch-22* exhibits certain characteristics of its period. The novel, for example, bases its narrative upon a fluctuating rhythm of crisis. One may observe a parallel development in the public's response to war as conveyed through the media and newspapers: many of the latter reserve a section of their foreign news pages for the coverage of wars abroad, and the most acclaimed newspaper men tend to be those frequently prominent in front-line action. Another obvious relation of Heller's narrative devices of concealment to external reality may be deduced from the curious public oxymoron of a 'balance of terror': such a euphemism does not conceal nuclear technology's proliferation of new horrors, the development of weapons like the neutron bomb recently created, for instance, which outrival avant-garde art in breaking with convention and rendering obsolete all that has come before. Whether one conceives of literature as a strictly determined ideological form or as a cultural product which retains a relative autonomy, it seems probable that such a history of war as continuing literary event informs Heller's novel. Heller's sustained satire against the dullness of maladministration, his post-absurdist lament for the disappearance of identity, suggests that the thrust of war writing in the sixties changed focus, from the heroic struggles of the battlefield to the absurdities of the communications process itself. The strains and confusions endured by American democracy, throughout Korea, the Cold War and McCarthyism, seem to have found subliminal articulation in the lunacy of Cathcart, Korn and Major and in the disordered narrative of the novel.

The chief thematic polarity in *Catch-22* is the struggle between the fetishistic, admired and worshipped for itself, and the soldier's counter attempt to hold fast to personal identity. An extended satire upon naming informs the novel at many levels. The case of Major Major Major Major, permanently trapped by his cumbersome names, illustrates such a predicament. Major Major, 'born too late and too mediocre', discovers that he is being utterly taken over by 'prolix bulletins', and so he 'grew despondent'. One day he signed Washington Irving's name to a document, an act of re-

bellion which functioned as catharsis: henceforth he exploits as a counter-strategy the names of other famous writers, notably John Milton, in order to fight back. Of course, Major Major's insubordination brings forth a plethora of activity from security men (whose bizarre activities seem to anticipate fictionally the historical reality of Watergate a decade or so later). The fetishistic status accorded to trivial memoranda in *Catch-22* signifies an entire military code, the collective voice of a self-perpetuating bureaucracy whose directives alter consciousness.

Modern war in *Catch-22* appears essentially to be an administrator's war, the focus having shifted from the exigencies of combat to the rampages of bureaucrats whose methods of communication imply a new species of epiphenomenalism; the end result is a situation where the liberal concept of identity is so far eroded that it eventually vanishes altogether. This finds outstanding comic expression in the novel when literal truth and the falsified bureaucratic version of reality clash head-on. Such disjunctures are strewn throughout *Catch-22*, in the strange figure of the soldier in white, a powerful image of anonymity, or the unknown soldier Mudd, who, blown to bits in the sky, generates a persuasive synecdoche for men at war. The two most celebrated paradigms are the cases of the dead man in Yossarian's tent, the soldier who died in a dogfight over Orvieto before he was officially reported missing and is, therefore, deemed never to have died; and the diametrically opposite fate of Doc Daneeka, who is deemed to be dead because he was supposed to be on flight duty in a plane that was destroyed. Doc Daneeka's living presence does nothing to contradict the authorised report of his death. With capacious irony Heller plots the repercussions of his figurative death—for example, the cumulative benefits bestowed upon his 'widow', who eventually refuses to accept his letters, preferring to disown him and accept the official version of his non-existence. The lieutenant who has been killed in action but never officially 'arrived" in the squadron was simply a 'replacement' pilot, whose belongings insist for Yossarian upon the recalcitrance of death, a reality closed to Major Major, who allows Sergeant Towser to report him as never having 'arrived' at all. Such depictions infer the nature of modern war where the substantive reality of combat death often becomes unknowable and its actuality concealed within the labyrinthine processes of modern technology—the circuitry of electronic media, for example—that produce new kinds of mystification.

The reader of *Catch-22* encounters one of the recurrent preoccupations of American war writers, the domination of combat men by unvalorous administrators. Sergeant Whitcomb, for example, feels delighted that twelve more men have been killed in combat (and they are sent duplicated 'personalised' letters of condolence) because his chances are increased of getting an article in *Saturday Evening Post* in praise of his commanding officer. The war increasingly becomes a publicity man's war where good aerial photographs rather than military tactics dictate the strategy of tight bomb patterns. Language uses, too, assume an important role in the mixed devices of concealment and self-advertisement employed by high-ranking officers: the officers most likely to succeed are those, such as General P. P. Peckem, who are highly sophisticated users of language, or those, such as Scheisskopf, whose crude instrumentation theories and encyclopaedic knowledge of trivial regulations result in promotion to the rank of general. An instance of Scheisskopf 's pedantic lunacy occurs in his admiration of parades, the most redundant part of military routine. Beneath Scheisskopf 's comic presentation, though, hides a sinister reality; his fixation upon swingless marching hints at a crucifixion mentality. Men, in Scheisskopf 's opinion, should ultimately become as precise as machines:

> Lieutenant Scheisskopf 's first thought had been to have a friend of his in the sheet metal shop sink pegs of nickel alloy into each man's thighbones and link them to the wrists by strands of copper wire with exactly three inches of play, but there wasn't time—and good copper wire was hard to come by in wartime. He remembered also that the men, so hampered, would be unable to fall properly during the impressive fainting ceremony preceding the marching and that an inability to faint properly might affect the unit's rating as a whole.

The literary technique deployed here characterises much of Heller's novel; it sustains awareness, through inventive distortion and departure from strictly literal truth, of the connotations of mechanised slaughter, the transformation of men into machines. As a hospital administrator says to Yossarian on another occasion, when considering the expendability of soldiers, 'one dying boy is just as good as any other or just as bad'. Yossarian learns, too, that his leg 'belongs' to the government.

Heller reveals an aesthetic predilection towards gradual revelation and partial disclosure: for example, the sparse and selective use of conventional literary realism heightens the reader's intuition of aerial combat, acting as a sharper lens. Such naturalistic scenes are framed in the novel, and their locations provide formal interplay within the overall strategy of derangement: they seem almost like set-pieces. The limited usage of 'realistic' presentation is also appropriate in a wider formal sense too, because in the institutionalised world of the novel traditional concepts of worth and epic heroism (which seem to emerge from such realistic presentation) prove obsolete and invalid. The environment of *Catch-22* spawns officers who act not out of moral considerations but only to defend or advance their own in-

terests (as in the ironic promotion of Yossarian for breaking orders). It is wholly consistent, then, that fictional structures and narrative plotting should display a commensurate problematic of evasiveness and disorientation; such a consideration is raised if one examines the relationship of the novel to earlier traditions of war writing. In *Catch-22* many of the familiar conventions of the war novel are transformed into preposterous jokes: even the arrangement of Heller's novel parodies an earlier type of war narrative and movie. The narrative, based on the adventures of a group of officers and men, is broken up into a series of discontinuous sections, each of which only tenuously conveys the experiences of a character, such as Hungry Joe or Nately's Whore. Heller observes few rules in burlesquing the method of earlier naturalistic writers, such as William March in *Company K,* or admired contemporaries, such as Norman Mailer in *The Naked and the Dead*. It is a technique that relies minimally upon plot, and thus allows great organisational flexibility.

Heller's characteristic method may be described as neo-satiric as he frequently shifts the position of attack through a sophisticated usage of fictional apparatus, the deployment of hallucinations, *déjà vu* visions, nightmares, flash-backs and mystical projections that cohere to cloak his characters and ironically imply their occultness in a world where everyday reality seems to imitate the supernatural. Several critics, including Joseph Stern and Brian Way, have written of the symbolic and traditional formulas in Heller's novel. The Soldier in White, for example, parodies the wounded soldier-hero, such as Dalton Trumbo's bandaged protagonist in *Johnny Got His Gun,* and also recalls Shakespeare's ghosts in striking the conscience. This fusion of the neo-satiric, a genre of avant-gardism, with the traditional distinguishes Heller as a war novelist. When Yossarian casts off his uniform and stands naked to receive his undeserved medal he is at one with such earlier deserters and rebels as Frederick Henry or John Andrews, but when he is absorbed into the Chaplain's mistaken vision, a naked man in a symbolic Tree of Life, he assumes briefly the aura of an Everyman, becoming part of a highly wrought pattern of imagery, like Hungry Joe's cat, which sleeps on his face and finally suffocates him. The planned obsolescence, redundancies and side-tracking in Heller's novel function in a similar manner; the reader can no longer cling to modes and assumptions of a well-tried kind; he finds himself in a satiric environment of constant confusion, and yet one which hints at the apocalyptic only to re-emphasise the material and the mundane, the impossibility of spiritual escape. (pp. 188-95)

Jeffrey Walsh, "Towards Vietnam: Portraying Modern War" in his *American War Literature, 1914 to Vietnam,* The Macmillan Press Limited, 1982, pp. 185-207.

SOURCES FOR FURTHER STUDY

Dickstein, Morris. "Black Humor and History: The Early Sixties." In his *Gates of Eden: American Culture in the Sixties,* pp. 91-127. New York: Basic Books, 1977.

Asserts that the black humor and disenchantment with authority that permeate *Catch-22* anticipated the mood of America from the 1960s onward.

Kiley, Frederick and Walter McDonald, eds. *A 'Catch-22' Casebook.* New York: Crowell, 1973, 403 p.

Selection of representative criticism that includes early reviews and analyses of form, structure, theme, and the relationship of *Catch-22* to absurdist literature.

Merrill, Robert. *Joseph Heller.* Boston: Twayne Publishers, 1987, 153 p.

Surveys Heller's works as they reflect the themes and techniques utilized most successfully in *Catch-22.*

Nagel, James, ed. *Critical Essays on Joseph Heller.* Boston: G. K. Hall, 1984, 253 p.

Anthology of criticism that includes essays by Kurt Vonnegut, Thomas LeClair, and John W. Aldridge, plus an annotated bibliography.

Seed, David. *The Fiction of Joseph Heller: Against the Grain.* London: Macmillan Press, 1989, 244 p.

Examines Heller's works from the early short stories to *Picture This.*

Seltzer, Leon F. "Milo's 'Culpable Innocence': Absurdity as Moral Insanity in *Catch-22.*" *Papers on Language & Literature* 15, No. 3 (Summer 1979): 290-310.

Contends that Heller employs the absurd world of Pianosa as a means to explore the inhumanity of contemporary society, particularly capitalism.

Ernest Hemingway

1899-1961

American short story writer, novelist, essayist, nonfiction writer, memoirist, journalist, poet, and dramatist.

INTRODUCTION

*H*emingway is lauded as one of the greatest American writers of the twentieth century. Considered a master of the understated prose style which became his trademark, he was awarded the 1954 Nobel Prize in literature. Although his literary stature is secure, he remains a highly controversial writer, and his novels and short stories have evoked an enormous amount of critical commentary. His narrow range of characters and his thematic focus on violence and machismo, as well as his terse, objective prose, have led some critics to regard his fiction as shallow and insensitive. Others claim that beneath the deceptively limited surface lies a complex and fully realized fictional world. Although Hemingway's literary achievement has been measured chiefly by his novels *The Sun Also Rises* (1926), *A Farewell to Arms* (1929), and *The Old Man and the Sea* (1952), his short stories have increasingly won critical acclaim. Today, works of both genres are widely read, and Hemingway remains one of the most imitated writers in modern literature.

Perhaps to a larger degree than that of any other twentieth-century writer, criticism of Hemingway's work has been colored by his own mythic persona. Indeed, he helped promote his larger-than-life reputation as a robust, belligerent American hero who sought to experience violence as well as write about it. He was a schooled expert in the arenas of war, bullfighting, deep-sea fishing, boxing, big-game hunting, and reckless, extravagant living—experiences that he often recounted in his fiction. Although he spent much of his life in foreign countries—France, Spain, Italy, and Cuba, in particular—he was, once established as a major writer, continually in the public eye. His passion for fistfighting and quarrels and his weakness for hard liquor became legendary, as did his ties to Hollywood personalities. Yet, beneath this flamboyance was a man who viewed writing as his sacred occupation, one which he strove always to master. Although he loved fame and never shunned his mythic status, he was disenchanted in his later years with the vulnerable position created by his literary success. His life was marred by three failed marriages, a debilitating addiction to alcohol, and marked periods of literary stagnation.

Born and raised in Oak Park, Illinois, by strict, Congregationalist parents, Hemingway led a fairly happy, upper-middle-class childhood. Scholars note, however, that as he grew older he felt bitter toward both his parents, particularly his mother, whom he viewed as selfish and domineering. By his teens he had become interested in literature, and he wrote a weekly column for his high school newspaper and contributed poems and stories to the school magazine. Upon his graduation in 1917, he took a junior reporter position on the *Kansas City Star,* covering the police and hospital beats and writing feature stories. Here he began consciously refining his prose according to the *Star's* guidelines of compression, selectivity, precision, and immediacy. In his journalism, Hemingway demonstrated a proclivity for powerful yet utterly objective stories of violence, despair, and emotional unrest, concerns that dominated his fiction. Of tremendous impact to Hemingway's development as a writer was his ensuing participation in World War I as a Red Cross ambulance driver in Italy. Wounded in both legs by a shrapnel explosion near the front lines, he fell in love with the American nurse who cared for him; however, she abruptly left Hemingway for an older man. He returned to the States a decorated hero, but his triumph was overshadowed by the disillusionment of his broken romance and a stifling relationship with his parents. At Oak Park, and also in northern Michigan where his family owned a summer cottage, Hemingway drafted stories drawn from boyhood, adolescence, and wartime experiences that captured his awakening realization of life's inherent misfortunes. He eventually returned to journalism to support himself, contributing features to the *Toronto Star.*

Following his first marriage in 1921, Hemingway returned to Europe to launch a writing career. Sherwood Anderson, who had met and befriended Hemingway earlier in Chicago, provided him with letters of introduction to several notable writers living in Paris, the literary capital of the twenties. For the next seven years, Hemingway resided principally in France, though he travelled frequently, covering the Greco-Turkish War of 1922 and writing special-interest pieces for the Toronto paper. During this period Hemingway matured as a writer, greatly aided in his artistic development by his close contact with several of the most prominent writers of the time, including Gertrude Stein, James Joyce, Ezra Pound, Ford Madox Ford, and F. Scott Fitzgerald. He eventually quit journalism, though he periodically returned to the medium, serving as a correspondent during several major wars.

Hemingway's first publication, *Three Stories and Ten Poems* (1923), included an Anderson-inspired story, "My Old Man," that Edward J. O'Brien chose for his *The Best Stories of 1923.* Hemingway's power and originality as a writer of compressed, impressionistic sketches became apparent with his next publication, *in our time* (1924). A series of eighteen brief untitled chapters stemming from Hemingway's war and journalistic experiences, this work was revised, greatly expanded, and published in America a year later as *In Our Time.* The American version included fifteen complete short stories with the remaining vignettes serving as interchapters. By the appearance of his next story collection, *Men without Women* (1927), Hemingway's literary reputation—as the author of *The Sun Also Rises* and consequent chronicler of the "lost generation"—was all but solidified. Following the immense success of *A Farewell to Arms,* he was recognized as a major force in literature.

While the 1930s was Hemingway's most prolific decade, he published little of lasting significance, save for the short story collection *Winner Take Nothing* (1933) and an assemblage of forty-nine stories, published with the play *The Fifth Column,* which incorporated such widely anthologized stories as "The Short Happy Life of Francis Macomber" and "The Snows of Kilimanjaro." The 1940s was a fallow decade for Hemingway. After the publication of his variously received long novel of the Spanish Civil War, *For Whom the Bell Tolls* (1940), his major achievement was his participation as reporter and paramilitary aide in the liberation of France from German occupation in 1944. The fifties was for Hemingway nearly as productive as the thirties, though most of the work from this period was published posthumously. By the middle of the decade, however, a variety of recurrent physical ailments had severely curtailed his creative energy. In 1960 Hemingway suffered a mental breakdown and was admitted to the Mayo Clinic for electrotherapy treatments. His depressive behavior and other illnesses persisted, and Hemingway committed suicide the following year.

Although Hemingway's most significant works include such renowned novels as *The Sun Also Rises, A Farewell to Arms,* and *For Whom the Bell Tolls*—as well as his Pulitzer Prize-winning novella, *The Old Man and the Sea*—critical response to these works has been varied. His short stories, however, particularly those in *In Our Time,* are consistently considered some of his finest efforts. The majority of these stories focus on Nick Adams, a protagonist often discussed as the quintessential Hemingway hero and the first in the line of the author's "fictional selves."

Like Hemingway, Nick Adams spent much of his early youth in the Michigan woods. The early stories set in Michigan, such as "Indian Camp," "The End of Something," "The Three-Day Blow," and "The Doctor and the Doctor's Wife," introduce Nick as a vulnerable adolescent attempting to understand a brutal, violent, and confusing world. On the surface, Nick, like all of Hemingway's protagonists, appears tough and insensitive. However, recent scholarship has determined that Nick's toughness stems not from insensitivity but from a strict moral code that functions as his sole defense against the overwhelming chaos of the world. Cleanth Brooks, Jr. and Robert Penn Warren, in their influential exposition of the short story "The Killers," noted that "it is the tough man, . . . the disciplined man, who actually is aware of pathos or tragedy." Though he seems to lack spontaneous human emotion, the hero "sheathes [his sensibility] in the code of toughness" because "he has learned that the only way to hold on to 'honor,' to individuality, to, even, the human order . . . is to live by his code."

The "code" hero is also found in Hemingway's most celebrated novels. Jake Barnes in *The Sun Also Rises* is both disillusioned and emasculated as a result of the war, and he establishes his own code of behavior because he no longer believes in the dictates of society. Frederic Henry in *A Farewell to Arms* finds order in his life through his love for a woman, maintaining his dignity even when she dies and the structure of his world collapses. Robert Jordan in *For Whom the Bell Tolls* is an American who dedicates himself to the Loyalist cause during the Spanish Civil War and ultimately dies for his convictions. These men demonstrate courage and perseverance in the face of adversity, thus exemplifying Hemingway's concern with fortitude and personal commitment.

With the novella *The Old Man and the Sea*, Hemingway turned from themes of love and war to focus on a lone fisherman's struggle to capture a large marlin. The protagonist, Santiago, heroically fights the elements, only to lose all but the fish's carcass to sharks.

Characteristic of Hemingway's fiction, the terse, almost journalistic prose, the compressed action, and the subdued yet suggestive symbolism in *The Old Man and the Sea* point to a deeper meaning than appears on the surface. Hemingway stresses Santiago's heroism through subtle allusions to Christ, and the simplicity of action serves to underscore the hero's nobility.

"The writer's job is to tell the truth," Hemingway once said. When he was having difficulty writing he reminded himself of this, as he explained in his memoirs, *A Moveable Feast* (1964): "I would stand and look out over the roofs of Paris and think, 'Do not worry. You have always written before and you will write now. All you have to do is write one true sentence. Write the truest sentence that you know.' So finally I would write one true sentence, and then go on from there. It was easy then because there was always one true sentence that I knew or had seen or had heard someone say." His endeavor to write "one true sentence" resulted in the creation of over twenty-five books. Summing up Hemingway's work and contribution to American literature, Robert P. Weeks concluded: "Hemingway has won his reputation as an artist of the first rank by operating within limits that would have stifled a lesser writer. But within and because of these limits, he has in his best work uttered a lyric cry that—although it may not resemble the full orchestra of Tolstoy or the organ tones of Melville—is nonetheless a moving and finely wrought response to our times."

(For further information about Hemingway's life and works, see *Contemporary Authors,* Vols. 77-80; *Contemporary Literary Criticism,* Vols. 1, 3, 6, 8, 10, 13, 19, 30, 34, 39, 41, 44, 50, 61; *Dictionary of Literary Biography,* Vols. 4, 9; *Dictionary of Literary Biography Documentary Series,* Vol. 1; *Dictionary of Literary Biography Yearbook,* Vols. 81, 87; and *Short Story Criticism,* Vol. 1.)

CRITICAL COMMENTARY

EDMUND WILSON

(essay date 1941)

[Wilson is considered one of America's foremost men of letters in the twentieth century. In the following excerpt, he surveys Hemingway's artistic development.]

Ernest Hemingway's *In Our Time* was an odd and origi-

nal book. It had the appearance of a miscellany of stories and fragments; but actually the parts hung together and produced a definite effect. There were two distinct series of pieces which alternated with one another: one a set of brief and brutal sketches of police shootings, bullfight crises, hangings of criminals, and incidents of the war; and the other a set of short stories dealing in its principal sequence with the growing-up of an

Principal Works

Three Stories and Ten Poems (short stories and poetry) 1923

in our time (sketches) 1924

In Our Time (short stories) 1925; revised edition, 1930

The Sun Also Rises (novel) 1926; also published as Fiesta, 1927

The Torrents of Spring: A Romantic Novel in Honor of the Passing of a Great Race (novel) 1926

Men without Women (short stories) 1927

A Farewell to Arms (novel) 1929

Death in the Afternoon (nonfiction) 1932

Winner Take Nothing (short stories) 1933

Green Hills of Africa (nonfiction) 1935

To Have and Have Not (novel) 1937

Fifth Column and the First Forty-Nine Stories (play and short stories) 1938; also published as First Forty-Nine Stories [abridged edition], 1956

The Spanish Earth (commentary and film narration) 1938

For Whom the Bell Tolls (novel) 1940

The Portable Hemingway (novels and short stories) 1944

The Essential Hemingway (novel, novel fragments, and short stories) 1947

Across the River and into the Trees (novel) 1950

The Old Man and the Sea (novella) 1952

The Hemingway Reader (short stories) 1953

The Snows of Kilimanjaro and Other Stories (short stories) 1961

The Wild Years (journalism) 1962

The Short Happy Life of Francis Macomber and Other Stories (short stories) 1963

A Moveable Feast (memoirs) 1964

By-Line: Ernest Hemingway: Selected Articles and Dispatches of Four Decades (nonfiction) 1968

Islands in the Stream (novel) 1970

The Nick Adams Stories (short stories) 1972

88 Poems (poetry) 1979

Ernest Hemingway: Selected Letters, 1917-1961 (letters) 1981

The Garden of Eden (novel) 1986

The Complete Stories of Ernest Hemingway (short stories) 1987

* Works after 1961 were published postumously.

American boy against a landscape of idyllic Michigan, but interspersed also with glimpses of American soldiers returning home. It seems to have been Hemingway's intention—*'In Our Time'*—that the war should set the key for the whole. The cold-bloodedness of the battles and executions strikes a discord with the sensitiveness and candor of the boy at home in the States; and presently the boy turns up in Europe in one of the intermediate vignettes as a soldier in the Italian army, hit in the spine by machine-gun fire and trying to talk to a dying Italian: *'Senta,* Rinaldi. *Senta,'* he says, 'you and me, we've made a separate peace.'

But there is a more fundamental relationship between the pieces of the two series. The shooting of Nick in the war does not really connect two different worlds: has he not found in the butchery abroad the same world that he knew back in Michigan? Was not life in the Michigan woods equally destructive and cruel? He had gone once with his father, the doctor, when he had performed a Caesarean operation on an Indian squaw with a jackknife and no anaesthetic and had sewed her up with fishing leaders, while the Indian hadn't been able to bear it and had cut his throat in his bunk. Another time, when the doctor had saved the life of a squaw, her Indian had picked a quarrel with him rather than pay him in work. And Nick himself had sent his girl about her business when he had found out how terrible her mother was. Even fishing in Big Two-Hearted River—away and free in the woods—he had been conscious in a curious way of the cruelty inflicted on the fish, even of the silent agonies endured by the live bait, the grasshoppers kicking on the hook.

Not that life isn't enjoyable. Talking and drinking with one's friends is great fun; fishing in Big Two-Hearted River is a tranquil exhilaration. But the brutality of life is always there, and it is somehow bound up with the enjoyment. Bullfights are especially enjoyable. It is even exhilarating to build a simply priceless barricade and pot the enemy as they are trying to get over it. The condition of life is pain; and the joys of the most innocent surface are somehow tied to its stifled pangs.

The resolution of this dissonance in art made the beauty of Hemingway's stories. He had in the process tuned a marvelous prose. Out of the colloquial American speech, with its simple declarative sentences and its strings of Nordic monosyllables, he got effects of the utmost subtlety. F. M. Ford has found the perfect simile for the impression produced by this writing: 'Hemingway's words strike you, each one, as if they were pebbles fetched fresh from a brook. They live and shine, each in its place. So one of his pages has the effect of a brook-bottom into which you look down through the flowing water. The words form a tesellation, each in order beside the other.'

Looking back, we can see how this style was already being refined and developed at a time—fifty years before—when it was regarded in most literary quarters as hopelessly non-literary and vulgar. Had there not been the nineteenth chapter of *Huckleberry Finn?*—'Two or three nights went by; I reckon I might say they swum by; they slid along so quick and smooth and lovely. Here is the way we put in the time. It was a monstrous big river down there—sometimes a mile and a half wide,' and so forth. These pages, when we happen to meet them in Carl Van Doren's anthology of world literature, stand up in a striking way beside a passage of description from Turgenev; and the pages which Hemingway was later to write about American wood and water are equivalents to the transcriptions by Turgenev—the *Sportsman's Notebook* is much admired by Hemingway—of Russian forests and fields. Each has brought to an immense and wild country the freshness of a new speech and a sensibility not yet conventionalized by literary associations. Yet it *is* the European sensibility which has come to Big Two-Hearted River, where the Indians are now obsolescent; in those solitudes it feels for the first time the cold current, the hot morning sun, sees the pine stumps, smells the sweet fern. And along with the mottled trout, with its 'clear water-over-gravel color,' the boy from the American Middle West fishes up a nice little masterpiece.

In the meantime there had been also Ring Lardner, Sherwood Anderson, Gertrude Stein, using this American language for irony, lyric poetry or psychological insight. Hemingway seems to have learned from them all. But he is now able to charge this naïve accent with a new complexity of emotion, a new shade of emotion: a malaise. The wholesale shattering of human beings in which he has taken part has given the boy a touch of panic. (pp. 174-76)

[In *Men Without Women*] Hemingway has mastered his method of economy in apparent casualness and relevance in apparent indirection, and has turned his sense of what happens and the way in which it happens into something as hard and clear as a crystal but as disturbing as a great lyric. Yet it is usually some principle of courage, of honor, of pity—that is, some principle of sportsmanship in its largest human sense—upon which the drama hinges. The old bullfighter in **"The Undefeated"** is defeated in everything except the spirit which will not accept defeat. You get the bull or he gets you: if you die, you can die game; there are certain things you cannot do. The burlesque show manager in **"A Pursuit Race"** refrains from waking his advance publicity agent when he overtakes him and realizes that the man has just lost a long struggle against whatever anguish it is that has driven him to drink and dope. 'They got a cure for that,' the manager had said to him before he went to sleep; " 'No,' William Campbell said, 'they haven't got a cure for anything.' " The burned major in **"A Simple Enquiry"**—that strange picture of

the bedrock stoicism compatible with the abasement of war—has the decency not to dismiss the orderly who has rejected his proposition. The brutalized Alpine peasant who has been in the habit of hanging a lantern in the jaws of the stiffened corpse of his wife, stood in the corner of the woodshed till the spring will make it possible to bury her, is ashamed to drink with the sexton after the latter has found out what he has done. And there is a little sketch of Roman soldiers just after the Crucifixion: 'You see me slip the old spear into him?—You'll get into trouble doing that some day.—It was the least I could do for him. I'll tell you he looked pretty good to me in there today.'

This Hemingway of the middle twenties—*The Sun Also Rises* came out in '26—expressed the romantic disillusion and set the favorite pose for the period. It was the moment of gallantry in heartbreak, grim and nonchalant banter, and heroic dissipation. The great watchword was 'Have a drink'; and in the bars of New York and Paris the young people were getting to talk like Hemingway. (pp. 178-79)

In [*Winner Take Nothing*] he deals much more effectively than in *Death in the Afternoon* with that theme of contemporary decadence which is implied in his panegyric of the bullfighter. The first of these stories, **"After the Storm,"** is another of his variations—and one of the finest—on the theme of keeping up a code of decency among the hazards and pains of life. A fisherman goes out to plunder a wreck: he dives down to break in through a porthole, but inside he sees a woman with rings on her hands and her hair floating loose in the water, and he thinks about the passengers and crew being suddenly plunged to their deaths (he has almost been killed himself in a drunken fight the night before). He sees the cloud of sea birds screaming around, and he finds that he is unable to break the glass with his wrench and that he loses the anchor grapple with which he next tries to attack it. So he finally goes away and leaves the job to the Greeks, who blow the boat open and clean her out.

But in general the emotions of insecurity here obtrude themselves and dominate the book. Two of the stories deal with the hysteria of soldiers falling off the brink of their nerves under the strain of the experiences of the war, which here no longer presents an idyllic aspect; another deals with a group of patients in a hospital, at the same time crippled and hopeless; still another (a five-page masterpiece) with a waiter, who, both on his own and on his customers' account, is reluctant to go home at night, because he feels the importance of a 'clean well-lighted cafe' as a refuge from the 'nothing' that people fear. **"God Rest You Merry, Gentlemen"** repeats the theme of castration of *The Sun Also Rises;* and four of the stories are concerned more or less with male or female homosexuality. In the last story, **"Fathers and Sons,"** Hemingway reverts to the Michigan woods, as if to take the curse off the rest: young Nick had once enjoyed a nice Indian girl with plump legs and hard little breasts on the needles of the hemlock woods.

These stories and the interludes in *Death in the Afternoon* must have been written during the years that followed the stockmarket crash. They are full of the apprehension of losing control of oneself which is aroused by the getting out of hand of a social-economic system, as well as of the fear of impotence which seems to accompany the loss of social mastery. And there is in such a story as **"A Clean, Well-Lighted Place"** the feeling of having got to the end of everything, of having given up heroic attitudes and wanting only the illusion of peace.

And now, in proportion as the characters in his stories run out of fortitude and bravado, he passes into a phase where he is occupied with building up his public personality. He has already now become a legend, as Mencken was in the twenties; he is the Hemingway of the handsome photographs with the sportsmen's tan and the outdoor grin, with the ominous resemblance to Clark Gable, who poses with giant marlin which he has just hauled in off Key West. And unluckily—but for an American inevitably—the opportunity soon presents itself to exploit this personality for profit: he turns up delivering Hemingway monologues in well-paying and trashy magazines; and the Hemingway of these loose disquisitions, arrogant, belligerent and boastful, is certainly the worst-invented character to be found in the author's work. If he is obnoxious, the effect is somewhat mitigated by the fact that he is intrinsically incredible. (pp. 182-84)

You may fear, after reading *The Fifth Column*, that Hemingway will never sober up; but as you go on to his short stories of this period, you find that your apprehensions were unfounded. Three of these stories have a great deal more body—they are longer and more complex—than the comparatively meager anecdotes collected in *Winner Take Nothing*. And here are his real artistic successes with the material of his adventures in Africa, which make up for the miscarried *Green Hills*: **"The Short Happy Life of Francis Macomber"** and **"The Snows of Kilimanjaro,"** which disengage, by dramatizing them objectively, the themes he had attempted in the earlier book but that had never really got themselves presented. And here is at least a beginning of a real artistic utilization of Hemingway's experience in Spain: an incident of the war in two pages which outweighs the whole of *The Fifth Column* and all his Spanish dispatches, a glimpse of an old man, 'without politics,' who has so far occupied his life in taking care of eight pigeons, two goats and a cat, but who has now been dislodged and separated from his pets by the advance of the Fascist armies. It is a story which takes its place among the war prints of Callot and Goya, artists whose union of elegance with sharp-

ness has already been recalled by Hemingway in his earlier battle pieces: a story which might have been written about almost any war.

And here—what is very remarkable—is a story, **"The Capital of the World,"** which finds an objective symbol for, precisely, what is wrong with *The Fifth Column*. A young boy who has come up from the country and waits on table in a pension in Madrid gets accidentally stabbed with a meat knife while playing at bullfighting with the dishwasher. This is the simple anecdote, but Hemingway has built in behind it all the life of the pension and the city: the priesthood, the working-class movement, the grown-up bullfighters who have broken down or missed out. 'The boy Paco,' Hemingway concludes, 'had never known about any of this nor about what all these people would be doing on the next day and on other days to come. He had no idea how they really lived nor how they ended. He did not realize they ended. He died, as the Spanish phrase has it, full of illusions. He had not had time in his life to lose any of them, or even, at the end, to complete an act of contrition.' So he registers in this very fine piece the discrepancy between the fantasies of boyhood and the realities of the grown-up world. Hemingway the artist, who feels things truly and cannot help recording what he feels, has actually said good-bye to these fantasies at a time when the war correspondent is making himself ridiculous by attempting to hang on to them still.

The emotion which principally comes through in **"Francis Macomber"** and **"The Snows of Kilimanjaro"**—as it figures also in *The Fifth Column*—is a growing antagonism to women. Looking back, one can see at this point that the tendency has been there all along. In **"The Doctor and the Doctor's Wife,"** the boy Nick goes out squirrel-hunting with his father instead of obeying the summons of his mother; in **"Cross-Country Snow,"** he regretfully says farewell to male companionship on a skiing expedition in Switzerland, when he is obliged to go back to the States so that his wife can have her baby. The young man in **"Hills Like White Elephants"** compels his girl to have an abortion contrary to her wish; another story **"A Canary for One,"** bites almost unbearably but exquisitely on the loneliness to be endured by a wife after she and her husband shall have separated; the peasant of **"An Alpine Idyll"** abuses the corpse of his wife (these last three appear under the general title *Men Without Women*). Brett in *The Sun Also Rises* is an exclusively destructive force: she might be a better woman if she were mated with Jake, the American; but actually he is protected against her and is in a sense revenging his own sex through being unable to do anything for her sexually. Even the hero of *A Farewell to Arms* eventually destroys Catherine—after enjoying her abject devotion—by giving her a baby, itself born dead. The only women with whom Nick Adams' relations are perfectly satisfactory are the little Indian girls of his boyhood who are in a position of hopeless social disadvantage and have no power over the behavior of the white male—so that he can get rid of them the moment he has done with them. Thus in *The Fifth Column* Mr. Philip brutally breaks off with Dorothy—he has been rescued from her demoralizing influence by his enlistment in the Communist crusade, just as the hero of *The Sun Also Rises* has been saved by his physical disability—to revert to a little Moorish whore. Even Harry Morgan, who is represented as satisfying his wife on the scale of a Paul Bunyan, deserts her in the end by dying and leaves her racked by the cruelest desire.

And now this instinct to get the woman down presents itself frankly as a fear that the woman will get the man down. The men in both these African stories are married to American bitches of the most soul-destroying sort. The hero of **"The Snows of Kilimanjaro"** loses his soul and dies of futility on a hunting expedition in Africa, out of which he has failed to get what he had hoped. The story is not quite stripped clean of the trashy moral attitudes which have been coming to disfigure the author's work: the hero, a seriously intentioned and apparently promising writer, goes on a little sloppily over the dear early days in Paris when he was earnest, happy and poor, and blames a little hysterically the rich woman whom he has married and who has debased him. Yet it is one of Hemingway's remarkable stories. There is a wonderful piece of writing at the end when the reader is made to realize that what has seemed to be an escape by plane, with the sick man looking down on Africa, is only the dream of a dying man. The other story, **"Francis Macomber,"** perfectly realizes its purpose. Here the male saves his soul at the last minute, and then is actually shot down by his woman, who does not want him to have a soul. Here Hemingway has at last got what Thurber calls the war between men and women right out into the open and has written a terrific fable of the impossible civilized woman who despises the civilized man for his failure in initiative and nerve and then jealously tries to break him down as soon as he begins to exhibit any. (It ought to be noted, also, that whereas in *Green Hills of Africa* the descriptions tended to weigh down the narrative with their excessive circumstantiality, the landscapes and animals of **"Francis Macomber"** are alive and unfalteringly proportioned.)

Going back over Hemingway's books today, we can see clearly what an error of the politicos it was to accuse him of an indifference to society. His whole work is a criticism of society: he has responded to every pressure of the moral atmosphere of the time, as it is felt at the roots of human relations, with a sensitivity almost unrivaled. Even his preoccupation with licking the gang in the next block and being known as the best

Hemingway on a hunting trip, ca. 1943.

basketball player in high school has its meaning in the present epoch. After all, whatever is done in the world, political as well as athletic, depends on personal courage and strength. With Hemingway, courage and strength are always thought of in physical terms, so that he tends to give the impression that the bullfighter who can take it and dish it out is more of a man than any other kind of man, and that the sole duty of the revolutionary socialist is to get the counter-revolutionary gang before they get him.

But ideas, however correct, will never prevail by themselves: there must be people who are prepared to stand or fall with them, and the ability to act on principle is still subject to the same competitive laws which operate in sporting contests and sexual relations. Hemingway has expressed with genius the terrors of the modern man at the danger of losing control of his world, and he has also, within his scope, provided his own kind of antidote. This antidote, paradoxically, is almost entirely moral. Despite Hemingway's preoccupation with physical contests, his heroes are almost always defeated physically, nervously, practically: their victories are moral ones. He himself, when he trained himself stubbornly in his unconventional unmarketable art in a Paris which had other fashions, gave the prime example of such a victory; and if he has sometimes, under the menace of the general panic, seemed on the point of going to pieces as an artist, he has always pulled himself together the next moment. The principle of the Bourdon gauge, which is used to measure the pressure of liquids, is that a tube which has been curved into a coil will tend to straighten out in proportion as the liquid inside it is subjected to an increasing pressure. (pp. 191-96)

Edmund Wilson, "Hemingway: Gauge of Morale," in his *The Wound and the Bow: Seven Studies in Literature*, 1941. Reprint by Farrar, Straus, and Giroux, 1978, pp. 174-97.

EARL H. ROVIT

(essay date 1969)

[In the following excerpt, Rovit offers a favorable review of *The Sun Also Rises*, noting that it is "a curious exception" among Hemingway's literary canon.]

Within the entire canon of Hemingway's works—some seven novels, fifty-odd short stories, a play, and several volumes of nonfiction—*The Sun Also Rises* is something of a curious exception. Published in 1926 while Hemingway was still in his twenties and relatively unknown, it was his first serious attempt at a novel; yet, in spite of the fact that it was to be followed by such overwhelming commercial successes as *A Farewell to Arms* (1929), *For Whom the Bell Tolls* (1940), and *The Old Man and The Sea* (1952), most critics agree that *The Sun Also Rises* is his one most wholly satisfying book. Here Hemingway indelibly fixed the narrative tone for his famous understated ironic prose style. And here he also made his first marked forays into an exploration of those themes that were to become his brand-mark as a writer and which were to occupy him throughout his career. The pragmatic ideal of "grace under pressure," the working out of the Hemingway "code," the concept of "style" as a moral and ethical virtue, and the blunt belief or determination that some form of individual heroism was still possible in the increasingly mechanized and bureaucratic world of the twentieth century: these characteristic Hemingway notions deeply inform the structure of *The Sun Also Rises*. And while Hemingway was to develop these ideas at much greater length and with perhaps more drama in his subsequent work, they achieve a balance and a cogency in *The Sun Also Rises* which, it seems to me, he never really equalled again except in some of his short stories.

At the same time, while *The Sun Also Rises* is characteristically Hemingway, it is radically different from Hemingway's typical fictions. Indeed, it may be precisely in the area of its differences that it attains its special quality and pertinence as a major American novel. For there are subtleties of tone and meaning in *The Sun Also Rises* which suggest a profounder confrontation with the ambiguities of the modern "experience" than Hemingway was ever to sustain again. Hemingway himself regarded this work not as "a hollow or bitter satire, but a damn tragedy with the earth abiding forever as the hero." Without worrying about Hemingway's use of the academically sacred word, "tragedy," I think he may be correctly pointing his reader to the general area where the complexities of the novel come into focus. *The Sun Also Rises* is a novel about loss. Most of Hemingway's work is about loss; the loss of one's desires, one's loves, one's life. But *The Sun Also Rises*, alone among Hemingway's novels, begins with the loss as a "given," as a fatal limitation on open possibilities and opportunities. As in the best of the Nick Adams stories, *The Sun Also Rises* is concerned with that moral space which remains for man's occupancy after necessity has effected its inexorable curtailment on his freedom. And the concentrated passion which gives this novel its tautness of structure and its authority of statement is its exploration of that diminished measure of dignity and endurance which a man may still strive for even while he is a captive in the nets of bleak fatality.

When one considers the gallery of the popular Hemingway heroes—and how difficult it is to refrain from imposing Hemingway's own photogenic features on those of his heroic characters—the composite image can almost be stereotyped in Hollywood terms. . . . As Sean O'Faolain has pointed out, Hemingway's concept of heroism is almost unique in serious modern literature in the mere fact that, as it is presented, it is a convincing possibility. Far from being a passive pawn, the Hemingway hero succeeds in maintaining his own initiative and momentum in those isolated pockets of endeavor such as sports and war, which he carves out for himself in a dehumanized world. At the end, of course, he loses; the winner is allowed to take nothing, nothing except a sense of moral success in knowing that he has lost on his own and not on the world's terms. The typical background for the hero's exploits is a technicolor adventure world. . . . [These settings] are appropriately epic as both foil for and projection of the hero's ritual gestures in his dramatic dance with fate. Nor were the critics slow to attack the validity of Hemingway's fictional world. Dazzled by the exotic color and the Horatio Alger bravura with which Hemingway painted his version of moral struggle, they accused him of a variety of artistic and philosophical sins, ranging from the venial sin of romantic primitivism to the mortal sin of arrant commercialism. But this is to read Hemingway with a malicious premeditated selectivity. It is to ignore the marvelous classic restraint of his prose style. It is to fail to measure the qualitative difference between his heroic "heroes" and his typical narrator-protagonists. And it is almost wholly to disregard *The Sun Also Rises* as a work of art in itself, as well as a radical metaphor in terms of which Hemingway fashioned the most effective and influential elements of his work.

To be sure, *The Sun Also Rises* has been the most variously interpreted of all Hemingway's fiction. Critics have failed to agree on where, if at all, the base of values resides in the novel. They have argued the importance of Pedro Romero as a "code-hero"; they have disagreed on the goodness or badness of Lady Brett; and they are far from unanimous on the meaning of Jake's role or experience. The causes of these confusions would seem to be inherent in the novel itself and not in the subjective predilections of the critics; but in this case, at least, the confusions attest to the vitality rather than the incoherence of the work of art. On its most accessible level, *The Sun Also Rises* is a novel of deceptively casual surfaces, a seemingly realistic *roman à clef*, narrated by Jake Barnes-Hemingway, which sketches several months in the lives of a not particularly prepossessing band of expatriated Bohemians in Paris in 1925. Nothing happens of much moment in the novel as the merrymakers drink, dance, arrange abortive liaisons, backbite, and generally fritter away their time in an empty irresponsible pursuit of joyless pleasure. The narration begins in the spring, builds up a small tension when Robert Cohn goes off to San Sebastian with Lady Brett, and comes to a climax at the final gathering and dispersion of the band in Pamplona for the July 6th Festival of San Fermin.

The critics who stress what Hemingway referred to as "the hollow or bitter satire" of the novel have had two options open to them. They can see the force of the novel's anger as directed against the characters in the novel who, for the most part, assume mawkish postures of self-pity and self-indulgence, while they excuse themselves from responsibility because they are all "a lost generation." From this viewpoint, *The Sun Also Rises* is a fictional extension of Hemingway's lifelong disgust with Bohemianism, tourism, amateurism, and lack of self-discipline. And certainly, narrated as it is by a character who stands off on the margins of the group, the novel supports this effect. The other option open to the critic of this persuasion is to view the satire in a larger, even a cosmic, dimension. The "dirty war" is the immediate historical antecedent behind the bombed-out lives of the expatriates. Jake Barnes has been rendered sexually impotent by his wound in the war. Brett Ashley's "true love" died of dysentery. The sustaining values of western civilization—religious, ethical, philosophical—have been exploded. The frenetic hedonism of the Bohemian group is only a desperate and hopeless complement to the futility and nihilism which the First World War has revealed as the essential element within which human beings have always lived when, for one reason or another, illusions are denied them. This critical view can treat the satire as historically contained—a condemnation of the shallow bourgeois Protestant ethic when it is tested by the absurd degradation of modern war; or, more ambitiously, as Hemingway's attempt to universalize the stark lessons of stoicism and philosophical resignation which have always ruled against man's attempts to impose transcendent meanings upon life. And again, the rhetorical resonance of the novel, as well as its ruthless, if muted, rejection of illusions, will offer a good deal to substantiate this position.

Probably, no interpretation will adequately capture the shifting nuances of meaning which generate the deeper energies in *The Sun Also Rises.* Satire, tragedy, even some variation of "romance" can find a supporting configuration in the novel, but only at the cost of deflecting the main thrust of the novel in an effort to make it amendable to the understanding. And the ultimate inconclusiveness of any interpretation will be almost entirely due to the ambiguous status of Jake Barnes. As the first-person narrator, he and only he is responsible for what the reader knows and what the reader can never know. But his reliability as a reporter is seriously affected by two factors: first, his inevitable physical and psychological passivity (unlike the popular Hemingway "hero," Jake is pre-eminently a man to whom things happen); and, second, his intense emotional involvement in the events that he describes, precisely because he is fighting as hard as he can to keep from succumbing to hysteria or despair. More than anything else, the novel is Jake's story, a blow-by-blow description, told from the inside, by a man struggling to catch his balance as he teeters on the edge of spiritual suicide. For Jake has already suffered his irreparable loss when the novel begins. Unusually responsive to physical sensation as are all Hemingway's heroes, Jake is continually beset by stimuli which mix a witches' brew of memory and desire in him. But he is not free to act upon his desires; the option of love is forever foreclosed in his life. *The Sun Also Rises* is a chronicle of Jake's attempt to live in a centerless world as a personality lacking a vital center. His dislocation is not single, but double, and it pervades his entire existence. Since Hemingway has chosen to locate the novel's viewing-point within a focus of such radical dislocation, we ought not to be surprised at the resultant confusion of interpretation because it is inherent in the internal dissociation of the narrative voice itself.

The point is that Jake cannot trust himself, nor can he even believe that he possesses or will ever possess a stable core of being which is potentially trustworthy. He must ignore his desires because they can only cause him anguish. He must try to bury his memories because they are only desires in a concealed guise. Even as he tries to maintain himself as a careful spectator in life, nurturing his epicurean satisfactions in the pleasures of trout fishing and watching bullfights, he finds himself acting the pander between Brett and Pedro Romero, and hence he betrays both his desired love and his hard-won *aficion*. He cannot trust himself because his grotesque wound has denuded him of man's most cherished illusion—the illusion that there is a center to one's life. It is in this context that Jake's often-quoted reflections during the fiesta should be interpreted:

> I thought I had paid for everything. Not like the woman pays and pays and pays. No idea of retribution or punishment. Just exchange of values. You gave up something and got something else. Or you worked for something. You paid some way for everything that was any good. . . . Either you paid by learning about them, or by experience, or by taking chances, or by money. Enjoying living was learning to get your money's worth. The world was a good place to buy in. It seemed like a fine philosophy. In five years, I thought, it will seem just as silly as all the other fine philosophies I've had.

> Perhaps that wasn't true though. Perhaps as you went along you did learn something. I did not care what it was all about. All I wanted to know was how to live in it. Maybe if you found out how to live in it you learned from that what it was all about.

This famous "exchange of values" philosophy is a movement from a concern with "essence" ("*what* it was all about") to a focus on "existence" ("*how* to live in it"). It is a movement which candidly rejects "centers" and transfers its interest to the peripheries of one's sensations. It suggests that life can be dealt with only as a system of transactions, a volatile sequence of energy-exchanges where the difference between life and death, value and worthlessness, being and nothingness, is dependent only on the capital reserve that is left in the credit column. And thus the structure of *The Sun Also Rises*, symmetrically but deceptively patterned in terms of the three acts of the classic bullfight, rests on a dynamically askew and radically dislocated, shifting basis.

This, it would seem, is the main source of the novel's strength and the root reason for Jake's moral success in achieving "a way to be" in the world. Without this eccentric focus, the novel would be little more than a banal variation of another "identity-quest," trite and pompous in its acquisition of platitudinous "truths." But Jake finds a different way out, or at least a viable technique of living within a world of inexorable loss. *Style* is what Jake resorts to after alcohol, religion, and philosophy have proved ineffectual in keeping him from crying at night in his room. Style of whatever kind is no more nor less than a manner, a system of rhythmic interrelationships, an achieved harmony of disparate movements, intentions, and effects. A "good" style is one which gives the impression of being inevi-

table and one which works; which, that is, accomplishes the job that it is set to do. And Hemingway's style in *The Sun Also Rises,* a style which is synonymous with Jake's voice, is the best documentation that we possess of Jake's success in working out for himself a psychological and spiritual balance without a center of gravity. Of all the characters in the novel, only he (and possibly Count Mippipopolous) achieve this order of style. Pedro Romero has an admirable style, of course, but it works only when he is fighting his bulls or Robert Cohn, and, at any rate, it is a "received," traditional style which is his by initiation and apprenticeship. Bill Gorton, Mike Campbell, and Brett also possess a style of sorts; but it doesn't work particularly well for them, nor does it seem inevitable and natural.

The general life-style of the rootless expatriate world, as Hemingway presents it, is like that of an endless costume party where the drunks get drunker and the cheap finery gets shabbier and shabbier under the harsh lights. And Robert Cohn, of course, is the horrible example in the novel of precisely "the way *not* to be." In some sense Jake's alter ego, Cohn is sensitive, intelligent, and desperately eager to discover meaning and value in experience. However he is basically dishonest in his keeping of the accounts of his energy-transactions—the cardinal sin of an exchange-of-values philosophy is falsification—and his various styles (the romantic artist, the unrequited lover, the self-pitying martyr) are a succession of ill-fitting, secondhand gestures and responses which fool no one and fail to work at all. Only Jake has the self-discipline, the honesty, and the driving need to achieve a thin sleeve of freedom in recognizing and accepting the limitations of his condition. The prose style of *The Sun Also Rises* and the moral style which Jake successfully strives for are what give this book its power and continued relevance.

Hemingway was not to follow up this direction in his later work. Probably such an effort would have required an expense of psychic energy which no human being could have long sustained. Instead, he held on to the prose style which was Jake Barnes's achievement of a *moral* style, but he employed it to narrate the stories of men in the process of suffering loss. . . . Only in some of the magnificent short stories like **"Big Two-Hearted River"** (1925), **"In Another Country"** (1927), **"The Clean Well-Lighted Place"** (1933), and **"The Snows of Kilimanjaro"** (1936), stories, incidentally, in which the loss has occurred *before* the narrative begins, do we find that conjunction of prose style and moral style which Hemingway forged in *The Sun Also Rises,* seemingly as a last-ditch strategy to cope with a world stripped of illusions where *nada* is omnipresent and well-nigh omnipotent.

It would be well to remember here that as significant as the novel may have been in the development of

Hemingway's work, *The Sun Also Rises* has enjoyed an importance of its own apart from Hemingway. What fortuitous conjunction of events it is that transforms a novel into a cultural document—what makes some works of art take on an additional life as expressions of an historical period or, indeed, a national life-style, we do not at all know. . . . At any rate, it is surely provocative to note that *The Sun Also Rises* was published within four years of such major American statements as Eliot's *The Waste Land,* Dreiser's *An American Tragedy,* and Faulkner's *The Sound and the Fury.* Certainly these four books are vividly independent, each pursuing its own content and creating its own form in terms of each individual author's unfathomable needs and artistic gifts. And yet there are curious similarities and parallels between these titles. If not one of them is a tragedy, still they all of them traffic surprisingly close to that mood of grotesque poignancy which may be the nearest our age can come to the spirit of the tragic. In Hemingway's and Eliot's works there is literal sexual impotence; in Dreiser's and Faulkner's books, a symbolic impotence is a major factor in the development of both plots. Further, all four books are, in their various ways, equally zealous at unmasking the social and metaphysical illusions which impose palpably false meanings on human experience.

Jake Barnes had suggested that "you paid some way for everything that was any good." "After such knowledge, what forgiveness?" asks Eliot's Gerontion, and, in a sense, all four of these books, foundering on the jagged intransigencies of payment and retribution, brood over the dark implications in those two statements: implications which challenge the very existence of moral impetus, responsibility, and the primal integrity of the human consciousness. The four authors differ greatly in the degree of intensity with which they suggest an ultimately nihilistic reality as the sole reality in the universe, and each, perhaps, offers his own tentative saving graces, but the void is frighteningly near to the surfaces of all of these texts. Most coincidentally of all, each of these books is fundamentally *uncentered* in a manner similar or analogous to the way *The Sun Also Rises* is uncentered. . . . [This] congruence of metaphor and structure in what are probably the four outstanding books of that great decade may indicate one reason why *The Sun Also Rises* has had a singular position among the scores of very good books that are part of the post-First World War disillusionment. These four works not only *reflect* the whirling frenzy of a culture in the midst of historical upheaval, but they also *project* metaphorical patterns of thought (specifically, those concerned with the most basic metaphor of all— the metaphor of man himself) that we are only now beginning to recognize and investigate with care.

Purely as a result of a geographical and a series of historical accidents, American culture has always been a "modern" culture; and its most basic and constant experience has been that of radical dislocation. Obviously this fact has been a source of both cultural strength and weakness. But one of the strengths has been the peculiar position accorded to the American writer within, as well as on the margins of, the western world. The American artist has enjoyed (or been burdened by) a special prescience, an almost preternatural and prophetic sensitivity to the major movements in modern life. Since his equilibrium has never come from traditionally supported bases of gravity, like a seismograph he has been inordinately receptive to the slightest of vibrations. . . . While Hemingway can be seen as at least a partial heir to that tradition, *The Sun Also Rises* is informed by an uncanny intuition of a new metaphor. As the Newtonian world-machine image of the eighteenth century gave way to the organic metaphor of the nineteenth century, so it is possible that the organic metaphor has already been supplanted by a new worldview, a view for which the most adequate metaphorical image may be that of explosion. If this is so, then it is likely that radically dislocated structures that are capable of functioning well, and personalities without a vital center that can maintain viable lives should have a special meaning for us today. And it is, finally, for this reason that *The Sun Also Rises* ought to continue to command our attention and provoke our thought. (pp. 303-12)

Earl H. Rovit, "Ernest Hemingway: 'The Sun Also Rises'," in *Landmarks of American Writing,* edited by Hennig Cohen, Basics Books, Inc., Publishers, 1969, pp. 303-14.

HERBIE BUTTERFIELD
(essay date 1983)

[In the following excerpt, Butterfield explores recurring themes in Hemingway's novels.]

[In the story that concludes *In Our Time,* **"Big Two-Hearted River"**, Nick Adams puts the] stuff of nightmares behind him, 'everything behind, the need for thinking, the need to write, other needs', . . . [and] heads away from the road for the woods and the river. Far from other human sound, he fishes, pitches his tent, builds a fire, cooks a buckwheat flapjack, brews coffee. 'He was there, in the good place. He was in his home where he had made it.'

It is a familiar American literary moment, this sealing of the solitary compact with nature, marked most famously amongst Hemingway's predecessors by Thoreau, in *Walden* and his other journals and natural histories. Thoreau was a writer who on the face of it

Major Media Adaptations: Motion Pictures and Television

A Farewell to Arms, 1932. Paramount. Director: Frank Borzage. Cast: Gary Cooper, Helen Hayes, Adolphe Menjou, Mary Philips, Jack LaRue, Blanche Frederici, Henry Armetta.

For Whom the Bell Tolls, 1943. Paramount (Sam Wood). Director: Sam Wood. Cast: Gary Cooper, Ingrid Bergman, Akim Tamiroff, Arturo de Cordova, Katina Paxinou.

To Have and Have Not, 1945. Warner (Howard Hawks). Director: Howard Hawks. Cast: Humphrey Bogart, Lauren Bacall, Walter Brennan, Hoagy Carmichael, Dolores Moran.

The Killers, 1946. Universal-International (Mark Hellinger). Director: Robert Siodmak. Cast: Burt Lancaster, Edmond O'Brien, Ava Gardner, Albert Dekker, Sam Levene, John Miljan.

The Macomber Affair, 1947. UA. [Adaptation of "The Short Happy Life of Francis Macomber"] Director: Zoltan Korda. Cast: Gregory Peck, Joan Bennett, Robert Preston, Reginald Denny, Carl Harbord.

The Breaking Point, 1950. Warner (Jerry Wald). [Adaptation of *To Have and Have Not*] Director: Michael Curtiz. Cast: John Garfield, Patricia Neal, Phyllis Thaxter, Wallace Ford, William Campbell.

The Snows of Kilimanjaro, 1952. Twentieth-Century Fox (Darryl F. Zanuck). Director: Henry King. Cast: Gregory Peck, Susan Hayward, Ava Gardner, Hildegard Neff, Leo, G. Carroll.

A Man Alone, 1955. Republic. [Television adaptation of "The Killers"] Director: Ray Milland. Cast: Ray Milland, Mary Murphy, Ward Bond, Raymond Burr, Lee Van Cleef.

A Farewell to Arms, 1957. Twentieth-Century Fox (David O. Selznick). Director: Charles Vidor. Cast: Rock Hudson, Jennifer Jones, Vittorio de Sica, Alberto Sordi, Kurt Kasznar.

The Sun Also Rises, 1957. Twentieth-Century Fox (Darryl F. Zanuck). Director: Henry King. Cast: Tyrone Power, Ava Gardner, Errol Flynn, Eddie Albert, Mel Ferrer, Robert Evans.

The Gun Runners, 1958. UA (Clarence Greene). [Adaptation of *To Have and Have Not*] Director: Don Siegel. Cast: Audie Murphy, Eddie Albert, Patricia Owens, Everett Sloane.

The Old Man and the Sea, 1958. Warner. Director: John Sturges. Cast: Spencer Tracy, Felipe Pazos, Harry Bellaver.

The Killers, 1964. Universal-International. Director: Don Siegel. Cast: John Cassavetes, Lee Marvin, Angie Dickinson, Ronald Reagan, Claude Akins.

---

would appear to have been unimportant to Hemingway. . . . However, that he sensed a kinship between himself and Thoreau can be gauged from the fact that in the first draft of **"The Snows of Kilimanjaro"** the names he gave to the dying writer, who, simply because he is a writer, is the closest representative in the fiction of Hemingway himself, were the determinedly significant ones of Henry Walden. He soon suppressed the association, but an underlying connection had briefly surfaced.

There were of course immense differences between the times and the lives and personalities of Thoreau and Hemingway. For Thoreau, self-encouragingly, 'the truest account of heaven is the fairest', where Hemingway had early on seen things that permanently disturbed his sleep, so that the dark was full of terrors and empty of God. Conversely, there were compensatory pleasures of the body, of board and bed, that Hemingway joyously rendered, but that Thoreau for whatever reason denied himself; just as, gregarious, amatory, and self-damagingly restless, Hemingway envied Thoreau's capacity for solitude. But at the core, at the still centre, as Hemingway recognized, there was affinity of spirit. In different accents each spoke the language of a radical, isolate individualism

that separated them from others, the mass of men leading lives of quiet, or hectic, desperation, and beckoned them towards an unpopulated nature. Each in fundamentally Protestant manner knew that what a man does with his solitariness is the true subject of philosophy. And each to be renewed, to be made whole, went home to nature, to earth and water, to Walden Pond and Big Two-Hearted River.

To be sure, where Thoreau levels a long, steady gaze at nature, Hemingway, as here with Nick, offers only brief homecomings; where Thoreau evolved into a herbivore, Hemingway remained a predator; and where Thoreau in his narratives has his solitude interrupted by only occasional or chance meetings, Hemingway's fictional world is often densely populated. But the important point is this, that whether the world be as uninhabited as Nick's in **"Big Two-Hearted River"**, or as crowded as the expatriate caravan of *The Sun Also Rises*, the essential condition of life for Hemingway is solitary, and the interesting, the properly serious business, is the management of that solitude.

Thus, in *The Sun Also Rises,* which was published exactly a year after *In Our Time,* Jake Barnes managerially 'did not care what it was all about. All I wanted to know was how to live in it', the primary characteristic of 'it' being a loneliness that is in fact in the general nature of things, though for Jake it has been given particular immediacy by the war-wound that has deprived him of the possibility of sexual love and comfort. To the problem of how to live in the days there are simple solutions; they can be filled with activity, people, laughter, and one more drink to fend off the night. 'It is awfully easy to be hard-boiled about everything in the daytime, but at night it is another thing.' There, alone, the dark is a place less of pointless yearning than of terror. . . . The fear is not of hidden presences, but of emptiness, universal absence, oblivion. It is of course a legacy of the war. . . . The war as a cause, though, is scarcely important; what matters is the reality of its effect, the knowledge of the fearful loneliness, the 'it' that must be lived in. There are the daytime distractions, which give to the novel such colour and movement; there are the natural world's healing balms (fishing at Burguete, bathing at San Sebastian, reestablishing footholds upon the earth that abideth forever); and for the nominally Catholic Jake there are some very flimsy 'consolations of religion'. But the continuing impression and the final picture (Jake sardonically puncturing Brett's wishful daydream of togetherness) is of a solitariness, that must be borne, coped with, lived in. And this is not just because of Jake's exceptional status, imposed upon him by the misfortunes of war. Other figures, central and peripheral, for whom we feel sympathy, are similarly marked, whether Brett in her loneliness of spirit careless and abandoned, or the Englishman Harris and fat Count Mippipopolous in theirs composed and dignified. Indeed, it is almost a precondition of our sympathy. Only the despised, those outside the circle, those who try too hard or not hard enough, seem not to know of such loneliness. (pp. 186-89)

[Hemingway's novels *Across the River and Into the Trees, To Have and Have Not,* and *For Whom the Bell Tolls*] all bear witness to . . . his obsession with death. All end or reach their climaxes with the death or impending death of the principal characters, figures as various as a small-time smuggler, an idealistic young guerrilla fighter, and a cynical middle-aged professional soldier. *Across the River and Into the Trees* (1950) closes with Colonel Cantwell, after a night of love and a day of duck-shooting, dying from the heart condition that has tracked and threatened him throughout. Cantwell is a representative Hemingway leading character, even if a rather coarse and unpleasant version, and as such he need not detain us here. The two earlier novels, however, offer the interesting difference of being consciously political in a way that his previous books had not been. *To Have and Have Not* (1937) is an emphatic protest against corruption, exploitation, political hypocrisy, and the immorality of gross inequality; while *For Whom the Bell Tolls* (1941) commemorates three days of a guerrilla action in the Spanish Civil War, on

which Hemingway had reported as a passionate adherent of the Loyalist cause. Hemingway's basic politics were consistent with his individualism, which is to say that they were anarchic, libertarian, and humanist. . . . On such grounds, entirely to his credit and in contrast to a notorious number of his literary contemporaries, he had early on laid his unambiguous opposition to Italian Fascism and his immediate hatred of Hitler. But if it was 'natural' for a libertarian individualist to detest totalitarianism, it was not 'natural' for one such to take up left-wing collectivist politics. And it is from the resultant uncertainty as to political identities that the relative failure of *To Have and Have Not* stems. Harry Morgan, named after the pirate Henry Morgan, is precisely piratical, a swashbuckling individualist, given to private criminal enterprise. He dies an appropriate violent, heroic death. What does not convince, though, what is not in character, is the swansong he utters while dying, the halting knell of that individualism: 'One man alone ain't got. No man alone now. No matter how a man alone ain't got no bloody chance.' The words may fumble towards a historical truth, but they have been learned in a politics lesson, rather than derived from Harry Morgan. The character and his incipiently political message have been separately conceived; and that absence of conceptual integrity accounts also for the clumsy obtrusiveness of the methods whereby elsewhere in the novel injustice is exposed. Hemingway's sentiments in this context are generous and admirable; but it did not come easily to him to give those sentiments a political cast. In fact, in the film made several years later, Faulkner in his script, Hawks in his direction, and Bogart in his starring role were between them, in being unfaithful to *To Have and Have Not,* being more faithful than Hemingway to himself.

For Whom the Bell Tolls is a greater work altogether, albeit an extraordinary combination of the exhilaratingly good and the embarrassingly bad. Neither for the first time nor for the last it is in the recreation of love that Hemingway goes astray. In the depiction of the loss of love that leaves a man bereft he excels; but in the description of lovers together he is ever liable to an excessive, distorting sentimentality that infantilizes, demeans, or renders ridiculous man and woman alike; never more so than here, with Jordan's and Maria's brief affair. Conversely, as in *A Farewell to Arms,* nearly all that has to do with war is excellently done: the characterization of the members of the guerrilla group; the comradeship, the hatred of enemies, the respect for enemies, the bravery, the brutality, the self-transcendence, the self-debasement. There are at least three permanently memorable narrative scenes: Pilar's tale of the murder of the Fascist civic leaders, El Sordo's last stand on the hill-top, and the mining and blowing up of the bridge. *For Whom the Bell Tolls* is a story of men and women in action together, dependent upon one another, fighting for a common cause; yet here again in its final picture the light falls not upon that cause, upon history and politics, but upon two lone individuals, both about to face their deaths; upon Lieutenant Berrendo, the decent Fascist, 'his thin face serious and grave', riding into Robert Jordan's range, and upon Jordan, dying for the cause, yes, but also dying for himself, alone, with courage and honour. Beneath the new political clothes, it is the same man.

We are each of us alone, then, at home in nature when we can find our way there, but amongst others solitary individuals rather than members of a community; alive, we suffer, in body and mind; and, knowing that we will die, we dwell upon death. That is the human condition as it appeared to Hemingway, or as it appeared important to him. The ways he proposed of meeting or managing this fate were various and distinct, so that in different aspects his values may seem, loosely, stoic, heroic, Protestant, or hedonistic. Pleasure, sensuous pleasure—food, drink, and all kinds of physical activity—he conveys with a rare, discriminating vividness, especially in the early writings and in the retrospective *A Moveable Feast* where, aided by his recently rediscovered notes, he shows a quite remarkable ability to recapture poignantly the look, smell and taste of things thirty and more years ago. If it is a world of pain, it is also one of pleasure, of visual beauties and tactile delights that ease our passage. (pp. 192-94)

The principal element, though, in Hemingway's imaginative world, the quality with which in some form or other virtually all his best writing is concerned is courage: simply, courage. If life is intrinsically painful, and the prospect of death omnipresent, the act of living becomes by definition a test of courage. The courage required may be moral, or mental, or physical; it may be passive or active; it may be as ostensibly minimal as bearing it, with or without grinning, or it may be the stuff of awards for gallantry. The active exemplars include the bullfighters, boxers, hunters, soldiers, and guerrilla fighters, men and women: Pedro Romero; Manuel Garcia; Jack Brennan; Wilson, the white hunter; Agustin; Pilar. The passive models cover a moral range from those who merely refuse self-deception . . . to those who exhibit varying degrees of what Hemingway famously termed 'grace under pressure'. Some are with faith, like the priest in *A Farewell to Arms* or Anselmo who was 'a Christian. Something very rare in Catholic countries'; some without faith, like Count Greffi who 'had always expected to become devout . . . but somehow it does not come', and the waiter of **"A Clean, Well-Lighted Place"**; but all are seen to bear with grace—it is a matter of courage and a quality of the spirit—the pressures that fate exerts upon them.

The last and longest test of courage, beyond which there was really no need of further testing, was that undergone by the fisherman Santiago in *The Old Man and the Sea,* who after months of failing to catch anything wrestles day-long and night-long with the great marlin, only to have his magnificent fish devoured by sharks. Published in 1952, the long story proves a splendid exception to the otherwise poor or drastically uneven writing that Hemingway was doing at this time; and with its knowledge of mystery and its natural reverence . . . it represents also a marvellous renewal after the morally and imaginatively dull record of competitive killing into which his previous saga of man and beast, *Green Hills of Africa,* had degenerated. *The Old Man and the Sea* is a story of skill, of all kinds of courage, of defeat in the flesh, of victory in the spirit, of pride humbled and self-respect earned, of suffering, and of final great peace of mind. It was the last fiction that he published.

The Old Man and the Sea is not a novel, but a long story, in its texture self-consciously and I think effectively poetic. The point has often been made, in one form or another, that Hemingway was essentially a poet rather than a novelist. . . . Certainly in his attitude to language and the tools of his craft Hemingway was far closer to many poets, especially amongst his contemporaries, than he was to at least the more utilitarian of novelists. What is the famous diatribe against the rhetoric of war in *A Farewell to Arms* but an emotionally charged, morally urgent elaboration upon Pound's Imagist dictate to 'go in fear of abstractions'? What is the lament in *Death in the Afternoon* that 'all our words from loose using have lost their edge' but a sparse precursor of the passage in Eliot's "Burnt Norton", where words 'slip, slide, perish, / Decay with imprecision, will not stay in place, / Will not stay still'? . . . Concentration, understatement, significant omission, antiphonal repetition and variation, austerity, verbal propriety: these are some of the technical devices or aesthetic values that he came to cherish, learned from others (Turgenev, Twain, Crane, and Conrad; Anderson, Stein, Ford, and Pound), but mastered for himself. With such literary priorities and with the priceless gift of his extraordinarily fine senses, especially of sight and taste, he developed an art capable of rendering outer and inner worlds alike, not with miniscule detail or complexity, but with startling, lucid simplicity. His achievements with language are on a par and of a kind with the great modernist poets of his generation. (pp. 195-97)

Herbie Butterfield, "Ernest Hemingway," in *American Fiction: New Readings,* edited by Richard Gray, Barnes & Noble, 1983, pp. 184-99.

FRANK McCONNELL
(essay date 1983)

[In the following excerpt, McConnell assesses Hemingway's contributions to contemporary American writing.]

In 1944 the Second World War was virtually over, the Axis will and neck all but terminally broken, Paris retaken, and Ernest Hemingway a picturesque but faintly absurd epiphenomenon of the tidal wave rolling toward Berlin. The most important American novelist of his time (but that time was passing), a sometime war correspondent (but his war correspondence was muddled), and a self-styled soldier on behalf of the civilized world altogether (though the civilized world, at that crucial moment, had very much larger things to worry about), he was lurching between bravery and silliness in a way that boded ill, indeed, for the remainder of his career. (p. 193)

For, just as the First World War virtually made Hemingway a serious writer—second only to T. S. Eliot as the chronicler and anthem-writer of a whole generation's despair—so the Second World War effectively marked the end of Hemingway's moment: or, at least, appeared to do so. 1944, the year of Allied victory and Hemingway foolishness was also the year of a new and startling talent in American letters. For while Hemingway was hoping to get into Paris without getting shot, Saul Bellow was publishing his first novel, *Dangling Man*. It is the fictionalized journal of 'Joseph', a Chicago-based intellectual and agonized draft-resister, a sensitive man who cannot even decide if he should enter the war to which Hemingway gave himself so enthusiastically. And it begins with what is essentially a refutation of the entire Hemingway mystique. . . . (p. 194)

In retrospect, there is something a little *too* cruelly parodic about . . . [the opening] sendup of the 'tough boy'. Much of our contemporary sense of Hemingway, after all, is precisely the sense of how far from 'tough' he really was, all along. Philip Young was probably the first critic to demonstrate compellingly what an ocean of self-doubt and vulnerability underlay that charade of gusto. But we do not, now, even need Young: we have the suicide. And in the glare of the suicide we can see that Nick Adams, Jake Barnes, Frederick Henry, Robert Jordan and the whole Hemingway crew were always, in one way or another, weak men overcompensating desperately for their weakness. Bellow goes on . . . to observe that the hardboiled writers tend to be deficient in the finer senses of despair and possibili-

ty. They are unpractised in introspection, he writes, 'and therefore badly equipped to deal with opponents whom they cannot shoot like big game or outdo in daring'.

Badly equipped, yes: but one wonders about that word, unpractised. Is anyone *well* equipped to deal with the monsters inside, as opposed to outside the head? And isn't the man who quests obsessively for beasts in view, for clear and evident monsters to kill, perhaps also the man who understands best how unkillable are the monsters within?

To ask such questions is, of course, to re-romanticize Hemingway, to return him—man and style—to the arena of melodrama he himself felt most comfortable in. But that itself might not be a bad thing to do. In the twenty-odd years since his death, Hemingway has been subjected to much more blatant, and much less understanding, kinds of parody than Bellow's treatment in *Dangling Man*. And most of the worst of it has come from the literary critics.

He was a sad man. His bluster, his bullying, his loud adventurism were a mask for a deep-seated insecurity. He was . . . a *miles gloriosus*, a braggart soldier who could be taken as a mere, absurd figure of fun. So much is true, and is eminently acceptable as an attitude to strike toward Hemingway in the American academy. For so much is, to put it bluntly, reassuring. One needn't fear the braggart soldier, just because he *is* only a braggart: we know that by the last act he will be revealed to be a coward, like us.

But, I want to suggest, Hemingway managed to be all those absurd, laughable things, and also to be something else, something permanently valuable for American letters. He managed to be a hero of consciousness, a writer and a stylist who made his cowardice, and his knowledge of his cowardice, the very stuff of his heroism and his endurance. This is, again, a cliché of a certain strain of romanticism: the Byronic. And yet the evidence of American fiction after Hemingway is that he, like Lord Byron, was the kind of truly great clown whose special talent is for making that kind of cliché vital and serviceable. (pp. 194-95)

Both Byron and Hemingway were dandies: ostentatious, elegantly vulgar men who made their insecure egotism the subject of their art. Hemingway's most lasting importance, indeed, may be that he was the first great American dandy of this century (only Whitman and Twain come to mind from the nineteenth century); and that, like all the truly valuable members of the sect (e.g. Byron, Baudelaire, Wilde, T. E. Lawrence), he shows us something of the cost, as well as the value, of the dandy's pose.

Francis Jeffrey wrote what is probably the definitive analysis of the literary dandy, in his review of Byron's *The Corsair;* and his analysis applies with striking appropriateness to the Hemingway persona, also. Why all this fascination, in a civilized country, with violence, adventure, and deep melancholia, he asks. Because the very civilization with which we have surrounded ourselves puts us out of touch with certain primal instincts, rages, and passions that are necessary to our souls. So that Byron's 'primitivism' is not primitivism at all, but the very sophisticated nostalgia of an over-complex victim of the modern age. (p. 196)

The dandy values style above substance . . . because he finds the world of substances empty, void, a sham. This is the Byronic abyss of cynicism, this is Lawrence's profound despair at politics, and this is Hemingway's celebrated *nada*. The dandy confuses the life and the work: to the degree that his heirs or his successors must laboriously separate the life from the work, in order to see the work afresh. The dandy loves to show off; loves to be sketched or photographed in the various poses and costumes of his dandyism: see the portrait of Byron in Albanian garb, or the photos of Hemingway, smiling over dead buffalo, in his white-hunter slouch hat and khaki.

And the dandy loves war. He loves war for the same reason he loves stylized brutality, because war *is* stylized brutality, the absolute triumph of technique over value and therefore the permanent, the true condition of humankind. Patton and Montgomery are two dandies *manqués*—neither wrote well—in that they both seemed to understand war as theatre, as a riotous backdrop for their own performing selves.

But the dandy loves war as he loves everything else: ironically. 'Abstract words such as glory, honour, courage, or hallow were obscene beside the concrete names of villages, the numbers of roads, the names of rivers, the numbers of regiments and the dates.' That, of course, is Frederick Henry in *A Farewell to Arms:* one of the most often-quoted, and one of the most crucial of Hemingway passages. Byronic romantic that he was, Hemingway believed in this wounded emptiness before he ever saw it manifested in the War (think about his jejune parody of Anderson's sentimentality in *The Torrents of Spring*). But he welcomed the War—and became its chief elegiac voice—just because it was the manifestation of the *nada* he carried inside himself.

And that gift of irony, that sublime hollowness, is his bequest to later American writers. (pp. 196-97)

Hemingway—as writer and as presence—broods with a particular urgency over the writers who come after him. I have said that the literary dandy confuses his life and his art. In Hemingway's case that confusion has been unusually productive, and unusually indicative of shifts in the national self-consciousness. We can take Hemingway as the first successful American romantic after Walt Whitman, the first man to identify a style of writing with a style of being in the world, and

Hemingway (age 5) fishing in Horton Creek in northern Michigan.

to make the indentification popular. He *was,* largely, the Byron of his age: so much so that 'Byronic' and 'Hemingwayesque' are the only two terms we normally apply as adjectives to the word, 'hero'. (p. 201)

If Hemingway is the American Byron, we might expect that his influence and his presence would be, like Byron's, both blatant and subtle. And so it has been. Indeed, like Byron, Hemingway has had at least as important an influence on so-called 'popular' culture as he has had on so-called 'serious' writing. His very short story, **"The Killers"**, from *In Our Time,* has provided a title and at least the bare bones of a script for two excellent gangster films (one directed by Robert Siodmak, 1946; one directed by Don Siegel, 1963). But beyond this explicit influence, it is also evident that Hemingway and the Hemingway style have exercised a strong, probably determinative, effect on the whole course of the American detective story in both film and literature.

Dashiell Hammett and Raymond Chandler are usually credited with being the originators of the American or 'hardboiled' style of detective writing. But, as the phrase itself, 'hardboiled' may indicate, both Hammett and Chandler—and their contemporary heirs, Ross Macdonald, John D. MacDonald, Lawrence Sanders, and Stuart Kaminsky—would not really be possible without Hemingway. Indeed, the Hemingway hero is, by and large, the classic American hardboiled private eye; and the prose style that goes along with that peculiar figure is, by and large, the prose style Hemingway developed for a very different kind of character: i.e. the wounded, disillusioned veteran of the First World War.

'Doctors did things to you and then it was not your body any more', thinks Frederick Henry in *A Farewell to Arms,* returning to the Front. 'The head was mine, and the inside of the belly. It was very hungry in there. I could feel it turn over on itself. The head was mine, but not to use, not to think with, only to remember and not too much remember.'

'Only to remember and not too much remember': that may be the distinctive definition of the Hemingway style. For at its best it is a style that places a screen of words, a screen of short, ritualistically declarative sentences between the narrator/perceiver of the action and the horrendous, tragic quality of the action itself. Jake Barnes *is* impotent; Frederick Henry *does* fail to make a 'separate peace'; Robert Jordan *does* die needlessly; Santiago *does* fail to catch and bring back the great fish. It is a universe of defeat and disillusionment, and yet that telegraphic style . . . almost reconciles us to the horror, since it all but masks the horror within an ironic, primitive, unremembering articulation.

This is to say that the Hemingway style is a direct equivalent of the celebrated 'code' of the Hemingway hero; for both are deliberate reductions of the flux of life to the dimensions of an elaborate game—the one in the world of behaviour, the other in the world of utterance. And that, of course, is precisely the tone of the classic American detective story, whether in film or in literature. It is a deliberate unremembering: a recapitulation of the violent past that filters the horror of the past—the horror of betrayal, of failure, of psychic impotence—through the obsessive detail of its descriptive style. In American film this is the tradition of the *film noir,* from classics of the '40s like *The Maltese Falcon* and *Double Indemnity* to recent attempts at recapturing that special tone like *Chinatown, The Godfather,* and *Body Heat.* What all these disparate films have in common is their celebration of a certain tender cynicism, a certain conviction that, rotten at the core and inevitably entropic as human history may be, there is a kind of existential toughness, a bullet-biting disengagement that can survive the ravages of time with something like dignity.

That is the Hemingway tradition at its most popular—and perhaps also at its most dangerous. The self-advertising 'toughness' . . . can also be adopted at its most vulgar and arrogant pitch of *machismo.* No one, for example, could seriously argue that the popularity of

the Hemingway hero is directly responsible for the obscene bullyism of America's venture into Vietnam. But, on the other hand, one could argue that the Hemingway vision is symptomatic of a certain strain of irresponsibility, of cruelty, of dangerously arrested adolescence that is a permanent flaw in human character and a fatal flaw of empires. (pp. 202-04)

If indeed there are two Hemingways, the self-aggrandizing man and the writer who was a hero of consciousness, it may be fair to say that his heirs have learned an important lesson that he never learned: how to keep the two separate. And they have learned it, of course, from his example. His presence grows increasingly analogous to Byron's presence in the nineteenth century: a sensibility and a style impossible to ignore, and a personality impossible to emulate.

The work of Thomas Pynchon is the best and richest place to track Hemingway's ghost. Pynchon's two massive novels, *V* and *Gravity's Rainbow,* and his novella, *The Crying of Lot 49,* may be the most important fictions produced in America after the Second World War; they are certainly the most apocalyptic. Pynchon's vision is of an absolutely paranoid universe, presided over by giant cartels and international war machines whose grand design is to turn human beings into mere mechanisms. It is a vision of plastic entropy very like Joseph Heller's vision of the War in *Catch-22,* except that its grimness is more unrelenting and its comedy even blacker. And it is, of course, a vision directly inherited from Hemingway. In the same paragraph where Jake Barnes reflects on not too much remembering, he meditates on the surgery that has been performed on his knee:

> Valentini had done a fine job. . . . It was his knee all right. The other knee was mine. Doctors did things to you and then it was not your body any more. The head was mine, and the inside of the belly. It was very hungry in there.

This very famous passage might almost be the epigraph for all of Pynchon's fiction. . . . Life is increasingly encroached upon by the technologies of war and healing, both of which have the effect of robbing life of its vitality, and the only escape from that warfare is into the Switzerland of 'the head and the inside of the belly'. Pynchon's heroes . . . are the contemporary reincarnations of this mode. Benny Profane in *V,* Oedipa Maas in *Lot 49,* Tyrone Slothrop in *Gravity's Rainbow*—they are all weaklings, wounded and put-upon losers who are shocked into rebellion and a separate peace by the discovery that they are being turned into *someone else's* creation.

Their retreat is into style, into canniness . . . and into the kind of bitter, end-of-the-world charity that also characterizes the best of Hemingway throughout his career. In *V* the jazz musician McClintic Sphere articulates, in a brief scene, what may be the summary statement of the dandy's ironic humanism: 'Keep cool, but care.' And in the toughness and tenderness of that short line one hears echoes of all the sensibilities we have been examining, but with Papa at the centre.

No final assessment of the Hemingway presence can really be made, of course. This has been a century of triumph of partial visions, all of which have left their mark on what comes after. But Hemingway more than any American novelist of the age represented and lived the vocation of art as *risk,* as a deliberate gamble with one's chances for sanity in a mad world. And in that he became a paradigm—something much larger and subtler than an 'influence'—for the most serious American writers of the post-War years. His ghost, the ghost of his finest perceptions and strongest acts of literary courage, is a very unquiet ghost indeed. And its rumblings are an inescapable part of the splendid dissonance that is contemporary American fiction. (pp. 210-11)

Frank McConnell, "Stalking Papa's Ghost: Hemingway's Presence in Contemporary American Writing," in *Ernest Hemingway: New Critical Essays,* edited by A. Robert Lee, Barnes & Noble, 1983, pp. 193-211.

SOURCES FOR FURTHER STUDY

Benson, Jackson J., ed. *New Critical Approaches to the Short Stories of Ernest Hemingway.* Durham, N.C.: Duke University Press, 1990, 512 p.

Collection of critical essays on Hemingway's short stories.

Donaldson, Scott. *By Force of Will: The Life and Art of Ernest Hemingway.* New York: Viking Press, 1977, 367 p.

Comprehensive biographical and critical study of Hemingway.

Flora, Joseph M. *Hemingway's Nick Adams.* Baton Rouge: Louisiana State University Press, 1982, 285 p.

Examines the character of Nick Adams, focusing on his development throughout Hemingway's literary canon.

Lee, A. Robert, ed. *Ernest Hemingway: New Critical Essays.* Totowa, N.J.: Barnes & Noble, 1983, 216 p.

Features ten commissioned essays on Hemingway, including Colin E. Nicholson's "The Short Stories after *In Our Time:* A Profile," Eric Mottram's "Essential History: Suicide and Nostalgia in Hemingway's Fictions," and Faith Pullin's "Hemingway and the Secret Language of Hate."

Wagner, Linda Welshimer. *Ernest Hemingway: Five Decades of Criticism.* East Lansing: Michigan State University Press, 1974, 328 p.

Contains essays on individual novels, on Hemingway's style and technique, on his work as a whole, and on his literary development. Of especial interest is George Plimpton's 1958 *Paris Review* interview with Hemingway on the theory and practice of his craft.

Young, Philip. *Ernest Hemingway: A Reconsideration.* University Park: Pennsylvania State University Press, 1966, 297 p.

Analyzes major traits in Hemingway's fiction, including: the Hemingway moral code, the wounded hero, and the Hemingway style.

O. Henry

1862-1910

(Pseudonym of William Sydney Porter) American short story writer, journalist, humorist, and poet.

INTRODUCTION

O. Henry is perhaps the most popular and widely known American short story writer of the twentieth century. During the eight-year period that he lived and wrote in New York City, the short story form was at the height of its popularity, and dozens of periodicals featuring short fiction competed for the works of celebrated authors. It was against this background that O. Henry quickly rose to become the most sought-after and acclaimed American short story writer by virtue of his distinctive works: typically brief stories characterized by familiar, conversational openings, circumlocutory dialogue, plots hinging on improbable coincidence, and variations on the surprise or twist ending. The highly ironic, sentimental, or unexpected story conclusion has been so closely identified with O. Henry that his name has become synonymous with fiction of this kind.

O. Henry was born William Sydney Porter, the second son of Dr. and Mrs. Algernon Sidney Porter of Greensboro, North Carolina. Following Mrs. Porter's death when O. Henry was three, Dr. Porter moved with his children into his mother's house, where the boys' grandmother and an aunt undertook their education and upbringing. As a teenager, O. Henry helped support his family by working as a pharmacist's assistant in an uncle's drugstore, and he obtained his pharmacist's license in 1881. Never in robust health, O. Henry worried particularly about contracting pneumonia, which had been the cause of his mother's early death. When at nineteen he developed a persistent cough, he sought a milder climate in southwest Texas, where he worked on a cattle ranch owned by family friends. His health improved gradually, and at twenty-two he moved to Austin, where he met his first wife and found work as a bank teller. In 1894 he purchased a weekly humor paper, retitled it *The Rolling Stone,* and supplied virtually all of the paper's content. When the periodical failed after a year's publication, he continued to submit humorous stories and articles to other newspapers. Also in 1894, O. Henry was dismissed from his bank post because of shortages in his accounts. When the case was reinvestigated in 1895, and embezzlement charges seemed imminent, he fled Austin for Houston and later New Orleans, sailing from there to Honduras. In 1897, after learning that his wife was seriously ill, he returned to Austin and surrendered to authorities. After his wife's death he was convicted of embezzlement and sentenced to five years in the Federal Penitentiary in Ohio, where he was assigned to the prison pharmacy's twelve-hour midnight shift. His duties included prescribing and administering medication and tending to injured prisoners. O. Henry had made his first professional story sale to a magazine shortly before his conviction, and he continued to submit short stories for publication, based on his experiences in the southwest, in Central America, and in prison, using his in-laws' Pittsburgh address as a screen for his actual circumstances.

O. Henry's criminal conviction and prison term was for some time the most uncertain and controversial aspect of his life. One of his biographers, Al Jennings, who was in the penitentiary with O. Henry, recounts that the writer's greatest fear was that he would be recognized and greeted by a former inmate while in the company of others. Many of O. Henry's closest acquaintances never knew that he had spent time in prison, and he often juggled dates to account for the years spent in prison. As a result there was some initial uncertainty about several important dates in his life, but biographers now believe that they have established an accurate chronology. It was common for early biographical essays to hotly debate the question of his innocence or guilt. Most modern biographers conclude that while O. Henry may have been technically guilty of embezzlement, he was almost certainly following the extremely lax bookkeeping policies of the Austin bank.

Obtaining an early release after serving three years of his sentence, O. Henry lived for a short time with his wife's parents, but moved to New York City in the spring of 1902 at the urging of *Ainslee's Magazine* editors Gilman Hall and Richard Duffy, who had been printing his stories and were confident that he could make a successful career writing for New York magazines. O. Henry began publishing stories in numerous periodicals under pseudonyms that included variations of his real name. He quickly gained fame under his most often-used pen name, O. Henry. A contract with the New York *Sunday World* for a weekly short story provided him with a steady income, while the *World's* circulation of nearly one-half million assured him a wide readership. O. Henry's remuneration from the periodical—one hundred dollars per story—was liberal for the

time, and he supplemented his income by selling stories to other magazines that were anxious to print his popular works. However, he was financially irresponsible and continually in debt. He loved to sit for hours in restaurants and bars, observing other patrons and constructing instantaneous fictions about them, and then leaving a tip that often exceeded his bill. He was also lavish in the handouts he dispensed to panhandlers and prostitutes who, he claimed, often provided him with the germ of a story whereby he more than recouped his initial investment. Increasingly, he turned out stories in haste to honor the generous advances he received from editors.

Biographer Richard O'Connor has written that "the year 1904 . . . was easily the busiest and most productive of [O. Henry's] career. As the price for his stories went up, he simply produced less. But that vintage year . . . saw him at the peak of his creative power." Since his arrival in New York two years earlier, O. Henry had been steadily gaining not only in popularity but also in critical regard as an important literary figure. In 1904, *McClure's Magazine* editor Witter Bynner suggested assembling O. Henry's stories with Central American settings as a novel under the title *Cabbages and Kings,* a work that most critics have regarded as a grouping of loosely connected short stories. His collection *The Four Million* followed two years later, and his works, rescued from the impermanence of periodical publication, became more widely known. Further compilations of his stories appeared yearly thereafter and for several years after his death. Plagued by a variety of health problems, including diabetes and cirrhosis of the liver exacerbated by alcoholism, O. Henry died in 1910 at the age of forty-seven.

O. Henry's fame rests upon the type of short story he wrote and not upon the distinction of any individual work. The archetypal O. Henry story is described by his biographer and critic Eugene Current-García as possessing several unmistakable characteristics: "the chatty, shortcut opening; the catchy, piquant descriptive phrasing; the confidential, reminiscent narrator; the chance meeting of old pals; and half a dozen or more variations of the surprise ending." His stories are often divided into five distinct groups according to their settings: the American South, the West, Central America, prison, and New York. By far the best known and most often reprinted are the stories set in New York City. These one hundred and forty stories, making up nearly half of his total output, capture the essence of early twentieth-century city life, and include the frequently anthologized "Gift of the Magi," "The Furnished Room," "A Municipal Report," "The Skylight Room," and "An Unfinished Story." Commonly recurring themes in O. Henry's short stories are those of deception, mistaken identity, the effects of coincidence, the inexorable nature of fate, and the resolution of seemingly insurmountable difficulties separating two lovers. In the stories that revolve around deliberate deception, O. Henry often used a plot contrivance that he called "turning the tables on Haroun Al-Raschid," the caliph from *The Arabian Nights' Entertainments* who disguised himself to mingle with the common people. In O. Henry's stories it is the common people—the clerks, salespeople, factory and office workers—who save assiduously for the infrequent evenings when they can dress in their finest and mix with the rich and powerful. A favorite device of O. Henry was to depict a poor working man or woman whose potentially romantic encounters come to nothing because of the ridiculous poses they feel obliged to adopt while pretending to be wealthy. Although plot resolutions of O. Henry stories often depend on improbable coincidence, some critics assert that the wealth of detail concerning characters and settings makes the stories appear naturalistic despite the sometimes fantastic plots.

During the last decade of his life and for about a decade following his death, O. Henry was the most popular and widely read American short story writer. He was commonly regarded as the modern American master of the short story form, ranked with Edgar Allan Poe, Nathaniel Hawthorne, and Bret Harte. His works were considered models of the genre and his short story techniques were taught in college writing courses. The growing tide of favorable assessments culminated in C. Alphonso Smith's *O. Henry Biography*, published in 1916. At about this time, however, O. Henry's critical reputation began to undergo reevaluation. Critics began to question the validity of the excessive praise that O. Henry had garnered in the previous two decades, and some—most notably Katharine Fullerton Gerould and Fred Lewis Pattee—dismissed his

work as facile, anecdotal, journalistic, and of little lasting literary value. Gerould went so far as to denounce O. Henry's pervasive influence on the modern short story as "pernicious," while Pattee questioned the moral basis of the works, writing that O. Henry's nonjudgmental portrayals of criminals amounted to an endorsement of lawless behavior. Other critics noted how quickly O. Henry stories seemed to date, and his trademark surprise endings were called overly sentimental and predictable.

Concurrent with the growth of negative criticism in the United States came the first translations of O. Henry's stories and the beginning of his great renown abroad. With the advent of experimental literary forms in American literature in the 1920s and 1930s, O. Henry's critical reputation reached its lowest point. The tendency of literary critics—when they mentioned O. Henry at all—was to relegate him to a minor place in American literary history. In the 1960s, however, another reevaluation began to take place, inspired largely by the fact that despite his decline in critical standing, O. Henry had always retained popularity with readers. Critics continue to reassess O. Henry's contribution to literature, with most maintaining that his characteristically brief, humorous, sometimes sentimental stories have earned him a permanent place as a skilled and inventive story writer who profoundly influenced the course of the American short story for half a century.

(For further information about O. Henry's life and works, see *Concise Dictionary of American Literary Biography, 1865-1917; Contemporary Authors*, Vol. 104; *Dictionary of Literary Biography*, Vols. 12, 78, 79; and *Twentieth-Century Literary Criticism*, Vols. 1, 19.)

CRITICAL COMMENTARY

CARL VAN DOREN
(essay date 1917)

[Van Doren is considered one of the most perceptive critics of the first half of the twentieth century. He worked for many years as a professor of English at Columbia University and served as literary editor and critic for the *Nation* and the *Century* during the 1920s. A founder of the Literary Guild and author or editor of several American literary histories, he was also a critically acclaimed historian and biographer. In the following excerpt, he discusses essential traits of O. Henry's personality and fiction.]

Mature when he found himself, allowed less than ten years of working life, O. Henry exhibited in his twelve volumes only one method, varied as his management of it was. His earlier stories, indeed, were written with a more careful finish than he found in demand upon Broadway, but his falling off in finish was in the interest of a quality which ruled his art. For O. Henry, among the fiction writers of his generation, was the raconteur. He is said on sound authority to have composed many of his stories to the last detail before writing a word. Whether or not this was his general practice, the fact remains that he was the literary quintes-

---

Principal Works

Cabbages and Kings (novel) 1904

The Four Million (short stories) 1906

Heart of the West (short stories) 1907

The Trimmed Lamp (short stories) 1907

The Gentle Grafter (short stories) 1908

The Voice of the City (short stories) 1908

Options (short stories) 1909

Roads of Destiny (short stories) 1909

Strictly Business (short stories) 1910

Whirligigs (short stories) 1910

Sixes and Sevens (short stories) 1911

Rolling Stones (short stories) 1912

Waifs and Strays (short stories) 1917

O. Henryana (sketches and poetry) 1920

Letters to Lithopolis (letters) 1922

Postscripts (humor) 1923

O. Henry Encore (humor) 1939

The Complete Works of O. Henry. 2 vols. (short stories and novel) 1953

---

sence of a type which flourishes in America, the man whom easy social boundaries have allowed to slip through all grades of experience and who finds himself called upon to render an account of his adventures to that very large body of his countrymen who stay at home and have yet the sharpest hunger for unusual incident and character. Such a man is not at all the instinctive autobiographer, whose capital is his own deeds and emotions. He is nearer the actor than the historian. His methods must be swift and easy, not too subtle. Even though he take the gravest topic, he must handle it a moment, lightly, and then be up and away to outrun boredom. Occasionally he may be sentimental, but he must insulate his sentiment with laughter. He must be colloquial, tactful, full of memories, inventive, pungent, surprising. He may speak as if he has been in every action he tells of, but he must speak as if the action no longer weighs upon him, as if his philosophy has conquered his past and made it all into material for art or mirth. (p. 250)

His method developed, so far as it can be said to have developed at all, chiefly in the direction of greater freedom for himself behind the raconteur. As he became more assured of his audience, he kept less out of sight. "Don't lose heart," he suddenly exclaimed in the midst of **"A Night in New Arabia,"** "because the story seems to be degenerating into a sort of moral essay for intellectual readers. There will be dialogue and stage business pretty soon." And again in **"Tommy's Burglar"**: "The burglar got into the house without much

difficulty; because we must have action and not too much description in a 2,000-word story." These are the perilous flippancies of a man among friends. But though O. Henry accepted more and more the insouciance of Broadway, he did not really give up his own secrets or visit his emotions upon the world. . . . The subtler moods, about which one learns either from others or from oneself, only by long brooding, O. Henry left untouched, partly because they are subtle and partly because they are private.

"If I could have a thousand years—just one little thousand years—more of life, I might, in that time, draw near enough to true Romance to touch the hem of her robe." These words [from the story **"He Also Serves"**] illuminate the mood and substance of O. Henry. The object of his vision was not history or morals, as with Hawthorne, or the world of dreams, as with Poe, but what he called adventure. "The true adventurer," he said in **"The Green Door,"** "goes forth aimless and uncalculating to meet and greet unknown fate." One need not be a hero or a philosopher to adventure thus. It is enough to keep an open and hopeful mind, a vigilant eye, and an unfading gusto for the prizes one takes on such a hunt. Like a scientist, the adventurer desires to find his facts in reality, but he wants to meet them at a time when the meeting will seem to have the significance of art. O. Henry was an adventurer of this type and a connoisseur of adventure whose restless avidity in exploring his field of romance appears in the astounding riches of his invention and illustration.

The first impression, indeed, which one is likely to take from a volume of his stories is of his high-spirited profusion. Images, turns, strange conceits, fantastic foolishness pour in upon him like a flood. He is gay, irresponsible, impudent, hoaxing; no writer in the language seems clever immediately after one has been reading O. Henry. Much of his ingenuity is verbal, but it seems almost exhaustless. (pp. 251-52)

[An] irrepressible opulence shows in his plots. Not ignorance of the austere bounds of probability but chuckling unconcern for the timid conventions of realism lies behind his romancing. Some have found in O. Henry's capricious plots the defect of the recluse who writes about a world of other men. There is no reason, however, to think that he regarded his strange tales as normal. He wrote to please himself and the magazines that paid him.

"A Night in New Arabia" thoroughly illustrates the point. Old Jacob Spraggins, a retired malefactor with a conscience which impels him to charity, has a daughter Celia, who loves the grocer's boy. This, of course, is only a new version of the case in [the early fourteenth-century metrical romance] *The Squire of Low Degree*. And O. Henry, like the nameless medieval poet, takes the wish of his readers for a guide. After a period of suspense much briefer than the Squire's seven years in Lombardy, the grocer's boy, having suddenly been made rich and worthy by certain expiatory thousands from his sweetheart's father, is made richer by the girl herself. Such an outcome is quite in the popular tradition; so is Celia's stooping to a parlor maid's cap and apron to conquer the modesty which she knew would never aspire to an heiress. Moreover, as the title of the story makes clear, O. Henry was deliberately parodying, with the sympathy of knowledge, *The Arabian Nights.* Indeed, that great fountain head of romance comes to one's mind again and again in a reading of O. Henry. Not only verbal reminiscences, which abound, and the atmosphere of the swarming city suggest it, but a certain popular quality in the plots, as if not a man but a generation had invented them. They seem too varied to have come from one head, and their bewildering conclusions, no matter by what breathless route arrived at, generally fulfill the desires of a whole populace.

This quality of fulfillment, of course, lies at the very heart of popular romance. It is the supernatural providence of the world of fiction, and the changes which have come over the fashions in heroes and manners have not essentially altered it. Heracles, happening by, wrests Alcestis from the death that has been decreed; St. George appears just at the moment of despair and defends the English against the horrible Saracens; exactly at the right instant, in **"The Church with an Overshot Wheel,"** the stream of flour sifts down through the gallery floor and reveals the lost Aglaia to her father. Deity, saint, coincidence,—something must furnish the element of wonder and the desired miracle. One should not be misled by the fact that new names have been given to the mysterious agent. Named or nameless, it has existed and exists to accomplish in art the defeated aspirations of reality. It is O. Henry's most powerful aid, brilliant in his endings, everywhere pervasive. His strong virtue was the genius to select from the apparent plane of fact whatever might bear testimony to the presence in life of this fiery spirit of romance. By this he spoke to the public with something of the authority of a priest of their well-trusted providence.

It would be easy, smiling at the thought of O. Henry in the rôle of priest, to dismiss him with the sharp charge of having suited the public, if that charge were a final condemnation. One must admit outright that his taste was often bad. . . . It has been urged that his bad taste, which was largely verbal, must be excused because slang was his normal idiom. . . . The fact that he wrote as he talked may explain why he wrote as he did, but it cannot justify his bad taste any more than it can avert its chief penalty, which is that in twenty years much of his work must appear tawdry or unintelligible. That price he paid for certain easily bought roars from his generation.

Thus in language, as in plots, it appears that he was close to the general audience which took his art for its amusement. And the evidences of that kinship have led many persons into cant about his universal humanity. As a matter of fact, it was his curious search for romance, quite as much as his humanity, which took him into every hole and cranny of the world he worked in. He was no indiscriminate lover of the human race, swollen to quick tears and tenderness at the mere proximity of a crowd. He was not even a hail fellow, backclapping and vociferous, but shy, chary of intimates, too much an ironist for general embraces. His whole life was a spectatorship. He was often obliged to deny what was said of him as soon as he took the public fancy, that he had been engaged in every calling he wrote about. Nor should critics who thus complimented him on his experience at the expense of his insight, have needed the facts of his career to obviate such a judgment. His work alone carries the proof that he was a spectator. Few workers could have mastered the details of so many crafts as he learned how to use, in fiction, by his observant loafing. Moreover, when one comes to think of it, almost all his stories have at least one end in the street or some public place, where he might have seen it and deduced the rest. And, finally, there was in his temper a certain balance arising out of a philosophy which, whether natural or deliberate, is invariably a detached philosophy, a spectator's reading of life.

With his wide, serious, shrewd experience, O. Henry was destined to clearness of vision. He had need of it, indeed, in the kaleidoscopic world which he dominated, for he was dealing with that uncharted thing which his generation called "real life." But he had no delusion regarding the value of promiscuous experiments in it. "Nearly everybody nowadays," he said, "knows too much—oh, so much too much—of real life." Nor did he mistake reality. Human beings naturally joined in orderly existence, he knew to be something real. He had been made too conscious of the social order ever to forget it. Again and again he expressed a sense of the instability of the spaces which lie outside human laws. (pp. 253-56)

To appreciate reality as he did is to be a moralist. Perhaps it is with surprise that one first realizes how thoroughly, in the midst of his world of gay and fascinating romance, under his sparkle and foam of cleverness, O. Henry exhibits the rules by which men live together. After half a dozen volumes one thinks less than at first of the crackle of the endings; they seem but the mannerism of a technique, like the resounding last lines of sonnets. Gradually then emerges O. Henry's true humanity, as skilled in detecting the real motives of men as in perceiving the romantic possibilities of their lives. Above all, it is intelligent. Except when he is farcical, and so legally without the law, he is almost unerring in the disposition of his sympathies. . . . He did not stop thinking to feel. Consequently he kept much of the improbability of his plots out of his characters, who, through the most bewildering dances of fortune, maintain a proportion and consistency which could have been imparted to them only by a mind conscious of some kind of order in human conduct. This order, his system of morality, pervades O. Henry's whole universe. It is not always according to statutes—in **"A Municipal Report,"** one of his truest stories, he condones a murder—and it is not always austere. Indeed, its basis seems to be largely the instinct for fair play which exists in all popular codes. It rounds out his plots with poetic, which is popular, justice. It makes him condemn certain offenders, outspokenly, beyond the need of art, that no one may miss the moral. But it does not afflict him with sentimentalism, mob judgment, or limp concession to popular prejudices. Stoutly as he stood by the world which he represented in his art, he preferred its sense to its nonsense when it came to judging life. Just as, in his invention, he sums up and a little transcends the romantic majority of the people, so, in his reading of life, he speaks for the undeceived minority of sensible men.

This is solid ground. But as the favored story teller of that substantial public which keeps alive public art O. Henry does not speak for too narrow a minority, for those rectangular realists, for example, who think they follow Mr. Bernard Shaw. This is to say, O. Henry was sensible but not speculative. To all appearances, he cared little for general ideas. Skeptical in religion, he rarely talked skepticism; sociology he avoided; his discussions of life seldom took him beyond the province of daily conduct. He was as content to handle the world before him as his more cosmopolitan, if less humane, contemporary, Mr. Kipling. And yet O. Henry's stories are alive with the sense of irony, of the constant meddling of the "little cherub who sits up aloft." One thinks of Mr. Hardy in this connection, and there opens up a world of contrast between the art of the populace and an art which has speculation at its roots. The irony of O. Henry is as impudent as Swift's, sometimes as cruel as that of Mr. Hardy, but it is too gaily, too briefly dealt with to become a real menace to the happiness of an irrepressible comic scene. The grinding spirit of irony which allows comedy to call tragedy cousin, O. Henry never took with full seriousness. Unlike Mr. Hardy, he never hunted for an agent, long and broodingly behind the ironic fortune which taunts human effort, never found a systematic malice, a diabolical providence, to which to ascribe all the acts of irony. Like the public he represented, he had comedy's short memory, which soon forgets the first biting impertinences of fate and greets new ones with a laugh. His comedy had and took no time to build up a principle that might account for the hostile facts it met. Satisfied that there lay in each of them a little mirth, this comedy gathered such

mirth where it found it, used it, flippant and prodigal, in the day's business, and pushed on to new enjoyment. Mr. Hardy's tragedy, following, gleaning, storing up, has the later and the impressive word. But the comedy of O. Henry, for all it speaks so lightly, has passed, it must still be remembered, with keen and open eyes, along the same highway. (pp. 256-59)

Carl Van Doren, "O. Henry," in *The Texas Review,* Vol. II, No. 3, January, 1917, pp. 248-59.

YEVGENY ZAMYATIN
(essay date 1923)

[Zamyatin is considered among the most influential twentieth-century Russian fiction writers and critics. He consistently employed new techniques in his art, and his work is recognized for its arresting language, fantastic imagery, and ironic viewpoint. Insisting that true art is created by rebels and heretics, Zamyatin urged young writers to remain independent of political pressures and to create a new reality through experimentation with form and language. In the following excerpt from his introduction to a 1923 Soviet edition of O. Henry's short stories, Zamyatin examines some reasons for O. Henry's popularity with Russian readers.]

Advertisements shout; varicolored lights blink, in windows, on walls, in the sky; trains clatter somewhere in the air overhead; floors madly climb on floors, each on the other's shoulders—the tenth, the fifteenth, the twentieth. It is London, Paris, Berlin, wound up ten times more feverishly: it is America.

At top speed, by telephone, by telegraph, one must make millions, swallow something on the run in a bar, and then—a ten minute rest over a book in a flying coach. Ten minutes, no more, and in those ten minutes one must have something complete, whole, something that will fly as fast as the one-hundred-mile-an-hour train, that will make one forget the train, the clatter, the whistles, everything.

This demand was met by O. Henry (William Sidney Porter . . .). His short, sharp, quick stories hold a condensed America. Jack London is the American steppe, its snowy plains, its oceans and tropical islands; O. Henry is the American city. It does not matter that London wrote *Martin Eden* and urban stories; and it does not matter that O. Henry wrote a book of the steppes, *The Heart of the West,* and a novel, *Cabbages and Kings,* depicting the life of some South American province. Jack London is still, first and foremost, the Klondike, and O. Henry is New York.

It is wrong to say that the cinema was invented

by Edison: the cinema was invented by Edison and O. Henry. In the cinema, the most important thing is motion, motion at any cost. And in O. Henry's stories the most important thing is dynamics, motion; hence his faults and his virtues.

The reader who finds himself in O. Henry's cinema will come out of it refreshed by laughter: O. Henry is invariably witty, amusing, youthfully gay—like A. Chekhonte who had not yet grown into Anton Chekhov. But occasionally his comic effects are overdrawn, far-fetched, somewhat crude. The feelings of the movie public must be touched sometimes: O. Henry stages charming four-page dramas for it. Once in a while these dramas are sentimental and cinematically edifying. But this happens seldom. O. Henry may wax emotional for a second, but immediately he rushes on again, mocking, laughing, light. A quick tongue, a quick wit, quick feelings—every muscle is in motion, very much as in the case of another American national favorite, Charlie Chaplin.

What does Charlie Chaplin believe in? What is Charlie Chaplin's philosophy? Probably nothing; probably none: there is no time. And the same is true of O. Henry, and of millions of New Yorkers. O. Henry begins one of his stories, **"The Higher Pragmatism,"** punning and playing with the sound of the words: "The ancients are discredited; Plato is boiler-plate; Aristotle is tottering; Marcus Aurelius is reeling; . . . Solomon is too solemn; you couldn't get anything out of Epictetus with a pick." And this is, perhaps, one of the few occasions when O. Henry speaks seriously. As a rule, when he is not afflicted with sentimentality, he laughs and jests. Even through his makeup, we occasionally catch a glimpse of the inimitable Charlie Chaplin. Smiling, he starves; smiling, he goes to prison; and he probably dies with a smile. Perhaps his only philosophy is that life must be conquered with a smile. O. Henry is one of those Anglo-Saxons who sang hymns on the *Titanic* as it was slowly sinking. He probably understood, or, at least, sensed remotely, that the huge, comfortable *Titanic* of nineteenth-century civilization had struck an iceberg and was majestically sinking to the bottom. But O. Henry was at home on his ship; he would not abandon it. With jests on his lips— sometimes frivolous, sometimes tinged with bitterness—he would die courageously, like Spengler's "Faustian" man.

This ineradicable, resilient vitality had been bred into O. Henry by his whole life: the hammer tempers the steel. He himself had lived in the shabby furnished rooms where he often brings his reader. He himself spent nights on park benches. He is the New York bohemian, the romantic American tramp. His biography would probably make an excellent motion picture: O. Henry the salesman in a tobacco shop; O. Henry the clerk behind a drugstore counter; O. Henry over a led-

ger in a business office; O. Henry the member of a gang of railway thieves in South America; O. Henry in prison for three years. And, after prison, not the "Ballad of Reading Gaol," but gay, light stories, splashed with laughter. The blow that broke the pampered, delicate Wilde struck the first creative spark from O. Henry.

Want, and the fever of the huge American city, drove him, whipped him on. He wrote too much— some years as many as fifty or sixty stories. This is why his work is uneven. True, even among his weakest lines there will be an occasional glint of true O. Henry gold. But then, the same carbon produces both coal and graphite and diamonds. At any rate, O. Henry has produced diamonds, and this brings him into the vicinity of such masters of the short story as Chekhov and Maupassant. And it must be said that O. Henry's technique—at least in his best works—is sharper, bolder, and more modern than that of many short-story writers who have already assumed their place as classics.

A pungent language, glittering with an eccentric and unexpected symbolism, is the first thing that captures the attention of O. Henry's reader. And this is not the dead, mechanical eccentricity found in the symbols of the Imagists. In O. Henry the image is always *internally* linked to the basic tonality of his character, incident, or entire story. This is why all his epithets or images, even when seemingly incongruous or far-fetched, are convincing and hypnotic. The housekeeper of a rooming house (in the story **"The Furnished Room"**) has a "throat lined with fur." At first the image is difficult to assimilate; but as the story proceeds, it is varied, becoming sharpened with each variation. Now it is simply a "furry throat," or "she said in her furriest tones"—and the cloying figure of the housekeeper, never described in detail as it would have been by the old narrative method, is etched in the imagination of the reader.

O. Henry achieves especially striking effects by employing the device which can most accurately be described as that of the *integrating image* (in analyzing literary prose we are compelled to create our terminology afresh). Thus, in the story **"The Defeat of the City,"** Miss Alicia Van Der Pool is "cool, white and inaccessible as the Matterhorn." The Matterhorn—the basic image—is developed as the story goes on; it becomes ramified and embraces almost the entire story broadly and integrally: "The social Alps that ranged about her . . . reached only to her knees." And Robert Walmsley attains this Matterhorn. But, even if he has found that the traveler who reaches the mountaintop finds the highest peaks swathed in a thick veil of cloud and snow, he manages to conceal his chills. "Robert Walmsley was proud of his wife; although while one of his hands shook his guests' the other held tightly to his alpenstock and thermometer."

Similarly, the story **"Squaring the Circle"** is permeated with the integrating image: nature is a circle, the city a square. In **"A Comedy in Rubber,"** the image is of the rubbernecks as a special tribe, and so on.

O. Henry's kind of story approaches most closely the *skaz* form (to this day, one of the favorite forms in the Russian short story): the free, spontaneous language of speech, digressions, purely American coinages of the street variety, which cannot be found in any dictionary. His, however, is not that ultimate, complete *skaz* form from which the author is absent, in which the author is but another character, and even the author's comments are given in a language close to that of the milieu depicted.

But all these are the static aspects of a work of art. The urban reader, who grew up in the mad whirl of the modern city, cannot be satisfied with only the static elements; he demands the dynamics of plot. Hence all that yellow sea of criminal and detective literature, usually crude and unartistic verbally. In O. Henry, brilliant language is usually combined with dynamic plot. His favorite compositional device is the surprise ending. Sometimes the effect of surprise is achieved by the author with the aid of what may be called the *false denouement:* in the plot syllogism, the reader is deliberately led to the wrong conclusion, and then, somewhere at the end, there is a sudden sharp turn, and an altogether different denouement reveals itself (in the stories, **"The Rathskeller and the Rose," "Squaring the Circle," "The Hiding of Black Bill"**). Very complex and subtle compositional methods may be found in O. Henry's novel, *Cabbages and Kings.*

Unfortunately, the composition of O. Henry's stories, especially in the endings, suffers from sameness. The chronic surprise loses its point; the surprise is expected, and the exception becomes the rule. The reader has much the same feeling as he experiences under Wilde's shower of paradoxes: in the end he sees that each paradox is but a truism turned inside out.

However, Tolstoy's Nekhludov did not love Katyusha Maslova a whit less because her eyes were just a little crossed. And his faults did not prevent O. Henry from becoming one of the most beloved writers of America and England. (pp. 291-95)

Yevgeny Zamyatin, "O. Henry," in his *A Soviet Heretic: Essays,* edited and translated by Mirra Ginsburg, The University of Chicago Press, 1970, pp. 291-95.

H. E. BATES
(essay date 1941)

[A master of the twentieth-century English short story, Bates is the author of *The Modern Short Story,* a highly regarded introduction to the history, development, and pioneering writers of this genre. In the following excerpt from that book, he illustrates O. Henry's attributes as both a literary "trickster" and a serious writer.]

If Sarah Orne Jewett was the painter of a certain section of American life, O. Henry strikes one as being the itinerant photographer who buttonholes every passer-by in the street, wisecracks him, snaps the camera, raises his hat and hands him the inevitable card. O. Henry has just the natural buoyancy, cheek, good-humour, wit, canny knowledge of humanity and its demands, and above all the tireless flamboyant gift of the gab that characterizes any seller of carpets, cure-alls, gold watches, and something-for-nothing in the open market place. O. Henry is not, and I think never was, a writer. He is a great showman who can talk the hind leg off a donkey and then proceed to sell the public that same donkey as a pedigree race-horse.

All this can be simply deduced from the stories. A life of hard facts, of great adversity, confirms it. O. Henry had little schooling, began work in a drug-store, was forced by ill-health to try his luck on a ranch, worked later in a bank, bought and edited a weekly paper, saw it fail, worked on another paper, and finished up in the Ohio State Penitentiary on a charge of embezzling funds. Contrast that with the calm fortunes of the Miss Austens and Miss Jewetts of this world. The wonder is not that O. Henry could not write, but perhaps that he was ever able to put a consecutive sentence together at all. Such adversity would have crushed into complete oblivion a lesser man, just as it might have turned a greater man into that all-American genius of realism for which America still waits. It simply made O. Henry into a trickster—the supreme example in the history of the short story of the showman "wrapping it up so that the fools don't know it."

But it would be the greatest injustice to O. Henry to leave it at that. The body of his work alone, the achievement of his colossal industry, entitles him to something more. His manipulation and marketing of a new type of story (in reality borrowed from others), whose chief effect was that of the surprise packet, entitles him to more again. For however you talk round O. Henry he still emerges, by his huge achievement and the immense popularity of his particular method, as an astonishingly persistent influence on the short story of almost every decade since his day.

O. Henry had many of the qualities that make a greater writer. His eye was excellent, and he was able to focus it on an immense variety of objects, and always, thanks to an immense experience, realistically; he was tirelessly interested in people and could make people tirelessly interesting; he had a certain sense of tragedy, a deep if sentimental sympathy for the underdog, was at his best a sublime humorist, and was blessed with that peculiar faculty of being able to impress the flavour of himself on the page. These qualities, backed by a stronger attitude of mind, a certain relentlessness, might have made O. Henry really great. They were backed instead by a showman who was also a sentimentalist. As a journalist O. Henry knew how to spread it on and spread it out; he knew all about the human touch; he knew, as Bret Harte did, all about the laughter behind the tears. What his work never had was reticence or delicacy; his poetry was that of the journalist who, unable to conceive a lyrical image and knowing that it would be wasted anyway, reaches for the book of *Metaphors and Phrases*. On anything like a real test his work will fail because of a certain shallowness, the eternal touch of the cheap-jack who palms you off with the imitation of the real thing.

Yet O. Henry, perhaps more than Maupassant, put the short story on the map. His brand of goods tapped a world market. And to-day you will still find him held in affection, as much as esteem, by a great many people who will not hear a word against his method and its results. For this reason I must not overlook a certain quality of lovableness about O. Henry—a quality well seen, I think, in such a story as **"The Cop and the Anthem."** But that quality alone could not, and does not, account for O. Henry's great popularity. That popularity sprang from a conjuring trick—the story with the surprise—or trick-ending.

This was nothing new. Some use of it may be seen in Poe and Bierce, and a good deal of use of it may be seen in Bret Harte, who apparently failed to grasp its greatest possibilities, as may be seen in the anti-climax of the last six lines of "The Iliad of Sandy Bar." But for some reason O. Henry's use of it captures the imagination not only of readers but also of writers, so that long after O. Henry's death writers like Maugham were still using it, though more perhaps on the Maupassant model than that of O. Henry. For to Maupassant, and not O. Henry, still belongs that supreme *tour de force* of surprise endings, "The Necklace," in which the excellence and the limitation of the method can be perfectly seen. Maupassant's story of the woman who borrows a diamond necklace from a friend, loses it, buys another to replace it, and is condemned to ten years' suffering and poverty by the task of paying off the money, only to make the awful discovery at last that the original necklace was not diamond but paste—this story, dependent though it is for effect on the shock of the last line, differs in one extremely important respect from anything O. Henry ever did. For here, in "The Necklace," trick and tragedy are one. By placing a certain strain on the credulity of the reader (why, one asks, was it not explained in the first place that the necklace was paste? or why, later, did not Madame Loisel make a clean breast of everything to a friend who had so much trusted her?), by the skilful elimination of probabilities, Maupassant is left holding a shocking and surprising card of which the reader is entirely ignorant. He is entirely ignorant, that is, *the first time*. Like a child who is frightened by the first sudden bo! from round the corner, but knows all about it next time, the reader of "The Necklace" can never be tricked again. For Maupassant is bound to play that card, which is his only by a process of cheating, and having played it can never again repeat its devastating effect. In story-telling, as in parlour games, you can never hope to hoodwink the same person twice. It is only because of Maupassant's skilful delineation of Madame Loisel's tragedy that "The Necklace" survives as a credible piece of realism. Maupassant, the artist, was well aware that the trick alone is its own limitation; O. Henry, the journalist, never was aware of it.

Yet by the use of the trick, by the telling of scores of stories solely for the point, the shock, or the witty surprise of the last line, O. Henry made himself famous and secured for himself a large body of readers. Apparently neither he nor they ever tired of this game of trick endings. Yet no one, so far as I know, has drawn attention to the technical excellence of O. Henry's trick beginnings. Mr. Ellery Sedgewick, following up his opinion that "a story is like a horse race, it is the start and finish that count most," goes on to say, "Of these two the beginning is the harder. I am not sure but it is the most difficult accomplishment in fiction."

O. Henry was well aware of that. In the marketplace the cheap-jack is confronted with precisely the same difficulty—the problem of making the public listen, even of making it listen, if necessary, against its will, since the nicely wrapped-up ending is entirely useless if the beginning has failed to attract the customer. And in reshaping the short story's beginning, in dispensing with its former leisureliness, its preliminary loquacity, and its well-balanced lead-up, O. Henry did a very considerable service to the short story. He recognized, as the following examples will show, the great value of an instant contact between reader and writer:

So I went to a doctor.

"How long has it been since you took alcohol into your system?" he asked.

Finch keeps a hats-cleaned-by-electricity-while-you-wait establishment, nine feet by twelve, in Third Avenue. Once a customer, you are always his. I do not know his secret process, but every four days your hat needs to be cleaned again.

The trouble began in Laredo. It was the Leano Kid's fault, for he should have confined his habit of manslaughter to Mexicans.

On his bench in Madison Square Soapy moved uneasily. When wild geese honk high of nights, and when women without sealskin coats grow kind to their husbands, and when Soapy moves uneasily on his bench in the park, you may know that winter is near at hand.

These are examples taken almost at random; there are many others. O. Henry rarely fumbles the beginning, and when he does so it is invariably by the two pieces of fancy irresistible to the journalist of his type: a desire to be moral, a desire to show that he knows all about poetry. Otherwise he can show a series of masterly lessons not only in how to begin a story but, perhaps more important, when to begin.

As a humorist O. Henry stands in the true line of what appears to be an essentially American tradition—the tradition in which Leacock, Thurber, and Runyon are true-blood descendants. That tradition appears to be largely the expression of the wider American revolt against the heavier values so held in esteem in the Old World: pomposity, class distinction, dignity, family tradition, and indeed almost anything liable to be taken over-seriously. By taking such things as pompous family tradition and treating them with levity (as in Leacock) or by taking trivialities and treating them with a language mixed into an affected combination of the academic and the vernacular (as in Runyon), American writers produce a high contrast that is, as in Wodehouse, very funny. In this method O. Henry, who excelled in the use of both vernacular and a certain pompous brand of journalese, was bound to be a success. (pp. 58-64)

H. E. Bates, "American Writers After Poe," in his *The Modern Short Story: A Critical Survey,* 1941. Reprint by The Writers, Inc., 1956, pp. 46-71.

V. S. PRITCHETT

(essay date 1957)

[Pritchett is a highly esteemed English novelist, short story writer, and critic. In the following excerpt, he discusses the relationship between O. Henry and his fiction.]

O. Henry is one of the many casualties of American literature. Original, inventive and prolific in his short stories, he is one of those writers of whom the critics say: Could have done better if he had tried. In his life and in his work there is a failure of the sense of responsibility. Chekhov's beginnings were just as difficult and commonplace as the American's. Like O. Henry, he began by writing crude comic sketches for popular papers, and had to be fished out of vulgar employ by discerning editors; but whereas O. Henry perfected only his craft, Chekhov (like all great artists) strenuously perfected himself as a means of seeing and feeling his subjects. Chekhov grew; O. Henry copied himself. Chekhov was concerned to write less and better. O. Henry certainly worked hard, but rather in the Puritan way that finds in work of any kind a drugging or redemption in itself. The result is that behind the laughter of O. Henry's caricatures and the wit of his invention, there is a sensation of moral exhaustion and personal lassitude.

O. Henry was a modest, fastidious, impenetrable character. He was enclosed, furtive and evasive. The fact is he was shut in by an amiable and undisquieting alcoholism; his secret was that he had served a prison sentence of three years for embezzlement. These two matters were symptoms rather than causes of much earlier cooling-off from life. (p. 697)

Mr Gerald Langford's new biography *Alias O. Henry,* goes thoroughly into [the confusing story of O. Henry's embezzlement conviction]. He finds it just as hard to make up his mind about O. Henry's guilt or innocence as others have done. O. Henry himself was evasive and self-contradictory; protesting his innocence, and yet clearly having no notion that what he was ready to admit displayed some kind of guilt. His attitude was ambiguous; and this ambiguity provides half the comedy of his tales of grafters and frauds. When the man becomes the artist, we see him converting what is a painful failure to face reality into low garrulous poetry of cunning and trickery. He becomes a fabulist. This is among the oldest delights of popular story-telling. O. Henry's enormous success with the great public does not depend on his shallowness and sentimentality, but on his sharing the common pleasure in watching people do each other down, in the outsmarting of the market. In his life, after he came out of gaol, O. Henry added incompetence to innocence. He shared Balzac's need of debt as a stimulus to work. He borrowed money incorrigibly and continuously, even when he was highly paid; he spent it or, rather, gave it away, absurdly. There are stories of him giving tips in restaurants many times larger than the bills. There is a drifting, indifferent quality in this carelessness. He was not the arrogant borrower; he was cringing, promising, sentimental, almost sobbing. We have the impression of a gentle, dandyish, pleasantly pickled man stuck in a dream and who soothed himself, when he woke up, by occasional fits of theatrical sentimentality.

O. Henry's earliest stories were written in prison. He emerged with a natural feeling for the lonely, the underdog and the rogue; also with a desire, not for security and affection, but for anonymity. For many writers the edge and freedom of the anonymous life have been indispensable. The security of his second marriage was intolerable to him. He was just the man to be lost with advantage in the streets of New York. He became domesticated to the backrooms of small hotels, the pavements, doorways, cheap bars, park seats of the city. He was a dedicated night wanderer—the habit was partly responsible for the breakdown of his second marriage. He hated literary society, preferring to talk with the shop girls, tarts, bar props and others who gave him his material. He was protected by his fastidiousness and by his work from the waste of literary Bohemianism. But, as Mr Langford says, when he attacked the sterility of literary company, he was not altogether sincere. Literary society is often sterile and too much of it is fatal, above all to short-story writers who use up their material more quickly than any other kind of writer. O. Henry needed the streets and the bars. But literary society of the right kind might have given O. Henry the impetus to go beyond the commonplace limitations of his work, to resist the downhill tendency of his talent. Occasional stories, like **"An Unfinished Story"** or **"A Municipal Report,"** show how it was well within his powers to go deeper than contrivance and anecdotal trickery. Clearly he felt exposed without them, but he could have been given the courage.

The sudden extinction of O. Henry's fame after 1910 is saddening but natural. By the Twenties a major literary movement had begun in the United States, and O. Henry was lost in the journalistic and characterless period that preceded it. He belongs to the vernacular tradition, though H. L. Mencken thought he perverted it with false and ornate Broadwayese. Yet the hostile critics, I think, are merely copying each other when they damn O. Henry for his use of coincidence and for snap-endings that trick the reader. (The trick was, in any case, part of the gaiety.) The hostile forget that O. Henry's virtue is his speed of narrative; it moves forward freely; it jumps with confidence. He is economical and at home in his tale.

This technical proficiency of O. Henry's is in itself delightful because it has the attraction of daring and impudence. His gaudy phraseology, his colliding metaphors, his brilliant malapropisms are not always in excess. We can at once picture the woman in **"Telemachus, Friend"** who would have 'tempted an anchovy to forget his vows' and who had an air of welcome about her that 'seemed to mitigate her vicinity'; we see her, after supper, when her two lovers find her, 'with a fresh pink dress on and cool enough to handle'. The low comedy of courtship is a traditional subject, and in handling it O. Henry brought the American talent for using metaphors grotesquely wide of the mark. He had the important comic gift of capping a good joke with an even more powerful riposte to it. In **"Telemachus, Friend,"** for example, we are not only told the wrong method of seizing a lady's hand—'Some men grab it so much like they was going to set a dislocation of the shoulder'—but we are told the right method which begins with splendid sentences, straight out of the Mark Twain tradition:

> I'll tell you the right way. Did you ever see a man sneak out of the backyard and pick up a rock to throw at a tom-cat that was sitting on a fence looking at him. He pretends he hasn't got a thing in his hand, and that the cat don't see him and that he don't see the cat.

A great deal of O. Henry is hilarious, school-boy stuff on the surface. He has not the polish or the maturity of a writer like W. W. Jacobs, but he has a far greater range. He has the blessed American gifts of economy and boldness in comic writing; the gift also of bouncing the reader. When we object to his exaggeration and caricature, we should discriminate. The impulse is fundamental to American folk comedy and corresponds to the native and traditional sense of the tall and fabulous. Much of American comedy consists of bluffing and counter-bluffing fantasy: the duke and king episode in *Huckleberry Finn,* for example. This quality comes out very strongly in O. Henry's Texan stories which—after excepting his masterpiece **"The Municipal Report"**—seem to me his richest. . . .

Mr Langford makes much of O. Henry's statement (made in his last year when he was planning to write a novel) that writers do not tell the truth. It is inferred that O. Henry was beginning to see through the haze in which he lived his stunned life and was about to face realities he had avoided. He was infantile about money, he was puritanical about sex: he disliked being compared with Maupassant who was a 'filthy writer'. We cannot imagine what O. Henry's 'truth' would have been, but we can guess that it would have been the end of him as a comic writer. It is fatal for the comics to resolve their problems; their only salvation lies in improving their jokes. Only serious writers seem to be able to get away, sometimes, with living above their moral means. It is unjust, but there it is. (p. 698)

V. S. Pritchett, "O. Henry," in *New Statesman,* Vol. LIV, No. 1393, November 23, 1957, pp. 697-98.

DONALD F. PEEL
(essay date 1961)

[In the following excerpt, Peel examines and defends O. Henry's use of the surprise ending.]

A valid surprise ending . . . should be plausible. Though it may be unnatural, in the sense that it seldom occurs in real life, it must seem natural to the reader. It should depend on the shifts and twists of human agents. Changes in circumstances should be intrinsic to the story.

On the other hand, the ending should not depend on arbitrary arrangement of external circumstances. One of O. Henry's weaknesses is the use of coincidences that seem almost incredible. . . . It is almost incredible that in a city of four million people a young man [in **"The Furnished Room"**] should come by chance to the same room in which his lost love had committed suicide. **"The Higher Abdication"** has another coincidence: A bum climbs into a wagon and goes to sleep. While sleeping he is driven to a ranch. It turns out that he is the son of the owner of the ranch who was lost or stolen from home at the age of two. **"The Church with an Overshot Wheel"** depends upon a similar coincidence. A little girl is lost from home at the age of four. She returns at the age of twenty and is recognized because she recognizes an old song her father sang when she was a child. Another of his famous stories, **"The Third Ingredient,"** rests upon a far-fetched coincidence. A young man rescues a girl who has jumped off a ferry boat. Out of all the rooming houses in New York he comes by accident to the one in which she lives.

There are other reasons for the failure of the surprise ending. One of the devices of O. Henry to achieve the surprise ending is the story within the story. The surprise ending comes at the external story's ending and is too often an inconsequential or trivial statement. As in the **"Halberdier of the Little Rheinschloss,"** the story begins with the question of why a cigar case was broken; this leads to another story which has no connection with the first; the surprise ending comes in the explanation of the cigar case which is completely inconsequential. A surprise ending that leaves the basic conflict unsolved may be regarded a failure. **"Hearts and Crosses"** is such a story; the husband and wife are brought back together by the birth of their child, but the conflict between them is not thereby solved, only delayed to a future date.

The surprise ending must be nearly the same as the single effect. When a story becomes too involved for a single effect, a surprise ending is almost impossible. In **"An Afternoon Miracle,"** O. Henry uses two involved stories, and tries to bring them together in a "surprise ending." First, there is a story about the hero, Bob Buckley, and his pursuit of an outlaw; then there is an account of the heroine, snake charmer Alvarita, who is in pursuit of one of her snakes. When hero and heroine get together, the "surprise ending" is that she screams at the sight of a caterpillar. This climax is rather a letdown after Bob Buckley has a barefisted fight with a knife-wielding outlaw. (pp. 11-13)

The surprise ending was the method of writing that O. Henry found to be most effective. He sacrificed reality no more than any artist must sacrifice reality. That one form of writing—realism, naturalism, surrealism—is closer to reality than another is at best a matter of opinion. (pp. 16-17)

One outstanding characteristic of O. Henry's work of which critics have taken little note is his use of the technique of "after the thunder, the still, small voice." This is the adding of a moral after the punch line or surprise ending, which we have already noted. O. Henry's stories are often didactic in this fashion. (p. 17)

Another favorite technique of O. Henry is that of storyteller. Someone has said that it is the old American game of "tell me another" or "I'll top that." Most of the stories in *The Gentle Grafter* are of this nature. He uses this method often to provide a surprise ending.

Besides these there are perhaps four main methods that O. Henry uses to bring about a surprise ending:

a. The withholding of information. An example of this is **"The Double Dyed Deceiver"** where we are not told the identity of the youth the Llano Kid murdered until the end of the story. The revealing of this information provides the surprise. There is a similar usage in **"A Municipal Report,"** and many other stories.

b. The angle of narration. This is not so much the withholding of information, as the telling of the story so that the information is not necessary until the denouement. This is the method used in **"Gift of the Magi," "The Love-Philtre of Ikey Schoenstein,"** and **"The Romance of a Busy Broker,"** among others.

c. Attempts to mislead. This is the old method of letting the reader tell the story. . . . If the surprise ending could ever be called a "trick plot" it is in this usage. Yet, the author does not mislead the reader so much as the reader misleads himself. In **"October and June"** O. Henry uses a conventional situation of a difference in age between a man and a woman. The reader assumes that the man is the older and is surprised (or should be) to learn that it is the other way around. In

H, odd words

The Friendly Call

by O. Henry

When I used to sell hardware in the West, I often "made" a little town called Saltillo, in Colorado. I was always certain of securing a small or large order from Simms Bell, who kept a general store there. Bell was one of those six-foot, low-voiced products, formed from a union of the West and the South. I liked him. To look at him, you would think he should be robbing stage coaches or juggling gold mines with both hands; but he would sell you

Page from the manuscript of "The Friendly Call."

"Girl" a conventional situation is used: a wealthy man is pursuing a girl; the reader assumes that he wants to marry her; actually he wants to hire her to be his cook.

d. The misunderstanding. This is an old device in fiction. A typical O. Henry example is "Hygeia at the Solito," in which a wealthy cattleman takes a sick man home to his ranch to recuperate; a doctor apparently examines the man and pronounces him well; the rancher puts him to work; the man does recover from his illness, and it turns out that the doctor examined the wrong man.

Possibly, there are other methods that could be mentioned, but most of O. Henry's stories could be classified under these headings. O. Henry found the surprise ending in use in fiction, made it his own, and passed it on to become one of the most popular short story devices.

The statement, in one form or another, has been made by critics that O. Henry was willing to sacrifice anything, even truth, for the sake of the surprise ending. The question of truth in fiction is one that has long vexed critics perhaps even before the Puritans charged that fiction was "lies." Porter was aware of the problem; he opens "The World and the Door" (*Whirligigs*) with the comment:

> As for the adage quoted above [truth is stranger than fiction], I take pleasure in puncturing it by affirming that I read in a purely fictional story the other day the line: "Be it so," said the policeman. "Nothing so strange has yet cropped out in Truth" [the capital T is Porter's].

This comment, of course, does not answer the question as to what is truth in fiction. Pattee's explanation as to O. Henry's failing is that he does not present "humanity as humanity actually is." This statement provides us with a guide that we can use in reaching a working definition. Pattee seems to suggest that there is a distinction between *fact, truth,* and *opinion. Fact* can be defined in terms of its roots; that is, a *fact* is something that is done (a definition preserved in "an accessory after the fact"), a deed. A *truth,* on the other hand, is a generalization deduced from a fact or facts, and is to be distinguished from *true.* Thus, "God exists" is a truth but not a fact; "God created the heavens and the earth," is a *fact,* a *true* statement but not a *truth.*

According to these definitions, fiction may contain *truth* even though it is not *fact.* For example, in fiction, a writer may put a rocket ship in orbit around Mars. Since what he writes is admittedly fiction no demand should be made that he treat of *fact.* As to truth, having his rocket ship in orbit, the writer must then make his characters act in accordance with known laws of human nature. (pp. 17-19)

Does O. Henry make his characters act in accordance with known laws of human nature? In "Gift of the Magi" Della and Jim each sacrifice a prized personal possession to give a gift to the other; this surely is in accord with the known actions of people in love. In "A Municipal Report" a man conceals what might have been evidence of a murder; considering the character drawn of the murdered man, the *persona* might well act as O. Henry alleges. Then there is Dulcie of "An Unfinished Story"; she spends her last fifty cents for an imitation lace collar to wear on her first date. True to human nature? Instances of such observation of human nature might be multiplied. (p. 20)

O. Henry's stories possess truth and reality (not *realism* by the technical definitions of that term). The story "The Third Ingredient" rests on a highly improbable coincidence, but truth does not depend on probability. *Truth* rests on the question: Do the characters in the writer's universe, i.e. the story in question, act as people have acted in the universe which the reader knows? And for "The Third Ingredient" the answer must be yes.

Hetty, the lead, when fired from her job goes home and in a matter-of-fact way begins to prepare lunch. She finds a girl preparing potatoes and invites her to contribute them to the beef stew; later she meets a young man who has an onion to contribute and invites him to join. Surely nothing in this violates human conduct. The story revolves around a young artist (miniature painter, more accurately) who has been rescued from a suicide attempt. She and her rescuer have fallen in love at first sight; this is not unusual psychology. Now granted that in a city of four million people it is improbable that these two people should be brought back together, would they still have this feeling of love? Records show that it is quite possible that the feeling would continue. The question of how long it would continue is not relevant since O. Henry does not attempt to answer that phase of the problem. O. Henry then does remain true to human nature. (p. 22)

William Sidney Porter was aware of his faults. He did protest the debasing of art and of literature. The artist, according to O. Henry's concept, has a responsibility to society and to his ideals.

The artist fulfills his responsibility to society by living up to his highest ideals. He has, according to Porter, no right to produce work simply because it will sell nor should he attempt to sell work for any reason other than its artistic excellence. Thus in *Heart of the West* he portrays a young cowpuncher as riding his horse through a picture he has painted rather than to allow the state legislature to purchase it for the deeds of his father (the cowpuncher's father).

An analysis of O. Henry's work will show that the writer did not always fulfill the critic's demands. Much of his work does not meet the highest standards of artistic excellence. Yet O. Henry should not be written off for this failure, anymore than Arnold and Wordsworth should be for their respective failures to live up to their respective written creeds. Much that O. Henry did write is of the highest quality.

Nor can O. Henry be summed up simply as a humorist. His best work is too profound for such a simple description; his best work has that mingling of comedy and tragedy that is the mark of great art.

Another reason for considering him as a great writer is that many of the objections to his work are not based on valid critical studies, but are rather expressions of the reaction against form and mechanics that began in the 'teens and which continues to a certain extent to the present time. Such transitory standards should not weigh heavily in judging an artist's work.

Therefore it seems likely that for his mastery of the surprise ending and for his insight into human nature William Sidney Porter will continue to rank as one of the masters of the short story. (pp. 23-4)

Donald F. Peel, "A Critical Study of the Short Stories of O. Henry," in *The Northwest Missouri State College Studies,* Vol. XXV, No. 4, November 1, 1961, pp. 3-24.

KAREN CHARMAINE BLANSFIELD

(essay date 1988)

[In the following excerpt, Blansfield explores O. Henry's role as a popular artist, employing the *auteur* theory of criticism, which she describes as an approach that examines an artist's "entire body of material to discover and analyze structural characteristics and stylistic motifs."]

As a popular artist, Porter shares company with a host of literary luminaries: Homer, Shakespeare, Twain, Hugo, Dickens, Melville, and innumerable others. Like them, he stirred the mass imagination, drawing for material from the world about him, probing the foibles, dilemmas, comedies, and tragedies of human existence, speaking in a voice that could be understood by the multitudes.

This communal kinship lies at the heart of Porter's popularity, as it does for any popular artist. The public could identify with and respond to the people, places, and situations Porter wrote about. His stories offered the escape from daily drudgery so desperately needed by "the four million" and fulfilled the fantasies—if only vicariously—they so often longed for. [In his essay "Oh What A Man Was O. Henry," published in the *Kenyon Review* (November 1967), William Saroyan stated]: "The people of America loved O. Henry. . . .

He was a nobody, but he was a nobody who was also a somebody, everybody's somebody."

Porter, of course, calculated this success to some degree; he knew his audience and gave them what they wanted. "We have got to respect the conventions and delusions of the public to a certain extent," he wrote to his prison comrade Al Jennings. "In order to please John Wanamaker, we will have to assume a virtue that we do not possess." Nevertheless, he perceived his subjects with a compassion and understanding that is unquestionably sincere. He specialized in humanity but did not exploit it. He accepted,

> with a mixture of irony, wit, and sympathy, the distressing fact that a human being can be a clerk, the remarkable fact that a clerk can be a human being. . . .

To O. Henry, . . . the clerk is neither abnormal nor subnormal. He writes of him without patronizing him. He realizes the essential and stupendous truth that to himself the clerk is not pitiable.

Besides, Porter spins a good yarn, and he can turn a phrase as few authors ever have, rambling on in an easy, neighborly manner that slaps the reader on the shoulder, bandying an insouciant humor, and displaying a verbal range and precision that is astounding. He is a born raconteur; to listen to him is irresistible.

Above all, he is a master of technique. Even his severest critics acknowledge that as a designer of stories Porter "ranked supreme." His manipulation of elements into a tight literary structure . . . is effective, if mechanical, and were one aspect of Porter's art to be held up as the most important or memorable, it would surely be this one. (pp. 28-9)

All of these characteristics—his empathy for his fellow man, his sharp scrutiny of public demand, and his skill at the narrative craft—contribute to Porter's vast popularity. Furthermore, one other feature essential to popular art—wide-spread distribution—also accelerated Porter's rise to literary fame. . . . [The] superfluity of magazines and the tremendous need for material were propitious conditions for the fledgling author; joined with his talents and the public's desire, they propelled Porter into a position as a popular and widely read writer.

In the decades since, his stories have been anthologized, collected, and reprinted; they have been translated into numerous foreign languages; they have been performed as radio, stage, and television drama, with some also made into films. (p. 29)

Such broad appeal is the domain of the popular artist, be he author, musician, performer, painter, or other creative type. Although he manifests a style distinctly his own and is recognizable by his particular manner, the popular artist conforms to certain expecta-

Porter in his teller's cage at the First National Bank of Austin. He was convicted in 1898 of embezzling funds from the bank, and served three years of a five-year sentence in the Ohio Penitentiary at Columbus.

tions, presenting his material in forms familiar to his audiences and mirroring the joys and frustrations, the excitement and ennui of their everyday lives. This direct, personal relationship is one which the popular artist strives for, aiming deliberately to reach and to please his readers or listeners. Unlike "elite" or "high" art, which springs from individual and aesthetic motives, or folk art, which tends to be anonymous and utilitarian, popular art purposely appeals to the masses, while displaying the unmistakable touch of a single creator. (p. 30)

The skills of Porter as popular performer fuse into a style as distinctive and memorable as Charlie Chaplin's or Alfred Hitchcock's, an indelible style which breathes "O. Henryism" into his tales. Two of the most predominant components of this style . . . are plot structures and character types. The most famous and easily recognized plot characteristic is, of course, the surprise ending, a trick which results from clever, careful strategy. Although Porter was certainly not the first writer to employ this device—de Maupassant being particularly inclined toward it—he popularized it and staked a peculiar claim upon it, so that it has come to be inextricably linked with him and dubbed "the O. Henry twist." In terms of characters, the most well-

known is probably the shopgirl, a type which, again, is invariably associated with the writer.

Other idiosyncrasies also contribute to the "O. Henryism" that generated such enthusiastic response: the folksy narrative voice, confidential asides to the reader, intricate and sometimes outrageous language and dialogue, full-blown metaphors, hyperbole, and copious allusions.

Porter embroiders all these elements together to form a personal style that distinguishes his work from that of other popular writers, even though such writers may employ similar or identical devices. Less skillful popular artists may depend so heavily upon story formula or character stereotypes to accomplish their purposes that individual artistry is obliterated; indeed, a whole slew of nineteenth-century fiction manufacturers churned out material in such quantity and such anonymity that their work "was more or less comparable to the product of machines," and authors were easily interchangeable—names like Horatio Alger, Jr., Laura Jean Libbey, Edward Stratemeyer, and Edward Judson pertain. But a popular artist like Porter is an essential creative force behind his products; his shaping hand is always apparent, and his presence within his work helps to establish the rapport so important to the popular artist. As one critic points out, "To read him is at times almost to feel his physical presence."

This unique style, a compilation of several elements, defines Porter's work internally as well as externally. Besides setting him apart from other popular writers, Porter's style constitutes a kind of formula which recurs within and defines his own body of work. This evolution of a personal, recognizable formula is intrinsic to popular art: "the quality of stylization and convention" that is so important "becomes a kind of stereotyping, a processing of experience, a reliance upon formulae." In other words, the artist employs his selected materials—characters, settings, plots, etc.— over and over again, so that they become familiar aspects within his work, yet he also imbues them with a flavor distinctly his own. (pp. 30-1)

In a sense, because of the personal style that emerges through his recurrent use of specific literary elements, Porter can be considered an *auteur,* and the proposal to examine his body of work in terms of these elements is essentially the approach of *auteur* criticism. Originating in the 1950s as a mode of film criticism, the *auteur* theory offers a worthwhile model for analyzing and interpreting popular culture in general, as John Cawelti suggests in his seminal essay on the subject:

The art of the *auteur* is that of turning a conventional and generally known and appreciated artistic formula into a medium of personal expression while at the same time giving us a version of the formula which is satisfying because it fulfills our basic expectations.

(p. 32)

For a popular artist like Porter, the *auteur* approach, with its emphasis on surveying an entire body of material to discover and analyze structural characteristics and stylistic motifs, seems particularly appropriate and useful. What is distinctive about *auteur* criticism is that it stresses "the whole *corpus*" of material rather than a single work, emphasizing recurring characteristics and themes; it "implies an operation of decipherment" and ultimately defines the *auteur*—the filmmaker, the author—in terms of these recurring elements, which come to be recognized as his particular style. "The strong director imposes his own personality on a film," [asserts Andrew Sarris in his *The American Cinema* (1968)], just as a writer can stamp his distinctive seal on his own creations. . . .

[Although not the *entire* body of Porter's work, the] New York stories form a singular portion of his literary output for several reasons: together, they comprise well over a third of his work; they are bound together by their urban characteristics; they were produced during the most significant period of his literary career; and they include most of the stories for which he is so well remembered. Furthermore, the recurring characteristics and themes which are discovered here through "an operation of decipherment" can then serve as models for examining Porter's other stories—of Texas, New Orleans, and South America—which display similar structural and character motifs though in different cultural contexts.

As a popular artist, Porter is similar to the type of filmmaker who emerges in *auteur* criticism, since the latter is essentially a cinematic popular artist. Both the *auteur* and the popular artist utilize formulaic elements of plot and character to create a personal, recognizable style, weaving new variations on old familiar themes. Both, in turn, develop this individual style into a kind of personal formula running through their work. Both are also confronted by similar restrictions—mainly, conventional limitations on characters, setting, and plots, and commercial demands in their given mediums. (p. 33)

[The patterns] in the plots and characters of Porter's urban stories draw upon conventional situations, reinforce conventional values and expectations, and embody recognizable cultural types. By occurring repeatedly within the body of Porter's work, these plots and characters define it internally; by emulating more universal, archetypal patterns and characters, they achieve a broader recognition and a similarity to other artistic products, while remaining distinctive to Porter's art.

This continual recurrence of specific motifs, so central to Porter's art, to popular art, and to the theory of *auteur* criticism, constitutes the element of formula. For Porter, as for any popular artist, formula provides the fundamental structure for his art, and not surprisingly, it also contributes to his popular appeal. For as a constant and predictable pattern, formula is inherent to the cycle of human existence, and it also characterizes the earliest forms of literature most people learn—myths, fairy tales, songs, etc. Because it is so elemental, formula is familiar and comforting; it is an artistic expression of the subliminal human need for security and certainty in a life that promises just the opposite, and to some extent at least, the presence of formula in popular literature satisfies that need.

"High" or "elite" art, unlike popular or even folk art, lacks these elements of predictability and standardization, so that popular art is, by and large, the type most accessible to the ordinary individual, relating more closely to the experiences of everyday life and to the rhythms of existence. (p. 34)

In his important study *Adventure, Mystery and Romance: Formula Stories As Art and Popular Culture,* John Cawelti defines a literary formula as, in general, "a structure of narrative or dramatic conventions employed in a great number of individual works." This is a broad, encompassing definition, but in it Cawelti sets forth the two major elements of formulaic literature: convention and repetition.

The first major element is convention. As opposed to invention, which refers to original creations, convention denotes elements familiar to both the author and the reader. Conventions "consist of things like favorite plots, stereotyped characters, accepted ideas, commonly known metaphors and other linguistic devices, etc." While inventions, Cawelti says, confront us with new, previously unrecognized perceptions, "conventions represent familiar shared images and meanings and they assert an ongoing continuity of value." Conventions therefore may be cultural elements and thus be limited in their effect to a particular time, place, and people, or they may be universal and thus transcend such limitations. Or they may be fusions of these two aspects, with the universally held conventions being presented in terms of a specific cultural convention; thus, for example, Porter may present the familiar, universal character of the outcast in the cultural garb of the tramp, a figure who will, in turn, also be shaped by certain expectations. These two aspects of convention are equivalent to the more familiar terms "archetype" and "stereotype," the only difference between them being the range of their focus and the extent of their appeal.

Cawelti makes the same kind of distinction in defining formula, breaking the term down into two usages which, taken together, adequately define a literary formula. The first usage of the term, he says, "denotes a conventional way of treating some specific thing or person," such as Homer's epithets, standard similes and metaphors; and by extension, "any form of cultural stereotype commonly found in literature." What is important about this usage is its limited nature: "it refers to patterns of convention which are usually quite specific to a particular culture and period and do not mean the same outside this specific context." Porter's shopgirl, for example, who assumes specific characteristics as a type within the context of the stories, is a conventional embodiment of the innocent, vulnerable orphan, the same kind of role a young male Dickens character might play. But removed from Porter's stories or from the context of America's social and industrial conditions in the early twentieth century, the shopgirl would not convey the same meaning, while in the literature of another time or culture, the character of the shopgirl may assume different characteristics altogether from those she displays in Porter's stories. As Boris Ejxenbaum points out [in his *O. Henry and the Theory of the Short Story*, 1968], "Tender stories about New York shopgirls have more appeal for the American reader" than for Russian readers.

The second usage of the term "formula" encompasses larger plot types, which are not limited to specific cultures. Rather, these plot patterns "seem to represent story types that, if not universal in their appeal, have certainly been popular in many different cultures at many different times." They are, in other words, archetypal patterns: the adventure story, the romance, and the quest are three examples.

The fusion of these two usages—that is, the "synthesis of a number of specific cultural conventions with a more universal story form or archetype"—constitutes a formula. Put another way, formula can be defined as "a conventional system for structuring cultural products."

The other major element of formula, repetition, involves, like the term "convention," distinctions of degree. Within the context of one author's work—in this case Porter's urban short stories—repetition involves the frequency with which the author employs specific plot patterns and specific cultural elements. It is through such repetition that the works assume a formulaic nature. (pp. 35-6)

Secondly, repetition involves the frequency with which the plot patterns and cultural elements have been employed outside the context of the author's works. This is the universal aspect of repetition and the means by which plot patterns and specific elements become archetypal and serve as models of comparison for specific works. The existence of a universal story pattern, or of a general element such as a character type defined only by human traits, not bounded by cultural details, provides the standard of comparison for an author's works and the framework on which he can, with specific cultural elements, construct a story which will be relevant and meaningful to a certain group of people in a certain place and time.

Elements of repetition are quite apparent in Porter's urban short stories, for he draws recurringly upon a number of basic plot patterns and character types. Variations occur, of course, and not every single story can be neatly categorized according to plot and character; such extremism threatens to squeeze the life out of the literature. Still, in the nearly one hundred stories that deal with the city, recurrent plot patterns and characters do emerge which can be identified and used as a means of classification.

The plots of these stories can be divided into four basic patterns, overlapping to some extent but nevertheless bearing distinguishing characteristics: they are the cross pattern, the habit pattern, the triangular pattern, and the quest pattern. All develop themes familiar to most readers: the cross pattern, for example, builds on the unexpected reunion; the habit pattern provides excitement by an unexpected change in routine; the triangular pattern inserts a new twist in the familiar love triangle, and the quest pattern is Porter's version of the adventure story. . . . Porter repeatedly uses these patterns, or some variation of them, in his stories.

The characters, too, can be divided into six basic types, although because they often play more than one role simultaneously, they are more difficult to classify definitively. These six types [are] the shopgirl, the habitual character, the lover, the aristocrat, the plebeian, and the tramp. . . . Each type is a composite of specific characteristics, such as appearance, lifestyle, and attitude—characteristics which identify the entire group, with little if any attention paid to individual tendencies. Furthermore, each character type responds to conventional expectations: the shopgirl is poor but brave; the habitual character sticks to the ordinary routine of domestic life; the lover places love above self-interest; the aristocrat places money below principle; the plebeian bears the standard marks of poverty; and the tramp sleeps on a park bench.

Thus, Porter draws upon a "conventional system" for structuring his stories. His plot patterns are formulaic within the context of his own works, for he uses a number of patterns repeatedly; they are also formulaic in their relationship to more standard universal models. His characters are formulaic because they appear repeatedly, as types, within the stories and also because they represent, underneath their garb of culture, more universal character types. This recurrence of character type and plot pattern, and the interweaving of specific cultural material with more universal standards, together form the basis of the formulaic art of Porter's urban short stories. (pp. 36-8)

Karen Charmaine Blansfield, in her *Cheap Rooms and Restless Hearts: A Study of Formula in the Urban Tales of William Sydney Porter*, Bowling Green State University Popular Press, 1988, 143 p.

SOURCES FOR FURTHER STUDY

Current-Garcia, Eugene. *O. Henry.* Boston: Twayne Publishers, 1965, 192 p.

> Thorough biographical and critical study that includes an examination of O. Henry's regional background and its influence on his works.

Davis, Robert H., and Maurice, Arthur B. *The Caliph of Bagdad: Being Arabian Nights Flashes of the Life, Letters, and Work of O. Henry.* New York: D. Appleton and Co., 1931, 411 p.

> Thorough biography quoting extensively from the letters and memoirs of friends, family members, and acquaintances of O. Henry as well as from his own letters.

Gallegly, Joseph. *From Alamo Plaza to Jack Harris's Saloon: O. Henry and the Southwest He Knew.* Paris: Mouton, 1917, 213 p.

> Historical study of the social conditions prevailing in the areas of the American Southwest where O. Henry spent much of his early life. Gallegly offers critical commentary on the stories that have Southwestern settings.

Harris, Richard C. *William Sydney Porter (O. Henry): A Reference Guide.* Boston: G. K. Hall, 1980, 229 p.

> Comprehensive annotated bibliography of writings about O. Henry.

O'Connor, Richard. *O. Henry: The Legendary Life of William S. Porter.* Garden City, N.Y.: Doubleday & Co., 1970, 252 p.

> Thorough critical and biographical study.

Rollins, Hyder E. "O. Henry." *The Sewanee Review* XXII, No. 2 (Spring 1914): 213-32.

> Discusses some characteristics of O. Henry's short stories.

Hermann Hesse

1877-1962

(Also wrote under pseudonyms Hermann Lauscher and Emil Sinclair) German-born Swiss novelist, poet, short story writer, editor, and critic.

INTRODUCTION

Recipient of the 1946 Nobel Prize for Literature, Hesse won critical esteem and popular success primarily for his novels, which he termed "biographies of the soul." A recurring theme in Hesse's work is the individual's search for truth and identity through what he called the "inward journey," and the intensely autobiographical nature of his writing reflects his self-introspection. Hesse's fiction received international attention during his lifetime, but beginning in the 1960s he attained a huge, cult-like readership among young people, who readily identify with his rebellious, passionately spiritual heroes and their struggle to transcend the materialism of society through art, mysticism, and love.

Born in Calw, Germany, Hesse was instructed from childhood to accept the tenets of his parents' devout Pietism, a religious movement which stressed Bible study and personal religious experience. He also had access to books on Eastern philosophy and religion, for his maternal grandfather was a missionary and Indologist. Hesse's readings in this area influenced his outlook and writing. As a youth Hesse was fond of eighteenth- and nineteenth-century German Romantic literature, and his early fiction reflects this affinity. The pieces in such short story collections as *Eine Stunde hinter Mitternacht* (1899) and *Hinterlassene Schriften und Gedichte von Hermann Lauscher* (1901) typically feature misunderstood outsiders who retreat from society and engage in melodramatic fantasies about love and death. Hesse also maintained a lifelong fascination with fantasy and folklore, an influence that surfaces in *Märchen* (1919; *Strange News from Another Star and Other Tales*) and *Piktors Verwandlungen* (1925; *Pictor's Metamorphoses and Other Fantasies*). In these volumes of fantasies, allegories, and fables, magic is part of reality as wish fulfillment, transformation, and the animation of objects occur as a matter of course. In 1916 and 1917, Hesse underwent psychoanalysis with Dr. Josef Lang, a disciple of Carl Jung, to cope with both an emotional crisis triggered by illness and death in his family and the horrors of World War I, which disturbed him as an avowed pacifist. He emerged from these sessions with the ambition to follow "Weg nach Innen," or an inward journey, which he hoped would result in increased self-knowledge and fulfillment of his artistic potential. Inspired also by the philosophy of Friedrich Nietzsche, Hesse vowed to reject traditional religion and morality and to lead a life of isolation and individualism.

Hesse's interest in Eastern philosophy and religion is most evident in the novellas *Siddhartha: Eine indische Dichtung* (1927; *Siddhartha*) and *Die Morgenlandfahrt* (1932; *The Journey to the East*). He conceived of *Siddhartha* in 1911 following an extended visit to southeastern Asia in search of the peace of mind that he believed Oriental religions could offer. Instead, Hesse found only abject poverty and vulgarized Buddhism, and he left Asia before reaching his final destination, India. In *Siddhartha,* the title character is an exceptionally intelligent Brahmin, a member of the highest caste in Hinduism, who seemingly has a well-ordered existence yet feels spiritually hollow. He renounces his life of ritual and asceticism to embark on a quest for wisdom and God. With his friend Govinda he seeks Gotama the Buddha, who reputedly has achieved perfect knowledge. After speaking with Buddha, however, Siddhartha realizes that he cannot accept the Buddhist doctrine of salvation from suffering. Siddhartha then immerses himself in material and carnal pursuits but comes no closer to knowledge. Disillusioned that all these paths have failed, Siddhartha becomes a ferryman, and during repeated crossings of a river he experiences total bliss. Bernard Landis commented: "[Siddhartha perceived the river] to be the mirror of all life, past, present, and future. All was One, and One was All. Spirit and flesh, mountain and man, blood and stone were all part of the one continuous flow of existence. True peace was obtained in the only way possible, through a unity of the self with the universal, eternal essence."

Another emotional and spiritual crisis in the late 1920s led Hesse to write *The Journey to the East.* In this novella, he hoped to overcome his fears about his life and art and to establish order in his being. The autobiographical hero, H. H., earns entrance into the Order of Eastern Wayfarers, a group of elite intellectuals and artists from the past and present who are engaged in a perennial pilgrimage to the East. Each member seeks the ultimate meaning of life, which assumes a different objective for every individual. H. H.'s aim is to see Princess Fatima, who is, in Inder Nath Kher's words, "his fate and *anima,* the archetypal mother who represents

the center . . . and the circumference of the psyche." When the esteemed community breaks up, H. H. loses contact with Leo, who is regarded as both servant and master of the circle and the embodiment of true friendship. After ten years of suffering and searching, H. H. again meets Leo and is allowed back into the Order. Leo gives H. H. his lost ring, which, Inder Nath Kher asserted, "symbolizes marriage and wholeness, self-illumination and grace." In *The Journey to the East,* Hesse reaffirmed what he considered the superiority of the timeless realm of art and thought.

The novel *Demian* (1919) launched the series of works that chronicle Hesse's inward journey. Set in Germany before World War I, *Demian* exhibits Jungian ideas about dreams and symbols in which Hesse had been deeply involved during his two years of psychotherapy. This work traces Emil Sinclair's self-exploration, which begins near the time of his confirmation as a Christian. Sinclair's inward journey is aided by fellow student Max Demian, who encourages Sinclair to question his traditional bourgeois beliefs regarding family, society, and faith. Sinclair suffers a crisis of identity while away at school and endures periods of decadence and despair until gaining better realization of his self through art. Demian and his mother, Frau Eva, appear in Sinclair's paintings and dreams, and some critics have interpreted these two characters as Jungian archetypes: Demian is thought to be Sinclair's imago or conception of the ideal self, while Eva is viewed as Sinclair's anima or soul, the unconscious with which he must become familiar in order to form an identity. A brief period of bliss ensues when Sinclair reunites with Demian and gains insight from Eva, but this is interrupted by the outbreak of World War I. Both Demian and Sinclair become soldiers, are wounded, and end up in a hospital together. Sinclair witnesses Demian's death and is reborn by it, as he realizes that Demian is within him as brother and master; thus, Sinclair can proceed to discover his true self.

Der Steppenwolf (1927; *Steppenwolf*), probably Hesse's best-known novel, arose out of a third major crisis in his life, the failure of his second marriage. Full of self-loathing and hungry for an uninhibited life, Hesse frequented the bars and dance halls of Zurich, Switzerland, in hopes of losing himself in alcohol, jazz, and sex. The protagonist of *Steppenwolf,* Harry Haller, goes through similar experiences, and like many other Hesse heroes, serves as the author's alter ego. A lonely, depressed 50-year-old writer who is alienated from the bourgeois society he disdains, Haller has fruitlessly pursued truth and spiritual fulfillment through asceticism. Late one night, unable to further tolerate his alienation, he decides to find relief in sensual experiences. He encounters Hermine, a free-spirited androgyne who teaches Haller to dance, laugh, and enjoy life. In return for this, she predicts that Haller will kill her. After introducing him to Pablo, a young jazz musician, Hermine shows Haller into the Magic Theater, a fantastic realm devoted to liberating the senses. During a series of phantasmagoric episodes in the Magic Theater, where one's deepest fantasies can be enacted, Haller finds Hermine and Pablo lying together in postcoital exhaustion, and he hallucinates that he stabs her in the heart. There occurs a trial in which Haller is sentenced to eternal life for his imaginary murder of an illusory person. He then engages in an imaginary conversation with the composer Wolfgang Amadeus Mozart about the importance of laughter and the primacy of the ideal. Mozart then transforms into Pablo, who disappears with Hermine, leaving Haller alone to contemplate his life. The novel concludes optimistically with Haller vowing to follow the examples of Immortals like Mozart and Goethe, to learn the value of pleasure and laughter, and to harmonize the intellectual, spiritual, and sensual aspects of life.

Many of Hesse's works focus on interactions between characters with opposing temperaments. In *Narziss und Goldmund* (1930; *Narcissus and Goldmund*), for example, the title characters represent, respectively, spirit and life, or mind and matter. Set in a medieval monastery, half of this novel follows the friendship of the introverted, ascetic Narcissus and the extroverted sculptor Goldmund; the other half chronicles the latter's hedonistic adventures outside the cloister. Goldmund moves from village to village, has numerous sexual partners, studies sculpture under Master Niklaus, is exposed to the plague, and finally returns to the monastery, where Narcissus saves him from death. G. W. Field observed: "Goldmund's adventures suggest two related themes: the awareness of transience, especially in the relationship of love and death, and secondly, his awakening to the power of art to stamp eternity on the ephemeral phenomena of the senses." Some commentators have interpreted Narcissus and Goldmund as symbols of Hesse's divided self, though they generally believe that, while advocating both, Hesse favors Goldmund's way of life, even if

in reality he was closer in spirit to Narcissus' monastic austerity.

Hesse's last major novel, *Das Glasperlenspiel* (1943; *Magister Ludi;* later translated as *The Glass Bead Game*), is often considered his most complex and ambitious work. Written as a historical biography of Josef Knecht in the year 2400 by an anonymous narrator, this work portrays Knecht's rise to Magister Ludi, or Master of the Glass Bead Game, in Castalia, a utopian province where artists and intellectuals strive to attain "perfection, pure being, the fullness of reality." Gary R. Olsen described the Game: "Generally, it represents a very complex and symbolic sign system designed to encompass and summarize all human knowledge around a central idea." Hesse visualized the Game as a panacea for the evils of modern civilization. Knecht, however, finally becomes disenchanted with the timeless, abstract, purely contemplative existence of Castalia and defects. Ironically, he finds a sense of identity and permanence within the ephemeral realm outside Castalia while tutoring a student. In *The Glass Bead Game,* Hesse rejects his long-held ideal of a cloistered community of intellectual elites and affirms the value of asserting one's creativity and individuality.

Hesse's fiction has profoundly affected readers worldwide, especially the young, who sympathize with many of his preoccupations: the quest for truth and self-discovery, the dualistic nature of existence, the conflict between spirit and flesh, the individual's need for freedom, and the primacy of art and love. Due largely to his ability to universalize personal crises and private torments, Hesse has remained one of the most popular German-language authors of the twentieth century.

(For further information about Hesse's life and works, see *Contemporary Authors,* Vols. 17-20; *Contemporary Authors Permanent Series,* Vol. 2; *Contemporary Literary Criticism,* Vols. 1, 2, 3, 6, 11, 17, 25, 69; *Dictionary of Literary Biography,* Vol. 66: *German Fiction Writers, 1885-1913; Short Story Criticism,* Vol. 9; and *Something about the Author,* Vol. 50.)

CRITICAL COMMENTARY

JOHANNES MALTHANER
(essay date 1952)

[In the essay excerpted below, Malthaner describes the spiritual journey of the title character in *Siddhartha* and suggests that his quest reflects Hesse's attempt to regain his harmonious relationship with the world.]

Herman Hesse, the German-Swiss poet and novelist, is relatively little known in this country although a good deal of publicity has been given him since he was granted the Nobel prize for literature in 1946. This "unpopularity" of Hesse is only partly due to the fact that he writes in a foreign tongue—until very recently only very few of his works have been available in English translations—, even now his books are little in demand outside of university circles. That means that Hesse has not caught the fancy of the American public, that he has so far no large popular following. The main reason for this is, as I see it, that his novels do not have a strong plot around which the action revolves and therefore lack suspense or excitement. They are largely autobiographical and deal with questions of "Weltanschauung", of a philosophy of life. The plot is used by Hesse to drape his thoughts around it, to have an opportunity to present his innermost thoughts and the struggle for an understanding of the great problems of life. Hesse is, and always has been, a god-seeker; he has a message for his fellow-men, but one must "study" him, read and reread his works carefully if one wants to get the full benefit of their message. His works are not so much for entertainment but rather want to give food for thought; they have therefore a very strong appeal for the serious-minded reader but not for the masses that crave excitement and entertainment instead of beauty and depth.

Herman Hesse's novel *Siddhartha* is just such a work of literature, and it is of special interest to the student of literature, and of Hesse in particular, because it marks an important step in the development of Hesse and is unique in German literature in its presentation of Eastern philosophy.

The novel is largely autobiographical and has a long and interesting history. It is no doubt true of all great works of art that they do not just happen, that they are not products of chance. Great works of literature have their roots way back in the life of their writers, they have grown out of life and are part of the life of their creators; great works of literature are not factory products but grow and ripen slowly to full bloom. This is especially true of *Siddhartha.*

Siddhartha was published in 1922 but has its roots in the earliest childhood of Hesse. His parents had been missionaries to India, his mother having been born in India of missionary parents; but on account of the poor health of Hesse's father the family had to return to Europe and came to Calw, a small Black Forest town, to help the maternal grandfather of Hesse, Dr. Gundert, the director of their mission and a famous Indian scholar and linguist. Indian songs and books, frequent discussions about India with visiting missionaries and scholars, a large library of Indian and Chinese writings, also many objects of Eastern art created great interest and left a deep impression on Hesse ever since his childhood.

The first part of *Siddhartha,* up to the meeting with the courtesan Kamala, was written before 1919 and was first published in the literary magazine *Neue Rundschau.* Siddhartha is the son of a rich Brahman of India. He is a good obedient son and the joy of his parents, but one day he awakens to the realization that his life is empty, that his soul has been left unsatisfied by his devotion to duty and the strict observance of all religious ordinances. He wants to find God who so far has been to him only a vague idea, distant and unreal, although he tried to serve him with sincerity of heart to the best of his understanding. Young Siddhartha realizes that he is at a dead end and that he must break away. So he leaves home leaving behind him all that he so far had loved and treasured, all the comforts, giving up his high social position, and becomes a Samana, an itinerant monk, with no earthly possessions anymore, accompanied by his boyhood friend Govinda who has decided to follow Siddhartha's lead. By fasting and exposing his body to the rigors of the weather, Siddhartha wants to empty himself completely of all physical desires so that by any chance he may hear the voice of God speaking to his soul, that he may find peace.

Hesse's books are confessions, and the story of Siddhartha is his own story describing his own doubts and struggle. He, too, had rebelled: against the pietistic orthodoxy of his parents and the strict school system in Germany that destroyed any attempt of independence in its pupils. So he ran away to shape his own life. Self-education is the main theme of most of the novels of Hesse, especially of the books of his youth.

Principal Works

Eine Stunde hinter Mitternacht (short stories) 1899

Hinterlassene Schriften und Gedichte von Hermann Lauscher (short stories) 1901

Peter Camenzind (novel) 1904
  [Peter Camenzind, 1961]

Unterm Rad (novel) 1906
  [The Prodigy, 1957; also published as Beneath the Wheel, 1968]

Gertrud: Roman (novel) 1910
  [Gertrud and I, 1915; also translated as Gertrude, 1955]

RoBhalde (novel) 1914
  [Rosshalde, 1970]

Demian: Die Geschichte einer Jugend von Emil Sinclair (novel) 1919
  [Demian, 1923; also published as Demian: The Story of a Youth, 1948; and Demian: The Story of Emil Sinclair's Youth, 1965]

Märchen (short stories) 1919
  [Strange News from Another Star, and Other Tales, 1972]

Siddhartha: Eine indische Dichtung (novella) 1922
  [Siddhartha, 1951]

Aufzeichnungen eines Herrn im Sanatorium (unfinished novel) 1925; also published as Haus sum Frieden: Aufzeichnungen eines Herrn im Sanatorium, 1947

Piktors Verwandlungen (short stories) 1925
  [Pictor's Metamorphoses and Other Fantasies, 1981]

Der Steppenwolf (novel) 1927
  [Steppenwolf, 1929; revised translation, 1963

Krisis: Ein Stück Tagebuch (poetry) 1928
  [Crisis: Pages from a Diary, 1975]

Narziss und Goldmund: Erzählung (novel) 1930
  [Death and the Lover, 1932; also published as Goldmund, 1959; Narziss and Goldmund, 1965; and Narcissus and Goldmund, 1968]

Die Morgenlandfahrt: Eine Erzählung (novella) 1932
  [Journey to the East, 1956]

Das Glasperlenspiel: Versuch einer Lebensbeschreibung des Magister Ludi Josef Knecht samt Knechts hinterlassenen Schriften. 2 vols. (novel) 1943
  [Magister Ludi, 1949; also published as The Glass Bead Game (Magister Ludi), 1969; and Magister Ludi (The Glass Bead Game), 1970]

Berthold (unfinished novel) 1945

Mein Glaube (essays) 1971
  [My Belief: Essays on Life and Art, 1974]

Self-education has been for centuries a very favorite theme in German literature and men like Luther, Goethe, Kant, and many other leading German writers and philosophers were the inspirers of German youth in their longing for independence.

It is significant that Hesse gave to a collection of four stories published in 1931, in which he included *Siddhartha,* the title of *Weg nach Innen, Road to Within.* Indeed, Siddhartha turns away from the outside observance of religious rituals and ordinances to a life of contemplation. So also does Hesse himself after the outbreak of World War I. Up to the war, Hesse had lived a rather quiet and self-satisfied life. After years of hard struggle to win recognition as a poet, he had found first success which brought him not only social recognition and financial security but also many friends and a home. But the war brought him a rather rude awakening out of his idylic life on the shore of Lake Constance where he had lived a rather happy and retired life. His apparently so secure and well-ordered world came crashing down over his head. The vicious attacks by the German press and by many of his former friends for his stand against the war psychosis—Hesse was living at that time in Switzerland although he was still a German citizen—forced him to reexamine the fundamental truths on which he had built his life. He had become distrustful of religion as he saw it practised, and of education which had not prevented the western world of being plunged into a murderous war. Where was the truth? On what foundation could a man build his life? All had been found wanting.

Siddhartha is Hesse's attempt to restore his faith in mankind, to regain his lost peace of mind, and to find again a harmonious relationship with his world. A new more spiritual orientation takes place. He does no longer believe in the natural goodness of man, he is thrown back unto himself and comes to a new concept of God: No longer does he seek God in nature but, in the words of the Bible, he believed that "the Kingdom of God's is within you".

Hesse confesses that he had been pious only up to his thirteenth year but then had become a skeptic. Now he becomes a believer again, to be sure it is not a return to the orthodox belief of his parents, he wants to include in his new concept of religion not only the teachings of Jesus but also those of Buddha and of the Holy Scriptures of India as well. (pp. 103-06)

Returning to our story, we find that Siddhartha also as a Samana has not come nearer his goal of happiness and peace. It seems to him that his religious fervor had been nothing but self-deception, that all the time he had been in flight from himself. The hardships which he had endured as a Samana had not brought him nearer to God.

At this period of his life, Siddhartha hears of Gotama Buddha of whom it was said that he had attained that blissful state of godliness where the chain of reincarnations had been broken, that he had entered Nirvana. Siddhartha goes to find him, hears him teach the multitude, and then has a private conversation with the Holy One; but it becomes clear to him that the way of salvation can not be taught, that words and creeds are empty sounds, that each man must find the way by himself, the secret of the experience can not be passed on. So he leaves also Gotama Buddha and all teachers and teachings. Govinda, his friend, stays with Gotama and so Siddhartha cuts the last link with his past. He is now all alone. And he comes to the sudden realization that all through the years so far he has lived a separate life, that he actually never had sought a real understanding of his fellow men, that he knew very little of the world and of life all about him. For the first time in many years he really looks about him and perceives the beauty of the world. The world about him, from which he had fled, he now finds attractive and good. He must not seek to escape life but face it, live it.

This is the startling new discovery Siddhartha makes and so he decides to leave the wilderness. He comes to the big city where he sees at the gate the beautiful Kamala, the courtesan. He finds her favor and she teaches him the ways of the world. He discards his beggar's clothes and becomes in short time a very successful merchant. But his heart is neither in his love nor in his business; all the pleasures of the world can not still the hunger of his soul. He finds the world wanting, too, and, moreover, he must realize after a few years that the worldly things, the acquiring of money, have gradually taken possession of his life, that he is being enslaved and harassed by the necessity of making money in order to satisfy his extravagant tastes, that he has become a busy and unfree man whose thoughts dwell less and less on the eternal things.

So he cuts himself lose from all that he had acquired, leaves once again everything behind him, and goes back to the river which he had crossed when he gave up his life as a Samana.

At this point there is a long interruption in the writing of *Siddhartha.* Hesse realized that his knowledge of Eastern philosophy was not sufficient; he devoted himself therefore to a very thorough study of Indian philosophy and religion. After a year and a half he takes up the writing of the story again. It is quite evident, however, that the emphasis has shifted. Description from now on is practically absent, and the tone is lighter, the language, too, is not so heavy, not so mystic

but transparent and more elevated. The whole concentration is on the spiritual element. Instead of long discussions of philosophies and systems, we find the emphasis now on Faith. He perceives that only through faith, not by doing or by teachings, can man penetrate to the source of light, can he find God.

At the bank of the river Siddhartha sits for a long time and lets his whole life pass in review before him. He finds that even the evil things which he had done lately had been necessary as an experience in order to bring him to an understanding of what life really was. But he also becomes discouraged because all his endeavors so far had not given him the desired insight and peace of soul. There was nothing left in life that might entice him, challenge him, comfort him; he finds himself subject to an unescapable chain of cause and effect, to repeated incarnations, each of which means a new beginning of suffering. Will he ever be able to break this chain? Will he ever be able to enter Nirvana? He doubts it and is at the point of drowning himself when the mysterious word "OM" comes to his mind. "OM" means "having completed," in German "Vollendung." He realizes the folly of his attempt to try to find peace and an end to his sufferings by extinguishing his physical being. Life is indestructible. Siddhartha realizes, too, that all life is one, that all creation is an indivisible one, that trees and birds are indeed his brothers; he sees his great mistake in trying always to do something instead of just to be.

He joins Vasudeva, the ferry man, who shows him the great secret of the river, namely that for the river the concept of time does not exist: The river just is, for the river there is no past, no future, no beginning, no end; for the river is only the presence. And for man, too, Vasudeva tells him, happiness is real only when causality—that is time—has ceased to exist for him. The problem is not, as Siddhartha had always understood it, to find perfection, but to find completion, "Vollendung."

One more lesson Siddhartha had to learn. When he left Kamala she had known that she would bear him a child, but she did not tell Siddhartha because she realized that she could not and must not hold him back, that Siddhartha had to go his own way. Later, too, she felt the emptiness of her life; so one day she decides to seek Gotama Buddha of whom she had heard. Her way leads her to the river where, unknown to her, Siddartha lived and stopping at the bank of the river to rest, she is bitten by a poisonous snake. Siddhartha finds her dying and recognizes her. After he had buried her, he takes his son, a boy of some twelve or fourteen years of age, to him. Siddartha feels keenly the loss of Kamala, but it is not sadness that is in his heart for he knows now that all life is indestructible, that Kamala has only entered a new life, life in a wider sense, that in every blossom, in every breeze about him there is Kamala. He is not separated from her, never will be, in fact she is nearer to him now than ever before.

Siddhartha devotes himself to the education of his son but must make the painful experience that his love is not appreciated and his endeavors are repulsed. His son does not want the life Siddhartha thinks best for him, he wants to live his own life, and thus breaks away from his father as Siddhartha in his own youth had broken away from his own father. With the loss of his son, there is nothing left that binds Siddhartha to this world. He realizes that this had to come, so that he would no longer fight what he considered fate but give himself unreservedly to his destiny; thus Siddhartha has overcome suffering at last and with it has attained the last step of his completion, he has entered into Nirvana; now peace has come to Siddhartha at last. (pp. 106-09)

Johannes Malthaner, "Hermann Hesse: 'Siddhartha'," in *The German Quarterly*, Vol. 25, No. 2, March, 1952, pp. 103-09.

COLIN WILSON
(essay date 1956)

[Wilson is an English novelist, critic, and philosopher. In the excerpt below from his *The Outsider*, he defines Harry Haller, protagonist of *Der Steppenwolf*, as a "tragically divided and unproductive" individual whose spiritual strength paradoxically reinforces bourgeois society.]

Steppenwolf is the story of a middle-aged man. This in itself is an important advance. The romantic usually finds himself committed to pessimism in opposition to life itself by his insistence on the importance of youth (Rupert Brooke is a typical example). Steppenwolf has recognized the irrelevancy of youth; there is a self-lacerating honesty about this journal of a middle-aged man.

In all externals, Steppenwolf (the self-conferred nickname of Harry Haller) is a Barbusse Outsider [the protagonist of Henri Barbusse's novel, *L'enfer*]. He is more cultured perhaps, less of an animal; the swaying dresses of women in the street do not trouble him. Also he is less concerned to 'stand for truth'; he allows his imagination full play, and his journal is a sort of wish-dream diary. But here again we have the man-on-his-own, living in rooms with his books and his gramophone; there is not even the necessity to go out and work, for he has a small private income. In his youth he considered himself a poet, a self-realizer. Now he is middle-aged, an ageing Emil Sinclair [a character in *De-*

mian], and the moods of insight have stopped coming; there is only dissatisfaction, lukewarmness.

The journal opens with an account of a typical day: he reads a little, has a bath, lounges around his room, eats; and the feeling of unfulfilment increases until towards nightfall he feels like setting fire to the house or jumping out of a window. The worst of it is that he can find no excuse for this apathy; being an artist-contemplative, he should be ideally contented with this type of life. Something is missing. But what? He goes to a tavern and ruminates as he takes his evening meal; the food and wine relax him, and suddenly the mood he has despaired of having pervades him:

> A refreshing laughter rose in me. . . . It soared aloft like a soapbubble . . . and then softly burst. . . . The golden trail was blazed and I was reminded of the eternal, and of Mozart, and the stars. For an hour I could breathe once more. . . .

But this is at the end of a long day, and tomorrow he will wake up and the insight will be gone; he will read a little, have a bath . . . and so on.

But on this particular evening something happens. The reader is not sure what. According to Haller, he sees a mysterious door in the wall, with the words 'Magic Theatre: Not for everybody' written over it, and a man with a sandwich board and a tray of *Old Moore's Almanacs* gives him a pamphlet called *A Treatise on the Steppenwolf*. The treatise is printed at full length in the following pages of the novel, and it is obviously Haller's own work; so it is difficult for the reader to determine when Haller is recording the truth and when he is playing a game of wish-fulfilment with himself.

The treatise is an important piece of self-analysis. It could be called 'A Treatise on the Outsider'. As Harry reads it (or writes it) certain convictions formulate themselves, about himself and about the Outsider generally. The Outsider, Haller says, is a self-divided man; being self-divided, his chief desire is to be unified. He is selfish as a man with a lifelong raging toothache would be selfish.

To explain his wretchedness, Haller has divided himself into two persons: a civilized man and a wolf-man. The civilized man loves all the things of Emil Sinclair's first world, order and cleanliness, poetry and music (especially Mozart); he takes lodgings always in houses with polished fire-irons and well-scrubbed tiles. His other half is a savage who loves the second world, the world of darkness; he prefers open spaces and lawlessness; if he wants a woman he feels that the proper way is to kill and rape her. For him, bourgeois civilization and all its inanities are a great joke.

The civilized man and the wolf-man live at enmity most of the time, and it would seem that Harry Haller is bound to spend his days divided by their squabbling. But sometimes, as in the tavern, they make peace, and then a strange state ensues; for Harry finds that a combination of the two makes him akin to the gods. In these moments of vision, he is no longer envious of the bourgeois who finds life so straightforward, for his own conflicts are present in the bourgeois, on a much smaller scale. He, as self-realizer, has deliberately cultivated his two opposing natures until the conflict threatens to tear him in two, because he knows that when he has achieved the secret of permanently reconciling them, he will live at a level of intensity unknown to the bourgeois. His suffering is not a mark of his inferiority, even though it may render him less fit for survival than the bourgeois; unreconciled, it is the sign of his greatness; reconciled, it is manifested as 'more abundant life' that makes the Outsider's superiority over other types of men unquestionable. When the Outsider becomes aware of his strength, he is unified and happy.

Haller goes even further; the Outsider is the mainstay of the bourgeois. Without him the bourgeois could not exist. The vitality of the ordinary members of society is dependent on its Outsiders. Many Outsiders unify themselves, realize themselves as poets or saints. Others remain tragically divided and unproductive, but even they supply soul-energy to society; it is their strenuousness that purifies thought and prevents the bourgeois world from foundering under its own dead-weight; they are society's spiritual dynamos. Harry Haller is one of these.

There is a yet further step in self-analysis for the Steppenwolf: that is to recognize that he is not really divided into two simple elements, man and wolf, but has literally hundreds of conflicting I's. Every thought and impulse says 'I'. The word 'personality' hides the vagueness of the concept; it refers to no factual object, like 'body'. Human beings are not like the characters in literature, fixed, made immutable by their creator; the visible part of the human being is his dead part; it is the other part, the unconditioned Will that constitutes his being. Will precedes essence. Our bourgeois civilization is based on personality. It is our chief value. A film star has 'personality'; the salesman hoping to sell his first insurance policy tries to ooze 'personality':

> The human merry-go-round sees many changes: the illusion that cost India the efforts of thousands of years to unmask is the same illusion that the West has laboured just as hard to maintain and strengthen.

The treatise comes to an end with a sort of credo:

> Man is not . . . of fixed and enduring form. He is . . . an experiment and a transition. He is nothing else than the narrow and perilous bridge between nature and spirit. His innermost destiny drives him on to the spirit and to God. His innermost longing

draws him back to nature . . . man . . . is a bourgeois compromise.
> That man is not yet a finished creation but rather a challenge of the spirit; a distant possibility dreaded as much as desired; that the way towards it has only been covered for a very short distance and with terrible agonies and ecstasies even by those few for whom it is the scaffold today and the monument tomorrow.

Steppenwolf knows well enough why he is unhappy and drifting, bored and tired; it is because he will not recoginize his purpose and follow it with his whole being.

'He is resolved to forget that the desperate clinging to the self, and the desperate clinging to life are the surest way to eternal death.' Haller knows that even when the Outsider is a universally acknowledged man of genius, it is due to 'his immense powers of surrender and suffering, of his indifference to the ideals of the bourgeois, and of his patience under that last extremity of loneliness which rarefies the atmosphere of the bourgeois world to an ice-cold ether around those who suffer to become men, that loneliness of the garden of Gethsemane'.

> This Steppenwolf . . . has discovered that . . . at best he is only at the beginning of a long pilgrimage towards this ideal harmony. . . . No, back to nature is a false track that leads nowhere but to suffering and despair. . . . Every created thing, even the simplest, is already guilty, already multiple. . . . The way to innocence, to the uncreated and to God, leads on, not back, not back to the wolf or the child, but ever further into guilt, ever deeper into human life. . . . Instead of narrowing your world and simplifying your soul, you will have at the last to take the whole world into your soul, cost what it may.

The last image of the treatise recalls an idea of Rilke's: the Angel of the Duinese Elegies who, from his immense height, can see and summarize human life as a whole.

> Were he already among the immortals—were he already there at the goal to which the difficult path seems to be taking him—with what amazement he would look back over all this coming and going, all the indecision and wild zigzagging of his tracks. With what a mixture of encouragement and blame, pity and joy, he would smile at this Steppenwolf.

The Outsider's 'way of salvation', then, is plainly implied. His moments of insight into his direction and purpose must be grasped tightly; in these moments he must formulate laws that will enable him to move towards his goal in spite of losing sight of it. It is unnecessary to add that these laws will apply not only to him, but to all men, their goal being the same as his. (pp. 57-61)

Logically, the 'Treatise on the Steppenwolf' should be the end of the book; actually, it is within the first hundred pages. Harry has only rationalized his difficulties; he has yet to undergo experiences that will make his analysis real to him. The *Bildungsroman* is only one-third completed.

After reading the treatise, he hits rock-bottom of despair; he is exhausted and frustrated, and the treatise warns him that this is all as it should be; he decides that this is the last time he allows himself to sink so low; next time he will commit suicide before he reaches that point. The thought cheers him up, and he lies down to sleep.

The treatise is the high point of the book from the reader's point of view, but Hesse still has a job to finish; he has to show us how Steppenwolf will learn to accept life again and turn away finally from the thought of cutting his throat. This comes about by a series of romantically improbable events. The man with the sandwich board has mentioned the name of a tavern; Haller goes there and meets a girl called Hermine. She takes him in hand; makes him learn ballroom-dancing and listen to modern jazz. She introduces him to the saxophone player, the sunburnt Pablo, and to the sensuously beautiful animal Maria, whom he finds in his bed when he returns home one night. Like Siddhartha, he goes through an education of the senses. In bed with Maria, he recovers his own past . . . and finds it meaningful.

> For moments together my heart stood still between delight and sorrow to find how rich was the gallery of my life, and how thronged the soul of the wretched Steppenwolf with high eternal stars and constellations. . . . My life had become weariness. It had wandered in a maze of unhappiness that led to renunciation and nothingness; it was bitter with the salt of all human things; yet it had laid up riches, riches to be proud of. It had been, for all its wretchedness, a princely life. Let the little way to death be as it might—the kernel of this life of mine was noble. It came of high descent, and turned, not on trifles, but on the stars. . . .

This experience can be called the ultimately valid core of romanticism, stripped of its externals of stagey scenery and soft music. It has become a type of religious affirmation. Unfortunately, there can be no doubt about the difficulty of separating it from the stage scenery: the overblown language, the Hoffmannesque atmosphere. Only a few pages later, Haller admits that a part of his new 'life of the senses' is smoking opium; and there is bisexuality too. (Pablo suggests a sexual orgy for three: himself, Harry and Maria; and Maria and Hermine have Lesbian relations.)

The book culminates with a dream fantasy of a fancy-dress ball in which Harry feels the barriers between himself and other people break down, ceases to feel his separateness. He kills (or dreams he kills) Hermine, and at last finds his way to the Magic Theatre, where he sees his past in retrospect and relives innocent dreams. After this scene, he has achieved the affirmation he could not make earlier in the book:

> I would sample its tortures once more and shudder once more at its senselessness. I would traverse not once more but often, the hell of my inner being. One day I would be a better hand at the game. . . .

Steppenwolf ends in the same romantic dream-haze that we have noted in the previous two novels; but in this case its effect is less irritating because the reader has already, as it were, granted Haller latitude to tell what lies he chooses. Nevertheless, it is not these last scenes that impress themselves on the mind (as it should be, since they are the climax of the novel); it is the pages of self-analysis, when there is no action taking place at all. Unlike his great contemporary, Thomas Mann, Hesse has no power to bring people to life; but his ideas are far more alive than Mann's, perhaps because Mann is always the detached spectator, while Hesse is always a thinly disguised participant in his novels. The consequence is that Hesse's novels of ideas have a vitality that can only be compared to Dostoevsky; the ideas are a passion; he writes in the grip of a need to solve his own life's problems by seeing them on paper.

In *Steppenwolf* he has gone a long way towards finally resolving them. In the final dream scene, Haller glimpses the words: Tat Tvam Asi—*That Thou Art*—the formula from the Upanishads that denotes that in the heart of his own being man discovers the godhead. Intuitively, Harry knows this. The path that leads from the Outsider's miseries to this still-centre is a path of discipline, asceticism and complete detachment. He shows himself aware of it in the 'Treatise on the Steppenwolf', but he admits that it is too hard a saying for him. By the end of the novel it would seem that he has found some of the necessary courage to face it. (pp. 62-4)

Colin Wilson, "The Romantic Outsider," in his *The Outsider*, Houghton Mifflin Company, 1956, pp. 47-69.

ESTHER C. GROPPER
(essay date 1972)

[In the following excerpt, Gropper discusses the appeal of Hesse's novels among contemporary youth.]

If *Future Shock* touches a raw nerve and compels the

young reader to make some searching inquiries into his social structure, how is it that they find *The Glass Bead Game* by Hesse so appealing? Against the bizarre tapestry of 2000 A.D. which Toffler weaves is one projected into 2500 A.D. by Hesse. Hesse "hears music and sees men of the past and future." He sees "wise men and poets and scholars harmoniously building the valued and vaulted cathedral of Mind." Symbolically, in a game performed according to the strictest rules with supreme virtuosity, the mandarins of a new culture work out a mental synthesis of all the spiritual values of all ages. Castalia, Joseph Knecht's sanctuary (clearly Hesse's in his own continuing search for a spiritual dimension of life) becomes a realm where all of the best thoughts and values are kept alive through the practice of the Glass Bead Game. It is a future society in which our youth has learned to distrust. The game is superbly constructed, a product of tremendous experience and imagination and, because it incorporates so much of our irrational behavior, engaging and funny. Not to see the humor is to miss the fun and to miss the irony with which it was written.

When we follow Joseph Knecht through his experiences at Mariafels, a remote monastery where the contemplative life is pursued—not a new idea, we find it in Platonic academies or yoga schools—we become aware of the "radicalization of the intellectual" who moves from isolation into a responsible action controlled by dispassionate reflection. It is essential to understand that Knecht's defection from Castalia, far from implying any repudiation of the spiritual ideal, simply calls for a new consciousness of the social responsibility of the intellectual. He warns these intellectuals to give up their arrogant and self-satisfying game which can lead only to inbreeding and destruction. He makes a commitment by putting spirit and intellect at the service of the world. Thematically, it seems to have much in common with *The Greening of America.*

Hesse's book fictionalizes the admonitions of an outsider who urges us to question accepted values, to rebel against the system that humiliates us, to challenge existing institutions in the light of higher ideas. Hesse's age rejected his criticisms; our age was oblivious to it; the new generation applauds it. They believe the only true culture is Joseph Knecht's which responds to the social demands and requirements of the times. They see Knecht's resolution as the answer to Toffler's computerized society, to impersonal bureaucracy, to a technologically controlled human—rather inhuman—culture. The longer we consider Hesse's novel, the more clearly we realize that it is not a telescope focused on an imaginary future but a mirror reflecting with disturbing sharpness a paradigm of present reality. (pp. 981-82)

Seeking a new morality, [the young] find a kindred wanderer in Siddhartha who, transcending the conventional dichotomy of good and evil, embraces all

extremes of life in one unified vision. His has been a pursuit of self identity which takes him to the shores of sensuality and of asceticism. With experience comes insight and Siddhartha learns to travel the river of life which touches both shores and which ultimately—after sorting out his values—offers harmony, knowledge, and perfection. He reaches a level of awareness where one is capable of accepting all being. Isn't that what our young seem to hope for?

Hesse succeeded as very few have, in capturing the frustrations and sexual fears of adolescents who are engaged in a pursuit for identity. And if tranquillity is what they need to reflect upon these questions, then Gautama Buddha offers them serenity and contemplation, a pause in their twentieth-century race. Some hope, some insight to the essence of life is offered.

This leads to another aspect of Hesse's writings; namely, the philosophical, poetical nature of it. He finds a language both personal and symbolic, a simple but highly lyrical language, which corresponds to the young person's own thoughts. It is Hesse's language and vision which excite his readers. It is his form, which however repetitive, is consistent. After reading a few of his books—for rarely does anyone stop at *Siddhartha*—the young reader recognizes a basic structure to Hesse's books. In Hesse's own essays he says that the child is born into a state of unity with all being. This is the young Siddhartha—dutiful, respectful, loving, happy. When he learns about good and evil, he advances to a second level of humanization characterized by despair and alienation, for he has been made aware of laws and moral codes. But he feels incapable of adhering to arbitrary standards established by conventional religious or moral systems because they exclude so much of what seems perfectly natural. Siddhartha finds his "self" submerged in a culture in which he sees injustices and imbalance. This second level of awareness is that in which most men are condemned to live. Those like Siddhartha who are not willing to accept the lies, who are troubled by elders, or teachers, who point out sense, happiness, and beauty, move on to the third level of a spiritual kingdom, to experience pure thought, to an emerging new culture. The same resolution reached in *The Glass Bead Game!*

It is in the mystique of *Demian* that the young feel Hesse is the interpreter of their innermost lives. Following the format, Sinclair is the young one born into an orderly world—unsullied, gentle, clean. He lives in this world but perceives the other. Inevitably, he is drawn into it and lives through the terrors of the streets. Alienated from the innocent world, he suffers terrible guilt for the pain he brings to his family. . . . Demian made Sinclair face his own weaknesses, his own cowardice. But there must be parting even with a good friend because that dependence can become exacting, repugnant, demoralizing. True independence, responsible action, means some isolation. Sinclair accepts that premise and ultimately achieves independence.

Hesse plays the theme through his hero in *Beneath the Wheel,* this time a tragic one. Caught up in the snarl of values, restricted by conventions which he does not dare to question, alienated in a society which doesn't respect his limitations, unable to find solutions, Herman Heilner commits suicide. So many students recognize their own sense of inadequacy, their own isolation from the world, the bitter disappointment in an education system, in this character. In this one pessimistic work—for all his others seem to reach more optimistic conclusions—there is strong, possibly too strong an identification. It helps to make students see that turning away from society, walking alone, leads to failure. He has to examine the complexity of the world; not to do so is suicidal.

Steppenwolf has extremely strong appeal for the young. Steppenwolf takes them into a mystical world and, admittedly in his magic theater sequence, into illusion that is produced by hallucination and drugs. Some have even criticized this book for young people because the fantasies, while bizarre, sound enticing. . . . Had they completed "the trip" recounted in this book for the truth, as I see it, they would see Steppenwolf emerge not half man and half wolf but as one with a unified vision of man who cannot hope for the answers in phantasmagoria but in a reality which takes all matters into account. Hesse, in this book, attacks the popular concept of the intriguing, mysterious duplicity of man. He discounts that as a deception. Man is not merely saint or profligate! . . . [As] Hesse said, there is not a single human being, not even the primitive, not even the idiot who is so conveniently simple that his being can be explained as the sum of two or three principal elements. No! Man consists of a hundred or a thousand selves, not two. His life oscilates, as everyone else's does, not merely between two poles, such as the body and the spirit, the saint and the sinner, but between thousands and thousands. (pp. 982-83)

From my point of view, *Narcissus and Goldmund* is the richest novel Hesse wrote. His keen insights to the complexities of life entice the reader to outward exploration of the whole range of beauty and depravity that man encounters; his understanding of man's emotional turmoil pulls inwardly towards a responsiveness to the symbolic truth of the search for meaning in a paradoxical world. Narcissus and Goldmund represent the basic worlds that Hesse plays out: the intellectual and the sensual, the possibilities of withdrawal or involvement, and the ultimate union of the aesthetic and the practical.

Man's life and terrors are explored in all of Hesse's works, but the strength in them is that he reaffirms some basic aspects which not only have served

humanity in the past but which are supportive for the future. He eliminates those that have hamstrung us to a feudal culture. He releases us for an attack upon technology which destroys individuality. He makes us believe there is hope for those who will not be button-controlled, gene-controlled, and that there may be a culture for the mandarins of the future. (p. 984)

Esther C. Gropper, "The Disenchanted Turn to Hesse," in *English Journal,* Vol. 61, No. 7, October, 1972, pp. 979-84.

RUSSELL A. BERMAN
(essay date 1986)

[In the following excerpt, Berman discusses the role of cultural modernism in bourgeois society in *Der Steppenwolf.*]

In *Steppenwolf,* Hesse presents the fictional notes of his hero, Harry Haller, a highly educated European intellectual troubled by the crisis of modern western culture. His essayistic reflections on the modernization of everyday life, the decline of the arts, and the flawed structure of the bourgeois personality are interspersed with a curious personal history. With the help of mysterious figures, Haller makes his way on a pilgrim's progress through a perfunctory established culture, devoid of meaning, to a new organization of cultural life.

In Hesse's account the reification of established culture encompasses both a monumentalization of the literary legacy and, as both cause and effect of this element, a mechanization of life forms. Cultural material loses its vitality, just as middle-class normalcy grows increasingly rigid. With his characteristic moroseness, Haller complains:

> All our striving, all our culture, all our beliefs, all our joy and pleasure in life—already sick and soon to be buried too. Our whole civilization was a cemetery where Jesus Christ and Socrates, Mozart and Haydn, Dante and Goethe were but the indecipherable names on moldering stones; and the mourners who stood round affecting a pretence of sorrow would give much to believe in these inscriptions that once were holy or at least to utter one heartfelt word of grief and despair about this world that is no more. And nothing was left them but the embarrassed grimaces of a company round a grave.

Cultural possessions exist solely as a petrified forest, hardened relics of a formerly vibrant world for which contemporary recipients cannot even mourn authentically, so desiccated has their affective sensibility become. Social life assumes a perfunctory character; its forms are maintained and respected, but they are devoid of immanent meaning, and the participants are "embarrassed" at their own acquiescence, even though they never call it into question. The mechanical constitution of society which systematically excludes emotional depth and genuine happiness goes hand in hand with the desecration of culture: in place of genuine holiness, Hesse pinpoints a sham cultic reverence.

Hesse concretizes this abstract diagnosis of contemporary society in the episode of Haller's visit to a professor, the representative of established culture. Haller leaves no doubt as to his contempt for the formal character of social life: "it is all compulsory, mechanical and against the grain, and it could all be done or left undone just as well by machines." The critique of merely formal existence that lacks inner substance or an authentically experiential dimension is repeated in the description of the host. Haller regards the invitation and the evening as fundamentally empty, and the professor himself becomes the cipher for a senseless activity carried on without reflection and without meaning. He pursues his arcane research with mechanical regularity. Now, however, Hesse augments the critique of formal existence with a specifically political dimension by presenting the professor as right-wing mandarin. He is not only the automaton of an absurd existence, hopelessly lost in books, but also the racist reactionary with a taste for culture:

> There he lives, I thought, and carries on his labor year by year, reads and annotates texts, seeks for analogies between western Asiatic and Indian mythologies, and it satisfies him, because he believes in the value of it all. He believes in the studies whose servant he is; he believes in the value of mere knowledge and its acquisition, because he believes in progress and evolution. He has not been through the war, nor is he acquainted with the shattering of the foundations of thought by Einstein (that, thinks he, only concerns the mathematicians). He sees nothing of the preparations for the next war that are going on all around him. He hates Jews and Communists. He is a good, unthinking, happy child, who takes himself seriously; and, in fact, he is much to be envied.

The text relies on the tension between the representation of bourgeois culture and the standards by which it is measured: not only allegedly superior values but a fuller and therefore superior sense of life. Hesse draws on a vitalist critique of Wilhelmine society, asserting that modern civilization has lost touch with the original, creative forces of life.

By holding up a purportedly empty scholarly rigor to derision, Hesse as Haller denounces the established wing of contemporary cultural life which still insists on an immanent significance to cultural production. Yet "mere knowledge," part of mere life, is not enough, and Hesse links it directly to two other implic-

itly anachronistic liberal values, progress and evolution. Furthermore, he underscores the conservative character of this knowledge, a remnant of Wilhelmine liberalism in the Weimar Republic, by having the professor ignore the intellectual force driving the modernization of culture, just as, in his ivory-tower manner, he ignores the imminent political catastrophe. Thus the cult of "mere knowledge," with its willingness to separate scholarly activity in particular and cultural activity in general from the allegedly more authentic concerns evident to the vitalist consciousness of the novel, leads first to an otherworldly naiveté and ignorance concerning contemporary developments, and then to an authoritarian personality and concomitant militarist politics. The same linkage that was apparent in a rudimentary form in [Robert Musil's] *Young Törless* is radicalized and made explicit here. Reified culture distorted Törless' growth and made him susceptible to the sadistic gang, while the professor, because of the mechanical culture of which he is a cipher, transforms that sadism into a real political program.

Hesse argues that monumental culture and ideology are interrelated. The culture industry is not a matter primarily of the mass-marketing of popular art but of the transformation of social relations through cultural objects in order to maintain the stability of postliberal capitalism. Culture loses its autonomous status and is integrated directly into the ideological apparatus, and this integration applies as much to the treasures of high culture as it does to popular forms. Its representations express the system of authority and the signs of power, while the purported cultural material itself sinks into the background. Consider Haller's account of a cultural icon in the professor's home:

> It was an engraving and it represented the poet Goethe as an old man full of character, with a finely chiseled face and a genius's mane. Neither the renowned fire of his eyes nor the lonely and tragic expression beneath the courtly whitewash was lacking. To this the artist had given special care, and he had succeeded in combining the elemental force of the old man with a somewhat professional makeup of self-discipline and righteousness, without prejudice to his profundity; and had made of him, all in all, a really charming old gentleman, fit to adorn any drawing room. No doubt this portrait was no worse than others of its description. It was much the same as all those representations by careful craftsmen of saviors, apostles, heroes, thinkers and statesmen. Perhaps I found it exasperating only because of a certain pretentious virtuosity. In any case, and whatever the cause, this empty and self-satisfied presentation of the aged Goethe shrieked at me at once as a fatal discord, exasperated and oppressed as I was already. It told me that I ought never to have come. Here fine Old Masters and the Nation's Great Ones were at home, not Steppenwolves.

The "Steppenwolves" are those who, like the narrator, have grown disaffected with middle-class society without having found a new home or a stable identity. Haller's hostility toward the professor and the portrait corresponds to Hesse's critique of an inauthentic bourgeois culture. Haller insults his host by articulating his contempt for the engraving, which turns out to be a family heirloom, and the incident quickly puts an end to the visit. In this passage, which moves from an aesthetic account of the representation of Goethe through comments on the genre in general to social and political conclusions, Hesse retraces the argumentative connection between cultural reification and social crisis. None of the features recognized in the image is treated as authentic; all are clichés, the obligatory emblemata of the patron saint of national culture: the "chiseled face," "genius's mane," "renowned fire of his eyes," and "lonely and tragic expression." Thus Hesse identifies this portrait with others of its ilk; Goethe hangs in all the drawing rooms of the bourgeoisie, and this is the way he always looks. This constant appearance has nothing to do with the historical personage or with the character of the literary texts, but solely with the bourgeoisie, which remakes its poets in its own image in order to reassure itself of its own legitimacy. Culture loses its authentic substance. Haller cries out against this insipid comprehension of literature when he rejects the "empty and self-satisfied presentation" of the poet. Yet the emptiness is no vacuum; the constellation of clichés sets up a formula for genius as the concurrence of discipline, fire, and tragedy, categories that slide from cultural representation into belligerent politics. Haller realizes as much in the insightful conclusion of the passage, where the ideological system transforms cultural material into an authoritarian cult of masters in which literary grandeur and political power converge. Literature becomes a cult object, and politics is aestheticized in a seamless mechanism of domination. Precisely here, however, the space for an alternative cultural practice begins to open up: established culture excludes Haller, just as the priestly teachers in *Young Törless* cast out the young prophet, and both can therefore explore counterinstitutional cultural possibilities.

The transition from the critique of established cultural forms to the investigation of a new practice occurs immediately after the departure from the professor's home. Haller's exit amounts to a denunciation of monumentalized culture which has no relation to the ultimate concerns of life, and his compulsive oscillation between contempt for the bourgeoisie and desire for its security seems to be finally broken. The exploration of an alternative organization of aesthetic experience ensues under the dual leadership of Hermine, Haller's female alter ego, who guides him through an artistic demimonde, and the musician Pablo, who introduces him to phantasy and hallucinations.

In place of the traditional values associated with the professor, Hesse attempts to redefine the character of culture in both its high and its low forms. In dreams and hallucinations, Haller confronts the prototypically canonic cultural figures of Goethe and Mozart, whom he discovers to be much less cumbersome and staid than their obsequious admirers would expect. Goethe explicitly exhorts Haller to cease approaching the grand figures with excessive respect and awe and to emancipate himself from the submissive patterns associated with such a reception. In a key passage, the poet first parodies Haller's reverence for an immortal culture and then appropriates the epithet in order to overcome the strictures of bourgeois temporality. In both cases, the monumentalization of culture is denounced and the previously serious recipient is urged to recognize the primacy of humor, which breaks the spell of time-bound existence. Here and in a similar Mozart passage, Hesse presents the prescription for Haller's recovery from the painful bifurcation of bourgeois subjectivity: release from encasement in the mundane concerns of the private ego and emancipation of the soul into the immateriality of atemporal being.

Hesse describes the popular culture corollary to this eternity by having Hermine introduce Haller to the world of dance and jazz. At first he expresses total disdain for this mass culture as a symptom of social conformism, Americanism, and tastelessness, allowing Hesse to parody the same middle-class conservatism inherent in his depiction of the professor. Haller rejects the popular culture of pleasure and entertainment, populated, in his view, by the unproductive, the flirtatious, and worst of all, the carriers of an elegance that is only "second-rate"; he looks at it with a corresponding mixture of contempt and desire. Yet just as the novel records the transformation of Haller's attitude toward high culture and his discovery of authentic culture's resistance to its bourgeois marmorealization, so too does his disdain for the jazz-filled dance hall end. Pleasure and entertainment are never accepted just as such, for Hesse is too much of a moralizer to allow for simple fun. Instead, he revises the initially negative judgment of dance as just so much pleasure by transforming it into a religious experience during which a new type of individual and a new sort of social bond come to the fore during the artists' ball:

> An experience fell to my lot this night of the Ball that I had never known in all my fifty years . . . the intoxication of a general festivity, the mysterious merging of the personality in the mass, the mystic union of joy . . . A hundred times in my life I had seen examples of those whom rapture had intoxicated and released from the self, of that smile, that half-crazed absorption, of those whose heads had been turned by a common enthusiasm. I had seen it in drunken recruits and sailors, and also in great artists in the enthusiasm, perhaps, of a musical festival;

and not less in young soldiers going to war . . . I myself breathed the sweet intoxication of a common dream and of music and rhythm and wine and women—I, who had in other days so often listened with amusement, or dismal superiority, to its panegyric in the ballroom chatter of some student. I was myself no longer. My personality was dissolved in the intoxication of the festivity like salt in water.

Haller goes on to describe the universality of the erotic experience. Dancing with one woman, he dances with all, while even the barriers against homoerotic love collapse. The experience of communion mediated by music and dance breaks down all borders and differences. Individuality loses its private character, as the contours of the personality expand, until the former subject becomes merely part of a new unity, an ecstatic community, no longer atomized by egoism, time, and material concerns. Thus popular music, like the music of Mozart or the poetry of Goethe, ultimately provides access to a qualitatively different experiential dimension, homologous to Musil's aesthetic state, where the practice of culture takes on a radically new character. Haller's assurance at the novel's end that both Mozart and Pablo would wait for him does not necessarily indicate an absolute convergence of high and low culture, for the precise musical forms may remain very different. Yet Hesse is certainly attempting to outline a tentative reinstitutionalization of culture in which the character of each is redefined: high culture loses its monumentality, while low culture ceases to be superficial. Each contributes in its own way to the destruction of the bourgeois personality with its impoverished binary structure, and each engenders instead the new cultural community, ecstatic and emotive, no longer rational or egocentric. More so than in *Young Törless,* the modernist revolt in *Steppenwolf,* which constitutes the substance of the novel's program, thematizes its social consequences as the search for a new type of collectivity, outside the logic of market exchange, carried by a charismatic spirit. In the enthusiasm of the dance, a utopian communism is inscribed, just as the thematic critique of individuality reflects the prevailing postliberal social forms. Against the background of the social crisis projected onto a single personality, the redefinition of cultural institutions as the project of modernism takes shape, and this redefinition has not only an individual-psychological but also a collective-social dimension, as modernism sets out to change the world through literary innovation.

In *Young Törless,* modernist innovation was grounded in a reorganization of the personality that Musil linked to a newly discovered aesthetic dimension. In *Steppenwolf,* this modernist subjectivity is radicalized. Instead of Musil's dual structure, Hesse advocates an infinitely shattered ego, which is linked to a renewed social collective. Modernism emancipates

the individual from the desiccation of a mechanized rationality and reinvigorates the charismatic community. Both transitions are mediated by aesthetic experiences: abstractly for Törless in the encounters with the aesthetic state, and concretely for Haller in the musical episodes. Yet modernism often defines this mechanism of transition precisely within itself: it describes itself as the agent of the renewal within its own texts in an inscribed aesthetics. Though self-defining elements are evident in all literary periods, they are particularly salient in modernism where literary self-consciousness and, especially, the recognition of the function of the opponent literature of the culture industry are strongly developed. (pp. 188-95)

Russell A. Berman, "The Charismatic Novel: Robert Musil, Hermann Hesse, and Elias Canetti," in his *The Rise of the Modern German Novel: Crisis and Charisma,* Cambridge, Mass.: Harvard University Press, 1986, pp. 179-204.

JANE M. DEVYVER

(essay date 1988)

[In the excerpt below, Devyver views the major theme of *Magister Ludi* as humankind's recurring search for peace.]

[*Magister Ludi*] may be regarded as the lyrical exposition of a multiplicity of variations on basically a single theme, where, like the complex contrapuntal voices of a Bach fugue, all the developments of the themes and variations are tightly interwoven and interrelated, contributing to the overall definition of the primary theme, and concluding with three codas which succinctly recapitulate the dominant themes in three brief and less elaborate statements.

The dominant theme upon which Hesse expounds is man's perennial and archetypal quest for that serenity which proceeds from his enlightenment and resultant harmonization of polar opposites, which no longer conflict, but are perceived and experienced as aspects of a single unified whole. Hesse's chief mode of developing this theme is through the archetype of the "Wise Old Man," who is approached by a young boy who desires to serve the master as a pupil and learn from him the secrets of his wisdom and serenity. The pupil then in turn becomes a master and successor of the wise old man, to whom pupils come. However, in the exposition and development of the themes and variations, Hesse artfully harmonizes lyrical beauty and that profound depth of insight and wisdom which could only be born out of his own inner suffering in the interminable quest, together with the superb skill of an expert storyteller. The consequent achievement is the transposition of the archetypal symbols from the realm of abstract forms onto the concrete tangible stage of human life where the reader may share and vicariously participate in the process and development of the attainment of spiritual enlightenment and its product, serenity.

Upon Hesse's stage of human life we encounter Joseph Knecht, who, through the special tutelage of the Magister Musicae and the pedagogy of the Castalian Order, attains to that spiritual unity that is the goal of the pure ideal world of Castalia. Then, as the Order's most perfect embodiment of its ideals, he becomes the Magister Ludi, the Master of the Bead Game (*Glasperlenspiel*), the highest office in Castalia. This game symbolizes the highest and the most sublime goal of the intellectual elite, the harmonization of all knowledge into the perfect unity, balance, and rhythm of the Glass Bead Game. However, having achieved the perfection for which the way of truth and meditation strives, Joseph Knecht must carry it a step further than Castalia allows, but which is the logical and inevitable progression of having attained the ideal perfection. Ultimately, he must seek to harmonize the outer reality (the world outside Castalia) with the inner reality (the pure cerebral world of the intellect and spirit), and therefore is inwardly compelled to leave Castalia in order to teach in that outer world from which Castalia has virtually isolated itself.

Let us briefly look at some of the subtleties and intricacies of the development of the various major and minor themes and variations of Hesse's musical composition.

According to Carl Jung, the archetype of the Wise Old Man is "the superior master and teacher, the archetype of the spirit, who symbolizes the pre-existent meaning hidden in the chaos of life." Certainly then the form of Hesse's story, revolving as it does around the various masters of the Castalian pedagogy—the Masters of music, of the bead game, of grammar, of mathematics, and so forth, is intrinsic to the intellectual search for meaning and the spirit. Symbolically, the spiritual-intellectual quest for truth, meaning, and understanding are equated and associated with the sun, light, enlightenment, wisdom, divine spirit, and the Word. Symbolizing the human who has achieved such wisdom and spirit are various archetypal figures—the Wise Old Man, the Sage, the Master, the Teacher, the King, the Yogi, the Medicine Man, the Shaman, the Philosopher.

However, the aged gray-beard Master is but one side of the dual and paradoxical nature of reality, for, as Jung instructs us,

Hesse working in his study in 1952.

archetypes are in principle paradoxical, just as for the alchemists the spirit was conceived as *"senex et iuvenus simil"*—an old man and a youth at once.

Thus the nature of the archetypal theme requires that the master have a young pupil-son-disciple-servant in order to provide the paradoxical balancing element.

The play on words and names by Hesse are artful and provide a more subtle harmony of paradox. The German word, *knecht*, means both servant and knave. Thus our author gives in his main character's name two opposing elements to the Wise Old Man archetype. As a servant, we have the pupil-youth-servant-famulus (Knecht's name in the second Incarnation, "The Father Confessor") counter-balancing the Wise Old Man, as well as the opposing component of the wise master— the trickster or knavish element. As a youth and pupil, Knecht provides the balancing factor for an external Sage, the Magister Musicae. In later life he symbolically expresses through his name the unity and harmony of the two opposites within himself when he becomes a Magister, and is simultaneously master and servant. Knecht is well aware of the ambiguous experience of becoming less free the higher one rises in the Castalian hierarchy, so that finally, as the perfect master he must become the perfect servant—Magister-Knecht. As Knecht struggles to bring into balance the master-servant polar opposites within himself, so does he correspondingly wrestle to reconcile the 'freedom' of the master with the 'slavery' of the servant. Likewise does he experience the natural paradox of the true magister-master's desire to teach and of the true magister-pupil's desire to learn. Knecht's post as Magister Ludi thwarted the balancing of the teacher-student duality and was one of the influencing factors in Knecht's leaving his high post and Castalia.

Hesse also displays subtle artistry in his choice of first name for his main character—Joseph. The Joseph prototype is Joseph in Egypt, who has a similar life story as Joseph Knecht. Joseph-ben-Jacob, more or less orphaned when sold by his brothers, was taken to a foreign country (Egypt/Castalia) as a servant to a Wise Old Man (the Pharoah/the Magister Musicae). There he resisted the temptations of the unenlightened worldly life (Pharoah's wife/doubts and disputes with Designori), and after he proved himself through the tests of the initiation experience of being plunged into the chasm of death and darkness (prison/elite schools), he re-emerged victoriously into the sunlight due to his inner superior spirituality and wisdom (perceiving the meaning hidden behind the veil—of the Pharoah's dream/of the Bead Game). Then, through wisdom, insight, and inner spirituality, he was elevated by the Master (the Pharoah/the magisterium, especially the Magister Musicae) to a high post in the hierarchy, where he excelled in the management of the affairs of the society in which he served as Master. Joseph in Egypt was reunited with his eleven brothers and his father Jacob. There is also a Jacob in Joseph Knecht's life, Father Jacobus, who sired Joseph's second birth into the world through the study of the history of the 'secular world' outside Castalia. A further paradox is implicit here, since the usual 'second birth' refers to a spiritual birth, but here it is the reverse. Joseph Knecht's return to the world outside Castalia is analagous to the other Joseph's being reunited with his biological family.

Hesse's choice of name for the elite Order and Province, Castalia, is also highly significant, for in its similarity to the word 'castle,' it points to both the positive and negative aspects of the elite distillation of the intellect in a community of scholars. What is the symbolism of a castle? Most everyone is charmed by a castle: usually elevated on a beautiful hill, it tempts by its cool, reserved isolation from the banalities of the world, by its self-sufficiency, strength, and endurance, and by the fanciful tales associated with a castle of knights and noble men and women. The castle, by its shape and location on a hill-top, shares symbolic value with menhirs, obelisks, columns, high towers, and the tops of sacred mountains, first as places where humans reach out towards the celestial and divine, seeking to communicate with and understand the unity of Cosmic Being, and second, as places where God talks with humans and veils/reveils-reveals his dazzling splendor which conceals him from humans, while seeking to illuminate people's mind and spirit. Nevertheless, a person cannot remain continually in the pure celestial light of the top of the holy mountain, for it is too dazzling. The person must return to the everyday life of the people below, to show them the way of enlightenment. Therefore, the inherent danger of Castalia is the sunstroke which blinds the inhabitants to its polar opposite—the people in the world—and how necessary it is to harmonize the two polarities. A castle may be enticing, but its very isolation can be suffocating, like a castle's dungeon or the abyss of the deep.

There remains for us to consider two very important expositions of Hesse's theme: the *Glasperlenspiel* and music. The original German title that Hesse gave to his novel was *Glasperlenspiel* (glass-pearls-game). What is glass? Glass is both reflecting and transparent. Glass reflects light and images, and thus, metaphorically, points to mental reflection and thought, and to the ascendancy of light and order over chaos—e.g., the state of darkness where no reflection is possible, and thus where there are no images, only disorder and the void of nonbeing. Glass, then, reflects the pure light of wisdom onto the beholder. Insofar as glass is also transparent, it further signifies the quality of enlightenment which sees through and penetrates the surface of things to see the inner light of spirit and meaning which resides in and permeates existence. Hesse connects 'glass' to 'pearls.' What is a pearl? A pearl is a round, white jewel, a gem of great treasure, whose existence is enigmatic and paradoxical, for it is seemingly mysteriously created in a sea shell as though by parthenogenesis. The pearl represents the enigmatic purity of the complete harmonization of opposite cosmic forces—of life/death, good/evil, male/female, parent/child, love/hate, suffering/joy. The pearl furthermore is the mystic center, the Self. In its roundness it symbolizes the perfect reconciliation of opposites, the round oneness from which all life emanates and to which all life is to return by traversing the path full circle. The round is the center point of the cosmic wheel, the center of the cosmic cross, and the *via crucis*. The pearl is the priceless treasure that resides within each person, the treasure given to the person who brings into unity the disparate warring forces within oneself, through the struggle which Jung calls the 'process of individuation.' This symbol of the unified self, the pearl, in the Bead Game is made of glass. There are two ways in which we may interpret this. We can combine the double symbolism of pearl and glass, and interpret the glass pearl to mean that the pearl of the Self, when claimed by the individual, is transparent, in that the light may pass outside oneself as the light of the world. Another interpretation is that since the pearls are not genuine, but artificially made of glass, we have an inherent and paradoxical warning that the game and Castalia are artificial and not all they appear to be.

But in what way are these pearls of glass a game? Many explanations come to mind. The *glasperlenspiel* of the Castalians was a microcosm in which the infinite varieties of perfect harmonious combinations of pure distilled knowledge danced and played a cosmic game in which all observers and participants joined in contemplation and meditation. The Game was the absolute pinnacle of Castalian existence at its best, but like all attempts to institutionalize—in order to preserve the pure distillation of divine wisdom, spirit, and light—it was a game, an esoteric and divine liturgy, a microcosmic crystallization of Reality, but ultimately a game, because it was not the goal itself, but pointed beyond itself to the Ultimate Reality—Cosmic Being. The subline *glasperlenspiel* symbolizes the divine light and points to and leads one to one's own pearl within oneself, but the game is dangerous when it comes to be regarded as an end in and of itself. Thus it is an esoteric game of the highest order, but ultimately dispensable, replaceable, and reformable. Such is what Joseph Knecht awesomely discovers when he becomes the Master of the (Glass) Bead Game, for he has to transcend even this, the sublimest of sublime cosmic games.

However, in a paradoxical way, can we not view the whole of learning and wisdom as a game in which the players are losers (*lusors* = players)? Just as the necessary polar components of wisdom and the master are folly and the knave/trickster, perhaps likewise the game is the necessary component of existence that keeps us from taking reality too seriously. Perhaps the problem of Castalia was that it forgot to play, and the higher up in the hierarchy one went, the more playfulness of heart was forgotten. Is *homo ludens* (playing man) ultimately ludicrous or of ultimate seriousness? Who is the most ludicrous—the one who plays at playing, or the one who plays too seriously?

Another concern of the highest magnitude in *Magister Ludi* and for the Magister Ludi is music. Music played an important role in the Bead Game. But whereas Knecht could imagine life without the Bead Game, without music life would not be possible. Music, indeed, is infinite in its ramifications and vast symbolism. It represents the cosmic harmony and unity inherent in its multiplicity of parts, yet somehow music also shares in that cosmic reality and imparts its serenity and balance to its listeners and players. Although all the various notes, intervals, and rhythms have specific symbolic values, mostly as associated with numerology, yet, without a doubt, the total sum of music transcends the sum of its components. Celestial beings play music continuously: music never ceases from the celestial sphere, for it is the harmonic rhythm of the ordered unity of the cosmos. Yet to terrestrial beings who void their lives of the secrets of music and have forgotten how to play, it is as though "the earth was without form and void, and darkness was upon the face of the deep" (Gen. 1:2). To such a person the *homo ludens* indeed appears as a ludicrous fool. Such a person could never be admitted as an initiate to the secret wisdom of play, music, or the Bead Game. It is appropriate, then, that the art of the Bead Game was a secret to which one could be initiated only after the many years it took to master its wisdom, much as it takes many years of apprenticeship to the secrets of music before one is transformed into a master of unified harmony and balance.

There is much more to be played with here, such as the dualities of Master and knave/trickster. Does a Master play tricks, or just play? If God is the supreme prototype of the Sage, does he play tricks on the world and on us humans? Does the Wise Old Man play tricks on God or humans—or on himself—with his artistry? Or could the trickster element be an earlier stage of the development of the Master which must be transcended by the Master, lest he remain simply a magician? On the other hand, perhaps the trickster element points to the essential need to maintain a playfulness of heart in order to attain to true wisdom. And the glass pearls—are they a trick? Only marbles? Are we being duped by a con-artist with his shell and bead game, which is nothing but walnut shells and a pea or marble? Are we duped into believing in such things as time, space, movement, reality, life, and death? Do they belong to the 'real' or 'fantasy' world? There are so many paradoxical questions. (pp. 487-95)

[There] is something strange and wrong about Castalia, we must remember. They were not allowed to create anything of their own—music, art, poetry, literature, or children (there were no women in Castalia). They could only vicariously partake of creativity through the creative anguish of others, through their cultural predecessors who lived and created prior to the ideal age of Castalia. Creativity is accompanied by suffering, or ecstasy and exhilaration, neither of which existed in Castalia, because passion did not exist in Castalia. Perhaps their creativity died because they took their games of glass beads so seriously that they forgot it was a game, and forgot to play. Perhaps it was because they got stuck at one place of the wheel—the cir-

cle of growth—and the game froze. Perhaps it was forgotten that one must continually transcend previous transcending, that once the goal is reached, it is immediately lost to a further goal, that the process is ever-becoming, ever-reforming/transforming, ever-transcending. Perhaps Joseph Knecht only truly became the wise master when he discovered that the play, the game, and the dance still go on—and he followed Sidney Carter's Lord of the Dance who sang: "Dance then, wherever you may be, I am the Lord of the Dance, said he, and I'll lead you all wherever you may be, and I'll lead you all in the dance, said he." (p. 496)

Jane M. Devyver, "Symbol and Paradox in Hermann Hesse's 'Magister Ludi'," in *The Midwest Quarterly,* Vol. XXIX, No. 4, Summer, 1988, pp. 487-96.

SOURCES FOR FURTHER STUDY

Boulby, Mark. *Hermann Hesse: His Mind and Art.* Ithaca, N.Y.: Cornell University Press, 1967, 338 p.

Contains detailed examinations of Hesse's major novels, emphasizing structural patterns and the importance of such early works as *Peter Camenzind* and *Unterm Rad.*

Field, George Wallis. *Hermann Hesse.* New York: Twayne Publishers, 1970, 198 p.

Critical and biographical study.

Freedman, Ralph. *Hermann Hesse: Pilgrim of Crisis.* New York: Pantheon Books, 1978, 432 p.

Attempts to demythologize Hesse by asserting that he "continues to be a force of considerable magnitude as he reflects the uncertainties and betrayals of our history from the late nineteenth century to the present—a poet of crisis who achieved his identity as a pilgrim into the inner life."

Mileck, Joseph. *Hermann Hesse: Life and Art.* Berkeley and Los Angeles: University of California Press, 1978, 397 p.

Attempts to reveal "Hesse the person and his world of ideas" by "characterizing his writings in both their substance and form, and drawing attention to the intimate relationship between his life and his art."

Rose, Ernst. *Faith from the Abyss: Hermann Hesse's Way from Romanticism to Modernity.* New York: New York University Press, 1965, 175 p.

Focuses on the relationship between Hesse's life and work.

Ziolkowski, Theodore. *The Novels of Hermann Hesse: A Study in Theme and Structure.* Princeton, N.J.: Princeton University Press, 1965, 375 p.

Structural and thematic analysis of Hesse's major novels, concentrating on his gradual shift from romantic aestheticism to "a new existential commitment to the world."

Gerard Manley Hopkins

1844-1889

English poet.

INTRODUCTION

*H*opkins, a crafter of both poetry and poetic theory, has elicited extensive study and appreciative criticism from a wide spectrum of scholars in the twentieth century. Frequently dealing with religious themes and evoking imagery from nature, the poems of Hopkins are distinguished by stylistic innovations, most notably his striking diction and pioneering use of a meter he termed "sprung rhythm." His radical departures from poetic traditions, coupled with his reluctance to publish his writings, caused his works to be almost completely unknown in the nineteenth century. However, critics today agree that Hopkins wrote some of the finest and most complex poems in the English language, and he is now firmly established as an outstanding innovator and a major force in the development of modern poetry.

The oldest of Manley and Kate Hopkins's nine children, Hopkins was born in Stratford, Essex, and raised in a prosperous and cultured environment. Beginning in 1854, he attended the Cholmeley Grammar School in Highgate, where he excelled in his courses and won a school poetry competition. In 1863 he obtained a scholarship to Balliol College at Oxford University. His experiences at Oxford had a profound influence on his life; there he pursued his interests in poetry, music, sketching, and art criticism, established important friendships, and, most importantly, came under the influence of John Henry Newman, a leading figure in the Oxford Movement and an important Catholic apologist and educator. In 1866, after months of soul-searching, Hopkins resolved to leave the Church of England and become a Roman Catholic. The following year he graduated from Oxford with high academic honors and accepted a teaching position in Birmingham. Then, in the spring of 1868, he decided to become a Jesuit priest. He burned all his early poems, vowing to give up writing and dedicate himself fully to his religious calling. He entered Manresa House in Roehampton in the fall of 1868 to undergo the rigorous training of the Jesuit novitiate, and in the following years went on to study philosophy at St. Mary's Hall, Stonyhurst, and theology at St. Bueno's College, Wales. After his ordination in 1877, Hopkins served as a priest in London, Oxford, Liverpool, and Glasgow parishes and taught classics at the Jesuit Stonyhurst College. In 1884 he was appointed a fellow in classics at the Royal University of Ireland and professor of Greek at the University College in Dublin, positions he retained until his death from typhoid in 1889.

Although he was a dedicated priest and teacher, most biographers agree that Hopkins was not temperamentally suited to his work assignments. As time passed, he became progressively more isolated, depressed, and plagued with ill-health and spiritual doubts, particularly during his years in Ireland. Many writers on Hopkins have suggested that a major source of his unhappiness was his difficulty reconciling his priestly duties with his poetic impulse. For several years after destroying his early poems, Hopkins wrote no poetry except for a few minor occasional pieces on religious themes. But in 1876, with the approval of his superior, he returned to writing verse, strictly limiting the time he spent on composition.

The first work Hopkins produced after he resumed writing, "The Wreck of the Deutschland," was an account of the widely publicized loss at sea of a German ship, in which he also examines his spiritual struggles. In this poem, Hopkins introduced the revolutionary sprung rhythm he is credited with originating. Unlike conventional poetic meter, in which the rhythm is based on regular alternation of stressed and unstressed syllables, the meter of sprung rhythm is determined by the number of stressed syllables alone. Thus, in a line where few unstressed syllables are used, the movement is slow and heavy, while the use of many unstressed syllables creates a rapid, light effect. Hopkins claimed that this irregular meter appears in classical literature, Old English and Welsh poetry, nursery rhymes, and the works of William Shakespeare and John Milton. Moreover, he valued it as "nearest to the rhythm of prose, that is the native and natural rhythm of speech." "The Wreck of the Deutschland" is generally considered the first English work written primarily in sprung rhythm.

In addition to experimenting with meter in this poem, Hopkins employed several other poetic techniques for which he is known. His diction is characterized by unusual compound words, coined phrases, and terms borrowed from dialect, further complicated by intentional ambiguities and multiple meanings. In addition, he frequently utilized elliptical phrasing, compression, internal rhyme, assonance, alliteration, and meta-

phor. "The Wreck of the Deutschland" also introduces the central philosophical concerns of Hopkins's mature poetry. The poem reflects both Hopkins's belief in the doctrine that humans are created to praise God and his commitment to the Jesuit practices of meditation and spiritual self-examination. The teachings of the thirteenth-century Franciscan scholar John Duns Scotus likewise influenced his works. From Duns Scotus's teaching of "haecceitas," or the "thisness" of all things, Hopkins developed the concepts of "inscape," a term he coined to describe the inward, distinctive, essential quality of a thing, and "instress," which refers to the force that gives a natural object its inscape and allows that inscape to be seen and expressed by the poet.

After completing "The Wreck of the Deutschland," Hopkins continued to experiment with style, language, and meter. He is perhaps most widely known for his shorter poems on nature, many of which were written in the early years of his priesthood. In such celebrations of natural beauty as "Spring," "Inversnaid," "Pied Beauty," "God's Grandeur," "The Starlight Night," and his best-known sonnet, "The Windhover," Hopkins strove to capture the inscape of creation as a means of knowing and praising God. Other poems, including "Felix Randal," "Tom's Garland," and "Harry Ploughman," examine the inscape of common working people, while an unfinished poem on Margaret Clitheroe and a drama fragment on St. Winefred deal with Christian martyrs. Hopkins's last works, known as the "terrible sonnets," express spiritual struggle. In "No Worst, There Is None," "Carrion Comfort," "I Wake and Feel the Fell of Dark, Not Day," and "Thou Art Indeed Just, Lord," Hopkins chronicled the sense of sterility, isolation, and despair he experienced toward the end of his life. In the sonnets "Spelt from Sibyl's Leaves" and "That Nature Is a Heraclitean Fire," he works toward a resolution of his spiritual questionings. Although Hopkins feared that his poetic power was declining in his final years, the terrible sonnets are highly regarded by critics for Hopkins's unguarded self-revelation and mastery of the sonnet form.

None of Hopkins's major works were published in his lifetime. He submitted "The Wreck of the Deutschland" to the Jesuit periodical the *Month* in 1876, but it was refused, as was his next offering, a simpler poem on a similar theme, "The Loss of the Eurydice." After the rejections of the "two wrecks," as he referred to them, Hopkins submitted a selection of his sonnets to an anthology but once again was refused. Despite the urgings of his friends, he was unwilling to make any further attempts to have his poems printed. Following Hopkins's death, Robert Bridges, his literary executor, arranged for a few of his simpler works to appear in verse anthologies. The selections by Hopkins in these works received little notice, however, except in Catholic circles where "Heaven Haven" and "The Habit of Perfection" were praised for their religious content.

In 1918 Bridges compiled and published *Poems of Gerard Manley Hopkins*, the first collection of the poet's works. Early critical response to the volume generally echoed Bridges's explanatory notes in which he condemned the "obscurities," "oddities," and "faults of taste" in Hopkins's verse. A few reviewers of the collection praised Hopkins's expression of religious feeling, but the predominant response was one of bewildered incomprehension. In the 1920s, the poems found a small but select following among such literary figures as Laura Riding, Robert Graves, I. A. Richards, and William Empson. Early proponents of a close reading of the poetic text, these critics valued the complexity of Hopkins's works and his stylistic originality. The 1930s saw an enormous growth of interest in Hopkins's works. In that decade his letters and personal papers were first published, together with a second, enlarged edition of the poems. Among the young poets of the 1930s, Hopkins was revered as a model; his influence is evident in the works of writers as diverse as Dylan Thomas, W. H. Auden, Cecil Day Lewis, and Robert Lowell. With the centenary of Hopkins's birth, numerous critical essays and appreciations appeared, and since that time his works have continued to attract extensive analysis. Hopkins's writings have proved highly suited to New Critical approaches emphasizing explanation and interpretation of individual poems with particular attention to their style, rhythm, and imagery. His poems have also received the scrutiny of poststructuralist and deconstructionist critics, who consider his use of deliberately ambiguous language of profound interest.

Hopkins has been the subject of numerous studies undertaken from a wide range of critical perspectives, and though a few commentators maintain that he is essentially a minor author because of the narrowness of his experience, he is now regarded as one of the greatest poets of the Victorian era. Acclaimed for his powerful influence on modern poetry, Hopkins continues to be praised as an innovative and revolutionary stylist who wrote some of the most challenging poems in the English language on the subjects of the self, nature, and religion.

(For further information about Hopkins's life and works, see *Dictionary of Literary Biography*, Vols. 35, 57; and *Nineteenth-Century Literature Criticism*, Vol. 17.)

CRITICAL COMMENTARY

HERBERT READ

(essay date 1933)

[Read was a prolific English poet, critic, and novelist. In the general comments on Hopkins's poetry excerpted here, he counters critical reservations expressed by Robert Bridges in his 1918 critical edition of Hopkins's poems and examines such central aspects of Hopkins's poetic philosophy as his metrical theory, vocabulary, imagery, and subject matter.]

Hopkins is only just emerging from the darkness to which his original genius condemned him. It is a familiar story; nothing could have made Hopkins's poetry popular in his day: it was necessary that it should first be absorbed by the sensibility of a new generation of poets, and by them masticated to a suitable pulp for less sympathetic minds. That process is going on apace now, and when the history of the last decade of English poetry comes to be written by a dispassionate critic, no influence will rank in importance with that of Gerard Manley Hopkins.

Hopkins himself was aware of the quality of his genius, and therefore knew what to expect from his contemporaries. (pp. 45-6)

Probably the only one of his small circle who understood him fully was his fellow-poet, Richard Watson Dixon. Dixon, writing to Hopkins to urge him to write more poems, refers to their quality as "something that I cannot describe, but know to myself by the inadequate word *terrible pathos*—something of what you call temper in poetry: a right temper which goes to the point of the terrible: the terrible crystal. Milton is the only one else who has anything like it, and he has it in a totally different way; he has it through indignation, through injured majesty, which is an inferior thing. . . . " Here is a full understanding which we do not find in the published letters and writings of others who knew Hopkins—not in Coventry Patmore, who floundered in deep astonishment, and not in his closest friend and final editor, the late Poet Laureate. To contend that Dr. Bridges did not understand the poetry of Hopkins would not be quite fair; he understood the craftsmanship of it, and was sensible to the beauty. But there seems to have been an essential lack of sympathy—not of personal sympathy, but of sympathy in

Principal Works

Poems of Gerard Manley Hopkins (poetry) 1918; also published as Poems of Gerard Manley Hopkins [enlarged editions], 1930, 1948, 1956, 1961, 1967

The Correspondence of Gerard Manley Hopkins and Richard Watson Dixon (letters) 1935

The Letters of Gerard Manley Hopkins to Robert Bridges (letters) 1935

The Notebooks and Papers of Gerard Manley Hopkins (diary, journal, and notes) 1937

Further Letters of Gerard Manley Hopkins (letters) 1938

The Journals and Papers of Gerard Manley Hopkins (diary, journal, and notes) 1959

The Sermons and Devotional Writings of Gerard Manley Hopkins (sermons, journals, and notes) 1959

The Poetical Works of Gerard Manley Hopkins (poetry) 1990

poetic ideals. The Preface to the notes which Dr. Bridges contributed to the first edition of the poems . . . is marked by a pedantic velleity which would be excusable only on the assumption that we are dealing with a poet of minor interest. That is, indeed, the attitude: "Please look at this odd fellow whom for friendship's sake I have rescued from oblivion." The emphasis on oddity and obscurity is quite extraordinary, and in the end all we are expected to have is a certain technical interest, leading to tolerance, and the discovery of "rare masterly beauties." Hopkins is convicted of affectation in metaphor, perversion of human feeling, exaggerated Marianism, the "naked encounter of sensualism and asceticism which hurts the **'Golden Echo',**" purely artistic wantonness, definite faults of style, incredible childishness in rhyming—at times disagreeable and vulgar and even comic; and generally of deliberate and unnecessary obscurity. Everything, in such an indictment, must depend on the judge's set of laws, and in criticising Dr. Bridge's treatment of Hopkins, I am wishing to say no more than that the Poet Laureate applied a code which was not that of the indicted. The lack of sympathy is shown precisely in this fact. Hopkins was a revolutionary; that is to say, his values were so fundamentally opposed to current practices that only by an effort of the imagination could they be comprehended. Once they are comprehended, many apparent faults are justified, and there is no reason to dwell on any of them.

Hopkins was serene and modest in his self-confidence. He could admit the criticism of his friends, and yet quietly persist in his perverseness. (pp. 46-8)

A full exposition of Hopkins's theories would take us far into a discussion of the historical development of poetry. Let me briefly indicate their main features. There is in the first place a metrical theory, of the greatest importance. Hopkins's poems are written in a mixture of what he called Running Rhythm and Sprung Rhythm. Running rhythm, or common English rhythm, is measured in feet of either two or three syllables, and each foot has one principal stress or accent. Hopkins preferred to take the stress always first, for purposes of scanning; but obviously that is only a question of convenience. To vary this running rhythm, poets have introduced various licences, of which the chief are reversed feet and reversed rhythm. If you pursue these variations far enough, the original measure will seem to disappear, and you will have the measure called by Hopkins sprung rhythm. In this measure each foot has one stress, which falls on the only syllable, if there is only one, or on the first if there are more than one. Normally there should not be more than four syllables to a foot, and the feet are regular measured in time. Their seeming inequality is made up by pause and stressing.

In general, sprung rhythm, as Hopkins claimed, is the most natural of things. He tabulated the reasons:

(1) It is the rhythm of common speech and of written prose, when rhythm is perceived in them.

(2) It is the rhythm of all but the most monotonously regular music, so that in the words of choruses and refrains and in song closely written to music it arises.

(3) It is found in nursery rhymes, weather saws, and so on; because, however these may have been once made in running rhythm, the terminations having dropped off by the change of language, the stresses come together and so the rhythm is sprung.

(4) It arises in common verse when reversed or counterpointed, for the same reason.

These reasons need no further comment; but there are two historical considerations to note. Sprung rhythm is not an innovation; it is the rhythm natural to English verse before the Renaissance. It is the rhythm of *Piers Ploughman* and of Skelton. Greene was the last writer to use it, and since the Elizabethan age, as Hopkins claimed, there is not a single, even short poem, in which sprung rhythm is employed as a principle of scansion. The other observation Hopkins could not make, because it is part of our history since his time. It is that the principles contended for by Hopkins on the basis of scholarship and original tradition (but only *contended* for on that basis: he actually wrote as he felt, and then went to history to justify himself) are in many essentials identical with the principles contended for by those modern poets already mentioned (whose advocacy and practice of 'free verse' is also based on feeling and intuition rather than historical analysis.)

A second characteristic of Hopkins's poetry which while not so original, is yet a cause of strangeness, may be found in his vocabulary. No true poet hesitates to invent words when his sensibility finds no satisfaction in current phrases. Words like 'shive-light' and 'firedint' are probably such inventions. But most of Hopkins's innovations are in the nature of new combinations of existing words, sometimes contracted similes, or metaphors, and in this respect his vocabulary has a surface similarity to that of James Joyce. Examples of such phrases are to be found in almost every poem: 'the beadbonny ash,' 'fallowbootfellow,' 'windlaced,' 'churlsgrace,' 'footfretted,' 'clammyish lashtender combs,' 'wildworth,' and so on. Commoner phrases like 'beetle-browed' or 'star-eyed' are of the same kind, made in the same way, and freely used by him. Here again an explanation would take us far beyond the immediate subject; for it concerns the original nature of poetry itself—the emotional sound-complex uttered in primitive self-expression. . . . Poetry can be renewed only by discovering the original sense of word formation: the words do not come pat in great poetry, but are torn out of the context of experience; they are not in the poet's mind, but in the nature of things he describes. (pp. 49-52)

Of Hopkins's imagery, there is not much in general to be said, but that 'not much' is all. He had that acute and sharp sensuous awareness essential to all great poets. He was physically aware of textures, surfaces, colours, patterns of every kind; aware acutely of earth's diurnal course, or growth and decay of animality in man and of vitality in all things. Everywhere there is passionate apprehension, passionate expression and equally that passion for form without which these other passions are spendthrift. But the form is inherent in the passion. For, as Emerson remarked with his occasional deep insight, "it is not metres, but a metre-making argument, that makes a poem—a thought so passionate and alive, that, like the spirit of a plant or an animal, it has an architecture of its own, and adorns nature with a new thing".

The thought in Hopkins's poetry tends to be overlaid by the surface beauty. But the thought is very real there, and as the idiom becomes more accepted, will emerge in its variety and strength. There is no explicit system, nor need there be in great poetry. Perhaps the only essential quality is a sense of values, and this Hopkins had in a fervid degree. He was a convert to Roman Catholicism, and might have ranged widely in intellectual curiosity had he not preferred to submit to authority. One of his contemporaries at St. Beuno's Theological College wrote of him:

I have rarely known anyone who sacrificed so much in undertaking the yoke of religion. If I had known him outside, I should have said that his love of speculation and originality of thought would make it almost impossible for him to submit his intellect to authority.

Perhaps in actual intensity his poetry gained more than it lost by this step, but one cannot help regretting the curtailment it suffered in range and quantity. After joining the Church, he applied to himself a strict ascetic censorship, and apart from what he may have destroyed, deliberately refrained from writing under every wayward inspiration. (pp. 52-4)

Herbert Read, in a chapter in his *Form in Modern Poetry*, Sheed & Ward, 1933, pp. 35-55.

W. H. GARDNER
(essay date 1949)

[In the following excerpt from the conclusion to his widely respected two-volume study of Hopkins, Gardner comments on Hopkins's status as a major poet.]

When this Epilogue was first written, some ten years ago, it included the following words:

The best of the later, deeply-pondered critical studies of Hopkins . . . have all sought to establish the fact that Hopkins was not merely an interesting experimentalist and innovator in the technique of poetry; they have proved that he is entitled to be acknowledged as a complete and successful poet.

That it should still be necessary to enunciate this claim points to an unhealthy state of criticism, a tendency to pay too much attention either to the manner and technique of poetry or to the matter alone—an extraordinary inability to comprehend poetry as it really is, that almost mystical *compositum* of thought, emotion, and form.

The many pages we have ourselves devoted to the formal aspects of Hopkins's verse have been justified (in as many more pages) by the clear assumption that the importance of his new and striking manner is dependent upon the supreme value of the total poetic effect. Apart from the rare and exalted pleasure to be derived from his work, the attitudes evoked are undoubtedly conducive to the social and spiritual welfare of mankind.

Too many of the critics who have written articles on Hopkins the Revolutionary Poet, the Innovator, or the Pioneer have created a false standard of assessment; they have, in Fr. Lahey's odd but true phrase, "prescinded from the well-spring of Hopkins's poetry". But this well-spring was not solely his religious ideals: it was that region in the subconscious mind where all the hidden tributaries of sensory experience met and mingled with his deepest intellectual convictions. To a degree not realized by many who have deplored his "frustration" and "self-laceration", the aesthetic and purely poetic values of Hopkins were ontologically or mystically bound up with his strong religious emotions.

Hence the poetic *compositum* or total poetic effect of Hopkins's work can be known and felt only by those who acknowledge God and the supernatural basis of life, and who at the same time appreciate the natural and traditional foundations of Hopkins's rhythm and style. All other readers may hold and cherish some *part* of this poet, but they cannot claim to comprehend and expound his complete personality, experience, and significance.

Hopkins's great work as a rhythmist has a unique absolute and historical value. Its unique absolute value lies in a variety, a subtlety, and a power of rhythmical effect which have never been surpassed and have probably never been equalled in any other poetry of comparable bulk. Its historical importance is that it proved, once for all, that the old native and popular stress-rhythms are as worthy to be considered the traditional rhythms of English poetry as the Romance syllabic metres which date from Chaucer. It is unlikely, however, that syllabic metres will be finally superseded; for the sprung, expressional, and cumulative rhythms of Hopkins demand a greater share of "auditory imagination", a more delicate sense of musical tone and timing, than are given to most poets. Sprung rhythm either succeeds perfectly or fails lamentably. . . . [Hopkins] triumphantly avoided all the pitfalls by combining what was healthy and robust in the native rhythms with the finest graces of the Greek melic poetry and Welsh *cynghanedd.*

As a master of poetic diction and of poetic 'linguistics' Hopkins again occupies a unique historical position. In an age of diffused Romanticism, he broke through the hidebound literary tradition which, save for brief exceptions in Wordsworth, Keats, and Browning, had for nearly two hundred years divorced the diction and phrasing of poetry from the direct perceptions of everyday life and language. Carefully avoiding the prosaism of Browning, the archaism of Swinburne, and (for the most part) the awkwardness of Doughty, Hopkins restored to poetry something like the fluidity and resourcefulness of Elizabethan English; by so doing he materially helped all later poets to reduce the gap which had always seemed to exist inevitably between the greatest master of poetic language, Shakespeare, and his successors.

Of almost equal importance is the mark left by Hopkins's powerful idiosyncrasy upon the *texture* of English poetry. The rich phonal qualities of his verse reinforce, and are themselves enhanced by, the flexible stress-rhythm; and all these auditory elements are at the same time skilfully modulated to suit the shifting phases of closely packed thought and developing emotion. Pre-eminently Hopkins's example has revived the tradition (long in partial abeyance) that poetry is to be read with the ear and not merely with the eye.

Hopkins, in fact, has set up a standard of poetic beauty which, for the many who now fully acknowledge its fascination, is profoundly disturbing. After an intensive reading of Hopkins, most other English poetry seems outwardly facile and in varying degrees inadequate: its harmonic pattern is too simple, too adventitious; it seems not to have advanced far enough along the road which leads from plain utilitarian prose to the purest of literary art-forms—to the "condition of music". This does not mean that the admirer of Hopkins can no longer enjoy other poets: his appreciation of Shakespeare, of Donne and the other early seventeenth-century poets, of Milton and Keats will probably be increased rather than diminished. It does mean, however, that the proportion of other poetry to which he can return with the old enjoyment will be noticeably smaller; his taste, sharpened and refined by Hopkins, will demand a more exquisite amalgam of thought and emotion, a more significant concentration and point, to make up for the lack of *inscape* and *instress* in the outward form.

Gathering and retwining so many straying strands of the European poetic tradition, Hopkins was a great eclectic who was also eminently creative and original. The total complex of his style is (to use his own expression) a poetic "species"; as such it can never recur—except by shameless imitation.

Our final estimate may in some measure be influenced by the answer we give to one outstanding question, namely, how far Hopkins can be said to reveal, through his poetry, a truly mystical vision. He knew the Purgative Life, and had glimpses of the Illuminative; but that last calm 'possession' of God was a consummation desired but never attained in this world. Nevertheless, his direct apprehension of the Infinite through the medium of His creation frequently assumes a mode of expression which is identical with that of the acknowledged mystics. . . . (pp. 368-70)

Current verdicts on Hopkins's ultimate status as a poet vary between the designations "minor" and "great". The former points to the relative smallness of his output,—for this, and this only, can provide reasonable grounds for calling him a *minor* poet. But the deficiency is more than compensated by the absolute merit and subsequent influence of those poems which will continue to be *read,* and not merely admired, as long as the English language endures. In some age not attuned to his peculiar music and message, his reputation may suffer temporary eclipse; but the re-emergence of his fame will be all the brighter.

Hopkins is already a 'classic'. In his poetry we recognize not only what he himself demanded—"a fine execution", but also what Joseph Warton rightly called the two chief nerves of all genuine poesy—the Sublime and the Pathetic. By both criteria Hopkins attains the heights, though not the long sustained flights, of the acknowledged great masters—of Dante, Shakespeare, Milton. It is this fact, coupled with his unique individuality, which sets him apart from and above the exquisite *minor* poets, like Herrick, Marvell, and Christina Rossetti.

We shall attempt to justify those critics who have already pronounced Hopkins a *major* poet. Firstly, the fact that a *Times* reviewer, in giving him this title, compared his achievement in "bulk and quality" with that of Matthew Arnold is significant: it would appear that Hopkins's fourteen hundred lines can make as deep an impression as the fourteen thousand of Matthew Arnold. Indeed, whether his work be considered from the point of view of matter, manner, or both, Hopkins is, for the present writer, the more important poet; though in saying this we do not call in question the *major* status usually assigned to Arnold, Swinburne, and D. G. Rossetti.

According to Dr. F. R. Leavis,

Hopkins was one of the most remarkable technical inventors who ever wrote, and he was a major poet. . . . He is likely to prove, for our time and the future, the only influential poet of the Victorian age, and he seems to me the greatest.

An Australian critic, D. P. McGuire, writes:

The genius of Hopkins comprehended, as none other has comprehended even to our own day, the characteristic features of the oncoming world: the still increasing tempo, the still increasing complexity of modern life. For the social philosopher as well as for the common reader he is the most important poet since Shelley.

Such judgments will not pass unchallenged; and it must be admitted in the best interests of Hopkins that each pronouncement contains an unfortunate touch of exaggeration. Surely Browning and Whitman cannot be dismissed as less influential than Hopkins; and surely those two very considerable poets, together with Tennyson, will in future times be of the highest importance to the social philosopher and probably also to the common reader.

D. P. McGuire's statement about the increasing tempo and complexity of modern life suggests a further relevant observation. The growing bulk of the best European literature makes it ever more difficult for people of culture to keep pace with it. If we must have specialization and ample scope for personal preferences, then Hopkins is certainly a major poet on the showing of the above representative critics; but if those who are to decide the value and status of a poet are to be conversant with all the best poetry of the modern world, then the significance of mere *quantity* in a poet's output must be held to be rapidly diminishing. For most readers, it is obviously more profitable to skim the cream of *two* famous poets than to imbibe all, good and indifferent, of either one. Even Hopkins, who urged Patmore to write more poetry for the sake of his fame, was slightly contemptuous of his laboriously prolific contemporaries: "Just think of the blank verse these people have exuded". And to-day Mr. T. S. Eliot is certainly not alone in thinking that the effect of some of the nineteenth-century poets was lessened by their bulk:

Who now, for the pleasure of it, reads Wordsworth, Shelley and Keats even, certainly Browning and Swinburne and most of the French poets of the century—entire?

Who, indeed? And why should Coleridge, Byron, Tennyson, and William Morris be excluded from the list? Stopford Brooke reduced Coleridge to "twenty pages of pure gold"; and if this sifting and refining process were extended to all the above poets, the result would be a series of selections each of which would be hardly larger (if not actually smaller) than the total output of Hopkins. Such selections are constantly being made, chiefly for educational purposes, and the editors show no great diversity of choice. It should therefore be frankly admitted that only by their best can the voluminous writers of the past be poetically and culturally active to-day. Such an admission would bring the self-winnowed Hopkins into line with most of the poets whose work now commands a much larger space in our libraries and academic literary manuals.

For some years to come the many alleged faults and errors of taste in Hopkins may seriously reduce the bulk of his 'active' poetry. Meanwhile, we may go back for reassurance to Longinus, who asked himself whether the greater number or the higher quality of excellences should bear the bell in literature. The higher natures, he said, are the least faultless. Major excellences, even if not uniformly present, should always carry the election; for their greatness of thought if for nothing else. According to Wordsworth, however, the emphasis in any assessment of poetry is to be placed not on 'thought' but on 'sensibility'. Of genius in the fine arts, he says,

the only infallible sign is *the widening the sphere of human sensibility*. . . . Genius is the introduction of a new element into the intellectual universe . . . the application of powers to objects on which they had not before been exercised, or the employment of them *in such manner as to produce effects hitherto unknown.*

By this criterion, too, Hopkins was undoubtedly a genius, and is certainly a major poet.

After a century of poetry in which the purely intellectual element was, to say the least, uncertain, diffused or exiguous, it is not surprising that to-day poets and critics alike are trying to redress the balance. In this respect, the scope and quality of Hopkins's work has provoked some adverse comparisons. The late W. J. Turner, for instance, said that Hopkins did not show the intellectual powers of Keats—that he had not the power of philosophic thought as manifested by Shakespeare, Milton, Donne, Keats, and Shelley.

Now although this opinion is true as regards the greater intellectual range of Shakespeare, Donne, and Milton, it contains, we think, a serious fallacy. W. J. Turner, like Dr. Richards and other agnostic critics, assumes too readily a position which would require volumes to 'justify', namely, that Christian beliefs and principles are mere emotional vagaries having little to do with intellection. It would be extremely difficult to prove that the free play of intellect in agnostic poets like Shelley and Keats has produced ideas and attitudes which are *more valuable* than those arising from the play of an intensely original mind and imagination among and around the matured tenets of Christianity. (pp. 370-73)

In the exercise of a mature intellect upon the raw materials of poetry, as also in the underlying and unifying metaphysic of his finished work, Hopkins must be pronounced equal and in some ways superior to both these earlier poets. Where they are promising and sometimes successful (in the invention of character and fable), Hopkins makes no claim to excellence; where they are really strong (in the speculative and meditative lyric), he is, we think, even stronger.

No informed critic would nowadays deny the major status of Donne, Baudelaire, and Walt Whitman. They are still living forces; though their influence is largely refracted through the minds of other writers, they continue to modify thought and action. Now for the present writer at least, Hopkins, in the sheer power or stress of his genius, has a real claim to rank with these three poets.

His affinity with Donne derives from the play of intellect on the problems of faith and religious endeavour—the yearning of imperfection towards perfection, the desire to know and hold God more closely—together with the play of individual sensibility upon the materials of poetry and on the conventional standards of diction and rhythm. In Donne, the clash between the 'man of the world' temper and the claims of a pious and ascetic calling did not admit of a poetic reconciliation so clear and sharp as that of Hopkins; for Donne never found, as Hopkins did in Catholicism, an interpretation of life which could be so flushed with

feeling as to become a complete and illuminating experience. Although Donne has the wider range of ideas, he is often fanciful, fantastic, and inconclusive; Hopkins, though hardly less 'cerebral' and exciting and frequently far more troubled, expounds on the whole the more rational and realistic world-view.

Baudelaire, too, was a poet who looked at human life and the universe with almost the same eyes as Hopkins; but the two men differed fundamentally in their interpretations of what they saw. Not always, however, in their reading of life: at times it seems to be rather a difference in the degree of will-power or moral consistency of which each was capable—the gift of grace not only of seeing what is best but of holding only to that. For instance, Baudelaire's *L'Horloge* expresses the same high and strict morality as Hopkin's **"To His Watch"**; *L'Avertisseur* and many other poems show the French poet's constant preoccupation with sin and redemption. In *Le Gouffre* (where the link is Pascal) we find that overwhelming sense of the simultaneous presence and absence of God, that apprehension of 'le vide et le néant' which only the mind capable of the fullest realization of the numinous can experience. What could be more like Hopkins than

> et sur mon poil qui tout droit se relève
> Mainte fois de la Peur je sens passer le vent,

and

> Sur le fond de mes nuits Dieu de son doigt savant
> Dessine une cauchemar multiforme et sans trêve.
>
> J'ai peur du sommeil comme on a peur d'un grand trou,
> Tout plein de vague horreur, menant on ne sait où;
> Je ne vois qu'infini par toutes les fenêtres,
>
> Et mon esprit toujours du vertige hanté
> Jalouse du néant l'insensibilité.—

and again:

> J'implore to pitié, Toi, l'unique que j'aime,
> De fond du gouffre obscur ou mon caeur est tombé?

Nevertheless, one great difference cannot be overlooked: Baudelaire's physical and mental morbidity made him the poet of *Les Litanies de Satan* and other works which must be read (if read at all) with the strictest caution. However much we admire the artist and pity the man, the sheer diabolism of much of his verse lowers the value of his achievement. By contrast, Hopkin's moral healthiness more than compensates for his smallness of output and frequent obscurity.

In his essential sanity Hopkins was closer to Whitman, whose impetuous rhythms, dynamic style, and pervasive nature-mysticism are often so like his own. Both poets expressed the "pure wild volition and energy of nature." As Mr. Charles Madge once pointed out in an illuminating short essay, there is a Corybantic strain in each one, much as the inhibited and obedient Jesuit differed from the broad-minded and broad-tongued Democrat. Hopkins's sky "all in a rush with richness" and his ecstatic "What is all this juice and all this joy"? are paralleled by Whitman's

> Hefts of the moving world at innocent gambols silently
> rising, freshly exuding,
> Scooting obliquely high and low. . . .
> Seas of bright juice suffuse heaven.

Both were fascinated by the infinite variety and laciness of natural beauty; as Whitman said:

> I effuse my flesh in eddies, and drift in lacy jags;

and Whitman, like Hopkins, knew the value of a strict asceticism in his private life. Yet here again there is a fundamental difference: it will redound, we think, to the Christian poet's credit that he shows a more pronounced "chastity of mind", a strength to resist the glib emotional generalization. The great friendly Whitman-arm thrown indiscriminately round the shoulders of Humanity may prove, in the end, a Judas-kiss. Instead of singing:

> None has begun to think how divine he himself is,
> and how certain the future is,

Hopkins was prophetically inclined to lament the fact that too many have arrogantly assumed divinity, while too few have begun to think how divine they might become and how desperately uncertain their souls' future may be.

We can agree with E. E. Phare when she says that the mere prose substance of Hopkins's poetry has more value than that of most avowedly didactic and philosophic poetry. The same critic asserts too that if all their respective poetical works were turned into prose paraphrases, Hopkins would have the better of Browning and possibly, also, of Wordsworth. Her doubt as regards Wordsworth is reassuring; for Wordsworth is, of course, the greater poet. But Miss Phare's opinion will not seem extravagant to anyone who sets the highest value upon the Christian faith and philosophy. Moreover her choice of Wordsworth and Browning in this context is a more extraordinary tribute to Hopkins's merit than at first appears; for of all nineteenth-century English poets, these two have probably given an intellectual stimulus, a more constructive and hopeful orientation, to the greatest number of intelligent people.

Before drawing our final conclusion we must say a last word about Hopkins's faults. That he left so many poems unfinished was partly his misfortune and partly to his credit: he refused to substitute putty and rubble for genuine inspiration. The peculiar nature of his mind and inner experience made it necessary for him to fuse, adapt, twist and sometimes distort the elements of his native language; and at rare times idiosyncrasy led him into oddity or extravagance. Yet the truth of Erigena's saying, that 'a vice is but a spoilt virtue and can have no separate existence', is in this case so curiously demonstrated that the task of absolute critical discrimination becomes well-nigh impossible: what seems good to one reader may seem bad to another. All the critic can do is to expound the processes of thought and expression, indicate the general solipsist tendency, and leave the individual educated reader to form his own judgment on this word or that construction. We must repeat, however, that most of this poet's awkwardness and difficulty disappears when we have taken the trouble to master his idiom. His style is not for imitation, because it is doubtful whether the same combination of qualities will ever be found again in one man.

When the clamour of protest and approval has died down, these facts about our subject will, we believe, emerge clearly: that by his unique personality and character, merging good living with high thinking; by his interpretation of beauty and duty, touching man to the very quick of his being; by his power of speech at once sweet and strong, melodic and harmonic; by his skill in architectonic and execution; by the stimulus he gave to the ethical and creative purposes of poets yet to be—by these and other qualities Gerard Manley Hopkins has certainly earned the distinction of being called a *major poet:* and in his finest moments he is assuredly one of our greatest. (pp. 374-78)

W. H. Gardner, in his *Gerard Manley Hopkins (1844-1889): A Study of Poetic Idiosyncrasy in Relation to Poetic Tradition, Vol. II,* revised edition, Yale University Press, 1949, 415 p.

ALAN HEUSER
(essay date 1958)

[In the following excerpt, Heuser outlines the artistic and philosophical movements that influenced Hopkins's life and poetry.]

In both art and religion Hopkins was closely linked with his times. The Oxford movement of Pusey and Newman overtook him in his pursuit of classical studies: he became first an Anglo-Catholic, then a Roman Catholic and a Jesuit. The Pre-Raphaelite movement of painters and poets, together with the critics Ruskin and Pater, gave him his artistic context: he became painter, poet, and critic too. Then, while the debate between science and religion was going on, Hopkins developed a theory of art using the best of both worlds—the laws of science and the life of religion—combining wild naturalism (type of Mary) with religious idealism (type of Christ). On the one hand, there was a Romantic return to primitive innocence of sensations; on the other, a Christian striving towards the perfect Manhood. Here was the peculiar Pre-Raphaelite tension between angelic heaven and fleshly earth, without any of its sickliness, for Hopkins' work was free from two Victorian diseases—subjective dream indulgence in vogues of escape and reverie, brooding exploitation of confused emotionalism and passive sensationalism. In Hopkins all had the immediacy and 'rash-fresh' clarity of authentic vision, the intensity of honest sensations and emotions.

The problem of the Victorian age was its divorce of ideal theory and practical vision, together with the substitution of ethical for religious and metaphysical values. In verse there was a double weakening: the blight of archaic diction (often pseudo-Elizabethan) and the effeminacy of exotic forms (French verse forms of the rondeliers). The triumph of Hopkins' achievement was a heightening of living language, a reinforcement of familiar forms by native stress, an illuminative integration of vision and theory, an exhilarating conquest of religious meaning, by which even failure (in the dark sonnets) was made victorious. Behind the vision of nature, under the wilderness and sufferings of the world, Hopkins discovered no dry theory but a lively one, echoing with the songs of creation and redemption. Nature rang with sympathetic analogies. As in George Herbert, all nature was seen in terms of a musical metaphor, and there was ultimate harmony, harmony of nature in grace where innocence and perfection were to be restored after the universal extension of sacrifice.

Beyond his fellow Victorians Hopkins was faithful to his poetic voice, sometimes denying it utterance, but never forcing it for the sake of mere writing, always relying upon genuine inspiration, always advancing in rhetorical technique. His lack of a reading public was an unforeseen advantage. Many other poets, writing on a par with prose writers, betrayed voice and vision to a mass audience, so that at the core of their works are found hesitancy and evaporation of meaning. The problem of private vision assuming public voice and aimed at a large, undefined audience made the longer works of Tennyson and Browning tedious (*Idylls,* the *Ring*) and actually put an end to the poet in Arnold. The problem of Hopkins was the reverse: public vision of creation and redemption revealed by private oracle and received by a very few, the audience widening only long after the death of the poet.

Placing Hopkins' poetry in the English poetic tradition has been found a difficult task. Various schools have been invoked along with his name—Wordsworthian, Miltonic, Keatsian or Pre-Raphaelite, the alliterative school of Middle English, the new metaphysical school of Patmore and Thompson. Each of these influenced Hopkins at some stage in his development; the Pre-Raphaelite school was the most significant. If a distinct label is needed, perhaps 'baroque' is almost satisfactory, expressing the vehement and fiery incarnation of idea in word-made-flesh, the word rendered sensational. Jesuit tradition in the baroque style links Hopkins directly to the seventeenth-century poetic experience of controlled violence and surprise, of Christian feeling infusing and commanding classical forms, and thus he recalls the poetry of Donne, Herbert, Crashaw, Quarles, and Benlowes. Yet how did this happen in the nineteenth century? It must not be forgotten that Pre-Raphaelite art arranged realistic detail of nature for ideal message-value, to tell a story or embody an idea, and that this technique carried on, in a new key, the old tradition of the baroque emblem-books. The verse-picture combination of the black and white emblem came to coloured life in the poetry-painting association of Pre-Raphaelite art: not only were pictures painted to illustrate poems and vice versa, but book-illustration in art and word-painting in literature were widely popular. In Hopkins Pre-Raphaelite symbolism and Jesuit emblem-tradition met in a new baroque, independent and fresh, for Hopkins remained deliberately his own species, unique, as he thought all poets should be.

Hopkins' three great technical advances were in diction, rhythm, and texture. For him poetic diction meant 'current language heightened'. He sought out provincialisms and coinages native to the concrete and living roots of language, combining these specific marks into alogical, co-ordinated, and exclamatory periods. Sprung rhythm derived force and flow, not from haphazard accents, but from high stresses important to 'fetch out' the sense by emphasis. The style was declamatory, interpretive, and followed a free pattern fitting the individual phrase or line of thought—reminiscent of Purcell's bold liberties and surprises threaded on a continuous melodic line. But the new metre and the new language would have been frigid innovations without the entire expressional texture fused with them—chiming of consonants and alliteration of vowels—a concatenation of syllables similar to Welsh systems of lettering. Neglect of this rich overlay of textural echo would result in a loss, not of a mere ornament, but of the very nature of sprung rhythm.

Along with advances in language and rhetorical technique, Hopkins left to the poetic tradition significant contributions in lyric form, especially in sonnet and ode. Concentrating on the Petrarchan sonnet, with its careful balance of octave and sestet, Hopkins experimented in contracted and expanded modes . . . , always maintaining basic rhymes and proportions. . . . Expanded sonnets were the more important, in order to make the English sonnet equal in length to the Italian. Lines were lengthened by extra stresses (to six or eight feet), by extrametrical syllables (outrides), or by additional half-lines (codas and burden-lines); sometimes all three methods were used. In each case Hopkins gave his sonnet the orchestral fullness and impact of an ode. He turned to the ode proper in either of two modes—the Horatian or the Pindaric—often with an elegiac intent in view. For the Horatian ode he kept to a series of quatrains written in compressed style of simple tetrameter and/or trimeter. For the Pindaric he maintained a strophic or stanzaic manner in elaborate metric, frequently dividing the ode into two parts.

Beyond technical advances in versification and contributions in lyric form, Hopkins' poetry wrestled with a strong core of thought (Christian ideas infused with Gothic feeling into classical forms). The three notes of his nature verse—joy, pity, and fear—came to him from his religious life: the joy of creative light in sacramental sonnets of nature, the pity of the compassionate cloud in poems of the pastoral care for men, and the fear of redemptive night in the dark sonnets of personal desolation. Over these notes—the exaltation of joy, the catharsis of pity and fear towards a new joy—was woven his characteristic spiritual imagery: images of the soul as angelic voice or bird (winged *eros* or *psyche*), with its activities of affection as love-lace (organic growth, binding *philia*) and of election as battle-armour (military combat, sacrificial *agape*), based on the mystery of the self (naval or racing course of pitch). Under the poetry there lay the foundations of a life truly lived in honesty with acceptance. (pp. 95-8)

[Hopkins' creative vision moved] from naturalistic idealism through a philosophy of inscape and instress to a Scotist voluntarism and a Pythagorean Platonism of music, memory, and number. Under the pressure of Greek and Pre-Raphaelite studies, Hopkins' concrete vision soon acquired an abstract theory. Vision and theory interlocked in his pursuit of the three

Hopkins's sketch of himself reflected in a lake, dated 1864.

arts of painting, music, and poetry. Principles learned from colour-music, from Pre-Raphaelite art and art-criticism, from plainchant and counterpoint in music, from Greek and Welsh studies in verse mutually enriched the poetry as well as the aesthetics behind the poetry. Hopkins was for ever reaching behind vision to theory. In his early years he turned from naturalistic idealism to set up a new Realism in Platonist terms—fixed types in a scale of nature—out of which emerged a philosophy of inscape and instress. In his maturity he developed the philosophy into a psychology, a verse theory, a theology, a moral idealism, and a Scotist scheme of salvation. Finally he speculated in the preconscious realm of memory and in number. In each case a musical metaphor lay at the base of creative vision. And at every stage of development there was renunciation and revival: when Hopkins gave up painting, he cultivated word-painting in journals; after he burnt his poetry, there was a long silence, followed by the discovery of a new verse theory; when he found poetry difficult in later years, he turned to musical composition. The death of an old art brought forth new life, and death passed into resurrection.

Vision and theory met in the interaction of poetry and spirituality, in the relationship between aesthetics and religion. Inspiration or desolation in Hopkins' prayer life gave in the poetry corresponding ejaculations of comfort or distress. His stylistic habit of invocation was the natural consequence of vocation directing frequent aspirations to God. Hopkins' life-long occupation with Greek scholarship maintained in him a Platonist view of reality, not always caught up by Scotism into a world of Christian truth, nor always turned into Christian poetry. There remained the underworld of the preconscious and primitive, ideal types and mirror images among pagan myths and Pythagorean numbers. Here in the storehouse of memory was the world of angelic possibles. It was in this way that Hopkins pursued his speculations.

What was the vision, its theory, its applications? The vision of creation was trinitarian—testifying to the fatherhood of being, the sonship of inscape, the spirituality of stress—and unitive through 'the stem of stress' or tangible finger of power in all creation. The theory centred on three key terms: inscape, the inward tongue-shape of the creature; instress, its inward stem-pressure of feeling and will; pitch, its directed singularity. The theory was extended to verse—'the inscape of spoken sound', quaint margaretting based on chime pattern and stress curvature; to human nature—a moral inscape forged by instress of will and fulfilled in the sacrificial Humanity of Christ; to psychic experience of lower heart—stress and slack of feeling, instress by association in the unconscious below reason; to the spiritual world of higher heart with levels of instress—affective will determined by nature, elective will free at pitch—and with focus on correspondence to grace in the line or stem of sequence of stress in the heart. Now, with the emergence of a doctrine of the self, with the Scotist distinction between individuality and nature, the developed theory elaborated echoes on levels of being—sakes as reflexions of individual pitch, keepings as reflexions of specific nature. Finally, the fixed points of Platonic Realism were defined in terms of Pythagorean numbers, and mathematics held out promise for a philosophical basis to metre and music. The Greek doctrine of music provided an important basis for the theory of pitch (degree of tuning on the string of being), stress (God's bow pressing on the string), and instress (man's bow responding). Yet the theory, however far abstracted, was ever brought home to the concrete through Hopkins' strong senses, his interest in primitive sensation breaking from the unconscious, in spiritualization of sensation. Furthermore, it must be remembered that the vision passed through four or five stages, that it was always in development. (pp. 98-100)

Alan Heuser, in his *The Shaping Vision of Gerard Manley Hopkins,* 1958. Reprint by Archon Books, 1968, 128 p.

WENDELL STACY JOHNSON
(essay date 1968)

[In the following excerpt, Johnson explores the significance of light and darkness in Hopkins's poems, briefly comparing his imagery with that of other Victorian poets.]

Images of light, of fiery sunlight, starlight, moonlight, are everywhere in Hopkins, contrasted with and complemented by the images of shadow and of night. The poet's love for painting, his early desire to emulate the Pre-Raphaelites in art, and Ruskin's influence on him may have something to do with his interest in precise description of light effects and visual phenomena. In fact, Hopkins can sometimes evoke a brightly lit and shaded landscape more vividly than the painter-poet Dante Rossetti does.

Of course, his concern for just how things are lit and how they look is by no means unique in his times; the criterion of exact fidelity to nature, applied to painter and poet alike, is generally accepted in Victorian criticism of the arts, and it is not only Ruskin who describes in words or represents in drawings how light and shadow define the forms of objects. It is a matter of visual accuracy, something that Tennyson, too, very much cares about.

While the imagery of light is literal for Hopkins and the poets of his century, it is also something more

for them: for Wordsworth, the essence of nature is revealed in a glorious light seen clearly only by the young and innocent; and for Tennyson, Arnold, and Swinburne, daylight, nature's light, may be literally but also metaphorically both creative and destructive. The special quality of Hopkins' poems about light is their way of distinguishing a devotion beautifully illuminated, to nature, which is to be represented faithfully, from a sense of nature's being fallen and alien, its light partly darkness. These two attitudes toward nature, toward the world of sunlight and stars, might be said to alternate in other Victorian poets; in Hopkins they occur simultaneously. . . . [One] of his favorite adjectives is *dappled;* his world is double in a pictorial sense and in a metaphorical one, always being dappled with sun and shadow. In ocean, in landscape, and in all creatures he finds harsh, fleeting beauty and imperfectly reflected, echoed power and grace. (pp. 125-27)

Hopkins uses darkness to describe the dreary and sometimes dreadful sense of being only oneself, cut off from the glory of heaven:

I wake and feel the fell of dark, not day.
What hours, O what black hours we have spent
This night!

So begin the most terrible of all his lines on being oneself. In **"Carrion Comfort,"** too, during inner tempest and suffering, the most the speaker can do is "wish day come" after the night "Of now done darkness [when] I wretch lay wrestling with (my God!) my God."

Yet, although man mourns his mortal self in darkness, as Margaret does in **"Spring and Fall,"** the darkness is ambiguous and intermittent. Light and darkness intertwined make up the major imagery of **"Spelt from Sibyl's Leaves,"** which is about the mixed nature of this mortal world. Heavy baroque lines describe the straining toward death of "hearse-of-all-night," but also the stars in "fire-featuring heaven." These lines concern the tendency of selves, of forms, to dissolve and be forgotten or dismembered—but also the oracular promise of something else. The dapple and the doubleness of earthly life seem to rush toward the singleness of night, of death; yet there remain two spools, two folds, two aspects of each reality, including self: light, white, right, as well as darkness, black, wrong. So "Selfwrung, selfstrung, sheathe- and shelterless, thoughts against thoughts in groans grind."

But behind the dappled world and its temporary darkness, and, at least in one sense, within the very darkness, Hopkins believes there is light. That is just the point that has been made by the language and imagery of **"The Deutschland."** In that poem there are three versions of light: the lovely light of nature represented by stars and the clear bright sky, sustained by the Holy Ghost; the fiery light of divine power represented by lightning and "fire of stress," or flames of grace, the working of God the Father; and the light of virtue or grace incarnate represented perfectly in Christ, the kindly "heart's light," but also reflected in Christ-like man seen as a "beacon of light." It is necessary to pass from the first stage through the instress demanded by the second before reaching the third stage, which allows a full recognition of human—and Christ-imitating—inscape. And this means discovering that, just as in thunder there is lightning, so above and acting through the fact of mortal darkness there is still the light of divine power: "Thou art above, thou Orion of light." Christ is re-born through darkness and drowning.

Because Hopkins is a poet of doubleness, a poet of Christian paradox, he is misread when these three stages are separated from each other, or when he is taken not to have a single and consistent imaginative scheme. There are urgent tensions within his art, and indeed there is at the center of it a seeming contradiction, because there is a seeming contradiction at the center of Christian thought. But the several elements are almost always present, at least implicitly, in his verse. Hopkins does not express the conflict between, and alternating of, priest and artist, or devotional writer and nature poet, or ascetic and aesthete; and he does not sometimes believe that the landscape in which men live is wholly dark, nor does he sometimes believe that it is wholly bright. (pp. 144-46)

The dappled imagery of light and darkness is, in fact, ubiquitous in Hopkins. For instance, "the fire that breaks from" the windhover relates that creature to the ploughed-down clods that shine and the galled embers that "gash gold-vermillion." It seems clear, however, and important, that the poet can distinguish several sorts of light: the light of earthly nature, as in **"God's Grandeur,"** which turns to darkness as it dies; the light of mortal human selves, as in **"To What Serves Mortal Beauty?"** which becomes dark only insofar as it is mortal and removed from a divine source; the light of God himself, the flame of the Father in **"The Deutschland"** that makes use of deadly darkness to evoke men's own bright inner lights, but also the milder light of the Son, which contends with the darkness in men and which is reflected by those inner lights flashing from the heroic nun and from the windhover.

One question the light imagery in Hopkins' poetry might be taken to pose is whether these several sorts of light form an imaginative pattern, whether they are related accidentally or essentially. . . . Hopkins, like other Victorian poets, both appreciates the beauty of natural light and recognizes its harshness. This can be a matter of mood. He can alternately derive hope and joy from daylight, as Tennyson does from the dawn in "The Two Voices," and see it as bafflingly irrelevant to his own inner darkness, as Tennyson does in the early lyrics of *In Memoriam*, where the dawn is "blank." He

can recognize the ambiguity of nature's light, its significance depending upon mood and point of view—as Tennyson perhaps does in "The Vision of Sin," which ends, "God made himself an awful rose of dawn," and as Arnold does in "The New Sirens" and Swinburne in "The Lake of Gaube," for examples. But Hopkins' thought is more systematic, being founded on dogma, than that of most other Victorian writers, and for him a proper response to the light of nature must distinguish it from but also specifically relate it to the fire which is human inscape—and to God the "Orion above." The problem is one of personal belief but also one of poetic imagery.

Victorian imaginations, still largely dominated by the grandeur and the difficulties of the Romantic temper, repeatedly brood upon the relation of man to external nature, of the human figure to the landscape. In Hopkins' scheme of imagery, this becomes specifically the problem of how the light of self, the flash of human inscape, is related to the natural lights and beauties of the world. Hopkins' answer can be given only by reference to the light of God in Christ. A relationship is definitely established in **"That Nature Is a Heraclitean Fire and of the Comfort of the Resurrection,"** the poem whose title both states a proposition and introduces a subject for contemplation. Joining the proposition about nature constantly inconstant and the contemplation of the fact of an unnatural or miraculous event breaking into the otherwise continuous natural flux, the poet can observe the supposed nature of men and assert the true state of mankind.

Like so many other lyrics about natural loveliness, this poem begins with a literal description of a scene. And, again characteristically, the poet is attracted by the sky and light effects. Clouds are like puffballs, or pillows, or groups of roisterers thronging the heavens, gleaming "in marches." They sparkle as they march or move along, or they brighten up large areas, territories in the sky. Bright rays of sun make strips of light (shives, which are slices or threads) and ropes of shadow (if "tackle" means rope) under the arches of elm trees. The light and shadow produce stripes, lacy patterns with lances or lashes of brightness on the ground, and when the bright and dark "pair," the landscape is literally seen as pied or dappled, as spotted. For the moment this seems like a delightful dappling, as it has been in **"God's Grandeur."** Still, the evidence is that storms occur in this world: yesterday's tempest has left some marks. And, precisely as in **"God's Grandeur,"** man's treading down and marking natural beauty also flaws it—even though ministering winds erase the marks as natural grandeur renews itself.

Delightfully the bright wind boisterous ropes, wrestles,
　　　　　　　　　　　　　　　　　　　　　　　beats
　　earth bare

Of yestertempest's creases; in pool and rutpeel parches
Squandering ooze to squeezed dough, crust, dust; stanches,
starches
Squadroned masks and manmarks treadmire toil there
Footfretted in it.

The boisterous wind moves in a current across the ground as if it were a rope pulled rapidly; in swaying things here and there it seems to be wrestling, and even to be beating against the earth in its playfulness, as it blows away or flattens out the litter left by yesterday's rain storm. The wind and sun dry up, or parch, into dusty peels the mud of pool and ditch (rut), making the ooze spend or squander its wetness and become damp earth like dough that can be kneaded—and, at last, become crisp dry dough, or crust, hard earth with a residue of dust. In fact, the wind appears not only to stanch wetness, as one would stop up a wound and dry it, but also, like an efficient servant, to starch and leave both clean and crisp the rumpled earth's very "masks and manmarks," those signs of human habitation that cover up the landscape. These are the artificially arranged (squadroned) signs of man's pedestrian toil on the boggy earth. "Treadmire toil" suggests also the futility of most human labor, the sense of man's being "bogged down." Man has "footfretted [marks] in it," has disturbed the earth, just as his tramping over any creature might "fret" it. The first sentence of the poem, then, four lines long, describes the sheer delight of sky, light, and earth. The second, just over four lines long, again shows nature renewing itself after man has marred its beauty. The third sentence, marking the end of a primary stage in the poem, sums up these meanings and implies much more, using the imagery of fire from the ancient philosopher Heraclitus: "Million-fueled, nature's confire burns on." In spite of men, it would seem now, the world of lovely things continues to exist. But even more than the clouds, the sunlight and the parching, starching wind do, all of them images that hint of change, the philosopher's image of the bonfire poses difficulties. All things are burning, Heraclitus said, and constant change is the only reality. Fire has to feed on fuel that cannot literally, like the mythical phoenix, renew itself; so the fire of nature is constantly renewed only as the millions of inscaped, individual, parts of nature are constantly consumed and utterly destroyed. The life of nature, then, means the endless death of all its parts. And, after all, like the elm tree and its leaves, the body of man is a part of nature, one of the fuels in its burning. For all the delight of this first stage and for all the excitement of the phrase, "nature's bonfire burns on," there is an uneasy undertone heard in the qualifying words, "million-fueled."

Even so, the first nine lines of the poem are mainly a celebration of natural vitality. Appropriately, the second stage is introduced as a contrast. For once, Hopkins marks his transition with the adversative, "but." If the **"Heraclitean Fire"** begins as a nature poem comparable with **"God's Grandeur"** and **"Pied Beauty,"** it proceeds as a reflection on man's mortality, and thus becomes rather like **"Spring and Fall."** It proceeds in sober, clear, and shorter sentences, with little of the playful echoing and verbal delight of the first section, where the poet has teased, tricked, skipped, and poured out his joy until he and his reader are breathless; and he has in fact written in "gay-gangs" of words, repeating sounds constantly in alliteration and internal rhyme just as the very life of bonfire nature repeats, sustains, always varies and yet constantly restates itself. Now, instead, the words move heavily. "Both are in an unfathomable, all is in an enormous dark / Drowned." And Hopkins' imagery, rather than one of skies and brightness, is one of light quenched, darkness, drowning, blurring, and emptiness. For now his subject is not aesthetic but moral, and the point of view is not the artist's so much as the mortal realist's. Once more the idea of inscape, of unique selfhood, provides for this shift. Seen only as a part of nature, man has the most fully developed individual identity in the landscape. And so, even if he litters and frets the rest of nature with his trash, with his marks, he himself is the finest mortal thing in a world of mortal things, the pride of all nature.

But quench her bonniest, dearest to her, her clearest-selved spark
Man, how fast his firedint, his mark on mind, is gone!

Man's mortal spark, his bodily beauty and natural grace, can be quenched by water, by tempest and wrecking, or merely by burning itself out. One way or another, it dies. And this fact is no less painful to Hopkins than it is to the Tennyson of *In Memoriam*. Now clearly, man's mark on mind is as dear as his mark on nature can be fretting: this "firedint" mark is his communicating of self to other selves, other minds. But, as **"The Lantern Out of Doors"** has put it, the bright mark of self is soon consumed by death or distance, as individual men soon die and are forgotten. The mortal brevity of nature's highest form makes both the form and all of nature seem now dark and melancholy:

Both are in an unfathomable, all is in an enormous dark
Drowned. O pity and indignation! Manshape, that shone
Sheer off, disseveral, a star, death blots black out; nor mark
      Is any of him at all so stark
But vastness blurs and time beats level.

Again darkness and drowning are opposed to light and vitality. But now manshape is merged into landshape, or landscape, and all is darkened, all is dead, all shape is lost. For Hopkins, life is defined by individual shape, by inscape, the unique shape naturally evolving from an inner principle of being that is precisely "disseveral" because it is one, not several, not general or typical. Like his much admired Duns Scotus, with his individuating principle of *haecceitas,* or concrete separate being, Hopkins can conceive of universal nature only as existing in shapes. Ironically, however, the very constancy and self-renewing of nature that the first stage of this poem celebrates—the fact that "nature is never spent"—is what has to destroy all forms, just as, biologically, birth has to imply death. Time "beats level" the very mark or memory of any man just as today's wind "beats earth bare" and stanches "manmark." What the speaker now sees is what he saw at first, but he sees with different eyes, from a different vantage point, or, one might say, in a different season of the mind, the season not of spring morning but of fall evening. He sees that life in space and time must mean, for men as well as for everything else, death in space and time. Seeing this, he imagines all space and time not as a bonfire really but as a shapeless, chaotic, great ocean of darkness: "Unfathomable," "enormous," vast.

The adverb "delightfully" gives a key to the first stage, the phrase "pity and indignation" sets the mood of the second, and the verb "to be" defines the sense of the third and final stage, the resolution. This begins "Enough!" The exclamation can be taken in the usual sense, "Enough of all this morbid reflection," meaning that it is nonsense or wrong to dwell on such melancholy thoughts. In fact, however, and the point is relevant to Hopkins' dark "terrible sonnets" of his very late period (this poem is, of course, one of his last), it can better be read to mean no more than what it literally says. The reflections on mortality have gone on not too long but simply long enough. It is good and necessary to think, even in pity and indignation, of how natural beings die, but one can dwell on such matters only so long. The first and second stages are both necessary to lead one on to the final stage. And this final reflection on what it means for man truly to *be* represents a higher version of the subject with which the poem began. For the subject now again is renewal, the renewal of life. First, nature renews itself after storms and pollutions. Second, since nature is like a great fire, in renewing itself it destroys all its individual forms; and from man's point of view this fact makes all of nature dark and terrible because within it shape, or specific being, is ephemeral. But, third, a man's shape, or being can be renewed as a fire is, and yet not destroyed, because it is more than natural. In nature's renewal of its fire there can be no resurrection, for nature consumes shape; the supernatural renewal restores and preserves shape, for it is precisely a resurrection of the body. So "the Resurrection" of Christ, which sets the pattern for an ultimate resurrection of all men's bodies, is a "heart's clarion" like the trumpet call of the angel Gabriel on the last day.

> Away grief's gasping, joyless days, dejection,
>   Across my foundering deck shone
> A beacon, an eternal beam. Flesh fade, and mortal trash
> Fall to the residuary worm; world's wildfire leave but
>   ash:
>   In a flash, at a trumpet crash,
> I am all at once what Christ is, since he was what I am,
>   and
> This Jack, joke, poor potsherd, patch, matchwood,
>   immortal
>
> diamond,
>   Is immortal diamond.

"Grief's gasping," the dejection of "joyless days," is what the darkest poems about the sense of self have expressed. But now, in this great and almost final poem, the imagery is echoed, and the themes are more succinctly developed, of Hopkins' most ambitious earlier work, **"The Deutschland."** . . . And in this final mood the poet is willing to let time and space blur, to let the flesh fade, the mortal body be consumed by worms and by the Heraclitean fire that leaves only ash, the literal dust to which mortal bodies return. For the flash of light reveals an inner shape that outlasts infinitely the splendid but brief natural form. A man, for Hopkins, is like the windhover and any other creature that reveals Christ's inscape, and yet he is much more than any other creature can be: he is what Christ is "in a flash." He is Christ-like when he flashes forth his own light all of a sudden. And he is what Christ is "at a trumpet crash," at the clarion call signalling the resurrection of all bodies on the day of judgment. The tenses—what Christ was on earth, what I am, what bodies will be at last—are all merged in an eternal present, a being essentially out of time. "I am," this body "is." Time is still kept in mind, as Christ "was what I am," a man incarnate in the flesh, at a point in history, but the meaning of all human history since that time—and "since" means both "because" and "ever since"—is eternal as well. Everything in time belongs partly to nature, but what is wholly natural is fuel in the temporal bonfire. Man exists not only in time, as Christ has been not only of the mortal flesh. Thus, a man, who appears to be and partly is common, "Jack" the common man, and trivial, a "joke," who appears to be mere clay, "potsherd," and fuel for the all-consuming fire of time, "matchwood," is really more than all this. Hopkins has used the term "Jack" several times before: in **"The Candle Indoors,"** in the lines (about "Jackself") **"My Own Heart Let Me Have More Pity On,"** and in the fragment that begins, **"The Shepherd's Brow, Fronting Forked Lightning,"** in which "Man Jack the man is, just." In each place the name suggests an everyman, a common and a dull sort of creature. In the **"Heraclitean Fire"** Jack the ordinary self becomes a diamond.

This last image carries the sense of infinite durability, for a diamond is the hardest of substances and is indestructible by fire. It also suggests the beauty of form that has been produced by stress, as the carbon of the jewel is like the earth and ember of **"The Windhover,"** flashing forth its brilliance only after having been submitted to intense pressure. And the diamond, for all its brilliance, is not so much the source as the reflector of light, catching it and flashing back. The immortal diamond is the creature and not the creator, even though at best it imitates and beautifully shows forth the divine and perfect light.

The **"Heraclitean Fire"** calls for such explication as this not because of its ambiguous phrasing and syntax, for it is less ambiguous than **"The Windhover"** and much of **"The Deutschland;"** and in fact the first part, its verbally most difficult one, has a total meaning extremely simple and obvious. Rather, the best of Hopkins' verse sustains a thinking-out of one's response to it, as the last part of this poem does, because for him art and thought are one. The rhyme, rhythm, and imagery *are* meaning, and it is as important in reading Hopkins to observe the ironic rhyming of "spark" and "dark," the change in speed of the sentences, from "all is in an enormous dark" to "a heart's clarion!" and the several implications of "dust," "bonfire," and "diamond," as it is to know the eschatology of the resurrection of the body.

In his thinking and feeling through images, often ambivalently, Hopkins is, again, as recognizably Victorian as Tennyson or Arnold. The difference is that his ambivalence is emotional but not, so to speak, intellectual; at best, his images both invite a double response and retain a single meaning. Men's inscapes are expressed in the observed lights of nature, as they are natural and mortal; yet the light that shapes an individual being is the reflection as well of divine light. And the image, of the body, the beacon, or the diamond, remains one. This is why, in spite of all his sufferings and anxieties—and he is quite as much in earnest about man's life, the beauty of nature, and the will of God as any other Victorian—Hopkins seems to have a more consistent imagination, in dealing with the largest of themes, than many of his contemporaries.

The danger of this consistency might be his striking the reader as narrow, as repetitive. Still, his imagery is specific and real, and his traditional response to Victorian questions about man and nature is as rich, complex, and personal as it is essentially paradoxical. He is more technically original and not much more limited by subject than George Herbert. Like Herbert and un-

like the Tennyson of the *Idylls,* who is also deeply concerned with spiritual self and physical nature, Hopkins has full intellectual control of his imagery and plot. For Tennyson's attempted image of Christ, a King representing pure spirit in conflict with the senses, is actually a Manichean anti-Christ who can only demonstrate how sterility and death, not marriage and its promise of birth, result from this conflict. If Hopkins' intellectual control of image and action is more consistent than Tennyson's, his point of view toward self and nature—as distinct from mood—is more consistent than, for instance, Arnold's; in Arnold's poetry, the ocean of external nature is sometimes man's exemplar of natural virtue and sometimes wholly alien to man. And although it is not necessarily a fault when a poet shifts the sense of a metaphor or symbol from poem to poem—with certain writers, one might argue, the result is freshness and variety—Arnold's shifting reveals an uncertainty about how to define or imagine man and nature, an uncertainty that makes the tone in his straightforward intellectual poems ring false by sounding either shrill or vague, as Hopkins' poetic statements of belief—even those that are relatively flat—virtually never do. Finally, Hopkins sustains his imagery within a poem much more consistently than Swinburne can, with his kaleidoscopic images of praise for freedom from all dogma and imposed forms. Tennyson writes poetry with more profoundly mysterious and more powerful symbolism; Arnold has a greater range and variety of mythic sources and ideas; and Browning has more dramatic force, more negative capability. Yet, compared with his major contemporaries, with whom he shares so many interests, Hopkins is more often able to concentrate into the brief lyric a clearly conceived, a coherently imagined, "philosophic" meaning. This is so because, as the consistency of his descriptive and metaphoric language from poem to poem may suggest, he maintains a central and single, if complex, idea of man and nature.

Not that Hopkins is in every respect superior to other Victorian poets. But within his range and at his best, his artist's imagination orders idea, plot, iconography, and tone in a way quite remarkable for his period, while using the themes of his period. Such poems, both personal and intellective or "objective," as **"The Windhover," "Spring and Fall,"** and, especially, **"That Nature Is a Heraclitean Fire"** are as luminous, as clear and whole, as any of the greatest English lyrics. (pp. 149-63)

Wendell Stacy Johnson, in his *Gerard Manley Hopkins: The Poet as Victorian,* Cornell University Press, 1968, 178 p.

SOURCES FOR FURTHER STUDY

Bottrall, Margaret, ed. *Gerard Manley Hopkins, Poems: A Casebook.* Casebook Series, edited by A. E. Dyson. London: Macmillan Press, 1975, 256 p.

> Reprints selected criticism important to the growth of Hopkins's reputation.

Bump, Jerome. *Gerard Manley Hopkins.* Boston: Twayne Publishers, 1982, 225 p.

> A biographical and critical survey.

Hartman, Geoffrey H., ed. *Hopkins: A Collection of Critical Essays.* Englewood Cliffs, N.J.: Prentice-Hall, 1966, 182 p.

> Includes essays on Hopkins's works by such critics as Hartman, Herbert Marshall McLuhan, J. Hillis Miller, and Walter J. Ong.

The Hopkins Quarterly I— (1974-).

> A quarterly journal devoted to Hopkins studies.

The Kenyon Critics. *Gerard Manley Hopkins.* The Makers of Modern Literature Series. Norfolk, Conn.: New Directions Books, 1945, 144 p.

> Influential essays by Austin Warren, Herbert Marshall McLuhan, Harold Whitehall, Josephine Miles, Robert Lowell, Arthur Mizener, and F. R. Leavis. Most of these essays first appeared in the *Kenyon Review* in 1944.

Weyand, Norman, S.J., ed. *Immortal Diamond: Studies in Gerard Manley Hopkins.* New York: Sheed & Ward, 1949, 451 p.

> A collection of essays by Jesuit scholars on various aspects of Hopkins's works.

Langston Hughes

1902-1967

(Full name James Mercer Langston Hughes) American poet, short story writer, novelist, dramatist, autobiographer, editor, translator, and author of children's books.

INTRODUCTION

A seminal figure of the Harlem Renaissance, a period during the 1920s of unprecedented artistic and intellectual achievement among black Americans, Hughes devoted his versatile and prolific career to portraying the urban experience of working-class blacks. Called "the Poet Laureate of Harlem" by Carl Van Vechten, Hughes integrated the rhythm and mood of jazz and blues music into his work and used colloquial language to reflect black American culture. Hughes's gentle humor and wry irony often belie the magnitude of his themes. Having been a victim of poverty and discrimination, Hughes wrote about being seduced by the American Dream of freedom and equality only to be denied its realization. He composed the poem "Dream Deferred" to express his frustration: "What happens to a dream deferred? / Does it dry up / like a raisin in the sun? / Or fester like a sore— / And then run? / Does it stink like rotten meat? / Or crust and sugar over— / like a syrupy sweet? / Maybe it just sags / like a heavy load. / Or *does it explode?*" Speaking of Hughes's wide-range of works, Theodore R. Hudson stated: "Dipping his pen in ink, not acid, [Hughes's] method was to expose rather than excoriate, to reveal rather than revile."

Hughes was born in Joplin, Missouri, to James Nathaniel and Carrie Mercer Langston Hughes, who separated shortly after the boy's birth. His father left the United States for Cuba and later settled in Mexico, where he lived the remainder of his life as a prosperous attorney and landowner. In contrast, Hughes's mother lived a transitory life, often leaving him in the care of his maternal grandmother while searching for a job. Following his grandmother's death in 1910, Hughes lived with family friends and various relatives in Kansas and, in 1914, joined his mother and new stepfather in Cleveland, Ohio. Hughes attended Central High

School, where he excelled academically and in sports. He also wrote poetry and short fiction for the *Belfry Owl,* the high school literary magazine, and edited the school yearbook. In the summer of 1919 Hughes visited his father in Mexico for the first time but soon became disillusioned with his father's materialistic values and contemptuous belief that blacks, Mexicans, and Indians were lazy and ignorant. Upon graduating from high school in 1920, Hughes returned to Mexico, where he taught English for a year and wrote poems and prose pieces for publication in the *Crisis,* the magazine of the National Association for the Advancement of Colored People. With the help of his father, who had originally urged him to study engineering in Switzerland or Germany, Hughes enrolled at Columbia University in New York City in 1921, favoring classes in English literature. Subjected to bigotry on campus—he was assigned the worst dormitory room because of his color—and teachers he found boring, Hughes often missed classes in order to attend shows, lectures, and readings sponsored by the American Socialist Society. Following his freshman year, Hughes dropped out of college and worked a series of odd jobs while supporting his mother, who had recently moved to Harlem. Hughes also published several poems in the *Crisis* during this period. In 1923 he signed on as a cabin boy on a merchant freighter en route to West Africa.

Hughes spent the majority of the following year overseas. After resigning his position on the *S. S. Mc-Keesport* in the Netherlands, he lived in virtual poverty in France and Italy. Returning to the United States in 1925, he resettled with his mother and half brother in Washington, D. C. He continued writing poetry while working menial jobs, experimenting with language, form, and rhythms reminiscent of the blues and jazz compositions he had heard in Paris nightclubs. In May and August of 1925, Hughes's verse garnered him literary prizes from both *Opportunity* magazine and the *Crisis.* In December, Hughes, then a busboy at a Washington, D.C., hotel, attracted the attention of poet Vachel Lindsay by placing three of his poems on Lindsay's dinner table. Later that evening Lindsay read Hughes's poems to an audience and announced his discovery of a "Negro busboy poet." The next day reporters and photographers eagerly greeted Hughes at work to hear more of his compositions.

Shortly thereafter, with the help of critic and art patron Carl Van Vechten, Hughes published his first book, *The Weary Blues* (1926), a collection of poems that reflect the frenzied atmosphere of Harlem nightlife. Most of the selections in this volume approximate the phrasing and meter of blues music, a genre popularized in the early 1920s by rural and urban blacks. In such pieces as "Jazzonia," "Cabaret," and "The Weary Blues," Hughes evoked the frenzied, hedonistic atmosphere of Harlem's famous nightclubs and speak-

easies, while "The Jester" and "Mother to Son" comment upon racial conflict. Hughes also included several pieces about his travels in Africa, as well as "The Negro Speaks of Rivers," a much-anthologized poem Hughes wrote during his second visit to Mexico in 1920. The lines "I bathed in the Euphrates when dawns were young / I built my hut near the Congo and it lulled me to sleep" foreshadow the nationalist writings later popularized by other writers of the Harlem Renaissance and by young militant poets of the Civil Rights era. *The Weary Blues* received mixed reviews, with some critics questioning the motives and appropriateness of using blues and jazz verse to describe Harlem life. Countee Cullen wrote: "I regard these jazz poems as interlopers in the company of the truly beautiful poems. . . . There is too much emphasis here on strictly Negro themes."

Shortly before the publication of *The Weary Blues,* Hughes enrolled at Lincoln University in Pennsylvania, where he continued publishing poetry, short stories, and essays in mainstream and black-oriented periodicals. In 1927, Hughes, Zora Neale Hurston, and other writers founded *Fire!,* a literary journal devoted to African-American culture. The venture was unsuccessful however, and a fire eventually destroyed the editorial offices. In the spring of the same year, Hughes published his second collection of verse, *Fine Clothes to the Jew* (1927). In this volume he included several ballads and chose Harlem's lower class as his principal subject. This approach dismayed several leading black intellectuals and critics, who felt that Hughes's depictions of crap games, street brawls, and other unsavory activities would undermine their efforts to improve race relations. Alain Locke, however, held an opposing view: "[*Fine Clothes to the Jew*] is notable as an achievement in poetic realism in addition to its particular value as a folk study in verse of Negro life." During the late 1920s Hughes met Mrs. R. Osgood Mason, an elderly white widow whom he called "Godmother" and who served as both his literary patron and friend. Strongly committed to developing the talents of young black artists, Mason supported Hughes while he wrote his first novel, *Not without Laughter* (1930). Following this book's publication, however, Hughes and Mason suffered a dramatic and bitter break in their relationship. Hughes later reconstructed these events in his short story "The Blues I'm Playing."

In 1932 Hughes traveled to Moscow with other black Americans on an unsuccessful filmmaking venture that nevertheless proved instrumental to his short story writing. While working as a journalist in Moscow, a friend loaned Hughes a copy of D. H. Lawrence's short story collection *The Lovely Lady.* After reading the title story, Hughes was struck by the similarities between Lawrence's main character and Mrs. Mason, his former Park Avenue patron. Overwhelmed by the power of Lawrence's stories, Hughes began writing short fiction of his own. By 1933, when he returned to the United States, he had sold three stories and had begun compiling his first collection, *The Ways of White Folks* (1934). Between 1933 and 1935 Hughes wrote the majority of his short stories, and, in 1943, the first of his Simple tales appeared in the black-owned *Chicago Defender* newspaper. His most noted short pieces, the Simple sketches center on Jesse B. Semple, known as Simple, who is a black Everyman. Simple is the quintessential "wise fool" whose experiences and uneducated insights capture the frustrations felt by black Americans. Arthur P. Davis declared that "Simple's honest and unsophisticated eye sees through the shallowness, hypocrisy, and phoniness of white and black America alike." The Simple sketches were very popular among black readers of Hughes's day, and they remain some of Hughes's best-loved works. The Simple stories are collected in *Simple Speaks His Mind* (1950), *Simple Takes a Wife* (1953), *Simple Stakes a Claim* (1957), and *Simple's Uncle Sam* (1965).

Although generally considered less significant than his poetry and prose, Hughes's work for the theater was also popular with black audiences. Using such innovations as theater-in-the-round and audience participation, Hughes anticipated the work of later avant-garde dramatists, including Amiri Baraka and Sonia Sanchez. In 1938 Hughes founded the Harlem Suitcase Theater and also helped establish the Los Angeles Negro Arts Theater and the Skyloft Players of Chicago. As with his work in other genres, Hughes's drama combines urban dialogue, folk idioms, and a thematic emphasis on the dignity and strength of black Americans. *Mulatto* (1935), his first play to be produced, *Little Ham* (1935), *Soul Gone Home* (1937), *Simply Heavenly* (1957), and *Tambourines to Glory* (1963) are among Hughes's most noted plays.

Despite his success in a variety of genres, Hughes considered himself a poet first. In the late 1930s, after producing numerous plays and short stories, he returned to writing poetry. These later collections of verse, however, show an increasingly bleak view of black America. In *Montage of a Dream Deferred* (1951) Hughes contrasted the drastically deteriorated state of Harlem in the 1950s to the Harlem he had known in the 1920s. The exuberance of nightclub life and the vitality of cultural renaissance had given way to an urban ghetto plagued by poverty and crime. Parallel to the change in tone was a change in rhythm: the smooth patterns and gentle melancholy of blues music were replaced by the abrupt, fragmented structure of postwar jazz and bebop. *Ask Your Mama: 12 Moods for Jazz* (1961) consists of twelve irreverent poems that comment on the political turbulence of the early 1960s. Intended to be read aloud with musical accompaniment, Hughes's verse offers acerbic solutions

to segregation and the plight of Southern blacks. He also rendered an imaginary South in which civil rights leader Martin Luther King, Jr., is elected governor of the state of Georgia, and Orval Faubus, the Arkansas governor who defied federal court orders to desegregate public schools, becomes a mammy in charge of rearing black children. Hughes's final collection of verse, *The Panther and the Lash: Poems of Our Times,* was published posthumously in 1967. In such pieces as "Black Panther" and "The Backlash Blues," Hughes wrote bitterly and angrily about race relations in America. This volume received scant critical attention upon its publication; some reviewers viewed the work as a polemical effort that surrendered to political fashion. W. Edward Farrison, however, considered *The Panther and the Lash* an appropriate conclusion to Hughes's career: "From the beginning of his career as an author, Hughes was articulate in the Negro's struggle for first-class citizenship. It is indeed fitting that this volume with which his career ended is a vital contribution to that struggle as well as to American poetry."

Throughout his career Hughes encountered mixed reactions to his work. Many black intellectuals denounced him for portraying unsophisticated aspects of lower-class life, claiming that his focus furthered the unfavorable image of his race. Hughes, however, believed in the inherent worth of the common people and in the need to present the truth as he perceived it: "I didn't know the upper class Negroes well enough to write much about them. I knew only the people I had grown up with, and they weren't people whose shoes were always shined, who had been to Harvard, or who had heard of Bach. But they seemed to me good people, too." As the struggle for American civil rights became increasingly widespread toward the end of his life, Hughes was also faulted by militants for failing to address controversial issues. Nevertheless, Hughes's reputation with black readers has remained consistently strong, chiefly due to his poetry and short stories. Despite the criticism, Hughes' position in the American literary scene seems to be secure. David Littlejohn wrote: "[Hughes is] the one sure Negro classic, more certain of permanence than even Baldwin or Ellison or Wright. . . . His voice is as sure, his manner as original, his position as secure as, say Edwin Arlington Robinson's or Robinson Jeffers'. . . . By molding his verse always on the sounds of Negro talk, the rhythms of Negro music, by retaining his own keen honesty and directness, his poetic sense and ironic intelligence, he maintained through four decades a readable newness distinctly his own."

(For further information about Hughes's life and works, see *Black Literature Criticism; Black Writers; Children's Literature Review,* Vol. 17; *Contemporary Authors,* Vols. 1-4, 25-28; *Contemporary Authors New Revision Series,* Vol. 1; *Contemporary Literary Criti-*

cism, Vols. 1, 5, 10, 15, 35, 44; *Dictionary of Literary Bi-
ography,* Vols. 4, 7, 48, 51, 86; *Poetry Criticism,* Vol. 1;
Short Story Criticism, Vol. 6; and *Something about the
Author,* Vols. 4, 33.)

CRITICAL COMMENTARY

EDWARD E. WALDRON
(essay date 1971)

[In the following excerpt, Waldron explores three
themes common in Hughes's blues poetry: love,
bad luck, and flight.]

As a form of folk expression, the blues has come to occupy a justly revered spot in American music; at long
last, recognition is being given to the artists—and the
audience—that were instrumental in creating this art
form. At the same time, many writers/poets have attempted for years to incorporate the essence of the
blues into works outside the reference of music—i.e.,
into stories and poetry. One of the most successful
poets in this endeavor was Langston Hughes, the "Poet
Laureate" of Black America. In his blues poetry Langston Hughes captures the mood, the feel, and the spirit
of the blues; his poems have the rhythm and the impact
of the musical form they incorporate. Indeed, the blues
poems of Langston Hughes *are* blues as well as poetry. . . .

[The] blues reflects the trials and tribulations of
the Negro in America on a secular level, much as the
spirituals do on the religious level. Both expressions
are, certainly, necessary releases. In one of his "Blues
for Men" poems in *Shakespeare in Harlem,* Hughes
dramatizes the necessity for this release. Lamenting the
dirty treatment he has received from his woman, the
singer of **"In a Troubled Key"** (the narrator of a blues
poem *is* a singer, in effect) sings:

> Still I can't help lovin' you,
> Even though you do me wrong.
> Says I can't help lovin' you
> Though you do me wrong—
> But my love might turn into a knife
> Instead of to a song.

Here we see the blues maker turning his despair into
song instead of into murder; and, one has the feeling
that the mood of the blues is often one step away from
death—either murder or suicide—and that the presence
of the blues form makes it possible for the anguished
one to direct his sorrow inward into song and find happiness in the release. (p. 140)

The blues, as any art form, has definite patterns
which are adhered to in its composition. In [an] introductory **"Note on Blues,"** . . . in *Fine Clothes to the
Jew,* Hughes gives us the most common pattern:

> The *Blues,* unlike the *Spirituals,* have a strict poetic
> pattern: one long line repeated and a third line to
> rhyme with the first two. Sometimes the second line
> in repetition is slightly changed and sometimes, but
> very seldom, it is omitted.

In order to maintain a closer semblance to poetic
form, Hughes breaks the first two lines into two lines
each and also divides the final line, creating a six-line
stanza. A typical stanza is this one from **"Po' Boy
Blues":**

> When I was home de
> Sunshine seemed like gold.
> When I was home de
> Sunshine seemed like gold.
> Since I come up North de
> Whole damn world's turned cold.

The second stanza of the poem illustrates the
change that often occurs in the repeated line(s):

> I was a good boy,
> Never done no wrong.
> Yes, I was a good boy,
> Never done no wrong.
> But this world is weary
> An' de road is hard an' long.

In the case of a line changed in repetition, sometimes a word of exclamation, such as the "Yes" of this
example, is added, and sometimes a word or two might
be omitted, if not the whole line. For example, consider
this stanza from **"Bound No'th Blues":**

> Goin' down de road, Lawd,
> Goin' down de road.
> Down de road, Lawd,
> Way, way, down de road.
> Got to find somebody
> To help me carry dis load.

Here we see both kinds of change taking place;
the repeated first line has dropped a word, and the repeated second line has changed by dropping one word

Principal Works

"Negro Artist and the Racial Mountain" (essay) 1926; published in periodical The Nation

The Weary Blues (poetry) 1926

Fine Clothes to the Jew (poetry) 1927

Not without Laughter (novel) 1930

Dear Lovely Death (poetry) 1931

The Negro Mother and Other Dramatic Recitations (poetry) 1931

The Dream Keeper and Other Poems (poetry) 1932

Popo and Fifina: Children of Haiti [with Arna Bontemps] (juvenilia) 1932

Scottsboro Limited: Four Poems and a Play in Verse (poetry and drama) 1932

The Ways of White Folks (short stories) 1934

Little Ham (drama) 1935

Mulatto (drama) 1935

Soul Gone Home (drama) 1937

Don't You Want to Be Free? (drama) 1938

A New Song (poetry) 1938

The Big Sea: An Autobiography (autobiography) 1940

Shakespeare in Harlem (poetry) 1942

Freedom's Plow (poetry) 1943

Jim Crow's Last Stand (poetry) 1943

Lament for Dark Peoples and Other Poems (poetry) 1944

Fields of Wonder (poetry) 1947

One-Way Ticket (poetry) 1949

The Barrier (libretto) 1950

Simple Speaks His Mind (short stories) 1950

Montage of a Dream Deferred (poetry) 1951

Laughing to Keep from Crying (short stories) 1952

Simple Takes a Wife (short stories) 1953

The Sweet Flypaper of Life [with Roy De Carava] (nonfiction) 1955

I Wonder as I Wander: An Autobiographical Journey (autobiography) 1956

Simple Stakes a Claim (short stories) 1957

Simply Heavenly (drama) 1957

The Langston Hughes Reader (poetry and short stories) 1958

*Tambourines to Glory (novel) 1958

Selected Poems of Langston Hughes (poetry) 1959

Ask Your Mama: 12 Moods for Jazz (poetry) 1961

The Best of Simple (short stories) 1961

Black Nativity (drama) 1961

Five Plays by Langston Hughes (dramas) 1963

Something in Common and Other Stories (short stories) 1963

Simple's Uncle Sam (short stories) 1965

The Panther and the Lash: Poems of Our Times (poetry) 1967

†Mule Bone: A Comedy of Negro Life [with Zora Neale Hurston] (drama) 1991

*This work was adapted for the stage in 1963.

†This comedy, completed by Hughes and Hurston in 1930, was first staged in 1991 with a prologue and epilogue by George Houston Bass.

---

and adding others in its place. This changing of lines helps keep the flow of the poem going, without ruining the effectiveness of the repetition. (pp. 141-42)

As with any poetic style, the blues' form is directly related to its content. Although what a particular blues is about may vary from blues to blues, the basic content of the blues usually has to do with some form of disappointment, most commonly in love, but also in other areas of life—or maybe in just plain living. [E. Simms] Campbell may be going a little overboard when he states that the blues " . . . are songs of sorrow charged with satire, with that potent quality of ironic verse clothed in the raiment of the buffoon." Yet, he is close to the same concept of the blues that Hughes voiced in the **"Note on Blues"** in *Fine Clothes to the Jew:*

The mood of the *Blues* is almost always despondency, but when they are sung people laugh.

This seemingly paradoxical statement reflects an

essence that is found in almost every facet of Black American expression: the duality of laughing and crying at the same time or, as Hughes says it, "laughing to keep from crying." Laughing at trouble is a concept we may all try to adopt at one time or another, but Black American writers have wrought this fine ability into a grand motif that consistently runs through their works; and Langston Hughes is certainly qualified as an artist in weaving this quality into his poetry and other works. (p. 142)

An extensive treatment of the man's side of the lost-love blues is found in the "Seven Moments of Love" section of *Shakespeare in Harlem,* which Hughes subtitled "An Un-Sonnet Sequence in Blues." This is a progressive series of seven poems dealing with a man's state of mind after his woman has left him. At first **("Twilight Reverie")** he wants to shoot her, but his loneliness begins to take away that mood. By **"Supper Time"** his despair has advanced to the point where he can hear his "heartbeats trying to think" and his "footprints walking on the floor." **"Bed Time"** is even worse; he wants to go out and have fun, but his habits of being with his woman won't let him go: "A human gets lonesome if there ain't two." He wakes up the next day **("Daybreak"),** miserable, and wonders "if white folks ever feels bad / Getting up in the morning lonesome and sad?" **"Sunday"** finds him thinking again about how "glad" he is to be "free"—"But this house is mighty quiet!" On **"Pay Day"** he recalls how he used to have to give his woman all the money, but now he is free to spend it all by himself. He is going to give up the furniture and things and go back to renting "a cubby-hole with a single bed." His dismay at his woman has the sound of frustrated humanity in it:

Women's abominations! Just like a curse!
You was the best—but you *the worst!*

Finally, he hears from Cassie and writes her a **"Letter"** telling her to come back: "I can't get along with you, I can't get along without." With this last echoing thought, a thought that permeates the blues of love, Hughes closes one of his more ambitious blues poetry experiments. Throughout this series of poems Hughes manages to maintain a sense of identity in the singer of the blues and keeps at work a progression that ties together all seven poems very neatly. (p. 143)

While men do get to sing some of the blues written by Langston Hughes, the women seem to find favor with the poet more frequently, and their reactions often are more severe. Two poems from *Fine Clothes to the Jew* state explicitly the blues singer's desire to kill herself. The first stanza in **"Suicide"** as well as the title itself, makes the singer's intent quite clear:

Ma sweet good man has
Packed his trunk and left.
Ma sweet good man has
Packed his trunk and left.
Nobody to love me:
I'm gonna kill ma self.

The river usually serves as the focal point for the suicide's thoughts of self-murder, although this woman does consider using a knife first. She rejects the blade, though, in favor of the water. . . . Of course, no one expects the blues singer to go out and commit suicide; after all, singing the blues is supposed to help relieve the hurt and act to channel the emotions away from self-directed or other-directed murder (see **"In a Troubled Key"** mentioned earlier).

In another woman's blues, **"Midnight Chippie's Lament"** (*Shakespeare in Harlem*), Hughes presents us with a blues person who seeks out the blues instead of death for her release:

I looked down 31st Street,
Not a soul but Lonesome Blue.
Down on 31st Street,

Nobody but Lonesome Blue.
I said come here, Lonesome,
And I will love you, too.

But "Lonesome Blue" rejects her offer, saying:

Woman, listen! Hey!
Buy you two for a quarter
On State Street any day.

Although Hughes ends this blues with a bit of sardonic humor ("Cry to yourself, girls, / So nobody can't low-rate you"), it still remains obvious that the woman singing this blues has reached a desperate level; she'd rather have the lonesome blues than *nothing* at all. (pp. 143-44)

[Love] is not the only subject of the blues, even though it does dominate as the main concern of the blues. Another common theme of the blues is bad luck. **"Hard Luck"** in *Fine Clothes to the Jew* is a good example of this kind of blues and gives the source of the title of that collection:

When hard luck overtakes you
Nothin' for you to do.
When hard luck overtakes you
Nothin' for you to do.
Gather up yo' fine clothes
An' sell 'em to de Jew.

"De Jew" here is, of course, the local pawnbroker, the man to whom the desperate must turn in order to scrape up a few pennies with the last of their possessions. That the amount given for the goods received is rarely considered equitable is reflected in the second stanza:

Jew takes yo' fine clothes,
Gives you a dollar an' a half.
Jew takes yo' fine clothes,
Gives you a dollar an' a half.
Go to de bootleg's
Git some cheap gin to make you laugh.

(p. 145)

A final dominant theme in blues poetry is the idea of moving, of traveling, of getting away. **"Six-Bit Blues,"** an early poem which appeared originally in *Opportunity* (February, 1939), has this idea as its central theme:

Gimme six-bits' worth o' ticket
On a train that runs somewhere.
I say six-bits' worth o' ticket
On a train that runs somewhere.
I don't care where it's goin'
Just so it goes away from here.

The urgent need to move and to escape does not precede the need for love, but it makes that need somehow less binding:

Make it short and sweet, your lovin',
So I can roll along.

I got to roll along!

The final "tag" line, italicized for emphasis, reinforces the singer's urgent desire to get away. No explanation is given about why he wants to leave, but an explanation really is not necessary. In fact, given the nature of the blues, the question is probably irrelevant. (pp. 146-47)

Humor dominates in a few of the blues poems of Langston Hughes. **"Crowing-Hen Blues"** (*Poetry,* September, 1943) is a blues that is also pure folk humor. The singer, after a rough night of drinking, swears he hears his cat talking:

I had a cat, I called him
Battling Tom Mc Cann.
Had a big black cat, I called him
Battling Tom Mc Cann.
Last night that cat riz up and
Started talking like a man.

Waking up his "baby" to tell her the news, he gets a skeptical reaction: "I don't hear nothin' / But your drunken snorin', dear." Undaunted, the singer stands up for his right to drink and hallucinate all he wants. . . . (p. 147)

Another humorous blues poem by Hughes is **"Morning After,"** from the "Blues for Men" section of *Shakespeare in Harlem.* The subject of this blues, again a hangover and its effect on the singer, seems more the subject of a standup comedian than a blues maker, but the blues form does suit this particular poem. The first stanza establishes the man's problem:

I was so sick last night I
Didn't hardly know my mind.
So sick last night I
Didn't know my mind.
I drunk some bad licker that
Almost made me blind.

The humor gets very heavy-handed in the last two stanzas, as the man laments that his baby's "mouth was open like a well" and made enough noise for "a great big crowd." While this type of blues may not be as common as other blues, it does illustrate the wide possibilities of the blues form. Clearly, the mood of this blues poem is *not* despondency.

In addition to the more common subjects for blues that Hughes makes use of in his poetry, he also uses other, less common, subjects. A natural disaster would most likely find its way into a blues or a folk ballad, and Hughes took a terrible flooding of the Mississippi as the subject for his **"Mississippi Levee."** In the poem the singer cries out in anguish as the flood-waters keep coming in spite of his efforts to stop them. . . . A sense of hopelessness dominates this poem and is made clear in the final stanza:

Levee, Levee,

How high have you got to be?
Levee, Levee,
How high have you got to be?
To keep them cold muddy waters
From washin' over me?

Folk material has always made use of local natural disorders as subject matter, and this poem is in keeping with that tradition.

Finally, the blues themselves serve as the subject for some of the blues written by Langston Hughes, and the best single example of this type of poem is the title poem from *The Weary Blues.* In this poem, Hughes sets up a "frame" wherein he recalls the performance of a blues singer-pianist "on Lenox Avenue the other night":

With his ebony hands on each ivory key He made that poor piano moan with melody—

. . . . .

Sweet Blues!
Coming from a black man's soul.

After an exhausting performance, one that both drains and relaxes the blues man as only a creative act can, he quits his playing and goes to bed:

While the Weary Blues echoed through his head.
He slept like a rock or a man that's dead.

This form proves quite effective, since in it the reader receives not only the blues of the singer, but also a look at the creation of this blues from an outside source—the poet. In this way we become totally involved in the creative blues process.

The blues poetry of Langston Hughes, then, has a great deal to offer. Within this limited source of Hughes's creativity alone, we confront many of the themes that he develops more fully in other works. Loneliness, despair, frustration, and a nameless sense of longing are all represented in the blues poetry; and, these themes dominate not only the works of Hughes but also those of most Black American writers.

What direction Hughes's poetry of the blues might have taken thematically were he writing today is hinted at in the one traditional-form blues included in his last collection of verse, *The Panther and The Lash:* **"The Backlash Blues."** Once again Hughes underscores his concern with the social plight of the Black man in America in this poem, which also warns—

I'm gonna leave you, Mister Backlash,
Singing your mean old backlash blues.

You're the one,

Yes, you're the one
Will have the blues.

While the blues traditionally have not concerned themselves *directly* with sociopolitical problems, and while Hughes follows this tradition fairly closely in his blues poetry, one sees in this, his final published blues poem the potential that Hughes might have developed in light of today's Black Power movement. Whether he would have gone in this direction or not is, of course, mere speculation, but his concern with the common man throughout his blues poetry—and other works—could have led him in this direction.

At any rate the blues poems we *do* have from this gifted poet illustrate quite well the effectiveness of this great American art form—even though his blues are read and not sung. Indeed, Hughes's sensitive reproduction of the language of the blues, which is the language of the common man/blues maker, and his ability to recreate the rhythmic effect of a sung blues make it difficult *not* to sing, however softly, the blues of Langston Hughes. (pp. 147-49)

Edward E. Waldron, "The Blues Poetry of Langston Hughes," in *Negro American Literature Forum*, Vol. 5, No. 4, Winter, 1971, pp. 140-49.

CARY D. WINTZ

(essay date 1975)

[In the following excerpt, Wintz traces Hughes's portrayal of the black working class from the Depression to the Civil Rights era.]

The Harlem Renaissance of the 1920's was the first major literary movement in the Negro's experience in America. As such it provides an important and well-developed statement of the Negro's attempt to come to terms with his experience in America. The Renaissance occurred at a critical moment in the history of the American Negro. On the one hand, during the 1920's the urban ghetto was rapidly replacing the rural South as the principal environment of blacks in this country. At the same time blacks were re-evaluating their approach to racial problems. The death of Booker T. Washington, the rise of the National Association for the Advancement of Colored People, and the postwar race riots signaled an increasing impatience with accommodation and the growth of racial pride. The black writers of the Harlem Renaissance gave expression to these feelings of social and political unrest, and they attempted to define the Negro experience in a manner which would integrate the Negro's rural heritage with his new urban existence.

Ironically, most of the black writers who participated in the Harlem Renaissance came from backgrounds that were far removed from the harsh but colorful life of the black ghetto. Langston Hughes, one of the most gifted writers of the period, spent his formative years in Topeka and Lawrence, Kansas, more than a thousand miles from the sidewalks and tenements of Harlem. Nevertheless, Hughes emerged as the most brilliant of Harlem's Renaissance poets, and as the one who created the most vibrant portrait of the Negro's urban experience.

The road from Lawrence, Kansas, to Harlem was a long one, and it would not have been unusual if Hughes had ignored his small-town background as he became a spokesman for the black metropolis. At first glance, Hughes's Renaissance poetry, with its emphasis on urban themes, seems to support this premise. However, at least during the 1920's he never completely severed his ties with the heritage of his childhood. Many of his values, particularly his interest in the common man and his racial pride, much of his intellectual curiosity, and his fascination with literature were born during his years in Kansas. And before he withdrew from involvement with the Harlem Renaissance, Hughes focused his literary talents on the experiences of his youth, and produced a rare picture of black life in Kansas. (p. 58)

In 1926 Hughes had published his first volume of poetry, *The Weary Blues.* This book, published with the assistance of novelist Carl Van Vechten, contained a sampling of much of the material he had written up to this point. The most outstanding feature in this volume was the use of Negro music as a model for a number of poems. The blues and jazz, the distinctive music of Negro life, provided the form for the title poem and several others. This stylistic experimentation was one of the major elements in Hughes's work. In this first volume the young poet also introduced the two major themes that would characterize his poetry throughout his long career. First, he expressed a deep commitment to the Negro masses. Years earlier he had learned from his grandmother the dignity and drama of the oppressed's struggle against injustice, and he had observed first hand the lives of the ordinary Negro working people. It is not surprising, then, that as a poet he consistently sang the song of the people. Most of his work focused on the men and women he saw around him—elevator operators, workers, cabaret dancers, prostitutes, and ordinary people walking down the street. His verses reflected a keen insight into the life of the Negro masses, including a vivid picture of the poverty and deprivation of their life. The poignant advice in **"Mother to Son"** captured this element in Hughes's work:

Well, son, I'll tell you:
Life for me ain't been no crystal stair.

It's had tacks in it,
And splinters,
And boards torn up,
And places with no carpet on the floor—
Bare.

The second theme that Hughes introduced in his first volume of poetry was Harlem. Although he depicted Negro life in the rural South, and occasionally in his native Midwest, Hughes was essentially an urban poet, and life in the Negro metropolis was a basic element in his work throughout his career. As Arthur P. Davis observed, "either stated or implied, used as subject or background or protagonist, and on occasion even as a symbol for Negroes everywhere, Harlem has been a constantly recurring theme in Langston Hughes' poetry." In every book except one, beginning with *The Weary Blues* and ending with *The Panther and the Lash* in 1967, Hughes examined life in Harlem.

In 1926 Hughes's Harlem was the Renaissance metropolis with the sounds of jazz floating down the streets and a club on every corner where "sleek black boys" and "shameless girls" found joy in a "whirling cabaret." Hughes, however, was also a realist. More clearly than most other Renaissance writers he saw that beneath Harlem's glitter was an oppressive, melancholy slum; the excitement of jazz contrasted sharply with the weary blues. . . . (pp. 60-1)

Hughes published his second volume of poetry, *Fine Clothes for the Jew,* in 1927. In this collection he continued to develop the themes that he introduced in the first volume. He felt that this book was better than *The Weary Blues* because "it was more impersonal, more about other people than myself, and because it made use of the Negro folk-song forms, and included poems about work and the problems of finding work, that are always so pressing with the Negro people." However, a number of black critics did not share this conviction. Many Negro intellectuals and much of the Negro press condemned Hughes for his preoccupation with the lower classes, and viewed his jazz and blues poems as a disgrace to the race and a return to the dialect tradition of Paul Dunbar. Most white critics liked the book, although a number of Jews were offended by the title. With his second volume of poetry Hughes established himself as one of the better young black poets, and as one of the most controversial. He had won the reputation of a talented but radical poet who flirted with the leftist political doctrines and opened his pages to the Negro proletariat. (p. 61)

Throughout the Renaissance Hughes continued to be preoccupied with the themes he had introduced in *The Weary Blues.* As he matured as a poet in the late 1920's he turned his attention more and more on the Negro lower classes, examining all aspects of their lives—joy, sorrow, pleasure, and poverty. In later years Hughes would refer to himself as a "social poet," and

note that he often focused his attention on the proletariat. However, as deep as his commitment was to the lower classes, he never lost touch with the individual, and his poetry remained on a personal level. During the Renaissance, at least, he always addressed himself to the problems of living, breathing individuals, not to the abstraction of a faceless social class. In an article written several years after the Renaissance Hughes looked back on his career and explained why he so often directed his art toward the life and social problems of the lower classes:

Beauty and lyricism are really related to another world, to ivory towers, to your head in the clouds, feet floating off the earth. Unfortunately, having been born poor—and also colored—in Missouri, I was stuck in the mud from the beginning. Try as I might to float off into the clouds, poverty and Jim Crow would grab me by the heels, and right back to earth I would land.

In addition Hughes believed that there was more vitality among the lower classes, and that this made them better material for literature. . . . (p. 62)

In *The Weary Blues* and especially in *Fine Clothes for the Jew,* Hughes's poetry reflected this preoccupation with the working class. In **"Elevator Boy,"** for example, he examined one of the menial jobs that many blacks drifted into and then quickly out of. Jobs, he observed, were closely related to luck—occasionally he would find a good one, but frequently he would hit a string of bad luck and drift from one poor job to another, earning barely enough to provide the necessities of life. . . . In **"Brass Spittoons"** Hughes exposed the oppressive nature of much of the work set aside for blacks. In this case the job was not only menial, it was also demeaning. . . . Like the elevator operator, the spittoon boy worked for the basic necessities of life— house rent, shoes for the baby, and gin on Saturday. For this he endured a distasteful job which was meaningful only in his fantasies. Always, though, his dreams evaporated with the rude snarl of his boss.

The life of the poor was not all work. Hughes also examined the ghetto night clubs and cabarets where he found blacks at play. . . . Unlike other black poets who often depicted only the glamorous side of the ghetto existence, Hughes never lost sight of the uncertainties of poverty. The pleasures and joy of the cabaret were at best only temporary rays of sunshine which brightened an otherwise bleak landscape. There were, of course, some pleasures that were less transitory:

When Susanna Jones wears red
Her face is like an ancient cameo
Turned brown by the ages.
Come with a blast of trumpets, Jesus!

These poems, and much of what Hughes wrote

during this period, reflected his second major concern, life in Harlem. The bars, streets, and tenements of the Negro metropolis formed a constant background for much of Hughes's work. This element in his poetry culminated in 1951 in a book-length epic discourse on Harlem, *Montage of a Dream Deferred.* During the Renaissance he carefully laid the foundations for this work with numerous poetic sketches of ghetto life.

As Hughes developed his portrayal of the black lower classes and their ghetto environment, he became more and more preoccupied with the question of the Negro's racial identity. Hughes had begun his search for the meaning of the racial experience in America shortly after he graduated from high school. In his first mature poem, **"A Negro Speaks of Rivers,"** he found an analogy between the river that flowed through his native Midwest and the ancient rivers that watered the lands where his race was born:

I've known rivers:
I've known rivers ancient as the world and older
   than the flow of human blood in human veins.
My soul has grown deep like the rivers

Hughes continued this investigation in several directions. First, like many of his contemporaries, he looked to Africa, where he found few answers but a great many questions. In 1923 he had visited Africa while working on an American freighter. At first he saw his ancient homeland as an exotic land of black, beautiful people, sensual women, and strong men laboring on the docks. Then, he found to his amazement that the Africans considered him white because of his light skin and straight hair. Finally he saw that the principal feature of Africa in the 1920's was its domination by Western imperialism. Even his own ship had come to carry away the wealth of the continent. In his poetry Africa became a symbol of lost roots, of a distant past that could never be retrieved. (pp. 62-4)

Except in his very early poetry Hughes did not devote as much attention to African roots as did several other Renaissance poets. As one who had grown up in America's heartland he seemed content with his conclusion that American blacks were Americans, not Africans, and consequently he focused his attention on the Negro's identity problems in this country. In particular, on several occasions he looked into the role of the mulatto in American society. In a number of poems, and in a play he wrote in 1935, he investigated the frustrations of those suspended between black and white America. **"Cross,"** which first appeared in the *Crisis* in 1925, was his simplest and most powerful statement of this dilemma:

My old man's a white old man
And my old mother's black.
If ever I cursed my white old man
I take my curses back.

If ever I cursed my black old mother
And wished she were in hell,
I'm sorry for that evil wish
And now I wish her well.

My old man died in a fine big house.
My ma died in a shack.
I wonder where I'm gonna die,
Being neither white nor black?

Very quickly, very directly, Hughes moved beyond anger and resentment to expose the isolation that was the real tragedy of the mulatto in a racist society. He followed this poem with an equally dramatic, but a more bitter examination in **"Mulatto."** Here he wove together two themes, an angry confrontation between an illegitimate youth and his white relatives, and a taunting description of the violent act of miscegenation. . . . Here were all the themes of racial sex exploitation. A black woman raped in the southern night, an angry mulatto disowned and mocked by his white father and half-brothers. The situation was both universal and highly personal. Hughes, however, carefully avoided the usual stereotypes which depicted the mulatto as the victim of a divided heritage, with intellectual ambitions contrasted with tendencies toward savagery. Instead he described him as an individual of divided heritage, unable to relate to either race in America.

Given Hughes's interest in the problems of the lower classes and his attempt to uncover the difficulties of being black in the United States, it is not surprising that he occasionally turned his pen against racial and social injustice. Fortunately his protest poetry did not succumb to bitterness. Perhaps because he had grown up in the Midwest where lynching and the other more violent expressions of racism were not common occurrences, his poems never seemed dogmatic or excessively propagandistic (at least during the Renaissance period). Instead, he approached the subject of racial oppression through satire, understatement, or wry, sardonic humor. The poem **"Cross"** was a clear example of his ability to expose an extremely controversial subject in a cool, matter-of-fact fashion. In **"Mulatto"** his language was angry and even inflammatory, but the impact of the poem remained controlled and powerful. This was also true of his most controversial protest poem, **"Christ in Alabama,"** which he wrote at the height of the Scottsboro case. . . .

Christ is a Nigger
Beaten and black—
O, bare your back.

Mary is His Mother—
Mammy of the South,
Silence your mouth.

God's His Father—

Hughes on race and poetry:

One of the most promising of the young Negro poets said to me once, "I want to be a poet—not a Negro poet," meaning, I believe, "I want to write like a white poet"; meaning subconsciously, "I would like to be a white poet"; meaning behind that, "I would like to be white." And I was sorry the young man said that, for no great poet has ever been afraid of being himself. And I doubted then that, with his desire to run away spiritually from his race, this boy would ever be a great poet. But this is the mountain standing in the way of any true Negro art in America—this urge within the race toward whiteness, the desire to pour racial individuality into the mold of American standardization, and to be as little Negro and as much American as possible.

Hughes, in *The Negro Artist and the Racial Mountain*, 1926.

White Master above,
Grant us your love.

Most holy bastard
Of the bleeding mouth:
Nigger Christ
On the Cross of the South.

Hughes described this piece as "an ironic poem inspired by the thought of how Christ, with no human father, would be accepted if he were born in the South of a Negro mother." Its power, like that of most of his poetry, came through using inflammatory images to produce a cool, controlled anger.

Perhaps the most interesting feature of Hughes's poetry was his innovative style. Throughout his literary career he experimented with adapting black musical forms to his work. It is not particularly surprising, given his commitment to the black masses, that he would use their art form, music, in his poetry. Beginning with *The Weary Blues* he experimented with blues, jazz, and folk forms in his writing. As a result, he emerged as one of the few truly innovative writers to come out of the Harlem Renaissance, and in the process he uncovered a poetic style that was adaptable to a variety of circumstances. The blues form, for example, with its repetitive reinforcement, was a very effective technique to impart a subtle sense of suffering and despondency:

When I was home de
Sunshine seemed like gold.
When I was home de
Sunshine seemed like gold.
Since I came up North de
Whole damn world's turned cold.

(pp. 64-5)

Hughes used jazz rhythms and the tempo of black

work music to achieve different effects. In **"Brass Spittoons,"** for example, work rhythms set the pace of the poem and captured the feeling of menial, methodical labor. In jazz he found a particularly fertile area for experimentation. Early in his career he observed that "jazz . . . is one of the inherent expressions of Negro life in America: the eternal tom-tom beating in the Negro soul—the tom-tom of revolt against weariness in a white world, a world of subway trains, and work, work, work; the tom-tom of joy and laughter, and pain swallowed in a smile." Hughes took this music with its choppy, breathless, almost chaotic tempo and recreated the bustling rhythms of city life and the boisterous atmosphere of the ghetto at night. An early example of this technique appeared in **"Lenox Avenue: Midnight":**

The rhythm of life
Is a jazz rhythm,
Honey.

The gods are laughing at us.

The broken heart of love
The weary, weary heart of pain—
Overtones,
Undertones,
To the rumble of street cars,
To the swish of rain.

Lenox Avenue,
Honey.
Midnight,
And the gods are laughing at us.

This was not one of Hughes's better pieces, but it demonstrated the possibilities of applying jazz structures in poetry about urban life. He refined this technique in his post-Renaissance poetry and applied it most successfully in his Harlem epic, *Montage of a Dream Deferred*, where he used jazz models to capture the full essence of Harlem life. (p. 66)

Here he examined the black metropolis that had become a slum, and concluded with the question:

What happens to a dream deferred?

Does it dry up
like a raisin in the sun?
Or fester like a sore—
And then run?

Does it stink like rotten meat?
Or crust and sugar over—
like a syrupy sweet?

Maybe it just sags
like a heavy load.
Or does it explode?

Hughes's poetry also shifted to the left during the

1930's. Although he always had been concerned with the problems of blacks and of the poor, during the depression years he moved closer to Communism in his personal beliefs, and his poetry became angrier and more inclined toward propaganda. Unfortunately, as Hughes became more political, the quality of his work declined.

In spite of his various shortcomings Missouri-born, Kansas-raised Langston Hughes was one of the most successful writers of the Harlem Renaissance. He was, for example, the only one who supported himself entirely through the income of his writing. Also, his literary career, which stretched into the 1960's, lasted long after his Renaissance colleagues had become silent. In fact, Hughes continued to write until his death in 1967. Finally, Hughes was the best known of all the Renaissance writers. For many who had never heard of the Harlem Renaissance, Hughes was the premier Negro poet in America. (pp. 68-9)

Cary D. Wintz, "Langston Hughes: A Kansas Poet in the Harlem Renaissance," in *Kansas Quarterly*, Vol. 7, No. 3, Summer, 1975, pp. 58-69.

ONWUCHEKWA JEMIE
(essay date 1976)

[In the following excerpt from his *Langston Hughes: An Introduction to the Poetry* (1973), Jemie summarizes Hughes's mission as a black writer.]

In his seminal essay **"The Negro Artist and the Racial Mountain,"** written as a rebuttal to [George S.] Schuyler and appearing in *The Nation* . . . Hughes contends that far from being totally assimilated into American life, blacks had in fact retained their ethnic distinctness. Hughes does not go into the historical reasons for this, but he welcomes it, regards it as an asset for black people and a boon to the black artist. For he sees it as one of the writer's challenges to translate into literature this ethnic distinctness, with its "heritage of rhythm and warmth, [and] incongruous humor that so often, as in the Blues, becomes ironic laughter mixed with tears." Whatever his medium, the work of the black artist who uses material from his own rich culture cannot but be identifiably racial. Therefore for him to wish to be regarded as an artist but not as a black artist—as though the two things were mutually exclusive—is, in Hughes's view, in effect to turn his back on his identity, to cast aspersions on his heritage, to wish to be other, to wish he were white. It is to accept the white world's definition of his people as ugly and inferior, unworthy of serious exploration in art.

Longstanding white prejudice against things black (Braithwaite's argument) is, in Hughes's view, no excuse for such abandonment of self. Prejudice has bred self-hate—"this urge within the race toward whiteness," this reaching for "Nordic manners, Nordic faces, Nordic art . . . and an Episcopal heaven" so common among the Negro middle and upper classes. But the artist's mission is to counter self-hate, not to pander to it.

> To my mind, it is the duty of the younger Negro artist, if he accepts any duties at all from outsiders, to change through the force of his art that old whispering "I want to be white," hidden in the aspirations of his people, to "Why should I want to be white? I am a Negro—and beautiful!"

The writer who accepts this mission will find a sturdy ally and positive example in the black masses, the "low-down folks," with their confident humanity, their indifference to white opinion, their *joie de vivre* amidst depressing circumstances. Unlike the middle and upper classes, the common folk "accept what beauty is their own without question." They are the uncontaminated reservoir of the strength of the race, the body and vehicle of its traditions. In their lives, and in black-white relations "with their innumerable overtones and undertones," the writer will find "a great field of unused material ready for his art. . . . an inexhaustible supply of themes." The writer will also find two temptations, two monsters conspiring to swallow him: he must steer a straight course between the scylla of stereotyped portraits of blacks so beloved by much of the white public who comprise the majority of his audience, and the charybdis of idealized and compensatory portaits sometimes demanded by vigorous defenders of the race. The transforming energy of his art would have to radiate from accurate representations of black people in all their human splendor—and human deformity. "We know we are beautiful. And ugly too." Like other races of mankind, the black race is neither uniformly admirable nor uniformly despicable. There is therefore no need either to apologize for it or to exaggerate its virtues. The artist's currency is reality and truth, and he should offer these "without fear or shame." He should create with an inner freedom, refusing to give in to pressure from any camp. . . . Succumbing to pressure from the racist majority is unthinkable. But it is equally important to avoid, on the one hand, artistic propaganda of the "best foot forward" type, and, on the other, the romanticism of the "primitivists" and bohemians for whom all things black or non-Western are beautiful and pure. Hughes calls instead for *critical realism*—a balanced presentation as free from chauvinism as from apology, a view in which blacks are neither monsters nor saints but richly and complexly human.

Hughes's essay amounts to a manifesto, an apolo-

Hughes with Mikhail Koltzov, Ernest Hemingway, and Nicolas Guillén in Madrid, 1937.

gia not only for his work but for the black art of his generation and the generations before and after him. It is an admonition to his fellow writers to "cast down your bucket where you are" (if I might quote Booker T. Washington in such an alien context). The creators of great black music and dance, including the blues and jazz artists of the day, invariably rooted themselves in black tradition. Naturally and without urging, they have utilized the vast cultural wealth into which they were born. This is what gives their music its depth and power. (pp. 9-11)

In his own work, Hughes attempted to follow the example of Dunbar and Chesnutt and the musicians: "Most of my own poems are racial in theme and treatment, derived from the life I know. In many of them I try to grasp and hold some of the meanings and rhythms of jazz." His "theme" (matter) is black people and their concerns; and for his "treatment" (manner, style, technique, point of view) he adopts the technical resources of the culture: black idiom and dialect; black folk humor, including the tragicomic irony of the blues; the form and spirit of jazz. The "meaning" of black life in America, Hughes implies, is to be found in black music: in the *blues,* a philosophy of endurance of the ap-

parently unendurable ("pain swallowed in a smile"); in *jazz,* subversion of the status quo ("revolt against weariness in a white world, a world of subway trains, and work, work, work"). *Black music, in short, is a paradigm of the black experience in America.* It is not only black America's most profound cultural expression and "product," but, in its most complex, representative contemporary forms of blues and jazz, it encompasses the polar extremes of that experience, namely: *resignation,* or the impulse towards assimilation; and *revolt,* or the impulse towards nationalism.

Implicit in Hughes's essay is a call for the reeducation not only of the black artist but of the black middle class public as well; a call for the emergence of a black audience that would take the initiative in recognizing and patronizing black talent, instead of waiting for white public approval first. To do this, of course, implies a proper valuation of black culture, the communal recognition, in other words, of a black esthetic. A critically alert black audience, Hughes seems to imply, might have been able to prevent the works of important artists, such as Dunbar and Chesnutt, from going out of print, or Jean Toomer's *Cane* from suffering so total a commercial failure. But of course what is involved here, among other things, is the ancillary issue of black control of black publishing, an issue which Hughes does not explore.

Hughes's insistence on a distinct black art utilizing black themes and styles is an affirmation of black existence, a recognition of the fact that Afro-Americans are a distinct people within the American nation, and an insistence on their continued ethnic distinctness. Hughes, in other words, could accurately be described as a nationalist although he did not articulate his position in those terms. The revolutionary potential which he perceives in black art will be redefined and given ideological direction in the following decade.

The 1930s was a Marxist decade for Hughes as it was for some other American writers. Communism promised an alternative to the capitalist order which feeds on racism and the exploitation of the working classes. It emphasized the identity of interests of all oppressed peoples, regardless of race or nationality, and called upon them to unite and overthrow their oppressors. Unlike Richard Wright, Hughes never specifically joined the Communist Party; but he found in its ideology a fresh perspective, an effective tool of social analysis, a broader conception of the black struggle as part of a world-wide struggle against oppression. (pp. 11-13)

[In his **"To Negro Writers"**] Hughes calls on black writers to address their work to the masses, both black and white, and seek to unify them, and to use their work to lay bare the true nature of America: the hypocrisy of philanthropy and of organized religion; the betrayal of workers by white labor leaders, and of the black masses by false Negro leaders who were controlled by the ruling class; the manipulation of patriotic sentiment in support of wars which destroy the citizenry and profit the ruling class. The black writer should use his art to expose "all the economic roots of race hatred and race fear."

In short, Hughes calls for a functional literature, or what Jean-Paul Sartre was to call a *littérature engagée,* a literature committed to revolution. As he sees it, the black writer has a clear and unequivocal role in the struggle for revolution, for that struggle is being waged for him and his. Writers who place themselves aloof from the struggle at best condemn themselves to social irrelevance; at worst, they are aiders and abetters of the status quo, partners in oppression, whether they are aware of it or not. In the literature of struggle there is no place for the romanticisms of the Harlem Renaissance which celebrated the gaiety and rhythm of black life; and the tragicomic laughter of the blues is to be transformed into laughter that "chokes the proletarian throat and makes the blood run to fists that must be increasingly, militantly clenched to fight the brazen terror" of capitalism. Black laughter has to become menacing, as in Burck's cartoons, foreshadowing "the

marching power of the proletarian future," a future which the oppressor cannot laugh off so easily. (pp. 13-14)

Hughes abandoned Marxist terms of rhetoric in his collected works, but not the principle of literature as an instrument of social change. On the contrary, as we have seen, he had enunciated this principle as early as **"The Negro Artist and the Racial Mountain,"** and only elaborated and extended it in his more specifically Marxist declarations. Indeed it would be fair to say that **"The Negro Artist and the Racial Mountain"** is the basic document of his esthetic, and future pronouncements are restatements and elaborations, footnotes and glosses. In subsequent statements he downplays the hortatory functions of literature and expands on the expository. He continues to stress the social responsibility of the black artist, and no doubt saw his own career as fulfilling that socially responsible role. In **"My Adventures As a Social Poet,"** his most important restatement of the 1940s, Hughes defines himself as a primarily social as distinct from a primarily lyric poet, thus giving formal recognition to a bias which became visible quite early in his career. "The major aims of my work have been to interpret and comment upon Negro life, and its relations to the problems of Democracy." Taking the American Dream as his cue, Hughes had developed his poetic metaphor of the dream, a concept which was to become a strategic theme, a major artery running through the body of his work. The dream is transmitted along two channels: first, as an assortment of romantic fantasies and desires, including the desire for a life rich in love and adventure; secondly, as the dream of political freedom and economic well-being. The latter is an extension of the former, and it is this latter that is the "dream deferred" of the black man and black race. Although he did not coin the phrase itself until *Montage of a Dream Deferred* (1951), which came in mid-career, his dual vision of the dream is introduced in his first book, *The Weary Blues.*

As might be expected, the theme of the "dream deferred" finds its fullest expression in his social poetry, whereas his lyric poetry is the particular vehicle of the dream as romantic fantasy ("love, roses and moonlight"). (pp. 15-16)

Hughes did not then cease writing lyric poetry, but the balance had tipped heavily in the direction of social poetry. In **"My Adventures as a Social Poet"** he explains why: much as he had stated in his Marxist essay, beauty and lyricism, or poems about love, moonlight, and roses, are "really related to another world, to ivory towers, to your head in the clouds, feet floating off the earth," rather than to the everyday world of poverty and Jim Crow in which he was born and bred and still lived. In his world, the sentiment of romantic love, for example, is all too often twisted and blasted by the economic imperative, as the ghetto wasteland of

Montage of a Dream Deferred was to demonstrate. Roses are fine, but "almost all the prettiest roses I have seen have been in rich white people's yards—not in mine." And as for moonlight,

> sometimes in the moonlight my brothers see a fiery cross and a circle of Klansmen's hoods. Sometimes in the moonlight a dark body swings from a lynching tree.

Roses and moonlight, yes, but their thorny dark sides. To Hughes's thinking, the social realities of black life in America are so overwhelming that the concerned black artist could not but make these realities the central matter of his art. Hughes is not attempting to legislate subject matter for the black artist; but he is insisting, stubbornly, that given the Afro-American situation, beauty and lyricism, love and moonlight and roses, are insufficient matter. Whether they are sufficient for the rich, middle class, comfortable and white, is something else.

Because he deals with sensitive public issues, the social poet invariably runs into censorship and confrontations with authority, with the upholders of the status quo. Hughes was no exception, and **"My Adventures as a Social Poet"** is, among other things, a humorous inventory of the unpleasantnesses he had been subjected to because of his poetry. (pp. 16-17)

The need for realistic portraiture of black life is a theme that Hughes returns to again and again. From his earliest days his own work had been repeatedly denounced by "respectable" Negroes for focussing on lower-class life and for daring to portray prostitutes, pimps, and other disreputable characters. But Hughes had always resisted the "best foot forward" argument. His theory and practice was to portray the ugliness as readily as the beauty of black life, the unsavory as readily as the admirable. Critical realism demanded both. However, toward the end of his career we find what on the surface might appear like a shift toward the position of his critics. Dismayed by the alienation and despair, foul language, and explicit sexuality with which so much of the literature of the early 1960s by and about blacks was replete, Hughes urged black artists

> not necessarily to put our *best* foot forward, but to try at least to put a balanced foot forward, so that we do not all appear to be living in a *Cool World* in *Another Country* in the *Crazy House of the Negro* in which the majority of *The Blacks* seem prone to little except the graffiti of *The Toilet* or the deathly behavior of a *Slow Dance on the Killing Ground*.

If there is a shift, it is more semantic than substantive, for the demand for "a balanced foot" is a demand for proportion, for an exacting fidelity to fact which would preclude biassed and exaggerated concern with either the unsavory aspects of black life, or the admirable. The politics of the civil rights era would, in his view, make such balance even more urgent:

> The Negro image deserves objective, well-rounded (rather than one-sided) treatment, particularly in the decade of a tremendous freedom movement in which all of us can take pride.
>
> (pp. 18-19)

Onwuchekwa Jemie, in his *Langston Hughes: An Introduction to the Poetry,* Columbia University Press, 1976, 234 p.

PETER BRUCK
(essay date 1977)

[In the following excerpt, Bruck provides a social, literary, and historical perspective on Hughes's short fiction, focusing on the black artist's relationship with white culture in the semiautobiographical "The Blues I'm Playing."]

Langston Hughes (1902-1967), according to many critics "poet laureate of Harlem" and "Dean of American Negro Writers," began his literary career by winning a poetry contest sponsored by the black magazine *Opportunity* in 1925. **"The Weary Blues"** was noted by Carl Van Vechten, through whose sponsorship Hughes was able to get his first contract with the noted publisher Alfred Knopf. Van Vechten, who acted as a main ambassadorial advisor and patron of black literature to white publishing firms during the 1920's, not only paved the way for Hughes' literary career but also became the "chief architect of his early success." Just as with [Paul Laurence] Dunbar and [Charles Waddell] Chesnutt, white patronage played a decisive role in the literary emergence of Langston Hughes. The omnipresence of the white patron with his significant socio-literary influence on the black author was a discovery that the young Hughes was still to make; his gradual and painstaking emancipation from the grip of such white patrons was to become the major concern of his early phase and to play a dominant theme in his short fiction.

Starting to publish in the midst of the 1920's meant for Langston Hughes to be intrinsically involved in a debate over the function, theme, and aesthetic form of black literature. The problem became even more urgent when the 'Harlem Renaissance' period began and, at the same time, the widely acclaimed emergence of the "New Negro" confronted the black writer with the task of defining his role as a literary artist. In order to foster a critical discussion of these questions, the leading black magazine *The Crisis* organized a symposium, "The Negro in Art: How Shall He Be Portrayed?," throughout the March-November issues of 1926. Prior to this, Alain Locke, "father of the 'New Negro' and the so-called Harlem Renaissance," had attempted to define the cultural stance of the 'New Negro' in the following manner:

> He [the New Negro] now becomes a conscious contributor and lays aside the status of a beneficiary and ward for that of a collaborator and participant in American civilization. The great social gain in this is the releasing of our talented group from the arid fields of controversy and debate to the productive fields of creative expression. The especially cultural recognition they win should in turn prove the key to that revaluation of the Negro which must precede or accompany any considerable further betterment of race relationships.

Locke, who clearly pursued [W. E. B.] DuBois' philosophy of a "talented tenth," aspired to an attitude of cultural elitism that envisioned art and culture to be a bridge across the racial barrier; hence his calling for a "carefully maintained contact between the enlightened minorities of both race groups." This philosophy of culture undoubtedly presented a challenge to all those young black writers who were primarily concerned with expressing the new feeling of ethnic identity and racial pride. One of those willing to face this challenge was the young Langston Hughes who, on June 23, 1926, published an essay [in the *Nation*] that may not only be viewed as an indirect reply to Locke but also became known as the first significant black literary manifesto.

The importance of the **"Negro Artist and the Racial Mountain"** for the evolution of black literature cannot be overstressed. In the words of Charles S. Johnson, former editor of *Opportunity,* none other than Hughes with this essay "so completely symbolized the new emancipation of the Negro mind."

In outlining his stance as a black writer, Hughes placed particular emphasis on racial pride and ethnic identity:

> To my mind, it is the duty of the younger Negro artists . . . to change through the force of his art that old whispering, "I want to be white," hidden in the aspirations of his people, to "Why should I want to be white? I am a Negro and beautiful."

Hughes' emphasis on blackness, which anticipated the present-day discussion of the possibilities of a black aesthetic, clearly signalled the renunciation of the well-known problem of "racial" vs. "universal" art. Instead Hughes turned to depicting the ordinary black American. . . . His extensive reliance on folk forms and rhythms and his application of oral folk culture to poetry highlight his innovating efforts and mark the beginning of the "reconciliation of formal black poets to their folk roots and grass roots audience." One of the most popular results of his preoccupations in terms of narrative fiction were the "Simple folk tales" that first appeared in the black weekly *Chicago Defender* in November 1942. (pp. 71-3)

From a socio-literary point of view, the Simple tales marked Hughes' first success in gaining a genuine black audience. In the late 1920's, however, this goal still proved utopian. . . . Whereas the bulk of his poetry is usually associated with the Harlem Renaissance, . . . [Hughes's] career as a short story writer did not begin before the wane of this epoch. Although his first stories, all reflecting the author's experiences as a seaman on a voyage along the West coast of Africa, were already published in Harlem's literary magazine *The Messenger* in 1927, it took another six years before Hughes really devoted himself to writing short fiction. From the spring of 1932 to the fall of 1933 he visited the Soviet Union and the Far East. It was during his stay in Moscow that he had a decisive reading experience [having read D. H. Lawrence's collection *The Lovely Lady*] which prompted him to devote himself to the short story. . . . The years to come were to see amazing results from this literary initiation. Between 1933 and 1934 he devoted himself exclusively to this genre. (pp. 73-4)

[*The Ways of White Folks*] which received rather favorable reviews, presents, thematically, a close examination of black-white relationships. Mostly satirical in tone, the stories try to unmask several manifestations of the Harlem Renaissance. Specifically, the theme of white patronage, as displayed in **"Slave on the Block," "Poor Little Black Fellow,"** and **"The Blues I'm Playing,"** is used to demonstrate the dishonesty of whites and the absurd notion of their paternalistic philanthropy. In this context, it is of particular socio-literary interest to note that Hughes' fictional treatment of the incipient dissociation from white predominance caused him no setback in magazine publication. Instead, his new literary efforts soon found their way into leading periodicals. Whereas Hughes' poetry was usually printed in such black journals as *Opportunity* and *The Crisis* (he had complained in 1929 that "magazines used very few stories with Negro themes, since Negro themes were considered exotic, in a class with Chinese or East Indian features), four out of his five stories written in Moscow were now accepted and published by such noted periodicals as *The American Mercury, Scribner's Magazine* and *Esquire.* This major breakthrough provided him with a nation-wide, non-parochial platform, allowing him to escape from his predicament, and opened up the opportunity of gaining a primarily white reading audience.

The reading of Lawrence's *The Lovely Lady* not only prompted Hughes to concentrate on the short story but also persuaded him to use the story's protagonist Pauline Attenborough as a model for the creation of Dora Ellsworth, the fictional representative of his former white Park Avenue patroness. **"The Blues I'm Playing,"** written after his return from the Soviet Union and first published in the May 1934 issue of *Scribner's Magazine,* was thus subject to an interesting combination of influence.

The impact of Lawrence's story becomes apparent when one compares the opening description of both women. Lawrence describes Pauline Attenborough as a women who "could still sometimes be mistaken . . . for thirty. She really was a wonderfully preserved woman, of perfect *chic.* . . . She would be an exquisite skeleton and her skull would be an exquisite skull." The narrator's mocking emphasis on her appearance, which she can change through a "mysterious little wire" of "will," exposes her artificiality. As a collector of art, Pauline is herself a "self-made object d'art." Dora Ellsworth is introduced in a similar way. Hughes' description, however, is more mocking and obviously aims at unmasking his character's self-deception from the very beginning. Hence one common denominator of both figures seems to be hypocrisy:

> Poor dear lady, she had no children of her own. Her husband was dead. And she had no interest in life now save art, and the young people who created art. She was very rich, and it gave her pleasure to share her richness with beauty. Except that she was sometimes confused as to where beauty lay. . . . She once turned down a garlic-smelling soprano-singing girl, who, a few years later, had all the critics in New York at her feet.

This passage reveals several central aspects of the narrative texture. The focus of interest, which is on Mrs. Ellsworth throughout the story, suggests that Hughes is primarily concerned with depicting the ignorance of the white philanthropist. This intention is underlined by authorial comments which, although sometimes quite devastating, are seldom strongly aggressive. Instead, Hughes pities his white character, thereby producing the particular reading process of **"The Blues I'm Playing."** By undermining the cultural status of his protagonist and exposing the absurdity of her judgements, Hughes creates in the reader's imagination the illusion of witnessing the forthcoming degradation of so-called superior white culture.

Satire hence sets the emotional tone throughout the story. Its function, autobiographically, is to unveil the devasting influence that Hughes' former patroness had on his creative impulses: "She wanted me to be primitive and know and feel the intuitions of the primitive. But, unfortunately, I did not feel the rhythms of the primitive surging through me, and so I could not live and write as though I did." On the cultural level, this conflict was representative of a whole range of dilemmas that had emerged during the Harlem Renais-

sance. The black writers' "search back to a national past," their literary journey of ethnic self-discovery, marked the beginning of a declaration of cultural independence, whose paradigm may be seen in Hughes' literary manifesto **"The Negro Artist and the Racial Mountain."** Satire as employed in **"The Blues I'm Playing"** signals the end of white paternalism, thereby demystifying the 'cult of the primitive Black' that many whites took for granted during the 1920's.

This historical conflict is reflected in the antagonistic relationship of Dora Ellsworth and her black protegée, the pianist Oceola Jones. Both women represent opposing points of view; [according to Robert Bone in his *Down Home*], this structural contrast manifests a clash between "two standards of morality," between a "white and a Negro code." The conflict itself evolves throughout five stages, each dramatizing their incompatible positions: the financial sponsorship is followed by increasing efforts on part of Mrs. Ellsworth to dominate the private life of her protegée; Oceola's return to Harlem and the announcement of her engagement to a black medical student cause a severe crisis and finally lead to a dissolving of their relationship.

The mocking irony with which the narrator emphasizes Mrs. Ellsworth's ignorance prevails through all these scenes. Her ignorance of art and artists is even excelled by her total lack of insight into black life and, in particular, Harlem: "Before going to bed, Mrs. Ellsworth told her housekeeper to order a book called *Nigger Heaven* . . . , and also anything else . . . about Harlem." Here Hughes tries not merely to unmask the fakery of white patronage; he also scores Carl Van Vechten's *Nigger Heaven.* This novel, published at the height of the Harlem Renaissance in 1926, served as a kind of guide-book to Harlem for many white readers and was mostly rejected by blacks. DuBois' review [in the *Crisis,* 1926] perhaps sums up best the black reaction of that time: "*Nigger Heaven* is a blow in the face. It is an affront to the hospitality of black folk. . . . It is a caricature. It is worse than untruth because it is a mass of half-truths." Although Hughes' own criticism of *Nigger Heaven* and Van Vechten [in his autobiography, *The Big Sea*] was rather friendly, the satirical connotation of the passage quoted above seems to suggest that by 1934 Hughes felt free enough do denounce Van Vechten's patronage in the same way as he did that of his former Park Avenue patroness.

Moreover, the same passage reveals another important feature of Mrs. Ellsworth's personality. Her reliance on books instead of personal experience, her preference for a substitute for reality, demonstrates that she is unable to differentiate between substance and appearance. This failure is particularly emphasized in the scene where she drives Oceola to her Harlem home:

Mrs. Ellsworth had to ask could she come in. "I live on the fifth floor," said Oceola, and there isn't any elevator," "It doesn't matter, dear," said the white woman, for she meant to see the inside of this girl's life, elevator or no elevator.

Devoid of any emotional and psychological perception, she mistakes the exterior for the interior, form for being, and thereby reduces life to a mere artefact. This attitude is equally apparent in her conception of art. Having substituted art for life, Mrs. Ellsworth, like Pauline Attenborough, becomes a self-made *objet d'art;* her stress merely on the refining, cultivating, and subli- mating function of art not only separates art from life, but also deprives it of its vitality and reduces it to a dead object.

Mrs. Ellsworth's attitudes contrast with Oceola's character and music. Having grown up in the musical tradition of the black church, Oceola's life is firmly rooted in jazz and the blues. Her music, which derives its strength from her cultural identity, distinctly sets her apart from Dora Ellsworth, who conceives of art as essentially classical. The evolving conflict thus centers around the clash of two antagonistic modes of life. In contrast to her patroness' understanding of music, Oceola has kept an original sense of it, one that "de- manded movement and expression, dancing and living to go with it." As an initial, spontaneous expression of black life and experience, the blues is devoid of "classi- cal runs or fancy falsities." Rather, it becomes, as Ralph Ellison once remarked, a form of individual therapy:

> The blues is an impulse to keep the painful details and episodes of a brutal experience alive in one's aching consciousness, to finger its jagged grain, and to transcend it, not by consolation of philosophy but by squeezing from it a near-tragic, near-comic lyri- cism. As a form, the blues is an autobiographical chronicle of personal catastrophe expressed lyrical- ly.

Oceola's music hence becomes not only an asser- tion and definition of her identity; it also links her, cul- turally, to that chain of black folklore tradition, which, as Ellison has pointed out, "announced the Negro's willingness to trust this own experience, his own sensi- bilities as to the definition of reality, rather than allow his masters to define these crucial matters for him." Oceola's "sheer love of jazz", her hatred of "most artists, . . . and the word art in French or English," gives voice to an attitude which considers music a man- ifestation of an experienced reality, thus merging both art and life. Her contempt for a philosophy that sepa- rates these two arises out of her primal emphasis on the affirmative and virile nature of music. . . .

The "bipàrtite structure" of this story, emphasiz- ing two opposing ethnic codes and philosophies of art, is also equally apparent in the different geographical settings of the various scenes. From the very beginning of their relationship, the Park Avenue patroness tries to alienate Oceola from Harlem: "I must get her out of Harlem at once. I believe it's worse than Chinatown." Her efforts finally result in Oceola's moving to Green- wich Village, and then for two years' study to Paris. The effects of her training in classical music are not, however, as sublimating as Mrs. Ellsworth had hoped. Returning from Paris, Oceola is determined more firm- ly than ever not to give up the black musical tradition. This is especially shown in her decision to move back to Harlem: "I've been away from my own people so long, I want to live right in the middle of them again." This symbolic rediscovery of her heritage, induced by a stay in Paris, is one of the earliest black reiterations of the Jamesian pattern. For it is in Europe that Oceola, to paraphrase a title of one of James Baldwin's essays, makes the discovery of what it means to be black.

The different settings hence express metaphori- cally the various stages of their relationship. The sym- bolic confrontation of Harlem with Greenwich Village and Paris ultimately demonstrates that the conflict is again dramatized on a personal as well as cultural plane. Her return to Harlem signals the attempt to preserve her black cultural identity. Significantly enough, it is only after she has accepted her lover's proposal that Oceola at a concert in a Harlem church suddenly lives up to her own musical intentions by "not sticking to the classical items listed on the program," for now she is able to "insert one of her own variations on the spiri- tuals."

The inevitable separation of Oceola and Mrs. Ellsworth takes place one evening in the patroness' apartment, where Oceola had come to play for the last time "with the techniques for which Mrs. Ellsworth had paid." Again, the conflict is described in the con- trasting images that are representative of the two dif- ferent cultural spheres. Dora Ellsworth's position is al- most entirely linked with exquisite, though lifeless an- tique objects, evoking the impression of her emotional sterility and deadness. These objects, acting as objec- tive correlatives of her emotional state, cannot be rec- onciled with life. The vital, life-promising nature of Oceola's music, which grew "into an earth-throbbing rhythm that shook the lilies in the Persian vases of Mrs. Ellsworth's music room," ultimately exposes her limit- ed point of view and suggests the final triumph, as it were, of black over white culture.

Because of her limited point of view, Dora Ells- worth remains unchanged. Even though she is dressed at the end in the same black velvet that Oceola used to wear, [James A.] Emanuel's reading this as "a symbolic fusion of herself and her protegée" seems to be an un- warranted conjecture. Rather, the story's ending calls for a reading [as Bone states] which views the two un- reconciled positions as a re-emphasis of "the theme of cultural dualism which is basic to the Harlem Renaissance" and Hughes' position therein.

Oceola's self-conscious revolt against her patroness, which has strong autobiographical parallels, underlines historically the black's incipient ethnic assertion, his pride in his race and the rediscovery of his cultural heritage. Within this cultural context, **"The Blues I'm Playing"** may be considered a two-fold satire. One of its objectives, of course, is to unmask the hypocrisy of white patronage. In addition to this, the philosophy of black cultural elitism and the 'New Negro' seems to be equally under attack. By refuting the 'high culture' of the Renaissance champions, Hughes satirizes through his fictional character those attempts to bridge the gap between the two races by means of art. For this must, as he demonstrates through Oceola, inevitably lead to servility and a loss of black identity. In contrast to Emanuel's general dictum that "Hughes as a writer cannot be explained by references to the Harlem Renaissance," this particular short story echoes, both on the autobiographical and cultural plane, historical problems that were firmly rooted in this period; thus Hughes' delineation of Oceola may ultimately be conceived as a fictional representation of his own literary manifesto and the story as a satirical reaction to the Harlem Renaissance.

Within the bulk of Hughes' sixty-six published short stories, **"The Blues I'm Playing"** holds a unique position. In keeping with Emanuel, who classified Hughes' short fiction thematically, this story turns out to be his only genuine artist story. It marks one of Hughes' outstanding achievements in this genre and established him as a serious writer of satirical short fiction. Most stories in the collection *The Ways of White Folk* are retrospective, looking back to the 1920's and trying to unveil many of the manifestations of the Harlem Renaissance. The date of publication, however, suggests a further significance. For the year 1934 signals the end of Hughes' early phase. (pp. 74-80)

Despite favorable reviews, the first issue of *The Ways of White Folk* sold only 2,500 copies. This meagre success may be accounted for not only by the fact that Hughes had not yet gained, as he was to do later with his "Simple Tales," a genuine black reading audience; the commercial failure also seems to demonstrate that with the end of the Harlem Renaissance the potential white audience no longer shared a larger enthusiasm in black literary products. From a historical and socio-literary perspective, however, the stories of *The Ways of White Folk* caused a major breakthrough in paving the way for a racially unrestricted audience. By re-examining the black-white relationships of the 1920's and by unmasking the falseness of the enthusiasm of whites for the 'New Negro,' [Donald C. Dickinson states that] Hughes "clarified for the Negro audience their own strength and dignity and . . . supplied the white audience with an explanation of how the Negro feels and what he wants." Six years after the publication of this collection, Richard Wright, in a review of Hughes' autobiography *The Big Sea,* perhaps summed up the importance of the early works of Hughes best. In his eyes, Hughes, on account of his extensive publications, had served as a "cultural ambassador for the case of the blacks." (pp. 80-1)

Peter Bruck, "Langston Hughes: 'The Blues I'm Playing' (1934)," in *The Black American Short Story in the 20th Century: A Collection of Critical Essays,* edited by Peter Bruck, B. R. Grüner Publishing Co., 1977, pp. 71-84.

SOURCES FOR FURTHER STUDY

Barksdale, Richard K. *Langston Hughes: The Poet and His Critics.* Chicago: American Library Association, 1977, 155 p.

> Surveys the critical reception of Hughes's works throughout his career.

Emanuel, James A. *Langston Hughes.* New Haven, Conn.: College and University Press, 1967, 192 p.

> Literary biography of Hughes.

O'Daniel, Therman B., ed. *Langston Hughes: Black Genius—A Critical Evaluation.* New York: William Morrow & Co., 1971, 245 p.

> Collection of thirteen critical essays on Hughes, with a selective bibliography of criticism.

Rampersad, Arnold. *The Life of Langston Hughes: I, Too, Sing America, Volume I, 1902-1941.* New York: Oxford University Press, 1986, 468 p.

> Literary biography of Hughes up to the publication of his autobiography *The Big Sea.*

——. *The Life of Langston Hughes: I Dream a World, Volume II, 1941-1967.* New York: Oxford University Press, 1988, 512 p.

> Continues discussion of Hughes's life and career up to his death.

Randall, Dudley. "The Black Aesthetic in the Thirties, Forties, and Fifties." In *The Black Aesthetic,* edited by Addison Gayle, Jr., pp. 224-34. Garden City, N.Y.: Doubleday and Company, Inc., 1971.

Examines black nationalism in Hughes's poetry and prose.

Victor Hugo

1802-1885

(Full name Victor Marie Hugo) French novelist, poet, dramatist, and critic.

INTRODUCTION

*H*ugo is considered one of the leaders of the Romantic movement in French literature, as well as its most prolific and versatile author. Although chiefly known outside France for the novels *Les misérables* (1862) and *Notre Dame de Paris* (1831; *The Hunchback of Notre Dame,* 1833), he is renowned in his own country primarily for his contributions as a Romantic poet. In his lifetime, Hugo also received acclaim for his extensive dramatic output, but critical opinion of his theatrical work has waned in this century, and his plays retain significance chiefly in scholarly circles. Regardless of the endurance of his individual works, Hugo remains an outstanding symbol of liberty and humanitarianism in France.

Born into a military family, Hugo traveled extensively during his childhood until, when he was twelve years old, his parents separated. He settled in Paris with his mother, attended school, and attained literary recognition at a young age. At the age of twenty, Hugo founded a prominent literary magazine, *Le conservateur littéraire,* and published his first volume of poetry, *Odes et poésies diverses* (1822). This earned him a pension from Louis XVIII and enabled him to marry his childhood sweetheart, Adèle Foucher. His home became a center of intellectual activity and he counted among his devoted friends Charles Sainte-Beuve and Théophile Gautier. During this period, Hugo wrote several novels and volumes of poetry that express the exoticism and youthful vigor that foreshadow his Romantic tendencies.

Hugo's dramatic work began with the publication of the controversial preface to his lengthy and unstageable verse-drama, *Cromwell* (1827). This preface sought to establish a new set of dramatic principles that were to become the manifesto of the Romantic movement. Hugo demanded a new form of verse drama that abandoned the formal rules of classical tragedy. One of the most important principles introduced in the preface concerns the necessity of portraying the grotesque as well as the beautiful. Hugo viewed the grotesque as the complement of the sublime and considered fidelity to the multifarious nature of creation to be an underlying tenet of literary composition. These precepts were put to the test in 1830, with the Comédie française's turbulent production of Hugo's *Hernani* (1830). Its debut was referred to as the "battle of *Hernani*" because of censorship difficulties and the heated reaction of the theatergoers. Groups of Romantic writers and artists attended performances to demonstrate support for Hugo's revolutionary use of language and innovative dramatic techniques; traditionalists attended in order to denounce Hugo's disregard of the classic precepts of drama, including unity of time, place, and action. Hoping to benefit from the publicity surrounding *Hernani,* Hugo's publisher pressed him for a novel, adding a clause to their agreement requiring Hugo to pay a considerable fine for each week the manuscript was overdue. Determined to meet his contractual responsibilities, Hugo returned to a novel he had begun researching in the late 1820s about Parisian life during the Middle Ages. He worked furiously, completing the book in January, 1831; it was published as *Notre-Dame de Paris* the following March.

Notre-Dame de Paris is recognized as an intellectually and emotionally powerful romantic tragedy. Critics have especially praised the novel for its masterful depiction of medieval Paris, its intricately ordered narrative, and its memorable portraits of such stock romantic characters as the gentle monster, the evil cleric, and the beautiful, orphaned heroine. The story concerns the lust of the evil archdeacon Claude Frollo for Esmeralda, an innocent gypsy dancing girl, who, through a simple but kind action, has gained the love of Quasimodo, the hunchbacked bell ringer of Notre-Dame cathedral. Conceived during a turbulent period in French history and completed in the months immediately following the tumultuous July Revolution of 1830, *Notre-Dame de Paris* also embodies Hugo's views on numerous social and political issues, most notably on the development of the common people as a significant political force. Contemporary French reviewers were generally unimpressed by the novel when it was published. Researcher Max Bach has attributed this unenthusiastic response to the partisan concerns of various groups of critics, including those who objected to the absence of religion in the novel and those who believed that Hugo had slighted the bourgeoisie. Nevertheless *Notre-Dame de Paris* gained a wide audience among the novel-buying public and followers of the Romantic movement, and soon garnered worldwide popular success, inspiring translations into more than twenty languages.

While Hugo's literary life flourished, his personal life deteriorated. Adèle Hugo fell in love with his best friend, Sainte-Beuve, and Hugo, devastated by his wife's infidelity, found solace in a number of romantic liaisons. He maintained a gallant exterior—possibly because of his professional tie to Sainte-Beuve—and, though Hugo and his wife lived thereafter in a state of platonic affection, the pain of her betrayal cast a melancholy tone on his later work.

Hugo's literary achievement was recognized in 1841 by his election to the Académie française and in 1845 by his elevation to the peerage. During the latter half of that decade, he devoted most of his time to politics. In accordance with his desire to represent "the camp of the convicts" rather than any political party, Hugo delivered a number of impassioned speeches in the Chamber of Peers in which he condemned the legal system and society's persecution of the poor—subjects he had treated in the novels *Le dernier jour d' un condamné* (1829; *The Last Day of the Condemned,* 1840) and *Notre–Dame de Paris.* These themes also dominated a work in progress whose title, *Les misères,* was eventually changed to *Les misérables.* As Hugo became increasingly disenchanted with monarchism, he interrupted the composition of *Les misérables* to participate in the revolution of 1848. In 1849, he was elected to the L'assemblée nationale and publicly espoused republicanism. Because of his uncompromising opposition to Louis Napoleon's dictatorial ambitions, he was forced to leave France following the *coup d' état* of 1851. He initially fled to Belgium, but finally settled on the island of Guernsey, where he remained until 1870. His first poetical work in exile, *Les châtiments* (1853), was a political indictment of Louis Napoléon. Tiring of overtly political topics, he next explored the metaphysical aspects of death and life in *Les contemplations* (1856). His use of symbol and metaphor to give new, sometimes obscure, meaning to poetic language, along with his often highly personal and reflective work, influenced the later Symbolist poets.

After publishing several volumes of poetry while still in exile, Hugo returned to the unfinished *Les misérables.* The work is now considered one of the most memorable novels in nineteenth-century literature and the maturest expression of Hugo's lifelong interest in the problems and sufferings of the poor. Described by Hugo as a religious epic "moving around a great soul, which is the incarnation of all the social misery of the time," *Les misérables* is the story of a released convict, Jean Valjean, who faces repeated hardships despite his efforts to reform. Valjean's tragic history is an indictment of unfair legal penalties, and his life in the underworld of Paris illustrates Hugo's conviction that social evils are created and fostered by existing laws and customs. Written in praise of the masses and offering the victims of society's injustice the hope of redemption,

Les misérables achieved international popularity and was influential in the movement for legal and social reform in nineteenth-century France.

Upon his return to France, Hugo received widespread recognition. Though nominated for public office, he took little further interest in national affairs. His final years were marked by personal loss and, though he continued to write prolifically, he became increasingly detached from the world around him. He died a national hero. Though he lay in state under the Arc de Triomphe and was buried in the Panthéon, his body was transported in the hearse of a poor man, in accordance with his last request.

Though critical attention to Hugo's work dimin-ished shortly after his death, modern critics consider him an outstanding poet whose technical virtuosity advanced French poetry. Hugo's reputation as a prose writer has waned in this century, but his work has proved a dominant force in French letters and he is remembered as an artist of great popularity and importance. Charles Baudelaire said of Hugo, "No artist is more universal than he."

(For further information about Hugo's life and works, see *Nineteenth-Century Literature Criticism*, Vols. 3, 10, and 21 and *Something about the Author*, Vol. 47.)

CRITICAL COMMENTARY

ROBERT LOUIS STEVENSON

(essay date 1874)

[Stevenson was a Scottish novelist, poet, and essayist. In the following excerpt from an essay that first appeared in *The Cornhill Magazine* in 1874, he discusses the varying tones of Hugo's romances.]

Victor Hugo's romances occupy an important position in the history of literature; many innovations, timidly made elsewhere, have in them been carried boldly out to their last consequences; much that was indefinite in literary tendencies has attained to definite maturity; many things have come to a point and been distinguished one from the other; and it is only in the last romance of all, *Quatre Vingt Treize,* that this culmination is most perfect. (p. 13)

The moral end that the author had before him in the conception of *Notre Dame de Paris* was (he tells us) to "denounce" the external fatality that hangs over men in the form of foolish and inflexible superstition. To speak plainly, this moral purpose seems to have mighty little to do with the artistic conception; moreover it is very questionably handled, while the artistic conception is developed with the most consummate success. Old Paris lives for us with newness of life: we have ever before our eyes the city cut into three by the two arms of the river, the boat-shaped island "moored" by five bridges to the different shores, and the two unequal towns on either hand. We forget all that enumeration of palaces and churches and convents which occupies so many pages of admirable description, and the thoughtless reader might be inclined to conclude from this, that they were pages thrown away; but this is not so: we forget, indeed, the details, as we forget or do not see the different layers of paint on a completed picture; but the thing desired has been accomplished, and we carry away with us a sense of the "Gothic profile" of the city, of the "surprising forest of pinnacles and towers and belfries," and we know not what of rich and intricate and quaint. And throughout, Notre Dame has been held up over Paris by a height far greater than that of its twin towers: the Cathedral is present to us from the first page to the last; the title has given us the clue, and already in the Palace of Justice the story begins to attach itself to that central building by character after character. It is purely an effect of mirage; Notre Dame does not, in reality, thus dominate and stand out above the city. . . . [But] it is an effect that permeates and possesses the whole book with astonishing consistency and strength. And then, Hugo has peopled this Gothic city, and, above all, this Gothic church, with a race of men even more distinctly Gothic than their surroundings. We know this generation already: we have seen them clustered about the worn capitals of pillars, or craning forth over the churchleads with the open mouths of gargoyles. About them all there is that sort of stiff quaint unreality, that conjunction of the grotesque, and even of a certain bourgeois snugness, with passionate contortion and horror, that is so characteristic of Gothic art. Esmeralda is somewhat an exception; she and the goat traverse the story like two children who have wandered in a dream. The finest moment of the book is when these two share with the two other leading characters, Dom Claude and Quasimodo, the chill shelter of the old cathedral. It is here that we touch most intimately the generative artistic idea of the romance: are they not all four taken out of some quaint

Principal Works

Odes et poésies diverses (poetry) 1822

Han d'Islande (novel) 1823

   [Hans of Iceland, 1845]

Bug-Jargal (novel) 1826

   [The Slave King, 1833]

Cromwell [first publication] (drama) 1827

   [Cromwell, 1900]

Le dernier jour d'un condamné (novel) 1829

   [The Last Day of a Condemned, 1840]

Les orientales (poetry) 1829

   [Eastern Lyrics, 1879]

Hernani (drama) 1830

   [Hernani, 1833]

Les feuilles d'automne (poetry) 1831

Marion de Lorme (drama) 1831

   [The King's Edict, 1872; also published as Marion de Lorme, 1934]

Notre-Dame de Paris (novel) 1831

   [The Hunchback of Notre Dame, 1833]

Le roi s'amuse (drama) 1832

   [The King's Fool, 1841]

Lucrèce Borgia (drama) 1833

   [Lucretia Borgia, 1842]

Ruy Blas (drama) 1838

   [Ruy Blas, 1861]

Les châtiments (poetry) 1853

Les contemplations (poetry) 1856

La légende des siècles. 3 vols. (poetry) 1859-83

   [The Legend of the Centuries, 1894]

Les misérables (novel) 1862

   [Les Misérables, 1862; also published as The Wretched, 1863]

William Shakespeare (criticism) 1864

   [William Shakespeare, 1864]

Les travailleurs de la mer (novel) 1866

   [The Toilers of the Sea, 1866]

L'homme qui rit (novel) 1869

   [The Man Who Laughs, 1869; also published as By Order of the King, 1870]

Quatre-vingt treize (novel) 1874

   [Ninety-three, 1874]

Choses vues (essays) 1887

   [Things Seen, 1887]

---

moulding, illustrative of the Beatitudes, or the Ten Commandments, or the seven deadly sins? What is Quasimodo but an animated gargoyle? What is the whole book but the reanimation of Gothic art?

It is curious that in this, the earliest of the five great romances, there should be so little of that extravagance that latterly we have come almost to identify with the author's manner. Yet even here we are distressed by words, thoughts, and incidents that defy belief and alienate the sympathies. (pp. 21-3)

In spite of the horror and misery that pervade all of his later work, there is in it much less of actual melodrama than here, and rarely, I should say never, that sort of brutality, that useless insufferable violence to the feelings, which is the last distinction between melodrama and true tragedy. Now, in *Notre Dame,* the whole story of Esmeralda's passion for the worthless archer is unpleasant enough; but when she betrays herself in her last hiding-place, herself and her wretched mother, by calling out to this sordid hero who has long since forgotten her—well, that is just one of those things that readers will not forgive; they do not like it, and they are quite right; life is hard enough for poor mortals, without having it indefinitely embittered for them by bad art.

We look in vain for any similar blemish in *Les Misérables.* Here, on the other hand, there is perhaps the nearest approach to literary restraint that Hugo has ever made: there is here certainly the ripest and most easy development of his powers. It is the moral intention of this great novel to awaken us a little, if it may be—for such awakenings are unpleasant—to the great cost of this society that we enjoy and profit by, to the labour and sweat of those who support the litter, civilisation, in which we ourselves are so smoothly carried forward. People are all glad to shut their eyes; and it gives them a very simple pleasure when they can forget that our laws commit a million individual injustices, to be once roughly just in the general; that the bread that we eat, and the quiet of the family, and all that embellishes life and makes it worth having, have to be purchased by death—by the death of animals, and the deaths of men wearied out with labour, and the deaths of those criminals called tyrants and revolutionaries, and the deaths of those revolutionaries called criminals. It is to something of all this that Victor Hugo wishes to open men's eyes in *Les Misérables;* and this moral lesson is worked out in masterly coincidence with the artistic effect. The deadly weight of civilisation to those who are below presses sensibly on our shoulders as we read. A sort of mocking indignation grows upon us as we find Society rejecting, again and again, the services of the most serviceable; setting Jean Valjean to pick oakum, casting Galileo into prison, even crucifying Christ. There is a haunting and horrible sense of insecurity about the book. The terror we thus feel is a terror for the machinery of law, that we can hear tearing, in the dark, good and bad between its formidable wheels with the iron stolidity of all machinery, human or divine. (pp. 23-4)

With so gloomy a design this great work is still full of life and light and love. The portrait of the good Bishop is one of the most agreeable things in modern literature. The whole scene at Montfermeil is full of the charm that Hugo knows so well how to throw about children. . . . Take it for all in all, there are few books in the world that can be compared with it. There is as much calm and serenity as Hugo has ever attained to; the melodramatic coarsenesses that disfigured *Notre Dame* are no longer present. There is certainly much that is painfully improbable; and again, the story itself is a little too well constructed; it produces on us the effect of a puzzle, and we grow incredulous as we find that every character fits again and again into the plot, and is, like the child's cube, serviceable on six faces; things are not so well arranged in life as all that comes to. Some of the digressions, also, seem out of place, and do nothing but interrupt and irritate. But when all is said, the book remains of masterly conception and of masterly development, full of pathos, full of truth, full of a high eloquence. (p. 25)

[And in *Les Travailleurs de la Mer*] once more the artistic effect and the moral lesson are worked out together, and are, indeed, one. Gilliat, alone upon the reef at his herculean task, offers a type of human industry in the midst of the vague "diffusion of forces into the illimitable," and the visionary development of "wasted labour" in the sea, and the winds, and the clouds. No character was ever thrown into such strange relief as Gilliat. The great circle of sea-birds that come wonderingly around him on the night of his arrival, strikes at once the note of his pre-eminence and isolation. He fills the whole reef with his indefatigable toil; this solitary spot in the ocean rings with the clamour of his anvil; we see him as he comes and goes, thrown out sharply against the clear background of the sea. And yet his isolation is not to be compared with the isolation of Robinson Crusoe, for example; indeed, no two books could be more instructive to set side by side than *Les Travailleurs* and this other of the old days before art had learnt to occupy itself with what lies outside of human will. Crusoe was one sole centre of interest in the midst of a nature utterly dead and utterly unrealised by the artist; but this is not how we feel with Gilliat; we feel that he is opposed by a "dark coalition of forces," that an "immense animosity" surrounds him; we are the witnesses of the terrible warfare that he wages with "the silent inclemency of phenomena going their own way, and the great general law, implacable and passive:" "a

conspiracy of the indifference of things" is against him. There is not one interest on the reef, but two. (p. 26)

But in *Les Travailleurs,* with all its strength, with all its eloquence, with all the beauty and fitness of its main situations, we cannot conceal from ourselves that there is a thread of something that will not bear calm scrutiny. There is much that is disquieting about the storm, admirably as it begins. I am very doubtful whether it would be possible to keep the boat from foundering in such circumstances, by any amount of breakwater and broken rock. I do not understand the way in which the waves are spoken of, and prefer just to take it as a loose way of speaking, and pass on. And lastly, how does it happen that the sea was quite calm next day? Is this great hurricane a piece of scene-painting after all? And when we have forgiven Gilliat's prodigies of strength (although, in soberness, he reminds us more of Porthos in the Vicomte de Bragelonne than is quite desirable), what is to be said to his suicide, and how are we to condemn in adequate terms that unprincipled avidity after effect, which tells us that the sloop disappeared over the horizon, and the head under the water, at one and the same moment? Monsieur Hugo may say what he will, but we know better; we know very well that they did not; a thing like that raises up a despairing spirit of opposition in a man's readers; they give him the lie fiercely, as they read. (p. 27)

In *L'Homme qui Rit,* it was Hugo's object to "denounce" (as he would say himself) the aristocratic principle as it was exhibited in England; and this purpose, somewhat more unmitigatedly satiric than that of the two last, must answer for much that is unpleasant in the book. The repulsiveness of the scheme of the story, and the manner in which it is bound up with impossibilities and absurdities, discourage the reader at the outset, and it needs an effort to take it as seriously as it deserves. And yet when we judge it deliberately, it will be seen that, here again, the story is admirably adapted to the moral. The constructive ingenuity exhibited throughout is almost morbid. (p. 28)

There is here a quality in the narration more intimate and particular than is general with Hugo; but it must be owned, on the other hand, that the book is wordy, and even, now and then, a little wearisome. Ursus and his wolf are pleasant enough companions; but the former is nearly as much an abstract type as the latter. There is a beginning, also, of an abuse of conventional conversation, such as may be quite pardonable in the drama where needs must, but is without excuse in the romance. (p. 29)

Romance is a language in which many persons learn to speak with a certain appearance of fluency; but there are few who can ever bend it to any practical need, few who can ever be said to express themselves in it. It has become abundantly plain in the foregoing examination that Victor Hugo occupies a high place among those few. He has always a perfect command over his stories; and we see that they are constructed with a high regard to some ulterior purpose, and that every situation is informed with moral significance and grandeur. Of no other man can the same thing be said in the same degree. His romances are not to be confused with "the novel with a purpose" as familiar to the English reader: this is generally the model of incompetence; and we see the moral clumsily forced into every hole and corner of the story, or thrown externally over it like a carpet over a railing. Now the moral significance, with Hugo, is of the essence of the romance; it is the organising principle. (pp. 32-3)

Having thus learned to subordinate his story to an idea, to make his art speak, he went on to teach it to say things heretofore unaccustomed. . . . There is no hero in *Notre Dame:* in *Les Misérables* it is an old man: in *L'Homme qui Rit* it is a monster: in *Quatre Vingt Treize* it is the Revolution. Those elements that only began to show themselves timidly, as adjuncts, in the novels of Walter Scott, have usurped ever more and more of the canvas; until we find the whole interest of one of Hugo's romances centring around matter that Fielding would have banished from his altogether, as being out of the field of fiction. . . . [For] Hugo, man is no longer an isolated spirit without antecedent or relation here below, but a being involved in the action and reaction of natural forces, himself a centre of such action and reaction; or an unit in a great multitude, chased hither and thither by epidemic terrors and aspirations, and, in all seriousness, blown about by every wind of doctrine. (pp. 33-4)

[*Notre Dame, Les Misérables, Quatre Vingt Treize, L'Homme qui Rit,* and *Les Travailleurs*] would have made a very great fame for any writer, and yet they are but one façade of the monument that Victor Hugo has erected to his genius. Everywhere we find somewhat the same greatness, somewhat the same infirmities. In his poems and plays there are the same unaccountable protervities that have already astonished us in the romances. There, too, is the same feverish strength, welding the fiery iron of his idea under forge-hammer repetitions—an emphasis that is somehow akin to weakness—a strength that is a little epileptic. He stands so far above all his contemporaries, and so incomparably excels them in richness, breadth, variety, and moral earnestness, that we almost feel as if he had a sort of right to fall oftener and more heavily than others; but this does not reconcile us to seeing him profit by the privilege so freely. We like to have, in our great men, something that is above question; we like to place an implicit faith in them, and see them always on the platform of their greatness; and this, unhappily, cannot be with Hugo. . . . If we look back, yet once, upon these five romances, we see blemishes such as we can

lay to the charge of no other man in the number of the famous; but to what other man can we attribute such sweeping innovations, such a new and significant presentment of the life of man, such an amount, if we merely think of the amount, of equally consummate performance? (p. 35)

Robert Louis Stevenson, "Victor Hugo's Romances," in his *The Essays of Robert Louis Stevenson,* MacDonald, 1950, pp. 13-35.

M. O. W. OLIPHANT
(essay date 1885)

[Oliphant was a Scottish novelist, biographer, and critic. In the excerpt below, she provides an overview of *Notre-Dame de Paris*, *Les misérables*, *Travailleurs de la mer*, *L'homme qui rit*, and *Quatre-vingt treize*.]

[The] great mass of the work which Victor Hugo has left behind him can be separated from the polemics of his troubled age and fiery temper. It is not in any sense a peaceful literature. Conflict is its very inspiration. The struggle of human misery with all the confusing and overbearing forces of life; of poverty with the requirements and oppressions of wealth; of the small with the great; of the people with tyrants; of Man with Fate: these are his subjects, and he is never an impartial historian. He is on the side of the weak in every combat, the partisan of the oppressed. But this does not detract from his work when his opponents are the oppressors of the past, or the still more subtle, veiled, and unassailable forces of Destiny. The poet's region is there: he is born, if not to set right the times, which are out of joint, at least to read to the world the high and often terrible lesson of the ages. But it vulgarizes his work when he is seen, tooth and nail, in violent personal conflict with foemen unworthy of his steel, embalming in poetry the trivial or the uncompleted incidents of contemporary warfare. (pp. 11-12)

Hugo has enough and to spare for all subjects that occurred to him. A sunset, a landscape, a love song, alternate in his pages with a philosophical discussion or a brief and brilliant scene snatched from history, from contemporary life, from his own inner existence, all clothed in the noblest verse of which the French language is capable. His power over that language is boundless, the wealth of an utterance which never pauses for a word, which disregards all rules yet glorifies them, which is ready for every suggestion and finds nothing too terrible, nothing too tender, for the tongue which, at his bidding, leaps into blazing eloquence, or rolls in clouds and thunder, or murmurs with the accent of a dove. Never had there been so great a gamut, a compass so extended. (p. 17)

It is impossible, or almost impossible, to convey through the medium of translation the melody and beauty of lyrical poetry from one language to another; it is even difficult for a foreigner to appreciate fully, though well acquainted with the language, that finer soul of verse which is dearest to the native ear. And we do not venture to attempt to explain and describe the indescribable. But yet there are many of Victor Hugo's most striking poems which might be translated with at least an approximate success. For that in which he is perhaps at his best is the delineation of a sudden scene, an incident in which human nature is seen at its highest or lowest, a spark struck out of the darkness in which history leaves the mass of humankind. (p. 18)

It is not, however, upon his poetry, either in the form of drama, lyric, or narrative, that his fame out of France, or at least in England, is founded. There is no more usual deliverance of superficial criticism in this country than that which declares French poetry in general to be either nought—which is still a not uncommon notion—or at least not great enough to be worth the study which alone could make it comprehensible. There are many good people who dare to say this yet live, audacious, and unconscious of their folly. We have now, however, to consider Victor Hugo on a ground which no one ventures to dispute. The great Romances—for which we should like to invent another name—which we cannot call novels, and which are too majestic even for the title of romance, though that means something more than the corresponding word in English—are in their kind and period the greatest works produced in his time. We are glad that we are not called upon to make any comparison of the Frenchman with our own beloved romancer, the master of all fiction in England, the name most dear in literature. Scott's noble, sober, temperate, and modest genius is in all things different from the tempestuous, fantastic, and splendid imagination—the nature fiery, violent, yet profound—of his successor in the field. That Hugo penetrates deeper, that the depths of that abyss of which he is so fond lie open before him, and that nothing in Scott gives the terrific impression which the dark and surging mass of vitality, misery, and crime lurking in the backgrounds of Paris both mediaeval and actual, conveys to us, we readily admit. (pp. 19-20)

Notre Dame de Paris, with all its strange learning and wonderful panoramic effects, is not like the work of a young man, or a first essay in the art of fiction. Yet [Hugo] was scarcely twenty-eight when it was written. It has nothing of the frank reality and open-air life of Scott. Its extreme elaboration and detail resemble more the work of Manzoni in the "Promessi Sposi," and it has evidently been the model, conscious or unconscious, of "Romola." George Eliot, who was not, so far

as we are aware, a disciple of Hugo, bears more resemblance to him than any other writer of historical romance. Scott has no object but that of telling his manful delightful story of times which charm him by their picturesqueness, which have seized upon his imagination in all their glory of arms and adventure, and with that advantage of distance which makes the past the true land of romance. Manzoni has no story to tell, nor spontaneous impulse like that of our great romancist, but the distinct and carefully worked out purpose of elucidating the Middle Ages in Italy, and laying before us the conditions of life in that departed condition of affairs. Victor Hugo adds something to both. He has his tale to tell, but the tale is a parable—he has his revelation to make, his old world to light up with a lurid illumination, which does not diffuse itself over the landscape, but lights up here and there with miraculous Rembrandt effects against the background of a world of shadows. With him there is meaning in everything, and the common struggle and conflict of humanity at large with the forces that oppress and enslave is never lost sight of, even when his principal object is to trace out some individual struggle against those awful powers of fate which have been the subject of so many dramas, and have affected the imagination of so many poets. (p. 20)

Victor Hugo makes no historical portraits. The group of beings round whose hapless feet he draws the coils of fate are all offsprings of his fancy. The dancing girl of the streets, an image most probably borrowed from the "Precioza" of Cervantes—if among such sovereigns of poetic inspiration there could ever be any question of borrowing—the frightful spectre of the priest, the deformed and formidable monster Quasimodo, with his hideous body and faithful soul, all linked together in fatal fortuitous combination, belong to the imagination alone. The *beau capitaine* has a certain footing on the solid earth, and is, indeed, a remorseless picture of the young libertine, handsome and heartless and beloved, with whom fiction is but too familiar. But all these figures are primitive, in the elementary stage of existence; they have no defence of character, of individual life or thought against the constraining force of the fatality which grasps them, and which they cannot escape. Even the girl, who is the image of purity and innocence amid all those sombre and terrible scenes, is pure only till temptation really touches her, and has in herself no protest against sin, but only against that to which she has no inclination. The priest in his vile soul has no pretence of a higher feeling. The passion that rages in him has no right to be called love; for it is the basest and most gross of animal desires. (p. 21)

According to his own explanation, it is the struggle of human nature with superstition which Victor Hugo has set himself to demonstrate in this book. But it is much more. Superstition is the feeblest of the forces in it. The condemnation of the hapless girl as a sorceress is little more than the framework of the drama. The sudden commotion of the fierce yet easily diverted crowd, the merciless apparition of Tristan L'Hermite and his soldiers, and the various scenes about the gibbet give but a superficial support to this theory. The picture is really more dark and fatal, less temporary and chronological. With greater reason it might be said that the *motif* of the sombre strain is that which plays so little part in ancient tragedy, but which is so great an actor in the modern. . . . The drama is, in fact, deeper and of far wider significance than the author claims for it. It is the errings and mistakes of the half-enlightened human creature, "moving about in worlds not realized," stumbling into paths discovered too late to be fatal, half seeing, not understanding, till time brings the terrible explanation. Superstition has not much more to do with it than has the grand shadow under which all is enacted: that magnificent Notre Dame which it is scarcely possible to think of, standing there, the central figure in the scene, as an inanimate thing.

This was Victor Hugo's *coup d'essai* in fiction, and it stands by itself a work, so far as we know, without parallel—a piece of mediaeval life and of universal tragedy, vivid, terrible, appalling. (p. 22)

There is no tenderness in *Notre Dame*. Love itself is a delirium, and pity is so qualified with horror that there is no softness in it. But when we come to the *Misérables*, all is pity and tenderness, and a compassion which melts the heart. To turn from Claude Frollo, and find ourselves suddenly in the presence of Bishop Myriel, is a change for which we can find no words. In the gloomy world, wherein the dark priest of Notre Dame represents religion, there is no repentance or power of betterment, nor healing touch of sympathy, but only fierce remorse and execration and terror. But when the great romancist begins his second chapter of human history and fate, the altered atmosphere makes itself felt in a moment. (p. 23)

The *Misérables,* is the story of [the] struggle in the soul and life of the rescued criminal, but it is also the story of the world that lies behind and around him. Again, that swarming, tumultuous Paris, with its suffering multitudes, its chaos of discordant elements, and the great stream of life that carries on all those contradictions and anomalies. No city was ever so overflowing with the sound of a multitude; every roof hides a little secondary conflict; everywhere there are the tokens of the struggle, not with the law only and its rigid rules, but of the nobler with the baser, of mercy with judgment. . . . Nothing is omitted in this wonderful book. If its chief subject is in the depths, it rises also to the serenest heights of imagination. It is the epic of the miserable; but since that great change which in the late twilight, among the wild freedom of the open moors,

we saw taking place in the soul of the miserable convict, it becomes also the romance of the happy. For that is the turning-point—not Javert and his needless pursuit, but the fact that Jean Valjean becomes the père Madeleine—the repentant, the sorrowful who has obtained mercy. There are many indications of vice, such as were indispensable to the subject; and there are also, as unfortunately in all Victor Hugo's works, much wild talk and rhapsodies which to the innocent may sound like blasphemy. But withal, the *Misérables* is the greatest of religious romances: a noble, modern, nineteenth-century legend of the saints.

The *Travailleurs de la Mer* is more strictly and formally true to the author's declared purpose. It is the struggle of Man with the forces of Nature in a clearer sense than the *Misérables* represents the struggle with Society. The fantastic character of that conflict, and of the devilish being with which it is made, is within the privileges of art, though not perhaps according to the laws of probability. . . . The concentration of the struggle with brute force, and the hideous, unreasoning will which seems to confront man in his attempts to subjugate the earth, and resist him to the death, in a malignant creature, is in this point of view quite justifiable. But here again the subject widens, and the larger atmosphere of humanity comes in. Gilliat's death struggle is not with the pieuvre, nor with the winds and seas, over which the resources and expedients of humanity (in his case naturally strained to extravagance) are always victorious in the end; but with a thing much slighter and much greater—a trifling thing, not worth counting in the history of the race—yet not to be overcome by those forces which can move mountains, or touched by the lever even which could upset the earth. It is the heart of another human creature, the foolish impulse of another's inclination, which is the object, unconquerable by any giant, and against which, with all his strength and patience and boundless resource, this conqueror of the seas is brought to shipwreck and destruction. (pp. 24-5)

[Hugo's] former works were full of night effects, strong contrasts of light and shade: but here the sky and horizon have all the largeness, the breadth and space which belong to the sea. The scene is larger, but it is less peopled, the actors in the drama are few, for a great part of the work Gilliat alone holds by himself the human side of the struggle, and all the uncertainty of incident and surroundings, which in the former works were so endless and varied, are here entirely laid aside. It is an epic rather than a tragedy, yet the most tragic epic: the story of our life. (p. 27)

We may permit ourselves to take the privilege of selection, and omit the next of his works, the *Homme qui Rit.* The book is an embodiment of all that is offensive in Hugo—extravagance, false taste, false rhetoric, and a choice of the painful, the horrible, and the grotesque, which in itself is a vice. He was weary of exile, of sorrow, of long waiting for the good to come, when he had this nightmare. His next great work of fiction was produced under happier auspices. It was intended to have been followed by two others, in which the story of the Revolution should have been repeated and summed up; but this intention was never carried out. As a matter of fact, a sequel to the portion of the work already before us would be little possible, since two of the chief personages, and these the typical leaders of the Revolution, had demonstrated the poetical impossibility of the undertaking by their tragic end.

In *Quatre-vingt-treize* we come back from the stillness of the island, the concentration of life within the surroundings of the seas, once more to the crowds and heat and conflict of tumultuous existence, into the bitter misery of civil war, and that desperate struggle for mastery which had not yet found a solution in Bonaparte. No scene in Victor Hugo's works is more characteristic than the scene in the ship with the cannon which has broken loose. The blind and fatal thing, simulating the struggles of a creature that has life and some sort of intelligence, is such a symbol as is dear to him. It is like the pieuvre, it is like Javert, an irresponsible instrument of evil; malign, yet innocent; striving to murder, yet without guilt. Its bounds and plunges are so many details in his parable—the man who stands with his life in his hands opposed to that threatening, redoubtable, lifeless monster, is man incarnate against the powers of destiny. (pp. 27-8)

[The charm of the sombre volumes of *Quatre-vingt-treize* is] also the charm of the poet's old age—the wonderful group of children which appears in the midst of all the fire and flame, the conflict of passions and elements. There is no chapter of the life of childhood in literature known to us which we could place beside the chapter entitled "Le Massacre de St. Barthélemy." The men outside may be types and symbols, the children live and breathe. . . . The little group altogether fills our eyes as we read with the moisture of delight, with something of that unspeakable tenderness, compassion, adoration, which is in the eyes of the writer. These little beings are in all the freshness of the inarticulate, creatures conceived, not described; fresh from the hand of God, not sullied by the touch of that reverent yet playful beholder through whom we see the blossoming of their unconscious life. Their seriousness, their busy-ness, their tremendous discoveries, their absorption in the little world about them, and indifference to all that passes outside; the masculine energy of René-Jean and Gros-Alain; the finer dreamer, twenty months old, not yet sufficiently entered in life to give her full attention to it—form such a picture as neither poet nor painter had dreamed of. The atmosphere about them is half heaven, half morning—the little comedy of their existence is full of a pathos which

is at once heartrending and delightful. Amid all the wonders of Hugo's genius, this is perhaps the most wonderful of all. (pp. 30-1)

M. O. W. Oliphant, "Victor Hugo," in *Contemporary Review*, Vol. XLVIII, July, 1885, pp. 10-32.

MADAME DUCLAUX
(essay date 1921)

[In the following excerpt, Duclaux addresses the genesis of *Les misérables* and comments on its literary models, elements of realism, and social implications.]

[*Les Misérables*] is conceived in the same key as [*La légende des siècles*]; it also is a progression towards an apotheosis. But where the poem is legend or prophecy, the prose epic touches reality and moves in our sphere. Marius, the hero, is the contemporary, and indeed the double, of Victor Hugo—the son of a Royalist mother and a father who had served in Napoleon's armies, like General Hugo.

Marius, too, had been young in 1830, had lived on the barricades of a revolution, had married, after endless difficulties, the girl whom all his young will and passion were bent on obtaining. Marius is an image of Hugo's youth. But is Marius the hero of *Les Misérables?* No. Evidently their real hero is Jean Valjean, the convict, the criminal who steals the cherished treasure of his benefactor, who cheats the boy-sweep of his florin; who then, repenting, is transformed into a man of honesty and honour. (p. 203)

There is, no doubt, a sort of moral paradox, an amplification like that produced by the fumes of opium, in this conception of a hardened criminal shattered by remorse because he has stolen two francs from a little boy, and giving himself up to justice in order to save an innocent man wrongly accused. Hugo is incurably sentimental. We must accept him as he is. His virtuous thieves and angelic prostitutes are, after all, but the transposition into modern art of figures sufficiently familiar in the Gospels. Hugo was as intimately convinced as any priest that the heart of man is complex, never wholly good nor wholly bad, and that there is no sin which may not be redeemed. In *Les Misérables* he gives life and substance to those theories of expiation and atonement which he has preached consistently enough in his play of *Marion de Lorme* and in his poems of *Les Contemplations*.

Jean Valjean is a double nature, such as suited the genius of Hugo, that unrepentant Manichee: Jean Valjean wears, as it were, two pouches; in one he has the experience of a convict, in the other the instincts of a saint; and his thoughts and deeds are extracted, as he goes through life, sometimes from the one, and sometimes from the other. . . . When Jean Valjean stole the Bishop's plate, there was something hidden with it in his sack, as surreptitiously as the silver cup in Benjamin's wallet; and that was Salvation. For kindness, charity, courtesy, though betrayed, and finally a free forgiveness, accomplished that which years of cruel repression had failed even to suggest. In an earlier book—which all lovers of *Les Misérables* should read—in *Claude Gueux*, Hugo had already incriminated the injustice of human justice. Tolstoi, I think, must have thought of *Les Misérables* when he wrote *Resurrection.*

In his former great novel, in that tragic, bitter, dilettante *Notre-Dame de Paris*, Hugo, his heart wrung by the deep disappointment of his marriage, had preached the hopeless doctrine of Fatality. We are all, said he, subject to Necessity. . . . But *Les Misérables* is a generous recantation, a palinody full of faith in the soul's liberty and in social progress. . . . Fatality is a monster of the Middle Ages. Monsters evolve and develop into angels. From the dead cocoon of Necessity a soaring and glittering being issues, shedding hope and love from its radiant wings; and Fraternity illuminates the Future. . . . [In *Les Misérables* Hugo] celebrates the times when there shall be no more wars, no more classes sunk in misery, no more ignorance, no more crime, no more indigence. Here Hugo wanders in Utopia; but he does not ignore, in his novel, the terrible problem of crime. Besides Jean Valjean, the criminal-made, he sets Thénardier, the criminal-born, whom nothing can redeem; who, when unexpected prosperity gives him, in a new country, a new lease of life, employs his unhoped-for capital as a fund to start himself in business as a slave-dealer. There is not one single noble instinct in Thénardier. . . . [Round] Thénardier gravitates a system of thieves and bullies, criminal by a bent of their nature, from laziness, or brutality, or sheer malice, as well as from mere love of adventure. For nine-tenths of these, surely, there is little to be hoped in this world or the next. All we can admit is their annihilation, since Evil has no immortal soul. Hugo the novelist knows the depths of human nature more profoundly than Hugo the philosopher. The root of Crime is not mere Ignorance. There exists a mysterious natural depravity. Was not the vile Thénardier, who had studied to be a priest, less ignorant than Jean Valjean? (pp. 204-05)

Misérables is a word with two meanings, for *misérable* means "wretch," and also merely "wretched"—wretchedly poor. Victor Hugo had never been able to forget the condition of Lazarus at his gates; pity for the poor no less than love of liberty had made him a revolutionary; and the question of how to purify the dregs of society was seldom long absent from his mind.

Something noble and magnanimous in his temper prevented him from acquiring the indifference of the pure artist, and at sixty years of age he rebelled as indignantly against injustice, oppression, or the hard and starving misery which infests the slums of great cities as any generous youth in his first fresh contact with reality. If I had to translate the title *Les Misérables,* I think I should call it: The Dregs of Society. In our common round of life we scarcely notice these dregs, fallen to the bottom; the draught we drink is clear and sweet. But sometimes the Hand of God takes up the glass and shakes it rudely. Then there is a revolution and the dregs mix with the wine, and give their acrid flavour to the whole.

Les Misérables is a study of those first years after 1830, when the people of France, resenting the tricks of legerdemain, thanks to which Louis-Philippe had put their revolution in his royal pocket, broke out again and again in useless insurrections. . . . It was [Hugo's] memories of the street-fighting of 1851 which enabled him in *Les Misérables* to vivify his picture of the life of a barricade, and to show that mutual exaltation, that more than individual existence, that incorporate and unanimous mind, in which a trench or a barricade—any body of men so much in earnest as to make light of death and pain—can live a sublimer life than their separate components ever know. *Les Misérables* is an epic of insurrection, the development of an obscure and immanent force, that tends to the light, striving to destroy the tyranny which would keep it plunged in the abyss. Both the tyranny and the resurgent force . . . are charged with the fetters of the Past. Their clash is the conflict of two powers alike doomed to perish; for who lives by the sword shall perish by the sword; but, out of their ruined violence, a new order shall arise, which shall not seek to repress or punish, but to reform and to elevate; which shall attempt not to grasp but to share, and not to dominate but to love.

Such is the gospel of *Les Misérables;* but a novel lives less by its general ideas than by the characters which it exhibits and the pictures it represents. Hugo has never been so happy in his personages as in these volumes. Marius and Cosette move through these scenes of riot and upheaval haloed in a blue and tender gleam as wonderful as that more golden haze which irradiates the figure of a girl in Rembrandt's "Ronde de Nuit"; for he sees them in the light of his own youth—still infinitely fair and intimately real, in spite of Life's disenchantment. Cosette is just a girl in love—a type more than an individual—and she has borrowed something from either of the two women that Hugo loved with the two valves of his double heart. . . . [It] is not so much the woman that we see as the charm that emanates from her, the dawn-like, delicious, girlish radiance that suddenly transfuses and transfigures the lean, lanky, sallow grasshopper of a girl to whom Marius had paid scant attention. Cosette is a haunting strain of music, an almond-branch in flower, a delight we should be sorry to have missed. But Marius is a person, for Marius is Victor Hugo, and the study of Marius unbares the poet's heart. (pp. 206-08)

There are pages in *Les Misérables*—the charming idyll of Marius and Cosette in the Luxembourg Gardens; the struggle in the soul of Jean Valjean when he hears that an innocent man has been arrested for his crime; his dream; his drive to Amiens; and the scene in the Courts; or again the magnificent recital of the suicide of Javert, with its view of Paris at night seen from the quai de la Mégisserie—there are pages which, I suppose, are unmatched in nineteenth-century fiction except perhaps by certain passages in the great novels of Tolstoi or George Eliot. And yet at this supreme point commences Hugo's decadence. For his age betrays him: that proliferation of tissue which is a sign of degenerescence, that senile amplification which more and more will gain upon our poet, are already incipient. . . . (p. 209)

Madame Duclaux, in her *Victor Hugo,* Henry Holt and Company, 1921, 268 p.

C. E. VAUGHAN

(essay date 1926)

[In the following excerpt, Vaughan addresses themes of conflict in Hugo's poetry.]

[Hugo is primarily] a poet; and it must now be our task to indicate the relation of his poetry to the idea which has hitherto been traced in his Drama and Romance. (pp. 424-25)

In political poetry, Hugo stands as much alone as in the writing of Romance. No poet, except Juvenal, has attempted a task resembling that which he has performed: and Juvenal, supreme as he is, could hardly claim to have struck so deep a chord as is struck in [Hugo's volumes]. The poetry of Hugo in this department may be compared, indeed, with the romances written by himself before and during the period of his exile. The idea which underlies it is identical: the treatment is, fundamentally, the same. In the poetry, as in the romances, there is a conflict; here, as there, all the light is on one side, nothing but darkness on the other. Of course the difference of form involves to a certain extent, a modification in the treatment of the idea. There can be no question here of the completeness which is given to the representation of society in *Les Misérables,* of nature in *Les Travailleurs de la mer.* But, what is lost in completeness is more than compen-

sated by the greater appropriateness of the setting in which the conception is put forth. *Les Misérables* claims to give a portraiture of society, as it always tends to be, as it actually was after the fall of the Empire and the Revolution of 1830 in modern France. (p. 425)

Satire and invective—which is a more direct, and therefore in worthy hands a nobler, form of satire—have never gone deeper and higher than in *L'expiation* and *La vision de Dante* on the one hand, and in *Le Te Deum du I er Janvier* and *Le Jour des rois* upon the other. The poet of conflict was never more in his element than when crusading against tyranny and superstition. The spirit of Voltaire might seem to walk the earth again; but of Voltaire raised and widened by the influence of the two movements, revolutionary and romantic, that since his death had renovated the world. The satire of Hugo—to use the word in a wider sense than above—is not less, but more, direct and uncompromising than that of Voltaire himself.

Nor is it only in the bare fact of writing satire that Hugo shows himself pre-eminently the poet of conflict. The specific form which his satire takes exhibits still more plainly the same tendency at work. Other satirists have branded what was unrighteous and contemptible. Hugo alone has confronted successful wickedness with the purity and justice which it had trampled under foot. No part of his satire is more characteristic, no part is more essential, than such poems as that on the child shot on the 4th of December, and the Hymn of those transported in *Les Châtiments,* or *Le Crapaud* and *Les pauvres gens* in *La Legénde des Siècles.* (p. 426)

In satire, as in Drama and Romance, conflict is the idea which underlies all that Hugo has produced. The idea is, as has been seen, carried a stage further, because it is worked out more consistently in satire than in Romance: but in both it is fundamentally the same.

In turning to Hugo's poetry of nature, we are, at first sight, met with a singular deviation from the conception which has so far been traced through the various divisions of his work. Occasionally, indeed, as in the *Toilers of the Sea,* man may be represented in the act of struggling with nature. But far more generally the very reverse of this is done. Nature is not commonly portrayed as the antagonist who wrestles with man, but as the superior who disdainfully mocks, or disdainfully instructs him. . . . (p. 427)

[What] induces Hugo to put nature above man, and by consequence instinct above reason, is zeal for the progress which, by so doing he seems to set aside, but which, only if set aside for the moment, could in his view be permanently ensured. The conflict is stayed for the instant, and in this region, that it may be fought more relentlessly in other fields. Man is bidden throw himself on the sustaining power of nature that from her breast he may drink fresh strength for the war which he is to wage with man and, when occasion calls, with nature.

The form which this conception takes in Hugo is either more or less explicit. In the earlier volumes of poetry it is less so, and its full scope is hardly recognised by the poet himself. It is true, indeed, that even here to him, as to Wordsworth, nature is greater and richer than man. What is wanting here, and what is present in the later poems, is the thought that what nature has to give to man is specifically combative energy and power of resistance. (p. 429)

In the poems written after the beginning of his exile all is changed. Nature is still the source of truth, but she is the source also of action, for men. And this implies an essential change in the conception of truth itself. It is no longer sought with groping steps, but with some measure of assurance. There is a certainty in the note which nature, as the organ of truth, gives out through the second volume of *Les Contemplations* and *La Légende des Siècles* which is wanting, as the titles might indicate, to the poems contained in *Les Chants de Crépuscule* and *Les rayons et les ombres*. "**Pensar, dudar**"—to think is to doubt,—the title of one among the greatest of Hugo's early poems, might be taken to give the keynote of the earlier period: to think is to believe and do is the fundamental conception of his later writings. And if there is a mystical strain about the later, which was absent or but seldom present in the earlier, poems, that is no contradiction but rather a confirmation of what has been said. (p. 430)

To Hugo it is the storm and tempest, the strength and fury which seem the essential thing in nature. In themselves they are indifferent; they inspire the horror of the storm-wind and the malignity of the Devil-fish in the *Toilers of the Sea* as much as the Lion of Androcles, and the waves that console the exile or the forests that rebuke the bandit in *Les Châtiments*. But, when swept into the circle of human life even at their wildest, even at what appears to be their worst, they may be an essential element in the mysterious "formation of the law of progress." And at certain crucial moments of history, to have committed himself trustfully to their rushing tide has been necessary to man that he may be saved from himself, and exchange the exhausted soil of an old world for the rich life of a new. Thus, it might be said, at the Christian era, man threw himself on nature, and received the gift of love: at the Renaissance, he threw himself on nature and received a new conception of God, and a new sense of life and knowledge; at the Revolution, he threw himself on nature, and received freedom. The second of these periods, under a grand figure, forms the subject of *Le Satyre*, which, if we are to take any one poem, gives probably the most complete and splendid expression to the genius of Hugo.

To describe that poem would be an impossible and, it may be supposed, a superfluous task. It affords, in truth, an apt symbol to represent the "new birth" which, in the language of Michelet, "discovered nature and re-discovered man," and which, it might be added, brought religion, as Socrates brought philosophy, down from heaven to earth, snatching it from the hand of a priestly caste to make it the common possession of mankind. But what most concerns us at the present moment to remark is the faith with which, in this poem, Hugo trusts himself to the undisciplined powers which start from the depth of nature to play their part in the changed order of the world. (p. 431)

[In the Drama,] the struggle was within the character of the individual: in Romance it was between the individual and the world without. Here the battlefield is still wider. The struggle is in nature; and nature is but that writ large which in man is written small; man therefore is ranged with nature in the fight which, in detail always, on a large scale at the turning-points of history, is being waged against the powers of darkness. Man and nature are associated, almost identified: together they fill the whole circle of life; and they in turn are filled with the spirit of conflict. And, to enlarge the stage of action still further, that against which the conflict lies is either kept out of sight or but darkly shadowed forth. . . . It is the application of the idea of conflict to history and nature, and the harmonisation of man, as of history, with nature that gives so wide a reach to the best of what Hugo has written on these two subjects. He is a great political poet, and he is a great poet of nature; and he is one because he is the other. The reflection of man in nature, and of nature into man, the recognition of the same law of conflict working out to the same end in both man and nature, opens out a possibility of wider issues, and a more intense life, in his treatment of either subject. . . . The humanisation of nature, the penetration of her forms with the idea of conflict, has for its result to raise the vitality of nature to the highest point which it can reach. Bird and beast, even wind and wave, become instinct with the life, and combative energy, which we are apt to regard as the property of man alone. To nature may be applied the figure which, in one of the poems in *La Légende des Siècles*, represents Hugo's conception of history. The outer coating of the blind wall that fronts man melts away; and the whole tissue behind, which he had taken for inanimate and dead, is seen to be built up from countless myriads of souls in ceaseless activity to weave "the web of being spun," in some cases blindly, in others with full consciousness. (pp. 432-33)

His conception of life does not stop with the component parts, but is extended to the whole. Each part of nature may have a separate life: but there is a life, a personality for the whole which, in his view, is still more essential. "If the world had no individual life, man, who has it, would be greater than the world"; or again, "I believe in nothing apart from God":—this thought lies at the root of Hugo's way of conceiving nature. . . . It is the chief work of his later years to have bridged the gulf between man and nature, and to have fused both from end to end with the idea of God, a living and loving God, who works both through man and nature, indifferently in the tempest and the calm. (pp. 433-34)

C. E. Vaughan, "Goethe and Hugo," in *Bulletin of The John Rylands Library*, Vol. 10, No. 2, July, 1926, pp. 407-34.

KATHRYN M. GROSSMAN

(essay date 1983)

[In the excerpt below, Grossman discusses major themes in *Notre-Dame de Paris*.]

At the end of "Paris à vol d'oiseau" [in Volume III of *Notre-Dame de Paris*], where fifteenth-century Paris is evoked from atop Notre-Dame in one of Hugo's great digressive *tours de force*, the reader finds himself listening to a symphony of bells pealing throughout the city:

D'abord la vibration de chaque cloche monte droite, pure, et pour ainsi dire isolée des autres dans le ciel splendide du matin. Puis, peu à peu, en grossissant elles se fondent, elles se mêlent, elles s'effacent l'une dans l'autre, elles s'amalgament dans un magnifique concert. Ce n'est plus qu'une masse de vibrations sonores qui se dégage sans cesse des innombrables clochers, qui flotte, ondule, bondit, tourbillonne sur la ville, et prolonge bien au-delà de l'horizon le cer-

cle assourdissant de ses oscillations. Cependant cette mer d'harmonie n'est point un chaos.

In this way, Hugo crowns his revelation of the "plan géométral" underlying the apparently chaotic disposition of the city's streets with the creation of yet another heterogeneous, but deeply harmonious, order. After unravelling the spatial labyrinth of Paris, he combines its many voices in the thunderous temporal articulation of a monumental "opéra."

This triumph of harmony over cacophony, of congruity over disorder, teases the reader with echoes of several patterns already established in the novel. For instance, the deafening noise of the bells, along with their uncoordinated ringing and the jumbled aspect of the city around them, reminds us of Quasimodo, whereas their lively dance and inarticulate song are the unmistakable hallmarks of la Esmeralda. By the same token, this symphony for a thousand voices has occurred previously, in the minor, comic mode, when Pierre Gringoire, "tout assourdi par la fatale vibration des mille sonnettes du mannequin," manages to orchestrate his own "redoubtable carillon" in the Cour des Miracles. And a static but equally magnificent version of this concert has just received extended treatment in the chapter on "Notre-Dame," the cathedral itself appearing as a "vaste symphonie en pierre." Like both Paris and the orchestra of bells, the cathedral gives an overall impression of harmony, despite its mixed origins: beneath "la prodigieuse variété extérieure de ces édifices . . . réside tant d'ordre et d'unité." Its mystery of the triune God, equally incongruous at first approach, adumbrates that of the symbiotic relationship between the "trois grandes divisions de Paris" developed at length in "Paris à vol d'oiseau." It seems evident, then, that a number of important structures and themes in the novel converge at the end of the third book. (pp. 205-06)

We shall start with the cathedral itself, backdrop for much of the main action of the novel. In "Notre-Dame," Hugo insists on its composite, transitional nature: "Notre-Dame de Paris n'est pas du reste ce qu'on peut appeler un monument complete, défini, classé. Ce n'est plus une église romane, ce n'est pas encore une église gothique. Cet édifice n'est pas un type." Such "constructions hybrides" defy convention because they can never be fully contained or explained by one set of rules. In fact, according to the author, convention has been the most ruthless enemy of the cathedral: in the guise of fashion it has done more to damage its majestic beauty than time and revolution combined.

Since the hybrid building cannot be subsumed by a higher aesthetic order, it must then be considered a law unto itself. But this does not necessarily imply disorder. In "Ceci tuera cela," Hugo is careful to show that "la fantaisie et le caprice" of Notre-Dame are firmly enrooted in its essentially lawful foundation: "on y sent partout l'autorité, l'unité, l'impénétrable, l'absolu. . . ." The Gothic springs forth from the Romanesque, the cathedral's "loi de poésie" is indissociable from its "loi de géométrie." Thus, whereas arbitrary rules imposed from without can only have a harmful effect, the grounding of the building in a certain "roideur du dogme" assures its basic solidity. It is the combination of this rigidity with the radical liberty of Gothic architecture that gives Notre-Dame its sublimely harmonious originality. (p. 206)

Hugo's reading of Notre-Dame, itself hardly conventional, also invites a radical exegesis of such major characters in the novel as Quasimodo, la Esmeralda, Pierre Gringoire, and Claude Frollo. The cathedral's specifically architectural mixed alliance presents, for example, an obvious parallel with that of the hunchback and gypsy dancer. Certainly the tragedy of their heterogenous and fruitless "mariage" in death at the close of the novel repeats that of the union *sui generis* of disparate elements in the cathedral. Moreover, Notre-Dame can be viewed as representing all the magnificent edifices of its age, doomed to die out by the advent of the printing press.

To begin with, one might attempt to derive a dualistic system whereby a grotesquely limited Quasimodo was juxtaposed to a purely free and sublime Esmeralda. Unfortunately, the book develops far too many parallels, rather than just contrasts, between these two personages to justify such a simplistic arrangement. The gypsy's characteristic "moue" is as much a "grimace" as the cripple's face, itself a "grimace sublime." Both are orphaned and adopted children, both subsist outside society, both transcend their situations to act spontaneously and generously toward each other. Quasimodo is, in fact, neither la Esmeralda's opposite nor her complement, as [Kathryn E. Wildgren] maintains, but her reverse image. According to Jeffrey Mehlman, the two characters, substituted for each other as children and bearing la Esmeralda's sobriquet of "Similar" (= "à peu près" = "Quasimodo") names, are to be considered equivalent: "The novel thus elaborates a surprising interchangeability between the epitomes of the sublime and the grotesque." Phoebus, who rechristens both outcasts with much the same irreverence and inattention, witnesses their tendency to displace one another the night of la Esmeralda's attempted abduction by Quasimodo at the behest of Claude Frollo. Like the girl's mother before him, he is left to complain: "Vous m'avez laissé en votre lieu, ma belle, . . . un assez rechigné drôle, borne et bossu. . . ." The parity that has proven so tragic for la Chantefleurie thus becomes, in the indifferent eye of Phoebus, a matter for flirtatious banter.

This fundamental identity, portrayed by their final union, is in part due to the nature of the aesthetic

Hugo in 1882.

principles they embody. Recent efforts at defining the grotesque, for instance, tend to agree that, in and of itself, it fuses several incongruous elements—the ridiculous and the horrible—which never quite achieve resolution. At the same time, the sublime has been deemed to surpass the merely beautiful by overcoming a sense of awe and fear before the seemingly limitless powers of the universe. The two experiences are thus, from the outset, equally impure in that they elicit responses from the ethical and aesthetic faculties alike. Their frequent interplay in melodrama, an important post-Revolutionary genre, stems from their simultaneous emergence in the modern consciousness as modes for dealing with the desacralized, and therefore potentially absurd and ambiguous, world around it.

The resemblance between Quasimodo and la Esmeralda thus contains ethical/political, as well as aesthetic, overtones. In this perspective, the chaste and compassionate relationship of these two "siblings" can be seen to foreshadow the notion of human confraternity embraced later on by the French Revolution. But this very synonymity—within the family or before the law—of highly disparate "equals" constitutes in turn a kind of metaphor, perhaps the greatest of all, namely that all men are brothers. The fact that the novel's most apparently dissimilar personages end by enduring quite analogous fates vigorously underscores the truly senseless ethos of their own era. For, as the *surdus* who is reduced to reading the world in terms of its explicit signs, the hunchback becomes the victim of an equally deaf judge. Likewise, la Esmeralda finds herself bound over to the same insouciant magistrate that her pet goat has learned to imitate. In other words, Jacques Charmolue's officiation at the trial of la Esmeralda is no less a parody of justice than his caricature as performed by Djali, or than the *dialogue de sourds* between Florian Barbedienne and Quasimodo, or than Pierre Gringoire's "trial" in the Cour des Miracles. This failure of the medieval legal structure to accommodate those who appear to be outlaws reveals its deepest flaws. It is, literally, *absurdus,* a grotesque system of justice, treating men with equal inequity. In order to be rectified, this methodical and paternalistic distribution of nonsense must await the Revolution, which inaugurates an entirely different vision of brotherhood. The higher order of resolution that will ultimately result from such political chaos is signaled by the very concert of bells, "cette symphonie qui fait le bruit d'une tempête," that Hugo seems so gratuitously to deploy in the midst of his novel.

As far as Gringoire and Frollo are concerned, they too can be read as a series of patterns which overflow their superficial psychological pretexts. An "esprit essentiellement mixte, indécis et complexe, tenant le bout de tous les extrêmes, incessament suspendu entre toutes les propensions humaines et les neutralisant l'une par l'autre," Gringoire remains all his life a completely sterile hybrid, one whose lukewarm "équilibre" is rarely disturbed. That he is perpetually threatened with hanging only reinforces this disengaged, tepid, amoral, "suspendu" side of his temperament. His ridiculous survival to write wretched epics and tragedies, while ignoring the suffering around him, serves to stress the truly dynamic tensions and relationships that comprise the drama in which the other characters are involved. As the writer's alter ego, Gringoire appears then as a "parodie de lien entre des irreconciliables," suggesting through the very emptiness of his eclecticism the qualities of the real artist. We come to recognize the features of that missing other through his inverted image Gringoire, just as turning Quasimodo inside out consistently reveals la Esmeralda. The absent, but sublime, author suddenly eclipses his negatively present counterpart.

Frollo, too, stands in opposition to the couple la Esmeralda/Quasimodo. As one whose outwardly ordered existence belies a terrible inner strife, he contrasts boldly with the crippled bellringer and errant gypsy, who reach superior orders of being through both their art and their compassion. In a way, he closely approximates Hugo's conception of the Romanesque: his rigidity, his adherence to "la théocratie, la caste, l'unité, le dogme, le mythe, Dieu," and his basic incorrigibility all associate the archdeacon with the dogmatic

foundations of his cathedral. Since he is literally overthrown by Quasimodo at the book's end, this may well signal the hunchback's corresponding identity with Gothic architecture. Such a designation would take into account not only Quasimodo's grotesque appearance and intellectual aberrations, but also his capacity for free moral and aesthetic expression. Moreover, it would explain his fervent adoration of the only mother he has ever known, Notre-Dame de Paris: "il y avait une sorte d'harmonie mystérieuse et préexistante entre cette créture et cet édifice." The oedipal overtones of Frollo's upset by his adopted "son" must thus infuse the Gothic triumph over Romanesque architecture as well. This modern example of "une architecture de peuple succédant à une architecture de caste" merely announces, however, that the people (Quasimodo) are destined eventually to supplant their king (Frollo).

Yet this is not the final reversal of authority. Relations already observed among the main protagonists and within the architectural world of the novel can be found on several other levels too. For Hugo's discussion of the Gothic in "Ceci tuera cela" is just part of a lengthy development by the author on the genealogy of the printed word itself. In this account, Gothic architecture assumes a striking resemblance to la Esmeralda's dance: "Les caractères généraux des maçonneries populaires . . . sont la variété, le progrès, l'originalité, l'opulence, le mouvement perpétuel." Notre-Dame's transitional nature may perhaps reemerge, albeit in a different form, in the homeless but profoundly principled gypsy. Certainly, she makes her ephemeral appearance on the eve of the revolution which inaugurates the supremacy of printing, a "révolution mère" that overturns architecture as ineluctably as the French Revolution will overturn the monarchy: "le livre de pierre . . . allait faire place au livre de papier. . . . Un art allait détrôner un autre art." Moreover, this aesthetic revolution seems to be linked to la Esmeralda's song. Printed thought, for Hugo, is "volatile, insaisissable, indestructible. Elle se mêle à l'air." The beauty and order beneath the wildness of la Esmeralda's singing and dancing, like that underlying the "prodigieuse variété extérieure" of the cathedral, point the way to "la seconde tour de Babel du genre humain": "Là chaque oeuvre individuelle, si capricieuse et si isolée qu'elle semble, a sa place et sa saillie. L'harmonie résulte du tout." Thus does the lost child end by bridging the gap between these two monumental artistic forms. Through the love that she inspires, she succeeds in permanently dissociating the Gothic bellringer from his Romanesque servitude and in orienting him toward the future.

This future contains, of course, one further major upheaval. Besides falling to both printing and the republic, it is also inherited by the Romantic movement, that other great French Revolution which Hugo, even as a young "ultra," was already associating with the literary efforts of his age as early as 1823. That is when he first mentions the "singulier phénomène littéraire né d'un autre phénomène politique, la révolution française. Il y a aujourd'hui en France combat entre une opinion littéraire encore trop puissante et le génie de ce siècle." Given this fundamental relationship between a politic and an aesthetic of freedom in Hugo, must we not review the function of the illegitimate—i.e., the unlawful, the unsanctioned—characters of *Notre-Dame de Paris?* Victor Brombert's assertion [in *The Romantic Prison: The French Tradition*] that the "restrictive rules of neo-classical tragedy (negative value)" are related to "monastic rules or values" is highly suggestive in this context. In other words, Claude Frollo may represent far more than just the Romanesque in Hugo's novel. When the author states that the "caractères généraux de toute architecture théocratique sont l'immutabilité, l'horreur du progrès, la conservation des lignes traditionnelles," he is indicting the weaknesses of Classicism itself. His praise, then, of Gothic buildings as "des édifices pénétrables à toute âme, à toute intelligence, à toute imagination, symboliques encore, mais faciles à comprehendre comme la nature" would therefore announce the triumph of Romantic popularism over the *hermétisme* of Neo-classical art.

Such a hypothesis seems to conform to the results of our study thus far. Frollo's alliance with the forces of inflexible rule–giving marks him as a symbol of the worst traits of French Classicism. . . . By the same token, the apparently chaotic, but ultimately ordered existence of Quasimodo and la Esmeralda invests them with the positive values of Romantic literature. The very incongruity of their relationship only adds to this link with Hugo's own aesthetics, Romanticism being above all a willed contamination, a *mélange des genres* which transcends dissonance to achieve a superior harmony. Finally, the discovery of the absent author through comparing Gringoire to this sublime/grotesque pair can be considered a paradigm for the parallel between the Romanesque/Gothic on the one hand and architecture/printing, then the more occulted monarchy/republic, and eventually Classicism/Romanticism on the other.

If we choose to read this seemingly universal history of supplanting, dethroning, and succeeding as analogous to the triumph of the son over the father, then the violence of such "progress" becomes rather disturbing. Hugo's assertion that : "Le livre imprimé, ce ver rongeur de l'édifice, la suce et la dévore" plainly depicts the new generation as a kind of parasite or vampire deriving strength from the old. Nevertheless, this repeating pattern need not be viewed in a purely negative manner. Reference to Hugo's treatment of Notre-Dame permits an entirely different perspective by providing one additional parallel between that edifice and

the author's conception of Romanticism. For, just as the cathedral's "poetic" side is grounded in its "geometry," so is Romantic freedom firmly founded on Classical lawfulness. The higher realm to which the one belongs comprehends (= understands and includes) the other. Once again we are dealing, not with a dualistic system, but with a more complex relationship between presumed opposites. Instead of being destroyed by the child, the parent is actually subsumed and perpetuated in an even more glorious form. In this context, Romanticism appears as the rightful heir of Classicism, rather than its mere usurper. When the young Hugo writes that "l'abbé d'Aubignac se bornait à *suivre* les règles; Racine *à ne pas les enfriendre*," he is establishing his own aesthetic genealogy, one which will be further explored several years later in *Notre-Dame de Paris.* The presence of guiding principles in post-Revolutionary literature—as well as politics—assures its divergence from pure anarchy and, therefore, its legal birthright. After the degenerative and destructive activities of the eighteenth century, the printed word, "au dixneuvième siècle, va reconstruire."

The novel itself supports this claim of an underlying unifying structure quite clearly. Its higher law, like that of the Gothic cathedral, is, of course, that of nature: "Les grands édifices, comme les grandes montagnes, sont l'ouvrage des siècles. . . . La chose s'accomplit sans trouble, sans effort, sans réaction, suivant une loi naturelle et tranquille. C'est une greffe qui survient, une sève qui circule, une végétation qui reprend." This analogy, already noted by Jean Gaudon, nevertheless leaves open the question of the book's "loi de géométrie," the "original well-disciplined and designed arrangement" that John Ruskin declares to exist at the center of every Gothic sculptor's elaboration of the Romanesque. This skeletal framework turns out to consist of an intricate but closely woven system of triads: the cathedral houses and expresses a triune God; Paris is composed of three basic neighborhoods, "la Cité, l'Université, et la Ville"; three suitors, the one grotesque, the other demonic, the third a dreamer (the famous "tres para una") pursue la Esmeralda; the plot unfolds on the three public "stages" of the Palais de Justice, the Place de la Grève, and the Parvis de Notre-Dame. In each case we find ourselves confronted by the essential mystery of *communication,* be it in the use of architectural symbol, in the network of streets such that "ces trois fragments de cité formaient un seul corps," in the mediation through one woman of the fates of three widely dissimilar men, or in the presence of connecting ropes or ladders between audience and participants at the three principal "theatres" where the narrative unfolds.

The pervasiveness of this structure, even down to the frequent tertiary rhythm of the sentences, suggests the existence of the same point of reference outside each of these particular cases. In fact, we need only re-examine both Hugo's own well-known statement defining the new novel as being "à la fois drame et épopée, pittoresque, mais poétique, réel, mais idéal, vrai, mais grand, qui enchâssera Walter Scott dans Homère" and his hints in the novel's preface about "la pensée d'esthétique et de philosophie cachée dans ce livre" to discover this triadic archetype—*Notre-Dame de Paris* itself. By harmoniously combing the three genres of drama, epic, and essay, Hugo's work aspires to the fundamental order and unity it continually claims for the cathedral whose name it bears.

That this cathedral serves as the nucleus of the glorious symphony previously referred to can be no accident, for it is there that the drama of communication (consonance) and non-communication (discord) between its various characters takes place. While edifice and novel alike may well play on the Pythagorean notion that nature and art can be reduced to a numerical order, they also insist on the Augustinean conception of harmony as emerging from an apparently discordant diversity. Notre-Dame orchestrates a great concert, despite the several kinds of dissonant relationships both within and around it. The poetic voice of *Notre-Dame de Paris* too is situated at its centre, "c'est-à-dire au lieu même d'une dialectique de la totalité," whereby it is attuned to the entire universe.

Notre-Dame, then, serves not so much as the book's main character, but as its very prototype. So that when, by an opposite movement, the literary work seems to incorporate and perpetuate the monument threatened by extinction, we must learn to read through such a superposition to the structure beneath. In 1825, Hugo's statement in **"Sur la destruction des monuments en France"** that: "Il faut qu'un cri universel appelle enfin la nouvelle France au secours de l'ancienne" may possibly refer to just architecture. However, given his respect for such "monumental" Classicists as Corneille and Racine, the figure of the cathedral definitely assumes still another dimension in 1831. The "old" France succored here by the "new" is the legacy of the Classical era, the challenge of creativity under law.

Thus do we begin to seize the dynamics of the genealogy of Hugo's novel. At once playing on its vir-gin birth by "Notre-Dame" and avowing the paternal influence of Classicism, *Notre-Dame de Paris* constitutes a search for origins and originality alike. La Esmeralda finds her mother and, despite the absence of the father, finally achieves legitimacy. Quasimodo abandons his mother / sweetheart, Notre-Dame, and his malevolent father, Claude Frollo, when he falls in love with the gypsy dancer. Unlike Hugo, neither succeeds in discovering the "good" father, the *deus absconditus* of the post-Sacred world. On the other hand, the union of these two characters at the novel's close reminds us that it is essentially their interaction which has engendered the book's dramatic movement and its most spectacular moments, much as the cathedral has supplied its basic formal pattern. The axis of interchangeability or brotherhood—that is, of metaphor—complements therefore at a fundamental level of the novel that of extension or paternity—that is, of metonymy. The intersection of both modes of substitution constitutes, in fact, the mainspring of Hugo's book, itself the replacement *and* the perpetuator of the celebrated cathedral.

In this way, the unique but theoretically infertile heterogeneity of Notre-Dame de Paris, reflected in that of the couple la Esmeralda / Quasimodo, does produce that one miraculous offspring which Hugo designates as his book. Even more wonderful, however, is the ultimate fate of his work as he predicts it. The last of one line, it will be the first of another, assuring thereby its continuity as well as its originality. Such is the heritage of an alliance between the "loi de géométrie" and the "loi de poésie" from which it springs. Its potential sterility will thus yield to a future of fruitfulness: "Un poète ne sera jamais réputé grand parce qu'il se sera contenté d'écrire suivant les règles. La morale ne résulte pas des lois, mais de la religion et de la vertu. La littérature ne vit pas seulement par le goût; il faut qu'elle soit vivifiée par la poésie et fécondée par le génie." Allied to both genius and the printing press, the creative function of Romantic art will, for Hugo, be marvelously (re)productive. (pp. 206-13)

Kathryn M. Grossman, "Hugo's Poetics of Harmony: Transcending Dissonance in 'Notre-Dame de Paris'," in *Nineteenth-Century French Studies*, Vol. XI, Nos. 3 & 4, Spring & Summer, 1983, pp. 205-15.

SOURCES FOR FURTHER STUDY

Brombert, Victor. *Victor Hugo and the Visionary Novel.* Cambridge: Harvard University Press, 1984, 286 p.

Focuses on the utopian and revisionary aspects of Hugo's novels.

Chesterton, G. K. "Victor Hugo." In his *A Handful of Authors: Essays on Books and Writers,* edited by Dorothy Collins, pp. 36-44. New York: Sheed and Ward, 1953.

> Discusses Hugo as representative of two nineteenth-century movements—Romanticism and democracy. This essay was written in 1902.

Grant, Richard B. *The Perilous Quest: Image, Myth, and Prophecy in the Narratives of Victor Hugo.* Durham, N.C.: Duke University Press, 1968. 253 p.

> Follows the development of Hugo's literary motifs.

Houston, John Porter. *Victor Hugo.* New York: Twayne Publishers, 1974, 165 p.

> Overview of Hugo's life and works.

Maurois, André. *Olympio: The Life of Victor Hugo.* Translated by Gerard Hopkins. New York: Harper & Brothers, 1956. 498 p.

> Definitive biography.

Ward, Patricia A. *The Medievalism of Victor Hugo.* College Station, Penn.: Pennsylvania State University Press, 1975. 134 p.

> Treats Hugo's use of medieval history and thought, especially in *Notre-Dame de Paris.*

Aldous Huxley

1894-1963

(Full name Aldous Leonard Huxley) English novelist, short story writer, poet, dramatist, scriptwriter, critic, essayist, and nonfiction writer.

INTRODUCTION

*H*uxley's prolific literary output reflects his constant search for alternatives to a perceived chaos of the modern world. He often blended sophisticated social and cultural commentary with a witty style to produce satires of modern values. Huxley, who underwent several phases of notoriety and neglect during the course of his career, is best known for his "dystopian" novel *Brave New World* (1932), in which he warns that new technology, social and scientific developments, and political manipulation could result in a dreadful future civilization.

Huxley was born into a family renowned for scientific and intellectual achievements. His father, Leonard, was a respected editor and essayist, and his grandfather, Thomas Henry Huxley, was a leading biologist during the advent of Darwinism. Huxley's brother, Julian, was a noted biologist, and his half-brother, Andrew, was awarded the Nobel Prize in 1963 for his work in physiology. As a young man Huxley received extensive training in medicine and in the arts and sciences; he expounded upon these topics throughout his literary career. V. S. Pritchett commented on Huxley's talent and inquisitive nature, describing him as "that rare being—the prodigy, the educable young man, the perennial asker of unusual questions."

After publishing three volumes of poetry and a collection of short stories to mild critical attention, Huxley gained wide recognition in England with his first two novels, *Crome Yellow* (1921) and *Antic Hay* (1923). The first novel is set on an estate where a number of scientists, artists, and aristocrats congregate for parties and conversation; in the second novel Huxley recreates the social atmosphere of the upper classes in post-World War I London. Often categorized as "novels of ideas" because the philosophical content dominates the style and structure, both of these works focus on eccentric characters who espouse fashionable sentiments. By including such characters in his early fiction, Huxley was able to compare various philosophical ideas while overtly satirizing pseudointellectual vanities. Another "novel of ideas," *Point Counter Point* (1928), is considered Huxley's finest accomplishment in this mode. Huxley draws upon his knowledge of music to create a novel that imitates a musical composition with many contrasting melodies; through the constant opposition of themes, moods, characters, and scenes, he portrays the varied and multifaceted nature of life. Primarily on the basis of his early novels, Huxley became a well-known literary figure who was especially popular among young people. Because his skeptical view of humanity pictured England of the 1920s as languishing in social and cultural malaise, Huxley was viewed by many as a rebel.

During the 1930s, Huxley's writings began to reflect his growing interest in politics. He won international fame with *Brave New World,* in which he shifts from his mildly satiric observations of a limited group of people to a broader and more ironic satire of a utopian society. *Brave New World* projects a future totalitarian state that is an extension of the values and trends of the modern world. The inhabitants of this society are free from war, disease, and suffering, and they enjoy an abundance of material and physical pleasures. In order to achieve such a state, human beings are conceived and mass-produced in test tubes and are genetically engineered with standardized traits. As children they are socially conditioned through technology and drugs; as adults they fulfill prescribed roles according to their predetermined social classes and enjoy promiscuous, carefree lives. Conflict arises when a young man named John, or "the Savage," who was raised in a more primitive society, is introduced into the new world. John, who is capable of expressing diverse emotions and who desires the many possibilities of life, rebels against the standardization and mass conformity of the new world. *Brave New World* ranks with George Orwell's novel *1984* as an archetypal work of dystopian literature.

Critics generally regard Huxley's fiction after *Brave New World* as less important than his previous works. However, Huxley drew consistent critical and popular attention with several volumes of essays. His early essays reflect many of his early fictional concerns; they typically project a skeptical outlook on society and demonstrate Huxley's tendency to present multiple points of view. Beginning in the late 1930s and coinciding with his relocation to California in 1937, Huxley became interested in such topics as mysticism, Eastern thought, parapsychology, and mind-altering drugs. In *The Perennial Philosophy* (1945), Huxley seeks means for mystic transcendence and concentrates on ideas that are common among various religions. *The Doors of Perception* (1954) recounts his heightened awareness and his perceptions during experiments with mescaline. In *Brave New World Revisited* (1958), Huxley reassesses the futuristic developments depicted in *Brave New World* and discusses what he considers to be the most urgent problems confronting the contemporary world: mind control, overpopulation, and environmental destruction. In *Literature and Science* (1963), Huxley reiterates his belief that the arts and sciences should work together to promote positive human values and practices. Several months after publishing *Literature and Science,* he died at his home in California, having spent the later years of his life in the United States.

Today, Huxley's early novels are read and discussed for their analyses of English life during the post-World War I era, and *Brave New World* is regarded as a classic examination of modern values and utopian vision. Although critics agree that Huxley was not a particularly innovative writer, his eloquent discussions of a wide range of ideas are consistently stimulating, and he is commended for his tireless search for and support of humanistic values.

(For further information about Huxley's life and works, see *Contemporary Authors,* Vols. 85-88; *Contemporary Literary Criticism,* Vols. 1, 3, 4, 5, 8, 11, 18, 35; *Dictionary of Literary Biography,* Vols. 36, 100; and *Something about the Author,* Vol. 63.)

CRITICAL COMMENTARY

THOMAS D. CLARESON
(essay date 1961)

[An American educator and critic, Clareson is an authority on science fiction. In the following excerpt, he analyzes *Brave New World* and praises the "universal" character of Huxley's futuristic society.]

The continued recognition given Aldous Huxley's *Brave New World,* including its widespread use in the classroom, certainly suggests that it be regarded as the classic anti-utopian novel. (p. 33)

Basic to the construction of Huxley's fable are three techniques: first, extrapolation; second, parody and juxtaposition of detail; third, sharp contrast of points of view. In both *Brave New World* and *Brave New World Revisited,* Huxley is a humanist horrified by the theories and accomplishments of extremists of his own time, but in the novel by using contrasting points of view, he makes no explicit statement of his own position. Only in later prefaces and *Brave New World Revisited* does his emotion overcome his artistry so that he underscores his own position by direct statement.

First, then, he extrapolates. By 1931 some factual basis lay behind each ingredient in his "perfect" world. The most obvious is, of course, Henry Ford. In 1914 Ford installed a conveyor-belt assembly line that has since become one of the corner stones of our technology. (p. 34)

In regard to Huxley's science, by the second decade of this century the German Nobel Prize winner, Hans Speman, made experimental embryology one of the most exciting areas of study. . . . Moreover, Pavlov and Watson had developed psychology into an experimental science. From 1902-03 to the late twenties Pavlov's experiments with the neural behavior of dogs established far-reaching principles. In 1913, from Pavlov's results and a smattering of his own data, Watson founded the Behaviorist School. He generalized about human behavior, reducing man to a complex network of stimuli and responses which could, of course, be formed into any end product the experimenter (conditioner) desired. He was of vast influence, though most psychologists never agreed with his sweeping declarations.

Actually, although Freud is mentioned explicitly only once in *Brave New World,* he is even more significant to the novel than Pavlov and Watson. With the possible exception of Mustapha Mond, Freudian concepts dominate the motivation of all the characters in the novel. The Savage, for example, is motivated fundamentally by the Oedipus Complex and by masochism. The passages that he quotes from *Hamlet* reinforce this interpretation.

As for the more obvious paraphernalia: hypnopaedia was a fad of the twenties and thirties. Since the development of the electroencyclograph which can measure depth of sleep, evidence of the effectiveness of sleep-teaching is largely negative. In *Brave New World* itself Huxley himself points out how inadequately it teaches information. Yet his suggestion that it be used to instill the moral conscience of a society may have something, for people "feel" what is right even when they do not know what is. The similarity between soma and modern tranquillizers seems obvious and needs no discussion, except to remind one that in *Brave New World Revisited,* Huxley points out that doctors now write prescriptions for tranquillizers at a rate of 48 million a year—most of them refillable. (pp. 34-5)

However intriguing these extrapolations, if the fable concentrated upon them only, it would lose much of its effectiveness. It would become a mere catalogue of "gadgets." Significantly—and I do not feel that drawing an analogy to Zola's *Germinal,* for example, is inappropriate—Huxley spends the first hundred pages of the novel creating his future world while minimizing plot action. Once this portrait has been drawn—by the time Bernard and Lenina leave for the Reservation in Chapter Six—the portrait of the Brave New World has been finished. No "gadgets" or problems that have *not* at least been referred to in this section are introduced later in the novel. In addition, unlike Zola, Huxley has little regard for verisimilitude; the Brave New World is portrayed selectively, non-representationally, with emphasis concentrated upon those aspects of the society he wishes us to remember. Basic here is his second technique—parody and juxtaposition of details. To aid our "willing suspension of disbelief" he includes a multitude of details common to our everyday knowledge, but he changes them, places them in new context and new combination so that while they remain familiar, they are also startlingly new. (p. 35)

In naming the citizenry, Huxley has paid tribute to all the scientists, industrialists, financiers, and Marxists responsible for creating the twentieth century. The

Principal Works

The Burning Wheel (poetry) 1916

The Defeat of Youth and Other Poems (poetry) 1918

Leda and Other Poems (poetry) 1920

Limbo (short stories and drama) 1920

Crome Yellow (novel) 1921

Antic Hay (novel) 1923

On the Margin (essays) 1923

Jesting Pilate: An Intellectual Holiday (travel journal) 1926

Point Counter Point (novel) 1928

Brave New World (novel) 1932

Eyeless in Gaza (novel) 1936

The Gioconda Smile (short stories) 1938

After Many a Summer Dies the Swan (novel) 1939

The Perennial Philosophy (essay) 1945

*Gioconda Smile (drama) 1948

The Doors of Perception (essay) 1954

Heaven and Hell (nonfiction) 1956

Brave New World Revisited (essay) 1958

Island (novel) 1962

Literature and Science (essay) 1963

The Collected Poetry of Aldous Huxley (poetry) 1971

*Adapted from the short story of the same name; also published as Mortal Coils.

most individual name is that of Mustapha Mond, and it is a pun. Yes, "Must staff a world."

Perhaps the most sustained and, for some, the bitterest irony occurs in the delineation of the Solidarity Service, which, of course, parodies Holy Communion, perhaps at a revival meeting. The significance of twelve in each group, of holding the service on Thursday, of the invocations—"I drink to my annihilation" and "I drink to the imminence of His Coming."—is obvious. . . . Notice the echo of Anglican and Presbyterian hymns throughout the service; notice the despair Bernard expresses when he "foresaw for himself yet another failure to achieve atonement." How out of place seems the word atonement. Yet after so serious and deliberate a detailing, Huxley rises to high artistry by suddenly changing his entire tone as he perverts a familiar nursery rhyme—"Orgy-porgy, Ford and fun / Kiss the girls and make them One / Boys at one with girls at peace; / Orgy-porgy gives release."

This often startling parody and juxtaposition obviously contributes to his third technique—contrast. Without its contrasts Huxley's fable would lose its dramatic and intellectual impact. . . . Most obviously there is the contrast of the Brave New World with contemporary society. In Chapter Three Huxley juxta-

poses the Freudian-motivated world of A.D. 1931 with that of A.F. 632. But structurally the fable is dominated by the contrast between the Savage and the "Utopia." First Huxley constructs civilization in its gaudy, pleasurable detail. Then against the naked rock of Malpais he etches the Savage. Only when the two stand face to face in the last half of the novel is there sustained dramatic conflict, culminating in the Savage's suicide. Most important, however, is the contrast, the conflict, of philosophies. The Brave New World chooses to know no pain; the Savage, to know no pleasure. Indeed, he commits suicide after he indulges in what is probably the first pleasurable act of his life.

By and large the citizens of the Brave New World are incapable of constructive, imaginative thought; Mustapha Mond asserts that they have been so conditioned—in order to preserve the stability of their world. On the other hand, with the exception of the incident in which he builds his bow and arrow and puts into practice the knowledge old Mitsima taught him, the Savage shows himself incapable of constructive, imaginative action. He can act only in a frenzy, as when he pointlessly destroys the Soma of the Delta workers. It is on the horns of this complicated dilemma that Huxley's thesis lies.

He built his society and his characters upon two principles with which few psychologists would argue. First, that pleasure—that is, whatever the individual finds pleasurable—is the most powerful motivator of man. Secondly, as Huxley himself puts it, "Feeling lurks in that interval of time between desire and its consummation. Shorten that interval, break down all those old unnecessary barriers." (pp. 36-7)

The dialogue between Mustapha Mond and the Savage . . . stands as the heart of the fable. (p. 37)

The Brave New World is mindless. The World Controller explains, however, that its citizens are "nice tame animals, anyhow." They have sacrificed the past and the future for the pleasure of the moment, shortening that time between desire and consummation to nothing, or escaping time and space with Soma. They have become, as Huxley symbolizes in Lenina, so much meat, however pneumatic. That is the price they have paid for "Community, Identity, Stability."

Amid this human debris it is perhaps tempting to call the Savage heroic and feel that he represents Huxley's point of view. To do so exposes our own conditioning rather than a close reading of the text. In any society in which he attempted to live, the Savage would commit suicide; even had he lived as a solitary in the hills near Malpais or at the lighthouse, eventually he would have tortured himself to death. . . .

Yet because his is the only voice protesting the infantilism of the Brave New World, the reader wants to sympathize with him—as Huxley undoubtedly intended, perhaps only so that his central theme could be more effectively realized. The scenes at the lighthouse crystallize Huxley's theme. There, in the final chapters, he literally destroys the Savage—ending with an artistic finality of incident and language matched in few works. (p. 38)

Such brutal and final destruction of the Savage hardly suggests that Huxley had sympathy for him. And this is as it should be, for the Savage is the second horn of the dilemma—"the choice between insanity on the one hand and lunacy on the other," as Huxley states in his preface. The fable must be interpreted as an attack upon both the "utopian" civilization and the Savage. On the one hand, Huxley projects the end of the great multitude of men who live for bread and pleasure; on the other, ironically using the label Savage, he attacks those intellectuals who are both incapable of taking a constructive role in society and, at least since Rousseau, have sought escape in the simplicity and alleged truth of a benevolent nature. And yet this statement oversimplifies, for through his Penitente-ism the Savage also represents those men whose harsh religiosity has rejected the physical world. In short, then Aldous Huxley's *Brave New World* dramatizes several of the conflicts that have haunted western civilization during the past centuries. Against a background of "gadgets" he thus gains a universality. (p. 39)

Thomas D. Clareson, "The Classic: Aldous Huxley's 'Brave New World'," in *Extrapolation,* Vol. III, No. 1, December, 1961, pp. 33-40.

V. S. PRITCHETT

(essay date 1963)

[Pritchett is a highly esteemed English novelist, short story writer, and critic. In the following excerpt, he praises Huxley's desire to shock and stimulate his audience in the name of intellectual freedom.]

In the Twenties, reading [Huxley's] first poems and the Peacockian novels, one had thought him an assertive and alarming figure. He was immediately an enormous success, a young man packed with brains, modish, the perfect embodiment of the new American word, 'highbrow'; so assured at once in scientific outlook and in his enormous knowledge of music, painting, architecture, history and most of the famous sites and museums of the world; more important to us, a ribald innovator in the modernities, blasphemies and iconoclasms of the period. One was overwhelmed. There was no need to be. Huxley was the most considerate, gentle, most softly and brilliantly conversable of men, in the simplest terms. . . . [He] was that rare being—the prodigy, the educable young man, the perennial asker of unusual questions.

For the artist in him this compulsion must have been a burden as well as an inborn exhilaration. Like Bacon's jesting Pilate, from whom he borrowed a title, he asked and did not stay for an answer. He moved on. Nothing short of universal knowledge was his aim. No traveller through cultures, no connoisseur of human habits, no asker had lapped up so much. As a writer, he became a mellifluous but active, ever-extending, ever-dramatising encyclopedia and he had the gaiety and melancholy of mind to put it out in novels, essays, plays and works of speculation and criticism. Endlessly educable, he was, in the family tradition, a hybrid—the artist-educator; an extraordinary filler-in of the huge gaps in one's mind. . . .

Aldous Huxley's spell was the old Arnold-Huxley spell of an education, disseminated with wit from above. It was imposed by his mastery of the art of conversation. He was a daring assimilator rather than an original creative mind; but if it is true to say that the exquisite *Crome Yellow* was a pastiche of Peacock, how brilliant to have spotted that Peacock was just the author for disordered times and that whole passages could be adapted for today. The other good novel, *Brave New World,* which time has caught up on, is a work of disgust. It suffers ultimately from a sort of horrific complicity on the part of the author. Swift believed in ordinary men; Huxley believed in reason and that can lead to intellectual self-indulgence. Huxley was not a novelist in the sense of being interested in how people live and what they are wholly like. He turned for inspiration to Gide, that other master of conversation and contemporary morbidities, and wrote *Eyeless in Gaza* and *Point Counter Point.* They were amusing *romans à clef* but were both too newsy and too stilted compared with *Les Faux-Monnayeurs.* The characters were simply the faces on a pack of cards, good for a rubber or two of talk and scandal, but too flat and crude when asked to be human beings. They were too brittle to stand up to the preposterous things he offered them.

There was, I have said, a touch of complicity in Huxley's disgust with human beings, in his eye for the grotesque, the vulgar and libidinous. They became less ribald and more savage as he moved skyward from the Twenties into his Californian Laputa where scientific rationalism and the perennial philosophy disputed for possession of the facts of Nature and the soul's perceptions.

Huxley's conversation still dazzled because he pursued the strange facts the sciences offer to anyone with a dramatic instinct. One got from him a stereoscopic view of the world. One can call his method popularisation; but really the attraction lay not only in the new facts, but in the opportunity for more speculation. Perhaps, after all, the sexual practices of the dotty Oneida community were better than our own? Was not the classical view of the 'eternal Mediterranean' a fraud? The olive groves of Cézanne and Renoir represent a benign pause in man's war against landscape. The mulberries were being replaced by the peach tree in the Rhône valley because of the invention of artificial silk. . . .

Whether such juxtapositions—and Huxley was expert in making them—are tenable, they are vivid, and more than vivid. They awaken. They disturb our settled superstitions. But even when we recognise this, we must inquire why superstitions exist, why they last and what estimable impulses of the human imagination they have both protected and perverted. Huxley enjoyed the follies of the human mind even as he stoically stood out against them.

His mind had, of course, the tricks of the man who knew too much and too well how to express it. He was one of the last of the Victorian liberals. He was totally pacifist. Logically he refused to be implicated. His manner had a lot of the old Bloomsbury in it. 'Significant. But significant of what?' 'Possibly. But possibly not.' The bomb explodes. One has not time to make the distinction. All the same these phrases were designed to drop us simple readers into a void where, defenceless, we were exposed to shock. Shock was one of the luxuries of the Twenties. But, for Huxley, perhaps the most accomplished educator of his generation, to shock was to ensure the course of intellectual freedom.

V. S. Pritchett, "Aldous Huxley," in *New Statesman*, Vol. LXVI, No. 1708, December 6, 1963, p. 834.

CHARLES M. HOLMES
(essay date 1966)

[In the following excerpt from an essay that first appeared in *Texas Studies in Language and Literature* in 1966, Holmes discusses Huxley's poetry, the themes and styles of which, he claims, anticipate the author's more successful and subsequent fiction.]

[Huxley's] early poetry is a record of the highly complicated inner struggle which influenced, even determined the theme and the shape of his much more popular, much more successful fiction. After *The Burning Wheel* he quickly produced *Jonah* (. . . 1917), *The Defeat of Youth* (. . . 1918) and *Leda* (. . . 1920), and he appeared several times in the annuals *Oxford Poetry* and *Wheels*. Although this work shows some development in technique, some improvement in quality, it illus-

trates more clearly Huxley's shifting and ambivalent attitude toward the very practice of literary art. Like his fiction, Huxley's verse embodies his need to express himself entangled inextricably with the problem of how to do so. From the earliest poems the crucial inner conflict appears; Huxley tries various styles to express it; the need to choose a style then intensifies the conflict as Huxley is forced to choose between sincere expression and effective poetry. It is this dilemma I have attempted to follow, up to the point where Huxley virtually abandoned verse for fiction.

The first sign of inner conflict is a startling inconsistency between poems expressing a rebellious desire to shock and other poems voicing merely conventional sentiment. Huxley's first published poem, **"Home-Sickness . . . From the Town,"** is as obviously anti-Victorian as anything he ever was to write. . . . As in so many of the novels, a deliberately shocking frankness about sex is combined with the makings of a new poetic style forged of knowing allusions and esoteric words. Yet in *The Burning Wheel* a few months later we find verses in the very manner Huxley seemed to have attacked, poems almost shockingly banal and stale where conventional phrases and worn-out notions abound. **"Escape"** begins like inferior Tennyson. . . . **"Philoclea in the Forest,"** an even staler poem, is set amidst Arcadian wood-moths, flowers, and lutes. **"Sentimental Summer"** is a maudlin poem of love. . . . (pp. 64-5)

Although there is something typically youthful in this inconsistency, in Huxley's case it was a most important symptom, not just the sign of an inevitable but temporary stage. His inconsistency in poetic attitude and style was rooted in deep and lasting inner conflict, a conflict destined to increase, to plague him for years, to become and remain the most important force in all his work. **"Home-Sickness . . ."** is an exaggerated recognition of the real, **"Escape"** and **"Sentimental Summer"** a sincere gesture toward the ideal. Like Shelley and other romantics of the century before, Huxley saw a clash between the two. He presented the ideal as beauty, as love, or as spirit, and the real as the disappearance or transcience of beauty, the loss of love, sometimes replaced by lust, or the ugly facts of the surrounding material world. Most important, not only is his own soul affected by this clash; it is also both a part and an illustration of it. . . . [Huxley] finds both the ideal and the real within himself. Only occasionally could he project a vision of the ideal untarnished by unpleasant actuality, seen residing outside, in others, or within. Though he has been called a "frustrated romantic," he was inwardly split as most of the romantics never were. . . . He visualized a purer love, a permanent beauty, a world deserving nothing but our devotion and his praise. But he recognized his own tendency toward such romantic flights of fancy, and he also understood the frequent sordidness of actuality, in the world, in others, but—most disturbingly—in himself. (p. 66)

But more surprising than these contradictions is his own reaction to them. His inconsistencies apparently leave him unperturbed. He can be disturbed, of course, by what he finds in the world and himself, but not by the pattern of contradictions in his response. Yeats, who was at least as sharply split as Huxley, began to search for "Unity of Being" and regularly found his art a way to resolve his inner tensions. Huxley was not so much trying to dissolve his inner conflict as attempting to express or project it in his verse. Though he may have been searching for inner harmony, he seems to have been more interested in something theoretically external—a usable, original, aesthetically pleasing style. *The Burning Wheel* not only shows that inner conflict exists, it shows Huxley trying several different poetic styles, several different ways of putting the conflict into words.

In the title poem, **"The Burning Wheel,"** an obviously symbolist style is used. The wheel of life, "Wearied of its own turning," painfully spinning "dizzy with speed," agonizingly yearns to rest. . . . The real-ideal conflict is seen here not through the specific emotions of the poet, but rather as symbolically generalized and abstract, as the opposition of life and death, the tension between activity and calm. The theme will find new symbols in the novels: the crystal of quiet described with such intensity in *Antic Hay,* and the connected pair of cones in *Eyeless in Gaza,* symbolizing the same quiet along with the flux of tortured lives. But Huxley immediately abandoned this kind of symbolism in his verse. Three other styles dominate the early poems.

"Escape," "Sentimental Summer," and their ilk are written in a "romantic" style, a diluted version of the manner perfected a century before, now superannuated though still so frequently used. It is easily recognized, in Huxley's early poems, by the direct, unguarded expression of emotion, by supposedly "poetic" phrases and words, by imprecise and worn-out metaphors. We find it, of course, when Huxley can believe in his ideal—when, for example, he can see love as untarnished by lust. . . . But just as frequently it expresses his disillusionment; his sense of the real, the unpleasant, the actual, victorious over the imagined, the ideal. . . . Most of the poetry in this romantic style is buncombe, soon to be parodied by Huxley himself in *Crome Yellow* when Denis Stone idealizes the older Anne in the lyric he calls **"The Woman Who Was a Tree."** Yet Huxley never abandoned either the romantic attitude or the corresponding style. They are important in almost all of his novels, from *Antic Hay* and its visions of young Gumbril to the synthesized utopia of Huxley's final statement, *Island.*

Huxley also tried a simple dialectic, a style embodying versified argument or discussion. Yeats had already begun to use it for expressing inner conflict, for presenting artistically his battles with himself. But Huxley was attracted by a curious potential unappealing to Yeats—the fact that two sides of his conflict could be expressed in dialectic with no demand that the conflict be resolved. . . . He frequently seems to be nurturing his conflict, almost preserving it as a subject for his poems.

Huxley was to transform his dialectic style into the sparkling conversations of the novels, the house party discussions of *Crome Yellow* and *Those Barren Leaves.* But his fourth, "ironic" style was an even more congenial voice, destined to be the one his public wanted to hear and most frequently heard. It became the characteristic trademark of his fiction, the tone of *Point Counter Point,* the very conception of *Brave New World.* Suggested as early as **"Home-Sickness . . . From the Town,"** with its "debile" women and allusions to Rousseau and Keats, the style depends on the ironic contrast provided by the unexpected, in the form of such learned allusions and esoteric words. Its irony also involves another favorite Huxley strategy, setting the real against the ideal by putting human beings into a zoo. (pp. 67-9)

When Huxley shifts in a single volume from one style to another, juxtaposing "treasured things" and "golden memories" with turd-kicking children and souls as elephants' snouts, he is obviously unsettled, perhaps thoroughly confused. Yet his experiments, his vacillations in style seem to have made his conflict even more severe. Faced with the dilemma, the conflict posed by the real and the ideal, Huxley had tried four different styles in attempts to express himself, to put the conflict into words. He found that sincerity asked for the use of one of his styles but poetic effectiveness called for the use of one of his styles but poetic effectiveness called for the use of another. To be candid about his state of mind, dialectic was the obvious choice, another. To be candid about his state of mind, dialectic was the obvious choice, and it dominates his contributions, a year after *The Burning Wheel,* to the 1917 volume of *Wheels.* (p. 70)

Huxley seems gradually to have realized that his dialectic style, burdened by such complexities and awkwardnesses as these, could never be as effective as his ironic style and its amusing human zoo. But the greater aesthetic discipline the ironic style imposed either inhibited or made impossible sincere and frank expression. As a result a new element of inner conflict appeared; the clash between sincerity and the desire to develop effective style became another dominant motif of his career. In a later essay, **"Sincerity and Art,"** Huxley tried to escape from the dilemma. Being sincere, he claimed, is not "a moral choice between honesty and dishonesty," but rather "mainly an affair of

Huxley about 1960.

talent." . . . The writer does not have to expose his feelings, to explore his deeper self, to heed the cries of his truest inner voice. He merely needs to use his talent, to compose the most skillful, the most carefully polished poems.

The slim, rare volume *Jonah* (1917) seems to demonstrate this conclusion in the craft so evident in the dozen poems it includes. The idealistic Huxley of the romantic style, the split Huxley of dialectic have all but disappeared. Instead of the self-conscious involutions of **"Retrospect,"** we find Huxley's ironic style prevailing again, this time reinforced by the influence of other poets. **"The Oxford Volunteers"** reflects the bitter manner of Wilfred Owen, but more frequently the poems echo the work of Arthur Rimbaud, whose startling imagination helped Huxley to fill his weird, ironical zoo. **"Behemoth,"** for example, is a Rimbaldien kind of fantasy. . . . Even more Rimbaldien is **"Zoo Celeste,"** one of the four *Jonah* poems actually composed in French. . . . The world of Rimbaud's famous "Après le Déluge" . . . is larger, more dazzling, more varied than Huxley's zoo, and his poem a more remark-

able imaginative achievement. But **"Zoo Celeste"** is hardly less fantastic and less odd.

Rimbaud suggested motifs and subjects, and ways of rendering ironically the imagined and the ideal. Another Frenchman, Jules Laforgue, helped Huxley to find a congenial tone and to apply his ironic style to himself. Temperamentally and stylistically the converse of the older symbolist, Laforgue developed a bored, self-deprecating irony as evident in *Jonah* as the fantastic imagery so clearly drawn from Rimbaud. . . . [*Jonah* itself is a] remarkable example of this peculiar, efficient, distinctive style, as Laforgue's ironic use of scientific and medical words is merged with the spirit of fantasy of Rimbaud. (pp. 71-3)

These unusual poems were produced by subjugating at least a degree of sincerity to talent. They do not represent, as Huxley's romanticism proves, the attitude he consistently really felt, nor do they even hint at the struggle raging within. But they involved or suggested a kind of compromise procedure, a strategy allowing Huxley to write effectively without completely stifling the voice of inner conflict. He could use his clever, ironical, exaggerated style as an inverse kind of "sincere" poetic mask. The poet, to a degree, is there for all to see. But his deeper concerns, his sensitivities are hidden; he is protected even in self-expression by the masking effect of his style. . . . *Jonah* shows Huxley grappling with the sincerity-art dilemma by developing a style that would serve him as a mask. Wearing it, he could make gestures toward the sincere while composing his best ironic poems.

Huxley never transformed his need for a mask into a theory, as Yeats was soon to do as part of his system in *A Vision.* His problem was too personal for such objective treatment, too elusive and complex for any highly organized plan. He preferred presenting himself in verses like **"The Contemplative Soul"** as a weird, deeply submerged, ship-inhabiting fish:

Fathoms from sight and hearing,
Where seas are blind and deaf,
My soul like a fish goes steering
Her fabulous gargoyle nef. . . .

Since a danger awaits if the soul-fish comes to the surface, it decides to remain far down below. . . . Perhaps Huxley is already aware of his future: the final images [of this poem] hint at the mysticism he will eventually pursue. But the secret, whatever it is, is only barely suggested beneath the comical, self-deprecating mask.

Though Huxley had formed a style useful for deceptively partial self-expression, he did not employ even it with any consistency. It was a limited, temporary resolution of his dilemma, even though it produced the best of his early poems. The style of his next group, for the 1918 cycle of *Wheels,* is merely the purest, clearest expression of the impact on him of Rimbaud. . . . Unlike the *Wheels,* 1917, selections they are not in dialectic, nor are they in any other previous Huxley style; they are prose poems in the manner of *Illuminations,* with something of the energy of Rimbaud's imagination. (pp. 73-5)

Rimbaud the visionary, who saw beyond sordid actuality to an ideal, inspired the most important of these poems. **"Beauty"** is a glowing, lyrical disquisition, and—for Huxley—a surprising autobiographical admission. The search narrated in the poem is not really for beauty itself but for a way of living in the world with minimum conflict, and at the same time for a posture that will help him to create. Like the Rimbaud of "Being Beauteous," Huxley sees a dazzling female image, a "perpetual miracle, beauty endlessly born." But whereas Rimbaud will fall "à traverse la mêlée." Huxley's much longer poetic search continues. . . . The only true poets are centaurs, he concludes [after his long search]; their bellies travel close to the ground but their heads are in the air.

As this final image hints, though **"Beauty"** is an idealistic, visionary poem, it is the vision of an idealism

severely challenged by actuality—so severely that it may corrode away. No mask, no ironical pose appears in the poem. The poet instead suggests that he is tempted to be a cynic—not to hide his idealism underneath a comic mask, but to flaunt his discovery that the ideal is mocked by the real. (pp. 75-6)

The idealist-turned-cynic accounts for Huxley's next book title, the volume he called *The Defeat of Youth and Other Poems.* The title refers to the volume's opening sonnet sequence, a group of poems directly avowing the cynical view. They redescribe Huxley's earlier idyllic view of love; reaffirm his idealized vision of true beauty; trace the change of love to lust in consummation; and leave the weary poet disillusioned, now in sight of a very different truth. The quest for the ideal, it appears, has been forsaken; the strategy of hiding conflict behind a mask has been abandoned; the poet has no choice but the cynical, tired view, and his earliest and least effective style, the romantic.

Yet the poems which follow **"The Defeat of Youth"** [in this volume] demonstrate that nothing could be farther from the truth. Cynicism is another alternative, another temporary phase. (pp. 76-7)

The Defeat of Youth is a more bewildering set of contradictions, of contrasts in attitude and of the various Huxley styles, even than those in Huxley's first book, *The Burning Wheel.* Yet this great variety apparently served as a kind of creative catharsis, a test which isolated the worst and the best and helped the vacillating poet to make his ultimate choice. In *Leda,* Huxley's last collection of early verse, and in the handful of poems for the last three collections of *Wheels,* the ironic style becomes once and for all Huxley's most frequent, most characteristic voice, and he regularly appears exposed and hidden with his mask. . . . [The] best and most typical are the four "Philosopher's Songs," the self-deprecating lyrics of a bard who continues to find the ridiculous or the grotesque in life and love. (pp. 77-8)

The conflict masked in the grotesquerie of poems such as these, Huxley's increasingly obsessive concern for love and lust, is a little more obvious in **"Morning Scene"** and **"From the Pillar."** In the first the poet sees, poised above Goya's image of scattered hair and tempting bosom, "a red face / Fixed in the imbecile earnestness of lust." In the other he seems to project an exaggerated version of himself [split by a mixture of hatred and envy]. . . . Huxley's desire both to accept and reject the flesh may account for yet another experiment, the final one before he virtually abandoned writing poems. All his poems before *Leda* had been short ones. He needed a more flexible, more extended mode of expression, especially to explore the continuing problem of the flesh. The temporary answer appears in the two poems which begin and end the volume, poetry in the form of narrative.

"**Leda,**" which has found many critical admirers, is a long, elaborate treatment of the myth so powerfully compressed in Yeats' sonnet "Leda and the Swan." . . . [Though expansively and elegantly composed of blank verse, the] poem is not only a polished handling of the myth, it is also an allegory of Huxley's plaguing concern. Leda is the ideal, another vision of "perfect loveliness." Jove, embodying superhuman, transcendent power, is driven like mere mortals by restlessness and an irresistible sensual itch. His possession of Leda is the rape of "almost spiritual grace." Like the parade of women who soon will people Huxley's novels, Leda is unable, unwilling to resist. . . . Even centuries ago, the implication is, the gross forces of life destroyed the virginal ideal.

"**Soles Occidere et Redire Possunt**" (Suns are able to set and to return) is a narrative in a less traditional, more flexible medium. In loosely rhymed stanzas with a line of varying length, Huxley traces a day in the life of a friend killed in the War. Yet just as the friend sounds very much like Huxley, the style combines the elements Huxley had already used before. John Ridley, the supposed subject of the poem, lies in bed engaging in dialectic with himself, an idealized dream battling with an approaching "quotidian" task. . . . Through Ridley, Huxley seems to project his own life once again, but at greater length than in any earlier poem.

"**Soles**" and "**Leda**" both were abortive efforts, however; neither was a final answer, a proper mode for self-projection. Blank verse, however well he could employ it, was obviously a style wedded to a remote past. The contrasting jerky, cacophanous rhythms of "**Soles**" were the work of a poet really out of his element, who seems to be writing for the first time all over again. Earlier, his work in dialectic had allowed him the freest self-expression, yet his self was often what he most deeply wanted to mask. The ironic style had provided the mask and produced his most effective poems, yet its very indirectness, with the brevity it encouraged, inhibited full expression of his themes. The long narrative poems had at least helped to suggest an answer. If no style of poetry would work, perhaps the combination of prose and narrative would. Huxley was not quite yet ready to publish his first novel, but he was more than ready to try to master the short story. Before 1920, the year of *Leda*, was over, he had in the stories of *Limbo* most auspiciously begun. (pp. 78-80)

Charles M. Holmes, "The Early Poetry of Aldous Huxley," in *Aldous Huxley: A Collection of Critical Essays*, edited by Robert E. Kuehn, Prentice-Hall, Inc., 1974, pp. 64-80.

LAURENCE BRANDER
(essay date 1970)

[In the following excerpt, Brander surveys Huxley's essays.]

The essay has become a neglected form. The rush of progress has made it too expensive to print what essayists have to say, and we regret it even more than the loss of the short story. For it cheers us to listen to an amusing man of great intelligence, especially when he talks about himself. Huxley satisfies this desire in ["**Along the Road**"] more than anywhere else. He is talking about the great things in his own civilisation and we shall see in ["**Beyond the Mexique Bay**"] that when he wanders in alien lands among peoples whose civilisations are remote, he loses something of his tone. (p. 121)

Huxley's normal tone in ["**Proper Studies**"] is well-mannered, straightforward and easy. The pace is equable, suitable to expository work; and he attracts us as an essayist should, because he is an interesting person, with sensible reactions to a difficult world. Society is in flux; a civilisation appears to be destroying itself, but is in fact becoming explosively something new, with almost limitless possibilities of social evolution. (pp. 132-33)

[The essays of "**Proper Studies**"] do not acquire the force of a connected argument, but a thread of connection runs through them, and this increases their impact. Their greatest interest is that they adumbrate the themes he will pursue in "**Ends and Means**" and "**The Perennial Philosophy.**" Everything in the later books is here in embryo. And here too are the ideas which will dominate his fiction. But the last essay enjoys a different mood, like the little comedy after a serious play. In this essay on our quite modern weakness for comfort, he exploits the gifts which entertained us so much in "**Crome Yellow.**" He is gay and mischievous; and innocently so. His prose dances along. He happens on a nonsense and develops it for all he is worth. It is clowning in the best sense. He pauses to think and races off in another cascade of agreeable nonsense. And back of it all is a good deal of good sense and truth. The preacher has relaxed. We have come back to the creative artist. (p. 139)

His approach [to "**Ends and Means**"] is patrician. In his opening pages he subscribes to the brahminical view of non-attachment. He is trying to find a word 'that will adequately describe the ideal man of the free philosophers, the mystics, the founders of religion'. He decides that 'non-attached' is perhaps the best. He is non-attached to his bodily lusts, his desire for power, his possessions, to anger and hatred, 'to his exclusive loves'. He is non-attached to wealth, fame, social position and even to science, art, speculation, philanthropy. And he is non-attached for a very positive purpose, so that he can properly exercise charity, courage and intelligence. (p. 140)

"Ends and Means," like **"Proper Studies,"** is about man in society, and the solitary, seeking ultimate reality, is only discussed in contrast. Only when he comes to **"The Perennial Philosophy"** is he mainly concerned with the solitude and silence of the ascetic, who withdraws completely from society in 'holy indifference' and affects the world of men by his remote and non-attached sanctity. (pp. 141-42)

All that Huxley says in this book is now generally known. But very little of it has been done; human prejudice and inertia have seen to that. . . . He wrote it in response to the knowledge explosion and its balancing horror, the emergence of Mass Man. It remains relevant. Its eloquence and eagerness will help us to make the ideas in it effective. (p. 151)

[The language of **"The Perennial Philosophy"** is] the language of sermons and many chapters of this book, especially the later ones, give us all the pleasures of an eloquent sermon, denouncing, explaining, exhorting. . . .

Huxley's wide reading and the exertions of many translators give us a book which attracts us to the study of the true end of man, the unitive knowledge of God. (p. 153)

It is an invitation rather than a handbook. The only sure and safe way to explore the further potentialities of our consciousness is with a guru, a teacher. Without personal guidance it is difficult to begin, and easy to fail. An oriental ascetic would probably find the book inadequate. (p. 154)

As we go through the book we can make for ourselves an anthology of Huxleyan *dicta* on contemporary societies and world affairs, those public evils against which he was continuously tilting. In these vigorous pages we do not live entirely on the frontiers of spiritual experience. The background must be prepared is what he implies, so that western man can seek the unitive knowledge of God. (p. 156)

[The brief essay **"Science, Liberty and Peace"**] is part of the agonised debate among scientists after the atom bombs had dropped. How could they make sure that their part of the knowledge explosion would never be used for the destruction of mankind? . . . The Tolstoyan theme of working in contact with the earth, of decentralising to save mankind from disaster, is developed throughout the essay. The argument is based firmly on what he had written in **"The Perennial Phi-**

losophy." As soon as he had worked into his subject, he echoes the Perennial theme. Human beings have basic physical and psychological needs; food, clothing, shelter, and the chance to develop their mental capacity. . . . His argument is that man has been used for applied science and not applied science for man. He regrets that it had not been used for the 'benefit of the individual men and women, considered as personalities, each one of which is capable, given suitable material and social conditions, of a moral and spiritual development amounting, in some cases, to a total transfiguration'. He is carried away. We have heard him argue before that it is not by material things that man will move forward towards his Final End. (pp. 160-61)

[Huxley's main theme is] the problems of the applied scientists. They 'have equipped the political bosses who control the various national states with unprecedentally efficient instruments of coercion', and he means everything from tanks and tear gas to television. By doing so, applied science 'has contributed directly to the centralization of power in the hands of the few'. There is another aspect of the battle between the few and the many which we have seen a great deal of since Huxley wrote. The few are determined to keep things going and to progress despite the many. (p. 162)

The problem of liberty and peace has been increased by Mass Man. If liberty is taken from him we can have peace; but our liberty goes too. (p. 164)

The purpose of [**"Heaven and Hell"**] is to examine the methods by which visions may be obtained. Huxley's analysis reminds us that during our knowledge explosion we have learned that life and happiness is very much a matter of chemical constitution. The line between sanity and insanity, health and malaise, may depend on the presence or absence of a trace element or a vitamin in our food. Huxley's concern here is not with the body in normal conditions but with the spirit when the body is tuned to allow it to explore 'the not too distant Virginias and Carolinas of the personal subconscious and the vegetative soul'. The exploration can be made in various ways, by the use of drugs and hypnosis among them. (pp. 194-95)

Like **"The Doors of Perception,"** this essay is a concentration of skill and experience. It is wonderfully suggestive, a fine example of the intellectual function of seeing hitherto unsuspected relationships.

When the climax comes, it is a rehearsal of what he had previously written on these topics: 'Of those who die an infinitesimal minority are capable of immediate union with the divine Ground.' The essay is the most compressed and mordant of his explorations of the mental phenomena by which we become conscious of a farther world. It reflects his immoderate hydroptic thirst for learned support from all ages and all civilisations; but it never grows heavy and it never grows dull. It illuminates a fascinating subject. (p. 195)

Laurence Brander, in his *Aldous Huxley: A Critical Study,* Bucknell University Press, 1970, 244 p.

MILTON BIRNBAUM
(essay date 1971)

[Birnbaum, a Polish-born American educator and critic, has stated: "Aldous Huxley has been my special interest because of his classical temper, his encyclopedic interests, and because his writing has always been concerned with trying to infuse life with greater meaning." In the following excerpt, he discusses the values and philosophy evinced in Huxley's works.]

Whether Aldous Huxley has been a force for good or evil, whether he is an artist more noted for his contributions to the novel of ideas or for the ideas themselves, whether he is chiefly a romantic or a neoclassicist—on these questions, critics have not agreed. He has been called a frustrated romantic by [David Daiches in *The Novel and the Modern World*]; he has been attacked because he has joined Freud, Jung, Adler, and Lawrence "to sow distrust of reason, and to represent it as a mere tool of the unconscious [by C. E. M. Joad in *Return to Philosophy*]. His view of life has been characterized as "essential sterility" [by Millett, Manly and Rickert in *Contemporary British Literature*], and his embracing of mysticism has been called "the rationalist's substitute for suicide" [by Edwin Berry Burgum in *The Novel and the World's Dilemma*]. But Huxley has had his defenders, too. His description of the modern world has been hailed as "far more honest and decent than the early Victorian age depicted in Bulwer Lytton's *Pelham*" [by Morris R. Cohen in *The Faith of a Liberal*]. Similarly, "despite the temptations which beset a successful author," he never "seriously compromised with his intellectual integrity" [Jocelyn Brooke in *Aldous Huxley*]. . . .

Wherein then lies the value in giving serious consideration to Huxley? Precisely in his being able to articulate the intellectual and moral conflicts being fought in the collective soul of the twentieth century. D. H. Lawrence would express his reactions viscerally but failed to look through a microscope, as Huxley reminds us. James Joyce could disentangle himself from the nets in which he felt caught, but he did not seem aware of the oases to be found in Eastern meditative systems. E. M. Forster knew of passages to other cultures but preferred to regard art as self-sufficient rather than as catalytic. Virginia Woolf knew the agony of private torment but did not realize the healing that can

emerge from societal involvement. It was Huxley of all these twentieth-century English writers who best reflected and coordinated the divisions of the modern world; he best expressed its *Weltanschauung* in its most universal sense. Thomas Henry Huxley, Aldous Huxley's grandfather, was called "Darwin's bulldog" because he so tenaciously clung to and advocated Darwin's theories; similarly, Aldous Huxley may become best known for being both an observer of and a contributor to the shifting values of our world.

That Huxley's works have always demonstrated a search for values can be shown by an analysis of his works from the very beginning. The novels published in the 1920's (*Crome Yellow, Antic Hay, Those Barren Leaves,* and *Point Counter Point*) were all concerned with showing how some of the traditional sources of value—religion, love, family life—were absent from the postwar generation. Most readers thought these books to be cynically entertaining and did not see their essentially moral undercurrent. (pp. 4-5)

He attacks the growing preoccupation with hedonism, materialism, technology, and false intellectualism in *Brave New World* (1932), *Eyeless in Gaza* (1936), *After Many a Summer Dies the Swan* (1939), *Time Must Have a Stop* (1944), and *Ape and Essence* (1948). He considers alternatives to materialism: mysticism (*The Perennial Philosophy,* 1946), an intelligent application of science (*Science, Liberty and Peace,* 1947), and a fusion of mysticism and science (*Island,* 1962). Occasionally, as in *The Doors of Perception* (1954) and *Heaven and Hell* (1956), he endorses the use of hallucinogenic drugs as a means of heightening one's spiritual and aesthetic awareness. *Brave New World Revisited* (1948) considers "the subject of freedom and its enemies." Even in books that are purportedly biographical, there is evident concern with moral directions; when he writes about the life of Father Joseph, adviser to Cardinal Richelieu, he deplores the evil mingling of spiritual and material values—saying, in effect, that Caesar and God cannot be served simultaneously. Similarly, in *The Devils of Loudun* (1952), he impregnates the biography of a seventeenth-century monk with meaning for this century. The life of Maine de Biran, the eighteenth-century French philosopher, occupies about half of *Themes and Variations,* but here again, as with the other subjects found in this 1950 volume, Huxley's observations are tinged with moral implications. (p. 7)

Huxley . . . prefers to consider his characters as states of being rather than what E. M. Forster would call "round characters." It is no wonder then that his characters can be classified under so many "humors." First, there is the intellectual who has developed his mentality but pathetically neglected the emotional and physical sides of life—people like Philip Quarles (*Point Counter Point*), Denis Stone (*Crome Yellow*), Bernard

Marx (*Brave New World*), Shearwater (*Antic Hay*), Anthony Beavis (*Eyeless in Gaza*). Then there is the sardonic cynic—people like Spandrell (*Point Counter Point*) and Mark Staithes (*Eyeless in Gaza*). There is the promiscuous female—characters like Mary Thriplow (*Those Barren Leaves*), Mrs. Viveash (*Antic Hay*), Lucy Tantamount (*Point Counter Point*), Lenina Crowne (*Brave New World*), and Virginia Maunciple (*After Many a Summer Dies the Swan*). The mystic began to appear in the novels of the 1930's—characters like Mr. Propter (*After Many A Summer Dies the Swan*), Dr. Miller (*Eyeless in Gaza*), and Bruno Rontini (*Time Must Have a Stop*). Other characters of humors could be listed to make the point that most of Huxley's characters are used to illustrate the values (or more often, the lack of values) of certain ways of life. (p. 8)

Despite his inclusion of a mystic character in all his novels beginning with *Eyeless in Gaza,* it is revealing that the characters who most closely resembled Huxley in those novels (people like Anthony Beavis in *Eyeless in Gaza* and Sebastian Barnack in *Time Must Have a Stop*) were not the mystics but those Hamlet-like individuals who were frozen into inaction by their excessive cerebration. The mystic characters, it would seem, typified the person whom Huxley would have liked to emulate. He still remained the person who found conflict between his ideals and reality; who preferred to detach himself from the torrent of life's paradoxes. . . . (p. 18)

Basic to any interpretation of Huxley's quest for values is an understanding of Huxley's conception of reality, for therein lie the causes for his seeming inconsistencies, his sardonic irony, his rejection of many of the traditional sources of meaning in life, his plunge from the fetters of self, time, and space into self-transcendent mysticism, and finally, his attempt in his last novel (*Island*) to attain heaven on earth by embracing the knowledge of science along with the wisdom of religion. . . .

Huxley's search for reality assumed three seemingly different directions. Until the 1930's, Huxley's books (both fiction and nonfiction) examined a world in which the traditional sources of value (Judeo-Christian religion, patriotism, the conventional frameworks of private and public morality, the "progress" concept derived from the findings of science) were either replaced by a moral vacuum or else privately violated while publicly espoused. Such books as *Crome Yellow, Antic Hay,* and *Point Counter Point* indicate Huxley's disillusionment with Western society. In the second stage, approximately from the publication of his *Eyeless in Gaza* (1936) through *The Perennial Philosophy* (1945), Huxley tried to embrace the reality offered by mysticism, especially that preached by Buddhism. Then, in the last decade and a half of his life, Huxley

tried to incorporate Buddhism within the framework of science (pp. 27-8)

Let us briefly review the path Huxley took before he embarked on the road to the ultimate reality as revealed by mysticism. He first found objective reality (the world of matter as measured and interpreted by science) both ugly and incomplete. Subjective reality (as explained by most philosophies of the Western World) he found equally objectionable because in most instances these philosophies were merely rationalizations of basic ugliness and selfishness. On the question of teleology, he found little to write about. On the problem of causality, he felt that hereditary and environmental forces are influential; at the same time, he believed, or at least hoped, that an assertion of will can do much to combat the determinism of heredity and environment. Looking at history, he found that the mistakes of the past tend to be repeated. This concept of reality led Huxley first to a kind of bitter cynicism. . . . Even the mystics found in Huxley's early works are somewhat cynical. Mr. Propter, in *After Many a Summer Dies the Swan,* tells Pete: "Most of the things that we're all taught to respect and reverence— they don't deserve anything but cynicism." It was almost inevitable, therefore, that the vacillations from despair to hope, from hope to cynicism again, vacillations which both objective and subjective reality engendered in Huxley, should yield to an attempt to find an absolute reality. This absolute reality Huxley found synonymous with the divine reality, or the divine Godhead. "Ultimate reality is at once transcendent and immanent. God is the creator and sustainer of the world; yet the kingdom of God is also within us . . ." (*Grey Eminence*). It is characterized by self-transcendence, that is, by anegation of the world of the ego, of animal desires, or carnal and material aspirations. The philosophy of this absolute reality is the perennial philosophy. . . .

This self-transcendence and loss of personality is the only effective cure for a world suffering from idolatry, stupidity, and cruelty. In the ultimate reality, we can find true salvation. This attainment of the divine Godhead, Huxley felt, can be facilitated by a strong determination to do so. (pp. 36-7)

Selfhood, time, space—these are the obstacles to attainment of self-transcendence. And yet, unless we achieve this state, Huxley warned us in *Themes and Variations,* we are slaves to sorrow, wars, barbarism, futility. . . .

Huxley did not believe that very many people are capable of achieving this self-transcendence, although there has always been yearning for self-transcendence because human beings are tired of themselves, their dreary lives, and their responsibilities. (p. 38)

Despite Huxley's passionate belief that the divine

reality is the only reality that can bring salvation, he was sufficiently pragmatic to recognize the limited appeal of such a philosophy of reality for most people. With the exception of the people in *Island,* all the mystics in his novels are, significantly enough, either old or else completely without any family responsibility. (pp. 38-9)

Possibly because Huxley realized that the life of self-transcendence could not be attained by very many people if will power were the only means utilized, Huxley began experimenting with certain drugs like mescalin. He found that the mystic euphoria could be reached not merely by a saintly self-transcendence, but by the taking of these drugs as well. Consequently, the books he wrote during the last decade of his life (*The Doors of Perception, Heaven and Hell, Brave New World Revisited, Island,* and *Literature and Science*) show an increasing respect for science as a means of ordering the chaos of reality into a sane existence. In the utopian society of Pala that he created in his last novel, *Island,* chemistry, physics, physiology, and other sciences are no longer satirized as they were in *Brave New World.* There is still, however, an occasional cynical echo from Huxley's early period. (pp. 39-40)

It should be fairly obvious, however, that Huxley's return to science and religion does not mean that he finally succeeded in his quest for truth. (p. 40)

Huxley began by trying to attain "Shanti." He ended by embracing the hallucinatory bliss of "*moksha-medicine.*" On his pilgrimage to reach the shrine of understanding the ultimate reality, he ended by embracing not reality but an escape from it. (p. 41)

Although Huxley has offered many suggestions to effect an ideal government and the establishment of peace, what underlies all his statements for reform is a current of pessimism about the ultimate efficiency of any attempt to ameliorate the evils of our society. This undercurrent of pessimism is perhaps responsible for the paradoxical juxtaposition of offering a cure in one book, and then satirizing it in the next. For example, although he will advocate the creation of bridge-builders to bring about a better understanding of the various countries and philosophies in the world, he will satirize such a bridge-builder as De Vries in *Time Must Have a Stop.* Similarly, although he mildly favors the establishment of a world government, he will say, in *The Perennial Philosophy,* that what is needed is more decentralization. . . . (p. 114)

Despite the lack of finality and absolute certitude in the reforms he suggests, the impression that clearly emerges from the reading of his works written prior to *Island* is that government per se cannot possibly serve as a source of permanent value. . . . (p. 115)

Little wonder that Huxley tried to resolve the mess of human problems by detaching himself from them; consequently, his penultimate solution for the problem which a consideration of government, war, and peace engenders is a life of mystical nonattachment and a striving for a unitive knowledge and love of God. (p. 116)

Whatever else Aldous Huxley may have been, he was not a romantic, at least not a dedicated one. The romantic preoccupation with love and Nature is manifestly absent from his writings. . . .

From his earliest novel, *Crome Yellow,* to his last, *Island* (in spite of his attempts there to preach the yoga of love), sexual relationships are never considered a source of value. His comments about love in his nonfiction works likewise treat physical love disparagingly. With the exception of several artifically delineated happy marriages in *Island,* there is not a single love affair in all of Huxley's novels that is successfully and satisfyingly consummated; the marital and extramarital relationships all lead to pain or frustration. (p. 119)

Up to the time that he embraced mysticism as a way of life, Huxley had been grappling with the problem of sex and love and had come up with no satisfying solution. (p. 128)

In Huxley's novels, Nature is almost completely absent; to this extent, he might be called an urban novelist. He is primarily concerned with the life in the cities, the sophisticated conversations held in drawing rooms. Nearly all his characters are members of the upper classes and of the genteel professions. There are no laborers or rustics in his works; his dialogue never has the Hardy earthiness; his characters speak aphoristically. The forces of Nature play no significant role either in the setting or the characterization of his novels. And yet, in a sense, Huxley does analyze Nature as a source of value: he first attacks the romantic conception of Nature which seeks to find in Nature the source of wisdom and beneficence; he also warns us that if we are to continue the callous exploitation of Nature's resources, then we are faced with a far graver crisis than the political struggle of opposing ideologies. (p. 133)

Huxley's objections to the encroachment of applied science upon our lives are twofold: first, applied science, he argues, has intensified standardized mediocrity and the loss of attention to intellectual and spiritual values; second, the technology of the scientist has contributed to the destructiveness of war and to the diminishing of individual freedom. (p. 144)

Has science, then, no value for man? Huxley tries to work out a kind of conciliatory compromise which would maintain the contributions of science in helping to solve man's ecological problems while it would also tend to eliminate some of the evils that an uncontrolled technology would create. He wants scientists to be more actively responsible for the technological improvements they help to bring into existence; in other words, he wants them to be morally responsible for their actions or, as has been the case in the past, for their lack of active protests against producing more destructive weapons of mass annihilation. He also wants people to recognize the fact that the advantages of technology also bring with them disadvantages. (p. 149)

In his evaluation of science as a source of value, Huxley assigns to science the same function he did to the arts: facilitating the apprehension of the nature of ultimate reality. Science, like the arts, should never become an end in itself; both science and the arts should not be worshiped as ultimately divine entities. Science and technology, unless carefully controlled, can cause many evils: increased mediocrity, rising unemployment, and the barbarisms of warfare and totalitarianism; science and technology can, however, help man wisely use the earth's natural resources and can even aid him in achieving "the end and ultimate purpose of human life: Enlightenment, the Beatific Vision" (*Doors of Perception*). (p. 151)

His search for ultimate answers led him, in his examination of religion, into all kinds of paradoxical complexities which were not resolved very clearly in his works and into all kinds of generalizations which have little meaning when subjected to detailed scrutiny. For example, he will sometimes speak of Christianity or Judaism as if they were monolithic entities. Furthermore, when he talks of Buddhism, Confucianism, Hinduism, or Mohammedanism, he does not consider the evolutionary changes that have been incorporated into these beliefs so that when he makes criticisms about them, one is not sure, for example, whether he is castigating the Mohammedanism of the late Middle Ages or the Mohammedanism of today. . . .

There are other difficulties besides trying to find specific meaning in the welter of generalizations one finds in Huxley's comments on religion. There is the difficulty in trying to grasp Huxley's attempts to reconcile religion with philosophy, aesthetics, ethics, and government. There is also the problem of endeavoring to find a relationship between religion considered as a metaphysical concept and religion considered as ritual and as a practical guide to mundane problems. (p. 154)

He found little to admire in the religions of Judaism, Christianity, and Islam. He blamed Judaism for narrowness of vision and excessive preoccupation with material success; he castigated Christianity for its cruel oppression of heresy, its occasional hypocrisy, its failure to object to the existence of wars; he criticized Islam for its pessimism and fatalism. It should be remembered, however, that what he was specifically rejecting in these three religions was the nonmystical element; wherever he found elements of mysticism, as he did in the Book of Ecclesiastes; in the writings of such mystic Christians as St. Augustine, St. Bernard of Clairvaux,

Meister Eckhart, Walter Hilton, William Law, St. Francois de Sales, Thomas Traherne, and others; in the Sufi books of Islam, he accepted their teachings of contemplation, renunciation of worldly preoccupation, and the practice of love. It is, therefore, not so much religion itself that he was rejecting but what he felt was the perversion of the religious essence. (p. 163)

Essentially, then, Huxley's religious quest has been paradoxical and tortuous. He began by mocking and rejecting the Judeo-Christian tradition (though accepting its occasional manifestations of mysticism), flirted temporarily with the Lawrentian doctrine of instinctive living and "blood consciousness," changed to contemplative investigation, turned to the East for further illumination, and died in the West trying to balance, in an uneasy syncretism, the Caliban of Western science with the Ariel of Buddhist mysticism. One is saddened to observe that the religious syncretism turned out to be a synthetic product, that his metaphysical quest ended with a pharmacological solution. (p. 174)

[Since] man lives in many compartments, Huxley also compartmentalized himself. His spiritual self sought value and meaning by turning ultimately to a unitive knowledge and love of God; his societal self realized that man does not live by spirit alone, and thus he wrote frequently about society's need to adopt rational and scientific approaches for its many problems such as an inadequate supply of food, overpopulation, and the threat of man's extinction by war. The inner search and external quest thus formed the two foci of his elliptical journey through life. It was a journey well taken. (p. 183)

Milton Birnbaum, in his *Aldous Huxley's Quest for Values,* University of Tennessee Press, 1971, 230 p.

GEORGE STEINER
(essay date 1975)

[Steiner is a French-born American critic, poet, and fiction writer. In the following excerpt, he harshly characterizes Huxley as a dated Victorian thinker.]

[The] greater part of Aldous Huxley's work is already stone-dead. He had a veritable genius for titles. *Crome Yellow, Antic Hay, Point Counter Point, Brave New World, Eyeless in Gaza* lead a brilliant, disembodied life in their own right, almost eclipsing the Shakespearean or Miltonic context from which they are taken. But what of the novels themselves? Why have they faded so quickly from imaginative authority? Why does *Point Counter Point* rely for what vitality it has on the presence among its characters of a distorted but suggestive portrayal of D. H. Lawrence? What has made of *Brave New World* and, even more emphatically, of Huxley's later utopian fantasy, *Island,* merely historical occasions in contrast to the urgent power of George Orwell's *1984* or, indeed, of the speculative fictions of H. G. Wells? (p. 103)

Though committed to the sharpest possible sense of the future—scientific, political, psychological—Huxley was perhaps the last of the Victorian sages. This may give a clue to our real problem: the mustiness, the datedness that hang like gentle dust over novels once so dashing, so up-to-the-minute.

Victorian sagacity will often have within it a streak of silliness. Probe the solid front of rational energy and you will turn up the faddist, the occultist, the practitioner of animal magnetism and cold ablutions. The genius of the Victorian middle class seems to contain an ineradicable retardment, a deliberately cultivated prolongation of childhood. We find it in Jowett, in Gladstone, even in Darwin. Nursery and school reach into adult existence with an unchallenged authority—part nightmare, part heart's longing. (Lewis Carroll precisely captures the ambiguous note.) . . .

Aldous Huxley's flash of intellect, his mental reach, his articulacy were legend. But the confident obtuseness, the immaturities are no less striking. ("The idea of using his knowledge in order to make himself better never seems to have occurred to him," says Huxley of Proust.) . . . Aldous Huxley's investments in [extraterrestrial theories and similar] matters are not accidental. On one level they reproduce, almost uncannily, the table-rapping, ectoplasmic, mesmeric trials of his Victorian forebears. The arrogant innocence that marks the relations of the Victorian agnostic to the charlatan carries over into the modern man. On another level, they are the touchstone of Huxley's radicalism, of his search for a "breakthrough" into new dimensions of understanding. The fineness and the silliness are inseparable. It was a recipe that drove D. H. Lawrence, toward whom Huxley was persistently generous, to black rage. (p. 104)

As modern research has revealed, narcotics and attempts to enlarge consciousness through hallucination played a large part in the Romantic movement and Victorian art and literature. Huxley was in this respect an heir to Coleridge, De Quincey, Baudelaire, and the *fin de siècle.* The utopian, socially directed aims of his explorations in "self-transcendence" were, on the other hand, entirely modern and prophetic. . . . The liturgical cadence, the paternalistic fervor [of his drug avocation] are unmistakable; they descend directly from Victorian evangelism or the robust confidence of the Victorian secularist in a sunrise future for mankind. We know now that Huxley's pharmacology was irresponsi-

ble and that *The Doors of Perception* is, at the very most, a profoundly ambiguous contribution. (p. 105)

It is, most likely, [his] cultivation of rootlessness, so contrastive with D. H. Lawrence's or James Joyce's anguish of exile, that makes much of Huxley's work brittle. He was, to use yet another late-Victorian idiom, marvellously clever rather than intelligent (the remark on Proust being a grim illustration of the difference). A giggly smartness turns up even in his most solid writings, such as *The Devils of Loudun.* It reduces a fair proportion—think of *The Gioconda Smile* and *The Genius and the Goddess*—to a novelettish, Hollywood level. He wrote too much, and under almost constant financial pressure. . . . Huxley's ability to make himself glossy, to deliver the scripts and the magazine articles, . . . points to an essential weakness. He may not have wished to end as a mass-media guru, but he filled the part all too well. (p. 106)

George Steiner, "The Last Victorian," in *The New Yorker,* Vol. L, No. 52, February 17, 1975, pp. 103-06.

MURRAY ROSTON
(essay date 1977)

[In the following excerpt, Roston examines the integration of form and theme in Huxley's *Point Counter Point.*]

[One] of the most impressive achievements of *Point Counter Point* lies within [the] area of experimentation with form and its close integration with the central theme of the novel. By placing within the story a writer who is jotting down notes for an essentially new type of novel the author openly acknowledges this intention, and his well-known Quaker Oats image of a novel about a novelist writing a novel underscores the point. . . . [The] novel being planned by Philip Quarles is actually the outer novel, *Point Counter Point,* in which he is a participant. Any innovations, therefore, which he suggests for his own projected book must be taken as applying directly to Huxley's own experiments with form.

The "multiplicity of viewpoint" which Philip decides to adopt for his novel has, of course, long been seen as in some way relevant to the main novel, but only in a very restricted sense, as helping to create those ludicrous juxtapositions and incongruous polarities which contribute to its wit. (pp. 378-79)

The reason for Philip's enthusiasm [for the concept of multiple viewpoints in a novel] is clear. Such an approach will enable him to explore the most perplexing element introduced by scientific thought—that, as the title of the novel suggests, no settled or controlling view seemed possible any longer. Each standpoint was cancelled out by a counter point. . . . From one standpoint we are shown the absurd untenability of the second; then the process is reversed and from the second standpoint we are shown the utter irrationality of the first. The result is spiritual paralysis, the conflict of reason and emotion symptomatic of that age for which Huxley became a spokesman. (p. 380)

It is here that the brilliance of the counterpoint technique can be seen at its best. For instead of offering us a single Prufrockian character, longing to be a Michelangelo or John the Baptist but left pinned and wriggling on the wall by the formulated phrases of psychology or biology which his intellect must affirm, he offers us here a series of different characters, each adopting one of the various possible responses to that dilemma and each failing to achieve any harmony or integrity of viewpoint which could satisfy the author or, indeed, the reader. (p. 381)

[One] should note how integral Huxley's literary innovation was to the artistic setting of his period. At exactly the same time as Huxley was writing *Point Counter Point,* Picasso was introducing into modern painting that same multiplicity of viewpoint. We are now so familiar with the device that we tend to forget how revolutionary it was when he began to present the human face, for example, viewed simultaneously both frontally and in profile on the assumption that if the eye may see only one view at a time, the mind is aware that other equally valid angles exist. (p. 382)

[Not] only Walter and Philip but almost every character in the novel can be seen as representing a different facet of the book's central concern, a different way of responding to that shared problem. Some of these responses seem absurd, some seem initially legitimate; but together, the bewildering variety, the contradictions they produce, and their ultimate failure to offer a solution make the choice of any final satisfactory view quite out of the question. . . .

Such characters may themselves be unaware of the absurdity of their positions, but the reader is left in no doubt. Illidge adopts the materialist ideology of communism to which he is fiercely dedicated, the principle that the individual is as nothing compared to the needs of the body politic; yet his heart and sentiments prompt him secretly to send a weekly allowance to his aged mother. This dichotomy of heart and intellect is dreadfully exposed as Spandrell drives him to political murder. (p. 383)

[These characters] are not, as has so often been argued, mere eccentrics pursuing their own idiosyncratic philosophies, but are far more intimately connected. Originally, it is true, Philip had thought of the contrapuntal technique almost as a joke, Jones murdering his wife juxtaposed to Smith wheeling a perambulator, but in its maturer and more developed form, as it functions in the outer novel itself, it is infinitely more subtle. There, presented in a natural setting with various people apparently engaged in interweaving social, marital, and amorous activities, we are in fact provided with a spectrum of the various responses to one central problem, the shared predicament of the age.

When Huxley presents that dilemma himself, not mediated through one of the characters, it is then that music performs its most prominent role in the novel. The two passages on Bach at the beginning of the work are delightfully written—amusing, ironical, and presented with the panache of the true satirist. Yet as one might expect from a true satirist, beneath the surface humor lies a deeply disturbing question. After warning us how each player in the orchestra imagines that his is the only true statement and, as that truth slides away and is replaced by another, leaves us bewildered by the complexity and variety of such supposed truths, he begins to describe the Bach fugue. For him such music represents not only absolute beauty, but also the supreme proof to the soul that there *is* an ultimate harmony, order, and goodness in the universe. But as the Walter-like heart responds to the romantic message, a Philip-like intellect interrupts in parenthesis to remind us of the harsh, incontrovertible facts which nullify that affirmation of splendor. (pp. 384-85)

The noble sound of Bach, wafted upwards to arouse ecstasy in the heart of Lord Edward, becomes in scientific terms merely a series of vibrations agitating the hairy endings of the auditory nerve by means of the *malleus, incus,* and stirrup bones. So much for the physicist. (p. 385)

Spandrell is a further variation on Philip and Walter, and with the climax of his story, the novel returns to the theme of music. The coldly analytical mind of Philip is here combined with a fervor of the heart, but this time religiously oriented. Had he been born in an earlier age, he could have lived contentedly as a scholastic dwelling within a monastery; but born into the twentieth century he cannot simply accept the firm conviction of his heart. He must have tangible or visible proof of God's existence before he can believe. The intellect, once again, is at war with the heart in this specifically scientific setting. . . . Here is the ultimate agony of the novel, as music, the symbol of the soul, is set against the intellectual's need for scientific proof—a need which Huxley himself seems to have recognized as valid. The heart yearns to believe in beauty and in the nobility of man, while the mind perceives the grotesqueness of his zoological or physiological state.

This is the theme which unifies the novel beneath the light banter, and once that theme has been perceived, the multiplicity of viewpoint emerges not as an entertaining trick but as an artistic tool for exploring the contradictory and diverse truths of the new era. To regard *Point Counter Point* as an aesthetic failure, as so many have, on the grounds that "the pattern promised by the title is never achieved," or even to argue that the dominant device is plot repetition with minor varia-

tions is, I think, to miss the extraordinarily subtle relationship between the characters, which counterpoint each other as in a fugue, each producing its own variation on the central tragic theme. (pp. 385-86)

Murray Roston, "The Technique of Counterpoint," in *Studies in the Novel*, Vol. IX, No. 4, Winter, 1977, pp. 378-88.

SOURCES FOR FURTHER STUDY

Bowering, Peter. *Aldous Huxley: A Study of the Major Novels.* New York: Oxford University Press, 1969, 242 p.

> Suggests that Huxley's work, fiction and nonfiction, is "most satisfactory when viewed as a synthesis." Thus, Bowering discusses the novels with "the widest area of reference, drawing freely on Huxley's non-fictional writings and source materials wherever possible."

Huxley, Julian, ed. *Aldous Huxley, 1894-1963: A Memorial Volume.* London: Chatto & Windus, 1965, 175 p.

> Collected personal tributes from "friends and admirers in many countries," including brother Julian Huxley, Stephen Spender, T. S. Eliot, Igor Stravinsky, Gerald Heard, and Christopher Isherwood.

Kuehn, Robert E., ed. *Aldous Huxley: A Collection of Critical Essays.* Englewood Cliffs, N.J.: Prentice-Hall, 1974, 188 p.

> Essays that comment on Huxley's work and raise crucial questions about the merits and defects of his writings. Kuehn's collection is "not meant to provide an historical summary of critical views of the past forty or fifty years."

May, Keith M. *Aldous Huxley.* London: Paul Elek Books, 1972, 252 p.

> Maintains that in Huxley's novels, "the diction and rhythms emerged involuntarily as a result of the particular attitudes which, at any given moment, he was constrained to formulate." Hence, May has selected from Huxley's novels what he deems the author's "peculiar and revealing" aspects of language for analysis.

Meckier, Jerome. *Aldous Huxley: Satire and Structure.* London: Chatto & Windus, 1969, 223 p.

> Isolates Huxley's major satiric themes and insists on their "perennial nature," adding that the governing purpose of this critical work is to "trace the relationship between these themes and the novelistic format Huxley uses to present them."

Watts, Harold H. *Aldous Huxley.* New York: Twayne Publishers, 1969, 182 p.

> Seeks to establish "the main tendencies of thought expressed in Huxley's early fiction" and to display the deepening of these earlier currents in Huxley's later, seemingly disparate works.

Henrik Ibsen

1828-1906

(Full name Henrik Johan Ibsen; also wrote under pseudonym Brynjolf Bjarme) Norwegian dramatist and poet.

INTRODUCTION

*H*ailed as one of the pioneers of modern drama, Ibsen broke away from the romantic tradition of nineteenth-century theater with his realistic portrayals of individuals, his focus on psychological concerns, and his investigation into the role of the artist in society. While initially utilizing conventions associated with the "well-made play," including exaggerated suspense and mistaken identity, Ibsen later used dialogue, commonplace events, and symbolism to explore the elusiveness of self-knowledge and the restrictive nature of traditional morality. Once writing that "I prefer to ask; 'tis not my task to answer," Ibsen did not establish distinct dichotomies between good and evil, but instead provided a context in which to explore the complexities of human behavior and the ambiguities of reality. Martin Esslin explained: "Ibsen can . . . be seen as one of the principal creators and well-springs of the whole modern movement in drama, having contributed to the development of all its diverse and often seemingly opposed and contradictory manifestations: the ideological and political theatre, as well as the introspective, introverted trends which tend towards the representation of inner realities and dreams."

Ibsen was born to wealthy parents in Skien, a lumbering town south of Christiania, now Oslo. The family was reduced to poverty when his father's business failed in 1834. After leaving school at age fifteen and working for six years as a pharmacist's assistant, Ibsen went to Christiania hoping to continue his studies at Christiania University. He failed the Greek and mathematics portions of the entrance examinations, however, and was not admitted. During this time, he read and wrote poetry, which he would later say came more easily to him than prose. He wrote his first drama, *Catilina* (*Catiline*), in 1850 and although this work generated little interest and was not produced until several years later, it evidenced Ibsen's emerging concerns with the conflict between guilt and desire. While *Catiline* is a traditional romance written in verse, Ibsen's merging of two female prototypes—one conservative and domestic, the other adventurous and dangerous—foreshadowed the psychological intricacies of his later plays.

Shortly after writing *Catiline,* Ibsen became assistant stage manager at the Norwegian Theater in Bergen. His duties included composing and producing an original drama each year. Ibsen was expected to write about Norway's glorious past, but because Norway had just recently acquired its independence from Denmark after five hundred years, medieval folklore and Viking sagas were his only sources of inspiration. Although these early plays were coldly received and are often considered insignificant, they further indicated the direction Ibsen's drama was to take, especially in their presentation of strong individuals who come in conflict with the oppressive social mores of nineteenth-century Norwegian society. In 1862, verging on a nervous breakdown from overwork, Ibsen began to petition the government for a grant to travel and write. He was given a stipend in 1864, and various scholarships and pensions subsequently followed. For the next twenty-seven years he lived in Italy and Germany, returning to Norway only twice. While critics often cite Ibsen's bitter memories of his father's financial failure and his own lack of success as a theater manager as the causes for his long absence, it is also noted that Ibsen believed that only by distancing himself from his homeland could he obtain the perspective necessary to write truly Norwegian drama. Ibsen explained: "I could never lead a consistent life [in Norway]. I was one man in my work and another outside—and for that reason my work failed in consistency too."

Ibsen's work is generally divided by critics into three phases. The first consists of his early dramas written in verse and modeled after romantic historical tragedy and Norse sagas: *Gildet paa Solhaug* (1856; *The Feast of Solhaug*), *Fru Inger til Østraat* (1857; *Lady Inger of Østraat*), *Haermaendene paa Helgeland* (1858; *The Vikings at Helgeland*) and *Kjaerlighedens Komedie* (1862; *Love's Comedy*). These plays are noted primarily for their idiosyncratic Norwegian characters and for their emerging elements of satire and social criticism. In *Love's Comedy,* for example, Ibsen attacked conventional concepts of love and explored the conflict between the artist's mission and his responsibility to others. *Brand* (1866), an epic verse drama, was the first play Ibsen wrote after leaving Norway and was the first of his works to earn both popular and critical attention. The story of a clergyman who makes impossible demands on his congregation, his family, and himself, *Brand* reveals the fanaticism and inhumanity of uncompromising idealism. While commentators suggest that Brand is a harsh and emotionally inaccessible character, they also recognized that this play reflects Ibsen's doubts and personal anguish over his poverty and lack of success. In comparison to Brand, the protagonist of Ibsen's next drama, *Peer Gynt* (1867), while witty, imaginative, and vigorous, is incapable of self-analysis. Although this play takes on universal significance due to Ibsen's use of fantasy, parable, and symbolism, it is often described as a sociological analysis of the Norwegian people. Harold Beyer explained: "[*Peer Gynt*] is a central work in Norwegian literature, comprising elements from the nationalistic and romantic atmosphere of the preceding period and yet satirizing these elements in a spirit of realism akin to the period that was coming. It has been said that if a Norwegian were to leave his country and could take only one book to express his national culture, [*Peer Gynt*] is the one he would choose."

Ibsen wrote prose dramas concerned with social realism during the second phase of his career. The first of these plays, *De Unges Forbund* (1869; *The League of Youth*), a caustic satire of the condescending attitudes of the Norwegian upper class, introduced idiomatic speech and relied upon dialogue rather than monologue to reveal the thoughts and emotions of the characters. Written, as Ibsen declared, "without a single monologue, or even without a single aside," *The League of Youth* evidenced Ibsen's shift from an emphasis on grandiose plot structures to characterization and interpersonal relationships. During his stay in Munich, when he was becoming increasingly aware of social injustice, Ibsen wrote *Samfundets Støtter* (1877; *The Pillars of Society*). A harsh indictment of the moral corruption and crime resulting from the quest for money and power, this drama provided what Ibsen called a "contrast between ability and desire, between will and possibility." The protagonist, Consul Bernick, while first urging his son to abide by conventional morality and become a "pillar of society," eventually experiences an inner transformation and asserts instead: "You shall be yourself, Olaf, and then the rest will have to take care of itself." Ibsen's next drama, *Et Dukkehjem* (1879; *A Doll's House*), is often considered a masterpiece of realist theater. The account of the collapse of a middle-class marriage, this work, in addition to sparking debate about women's rights and divorce, is also regarded as innovative and daring because of its emphasis on psychological tension rather than external action. This technique required that emotion be conveyed through small, controlled gestures, shifts in inflection, and pauses, and therefore instituted a new style of acting. *Gengangere* (1881; *Ghosts*) and *En Folkefiende* (1882; *An Enemy of Society*) are the last plays included in Ibsen's realist period. In *Ghosts* Ibsen uses a character infected with syphilis to symbolize how stale habits and prejudices can be passed down from generation to generation; *An Enemy of Society* demonstrates Ibsen's contempt for what he considered stagnant political rhetoric. Audiences accustomed to the Romantic sentimentality of the "well-made play" were initially taken aback by such controversial subjects. However, when dramatists Bernard Shaw and George Brandes, among others, defended Ibsen's works, the theater-going public began to accept drama as social commentary and not merely as entertainment.

With *Vildanden* (1884; *The Wild Duck*) and *Hedda Gabler* (1890), Ibsen entered a period of transition during which he continued to deal with modern, realistic themes, but made increasing use of symbolism and metaphor. *The Wild Duck,* regarded as one of Ibsen's greatest tragicomical works, explores the role of illusion and self-deception in everyday life. In this play, Gregers Werle, vehemently believing that everyone must be painstakingly honest, inadvertently causes great harm by meddling in other people's affairs. At the end of *The Wild Duck,* Ibsen's implication that humankind is unable to bear absolute truth is reflected in the words of the character named Relling: "If you rob the average man of his illusion, you are almost certain to rob him of his happiness." *Hedda Gabler* concerns a frustrated aristocratic woman and the vengeance she inflicts on herself and those around her. Taking place entirely in Hedda's sitting room shortly after her marriage, this play has been praised for its subtle investigation into the psyche of a woman who is unable to love others or confront her sexuality.

Ibsen returned to Norway in 1891 and there entered his third and final period with the dramas *Bygmester Solness* (1892; *The Master Builder*), *Lille Eyolf* (1894; *Little Eyolf*), *John Gabriel Borkman* (1896), and *Naar vi døde vaagner* (1899; *When We Dead Awaken*). In these final works, Ibsen dealt with the conflict between art and life and shifted his focus from the individual in society to the individual alone and isolated. It is speculated that *The Master Builder* was written in response to Norwegian writer Knut Hamson's proclamation that Ibsen should relinquish his influence in the Norwegian theater to the younger generation. Described as a "poetic confession," *The Master Builder* centers around an elderly writer, Solness, who believes he has misused and compromised his art. *Little Eyolf,* the account of a crippled boy who compensates for his handicap through a variety of other accomplishments, explores how self-deception can lead to an empty, meaningless life. The search for personal contentment and self-knowledge is also a primary theme in *John Gabriel Borkman,* a play about a banker whose quest for greatness isolates him from those who love him. In his last play, *When We Dead Awaken,* subtitled "A Dramatic Monologue," Ibsen appears to pass judgement on himself as an artist. Deliberating over such questions as whether his writing would have been more truthful if he had lived a more active life, *When We Dead Awaken* is considered one of Ibsen's most personal and autobiographical works.

After completing *When We Dead Awaken,* Ibsen suffered a series of strokes that left him an invalid for five years until his death in 1906. Although audiences considered Ibsen's dramas highly controversial during his lifetime because of his frank treatment of social problems, present scholars focus on the philosophical and psychological elements of his plays and the ideological debates they have generated. Ibsen's occasional use of theatrical conventions and outmoded subject matter has caused some critics to dismiss his work as obsolete and irrelevant to contemporary society, but others recognize his profound influence on the development of modern drama. Haskell M. Block asserted: "In its seemingly limitless capacity to respond to the changing need and desires of successive generations of audiences, [Ibsen's] work is truly classic, universal in implication and yet capable of endless transformation."

(For further information about Ibsen's life and works, see *Contemporary Authors,* Vol. 104; *Drama Criticism,* Vol. 2; and *Twentieth-Century Literary Criticism,* Vols. 2, 8, 16, 37.)

CRITICAL COMMENTARY

JAMES HUNEKER
(essay date 1929)

[Huneker was an American biographer, short story writer, novelist, and critic. In the following excerpt, he examines Ibsen's development as a dramatist and outlines the eclectic features of his plays.]

Henrik Ibsen was the best-hated artist of the nineteenth century. The reason is simple: He was, himself, the arch-hater of his age. Yet, granting this, the Norwegian dramatist aroused in his contemporaries a wrath that would have been remarkable even if emanating from the fiery pit of politics; in the comparatively serene field of aesthetics such overwhelming attacks from the critics of nearly every European nation testified to the singular power displayed by this poet. (p. 302)

The mixed blood in the veins of Ibsen may account for his temperament; he was more Danish than Norwegian, and there were German and Scotch strains in his ancestry. Such obscure forces of heredity doubtless played a rôle in his career. Norwegian in his love of freedom, Danish in his artistic bent, his philosophic cast of mind was wholly Teutonic. Add to these a possible theologic prepossession derived from the Scotch, a dramatic technic in which Scribe and Sophocles are not absent, and we have to deal with a disquieting problem. . . . There were in him many contradictory elements. Denounced as a pessimist, all his great plays have, notwithstanding, an unmistakable message of hope, from *Brand* to *When We Dead Awake.* An idealist he is, but one who has realized the futility of dreams; like all world-satirists, he castigates to purify. His realism is largely a matter of surfaces, and if we care to look we may find the symbol lodged in the most prosaic of his pieces. (pp. 304-05)

Ibsen can hardly be called a philosophic anarch, for the body of doctrine, either political or moral, deducible from his plays is so perplexing by reason of its continual affirmation and negation, so blurred by the kaleidoscopic clash of character, that one can only fuse these mutually exclusive qualities by realizing him as a dramatist who has created a microcosmic world; in a word, we must look upon the man as a creator of dramatic character, not as a theorist. And his characters have all the logical illogicality of life.

Several traits emerge from this welter of cross-purposes and action. Individualism is a leading motive from the first to the last play; a strong sense of moral responsibility—an oppressive sense, one is tempted to add—is blended with a curious flavor of Calvinism, in which are traces of predestination. . . . Search Ibsen throughout and it will be found that his subject-matter is fundamentally the same as that of all great masters of tragedy. It is his novel manner of presentation, his transposition of themes hitherto treated epically, to the narrow, unheroic scale of middle-class family life that blinded critics to his true significance. This tuning down of the heroic, this reversal of the old aesthetic order extorted bitter remonstrances. If we kill the ideal in art and life, what have we left? was the cry. But Ibsen attacks false as well as true ideals and does not always desert us after stripping us of our self-respect. A poet of doubt he is, who seldom attempts a solution; but he is also a puritan—a positivist puritan—and his scourgings are an equivalent for that *katharsis,* in the absence of which Aristotle denied the title of tragedy.

Consider, then, how Ibsen was misunderstood. Setting aside the historical and poetic works, we are confronted in the social plays by the average man and woman of everyday life. They live, as a rule, in mediocre circumstances; they are harried by the necessities of quotidian existence. Has this undistinguished *bourgeoisie* the potentialities of romance, of tragedy, of beauty? Wait, says Ibsen, and you will see your own soul, the souls of the man and woman who jostle you in the street, the same soul in palace or hovel, that orchestra of cerebral sensations, the human soul. And it is the truth he speaks. We follow with growing uneasiness his exposition of a soul. The spectacle is not pleasing. In his own magical but charmless way the souls of his people are turned inside out during an evening. No monologues, no long speeches, no familiar machinery of the drama, are employed. But the miracle is there. You face yourself. Is it any wonder that public and critic alike waged war against this showman of souls, this new psychologist of the unflattering, this past master of disillusionment? (pp. 305-07)

This psychological method was another rock of offense. Why transform the playhouse into a school of metaphysics? But Ibsen is not a metaphysician and his characters are never abstractions; instead, they are very lively humans. They offend those who believe the theatre to be a place of sentimentality or clowning; these same Ibsen men and women offend the lovers of Shakespeare and the classics. We know they are real,

Principal Works

*Catilina [as Brynjolf Bjarme] (drama) 1850
  [Catiline, 1921]

*Kjaempehøien (drama) 1850
  [The Warrior's Barrow, 1921]

†Gildet paa Solhaug (drama) 1856
  [The Feast at Solhaug, 1906]

*Olaf Liljekrans (drama) 1856
  [Olaf Liljekrans, 1921]

†Fru Inger til Østraat (drama) 1857
  [Lady Inger of Østraat, 1890]

Haermaendene paa Helgeland (drama) 1858
  [The Vikings at Helgeland, 1890]

Kjaerlighedens Komedie (drama) 1862
  [Love's Comedy, 1894]

Terje Vigne (poetry) 1862
  [Terje Vigne, 1917]

Kongsemnerne (drama) 1863
  [The Pretenders, 1890]

Brand (drama) 1866
  [Brand, 1894]

Peer Gynt (drama) 1867
  [Peer Gynt, 1892]

†De Unges Forbund (drama) 1869
  [The League of Youth, 1890]

Digte af Henrik Ibsen (poetry) 1871
  [Lyrics and Poems from Ibsen, 1912]

Kejser og Galilaeer (drama) 1873
  [The Emperor and the Galilean, 1876]

‡Samfundets Støtter (drama) 1877
  [The Pillars of Society, 1888]

Et Dukkehjem (drama) 1879
  [Nora, 1880; also published as A Doll's House, 1885]

‡Gengangere (drama) 1881
  [Ghosts, 1888]

‡En Folkefiende (drama) 1882
  [An Enemy of Society, 1888]

†Vildanden (drama) 1884
  [The Wild Duck, 1890]

†Rosmersholm (drama) 1886
  [Rosmersholm, 1891]

Fruen fra Havet (drama) 1888
  [The Lady from the Sea, 1890]

Hedda Gabler (drama) 1890
  [Hedda Gabler, 1891]

Bygmester Solness (drama) 1892
  [The Master Builder, 1893]

Lille Eyolf (drama) 1894
  [Little Eyolf, 1895]

John Gabriel Borkman (drama) 1896
  [John Gabriel Borkman, 1897]

Naar vi døde vaagner (drama) 1899
  [When We Dead Awaken, 1900]

Breve fra Henrik Ibsen (letters) 1904
  [Letters of Henrik Ibsen, 1905]

Samlede Vaerker 21 vols. (dramas, poetry, and scenarios) (1928-57)

*Translated and published in Early Plays: Catiline, The Warrior's Barrow, Olaf Liljekrans by Henrik Ibsen, 1921

†Early unpublished translations later collected in William Archer's The Collected Works of Henrik Ibsen, 1906-12

‡Translated and published in The Pillars of Society and Other Plays, 1888

yet we dislike them as we dislike animals trained to imitate humanity too closely. (pp. 307-08)

Protean in his mental and spiritual activities, a hater of shams—religious, political, and social shams—more symbolist than realist, in assent with Goethe that no material is unfit for poetic treatment, the substance of Ibsen's morality consists in his declaration that men to be free must first free themselves. (p. 310)

Perhaps the main cause of Ibsen's offending is his irony. The world forgives much, irony never, for irony is the ivory tower of the intellectual, the last refuge of the original. It is not the intellectual irony of Meredith, nor the playful irony of Anatole France, but a veiled corrosive irony that causes you to tread suspiciously every yard of his dramatic domain. (p. 311)

For the student there is a fascination in the cohesiveness of these dramas. Ibsen's mind was like a lens; it focussed the refracted, scattered, and broken lights of opinions and theories of his day upon the contracted space of his stage. In a fluid state the ideas that crystallized in his prose series are to be found in his earliest work; there is a remorseless fastening of link to link in the march-like movement of his plays. Their author seems to delight in battering down in *Ghosts* what he had preached in *A Doll's House; The Enemy of the People* exalted the individual man, though *Ghosts* taught that a certain kind of personal liberty is deadly; *The Wild Duck,* which follows, is another puzzle, for in it the misguided idealist is pilloried for destroying homes by his truth-telling, dangerous tongue; *Rosmersholm* follows with its portrayal of lonely souls; and the danger of filling old bottles with the fermenting wines of new ideas is set forth; in *The Lady from the Sea* free-will, the will to love, is lauded, though Rebekka West and Rosmersholm perished because of their exercise of this same will; *Hedda Gabler* shows the converse of Hilda Wangel's "will to power." Hedda is a creature wholly alive and shocking. Ibsen stuns us again, for if it is healthy to be individual and to lead your own life, in neurasthenic Hedda's case it leads to a catastrophe which wrecks a household. This game of contradiction is continued in *The Master-Builder,* a most potent exposition of human motives. (pp. 311-12)

The immorality of these plays is so well concealed that only abnormal moralists detect it. It may be admitted that Ibsen, like Shakespeare, manifests a preference for the man who fails. What is new is the art with which this idea is developed. The Ibsen play begins where other plays end. The form is the "amplified catastrophe" of Sophocles. After marriage the curtain is rung up on the true drama of life, therefore marriage is a theme which constantly preoccupies this modern poet. He regards it from all sides, asking whether "by self-surrender, self-realization may be achieved." His speech delivered once before a ladies' club at Christiania proves that he is not a champion of latterday woman's rights. "The women will solve the question of mankind, but they must do so as mothers." Yet Nora Helmer, when she slammed the door of her doll's home, caused an echo in the heart of every intelligent woman in Christendom. It is not necessary now to ask whether a woman would, or should, desert her children; Nora's departure was only the symbol of her liberty, the gesture of a newly awakened individuality. Ibsen did not preach—as innocent persons of both sexes and all anti-Ibsenites believe—that woman should throw overboard her duties; this is an absurd construction. As well argue that the example of Othello must set jealous husbands smothering their wives. *A Doll's House* enacted has caused no more evil than Othello. It was the plea for woman as a human being, neither more nor less than man, which the dramatist made. (pp. 312-13)

Without exaggeration, he may be said to have discovered for the stage the modern women. No longer the sleek cat of the drawing-room, or the bayadere of luxury, or the wild outlaw of society, the "emancipated" Ibsen woman is the sensible woman, the womanly woman, bearing a not remote resemblance to the old-fashioned woman, who calmly accepts her share of the burdens and responsibilities of life, single or wedded, though she insists on her rights as a human being, and without a touch of the heroic or the supra-sentimental. (p. 313)

Idealistic, symbolistic, moral, and ennobling, the Ibsen drama was so vilified by malice and ignorance that its very name was a portent of evil. Mad or wicked Ibsen is not. His scheme of life and morals is often oblique and paradoxical, his interpretation of truths so elliptical that we are confused. But he is essentially sound. He believes in the moral continuity of the universe. His astounding energy is a moral energy. Salvation by good works is his burden. The chief thing is to be strong in your faith. He despises the weak, not the strong sinner. His Supermen are the bankrupts of romantic heroism. His strong man is frequently wrong-headed; but the weakling works the real mischief. . . . Bad as is mankind, Ibsen, who was ever in advance of his contemporaries, believed in its possibility for betterment. Here the optimist speaks. Brand's spiritual pride is his downfall; nevertheless, Ibsen, an aristocratic thinker, believes that of pride one cannot have too much. He recognized the selfish and hollow foundation of all "humanitarian" movements. He is a sign-post for the twentieth century when the aristocratic of spirit must enter into combat with the herd instinct of a depressing socialism. His influence has been tremendous. . . . He brought to the theatre new ideas; he changed forever the dramatic map of Europe; he originated a new method of surprising life, capturing it and forcing it to give up a moiety of its mystery for the uses of a difficult and recondite art. He fashioned character anew. And he pushed resolutely into the mist that surrounded the human soul, his Diogenes lantern glimmering, his brave, lonely heart undaunted by the silence and the solitude. His message? Who shall say? He asks questions, and, patterning after nature, he seldom answers them. When his ideas sicken and die—he asserted that the greatest truth outlives its usefulness in time, and it may not be denied that his drama is a dissolvent; already the early plays are in historical twilight and the woman question of his day is for us something quite different—his art will endure. Henrik Ibsen was a man of heroic fortitude. His plays are a bold and stimulating spectacle for the spirit. Should we ask more of a dramatic poet? (pp. 325-26)

James Huneker, "Ibsen," in his *Essays by James Huneker,* Charles Scribner's Sons, 1929, pp. 302-26.

ERIC BENTLEY

(essay date 1946)

[Bentley, an American drama critic, introduced Bertolt Brecht, Luigi Pirandello, and other European playwrights to American audiences through his studies, translations, and stage adaptations of their plays. In the following excerpt, he surveys Ibsen's development as a dramatist, specifically his shift from naturalism to mysticism.]

Ibsen is in the tradition of "bourgeois tragedy," but he learned more from Romanticism, both from its high poetry and from its popular manifestations. We should stress the debt of Wagner and Ibsen to popular romanticism: Eugène Scribe and all he represents stand between the eighteenth century on the one hand and Wagner and Ibsen on the other. When Ibsen was appointed theater poet at Bergen in 1851 he proceeded to direct 145 plays, of which more than half were light plays from the French, 21 being by Scribe himself.

Ibsen's first play came out in 1850, his last in the last month of the century. The fifty years of his creative life were planned with the skill and precision of a master builder. Half of them were spent in trying out different styles, from Shakespearean fantasy to Roman tragedy, from light verse comedy to "world-historical drama," from Scribean "well-made play" to philosophic-dramatic poem, from prose satire to national myth. I have claimed that two of the "experiments" of this period—*Brand* and *Peer Gynt*—form a kind of bank for Ibsen to draw on in all his later plays. Although *Peer Gynt* is perhaps Ibsen's greatest work, it can, in relation to his career, be regarded as an experiment, for Ibsen came to consider the style of *Peer Gynt* quite wrong for himself and the age. "Verse," he wrote in words whose assertiveness may indicate diffidence, "has been most injurious to dramatic art. . . . It is improbable that verse will be employed to any extent worth mentioning in the drama of the future; the aims of the dramatists of the future are almost certain to be incompatible with it. It is therefore doomed." There could be no clearer proof of the strength of naturalism in late nineteenth-century culture, nor of Ibsen's desire to be naturalistic—or at least to make his peace with naturalism—in a naturalistic age.

The second quarter-century of Ibsen's work—beginning with [*Pillars of Society* and *A Doll's House*] . . . —is a steady development of the naturalistic form of play. The Ibsen of these plays—and of *Ghosts* . . . and its angry appendix *An Enemy of the People* . . . —is what one of his best commentators calls the "modern Ibsen." . . . The Ibsenite Ibsen seemed to belong not only to the general naturalist army, but to its extreme wing—Zolaist Naturalism. Calling attention to the rotten bottoms of ships, the subjection of Victorian wives, the ravages of syphilis, and the corruption of municipal politics and journalism, he made himself the father of the reformist drama of the end of the century—the drama of Brieux in France, of Galsworthy in England. But it is only by false association with these gentlemen that Ibsenism can be considered the quintessence of Ibsen.

Ibsen adopted a naturalistic form of play, and it is this naturalistic form that gives the "modern Ibsen" his character of an Anti-Wagner, a prosaic, restrained, dry-spoken, hard-bitten ironist. It gives him the opportunity for those clever expositions by innuendo and developments by nuance which many readers today find excessively elaborate or even completely gratuitous. To write *The League of Youth,* a heavy, creaking prose comedy in the manner of Scribe, *after* writing *Peer Gynt,* could give the impression that Ibsen had abandoned dramatic art for the commercial theater. It could rejoice those who wish playwrights to come to terms with their time as much as it could annoy those who want the artist to stick to art. The rejoicing and the annoyance would, however, be equally premature. The truth is that after the initial fumbling of two plays—*The League of Youth* and *Pillars of Society* (to which I am tempted to add *A Doll's House*)—Ibsen made out of his naturalism an instrument as personal and subtle—if not as attractive—as the Romanticism of Peer Gynt. In fact he made out of his naturalism a new and much less overt Romanticism.

This is not juggling with terms. If no art, and no artist, can be *wholly* naturalistic, it is always important to see in a work of naturalism what the non-naturalistic elements are. When the "modern Ibsen" is on the stage we see the heavy Victorian furnishing, the heavy Victorian costumes, the heavy Victorian beards and coiffures. These things, plus a sordid subject matter and technical virtuosity, are what many people think of as Ibsen. These things, however, are obviously not what make of Ibsen's plays the crowning glory of tragedy in modern dress. No. The paradox of Ibsen's naturalistic tragedy is that it depends so much on the non-naturalistic elements for its success. Inside the skins of these prim-looking women and beefy-looking men lurk the trolls and devils of *Peer Gynt,* that is to say, the trolls and devils of Norse folk tale, the trolls and devils of Ibsen's inner consciousness. Ibsen may pretend to be an utter Realist in the manner of midcentury France or a Naturalist in the manner of late-century France. He began, however, as a Romanticist—and not a Romanticist out-of-season, not a Neo-Romanticist either. In Ibsen's youth—a generation after the Romantic Revolt in western Europe—Romanticism was still fresh and flourishing in Scandinavia, for Norway is a suburb of Europe and there is a lag between the mode in Paris and the mode in Oslo. It is true that Ibsen was later embarrassed by the provinciality of his native land. He doffed his Romantic viking robes and began to think of himself as a cosmopolitan. He drew heavily on the resources of French and German culture. But his Romanticism was no less persistent for being driven underground. It was only concealed, not eliminated, by Victorian costume, upholstery, and conversation, and by the techniques and subject matters of the boulevards. The Ibsen Secret, if there was one, was that the archnaturalist remained to the end an arch-Romanticist too. (pp. 119-21)

Ibsen is difficult. He pretends to be easy, and is

hard. He pretends to write a dull, characterless dialogue. He pretends to be utterly usual in his plots, dishing up a "well-made play" (*An Enemy of the People*), a Naturalistic version of heredity (*Ghosts*), a sensational study of a *femme fatale* (*Hedda Gabler*) or anything at all which an enthusiast for Dumas *fils* or Zola would have required. In his last years he became, outwardly, an almost official figure in Norway; he attended banquets, wore decorations, and was the cultural father of his country. During all this he wrote works which were more and more subjective and difficult and which bore within them a concealed condemnation of modern men, including the poet himself. . . . [Ibsen] ended his artistic career with a portrait—in *When We Dead Awaken*—of an elderly sculptor at a health resort. The project seemed so inoffensive that no one winced when the sculptor spoke of the naturalism of his portrait busts:

> . . . it amuses me unspeakably. On the surface I give them striking likenesses, as they call it, so that they all stand and gape in astonishment (*lowers his voice*) but at bottom they are all respectable, pompous horse-faces, and self-opinionated donkey-muzzles. . . . And it is these double-faced works of art that our excellent plutocrats come and order of me. And pay for in good faith—and in good round figures too—almost their weight in gold . . .

This passage is the best available statement of Ibsen's own attitude to Ibsenite naturalism. . . . Ibsen pretends to write flat dialogue but the opaque, uninviting sentences carry rich meanings which are enforced only by their context. An Ibsenite sentence often performs four or five functions at once. It sheds light on the character speaking, on the character spoken to, on the character spoken about; it furthers the plot; it functions ironically in conveying to the audience a meaning different from that conveyed to the characters (and it is not merely that the characters say things which mean more to the audience than to them, but that they also say things which, as one senses, mean more to the characters than to the audience); finally, an Ibsenite sentence is part of the rhythmic pattern which constitutes the whole act. The naturalistic prose, then, is not there for its own sake. It is not there to display Ibsen's ability to write "natural" conversation. It is as rich in artifice as the verse of *Peer Gynt*. Its very naturalness is the final artifice, the art that conceals art. It is—above all—a way of giving concreteness and immediacy to themes that might have led a lesser artist into grandiosity and abstraction. It is anti-Wagnerite. (pp. 123-25)

Ibsen's naturalistic period, say the textbooks, begins with *The Pillars of Society* . . . , his "Symbolism," his "Neo-Romanticism" with *The Master Builder*. . . . But the symbolism which is the most tangible sign of the antinaturalistic or Romantic Ibsen is present in each of the naturalistic plays. Not to mention the

rather rudimentary symbolism of the titles *Pillars of Society* and *A Doll's House,* the ships in the former play and the tarantella in the latter are symbols central to the theme. The title *Ghosts* is a much better guide to the play than any discussion of syphilis. Nearly every "naturalistic" play of Ibsen's contains a central symbol whose significance spreads over the whole play.

From *The Wild Duck* . . . on, Ibsen becomes more and more what has been called mystical—meaning, I suppose, edifying though unintelligible. The truth is that the world of trolls and goblins comes thronging back into his work, that the naturalism becomes less the substance and more of a mask, that a complex, shifting symbolism is employed—to the dismay of those who expect symbolism to be either purely decorative or purely allegorical. A generation before Ibsen had begun to seem solid, Victorian, and safe—something, perhaps, to set up against the precious, obscure, and pessimistic moderns. The first generation of Philistines—such men as Ibsen named Manders, Kroll or Brack—tried to break Ibsen with their hatred; the second generation almost did kill him with their friendship. One should turn freshly to the plays of Ibsen's last period to rediscover a tortured, introverted, clever, repellent, oblique, and subtle genius.

The Master Builder, for example, shows exactly what kind of a playwright Ibsen is and is not. The starting point is a ballad which Ibsen wrote in the folk manner. "He" and "she" lose a jewel in a fire which burns down the house. Even if they find the jewel, says Ibsen, "she" will never recover her faith, nor "he" his happiness. The symbols are characteristic of the man who spoke of torpedoing the ark, of a corpse hidden in the cargo, the man who kept as a pet a poison-spitting scorpion. The ballad is indeed the nearest thing to an Ibsen play in all earlier literature. A ballad celebrates a recent disaster. An air of fatality broods over it. It is compressed. It is all catastrophe. Upon such a mythic pattern Ibsen built a naturalistic superstructure.

The base and the superstructure interact like significantly juxtaposed colors. It would be impossible to say which is more important, or which is the prime meaning of the play, for one takes meaning from the other. On the natural level, the play is about an aging architect who, growing jealous of his younger rivals, is egged on by a neurotic young woman to an athletic feat which proves his downfall. It could be a story by a French realist. If we add that the young woman's sexual life seems to have been perverted by first experiencing orgasm from the autoerotic experience of seeing the Master Builder climb a Tower, we have a story for a clinical Naturalist. Ibsen adds the myth. Underlying the play is the theme of *hubris,* the heroic rashness of ancient tragedy which brings retribution to the hero. Hilda Wangel, the neurotic young woman, represents the troll world, the world of the chaotic, tempestuous Id; she is a counterpart of the male troll who haunts her mother, who is Ibsen's main character in *The Lady from the Sea.* Hilda is not immoral, for she disapproves of Solness' harsh treatment of his assistant. She is amoral. She is a daemonic force playing upon the *hubris* of the hero.

Mythic theme and clinical story combine in Ibsen not as a vast Composite Art Work but as a highly specialized study of a very limited subject, the mind of Ibsen. Solness is the aging playwright who feels his powers slipping away, who wonders if in being so wholly an artist he has ceased to be a man, or if in appointing himself preceptor of mankind he has not built higher than he himself can stand. Cowardice or avoidance was Ibsen's besetting sin or at least his besetting fear, as we first see at the time when he declined to fight in the war against Bismarck in 1864. The fear is projected into *The Master Builder,* split into many colors like a spectrum; and the result is a symbolic drama that is rich, complex, strange, and by no means to be dismissed as mysticism.

The Master Builder and *When We Dead Awaken* are about Ibsen and nothing else. Does this mean that they are limited and narrow? Limited in their appeal they will always be. They are too difficult for any conceivable large audience to follow and enjoy. (pp. 126-28)

Limited in their appeal, are these increasingly subjective plays limited in their value, limited, that is, by their very subjectivity? No. Ibsen's subjectivity is not a failure to communicate. Nor is it egotism. It springs from his belief that "the highest attainment possible to a human being" is "so to conduct one's life as to realize one's self." The artist, Ibsen believed, should limit himself to what he has experienced. "All that I have written these past ten years," he told the Norwegian students, "I have mentally lived through." (p. 128)

Yet Ibsen did not stop at the individual. To his statement to the students he added: "But no poet lives through anything isolated. What he lives through all of his countrymen live through together with him. For if that were not so, what would establish the bridge of understanding between the producing and receiving mind?" (p. 129)

The modern intellectual oscillates between the two extremes of self-abandonment. Ibsen felt the pull of both, and, like Walt Whitman, he managed to avoid alike the fear of self that produces the sickly, eager radicalism of the carpet communist, and the fear of society and history that reinforces the natural egoism of the aesthete. The commissar-type he portrayed—not unsympathetically—in Peter Mortensgaard. He himself was Rosmer and Solness and Rubek. Or rather, the cre-

ation of these men was the way he purged himself of their faults. As one threw himself into a millrace and another fell headlong from a tower and the third was swept away by an avalanche, Ibsen could say: There but for the grace of God go I. And so it comes about that the late subjective plays are broadly significant, perhaps more broadly significant than anything Ibsen had written since *Peer Gynt.* After a performance of *The Wild Duck,* the poet Rilke wrote in a letter: "There was something very great, deep, essential. Doomsday and judgement. Something ultimate. And suddenly, the hour had come when Ibsen's majesty deigned to look upon me, for the first time. A new poet to whom we shall go by path after path now that I know one. And again a man misunderstood in the midst of fame. An entirely different person from what one hears." Exactly! (pp. 129-30)

Eric Bentley, "Wagner and Ibsen: A Contrast," in his *The Playwright as Thinker: A Study of Drama in Modern Times,* Reynal & Hitchcok, 1946, pp. 103-36.

RICHARD GILMAN
(essay date 1969)

[Gilman is an American drama critic and editor who has written extensively on the modern theater. His best-known works include *Common and Uncommon Masks: Writings on Theatre 1961-70* (1970) and *The Making of Modern Drama* (1974). In the following excerpt, he provides a thematic overview of Ibsen's plays.]

When Ibsen, believing, correctly as it was to turn out, that the era's stages were closed to any further movement in the line of his own earlier dramaturgically open and poetic plays, *Brand* and *Peer Gynt,* turned from epic historical dramas to begin his cycle of so-called social plays, his shift in strategy was extreme. But it was not likely in the nature of things to have been quickly detected for what it was. Along with Zola, although with far less "scientific" fervor and methodology, Ibsen appeared to be engaged in moving drama into participation in the naturalistic movement that had overtaken large sectors of fiction and compelled its attention to society's immediate dilemmas, maladies, disjunctions and distempers. Diagnostic, prophetic and hopefully purifying, the new drama banked on a recovered honesty of imagination and sight after the reign in the theater of evasion and more or less elegant artifice.

Issuing from a greatly reduced surface, one of bare planes and unresonant corners, commonplace, quotidian and "life-like" in their materials, Ibsen's plays of the 1870's and 1880's caught the half-horrified attention of audiences by their aggressive thrusts into public domains and their disturbing analyses of contemporary behavior. They carried with them and seemed to rise out of a heavily breathed air of topicality. And yet everything that seemed new and sensational, all the muckraking, the advanced ideas and calls to order, the assaults on public hypocrisy and private deceit, were fundamentally pretexts and sheathings for something else.

It was Eric Bentley who first undertook, in America at least, to rescue Ibsen from the soapbox or dais on which his statue—his decided-upon position in the life of culture—has so long rested. *A Doll's House,* Bentley demonstrated in *The Playwright as Thinker* is not really about women's rights, the theme that had so exercised the Victorian audience and that continues to reign in the textbooks, but about human appetites for power and exploitation. If Nora had been the husband and Thorwald the wife, Bentley argued, the theme and music of the play would have been the same. (pp. 172-73)

Our habit of not looking at Ibsen as an artist but as a sort of grim or splendid fulminator, an ideologue, or else as a kind of superior carpenter, has done more than obscure the aesthetic reality of his plays; it has

Caricature of Ibsen.

prevented us from seeing him as a crucial figure in the dialectic between art and life, artist and man, which has more than ever become the subject of art itself and the ground on which it takes shape. (p. 175)

The surfaces of his ostensibly naturalistic plays, their domestic and civic details and their apparent concern with conscious issues, had of course made it possible for people to go to them in the wrong way. (p. 176)

It was highly possible then and remains possible now, for example, to think of Hedda Gabler as a decadent aristocrat chafing under the encroaching pettiness of her bourgeois surroundings, or as a neurotic woman moving forward with sexual aggressiveness in order to mask a radical frigidity. When Bernard Shaw wrote that the trouble with such women is that they *don't* kill themselves, he was of course partly subscribing to these views of the play as character study. Yet it is much more mysterious than that. Beneath the surface of the play, under the merciless portraits and the exact iconography of domestic crisis, Ibsen was trying to fashion something else: a new kind of tragicomedy, more metaphysical than is comfortable for us to think, whose elements were energy turned in on itself and being struggling against its tendency to nonbeing, to dissolution.

From one point of view Hedda is indeed neurotic and the play does suggest a cold view of bourgeois propriety. But Hedda's revenge upon Lovborg, her destruction of his manuscript and then of herself, are actions in a dimension beyond pathology, whether social or psychological. Hedda cannot *live:* she is caught at the deepest level not so much in a particular set of circumstances as in human circumstance itself; she is a victim of the way things are. She is a fish in Ibsen's great, polluted, boiling sea, where creatures, ill-adapted at best, struggle to know what to do. (pp. 176-77)

To achieve this drama which was more than a conflict on a representational plane but which first had to represent in order to be anything at all, Ibsen rooted his methods in a poetry which was informal, hidden and besieged by the guardians of the surface, who drove it down into the depths beyond the audience's immediate eye. It was a poetry lying beyond the grasp of paraphrase and exploitable "meaning"; the conscious, public, assimilable events of the play would have to serve for that.

It was Henry James . . . who saw his real accomplishment by seeing through him, that is to say, through the ruse and the strategy. (p. 177)

When James wrote of Ibsen's "smoky rooms" with their "odor of spiritual paraffin" and spoke of his being "massively common and middle-class," he was indicating his distance from Ibsen's appearances, the very constituents of what was being taken for his substance. James could see beneath these appearances, however, to Ibsen's "independence, his perversity, his intensity, his vividness, the hard compulsion of his strangely inscrutable art." That the art should be "strangely" inscrutable was due to just that discrepancy between what Ibsen proposed as dramatic values and what he chose for these propositions' public life which James noted everywhere in his work. The art should have been entirely available; if it was all politics and all moral study, if its energies were essentially forensic, why should it resist analysis and clarifying study? The truth, it has turned out, is that with the possible exception of Chekhov, no modern playwright is more deceptive than Ibsen, more resistant to the easy triumphs of historical method and of a criticism which regards art as itself an aspect of history. (p. 178)

Hedda Gabler was the last of the social plays. . . . From then on, during the last nine years of his productive life . . . , the old and now unaccommodating Ibsen wrote four more plays. These are the so-called symbolic dramas which Mary McCarthy found inflated and which have figured in most histories of contemporary drama as aberrations. Although some critics have found them strangely beautiful, to the majority they were out of the main line of Ibsen's career and therefore cut off from the body of values and intentions by which he is most comfortably defined and located. . . .

With the exception of *Little Eyolf,* which seems to lie outside the main movements of Ibsen's imagination not so much because of its nonsocial and nonpsychological subject matter as through its narrowly mystical disposition of domestic event, the last plays strip themselves more and more of that skin of verisimilitude, that elephant trap, which had been stretched over the preceding ones. In so doing they seem to have provided for symbolmongers (or decriers) a series of *mises en scène*—the high tower of *The Master Builder,* the mysterious upper room of *John Gabriel Borkman,* the wind-swept mountaintop of *When We Dead Awaken*—which contain nearly all the material needed for their misapprehension. (p. 180)

Ibsen's last plays are not symbolic, nothing in them stands for anything else, and they are marvelously true and convincing dramas. What we take for symbolism in them is their having moved away from one kind of representation, from recognizable, predictable social and psychological life and behavior, from traditional *historical* human action. (p. 181)

From *The Master Builder* through *John Gabriel Borkman* to *When We Dead Awaken,* Ibsen moved step by step across a perilous region of the dramatic imagination where the task imposed was to create new myths—myths of art—for the most central and unlocalized human conditions. The kind of play he had been writing was far too limited for these new purposes and ambitions. His subject, as James had said, was an

idea, and now this idea threw off most of its particularities, or rather those particularities of social setting, psychological causation, the knowable relationships of lovers, citizens or family members, which had seemed to be the very arena of Ibsen's activity and had thus lent themselves to the misreading of him as a social philosopher rather than a poet.

In their different ways the three great last plays are myths of the individual caught in the fact, but now the fact has expanded toward a metaphysical dimension; it is mortality, finiteness, the ineluctability of death and the irretrievability of the past that press down on those points of consciousness, those arenas for struggle, which his characters have now more than ever become. It is greatly significant that all the protagonists are old or aging, for this is one of the means of their extrication from the limiting social milieus of the earlier plays; like their creator, they have been carried by time past the stage where social reality and social behavior are more or less decisive for moral and psychological leverage and revelation. They have in this way been liberated into more purely aesthetic functions. (p. 183)

Having in a sense dispersed himself among and embodied himself in his characters all along—in Brand, Peer Gynt, Mrs. Alving, Gregor Werles, Rosmer and Rebekka West, Hedda—he now entered the final and most rigorous process of purification through his own created surrogates. Through Solness, Rosmer and Rubek he broke into an expanded tragic awareness, one that in testing the limits of human existence also tested the limits and justifications of art and at the same time threw into final question the kind of play he had written before and that was to continue its domination of the stage long after his death, retaining to this moment its power as norm and model. (p. 184)

[This was] his way of being an artist involved with the world. More than most innovators Ibsen felt a need to *count,* to be immediately effective, so that his struggle with his art was seldom clearly separated from his battle to find a place, a large high position within the main enterprises of European civilization in his time. (p. 185)

We have seen something of how under the surface of Ibsen's social plays elements of a far-reaching tragic vision endeavor to shape themselves. Yet all the machinery of plot in the plays of his middle period works to the accompaniment of a hum of imaginative activity separate from the straightforward sounds of its wheels and gears: moral quests spread past the incidents arranged for their unfolding; metaphysical and spiritual actions take place in imperfect collaboration, sometimes in acute disharmony with the physical details of their stage life and the obligation to fashion recognizable portraits. (p. 188)

Most egregiously in plays like [*Pillars of Society*], *A Doll's House* and *Ghosts,* but also in more complex works like *Rosmersholm* and *Hedda Gabler,* the machinery of plot works logically to establish necessary physical connections, narrow sequences of cause and effect which propel the action forward and against which poetic event has to compete for a place, literally for "a piece of the action." Almost all these chains of physical event originate in the prehistory of the plays; fatality emerges like the visible segment of an iceberg or like a fist thrust through a wall by a hidden arm. Or rather these similes describe what Ibsen would have wanted the process of fate to have been like in his social plays.

In actuality their denouements have issued from mechanical rather than organically imaginative progressions, from an inevitability of physical causation resembling the causation we illusorily feel in real life, in life outside art. The famous letter in *A Doll's House,* Osvald's inherited illness in *Ghosts,* Lovborg's manuscript in *Hedda Gabler*—quintessential objects and data of the well-made plot—have the effect of imposing on the plays a stringency, an inevitability of a smaller and much more limited kind than the action of the imagination, and this is due to their need to reproduce ordinary causation, their obligation to resemble the inevitabilities of physical and social existence.

There has been little room for choice, the kind of choice by which a character is shown to "elect" his own fate, as Oedipus or Macbeth does, as a consequence of his own nature and existential situation and as an image of these things, instead of having his fate thrust on him by more or less arbitrary circumstances, by a logic of happenstance. However much those happenings strive to attain the condition of fatality itself, they remain incommensurate with the characters, too local, specific and literal to contain all their meanings and implications or to support fully their stature as freely imagined beings in an aesthetic environment and dimension. Thus once the letter is in the box, Nora is compelled, by the logic of the plot-as-fate, to act on the coercive knowledge of what its discovery by her husband will bring about; once Rosmer has learned of Rebekka West's machinations, he is propelled by this knowledge (as by literal machinery) to a death intended partly to atone for them and on that account smaller in implication and in metaphoric density than Ibsen was striving to create for him. (pp. 188-89)

The individual caught in the fact . . . has always been Ibsen's subject, his basis for aesthetic appraisal of his task. But in [*The Master Builder*] both individual and fact undergo a change toward a suggestive indefiniteness, a mysterious transcendence of milieu and era. In a way that looks back to *Brand* and *Peer Gynt, The Master Builder* rises to a more complete and self-contained metaphorical status than had been possible

for Ibsen to achieve as long as he was under the full exigencies of his entente with the naturalistic theater and its methods. His meanings and implications, the images and vocabularies from which they radiate, the objectifications of his intuitions, all exist now within an aesthetic environment that is more completely outside history; their disposition is more directly toward the service of his double task: to effect his own spiritual emancipation and purification, and to erect a sensual, histrionic equivalent and housing for that existential action. (pp. 190-91)

Solness, the protagonist, is a field of action within a field of action; he is the incarnation and arena of qualities and conditions in conflict, elements which we tend to isolate as "themes" but which are really ideas and intuitions brought together in an active, a dramatic, *instance.* For Ibsen the problem was how to make these ideas and intuitions, these experiences halfway between actuality and their potential new guise as art, issue in a work that would transcend personal, limited fate, that would be exemplary for a condition of existence and not a mere career; it was the problem of how to make fate universal and perennial in a bourgeois age in which the only accepted fatalities were social and what we might call *technical.* (pp. 191-92)

The Master Builder . . . expands the space available to its protagonist for the discovery and assumption of his destiny by converting much of the machinery of plot from the order of physical contingency and necessity to that of ontological urgency and spiritual choice. Solness is not free of course to evade his fate—that he has one means that the play exists—but he is free, within the dramatic narrative, to choose the events that will reveal and constitute it, in a way that has not been possible for any other Ibsen character since Brand and Peer. For the tyranny of the past, to have dealt with which was Ibsen's chief means of extending the well-made play into metaphysical areas, is no longer absolute; no longer does it act as a remorseless sequence of cause and effect. . . .

The "cause" of the culminating action of *The Master Builder* is an effect of choice, not the result of coercion by a logic of physical event. When Solness climbs up the tower for the traditional wreathing ceremony, he has been led to it by an act of will which he is free to repudiate at any time. That we feel his decision to be inevitable is not the result of his having been caught by circumstances, hooked in the mouth by plot, but because of Ibsen's successful creation of a world of inevitability built up from psychological and ontological materials under enormous pressure to find just such an aesthetic resolution. Solness, as a character, that is to say as a person brought into being for just this drama, this specific aesthetic use, has gathered in himself Ibsen's consciousness and intuitions of the grandeur and futility of art, of the terrible burdens it lays on the artist's ordinary life and of the doubts it perpetually raises about its agency in the world.

And along with this awareness of art as the necessary but disastrous "dream of the impossible" is consciousness of another and related realm of besieged being: human existence in time, the tyranny of aging and the loss of the self through the erosions of time. (p. 193)

Unlike any of Ibsen's other social protagonists, Solness has gone to the end of his possibilities with internal assent if not with full consciousness, and above all with freedom from mechanical plotted pressure. His decision to climb the tower has arisen from his original promise to Hilde of a "kingdom" for her, a promise which, since he had made it as nothing more than a flirtatious utterance to an enchanting child, puts him outside any rigorous moral or social necessity to fulfill. Yet he will give her her kingdom, since that is the only way he can assume his destiny.

Again, not since *Brand* and *Peer Gynt* has Ibsen made such complex and resourceful use of a controlling image. Beginning with its narrower function as a figure for romantic aspiration in general and for sexual promise, the notion of kingdom is steadily developed into a resonant metaphor for the life of art and, beyond that, for the ways in which existence presses toward its limits and discovers them in a dialectic of necessity and disaster. (p. 194)

When Hilde, in "quiet, crazed triumph," cries out at the moment of Solness' death that she has heard "harps in the air" and apostrophizes him as *"my—my master builder!"* she gives a home in consciousness to his lucid, insane act, one that contains all the brilliance and dementedness of men's efforts at transcendence. Solness has gone too far, which means that he has reached the tragic condition, something that Ibsen has not for a dozen plays been able to achieve for his protagonists. But he has been able to achieve it for this one only as the outcome of a major shift in dramaturgical procedure and not, as is so often taught, as the simple result of a change of values or of cultural ambition. (pp. 194-95)

Ibsen's two last plays are filled with an even greater anguish than *The Master Builder,* yet they are even sterner, more sparing of means, less dependent on an intricate narrative structure and on sequential action. For these final testaments he reached a condition of lyric expressiveness that sharply reduced the plays' reliance on linear movement, on progression of causally related events. (p. 195)

The last plays are not so much descriptions of Ibsen's state of being at the time he wrote them as new constructions which rescue the materials of that state from formlessness, abstraction and the destructions of time by placing them in the imagination. They are essentially static creations, informed by pure radical moral and ontological perceptions and intuitions, and what is needed for their dramatic viability is a form extensively different from anything Ibsen had thus far been able to control. He would not of course have called it "spatial form," that modern intellectual construct, but something of what the term suggests was surely the thing he was seeking. For the fact that almost all the crucial "action" the plays contain has been completed before the stage life has been set in motion, the two protagonists moving toward their deaths not as the result of a traditional dramaturgical development but out of recognitions that have been almost wholly present throughout, means that development will have to take place in some other fashion. Something other than a chain of causally linked occurrences will have to generate the necessary interest, that suspensefulness without which no drama can be said to exist.

The suspensefulness is in fact mostly created by the poetry, that web and mesh of implication, cross reference, image and suggestion which had been the subtext of all the social plays but which here, to an even greater degree than in *The Master Builder,* moves forward to become very nearly the whole drama itself. It is a poetry of discovery and lamentation, of cold recognition that the cost of everything is everything, and of dark, strangely exultant, lyric crystallizations of the sense and emotion of finality, of the irretrievability of the self's beautiful and catastrophic ambitions. (pp. 196-97)

[The] problem for Ibsen was to make things "happen" within a structure of plausibility such as the well-made play and his own temperament and training as a playwright required but that could scarcely be sustained now by the kind of linked events, replicas of "stories" from the self-dramatizing world outside art, such as he had been forced to devise for the past twenty-five years. His main instrument, the past, is no longer the principle of active dramatic pressure, one that brings about the revelations and denouements of the plays as physical consequences or even, as in *The Master Builder,* as spiritual ones in a sequential line. For both Rubek and Borkman have already reached their recognitions, and the plays, instead of being the unfolding process of these recognitions, are their swift flowerings. In a brilliant stroke Ibsen anticipated and partly inspired an entire milieu of plays to come by placing his protagonists as already "dead," as they are told by others, that is to say already in the condition to which ordinary drama must lead with all its parade of events. (pp. 197-98)

What marks *John Gabriel Borkman* and even more *When We Dead Awaken* as transitional plays (although nonetheless masterpieces for that; in Joyce's ecstatic opinion *When We Dead Awaken* was Ibsen's greatest work) and brings down on them the accusation of being "symbolic" is their settings, the wrapping of images—mysterious rooms, snow, storms, mountains, avalanches—within which the true poetic body of the plays forms itself. (p. 198)

Ibsen . . . brought into both plays [the] apparatus of external scene and suggestive setting, partly in order to accomplish physically the deaths of his protagonists, but more subtly because he could not yet imagine how a play whose ambition was nothing less than to exist immediately, all at once, causing itself and not being instigated by anything outside itself, and therefore existing as a poem does, whose passage through time is a concession to physical laws but whose end is really in its beginning—how such a play could be written and staged. Nevertheless, great mind and tireless spirit that he was, he remarked after writing *When We Dead Awaken,* when he was well past seventy and had not yet had his stroke, that he was ready now to strike out into wholly new regions. (pp. 198-99)

In *John Gabriel Borkman* and *When We Dead Awaken* he had written plays whose plots were fundamentally static, given so to speak all at once, whose characters underwent almost no "development" and whose thought, generalized perceptions of a moral and poetic kind, resisted more strongly than had any of his work since *Peer Gynt* a process of extrapolation and codification into "ideas."

But long before that he had been moving against the entrenchments of traditional dramatic method, more specifically the traditions that had become solidified during the century and a half or so before he began his career: the belief in stage characters as participating coherently in a recognizable typology drawn from "life," the belief in plot as a series of causally connected, physically logical incidents. Ibsen had shaken the foundations of reigning dramatic art as far back as *A Doll's House* when in a stroke that was more significant as a subterranean technical upheaval than as an open moral one he had kept Nora from coming back on stage after she had slammed the door on her husband. The play's first audiences had continued to sit and wait for it really, *properly,* to end until it was finally understood that this was in fact the ending the author had intended. (pp. 201-02)

What most profoundly disturbed the first audiences of *A Doll's House,* however unconscious they may have been of it, was not so much Nora's "immorality" as the fact of her absence, the fact that she had stepped outside the framework in which characters were supposed to be contained on the stage. The upheaval that had occurred is that which takes place whenever an art breaks with its immediate past, having been brought to it by the art's having stiffened into repetition and cliché, which means that it has become a confirmation of illusion rather than an accession to experience.

The prevailing illusion of the period was that life worked toward neat conclusions, and art, from which this sentiment had ironically enough been derived, was supposed to go on reflecting this. And so the audiences were unhappy, as other audiences were to be unhappy generations later when Godot failed to come, because they were not allowed to find out—fatal condition for the old easygoing entente between playwright and spectator—what had happened to Nora, what she was *now;* the play hadn't fulfilled drama's traditional task, which was to take characters along a fixed journey, to bring them from *one known place to another.* (pp. 202-03)

His aims were almost wholly different from those of what we might call the School of Paris, for which dramatic events on the level of mere cleverly arranged events and recognizable psychology made up most of the art of the stage. . . . But while he was fighting to make room within the well-made structures for his moral and poetic schemes, Ibsen, master builder, was at the same time extending the life and deceptive prowess of the genre by adding to its technical means. This is one source of his being confined, in our general consideration now, to a dated and narrow achievement. (pp. 203-04)

Richard Gilman, "Ibsen and Strindberg," in his *The Confusion of Realms,* Random House, 1969. Reprint by Vintage Books, 1970, pp. 172-218.

MARTIN ESSLIN

(essay date 1980)

[Esslin is an English drama critic who has written works on the Theater of the Absurd and dramatists Bertolt Brecht and Harold Pinter. In the following excerpt, he examines Ibsen's influence on modern theater.]

In the English-speaking world today Henrik Ibsen has become one of the three major classics of the theatre: Shakespeare, Chekhov and Ibsen are at the very centre of the standard repertoire, and no actor can aspire to the very first rank unless he has played some of the leading roles in the works of these three giants. Among this triad, Ibsen occupies a central position which marks the transition from the traditional to the modern theatre. While Ibsen, like all great dramatists who came after him, owed an immense debt to Shakespeare, Chekhov (who regarded Ibsen as his 'favourite writer') was already writing under Ibsen's influence. Ibsen can thus be seen as one of the principal creators and well-springs of the whole modern movement in drama, having contributed to the development of all its diverse and often seemingly opposed and contradictory manifestations:

the ideological and political theatre, as well as the introspective, introverted trends which tend towards the representation of inner realities and dreams.

Ibsen's first and most obvious impact was social and political. His efforts to make drama and the theatre a means to bring into the open the main social and political issues of the age shocked and scandalised a society who regarded the theatre as a place of shallow amusement. And Ibsen's position seems unique in the history of drama in that he seems to have been the only playwright who, in his lifetime, became the centre of what almost amounted to a political party—the *Ibsenites* who in Germany, England, and elsewhere appear in the contemporary literature as a faction of weirdly dressed social and political reformers, advocates of socialism, women's rights, and a new sexual morality (as in the Ibsen Club, in Shaw's *The Philanderer*). Again and again one can find, in the contemporary literature, the anxious father who inquires of his daughter about to introduce him to her fiancé-to-be whether by any chance the young man reads Ibsen and Nietzsche, thus *revealing* himself to be a dangerous subversive element. And the fact that Ibsen had become the symbol and figurehead of what amounted to a counter-culture has had a very considerable influence on the subsequent fluctuations of his posthumous fame and the appreciation of his plays by both the critics and the public.

It was not Ibsen himself, who greatly disliked this development, but a number of his early critics, admirers, and followers—Shaw, Archer, Brandes, Gosse, and others—who formulated the doctrines of Ibsenism which persisted for a long time and indeed still persist, inasmuch as Shaw's *The Quintessence of Ibsenism* is still (and deservedly) read as a masterpiece of Shavian polemical writing. The effect of this phenomenon was that Ibsen could, for a long time, be regarded as a principally political playwright commenting on topical social and moral issues. As a result, when some of the main objectives of what had been regarded as his closest concerns had been attained (for example: women's suffrage, a more tolerant attitude to sexual conduct, and the rejection of religious intolerance) the view spread that Ibsen had outlived his fame and become thoroughly out of date. Brecht expressed this view in 1928 when he declared that Ibsen's *Ghosts* had become obsolete through the discovery of Salvarsan as a remedy against syphilis. Yet the very fact that a playwright's work could be seen as having played a vital part in bringing about a change in public opinion and social attitudes had an immense effect on the status of drama as a medium of expression, and its status as an experimental laboratory for social thought and social change. As Brecht put it in 1939: 'The drama of Ibsen, Tolstoy, Strindberg, Gorki, Chekhov, Hauptmann, Shaw, Kaiser and O'Neill is an experimental drama. These are magnificent attempts to give dramatic form to the problems

of the time.' It will be noticed that Ibsen's name comes first in Brecht's list of the masters of the new kind of serious, experimental drama. And deservedly so: it was Ibsen who established that tradition, and proved that the theatre could be a forum for the serious consideration of the problems of the age. He is thus the founder and source of the whole strand of modern political and ideological theatre. Brecht himself, who developed a style of playwriting which radically rejected the convention of drama that Ibsen used, can thus be seen to have followed a trail blazed by Ibsen. And indeed, Brecht did acknowledge a direct indebtedness to Shaw who in turn was a professed follower of Ibsen.

This is one of the lines of descent of the contemporary drama we can clearly derive from Ibsen. It was Ibsen whose revolutionary impact and ultimate success showed that drama could be more than the trivial stimulant to maudlin sentimentality or shallow laughter which it had become—at least in the English-speaking world—throughout the nineteenth century.

It is usually assumed that the shock caused by Ibsen, and the furiously hostile reaction his early plays provoked, were due to this political and social subversiveness. But that is only one part of the truth. Another important cause of this virulent reaction by audiences and critics alike lay in the revolutionary nature of Ibsen's dramatic method and technique. This is an aspect which is far more difficult for us to comprehend today as we have become completely conditioned to precisely this then 'revolutionary' convention. Much of the fury directed at the time against Ibsen had nothing to do with his supposed obscenity, blasphemous views, or social destructiveness. What was criticised above all was his *obscurity* and *incomprehensibility*. Ibsen, it was said again and again, was a *mystificateur* who was obscure on purpose in order to mask the shallowness of his thinking, and whose dark hints and mysterious allusions were never cleared up in his plays. This view is perfectly expressed in a notice of *Rosmersholm* by Clement Scott in the London *Daily Telegraph* (19 February 1891):

> The old theory of playwriting was to make your story or study as simple and direct as possible. The hitherto accepted plan of a writer for the stage was to leave no possible shadow of a doubt concerning his characterisation. But Ibsen loves to mystify. He is as enigmatical as the Sphinx. Those who earnestly desire to do him justice and to understand him keep saying to themselves: granted all these people are egotists or atheists, or agnostics, or emancipated, or what not, still I can't understand why he does this or she does that.

The matter could not be put more clearly: in the then traditional convention of playwriting (a convention which, indeed, had existed from the very beginnings of dramatic writing) not only was every character labelled as either a villain or a hero, but was also—through soliloquies, asides, or confessions to a confidant—constantly informing the audience of his most secret motivations. The audience therefore did not have to deduce the motivations of the characters from their actions; they *knew* what their motivations were *before* they acted. Playgoers had been used to this convention for centuries. It was only when the demand for realism, of which the later Ibsen was the principal exponent, closed these windows into the inner world of the characters that the audience was faced with the problem of having to decide for themselves what the motivations of many of the characters' otherwise unexplained actions might be. No wonder that audiences unprepared for a manner of presentation that confined itself to the simulation of ordinary, everyday conversation, which hardly ever includes the full disclosure of hidden desires or deep motivations, could not make head or tail of what was supposed to be happening. Moreover, this development coincided in time with the discovery of the unconscious portion of the human psyche—the recognition that in most cases people do not even *know* their own motivations and could thus not express them even if the dramatic convention allowed them to do so. The modern convention of dramatic dialogue is, accordingly, diametrically opposed to the classical one. Now the art consists precisely in opening insights into the characters' unconscious motivations and feelings through the interstices between the most trivial everyday exchanges of small talk.

While Ibsen was by no means the only, or even the first, naturalistic playwright to apply this technique, he was certainly regarded as the most representative and also the most extreme in its application—quite apart from obviously being the greatest master practitioner of it in his own time. The introduction of this *principle of uncertainty* into drama certainly represents a fundamental revolution in dramatic technique, a revolution which is still with us and continues to dominate dramatic writing of all kinds, including the dialogue techniques of avant-garde cinema (as in the work of Robert Altman or John Cassavetes, where the dialogue is out of focus and overlaps so that no more than a general sense emerges). So far has this technique been developed that Ibsen now tends to appear to us overmeticulous and obvious in motivating his characters, however daring in breaking entirely new ground he might have appeared to his contemporaries. What is beyond doubt is that the line of development extends directly from Ibsen to Chekhov, who refined the technique of oblique or indirect dialogue and evolved the concept of the sub-text hidden beneath the explicit language of the dialogue, as well as to Wedekind who was the first to employ deliberately non-communicating dialogue so that the characters—too involved in themselves to listen to what their partners say—deliver what amounts to two monologues in par-

allel. And it is from Chekhov and Wedekind that the masters of contemporary non-communicating dialogue, such as Harold Pinter and Eugène Ionesco, can trace their ultimate descent.

To illuminate how direct this line of descent is, one has only to point out that James Joyce was not only an enthusiastic admirer of Ibsen in his youth but that he also wrote a very Ibsenite play—the much undervalued and neglected *Exiles*—which, in fact, makes this principle of uncertainty of motives its main theme. It is the subject raised in the final dialogue between Rosmer and Rebecca West in *Rosmersholm:* that one can, in fact, never know another human being's true motivation. Rosmer and Rebecca, because of the impossibility of any full and final awareness that the other's love is pure, can confirm their devotion to each other only in their willingness to die for love—whereas Richard Rowan, the highly autobiographical hero of Joyce's play, admits: 'I can never know, never in this world. I do not wish to know or to believe. I do not care. It is not in the darkness of belief that I desire you. But in restless, wounding doubt . . . ' Here this modern *principle of uncertainty* in human motivation is not only offered to the spectators, left in doubt about the characters' true feelings, but to the characters themselves whose love in fact is seen to spring directly from that very uncertainty; for full knowledge and total security would be an endpoint, the beginning of stagnation and complacency and thus the death of love, which must constantly renew itself out of risk and uncertainty. It is no coincidence that Harold Pinter adapted this play and twice directed performances of it. His deliberate abandonment of supplying motivations of any kind to his characters in plays like *The Homecoming, Old Times* or *No Man's Land* might be regarded as continuing the practice of Joyce and thus, ultimately, of Ibsen.

Affinities and organic evolutionary links in technique between writers like Ibsen, Joyce, and Pinter also highlight the close connection between the technique and form of their work and its subject matter. The method of writing dialogue itself opens up the problem of human communication, motivation, and the nature of the personality—the self. Here to Ibsen stands at the very wellspring of modern literature. And even writers whose technique has very little in common with that of Ibsen are organically linked with him in this respect. James Joyce, the dedicated Ibsenite, links Ibsen with another great writer of our time, Samuel Beckett—in spite of the fact that Beckett's anti-illusionist and non-realist techniques are diametrically opposed to those of Ibsen's plays. For, I venture to suggest, both Beckett and Ibsen are ultimately deeply concerned with a subject matter of fundamental modernity: the problem of *Being,* the nature of the self, with the question of what an individual means when he uses the pronoun *I.* How can the self be defined? Can one even speak of a consistent entity corresponding to an individual's self ? This, it seems to me, is the fundamental and underlying subject matter of Ibsen's *oeuvre* which was masked, for his contemporaries, by its surface preoccupation with social and political questions. Moreover, it is this problem which links Ibsen's earlier poetic drama with his later prose plays.

Here again Ibsen's uncanny ability to reflect the main currents of thought of his time emerges; for the problem of human identity, the nature of the self, seems to derive directly from the decline of religious belief which was the mainspring of the intellectual upheavals and revolutions of the nineteenth century to which Ibsen's entire *oeuvre* responded. As long as man was deemed to have an eternal essence, a soul which had been especially created for him by God and destined to persist—in Heaven or Hell—for all subsequent eternity, there was no problem about the nature of human identity. Each individual was believed to have his own special character and potential, which he might or might not fully develop to its utmost realisation, but which eventually would emerge into eternity. Swedenborg saw each individual in *Heaven and Hell* as bearing the outward form and features of his or her deepest nature. It was with the loss of transcendental beliefs of this nature that human identity became a problem. Was man the chance product of his genetic inheritance or of his environment? And if so, what was the true inner core of his self, its permanent component, as against the multitude of contradictory impulses which at any moment pull him in this or that direction?

Ibsen, although he insisted that he read few books and confined himself to reading the newspapers right down to the advertisements, was a brilliant sounding-board for all the philosophical cross-currents of his time, whatever the means by which he might have become aware of them. Already the protagonists of *The Pretenders*, or Julian in *Emperor and Galilean*, reflect the problem of the self, the need to search for the self 's real core, and the awareness that the realisation of one's true self is the highest human objective. Brand, who is torn between the abstract dictates of his faith on the one hand (a faith he experiences as an implacable imperative existing outside himself), and his impulsive human instincts towards his child and his wife on the other, brings this problem of identity into particularly sharp focus. So also does Peer Gynt, who realises that being sufficient to oneself (that is, merely living by one's contradictory, momentary, instinctive, sensual impulses) actually leads to failure in developing a self. The image of the onion with its core of nothingness is indeed very Beckettian, which is another way of saying 'existentialist'.

For the nothingness at the centre of our own perception of ourselves is, with Kerkegaard (whom Ibsen, even if he had never read him, must have understood

intuitively from the climate of discussion around him) and with Sartre, precisely the realisation of human *freedom*. The scene, at the end of *The Lady from the Sea* where Ellida has to be given her total freedom by her husband before she can freely decide to commit herself to him, seems to me the perfect expression of the existentialist position in drama (rivalled only by another great and even earlier proto-existentialist play, Kleist's *Prince of Homburg*). Here a character, Ellida, finds her true self by an act of her own will. Self-realisation as the creation of an integrated self out of nothing—the mere welter of instinctive drives—is the way out of the despair engendered by the disappearance of the notion of a God-centered and pre-ordained selfhood. In the case of Ellida, her encounter with the Stranger had conjured up before her a *false self-image* dictated by her animal attraction to him. And here again we are in a very modern field of ideas, the idea of *false consciousness*—a self-image which could easily have become destructive by preventing the potential integration of the personality in a harmonious balance between conflicting drives and needs, just as Brand's and Julian's false self-images ultimately lead to their downfall, or as Peer Gynt's failure to transcend the mere indulgence of his sensuality probably does (for, surely, the final vision of Peer's return to Solveig is no more than a fantasy, a dream image). Ellida's decision to commit herself—in full freedom—to Wangel seems to provide her with a valid, workable and harmoniously integrated self which, however, still remains precarious and problematic.

It is curious that the part of the Stranger, that giver of a false and destructive self-image to Ellida is, in another play, *The Master Builder*, played by Ellida's own step-daughter—Hilda Wangel. There Solness has transmitted his own false (because self-deceptive) self-image to Hilda who, years later, returns to confront him with it and to demand its realisation in action. Here the problematic nature of the human self is posed in a particularly brilliant dramatic form: Solness is faced with the reflection of his own now certainly obsolete idea of himself (which was a falsehood even at the time when he implanted it in Hilda's mind) in a manner which is reminiscent of the way Krapp is brought to confront his former and falsely romantic self in Beckett's play *Krapp's Last Tape*. The dramatic techniques could not be more different, but in substance the two plays resemble each other very closely. In Ibsen's play it is Hilda's memory which plays the part of the tape-recorder in Beckett's bleakly economical recreation of the same situation.

False consciousness, deceptive self-images, the *I* experiencing itself as the *Not-I* (to quote a Beckettian expression which has become the title of one of his plays)—these are expressions of a twentieth century cluster of problems for which Ibsen had his own terminology: he called this syndrome the *Life-lie* or, in a different perspective, the *lure of the ideal*. Peer Gynt's self-indulgence is, in this context, akin to Hjalmar Ekdal's complacency and self-deception—and the destructiveness of commitment to an abstract ideal on the part of Gregers Werle, to Brand's rigidity in blindly following the dictates of an abstract, revealed faith. John Gabriel Borkman, who has sacrificed his capacity for love, his human sensuality, to a Napoleonic self-image to which he still clings long after it has lost all reality, puts the problem of the self to discussion as much as the figure of Rubek, who betrayed both his capacity for love and for real greatness as an artist by opting for the compromise of worldly success and wealth—Peer Gynt's sufficiency to one's baser impulses. Always there is a conflict between irreconcilable aspects of the self, which the individuals concerned have failed to integrate into an harmonious, well-balanced whole.

If one looks at the underlying theme of Ibsen's *oeuvre* in this way, his preoccupation with the problem of women's rights, which so scandalised his contemporaries, also appears in a different perspective: Ibsen himself repeatedly insisted that in writing *A Doll's House* he had not, basically, been concerned with feminism, but merely with the problem of Nora's self-realisation as a human being. If Hilda Wangel destroys Solness by imposing upon him the self-image of a conquering hero unafraid to ascend the highest tower, so Helmer has imposed upon Nora the degrading role and self-image of a child-wife; and in walking out of the marriage she merely—that seems to have been the point Ibsen was concerned with—asserts her human rights to fashion her own self-image and to create her own integrated self.

Conversely, in what I feel is Ibsen's most 'modern' play, *Hedda Gabler,* we are presented with a character whose self-realisation is made tragically impossible by a number of external factors beyond her control. Hedda is basically a creative personality who cannot realise her potential in a society which does not allow women to live as independent human beings, while her sexual drive towards Løvborg cannot come to fruition because her rigid conditioning by having been brought up as an upper-class lady makes it impossible for her to defy convention by becoming Løvborg's mistress (as Thea, who has not been so conditioned, does). Thus Hedda is trapped in a truly tragic dilemma. Her seeming wickedness results from the confusion and contradictions within her own self-image between, on the one hand, her need to reject the role into which her upbringing and society have forced her (the dutiful and middle-class housewife and mother-to-be) and, on the other, her inability to do so because of the strength of her conditioning and the pressure of public opinion. Her destructiveness is thus merely her creativeness gone wrong, her tragic failure to achieve true selfhood.

Sexuality, and especially female sensuality,

which did not officially exist at all for the Victorians, was seen by Ibsen as one of the dangerous instincts insofar as its suppression by the demands of society forced the individual into false or inadequate integrations of his self. Mrs Alving's failure to break out of her marriage in *Ghosts* foreshadows Hedda Gabler's inability to give herself to Løvborg, and is shown by Ibsen to elicit similarly tragic results. In *Little Eyolf* the conflict is between motherhood and uninhibited female sensuality. Rita Allmers is the most openly sexually voracious character in Ibsen's plays: here the rejection of motherhood derives from an undue concentration on the sensual aspect of sex. The child is maimed because the mother neglected him while engaged in the sexual act; and Eyolf ultimately dies because his mother wishes him dead as an obstacle to her uninhibited indulgence of sexual activity. But Rita's exaggerated sexual drive may well spring from her husband's equally disproportionate commitment to his ideal, his work as a philosopher, which has led him to neglect both her sexual needs and their child's emotional and educational demands.

Ultimately this problem of the self is that of the missing core of the onion, the ultimate nothingness at the heart of the personality, the absence of a pre-ordained integrating principle which would automatically harmonise the conflicting drives and instincts that propel the individual in a multitude of centrifugal, disintegrating directions. That is why self-realisation, the creation of such an integrating principle by an act of will has become the task which confronts all of Ibsen's heroes. Seen from this angle, the problem of guilt in a play like *Rosmersholm* also appears in a new and more contemporary light. Here the false solutions arrived at in the past, the false self-images they have created, come between the individual and the ultimate realisation of his or her true self-image. The tradition of the Rosmers is as stifling as the upper-class rigidities of General Gabler's family; and false concepts of duty, on the one hand, and Rebecca's admittedly selfish instinctive sexuality, on the other, create what to these characters must appear as a situation without a way out. Whether, as Freud suggested, Rebecca West felt guilty under the curse of Oedipus (just having learned that she had committed incest with her father) or whether she felt that she had attained to a love of such purity that she could not, under the pressure of Victorian ideas, contemplate its sexual consummation—these characters are trapped in veritable labyrinths of false consciousness.

These are the thematic elements in Ibsen's *oeuvre* which, in my opinion, not only link him to the main preoccupations of contemporary drama but also constitute his continued relevance to the concerns of our time.

There is, however, another aspect of his work

which makes Ibsen peculiarly relevant to the dramatic literature of our time. Contemporary drama—whether it is the *epic theatre* created by Brecht; the *absurdist* strain represented by playwrights like Beckett, Genet, Ionesco, and Pinter; or the *documentary* strain of contemporary political theatre—is essentially anti-illusionist, anti-realistic (if realism is understood as the quasi-photographic reproduction of the external appearance of the phenomenal world). Ibsen is generally regarded as the antithesis of this position, as a realist, even a naturalist, who in the most influential phase of his activity strove for complete photographic verisimilitude: a world of rooms without a fourth wall.

This view of Ibsen is correct, up to a point. But Ibsen's essentially poetic genius also propelled him away from photographic realism. That there are dream-like elements, highly reminiscent of the introspective fantasy world of the Absurdists, in Ibsen's earlier plays, in *Brand* and *Peer Gynt*, that there is a vast epic sweep that transcends all realism in *The Pretenders* and *Emperor and Galilean*, is only too obvious. Again and again in these plays the action shifts from the external world into the protagonists' dreams or fantasies: the voice from the avalanche in *Brand*, the Troll scenes in *Peer Gynt*, Peer Gynt's shipwreck, the whole Button Moulder sequence and, indeed, the final vision of Solveig, are dreamlike projections of the characters' inner visions. When Ibsen made the decision to devote himself to realistic prose drama these dream and fantasy elements were—on the surface—suppressed. Yet they are continuously present, nevertheless. They emerge above all in what has come to be regarded as Ibsen's increasing resort to symbolism. Having renounced the use of *poetry in the theatre* (in the form of verse or grandly poetic subject matter) Ibsen made more and more use of *poetry of the theatre* which emerges from the sudden transformation of a real object into a symbol, from the metaphoric power of an entrance or an exit, a door opening or closing, a glance, a raised eyebrow or a flickering candle.

It is my contention—and conviction—that the continuing power and impact of Ibsen's plays spring from precisely this poetic quality. If we accept that all fiction, however realistic its form, is ultimately the product of the imagination, the fantasy-life, the day-dreaming of its author, then even the most realistic drama can be seen, ultimately, as a fantasy, a day-dream. The more creative, the more complex, the more original, the more poetic the imagination of the writer, the greater will be this element in his work. It is one of the hallmarks of the best work of some of our foremost contemporary playwrights that they are conscious of this position and make use of it. The plays of Edward Bond and Harold Pinter, to name but those who most readily come to mind, are examples of this tendency: they are conceived as working both on the level of ex-treme realism and at the same time on that of fantasy and dream. In this they have surely been anticipated by Ibsen. The continued and undiminished impact of even Ibsen's most seemingly political plays owes, in my opinion, a great deal to that immense hidden and mysterious power which springs from the co-existence of the realistic surface with the deep subconscious fantasy and dream elements behind it: the simulated forest wilderness in the attic of *The Wild Duck*, the white horses of *Rosmersholm*, the ghosts that haunt Mrs Alving, the mysterious Stranger of *The Lady from the Sea*, the spectral Rat Wife of *Little Eyolf*, Borkman's self-created prison, Løvborg's manuscript as Hedda's aborted dream-child, the haunting appearance of the destructive and seductive Hilda Wangel in *The Master Builder*, Aline's dolls in the same play—they all are powerful poetic metaphors, fantasy-images as well as real objects and forces which can be perceived in a sober, factual light.

For, ultimately, the power of all drama springs from its innermost poetic nature as a metaphor of reality, a representation of the whole of reality which of necessity must include the internal world, the world of the mind (both conscious and subconscious), as well as the external reality of rooms, furniture, and cups of coffee. As soon as that external reality is put on the stage it becomes, by the very nature of the theatrical phenomenon, an image, a metaphor of itself: *imaged,* imagined, and by that very fact a mental, a fantasy phenomenon. *'Alles Vergaengliche ist nur ein Gleichnis'*, as Goethe puts it in the final scene of *Faust:* all our ephemeral, evanescent reality is itself, ultimately, merely metaphor, symbol.

It is this quality of the metaphorical power, the poetic vision behind the realistic surface of Ibsen's later plays—their impact as images, and the complex allusive representations of those aspects of human existence, those problems that lie beyond the expressive resources of merely discursive language—in which their real greatness and enduring impact lies. And these, precisely, are the elements in Ibsen which are both highly traditional as well as continuously contemporary, continuously modern. (pp. 71-82)

Martin Esslin, "Ibsen and Modern Drama," in *Ibsen and the Theatre: The Dramatist in Production,* edited by Errol Durbach, New York University Press, 1980, pp. 71-82.

IRVING DEER
(essay date 1986)

[Deer is an American drama critic, editor, and educator whose works include *Ibsen: A Collection of Critical Essays* (1965). In the following excerpt, he asserts that *A Doll's House* shows a shift in Ibsen's artistic intentions.]

Despite the fact that a number of Ibsen's protagonists are artists or surrogate artist figures, little consideration has been given to his work as art about art, or, more specifically, drama about drama. This neglect may result partly from the fact that Ibsen is generally considered a kind of social problem writer, someone who is quintessentially concerned, at least in his plays, with the world, not with his own artistic problems. His status as the "father of modern drama," meaning the creator of realistic drama, promotes the same "blindness" to the possibility that he could be writing plays both about their own genesis and about the world.

I want to argue that such a paradox, both an inward and an outward focus, is precisely one of Ibsen's main concerns and achievements. His best plays are both about themselves and about the world, and perhaps most interestingly, about their own struggle to achieve that paradoxical state. (p. 35)

For those of us who have seen performances of *A Doll's House* by Claire Bloom or Jane Fonda on stage, screen or television in the last decade, there is little difficulty in understanding Ibsen's reputation as a writer of social problem plays. Most people still see the play as one about a heroic young woman's victorious struggle for freedom from repressive social conventions. Some, however, like Hermann Weigand in the twenties, see Nora as a deceptive, selfish, intriguing young woman bent only on having her own way. These critics believe Ibsen is satirizing and debunking her rather than, as the other critics believe, holding her up as virtue incarnate.

Whichever interpretation you favor, the play comes out to be about social problems, about the problems of the individual's responsibility to society and conversely, of society's responsibility to the individual. When the play first came out conventional audiences favored emphasizing the individual's responsibility to society. More liberal audiences since have emphasized the play's concern with society's responsibility to the individual. Although the liberal view has been dominant for years now, some such alignment still persists.

The problem from the point of view of my subject is not then one of showing Ibsen's concern with relating *A Doll's House* to society. That is obvious. What is more difficult is to show that the play is also about playing, that it is, in other words, a kind of self-conscious drama about drama itself. The illusion of objective realism Ibsen achieved with the play, its apparent photographic objectivity, seems to most people to deny the possibility of the kind of self-conscious subjectivity I am looking for in the play. Yet there is an almost obvious sense in which the play is about characters playing roles, clearly pretending, performing for others. This is most obvious with Nora herself. It is also perhaps one of the main reasons those in the Weigand camp see her as an intriguer and plotter rather than as the virtuous heroine for whom she is more often taken. From the beginning of the play she engages in little intrigues, pretending to Torvald she has been obeying him about not eating macaroons, when we just saw her eat some before he entered the room, performing like a squirrel for him to get him to give her some money so, as we later learn, she can engage in her greatest intrigue of all, the plot to cover up the loan she has been paying off in this way to Krogstad for years. Later when Krogstad threatens to write her husband not only about the loan but about her having forged her dead father's signature to get it, she gives a frenzied, desperate performance, a literal performance, dancing a tarantella at a party upstairs, to try to keep Torvald from going back to their apartment where he will pick up the mail with Krogstad's letter.

Performance, role-playing, is thus for the central figure in the play a necessary form of action, perhaps the main form her struggles take. But there is also another sense in which Ibsen's subject is drama itself. Most of the characters are conceived of as playing roles drawn from the kinds of Danish and French romantic melodramas from which Ibsen learned his craft. As Raymond Williams points out, there is "the innocent child-like woman, involved in a desperate deception, the heavy insensitive husband; the faithful friend." "Similarly," Williams continues, "the main situations of the play are typical of the intrigue drama: the guilty secret, sealed lips, the complication of situations around Krogstad's letter . . . Krogstad at the children's party . . . the villain against a background of tranquility. . . ." For Williams all of this is an indication of the play's weaknesses: "None of this is at all new," he says, "and it is the major part of the play."

His view would be true if the play were not self-conscious, that is, if it were not about the limitations of playing such roles in life as well as in drama. As I see the play, it is centrally about Nora's discovery of how limited her romantic role-playing has been, how it was not only imposed on her by society, but willingly accepted by her. I believe in fact that the main reason she is taken by one group as the embodiment of modern heroism and by another as villainy personified is that Ibsen shows us that each of those views is a fragment of the truth. Both constitute partial views of Nora. She did save her husband's life, she is willing to commit suicide like some Isolde to save her husband and family from ruin, but she also did naively forge her father's signature on a loan, and innocently expects Torvald to act like a storybook lover who takes all her shame on himself. She sees herself as the romantic heroine of the types of plays from which Ibsen learned his craft, the Danish historical romances and the French melodramas he imitated and directed. The liberal perspective supports her view. However, a shift to a more conservative perspective, one that emphasizes her responsibility to her husband, children, and society, can easily emphasize her similarity to the intriguing, villainous women of the French melodramas. From such a perspective, she lies, postures and intrigues about everything, and when found out, runs off, dropping all her responsibilities. Both these views of Nora, as the romantic heroine or the intriguing villain, are extremely limited, melodramatic views. As she is beginning to discover by the end of the play, by having accepted either of such limited views of herself, or having allowed society to impose one on her, she has contributed to her own frustration as a person who is trying to express more of herself than society allows. By showing us one melodramatic view of Nora, then the opposite melodramatic view, Ibsen is pointing out both the limitations of melodramatic ways of seeing and of writing.

We can see this in Ibsen's treatment of situations drawn from the popular Scribean intrigues he knew so well. The whole letter situation, for example, is given a new twist, not accepted in its mechanical conventional form as Williams seems to think. Nora does everything to try to divert Torvald's attention from the letter box. When he finally gets Krogstad's first letter and reads it, he acts as a character would in Scribe. The world turns in Scribe's plays on glasses of water, handkerchiefs and letters. Everything stops with them. The world is saved. The lovers are united. Virtue triumphs. The play ends. Nurtured by society on such forms of expression, Torvald reacts appropriately. He feels his life has been ruined by his stupid wife, just when he has become an important bank manager. In retribution, he in effect stops Nora from functioning. He tells her she can no longer be a real wife or mother to their children, that she will corrupt them as she is corrupted. Since the only roles society has allowed her have been those of child, lover, wife and mother, the only two roles she has left by which to express herself are those of wife and mother. Now Torvald has taken those away from her.

True, he returns them a few minutes later when Krogstad's second letter comes. Since Krogstad has returned the incriminating loan papers, Torvald is no longer in danger. He would like to forget the whole thing, to get back to where he and Nora were before he castigated her as innately corrupt. As he sees it, he is generously returning her to her status as wife and mother. She, however, sees the sequence of events somewhat differently. She see how limited and arbitrary have been the roles society has assigned her and she has accepted.

Nora now sees the need to find new ways of relating to society. She has also seen the possibility of finding new ways. She has seen her friend Christine become a widow, a working woman surviving on her own, a woman who goes into an unmarried, permanent relationship with a man, the choice which also makes the man, Krogstad, see that he is not doomed to isolation and to the intrigues he felt conventional society had forced on him. Just as Nora now sees the need and the possibility of finding new ways of relating to society, so does Ibsen as a writer of a new kind of drama. He was with *A Doll's House* creating the realistic drama that was to make him world famous. This new kind of drama constituted his attack on the conventional romantic and intrigue drama and vision he had inherited. It was the first step among several important ones he would take in experimenting with new, more contemporary possibilities for drama. (pp. 36-9)

Irving Deer, "Ibsen's Self-Reflexivity in 'A Doll's House' and 'The Masterbuilder'," in *Within the Dramatic Spectrum, Vol. VI*, edited by Karelisa V. Hartigan, University Press of America, 1986, pp. 35-44.

SOURCES FOR FURTHER STUDY

Byran, George B. *An Ibsen Companion: A Dictionary-Guide to the Life, Works, and Critical Reception of Henrik Ibsen.* Westport, Conn.: Greenwood Press, 1984, 437 p.

Includes a detailed chronology of Ibsen's life, original publication and production information, and plot synopses.

Downs, Brian W. *Ibsen: The Intellectual Background.* Cambridge: Cambridge University Press, 1946, 187 p.

An account of the artistic conventions and historical events that influenced Ibsen's dramas.

Gosse, Edmund W. *Henrik Ibsen.* New York: Charles Scribner's Sons, 1908, 244 p.

Biography that includes character descriptions and plot outlines of Ibsen's plays.

Lavrin, Janko. *Ibsen: An Approach.* London: Methuen & Co., 1950, 139 p.

Discusses Ibsen's process of composition and his development as a dramatist.

Meyer, Michael. *Ibsen: A Biography.* New York: Doubleday & Co., 1971, 865 p.

In-depth biography.

Scandinavian Studies 51, No. 4 (Autumn 1979): 343-519.

Special issue devoted to Ibsen, including articles by such critics as Einer Haugen, Evert Sprinchorn, and Yvonne L. Sandstroem.

Eugène Ionesco

1912-

Rumanian-born French dramatist, essayist, scriptwriter, novelist, and short story writer.

INTRODUCTION

A major figure in contemporary drama, Ionesco is linked by the themes and techniques of his plays to the Theater of the Absurd. He creates darkly comic portraits of the human condition by exploring such themes as alienation, the impossibility of communication between human beings, and the destructive forces of modern society. As is characteristic of the Theater of the Absurd, Ionesco's drama is experimental. He replaces the traditional structure of plot, action, and denouement with an oneiric drama composed of contradiction, nonsensical dialogue, and bizarre images and situations. Ionesco often draws upon his own dreams for dramatic material, and has stated that dreams "are reality at its most profound, and what you invent is truth, because invention, by its nature, can't be a lie."

The problematic nature of language and communication is a dominant theme in Ionesco's early works, including his first two plays, *La cantatrice chauve* (1950; *The Bald Soprano*) and *La leçon* (1951; *The Lesson*). In the first play Mr. and Mrs. Smith engage in a cliché-ridden conversation, while their visitors, Mr. and Mrs. Martin, speak as though they are strangers until realizing that they share the same home and child. The dialogue among the four characters eventually disintegrates into meaningless sounds. In the second play, a professor tutors a female student in several subjects, ranging from the logical constructs of mathematics to the less rigid rules of language. As the language lesson progresses, the professor becomes increasingly agitated, and the play climaxes when he stabs the student during a discussion of the word "knife." Both works end as they began, the only difference being that the two couples in *The Bald Soprano* exchange roles. The circular structure of these two plays has contributed to critics' perception of Ionesco's works as essentially pessimistic. As his career progressed, Ionesco began to use multiplying objects as a metaphor for the absurdity of life. In one of his most acclaimed works, *Les chaises* (1952; *The Chairs*), an elderly couple serve as hosts for an audience who assemble to hear an orator deliver a message that will save the world. As the couple arrange seating for their guests, the stage becomes crowded with chairs. Other plays demonstrate a similar proliferation of objects: in *Victimes du devoir* (1953; *Victims of Duty*), coffee cups multiply and in *Le nouveau locataire* (1957; *The New Tenant*) the protagonist's apartment eventually becomes filled with furniture. Critics frequently observe that the increasing number of objects in these works suggests the alienation and loss of identity experienced by people in modern society.

Beginning in the late 1950s, Ionesco wrote a number of plays that center on Bérenger, a modern-day Everyman. The best known of these works is *Rhinocéros* (1959), which is considered one of Ionesco's most accessible plays. During the course of the play everyone except Bérenger is transformed into a rhinoceros. Bérenger questions whether he should join them, but when he realizes he cannot, he decides to fight them. While the inspiration for this work came from Ionesco's reaction to a friend who joined the Nazi party, the play's significance extends beyond the confines of any single ideology to denounce mindless conformity and mob mentality. Other Bérenger plays include *Tueur sans gages* (1958; *The Killer*), in which Bérenger searches for a nameless killer to whom he falls prey, and *Le roi se meurt* (1962; *Exit the King*), in which Bérenger is a king who is told he will soon die.

The subject of death becomes an overriding concern in many of Ionesco's later plays. For example, in *La soif et la faim* (1964; *Hunger and Thirst*), the protagonist attempts to escape death as represented by his wife and child, and in *Jeux de massacre* (1970; *Killing Game*), an epidemic kills the inhabitants of a village. Charles I. Glicksberg explained: "Death for Ionesco represents the upsurge of the uncanny, the threat of nothingness, the quintessence of the Absurd." The dream-like images that pervade Ionesco's drama also become more prominent in his later works. In *L'homme aux valises* (1975) and *Voyages chez les morts* (1980; *Journey among the Dead*), the protagonists engage in conversations with the dead. The episodic nature of these plays, coupled with their fantastic elements, creates the impression of a dream. Commenting on the influence of dreams on Ionesco's work, Rosette Lamont stated: "Ionesco believes that an interpenetration occurs between the conscious day life and the subconscious night existence, for dreams contain fragments of the day's impressions, and the latter are encrusted with bits and pieces severed from the psyche's intense activity in its nightly revels."

Best known as a dramatist, Ionesco has also written a novel, *Le solitaire* (1972; *The Hermit*), and several volumes of essays and criticism. These works, like his drama, are marked by a sense of anguish and a vehement opposition to totalitarianism and oppression. Many of his essays offer incisive comments on his drama. Faulted as obscure by many critics at the beginning of his career, Ionesco's innovative drama has gained international acclaim, and a number of his works are now considered seminal pieces of the Theater of the Absurd.

(For further information about Ionesco's life and works, see *Contemporary Authors*, Vols. 9-12; *Contemporary Literary Criticism*, Vols. 1, 4, 6, 9, 11, 15, and 41; *Something about the Author*, Vol. 7; and *Major Twentieth-Century Writers*.)

CRITICAL COMMENTARY

JACQUES GUICHARNAUD AND JUNE BECKELMAN

(essay date 1961)

[In the essay below, Guicharnaud and Beckelman survey Ionesco's dramas, concluding that Ionesco's "liberated theatre" is a "mirror of the world as a nonsensical mechanism."]

Sketchy characters carried away by words, changing identities, having three noses, laying eggs, talking without communicating, preys to organized disorder, murder, the most grotesque cruelty, living out directed dreams, being transformed into rhinoceroses—indeed Ionesco's plays seem rather baffling at first. Despite the direct language and somewhat dreary realism of the settings, his works—sometimes called "characterless theatre," sometimes "tragic farce" or "metaphysical farce" or "anti-theatre"—are above all poetic. They present a concrete realization of metaphors and an im-

---

Principal Works

La cantatrice chauve (drama) 1950
  [The Bald Soprano, 1958; also translated as The Bald
  Prima Donna, 1958]
Le leçon (drama) 1951
  [The Lesson, 1958]
Les chaises (drama) 1952
  [The Chairs, 1958]
Victimes du devoir (drama) 1953
  [Victims of Duty, 1958]
Amédée; ou, Comment s'en débarrasser (drama) 1954
  [Amédée, 1958; also translated as Amédée, or How to
  Get Rid of It, 1961]
Jacques; ou, La soumission (drama) 1955
  [Jack; or, The Submission, 1958; also translated as
  Jack, or Obedience, 1958]
Le nouveau locataire (drama) 1957
  [The New Tenant, 1958]
Tueur sans gages (drama) 1958
  [The Killer, 1960]
Rhinocéros (drama) 1959

[Rhinoceros, 1960]
Notes et contre-notes (essays, addresses, and lectures)
  1962
  [Notes and Counter-notes, 1964]
Le piéton de l'air (drama) 1962
  [A Stroll in the Air, 1965]
Le roi se meurt (drama) 1962
  [Exit the King, 1963]
La soif et la faim (drama) 1964
  [Hunger and Thirst, 1968]
Présent Passé, Passé Présent (autobiography) 1968
  [Present Past, Past Present, 1971]
Jeux de massacre (drama) 1970
  [The Killing Game, 1974]
Le solitaire (novel) 1972
  [The Hermit, 1974]
L'homme aux valises (drama) 1975
Voyages chex les morts (drama) 1980
  [Journeys among the Dead, 1985]

---

mediate experience of existence, grasped in the relations of the individual to his surrounding world.

Like many of the French poet-playwrights, Ionesco brings the intangible elements of his vision of the world to the stage in the concrete form of objects or acts. But by going beyond a representation of his private imagery, he succeeds in giving a metaphysical impression, elementary enough to have universal value, at least in our times, and faces the spectator with a direct metaphor of the horror of the modern world, sending him back to his own anguish instead of drawing him into the mysteries of a privileged imagination.

The revolutionary aspect of his plays, denying the traditional flow of action and traditional concept of characters, plus the often incoherent or disconnected appearance that results makes them seem like parodies of the real world. Here fantasy is not a door opened onto a beyond; it is the source of a farcical universe parallel to traditional reality.

By presenting his inner fantasies with the objectivity of realism, Ionesco creates a dream-like atmosphere reminiscent of both Kafka and Strindberg. Within the worlds of his plays either the insignificant takes on the greatest importance and becomes the object of infinite discussion, or plans are delayed indefinitely and thwarted to the point of frustration and exasperation. In addition, certain Freudian themes recur frequently, especially the image of the Mother. Directed dreams, substitution of characters, changes of iden-

tity, abortive acts, all contribute to the general nightmarish quality of the whole. Nor is it difficult to interpret the actualized metaphors in such terms. In *Amédée ou comment s'en débarrasser,* the growing corpse and the mushrooms might be considered as part of an arsenal of dream symbols referring to a guilt complex. And most of the characters themselves can be compared to dreamers who have no idea that they are dreaming. For the spectator, the flow of events is absurd or incoherent, but it is accepted as real by the characters, just as in our dreams, we consider the most delirious wanderings as the only possible logic of the world.

But to consider Ionesco's theatre as merely the actualization of nightmares would be to limit it unjustly. Freudian symbolism may be a part of the playwright's world, but it is not the key to it. The elements of dream are simply given elements of an inner world, used and rearranged, not to define man by his obscure psychology, but to complete a perceptible image of the human condition in its totality.

Most important is the idea of totality. It includes the refusal to limit man's condition to one level, the political level in particular. There is no positive *engagement* in Ionesco's theatre. In fact he vigorously protested against any such attitude. As far as he is concerned, despite its pretensions at demystification, it merely falls back into or sets up new mystifications. Even his last play *Rhinocéros,* in which we see all humanity transformed into rhinoceroses and which ends with the hero's refusal to become a rhinoceros like the others, is less an attack on totalitarian regimes (obvious though it may be on one level) than a personal refusal of any political or social involvement.

Not that Ionesco's disengagement excludes a strong position of denunciation. Although his theatre could hardly be considered as belonging to a literature of *praxis,* it does offer a judgement on the world in the name of certain non-esthetic values. On the most superficial level, he has written a ferocious social satire and it constitutes the most obvious element of his "dark" humor. By substituting imaginary behavior patterns for real ones, yet keeping the general logic of the real, Ionesco reveals the ridiculous, absurd, and even monstrous aspects of social habits and customs. The madly delirious conversations in *la Cantatrice chauve* and the fiancée's two or three noses in *Jacques ou la soumission* are not there only to provoke the joys of the absurd or to recreate an atmosphere of nightmare: they are analogous to the facts of real life, and the destructive laughter they provoke reflects on their real correlatives. Ionesco creates a universe parallel to ours which, presented with the greatest objectivity and in the terms of realism, enjoys the same right to exist as our world. By extension, our world is neither more nor less justified than what unfolds on stage and can be considered quite as ridiculous.

Ionesco thus uses nonsense as a counterpart of reality. The spectator bounces back from the play into his own universe with the greater knowledge that one system is worth another on the level of underlying justifications and reasons for being. Indeed Ionesco's satire is total in that it results in the rejection of any belief in the reasonable justification for behavior, institutions, or values. His theatre gives men no opportunity to take themselves seriously. In fact in *l'Impromptu de l'Alma,* after having ridiculed theoreticians of the theatre and philosophers, he ridicules himself when, at the end of the play, he begins to expound his own theories.

In *Tueur sans gages,* Ionesco leads his hero Bérenger toward a final scene in which the process of complete demystification is explicitly developed. Bérenger finds himself alone with a killer and tries to convince him of the criminal and useless nature of murder. In his long monologue, he gives the arguments both for and against, discovering simultaneously that although there is no reason to kill, there is no reason *not* to kill. Happiness, the brotherhood of man, all the good reasons are destroyed even in Bérenger's mind by the Killer's silence or derisive laughter, especially because, getting no response at all, Bérenger himself goes beyond the reasons he presents in order to find more convincing ones, and in fact only ends in confusion:

I don't know anymore, I don't know anymore. Maybe you're wrong, maybe wrong doesn't exist, maybe it's we who are wrong to want to exist . . . Explain. What do you think? I don't know, I don't know. (The Killer sneers.)

The Killer's "infinite energy of obstinacy" wins over all the values, even over Bérenger's instinct of preservation. For Bérenger drops his pistols and lets himself be knifed, muttering: "What can we do . . . What can we do. . . . "

Tueur sans gages is a perfect example of Ionesco's vision of the world and, by extension, clarifies all his preceding works. Ionesco began in being irreverent with regard to the daily routine of life and gave new form to a hackneyed theme. Actually his irreverence was aimed at all action and all behavior, and the whole of his works is a cluster of metaphors illustrating Bérenger's final idea: "Maybe it's we who are wrong to want to exist." But when he questions the existence of human beings themselves instead of merely that of their behavior, Ionesco's tone changes from farce to pathos and we stop laughing. For here more is at stake than just reasons. A feeling of *Grand-Guignol* takes the place of humor, and Bérenger's fall is seen not as the well-deserved punishment of a fundamentally grotesque character, but as the result of a frightful revelation within a sympathetic character.

The richness of Ionesco's theatre—and also what makes it confusing—comes from the mixture of the domains he puts under question. All the absurdities are given equal importance, whether they be the presence of things, man's decisions, social disorder, social conventions, psychological impulses, old age, or the problems of city traffic. The world is seen simultaneously on all levels, with the result that the main problem or subject does not exclude the other levels. *La Leçon* is at the same time a quasi-surrealistic use of certain textbooks, a satire on teaching, and a terrifying psycho-drama. In *Tueur sans gages* a tableau of everyday life is mixed with the nightmare of organized disorder in a large modern city, a psychological study, and the tragedy of Bérenger in search of and then faced with the Killer. By juxtaposing themes as disparate as the satire of big city traffic and the failure of Bérenger's reason, a universe is evoked in which any hierarchy of levels is suppressed. Ionesco's theatre is the image of a world where everything is equally important—and, by the same token, unimportant.

All that can be said for this universe is that facts, events, beings, and things exist. And indeed they exist in abundance. One of the authentically dramatic dimensions of Ionesco's theatre lies in the tension between a superabundance of being and the absolute impossibility of justifying the fact of being. It is therefore metaphysical drama to the extent that it reveals existence as having no reason to exist and the unjustified as existing in superabundance. In short, the world is superfluous.

Visually, the feeling is communicated by an overcrowding of the stage, an accumulation of objects or their increase in size. On the most elementary level, *l'Avenir est dans les oeufs* merely has the stage fill up with millions of eggs until it finally collapses. In an ironic tone, the protagonist of *le Nouveau Locataire* willingly imprisons himself in the midst of endless pieces of furniture which he has brought to his room. More subtly, the two old people's imaginary world in *les Chaises* is overpopulated, and the crowd is visually suggested by empty chairs which multiply on stage. In addition to things and beings, there is also a superabundance of words themselves. The dialogue is drawn out for no particular reason and filled with repetitions that end by producing a kind of incantation, as in the case of *les Chaises.*

There are doubtless similarities between Ionesco's conception and certain passages of Sartre's *la Nausée.* But where, in Sartre, the impression is qualitative, in Ionesco it is quantitative. The viscous substance of existence is replaced by an accumulation of individual things or beings, a numerical or measurable (as in the case of the corpse in *Amédée*) superabundance.

The quantitative aspect of such devices makes it possible to establish a simple form of comedy, not far from Bergson's definition of the mechanical imposed upon the living. When the mechanism is applied to the phenomena of daily life, to insignificant activity, to the many domains we habitually think of in nonmechanical terms, it touches the essence of both comedy and laughter. When in a conversation about members of a family, their births, marriages, jobs, and deaths, Ionesco gives all the members the name of Bobby Watson, he is certain to get a dual effect: comedy in the contrast between what a family should be and the incongruity of the Watson family, supposedly typical—in other words, the classic device of revealing the truth behind appearances previously considered as the norm; and laughter because the truth behind the accepted conception of the family is found to be rigorously mechanical (*la Cantatrice chauve*).

Not only is a mathematical rigour imposed on human phenomena, but it is completed by a process of geometric progression or acceleration. Machines are slow and regular at first, in the same way as the corpse's growth in *Amédée,* the production of eggs in *l'Avenir est dans les oeufs,* the arrival of the furniture in *le Nouveau Locataire,* the repetition of dialogue in *les Chaises,* the professor's nervous irritation and confusion in *la Leçon,* and the multiplication of rhinoceroses in *Rhinocéros.* Then the growth or accumulation gathers speed until it reaches a mad precipitation. Here, in addition to the influence of gags such as those of the Marx Brothers, we feel that of the technical acceleration of the motion picture image itself.

The general impression, dominating certain plays and constituting their rhythm, is that of a machine out of control. The variations of speed lead to some pauses, but as in *le Nouveau Locataire* or *Rhinocéros,* they are more comparable to a shifting of gears than to the slowing down of a machine or the return to a more human perspective. As the acceleration is always cumulative and applied to both the speed and the object's increase in number, the loss of control finally applies to the very phenomenon of *being.* Ionesco's theatre is the comedy, both laughable and terrifying, of man transcended by being itself.

According to the so-called existentialist theatre, man has the freedom and indefeasible power to make himself and make the world. Ionesco's theatre is one of disenchantment. His vision is somewhat similar to the existentialists' but only in certain themes relevant to early phases of the philosophy: the isolation of the individual consciousness in our absurd universe, the unjustified presence of the being of things, the unbearable fact of existence itself—such as they appear in Sartre's *la Nausée* and Camus' *l'Etranger.* But where both writers developed their themes toward reasons for action, Ionesco—one literary generation younger—marks the failure of any such ambition.

Ionesco's theatre then is in many ways a return to the well-known nihilism of which existentialism, and in fact any exercise of lucidity, has so often been accused. Ionesco went deep into the immediate experience of the metaphysical absurd by isolating and objectifying it. No magic, no divinity with impenetrable ways is held responsible. Nor are any psychological or sociological explanations given. Ionesco quite simply communicates the bewildering paradox of man's life and the complete absurdity of the mechanism of being.

Those who have termed such theatre a "theatre of the atomic age" are right in that any hope in an efficacious *praxis* has been considerably shaken by a consciousness of the possibility of total destruction. Faced with total destruction, not only do the problems of modern naturalism (homosexuality, drugs, conflicts limited to the levels of family and society) have little weight, but the theme of political revolution loses its acuity and is leveled to the rank of the others. Sartre and Camus needed great exemplary acts to describe the human condition more effectively in their plays. But in the perspective of absolute annihilation, all acts are equalized, in Ionesco as in Beckett.

Not that the end-of-the-world atmosphere is always explicit. Although it is easy to interpret the setting of Beckett's *Fin de partie* as a symbol of the world after the H-bomb, in Ionesco there is but one precise suggestion of it in *les Chaises:*

THE OLD LADY. Paris never existed, my dear.

THE OLD MAN. It must have existed, since it collapsed. It was the city of light, since the light has been out, out, for 4,000 years. . . .

Even if the image is a product of the Old Man's delirium, it still reveals the psychosis of A.D. 1000, an obsession with universal catastrophe—but this time there is no Last Judgement and therefore no hope of redemption in a beatific beyond.

Ionesco never conceptualized the feeling or philosophized on it. He translated it directly into concrete images which the spectator must accept without argument. The "stories" he tells on stage, often parallel to reality, are meant to make the spectator feel it in a particularly vivid and one might say pure way. Both he and Beckett succeeded in recreating a metaphysical atmosphere through intensification. They also succeeded in making that atmosphere the source of two contrary reactions: laughter and pathos.

Ionesco's "tragic farce" is often funny, not only because of its mechanical elements, but because of the application of those elements to apparently trivial situations: the boredom of bourgeois life, the fiancée's three noses, the arrangement of a room. The entire universe may be questioned, but on the individual level, there is no danger of any serious catastrophe. In other situations, when the danger of death becomes evident, all laughter stops and pathos takes over. And the laughter stops—which is not the case even during murder in a play like Jarry's *Ubu Roi*—because the characters are endowed with enough density and humanity to cause an identification with the general vision of the world and individual suffering.

Indeed in this universe, where individuals never communicate among themselves and acts are ineffectual, there is often a desire for communication, an appeal for tenderness expressed in normal terms. The Old Man's whining in *les Chaises* and Bérenger's awkward good will in *Tueur sans gages* and *Rhinocéros* are of that order. From minute to minute the characters' psychological makeups are revealed and, without taking the center of the play, bring the spectator closer to them. Ionesco keeps that one traditional element which enables him to work on both levels (farcical exteriorization and inner psychology) at the same time.

Ionesco claims to have written plays that exclude any traditional psychology:

We will give up the principle of identity and unity of character for the benefit of movement, a dynamic psychology . . . We are not ourselves . . . Personality doesn't exist. Within us, we have merely contradictory and noncontradictory forces.

So declares Nicolas d'Eu in *Victimes du devoir*. He adds further on: "We have Ionesco, and Ionesco is enough!" Here Ionesco presents himself as inventor of the new theatre. But Nicolas' comments are parodic and through them Ionesco simultaneously theorizes about his own works and destroys his theories by ridiculing them. In any case, neither the comments nor the plays eliminate *all* psychology. The psychology he works with is simply new, corresponding to that found in many contemporary French novels. The characters are defined both by their function in the mechanism that surrounds them and by the inner play of their "contradictory and non-contradictory forces." In *Amédée* the cancer of guilt is represented objectively by the ever-growing corpse and the mushrooms that grow in the parlor, and also expressed in psychological terms through the dialogue. In *Tueur sans gages* Bérenger's desires are represented both by the real existence of a modern sun-lit city and the analysis of his inner necessity, and both are combined in the remark:

In short, inner and outer world are bad expressions; there are no boundaries between those so-called two worlds. There is a fundamental impulse, obviously, which comes from us, and when it can't be exteriorized, when it can't be objectively realized, when there is no complete accord between my inner me and my outer me, the result is catastrophe, universal contradiction, the final break.

Bérenger never succeeds in communicating his analysis to the Architect, and there we have a first drama or conflict. But on a deeper level, his comments potentially contain an adventure to come and one he has already gone through within himself, the abrupt transition from joy to melancholy, a "kind of tumultuous vacuum—like at the moment of a tragic separation, intolerable." Just as the new city is the hyperbolic realization of the force of joy within him, so the presence of the Killer and the final murder will be the amplified and extreme realization of the opposite force. Bérenger's inner struggle, given in terms of psychological analysis, is represented in concrete and objective acts and objects. The play is complete and rich because of Ionesco's skill in playing with the four elements of the drama: inner joy, inner vacuum, City of the Sun, Killer—inserting "breaks," as Bérenger calls them, at given points between the subjective and the objective, not relating them symbolically but concomitantly.

A meeting point of contradictory forces, each character carries his universe about with him and goes on with his series of metamorphoses independent of the others. The agonizing drama comes when the character becomes conscious of his solitude and tries to cling to others, like the old people in *les Chaises* or

Bérenger in *Tueur sans gages* and *Rhinocéros*. But whether the character be unaware or anguished, he is always a moving and incoherent being without any real communication with others. In rejecting conventional psychology, which has been transcended by modern science and no longer corresponds to living experience, Ionesco once again presents the chaos and mystery of the individual.

Absence of communication in the actual farces is expressed by all types of puns, long automatic speeches, meaningless dialogue in which the characters answer *as if* they were communicating. In the more serious plays, the drama is based in part on the hero's desperate attempts to communicate. In *Tueur sans gages* Bérenger confides in the Architect but his words fall on deaf ears, and his long final monologue never gets through to the Killer and ends destroyed by its own logic. The same Bérenger in *Rhinocéros* watches his friend Jean and the woman he loves gradually escape from him, moving further and further away as they are transformed into rhinoceroses. In addition to the many themes it symbolizes, the herd of rhinoceroses at the end represents the vague mass of the *Others*, with whom the hero can no longer communicate.

Ionesco does no more than portray the situation. But his portrayal has a special meaning. As Rosette Lamont notes with regard to *les Chaises:* "It is a twentieth century morality play which does not preach. The message of the play is an anti-message: speech, art, communication of any sort, are the illusions man needs while there is breath." At the end of *les Chaises* the Orator entrusted with communicating the Old Man's message is able only to emit "the gutteral sounds of a mute" and writes an obscure word on the blackboard, disconnected letters from which the word "Adieu" is finally made out. Ionesco thus emphasizes the vanity or vacuity of what everyone is trying to communicate.

This point of view has led Ionesco to a special attitude with regard to his own works. Having produced a meaningless mirror of a meaningless world, it would be impossible for him to take the first any more seriously than the second. Whence a general indifference to what the director does or could do to the text of his plays. As his aim is to represent the absence of gravity and justification as effectively as possible, only the effect counts, and the playwright himself shows no great respect for his own text. One has only to read Ionesco's ironic notes on Nicolas Bataille's changes for the staging of *la Cantatrice chauve,* or his "indications" for the staging of *Tueur sans gages,* in which he authorizes "all the cuts needed" in the second act, or the different possibilities of ending *l'Avenir est dans les oeufs.* When he carefully gives details on how to stage his plays, on the rhythm to follow, etc., he does so either to make the director's job easier or to make certain of a particular ef-

fect on the spectator, and not in the name of his sovereignty as a poet or the esthetic perfection of his play.

As Ionesco's message is that there is no message, he would never think of transforming his feelings into dogma. What he tries to do is reproduce on stage the tension between the individual's activities and fantasies and the vacuum in which they are suspended. The elements he embodies them in *directly*—that is, without arguments, theories, or abstractions—come from his inner imagery.

> Theatre for me is the projection on stage of the inner world. I reserve the right to take this theatrical material from my dreams, my obscure desires, my inner contradictions.

Such are Ionesco's words in *l'Impromptu de l'Alma* before he mocks his own serious and academic tone. The "material" itself is held up to ridicule, exploded by its own contradictions, or shown as absurd. What remains is a brutal and simple image, objective and concrete, which shows either a return to his original anguish (the sneers of an invisible mob in the empty décor of *les Chaises*), or annihilation (the final collapse in *l Avenir,* Bérenger on his knees before the Killer in *Tueur sans gages*), or the stabilization of an inexorable and unjustified mechanism (end of *Victimes du devoir, la Leçon,* and in a comic vein, *la Cantatrice chauve*), or in grotesque and spectacular fantasy (end of *Amédée*).

Ionesco's conclusions, usually theatrical, are a kind of negation of everything that went before, with either the tragic situation held up to ridicule or "annihilated," or its adventurous quality negated by the idea of beginning again, making it an interchangeable link in an undefined chain which relates to nothing. However the end of *Rhinocéros* is somewhat ambiguous. As all humanity is transformed into rhinoceroses, Bérenger, the only remaining man, surrounded by the rhinoceroses, and after having gone through the temptation of also becoming transformed, cries out: "I am the last man, I will remain so to the end! I will not surrender!" His refusal could be compared to the "no" of Anouilh's heroes—Antigone, Joan of Arc. And indeed instead of accepting defeat as in *Tueur sans gages,* Bérenger protests. His protest might be seen as Ionesco's first positive "message." But could it not also be interpreted as a standstill more than a victory? The curtain goes down on an immobilization and not a solution of the conflict between the desperate resistance of an individual to the superabundance of massive and mechanical being, presented in an extreme form.

A new psychology, absence of communication, the anti-message, unresolvable agony—such elements of seriousness and pathos do not keep Ionesco's theatre from being closely related to farce. For whether they be considered "tragic" or "metaphysical," Ionesco's plays present characters that are not on the same level as the spectator, that is, their existence is inferior to what the spectator considers his own. Whereas serious theatre stylizes man, traditional farce partly humanizes objects. The spectator's laughter and satisfaction come from the humanized object's failure to imitate life. The clown imitating a man of the world, the marionette aping a lover, the puppet Ubu imitating Macbeth or Richard III, are so many silhouettes, inferior forms that never succeed in being equal to their own ambitions and never reach the consistency and weight of their human objective's existence. The puppet is constantly called to order by a continual resurgence of mechanical forces that limit his imitation, thus provoking laughter.

And so it is in the works of Ionesco. Yet his true farcical moments have a very special flavor in that, while the mechanism, object, or puppet is given in advance, the human element is given as a *real* dimension—however stifled and impossible, or almost impossible, to bring out. Where the hero of traditional farce is satisfied with himself and believes in his own success, the hero of modern farce is conscious of his failure. At that level, the laughter stops and the farce becomes "dark." In a Romantic world, the laughter stops when the clown starts to cry; but Ionesco has replaced sentimentality by an anguish which excludes self-pity through protest. Using the mechanism of objects, expressionistic masks, and schematic and fantastic worlds, he has created a farce in which an embryonic humanity is unsuccessful in transcending the anguished consciousness of an inferior existence.

Even "darker" is the implication that Creation itself is nothing other than the mechanical ballet of sorrowful and grotesque masks, continuing on its own momentum, without justification and without control. Called anti-theatre by many critics, despite the fact that all the theatrical elements are included, such farce might be better termed *Théâtre en liberté* or liberated theatre, the mirror of the world as a nonsensical mechanism, mad in its ways, and thus giving the playwright complete freedom to indulge his fantasies. (pp. 178-92)

Jacques Guicharnaud and June Beckelman, "A World Out of Control: Eugene Ionesco," in their *Modern French Theatre from Giraudoux to Beckett,* Yale University Press, 1961, pp. 178-92.

EUGÈNE IONESCO WITH RONALD HAYMAN

(interview date 1972)

[The following interview was first published in *Transatlantic Review* in 1972. Here, Ionesco and Hayman explore several of Ionesco's works, noting the theo-

logical, psychological, and philosophical theories behind them.]

[Ronald Hayman]: *In* **The Bald Soprano** *and* **The Lesson** *you seem to have been writing dialogue without visualizing the room in which the action was taking place. Would it be fair to say that you started thinking about the decor around the time of* **Jacques** *and* **The Chairs?**

[Eugene Ionesco]: Yes, there was already some visualization in *Jacques,* the third play, and certainly in the following plays. In *Amédée* there is the corpse which grows, and in *The Chairs* it was a visualization of my angst. In the first two plays there was no need for scenery, except for some sort of bourgeois interior for *Soprano.* For me, all that mattered was the dialogue, but then I came to understand that dialogue is only a small part of a play.

Did the experience of acting in The Possessed *make much difference to you?*

That was very unpleasant.

Why?

Because I had the impression of being someone else. An actor needs a certain generosity. He needs to be able to forget himself and lend his own personality to the imaginary character, and I felt alienated. And recently, in September and October of last year (1970) I made a film based on a short story I wrote called *La vase.* I played my own character but even then I felt uncomfortable. I had the impression of being a prisoner of my own character. Acting is a sort of exhibitionism I do not like. I am an exhibitionist but through other people. Perhaps it's hypocrisy or modesty. But modesty is hypocrisy. In any case, I prefer writing for other people to play my lines.

In the first two plays there is no character with any resemblance at all to you. Then **Amédée** *has a little, not very much.*

I don't think so, he's an invented character.

What about Bérenger?

Perhaps there's some resemblance there. I spoke to the audience more directly.

You've cited the distinction Croce made between intuitive thought and discursive thought and you've said that discursive thought should be prevented from intervening in drama . . .

Croce said that intuitive thought is thought which is specific to literature and art, etc. Art is the expression of intuitive thought and what interested me about Croce is that he provided, perhaps for the first time, a more secure means of knowing whether a work of art is valid or not. He provided a more precise criterion by saying that each time there is something new in the expression—each time there is originality—there's probably merit. The history of art is the history of expression, expression being form and substance at the same time.

But the way that ideas come into Bérenger's dialogue in plays like **A Stroll in the Air** *is very different from the presentation of banal ideas in the early plays.*

Yes, they're plays which give the impression of being more ideological than the others, but it's not the ideology that's important. If you take Pirandello's plays, you see that the psychological theories are very out of date but it's not the ideas that count, it's the passions which the ideas clothe. You can create a very valuable work with a bad ideology, even with banal philosophical ideas. The most important example is Shakespeare himself. His philosophy had been familiar since the time of King Solomon, who said that all is vanity, but what matters is the way the ideas are lived and become flesh and blood.

Was there any particular reason for dropping the name Bérenger after **A Stroll in the Air?**

Just to make a change.

When did you first get interested in [Alfred] Jarry and 'Pataphysics?

Jarry since I was fifteen; 'Pataphysics more recently because it didn't exist—at least not in a visible form—until about 1948 or '50 with the College of 'Pataphysics. But of course 'Pataphysics existed before, it exists now and it will exist tomorrow. Everything's 'Pataphysics. What we're saying now is 'Pataphysics.

Richard Coe said that with **A Stroll in the Air** *you moved further away from 'Pataphysics.*

Yes, it's less important for me now, I think. That's 'Pataphysics without 'Pataphysics. I catch myself at the game of message bearing. I have always been against message in literature because I believe, as Nabokov put it, that the writer shouldn't deliver messages because he isn't a mailman. But I notice there are messages in what I wrote, though not the messages that people expect of me. Critics reproach me for not having a social or Marxist or Brechtian message.

You have a sympathy with [Emmanuel] Mounier's personalism?

Yes, to a certain extent. Especially around 1938 when I knew him, there was reason to be afraid of totalitarianism and Mounier's attitude was interesting. To be humane, the individual has to give himself to others. In face of the enemies of humanity, human society preserves its individuality but justifies it socially . . .

What about [Martin] Buber and Hasidism?

That's something quite different. That's my penchant for metaphysics. I don't know whether there are any signs of Buber's influence in my plays.

There are critics who say you are serious about the ideas of the antiworld that Bérenger puts forward in **A Stroll in the Air.**

In physics there is still talk of the antiworld and of antimatter. Heisenberg for example . . .

In **Fragments of a Journal** *you talk a great deal about dreams.*

It isn't the unconscious that dominates in dreams, it's a sharper form of consciousness. Dreaming is a sort of thinking in words and images, and precisely because the external world is no longer there, one can fall back on oneself. It's a moment of meditation. Dreams are always dramas; one is always in a situation. Jung said that the dream is a play in which one is author, actor and audience. It's total theatre.

But you believe that what is said in dreams is true?

Certainly consciousness is censored by the unconscious and vice versa. You can have very precise insights in dreams. Things appear in them with great clarity. There's a lot of talk about dreams but we don't trust them. We hear about the dreams of Descartes and it seems that the French physician Lucien Poincaré invented his theory when he was dreaming. One communes with oneself. Now, with psychoanalysis we interpret dreams but it seems to me that dreams themselves are an interpretation. It can be the truth.

You prefer Jung to Freud?

Yes.

Because he leaves the door open for religion?

Yes, he doesn't exclude it. He says that it's an imperative need. He makes no religious pronouncements himself but psychologically one needs God and no doubt that corresponds to a certain reality.

But that doesn't prove that God exists?

We don't know. That's where the betting begins.

Already in **The Lesson** *the Maid becomes motherly towards the Professor and in several of your plays, from* **The Chairs** *to* **Hunger and Thirst,** *the wife seems to be capable of mothering the man.*

She is. By her nature. We are all sons of woman . . .

The concierge who figures in so many of your plays has been called a symbol of the bourgeoisie.

Yes. The universal bourgeoisie.

It is possible to read into **The Lesson**—*among other things*—*a criticism of the conventional educational system.*

You can draw a lesson from anything. Even from a lesson. And you can find things of which the author was not conscious. For me, it was a game—games with words—but perhaps there are some memories, more or less conscious, of the difficulties I had when studying philology. But the purpose is also different . . . This language is empty. It no longer corresponds to anything. A sort of emptiness of language and a refusal of its call to culture. For the Professor words are just means of taking possession of a human being and through all his verbiage and word play, underneath this superficial culture, there is instinctual reality which this language masks or unmasks.

There's a very interesting connection between the Professor and the Monks in **Hunger and Thirst.**

Perhaps . . .

It's sometimes said that your plays are better without intermissions.

Yes, I've never liked intermissions because I think one should be able to move a play from one point to the next without interruption. There is a sort of progression in my plays which shouldn't be broken. In *The Killer* there was no intermission because it is a very short play, but *Exit the King* lasts one and a half hours without intermission. *Killing Game* lasts two hours or one hour fifty minutes without intermissions. In the eighteenth century the intermission was indispensable. In Racine's plays each act lasts for twenty-five minutes for the simple reason that the candles had to be renewed. And in the nineteenth century there were intermissions because theater was mundane and bourgeois and people needed to see each other and chat as if they were at a party. But the Greeks had no intermissions and the Japanese Noh Theater has no intermissions.

And in **Hunger and Thirst** *the intermissions are one of the reasons you constructed the play in the way you did.*

Exactly. Each act was constructed to some extent separately from the others, constituting a little play in itself.

For instance, it is difficult to see any relationship between Aunt Adelaide in Act One and Brechtoll and Tripp in Act Three.

Yes, you're right. I think that *Hunger and Thirst* is the only play to have been constructed with a view to intermissions. Certainly one doesn't see the relationship between the three acts and it's a bit like three plays but after the departure from the house it's a sort of quest, which becomes visible in Act Two and is concluded in Act Three. But in my opinion, if you have several intermediate acts, not just one, the play regains a certain unity. I wrote another act to put between the second and third (which would become the fourth). In the second act it's an amorous quest and in the act I wrote later to be inserted, it's a quest for consciousness, for example. You could have several quests. In fact I think I was a bit influenced by a play like Claudel's *Le soulier de satin.* It's a long quest. The first act and the last act remain as they are, but one could have in between several acts or several scenes. . . .

You once said that what we need is a new surrealism.

Yes, certainly, because most of the surrealists have become writers with a message, while others have been more or less suffering from hardening of the arteries. That's to say that automatic writing has become very automatic. The surrealists have got into bad ethical habits. What we need is a new thrust. The barriers

need to be broken all over again for the interior world to come out into the open, to demolish the barriers of conscience and prejudice. The stream of consciousness has to overflow.

It's odd that no one before you made surrealism viable in the theater.

There have been surrealist plays. There was Vitrac and there were plays I do not know by Breton and Soupault. And I think there was even a dadaist play. But surrealism became formalist; the avant garde fell into academicism.

It was interesting in **Fragments of a Journal** *you found five distinct meanings for the word "absurd." I often think that the playwrights of the so called theater of the absurd have very little in common.*

Yes. I find that the name "theater of the absurd" which has been glued on to us is absolutely meaningless. All theater is absurd. Shakespeare makes Macbeth say life is a tale told by an idiot, signifying nothing. It seems to me that there are only two possibilities if you want to write drama which bears on fundamental problems: either it is agnostic, which isn't the same as absurd, or it's religious, like the theater of Claudel. It must say either yes or no to religion. . . .

In **Notes and Counter Notes** *you say that since we don't want to die we must be* intended *to be immortal.*

Yes, I think we should be immortal. That's why we are afraid of dying. We feel that we should be made to be immortal.

But if mortality is the fundamental fact of human, animal and vegetable existence . . .

You can accept, you can resign yourself, you can have some faith or other in obeying the rules of what is called nature. But the human condition is inadmissible.

Having to get older, being diminished—it's inadmissible. Having to die is a condition which I reject.

You say that it's incredible that man has accepted it for centuries but what else is there to do?

One rejects it uselessly, I admit, but it's a law I won't accept.

If only there were a way of disobeying it . . .

Yes.

You say that since you were young you have had very little contact with the young and especially when you were young yourself.

Yes. My youth was spent partly in France, partly in Romania, where I saw the hatching of the Nazi movement. At that time everybody was a Nazi just as today everybody is an extreme leftist. If someone said he was a democrat then, he would have been lynched and the best spirits of the time, the intellectuals, were fascists, just as the intellectuals of today are leftists.

Zero Mostel as John and Eli Wallach as Bérenger in a 1961 production of *Rhinoceros.*

The banners are different but the fanaticism is the same. Books are even being burned, as in the old days, and there's antisemitism under cover of anti-Zionism. If you are against communism you are against democracy. Anglo-Saxons are detested, just as in the Nazi times. I find that very disquieting. You cannot read *Mein Kampf* today in the way that Mao's little red book is read, but the little red book is even worse than *Mein Kampf.* To me it seems there's a certain diabolical aggressiveness, a fanaticism which just changes its banner.

I very much like what you've said about politics as being a means of keeping people apart rather than bringing them together.

Yes, I felt very ill at ease then, in the same way as I do today. Now, as then, there's no friendship among the young, only camaraderie. And camaraderie is finally solitude in common. The world suffers from the fact that people cannot assume the right to be solitary. In the past there were solitaries. Now solitude is a catastrophe, a trauma. But people don't escape into themselves and even if one is with other people who march in rhythm, the fashion is to hide one's own solitude—but without escaping it . . .

You have said that it's out of fear of death that people kill each other.

I think it is that. It's to be ahead of death. And

then there are other reasons. People detest themselves and they kill themselves in others. They kill the other so as not to have to kill the self. The vitalism we saw earlier in German youth—their *élan vital*—was finally seen to be an enormous collective suicide. There are many reasons for suicide and fear of death is an important one. There are characters in Dostoevsky who were afraid of death but still wanted to kill themselves—perhaps for other reasons too—because they wanted to be free vis-à-vis God—to be stronger than God, not to accept the power of God. Kirilov in *The Possessed* kills himself because life is a sort of death . . .

In **Hunger and Thirst** *you obviously intend Brechtoll to be a representative of left wing totalitarianism and Tripp to be a fascist.*

Yes, but the most exploratory totalitarianism is that of the monks. Brechtoll and Tripp still think. They're ideologues and the dogmas of one neutralize the dogmas of the other, and it all ends by drowning itself in an impersonal totalitarianism which spies on us.

You have used the word nihilism but surely it isn't nihilistic to insist that neither form of belief is worth dying for?

Death is unacceptable and the conditions existing in heaven are almost equally unacceptable if our condition is reflected in that of heaven. You feel the malaise everywhere. It is the reason there have been so many social reformers, so many prophets. That's the reason for what is called progress. We are all unsatisfied with our condition and want to change it, so we follow this or that prophet or ideologue or revolutionary . . .

What is your attitude to existentialism?

I am not against existentialism. I am against the fact that Sartre, out of hatred for what he calls the bourgeoisie, destroyed documentary evidence he had about Soviet concentration camps. Which was very serious, because he had a great influence at that time. His political behavior was irresponsible, childish, and criminal at the same time.

But you don't agree with existentialism, do you? You're an essentialist, aren't you?

Yes. I am not enough of a specialist in philosophy to have precise ideas.

You have said "Nothing can change what I am but I exist in different fashions."

I had forgotten what I'd written. One's life changes every two weeks or so and it isn't coherent philosophies I've been presenting but passions and desires. I have found support in one idea and another according to the inclination of the moment. I am agnostic and desperate at not having some faith or other. (pp. 5-16)

Eugene Ionesco and Ronald Hayman, in an interview in *Eugène*

Ionesco by Ronald Hayman, Frederick Ungar Publishing Co., 1976, pp. 5-16.

ROSETTE C. LAMONT
(essay date 1973)

[In the excerpt below, Lamont examines Ionesco's varied dramas, asserting that "there are a number of different Ionescos."]

In June 1959 in the course of a talk that inaugurated the *Helsinki Debates on the Avant-Garde Theatre,* Ionesco made the following declaration:

> It has been said that what distinguishes man from the other animals is that he is the animal that laughs; he is above all the animal that creates. He introduces into the world things which were not there before: temples and rabbit hutches, wheelbarrows, locomotives, symphonies, poems, cathedrals and cigarettes. The usefulness of all these things is often only a pretext. What is the use of existing? To exist. What is the use of a flower? To be a flower. Of what use is a temple or a cathedral? To house the faithful? I doubt it, since the temples are no longer used and we still admire them. They serve to reveal to us the laws of architecture, and perhaps of universal construction, which are apparently reflected in our mind since the mind discovers these laws within itself.

For the playwright, a work of art is an autonomous universe, governed by its own laws. It is not an imitation of what we call our world, nor is it totally unlike that world; one could say that it is a self-contained construct, parallel to ours.

How do we as readers, or viewers of plays, approach and understand this strange world? It could be said that we are like a person who enters an unfamiliar house. We wander from room to room, floor to floor, sometimes in the dark, till, gradually, we get to know where the hallway leads, what is behind each door, how the architect has apportioned space, and what materials he has used. If this house is well put together we may linger, and if it speaks to us, fills us with its peculiar charm, we may be inclined to dwell there forever, or at least to return to it frequently. If we are teachers, or critics, or both, we will describe this home, lovingly, wishing to draw our friends' attention to cunning detail of the moulding, to a secret passage between rooms, or simply to the soundness of the whole construction.

On the surface Ionescoland is deceptively like our own. The modest clerks, mailmen, police officers, *concierges,* maids, married couples, maidens to marry, and apprehensive bachelors are the very people we see and overhear on the streets of Paris every day. We are lulled into believing there will be no surprises. One of the creators of Surrealism, Philippe Soupault, writes in a special Ionesco issue of *Les Cahiers des Saisons* (Hiver 1959) of Ionesco's "natural tone." The same Soupault, however, recognizes a younger brother, or an heir, when he suggests: "Eugene Ionesco, perhaps without meaning to, unleashes something scandalous the moment actors agree to speak his lines as he has written them." Is it because of the playwright's inner search for sincerity, his desire to reach a truth beyond that of so-called reality? Is it because, as Pierre-Aimé Touchard says in the same issue of the review, Ionesco has re-invented and resurrected myths? At any rate, we realize quite soon that the overstuffed pieces of furniture so much like the ones we inherited from aunt Marie, the clichés which pass for conversation, have deceived us into believing we knew exactly where we were. We are actually on the other side of the looking glass. There, one is condemned to run as fast as one can just to stay in place. Under our feet the earth sinks, the air sucks us up. The low fire we started in the fireplace to warm our bones becomes a conflagration, engulfs our planet. A little affection turns into an ocean of eros and drowns us. The four elements fuse into "deserts of ice, deserts of fire battling with each other and all coming slowly towards us . . . " (*The Stroller in Air*). We have awakened in the world of our private nightmares, issuing from a very ancient deposit to which all mankind may lay claim. This universe of myth, the crystallization of a poet's meditation, is as intimate as the secret recesses of our bodies, and as wide as the unconfined reaches of our dreams.

It took a while for Eugene Ionesco to become Ionesco. He was thirty-eight years old when his first play, *The Bald Soprano,* was presented to a very small public at the *Noctambules* theatre. It was not written as a play, but as a kind of exercise coming out of the future playwright's painful attempts to master the English language. Using the *Assimil* conversation method, Ionesco found himself in the company of an English couple, Mr. and Mrs. Smith. The Smiths seemed to find it necessary to inform one another that the ceiling was overhead, the floor underfoot, the week made up of seven days, and that they were having a fine English meal served by their maid Mary. It was at this point in the textbook reading that Ionesco was possessed by a strange excitement, utterly out of proportion either with the discussion held by this dull couple, or the task of learning English. Dizzy, as though he had received a solid knock on the head, the would-be student had to lie down, and not unlike the narrator of Proust's *A la recherche du temps perdu,* turn within in search of reasons for his rapture. Intelligence soon registered that what had happened was a take-over by the characters of *L'Anglais tel qu'on le parle;* the latter were writing their own lines. Thus what had begun as a didactic form of plagiarism obeyed, all of a sudden, mysterious laws surging from some dark night of the soul. Ionesco's *Discours de la Méthode* which he had considered calling *English Made Easy* or *The English Hour* kept on growing into a distorted vision: worthy bourgeois couples, struck with amnesia, failed to recognize one another even upon discovering they shared the same room and bed; inhabitants of a city—"men, women, children, cats and ideologists"—were all called Bobby Watson. To add to this confusion, "a fifth and unexpected character turned up to cause more trouble between the peaceable couples: The Captain of the Fire Brigade." The announcement of this emergence must have failed to surprise Ionesco's Italian audience at the French Institute where he was explaining, in 1958, the genesis of his play. In Italy the Captain of the Fire Brigade has a famous predecessor. Madame Pace, a dressmaker in *Six Characters in Search of an Author* whose shop is also a brothel, appears out of nowhere at the moment the Daughter relives before us the incestuous encounter with the Stepfather. Pirandello's character "comes to birth," evoked by the sheer magic of dramatic re-enactment. In *The Bald Soprano,* as in Pirandello's play, the strange happenings serve to sever the drama and the author from the habitual, an element in which most of us are constantly immersed as in some tepid bath. To be "bludgeoned" (*Notes and Counter Notes*) out of our natural mental sloth, we must be ready to endure the dangers of anarchic humor whose cathartic violence mingles with that brought about by the feelings of pity and terror. From then on, Ionesco was committed to the wild exaggerations of parody, for in the creation of what he had assumed was "a comedy on comedy," he had actually written "the tragedy of language."

Ionesco's plays are neither tragedies nor comedies but tragi-comedies or comitragedies. Since 186 B.C., when Plautus spoke of *tragicocomoedia* in his *Amphitryon,* the clearly separated genres began to come together. Till our own era, however, this meant that comic scenes came to relieve tragic events. Today, an interfusion has occurred lending comic coloring to tragic happenings and somber coloring to comic ones. Like Gogol's *Dead Souls,* the anti-plays of Beckett, Ionesco, Adamov, Dubillard, Arrabal, and Weingarten elicit "laughter through tears." In his essay, **"Experience of the Theatre,"** published in *Notes and Counter Notes,* Ionesco states:

> It seems to me that the comic is tragic, and that the tragedy of man is pure derision. The contemporary critical mind takes nothing too seriously or too lightly. In *Victims of Duty* I tried to sink comedy in tragedy: in *The Chairs* tragedy in comedy, or, if you like, to confront comedy and tragedy in order to link them in a new dramatic synthesis. But it is not a true synthesis for these two elements do not coalesce,

they coexist: one constantly repels the other, they show each other up, criticize and deny one another and, thanks to their opposition, thus succeed dynamically in maintaining a balance and creating tension.

It is becoming increasingly evident that this tragi-comic mode expresses our ironic age. Comedy, which traditionally involved detachment and even a sense of superiority on the part of the viewer, who was not forced to imagine that such absurd reverses of fortune could happen to him, seems less and less likely to speak to a generation that has witnessed shifts in political ideologies, violent upheavals, the disappearance of societies, the genocidal annihilation of millions. We can no longer afford to be detached from the rest of humanity, though we tend to be detached from ourselves. This brings us closer to tragedy which, traditionally, presents to the viewer the fate of individual human beings, and thus an image of his own destiny. At the same time we are distanced from it by the fact that its usual hero, the personage in high position, is one that our modern era is wary of, seeing in him or her more often than not the destroyer, the embodiment of tyranny. Tragicomedy, on the other hand, presents basically ordinary characters, types we can identify with. Thus when Ionesco writes—"When the fallen Richard II is a prisoner in his cell, abandoned and alone, it is not Richard II I see there, but all the fallen kings of this world; and not only fallen kings, but also our beliefs and values, our unsanctified, corrupt and worn-out truths, the crumbling of civilizations, the march of destiny. When Richard II dies, it is really the death of all I hold most dear that I am watching; it is I who die with Richard II" (*Notes and Counter Notes*)—he gives a perfect definition of the meaning of tragedy. His own dying king, Bérenger I, is a mixture of grotesque dignity and clownish fears; he is the common man facing dissolution. We laugh not *at* Bérenger but at ourselves; we share his anxieties, his desperate clinging to life; we cry because he must die at the end of the play, and because we must die at the end of the play which is our life.

Ionesco's *Exit the King* is a triumphant example of the tragicomic mode. It is a play about the apprenticeship of death which provides an affirmation of the act of living. This farce manages to blend humor and anguish, echoing at the same time the fear and trembling of Pascal and Kierkegaard, and the patient wisdom in regard to physical suffering of the Montaigne of *De l'Expérience.* It is a philosophical cartoon, bitter, yet immensely tender.

Nor does the playwright limit himself to portraying a dying man; he depicts a dying world, and the ultimate, apocalyptic disappearance of our planet. Scientific progress and the development of civilization are brilliantly derided in this play. The King, we are told by the Guard who serves as chorus, has lived for hundreds of years, not unlike Rabelais' giants. During that time he has invented steel, balloons, airplanes, has built Rome, New York, Paris, and Moscow. He has made revolutions and counter-revolutions, Reformation and Counter-reformation. He has created literature by writing *The Iliad* and *The Odyssey,* and it is he, not Bacon, who composed the tragedies and comedies of Elizabethan England under the pseudonym of Shakespeare. Yet, after his death, he will be only a page in a book of ten thousand pages, in a volume placed in a library among a million libraries. Then the books will yellow, the pages turn to dust. The planet will grow cold and die. All so-called immortality is temporary, and thus relative. "What must come to an end is already ended," cries out Bérenger. The unavoidable truth is man's mortality, and by making this the theme of one of his greatest tragicomedies, Ionesco has also written one of the most profound dramatic poems on death and dying in our century.

There are a number of different Ionescos. The author of *The Bald Soprano, The Lesson, Jack or Submission* sets in motion the mechanism of the theatre to portray aimless passions. Later in *Amédée,* even in *The Chairs,* metaphysical considerations are expressed by the motion of objects, the proliferation of matter. *Victims of Duty,* Ionesco's favorite drama, is confessional, *Hunger and Thirst,* allegorical. The most philosophic of Ionesco's plays is *Exit the King. Rhinoceros, The Killer,* and *Macbett* are mostly political.

Ionesco says over and over again that he is not a political writer. In "The London Controversy" which opposed Ionesco and Kenneth Tynan, one can follow the outlines of two programs. Tynan expresses fear at the thought that Ionesco's bleak new world may infect the age. An admirer of Brecht's Marxist theories, Tynan believes that art and ideology interact and "spring from a common source." In an answer which was never published by *The Observer* but which appears in *Notes and Counter Notes,* Ionesco makes his position clear: Tynan defends a narrow realism, socialist realism. True society is extrasocial. Socialist paradises have not been able to abolish, or even diminish the pain of living, the pain of death. What we have in common is our human condition. A revolution is a change in mentality; a language must be created to convey this change. Gradually what Tynan "calls anti-reality (becomes) clear, . . . the incommunicable (is) communicated." Man is not a social function; he is a solitude. Only by probing that solitary state, and bringing to the stage some of the images crystallizing at the bottom of the soul, do we rejoin other human beings.

Though Ionesco may not admit to it, he is passionately interested in politics. His view is not narrow; he neither preaches nor teaches, but he is always ready to denounce the cruelties of so-called ideologies, the inhumanity of man to man, in the name of future generations. His *Journals (Fragments of a Journal, Present Past Past Present*), the numerous articles he has written for *Le Figaro,* testify to his gifts as a pamphleteer, and to his commitment to fighting oppression, or the more subtle pressures of cliché opinions. It will become obvious as one looks back upon his body of work that Ionesco has written some of the most potent political satires of the second half of the twentieth century.

"My hero, if you can call him that," says Ionesco in conversation, "is not so much an anti-hero as a hero in spite of himself. When I was a young man in Rumania—that was after I left France to spend some time with my father—I remember how everyone around me converted to fascism, till it seemed to me that I was the only one left in the world. My own father had chameleonic gifts, and could always persuade himself that the present government was in the right. After all, History knew where it was going. It seemed to me at the time that although I was the most insignificant of creatures a terrible responsibility had befallen me, and that, somehow, I would have to do something, or rather *everything.* Isn't this the plight and privilege of the modern hero?"

Ionesco's Bérenger, the protagonist of *The Killer* and of *Rhinoceros* is indeed that hero-in-spite-of-himself who has become the central figure of much of our contemporary literature. He is the common man— "Bérenger, an average, middle-aged citizen." Unlike Molière's *raisonneur,* he speaks for unreason; for however modest or even humble he is, he thinks and feels as poets do. Patience, passive resistance, the silent rebellion of the spirit are his virtues.

Rhinoceros shows an entire community afflicted with *rhinoceritis,* the malady of conformity. Average men and women, but also philosophers, intellectuals, all catch the bug. Only Bérenger retains his humanity, and towards the end, when he is all alone, he begins to feel most uncomfortable with his white, human skin covered with light body hair since the brutes around him seem to rejoice in their thick, green hides.

The protagonist of *The Killer* (The French title is *Tueur sans gages* which is a reversal of the expression *tueur à gages,* hired assasin, thus stressing the gratuitous quality of this murder) tries to make his way to the police station through the goose-stepping throngs of Mother Peep's followers. Mother Peep, the new leader, who bears a disturbing resemblance to the *concierge* of Act I, shouts: "We'll replace the myths by slogans." Bérenger must reach the police, for he has found in the briefcase of his office friend, Edouard, the plans of the murderer who is destroying the citizens of the "radiant city." A weak, sickly man, Edouard denies any knowledge of the documents found among his papers; the killer's schedule second by second, the colonel's picture the murderer uses as bait, the complete list of his victims—all these have just slipped in among other plans.

When Bérenger says with some indignation: "After all you don't mean to say that these things got here all by themselves!" Edouard answers, not unlike Eichman at his trial: "I can't explain, I don't understand." Edouard believes that these documents, which were handed to him with a view towards publication, were "only projects, imaginary projects." So was *Mein Kampf!* At the end of the play, in an empty lot, Bérenger meets the killer, face to face. In a soliloquy which seems to be half of a dialogue—but the assassin's only answer is a shrug of the shoulders, a snicker, the flicker of a knife—Bérenger attempts to reason with the killer. Does he hate all human beings? Does he have any conception of happiness? Soon, it becomes clear that communication with such a creature is impossible. To take life is an absurd action. To argue with absurdity is to deliver oneself to its blind forces. Bérenger finds that he is driven to argue not against the murderer but with him, for him; the more he talks, the more reasons he finds for killing, or rather being killed. Though he is armed, Bérenger knows that he, a humanist, will not be able to bring himself to shoot even an enemy who means to destroy him. He says: "And what good are bullets against the resistance of an infinitely stubborn will?" He lays down his pistols, accepting his demise with a strange dignity and despair. In his *Journals* Ionesco writes:

> The greatest crime of all is homicide. Cain kills Abel. That's the crime *par excellence.* And we keep on killing. I have to kill my obvious enemy, the one who is trying to put me to death, in order that he shall not kill me. In killing him I find relief, for I am obscurely aware that I have killed death; I am not responsible for his death, I can feel no anxiety on that account, if have killed my adversary with the approval of the community; that's what wars are for, to enable one to kill with a clear conscience. By killing I exorcize my own death; the act of killing is part of a magic rite. (*Fragments of a Journal*)

Does Bérenger realize that he is the sacrificial victim of a magic rite? At least, we can say that Ionesco knows that our society is based on the ruthless eradication of individuals, sometimes of a whole class. Yet, "History is shrewd" as Lenin said. This is the *leitmotiv* of many of Ionesco's *Journal* entries. It reappears in his *Macbett*.

Ionesco's cartoon version of *Macbeth* is a witty exposition of that well-known fact that absolute power corrupts absolutely. In this great mechanism put together by Ionesco "to make you laugh for fear you'll weep instead," rulers and their generals are strapped to the tiny wheels of the infernal machine of power. Sovereigns, barons, princes of the church, those in power and those who seek that power pursue each other, dethrone one another, slaughter enemies, former friends and allies, entire nations. A king falls; another takes his place and his wife. Le Roi est mort, vive le Roi! Each

succeeding sovereign is more blood-thirsty than his predecessor, grown monstrous through the pursuit of power, and the desire to retain what he has gained at the price of his former virtue, his loyalty, his innocence. Ionesco, by his own admission, is giving us a re-reading of *Macbeth* filtered through the grotesquely ironic text of Jarry's *Ubu.*

Jarry, the inventor of Pataphysics—the science of imaginary solutions—is in more ways than one Ionesco's spiritual ancestor. Ubu the King is the first destroyer of language. His expressionistic opening word, a variation on a famous curse word, marks the beginning of that malady the philosopher Brice Parain diagnoses as "word ache." The new idiom of the avant-garde theatre is the result of the inflation suffered by language after the First World War. Inflation, as we know, is characterized by the fact that although prices remain the same currency decreases in value. Language suffered a similar crisis. War, with its inflated rhetoric, its propaganda, its diplomatic double talk allowing for broken promises, sapped the very essence of communication. In the lull between two world wars, Communism and Fascism flowered upon the debris of words and ideas. They made a meal of the clichés available to them while clamoring that words should be action. The Dadaists during the war of 1914, the Surrealists in the twenties were the first to realize the state of bankruptcy that had befallen language. They sought to create works which would be adventures in linguistic terrorism. Words would have to be destroyed by words. To perform this task the poet had to place side by side words which would ignite one another and be consumed. These exiled humanists, whose hatred for language is a disguised form of longing and love, admit that man, the only animal who speaks, *is* his language; that man secretes words to make of them his protective shell. Left with clichés, empty words for empty minds, the contemporary dramatists use them with a vengeance, not unlike the way in which Pop artists make use of Coca-Cola bottles, or Campbell soup cans. Thus the new writers weave from the web of commonplace expressions a language whose new synthetic texture reveals the monstrous realities of our atomic age.

Did Ionesco invent a new language or was he invented by it? The question need not be answered though it must be posited. "I write to know what I am thinking," he likes to proclaim. But the manner in which one writes alters one's thought patterns. "Man is language" affirms the poet Francis Ponge, while the young American poet, Robert Sward writes: "A dog is said Dog! Or by name." Once a writer has given an object a name, the word becomes the thing. Poets knew this before it was stated by the philosopher Wittgenstein, for the poet must constantly give birth to language anew, and thus reinvent his basic tools. Words are charged with previous associations. To free himself of dead images, to fight his way through the tangle of signs, the writer must strip words of the layers of filth which obscure their meaning, lifting the filmy surface as skillfully as a surgeon removes cataracts. In his essay on the poet Ponge, Jean Paul Sartre says that one must learn to "décrasser les mots" (scrub words clean). Once this is done a private vocabulary is formed, what we call style, or literary form. The reader who is invited to enter a private universe is like the child invited to enter a game the rules of which he must learn. These rules create boundary lines, visible only to the initiate, and serve to isolate the magic world created by the artist-magician. The writer may appear to speak the language of everyday life, but actually he never does; the artist's vocabulary is always a language within language.

In *Notes and Counter Notes* Ionesco states: "Each new author seeks to fight in the name of truth. Boileau wished to express truth. In his Preface to *Cromwell,* Victor Hugo considered that romantic art rather than classical contained more truth and was more complex. The aim of realism and naturalism was also to extend the realms of reality or reveal new and still unknown aspects of it. Symbolism and later surrealism were further attempts to reveal and express hidden realities. The question then is simply for an author to discover truths and to state them. And the manner of stating them is naturally unfamiliar, for this statement itself is the truth for him. He can only speak it for himself. It is by speaking it for himself that he speaks it for others. Not the other way around." In the same talk about the avant-garde, Ionesco calls the latter a "prestyle." You cannot see the avant-garde, he explains, until it has taken place, has turned in fact into the rear guard. (pp. 1-10)

[We] can, at this point, look back upon a body of work and begin to see the outlines of a face. The portrait is unfinished, but an expression has been caught. The face appears to be that of a melancholy but smiling clown. The eyes are bemused. A finger is held up to the lips as though the man in the picture were sharing a secret with himself. The round head reminds one of Socrates, and the folds of the flesh, apparent even under the clown mask, reveal that the taste of hemlock is not unfamiliar. The man is poised amid the moving architecture of his newly erected environment. The lower part of his body is embedded in what he calls "the warm slime of the living," partaking of the heaviness of matter, but the torso is stretched up, ready for flight. Under his feet, over his head, yawn Pascal's abysmal, silent spaces. To his right and left stand open-mouthed monstrous creatures who have retained in their state of metamorphosis something of the human traits they once possessed. The man in the unfinished portrait is alone, but knowing the depths of his solitude, he has formed a world, consubstantial with himself, which we can . . . explore. (p. 10)

Rosette C. Lamont, in an introduction to *Ionesco: A Collection of Critical Essays,* edited by Rosette C. Lamont, Prentice-Hall, Inc., 1973, pp. 1-10.

CHARLES I. GLICKSBERG
(essay date 1975)

[Glicksberg is an American educator and critic. In the excerpt below, he focuses on *Exit the King* as representative of Ionesco's thematic preoccupation with the inevitability of death.]

Like Beckett, [Ionesco] does not take literature seriously, though he keeps on writing plays. He acknowledges his indebtedness to Kafka, who shared his obsessions. His plays, like the fiction of Kafka, are not intended to convey a message, a rationally defined meaning. He composed *The Bald Soprano* in order "to prove that nothing had any real importance." . . . He finds existence "sometimes unbearable, painful, heavy and stultifying, and sometimes it seems to be the manifestation of God himself, all light." . . .

It must take a great deal of courage for a dramatist of the absurd to write at all. He must fight his own battle of the mind against the enervating feeling of futility. He is caught in the meshes of the destructive logic that supports his aesthetic of the absurd. If life, insofar as he can make out, is without meaning or purpose, then why take the trouble to repeat the lugubrious theme that life is without meaning or purpose? If, however, he is not bothered by the need to justify his creative venture, he is brought up short by the difficulty of embodying his vision of a reality that cannot be framed in words. How, as he practices the art of the absurd, can he name the unnameable? How give flesh and form to the ineffable experience of nada? (p. 223)

In order to capture the elusive features of the Absurd, Ionesco focuses on the elements of the comic, the grotesque, and the contingent in the life of man. Death for Ionesco represents the upsurge of the uncanny, the threat of nothingness, the quintessence of the Absurd. He protests against the fate of death, though he realizes that his protest is but an ineffectual gesture, an empty outburst of rhetoric. The finality of death reveals the distinctive character of the Absurd. The tragic and the comic interpenetrate. The drama of the Absurd is born of the dismaying insight that modern man, despite all his technological conquests, cannot escape his mortal lot. . . . The absurdist hero struggles fiercely against annihilation, but in the end, as in Ionesco's *The Killer,* he is overcome.

The type of drama called forth by this numinous encounter with the Absurd eliminates the possibility of tragic affirmation in the manner of the ancient Greeks. The absurd is simply there, a *tremendum mysterium* that is neither to be worshiped as divine nor assailed as diabolical; it is a haunting consciousness of the nothingness that waits for man. The tragedy of the absurd, like the nihilistic tragedy, seems to be a contradiction in terms. There is nothing the dramatist of the Absurd can affirm. Born of paradox and culminating in paradox, his plays abandon all illusion, though he is aware that these illusions constitute the essential humanity of man, his never-ceasing search for transcendence. The intimations of the Absurd emerge from this conflict between these all-too-human illusions and the adamantine indifference of the universe. The absurdist hero is defeated and dragged under, but he never pretends that the outcome will be other than it turns out to be. A dauntless truth-seeker, he prefers, like Bérenger, the protagonist of *The Killer,* to know the worst that will befall him rather than to remain deluded. He is able to endure the wounds that existence can inflict upon him and laugh at his mortal predicament. (pp. 224-25)

[Ionesco] is the visionary poet who can never get used to the strangeness of existence. He can make no sense of this phantasmagoric universe, these phantom presences that represent people, these moving lights and shadows and the all-enveloping curtain of darkness. He looks on the world as a rare spectacle, an incomprehensible and yet amusing show and he reacts to it with a sense of wonder, but it also induces anxiety and dread. He is caught in a series of irreconcilable contradictions. "Nothing is atrocious, everything is atrocious. Nothing is comic. Everything is tragic. Nothing is tragic, everything is comic, everything is real, unreal, possible, impossible, conceivable, inconceivable." His work, despite its exploitation of the comic vein, gives expression to an obsessive pessimism. Death is the epitome of the Absurd. . . . Death overtakes all men, regardless of their merit, and if that is so, then what is the purpose of living? Ionesco remarks: "We are made to be immortal, and yet we die. It's horrible, it can't be taken seriously." He cannot forget himself because he cannot forget that he must die, those he loves will die, and the world will ultimately come to an end.

Death is the supreme humiliation man is made to suffer, the outrage he is powerless to prevent. Death is meted out to all; and it is this knowledge that leads Ionesco to stress the vanity of life. All his reading, all the works of art he has studied, emphasize the implacable truth he perceived early in life: the inevitability of death. Why should he concern himself with the social, economic, and political problems of the hour when he knows that we are slated to die and that no revolution can save us from death. (p. 227)

Though Ionesco's obsession is fixed on death, it is not, like the work of Edward Young and Thomas L. Beddoes, morbid in content. It voices a universal

theme. It is a source of anguish, and it is this metaphysical anguish, which never lets up, that incites him to creativity. By writing he keeps the issue of mortality alive even though this intensifies the anguish he feels, anguish born of the "fear of nothingness." . . . It is this accursed knowledge that we are doomed to die that turns us into killers. Death is the tormenting question mark for which we can find no answer. Though this perpetual "Why" that we ask gets us nowhere in the end, we continue to interrogate the world of being. Why for millennia should the sons of Adam resign themselves to the intolerable imposition of death? If they begin to love life, they are soon overcome by the certainty that it will shortly be taken away from them. "This is the incredible thing: to love a life that has been thrust upon me and that is snatched away from me just when I have accepted it." . . . He is afraid that in dwelling repeatedly on this archetypal theme he may yield to the vice of self-pity or indulge in sentimentality. He writes: "I have been, I still am tormented at once by the dread of death, the horror of the void, and by an eager, impatient desire to live. Why does one long to live, what does living mean?" . . . He does not know the answer. It is the thought of death that makes living an impossible burden to bear. Like Camus, Ionesco rejects suicide as "unforgivable failure; and we must not fail." . . .

Ionesco comes to grips with the theme of death in *The Killer* and, later, in *Exit the King.* (p. 228)

Offhand no theme seems less promising than the one Ionesco has chosen to deal with in [*Exit the King.*] What dramatically fruitful results can be derived from the thanatopsian motif? The agonizing struggle to cling to life of a king who is dying and knows he is dying—what, after all, can the most gifted and original playwright do with such refractory material? The words of the Preacher in *Ecclesiastes,* the poignant cry of *memento mori,* the Dance of Death, the sermons and sonnets of John Donne, the lucubrations of the Graveyard School of poets—the potentialities of such an essentially static and sterile theme have already been exhausted. Nothing new can be added; no genuine conflict can possibly arise. The battle the condemned person wages is cruelly unjust. As in Andreyev's play *The Life of Man,* Death is always the winner. There is never a moment of doubt as to the final outcome. However desperate his resistance, the chosen victim must give in. It is only a matter of time. Here is the grim drama each man acts out at the end of his life: a drama that lacks the element of suspense. The plot must, of necessity, follow a pre-established pattern. Why did Ionesco revert to this theme that he had already sounded in *The Killer?*

Because it sums up the distinctive aesthetic of the Absurd. Because . . . death is Ionesco's constant obsession, the primary source of his inspiration. In *Exit the King* he is writing a twentieth-century version of *Every-*

man, in which the theological and moral gloss is left out. There is no God to pass judgment on life or to intercede for the dying man. Heaven and hell no longer exist. After death, there is—nothing.

Ionesco invests the theme with universal overtones. Each man is the virtual ruler of a kingdom, his body, which he is forced to surrender after a comparatively brief reign. The outlying provinces renounce their allegiance; the parts of the internal kingdom refuse to obey their sovereign. Or they break down, one by one, and are no longer capable of responding to his commands. He ceases to be in control of his subjects; he lacks the strength to support his crown and scepter. (pp. 229-30)

Charles I. Glicksberg, "Ionesco and the Comedy of the Absurd," in his *The Literature of Nihilism,* Bucknell University Press, 1975, pp. 222-33.

SOURCES FOR FURTHER STUDY

Coe, Richard N. *Eugène Ionesco.* New York: Grove Press, 1968, 129 p.

> Divides Ionesco's output into the early plays, which are characterized as "farces that somehow, after the astonishment had subsided into uneasy silence, demanded to be taken seriously," and the later plays, described as "desperately serious dramas hoping against hope to be received with laughter."

Esslin, Martin. "Eugène Ionesco: Theatre and Anti-Theatre." In his *Theatre of the Absurd,* pp. 79-139. Garden City, N. Y.: Doubleday & Co., 1961.

> Details Ionesco's life and literary career, suggesting that "his work constitutes a truly heroic attempt to break through the barriers of human communication."

Guppy, Shusha. "The Art of Theater VI: Eugène Ionesco." *The Paris Review* 26, No. 93 (Fall 1984): 53-78.

> Interview in which Ionesco discusses his works, influences, and views on modern theater.

Lamont, Rosette C. and Friedman, Melvin J. *The Two Faces of Ionesco.* Troy, N. Y.: The Whitston Publishing Co., 1978, 283 p.

> Collection of critical essays designed to illustrate the multifaceted nature of Ionesco's dramas.

Lewis, Allan. *Ionesco.* Boston: Twayne Publishers, 1972, 119 p.

> Comprehensive examination of Ionesco's life and works, asserting that in his dramas "Ionesco has touched something deep in contemporary malaise against which tradition cannot provide a protective sanctuary."

Pronko, Leonard C. *Eugène Ionesco.* New York and London: Columbia University Press, 1965, 47 p.

> Traces the development of Ionesco's dramas.

Washington Irving

1783-1859

(Also wrote under pseudonyms Geoffrey Crayon, Diedrich Knickerbocker, Jonathan Oldstyle, and Launcelot Langstaff) American short story writer, essayist, historian, journalist, and biographer.

INTRODUCTION

Considered the first professional man of letters in the United States, Irving was influential in the development of the short story form and helped to gain international respect for fledgling American literature. Following the tradition of the eighteenth-century essay exemplified by the elegant, lightly humorous prose of Joseph Addison and Oliver Goldsmith, Irving created endearing and often satiric short stories and sketches. In his most-acclaimed work, *The Sketch Book of Geoffrey Crayon, Gent.* (1819-20), he wove elements of myth and folklore into narratives, such as "Rip Van Winkle" and "The Legend of Sleepy Hollow," that achieved almost immediate classic status. Although Irving was also renowned in his lifetime for his extensive work in history and biography, it was through his short stories that he most strongly influenced American writing in subsequent generations and introduced a number of now-familiar images and archetypes into the body of the national literature.

Irving was raised in New York City, the youngest of eleven children of a prosperous merchant family. A dreamy and ineffectual student, he apprenticed himself in a law office rather than follow his elder brothers to nearby Columbia College. In his free time, he read avidly and wandered when he could in the misty, rolling Hudson River Valley, an area steeped in local folklore and legend that would serve as an inspiration for his later writings.

As a nineteen-year-old, Irving began contributing satirical letters under the pseudonym Jonathan Oldstyle to a newspaper owned by his brother Peter. His first book, *Salmagundi; or, The Whim-Whams and Opinions of Launcelot Langstaff, Esq., and Others* (1807-08), was a collaboration with another brother, William, and their friend James Kirke Paulding. This highly popular collection of short pieces poked fun at the political, social, and cultural life of the city. Irving enjoyed a second success in 1809 with *A History of New York, from the Beginning of the World to the End of the Dutch Dynasty*, a comical, deliberately inaccurate account of New York's Dutch colonization narrated by the fictitious Diedrich Knickerbocker, a fusty, colorful Dutch-American. His carefree social life and literary successes were shadowed at this time, however, by the death of his fiancée, Matilda Hoffmann, and for the next several years he floundered, wavering between a legal, mercantile, and editorial career. In 1815 he moved to England to work in the failing Liverpool branch of the family import-export business. Within three years the company was bankrupt, and, finding himself at age thirty-five without means of support, Irving decided that he would earn his living by writing. He began recording the impressions, thoughts, and descriptions which, polished and repolished in his meticulous manner, became the pieces that make up *The Sketch Book*. The volume was brought out under the pseudonym of Geoffrey Crayon, who was purportedly a good-natured American roaming Britain on his first trip abroad.

The Sketch Book comprises some thirty parts: about half English sketches, four general travel reminiscences, six literary essays, two descriptions of the American Indian, three essentially unclassifiable pieces, and three short stories: "Rip Van Winkle," "The Legend of Sleepy Hollow," and "The Spectre Bridegroom." Although only the last-named tale is set in Germany, all three stories draw upon the legends of that country. The book was published almost concurrently in the United States and England in order to escape the piracy to which literary works were vulnerable before international copyright laws, a shrewd move that many subsequent authors copied. The miscellaneous nature of *The Sketch Book* was an innovation that appealed to a broad range of readers; the work received a great deal of attention and sold briskly, and Irving found himself America's first international literary celebrity. In addition, the book's considerable profits allowed Irving to devote himself full-time to writing.

Remaining abroad for more than a decade after the appearance of *The Sketch Book*, Irving wrote steadily, capitalizing on his international success with two subsequent collections of tales and sketches that also appeared under the name Geoffrey Crayon. *Bracebridge Hall; or, the Humorists: A Medley* (1822) centers loosely around a fictitious English clan that Irving had introduced in several of the *Sketch Book* pieces. *Bracebridge Hall* further describes their manners, customs, and habits, and interjects several unrelated short stories, including "The Student from Salamanca" and "The Stout Gentleman." *Tales of a Traveller* (1824) consists entirely of short stories arranged in four categories: European stories, tales of London

literary life, accounts of Italian bandits, and narrations by Irving's alter-ego, Diedrich Knickerbocker. The most enduring of these, according to many critics, are "The German Student," which some consider a significant early example of supernatural fiction, and "The Devil and Tom Walker," a Yankee tale that like "Rip Van Winkle" draws upon myth and legend for characters and incident. After 1824 Irving increasingly turned his attention from fiction and descriptive writing toward history and biography. He lived for several years in Spain, serving as a diplomatic attache to the American legation while writing a life of Christopher Columbus and a history of Granada. During this period he also began gathering material for *The Alhambra* (1832), a vibrantly romantic collection of sketches and tales centered around the Moorish palace in Granada.

Irving served as secretary to the American embassy in London from 1829 until 1832, when he returned to the United States. After receiving warm accolades from the literary and academic communities, he set out on a tour of the rugged western part of the country, which took him as far as Oklahoma. The expedition resulted in three books about the region, notably *A Tour on the Prairies* (1835), which provided easterners with their first description of life out west by a well-known author. Irving eventually settled near Tarrytown, New York, at a small estate on the Hudson River, which he named Sunnyside. Apart from four years in Madrid and Barcelona, which he spent as President John Tyler's minister to Spain, Irving lived there the rest of his life. Among the notable works of his later years is an extensive biography of George Washington, which Irving worked on determinedly, despite ill health, from the early 1850s until a few months before his death in 1859.

The Sketch Book prompted the first widespread critical response to Irving's writings. Reviewers in the United States were generally delighted with the work of their native son, and even English critics, normally hostile in that era to American authors, accorded the book generally favorable—if somewhat condescending—notice. Among the pieces singled out for praise in the early reviews were most frequently the three short stories, particularly "Rip Van Winkle." Critics found Irving's style pleasingly elegant, fine, and humorous, although some, including Richard Henry Dana, perceived a lack of intellectual content beneath the decorative surface. Dana also observed that in adopting the authorial persona of Geoffrey Crayon—with his prose style modeled after the eighteenth-century essayists—Irving lost the robustness, high color, and comic vigor of his previous incarnations as Jonathan Oldstyle, Launcelot Langstaff, and Diedrich Knickerbocker, an observation that was echoed by later critics. Subsequent "Crayon" works, such as *Bracebridge Hall*, *Tales of a Traveller*, and *The Alhambra*, while generally valued for their prose style, tended to prompt such complaints as that by the Irish author Maria Edgeworth that "the workmanship surpasses the work."

Beginning in the 1950s, however, critics began to explore technical and thematic innovations in Irving's short stories. These include the integration of folklore, myth, and fable into narrative fiction; setting and landscape as a reflection of theme and mood; the expression of the supernatural and use of Gothic elements in some stories; and the tension between imagination and creativity versus materialism and productivity in nineteenth-century America. Many critics read Rip's twenty-year sleep as a rejection of the capitalistic values of his society—ferociously personified by the shrewish Dame Van Winkle—and an embracing of the world of the imagination. Ichabod Crane, too, has been viewed by such critics as Robert Bone as representing the outcast artist-intellectual in American society, although he has been considered, conversely, as a caricature of the acquisitive, scheming Yankee Puritan, a type that Irving lampooned regularly in his early satirical writings.

Today, many critics concur with Fred Lewis Pattee's assertion that the "American short story began in 1819 with Washington Irving." Commentators agree, moreover, that in "Rip Van Winkle" and "The Legend of Sleepy Hollow," Irving established an artistic standard and model for subsequent generations of American short story writers. As George Snell wrote: "It is quite possible to say that Irving unconsciously shaped a principal current in American fiction, whatever may be the relative unimportance of his own work." In their continuing attention to the best of Irving's short fiction, critics affirm that while much of Irving's significance belongs properly to literary history, such stories as "Rip Van Winkle" and "The Legend of Sleepy Hollow" belong to literary art.

(For further information about Irving's life and works, see *Concise Dictionary of American Literary Biography, 1640-1865; Dictionary of Literary Biography,* Vols. 3, 11, 30, 59, 73, 74; *Nineteenth-Century Literature Criticism,* Vols. 2, 19; and *Short Story Criticism,* Vol. 2.)

CRITICAL COMMENTARY

RICHARD HENRY DANA

(essay date 1819)

[Dana was an American poet and critic and co-founder of the *North American Review*. In the following excerpt from a review of *The Sketch Book of Geoffrey Crayon, Gent.*, he examines Irving's work to date and assesses his place in nascent American literature.]

[We] have to thank Mr. Irving for being the first to begin and persevere in works which may be called purely literary. His success has done more to remove our anxiety for the fate of such works, than all we have read or heard about the disposition to encourage American genius.

Mr. Irving's success does not rest, perhaps, wholly upon his merit, however great. *Salmagundi* came out in numbers, and a little at a time. With a few exceptions it treated of the city—what was seen and felt, and easy to be understood by those in society. It had to do with the present and real, not the distant and ideal. It was exceedingly pleasant morning or after-dinner reading, never taking up too much of a gentleman's time from his business and pleasures, nor so exalted and spiritualized as to seem mystical to his far reaching vision. (p. 334)

Mr. Irving has taken the lead [in *The Sketch Book of Geoffrey Crayon, Gent.*], in the witty, humourous and playful cast of works—those suited to our happier feelings. . . . He has not modelled himself upon any body, but has taken things just as he found them, and treated them according to his own humour. So that you never feel as when looking at [*The Sketch Book*], that you have gotten a piece of second-hand furniture, scraped and varnished till made to look fine and modern, that it may be put to a new use. His wit and humor do not appear to come of reading witty and humorous books; but it is the world acting upon a mind of that cast, and putting those powers in motion. There are parts, it is true, which remind you of other authors, not, however, as imitations, but resemblances of mind. (pp. 335-36)

Amidst the abundance of his wit and drollery, you never meet with any bilious sarcasm. He turns aside from the vices of men to be amused with their affectation and foibles; and the entertainment he finds in these seems to be from a pure goodness of soul—a sense that they are seldom found in thoroughly depraved and hardened hearts. (p. 336)

Amiableness is so strongly marked in all Mr. Irving's writings as never to let you forget the man; and

Principal Works

Salmagundi; or, the Whim-Whams and Opinions of Launcelot Langstaff, Esq., and Others [with William Irving and James Kirke Paulding] (satirical essays) 1807-08

A History of New York, from the Beginning of the World to the End of the Dutch Dynasty [as Diedrich Knickerbocker] (historical parody) 1809

The Sketch Book of Geoffrey Crayon, Gent. [as Geoffrey Crayon] (essays and short stories) 1819-20

Bracebridge Hall; or, the Humorists: A Medley [as Geoffrey Crayon] (short stories) 1822

Tales of a Traveller [as Geoffrey Crayon] (travel sketches and short stories) 1824

A History of the Life and Voyages of Christopher Columbus (biography) 1828

A Chronicle of the Conquest of Grenada (history) 1829

The Alhambra [as Geoffrey Crayon] (essays and short stories) 1832

The Crayon Miscellany [as Geoffrey Crayon] (essays and short stories) 1835

A Tour on the Prairies (travel sketches) 1835

The Works of Washington Irving. 15 vols. [author's revised edition] (essays, short stories, history, and biography) 1848-51

Oliver Goldsmith (biography) 1849

The Life of George Washington. 5 vols. (biography) 1855-59

the pleasure is doubled in the same manner as it is in lively conversation with one for whom you have a deep attachment and esteem. There is in it also, the gayety and airiness of a light, pure spirit—a fanciful playing with common things, and here and there beautiful touches, till the ludicrous becomes half picturesque.

Though many of the characters and circumstances in *Salmagundi* are necessarily without such associations, yet the Cocklofts are not only the most witty and eccentric, but the most thoroughly sentimental folks in the world. . . . With a very few exceptions, [Irving's] sentiment is in a purer taste, and better sustained, where it is mixed with witty and ludicrous characters and circumstances, than where it stands by itself. He not only shows a contemplative, sentimental mind, but what is more rare, a power of mingling with his wit, the wild, mysterious and visionary. (pp. 336-37)

It looks a little like impertinent interference to advise a man to undertake subjects of a particular sort, who is so well suited for variety in kind. Nor do we wish that Mr. Irving should give up entirely the purely witty, of humorous, for those of a mixed nature. We would only express our opinion of the deep interest

which such writings excite, and of his peculiar fitness for them; and at the same time suggest to him the great advantages he gains by changing from one to the other. For ourselves, we have no fear of being tired of his wit or humour, so long as they come from him freely. He is much more powerful in them, than in the solely sentimental or pathetic.

We give him joy of making his way so miraculously, as not to offend the dignity of many stately folks, and pray him go on and prosper. It was a bold undertaking in a country where we are in the habit of calling humour, buffoonery—and wit, folly. (p. 337)

Mr. Irving's style in his lighter productions, is suited to his subject. He has not thought it necessary to write the history of the family of the Giblets as he would that of the Gracchi, nor to descant upon Mustapha's Breeches in all the formality of a lecture. He is full, idiomatic and easy to an uncommon degree; and though we have observed a few grammatical errors, they arc of a kind which appear to arise from the hurry in which such works are commonly written. There are, likewise, one or two Americanisms. Upon the whole, it is superior to any instance of the easy style in this country, that we can call to mind. That of the Foresters is more free from faults than Mr. Irving's, but not so rich. The principal defect in his humorous style is a multiplying of epithets, which, making no new impression, weaken from diffusion. It is too much like forcing a good thing upon us till we think it good for nothing. We make no objection to a style rich with epithets, which have fitness and character, unless they are strung along so as to look like a procession. But Mr. Irving's are sometimes put upon a service for which they were never intended, and only occasion confusion and delay.

Another fault, and one easily to be avoided, is the employing of certain worn out veterans in the cause of wit. Indeed, we owe it to him to say, that we believe he has now dismissed them, as we do not meet with them in the *Sketch Book.* (p. 338)

Another fault, which is found principally in *Knickerbocker,* is that of forcing wit as if from duty—running it down, and then whipping and spurring it into motion again—as in that part upon the different theories of philosophers. Wit must appear to come accidentally, or the effect is lost. (p. 339)

Salmagundi is full of variety, and almost every thing good of its kind. Though upon an old plan, nothing can be better done than some of Mustapha's letters, particularly those upon a Military Review, and the City Assembly. (p. 342)

At parting company with *Salmagundi,* we cannot but say again, that though its wit is sometimes forced, and its serious style sometimes false, upon looking it over, we have found it full of entertainment, with an infinite variety of characters and circumstances, and with that amiable, good natured wit and pathos, which show that the heart has not grown hard while making merry of the world.

There is but little room left for *Knickerbocker*, of which we are glad to say, a third and very neat edition has lately been put out. As our remarks upon *Salmagundi* will apply equally well to this work, and an analysis of a story, which every one has read, is dull matter, we the less regret it. It has the same faults and same good qualities in its style, its wit and humour; and its characters are evidently by the same hand as the leading ones in *Salmagundi*, though not copies from them. They are perfectly fresh and original, and suited to their situations. Too much of the first part of the first volume is laborious and up hill; and there are places, here and there, in the last part to which there is the same objection. (pp. 344-45)

It was delightful meeting once more with an old acquaintance who had been so long absent from us; and we felt our hearts lightened and cheered when we, for the first time, took the *Sketch Book* into our hands. Foreigners can know nothing of the sensation; for authors are as numerous and common with them, as street acquaintances. We, who have only two or three, are as closely attached to them, as if they were our brothers. And this one is the same mild, cheerful, fanciful, thoughtful, humorous being that we parted with a few years ago, though something changed in manner by travel. We will be open with him, and tell him that we do not think the change is for the better. He appears to have lost a little of that natural run of style, for which his lighter writings were so remarkable. He has given up something of his direct, simple manner, and plain phraseology, for a more studied, periphrastical mode of expression. He seems to have exchanged works and phrases, which were strong, distinct and definite, for a genteel sort of language, cool, less definite, and general. It is as if his mother English had been sent abroad to be improved, and in attempting to become accomplished, had lost too many of her home qualities. . . . He too often aims at effect by a stately inversion of sentences. Another and a greater error, which is found principally in his serious and sentimental writings, is an incorrect use of figurative language, which is, frequently, from connecting a word, strictly an image, with one which is not, so as to present a picture to the mind's eye, and the next moment rub it out. This appears to be owing to a mere oversight, a want of considering that any figure was used. Another is, connecting two words which are figures, but quite hostile to one another, so that they seem brought together for no other purpose than to put an end to each other. (pp. 348-49)

We have made these short remarks, and given these few instances, because it is faults of this kind which make our style feeble and impure, rather than

the use of Americanisms, as they are called. . . . This defect of vision in picturesque language is the more singular in Mr. Irving, as he has an eye for nature, and all his pictures from it are drawn with great truth and spirit. *The Sketch Book* is extremely popular, and it is worthy of being so. Yet it is with surprise that we have heard its style indiscriminately praised.

We have already stated, why we consider Mr. Irving's former works, though more obviously bad in places, still, as a whole, superior in point of style to the *Sketch Book*. The same difference holds with respect to the strength, quickness and life of the thoughts and feelings. The air about this last work is soft, but there is a still languor in it. It is not breezy and fresh like that which was stirring over the others. He appears to us to have taken up some wrong notion of a subdued elegance, as different from the true, as in manners, the elegance of fashion is from that of character. There is an appearance of too great elaboration. (p. 350)

"The Broken Heart" has passages as beautiful and touching as any that Mr. Irving has written, but they are frequently injured by some studied, unappropriate epithet or phraseology which jars upon the feelings. The general reflections have a deep and tender thoughtfulness in them, and are much too good for the story. It is enough to meet in life with those who can make themselves over to one man, for lucre, or something worse or better, while their hearts are with another; but in a work of sentiment it is revolting. (p. 352)

Another fault—which is from the same false theory—is laying open to the common gaze and common talk, feelings the very life of which is secrecy. (p. 353)

"Rip Van Winkle" is our favorite amongst the new stories. We feel more at home in it with the author, than in any of this collection. Rip's idle good nature, which made him the favorite of the boys—his 'aversion to all kinds of profitable labour,' 'thinking it no use to work upon his own farm because every thing about it went wrong, and would go wrong, in spite of him,' yet always ready to help his neighbours—'the foremost at husking frolics, and building stone fences,' and ready at running errands for all the old wives in the village—and toiling all day at fishing and shooting—these show a thorough understanding of the apparent contradictions in character, and are set forth in excellent humour. . . . The mountain scenery is given with great beauty, and the ghostly party at ninepins is at the same time laughable and picturesque. The author's mind is highly fanciful and exactly suited to such scenes. (pp. 353-54)

Mr. Irving's scenery is so perfectly true—so full of little beautiful particulars, so varied, yet so connected in character, that the distant is brought nigh to us, and the whole is seen and felt like a delightful reality. It is all gentleness and sunshine; the bright and holy influences of nature fall on us, and our disturbed and lowering spirit is make clear and tranquil—turned all to beauty, like clouds shone on by the moon. Though we see in it nothing of the troubles and vices of life, we believe Mr. Irving found all he has described. If there be any thing which can give purity and true dignity to the character of man, it is country employments and scenery acting upon a cultivated mind. (p. 355)

Richard Henry Dana, in an originally unsigned essay titled, "The Sketch Book of Geoffrey Crayon, Gent.," in *The North American Review and Miscellaneous Journal,* Vol. IX, No. 2, September, 1819, pp. 322-56.

FRED LEWIS PATTEE
(essay date 1923)

[In the following excerpt, Pattee considers Irving as the progenitor of the American short story and discusses his positive and negative contributions to the development of the genre.]

The American short story began in 1819 with Washington Irving. Short fiction there had been in America before *The Sketch Book,* some of it written by men of significance—Franklin, Freneau, Charles Brockden Brown—but from the standpoint of the modern short-story form none of it need detain us. . . . A study of the form in its American phases begins with Irving.

The first observation to be made upon Irving concerns the fact that he was born in New York City of British parentage, and therefore was untouched by New England. The Puritan age had been introspective, and the New England of the early nineteenth century was still basically Puritan; the eighteenth century of Addison and Fielding and Goldsmith had been circumspective, and the New York of Irving's boyhood was a prolongation of it: worldly, cosmopolitan, it was even then absorbed in an all-engrossing present; the romantic age that was to dominate the opening years of the new century was to be retrospective, unmindful of voices within and clamor without, while it created for itself an ideal world out of its dreams of a vanished past. Of all that savors of introspection and New England Puritanism, Irving had no trace. The grim shadows of conscience and that chilling religious which in New England killed all early attempts at fiction and which in later days could render pale and often unearthly the work of a genius like Hawthorne, touched him not at all. Like Cooper, he could be lawless without a qualm. It is worth while to dwell upon this: it was inevitable that American fiction should have had its beginnings in New York, and especially inevitable was it that the short story should have sprung from its soil.

It would have withered and died in the shadow of early New England Brahminism, for it is a thing of this world; it breathes worldliness or it perishes.

Irving's birth in New York had another effect. Unlike the Boston of the period, the city had no intellectual atmosphere, no traditions of a scholarly past, no Brahmin caste, and as a result the lad, naturally bookish, was forced in upon himself and in upon his father's library, which had stopped growing at a period antedating the Revolution. To the eager boy, marooned in a literary desert, the volumes of the eighteenth-century writers came as something new and vital. The then comparatively recent advice of Dr. Johnson to give one's days and nights to the volumes of Addison was authoritative and compelling. As a result Irving prolonged the eighteenth century. Ignorant of the new literary tides that were rising to sweep away old things, he began deliberately to write as Addison would have written had he been born into the New York of the dying eighteenth century. The Jonathan Oldstyle papers, which appeared in the *Morning Chronicle* when Irving was nineteen, are of the age of Queen Anne rather than of the second decade of the lusty young American Republic. So, too, with the *Salmagundi* papers that followed in 1807. This basis of classicism, which in a way he had been forced upon, was, as we see it now, tremendously important to the young writer: it came first, it came in his impressionable years; he never wholly left it. It gave him stability while others went to extremes, it compelled restraint, it rendered impossible anything save beauty of style and perfect clearness, and it made him observant of men and manners and times.

But the eighteenth century was dead: even while Irving was writing his Oldstyle papers the reaction against all it had stood for had become a revolution. Already had come what Carlyle was terming "the sickliest of recorded ages, when British literature lay all puking and sprawling in Werterism, Byronism, and other sentimentalism, tearful or spasmodic (fruit of internal wind)." That the impressionable young New-Yorker sooner or later should have been affected was inevitable. How the new forces laid hold upon him and modified his classicism is a problem tremendously important, for it is at this point, where in him the Addisonian Arctic current was cut across by the Gulf Stream of romanticism, that there was born the American short story, a new genre, something distinctively and unquestionably our own in the world of letters. (pp. 1-3)

Excluding such rambling character sketches as **"The Wife"** and **"The Widow and Her Son"** in *The Sketch Book,* and such abandoned fragments as **"Buckthorne and His Friends"** and **"Ralph Ringwood"** in his later collections, Irving wrote something like forty-eight narrative pieces that, in a general way, we may call short stories. Roughly we may classify them under four heads: first, sentimental tales in the conventional manner of the time, like **"The Pride of the Village,"** **"Annette Delarbre,"** and **"The Widow's Ordeal"**; second, seven Knickerbocker tales—**"Rip Van Winkle,"** **"The Legend of Sleepy Hollow,"** **"Dolph Heyliger,"** **"The Devil and Tom Walker,"** **"Wolfert Webber,"** and **"The Adventure of the Black Fisherman,"** and **"Guests from Gibbet Island"**; third, other tales touched by German romance, like **"The Spectre Bridegroom"** and Parts I and III of *Tales of a Traveller;* and, fourth, Arabesque tales and sketches of Spanish romance, like those in *The Alhambra, Legends of the Conquest of Spain,* and *Wolfert's Roost.*

Arranged in chronological order, the tales reveal an evolution that is most instructive. The *Salmagundi* papers are of the eighteenth century: only one of them by any stretch may be called a short story. **"My Aunt"** is a whimsical anecdote, **"My Uncle John"** is an Addisonian sketch of character and manners, but **"The Little Man in Black"** has elements in it that are new: it is the transition link between the *Spectator* sketches of the book and the Germanized **"Rip Van Winkle"** that was to follow ten years later. So redolent of the eighteenth century is it that John Neal could declare it a direct imitation of Goldsmith's "Man in Black" in No. 26 of *The Citizen of the World,* yet it is not a study of manners or of character, and it is not an apologue—it has no moral. It is a graphic picture—the man is alive and he is presented not to make the reader think, but to make him feel. It has dialogue, characterization, but no development of character, and it has verisimilitude. The author's whole object is to entertain: to surprise, indeed, the reader. The little man is the first shadow of the coming Knickerbocker, and the first shadow also of the coming of the romantic into its author's work. In the story there is first a mystery, then a seeming solution, then a surprise-ending almost of the modern type: the little man is no other than a descendant of the erudite Linkum Fidelius who has been so whimsically and so ponderously quoted through the volume just as the Little Man in Black runs through *The Citizen of the World,* to be revealed at the end. A stupendous tome, the labor of a lifetime, has been left in the hands of the author and the source of his learned quotations is now plain. The reader is left with the impression that the tale was told with no other purpose than to set the stage for this surprise.

The Sketch Book, which came a decade later, after Scott and romanticism had come into Irving's life, marks the boundary line between the new and the old. The first critic clearly to recognize that a new literary form had arisen was Prescott, the historian, who under the title "Essay Writing" made, in *The North American Review* as early as 1822, this remarkable analysis:

> *The Sketch Book* certainly forms an epoch in the history of this kind of literature; for, although of the same generic character with the British essayists, it

has many important specific peculiarities. The former were written . . . with a direct moral tendency, to expose and to reform the ignorance and the follies of the age. *The Sketch Book,* on the other hand, has no direct moral purpose, but is founded on sentiment and deep feeling. . . . In one word, the principal object of the British essayists was to instruct, so they have for the most part given a picture of common life, in simple language; while the principal object of *The Sketch Book,* being to delight, scenes only of exquisite emotion are selected, and painted in the most exquisite, but artificial language.

Irving touched the eighteenth-century apologue with emotion, stripped it of its obvious moral, and reduced it from the general to the particular. Addison saw the type, Irving the individual; Addison aimed at the head, Irving at the heart; Addison lighted his work with flashes of wit, Irving suffused his with the mellow glow of humor.

From *The Sketch Book* the progress of Irving into the full stream of romantic fiction was rapid, until, indeed, his *The Alhambra* sketches are all picture, all emotion, sentiment, entertainment. Save in their restraint, their beauty of style, their clearness and simplicity, there is little in all of his later tales to remind us that their author had once been completely under the spell of the eighteenth century.

For the short story as we know it to-day Irving performed perhaps nine distinctive services:

1. He made short fiction popular. He was peculiarly endowed for writing the shortened form and he used it exclusively. After the sensational triumph of *The Sketch Book,* a success that stirred greatly the imagination of the younger seekers for literary recognition, sketches and tales became the literary fashion in America, and in such volume did they come that vehicles for their dissemination became imperative. The annual, the gift book, and lady's books like *Godey's* and *Graham's,* and the various popular magazines that sprang up in the 'thirties and 'forties—nurseries for the short story—were thus indirectly the fruit of Irving's success as a sketch writer. He set the bells ringing.

2. He was the first prominent writer to strip the prose tale of its moral and didactic elements and to make of it a literary form solely for entertainment. Knowing the fashions of his day, he was constantly apologizing for his lack of didactic basis. (pp. 18-21)

3. He added to the short tale richness of atmosphere and unity of tone.

4. He added definite locality, actual American scenery and people. Though only seven of his forty-eight tales are native in setting, these seven have been from the first his best loved and most influential work. They were the result of no accident. Deliberately he set out to create for his native land that rich atmosphere which

poetry and romance had thrown over the older lands of Europe, or, to quote his own words, "To clothe home scenes and places and familiar names with those imaginative and whimsical associations so seldom met with in our new country, but which lie like charms and spells about the cities of the Old World." He was the pioneer, therefore, in that new school that demanded an *American* literature, an art that would work in native materials in an original manner.

5. He was the first writer of fiction to recognize that the shorter form of narrative could be made something new and different, but that to do it required a peculiar nicety of execution and patient workmanship. (p. 21)

6. He added humor to the short story and lightness of touch and made it human and appealing. A pervasive humor it was, of the eighteenth-century type rather than of the pungent American type that was to be added by Aldrich and his generation, but nevertheless something new and something attractive.

7. He was original: he pitched the short story in a key that was as new to his generation as O. Henry's was to his. He constantly avoided, as he expressed it, the "commonplace of the day": "I choose to take a line of writing peculiar to myself, rather than to fall into the manner or school of any other writer." (p. 22)

8. Though his backgrounds may often be hazy, though the complaint of the early *Blackwood's* critic that there is "no reality about his Yorkshire halls" has a basis of truth, his characters are always definite individuals and not types or symbols. Rip Van Winkle and Ichabod Crane are more vividly real as human personages to-day than is George Washington, their contemporary. Even **"Mountjoy,"** a complete failure as a short story, has a character in it that is most decidedly alive, that is, indeed, a study in adolescence worthy even of a Henry James.

9. And finally, he endowed the short story with a style that was finished and beautiful, one that threw its influence over large areas of the later product. To many critics this was Irving's chief contribution to American literature, and to some New Englanders at least it was his only contribution. To Emerson, Irving was "only a word-catcher." Perhaps he was, and yet it is by no means a calamity that our pioneer short-story writer should have begun with a literary style that has been the despair of all of his followers. It would have been well if many others who have practiced the art, especially some in recent days could have learned Irving's secret of a distinctive and beautiful style.

But in many respects Irving was a detriment to the development of the short story. So far as modern technique is concerned he retarded its growth for a generation. He became from the first a model followed by all: unquestionably he was in America the most influ-

ential literary figure of the nineteenth century. To him as much as even to Scott may be traced the origin of that wave of sentimentalism and unrestrained romance that surged through the annuals and the popular magazines for three decades. . . . Everywhere in the mid-century [was] the softness and sentiment of this first great leader. . . . One may skip a generation and still be in the presence of the great romancer: Harte, the leader of the new school of short story writers after the war, began by writing legends modeled after the legends of the Hudson. Poe was powerless in the 'thirties and 'forties in his attempts to change the technique of the form. His careful analysis was either unread by his generation or else unheeded because it was a revolt from Irving.

Of form as we know it to-day the tales of Irving, even the best of them, have little. He had begun as an eighteenth-century essayist, and according to Dr. Johnson an essay is "a loose sally of the mind, an irregular, undigested piece; not a regular or orderly composition"; he had ended as a romanticist, and romanticism may be defined as lawlessness. His genius was not dramatic. He delighted to saunter through his piece, sketching as he went, and chatting genially about his characters. **"Rip Van Winkle"** has six pages of material before there is any movement. . . . A study of what the dramatist [who adapted the story for the stage] added to the tale and what he left out will reveal how far it falls short of modern short-story requirements. There is lacking sprightly dialogue, movement unimpeded by description or exposition, additional characters with more collisions and more contrasts, and finally a swift culmination involving all the *dramatis personae*.

To Irving plot seemed unessential. He had evolved with deliberation a form of his own that fitted him perfectly. In a letter to Brevoort he explains its characteristics:

> For my part, I consider a story merely as a frame on which to stretch my materials. It is the play of thought, and sentiment, and language; the weaving in of characters, lightly, yet expressively delineated; the familiar and faithful exhibition of scenes in common life; and the half-concealed vein of humor that is often playing through the whole—these are among what I aim at, and upon which I felicitate myself in proportion as I think I succeed.

Of **"The Legend of Sleepy Hollow"** he could say: "The story is a mere whimsical band to connect descriptions of scenery customs, manners, etc."

But there is a more serious indictment. *Blackwood's* mentioned it as early as 1824. About all of Irving's writings, the reviewer had complained, there is a languorous softness that relegated them almost to the realm of feebleness. . . . Irving lacked robustness, masculinity, "red-bloodedness." He was gentle to the verge of squeamishness. . . . Beyond a doubt this lack of robustness in Irving must be reckoned with as one cause of the general effeminacy and timid softness that characterized so much of American fiction during the greater part of the century.

But criticism of Irving's defects is thankless labor. It is best to overlook his faults and be profoundly thankful for him, for with him began American literature. He brought with him wholesomeness and distinction of style and careful workmanship; he introduced to us the form that has become our most distinctive literary product. . . . (pp. 22-5)

Fred Lewis Pattee, "Washington Irving," in his *The Development of the American Short Story: An Historical Survey,* Harper & Brothers Publishers, 1923, pp. 1-26.

HENRY SEIDEL CANBY

(essay date 1931)

[An American critic and editor, Canby was a founder of the *Saturday Review of Literature.* In the following excerpt, he explores the importance of style in Irving's literary works.]

Irving's reputation is the remarkable achievement of a style that sometimes rests upon little else than its own suavity. (p. 70)

[Irving] was not a man of letters who wrote history, he was a chronicler-historian who wrote like a man of letters. He was not creative, a fact that has been obscured by his successful use of legend and anecdote. He was more dependent upon his style than his famous predecessors, to whom he gladly admitted his debt, because the congenial task he chose for himself was to illumine history, myth, and character that appealed to him, by romance and wit gracefully expressed. In his authentic history—of Columbus and his companions, of Granada, of George Washington—he merely adds color to an assemblage of facts, which he brings together in a skilful narrative order without the slightest evidence of a trained historian's power of criticism and interpretation. Myth, anecdote, and picturesque historical incident he suffuses with his own romantic sentiment or with ironic humor, according to the subject and his mood, and with real imagination builds into charming edifices of style. The Knickerbocker *History, The Alhambra,* and **"Rip Van Winkle"** are masterpieces of this kind. Real life he sometimes quite literally transcribed, as in the *Tour on the Prairies,* sometimes suffused with sentiment and handled freely as in the feudal scenes of *Bracebridge Hall.* When he tells stories of contemporary life, as in **"The Wife"** and that one-time favorite, **"The Broken Heart"** in *The Sketch Book,* he is an arrant sentimentalist and conventional also, with no compensation for his lachrymosity except the unfailing suavity of his style.

To sum up, with no real power of character analysis, with no originality of thought, with no sense either of horror or pathos (his battles are usually humorous), quite immune to the great ideas sweeping through his world, Washington Irving relied upon a humorous, romantic temperament that mirrored with a difference the scenes that attracted such a mind—and upon a style. He was right, and he knew that he was right. (pp. 71-2)

It was only when his style became as easy as penmanship that Irving attempted long books—and they were formal, second-hand histories.

These histories, which Irving attempted in the hope that large, solid books would bring him in a steady income, did little for his reputation, which rests as he foresaw upon his miniatures and vignettes. . . . The enormous achievements of his elder contemporaries, Jefferson and Hamilton, are at the very base of American life, political, social, economic, but who reads their works? And who ever read **"Rip"** without pleasure, or missed a word! It is as fresh as the day it was written, and as indisputably a work of genius as it is certainly in thought and subject the "bagatelle" that Irving called it. *The Alhambra* deserves the word "charming" as richly as the essays of Lamb. I can think of few books of prose that in this attribute excel it. If Irving is often *vox et praeterea nihil,* and never more sonorous in the literary orchestra than his own favorite flute, yet in the earthy paradise of Sleepy Hollow, or the martial romance of the Moors, or the humors of Bracebridge Hall, he is a master of lovely rhythm. If his style gilds fustian, it can ornament the occasional nuggets of gold, and if it is monotonous, it is the monotony of fair weather. (p. 73)

Style always has its secret, and the secret of Irving's suavity is well hidden in that native environment which through all his years abroad he professed to love, and did love, best. The student of sources has had his say, and it has not been enough. Irving is more than Goldsmith served cold, and far more than German romanticism brought overseas. He owes much to Goldsmith, but he is not cold. He is a romantic, but very definitely not German. (p. 74)

[It was] no blighted heart but something much more common that made Irving a ready victim of the fashionable melancholy of the period and touched with the grace of sincerity the gentle sadness of his prose. It is clear that he was homesick, in the literal sense of the word. In all his books there is a longing for stability, for ease in surroundings to his taste, and for a home, which he never possessed until well into middle age. He makes the Alhambra domestic, and has drawn the classic picture of home life in the English country. Yet both ambitious poverty and the exigencies of his career compelled him to wander, and to wander single. . . . [The] pathos, the loneliness, the love, the tragedy in Irving's books reflect the emotions of a wandering bachelor deprived of an ideal domesticity, which he first dared not attempt lest something he valued more should be lost, then could not find. (p. 76)

If any outside influence is to account for Washington Irving's really remarkable success with only a humorous temperament and a sensitive soul to go on, then that influence will be found in American Federalism. For Irving, so far as his instrument permitted, represented the Federalist spirit in American literature, and this relationship is the key to much that is otherwise puzzling in a man at the same time so gentle and so famous. Not that Irving was ever interested in politics. He loathed them consistently through a long life in which he owed more to politics than most men. . . .

And yet, if Federalism as an ideal of living was to find literary expression, it was bound in that age of the romantic movement to have its Irving. For Federalism was essentially an aristocratic ideal struggling to adapt itself to the conditions of a republic and the equalities of a new country. (p. 77)

Irving was not interested in the political aims of either [the Republican or Federalist parties]. In his letters and occasional writings he calls a plague on both their houses every time an election stirs the muddy minds of the populace. . . . [A] young wit and beau, pretending to read law in a worldly little seaport where polite affiliations were almost as much European as American, could not be expected to sympathize either with ward politics, or with the moral intensities of a Dwight who believed that God had given America into the government of respectable church members, or with that Virginia idealism which proposed to erect a newfangled state utterly different from anything in the romances of Sir Walter Scott. In the England of Coleridge, Shelley, Byron, Wordsworth—to cite literary names merely—he was to see nothing but the picturesque, and the relics of Moorish Spain were to mean far more to him than Germany in its golden age. The ideas, great and small, of the formative period of the United States naturally passed over his head.

Indeed, when he does defend the American system he is a little absurd. . . . It was not merely old age that led him to end the *Life of Washington* at the moment when a heroic life of glory became involved in questions of domestic politics and a great career was used by partisans for their not very creditable purposes. Politics, for Irving, were New York politics, which meant a squabble between the ins and the outs.

And yet Irving, in spite of his indifference to

party, was more Federalist than the Federalists, more Federalist essentially than the Hartford wits, who adumbrated in their vast poems a government by moral didacticism that was New Englandism rather than aristocracy. He was keenly aware of the deeper struggle of which the brawls of politicians and the ideology of statesmen were only symptoms. . . . *Salmagundi,* like the "Spectator," and still more curiously like the "columns" of modern New York papers, is an onslaught upon manners, an attempt to give detachment, gaiety, civility, to a sodden town. Diedrich Knickerbocker's *History of New York* in its purely Dutch aspects is a satire upon a thoroughly bourgeois civilization, in its attacks upon the Yankees a satire on the ideals of traders and business men. . . . Half of Irving's heart is in **"Rip Van Winkle,"** where the picturesque Rip and his cronies, so full of humor and honest if stupid happiness, are set in contrast to the shabby pretentiousness of the village twenty years later. And the other half is in *Bracebridge Hall* and *The Alhambra,* for in each is a life tinged with the melancholy of departing, yet rich in loyalty, solidity, and human worth instead of human rights. (pp. 78-81)

America of the early eighteen hundreds was alive in all its parts, perhaps more so than the standardized and accomplished America of the twentieth century. Pathetic, from this point of view, is the young Irving's illusion that he and the few like him could create and keep a milieu of taste in hustling young New York, but strong the pressure, far stronger than if he had lived in contemporary Europe, to do something, be something, that expressed his loves and his hates. . . . But what could he do that he wanted? The answer was to write, to write like an aristocrat, like a gentleman, like a Federalist.

For Federalism . . . was much more than a political and economic system. It was a government by the best, the ideal to which all philosophic statesmen have aspired. It was, more specifically, an aristocracy, not of birth or of privilege, but of achievement, with the entrance door always open but a censor of manners, of morals, of capability, at the threshold. (p. 82)

It was to this intangible spirit of Federalism that Irving owed allegiance, a spirit deeper than economic theory, deeper than the struggle for power, a spirit which outlived the party that professed to represent it, so that it is still possible to call a man or a book Federalist in the United States. Irving shared the Federalist respect for the tried, its distrust of the new, its hatred of the vulgar. . . . Irving's feeling for England was magnified by his love for English literature, which was the basis of his education. . . . [If] George Washington was an English country gentleman, with a difference, Irving was an English man of letters, with a difference, who turned in disgust from the sprawlings for food and water of the gigantic infant, his country, and in protest against the crude and new sought to write as elegantly as he could. Yearning for civilized urbanity in a continent designed to be great in quite another fashion, he perfected a style, and only then ceased to feel beaten, discouraged, and futile.

Irving as the arch-Federalist of American literature is much more interesting than Irving as a custodian of the romantic movement in America. . . . It is true that the romantic haze that still hangs over the noble estuary of the Hudson rose from his pen, and the romantic past of that least romantic of American cities, New York, is his contriving. True, too, that he made Europe picturesque for Americans. England was not picturesque to Richard Mather, or to Benjamin Franklin, but Irving imbued it with all that the rest of us have ever since felt of romantic veneration. Yet, although as a maker of glamour he was a pupil of Walter Scott, his inspiration was not all literary. He spoke for the nostalgia of the Federalists, for the decorum, the stability, of colonial days, for the richness of living of the mother country. . . . The best of all this, and very little of the worst, is in Irving. As a romantic among the greater romantics of Europe he is humble and usually derivative, but as an American and as a Federalist he speaks in his own right, and had a motive to speak well.

To read Irving's works again with these facts in mind is to form a new estimate of the man as a writer. When he was young and heady . . . there was more edge than sentiment in his romance. . . . It is only when the Dutch come to New Amsterdam that [*A History of New York*] takes life, and why? Because these stupid Dutch with their sluggish bourgeoisity, their absurd parodies of courage, the "happy equality" of their intellects, their lack of fire, energy, grace, are perfect symbols of that sodden materialism which Irving found ridiculous in others and hated for himself. In spite of its comforts, which he did not disdain, it was the very opposite of all qualities of romance. . . . Indeed, if the *History* is, as I believe, the meatiest of Irving's books, and excelled in style only by a few of the best of his later sketches, the reason is that never again did he have so much of his own observation, his own prejudice and rooted dislike, to add to the documents he drew upon. (pp. 83-6)

The Knickerbocker *History,* erudite, polished, suave, antibourgeois, a satire upon the unromantic, an

A drawing by F.O.C. Darley of Ichabod Crane's schoolroom.

attack upon democracy, a challenge to all ideologues, pedants, moralists, fanatics, a lampoon on besotted commercialism, stands at the head of Federalist literature. (pp. 86-7)

His histories are admirable for style, but they are not literature, though often more literature than history. Indeed, Irving if he had lived in the twentieth century would have been a magazine writer, if not a columnist. . . . *The Sketch Book* is a miscellany, a travel book, sweetened to the taste of the times by romantic sugarplums, and rising to literature only when Irving was more Federalist than romanticist, or more storyteller and essayist than an adorner of sentiment by style.

There was of course some truth, and a good deal of insight, in the romanticizing of jolly old England that makes up so much of *The Sketch Book.* And it is Irving, not Dickens, who is chiefly responsible for the glamour that ever since his day has hung about Christmas in the old hall, the stagecoach, the waits, the loyal tenantry, and all the paraphernalia of merry England. It is only romantic truth, as can readily be ascertained by reading in order from *The Sketch Book* and from the contemporary pages of Jane Austen. Nevertheless, the literary symbolism that he found for the picturesque as he saw it at Abbotsford and Newstead Abbey took such hold on his readers on both sides of the water that it became to them history, and is as vivid in the imagination of the American tourist as manor houses and crumbling castles to his eye. (pp. 87-8)

Without the two Dutch stories, however, *The Sketch Book* would not have worn so well. They are perfect examples of what Irving best loved to do, and naturally he did them well. **"Rip Van Winkle"** and **"The Legend of Sleepy Hollow"** are history of that legendary character which he fed upon—history that preserves, with little care for too minute reality, the memories of a period. . . . He himself, in *The Sketch Book,* was Rip, gentle, pleasure-loving, inadaptable to the crudities of business and family support. He loved the rascal because he was as Irving might have been without brothers and friends. Dame Rip was the urge of hustling, unsubtle America that threatened to drive him away from the pleasant loafing that he loved into a mode of life he most philosophically disapproved of. The Catskills were those hills of romantic dreaming in which he wandered seeking the future—and the harsh disillusion of the bustling ugly village of twenty years afterward, where no one knew Rip, or wanted him, was no bad similitude of the future in those depressing years from 1816 to 1819 when the failure of his brother's business roused in his imagination the spectre of a return, *auctor ignotus,* to job-hunting in New York. No such symbolism, I suppose, was in Irving's consciousness, but he wrote these humorous idylls of picturesque living from his heart, and told them superbly in a prose

so pure and harmonious as to speak of a master at his best. (pp. 88-9)

The sense for style in 1819-20 had not yet been sicklied by the welter of romanticism. Houses were still being built with that easy mastery of form and proportion which was the gift of the eighteenth century, and if the crisp outlines of English prose were blurring under the pen of a Walter Scott, and if the quaintness of Charles Lamb and the profuseness of De Quincey were beginning to be preferred to the cool clarity of Goldsmith, the conception of measure, harmony, restraint, was to last as long as good architecture. Indeed, it is perhaps not altogether a coincidence that Irving and good architecture died in the same decade in America. A delightful temperament, a pleasing play of sentiment and humor upon fortunate themes, and a triumph of style—this was the current estimate of *The Sketch Book.* And it remains our estimate, except that the "sob stories," as they would be called in the modern vernacular, can no longer be regarded as fortunate.

The rest of Irving that really matters is implicit in the books I have already discussed. *The Alhambra,* that romance of history mellowed in a style that is too pure and clear to permit of turgid extravagance, is of course another *Sketch Book,* with the single theme of a lost and beautiful civilization. The earlier *Tales of a Traveller* are less admirable because, paradoxically, they are more original. Here Irving trusted too much to invention, and when he left legend and history and scenes that he knew by deep experience he fell almost invariably into mawkishness or into rhetorical display. Irving could write well on any theme, but rhetoric alone never turned a bad theme into literature. . . . *A Tour of the Prairies,* a work that deserves more reputation, was conceived as another *Sketch Book,* with included stories, and, like *The Alhambra,* with a single romantic theme—the march of the Rangers through the Indian country. But here Irving was too close to his subject. The Indian stories were not in his vein, the companions of his voyage did not project their shadows against historic backgrounds. . . . The material that Cooper found so rich was, for him, too thin. . . . He was, after all, a bookish writer, and the life he best interpreted was seen through books or under their influence. For the frontier he had no books with the flavor of history and hence no perspective. (pp. 89-91)

He did little to illumine American life and character although so much to enrich the American romantic imagination. He endowed the Hudson Valley with a past of legend and fable borrowed from the old world, but his Dutch are quite false, except as satire, his Yankees no more true than Yankee Doodle, his New Amsterdam a land of Cocaigne, which has bequeathed to posterity an idea that New Netherlands was the comic relief of colonial history.

He was not a great romantic, if Scott and Byron

and Shelley be taken as models of romanticism. His gentle melancholy is more akin to Collins, and his humor to Goldsmith. In truth, where Irving was most eighteenth century in manner he has best survived, for his humor, his sense for the quaint, and his admirable feeling for proportion are more valuable than his attempts at pathos, terror, and grandeur in the style of the Teutonized romance of his own period. (p. 91)

The romanticist in Irving powerfully influenced a century of American writers (*The Sketch Book* was Longfellow's first school of literature) and usually to their hurt. They sucked sentiment from him and left the humor behind. But equally strong, and much more fortunate, has been the ideal of excellence set up by his style. Every American writer who has cherished the Federalist hope of urbanity and a counsel of perfection in the midst of democratic leveling may claim Irving as his spiritual father.

The textbooks call him the first ambassador of the new world to the old. That is to look at him through English eyes and is in fact a repetition of his first authentic praising, which came from abroad. . . . Call him rather an American Marco Polo, bringing home the romance of other countries, bearing their gifts of suavity, detachment, ease, and beauty to a raw country dependent upon its vulgar strength, stronger in brains than in manners, yet not devoid of a craving for civility. (p. 92)

Irving might well have written, for his own epitaph, that his writings belonged to the best school of English prose. . . . Great American themes, native to our development, were later to find both prose and verse; they are not in Irving. He was the type of that American, always commoner than Europe believes, whose nostalgia in the midst of prosperity, strenuosity, and progress is genuine and enduring. (p. 94)

He wrote like a European, but with the desires, the mentality, the outlook (already defined), of an American. His style is English, but made in America, for an American need.

And because in order to speak for Federalist America he learned to write with a vanishing grace and a suavity not again to be attained on this side of the Atlantic, his future is more secure than that of his successors in the historical vein. . . . Irving's lighter craft is well trimmed for the shifting gales of fame. He had a style, he had a temperament, he had an eye for the humors, he was born a New Yorker, he could say, as New Englanders would not say, as Philadelphians and Virginians and Carolinians could not say effectively: While we create a new society in a new republic, let us not forget the mellowness of the age we have left behind us overseas, let us not forget the graces of life, let us not forget to be gentlemen. And if this was all he said, it was put admirably, in a time of need, and with

apposite and succinct example. He made Spain glamorous, England picturesque, and his own land conscious of values not to be found in industry, morals, or politics. A slight achievement beside Wordsworth's, a modest ambition by comparison with Byron's, but enough. Not a great man, not even a great author, though a good chronicler, an excellent storyteller, a skilful essayist, an adept in romantic coloring; not in accord with progress in America but the most winning spokesman for the Federalist hope; a musician with few themes, and the minor ones the best, and many played perfectly—that is Washington Irving. (pp. 95-6)

Henry Seidel Canby, "Washington Irving," in his *Classic Americans: A Study of Eminent American Writers from Irving to Whitman, with an Introductory Survey of the Colonial Background of Our National Literature,* 1931. Reprint by Russell & Russell Inc., 1959, pp. 67-96.

EDWARD WAGENKNECHT

(essay date 1962)

[An American scholar of nineteenth-century literature, Wagenknecht wrote noted biographies of such authors as Charles Dickens, Mark Twain, and Henry James. In the following excerpt, he provides an overview of Irving's fiction, examining strains of romanticism and realism in his work.]

[What of Irving] remains today as living literature?

"Rip Van Winkle," "The Legend of Sleepy Hollow," "The Devil and Tom Walker," "The Stout Gentleman," and a few more tales, plus the best of the essays in *The Sketch Book,* outstandingly those which, like **"Westminster Abbey,"** sound the note of mutability which he never failed to strike with practiced hand—this much all would grant. There would be general agreement, too, upon the beauty of his style; whether or not you are interested in what he is saying, you can hardly fail to be pleased by his way of saying it. Canby, to be sure, finds the style "a patina upon the metal of his thought rather than the flexible soul of the thought itself," but this does not cancel out either the finish or the charm. And, for all his elegance, he was not verbose. "Had I more time," he once wrote Storrow about a manuscript submitted to him, "I should have taken the liberty occasionally of shaking some superfluous words out of the sentences, which weaken them."

The sentence quoted is not a model of construction; it may, therefore, conveniently illustrate the point that Irving's stylistic accomplishments are not wholly, or perhaps even basically, a mechanical matter. His editors tried to take care of his rackety spelling, but they were not able to do anything with the incurable addiction to the dangling modifier which sometimes turned him into a unconscious humorist. "Alas!" he cries in *Columbus,* "while writing that letter, his noble benefactress was a corpse!" And in *Mahomet* faulty syntax even drives the Deity into evil ways: "Having fallen into blind idolatry, God sent a prophet of the name of Saleh, to restore them to the right way." In his journals he writes of Dante's "L'Inferno," and misspells the names of intimate friends.

Jonathan Oldstyle and *Salmagundi* may by common consent be passed over; they presaged a rather extraordinary number of themes afterwards developed, but they are not in themselves extraordinary supporters of reputation. *Knickerbocker's History* is another matter. Probably not many of us today nearly kill ourselves laughing at it as Fanny Kemble said she did, or even make our sides sore as Scott did his. But as a sustained imaginative effort it is still Irving's greatest book. . . . (pp. 169-70)

[The] common view that Irving was neo-classical up to *The Sketch Book* and romantic thereafter is much too simple to be maintained; it is true, however, that, once having begun to do his writing in a foreign land, he was less encouraged to develop that side of his talent which inclined him toward social and political satire. Publishing as he did on both sides of the Atlantic, he must appeal to two reading publics. When he wrote down what he observed in English villages, for example, he was as realistic as he could have been in America; he "added greatly to . . . [his] stock of knowledge, by noting down . . . habits and customs." Had he been merely a lover of fine scenery, he tells us, there would have been no need to leave his own country. "But Europe held forth the charms of stories and poetical associations."

Realism and romanticism can be much more easily separated in theory than in practice; there cannot have been many works of literature that were wholly one or the other. It is quite natural that there should be differences of opinion about these matters in Irving. Thus McDermott finds him reducing even the people he knew on his Western journey to literary types— "Irving is not a traveler reporting what he sees; he is ever the self-conscious literary man, the feature-story writer who, by the ready use of his imagination, makes a little fact go a long way"—while Nathalia Wright is so much impressed by his tendency to tie himself down to actual localities, even in such highly romantic stories as the banditti yarns in *Tales of a Traveller,* that she is willing to credit him with beginning a tradition in the American novel about Italy, "the chief characteristic of which, in contrast to the Gothic tradition, was an essential realism of background." Nobody can doubt that *The Sketch Book* has its romantic elements, but we can think of it as all romantic only by concentrating wholly

upon **"Rip Van Winkle," "The Legend of Sleepy Hollow,"** and **"The Spectre Bridegroom"** and ignoring everything else.

All three of these stories have been derived from German sources, but the first two—the great ones—have been ingeniously transplanted to the Hudson River country. "When I first wrote the Legend of Rip Van Winkle," so Irving remembered it in 1843, "my thoughts had been for some time turned towards giving a color of romance and tradition to interesting points of our national scenery which is so generally deficient in our country." He succeeded so well that translators have always had trouble with the story.

Irving's **"Rip Van Winkle"** is four times the length of Otmar's "Peter Klaus." He changes Otmar's knights to the ghosts of Henrik Hudson and his crew; he localizes; he characterizes Rip in his own manner, builds up his domestic background, and tells what happened after his return. If this is not a legitimate way to create literature, then Chaucer and Shakespeare will have to be cast into the outer darkness. As Longfellow once remarked, a modern writer cannot strike a spade into Parnassus anywhere without disturbing the bones of a dead poet. (pp. 173-74)

After the three stories, the part of *The Sketch Book* that is most read today comprises the several papers describing English Christmas celebrations. It should be remembered that this is pre-*Christmas Carol* material, though of course Addison had already described Sir Roger de Coverley's Christmas in *The Spectator.* But there are twenty-six papers altogether in *The Sketch Book* which concern English themes, and all but six of them have their scene outside of London. Irving catches the atmosphere of English rural life and the English Sunday as well as he catches the Christmas spirit. There is an essay about King James I of Scotland, the author of *The King's Quair,* and there are two papers about Shakespeare, one describing a visit to Stratford, and the other on Falstaff and the Boar's Head Tavern. There is also an essay on **"The Mutability of Literature,"** which is developed fancifully and imaginatively. The same melancholy which the thought of time's triumph over everything that is mortal calls forth here appears again in the famous paper on **"Westminster Abbey."** "The coffin of Edward the Confessor has been broken open, and his remains despoiled of their funeral ornaments; the sceptre has been stolen from the hand of the imperious Elizabeth, and the effigy of Henry the Fifth is headless." And I suppose no reader of *The Sketch Book* ever forgets the passage in which Irving muses over the neighboring tombs of "the haughty Elizabeth" and "her victim, the lovely and unfortunate Mary." Despite his penchant for the picturesque, Irving's English papers are not mere antiquarianism: he was also seeking to understand the British character, as the essay on **"John Bull"** shows. **"The Wife," "The**

Widow and Her Son," and "The Pride of the Village" have too much eighteenth-century sentimentalism to interest modern readers very deeply, but they are all based on realistic, not legendary, materials, and the incidents on which **"The Wife"** rests involved two of Irving's friends.

Of *Bracebridge Hall* Osborne has remarked that as Irving "had built *A History of New York* out of parts of *Salmagundi,* so he built *Bracebridge Hall* out of parts of *The Sketch Book.*" But Osborne knows better than anybody else, and has clearly demonstrated, that *Bracebridge Hall* itself also descends not only from *Salmagundi* but even from *Jonathan Oldstyle.* Except for the four stories included (Irving finds a place for them on the pretext that they were told at the Hall), the book is considerably more unified than its predecessor. It is an attractive picture of English rural life, viewed from the upper-class standpoint, but the author does not neglect rural superstitions and May Day customs; this side of the volume is further developed through the device of bringing in a band of gypsies. It is clear that the old folk beliefs appealed to Irving by reason of their picturesqueness, and that he would like to accept them, but his usual balance and common sense do not desert him; he knows, for example, that in their time the May Day games were considerably less innocent than those who cherish them merely because they are old would like to believe.

As for the stories: **"The Stout Gentleman"** contains one of the most artful uses of anti-climax in literature. **"Dolph Heyliger,"** a story of old New York, involves a doctor's idle apprentice and a search for buried treasure, and is one of the best of Irving's longer tales. **"The Student of Salamanca"** is pleasant enough reading about love, alchemy, intrigue, and the Inquisition. **"Annette Delarbre,"** the least substantial of the four, is another nineteenth-century tale about the tender-hearted maiden who could not distinguish between fidelity and fixation. Among them all, only *Evangeline* survives.

Irving himself thought *Tales of a Traveller* his best book, and his judgment was not absurd, for this was the only volume he had devoted entirely to fiction, and he was developing a new theory of narrative form which might have come to more than it did if further experiments had not been discouraged by the savage press which the book received. Poe, Longfellow, and Stevenson all loved it; perhaps Irving might find comfort here against not only the insensitiveness of contemporary reviewers but even the deplorably unimaginative tendency of many modern writers to echo them. It is true of course that the book lacks unity—but then it is called *Tales of a Traveller*—being divided into four parts: **"Strange Stories by a Nervous Gentleman," "Buckthorne and His Friends," "The Italian Banditti"** and **"The Money-Diggers."** (pp. 175-77)

"The Italian Banditti" is made up of conventional romantic materials of the kind one might expect to encounter under that title, not particularly distinctive perhaps but thoroughly enjoyable; the plots seem to be Irving's own. **"The Money Diggers"** is American material again, centered on the ideas of digging for pirate gold or gaining wealth through diabolical means. **"The Devil and Tom Walker"** is, of course, the finest narrative in this part of the book—and in the book in general—but **"Wolfert Webber"** is still well worth reading. (pp. 178-79)

[*The Alhambra*] combines *Arabian Nights* material, in the stories told, with honest, straightforward description of the place as it was in Irving's time, and of the people he encountered there. As he himself says, "Every thing in the work relating to myself and the actual inhabitants of the Alhambra is unexaggerated fact; it was only in the legends that I indulged in *romancing.*" As romancing it was very good.

The rest of Irving's work was repetition and addenda, or else it was factual and historical writing. Though not widely or intensively read today, it still commands considerable respect. (p. 179)

Modern detractors of Irving, like modern detractors of Longfellow, have generally been distressed over the fact that he was neither Herman Melville nor Ernest Hemingway. This much is undeniable, but why it should occasion so much distress is not quite clear. That he was a "genteel" writer admits of no doubt, but in his time "genteel" was not a dirty word. When he was seventy-five years old, he wrote a letter to a young relative not yet out of his teens, in which he described the personal qualities he admired:

> I have always valued in you what I considered to be an honorable nature; a conscientiousness in regard to duties; an open truthfulness; an absence of all low propensities and sensual indulgences; a reverence for sacred things; a respect for others; a freedom from selfishness, and a prompt decision to oblige; and, with all these, a gayety of spirit, flowing, I believe, from an uncorrupted heart, that gladdens everything around you.

His own possession of all these qualities was far above the average. And he valued their manifestation of themselves in books as well as in men.

It was not his function either to scale the heights or sound the depths of life; neither did he ever pretend to be able to do so. Though he was never so indifferent to either ideas or social evils as his critics would have us believe, he consistently inhabited a middle region which he surveyed and described with a winning, companionable charm. If you must have death in the afternoon and an orgy at night, he has nothing for you. And if life is flat and meaningless to you except in moments of rare spiritual ecstasy, he has nothing for you either.

Between the heights and the depths, however, there still lies a very wide and attractive area. The reading public which dwells there may be smug, and it may be dull, but it does not need to be kicked every few minutes to stay awake, and it is possible that the tides of life run higher and stronger here than in many other publics, and that it will survive longer. This is the area that Irving inhabits, and whatever other shortcomings it may have, there can be no question that it embraces a good deal of what we generally mean to indicate when we speak of civilization. (pp. 188-89)

Edward Wagenknecht, in his *Washington Irving: Moderation Displayed,* Oxford University Press, Inc., 1962, 233 p.

ROBERT A. BONE
(essay date 1963)

[In the following excerpt, Bone examines "The Legend of Sleepy Hollow" as an allegory of the conflict between materialism and the imagination in American society.]

Increasingly [in the early nineteenth century] the American writer found himself in an atmosphere of trade and commerce profoundly hostile to his art. In self-defense he turned to the Romantic movement, at the heart of which lay a spirited defense of the imagination.

During the Romantic period, the concept of imagination was itself transformed. Closely associated with devotional practices in the past, it now became more or less secularized. . . . As the role of the artist became increasingly differentiated from that of the clergyman or philosopher, the stage was set for a new phase in the history of the American imagination. *Henceforth the pressure of commodities would be experienced as a threat to the artistic process as such.*

It is Washington Irving's distinction first to have explored this theme. His interest in folklore, myth and legend provides him, in his best work, with a means of confronting the prosaic temper of his time. The folk tale, with its elements of fable and of fantasy, is an ideal medium, and it is here that Irving's creative powers reach fulfillment. **"The Legend of Sleepy Hollow"** is at once his finest achievement and his most enduring contribution to our literary history. For in the mythic encounter of Ichabod Crane and the Headless Horseman, the crisis of the modern imagination is first revealed.

The story begins with an epigraph from "The Castle of Indolence," by the Scottish poet James Thomson:

A pleasing land of drowsy head it was,
  Of dreams that wave before the half-shut eye;
And of gay castles in the clouds that pass,
  For ever flushing round a summer sky.

These lines serve primarily to establish the drowsy atmosphere of Sleepy Hollow, but are not without thematic relevance. "Dreams," "castles in the clouds," are suggestive of the imaginative faculty which is Irving's real concern. Moreover, the poem deals at length with the economic foundations of the arts; that is, with the question of patronage. This is one of the central issues which Irving means to raise.

Thomson is a spiritual cousin of Ben Franklin, and the poem amounts to a Calvinist homily on work. It is an allegorical attack on the slothful propensities of the leisure classes, and a sturdy defense of the Protestant ethic. Thomson is a poet, however, and he cannot suppress certain misgivings about the benefits of industry and progress. In particular, he deplores the loss of patronage which attends the passing of a cultured aristocracy. A jarring note thus intrudes upon his celebration of the Protestant virtues. In the old order, indolence brought social stagnation, but afforded a leisurely pursuit of art. The rise of the middle class portends great material prosperity, but leaves the fate of the poetic imagination in doubt.

This is precisely the mood of **"The Legend of Sleepy Hollow."** Dimly, uneasily, Irving sees the precarious position of the artist in bourgeois society. He is therefore of two minds as he contemplates the demise of Dutch colonial America. Fundamentally he approves of movement, activity and progress. Yet the story is saturated with nostalgia for the sheltered, protected, *embosomed* world of Sleepy Hollow, where dreams and reveries, ghosts and apparitions, still nourish the "visionary propensity."

Tarry Town emerges as a symbol of the colonial past, in which we tarry for a moment before moving on. The atmosphere is simple, uncomplicated, pastoral. It is established by such adjectives as quiet, listless, drowsy, dreamy, and such nouns as murmur, lull, repose, tranquillity. Captivated by the mood he has created, the narrator recalls his first exploit in squirrel hunting:

I had wandered into [a walnut grove] at noon time, when all nature is peculiarly quiet, and was startled by the roar of my own gun as it broke the Sabbath stillness around, and was prolonged and reverberated by the angry echoes.

It was a shot heard round the world. The disruptive roar of the gun heralds the introduction of the Hessian trooper, "whose head had been carried away by a cannon-ball, in some nameless battle during the Revolutionary War." To the quiet repose of the opening pages, Irving counterposes the furious speed of the galloping Hessian. He is seen "hurrying along in the gloom of the night, as if on the wings of the wind." He embodies the sudden violence of the Revolution, which brought the pastoral phase of the national life to an end. A new spirit is abroad in the land, the mercenary spirit of a Hessian soldier.

At this point it may be well to review the basic features of the plot, so as to establish a solid foundation for a symbolic interpretation. In essence, we have a romantic triangle. Ichabod Crane and Brom Bones are rivals for the hand of Katrina Van Tassel, the daughter of a prosperous Dutch farmer. Ichabod is defeated under comic circumstances, and as a result, his values are profoundly altered. Humiliation and defeat transform his life, but what is the inner meaning of these events?

As the three principals are introduced, certain details of characterization point to Irving's theme. To begin with, Ichabod's New England origins are heavily underscored:

> He was a native of Connecticut, a state which supplies the Union with pioneers for the mind as well as for the forest, and sends forth yearly its legions of frontier woodsmen and country schoolmasters.

His favorite book is Cotton Mather's *History of New England Witchcraft*. Great stress is laid upon his appetite, which is at once natural and supernatural, encompassing both the gustatory and the marvellous. In this he reflects the dilemma of his Puritan ancestors: the contest in his soul might be said to turn upon the question of which appetite will come uppermost.

The ascetic circumstances of his existence are suggested by the shabbiness of his schoolhouse and the itinerant character of his life. As he moves from home to home among his pupils' families, he carries "all his worldly effects tied up in a cotton handkerchief." His poverty, however, is not without its compensations. Because of his itinerant habits, he is welcomed as a bearer of news and gossip. He is esteemed by his neighbors as a man of letters, "for he had read several books quite through." He instructs the young people in psalmody, and his tales of the supernatural are a popular feature of village entertainment. Ichabod embodies, in short, the primitive impulse of a frontier society toward culture.

Since culture is viewed with suspicion in frontier communities, Ichabod is thought, "by all who understand nothing of the labor of headwork, to have a wonderfully easy time of it." Highly vulnerable to criticism, he is forced to justify his existence on utilitarian grounds:

> That all this might not be too onerous on the purses of his rustic patrons, who are apt to consider the costs of schooling a grievous burden, and school-

masters as mere drones, he had various ways of rendering himself both useful and agreeable.

There is something in the comic absurdity of Ichabod's situation which raises echoes of Cervantes. At one point, in fact, Ichabod rides forth "like a knight-errant in quest of adventures," astride a broken-down plough horse. In the light of these allusions, the character of Ichabod acquires a new dimension. Like Don Quixote, he is comic in appearance and behavior, but he must be taken seriously as a symbol of man's higher aspirations. Such a portrait requires a certain complexity of tone. For Ichabod is at once a comic and a tragic figure; he is, in Wallace Stevens' phrase, "A clown, perhaps, but an aspiring clown." In a portrait which is permeated with self-irony, Irving caricatures the position of the artist-intellectual in American life. Ichabod Crane is the first example in our literature of the comedian as the letter C.

Ichabod's antagonist is Brom Bones, "the hero of the country round." Brom's symbolic role is defined by a series of associations with the Headless Horseman. He is linked to the goblin rider by his skill in horsemanship and by the hurry-scurry of his midnight escapades. Like the Hessian, he scours the countryside with a squad of hard riders who dash about "like a troop of Don Cossacks." As the story reaches a climax, Brom becomes the literal incarnation of the Hessian trooper, for it is he, disguised as the Headless Horseman, who pursues Ichabod to his doom. Symbolically, Brom is the embodiment of the Hessian spirit, of mercenary values which threaten to engulf the imagination.

While Ichabod exists on the periphery of his culture, Brom occupies the very hub. Invisible spokes radiate from him to the entire male population of Sleepy Hollow. What is the "tough, wrong-headed, broad-skirted Dutch urchin who sulked and swelled and grew dogged and sullen beneath the birch" but a schoolboy version of Brom Bones? Brom's gang, whose behavior suggests the juvenile-delinquent phase of male development, harries the schoolmaster by smoking out his singing school and breaking into his schoolhouse after dark. (pp. 168-72)

Katrina is a pivotal figure; she provides the measure of Ichabod's social worth. The bestowal of her favors amounts to a kind of community sanction, for if Ichabod's society takes him seriously it must supply him with a wife. It is of course Brom Bones that she chooses; she has been flirting with the schoolmaster only to arouse the jealousy and ardor of his rival.

Irving's sketch of Katrina blends humorously with his description of her father's farm. She is "plump as a partridge; ripe and melting and rosy cheeked as one of her father's peaches." She wears "ornaments of pure yellow gold" whose colors call to mind the golden ears of Van Tassel corn, and "the yellow pumpkins . . .

turning up their fair round bellies to the sun." As Ichabod surveys his future prospects, the metaphors proclaim his gustatory love:

> In his devouring mind's eye . . . the pigeons were snugly put to bed in a comfortable pie, and tucked in with a coverlet of crust; the geese were swimming in their own gravy; and the ducks pairing cosily in dishes, like snug married couples, with a decent competency of onion sauce.

Faced with such temptations, Ichabod is defeated from within. Consider the implications of his name. "Ichabod" is from the Hebrew; it means "inglorious," or literally, "without honor." Ichabod is a turncoat; in pursuit of material comfort, he betrays a spiritual tradition. Confronted with the opulence of the Van Tassels, he succumbs to the sins of covetousness and idolatry. His imaginative faculty is perverted, deflected from its proper object:

> . . . his busy fancy already realized his hopes, and presented to him the blooming Katrina, with a whole family of children, mounted on the top of a wagon loaded with household trumpery, with pots and kettles dangling beneath; and he beheld himself bestriding a pacing mare, with a colt at her heels, setting out for Kentucky, Tennessee, or the Lord knows where.

Here is the New England imagination turned mercenary, placed in the service of the westering impulse. Brom Bones has only to bury the body.

Ichabod's encounter with the Headless Horseman is the dramatic climax of the story. The stage is set so carefully, however, that a closer look at the backdrop is in order. Dominating the landscape is an enormous tulip tree known in the neighborhood as Major André's tree. André was a young British officer, appointed by his superiors to consummate with Benedict Arnold negotiations for the betrayal of West Point. Captured by American militiamen after a midnight interview with Arnold, he was executed as a spy. In effect, he was a scapegoat, hanged for Arnold's crime. As a result, he occupies an ambiguous position in American history. This ambiguity seems to be the point so far as Irving is concerned:

> The common people regarded [Major André's tree] with a mixture of respect and superstition, partly out of sympathy for the fate of its ill-starred namesake. . . .

It is just this note of sympathy which Irving means to strike. Systematically he links "the unfortunate André" with "the unfortunate Ichabod," using the historical figure to control his tone. Let there be no mistake: Ichabod betrays the race of Cranes. The betrayal occurs at the quilting party, as he contemplates the possibility of becoming lord of the Van Tassel manor:

Then, he thought, how soon he'd turn his back upon the old schoolhouse; snap his fingers in the face of Hans Van Ripper, and every other niggardly patron, and kick any itinerant pedagogue out of doors that should dare to call him comrade!

But Irving wishes to soften the effect of this betrayal by shifting the burden in large part from Ichabod to his society. The reader is to respond to Ichabod rather as an André than an Arnold: not entirely guiltless, but largely the victim of circumstance. Yet the veiled threat remains. Irving recalls, by his allusion to Arnold, a famous episode in which the nation's neglect and ingratitude was repaid by treason. Be niggardly with your patronage, he warns the Hans Van Rippers, and your artists will desert to the enemy camp.

At the very spot where Major André was captured, Ichabod is accosted by the Headless Horseman. The schoolmaster is an unskillful rider; he attempts an evasive maneuver, but to no avail. With a fizzle and a sputter, Gunpowder ignites from the spark of his rider's fear, and off they fly, with the apparition in hot pursuit. As they near the safety of the bridge, the goblin rider rises in his stirrups and hurls his head at Ichabod, tumbling him into the dust.

What is the meaning of this parable? Ichabod is overwhelmed by the new materialism, but at an awesome price to society. For in order to conquer, the Hessian must throw away his head. The next morning a shattered pumpkin is found in the vicinity of the bridge. The organ of intellect and imagination has become an edible. The forces of thought have yielded to the forces of digestion.

Defeated by the spirit of the age, Ichabod reconstructs his life along more worldly lines. As rumor has it,

> . . . he had changed his quarters to a distant part of the country; had kept school and studied law at the same time, had been admitted to the bar, turned politician, electioneered, written for the newspapers, and finally had been made a justice of the Ten Pound Court.

It is hardly necessary to recall the unfortunate Irving's legal career to sense the diminution of spirit which the author intends. "The Ten Pound Court" unmistakably conveys the pettiness and triviality of Ichabod's new occupation. The community suffers a loss, the nature of which is defined by Ichabod's curious estate. A book of psalm tunes, a broken pitch pipe, Cotton Mather's *History of Witchcraft*, a book of dreams and fortune-telling, and an abortive attempt at verse in honor of Katrina: these crude tokens of the imaginative life are left behind as the schoolmaster vanishes from Sleepy Hollow.

The postscript is an ironic defense of the literary

imagination. The time is "the present," and it is clear that the descendants of Brom Bones are in the saddle. Folklore and legend, ghost stories and old wives' tales, have been superseded by an age of reason and common sense. Fiction itself has become suspect. Writing in a hostile climate, Irving supplies his fictional world with the trappings of historical research and objectivity. Hence the **"Postscript, Found in the Handwriting of Mr. Knickerbocker."**

This postscript recapitulates the theme; the dramatic situation alone has changed. The scene is "a Corporation meeting of the ancient city of Manhattoes, at which were present many of its sagest and most illustrious burghers." The role of Ichabod-Irving is played by a shabby narrator with a sadly humorous face, who is an entertaining storyteller, but is "strongly suspected of being poor." He has just told a tale called **"The Legend of Sleepy Hollow."** The role of Brom-Hessian is assumed by the sleepy aldermen who comprise his audience, and in particular by a literal-minded burgher who inquires as to the moral of the story, and what it goes to prove?

The narrator avoids a direct reply. The meaning of the story, Irving intimates, will not yield to purely logical methods. The art of fiction has nothing to do with "the ratiocination of the syllogism." The reader's imagination must supply the moral:

> The story-teller, who was just putting a glass of wine to his lips, as a refreshment after his toils, paused for a moment, looked at his inquirer with an air of infinite deference, and, lowering the glass slowly to the table, observed, that the story was intended most logically to prove:—
>
> That there is no situation in life but has its advantages and pleasures—provided we will but take a joke as we find it:
>
> That, therefore, he that runs races with goblin troopers is likely to have rough riding of it.
>
> Ergo, for a country schoolmaster to be refused the hand of a Dutch heiress, is a certain step to high preferment in the state.
>
> (pp. 172-75)

Robert A. Bone, "Irving's Headless Hessian: Prosperity and the Inner Life," in *American Quarterly*, Vol. XV, No. 2, Summer, 1963, pp. 167-75.

SOURCES FOR FURTHER STUDY

Aderman, Ralph M., ed. *Washington Irving Reconsidered: A Symposium.* Hartford, Conn.: Transcendental Books, 1969, 66 p.

Includes twelve articles on various aspects of Irving's career.

Bowers, Claude G. *The Spanish Adventures of Washington Irving.* Boston: Houghton Mifflin, 1940, 306 p.

Biography focusing on Irving's years in Spain, with extensive discussion of *The Alhambra.*

Hedges, William L. *Washington Irving: An American Study, 1802-1832.* The Goucher College Series. Baltimore: Johns Hopkins Press, 1965, 274 p.

A study of Irving's relevance to American literary history, examining his work and its relation to the intellectual character of his time.

Roth, Martin. *Comedy and America: The Lost World of Washington Irving.* Port Washington, N.Y.: Kennikat Press, 1976, 205 p.

Discusses the use of humor in Irving's writing. Roth also disputes the contention of Robert A. Bone that Irving personified the artistic imagination in Ichabod Crane (see excerpt dated 1963), arguing instead that Irving uses Crane to satirize the Yankee-Puritan element of New England society.

Springer, Haskell. *Washington Irving: A Reference Guide.* Boston: G. K. Hall, 1976, 235 p.

Lists secondary materials concerning Irving published between 1807 and 1974.

Williams, Stanley T. *The Life of Washington Irving.* 2 vols. New York: Oxford University Press, 1935.

The standard biography.

Shirley Jackson

1919-1965

American novelist, short story writer, and nonfiction writer.

INTRODUCTION

Jackson wrote several best-selling novels, but she is usually identified with "The Lottery," a classic short story that established her literary reputation as an author of gothic horror fiction. This frequently anthologized tale of victimization exemplifies the central themes of Jackson's fiction, which include such ordinary yet grotesque realities as prejudice, psychological malaise, loneliness, and cruelty. In works that often contain elements of conventional gothic horror, Jackson chronicles the universal evil underlying human nature. Her relatively impassive prose style belies the nihilism of her outlook; similarly, the charming hamlets that serve as settings for her tales contrast with the true malevolence of their inhabitants. Mary Kittredge asserted: "[Jackson's fiction] was the result of an exquisitely sensitive double vision that would have seemed an affliction to a less determined or talented writer. She saw the magic in the mundane, and the evil behind the ordinary. She saw that the line between the cruel and the comedic is sometimes vanishingly narrow."

Born into an affluent family in San Francisco, California, Jackson rebelled against her parents' superficial lifestyles and the restrictions that were placed upon women of her social class, and chose to spend much of her time alone writing in journals. Beginning in early childhood, Jackson claimed to possess psychic abilities and to be acutely aware of the clandestine thoughts and thinly-concealed viciousness of her upper-class community. In her first novel, *The Road through the Wall* (1948), she wrote of a snobbish neighborhood in suburban San Francisco and sketched its moral collapse as a result of prejudice and murder. This work affirmed Jackson's loathing of intolerance and bigotry. A plain, overweight woman, Jackson continually embarrassed her socially conscious mother, and further disgraced her Protestant family by marrying Stanley Edgar Hyman, a left-wing Jew and fellow student from Syracuse University who later became an eminent literary critic.

Following their marriage, the couple moved to North Bennington, Vermont, where Hyman taught English at the town's prestigious college and Jackson began publishing stories in various magazines. The diversity of her popular stories in such periodicals as *The New Yorker, Good Housekeeping, The Hudson Review, Woman's Day,* and *The Yale Review* thwarted the efforts of most critics to fit her work into any neat category. After her death, Hyman explained his wife's eclectic work: "Shirley Jackson wrote in a variety of forms and styles because she was, like everyone else, a complex human being, confronting the world in many different roles and moods. She tried to express as much of herself as possible in her work, and to express each aspect as fully and purely as possible." Despite general critical indifference, reviewers cite several enduring characteristics in Jackson's works. By omitting specific mention of such technical aspects as time and place, for example, Jackson shifted her thematic focus to universal human problems. Her style is compared to that of nineteenth-century author Nathaniel Hawthorne, who, like Jackson, disguised actual motives in rudimentary plotlines and sketched deceptively simple characters who reveal their true natures through gestures and mannerisms. Also as in Hawthorne's fiction, Jackson's works reveal the pressures exerted upon individuals by society. Carol Cleveland maintained: "In Jackson's world, the guilty are not greedy or crazy individuals, but society itself acting collectively and purposely, like a slightly preoccupied lynch mob." This belief is manifested in the short story, "The Lottery," originally published in 1948 in *The New Yorker.*

Described by Mary Kittredge as "beautifully imagined, sparely and gracefully written, a one-two punch of a story," "The Lottery" is invariably regarded as Jackson's most notorious work. On a lovely June morning, the citizens of a tranquil village gather in the town square for an annual drawing. Amidst laughter and gossip, families draw slips of paper from a ballot box until housewife Tessie Hutchinson receives the paper with a black mark on it, and the villagers stone her to death as a ritual sacrifice. The shocking impact of this unanticipated ending is intensified by Jackson's casual, detached narrative and serene setting. After publishing the story, *The New Yorker* received hundreds of letters and telephone calls expressing disgust, consternation, and curiosity, and Jackson herself received letters concerning "The Lottery" up to the time of her death. Many readers asked that Jackson interpret the theme, while some macabre individuals requested directions to the fictional town to observe the event. The latter people, Jackson later noted, embodied the human depravity depicted in her story.

Following "The Lottery," Jackson wrote dozens of stories, refining her emphasis on the need for individual identity in a repressive society. Many of her works have never been collected, but *The Lottery; or, The Adventures of James Harris* (1949) compiles several early short stories. Jackson twice received the Edgar Allan Poe Award, first for "Louisa, Please Come Home" in 1961 and again for "The Possibility of Evil" in 1965. The first story revolves around Louisa, a young woman who leaves home on her sister's wedding day, ignoring her family's pleas that she return. After four years, she relents, but has changed so drastically that the family cannot recognize her. Her very identity seems to have disappeared. "The Possibility of Evil" centers upon Adela Strangeworth, an elderly woman who enjoys sending slanderous and erroneous notes to people in her small town, anonymously informing them of their "wickedness."

Jackson was perpetually intrigued with the powers of the mind, and her fiction is replete with psychological insights. Her protagonists are frequently forlorn, socially misfit young women who undergo turbulent passages into adulthood. In Jackson's second novel, *Hangsaman* (1951), seventeen-year-old Natalie Waite mercifully escapes her father's oppression by leaving home to attend college. She does not have the social skills to adjust to the uninhibited environment, however, and so she invents Tony, an imaginary female friend. Tony soon becomes more frightening than friendly, and in a climactic scene, Natalie is forced to choose between reality and her imaginary friend. Many critics viewed Tony as Natalie's *doppelgänger,* regarding Natalie's rejection of her as an imperative step toward maturity and sanity. Jackson's next novel, *The Bird's Nest* (1954), is a psychological study based on a true case of multiple personality. Jackson's protagonist, Elizabeth Richmond, a somber, bland woman who is convinced she is responsible for her mother's death, invents alternate personas as a result of being unable to deal with guilt. With the help of a psychiatrist and an eccentric aunt, Elizabeth gradually regains control of her psyche. Generally regarded as Jackson's wittiest novel, *The Bird's Nest* was lauded for its comic yet compassionate treatment of mental disorder.

Jackson's next work, an apocalyptic, satirical novel titled *The Sundial* (1958), centers upon eleven boorish people who believe that the end of the world is near. Seeking sanctuary in a sprawling gothic estate, they burn the books in the library, irrationally stock the shelves with canned olives and galoshes, play cards, and bicker endlessly. At the novel's conclusion, the group is still waiting for Armageddon. Although Jackson presents the ironic possibility that these narcissists will spawn a new generation, critics generally felt that the repugnance of the characters overwhelmed the book's thematic content. A gothic manor again plays a crucial role in *The Haunting of Hill House* (1959). This work concerns an experimental psychic study held at Hill House, an eerie edifice that is presumed to be haunted. Research participants include Eleanor Vance, a timid, repressed woman with astonishing psychic powers. The other people brought to Hill House are confident and self-centered and soon alienate Eleanor from the only environment in which she was ever comfortable.

Jackson's last novel, *We Have Always Lived in the Castle* (1962), combines many of her most vital concerns—psychology, isolation, and evil—with a curiosity in black magic. Jackson possessed more than 200 books on the subject and seriously considered herself a witch, as did her friends and family. The resulting ostracism she endured from her community in North Bennington informs *We Have Always Lived In the Castle*, the story of two sisters victimized by their small New England village because of the unsolved mass murder of their family. Although neighbors believe the murder was committed by Constance, the older sister, Constance knows that her psychopathic younger sister Merricat poisoned the family by putting arsenic in the sugar bowl. In return for her sister's protection, Merricat shrouds Constance from the villagers' hostility and from the outside world. When their cousin Charles arrives hoping to collect the family fortune, the sisters' close alliance begins to crumble and Merricat burns down the house in a desperate attempt to kill Charles. After the fire, the neighbors stone the house and its inhabitants, and Charles departs, leaving Merricat and Constance to seek refuge in their burned-out mansion. Here Jackson questions the traditional definition of normality, suggesting that the villagers' violence is deviant behavior, while Merricat's actions are prompted by a psychological disturbance that should evoke sympathy and understanding. *We Have Always Lived in the Castle* was nominated for a National Book Award, and remains Jackson's most critically acclaimed novel.

Following the publication of *We Have Always Lived in the Castle*, Jackson began to suffer from severe mental and health problems. She sensed stronger animosity from the Bennington villagers, a justifiable fear since she had publicly admitted that they were the archetypes for the characters in "The Lottery." Her acute anxiety was aggravated by colitis, asthma, and agoraphobia, and she died of heart failure in 1965. After her death, Hyman published two omnibus volumes of her works, *The Magic of Shirley Jackson* (1966) and *Come along With Me* (1968). Both are notable for amassing previously uncollected stories, but *Come Along With Me* is especially significant for its title work, a comic novel that remained unfinished at the time of Jackson's death. The protagonist, a recently-widowed woman with a penchant for sorcery, embarks on a new life in the city. Carol Cleveland asserted: "This fragment has humor, verve, an undercurrent of eeriness, an appreciative echo of Flannery O'Connor, and is quite unlike any novel Jackson had yet published. *Come Along with Me* demonstrates that from the beginning to the end of her writing career, Shirley Jackson was at work mixing genres, confounding the expectations of the self-righteous and the placid."

(For further information about Jackson's life and works, see *Concise Dictionary of American Literary Biography, 1941-1968; Contemporary Authors*, Vols. 1-4, 25-28 [obituary]; *Contemporary Literary Criticism*, Vols. 11, 60; *Dictionary of Literary Biography*, Vol. 6: *American Novelists Since World War II*; and *Something about the Author*, Vol. 2.)

CRITICAL COMMENTARY

GEOFFREY WOLFF

(essay date 1968)

[The essay below is excerpted from a laudatory review of *Come Along with Me*, a posthumous collection of Jackson's short stories, lectures, and an unfinished novel. The collection was prepared by Jackson's husband, the eminent critic Stanley Edgar Hyman.]

"It has always been a comfort to me to make stories out of things that happen, things like moving, and kittens, and Christmas concerts at the grade school, and broken bicycles. . . . " This is the chattily domestic assurance of a lady whose most celebrated novel is narrated by an 18-year-old girl who poisoned to death her brother, her aunt, her mummy and her daddy at the age of 12. And whose best-known story is about a harmonious, happy village that each year chooses by lot a townsman to murder with stones.

Yet, *We Have Always Lived in the Castle* and "**The Lottery**" notwithstanding, Shirley Jackson was

---

Principal Works

The Road through the Wall (novel) 1948

The Lottery; or, The Adventures of James Harris (short fiction collection) 1949

Hangsaman (novel) 1951

Life among the Savages (nonfiction) 1953

The Bird's Nest (novel) 1954

Witchcraft of Salem Village (juvenile nonfiction) 1956

Raising Demons (nonfiction) 1957

The Sundial (novel) 1958

The Haunting of Hill House (novel) 1959

We Have Always Lived in the Castle (novel) 1962

The Magic of Shirley Jackson (short stories and novels) 1966

Come Along with Me (short stories, novel, and lectures) 1968

---

not being ghoulishly macabre, or even ironic, when she spoke of her comfort in making stories out of things that happen. The occasion for her remark was a lecture called **"Experience and Fiction"** (1958), during which she also said ". . . nothing is ever wasted; all experience is good for something; you tend to see everything as a potential structure of words."

Shirley Jackson's particular genius was to discover the commonplace details that co-exist with poisonous events, and the deadly, supernatural possibilities that agitate the commonplace. Her characteristic manner was to compose a tale of rather ordinary occurences so that it gradually began to radiate menace and corruption. She did this not by writing on several levels—hiding, as Hawthorne often did, her "real" intention—but by permitting a character's psychic life to reveal itself through representative gestures. Her stories seem ingenuous, yet they are impacted, implacably *written.* "Magic" is a word so commonly abused to modify "style" that it has lost its minted look. But if there is still any excuse to couple the two words, Shirley Jackson's effects provide it. The reader is moved beyond his expectations by some manipulation of his understandings that is complex and artful.

Now, three years after Shirley Jackson's death, her husband, the critic Stanley Edgar Hyman, has edited a collection of her writing [*Come Along With Me*]. Besides the title piece, a lamentably short first section of an unfinished novel, the collection includes 16 stories and three lectures.

Come Along With Me presents samples of Miss Jackson's work from 1938 to 1965. They are invariably about women, and usually about women trying to escape: from their parents or their husbands or the mem-

ory of their dead husbands. Typically, the heroine is described after she has run away; her motives for fleeing are lightly sketched or left entirely unrevealed. The story usually concerns itself with how she is affected by the liberation she sought.

In **"A Day in the Jungle"** (1952) a wife has fled her (presumably) ordinary husband to hole up in a hotel, which he locates without difficulty. When he telephones to reason with her, she agrees to meet him for dinner, but insists that for her it shall be no more than one way among many to pass the evening, that she will not return to him. Starting out for the restaurant, she is ". . . very much aware of the fact that for the first time she moved knowingly and of choice through a free world, that of all her life this alone was the day when she had followed a path she made alone . . . "

One paragraph later, as she walks along the street, fear begins to tug at her sleeve:

> The loving concern with which she put her feet down one after another on the sidewalk became without perceptible change, terror—was the cement secure? Down below, perhaps no more than two or three feet below, was the devouring earth, unpredictable and shifty. The sidewalk was set only upon earth, might move under her feet and sink, carrying her down and alone into the wet choking ground, and no one to catch her arm or a corner of her coat and hold her back.
>
> (p. 18)

Although very short, this story does many things. The plot describes a separation and a reconciliation. The underlying "meaning" concerns the danger of freedom from the known. Yet without at all straining for effect or implication, the story manages to substantiate paranoia, to invest objects with supernatural energy.

In **"The Lottery"** (1948) the environment is comforting and fruitful. The village is imagined as the apotheosis of the concept of community. Friendship and trust and good will are everywhere evident. There is solace in the gentle weather, the green trees, the ordered town—a town that must be the ideal of all in this country who would maintain law and order, who would resurrect the old values. Just one thing (often with Miss Jackson it is *just one thing*): to cultivate this paradise the good citizens must ritually sacrifice one of their number every year. This barbarism, too, is carried out in both a democratic and civilized manner. A family, and within that family one person, is chosen by lot.

To be told of **"The Lottery"** is doubtless to suspect it of the worst kind of sham and artifice. To read it is to know that it does not unappropriately join a brutal action to a pastoral setting. The story seems perfectly true. A sense of community is won at a price, and communal guilt and fear are seen as more binding than communal love.

We Have Always Lived in the Castle (1962—not in this volume) is Miss Jackson's most justly famed exploration of the nature of *communitas*, family unity, guilt and inheritance. It is, without qualification, the darkest, most sinister novel I have read. Mary Katherine Blackwood is mad, a murderer, a witch, and a child. Her sister, Constance, is a beautiful girl, 10 years older than "Merricat," teetering between madness and self-understanding. The girl's uncle, Julian, an urbane old man who is the only survivor of Merricat's remarkable crime besides Constance, similarly rocks back and forth from lunacy to wholesome good sense. The three live in a beleaguered old mansion. The townspeople suspect gentle Constance of the crime and are unnaturally cruel to the Blackwoods. A series of quite unbelievable crises end in the death of Uncle Julian, the grotesque mob insanity of the villagers, the partial burning of the house, and the complete self-isolation of the sisters in crazed retreat from a hostile world outside their boarded-up windows.

We Have Always Lived in the Castle forever verges toward Gothic Romance but never surrenders to it. The murder six years before, centerpiece of Merricat's narrative, is understood as at once a parable of supernatural power and a real event, heavy with expected consequence. Magic and witchcraft exist wholly in the mind: The tale does not indulge that impossible mix of the physical and the surreal characteristic of James' *The Turn of the Screw*. Miss Jackson's way, open and straightforward, is much more chilling.

The secret of her art in this novel is her "comfort" in describing "those things that happen." Food is important to the Blackwoods, and gardening, and household neatness and hospitality and good manners and straight talk. It is the perversion of these qualities (poison in the family's sugar) that so unnerves us. The madness is so tangled with the ordinary that we cannot shrug it away or hide from it. The blatant symbols—poison, the garden, the collective will of the community, the inherited house cleaned by fire—are not things and ideas that stand for something other than themselves. Rather they are the life of the novel.

In Freud's lexicon, the dream, or nightmare, is an allegory of hidden motives. In Miss Jackson's great novel, the nightmare lives on the surface, so terrifying because it seems so ordinary.

In none of Miss Jackson's tales that I have read is there an overt suggestion of sexuality. A very early story, **"A Cauliflower in Her Hair"** (1943), hints, in a kind of premonition of *Lolita*, at a father's desire for his young daughter's casual school acquaintance and at the child's sophistication. It is impossible for me to tell whether Miss Jackson's repression of explicit sexuality was a function of personal nicety or aesthetic intention, but it is a strange omission. It is also, intentionally or not, very sexy. One wonders what the 18-year-old murderer looks like, feels like. Physical touch is all Miss Jackson leaves unnamed and unexplored; we are made very alive to its absence. (pp. 18-19)

Come Along With Me would, I presume, have been a very funny novel. It is about a widow who buried her artist husband and moves to a rooming house in a strange city. (Miss Jackson sets many of her stories in rooming houses of strange cities.) Aside from *We Have Always Lived in the Castle,* the unfinished book exhibits Shirley Jackson's best prose. By 1965 she had mastered the kind of nutty-serious dialogue that she had tended toward for a long while. The heroine meets her landlady for the first time and is asked:

"And what do you do, Mrs. Motorman?"

"I dabble in the supernatural. Traffic with spirits. Seances, messages, psychiatric advice, that kind of thing."

There it is: the casual voice describing, comfortably, as though it were commonplace, the incredible. We hear the voice again in my favorite of Mrs. Motorman's many marvelous lines. "Once an old man followed me, but he turned out to be real." That "but" is astonishing—wonderful—but of course . . . (p. 19)

Geoffrey Wolff, "Shirley Jackson's 'Magic Style'," in *The New Leader,* Vol. LI, No. 17, September 9, 1968, pp. 18-19.

LYNETTE CARPENTER
(essay date 1982)

[The essay excerpted below was originally presented as a paper at a writer's conference at Hofstra University in November 1982. Carpenter asserts that the critical neglect of Jackson's wide variety of works is due to the inability of "traditional male critics . . . [to] reconcile genre with gender."]

Shirley Jackson's short story, **"The Lottery,"** published in 1948, was responsible for the greatest amount of mail ever received by *The New Yorker* up to that time in response to a piece of fiction. Jackson herself once said, "It was not my first published story, nor my last, but I have been assured over and over that if it had been the only story I ever wrote or published, there would be people who would not forget my name." Now, seventeen years after her death in 1965, an informal survey will indicate that most people remember neither Jackson's name nor the name of her famous story, although most people can, with a little prodding, reconstruct a fairly accurate plot summary out of their memories of high school or college English. Jackson's story has become a part of our educational, and therefore cultural, heritage; her name has been forgotten. And despite her remarkable achievement of both critical acclaim and popular success during her lifetime, she has been virtually ignored by critics and written out of literary history since her death. I would like to suggest that the reasons for this neglect are also reasons for the reevaluation of Shirley Jackson by feminist critics. I will argue that traditional male critics could not, in the end, reconcile genre with gender in Jackson's case; unable to understand how a serious writer of gothic fiction could also be, to all outward appearances, a typical housewife, much less how she could publish housewife humor in *Good Housekeeping,* they dismissed her. Feminist critics, on the other hand, should be able to appreciate the variety of Jackson's writings and the range of her experiences as wife, mother, and Great American Novelist.

To the extent that she is remembered at all, Jackson is remembered for her gothic fiction or psychological thrillers, and one might well contend that writers of gothic fiction have rarely held a secure place in literary history. Worse for Jackson, she was a humorist as well; one of the distinguishing features of her work is a delicate balancing of humor and horror that is bound to make the reader uneasy. In *The Road through the Wall* (1948), for example, when the comically portrayed thirteen-year-old neighborhood outcast hangs himself, our shock is compounded by our previous guilty participation in laughter at his expense. We may even feel betrayed because the author induced us to laugh at a character she knew to be tragically doomed. A similar situation occurs in *The Haunting of Hill House* (1959), in which the narrative's gentle mockery of the main character does not prepare us for her suicide at the end. Jackson's habit of mocking the doomed must have seemed to many traditional readers decidedly unfeminine.

Still, perhaps the literary historians would have accepted Jackson had she led the ill-fated life of an Edgar Allan Poe. But she did not conform to stereotype. Married to distinguished critic Stanley Edgar Hyman, she was, by published accounts, a model mother, hostess, PTA activist, cookie baker, and faculty wife. And if, in the end, she fell victim to severe nervous depression, no one considered it madness, since model wives and mothers did not, in those days, go mad. How could such a woman write stories about thirteen-year-old suicides, human sacrifice rituals, twelve-year-old girls who dispatched their families with arsenic? To make matters worse, she called herself a witch.

Historians might know less about Jackson's life had she not published numerous domestic sketches throughout her career, collected in *Life among the Savages* (1953) and *Raising Demons* (1957). Although Jackson herself never called these sketches autobiographical, most readers take them to be slightly modi-

fied accounts of actual events. . . . They are humorous tales in the vein of Jean Kerr and Erma Bombeck about the everyday trials of managing a household and raising children. Stanley Edgar Hyman once wrote that critics did not understand Jackson because they could not reconcile these stories, published in such magazines as *Good Housekeeping, Woman's Day,* and *Woman's Home Companion* with what they considered her more serious work, published in such journals as the *Hudson Review,* the *Yale Review,* and *The New Yorker.* In fact, the sketches display some of the same preoccupations as Jackson's fiction—her interest in the psychology of women and children, her fascination with fantasy worlds and characters, as well as with split or multiple personalities, and her appreciation of irony—but the tone is clearly different. Hyman's comment suggests that since critics were at a loss to explain how one writer could produce both gothic horror and cheerful housewife humor, they gave her up. We might also ask whether writers of domestic sketches have ever been taken seriously as writers. Is it not possible that Jackson's publication of housewife humor in the *Woman's Home Companion* hurt her literary reputation, caused critics, in the last analysis, to reconsider their estimation of her other work? If so, Jackson is overdue for a feminist reevaluation. (pp. 143-44)

In fiction, she writes most often about women. The typical Jackson protagonist is a lonely young woman struggling toward maturity. She is a social misfit, not beautiful enough, charming enough, or articulate enough to get along well with other people, too introverted and awkward. In short, she does not fit any of the feminine stereotypes available to her. She is Harriet Merriam in *The Road through the Wall* (1948), an overweight teenager who thinks to herself, "You'll always be fat, . . . never pretty, never charming, never dainty," and who may have been the one to murder pink and white, doll-like Caroline Desmond because the little girl was everything Harriet was not. She is Natalie Waite in *Hangsaman* (1951), whose feelings of isolation and alienation during her first few months away at college generate a fantasy other, an imaginary friend. She is Elizabeth Richmond in *The Bird's Nest* (1954), whose adolescent confusion about her mother and her mother's lover splits her at last into a tangle of discrete personalities. She is Eleanor Vance in *The Haunting of Hill House* (1959), whose feelings of rejection and social displacement ultimately lead her to suicide. She is Mary Katherine Blackwood in *We Have Always Lived in the Castle* (1962), who lives with her sister in a state of siege, barricaded against a town's hostility. She is Mrs. Angela Motorman in *Come Along With Me* (unfinished, 1965), whose world has always been peopled by creatures no one else can see. She is even Aunt Fanny in *The Sundial* (1958), whose life of uselessness as a maiden aunt is vindicated by a vision of doomsday.

These women are all victims, and several are clearly victimized by men. Elizabeth Richmond's split personality in *The Bird's Nest* is a result of her mother's neglect, but also of sexual exploitation by her mother's lover. Patriarchs, however, are often the villains. Natalie Waite's father in *Hangsaman* attempts to continue his proprietary control of her intellectual development even after she has gone off to college, just as Aunt Fanny's father presides over her life from beyond the grave by sending her visions of Armageddon. Mary Katherine Blackwood of *We Have Always Lived in the Castle* is the strongest of Jackson's heroines: she retaliates against her tyrannical father by poisoning him, along with most of the rest of her family. Patriarchy is not beside the point in this novel; Mary Katherine's brother, heir to Blackwood male power, gets the most arsenic. The climax of the novel occurs when a male cousin, supported by the men of the town, attempts to assume her father's role as family head and dictator.

Equally interesting to the feminist critic should be Jackson's portrayal of women's relationships to other women, beginning with her portrayal of adolescent friendships in *The Road through the Wall.* For most of the girls on Pepper Street, allegiances are drawn by intimidation; the most outspoken and audacious girls attract followers, until a tacitly understood hierarchy exists. Overweight Harriet Merriam, however, manages to develop a close friendship with the Jewish outcast Marilyn Perlman, until Mrs. Merriam intervenes. Without someone to share her ostracism, Harriet falls victim to despair. In *The Haunting of Hill House,* the lonely Eleanor Vance becomes infatuated with the beautiful Theodora when both are invited to a haunted house by a psychic investigator. The appearance of a young man introduces rivalry, tension, and cruelty into the relationship, as Eleanor struggles to maintain her favored status with Theodora. Eleanor kills herself when she is sent away and perceives that she is again to be excluded.

But the closest female friendship is that between the sisters, Mary Katherine and Constance Blackwood, in *We Have Always Lived in the Castle.* With all of the family dead from arsenic poisoning except Uncle Julian, who has been left a feeble-minded invalid by the attack, the Blackwood patriarchy has evolved into a matriarchy, and Constance Blackwood is its benign ruler. Mary Katherine, or Merricat, the narrator, says of her older sister, "She was the most precious person in my world, always," and the narrative is punctuated by their declarations of love for each other. Although Constance mothers Merricat, Merricat tries to protect Constance from the townspeople, who believe that Constance was the murderer despite her acquittal. The visit from a male Blackwood cousin signifies more than an attempt to reinstate the Blackwood patriarchy; it is also an attempt to undermine the love between the sisters upon which their matriarchal harmony depends. Cousin Charles tempts Constance with a romantic illusion of heterosexual happiness, a life more natural, in his eyes and in the eyes of the townspeople, than the life she is living with her sister. Merricat fights back and wins. After a cataclysmic confrontation which exposes Cousin Charles' greed and the murderous hostility of the townspeople, and which leaves Uncle Julian dead of a heart attack, the two women resolve to spend the rest of their lives together in isolation, and barricade themselves against intrusion from the outside world. In the final pages of the book, Constance tells her sister, "I am so happy."

The story about the persecution of two women who choose female companionship over heterosexual romance will sound familiar to many readers familiar with feminist writings on witchhunts and witchhunters. The connection is made explicit in the novel: Merricat aspires to be a witch, constantly devising spells and charms, but it is Constance who possesses the wise woman's knowledge of plants and their properties. Jackson herself owned a large collection of works on demonology. In the mid-fifties, she wrote *The Witchcraft of Salem Village* (1956). Yet even earlier, Jackson had established herself as a champion of the persecuted and the oppressed. At Syracuse University in the late thirties, she and Hyman had waged a bitter campaign against racial discrimination in campus housing. Her first novel, *The Road through the Wall,* portrays discrimination against Jews and Orientals. (pp. 145-47)

Finally, a feminist critic should be better able to piece together Jackson's life and art than a traditional critic. . . . After Betty Friedan's analysis of the pathology of the feminine mystique, or even Erma Bombeck's witty commentary on Supermoms, how can we read a catalogue of Jackson's virtues as wife, mother, and great American writer without wondering how she kept her sanity? She was chauffeur to a family of six (her husband did not drive), PTA mother, Little League supporter, a wonderful cook, an energetic hostess, and a one-time president of the faculty wives' club at Bennington College. But she was also a prolific writer, and wrote every day, taking time out to serve refreshments at regular Thursday night poker games. *We Have Always Lived in the Castle* was written during the early years of Jackson's illness, when she found the company of others increasingly difficult to bear and began to withdraw into seclusion. She created Mary Katherine Blackwood, a narrator all contemporary reviewers labeled mad, shortly before beginning psychiatric treatment for her own anxieties. (p. 147)

When she died of heart failure in 1965, she was working on a new novel, *Come Along with Me*—apparently a "happy book." It was the first Jackson novel to feature a female protagonist close to Jackson's own age. The narrator is a recent widow who buries her husband, sells her house, picks a city at random, and gleefully starts off for a new life under a new name. The book can be seen as a celebration of new beginnings. Ironically for Jackson, however, who had once been assured that her name would not be forgotten, the book marks the end of a distinguished career and the beginning of critical forgetfulness. Writing is the way out. (pp. 147-48)

Lynette Carpenter, "Domestic Comedy, Black Comedy, and Real Life: Shirley Jackson, a Woman Writer," in *Faith of a (Woman) Writer,* edited by Alice Kessler-Harris and William McBrien, Greenwood Press, 1988, pp. 143-48.

JOHN G. PARKS
(essay date 1984)

[In the following excerpt, Parks examines Jackson's use of gothic conventions in her novels.]

Mrs. Arnold of Shirley Jackson's story **"Colloquy"** (1944) feels driven to see a psychiatrist because of her confusion and bewilderment over her loss of " 'a world where a lot of people lived too and they all lived together and things went along like that with no fuss.' " The psychiatrist tries to get her to accept "reality," which to him means to accept and adapt to a world with "cultural patterns rapidly disintegrating." Mrs. Arnold refuses to adapt to the doctor's "disoriented world" and leaves his office. But the reader senses that the price for her refusal to accept the doctor's, and the rest of society's, definition of reality will be loneliness and madness. This story is in many ways representative of the concern of most of Jackson's fiction, which is to reveal and chronicle the outrage, at times tempered with laughter, stemming from the violation of the self by a broken world. Through the effective use of gothic conventions Jackson reveals the contours of human madness and loneliness in a disintegrating world generally bereft of the meliorating power of love and forgiveness. (p. 15)

[Very] few of her protagonists achieve much of a victory over oppression. Indeed most of Jackson's protagonists are emotionally violated and must struggle desperately to overcome their estrangement and dislocation, and most of them fail.

Appearing in the same year as her famous story **"The Lottery,"** Jackson's first novel, *The Road through the Wall* (1948), chronicles the collapse of a small community due to its own inner demonic contradictions. By focusing upon a whole neighborhood, rather than

upon a single violated protagonist as in her other novels, the novel creates an effective metaphor or microcosm for the tensions inherent in the culture in the postwar period. Moreover, whether the protagonist is individual or collective, the novel adumbrates and begins exploration of one of Jackson's primary concerns throughout her career: the dark incomprehensible spot or stain upon the human soul and our continuing blindness and, hence, vulnerability to it. Jackson's fiction refuses to compromise with the glib psychologies of our therapeutic age.

The story takes place in Cabrillo, a fictitious suburb of San Francisco, in 1936. It concerns a group of families and single individuals who live side by side in relative privacy and in apparent harmony, a kind of cross section of middle-class and upper-class aspiring families. Their children attend school together and share the street in play. Some of the parents gather weekly for sewing, and less frequently for parties. The apparent security and equilibrium of this community are broken and destroyed by a series of events. The first important event is the tearing down of the wall in order to extend and join Pepper Street with the one beyond the wall. This serves as a kind of catalyst for the rest of the action and the climax of the story. A three-year-old girl is discovered missing from a party at one of the homes, necessitating an all-out search. Missing also is a thirteen-year-old boy who "acted funny." Panic and wild imaginings spread. The little girl is soon found dead, her head smashed in by a rock. The boy is accused of murder, but before anything is found out he hangs himself. The important thing about the novel is not the plot, but, rather, as in most of Shirley Jackson's stories, the gradual unfolding of the layers of human personality, sometimes in response to, other times causative of, events.

The novel operates on two complementary levels. On one level the novel presents an exposure and examination of the social morals and manners of a community. The presence of a Jewish family and the incipient and, at times, outright anti-Semitism of the community, and the hidden envies due to economic differences are instances of this. These are symptomatic of what is going on at a deeper level—the level of the inner workings of the personality, and this is ultimately what the novel is seeking to delineate. The real world of the novel is not the world of social realism. There are enough features about it to indicate otherwise. The way the novel begins gives it the quality of the fairy tale or fable: "The weather falls more gently on some places than on others, the world looks down more paternally on some people. Some spots are proverbially warm, and keep, through falling snow, their untarnished reputations as summer resorts; some people are automatically above suspicion." And the use of the old gothic convention of the old woman making prophecies is further evidence that the novel is not just concerned with social conflicts. Its concern is with the inner demonic cancer of the community and how it eats away and destroys not only individuals, but families and the social unit as a whole. In short, beneath the mask of the ordinary lies unrecognized terror.

The Road through the Wall exemplifies what Irving Malin calls the "new American gothic" [in his book of the same title], in which the psyche is given priority over society, or, in Malin's words, "the disorder of the buried life must be chartered." The new American gothic employs a microcosm, with love as a primary concern. The weakling characters struggle with narcissism which often destroys others as well as themselves. Their narcissism leads them to make reality into a reflecting mirror of their own compulsions. The chief microcosm is the family, which "dramatizes the conflict between private and social worlds, ego and super-ego." In new American gothic, as in old gothic, there is often a confused chronology and dream quality about the narrative. The old conventions of the gothic—the haunted castle or house, the voyage or flight, and the reflection—function now as images of narcissistic love and antagonism. Nearly all journeys end in failure or disaster. The narcissism of the characters intensifies their isolation and loneliness, creating a kind of vicious, self-destructive cycle.

Using the neighborhood as her microcosm, Jackson presents a series of short glimpses into the households on the street—the tangled relationships, the lovelessness which produces its own poison that strangles and chokes off spontaneous life. The youngster accused of murdering the three-year-old girl is a victim of familial lovelessness. The evidence against him is circumstantial at best, but, with few exceptions, the street accepts his guilt. The crime or accident raises the larger issue of human responsibility. The novel depicts a community so fragile and sick that the ultimate responsibility is diffuse and all are implicated, no one is innocent. That few even glimpse this possibility betokens a community bereft of imagination and morally bankrupt.

Against this background of communal failure, Jackson moves in her second novel, *Hangsaman* (1951), into an initiation story tracing the descent into madness of an individual protagonist and her apparent return to a tenuous grasp upon reality. Natalie Waite, a college freshman, spends half her time in an imaginary world where she is being questioned by a detective regarding a murder, leaves family and home for college, and faces loneliness, hostility, and rejection by most of her peers, encounters the duplicity of institutions and adult life, falls into a relationship with a strange girl named Tony, who may herself be wholly imaginary, and comes near to a loss of self through absorption or suicide before finally emerging from the woods, literally as well as figu-

ratively, to a new self-understanding and a new approach to tangible reality. Natalie does, however, make the frightful transition from innocence of a sort, to experience, to the beginning of adult life. (pp. 16-19)

Natalie needs to escape from the heavy dominance of an egotistical and narcissistic father who seeks to create Natalie in his own image. Her mother has escaped from her dominating husband by fleeing into drink so that she offers no solace to Natalie in her time of need. (p. 19)

Out of desperation and loneliness, Natalie retreats deep into herself and her rich fantasy life. Writing fervently in her secret journal, she dreams of a time when people will fear her and she will be revered and respected. She lives with the feeling that something momentous is about to happen to her. She develops a close relationship with Tony, another despised girl on campus. To Natalie, Tony is exotic, clever, intelligent, and self-possessed. However, it is not clear throughout the novel whether Tony is real or an imagined creation that fulfills Natalie's need. In any case, Tony functions as Natalie's *Doppelgänger,* and as such represents Natalie's own growing fragmentation and self-alienation. Together they read the Tarot cards, and walk about the town like two Alices in a Wonderland of their own making. From the significantly named "Paradise Park," the winter-abandoned recreation area, Tony leads Natalie into the woods for a decisive encounter. If Tony is real, the scene may suggest a homosexual seduction or a kind of vampirism by her dark double, as in some of Poe's stories, or possibly even suicide. As a fantasy projection, the threat is psychic destruction through narcissistic nihilism. In either case, Natalie loses self and retreats from reality. But at the last moment, Natalie repels the dark other's embrace and returns to the school and to a renewed sense of reality. Out of her own inner resources, Natalie is able to repel the threat of her "dark lady" and make a successful, though perilous, passage to the world of experience and the knowledge of good-and-evil.

Shirley Jackson's fiction is filled with lonely, desperate women who reflect the disintegrations of modern life. This is seen quite clearly in Elizabeth Richmond, the disintegrating protagonist of *The Bird's Nest* (1954), Jackson's third novel. She is twenty-three years old when we first meet her in the novel, and lives with her eccentric maiden aunt, Morgen Jones, in an ugly, almost gothic, house. Her mother died when Elizabeth was nineteen, and since that time she has not spoken intimately with anyone; her life has become a virtual blank. She works in the upstairs office of the local museum because her aunt felt the job would give Elizabeth a more definite identity. But when the museum begins to undergo renovation, Elizabeth's precarious hold on reality slips, and she falls prey to a form of "possession" all too common in the modern world. As Rollo

May describes it [in *Love and Will*]: "Loneliness and its stepchild, alienation, can become forms of demon possession. Surrendering ourselves to the impersonal daimonic pushes us into an anonymity which is also impersonal; we serve nature's gross purposes on the lowest common denominator, which often means with violence." The violence in which Elizabeth indulges, as her demons come to the surface to haunt her, is a convoluted kind turned against her own fragile self.

While Shirley Jackson was a lifelong student of mental illness, and all of her novels explore some aspect of the inner life, *The Bird's Nest* is doubtless her most overtly psychological novel. She got the idea for the novel in part from reading Morton Prince's 1905 study entitled *The Dissociation of a Personality*, which records the case of a person with several successive personalities. Besides the complex psychic struggles of the patient, Jackson was also struck by the role of the psychiatrist, and how oblivious he appeared to the possibility that the various personalities of his patient might be creations of his own imagination. This same obtuseness is made a part of the character of the novel's Dr. Victor Wright, the rather oddball meta-psychiatrist who patterns himself after Thackeray. This purblind but essentially benevolent doctor treats Elizabeth for two years with the use of hypnosis. When he discovers four competing personalities in Elizabeth, he gives each one a name and sets out to fulfill the godlike role of creating a new person. He definitely likes some of the personalities better than others; indeed, he recoils instinctively from the demonic aspects of Elizabeth's psyche and seeks to destroy them in the name of his self-declared superior judgment and goodness. Despite his benevolence, it is quite clear that the pretentious good doctor is not aware of the implications of his treatment. (pp. 19-21)

Unlike Natalie of *Hangsaman,* who had no adult guides to turn to in her journey, Elizabeth is aided by the eccentric Aunt Morgen, whose quick, but masculine and coarse, wit makes her a perfect foil for the pompous Dr. Wright. It is from Aunt Morgen that Elizabeth learns the truth about her mother's death— Elizabeth was not to blame for it as she had believed. With the release from guilt, Elizabeth is able to make the journey back to wholeness—her four personalities disappear and a new one emerges. At the end the doctor and Morgen assign her a new name, Victoria Morgen, thus making her a product of both their imaginations, an ending not without irony and ambiguity.

The novel, as the first two, employs several features of the gothic. While the gothic mansion is not given much prominence, it is described as an ugly monstrosity well suited to an eccentric maiden aunt. There is the journey or flight from imprisonment when Elizabeth escapes to New York in search of her mother. And there is the reflection when the disintegrating Elizabeth sees her image in all the shiny surfaces of a room, symbolizing her growing schizophrenia and loss of control, and there are the split personalities which were always cropping up in Poe and the vampire novels.

The gothic house is a prominent feature of Jackson's last three novels. It serves not just as the focus of action or as atmosphere, but as a force or influence upon character or a reflection of character. . . . The house not only reflects the insanities of its occupants, but serves as a fitting microcosm of the madnesses of the world.

One is used prominently in *The Sundial* (1958), which employs all the gothic conventions for comic and satiric purposes. (pp. 21-2)

Showing her ability to find pity and terror in the ludicrous and the ludicrous in terror, Jackson created a fantasy of the end of the world which parodies the apocalyptic imagination, while at the same time portraying it. The novel is a full exposition of the poem by William Empson entitled "Just A Smack at Auden," especially this verse:

Shall we go all wild, boys, waste and make them lend,
Playing at the child, boys, waiting for the end?
It has all been filed, boys, history has a trend,
Each of us enisled, boys, waiting for the end.

At the end of the novel eleven self-elected survivors of the imminent end of the world are all there waiting, with Mrs. Halloran dead and propped up against the sundial on the lawn of the great Halloran estate, the windows and doors battened down from the inside as protection against the growing winds of doom. Some play bridge. Others talk of the realism of a recent movie. A few drink scotch and yawn in anticipation. " 'My,' Mrs. Willow stretched, and sighed. 'It's going to be a long wait,' she said." Indeed it is, for we leave them feeling that they will still be waiting to enter their hoped-for brave new world when the supplies they have stored in the library have been used up. The disconfirmation of apocalypse will doubtless lead only to new "revelations" and to new calculations for their waiting game. No matter, for they have already sealed their doom, which this grisly tale of comic horror and fantasy reveals.

The novel is concerned with the nature of belief, with the way desperate people grasp a belief and make it their truth, with how belief and madness combine, in turn, and lead to more desperate behavior, with how belief can be a form of madness itself, making people into grotesques. Jackson portrays twelve people who become grotesques because they need, and desperately want, to believe in the apocalyptic revelations of the mad spinster Aunt Fanny, who herself is in a desperate contest, a power struggle for control of the massive Halloran estate with the matriarch Mrs. Halloran. Before Mrs. Halloran can gain total control of the estate and carry out her threatened banishments, Aunt Fanny has a "revelation" from her dead father of the impending end of the world. The only survivors, he reveals, will be the residents of the Halloran mansion, who will enter a new and better world. Because everyone else longs to accept the revelations as fact, Mrs. Halloran is forced to concede to their belief and attempts to control a household of people who now regard themselves as a new chosen race.

In preparation for the new day, the Halloran clan burn all the books in the library and stock it with tons of food and supplies, and, remembering Robinson Crusoe, a grindstone, several shotguns, and hunting knives. Mrs. Halloran draws up a list of rules for conduct in the new era, setting herself as the sole monarch. But Mrs. Halloran fails in her attempt to control both present and future, for on the night before the expected new day, she falls or is pushed down the stairs, and her corpse is propped up against the sundial on the lawn.

The insane revelations of Aunt Fanny speak to a sense of loss and of the possibility of recovery that each within the house feels. Each is filled with what one of the characters calls "a kind of unholy, unspeakable longing." It takes over the self: "It is a longing so intense that it creates what it desires, it cannot endure any touch of correction. . . . This longing feeds the need to believe, no matter how bizarre the belief. And yet, at one point in their preparations, Mrs. Halloran remarks: "I wonder what nonsense we would be engaged in, if we were not doing this," to which her courtier, Essex, replies: " 'It is probably just as well that we have some nonsense to occupy us; just think of the harm we could do if we were bored.' " Mrs. Halloran and Essex, on one level at least, still realize that what they are engaged in is a fiction, a masquerade, a game, and can indulge in irony about it. But as they continue to play, the game becomes reality, each player acts in deadly earnest, and they become trapped in their own fiction and lose the capacity to change it. What begins as "harmless nonsense" evolves into a game involving unimagined consequences. The novel satirizes a human condition in which gullibility, cupidity, and culpability reign virtually unrestrained by moral principle, and create a community of the survival of the worst.

In *The Sundial* Shirley Jackson portrays the elitism of the apocalyptic mind that sees only itself as being worthy of survival and salvation. It is an imagination which accepts powerlessness and surrenders human responsibility to what it regards as an overpowering destiny, in the name of which any crime is possible. To the Halloran household the world will end and begin again with itself as the inheritor. (pp. 22-4)

While a setting for what begins as a mad masquerade party in *The Sundial,* the gothic house in a real sense is the chief character of *The Haunting of Hill House* (1959), Jackson's fifth and probably most popu-

lar novel. Its presence is felt on nearly every page. The house is over eighty years old and carries the unsavory reputation of death, madness, revenge, and suicide. It is marked by "clashing disharmony," everything off center, made entirely at "wrong angles," all the small aberrations adding up to a rather large distortion. Its basic structure is laid out in concentric circles, with rooms surrounded by other rooms—a "mother house." It is a fitting metaphor for madness, for the irrational, for an illogic that perversely coheres. . . . It is this house which welcomes home the utterly guilt-ridden, lonely, and loveless protagonist, Eleanor Vance, who surrenders willingly to its dark embraces, her own fragile self dissolving and fusing with the substance of Hill House.

Eleanor Vance, another of Jackson's violated women, is brought to Hill House as part of a scientific experiment into psychic phenomena. She is so fragile and vulnerable that her survival is questionable from the beginning. Her chief foil, reminiscent of Dr. Wright of *The Bird's Nest,* is Dr. Montague, a pompous academic representing scientific rationalism and logic. He is little more than an intellectual voyeur, knowing very much, but really understanding very little, especially when it comes to the mysteries of the human personality and the human heart. Terror and fear, the fatuous doctor believes, can be explained and controlled in terms of logic and will: " 'Fear . . . is the relinquishment of logic, the *willing* relinquishment of reasonable patterns. We yield to it or we fight it, but we cannot meet it half way.' " This militant rationalist shows little compassion for Eleanor's loss of sanity and banishes her from the house to protect his so-called experiment.

The character Theodora is another of Jackson's "dark ladies," recalling the figure of Tony in *Hangsaman.* She is the opposite of Eleanor. She is secular and much experienced, exotic and exciting, representing, in part, what Eleanor might have been if her life had not been so restricted and inhibited. At times Theodora's ministrations to Eleanor verge on the lesbian. At other times she ridicules Eleanor, and when Eleanor desperately reaches out for help, Theodora turns away abandoning her to her lonely dissolution. (pp. 24-5)

There is no place in the world for Eleanor. Unlike the Apollonian Dr. Montague, the Dionysian and cynical Theodora, Eleanor has no resources to call upon for survival. Her loneliness and schizophrenia find a welcome in the chaos of Hill House. If Eleanor is abandoned to suicide, the house remains unconquerable, eluding the vain assaults of rationality and pointing to the mysterious and incomprehensible.

The gothic mode serves well Jackson's purpose to explore the depths and contours of female violation in the modern world. Alfred Kazin writes [in his *Bright Book of Life*] that " 'woman's fiction' exists not as writing by women but as inordinate defensiveness against a society conceived as the special enemy of the sensitive." In Jackson, he says, the stories reveal a pattern of "assault, deception, betrayal," where a woman as victim is the protagonist and her defenselessness is the story. While we may disagree with his assessment of "woman's fiction," his suggested pattern applies well to most of the protagonists of Jackson's novels.

Violation, in the sense of assault, deception, and betrayal, is the concern of Jackson's sixth and last complete novel *We Have Always Lived in the Castle* (1962). Here also, as in so much of Jackson's work, there is a sense of primal sin and darkness pervading a world where forgiveness is lacking, where love is ambiguous, where hatred and hostility are all too ready to surface into action. (pp. 25-6)

For the first time in Jackson's novels, the tale of violation and defenselessness is told by a first-person narrator, the mad eighteen-year-old Merricat Blackwood, who murdered four members of her family with arsenic six years before the story starts. Merricat's older sister, Constance, was accused but acquitted for lack of evidence. For six years they have lived in constant tension with the villagers, who resent the Blackwoods for their wealth and for the fact that a mass murder went unpunished. To Merricat the village is a wasteland filled with gray, drab, and hateful people, while her "castle" is a place of peace, light, and harmony. Constance is a virtual handmaiden of nature, raising and canning fruits and vegetables, and tending flowers all over the estate.

The volatile tension between the lovely pastoral Blackwood home and the hostile, resentful village wasteland breaks into violence soon after cousin Charles Blackwood comes to visit. Ostensibly coming to help Constance, it is clear that he is really after the Blackwood fortune. Merricat senses his threat to their idyllic existence and seeks to purge the estate of his presence. When a fire breaks out, cousin Charles brings in the villagers to help. In a scene of terror reminiscent of Hawthorne's witches' Sabbath in "Young Goodman Brown," the villagers go on a rampage through the house and Merricat and Constance flee to the woods. When they return the next morning their proud mansion is a gutted ruin, but the two women close themselves in to create a new life in the remaining rooms. Some people come to help but are not received. Many of the villagers return at night and leave baskets of food with notes of apology.

The novel closes with the image of a ruin nearly completely covered with vines with two sisters huddled in fragile happiness within it. . . . In a very real sense, the Blackwood sisters are children of nature, though not in perfect harmony with it because of the lingering guilt-burden of the murders. The ruin symbolizes not only their crime, but also the crime of dark retribution perpetrated against them in anarchic pas-

sion by the maddened villagers. The real horror of the novel comes not so much from the unpunished murders by a twelve-year-old child, but largely from the inexplicable madness and violence of the so-called normal and ordinary people of the world outside the Blackwood home.

Like her story "The Lottery," *We Have Always Lived in the Castle* has to do with a kind of primordial sense of sin and defilement, which casts an ambiguous character upon love and forgiveness. The novel explores the dark dynamics of a virtually pre-ethical level of human experience—defilement, dread, retribution, revenge. This is the level where evil and personal suffering are still connected. Fault gives rise to the anticipation of punishment, which strengthens the bond between doing evil and suffering ill. This pre-ethical sense of defilement and vengeance is opposed in the novel by an ethical order of innocent sacrificial love and forgiveness, as seen in the figure of Constance and the world she creates. The villagers, representative of the world, cannot or will not forgive without an act of vengeance or retribution—hence, the mindless outbreak of violence and rage against the helpless Blackwood sisters. Perhaps this violence is somehow necessary; it has its role, its part to play in the mysterious dynamics of forgiveness and atonement. It did lead to a new order of love, though fragile and precarious because the world about it is still uncomprehending and unable to accept a world where forgiveness obviates retribution. Love seeks to bring order out of chaos and strength out of weakness, and perhaps the ruin of the castle will symbolize that, as well as the shame of lovelessness.

Shirley Jackson's gothic fiction is an effective mode for her exploration of the violations of the human self—the aching loneliness, the unendurable guilt, the dissolution and disintegrations, the sinking into madness, the violence and lovelessness. Her fiction fits well the description John Hawkes gives of several modern authors. There is

> a quality of coldness, detachment, ruthless determination to face up to the enormity of ugliness and potential failure with ourselves and in the world about us, and to bring to this exposure a savage or saving comic spirit and the saving beauties of language. The need is to maintain the truth of the fractured picture; to expose, ridicule, attack, but always to create and to throw into new light our potential for violence and absurdity as well as for graceful action.

This applies well to many of Jackson's fictions, especially to *We Have Always Lived in the Castle*, where disorderly or mad love summoned up evil darkness, setting in relief the bright light of forgiveness. . . . In the tales of Shirley Jackson, poetic justice and moral virtue do not win out as in many popular gothics and fairy tales, for she is true to her vision of the evil of our time. And she places her trust in the fact that if a tale is good and powerful, one need not explain or defend it, one need only tell it. (pp. 26-8)

John G. Parks, "Chambers of Yearning: Shirley Jackson's Use of the Gothic," in *Twentieth Century Literature,* Vol. 30, No. 1, Spring, 1984, pp. 15-29.

PETER KOSENKO

(essay date 1985)

[In the essay below, Kosenko presents a Marxist reading of "The Lottery."]

In her critical biography of Shirley Jackson, Lenemaja Friedman notes that when Jackson's story **"The Lottery"** was published in the June 26, 1948 issue of the *New Yorker* it received a response that "no *New Yorker* story had ever received": hundreds of letters poured in that were characterized by "bewilderment, speculation, and old-fashioned abuse." It is not hard to account for this response: Jackson's story portrays an "average" New England village with "average" citizens engaged in a deadly rite, the annual selection of a sacrificial victim by means of a public lottery, and does so quite deviously: not until well along in the story do we suspect that the "winner" will be stoned to death by the rest of the villagers. One can imagine the average reader of Jackson's story protesting: but we engage in no such inhuman practices. Why are you accusing us of *this?*

Admittedly, this response was not exactly the one that Jackson had hoped for. In the July 22, 1948 issue of the *San Francisco Chronicle* she broke down and said the following in response to persistent queries from her readers about her intentions: "Explaining just what I had hoped the story to say is very difficult. I suppose, I hoped, by setting a particularly brutal ancient rite in the present and in my own village to shock the story's readers with a graphic dramatization of the pointless violence and general inhumanity in their own lives." Shock them she did, but probably owing to the symbolic complexity of her tale, they responded defensively and were not enlightened. (p. 27)

A survey of what little has been written about **"The Lottery"** reveals two general critical attitudes: first, that it is about man's ineradicable primitive aggressivity, . . . ; second, that it describes man's victimization by, in Helen Nebeker's words, "unexamined and unchanging traditions which he could easily change if he only realized their implications." Missing from both of these approaches, however, is a careful analysis of the abundance of social detail that links the lottery to the ordinary social practices of the village. No mere "irrational" tradition, the lottery is an *ideological*

mechanism. It serves to reinforce the village's hierarchical social order by instilling the villagers with an unconscious fear that if they resist this order they might be selected in the next lottery. In the process of creating this fear, it also reproduces the ideology necessary for the smooth functioning of that social order, despite its inherent inequities. What is surprising in the work of an author who has never been identified as a Marxist is that this social order and ideology are essentially capitalist.

I think we need to take seriously Shirley Jackson's suggestion that the world of the lottery is her reader's world, however reduced in scale for the sake of economy. The village in which the lottery takes place has a bank, a post office, a grocery store, a coal business, a school system; its women are housewives rather than field workers or writers; and its men talk of "tractors and taxes." More importantly, however, the village exhibits the same socio-economic stratification that most people take for granted in a modern, capitalist society.

Let me begin by describing the top of the social ladder and save the lower rungs for later. The village's most powerful man, Mr. Summers, owns the village's largest business (a coal concern) and is also its mayor, since he has, Jackson writes, more "time and energy [read money and leisure] to devote to civic activities" than others. (Summers' very name suggests that he has become a man of leisure through his wealth.) Next in line in the social hierarchy is Mr. Graves, the village's second most powerful government official—its postmaster. (His name may suggest the gravity of officialism.) And beneath Mr. Graves is Mr. Martin, who has the economically advantageous position of being the grocer in a village of three hundred.

These three most powerful men who control the town, economically as well as politically, also happen to administer the lottery. Mr. Summers is its official, sworn in yearly by Mr. Graves. Mr. Graves helps Mr. Summers make up the lottery slips. And Mr. Martin steadies the lottery box as the slips are stirred. (pp. 27-8)

However important Mr. Graves and Mr. Martin may be, Mr. Summers is still the most powerful man in town. Here we have to ask a Marxist question: what relationship is there between his interests as the town's wealthiest business man and his officiating the lottery? That such a relationship does exist is suggested by one of the most revealing lines of the text. When Bill Hutchinson forces his wife, Tessie, to open her lottery slip to the crowd, Jackson writes, "It had a black spot on it, the black spot Mr. Summers had made the night before with [a] heavy pencil in [his] coal-company office." At the very moment when the lottery's victim is revealed, Jackson appends a subordinate clause in which we see the blackness (evil) of Mr. Summers' (coal) business being transferred to the black dot on the

Jackson at age three, with her younger brother Barry, in front of their San Francisco apartment, 1922.

lottery slip. At one level at least, evil in Jackson's text is linked to a disorder, promoted by capitalism, in the material organization of modern society. But it still remains to be explained *how* the evil of the lottery is tied to this disorder of capitalist social organization.

Let me sketch the five major points of my answer to this question. First, the lottery's rules of participation reflect and *codify* a rigid social hierarchy based upon an inequitable social division of labor. Second, the fact that everyone participates in the lottery and understands *consciously* that its outcome is pure chance gives it a certain "democratic" aura that obscures its first codifying function. Third, the villagers believe *unconsciously* that their commitment to a work ethic will grant them some magical immunity from selection. Fourth, this work ethic prevents them from understanding that the lottery's actual function is not to encourage work *per se* but to reinforce an inequitable social *division* of labor. Finally, after working through these points, it will be easier to explain how Jackson's choice of Tessie Hutchinson as the lottery's victim/scapegoat reveals the lottery to be an ideological mechanism which serves to defuse the average villager's deep, inarticulate dissatisfaction with the social order in which he lives by channeling it into anger directed at the *victims* of that social order. It is reenacted year after year, then, not because it is a mere "tradition," as Helen Nebeker argues, but

because it serves the repressive ideological function of purging the social body of all resistance so that business (capitalism) can go on as usual and the Summers, the Graves and the Martins can remain in power.

Implicit in the first and second points above is a distinction between universal participation in the lottery and what I have called its *rules* of participation. The first of these rules I have already explained, of course: those who control the village economically and politically also administer the lottery. The remaining rules also tell us much about who has and who doesn't have power in the village's social hierarchy. These remaining rules determine who gets to choose slips in the lottery's first, second and third rounds. Before the lottery, lists are "[made] up of heads of families [who choose in the first round], heads of households [who choose in the second round], [and] members of each household in each family [who choose in the last round]." The second round is missing from the story because the family patriarch who selects the dot in the first round—Bill Huchinson—has no married male offspring. When her family is chosen in the first round, Tessie Hutchinson objects that her daughter and son-in-law didn't "take their chance." Mr. Summers has to remind her, "Daughters draw with their husbands' families." Power in the village, then, is exclusively consolidated into the hands of male heads of families and households. Women are disenfranchised.

Although patriarchy is not a product of capitalism *per se,* patriarchy in the village does have its capitalist dimension. (New social formations adapt old traditions to their own needs.) Women in the village seem to be disenfranchised because male heads of households, as men in the work force, provide the link between the broader economy of the village and the economy of the household. (pp. 28-9)

[Women] have a distinctly subordinate position in the socioeconomic hierarchy of the village. They make their first appearance "wearing faded house dresses . . . [and walking] shortly after their menfolk." Their dresses indicate that they do in fact work, but because they work in the home and not within a larger economy in which work is regulated by finance (money), they are treated by men and treat themselves as inferior. When Tessie Hutchinson appears late to the lottery, other men address her husband Bill, "Here comes your Missus, Hutchinson." None of the men, that is to say, thinks of addressing Tessie first, since she "belongs" to Bill. Most women in the village take this patriarchal definition of their role for granted, as Mrs. Dunbar's and Mrs. Delacroix's references to their husbands as their "old [men]" suggest. Tessie, as we shall see later, is the only one who rebels against male domination, although only unconsciously. (p. 29)

On its surface, the idea of a lottery in which everyone, as Mrs. Graves says, "[takes] the same chance" seems eminently democratic, even if its effect, the singling out of one person for privilege or attack, is not.

One critic, noting an ambiguity at the story's beginning, has remarked that "the lottery . . . suggests 'election' rather than selection," since "the [villagers] assemble in the center of the place, in the village square." I would like to push the analogy further. In capitalist dominated elections, business supports and promotes candidates who will be more or less atuned to its interests, multiplying its vote through campaign financing, while each individual businessman can continue to claim that he has but one vote. In the lottery, analogously, the village ruling class participates in order to convince others (and perhaps even themselves) that they are not in fact *above* everyone else during the remainder of the year, even though their exclusive control of the lottery suggests that they are. Yet just as the lottery's black (ballot?) box has grown shabby and reveals in places its "original wood color," moments in their official "democratic" conduct of the lottery—especially Mr. Summers' conduct as their representative—reveal the class interest that lies behind it. If Summers wears jeans, in order to convince the villagers that he is just another one of the common people, he also wears a "clean white shirt," a garment more appropriate to *his* class. If he leans casually on the black box before the lottery selection begins, as a President, say, might put his feet up on the White House desk, while leaning he "talk[s] interminably to Mr. Graves and the Martins," the other members of his class, and "seem[s] very proper and important." (Jackson has placed these last details in emphatic position at the end of a paragraph.) Finally, however democratic his early appeal for help in conducting the lottery might appear—"some of you fellows want to give me a hand?"—Mr. Martin, who responds, is the third most powerful man in the village. Summers' question is essentially empty and formal, since the villagers seem to understand, probably unconsciously, the unspoken law of class that governs who administers the lottery; it is not just *anyone* who can help Summers.

The lottery's democratic illusion, then, is an ideological effect that prevents the villagers from criticizing the class structure of their society. But this illusion alone does not account for the full force of the lottery over the village. The lottery also reinforces a village work ethic which distracts the villagers' attention from the division of labor that keeps women powerless in their homes and Mr. Summers powerful in his coal company office.

In the story's middle, Old Man Warner emerges as an apologist for this work ethic when he recalls an old village adage, "Lottery in June, corn be heavy soon." At one level, the lottery seems to be a modern version of a planting ritual that might once have prepared the villagers for the collective work necessary to

produce a harvest. (Such rituals do not necessarily involve human sacrifice.) As magical as Warner's proverb may seem, it establishes an unconscious (unspoken) connection between the lottery and work that is revealed by the entirety of his response when told that other villages are considering doing away with the lottery:

> Pack of crazy fools . . . listening to the young folks, nothing's good enough for *them*. Next thing you know, they'll be wanting to go back to living in caves, nobody work any more, live *that* way for a while. Used to be a saying about 'Lottery in June, corn be heavy soon.' First thing you know, we'd all be eating stewed chickweed and acorns. There's *always* been a lottery.

But Warner does not explain *how* the lottery functions to motivate work. In order to do so, it would have to inspire the villagers with a magical fear that their lack of productivity would make them vulnerable to selection in the next lottery. The village women reveal such an unconscious fear in their ejaculatory questions after the last slip has been drawn in the first round: "Who is it?" "Who's got it?" "Is it the Dunbars?" "Is it the Watsons?" The Dunbars and the Watsons, it so happens, are the least "productive" families in the village: Mr. Dunbar has broken his leg, Mr. Watson is dead. Given this unconscious village fear that lack of productivity determines the lottery's victim, we might guess that Old Man Warner's pride that he is participating in the lottery for the "seventy-seventh time" stems from a magical belief—seventy-seven is a magical number—that his commitment to work and the village work ethic accounts for his survival. Wherever we find "magic," we are in the realm of the unconscious: the realm in which the unspoken of ideology resides.

Old Man Warner's commitment to a work ethic, however appropriate it might be in an egalitarian community trying collectively to carve an economy out of a wilderness, is not entirely innocent in the modern village, since it encourages villagers to work without pointing out to them that part of their labor goes to the support of the leisure and power of a business class. Warner, that is to say, is Summers' ideologist. At the end of his remarks about the lottery, Warner laments Summers' democratic conduct: "Bad enough to see young Joe Summers up there joking with everybody." Yet this criticism obscures the fact that Summers is not about to undermine the lottery, even if he does "modernize" it, since by running the lottery he also encourages a work ethic which serves his interest. Just before the first round drawing, Summers remarks casually, "Well, now . . . guess we better get started, get this over with, so's we can go back to work." The "we" in his remark is deceptive; what he means to say is "so that you can go back to work for me."

The final major point of my reading has to do with Jackson's selection of Tessie Hutchinson as the lottery's victim/scapegoat. She could have chosen Mr. Dunbar, of course, in order to show us the unconscious connection that the villagers draw between the lottery and their work ethic. But to do so would not have revealed that the lottery actually reinforces a *division* of labor. Tessie, after all, is a woman whose role as a housewife deprives her radically of her freedom by forcing her to submit to a husband who gains his power over her by virtue of his place in the work force. Tessie, however, rebels against her role, and such rebellion is just what the orderly functioning of her society cannot stand. Unfortunately, her rebellion is entirely unconscious.

Tessie's rebellion begins with her late arrival at the lottery, a *faux pas* that reveals her unconscious resistance to everything the lottery stands for. She explains to Mr. Summers that she was doing her dishes and forgot what day it was. The way in which she says this, however, involves her in another *faux pas:* the suggestion that she might have violated the village's work ethic and neglected her specific job within the village's social division of labor: "Wouldn't have me leave m'dishes in the sink, now, would you Joe?" . . . When Mr. Summers calls her family's name, Tessie goads her husband, "Get up there, Bill." In doing so, she inverts the power relation that holds in the village between husbands and wives. . . . Her final *faux pas* is to question the rules of the lottery which relegate women to inferior status as the property of their husbands. When Mr. Summers asks Bill Hutchinson whether his family has any other households, Tessie yells, "There's Don and Eva. . . . Make them take their charge." Tessie's daughter Eva, however, *belongs* to Don and is consequently barred from participating with her parents' family.

All of these *faux pas* set Tessie up as the lottery's likeliest victim, even if they do not explicitly challenge the lottery. That Tessie's rebellion is entirely unconscious is revealed by her cry while being stoned, "It isn't fair." Tessie does not object to the lottery *per se*, only to her own selection as its scapegoat. It would have been fine with her if someone else had been selected.

In stoning Tessie, the villagers treat her as a scapegoat onto which they can project and through which they can "purge"—actually, the term *"repress"* is better, since the impulse is conserved rather than eliminated—their own temptations to rebel. . . . But ultimately these rebellious impulses are channeled by the lottery and its attendant ideology away from their proper objects—capitalism and capitalist patriarchs—into anger at the rebellious victims of capitalist social organization. Like Tessie, the villagers cannot articulate their rebellion because the massive force of ideology stands in the way.

The lottery functions, then, to terrorize the village into accepting, in the *name* of work and democracy, the inequitable social division of labor and power on which its social order depends. When Tessie is selected, and before she is stoned, Mr. Summers asks her husband to "show [people] her paper." By holding up the slip, Bill Hutchinson reasserts his dominance over his wayward wife and simultaneously transforms her into a symbol to others of the perils of disobedience.

Here I would like to point out a curious crux in Jackson's treatment of the theme of scapegoating in **"The Lottery"**: the conflict between the lottery's literal arbitrariness and the utter appropriateness of its victim. Admittedly, Tessie is a curious kind of scapegoat, since the village does not literally choose her, single her out. An act of scapegoating that is *unmotivated* is difficult to conceive. This crux disappears, however, once we realize that the lottery is a metaphor for the unconscious ideological mechanisms of scapegoating. In choosing Tessie through the lottery, Jackson has attempted to show us whom the village might have chosen if the lottery had been in fact an election. But by presenting this election as an arbitrary lottery, she gives us an image of the village's blindness to its own motives.

Possibly the most depressing thing about **"The Lottery"** is how early Jackson represents this blindness as beginning. Even the village children have been socialized into the ideology that victimizes Tessie. When they are introduced in the second paragraph of the story, they are anxious that summer has let them out of school: "The feeling of liberty sat uneasily on most of them." Like their parents, they have learned that leisure and play are suspect. As if to quell this anxiety, the village boys engage in the play/labor of collecting stones for the lottery. Moreover, they follow the lead of Bobby Martin, the one boy in the story whose father is a member of the village ruling class (Mr. Summers and Mr. Graves have no boys), in hoarding and fighting over these stones as if they were money. While the boys do this, the village girls stand off to the side and watch, just as they will be expected to remain outside of the work force and dependent on their working husbands when they grow up.

As dismal as this picture seems, the one thing we ought not do is make it into proof of the innate depravity of man. The first line of the second paragraph— "The children assembled first, of course"—does not imply that children take a "natural" and primitive joy in stoning people to death. The closer we look at their behavior, the more we realize that they learned it from their parents, whom they imitate in their play. In order to facilitate her reader's grasp of this point, Jackson has included at least one genuinely innocent child in the story—Davy Hutchinson. When he has to choose his lottery ticket, the adults help him while he looks at them "wonderingly." And when Tessie is finally to be stoned, "someone" has to "[give] Davy Hutchinson a few pebbles." The village makes sure that Davy learns what he is supposed to do before he understands why he does it or the consequences. But this does not mean that he could not learn otherwise.

Even the village adults are not entirely hopeless. Before Old Man Warner cuts them off, Mr. and Mrs. Adams, whose last name suggests a humanity that has not been entirely effaced, briefly mention other villages that are either talking of giving up the lottery or have already done so. Probably out of deepseated fear, they do not suggest that *their* village give it up; but that they hint at the possibility, however furtively, indicates a reservation—a vague, unconscious sense of guilt—about what they are about to do. The Adamses represent the village's best, humane impulses, impulses, however, which the lottery represses.

How do we take such a pessimistic vision of the possibility of social transformation? If anything can be said against **"The Lottery,"** it is probably that it exaggerates the monolithic character of capitalist ideological hegemony. No doubt, capitalism has subtle ways of redirecting the frustrations it engenders away from a critique of capitalism itself. Yet if in order to promote itself it has to make promises of freedom, prosperity and fulfillment on which it cannot deliver, pockets of resistance grow up among the disillusioned. Perhaps it is not Jackson's intention to deny this, but to shock her complacent readers with an exaggerated image of the ideological *modus operandi* of capitalism: accusing those whom it cannot or will not employ of being lazy, promoting "the family" as the essential social unit in order to discourage broader associations and identifications, offering men power over their wives as a consolation for their powerlessness in the labor market, and pitting workers against each other and against the unemployed. It is our fault as readers if our own complacent pessimism makes us *read* Jackson's story pessimistically as a parable of man's innate depravity. (pp. 29-32)

Peter Kosenko, "A Marxist/Feminist Reading of Shirley Jackson's 'The Lottery'," in *New Orleans Review*, Vol. 12, No. 1, Spring, 1985, pp. 27-32.

MARY KITTREDGE

(essay date 1985)

[In the following excerpt, Kittredge offers an overview of Jackson's short stories and novels, focusing especially on elements of fantasy and gothic horror.]

No one, I think, was better than . . . [Shirley Jackson] at skewering an emotion, a setting, or a small event on a sharply-honed turn of phrase, then holding it up to the clearest light where it could be seen wriggling, humorously or horribly as the occasion required.

In addition to imagination, industry, and acute insight, she developed, by the "simple" method of daily practice, a pyrotechnical command of ordinary language, which she used economically but to spectacular effect. Whether in her domestic comedies or her stories and novels of psychological horror, she combined acute observation with absolute mastery of tone and clarity of expression. (pp. 3-4)

Her two "fictionalized" accounts of . . . domestic life convey a happiness that could not have been entirely invented; family love fairly shines through the pages of *Raising Demons* and *Life among the Savages.* (p. 5)

Raising Demons, at first glance, could not have sprung from the same consciousness as the doomed-dog story, **"Renegade."** But on closer inspection all Jackson's work shows a single theme, and that theme is magic.

Here is the small town of the 1950s, where the soda-fountain owner will hand you a blank check to pay for your childrens' lunches.

Here is that same town again, getting ready to murder your family's pet with a nail-studded choker.

The visions seem equally clear and true. There is some evidence that Shirley Jackson regarded her humorous books as "potboilers," but from this distance it is not so easy to dismiss them. They are the other side of horror; they show us what life is like when the magic works, when the good spells hold. The domestic rituals described in them are the routines that keep life from disintegration.

In *Raising Demons* and *Life among the Savages,* the horror is not absent; it is merely held at bay, as the titles themselves forcefully hint. If we pour in energy enough, these books suggest, we can hold off entropy for a while. With casseroles and shopping trips, coin collections and Little League, we may ring ourselves with the common charms that keep madness away. One thinks of the praying maiden in the Thurber cartoon: "Lord, please let me be just an ordinary girl."

But she was not. She was a writer of skill and vision, who saw that without constant and energetic applications of magic, things come apart, we shatter and fall. In her tales of haunting, madness, and murder, she described the disorder that may result when magic is ignored, or badly used, or mistaken through carelessness, lack of imagination, laziness, or simple bad luck.

In most of the novels, disorder is characterized by mental instability, a difficulty with which Shirley Jackson was familiar, and in all of them the main character retreats or is driven from the real world, into a life of the imagination. The heroine's perceptions, however mad, are presented as reasonable and her actions as well-justified.

The continuing conflict, Real World vs. Imaginary life, surfaces in each of Jackson's horror novels, and in each it is more completely developed. In each, the grasping tentacles of madness and the anatomy of magic—white, black, and the shades between—are drawn in more delicate detail.

Her first novel, *The Road through the Wall,* contains no supernatural elements but does contain at least one precursor of the oddness that will be developed in her later books; the story that ends with the murder of a child and the suicide of another takes place in a California suburb where many of the streets have no names, and the houses are unnumbered.

In *Hangsaman,* a college student suffers a mental breakdown and creates an imaginary friend to help her cope. But the friend's unreality makes her dangerous and as she becomes more uncontrollable and malicious, the heroine realizes that in order to regain sanity she must resist the lure of the unreal. To regain health, she must find and use the force of her own personality, integrate her own magic with the pleasures and obligations of real life.

In *The Bird's Nest,* the conflict is heightened; the "imaginary friends" are not imaginary. They are real personalities, not creations of the character's mind but truly existing facets of it, and they do not want to die. They want to do mischief, and they are vociferous about their "rights." Through them, mental disorder takes on dimension and pathos, and demonstrates willful malevolence against a haplessly passive victim-heroine.

In this novel, too, the heroine (with the help of a suggestively witch-doctorish psychiatrist) must cast off her passive victim's status, find her own "powers" (of will) and stand up to the real world, partly symbolized here by a wellmeaning but dragonish aunt. As she did in *Hangsaman,* Shirley Jackson demonstrated in *The Bird's Nest* that magical thinking and magical fantasies by themselves are not only useless but dangerous; to bring happiness, the real magic of the human personality must be purposefully grasped and wielded with determination.

Jackson's next novel was *The Sundial,* a story of magic in the hands of fools. The supernatural events and odd occurrences in it are interpreted by the novel's characters as messages from the late Mr. Halloran, whom they believe is warning them of the end of the world. Once again, Jackson seems to be saying that magic is as magic does, for the characters and especially Mrs. Halloran take the coming "end of the world" as

an opportunity to demonstrate small-mindedness, antiintellectualism, ambition, and simple greed. Luckily, the book was written in a comic style and many of its episodes are quite funny; otherwise the characters would be difficult to endure.

The Sundial offers no psychological explanations of the numerous supernatural events that occur in it, and in this respect represents a shift in Shirley Jackson's treatment of the subject. In previous books, weird happenings grew out of weird psyches; here, however, they occur independently and are apparently meant to be taken at face value; the snake that appears in the house, for example, is no ordinary snake, but it is quite real and not a figment of madness or imagination.

In *The Haunting of Hill House,* Jackson takes this shift a step further, giving the evil force not just reality, but personality and purpose. As in *The Sundial,* the supernatural in *Haunting* is neither product nor facet of the main character's mind; it is outside her, and independently real. It does not occupy her; rather, it lures and seduces her away from the pains and problems of the real world into a ghostly existence as another haunting spirit. In *Haunting,* the evil is developed to the point of winning the conflict; there is no happy ending for the heroine, because her character is too weak for the battle. She does not choose madness, but is overwhelmed by it.

In *Haunting,* the most "supernatural" of her full-length works, Shirley Jackson for the first time gives the devil his due. She puts her damsel into mortal distress and leaves her there, completely unrescued. The potential for disaster is fully explored; the evil force is developed into a completely independent and alien entity, and is shown to be a power that can triumph.

In this bleak and chilling twist on the house-with-the-terrible-secret gothic, the heroine dies. While she is the most psychically sensitive of the guests at Hill House, she is also the most susceptible to the forces there. Her personality is weak and poorly integrated; her "magic," the magic of life, is not sufficiently developed to survive a confrontation with the magic of death. With few satisfactions of her own, she has throughout her peril been wishing to merge herself with someone else, so that she will not have to make a life for herself. She harbors also the expectant fantasy that she will be rescued.

But the rescuing prince never appears. Unable to rescue herself, she succumbs to the power of the house, which chillingly grants her desire and makes her life part of its own.

Shirley Jackson's last completed novel was *We Have Always Lived in the Castle,* a book which embodies a twist of another kind. In it, the magic is unaligned, chaotic; the setting combines the comfortable domestic rituals of Jackson's comedies with the desperate strategies of an unrepentant arsenic-murderer. Within a rigidly constructed routine designed to ensure the antiheroine's security, a scenario of the most chillingly amoral madness is played.

Like the mother in *Demons* and *Savages,* the mad girl in *Castle* is a strong and determined user of domestic magic; in *Castle,* however, the forms and rituals of daily life are not allowed their own organic development. They are as rigid—and as brittle—as old grave markers. In Jackson's comedies, growth and change are regarded as necessary if inconvenient elements of life; in *Castle,* the antiheroine's main objective is to keep everything just as it is, for only in an unchanging static world can she protect her bizarre and fragile persona.

The attack of reason on madness is personified in *Castle* by a young man who arrives unexpectedly to challenge the status quo, and his underestimation of the antiheroine's mad magic is the second tragedy of the book. His practical sanity is a pitifully poor weapon against the murderer's elaborate, ritualistic system of defense. Like the heroine in *Haunting,* he just doesn't understand what he's up against, until it is too late.

In *We Have Always Lived in the Castle,* strong magic is not enough to fend off chaos, for magic has no moral alignment of its own. In the domestic comedies, Shirley Jackson's magic is a force in the service of love; in *Castle,* magic takes on the chaotic nature of the book's mad anti-heroine, losing its beauty but retaining its power.

Finally, among the novels there remains a fragment entitled *Come Along with Me,* about a woman who has cast off the obligations and guilts of the past, but who receives intermittent communications from the dead. Unfortunately, Shirley Jackson was unable to complete the book before her own death. (pp. 6-9)

Shirley Jackson's short stories differ from her novels mainly in that their thematic conflict is generally resolved when the story opens. Many of them are vignettes demonstrating the barrenness of lives devoid of magic, or in which it has been misperceived; in **"Elizabeth,"** for example, the main character fantasizes that her life will be transformed as if by magic. Under her armor of cynicism, she is as childish as the victim in *Haunting,* dreaming of rescue while failing to understand that she must break the spell of passivity for herself.

Some of the stories demonstrate the arbitrariness of luck; in **"The Tooth,"** a sane and sensible woman takes a painkiller, loses her mental equilibrium, and through no fault of her own is unable to find her way back to sanity.

In **"The Demon Lover"** a lonely woman is seduced into madness by the man of her dreams, her rescue fantasy smashed just as it seemed realized. Whether or not he ever existed outside her dreams is a question left for the reader to decide.

A few of the stories feature blithe survivors, like the unfinished heroine of *Come Along with Me.* **"My Life With R. H. Macy"** is a short romp with a girl who refuses to be reduced to a number. **"One Ordinary Day, With Peanuts,"** features a suitably nutty married couple, one of whom dispenses serendipity while the other doles out irritations to the world.

In the Edgar Allan Poe Award-winning story, **"Louisa, Please Come Home,"** a young woman deliberately transforms herself into a survivor, then discovers that she has done the job too well, changing herself so thoroughly that her family no longer recognizes her when at last she does respond to their plea.

"The Lottery," by which Shirley Jackson's work was introduced to a wide readership, has been subjected to so much interpretation and amateur psychologizing that it would be too bad to subject the poor battered object to any more comment. Suffice it to say that something about that story really got to people; in the first weeks after it appeared in the *New Yorker,* upwards of three hundred readers of the story wrote to the magazine, mostly in protest or to cancel their subscriptions.

It was, and is, a shocking story. It is also beautifully imagined, sparely and gracefully written, a one-two punch of a story. . . . (pp. 9-10)

The story has been anthologized so thoroughly that anyone who recognizes Shirley Jackson's name at all says, **"The Lottery,"** in an almost Pavlovian response. It was dramatized for the stage, and for television, and in one particularly unlikely adaptation was transformed into a ballet. It has been read in English textbooks by generations of high-school students, and if my informal survey has any validity, it is the only thing many people remember of what they read in that period. It made her fame, and surely assisted in making what was to be her fortune. Despite the anger and suspicion with which it was originally met, it has jolted hundreds of thousands, perhaps millions, of readers.

In its history, in its subject and theme, in its manner of production, and in its effect on Shirley Jackson's life and career, **"The Lottery"** at once demonstrates and validates the major theme of the author's life and work:

If you practice the ritual, you'll get the magic. (pp. 10-11)

In all the aspects of her life, . . . [Jackson] fought whatever obstacles she encountered at least to a draw. Her success in the horror genre, like her successful domestic comedy, was the result of an exquisitely sensitive double vision that would have seemed an affliction to a less determined or talented writer. She saw the magic in the mundane, and the evil behind the ordinary. She saw that the line between the cruel and the comedic is sometimes vanishingly narrow.

She wrote it all down, day after day, on good days and bad, creating enormous pleasure for her contemporary audience and contributing at least one story to the ranks of the best horror that has been written. Perhaps the worst that can now be said about Shirley Jackson's work is that there simply was not enough of it.

But then, there is never enough of that brand of magic. (p. 12)

Mary Kittredge, "The Other Side of Magic: A Few Remarks About Shirley Jackson," in *Discovering Modern Horror Fiction,* edited by Darrell Schweitzer, Starmont House, 1985, pp. 3-12.

SOURCES FOR FURTHER STUDY

Breit, Harvey. "Talk with Miss Jackson." *The New York Times Book Review* (26 June 1949): 15.

Interview conducted following the publication of "The Lottery" in which Jackson discusses her writing techniques and favorite authors.

Friedman, Lenemaja. *Shirley Jackson.* Boston: G. K. Hall & Co., 1975, 182 p.

Biographical and critical study in which Friedman scrutinizes Jackson's short stories and novels. Includes extensive bibliography.

Hyman, Stanley Edgar. "Shirley Jackson: 1919-1965." *Saturday Evening Post* 238, No. 25 (18 December 1965): 63.

Posthumous tribute by Jackson's husband.

Nebeker, Helen C. " 'The Lottery': Symbolic Tour de Force." *American Literature* 46 (March 1974): 100-07.

Highly regarded essay examines the various levels of symbolism in "The Lottery."

Oppenheimer, Judy. *Private Demons: The Life of Shirley Jackson.* New York: G. P. Putnam's Sons, 1988, 304 p.

Excellent, detailed biography containing extensive interviews with Jackson's children and friends and including many photographs.

Woodruff, Stuart C. "The Real Horror Elsewhere: Shirley Jackson's Last Novel." *Southwest Review* 52 (September 1967): 152-62.

Maintains that the true madness of *We Have Always Lived in the Castle* exists in the supposedly "normal" facade of the outside world.

Henry James

1843-1916

American novelist, short story and novella writer, essayist, critic, biographer, autobiographer, and dramatist.

INTRODUCTION

James is considered one of the greatest novelists in the English language. From the very beginning of his career he placed his individual stamp on the art of fiction: he enlarged the scope of the novel, introduced dramatic elements to the narrative tale, and developed the point of view technique to a level unknown before his time. His highly self-conscious narrators prepared the way for the interior monologues of such later writers as James Joyce and Virginia Woolf. Most importantly, James was a leading advocate of realism in American literature, evidenced particularly in his criticism and essays on the art of fiction. Besides matters of technical innovation, he brought a number of original themes to American literature. Perhaps the most obvious is the myth of the American abroad—the encounter of the New World with the Old. James incorporated this myth into the "international novel" genre, of which he was both originator and master. But he also dealt with other social and psychological concerns, such as the artist's role in society, the need for both the aesthetic and the moral life, and the benefits of a developed consciousness receptive to the thoughts and feelings of others. According to Van Wyck Brooks, James was most of all a "historian" of his age—an author who interpreted a generation of people on both sides of the Atlantic.

James was born in New York City, the second son of well-to-do, liberal parents. Because of his grandfather's wealth, James's father never had to work. Henry James, Sr. was an intellectual man of his day, a devotee of the philosopher Emanuel Swedenborg and an occasional theorist on religion and philosophy. James himself was a shy, bookish boy who assumed the role of a quiet observer beside his active elder brother William, who later became the founder of psychological study in America and the prominent formula-tor of the philosophy of pragmatism. Both Henry and William spent much of their youth traveling between the United States and Europe and were schooled by tutors and governesses in such diverse environments as Manhattan, Geneva, Paris, and London. This constant oscillation between two worlds had a profound effect on James: it became the major theme of his fiction.

At the age of nineteen James enrolled at Harvard Law School, briefly entertaining thoughts of a legal career. However, he soon began devoting his study time to reading literature, particularly the works of Honoré de Balzac and Nathaniel Hawthorne. Inspired by the literary atmosphere of Cambridge and Boston, James wrote his first fiction and criticism, his earliest works appearing in the *Continental Monthly, The Atlantic Monthly,* and *The North American Review.* He met and formed lifelong friendships with William Dean Howells—then assistant editor at *The Atlantic*—Charles Eliot Norton, and James Russell Lowell. Howells was to become James's editor and literary agent, and together the two are considered the chief proponents of realism in American literature. In 1869 James went abroad for his first adult encounter with Europe. While in London he was taken by the Nortons to meet some of England's greatest writers, including George Eliot, John Ruskin, Dante Gabriel Rossetti, and Alfred, Lord Tennyson. The year 1869 also marked the death of James's beloved cousin Minny Temple, for whom he had formed a deep emotional attachment. This, as well as his experiences in Europe, provided much of the material that would figure in such later works as *The Portrait of a Lady* (1881) and *The Wings of the Dove* (1902).

James returned to the United States in 1870 to live and write in his native country. During this time he wrote his first novel, *Watch and Ward* (1878), and his first significant American-European tale, "A Passionate Pilgrim." However, after a winter of unremitting hackwork in New York, James became convinced that he could write better and live more cheaply abroad. In 1875 he moved permanently to Europe, settling first in Rome, then in Paris, and eventually in London, where he found the people and conditions best suited to his imagination, producing the early novels which would establish his reputation—*Roderick Hudson* (1876), *The American* (1877), and *The Europeans* (1878). Though James earned recognition with his first European novels, it was not until the publications of *Daisy Miller* (1879) and *The Portrait of a Lady* that he gained popular success. The latter marked the end of what critics consider the first period in his career.

The years 1898 to 1904 were the most productive of James's literary career. During this period he brought out several volumes of stories as well as the consummate novels of his late maturity—*The Wings of the Dove* (1902), *The Ambassadors* (1903), and *The Golden Bowl* (1904). After 1904 James's health and creativity began to decline. Though he still produced a sizeable amount of work, consisting mainly of his autobiographies, essays, and criticism, he finished only one novel, *The Outcry* (1911). After the outbreak of the First World War, James devoted much of his remaining energy to promoting the Allied cause, and when the United States did not immediately back the Allies he assumed British citizenship in protest against his native land. On his deathbed the following year he received the British Order of Merit.

Most critics divide James's career into three periods. In the first, from 1876 to the mid-1880s, he established himself as the originator of the international novel and a masterful portrayer of the American character. In such early works as *Roderick Hudson, The American,* and *The Europeans,* James explored the effects of European civilization—with its rich mixture of history and art, sophistication and corruption—on the naive American. The tragedy, as well as the humor, in this situation—as James fully discovered—consists in the protagonists' insistence on partaking of the European experience without sacrificing their New World innocence. Numerous critics have interpreted the story of James's protagonists as a quest for identity, or, more specifically, as a deep passion to enter into the history of civilization. In all meanings of the word, his heroes and heroines become "civilized"—both morally and aesthetically fulfilled. It was also in *Roderick Hudson,* perhaps the best of these three novels, that James first developed his concern with the artist's role in society, a theme which pervades much of his middle and late fiction. Here the European experience is merged with the story of a young American sculptor who struggles between his art and his passions. Considered the most balanced of all his novels, *The Portrait of a Lady,* is a picture of Americans living in the expatriate society of England and Italy. It is a profound study of a young woman from upstate New York who brings to Europe her provincialism and moral pretensions, while also demonstrating a sense of sovereignty and a "free spirit" capable of living greatly at odds with the Victorian world. *The Portrait of a Lady* is a convincing demonstration of James's shrewd insight into American character and his understanding of the role social and financial power play in personal relations.

The second period, from the mid-1880s to 1897, is often considered the transitional phase in James's career. Many of the novels and stories written during this time show a marked advance in form and narrative technique: James began experimenting with point of view and with poetic elements, such as symbolism and recurring motifs. He also abandoned his international theme and began focusing on the conflict between art and life, aesthetics and social morality—particularly in such short stories as *The Aspern Papers* (1888). The

1880s also saw the publication of two novels dealing specifically with contemporary social issues: *The Bostonians* (1886), which depicts the struggle between a conservative Southerner living in New England and a man-hating suffragette, and *The Princess Casamassima* (1886), in which James portrayed the downward path of a young man who toys with revolution and is eventually destroyed by it. Perhaps the most significant work of this period is *The Tragic Muse* (1890), not because of its treatment of the artist in philistine London, which critics consider rather poorly presented, but because it signified James's growing interest in the world of drama. Stung by the neglect of his once-large reading public, he turned to the theater during the 1890s in hope of regaining his popularity. His dramatization of *The American* was a modest success, but his attempts at comedy, and his one historical play—*Guy Domville* (1895)—proved that James lacked the qualities to become a successful dramatist. However, from these experiences he brought back to his novels a new commitment to economy in writing and an extraordinary aptitude for framing fictional situations in a scenic and dramatic manner.

The third and final period of James's career, from 1897 to his death, saw the full development of techniques he had begun using during the 1880s. With the publication of such works as *The Spoils of Poynton* (1897), *What Maisie Knew* (1897), *The Turn of the Screw* (1898), and *The Awkward Age* (1899), he refined the methods of "scenic" progression, the point of view narration—which he narrowed to a single angle of vision—and the art of "indirect suggestion." The subjects of this period are the expanding consciousness of the individual, the moral education of children, and the clash between subjective and external realities. James even experimented with psychic phenomena—such as projected fantasies and repressed hysteria—and the reliability of language in *The Turn of the Screw.* However, the most important works of this final period are the three novels written at the beginning of the twentieth century: *The Wings of the Dove, The Ambassadors,* and *The Golden Bowl.* The first of these is the story of a dying American heiress, and, more specifically, of those characters who seek to inherit her millions. In *The Wings of the Dove* James created a moving study of a well-intentioned individual who becomes the victim of her own graces. Most critics view the character of Milly Theale as the apogee of James's American innocent, a figure so weak and pure that she suggests the Christ-like heroines in Fyodor Dostoyevsky's stories. *The Ambassadors* shows James's talent for investing a limited plot with grandeur and elegance. The novel is essentially a high comedy of American and European manners, as a middle-aged, self-satisfied American named Lambert Strether undertakes a mission to Paris to bring back the son of a wealthy provincial family. The irony of the story turns on Strether's accomplishing his mission against his will, for the young man agrees to return home even though Strether, now captivated by Parisian life, urges him to stay. *The Ambassadors* is often considered the most finely wrought of James's novels. The narration as well as the blossoming of Strether's consciousness are skillfully rendered, and the climax and conclusion are the most satisfying of all his works. *The Golden Bowl,* James's final work, is also regarded as the most symbolic and richest in poetic imagery of all his novels. It incorporates a number of Jamesian themes: the marriage of American and European cultures, the conflict between innocence and experience, and the redemption—specifically through the character of Maggie Verver—of moral order.

Throughout much of his career James was regarded as a "writer's writer," particularly during his middle and mature years. The average reader was, and often still is, apt to find him verbose, excruciatingly complex, and overly concerned with matters of social propriety. Many early critics held that his stories lacked the necessary amount of action to sustain interest and, more seriously, that they presented an inaccurate portrayal of social situations and events. These criticisms resulted in the author's near obscurity following the First World War, a period when the emphasis of his novels and stories seemed particularly trite. A revival of interest in James's work took place in the 1940s and 1950s. Critics such as F. O. Matthiessen, F. W. Dupee, and Leon Edel examined the technical skill and masterful character development in James's works. By the 1960s most critics acknowledged the depth of James's fiction. No longer were his plots considered mere contests between innocent Americans and corrupt Europeans; discerning readers found a broad philosophical and psychological basis in his fiction. Many critics interpreted James's novels and stories according to previously established myths, such as the Fall of Man, the figure of Christ, the Nietzschean notion of the "created self," and the famous battleground of the conscious ego and subconscious alter ego. Quentin Anderson has posited that James's fiction incorporated a detailed exposition of his father's Swedenborgian philosophy.

European and American critics are unanimous in placing James among the most imposing figures in twentieth-century literature, influencing such diverse writers as James Joyce and Graham Greene, Virginia Woolf and Joseph Conrad. His originality, his stylistic distinction, and the psychological complexity of his characters have led many critics to regard him as one of the subtlest craftsmen who ever practiced the art of fiction.

(For further information about James's life and works, see *Concise Dictionary of American Literary Bi-*

ography,1865-1917; *Contemporary Authors*, Vols. 104, 132; *Dictionary of Literary Biography*, Vols. 12, 71, 74; and *Twentieth-Century Literary Criticism*, Vols. 2, 11, 24, 40.)

CRITICAL COMMENTARY

JOSEPH CONRAD
(essay date 1905)

[Conrad is considered an innovator of novel structure as well as one of the finest stylists of modern English literature. In the excerpt below from a 1905 essay, he explores James as artist and historian.]

[Mankind] is delightful in its pride, its assurance, and its indomitable tenacity. It will sleep on the battlefield among its own dead, in the manner of an army having won a barren victory. It will not know when it is beaten. And, perhaps, it is right in that quality. The victories are not, perhaps, so barren as it may appear from a purely strategical, utilitarian point of view. Mr. Henry James seems to hold that belief. Nobody has rendered better, perhaps, the tenacity of temper, or known how to drape the robe of spiritual honor about the drooping form of a victor in a barren strife. And the honor is always well won; for the struggles Mr. Henry James chronicles with such subtle and direct insight are, though only personal contests desperate in their silence, none the less heroic (in the modern sense) for the absence of shouted watchwords, clash of arms and sound of trumpets. Those are adventures in which only choice souls are ever involved. And Mr. Henry James records them with a fearless and insistent fidelity to the *péripéties* of the contest, and the feelings of the combatants.

The fiercest excitements of a romance *"de cape et d'épée,"* the romance of yard-arm and boarding-pike so dear to youth, whose knowledge of action (as of other things) is imperfect and limited, are matched, for the quickening of our maturer years, by the tasks set, by the difficulties presented, to Mr. Henry James's men's and women's sense of truth, of necessity—before all, of conduct. His mankind is delightful. It is delightful in its tenacity; it refuses to own itself beaten; it will sleep on the battlefield. . . . All adventure, all love, every success is resumed in the supreme energy of an act of renunciation. It is the uttermost limit of our power; it is the most potent and effective force at our disposal. . . . [No] man or woman worthy of the name can pretend to anything more, to anything greater. And Mr. Henry James's men and women are worthy of the name, within the limits his art, so clear, so sure of itself, has drawn round their activities. He would be the last to claim for them Titanic proportions. The earth itself has grown smaller in the course of ages. But in every sphere of human perplexities and emotions there are more greatnesses than one—not counting here the greatness of the artist himself. (pp. 13-15)

Fiction is history, human history, or it is nothing. But it is also more than that; it stands on firmer ground, being based on the reality of forms and the observation of social phenomena, whereas history is based on documents and the reading of print and handwriting—on second-hand impression. Thus fiction is nearer truth. But let that pass. A historian may be an artist too, and a novelist is a historian, the preserver, the keeper, the expounder, of human experience. As is meet for a man of his descent and tradition, Mr. Henry James is the historian of fine consciences. (p. 15)

The range of a fine conscience covers more good and evil than the range of a conscience which may be called, roughly, not fine; a conscience less troubled by the nice discrimination of shades of conduct. A fine conscience is more concerned with essentials; its triumphs are more perfect, if less profitable in a worldly sense. There is, in short, more truth in its working for a historian to detect and to show. It is a thing of infinite complication and suggestion. None of these escape the art of Mr. Henry James. He has mastered the country, his domain, not wild indeed, but full of romantic glimpses, of deep shadows and sunny places. There are no secrets left within his range. He has disclosed them as they should be disclosed—that is, beautifully. And, indeed, ugliness has but little place in this world of his creation. Yet it is always felt in the truthfulness of his art; it is there, it surrounds the scene, it presses close upon it. It is made visible, tangible, in the struggles, in the contacts of the fine consciences, in their perplexities, in the sophism of their mistakes. For a fine conscience is naturally a virtuous one. What is natural about it is just its fineness, an abiding sense of the intangible, everpresent, right. It is most visible in their ultimate triumph, in their emergence from miracle, through an energetic act of renunciation. Energetic, not

Principal Works

A Passionate Pilgrim, and Other Tales (short stories) 1875	The Awkward Age (novel) 1899
Roderick Hudson (novel) 1876	The Sacred Fount (novel) 1901
The American (novel) 1877	The Wings of the Dove (novel) 1902
The Europeans (novel) 1878	The Ambassadors (novel) 1903
Watch and Ward (novel) 1878	The Golden Bowl (novel) 1904
Daisy Miller (novel) 1879	The American Scene (travel essays) 1907
The Portrait of a Lady (novel) 1881	The Novels and Tales of Henry James. 24 vols. (novels, novellas, and short stories) 1907-09
Washington Square (novel) 1881	
The Bostonians (novel) 1886	The Outcry (novel) 1911
The Princess Casamassima (novel) 1886	A Small Boy and Others (autobiography) 1913
The Aspern Papers. Louisa Pallant. The Modern Warning (novellas) 1888	Notes of a Son and Brother (autobiography) 1914
	Notes on Novelists, with Some Other Notes (criticism) 1914
The Tragic Muse (novel) 1890	
The Real Thing, and Other Tales (short stories) 1893	The Letters of Henry James. 2 vols. (letters) 1920
Guy Domville (drama) 1895	The Art of the Novel (criticism) 1934
The Spoils of Poynton (novel) 1897	The Notebooks of Henry James (notebooks) 1947
What Maisie Knew (novel) 1897	The Complete Plays of Henry James (dramas) 1949
The Two Magics: The Turn of the Screw, Covering End (novellas) 1898	

violent: the distinction is wide, enormous, like that between substance and shadow.

Through it all Mr. Henry James keeps a firm hold of the substance, of what is worth having, of what is worth holding. . . . One is never set at rest by Mr. Henry James's novels. His books end as an episode in life ends. You remain with the sense of the life still going on; and even the subtle presence of the dead is felt in that silence that comes upon the artist-creation when the last word has been read. It is eminently satisfying, but it is not final. Mr. Henry James, great artist and faithful historian, never attempts the impossible. (pp. 16-17)

Joseph Conrad, "Henry James: An Appreciation," in *Henry James: A Collection of Critical Essays*, edited by Leon Edel, Prentice-Hall, 1963, pp. 11-17.

PELHAM EDGAR
(essay date 1927)

[The following survey of James's early novels is taken from Edgar's *Henry James: Man and Author*, an important study of James's work as a novelist, short story writer, critic, and dramatist.]

Like many another first novel, *Roderick Hudson* . . . is too ambitiously planned, but its author has more art than the ordinary beginner to make a failure interesting, and to beguile his readers with a fallacious sense of effortless ease when he was really floundering through difficulties and labouring for breath. [James's] design was to portray a man of genius, and to reveal him to us in his formative period, in the moment of his success and in the decline of his intellectual and moral nature. Fiction shows few examples of artistic or literary genius convincingly displayed, and for a young writer to attempt the task and complicate it by a representation of the decay of these abnormal powers was to invite almost inevitable failure.

The peculiar distinction of James in his maturer work is his competence to occupy the whole scope of his design. His books are so planned that his intentions are amply fulfilled; and though he may drive his road through hazardous country, he never advances without a preliminary survey and measures taken for the surmounting of all engineering difficulties. In *Roderick Hudson,* by throwing pontoon bridges across the rivers and rope ladders across the gorges, he gets us precariously to the end of our journey; but lest these metaphors should mislead us into the assumption that the book is complicated by dangers of flood and fire and sword, I hasten to add that the processes of Roderick's decay are attended with singularly few incidents of an adventurous kind. He escapes from Rowland Mallet's oppressive company, but his borrowing of a few hundred pounds is our only indication that he has enjoyed himself in Baden-Baden. There he meets the balefully beautiful Christina Light, who completes what Rome had already begun—his alienation from his native country, and his abnegation of all the sentimental ties that bind the ordinary man to his home. (pp. 232-33)

[James] felt that he had failed in vividness on the American side of the picture, but, after all, the volubly vulgar Mr Striker and Mary Garland hemming her coarse kitchen towel sufficiently meet the realistic demands of the reader. More important is the failure of perspective he notes in the abruptly foreshortened account of Roderick's moral collapse. Revolutions of character are not often so catastrophic as James has made this particular one appear, and the author further involved himself in the equally difficult task, which confronted him later in Miriam Rooth, of accounting also for the sudden development of power that preceded the decay. Genius is a word to conjure with, but even genius requires some preparation, and must use ladders like the humblest talent. If, for Roderick's development, we are willing to accept mere affirmations for demonstration, the process of sudden decay is still to be accounted for. James has recourse in his dilemma to the old convention of the wild irregularity of genius, its inborn contempt of prescription, its rudderless reliance on impulse. Artistic conscience is allowed also to exercise its pressure, and Roderick is given us as an example of a creative genius whose technique, however wonderful, is incompetent to register his dreams of ideal perfection. But the great instrument of his moral decay was a woman of devastating beauty and diabolic charm, and James exerts himself to the utmost to represent the personality and influence of the enigmatic Christina Light. It was reserved for a later book [*The Princess Casamassima*] to reveal her more completely. In the early novel, not only was his knowledge of the sex less profound, but his hands were tied by his method, since we are dependent for our knowledge of her complexity on Rowland Mallet's unsupported testimony, and Rowland does not impress us as possessed of he requisite subtlety or depth for his task. (pp. 234-35)

The American, like *Roderick Hudson*, was subjected by James to a rigorous verbal revision before being admitted into the New York edition of his works. . . . There is hardly, I imagine, a page in either book that was allowed to remain precisely as it was written. (p. 237)

The situation that our author works out in this book he carried in his mind for years before he had the courage to attack it. In so far as the surmounting of difficulties is concerned he might as well have tackled the theme in the first flush of his invention, or have given himself the luxury of a longer incubation. He admits the falseness of the central conception—that is, the ascription of a dastardly and motiveless crime to Madame de Bellegarde and her eldest son; but he flatters himself

that he has made a merit of his defect by creating for his book an atmosphere of romantic mystery and suspense. Now James, and to his ultimate advantage, was very imperfectly endowed to explore the possibilities of adventurous romance—the romance of the dagger and the cowl, of dark, mysterious chambers and subterranean caves. His earliest efforts, and weak and groping they were, abound in melodramatic situations and overflow with effusive descriptions; but a chastening process gradually mitigated this exuberance, and by the time *The American* was written he had already achieved his emancipation from romantic extravagance. Christopher Newman has no impulse, for example, to scale the walls of the convent of the Rue d'Enfer, but paces the streets instead like an ordinarily disappointed man. The virtues or demerits, therefore, that attach to romanticism are not in question here, and we accept the crime as a somewhat clumsy expedient for precipitating the crisis that his plot demanded. (pp. 241-42)

[*The American*] is sufficiently commonplace, and is only inadequately relieved by the subordinate episode of the Nioches, which has the slenderest connection with the main story. The saving element that . . . enters is Claire's younger brother, the superlatively attractive Valentine, in whose life the book lives, and in whose death it dies. And truly the book was in full need of enlivenment, for Christopher was not born under the planet Mercury, and tradition and authority have set their killing weight on any natural spirits that Claire might normally have had. (p. 244)

With Valentine out of the story, James falls back for the sustainment of interest upon the elaboration of his original first conception—a guileless yet strongwilled American, the suitor of a woman of high birth, infamously rejected by the family that has accepted him, and presently possessed of information that would utterly discredit them. The theme is not adapted to his genius, yet working with alien material he does not wholly fail of his effects. A dozen contemporary writers could have manipulated more skilfully the element of suspense, but we cannot be certain that they would have divined the quite special value that might be elicited from the ultimate renunciation of revenge. This and the Valentine portrait are the redeeming features of a faulty book. I rank it for importance not above *The Bostonians,* and its reperusal satisfies me that the alteration of manner and method that begins to be so marked towards 1890 was prompted by an instinct wholly sound. James was not completely himself until he discovered that he was totally unlike everybody else. It has happened before in literary history that sincerity and naturalness have suffered rebuke as pose and affectation. The truth about James is that his particular form of sincerity and naturalness has never formed a working alliance with simplicity.

We now arrive at *The Portrait of a Lady* . . . , which is a book fortunate amongst its fellows in having enough of the obvious to recommend it to the casual reader, and enough subtlety to recompensate attentive perusal. (p. 245)

The theme of the book is clearly enough the career of an attractive girl who fronts life confidently, gains a few small triumphs, inspires a few loyal affections, yields to the weakness of a momentary infatuation, is miserable, escapes, and returns under compulsion of her sense of duty to the life of torture, for which there seems now no alleviation, and from which only the accident of death may set her free. (p. 249)

There is not much to be gained by portraying a woman with a mind, if that mind is ultimately to be cramped in its opportunity for growth, nor in emphasising the value of experience, if experience is to lead in the end to a spiritual prison in which the natural impulses of the heart must suffer an inevitable decay. We do not exact from a great artist a comfortable ending. It is not customary to approve Dr Johnson's reproach to Shakespeare for his disregard of poetic justice, and James has high enough sanction for his neglect of that same principle. But the ends of art might have been served, and one's sense of inevitable sequence might have suffered no injury, if some more immediate vista of escape had been granted to Isabel Osmond. This, after all, is not a Hardyesque tragedy, where everything co-operates to precipitate the impending doom, and where the gateless, unscalable wall of circumstance hems us in. It is the story of a girl of quick and eager mind, of affections and impulses equally quick and eager; and if I read the author's intention aright, he desired to illustrate the growth and not the paralysis of all these bounding energies. If there is one lesson that James, ordinarily so little dogmatic, is still inclined to emphasise, it is the value of abundant living. "Live as you like best," Ralph Touchett once told Isabel, "and your character will take care of itself." We know that there is nothing Rabelaisian involved in this prescription of conduct. There is always for James the check of moral decency, and to live abundantly implies with him always to live beautifully as well. But here is a character for whom fullness of life spells disaster, and whose determination to live beautifully seems to lead to no serener fate. Our difficulties in Isabel's case are not to supply explanations for her ultimate decision. These James marks out for us with sufficient clearness. . . . She had wilfully followed her unsupported judgment in choosing her husband, and she is equally wilful now in her determination to accept the consequences. All this I say is clearly enough expressed, but the flaw in the conclusion still remains. We are cheated of our desire to see an abundant nature expand, and we are not permitted to witness in exchange for this extinguished hope her recovery of strength through suffer-

ing. James wrote a later book, *The Golden Bowl,* to prove how a wife, by the exercise of no gross efforts, may redeem a situation that a husband has put in jeopardy. But Amerigo was amenable and affection had not died. Neither condition exists in our present book, where we do not experience the justifiable satisfaction of seeing an impossible situation adjusted, nor entertain even the remote hope of its amelioration. We readily grant the effective manner in which James has represented the actual suffering. The art he displays in the whole second part of the story marks a distinct advance on anything he had hitherto done and points in the direction of his later subtlety and power. (pp. 249-51)

It is quite possible . . . to read *The Portrait of a Lady* with no consciousness of innovation; but we are not doing the book full justice until we realise that the author is tentatively striving after a new method of romantic expression. If, as our self-complacency assures us, we belong to the class of readers who, as James says, insist on shaking his tree for him, and are therefore as much interested in the way situations are presented as in the story itself, *The Portrait* will have merits, and imperfections even, that will reward our closer attention.

I have quarrelled with the book perhaps quite irrationally for what it does not contain, and have recorded a disappointment that is possibly only personal at the abortive ending. Coming to the actual substance of the story, we realise that it has all the elements of a transitional work, and if we rank it only short of James's best efforts in fiction, it is because we feel that the old and the new methods of composition are not perfectly fused. James thought it the most symmetrical of all his productions except *The Ambassadors,* but for many readers the combination of two compositional styles will have the effect of roughening the surface, so to speak, and the book as a result will seem to lack the smoothness of finish and harmony of tone that characterise perhaps even to excess the novels of his full maturity. (p. 252)

The Bostonians is of the year 1885, and we gather from several references in the letters that only exigencies of space induced James to omit it from the New York edition of his works. He considered the book to possess merely a secondary value, but he was willing to let it stand for the best sort of thing he could produce in the old-fashioned manner. . . . The processes of its design are so clear as to seem almost mechanical in their artifice. The author's intention is evident in every line. Everything that has happened is carefully explained, and we are as carefully prepared for everything that is about to happen. When a new character appears he is neatly labelled and docketed. A few pages suffice to put us in complete relation with Olive, with Mrs Luna, Miss Birdseye, the Tarrants, the Burbages and Basil Ransom. Verena is the only character who is not fully revealed to us from the outset, but in her case the mystery is legitimately due to the fact that hers is the only character that has not taken its mould. She is obviously in process of transformation, and we are permitted to gain our estimate of her from a series of anticipatory hints which, but for their inferior subtlety, suggest the art of preparation and gradual revelation that is to signal a virtue in his later work. (pp. 256-57)

In the work of his later prime [James] was never in doubt as to what his principal theme might be. Here there is some confusion of background and foreground, for even in his own mind he was not clear whether his main purpose was to give a fantastic account of the feminist movement at a time when it was more comical than effective, or to tell the love story of Verena and Basil Ransom. He solved his doubts by blending the two themes, and thus gave himself the licence to wander to the prejudice of unity and concentration. (p. 265)

Reading this novel, where all the old devices abound, we find it difficult to realise that he was so soon and so radically to change his methods of expression, and even, so it would seem, the very texture of his thought. Between *The Bostonians* and *The Ambassadors* there is a wider gulf than is indicated by the space of years.

The Princess Casamassima . . . , which was concurrently written, is separated by a notably narrower margin. It was an audacious thing for James to attempt a novel treating of social conditions with which he was incompetent to cope, and we are uneasily aware that in *The Princess Casamassima* he is conscious of his difficulties, and is seeking to avoid them by the evasion of the central issues. If this were a book purporting to reveal the acute distress of a great city like London, and the revolutionary activities that misery engenders, it would be a patent and palpable fraud upon our intelligence. If, on the other hand, the amenities of life and the aesthetic conquests of civilisation may be shown to rest inevitably upon a *vague* basis of wretchedness, the author then will be under no constraint to establish a clear case for human misery, and so far as the artistic purposes of his book are concerned these evils may remain inferential and undetermined. There are writers of course for whom the social problem imposes more exacting conditions. Mr Galsworthy, for example, would have felt himself compelled to a much more exact notation of the facts, and we should have had a realistic novel in which the artistic and propagandist intention would have striven, perhaps in vain, for reconciliation. James was saved from this dilemma both by the absence in him of all dogmatic tendencies and by his defective knowledge of the actual facts. The reasons, however, that he advances for dodging these latter will not satisfy the most indulgent reader. We might have been contented had he said that he wished to relieve his book as far as possible of controversial matter,

or had he confessed frankly his inability to cope with subterranean conditions. It was somewhat disingenuous of him to say: "I felt in full *personal* possession of my matter; this really seemed the fruit of direct experience. . . . " (pp. 268-70)

The Lomax Place life is observed and rendered so vividly as to suggest the results of "direct experience," which in the case of an author so fastidious is the equivalent merely of imaginative contact. But in the later foreground of the picture, where we are entitled to expect a definite delineation of revolutionary figures, we are fobbed off with "loose appearances—just perceptible presences and general looming possibilities." We cannot take the fastidious slumming of the Princess very seriously; Hyacinth recoils from the besotted intelligence of the submerged masses; and only Lady Aurora would be competent to speak from actual experience of the horrors of the pit, which, for her gentle nature, are an opportunity for hard sacrificial work rather than an occasion for theorising. It is this failure on the author's part to face ultimate facts that accounts for our incomplete sympathy with his hero, and robs his tragedy of its full appeal to our imagination. If a tragedy misses poignancy it misses everything; and when we come to examine into the motives that precipitate Hyacinth into his fatal revolutionary activity, we shall realise why he succeeds in being futile and fails to be impressive. His early history is admirably conveyed, and so successfully is the boy of ten launched that we are keyed up to a high pitch of expectation for the incidents of his subsequent career. The prison scene is one that Dickens or Gissing would have seized upon with avidity, and it is not certain that either of them would have produced a more impressive result. The episode is at least as tender and penetrating as anything that James has given us, and it is a scene that will project its lurid light through all the years of the boy's growing consciousness—the puzzled, shrinking child himself, the timid Pinnie, the inexorable Mrs Bowerbank, and the fevered, yearning mother babbling French phrases. The pity of it is that the author does not carry to its logical conclusion this rankling sense of the world's injustice that had been so powerfully stimulated in the child. Pinnie is for ever there to remind him that he is a little aristocrat; and what ultimately moves him to act is less sympathy for the downtrodden poor than annoyance at being debarred from access to the fuller life to which his father's blood flowing in his veins impelled, if not entitled, him. (pp. 270-71)

James has told us that the history of little Hyacinth sprang up for him out of the London pavements. Many and fine though the passages are that render the life of the teeming city, we yet do not obtain from his pages the acrid savour of reality that we taste in Dickens or Wells. He is not willing to sacrifice an orotund fullness for the sake of vividness, and the art of representation is better served—the confession must be made—by their coarser, staccato methods. The passion that actually propelled the story was the sense, so prepotent in our author's mind, of the accumulated values which the past has stored up for our present use, and he merely amused himself with the palpable fiction of an aesthetic anarchist and a revolutionary princess, the one halted on the frontiers of the world of beauty and the other free of that region, yet wantonly forsaking it. (p. 280)

The Princess Casamassima . . . appeared concurrently with *The Bostonians* and five years later than *The Portrait of a Lady.* James's art was obviously in these years in a state of transition, when he was tentatively feeling his way, and was not yet certain which devices of the older method to reject and which to retain. *The Portrait of a Lady* is almost as advanced in its manner as *The Princess,* whereas *The Bostonians* is puzzlingly retrogressive, which means nothing more than to say that it is a plain straightforward romance of the traditional English type, with all the characters honestly labelled and classified on their first appearance. In the comparatively early *Roderick Hudson* James had adopted somewhat cautiously the more artistic device of presenting his personages by a process of gradual revelation. *The Portrait* utilises the same method with greater success, but the book is weighed down with a great amount of preliminary biographical material that his maturer art would have absorbed into the narrative. Then five years later comes *The Bostonians,* with a return to the older treatment, and simultaneously *The Princess Casamassima,* which, though a less attractive book than *The Portrait of a Lady,* for reasons that I have endeavoured to make clear, possesses certain formal advantages. The biographical antecedents of Hyacinth are not more suppressed than they were with Isabel Archer, and if it is a fault to supply such a background, which James asserts and many readers deny it to be, then both books stand upon a level, and from the standpoint of construction are equally defective. But the innovation making for advance in the later book is the Princess herself, whose qualities are never categorically presented to us, and who is studied by the method not only of gradual but also of indirect revelation. . . . [James] admits that he "goes behind" right and left in *The Princess Casamassima,* but the Princess herself he never goes behind, and what we learn of her is never gained from her own reflections upon her case. The pity of it is that we learn nothing definite of her from any other source, unless to be enigmatic is to be definite, and consequently for this negative result the method is not to be blamed. There would seem to be a certain degree of indecision even with James, who pondered these questions more deeply than other haphazard writers, as to when he shall have recourse to the direct and when to the indirect process. Minor characters of

course must not be given the privilege of self-analysis, but with the major ones also there seems to be no settled law. And we must further note that even when James had obtained a greater mastery of the method of indirection than he was possessed of in our present novel, the zest of experimentation was so strong in him that he occasionally flung his system overboard and produced a novel like *The Awkward Age,* in which everybody "goes behind" everybody else and no one behind himself. *The Princess Casamassima,* we conclude, was a sort of *ballon d'essai* to test the upper rarer air in which its author was ambitious to spread his wings. Without denying the validity of his theories one must permit oneself the ironical observation that his successes in this book lie with characters and situations delineated and described after the old fashion, with Miss Pynsent and Mr Vetch rather than with Hyacinth and the Princess; and that even when he was borrowing a leaf from the book of Dickens or Daudet, as witness the descriptions of Mrs Bowerbank and Rose Muniment, his success is not inconsiderable. I am not sure that his most delicate triumph of observation was not achieved in the diffident, dowdy, and wholly delightful Lady Aurora. (pp. 281-83)

Pelham Edgar, in his *Henry James: Man and Author,* 1927. Reprint by Russell & Russell, Inc., 1964, 351 p.

ANDRÉ GIDE

(essay date 1930)

[Gide was one of France's most influential thinkers and writers of the twentieth century. In the following excerpt, he voices a common criticism of James's art: that the author failed to "commit" himself to the lives of his characters.]

[James] lets only just enough steam escape to run his engine ahead, from page to page: and I do not believe that economy, that reserve, has ever sagaciously been carried further. The proportion remains perfect between the propulsive force and the drawing out of the narrative. No wonder, since nothing really alive nourishes him, and James only extracts from his brain what he knows to be there, and what his intelligence alone has put there. The interest is never in the outpouring, but is solely in the conduit. His work is like that of the spider, who ceaselessly widens her web by hanging new threads from one chosen support to another. Doubtless I shall praise him for taking his stand always on the same data of a problem. The skilfully made network spun out by his intelligence captivates only the intelligence: the intelligence of the reader, the intelligence of the heroes of his books. The latter seem never to exist except in the functioning of their intellects, they are only winged busts; all the weight of the flesh is absent, and all the shaggy, tangled undergrowth, all the wild darkness. . . .

Another thing: these characters never live except in relation to each other, in the functioning of these relations: they are desperately mundane; I mean by this that there is nothing of the divine in them, and that intelligence always explains what makes them act or vibrate. I do not feel so much that the author is snobbish as *profane:* yes profane, incurably so. To tell the truth, he does not interest me at all; or rather, it is his *métier* that interests me, his *métier* only, the prodigious virtuosity. But here also, there would be a great deal to say, and say again: this need of delineating everything, this conscience even, this scruple against leaving anything in the shadow, this minuteness of information, all this fatigues me, wears me out; his narratives are without color, without flavor; I hardly ever feel behind his figures, which are lighted from every side, that cone of unexplorable shadow where the suffering soul lies hidden, but his characters have no need of shelter—they have no souls. And I have not succeeded in persuading myself that this patience, this meticulousness . . . no, that is not great art; his strokes are too fine; he is afraid of the robust touches; he proceeds through subtleties.

Henry James in 1898.

And, again, this distresses me: he dominates his narrative from too great a height; he does not commit himself to it, nor compromise himself; it is as if he himself had perhaps nothing to confess to us. I notice incidentally that a character never interests me so greatly as when it is created—like Eve—from the very flesh of the author; when it is not so much observed as invented—and there indeed is the secret of the profoundest "analysts." . . . James, in himself, is not interesting; he is only intelligent; he has no mystery in him, no secret; no "Figure in the Carpet." At the most, he does at moments hoodwink us, as happens with the author hero of that specious narrative. Yes, this is exactly what distresses me—and what distresses me also in Meredith— to feel the author dominate, glide above the conflict that he invents, pull from too great a height the wires that make the actors move. (It seems to me that the value of Fielding, of Defoe, of Dickens, of George Eliot, of Hardy, comes from the fact that they never believe themselves, never show themselves, superior.)

Never do I feel that James is "in" with any one of them—and I am most certainly grateful to him for being impartial: but Dostoievsky, for example, finds a way of being impartial and committing himself at the same time to the most contrary, the most contradictory characters, who make him enter the heart of life, and us after him. Yes, it is just that; the secret of the great novelist is not in the domination of situations, but rather in the multiplicity of his intimate connivances. Undoubtedly these novels of James are marvels of composition; but one might say as well that the qualities of his narratives are always, are never anything but, the qualities of composition. We can marvel at the delicacy, at the subtlety of the gear wheels, but all his characters are like the figures of a clock, and the story is finished when they have struck the curfew; of themselves they return to the clock-case and to the night of our forgetting.

It goes without saying, nevertheless, that I am aware of all the importance of H. James; but I believe him more important for England than for France. England has never sinned up to the present by too much good cooking; James is a master-cook. But, as for me, I like precisely those great untrimmed chunks that Fielding or Defoe serves us, barely cooked, but keeping all the "blood-taste" of the meat. So much dressing and distinction, I am satiated with it in advance; he surpasses us in our own faults. (pp. 641-43)

André Gide, "Henry James," in *The Yale Review,* Vol. XIX, No. 3, March, 1930, pp. 641-43.

JOYCE CAROL OATES
(essay date 1974)

[Oates is an American fiction writer and critic. In the excerpt below, she contends that James failed in his attempts to present the "real" world in his fiction.]

It is felt generally, even by admirers, that in the novels of James and Woolf the aesthetic sensibility has so constricted life as to distort or pervert it, taking into account little of the richness and the vulgarity of the real world. It is not my suggestion that James and Woolf are similar in many important aspects; surprisingly enough, they seem quite clearly unrelated in matters of form, since James prepares forms quite as rigorous, though not as visible, as the plots of the traditional novel, and Woolf seeks to discover, along with her characters, design in the free flux of life; thematically, James is obsessed with the moral education of pastoral creatures—whether princesses or hardy Adamic voyagers from America—while Woolf is concerned with the necessary though doomed attempt to forge out of daily life a meaning that will somehow transcend it.

They are related, however, in their creation of subjective worlds that seek to define themselves in relationship to the larger, "real" world, the process often bringing with it annihilation, as in *The Voyage Out* and *The Wings of the Dove.* They are related most clearly in their use of minute psychological observations, Woolf casting about much more freely and inventively than James; and in their deliberate, unhurried, at times relentless faithfulness to these observations. What is most interesting about their art, however, is that it seems dehumanized to the ordinary intelligent reader. One cannot abstract from their worlds characters who are able to survive in an alien environment, as it would seem one might with other novelists—Dickens, Austen, Twain, Joyce. But this apparent weakness, however, may be seen as a necessary part of their literature.

One need only think of representative novelists—Thackeray and Conrad, for instance—to see that the vision of reality accepted by James and Woolf is severely different. For Thackerary and Conrad, unrelated though they are in most respects, reality is set and may be defined objectively, as history; for James and Woolf reality is a subjective phenomenon—more accurately, an endless series of subjective phenomena that may or may not be related. The secret lives of other people remain secret; one cannot penetrate into them, and the few flashes of rapport between people are perishable and cannot be trusted. Even the dead are mysterious.

Milly Theale and Mrs. Ramsay influence "reality" after their deaths, but their effect on others does not bring with it any sudden understanding on the part of their survivors. Human essences, shrouded in mystery, are forever one with the single existing moment in which they are expressed—they cannot be abstracted out of it; they cannot be summed up, understood, even forgotten. If, in modern art, it is a truism that things do not exist and relationships alone exist, this observation will work well in explaining the literature of James and Woolf. Their concern is primarily with the mystery and beauty and tragedy of human relationships, not with the depths of reality that constitute individual "personality." The creation of characters as ends in themselves, complete without functioning in a social or psychological equation with other characters, implies a metaphysical basis that is apparently not available to, or not chosen by, James and Woolf. Their metaphysics has in common the suggestion that man gains his identity, experiences his "life," in terms only of other people—other intelligent consciousnesses with whom he can communicate. Moreover, an individual's "reality" as an individual is determined by these relationships, which are entirely temporal and, especially in Woolf, undependable. The older sense of man defining himself in terms of God or of country or of family "history" has been replaced in James and Woolf by the sensitivity of the modern secular intellectual who admits of no reality beyond that experienced by the mind.

James's great myth is essentially the myth of the Fall: to James, heir of his Puritan ancestors as were Hawthorne and Melville, the fall is unfortunate in that it brings with it the mortal taint of decay as well as the "education" that is supposed to constitute a kind of minor, compensatory victory. One needs, then, to define James's world as essentially pastoral: an extension, into a more recognizable social *donnée,* of the blighted Eden of *The Turn of the Screw.* The paradise of innocence is carried precariously within a series of virginal heroines who are rounded, humanized descendants of Hawthorne's Hilda rather than Richardson's Clarissa— American purity typifying a spiritual purity that extends to mythic proportions, rather than being a reality, an end in itself as it is in the English novel. So we have Isabel Archer, the betrayed child Maisie, the children Miles and Flora, Maggie Verver, Milly Theale, and Fleda, who loses the spoils of Poynton because she is "too good" to compete for them. We also have Lambert Strether, the ambassador from Woollett, Massachusetts (innocence hardened into sterility, banality), to Paris (intuitive life hardened into sordidness), who is a widower, has experienced his only child's death, yet is seen to be unfulfilled until he comes to terms not simply with the richness of life Europe appears to offer but with the devastating underlying suggestion of evil this "real" life hides. In *The Ambassadors* . . . James refines experience so that it takes on the quality of thought rather than life. . . . [At] the same time, James develops to perfection the art of narrative by point of view, third-person restrictive, telling the story only through Strether's limited, though expanding, consciousness. The novel may be defined as a minute recording of an education into the reality of the self and the world entirely through the hero's deciphering of his relationships to other people and their relationships with one another. One is reminded of music cast into visible forms: of the dance, the changing and rechanging of partners, not, as in Austen, the gravitational pull toward "truth" and the "good," which are one, but the relentless pull toward knowledge. One cannot feel that Strether can be imagined apart from the novel; his psychic environment defines him, becomes him. For a man of Strether's sensitivity, by no means rare in our time, it is the consideration of what is not immediate that blights or undermines the present: "The obsession of the other thing is the terror," he says. Is the reality of this world of endless qualifications less legitimate than the reality of violence in the American novel, the one so committed to the mind, the other so committed to the body? James was surely influenced by the transcendentalists in his understanding of and insistence upon the legitimacy of psychic experience as total reality in the face of opposition by such critics as H. G. Wells. In an important sense all art is pastoral, its exclusions being at least as significant as its inclusions. For James the technique necessary to investigate reality to its depths is so precise, so fine, that the range investigated must be limited. The Jamesian technique cannot effectively be fused with the novel of action, nor is there any reason why it should be or why, failing its involvement in "total life," it should be considered somehow incomplete. . . . (pp. 12-16)

In James as well as in Woolf there is the suggestion that art controls life, that the demands of the "architecturally competent" novel must alter the free flow of life and that, in Woolf especially, the exquisite epiphany becomes an end in itself rather than a means of illuminating character: as if the novel were a novel only of "character" in the old-fashioned sense. If James's most satisfactory and perhaps most Jamesian work, *The Wings of the Dove* . . . , is considered in some detail, however, it will be seen to give us what must surely be the most exhaustive attempt ever made of rendering the sensitivity or reflection of a tragic experience. It is the experience that matters; the aesthetic achievement is secondary. The plot of the novel sounds legendary: a dying American heiress, Milly Theale, is betrayed by her "lover," Merton Densher, who is in love with another woman. This woman, the beautiful and powerful Kate Croy, has directed the love affair in the hopes that with the marriage of Milly and Densher, and Milly's expected death, Milly's fortune will come

to them and complete their lives. Milly learns of the plot, her death is hastened, but she wills her money to the young man just the same: by this act forcing in her betrayers a moral sense so violent as to change their lives. Milly reminds us of the passive victims in Dostoyevsky—the saintly, the weak, the helpless, who possess paradoxically, as Dostoyevsky thought, the greatest power in the world. It is Milly's submission to her "fate" that secures her power; but it is not a perverse masochistic submission as Dostoyevsky's women sometimes exhibit—for instance, the suicidal Nastasia Philipovna of *The Idiot*—so much as a Christlike surrender of the self to the sins of others, in this way bringing about a moral transformation in the sinners. Not that James was Christian, or even ostensibly concerned with religious problems. But the movement of the novel, its very rhythm of sacrifice and moral self-realization, the theme of the power of selfless love—all are unmistakable parallels with the religious experience, whether Christian or tragic in the Greek sense. Milly embodies the symbolic roles of the Adamic innocent and the savior, the transition from the one to the other being precipitated by her encounter with evil; she is the dove whose wings spread to enclose the soiled, to carry her innocence away into the safety of death. (pp. 16-17)

It is not, crudely synopsized, a working out of the conventional fear Milly has at the beginning of Book Three when we first meet her—the fear that the two lone women, touring Europe together, "were apt to be beguiled and overcome"? Precisely: but the brute experience itself is not what is important. It is Milly's consciousness of her experience, and the consciousness of sin on the part of Kate and Densher, that make the novel great. It is an education, a growth of the moral sense in all involved, that is the "reality" of the novel. Milly is the instrument by which we are shown the tragic knowledge of the relationship between life and death, life being fulfilled only through death (knowledge), the dove becoming the symbol—and James makes us see the rather trite image in the actual process of *becoming* symbol—of death-in-life, life-in-death. The Greek *ate* is here defeated, for the assimilation of evil by the innocent, the refusal to continue the power of evil by passing its suffering along to others, are affected by Milly's silence: in the clichéd sorrow of Mrs. Stringham's remark, "She has turned her face to the wall." The beauty of the spirit overshadows the "talent for life" of Kate Croy, Milly's opposite; the power of the dove overshadows that of the panther. (pp. 18-19)

The Golden Bowl . . . continues the theme of innocence accosted by evil, or the world, the essential—and rather surprising—difference here being that where the earlier heroines were defeated because of their innocence, the young heroine Maggie Verver is able to achieve a victory by way of her innocence. It is most clearly the story of an education, more faithful to life perhaps in its refusal to surrender life along with "innocence," less effective as art than *The Wings of the Dove,* which tends to equate (one is reminded of *Billy Budd*) purity and life itself. It involves the awakening of a "moral sense" adumbrated in the earlier *What Maisie Knew* and, though the parallel is rather sinister, in *The Turn of the Screw.* (pp. 19-20)

Essentially the story of a family, the novel's movement is determined by the changing of individuals into roles, the discovery of individuals that they are participants in a drama that has rich and threatening implications for them all. . . . The conclusion of the novel involves, depends upon, a re-establishment of *order* not on a moral level but on a social level, a preservation of something rather like an institution—the institution of marriage, of "love," of civilization—not of the individual. If James's work contains any single great irony, it is the irony of the imprisonment of the individual in relationships and forms precisely at the moment of his "illumination." James's people are usually wealthy, bathed in riches as the lambs and children of Blake's pastoral are bathed in sunshine, and they are wealthy for the same reason that Shakespeare's tragic figures are kingly: their economic freedom assures them moral freedom. (pp. 20-1)

The reader feels constantly the mercenary shallowness of both the Prince and Charlotte, so that James's refusal to concern himself with the morality—and good taste—of the transaction is puzzling. That he does not do so seems clear by his complete absorption in the character of Maggie, who begins as a shadow, a pronouncer of the customary, proper remarks, and who ends as the "creator" of her world—she has nearly acquired omnipotence by the end of the novel. That her fight for her husband must be waged behind social forms makes the struggle more difficult and, for the loser, Charlotte, who never learns how much anyone knows about her adultery, more cruel. Neither Maggie nor James shows any remorse. Maggie is the victor, having surrendered a father and chosen a husband; she enters history; it seems perhaps a regrettable flaw that the man for whom she sacrifices her innocence is not worth her sacrifice, since a better man would not have betrayed her—would not have necessitated her education. The novel ends with Maggie's father taking Charlotte to America, leaving Maggie with her husband, whom she both pities and dreads. She has learned to deceive in order to impose her will upon the world. . . . (pp. 22-3)

James must be understood . . . , in his later novels especially, as a creator of relationships; the actors—the fictional "characters"—come second. Though we may agree in part with his brother, William, when he criticized what he saw to be a "method of narration by interminable elaboration" . . . we must see that his apparent sacrifice of life to art is necessary for his vision

of character *as* art. Like the medieval alchemists, whom he may resemble in other ways also, James transformed himself into a lifework, and each of his characters carries the transformation further. His main characters are artists, and the art they create is their own lives. (pp. 23-4)

Joyce Carol Oates, "The Art of Relationships: Henry James and Virginia Woolf," in her *New Heaven, New Earth: The Visionary Experience in Literature,* Vanguard Press, 1974, pp. 9-35.

LOUIS AUCHINCLOSS
(essay date 1975)

[Auchincloss is an American novelist and critic. In the following excerpt, he discusses James's short stories and travel writing.]

James's first attempts [to deal with his American tour] were in three short stories, **"A Round of Visits," "Julia Bride,"** and **"Crapy Cornelia."** In all of these the American experience is insufficiently digested, as shown by the rather crude satire, which has some of the same shrill note that we find in Edith Wharton's later fiction. . . .

It was not until **"The Jolly Corner"** that James dealt with the American experience with a firm hand. Here he abandoned petty bickering and aimed his gun at what he conceived to be the basic evil in the heart of the American scene. (p. 46)

The story has a very nasty implication, which is that Spencer Brydon is a bigger man for having spent his life as a dilettante in Europe than he would have been for spending it as a successful man of affairs at home. America, in other words, is to be avoided at almost any price. . . . [The] story, based as it is upon James's real feelings and not upon surface irritations, is a great one.

In the novel which he left unfinished at his death, **"The Ivory Tower,"** James was still experimenting with the impressions of his American tour and the problems of the repatriated. (p. 47)

Perhaps the only really safe thing [one concludes from the fragment of **"The Ivory Tower"**], is to live in Europe with the aid of a small, respectable trust fund, one that dates far enough back to be free of the smirch of modern mercantilism.

In **"The Ivory Tower"** some of the triviality of the satire of the three American stories seems to have affected the central theme. On the other hand, the observation of the American characters is vastly strengthened over that of the stories. James, in dealing fiction-ly with the material of his American tour, had been unable to unite a strong theme with strong treatment.

Much more successful was his volume of travel reminiscences, **"The American Scene,"** a brilliant combination of prose that rises to the level of poetry and language that contains his most convoluted and intricate sentences. James in this book shows himself something of a prophet. There are passages where he foretells nothing less than the current destruction of our environment and the horrors of ethnic struggles. It is astonishing how much he was able to make out of a countryside viewed from the moving windows of Pullman cars and the wide verandas of summer houses. But, of course, he was a veteran tourist.

There are moments when the triviality of the personal note mars the elegiac invocation of the atmosphere. . . . But there are other times when he uses the personal grudge or inconvenience as a source of illumination of the entire horizon. Thus, at the end of the book when he arrives at The Breakers in Palm Beach, the Ultima Thule of the American boardinghouse ideal, and finds at ten o'clock in the evening, after a weary day on a train without a dining car, that he cannot order a bite to eat, he uses the episode as a brilliant demonstration of the essential rigor, the cruel uniformity, the lack of any real taste which underlies the gaudy, glittering, heartless American world of hotels.

I do not think it is going too far to suggest that in *The American Scene* James was trying his hand at what was—at least for him—a new writing method, a sort of literary impressionism. The book at times becomes almost a novel—at least a novel in the sense used today by Nathalie Sarraute. (pp. 49-50)

He was not afraid to face unpopular facts. He pointed out that the masses pouring into America from the slums of Europe could never be truly assimilated and that the price of continued immigration would be the loss of the national character and speech as his generation had known it. He saw, too, that the "Americanization" of Europeans, particularly Italians, tended to strip them of their native charm. And he was under no illusion about the racial hatred which smouldered under the dull calm of the Southern states. If the handsome and engaging young man who guided him through the Civil War Museum in Richmond was "incapable of hurting a Northern fly," he was still not to be trusted with a Southern Negro.

But his deepest divination was of the close connection between American democracy and materialism. He saw that even the snobbishness of the country club was basically superficial, that this curious institution represented the "people," freed from the shackles of European feudalism, enjoying themselves. Such was the true secret of America. The masses *liked* the crowding, the hubbub, the noise, the rush, the money, the glitter. America represented what they had always dreamed of, and they were not disappointed. James, emotionally identifying himself with the aristocracy of the past with all its traditions and disciplines, felt bewildered and left out. But he never apologized for not liking America. He did not trust it, and he had no faith in its future. (p. 51)

Many critics get in trouble when they turn their backs on the problem and put him on a pedestal as an unflawed genius. Behind the great writer who in cathedral tones denounced the materialism and wastefulness of his native land, there always lurked the fretful expatriate who scolded the beaches of Florida for their lack of history. (p. 52)

Louis Auchincloss, "Henry James's Literary Use of His American Tour (1904)," in *South Atlantic Quarterly*, Vol. 74, No. 1, Winter, 1975, pp. 45-52.

EDWARD WAGENKNECHT
(essay date 1983)

[Wagenknecht is an American biographer and critic. His works include critical surveys of the English and American novel and studies of Charles Dickens, Mark Twain, and Henry James. Here, he surveys James's middle, or "transitional," novels.

Compared to the three great monuments of James's "later manner"—*The Ambassadors, The Wings of the Dove,* and *The Golden Bowl*—*What Maisie Knew* is still a "short" novel (361 pages of the New York Edition . . .), but although it was written not long after its predecessor [*The Spoils of Poynton*], it is considerably more "advanced." It is also more difficult. Thus while there is no excuse whatever for the eccentric readings of *Poynton* with which we have been blessed of late, it is only fair to say that James must bear some share of responsibility for the less extensive mauling to which *Maisie* has been subjected, for he has left in shadow a number of matters about which he might, without injury to his story or his method, have been more explicit. As with *Hamlet,* so with *Maisie;* one may find a sentence somewhere to bolster almost any misreading, however obtuse, and James is without Shakespeare's excuse that we have three texts of his play but no authorized text. (p. 152)

In *What Maisie Knew* James attempted to paint a picture of a corrupt society as seen by a child and at the same time to trace the child's own development toward spiritual maturity. His original idea was to limit his presentation to what Maisie "might be conceived to have *understood*," but he soon realized that she was too young for that; consequently, although his *"line"* remained her "dim, sweet, sacred, wondering, clinging perception," he included also what she *saw* without understanding and employed a variety of devices to supplement and interpret her perceptions. Although there are still a few glaring instances of old-fashioned direct authorial comment ("Oh, decidedly I shall never get you to believe the number of things she saw and the number of secrets she discovered!"), such passages stand in the sharpest possible contrast to his highly sophisticated employment of "suppressed scenes and indirect discourse" to achieve "variety in his handling of scenes."

One asks oneself whether all the relationships portrayed in this novel, all the minute reactions of the characters, and all their kaleidoscopic regroupings are convincing. Personally I do not believe they are, but I am not sure the question is relevant. James admits in his preface that it was in the interest of symmetry that he had *both* Maisie's parents remarry. We are, I think, never made to feel what it was in Ida that attracted so many lovers nor how she could have enthralled such decent men as Sir Claude and the unnamed Captain, and it is equally hard to believe that both she and Sir Claude and Beale and Miss Overman should begin to be estranged from each other almost as soon as they are married. If we must have literary analogues for the kind of pattern James seems to be working out, let them be sought not in the realistic novel but in Restoration comedy or French classical tragedy or, better still, in the formations and figurations of classical ballet.

The attempts which F. R. Leavis and others have made to interpret *Maisie* as essentially comic are hopelessly one-sided; a book which eventuates in spiritual victory for the heroine and spiritual failure for almost everybody else can amuse neither God nor the devil. Nevertheless, the author has made abundant use of subordinate comic devices, sometimes embracing broad caricature. . . . Aside from one of Ida's lovers, Mr. Perriam, whom we glimpse only in passing, the most daring caricature is that of the "brown" countess whom Beale has descended to living upon at the end. . . . But caricature appears also in the description of Maisie's parents. (pp. 154-56)

Maisie's governess, Mrs. Wix, is, however, in this novel, James's greatest grotesque. . . . James uses every device Dickens would have used in describing Mrs. Wix except one; he does not invent a distinctive speech for her. . . . Mrs. Wix has her limitations as both an intellectual and a moral guide, but when the chips are down, she stands with the sheep, not the goats; it is all the more interesting, then, that James should not have refused to see the comic side of either her much-vaunted "moral sense" or her devotion to the memory of her daughter, Clara Matilda, who had been killed in traffic and for whom Maisie must in a measure act as surrogate. (pp. 156-57)

But what, then, *did* Maisie know? James plays a cat-and-mouse game with the idea, comparable to that of Henry Adams with education. And this not only makes for the difficulty of the book but determines its method. From first to last, the pages of the novel are studded with passages reflecting childish innocence. (p. 158)

On the other hand, she sometimes shows an insight and even prescience that reveals her as being in unconscious possession of a wisdom as old as the everlasting hills. The most touching example is in the great, powerfully underplayed scene in Chapter 17 in which she has her only encounter with the Captain, who seems to have been the most decent and deluded of her mother's many lovers. Having learned that he thinks Ida an angel and likes her better than any other woman, Maisie begs him not to love her "only for just a little," like "all the others," but to "do it always." This wonderful hit seems to have killed two birds with one stone, for when Maisie innocently mentions the Captain to Ida in Chapter 21 and Ida must make an effort to recall him as "the biggest cad in London," the reader understands that the girl has done both his and her mother's business for them. (p. 159)

What Maisie Knew ends when Sir Claude asks Maisie whether she would give up Mrs. Wix to live with him and Mrs. Beale. Being afraid of herself, she first asks time to consider and then declares that she will not go with him unless he gives up Mrs. Beale. (p. 160)

If the illicit nature of the tie between Sir Claude and Mrs. Beale has created the problem Maisie faces at the end, it must be understood both that she is not yet fully aware of all the implications of this and that her judgments, unlike those of Mrs. Wix, do not rest upon a strictly legalistic basis. By this time her "moral sense" has developed beyond that of her preceptress, whom she now needs only for mothering. James says that at last she knew what she wanted; I should say rather that she knows what she *needs*. There is more intuition than reason in her judgments, and being still a child, she could not be expected to explain them fully. But she *has* learned that people go together in twos, not threes, and (as her conversation with the Captain shows) that a dignifying and satisfactory relationship can exist only on a basis of permanency and fidelity. These qualities may be lacking, of course, in legalized as well as unlegalized relationships, as, notably, in those which Maisie has known thus far. She has already been disillusioned about Mrs. Beale, and she is in the process of being disillusioned about her erstwhile knight in shining armor, Sir Claude. In a sense, the proposition she places before him, is, whether she realizes it or not, part of a testing process. She has no desire to become part of a setup which would share the characteristics of those of which she has already seen far too much. (pp. 161-62)

Like its two immediate predecessors, [*The Awkward Age*] was conceived as a short story, but this time the beginning was not an anecdote or a situation but merely an idea and what must strike us today as a trifling, snobbish, and hypocritical idea at that. What happens to the "good talk" in the fashionable drawing room when the adolescent daughter, having outgrown the nursery, begins to "sit downstairs" but being still unmarried, is not supposed to know what her elders are talking about? Must the good talk be so expurgated to avoid bringing what Mr. Podsnap called the blush to the cheek of the young person? If so, what becomes of the level of sophistication? And if not, what becomes of her innocence? In France the problem could not arise, for the girl would be in a convent school until she was married and so passed at a bound from knowing nothing to knowing everything, nor yet in America, where talk was never "good" in the sophisticated English fashion. (pp. 162-63)

The Awkward Age represents the height of James's interest in "method," and his satisfaction in it seems to have derived from the conviction that he had so triumphantly brought it off. It is divided into what [Oscar] Cargill calls "ten books or acts and thirty-eight scenes" (James planned it all out almost mathematically), and there is no central reflective consciousness. Instead each book is named for one of the characters, intended to furnish what James calls a "lamp" to illuminate the action. (pp. 164-65)

In the predecessor of this novel, James had tormented his readers with the riddle of what Maisie *knew*. Here we are not so much concerned with that (Nanda obviously knows everything) as with whether she has been corrupted by what she knows and her contacts with immoral people, and even more with what must be the effect of all this upon her eligibility as a *parti* in the marriage market. Since nobody has ever suggested that she is either dishonest or unchaste, this may well strike modern readers as even more much ado about nothing than the basic problem or situation with which James began. The only thing Nanda is ever convicted of in the course of the action comes when her mother forces her to admit that she had read what was considered an indecent French novel, and since she did that only to find out whether it was fit to be read by her friend Tishy Grendon, who certainly needed no protection from her, this act shows her up as rather naive than corrupted. (pp. 166-67)

James deliberately deglamourizes Nanda. She has "no features" unless she has "two or three too many," and it is a question whether she is pretty at all. She lacks not only her mother's grace but humor and brightness also; at one point Mrs. Brook calls her "as bleak as a chimney-top when the fire's out." But her loyalties are absolute; degradation in others does not repel her; neither does she resent slights that have been shown to herself. Nanda does not love sinners for their sins but because they need loving. Her plea to Van not to desert her mother because "she's so lovely" and "so fearfully young" is even more touching because she is more fully aware of what she is saying than Maisie in her plea to the Captain. . . . She even begs Mr. Longdon to see to it that Van shall not lose financially by having turned down the endowment Mr. Longdon proposed to supply him with because he could not bring himself to take her along with the money! And it is quite clear that young as she is, she is going to be a mother to Mr. Longdon quite as much as he will be a father to her.

Mitchy's marrying Little Aggie to please Nanda would be more at home in a book like *Wuthering Heights,* where Cathy marries Linton to help Heathcliff, than in the at least outwardly realistic *Awkward Age,* but although Mitchy is not so "pure" as Nanda, he does share her charity. . . . Van is another story; for all his charm, his behavior at the end leaves room for nothing but contempt. . . . Although he quite lacks Gilbert Osmond's capacity for deliberate cruelty, he is like him in his hopeless conventionality and his inability to distinguish between the real and the apparent, and Dorothea Krook may well be right when she suggests that he would not be capable of living with a woman whose judgment and sense of values were superior to his own. What he really likes is the old-fashioned girl, but it is his pride, not purity, that causes Nanda to repel him; he could not bear to mate with a girl coming out of her environment so precious a creature as himself.

One of James's most surprising self-judgments is his special enthusiasm over Mrs. Brook, whom he . . . considered the best thing he had ever done, and some of the critics have been eager to outdo him on this score, comparing her to the great ladies of Restoration comedy and seeing her as an artist molding her environment into a work of art. It is true that Mrs. Brook is not the worst member of her circle; I agree that she is almost certainly not an adulteress (most of the adultery in this novel is committed by characters on the border of the circle); neither is she personally unsympathetic or cruel. But the higher one rates her potentialities, the deeper must be the condemnation she incurs for her useless life; indeed, as she herself perceives at one point, the fact that passion is absent even deprives her of an excuse she might otherwise have had. Surely those who have praised the intellectuality of her circle are easily impressed in this area. The only justification for such a judgment is that these people are all immensely preoccupied with analyzing each other's motives and reactions, often in disreputable situations. There is never the slightest suggestion that any of them ever had what could be called an idea in their lives or that they had ever manifested any interest in anything affecting the vital interest or general welfare of mankind. Mrs. Brook is greedy and morally indifferent (she even wants her daughter's life "to be as much as possible like my own") and her only real concern is to keep intact a circle of friends, if you can call them that, most of whom are even more useless than herself.

The basic idea for *The Sacred Fount* . . . posited a marriage between a young man and older woman, after which she bloomed and he languished, growing progressively older and weaker as she grew younger, stronger, and prettier. James promptly considered combining this with the experience of a second pair of this time unmarried lovers, exhibiting a once dull man who has drained the wit from a clever woman, the transformation in both persons being the means through which the liaison comes to light. (pp. 167-70)

The Sacred Fount resembles *The Awkward Age* in being developed largely in terms of a series of dialogues but differs from it in that these interchanges are both linked and interpreted by the unnamed narrator (it is the only novel by James, as distinguished from many short stories, written in the first person). This aids our understanding if we are willing to be guided by him but increases our difficulty if, with his antagonist Mrs. Brissenden (generally called Mrs. Briss), we think or pretend to think him crazy or, with some of the critics, envisage James as a concocter of puzzles who entrusted his readers only to guides who might lead them astray. Although J. A. Ward goes entirely too far when he tells us that we cannot even be sure whether the narrator is a man or a woman, it is true that we receive no information that has not been filtered through his consciousness; we have only his word not only for what the others do but for much of what they say, for he tells his story in retrospect and, as he informs us, sometimes paraphrases. (p. 172)

The Sacred Fount is generally regarded as James's most difficult novel, and even some of his admirers have called it unreadable. . . . The difficulty has been much exaggerated, however. It arises not from the style, which is clear enough, but from the intense concentration demanded and from James's insistence that readers interpret for themselves phenomena which admit of more than one interpretation instead of depending upon the author to do it for them. Consequently, the novel has been read as a vampire story . . . a spiritual detective story, and a study of how fiction is created, this last sometimes running over into the absurd notion that the author is burlesquing himself. (p. 174)

If there is any one thing in the novel that is more obscure than everything else, it is the haunting, sinister picture of "The Man with the Mask." . . . (p. 175)

This surely is an impressive use of symbolism which might well hold the key to the meaning of the book, but if so, neither the characters nor the critics have been able to turn the lock. The people looking at the picture seem agreed at least that the man looks like "poor Briss" and the mask like May Server, but there is no agreement as to whether the man is life and the mask death, if that is what they mean, or vice versa; Mrs. Server takes the first view, and the narrator the second. In any case the scene has a strange and eerie power. It seems odd that the reader should be so much affected by something so opaque—unless indeed that is the very reason.

The unnamed narrator is by all means the most important character, and since we know about the others only through him, perhaps it is not surprising either that there should be such a wide range of opinion about him or that so many should have made a pretty good job out of judging themselves through attempting to judge him. The range is indeed extraordinary, stretching all the way from the notion of a sneaking, sniveling Paul Pry or voyeur, through a deluded, pride-blinded fool attempting to play providence, or even, as Mrs. Briss, almost certainly insincerely, puts it at last, a lunatic, to an embodiment of the creative spirit of the artist. (pp. 175-76)

Our attitude toward the narrator necessarily determines what we believe about his antagonist, Mrs. Briss, and our interpretation of the interview between them which fills the last three of the book's fourteen chapters. To me nothing is clearer than that Mrs. Briss is another of James's great evil women and that in this scene she is completely mendacious and insincere. She denies everything she had previously affirmed and affirms everything she had previously denied. She now describes Gilbert Long as the same "poor fool" he had always been, although she had remarked the change in him even before the narrator noticed it, and denies that May Server had ever had any connection with him. (p. 179)

If the narrator is right in his hypothesis that May Server has been used as badly by Long as "poor Briss" has been used by his wife, that the two victims have now turned to each other for comfort while the two victimizers have embarked upon a fresh liaison with each other (which would be as neat a piece of Jamesian symmetry as anything in *What Maisie Knew*), and if Mrs. Briss now feels reasonably certain that the narrator is in the process of figuring all this out (he has certainly been giving her daring though ambiguous hints in this direction for some time), she has abundant reason for seeking the midnight interview with her antagonist, for her complete change of front when she encounters him, and for her bad manners toward him. Otherwise the whole situation is inexplicable.

But why, then, it may be asked, the contrived ambiguity of the ending? Why especially the last two sentences: "I *should* certainly never again, on the spot, quite hang together, even though it wasn't really that I hadn't three times her method. What I fatally lacked was her tone." This need not necessarily mean anything more than, as Ora Segal suggests, that "all the narrator admits is that he cannot match her brashness, insolence, and effrontery." Joan of Arc, I suppose, lacked the "tone" of the tribunal that sent her to the stake, but that did not prove them right nor her wrong. We must face the fact that there are many circumstances under which the children of light cannot look for anything but defeat by the children of darkness, simply because there are weapons that the children of light cannot use without undoing themselves. (pp. 180-81)

Edward Wagenknecht, in his *The Novels of Henry James,* Frederick Ungar Publishing Co., 1983, 329 p.

SOURCES FOR FURTHER STUDY

Anderson, Quentin. *The American Henry James.* New Brunswick, N.J.: Rutgers University Press, 1957, 369 p.

Biographical and critical examination that attempts to show that James's work was greatly influenced by his father's philosophical thought.

Beach, Joseph Warren. *The Method of Henry James.* Philadelphia, Penn.: Albert Saifer, 1954, 289 p.

One of the earliest full-length critiques of the narrative technique of James's major novels.

Edel, Leon. *Henry James.* 5 vols. Philadelphia and New York: J. B. Lippincott Co., 1953-72.

Definitive biography. Edel's five-volume biography, for which he was awarded the Pulitzer Prize, traces James's life and career as a writer in five separate stages: 1843 to 1870, 1870 to 1881, 1882 to 1895, 1895 to 1901, and 1901 to 1916.

Holland, Laurence Bedwell. *The Expense of Vision: Essays on the Craft of Henry James.* Princeton, N.J. Princeton University Press, 1964, 414 p.

Examines the manner in which James's imagery, his plots, his symbolism—in short, his imagination—defines the structure and development of his stories.

Poirier, Richard. *The Comic Sense of Henry James: A Study of the Early Novels.* New York: Columbia University Press, 1960, 260 p.

Focuses on James's dependence on "melodrama" and "comic extravagance" in such early works as *Roderick Hudson, The American, Washington Square,* and *The Portrait of a Lady.*

Veeder, William. *Henry James—The Lessons of the Master: Popular Fiction and Personal Style in the Nineteenth Century.* Chicago and London: The University of Chicago Press, 1975, 287 p.

Discusses the different literary traditions that influenced James and analyzes the manner in which "he transformed those materials into great art."

Robinson Jeffers

1887-1962

(Full name John Robinson Jeffers) American poet, dramatist, essayist, nonfiction writer, and short story writer.

INTRODUCTION

Jeffers is an important figure in twentieth-century American poetry whose prophetic admonitions against modern civilization and human selfishness have attracted both critical censure and admiration. He is perhaps best known for long dramatic narrative poems in which he combined violent imagery with a somber tone and dense syntax to explore unsettling topics. Guided by his philosophy of inhumanism, which he defined as "a shifting of emphasis and significance from man to not-man; the rejection of human solipsism and recognition of the transhuman magnificence," Jeffers contrasted the strength and enduring beauty of nature with a tragic vision of human suffering and relative inconsequence. Incorporating structures and themes from classical Greek drama, the Bible, and Eastern mysticism, and influenced by such thinkers as Lucretius, Arthur Schopenhauer, and Friedrich Nietzsche, Jeffers drew upon science, history, nature, and contemporary events for subject material. Jeffers was also inspired by the landscape and inhabitants of Southern California's Monterey coast, where he lived throughout his adult life.

The son of a Presbyterian preacher and theologian, Jeffers was born in Pittsburgh, Pennsylvania. He was tutored by his father in various languages, the classics, and the Bible before being sent to boarding schools in Switzerland and Germany. Following his graduation from Occidental College in 1905, Jeffers earned a masters degree in literature from the University of Southern California; he later spent several years studying medicine at USC and forestry at the University of Washington. After a modest inheritance freed him from the necessity of earning a living, Jeffers and his wife settled on an isolated plot of coastal land in Carmel, California, where he built a stone house and tower overlooking the Pacific Ocean. This rustic setting and

Jeffers's ensuing austere lifestyle suggested both the dominant imagery and tone of his poetry.

Jeffers's first two books, *Flagons and Apples* (1912) and *Californians* (1916), are generally considered conventional and undistinguished. In the poems collected in these volumes, Jeffers employs traditional structures, rhyme schemes, and diction, using the natural world as a backdrop for his semiautobiographical lyrics of frustrated love. *Roan Stallion, Tamar, and Other Poems* (1925; revised, 1935), which was originally published at Jeffers's own expense as *Tamar and Other Poems* (1924), exhibits a significant advance from his earlier work. Eschewing traditional modes, Jeffers utilizes simple, declarative, and often colloquial language, as well as long narrative forms, while exploring sexual themes that display the influence of Sigmund Freud, Carl Jung, and Havelock Ellis. "Tamar," for example, is based upon a story from the second book of Samuel. A tragedy involving incest between a sister and her brother, "Tamar" combines California locales with biblical diction and symbolism. "Roan Stallion" centers upon a woman whose abusive husband is killed by her horse when she flees to the animal for protection. After slaying the horse in retaliation for the death of her husband, the woman realizes that she has destroyed the embodiment of her freedom. Her subsequent anguish symbolizes the suffering that humanity inflicts upon itself when it squanders opportunities for change and improvement. "The Tower beyond Tragedy" is drawn from Aeschylus's *Oresteia,* in which Orestes kills his mother to avenge her murder of his father, Agamemnon. In his version, Jeffers focuses on the character of Cassandra, whom Agamemnon obtains as spoil from his victory at Troy and who prophesies many of the grim events that follow. Jeffer's Cassandra foretells not only the fall of old empires, as in the Greek myth, but that of future civilizations. Some of the shorter lyrics in this collection describe Southern California's terrain and display Jeffer's knowledge of biology, astronomy, and physics.

The Women at Point Sur (1927; revised as *The Women at Point Sur and Other Poems,* 1977) is an ambitious and complex dramatic narrative poem that is considered one of Jeffers's most controversial works. Described by Dwight Mcdonald as "a witches' dance of incest, suicide, madness, adultery and Lesbianism," this piece relates the story of Barclay, a Christian minister whose disillusionment with the war that claimed his only son turns him from theology. Abandoning his wife and church, Barclay withdraws to the Carmel coast, where he seeks to establish a new religion based upon the external world. He is distracted from his intention, however, by overbearing narcissism and lust for his daughter. Barclay eventually goes insane, and following an orgy of destruction, he wanders off to die in the hills. Modern in its use of science for poetic material

and its candid, realistic concern with sex, *The Women at Point Sur* satirizes human self-importance and explores harmful aspects of civilization.

Cawdor and Other Poems (1928) is regarded by some critics as Jeffers's finest single volume. The title poem of this collection is based upon the plot of Euripides's *Hippolytus,* in which Hippolytus is cursed by Aphrodite with the physical love of Phaedra, his stepmother. When Phaedra hangs herself in grief over her stepson's resistance to her advances, Hippolytus is driven from Athens by his father, whose prayers are fulfilled when his son is dragged to death by his own horses. This book also contains several short unrhymed verses that focus upon the benefits of death over life. The title piece of *Dear Judas and Other Poems* (1929) dramatizes the crucifixion of Jesus Christ by adapting elements of Japanese Noh theater. Narrated by the ghosts of Jesus, the Virgin Mary, and Judas Iscariot, "Dear Judas" exhibits Jeffers's most sustained concern with human emotion. Stage adaptations of "Dear Judas," first produced in 1947, have been banned on various occasions for allegedly sacrilegious subject matter. This volume also includes "The Loving Shepherdess," a dramatic narrative about a long-suffering young woman who roams the Southern California coast through settings reminiscent of those in other works by Jeffers. During her travels, she encounters a friendly vaquero to whom she relates the events which have led to her tragic predicament. *Descent to the Dead: Poems Written in Ireland and Great Britain* (1931) contains sixteen short poems written in stately verse that feature a wealth of local color and lore. In the title piece of *Thurso's Landing and Other Poems* (1932), Jeffers recounts the tale of an unhappily married couple whose passion is unable to save them from misery and confusion. In *Give Your Heart to the Hawks and Other Poems* (1933), Jeffers presents a psychological portrait of a strong-willed man who is driven insane by remorse for the murder of his brother. This volume also includes several short pieces that are predominantly concerned with themes of death and resurrection, poems from *Descent to the Dead,* and "At the Fall of an Age," which concerns the death of Helen on the island of Rhodes twenty years after the fall of Troy.

In *Solstice and Other Poems* (1935), Jeffers presents a modern version of the Greek legend of Medea founded upon an account by Euripides. This volume also contains the long narrative "At the Birth of an Age." Derived from the final sections of the Teutonic epic the *Nibelungenlied,* this poem portrays a petty argument between three sibling leaders of a small Germanic tribe and their sister that contributes to the defeat of Attila and the Huns during an invasion of Europe in 451 A. D. Jeffers overshadows the individual personalities of his characters by emphasizing the enormous consequences of their small-minded conduct. The title piece of *Such Counsels You Gave to Me and Other Poems* (1937) features a modernization of a traditional Scottish ballad in which the protagonist's medical acumen provides Jeffers with a vehicle for demonstrating his knowledge of science. Also included in this volume are short poems concerning Jeffers's refusal to align himself with any particular economic, social, or political movement, a position for which he was frequently criticized. *Be Angry at the Sun* (1941) contains several controversial portraits of Adolf Hitler, whom Jeffers considered historically necessary and simultaneously fascinating and disgusting. In *The Double Axe and Other Poems* (1948; revised, 1977), Jeffers utilizes elements of Eastern ideology to convey the alienation and hatred experienced by many veterans of war. The title poem of this collection is a tale of a young soldier who returns from the dead to confront and kill his father, who had sent him into battle during World War II. This volume also features the philosophical poem "The Inhumanist," in which Jeffers expounds his fundamental convictions. In the final collection published during his lifetime, *Hungerfield and Other Poems* (1954), which was inspired by his wife's death in 1950, Jeffers portrays death as a welcome respite from life's distress.

Several compilations and posthumous publications of Jeffers's poetry have been issued, including *Selected Poems of Robinson Jeffers* (1963) and *Rock and Hawk: A Selection of Shorter Poems* (1987). *The Beginning and the End and Other Poems* (1963) collects verse that Jeffers composed following *Hungerfield*, while the works assembled in *The Alpine Christ and Other Poems* (1973) were written between 1916 and 1924. The longest single poem that Jeffers composed, "The Alpine Christ" opens with a conference in heaven during which Satan compliments God for allowing World War I to exceed the horrors of hell. As a result, Jesus Christ returns to earth to redeem humankind but is unsuccessful and departs as the war continues. *Brides of the South Wind: Poems, 1917-1922* (1974) gathers verse that Jeffers composed immediately after the publication of his first two books, and *What Odd Expedients and Other Poems* (1981) contains many pieces concerning war.

Jeffers adapted several of his long dramatic narrative poems for the theater. The title character of *Medea: Freely Adapted from the Medea of Euripides* (1947) is a woman of elemental passions whose tendency toward violence illuminates humanity's need to surmount the limitations of mere emotion. *The Tower beyond Tragedy* (1950), like Jeffers's poem of the same name, is a rendering of Aeschylus's *Oresteia* in which Orestes rejects vanity and identifies himself with the divine nature of all things. In *The Cretan Woman* (1954), the text of which is included in *Hungerfield and Other Poems*, Jeffers borrows from his poem "Cawdor" to rework the plot of Euripides's *Hippolytus*. Although Jeffers wrote little criticism, he occasionally composed pieces that endeavored to express or clarify his beliefs. *Poetry, Gongorism, and a Thousand Years* (1949) was originally published as an essay, and *Themes in My Poems* (1956) was written to promote a lecture tour. Much of Jeffers's personal correspondence is compiled in *The Selected Letters of Robinson Jeffers, 1897-1962* (1968).

Critical reception of Jeffers's work has fluctuated greatly. During the 1920s and early 1930s, Jeffers was hailed as among the greatest living American writers; *Time* magazine, which is often considered a barometer of popular achievement, portrayed him on its cover in 1932. During subsequent years of the Depression and World War II, however, Jeffers suffered a reversal of literary reputation which critics variously attribute to his unpopular social and political views and the diminishing quality of his verse. Since his death in 1962, Jeffers's work has undergone extensive reevaluation, and several of his shorter poems, including "Shine, Perishing Republic," "Boats in a Fog," and "To the Stone-Cutters," remain essential to anthologies of American verse. Mercedes Cunningham Monjian concluded in 1958: "Whatever the future holds for this poet, our own age is still awed by the magnificent talent and effort of a burdened mind struggling to free humanity from the shackles of an impoverished self-love, and the myths to which he believes it gave birth."

(For further information about Jeffers's life and works, see *Contemporary Authors*, Vols. 85-88; *Contemporary Literary Criticism*, Vols. 2, 3, 11, 15, 54; and *Dictionary of Literary Biography*, Vol. 45: *American Poets, 1880-1945*.)

CRITICAL COMMENTARY

YVOR WINTERS
(essay date 1937)

[A prominent American poet and critic, Winters maintained that all good literature must serve a conscious moral purpose. In the following excerpt from an essay first published in 1937, he claims that Jeffers's poetry lacks a firm ethical grounding and shows little grasp of poetic technique.]

The method of repetition is essentially the same today as it has always been, if we confine our attention to the short poem. Of recent years, however, there has been a tendency to extend it into longer forms, with unfortunate results. Such extension is the chief method of Whitman, and results in a form both lax and diffuse. Such extension occurs even in many modern attempts at narrative, both in prose and in verse. To illustrate what I say, I shall venture to summarize the structural defects of the narrative poetry of Robinson Jeffers:

Mr. Jeffers is theologically some kind of monist. He envisages, as did Wordsworth, nature as Deity; but his Nature is the Nature of the text-book in physics and not that of the rambling botanist—Mr. Jeffers seems to have taken the terminology of modern physics more literally than it is meant by its creators. Nature, or God, is thus a kind of self-sufficient mechanism, of which man is a product, but from which man is cut off by his humanity (just what gave rise to this humanity, which is absolutely severed from all communication with God, is left for others to decide): as there is no mode of communication with God or from God, God is praised adequately only by the screaming demons that make up the atom. Man, if he accepts this dilemma as necessary, can choose between two modes of action: he may renounce God and rely upon his humanity, or he may renounce his humanity and rely upon God.

In the narratives preceding *Cawdor* and in most of the lyrics, Mr. Jeffers preaches the second choice. In *Cawdor* and in *Thurso's Landing,* he has attempted a compromise: that is, while the tragic characters recognize that the second choice would be the more reasonable, they make the first in a kind of half-hearted stubbornness. They insist on living, but without knowing why, and without any good to which to look forward save the final extinction in God, when it comes in God's time. Their stubbornness is meaningless.

Life as such is incest, an insidious and destructive evil. So much, says Mr. Jeffers by implication, for

Greek and Christian ethics. Now the mysticism of such a man as San Juan de la Cruz offers at least the semblance of a spiritual, a human, discipline as a preliminary to union with Divinity; but for Mr. Jeffers a simple and mechanical device lies always ready; namely, suicide, a device to which he has, I believe, never resorted.

In refusing to take this step, however, Mr. Jeffers illustrates one of a very interesting series of romantic compromises. The romantic of the ecstatically pantheistic type denies life yet goes on living; nearly all romantics decry the intellect and philosophy, yet they offer justifications, necessarily incoherent but none the less rational in intention, of their attitude; they are prone to belittle literary technique, yet they write, and too often with small efficiency; they preach, in the main, the doctrine of moral equivalence, yet their every action, whether private or literary, since it rests on a choice, is a denial of the doctrine. Not all romantics are guilty of all these forms of confusion, but the romantic who is guilty of all is more consistent than is he who is guilty only of some, for all inhere in each from a rational standpoint. And Mr. Jeffers, having decried human life, and having denied the worth of the rules of the game, endeavors to write narrative and dramatic poems, poems, in other words, dealing with people who are playing the game. Jesus, the hero of *Dear Judas,* speaking apparently for Mr. Jeffers, says that the secret reason for the doctrine of forgiveness is that all men are driven to act as they do, by the mechanism-God, that they are entirely helpless; yet he adds in the next breath that this secret must be guarded, for if it were given out, men would run amuck—they would begin acting differently.

The Women at Point Sur is a perfect laboratory of Mr. Jeffers' philosophy and a perfect example of his narrative method. Barclay, an insane divine, preaches Mr. Jeffers' religion, and his disciples, acting upon it, become emotional mechanisms, lewd and twitching conglomerations of plexuses, their humanity annulled. Human experience in these circumstances, having necessarily and according to the doctrine, no meaning, there can be no necessary sequence of events: every act is equivalent to every other; every act is devoid of consequence and occurs in a perfect vacuum; most of the incidents could be shuffled about into different sequences without violating anything save Mr. Jeffers' sense of their relative intensity.

Principal Works

Flagons and Apples (poetry) 1912

Californians (poetry) 1916

Tamar and Other Poems (poetry) 1924; also published as Roan Stallion, Tamar and Other Poems, 1925

The Women at Point Sur (poetry) 1927; also published as The Women at Point Sur and Other Poems [enlarged edition], 1977

Cawdor and Other Poems (poetry) 1928

Dear Judas and Other Poems (poetry) 1929

Descent to the Dead: Poems Written in Ireland and Great Britain (poetry) 1931

Thurso's Landing and Other Poems (poetry) 1932

Give Your Heart to the Hawks and Other Poems (poetry) 1933

Solstice and Other Poems (poetry) 1935

Such Counsels You Gave to Me and Other Poems (poetry) 1937

Be Angry at the Sun (poetry) 1941

Medea: Freely Adapted from the Medea of Euripides (drama) 1947

The Double Axe and Other Poems (poetry) 1948

Poetry, Gongorism, and a Thousand Years (essay) 1949

The Tower Beyond Tragedy (drama) 1950

The Cretan Woman (drama) 1954

Hungerfield and Other Poems (poetry) 1954

Themes in My Poems (essay) 1956

The Beginning and the End and Other Poems (poetry) 1963

Selected Poems of Robinson Jeffers (poetry) 1963

Robinson Jeffers: Selected Poems (poetry) 1965

The Selected Letters of Robinson Jeffers, 1897-1962 (letters) 1968

The Alpine Christ and Other Poems (poetry) 1973

Brides of the South Wind: Poems, 1917-1922 (poetry) 1974

What Odd Expedients and Other Poems (poetry) 1981

Rock and Hawk: A Selection of Shorter Poems (poetry) 1987

Since the poem is his, of course, this sense may appear a legitimate criterion; the point is, that this is not a narrative nor a dramatic but is a lyrical criterion. A successful lyrical poem of one hundred and seventy-five pages is unlikely, for the essence of lyrical expression is concentration; but it is at least hypothetically possible. The difficulty here is that the lyric achieves its effect by the generalization of experience (that is, the motivation of the lyric is stated or implied in a summary form, and is ordinarily not given in detailed narrative) and by the concentration of expression; lyrical poetry tends to be expository. Narrative can survive fairly well without distinction of style, provided the narrative logic is complete and compelling, as in the works of Balzac, though this occurs most often in prose. Now Mr. Jeffers, as I have pointed out, has abandoned narrative logic with the theory of ethics, and he has never, in addition, achieved a distinguished style: his writing, line by line, is pretentious trash. There are a few good phrases, but they are very few, and none is first-rate.

Mr. Jeffers has no method of sustaining his lyric, then, other than the employment of an accidental (that is, a non-narrative and repetitious) series of anecdotes (that is, of details that are lyrically impure, details clogged with too much information to be able to function properly as lyrical details); his philosophical doctrine and his artistic dilemma alike decree that these shall be at an hysterical pitch of feeling. By this method, Mr. Jeffers continually *lays claim* to extreme feeling, which has no support whether of structure or of detail

and which is therefore simply unmastered and self-inflicted hysteria.

Cawdor contains a plot which in its rough outlines might be sound, and *Cawdor* likewise contains his best poetry: the lines describing the seals at dawn especially, are very good. But the plot is blurred for lack of style and for lack of moral intelligence on the part of the author. As in *Thurso's Landing,* of which the writing is much worse, the protagonists desire to live as the result of a perfectly unreasoning and meaningless stubbornness, and their actions are correspondingly obscure. Mr. Jeffers will not even admit the comprehensible motive of cowardice. In *The Tower beyond Tragedy,* Mr. Jeffers takes one of the very best of ready-make plots, the Orestes-Clytemnestra situation, the peculiar strength of which lies in the fact that Orestes is forced to choose between two crimes, the murder of his mother and the failure to avenge his father. But at the very last moment, in Mr. Jeffers' version, Orestes is converted to Mr. Jeffers' religion and goes off explaining to Electra (who has just tried to seduce him) that though men may think he is fleeing from the furies, he is really doing no more than drift up to the mountains to meditate on the stars. And the preceding action is, of course, rendered meaningless.

Dear Judas is a kind of dilution of *The Women at Point Sur,* with Jesus as Barclay, and with a less detailed background. *The Loving Shepherdess* deals with a girl who knows herself doomed to die at a certain time in child-birth, and who wanders over the countryside caring for a small and diminishing flock of sheep in an anguish of devotion. The events here also are anecdotal and reversible, and the feeling is lyrical or nothing. The heroine is turned cruelly from door to door, and the sheep fall one by one before the reader's eyes, the sheep and the doors constituting the matter of the narrative; until finally the girl dies in a ditch in an impossible effort to give birth to her child. (pp. 31-5)

Yvor Winters, "Primitivism and Decadence: A Study of American Experimental Poetry," in his *In Defense of Reason,* The Swallow Press Inc., 1947, pp. 15-150.

AMOS N. WILDER
(essay date 1940)

[In the essay excerpted below, Wilder examines Jeffers's philosophy of Inhumanism, concluding that Jeffers is a misanthrope and a nihilist.]

The satisfaction that men take in evidences of the life of nature and especially in its power, and above all in surpassing manifestations of that power, is one of the perennial roots of religion. If it has been the ground of world-wide primitive religion, or one of its grounds, we may be sure that it reappears today among sophisticated minds. And this especially where such minds turn from habits of intellectualism or mechanism to rediscover vital moods. (p. 141)

It is some such sense of the greater and more elemental forces of nature which supplies one of the most powerful attractions in the work of Robinson Jeffers. . . . [It] is in the elemental and untamed in nature that he finds the clues of salvation, of what lies behind and before the human consciousness.

Here, then, he rejoins the tendency . . . to seek out and beyond the human for a solution, and to find the symbols for this in those apparitions of nature that are most alien. . . . One may not speak finally about any particular credo of this poet. There is occasional contradiction of his themes, but the ones we stress will be found to recur.

Apart from the lyrics the work of Jeffers consists of narrative poems of some length written in a Whitmanesque line presenting dramas or rather melodramas of more than usually violent and repellent character. Often the characterization and action is cloudily presented and the style loose, but in the best poems, **"Roan Stallion," "The Tower Beyond Tragedy," "Cawdor," "Give Your Heart to the Hawks,"** these become sharper and more powerful, and one recognizes in any case that the poems are not to be judged first of all as narratives. (pp. 142-43)

The literary interest of the poems is comparatively minor. It comes out occasionally in the eloquent passages on nature or comparing nature and man, or in the occasional lyric philosophy, or in the powerful utterances of remorse and alienation. But the chief interest of the work is its philosophical attitude and for this purpose much is of interest which is poor literature. The case is much the same with D. H. Lawrence, not to say Walt Whitman, though the credos are different. The question is asked, Why should a person with an allegedly "normal" view of life be interested in the view presented by Jeffers? The only answer can be that whole races of men have thought and felt similarly, that many of our own time undoubtedly have hauntings of this kind, and that nothing human is alien to us. Moreover if we would change such a world view we must understand it.

The reason for the repellent themes of crime and incest is found stated in a passage from **"Roan Stallion."** It is indicated that revelation and clues of the superman come not from the usual and conventional experiences but from the exceptional and rebellious. We are reminded of Rimbaud's search for illumination, and can recognize a kind of travesty of the myth of Prometheus or the doctrine of the Cross. . . . (pp. 144-45)

The theme is that man has a best chance often to be stung awake by experiences that force him beyond himself. To create situations that present this kind of possibility Jeffers recurs to the drastic experiences of unnatural crime, incest or matricide, and to their consequences of remorse and the struggle with remorse. Only so does he come to the frontiers of the nonhuman, realizing the insignificance of man, reason, conscience and law. He apparently has an acute sense of the horrible sufferings that can be occasioned by blame, by the sense of guilt, and he would relieve men of that. . . .

Jeffers gets his sense of the comparative inconsequence of man particularly from the contrast with nature to which we have referred. Living in his stone tower over Monterey Bay he has before him the Pacific Ocean, on which, as he says, a thousand-mile hurricane is only a shadow. About him are the crags of the shore and behind him the austere granite ranges. (p. 146)

But men are not only insignificant, they are corrupt. Despite the occasions when a doctrine of moral equivalence appears to be taught, those that argue original sin will find their testimony here as in other of the new poets. The human heart is vile, the human mind is a spider weaving treacheries. Man has corrupted himself in his societies, in his taboos and in his laws. . . .

Thus for every reason death or the discovery of the sense of death in nature is to be desired. It is to life as "heaven over deep hell." Who once being dead would rise again? . . .

The positive teaching of Jeffers offers an escape for man from this condition into a nihilist Nirvana—a return through the original fountain. Nature is only a symbol for that which is not consciousness, not mind, not man. We are . . . on the ground of the Upanishads in the aspect described. The Sierras and the stars and prehistoric cromlechs of Ireland and the life of the eagle have signified to him that there is an "unstated being" in the universe that is everything that man is not. (p. 147)

Jeffers' conception is represented very often in terms of the life of wild creatures as well as of inanimate nature. . . . The mystery of life is often felt with peculiar force in these creatures that live, but that live in ways so alien to men and often so independently of men. This thought is stressed in the speech of God in the climax of the Book of Job, to bring home to him that "the Eternal hath his own purposes" and that existence has other concerns than human. Of course in the Book of Job important complementary attributes of Deity are assumed which give a totally different final picture of him.

But Jeffers not only recurs again and again to these creatures; he seems to have a perverse interest in showing them under torture. A deer caught in barbed wire, a rabbit aflame from the prairie fire, lobsters cooking alive, a wounded Cooper's hawk fighting a gamecock to death, a coyote caught in two steel traps at once so that it cannot stand or lie, a yearling colt swollen with the sting of a rattler—we are apt to say masochism or sadism and satisfy ourselves with that. There is probably no one writing today that is so cruel, with the possible exception of Faulkner. But Jeffers is at least consistent. For his conception of life is of a prodigiously beautiful force that makes its way through shining and splendid creations (man apart), but bleeds as it goes. . . . It is never safe to pin this writer down to a given sentiment as is so unjustly done. . . . But it can be concluded that there is a disgust with man and an exaltation of that which is beyond life which leaves him "numb to the intricacies of human feeling," which as [Yvor] Winters says is a limitation of all mystical poetry. The person who is concerned with ethical and personal values will query as to the conditions that lead our contemporaries to such misanthropy. (pp. 148-49, 151)

Amos N. Wilder, "The Nihilism of Mr. Robinson Jeffers," in his *The Spiritual Aspects of the New Poetry,* Harper & Brothers Publishers, 1940, pp. 141-52.

HENRY STEELE COMMAGER
(essay date 1950)

[In the following excerpt, Commager places Jeffers within a tradition he terms "the cult of irrationality," finding in his poetry the paradox of religious mysticism alongside the scientific denial of Christian beliefs.]

"Finding their intelligence enslaved," wrote George Santayana in that remarkable essay on the "Intellectual Temper of the Age" which indicted alike evolution and pragmatism, determinism and irrationalism,

> our contemporaries supposed that intelligence is essentially servile; instead of freeing it, they try to elude it. Not free enough themselves morally . . . they cannot think of rising to a detached contemplation of earthly things, and of life itself and evolution; they revert rather to sensibility, and seek some by-path of instinct or dramatic sympathy in which to wander. Having no stomach for the ultimate, they borrow themselves downwards towards the primitive.

It was a just indictment of the irrationalists and the primitivists, of that whole school of thought and emotion represented variously by Sherwood Anderson and Ernest Hemingway, Gertrude Stein and Ezra Pound, Henry Adams and Robinson Jeffers. (p. 120)

The sources of the new irrationality were largely modern and exclusively European, and it is suggestive that where American literature was most derivative it was least articulate and where it was least mature it was most decadent. It owed something to the French—to the Symbolist poets, Mallarmé, Verlaine, Rimbaud, Valéry, Laforgue, and Paul Fort, to critics like Rémy de Gourmont and philosophers like Henri Bergson with his apotheosis of the *élan vital,* to novelists like André Gide and, above all, Marcel Proust. It owed more to Freud of Vienna and Jung of Zurich and the Russian Pavlov who made the western world not only conscious but self-conscious of the subconscious. It owed most of all—doubtless through the accident of language—to the philosophers, poets, and novelists from the British Isles: pioneers in the scientific study of the psychology of sex like Edward Carpenter and the magisterial Havelock Ellis; novelists like the indefatigable Dorothy Richardson and the brilliant Aldous Huxley and the brooding D. H. Lawrence and Virginia Woolf, not only practitioner but critic; the Irish experimentalists, William Butler Yeats and George Moore and Oscar Wilde and, above all, James Joyce, most successful of all those who floated their literary barks down the stream of consciousness.

What were the stigmata—for we can scarcely use the term principles for a persuasion that rejected the very concept of principle—of the new school? First, the rejection—on pseudoscientific grounds—of reason, meaning, normality, morality, continuity, and coherence, the rejection of civilization itself as eccentric and decadent. Second, a passionate interest in the subconscious and the unconscious and an enthusiasm for emotion rather than thought, instinct rather than reason, anarchy rather than discipline. Third, an obsession with sex, especially in its abnormal manifestations, as the most powerful and pervasive of all the instincts and the interpretation of all conduct in terms of sex. Fourth, a weakness for the primitive, for primitive people such as Africans, Indians, peasants, and children, for primitive emotions and activities—eating, drinking, sleeping, fighting, making love—and closely connected with this a predilection for violence in all forms. Fifth, the unqualified repudiation of all orthodox moral standards, all conformities and conventions, and acquiescence in a perverse amorality in which submission to instincts became the highest virtue. And, finally, the formulation of a new language and a new grammar to express more faithfully the fitful impulses emanating from the subconscious. (pp. 121-22)

The cult of irrationality was, from the beginning, doomed to self-destruction, for no literature built upon the quagmire of futility can survive. The attack upon reason, which flourished so furiously in the second and third decades of the [twentieth] century, was designed to pronounce the ultimate degradation of man—a degradation which reduced man, in the end, to gibbering. It carried to logical conclusion the findings of the naturalists and the determinists and revealed, more dramatically than any other inquiry, the bankruptcy of determinism. It was nihilism, but it was nihilism which proved its impotence by its very proclamation. It was the palpable insincerity of the revolt against reason which was, in the end, its most encouraging feature, for revolt is an act of will—even of free will—and those writers who engaged in it confess their inconsistency. They confess faith in their own reason by the act of composition, social consciousness by their appeal for a hearing, and recognition of a moral order by the establishment of standards, however eccentric, and the insistence upon values, however esoteric.

Robinson Jeffers is peculiarly the victim of this paradox, though his statement of it is more eloquent and more dignified than that of most of the irrationalists, as his logic—or his illogic—is more thorough. The most uncompromisingly scientific of the literary spokesmen of determinism, Jeffers is, at the same time, the most romantic. Trained to medicine, familiar with psychiatry, biology, geology, and physics, living, by

choice, close to nature and acknowledging no obligation but to nature, his affluent poetry is a scientific as well as a philosophical commentary on the life of man.

So completely does nature fill his poetic vision that man is scarcely admitted even as a part of nature. The men and women who infect his pages are so vile and perverse that they seem to contaminate nature herself. For aeons nature did not know man, and in a short time she will forget the stain he has put upon her. . . . For man is born to pain, as are all living things, but man alone adds moral depravity to physical torture: human beings alone are inhuman. (pp. 128-29)

From *Tamar* to *The Double Axe* Jeffers spreads before us such a pageant of violence, cruelty, bloodshed, depravity, and perversion as we have not heretofore encountered in our literature—not even in Faulkner or Caldwell. He violates our innocence and confounds our philosophy with a picture of unmitigated evil, or of evil mitigated only by endurance. Life is one long agony of pain, interrupted by pleasure that is fleeting and ecstasy that turns upon us and wounds us. . . . Only Nature is worthy of our contemplation, for only Nature has beauty and endurance. . . . The mountains, the sea, granite boulders, the redwood and the cypress trees, the eagle and the hawk—give your heart to these, says Jeffers, but not to men. (pp. 129-30)

What we have here, to be sure, is a scientific version of the Christian view where every prospect pleases and only man is vile. And for all his desperate repudiation of orthodox religion, there is a strain of religious mysticism in Jeffers. He, too, lifts up his eyes unto the hills from whence cometh his help; he confesses, on behalf of ruined man, that we have followed too much the devices and desires of our own hearts and there is no health in us. The mortal flaw, the fatal stain, is introversion—"man regarding man exclusively, founding his values, desires, his picture of the universe, all on his own humanity." . . . And it is as a symbol of this suicidal introversion that he uses incest again and again.

Yet for all his scientific and psychiatric vocabulary, Jeffers lingers in the romantic tradition, closer to Wordsworth and Arnold than to Haeckel or even to Freud and Jung, whose books, we are assured, adorn his shelves. What could be more romantic than this passion for the mountains and the sea and for granite boulders? For to impartial nature the loftiest peak of the Sierras is no nobler than a ditch, or the heaving Pacific than a stagnant pool, and in the long catalogue of time Hawk Tower will have no more permanence than a soap bubble. So, too, with the habit of ascribing dignity and nobility to birds and beasts; the concepts themselves are but tributes to man. Mankind, says Jeffers, has turned inward, and is corrupt. But what more shameless conceit than to ascribe human values to the works of nature, what more extreme introversion than to subject the universe to man's secular judgment?

Romantic though he is, Jeffers does not permit himself the recourse of earlier romantics, of Shelley whom he imitates or Arnold whom he recalls. There is no room in his cosmic philosophy either for Promethean defiance or for escape. Death alone can solace man, death and annihilation and the assurance that this is the fortunate destiny of all living things. (pp. 130-31)

This is nihilism, and it is a logical conclusion to scientific determinism, its consistency flawed only by the subjective view of nature that permeates every line and—it must be added—by the particular inspiration for the outbursts of despair. Thus, apropos the American participation in the second World War—Nazi guilt gave him no concern—Jeffers tells us that

. . . the whole human race ought to be scrapped and is on the way to it; ground like fish-meal for soil-food.
What does the vast and rushing drama of the universe, seas, rocks, condor-winged storms, icy-fiery galaxies,
The flaming and whirling universe like a handful of gems falling down a dark well,
Want clowns for?
("The Inhumanist," *The Double Axe*)

With Jeffers, the philosophical reaction to the world of science opened up first by Darwin came full circle. Man, the last born of nature's long travail, was seen not as her chiefest glory but as her most cruel blunder, because having endowed man with the critical faculty, she enabled him to realize the futility and horror of his existence. (pp. 131-32)

Henry Steele Commager, "The Cult of the Irrational," in his *The American Mind: An Interpretation of American Thought and Character since the 1880's,* Yale University Press, 1950, pp. 120-40.

JAMES G. SOUTHWORTH
(essay date 1950)

[In the following excerpt, Southworth admires Jeffers's thematic application of Inhumanism in his poems but finds that Jeffers has neither the sense of humor nor the technical mastery of a major poet.]

Mr. Jeffers is . . . much admired by Californians for the beauty of his California landscape-painting. What Wordsworth has done for the Lake District, Frost for New England, Shelley for the Italian sky, he, they feel, has done for California, particularly for the Monterey coastal mountain region. Descriptions of this locale are the sole subject of many short poems and provide the setting in which his dramas are played. Nowhere else in his work is he so attuned to his subject-matter.

Nothing else is so important to him. 'There is,' he says in **'Contrast,'** 'not one memorable person, there is not one mind to stand with the trees, one life with the mountains.'

He is not interested in the veins of a leaf, although he has noticed them. He prefers nature's grander aspects. He is Byron rather than Wordsworth, although at times he seems to share the latter's mystical association with nature. He senses decadence, however, in the quiet English landscape. Only in his Monterey country does he breathe freely. The landscapes of his poems are, one often feels, the chief actors, the chief moulding forces of his characters. He likes high plateaus, whale-backed hills, rock heads and precipitous cliffs, the gorges where they fall to the rocky or sandy shore, and what he calls the mysticism of stone. He rarely admires any of these in their serene and gentle moods, but prefers them licked by the sea-fog, in terrific storms, or on a hot day when the sun burns the water. His sunsets over the sea, like his pictures of the coast itself, are riots of colour, and the mere juxtaposition of colour words from the entire spectrum on vast and awe-inspiring objects plunges the reader into a different world, particularly into a different world of feeling. It is the proper setting for the Manfreds that throng his poems. Even when he describes the 'vast calm vaulting glory of the afterglow' the birds returning to their nests are cormorants. His favourite bird is the hawk. He likes everything it typifies: freedom, wildness, and cruelty. . . .

It is his landscapes that are responsible for the plots of his long poems and for the characters that resolve the plots. However superficially the characters might give the impression of being drawn from life their inspiration is almost wholly literary. He conceals this beneath his over-complicated plots—plots as involved as those in the early Hardy novels. The subject-matter is essentially what Mr. C. S. Lewis would call the 'primary' rather than the 'secondary' material of epic. He is chiefly concerned, that is, with the family rather than with national themes as in the *Aeneid* or super-national as in *Paradise Lost;* and then with the family whose members are in bitter conflict. He is concerned with violence rather than with genuine tragedy. . . .

Jeffers' characters are devised rather than real. Besides being devised to resolve the intricacies of the plot they are all projections, often compensatory ones, of the poet himself. His all too obvious lack of any sense of humour permits him to see nothing in its true focus. Distortion rules his pages. His characters are such persons as Mr. Jeffers, had he been born and bred in this isolated region, would have liked to be. His women are wild and free like the hawks with an elemental passion that makes the ordinary episodes of sex in fiction or real life pallid and anaemic. His young heroes are primitive, and strong and willing to fight for their women as viciously as beasts; his older men are patriarchal and resemble the Biblical old men in that retention of their potency past the age when a civilized man is willing to take his warm place in the chimney corner and stroke the cat. His sensitive young idealists succeed in winning nothing but disillusionment and release in death. These latter are probably most nearly Mr. Jeffers. . . .

He believes that professed Christianity with its doctrine of love for the common man is dangerous. It is, he says, the degradation of life and its eventual dissolution. 'The Apes of Christ lift up their hands to praise love,' but the present saviour of mankind is 'wisdom without love.' More important is 'power without hatred, mind like a many-bladed machine subduing the world with deep indifference.' Pity is unnecessary; love is dangerous because it is a clever servant, and insufferable master, and the trap that caught Christ. . . . Humanity, he adds elsewhere, 'is the mould to break away from, the crust to break through, the coal to break into fire, the atom to be split.' Because peace is such a personal, unique quality, he who has found it for himself cannot help others to find it. The masses will find salvation in death; all each can do while he lives is to 'make his health in his mind, to love the coast opposite humanity.' . . .

Where some see progress, Jeffers sees decay. Our rapidly expanding consciousness of empire is the decay that will lead America to dissolution. To avert that dissolution he would have man return to vision, desire, unnatural crime, inhuman science, wild love—all of which would 'slit eyes in the mask.' . . . The 'communal people' do not know 'the wild God of the world.' The hawk, however, remembers and with the blue-heron and the red-shafted woodpecker 'live their felt natures; they know their norm and live it to the brim; they understand life. While men moulding themselves to the anthill have choked their natures until their souls die in them; they have sold themselves for protection.' Such people are 'fractional' with no centre 'but in the eyes and mouths that surround them, having no function but to serve and support civilization, the enemy of man.' After further excoriation, he finally admits, however, that 'it is barely possible that even men's present lives are something.' . . .

Figures of speech thickly stud his work, similes and metaphors being applied with so lavish a hand that one is reminded of a young poet at work rather than an artist who has learned to use his ornamentation sparingly. Passages abound in which every line contains a metaphor or simile. . . . Subtlety is absent and rightly so. Mr. Jeffers seeks the larger effects, and from the point of view of the general reader, probably finds them, although the serious student of poetry remains unimpressed. Metaphors, too, are thickly strewn throughout the poems. Those arising from implied biological comparisons are scientifically accurate. . . .

In Mr. Jeffers' earliest volumes he used traditional verse-patterns which he discarded simultaneously with his early idealism. . . . [He] practically abandoned rhyme and developed the long unrhymed line that he has often used with outstanding effectiveness; often but not invariably. Too frequently this line degenerates into prose, and were it printed as such, few would suspect from its inner tension that it was meant to be anything else. He sought a rhythmic line 'moulded more closely to the subject' than was the older English poetry. The rhythm came from many sources: 'physics, biology, beat of blood, the tidal environments of life.' . . .

What his isolation gave him in one way it took from him in another. He detached himself from the important things of earth at the moment he sought to come closer to earth. His work can never be thought of as a reading of life. In seeking the permanent he has missed it. Had he had the saving grace of humour he might have been more successful, but in the writing of no poet of geniune importance are there less visible signs of humour, that saving grace which enables a man to see himself in perspective. Mr. Jeffers takes himself far too seriously. On the other hand, were he not always so intensely serious his rhetoric would degenerate into burlesque.

James G. Southworth, "Robinson Jeffers," in his *Some Modern American Poets*, Basil Blackwell, 1950, pp. 107-21.

JAMES DICKEY

(essay date 1964)

[Dickey is an American novelist, poet, and critic. In the following excerpt from a 1964 review, he reveals a reserved respect for Jeffers as a poet. Yet while perceiving "plenty to carp about" in Jeffers's verse, he also admires "the sheer power and drama of some" of his writing.]

Now that Robinson Jeffers is dead, his last poems have been issued [in *The Beginning and the End and Other Poems*], culled from handwritten manuscripts by his sons and his secretary. Though some of the pieces were obviously left unfinished—there are several different ones which have the same passages in them—it is worth noting that they are actually no more or less "finished" than the poems Jeffers published in book after book while he lived. This is typical of Jeffers's approach to poetry, I think; he had, as someone remarked of Charles Ives, "the indifference of greatness." Yet now, in some fashion, we must come to terms with Jeffers, for he somehow cannot be dismissed as lesser men—and no doubt better poets—can. As obviously flawed as he is, Jeffers is cast in a large mold; he fills a position in this country that would simply have been an empty gap without him: that of the poet as prophet, as large-scale philosopher, as doctrine-giver. This is a very real, very old and honorable function for poets, and carries with it a *tone* that has, but for Jeffers, not been much heard among us, in our prevailing atmosphere of ironic shrugs and never-too-much. Admittedly a great deal of bad poetry in all ages has been written from such a stance, but that does not invalidate the idea, or take from Jeffers the credit that is duly his. Surely he provides us with plenty to carp about: his oracular moralizing, his cruel and thoroughly repellent sexuality, his dreadful lapses of taste when he seems simply to throw back his head and howl, his slovenly diction, the eternal sameness of his themes, the amorphous sprawl of his poems on the page. The sheer power and drama of some of Jeffers's writing, however, still carries the day despite everything, and this is not so much because of the presence of the Truth that Jeffers believes he has got hold of but because of what might be called the embodiment of that Truth: Jeffers's gorgeous panorama of *big* imagery, his galaxies, suns, seas, cliffs, continents, mountains, rivers, flocks of birds, gigantic schools of fish, and so on. His Truth is hard to swallow—try looking at your children and drawing comfort from Jeffers's "inhumanism"—but one cannot shake off Jeffers's vision as one can the carefully prepared surprises of many of the neatly packaged stanzas we call "good poems"; it is too deeply disturbing and too powerfully stated. One thinks, uneasily, that the prophetic tone may be more than just a tone, remembering that Jeffers was telling us long before Hiroshima that the ultimate end of science, of knowledge and tool-using, is not comfort and convenience (how he despises such ideals!) but unrelieved tragedy. It is extraordinarily strange how the more awful and ludicrous aspects of the atomic age have come to resemble Jeffers's poems. In a film like *Mondo Cane,* for example, one sees the dying sea turtles, disoriented by the Bikini blasts until they cannot even find the Pacific Ocean, crawling inland to die in the desert, in the blazing sand they think is water, and the hundreds-of-miles-long trail of dead butterflies, the seabirds trying to hatch atom-sterilized eggs, and one thinks compulsively of Jeffers. Few visions have been more desperate than his, and few lives organized around such austere principles. It seems to me that we must honor these things, each in his own way. (pp. 187-89)

James Dickey, "Poets and Poetry Now," in his *Babel to Byzantium: Poets & Poetry Now,* 1968. Reprint by The Ecco Press, 1981, pp. 3-232.

ROBERT BOYERS
(essay date 1970)

[In the following excerpt, Boyers explores Jeffers's use of images culled from nature as metaphors for human shortcomings.]

In a way it is unfortunate that Jeffers wrote any long narratives at all, for none succeeds, and for reasons that need hardly be elaborated in detail. Structurally, they are sound enough, but the texture of these poems is swollen by effusions of philosophizing and by attempts to impose representative signification on characters and actions which are so extraordinary as to be either ludicrous or simply shocking. Not that any serious reader is going to rush shrieking from the room at the mention of a little incest at a time when every perversion has been relieved by repetition and familiarity of its capacity to extract from readers even a bit of a chill. What is shocking in Jeffers' narratives, from *Tamar* through the later poems, is the author's contentions of symptomatic and representative status for the perverse obsessions of his characters. Obviously the single-mindedness of Jeffers' pursuit of his themes in the long poems ought to dispel any notion that he indulged his fantasies in the interests of melodrama alone, as Rexroth claimed. Jeffers simply thought he had hit upon a fruitful means for engaging the most profound problem he could imagine: the relationship of the individual to his time, and the uses and limitations of human freedom. Jeffers was mistaken in that his means were not adequate to the task he set himself. Never a good judge of the work of other poets, Jeffers really was incapable of criticizing his own poetry, even after a period of years had gone by to provide a measure of detachment. Attempts to justify the narratives on philosophical grounds held but mild interest for Jeffers, who could barely force himself to breeze through books written on his work, and none of these succeed in justifying the narratives as poetry in terms that Jeffers himself could have admired. . . .

Only **"Roan Stallion"** among Jeffers' narratives would seem to provide the consistently varied texture that is requisite in a long poem, but even here one finds it difficult to accept Jeffers at his own estimate and in the terms of his advocates. While the entire poem is powerful and not at all absurd, as some have claimed, the whole fails to sustain particular elements in the imagery. The magnificent evocation of the roan stallion as a symbol of male potency is quite as fine in its way as D. H. Lawrence's comparable use of horses in his novel *The Rainbow,* published ten years before Jeffers' poem.

But the eroticism in these passages of **"Roan Stallion"** is not clearly related to the basic thrust of the poem, which cannot be taken to be an indictment of male potency in general. . . . Familiarity with Jeffers' universe, with the universe created by his many poems, suggests that the stallion was to call to mind qualities quite distinct from pure sexuality, though related, and yet these qualities are never sufficiently identified. The figure refuses to yield its latent connotations and is distinguished by an opacity that characterizes the image rather than the symbol. In this respect Jeffers' failure has a good deal in common with much of the narrative poetry produced in the Romantic period. In each there is a strong lyrical element which calls into question the poet's center of interest and the consequent interest of readers. While the structure of the work naturally tends to focus attention on the unfolding of events in the phenomenal world, the poet's interest seems always elsewhere, in the emotions that give rise to action, and in abstract conceptions of fate and will. Poets find themselves more immediately and intimately involved in their characters than they ought to be in narrative poems, unable to decide where their creations begin and they leave off. . . .

In short, then, for a number of reasons, Jeffers devoted a great deal of his time and energy to the cultivation of a subgenre—narrative poetry—to which his gifts were not especially adaptable. What is also distressing, though, is that the attention Jeffers has received has been so disproportionately weighted in the direction of these failed narratives and that his stock has fallen so badly as a result. What more signal instance have we of the capitulation of criticism to what is most gross and obvious in a man's work. . . .

It is as though there had been a tacit agreement among all influential parties that Jeffers' shorter poems should be looked upon as nothing more than an adjunct to the narratives, perhaps even as something less, as filler for the volumes his publishers issued with remarkable regularity for so many years. As it is, Jeffers' short poems, many of them rather lengthy by standards of the conventional lyric, will fill an enormous volume when they are collected, and an impressive volume it will be; for at his best Jeffers could blend passion and restraint, image and statement, contempt and admiration, as few poets of any time have been able to, and often with a music so ripe and easy that it is able to impress itself upon our senses without our ever remarking its grace and majesty, its sureness of touch. . . .

How much less we are disposed to object to Jeffers' poetry when he reminds us of his mortality. We remain wary of prophecy in general, and of false prophets in particular, but we consent nonetheless to attend to Jeffers' prophetic rigors on occasion, perhaps even to be a little moved by the spectacle of a man obviously concerned for a purity of spirit, an integrity so hard for any man to come by. We are moved, for example, by **"Shine, Perishing Republic,"** a poem too familiar to quote. It is not one of Jeffers' best things, but there is a fine tolerance for humankind in this poem that is attractive and that we respond to repeatedly. The theme of the poem is, after all, not so very new or terrible, having to do with the corruption of institutionalized life in the modern world, the tendency of mass culture to absorb protest and distinction and to heighten vulgarity in its citizens. . . .

Who among us that has read Jeffers with devotion, though critically, will not confess to an admiration for a man who could so charge a created universe with a network of images so consistently developed, so densely woven into the very fabric of the verse? Who more earnestly than Jeffers has confronted the frailty of our lives and engaged more desperately the attempt to reorient our customary perspectives, to take us beyond pain into praise and wonder? Jeffers knew all too well how men could suffer, and did; and he knew why they suffered, and his awareness rarely failed to leave him either angry or amused, or both, for he felt that most human suffering was the result of unwarranted expectations, foolish illusions. His entire career was dedicated to the chastisement of a pity he felt and knew others felt, for he did not believe that pity was an essentially human quality, though for the most part peculiar to our kind. He felt that pity, and the suffering it often implied, was a product not of human emotion, but of human civilization, and with this he had no sympathy at all. Against this civilization, the pride of Western man with its "little empty bundles of enjoyment," Jeffers set the figure of the hawk, the eagle, the falcon, the vulture, predators all, and cast them winging alternately amidst towering rocks and seething waters, landscapes of permanence and of violent energy. The ambience of Jeffers' poems is characteristically stark, though rarely barren, and one has in them a sense of granitic harshness, as of objects tempered in a flame so blazing as to burn away all that is ephemeral and soft and pitying—everything, in a word, that is simply and merely human. But Jeffers' poetry is neither antihuman nor inhuman. It plainly works itself out within a system of values which includes much that is human, in terms of what we are capable of responding to at our most intense. As one would expect in a created universe of considerable density, though not of great complexity, there is a recurrence of specific symbols within the pervasive imagery of the poems and a consequent cross fertilization of meanings, so that we are presented a vision of experience that is everywhere interfused, a frame of reference that cuts across entire groups of poems. Everywhere meanings seem to beckon away beyond themselves, so that in Jeffers' achieved works there is rarely an impression of a static quality, despite the weight of particular images. . . .

For Jeffers the god who creates and observes his universe cares not what we do, so long as we do it well, so long as life is clean and vibrant with energy and possibilities of renewal, so long as it is whole, sufficient unto itself like the rocks Jeffers loved to contemplate, like the white bone of the desert skull in his poem, freed of gross desire, liberated to "lonely exultations."

If Jeffers is truly a religious poet, he can be said to worship largely at the altar of art, for his resolution of the problems of spirit is really an aesthetic resolution, just as his politics, if he did indeed have a politics, is fundamentally determined by an aesthetic response to the world. Jeffers disparaged not human life, but the ways in which human beings could destroy their world and each other. . . .

Jeffers' exaltation of the hawk . . . is not an exaltation of a naked violence that will see the destruction of man by man, but an exaltation of nature, of need, of instinct. For Jeffers the instinct of the hawk is tolerable, even majestic, because it does not seek to aggrandize itself at the expense of creation—it strikes according to its need and within a framework that does not threaten the fundamental harmony of other things. Its rarity he saw as a quality intrinsic to its nature, associated also with its reasonable relationship to its surroundings. At the point where the environment could not support increasing numbers of the species, the species by a law intrinsic to its nature would cease to multiply: not a matter of will but of nature. How different is man, clamoring for a little space, killing for programs and ideologies. And anthropological investigations into the similarity of human and animal agressions, explanations of territoriality as a fundamental impulse of all life, would have left Jeffers no less secure in his mounting of the distinction, for Jeffers' thesis was not developed as fact, but as intuition. In the development of an ideal of what is beautiful and can authentically be meaningful to men, Jeffers' vision resists the disparagements of scientific critiques.

Jeffers does not succumb, it must be said, to pure aestheticism. His indictments of mass man, which is to say of man in our time, are not without a measure of conventionally *human* sentiment, and a number of the poems evoke a tension in which the resort to aestheticism is viewed as an element of necessity rather than of will or choice. The conflict in Jeffers is powerfully dramatized in the poem **"Rearmament"**—a poem in whose broadly undulating rhythms and the sweep of its long line the very quality and substance of Jeffers' message is embodied and reflected. . . .

Throughout his career Jeffers tried to resolve the ambiguities of his vision in a direction that would take him further and further from concern with his fellows. How successful he was we can see in **"Rearmament,"** with its persisting ambiguities and unresolved tensions. What is unmistakable, though, is the poet's steadfast refusal to counsel violence among men and his ability to achieve a perspective wherein the violence men would and did commit could be made tolerable, in a way even absorbed into the universe as an element of necessity. It is nothing less than a tragic vision; and if Jeffers in his poetry could not sufficiently examine and evoke the larger potentialities of man within his limitations, as could a Shakespeare and a Yeats, he did at least project a vision worthy of our attention and capable of giving pleasure. The felicities of Jeffers' poetry ought no longer to be denied, but received with gratitude. If he was not among our supreme poets, they have been few who were his equals.

Robert Boyers, "A Sovereign Voice: The Poetry of Robinson Jeffers," in *Modern American Poetry: Essays in Criticism,* edited by Jerome Mazzaro, McKay, 1970, pp. 183-203.

FREDERIC I. CARPENTER
(essay date 1977)

[An American educator and critic, Carpenter edited the *New England Quarterly* from 1929 to 1937. He is the author of *Emerson and Asia* (1930) and *American Literature and the Dream* (1955), as well as a book and several essays on Jeffers. In the article excerpted below, he states that he prefers Jeffers's early narratives because they distinguish between "good" and "evil."]

On March 3, 1941, Robinson Jeffers read from his poetry to a large audience in Emerson Hall, Harvard University. The room seated four hundred, but many more crowded the halls outside. The next day I drove Jeffers to visit Emerson's Concord and Walden Pond, and in conversation inquired the title of his next book. "Beyond Good and Evil," he replied; and when I did not hear well, he added: "Nietzsche." Nine months later his new book bore the title, *Be Angry at the Sun;* and on December 7 Pearl Harbor exploded.

At that time the incident did not seem very important. The title poem of the new volume translated the Nietzschean idea into poetic language, while it recalled the German of Spengler (mentioned in another poem), whose *Untergang des Abendlandes* announced the setting sun of all Western civilization. But after Pearl Harbor the new volume seemed almost treasonous: one poem coupled Roosevelt with Hitler as equal instigators of the new world war. . . . (p. 86)

Now more than a generation later, 1941 looms as a watershed in American history. But it also marks a watershed in the history of Jeffers's reputation. In March, 1941, his popularity had reached its highest point (although some critics had been denouncing him since the publication of *The Women at Point Sur* in 1927). But after Pearl Harbor his attempts to argue that "The cause is far beyond good and evil, / Men fight and their cause is not the cause," effectively destroyed his reputation. At the very moment when Americans most needed to believe in the absolute goodness of their cause, Jeffers denied them. And when he refused to describe their arch-enemy Hitler as absolutely evil, they called him fascist.

From 1941 until his death in 1962, Jeffers's reputation suffered eclipse. . . . But beginning with the poet's death in 1962, a gradual reversal set in, causing his reputation to increase. Now in 1977 a new publisher . . . has reissued three of his least popular volumes (*The Women at Point Sur, Dear Judas,* and *The Double Axe*). . . . (pp. 86-7)

[The worst of the volumes, *The Double Axe,*] certainly deserves reprinting, because the second of its narrative poems, **"The Inhumanist,"** has always been recognized as a thoughtful and original philosophic poem. But **"The Love and the Hate,"** which introduces the volume, has been condemned from the beginning.

"The Love and the Hate," on rereading, seems almost as bad as when first published. The story of the young soldier who returns from the dead to confront and kill the father who had sent him out to die in World War II remains both unbelievable and repulsive. But after rereading, the emotions of alienation and hatred which the poem projected seem to have been realized in the experiences of veterans of the Vietnam War. Recent novels and plays dealing with prisoners of that war who have returned verify the emotions which Jeffers had imagined a generation before. Although sometimes a bad poet, Jeffers was usually a good prophet.

The second volume of poetry now reprinted, *Dear Judas,* seems to me the best. The conflicts are always believable, and the poetry sometimes achieves magnificence. (p. 92)

The Women at Point Sur is the last of the volumes now reprinted, and the most controversial. It is the most complex, and in many ways the most interesting. Antoninus calls it "the most difficult and forbidding of all his poems," yet believes it to be his best. When first published in 1927, its extremes of plot and emotion so shocked many readers that they rejected it, while some turned against the poet entirely. Fifty years later we may confront the problems which it created.

The plot is simple and stark: a Christian minister renounces his faith and proclaims that "what was wrong's right, the old laws are abolished / . . . there is nothing wicked. What the heart desires, or any part of the body / That is the law." To symbolize his apostasy he commits incest with his daughter, April. Then in the second half of the poem he leads his demented followers through episodes of mounting violence and

perversion, until at the end he lies down "in the mouth of the black pit." The plot illustrates the total destruction which results from the total denial of moral law. And the first part of the narrative develops this plot logically, with passages of magnificent poetry. (p. 93)

In the second half of *The Women,* Jeffers "suspends what Freud called the censor"—and I, for one, cannot follow him. But others may. And certainly there exists a strange kind of illogic in madness. . . . The point is that the archetypal plot-patterns of *Tamar* and *The Women at Point Sur* follow a different logic from that of Aristotelian tragedy or of narrative realism. They go beyond the human laws of good and evil to imagine the timeless patterns of inhuman nature. And in so doing they enter the realm of myth. (p. 94)

In all his mature poetry Jeffers sought to explore the realm beyond good and evil. In *The Women at Point Sur* his Barclay specifically announced this purpose. But in this realm there are no roads or reasons, and half-way through this poem Jeffers proclaimed that "these here have gone mad." In their belief that they could live beyond evil, these characters became alienated from the world of reason and law. And this is the fate of all who believe that to go beyond evil means to deny the reality of evil. Barclay proclaimed that there is no evil. . . . (p. 95)

Obviously this extremism is absurd. . . . In *The Women* he put this extreme statement in the mouth of his Barclay, then emphasized that it resulted in madness, and finally dramatized the destruction that it produced. But the emotional intensity with which he realized his characters, and the poetic eloquence with which he described their actions, have tended to make the absurd seem almost reasonable and the evil seem almost acceptable. After *The Women,* therefore, he wrote his **"Apology for Bad Dreams"** in a conscious attempt to make his own nightmares make sense.

The problem, I would suggest, is one of perspective. These poems literally describe bad dreams—but so vividly that the dreams seem to become realities. By suspending what Freud called the censor, these poems force the reader to realize that the impulses which civilization has repressed remain powerful. They still lurk below the level of consciousness, and if acted upon, result in evil. But his **"Apology"** warns that "it is not good to forget. . . ."

The world which Jeffers's poetry explores is not beyond evil, but beneath (or before) evil. . . . All his poems, in Santayana's phrase, "stir the sub-human depths of the spirit." They recall those impulses which primitive myth once celebrated, and which early civilization sometimes practiced (the early Pharaohs practiced royal incest), but which modern civilization has put down. Buried beneath the level of modern consciousness, these impulses still exist beneath evil, "at the muddy root of things." Only if the author fails to distinguish between the two realms do problems develop. Jeffers's early poetry had distinguished clearly: "for goodness and evil are two things and still variant, but the quality of life as of death and of light / As of darkness is one, one beauty . . . " (**"Point Pinos and Point Lobos"**). But his later poetry concerned itself more with the "one." (pp. 95-6)

Frederic I. Carpenter, "Robinson Jeffers Today: Beyond Good and Beneath Evil," in *American Literature,* Vol. 49, No. 1, March, 1977, pp. 86-96.

SOURCES FOR FURTHER STUDY

Bennett, Melba Berry. *The Stone Mason of Tor House.* Los Angeles: Ward Ritchie Press, 1966, 264 p.

Biography of Jeffers that includes chronological table of publications and bibliography.

Brophy, Robert J. *Robinson Jeffers.* Boise State University Western Writers Series, edited by Wayne Chatterton, James H. Maguire, and Dale K. Boyer, No. 19. Boise, Idaho: Boise State University, 1975, 49 p.

Brief overview of Jeffers's life and works, focusing on recurring themes, motifs, and images.

Carpenter, Frederic I. *Robinson Jeffers.* New York: Twayne Publishers, 1962, 159 p.

Detailed discussion of Jeffers's narrative and lyric poetry.

Coffin, Arthur B. *Robinson Jeffers: Poet of Inhumanism.* Madison: University of Wisconsin Press, 1971, 300 p.

Studies major themes in Jeffers's works.

Morris, Lawrence S. "Robinson Jeffers: The Tragedy of a Modern Mystic." *The New Republic* LIV, No. 702 (16 May 1928): 306-90.

Seminal essay positions Jeffers within a literary tradition of mystic poets which includes William Blake and Walt Whitman.

Powell, Lawrence Clark. *Robinson Jeffers: The Man and His Work.* Pasadena: San Pasqual Press, 1940, 215 p.

Respected introduction to Jeffers's themes and philosophy of inhumanism.

Samuel Johnson

1709-1784

English essayist, lexicographer, critic, poet, and dramatist.

INTRODUCTION

*P*erhaps the best known and most often-quoted English writer after Shakespeare, Johnson ranks as the major literary figure of the second half of the eighteenth century. Yet the large and varied canon of his writings has often been overshadowed by his personality. Thus he is remembered as the witty conversationalist who dominated the literary scene of London—the man immortalized by James Boswell in *The Life of Samuel Johnson, LL.D.* (1791). Known in his day as the Great Cham of Literature, Johnson displayed a vigorous reasoning intelligence, a keen understanding of human frailty, and a deep Christian morality. These traits are especially evident in works as diverse as the poem "The Vanity of Human Wishes" (1749) and the prose narrative *The History of Rasselas, Prince of Abissinia* (1759), as well as in his *Dictionary of the English Language* (1755) and his *Prefaces, Biographical and Critical, to the Works of the English Poets* (1779-81), a work better known as *The Lives of the Poets.* Wrote nineteenth-century English critic William Hazlitt: "[Johnson] left behind him few wiser or better men." Today he may be considered the quintessential embodiment of English letters.

Born in Lichfield in 1709 to Sarah Ford and Michael Johnson, a bookseller, Johnson suffered from scrofula, which seriously affected his eyesight and disfigured his face. He was educated at Lichfield Grammar School and later at Pembroke College, Oxford, but a shortage of money forced him to leave the latter institution without a degree in 1729, after a residence of only thirteen months. After his father's death in 1731 Johnson lived in Birmingham, where he translated the French version of *A Voyage to Abyssinia,* by Father Jerome Lobo, which he published anonymously in 1735. The same year he married Elizabeth Porter, a widow twenty years his senior. After a failed attempt at running a boarding school, Johnson went to London to make a career as a man of letters. Once in London, he performed editorial work for Edward Cave's *Gentleman's Magazine,* to which he submitted essays, poems, reviews, and a series of brief biographies. His most notable contributions appeared between 1740 and 1743 and were entitled "Debates in Magna Lilliputia." These essays eloquently—perhaps too eloquently—recreate parliamentary proceedings and were widely accepted as authentic speeches of the great politicians of the day. In 1738 Johnson anonymously published his immediately successful *London: A Poem, In Imitation of the Third Satire of Juvenal,* which contains protests against political corruption, the dangers of the London streets, and the miseries of the unknown and impecunious author. His *Account of the Life of Mr. Richard Savage,* published anonymously in 1744, was the first of his prose works to captivate the public. Today, it is admired for its lively depiction of Grub Street life and is considered a milestone in the art of biography. Johnson next turned to Shakespearean work, publishing his *Miscellaneous Observations on the Tragedy of Macbeth* in 1745. *Miscellaneous Observations* also contains a preliminary proposal for a new edition of Shakespeare's plays, but Johnson laid that project aside after it was suggested that he compile a dictionary of the English language. In 1747 he published his *Plan of a Dictionary of the English Language,* dedicating the work to Lord Chesterfield—who, in fact, cared little about the project. In 1749 Johnson published his second Juvenalian imitation, "The Vanity of Human Wishes," in which the personal vicissitudes of scholars, philosophers, and legislators from the modern and ancient worlds are used to illustrate the pitfalls of political ambition, the uselessness of military conquest, and the anguish that accompanies literary production.

Beginning in 1750, Johnson published a semi-weekly periodical, the *Rambler,* each issue of which comprised a single anonymous essay on contemporary literary and social conditions. Fervently believing that it is the writer's duty to make the world a better place, to "redeem the time," Johnson crafted these essays in various forms: allegories, sketches of archetypal humans, literary criticism, and lay sermons. A few days after the last number of the *Rambler* appeared in 1752, Johnson's wife died. During the next few years he confined his literary efforts to work on the *Dictionary* and irregularly contributed to another weekly periodical, the *Adventurer,* published by John Hawkesworth. In 1755 Johnson and his secretaries finally finished the 40,000-word *Dictionary,* which surpassed earlier dictionaries of its kind, primarily in precision of definition. Johnson's lexicographical work is particularly esteemed for the literary illustrations that distinguish subtle nuances of meaning for particular words. Johnson,

however, was acutely conscious of its imperfections: refutable orthography, uncertain etymology, and the fact that, as he said, some words were budding and some were falling away. Nonetheless, the *Dictionary* firmly established Johnson's literary reputation and led to his receiving an honorary M.A. degree from Oxford University. Lord Chesterfield, striving to make amends for his previous lack of regard, hailed Johnson as the supreme dictator of the English language—only to provoke what is perhaps the most famous of Johnson's letters: a scornful rebuke of Chesterfield's self-serving praise and a defense of his own initiative and industry without the assistance of a patron. Soon thereafter, Johnson once again focused his attention on Shakespeare, formally issuing his *Proposals for Printing the Dramatick Works of William Shakespeare* in 1756. Despite the commercial success of the *Dictionary,* which nevertheless failed to relieve his money problems, Johnson continued to write essays, reviews, and political articles for various periodicals. From 1758 to 1760 Johnson contributed a regular weekly essay to the *Universal Chronicle.* These essays, appearing under the heading "The Idler," exhibit the moralist and social reformist perspectives of the *Rambler* pieces but also treat the lighter side of the human condition through comical character sketches. In 1759, informing his printer that he had "a thing he was preparing for the press" to defray the expense of his mother's impending funeral, Johnson wrote *The History of Rasselas, Prince of Abissinia* in the evenings of one week. Essentially an essay on "the choice of life," *Rasselas* tells the tale of an innocent young man's quest for the secret of happiness. With his sister and Imlac, a poet-philosopher, Rasselas contemplates fundamental problems of life and art, but the conclusion—"a conclusion, in which nothing is concluded"—resolves little. This work also contains Johnson's celebrated definition of the "business of the poet." According to Imlac, the poet inspects "not the individual, but the species . . . he does not number the streaks of the tulip;" and the poet writes "as the interpreter of nature, and the legislator of mankind . . . presiding over the thoughts and manners of future generations." Some critics view *Rasselas* as Johnson's spiritual autobiography.

In 1762 George III conferred upon Johnson a pension of £300 a year, thereby relieving him the drudgery of hackwork. The next year his accidental meeting with Boswell in Thomas Davies's bookshop in Covent Garden inaugurated one of the most famous literary companionships in history. Boswell's diary entry recording the event noted that Johnson's "conversation is as great as his writing." In 1764 Johnson gladly concurred with Joshua Reynolds's proposal for the founding of what still ranks as the most famous London dining club of all time. Simply called "The Club," it was later known as The Literary Club. Among the original members, besides Johnson and Reynolds, were Edmund Burke, Topham Beauclerk, Bennet Langton, and Oliver Goldsmith; eventually Boswell, Edward Gibbon, Charles James Fox, and several others were admitted to membership. It was at meetings of the Club that Johnson uttered many of his renowned epigrams and opinions. Indeed, Reynolds once admitted that the Club was formed primarily to give Johnson a forum to express himself verbally and in company. The following year Johnson's *Plays of William Shakespeare* appeared in eight volumes—eleven years after being proposed. A lifelong student of Shakespeare, Johnson corrected textual corruptions, elucidated obscurities of language, and examined Shakespeare's textual sources. For his Shakespearean work Johnson received the degree of LL.D. from Trinity College, Dublin, and a similar honor ten years later from Oxford. Although he continued writing prologues and dedications for friends, Johnson no longer devoted his work exclusively to problems of literature and ethics. Instead he expounded his essentially pragmatic political philosophy in a series of pamphlets on the power politics of English and French colonialism, most notably in *The False Alarm, The Patriot,* and *Taxation No Tyranny.* The last-named polemic, perhaps his most vociferous outburst against colonial American claims, was written in reply to the resolutions passed by the American Continental Congress of 1774. Enjoying unprecedented leisure in the mid-1770s, Johnson extensively toured Great Britain and visited the Continent. Having traveled to Scotland and the Hebrides with Boswell in 1773, Johnson published his impressions two years later in *A Journey to the Western Islands of Scotland,* which describes the customs, religion, education, commerce, and agriculture of eighteenth-century Highland society. Johnson also traveled with his good friends Henry and Hester Thrale to North Wales in 1774 and to France in 1775.

In 1777 Johnson agreed to write biographical prefaces for an "elegant and accurate" edition of the works of English poets, ranging from the time of John Milton onwards; instead, his prefaces were separately issued as *The Lives of the English Poets.* Completed in 1781, this ten-volume work contains fifty-two essays and a wealth of biographical material. Critics have charged, however, that in some cases the criticism is ill advised, even unfair, particularly in the cases of the Metaphysical poets, Milton's "Lycidas," and Thomas Gray's "Odes." Johnson's criticism in the *Lives* generally reflects such neoclassical tendencies as "good taste," polish, "common sense," and reason. Johnson himself said that he best loved the biographical part of literature—a fact especially apparent in the *Lives*—and claimed that he came nearest to actual enjoyment of writing while composing the *Lives.* However, his per-

sonal prejudices about any given poet's life influenced his critical assessment of the poet's works—he made no attempt to separate the poetry from the poet. In 1783 Johnson had a paralytic stroke that left him seriously debilitated until the spring of the following year. After visiting his native Lichfield for the last time in the summer of 1784, he returned to London in November, and although his physical condition had considerably worsened, his mind remained alert. Johnson died on 13 December 1784 and was buried in Westminster Abbey.

Johnson's reputation as a man of letters rests as much on his life and personality as it does on his writings. This is evidenced by the scope, depth, and sheer bulk of the corpus of Johnsonian criticism, much of which is pure character analysis. Boswell's account of his life, particularly from the time of their meeting onwards, was perhaps most responsible for "Johnsonizing" England, and it fostered an image of Johnson as a gifted and original writer and masterful conversationalist. Nonetheless, Johnson was revered by his contemporaries as a skilled poet, brilliant lexicographer, and sensitive moralist. Critics hailed him as the "new" Alexander Pope upon publication of "The Vanity of Human Wishes," and the *Dictionary,* initially well received, remained a standard until the appearance of the *Oxford English Dictionary* well over a century later. Equally, *Rasselas* supplemented the popular moral themes of Johnson's earlier *Rambler* and "Idler" essays while satisfying the tastes of eighteenth-century readers for what Pope termed "impressive truth in fashion drest."

Critics continued to admire most of Johnson's works in the decade following his death, but in time commentators began to fault Johnson for what they considered his highly Latinate, formal, and overly balanced prose style as well as for his wordiness and narrow critical method. Some critics singled out *Lives of the Poets,* chastising Johnson for his harsh appraisal of Milton and his prejudicial assessments of other works and authors, notably Thomas Gray and his "Odes." By the early nineteenth century Johnson's folk image—the man of Boswell's *Life*—had come to dominate critical thinking, leaving little room for studies of the works themselves. William Hazlitt evidenced this approach when he wrote in 1818: "His good deeds were as many as his good sayings . . . all these, and innumerable others, endear him to the reader, and must be remembered to his lasting honour." Indeed, this sort of assessment was typical until the last years of the nineteenth century. When critics did focus on Johnson's works, they generally turned to his *Dictionary* and *Lives of the Poets.* Leslie Stephen favorably remarked that the *Dictionary* "was a surprising achievement, and made an epoch in the study of language," while Thomas Babington Macaulay mirrored the views of his contemporaries when he appraised

Lives of the Poets: "They are the judgments of a mind trammelled by prejudice and deficient in sensibility, but vigorous and acute." Similarly, the *Rambler* essays were dismissed as didactic lay sermons, and other prose works were labeled "unreadable." Thus, by the turn of the century, interest in Johnson's literary works was at a low point, but the man himself continued to loom large in the minds of readers.

The bicentenary of Johnson's birth in 1907 sparked a major revaluation of the Johnson canon. Throughout the twentieth century, critical emphasis shifted from the amusing idiosyncrasies and the pointed commentaries of the man to his ethical and moral standards, his appraisals of the human condition, and the compass, strength, and method of his reasoning. Some scholars noted that Johnson's writings on morals closely anticipated the theories, if not the language, of Austrian neurologist Sigmund Freud, while others ranked Johnson just below Pope and John Dryden as masters of heroic-couplet verse. Even *Lives of the Poets,* the most favorably received of Johnson's works, was reconsidered. No longer perceiving Johnson as a strictly neoclassical critic, scholars contended that he employed an empirical approach in his criticism; some critics have even cited Johnson as the father of New Criticism. Recently, commentators have turned to Johnson's Shakespearean work, countering a common nineteenth-century claim that, in the words of Heinrich Heine, "Garrick got a better hold of Shakespeare's thought than Dr. Johnson." Likewise, Johnson's political tracts, long viewed as abusive expressions of his conservative prejudice against the rights of the people, are seen today as an extension of his lifelong concern with political morality and order.

Today, after a long eclipse, Johnson is once again preeminent in the history of English letters, and mention of his name commands reverence in the English-speaking world. According to Malcolm Muggeridge: "Dr. Johnson will go on being remembered, not so much for his achievements as a writer as for the mysterious quality of greatness that he exudes."

(For further information about Johnson's life and works, see *Dictionary of Literary Biography*, Vols. 39, 95 and *Literature Criticism from 1400-1800*, Vol. 15.)

CRITICAL COMMENTARY

HORACE WALPOLE

(essay date 1779?)

[An English author, politician, and publisher, Walpole is best known for correspondence that provides revealing glimpses of life in England during the last half of the eighteenth century. In the following excerpt from a short study possibly written in 1779, he comments on Johnson's style and manner of writing, noting that both "are uncommonly vicious and unworthy of imitation."]

Dr. Johnson's works have obtained so much reputation, and the execution of them, from partiality to his abilities, has been rated so far above their merit, that, without detracting from his capacity or his learning, it may be useful to caution young authors against admiration of his *style* and *manner;* both of which are uncommonly vicious, and unworthy of imitation by any man who aims at excellence in writing his own language.

A marked *manner,* when it runs through all the compositions of any master, is a defect in itself, and indicates a deviation from nature. The writer betrays his having been struck by some particular tint, and his having overlooked nature's variety. It is true that the greatest masters of composition are so far imperfect, as that they always leave some marks by which we may discover their *hand.* He approaches the nearest to universality, whose works make it difficult for our quickness or sagacity to observe certain characteristic touches which ascertain the specific author.

Dr. Johnson's works are as easily distinguished as those of the most affected writer; for exuberance is a fault as much as quaintness. There is meaning in almost every thing Johnson says; he is often profound, and a just reasoner—I mean, when prejudice, bigotry, and arrogance do not cloud or debase his logic. He is benevolent in the application of his morality; dogmatically uncharitable in the dispensation of his censures; and equally so, when he differs with his antagonist on general truths or partial doctrines.

The first criterion that stamps Johnson's works for his, is the loaded style. I will not call it verbose, because verbosity generally implies unmeaning verbiage; a censure he does not deserve. I have allowed and do allow, that most of his words have an adequate, and frequently an illustrating purport, the true use of epithets; but then his words are indiscriminately select, and too forceful for ordinary occasions. They form a hardness of diction and a muscular toughness that re-

Principal Works

A Voyage to Abyssinia. By Father Jerome Lobo, A Portuguese Jesuit [translator] (travel essay) 1735

London: A Poem, In Imitation of the Third Satire of Juvenal (poetry) 1738

"Debates in the Senate of Magna Lilliputia" (essays) 1740-43; published in periodical The Gentleman's Magazine; also published as Debates in Parliament by Samuel Johnson, LL.D., 2 vols., 1787

An Account of the Life of Mr. Richard Savage, Son of the Earl Rivers (biography) 1744

Miscellaneous Observations on the Tragedy of Macbeth (criticism) 1745

The Plan of a Dictionary of the English Language; Addressed to the Right Honourable Philip Dormer, Earl of Chesterfield (essay) 1747

Irene: A Tragedy (drama) 1749

The Vanity of Human Wishes (poetry) 1749

*The Adventurer. 2 vols. [with Richard Bathurst, John Hawkesworth, Joseph Warton, and others] (essays) 1753-54

†The Rambler. 2 vols. (essays) 1753

A Dictionary of the English Language: in which The Words are deduced from their Originals, and Illustrated in their Different Significations by Examples from the best Writers. 2 vols. (dictionary) 1755

Proposals for Printing the Dramatick Works of William Shakespeare (essay) 1756

"A Free Inquiry into the Nature and Origin of Evil by Soame Jenyns" (criticism) 1757; published in periodical The Literary Magazine, or Universal Review

The Prince of Abissinia. 2 vols. (prose narrative) 1759; also published as The History of Rasselas, Prince of Abissinia, 1787

‡The Idler. 2 vols. (essays) 1761

The Plays of William Shakespeare, in Eight Volumes, with the Corrections and Illustrations of Various Commentators; To which are added Notes by Sam. Johnson. 8 vols. [editor] (dramas) 1765

A Journey to the Western Islands of Scotland (travel essay) 1775

Prefaces, Biographical and Critical, to the Works of the English Poets. 10 vols. (criticism) 1779-81; also published as The Lives of the English Poets, and a criticism of their works, 3 vols., 1781

Prayers and Meditations, composed by Samuel Johnson, LL.D. (meditations) 1785

The Works of Samuel Johnson, LL.D. 11 vols. (criticism, drama, essays, poetry, prose narrative, and travel essays) 1787

A Diary of a Journey into North Wales, in the year 1774; By Samuel Johnson, LL.D. (diary) 1816

The Yale Edition of the Works of Samuel Johnson. 14 vols. (criticism, diaries, drama, essays, letters, meditations, poetry, prose narrative, travel essays, and sermons) 1958-78

§The Letters of Samuel Johnson. 4 vols. (letters) 1992-

*Originally published as individual numbers from 7 November 1752 to 9 March 1754.

†Originally published as individual numbers from 20 March 1750 to 14 March 1752. Johnson did not write Nos. 10, 15, 30, 44, 97, 100, and 107.

‡Originally published in 104 numbers of The Universal Chronicle, or Weekly Gazette. Johnson did not write Nos. 9, 15, 33, 42, 54, 67, 76, 79, 82, 93, 96, and 98.

§This edition of Johnson's letters is known as the Hyde Edition. Volume 4, a comprehensive index, is forthcoming.

---

sist all ease and graceful movement. Every sentence is as high-coloured as any: no paragraph improves; the position is as robust as the demonstration; and the weakest part of the sentence (I mean, in the effect, not in the solution) is generally the conclusion: he illustrates till he fatigues, and continues to prove, after he has convinced. This fault is so usual with him, he is so apt to charge with three different set of phrases of the same calibre, that, if I did not condemn his laboured coinage of new words, I would call his threefold inundation of synonymous expressions, *triptology.*

He prefers learned words to the simple and common. He is never simple, elegant or light. He destroys more enemies with the weight of his shield than with the point of his spear, and had rather make three mortal wounds in the same part than one. This monotony, the grievous effect of pedantry and self-conceit, prevents

him from being eloquent. He excites no passions but indignation: his writings send the reader away more satiated than pleased. If he attempts humour, he makes your reason smile, without making you gay; because the study that his learned mirth requires, destroys cheerfulness. It is the clumsy gambol of a lettered elephant. We wonder that so grave an animal should have strayed into the province of the ape; yet admire that practice should have given the bulky quadruped so much agility.

Upon the whole, Johnson's style appears to me so encumbered, so void of ear and harmony, that I know no modern writer whose works can be redde aloud with so little satisfaction. I question whether one should not read a page of equal length in any modern author, in a minute's time less than one of Johnson's, all proper pauses and accents being duly attended to in both.

His works are the antipodes of taste, and he a schoolmaster of truth, but never its parent; for his doctrines have no novelty, and are never inculcated with indulgence either to the froward child or to the dull one. He has set nothing in a new light, yet is as diffuse as if we had everything to learn. Modern writers have improved on the ancients only by conciseness. Dr. Johnson, like the chymists of Laputa, endeavours to carry back what has been digested, to its pristine and crude principles. He is a standing proof that the Muses leave works unfinished, if they are not embellished by the Graces. (pp. 361-62)

Horace Walpole, "General Criticism on Dr. Johnson's Writings," in his *The Works of Horatio Walpole, Earl of Orford, Vol. IV,* G. G. and J. Robinson, 1798, pp. 361-62.

JAMES BOSWELL
(essay date 1791)

[A Scottish diarist, biographer, and man of letters, Boswell is one of the most colorful and widely read figures in eighteenth-century English literature. Labelled the greatest of English biographers and best known for his *Life of Samuel Johnson* (1791), Boswell firmly established biography as a leading literary form through a conscious, pioneering attempt to recreate his subject by combining life history with anecdote, observation, dialogue, theme, and plot. In the following excerpt from the *Life*, he gives an account of Johnson's *Lives of the Poets* and describes the reception given the work.]

In 1781, Johnson . . . completed his *Lives of the Poets,* of which he gives this account: "Some time in March I finished the *Lives of the Poets,* which I wrote in my usual way, dilatorily and hastily, unwilling to work, and working with vigour and haste." In a memorandum previous to this, he says of them: "Written, I hope, in such a manner as may tend to the promotion of piety."

This is the work, which of all Dr. Johnson's writings will perhaps be read most generally, and with most pleasure. Philology and biography were his favourite pursuits, and those who lived most in intimacy with him, heard him upon all occasions, when there was a proper opportunity, take delight in expatiating upon the various merits of the English Poets: upon the niceties of their characters, and the events of their progress through the world which they contributed to illuminate. His mind was so full of that kind of information, and it was so well arranged in his memory, that in performing what he had undertaken in this way, he had little more to do than to put his thoughts upon paper;

exhibiting first each Poet's life, and then subjoining a critical examination of his genius and works. But when he began to write, the subject swelled in such a manner, that instead of prefaces to each poet, of no more than a few pages, as he had originally intended, he produced an ample, rich, and most entertaining view of them in every respect. In this he resembled Quintilian, who tells us, that in the composition of his Institutions of Oratory, *"Latiùs se tamen aperiente materiâ, plus quàm imponebatur oneris sponte suscepi."* The booksellers, justly sensible of the great additional value of the copy right, presented him with another hundred pounds, over and above two-hundred, for which his agreement was to furnish such prefaces as he thought fit.

This was, however, but a small recompence for such a collection of biography, and such principles and illustrations of criticism, as, if digested and arranged in one system, by some modern Aristotle or Longinus, might form a code upon that subject, such as no other nation can shew. As he was so good as to make me a present of the greatest part of the original, and indeed only manuscript of this admirable work, I have an opportunity of observing with wonder the correctness with which he rapidly struck off such glowing composition. (p. 339-40)

While the world in general was filled with admiration of Johnson's *Lives of the Poets,* there were narrow circles in which prejudice and resentment were fostered, and from which attacks of different sorts issued against him. By some violent Whigs he was arraigned of injustice to Milton; by some Cambridge men of depreciating Gray; and his expressing with a dignified freedom what he really thought of George, Lord Lyttelton, gave offence to some of the friends of that nobleman, and particularly produced a declaration of war against him from Mrs. Montagu, the ingenious Essayist on Shakespeare, between whom and his Lordship a commerce of reciprocal compliments had long been carried on. In this war the smallest powers in alliance with him were of course led to engage, at least on the defensive, and thus I for one, was excluded from the enjoyment of "A Feast of Reason," such as Mr. Cumberland has described, with a keen, yet just and delicate pen, in his "OBSERVER." These minute inconveniences gave not the least disturbance to Johnson. He nobly said, when I talked to him of the feeble, though shrill outcry which had been raised, "Sir, I considered myself as entrusted with a certain portion of truth. I have given my opinion sincerely; let them shew where they think me wrong." (p. 360-61)

James Boswell, in his *The Life of Samuel Johnson,* 1906. Reprint by J. M. Dent & Sons, 1978, 646 p.

EDMUND GOSSE

(essay date 1888)

[Gosse, an English translator and critic of Scandinavian literature, was responsible for introducing Henrik Ibsen's "new drama" to English audiences. He also wrote studies of John Donne, Thomas Gray, Sir Thomas Browne, and important articles about French authors of the late nineteenth century. In the following excerpt from a work originally published in 1888, he provides a critical chronology of Johnson's writings.]

All that [Bishop William] Warburton fancied himself to be, Dr. Samuel Johnson was. In the person of this ever-fascinating hero of the world of books we find the dictator of letters, the tyrant over the consciences of readers, that the militant bishop of Gloucester was too ready to conceive himself to be. Johnson holds a place in some respects unique in literature. Other writers, however sympathetic or entertaining their personal characters may have been, live mainly in their works; we read about them with delight, because we have studied what they wrote. But with Johnson it is not so. If we knew nothing about his career or character, if we had to judge him solely by the works he published, our interest in him would shrink to very moderate proportions. Swift and Pope, Berkeley and Gray, Burke and Fielding, have contributed more than Johnson to the mere edifice of English literature. But, with the exception of Swift, there is no one in the eighteenth century who can pretend to hold so high a place as a man of letters. The happy accident by which he secured the best of all biographers is commonly taken to account for this fact, but the character, the wit, the vigour, must have first existed to stimulate a Boswell and to entrance generation after generation. The fact is that Johnson's indolence and the painful weight of his physical temperament prevented his literary powers from being fully expressed in the usual way; but they were there, and they found a vehicle in speech at the dinner-table or from his tavern-throne. He talked superb literature freely for thirty years, and all England listened; he grew to be the centre of literary opinion, and he was so majestic in intellect, so honest in purpose, so kind and pure in heart, so full of humour and reasonable sweetness and yet so trenchant, and at need so grim, that he never sank to be the figure-head of a clique, nor ever lost the balance of sympathy with readers of every rank and age. His influence was so wide, and withal so wholesome, that literary life in this country has never been since his day what it was before it. He has made

the more sordid parts of its weakness shameful, and he has raised a standard of personal conduct that every one admits. He was a gruff old bear, "Ursa Major," but it would surely be hard to find the man or woman, whose opinion is worth having, who does love almost more than revere the memory of Sam Johnson. (pp. 282-83)

[In] 1735 he performed a piece of hack-work for a Birmingham bookseller, *A Voyage to Abyssinia,* from a French abridgment of Father Lobo's Portuguese travels. The anonymous preface to this translation is Johnson's earliest original publication. This preface is written in a very characteristic style, though not, as has been carelessly stated, in his more pompous manner. (p. 283)

From this time, for twenty years, Johnson was more or less dependent for support on the labours of his pen, and the iron entered deeply into his soul. He suffered from a physical inability to prolong the effort of writing, and he absolutely required leisurely intervals of repose and meditation. Hence, even when employment was abundant, he often failed to take full advantage of it, and not less often the work he did gave dissatisfaction to his stupid taskmasters. As a schoolmaster he had already failed because he had "the character of being a very haughty, ill-natured gent, and had such a way of distorting his face" that it frightened the lads. (p. 284)

In May of [1738] S. J. published, in folio, an imitation of the Third Satire of Juvenal, under the title **"London,"** for which he received ten guineas. This poem, though to be somewhat eclipsed by a later success, enjoyed the favour of the town. It was a vigorous but certainly not an inspired study in heroic couplets in the manner of Pope, who was still before the public as a living force, one of whose satires appeared on the very same day as **"London."** The latter poem is not always marked by the author's later seriousness of purpose; Johnson affects in it to scorn and puff away the city which he had really learned to find already indispensable, and which he was presently to love with passion. After the thirty-fourth line the sentiments of **"London"** are placed in the mouth of "indignant Thales," in whom the person of Savage has been usually recognised; he is represented as seeking retirement in Wales. There is pathos in the nervous lines in which the poet expresses the misery of those who, poor and enlightened, are obliged to endure the insolence of blockheads; Johnson, here at least, speaks from the heart, and not less when he asks the question, "When can starving merit find a home?" The Orgilis passage is the best in the poem, which only extends to about two hundred and sixty lines.

Two trifling publications belong to the year 1739, *The Complete Vindication,* an ironical defence of the licensers for suppressing Brooke's tragedy of *Gustavus Vasa,* and a satire, **Marmor Norfolciense,** for which latter it was absurdly rumoured afterwards that Johnson suffered a state prosecution. For the next four years he was busy in writing out the reports of the parliamentary debates for *The Gentleman's Magazine,* under the transparent disguise of **"Debates in Magna Lilliputia."** . . . *The Account of the Life of Mr. Richard Savage* appeared in 1744; it is the longest and most elaborate of Johnson's essays in biography, and may still be read with great pleasure, in spite of various patent faults. It recounted, with all detail, a scandal, into the truth of which Johnson had not taken the pains to inquire; it was but careless in the statement of facts which lay easily within the writer's circle of experience; and it treated with extreme indulgence a character which, in a stranger, would have called down the moralist's sternest reproof. The critical passages now escape censure only because so few in the present day read the works examined. But the little book was undeniably lively; it contained several anecdotes admirably narrated, and its graver parts displayed the development of Johnson's studied magnificence of language. Good biography was still rare in England, and *The Account of Savage* attracted a great deal of notice. (pp. 284-86)

In 1745 he printed a pamphlet on *Macbeth* [*Miscellaneous Observations on the Tragedy of Macbeth*], and in 1747 the prospectus of a vast scheme which he had formed, that of an English Dictionary, on a scale hitherto unattempted. He dedicated his *Plan of a Dictionary* to Lord Chesterfield, who sent him ten pounds, and then took no further interest in the matter, to his own lasting misfortune. For eight years no more was heard of this projected work. In 1748 Johnson spent a short holiday at Hampstead, where he wrote his longest and best poem, **"The Vanity of Human Wishes,"** published in 1749. This is a study in heroic verse, like **"London,"** but it extends to another hundred lines, and is, moreover, a much finer and more accomplished production. It is an imitation of the Tenth Satire of Juvenal, and is written in a very grave and even melancholy vein, though without unseemly bitterness. It was not much liked when it appeared; Garrick declared it was "as hard as Greek." The public had become accustomed to a thinner and smarter kind of satire, to the lucid snip-snap of the immediate followers of Pope, and **"The Vanity of Human Wishes"** was voted obscure. It is certainly weighted with thought, and the closeness with which the Latin original is followed gives a certain tightness of phrase, the result of a meritorious concentration. But it is perhaps the most Roman poem in the language, the one which best reflects the moral grandeur of Latin feeling and reflection; and it has contributed more familiar quotations to the language than any other work of Johnson's. Such a passage as the following gives a very favourable notion of Johnson as a didactic poet:

On what foundation stands the warrior's pride,

How just his hopes, let Swedish Charles decide;
A frame of adamant, a soul of fire,
No dangers fright him and no labours tire;
O'er love, o'er fear, extends his wide domain,
Unconquer'd Lord of passion and of pain;
No joys to him pacific sceptres yield,
War sounds the trump, he rushes to the field;
Behold surrounding kings their power combine,
And one capitulate, and one resign;
Peace courts his hand, but spreads her charms in
   vain,
'Think nothing gained,' he cries, 'till nought re-
   main;—
On Moscow's walls till Gothic standards fly,
And all be mine beneath the polar sky.'
The march begins in military state,
And nations on his eye suspended wait;
Stern Famine guards the solitary coast,
And Winter barricades the realms of Frost;
He comes, nor want nor cold his course delay,—
Hide, blushing glory, hide Pultowa's day.

A pleasing incident now broke into the monotony of Johnson's gray and laborious existence. His old pupil, David Garrick, had risen into success more rapidly than Johnson had, and was now manager of Drury Lane Theatre. When he was keeping school at Edial Hall, in 1736, Johnson had written a blank verse tragedy on a Turkish subject, but had vainly attempted, in later years, to get it acted. Garrick loyally determined that he would produce it, and after some obstinate struggles with the author, who could not be brought to yield willingly to any stage requirements, *Mahomet and Irene* was acted on the 6th February 1749. Johnson was present, and did not, on this occasion, "suspend the soft solicitudes of dress." He gained nearly £300 by the play, which, however, did not run for more than nine nights, and was never revived. Garrick had introduced the incident of Irene's being strangled on the stage, and to Johnson's mingled mortification and satisfaction, the audience hissed and called out "Murder! murder!" In future, on the stage, as in the printed play, the heroine was forced out by the mutes, crying for mercy, and was seen no more. The tragedy was presently published under the title of *Irene.* Johnson's solitary play labours under the disadvantage of being perfectly uninteresting. It was founded on a tragedy, by one Charles Goring, that had been acted at Drury Lane forty years before; there was no plot worth mentioning, no development of characters, no bustle or intrigue. The conduct of the speeches and the versification is closely modelled on that of the sentimental tragic poet Rowe, whose plays had been popular in Johnson's early youth; what Johnson said of Rowe's plays, long afterwards, might be repeated almost verbally as a criticism of *Irene.* The most amusing thing about the whole incident of this play is Johnson's odd remark to Garrick about the white stockings of the actresses.

Posterity is more ready to realise the Sage in the

character of "a majestic teacher of moral and religious wisdom" than as one whose scarlet waistcoat fluttered the dovecotes of Drury Lane. Since the days of Addison and Steele, or since, to be more exact, the *Guardian* of 1713, there had been made many attempts to rival the great social newspapers of the reign of Anne. But none of these had been successful, and Johnson, finding himself now moderately famous, determined to issue a new periodical. It was difficult to find a name; but one night he sat down on his bed, and determined not to go to sleep till he had thought of a title. The *Rambler* occurred to him at last, and he sank to rest contented. On the 20th of March 1750 the first number of this little newspaper appeared, and it closed on the 14th of March 1752. The death of his wife, a few days after the latter date, has been given as the cause of Johnson's discontinuance of a periodical of which he was probably weary. He wrote the *Rambler* unaided, with the exception of five numbers—of these one was written by Richardson; two by Elizabeth Carter (1717-1806), the translator of Epictetus; one by Hester Mulso, better known as Mrs. written by Richardson; two by Elizabeth Carter (1717-1806), the ladies deserve mention, not merely as dear and lifelong friends of Johnson, but as apt disciples of his moral manner. Johnson's authorship was at first kept secret, but his style was now familiar to careful readers, and was promptly recognised. The publisher complained that "the encouragement as to sale" was not in proportion "to the raptures expressed by the few that did read it." The *Rambler* is "too wordy," as the author confessed; he tried to be a little lighter in manner in the twenty-nine papers he contributed in 1752 and 1753 to Hawkesworth's *Adventurer,* and somewhat later we shall be called, in describing the *Idler,* to speak of him as a periodical writer at his best.

Meanwhile the mighty *Dictionary* had been slowly progressing, and in April 1755 it was published in two folio volumes. It hardly belongs to literature, except in connection with two short essays, in which Johnson shows himself at his best as a prose-writer, namely, the dignified and pathetic preface, which can scarcely be read to the close without emotion, and the astonishing letter, on the subject of a patron's duties, which he addressed to Chesterfield on the 7th of February 1755. In these two short compositions, in each of which the author is singularly moved, his English, though always stately and formal, is lifted out of the sesquipedalian affectation of magnificence which has amused the world so much, and which was beyond question a serious fault of Johnson's style. Here, and especially in the letter to Chesterfield, he is simple, terse, and thrilling, and, as the occasion was a private one, we may take it that in the extraordinary fire and pungency of the sentences we have something like a specimen of that marvellous power in conversation which made Johnson the wonder of his age. (pp. 286-89)

There is something of the same brightness and ease in the papers of the *Idler,* a series of essays published by Johnson from the 15th of April 1758 to the 5th of April 1760 in a newspaper called the *Universal Chronicle.* He took less trouble with his *Idlers* than with his *Ramblers,* and the result is more pleasing. Johnson as an essayist is most happy when he analyses a character, in the manner of La Bruyère, mingling criticism with narrative; the best example is the sketch of Dick Minim. He possessed shrewdness, judgment, singular knowledge of human nature, and plentiful wit; somehow all these qualities, though fused by his literary genius, did not quite produce a great essayist.

Perhaps it might be said that the best of Johnson's *Idlers* was the long apologue which appeared in book form while he was publishing his shorter weekly essays. The agreeable story of *The Prince of Abyssinia* (known from the seventh edition onwards by the name of its hero, *Rasselas*) was composed in the evenings of one week, to defray the expenses of his mother's funeral and to pay her debts. He received one hundred pounds as the first payment for this book, which appeared in April 1759, about three weeks after Voltaire's *Candide.* Johnson was interested in this latter fact, and said that "If they had not been published so closely one after the other . . . it would have been in vain to deny that the scheme of that which came latest was taken from the other." The resemblance, however, appears somewhat slight to a modern reader; Johnson has all the advantage in health and profundity, Voltaire in wit and intellectual daring. *Rasselas* is not a brilliant romance; the artless young person who flies to it as a story of African adventure will be sadly disappointed. It is a description in measured and elegant prose of how Rasselas became discontented in his Happy Valley, how he fled from it, in company with his sister Nekayah, under the guidance of an old man of infinite resource named Imlac, and how, after some mild and incredible incidents, they resolved to return to Abyssinia. The charm of the book is its humanity, the sweetness and wholesomeness of the long melancholy episodes, the wisdom of the moral reflections and disquisitions; nor is there wanting here and there the gentle sunshine of a sort of half-suppressed humour. *Rasselas* enjoyed an instant success, and was reprinted seven or eight times before Johnson died.

The toilsome part of Johnson's life closed with the publication of the *Dictionary;* and with his acceptance of a pension of £300 from the king a few years later he attained positive ease. . . . In 1764 the "Club" was created; among its original members were—besides Johnson—Reynolds, Burke, Goldsmith, and Hawkins. Garrick, C. J. Fox, and Boswell were soon added. To Johnson his semi-presidential chair at the Club was, as he said, "the throne of human felicity," and it was from this social palace that his edicts went forth to the world. He was no longer anxious to write. He loitered for nine years over a very perfunctory edition of Shakespeare, which finally appeared in 1765. For five years more he was silent, until in 1770 he contributed to the Wilkes controversy a tract, *The False Alarm,* on the Tory side. Having once plunged into the giddy waters of political pamphleteering, the old Tory veteran could not induce himself to withdraw. He published in 1771 *Thoughts on the late Transactions respecting the Falkland Islands,* which was geographical as well as polemical. In 1774 he attempted to stem the tide then flowing against the court party by a tract entitled *The Patriot,* and in 1775 he took the wrong side about America in *Taxation no Tyranny.* In 1776 these four treatises were issued in one volume, as *Political Tracts,* by S. J. It may be noticed that Johnson's full name appeared on no title-page during his lifetime. Of the political pamphlets it may be said that they were forcible, but entirely without historical breadth or sympathy. (pp. 290-92)

Late in the year [1774] appeared his *Journey to the Western Islands,* which is not to be compared for interest with Boswell's later work on the same theme. It was, however, read with curiosity and respect, for Johnson's reputation was now in its full splendour. In 1775 Oxford made her old disciple an LL.D., and Johnson a few months later entered into controversy with the "foolish and impudent" James Macpherson, whose version of Ossian he regarded with contempt. Johnson properly mistrusted the literary honesty of Macpherson, and openly told him that his book was an imposture in a letter only less famous than the Chesterfield specimen.

Johnson's literary work now seemed to be well-nigh ended, but in 1777 he undertook a labour of biography and criticism, which was perhaps, had he considered his responsibilities, the most arduous he had ever thought of. This is the book usually reprinted as *Lives of the English Poets,* but published in 1779-1781 as *Prefaces, biographical and critical, of the most eminent of the English Poets.* The life of Savage, though too long for the system of the book, was worked in, and so were other lives that Johnson had already written. The poets themselves appeared in sixty-eight volumes, and Johnson's *Lives* in a special edition of four volumes. The selection was arbitrary, although there was no intention of throwing scorn on Chaucer and Spenser by opening the roll of fame with Cowley. This was done merely to suit the convenience of the publisher. The *Lives* are of very various interest and value. Some of the worst are those in which Johnson deals with great men, such as Milton and Gray; some of the best are those in which he allows himself to meditate around very little men, as in the case of Edmund Smith. . . . The book is full of wit and thought, but al-

though a charming companion it is one of the worst of guides. Johnson was a competent critic only within a certain sharply-defined groove.

In 1782 the death of his old dependant, the "useful and companionable" Robert Levett, called forth what is certainly the most tender, and towards close the most admirable of Johnson's minor poems:

> His virtues walked their narrow round,
> Nor made a pause, nor left a void;
> And sure the Eternal Master found
> The single talent well employed.
>
> The busy day, the peaceful night,
> Unfelt, uncounted, glided by;
> His frame was firm, his powers were bright,
> Though now his eightieth year was nigh.
>
> Then with no fiery throbbing pain,
> No cold gradations of decay,
> Death broke at once the vital chain,
> And freed his soul the nearest way.

These stanzas might have been signed by Matthew Arnold, so modern are they in their workmanship. (pp. 292-94)

After Johnson's death every scrap of his manuscript that could be found was printed, his *Prayers and Meditations* in 1785, his *Sermons* in 1788-89, his *Diary in North Wales* in 1816; and in 1791 Boswell set the topstone to the edifice of Johnson's glory by his immortal biography. (pp. 294-95)

Edmund Gosse, "Johnson and the Philosophers," in his *A History of Eighteenth Century Literature (1660-1780),* The Macmillan Company, 1924, pp. 273-309.

LYTTON STRACHEY
(essay date 1906)

[Strachey was a twentieth-century English literary critic and biographer whose iconoclastic reexaminations of historical figures helped change the course of modern biography. In the following excerpt from an essay originally published in the *Independent Review* in 1906, he considers the overall "good quality" of Johnson's criticism in *The Lives of the Poets* but notes that the individual critical portraits "are never right."]

No one needs an excuse for re-opening the *Lives of the Poets;* the book is too delightful. It is not, of course, as delightful as Boswell; but who re-opens Boswell? Boswell is in another category; because, as every one knows, when he has once been opened he can never be shut. But, on its different level, the *Lives* will always hold a firm and comfortable place in our affections. After Boswell, it is the book which brings us nearer than any other to the mind of Dr. Johnson. That is its primary import. We do not go to it for information or for instruction, or that our tastes may be improved, or that our sympathies may be widened; we go to it to see what Dr. Johnson thought. Doubtless, during the process, we are informed and instructed and improved in various ways; but these benefits are incidental, like the invigoration which comes from a mountain walk. It is not for the sake of the exercise that we set out; but for the sake of the view. The view from the mountain which is Samuel Johnson is so familiar, and has been so constantly analysed and admired, that further description would be superfluous. It is sufficient for us to recognise that he is a mountain, and to pay all the reverence that is due. In one of Emerson's poems a mountain and a squirrel begin to discuss each other's merits; and the squirrel comes to the triumphant conclusion that he is very much the better of the two, since he can crack a nut, while the mountain can do no such thing. The parallel is close enough between this impudence and the attitude—implied, if not expressed—of too much modern criticism towards the sort of qualities—the easy, indolent power, the searching sense of actuality, the combined command of sanity and paradox, the immovable independence of thought—which went to the making of the *Lives of the Poets.* There is only, perhaps, one flaw in the analogy: that, in this particular instance, the mountain was able to crack nuts a great deal better than any squirrel that ever lived.

That the *Lives* continue to be read, admired, and edited, is in itself a high proof of the eminence of Johnson's intellect; because, as serious criticism, they can hardly appear to the modern reader to be very far removed from the futile. Johnson's aesthetic judgments

Walking up High Street: Johnson and Boswell experience life in Edinburgh by night.

are almost invariably subtle, or solid, or bold; they have always some good quality to recommend them—except one: they are never right. That is an unfortunate deficiency; but no one can doubt that Johnson has made up for it, and that his wit has saved all. He has managed to be wrong so cleverly, that nobody minds. When Gray, for instance, points the moral to his poem on Walpole's cat with a reminder to the fair that all that glisters is not gold, Johnson remarks that this is 'of no relation to the purpose; if *what glistered* had been *gold,* the cat would not have gone into the water; and, if she had, would not less have been drowned.' Could anything be more ingenious, or more neatly put, or more obviously true? But then, to use Johnson's own phrase, could anything be of less 'relation to the purpose'? It is his wit—and we are speaking, of course, of wit in its widest sense—that has sanctified Johnson's perversities and errors, that has embalmed them for ever, and that has put his book, with all its mass of antiquated doctrine, beyond the reach of time.

For it is not only in particular details that Johnson's criticism fails to convince us; his entire point of view is patently out of date. Our judgments differ from his, not only because our tastes are different, but because our whole method of judging has changed. Thus, to the historian of letters, the *Lives* have a special interest, for they afford a standing example of a great dead tradition—a tradition whose characteristics throw more than one curious light upon the literary feelings and ways which have become habitual to ourselves. Perhaps the most striking difference between the critical methods of the eighteenth century and those of the present day, is the difference in sympathy. The most cursory glance at Johnson's book is enough to show that he judged authors as if they were criminals in the dock, answerable for every infraction of the rules and regulations laid down by the laws of art, which it was his business to administer without fear or favour. Johnson never inquired what poets were trying to do; he merely aimed at discovering whether what they had done complied with the canons of poetry. Such a system of criticism was clearly unexceptionable, upon one condition—that the critic was quite certain what the canons of poetry were; but the moment that it became obvious that the only way of arriving at a conclusion upon the subject was by consulting the poets themselves, the whole situation completely changed. The judge had to bow to the prisoner's ruling. In other words, the critic discovered that his first duty was, not to criticise, but to understand the object of his criticism. That is the essential distinction between the school of Johnson and the school of Sainte-Beuve. No one can doubt the greater width and profundity of the modern method; but it is not without its drawbacks. An excessive sympathy with one's author brings its own set of errors: the critic is so happy to explain everything, to show how this was the product of the age, how that was the product of environment, and how the other was the inevitable result of inborn qualities and tastes—that he sometimes forgets to mention whether the work in question has any value. It is then that one cannot help regretting the Johnsonian black cap.

But other defects, besides lack of sympathy, mar the *Lives of the Poets.* One cannot help feeling that no matter how anxious Johnson might have been to enter into the spirit of some of the greatest of the masters with whom he was concerned, he never could have succeeded. Whatever critical method he might have adopted, he still would have been unable to appreciate certain literary qualities, which, to our minds at any rate, appear to be the most important of all. His opinion of *Lycidas* is well known: he found that poem 'easy, vulgar, and therefore disgusting.' Of the songs in *Comus* he remarks: 'they are harsh in their diction, and not very musical in their numbers.' He could see nothing in the splendour and elevation of Gray, but 'glittering accumulations of ungraceful ornaments.' The passionate intensity of Donne escaped him altogether; he could only wonder how so ingenious a writer could be so absurd. Such preposterous judgments can only be accounted for by inherent deficiencies of taste; Johnson had no ear, and he had no imagination. These are, indeed, grievous disabilities in a critic. What could have induced such a man, the impatient reader is sometimes tempted to ask, to set himself up as a judge of poetry?

The answer to the question is to be found in the remarkable change which has come over our entire conception of poetry, since the time when Johnson wrote. It has often been stated that the essential characteristic of that great Romantic Movement which began at the end of the eighteenth century, was the reintroduction of Nature into the domain of poetry. Incidentally, it is curious to observe that nearly every literary revolution has been hailed by its supporters as a return to Nature. No less than the school of Coleridge and Wordsworth, the school of Denham, of Dryden, and of Pope, proclaimed itself as the champion of Nature; and there can be little doubt that Donne himself—the father of all the conceits and elaborations of the seventeenth century—wrote under the impulse of a Naturalistic reaction against the conventional classicism of the Renaissance. Precisely the same contradictions took place in France. Nature was the watchword of Malherbe and of Boileau; and it was equally the watchword of Victor Hugo. To judge by the successive proclamations of poets, the development of literature offers a singular paradox. The further it goes back, the more sophisticated it becomes; and it grows more and more natural as it grows distant from the State of Nature. However this may be, it is at least certain that the Romantic revival peculiarly deserves to be called Naturalistic, because it succeeded in bringing into vogue the

operations of the external world—'the Vegetable Universe,' as Blake called it—as subject-matter for poetry. But it would have done very little, if it had done nothing more than this. Thomson, in the full meridian of the eighteenth century, wrote poems upon the subject of Nature; but it would be foolish to suppose that Wordsworth and Coleridge merely carried on a fashion which Thomson had begun. Nature, with them, was something more than a peg for descriptive and didactic verse; it was the manifestation of the vast and mysterious forces of the world. The publication of *The Ancient Mariner* is a landmark in the history of letters, not because of its descriptions of natural objects, but because it swept into the poet's vision a whole new universe of infinite and eternal things; it was the discovery of the Unknown. We are still under the spell of *The Ancient Mariner;* and poetry to us means, primarily, something which suggests, by means of words, mysteries and infinitudes. Thus, music and imagination seem to us the most essential qualities of poetry, because they are the most potent means by which such suggestions may be invoked. But the eighteenth century knew none of these things. To Lord Chesterfield and to Pope, to Prior and to Horace Walpole, there was nothing at all strange about the world; it was charming, it was disgusting, it was ridiculous, and it was just what one might have expected. In such a world, why should poetry, more than anything else, be mysterious? No! Let it be sensible; that was enough. (pp. 59-63)

Lytton Strachey, "The Lives of the Poets," in his *Books & Characters: French & English,* Chatto & Windus, 1922, pp. 59-64.

JOHN WAIN
(essay date 1959)

[Wain is an English critic, novelist, and poet. In the following excerpt from an essay originally published in the London *Observer* in 1959, he attempts to explain the 'reverence' that Johnson commands in the English-speaking world.]

Dr. Johnson is one of those myth-figures, like King Alfred or Nelson, of whom virtually every English person has heard. Most people think of him as an intellectual version of John Bull (a character invented by Arbuthnot some years before Johnson was born, and very much of the period). At school they read a few extracts from Boswell's *Life,* and get from it the impression that Johnson began every sentence with 'Sir' and contradicted every remark addressed to him. This is the sum of their knowledge.

For a myth-figure, this will do, being quite as substantial as Lady Hamilton or the burnt cakes, but it is as well to remind ourselves that behind the two-dimensional popular image stands a great and tragic character, full of paradox and enigma, calling out passionate loyalty and strong dislike not only during his lifetime but unbrokenly ever since. (pp. 171-72)

It used to be the fashion to decry Johnson's powers as a writer and claim that he was important solely as a character. In fact, by any objective standard he was one of the best writers of the eighteenth century; whether or not he was what people now understand by the word 'poet', he could write movingly and memorably in verse; if **"The Vanity of Human Wishes"** is not a poem, it is hard to know what else to call it. And Johnson's prose, grave, sonorous, heavily charged with meaning, gives the lie to the slander of 'Johnsonese', by which the Victorians meant an emptily inflated style. This prose is heavy because it is densely packed.

As a literary critic, Johnson was a conservative. His sensibility was formed during the first half of the eighteenth century, a period that was itself backward-looking and time-marking; and, though his working life stretched through the years that saw the rise of the novel, the renewed interest in mediaeval literature, balladry, and primitive art, and the shift from classic to romantic generally, he remained, like most critics, faithful to the taste of his early days. In the *Lives of the English Poets*, his most formidable repository of critical judgments, he is usually at his best in dealing with writers whose vogue passed away with his own youth.

The *Lives* may be Johnson's major critical work, but his most delightful critical writing occurs in the notes to his edition of Shakespeare. This took nine years to prepare and was published when Johnson was fifty-six, so that the notes show the working of his mind during the hardpressed years when he laboured in the heat of the day, whereas the *Lives* are the fruit of his lionised old age.

These notes show the force and freshness of Johnson's intelligence better than anything except the very best pages of Boswell. The stage direction 'Exit Pistol' in *Henry V* may not seem to call for a footnote: but it moves Johnson to write, with loving sadness:

> The comick scenes of the history of Henry the fourth and fifth are now at an end, and all the comick personages are now dismissed. Falstaff and Mrs. Quickly are dead; Nym and Bardolph are hanged; Gadshill was lost immediately after the robbery; Poins and Peto have vanished since, one knows not how; and Pistol is now beaten into obscurity. I believe every reader regrets their departure.

Such a comment reveals Johnson's loving absorption in the play. At other times his remarks show a vigilant desire to make Shakespeare's work directly available to the reader's moral life, by pointing out the lessons to be learnt from seemingly trivial lines. In *Much Ado About Nothing,* Leonato, the father of the wronged girl Hero, is so stunned by the brutal scene of rejection at the altar that he acquiesces in the friar's counter-scheme with the numb, almost indifferent words

> Being that I flow in grief,
> The smallest twine may lead me.

Johnson is ready with the comment:

> Men overpowered with distress eagerly listen to the first offers of relief, close with every scheme, and believe every promise. He that has no longer any confidence in himself, is glad to repose his trust in any other that will undertake to guide him.

The impression is of reading Shakespeare in company with a man who is prepared at every turn to weigh the author against his own long and rugged experience of life.

As writer and critic, then, he is still interesting. Nevertheless, it is true that Johnson's chief hold over our minds is as a moral hero, a great personal example. With all his faults and foibles, he lived a brave and unselfish life. Starting with every handicap—bad sight, poor health, no money, and uncouth appearance and uncontrollable nervous habits—he fought his way up to recognition as one of the great men of his time. Once there, he made no effort to turn his reputation to worldly advantage in pursuit of money or power; he gave away most of what he earned, keeping back only enough to supply his basic needs, and filled his house with a crowd of peevish old creatures who could not look after themselves.

All this was visible to the world. But the real heroism of Johnson's life lay in his unceasing struggle against the darkness within his own mind. Physically he never knew fear, but on another level he was haunted by neurotic guilt and the dread of eternal punishment. In the year of his death, a friend, trying to reason him into calmness, asked what precisely he understood by the term 'damned'. Johnson burst out passionately: 'Sent to Hell, Sir, and punished everlastingly!' When urged to rely on the merciful nature of God, he pointed out that, since Hell undoubtedly existed, it was part of the wisdom of God that some souls should be sent there, and why not his?

A man of strong passions and appetites will easily fall into temptations, and Johnson's *Prayers and Meditations* are full of piteous appeals for leniency from God and promises to amend ('O Lord, let me not sink into total depravity; look down upon me, and rescue me at last from the captivity of sin'). At times his reason threatened to give way; when he was living in Mrs. Thrale's house at Streatham, which he did intermittently for twenty years, he appears to have made her promise to lock him up, and even put him in irons, if he actually ran mad; among her effects, sold off at her death in 1823, was 'Johnson's padlock, committed to my care in 1768'.

Partly because he could never get the fear of Hell out of his mind, and partly because he had suffered and come through such desperate privations, Johnson was extremely hardhearted about trivial sufferings. In a world where many poor wretches were starving, and where the gates of Hell might at any moment yawn beneath one's feet, it seemed to him impious and wicked to complain about boredom, or a headache, or the spiteful remark of an acquaintance. He was also very suspicious of Utopians who claimed that with a little engineering human life could be made happy. To him, unhappiness was the permanent normal condition of human life, and this inclined him to political conservatism, since to throw over existing institutions in the belief that new ones would bring happiness seemed to him a self-indulgent folly. As he declared in *Rambler* No. 32:

> The cure for the greatest part of human miseries is not radical but palliative. Infelicity is involved in corporeal nature, and interwoven with our being; all attempts therefore to decline it wholly are useless and vain: the armies of pain send their arrows on every side, the choice is only between those which are more or less sharp, or tinged with poison of greater or less malignity; and the strongest armour which reason can supply will only blunt their points, but cannot repel them.

Johnson's whole way of life, as well as his intellectual position, can be deduced from that passage. Human suffering could be met, but only by putting on armour supplied by 'reason', and taking reasonable advantage of the 'palliative' cures, innocent diversions which enabled a man to forget his unhappiness. No one ever threw himself into blameless enjoyments with more zest than Johnson, who loved a good dinner and an evening's talk so well that he declared 'a good tavern or inn' the happiest invention of the human mind. Mrs. Thrale, who saw his domestic side, said that he 'always hated to be left out of any innocent merriment that was going forward. . . . I verily think, if he had had good eyes, and a form less inflexible, he would have made an excellent mimic.'

Conviviality, even 'buffoonery', were one side of Johnson; neurotic dread and melancholia were another; the strong, rapid play of a masterly intelligence was a third. But none of these quite explains the reverence in which he was held. As Johnson lay dying, Fanny Burney sat for hours in tears on the stairs leading up to his room, hoping that she might be called in to receive his blessing. No mere John Bull, intellectual or otherwise, inspires that kind of devotion. Johnson had a greatness of mind, a tragic and heroic stature, that we can feel across two hundred and fifty years. (pp. 173-76)

John Wain, "Samuel Johnson," in his *Essays on Literature and Ideas,* Macmillan and Co. Ltd., 1963, pp. 171-76.

GEOFFREY TILLOTSON
(essay date 1961)

[Tillotson was an English educator, author, and critic. In the following excerpt, he extols Johnson's linguistic insights as stated in his *Dictionary* and related writings.]

There are two pieces of extended writing connected with the *Dictionary.* The body of the *Dictionary* could not, in its very nature, be more than a series of short items, but as usual Johnson took the opportunity to deliver himself at large on the principles of the work he was concerned in doing. Eight years before the *Dictionary* was published, he brought out his **"Plan of an English Dictionary"**, and when the work was completed he affixed to it a **"Preface."** The **"Plan"** is enough to show that Johnson had been conscious of the nature of English words long before there had been any question of his making a dictionary. It shows a magnificent grasp of what lay ahead. When the time came for him to write his **"Preface"** he did not need to supersede the **"Plan"** at any important point. **"Plan"** and **"Preface"** together are two of the most remarkable writings we have about the matters they treat of.

The **"Plan"** and the **"Preface"** show that Johnson saw his work as concerned not so much with words as with language. That is one of the supreme merits of the *Dictionary.* It is possible for a dictionary-maker to do his work quite happily on a much lower plane. He is paid to take the words of the language, to arrange them in alphabetical order and to give us an account—some account—of their meaning. And this had been what dictionary-makers up to that time had felt to be all that was expected of them. But Johnson came to see that to isolate a word in dictionary fashion was to destroy something essential in its nature. He saw English words as things belonging to what he called 'a living tongue', and he saw that the advantage of belonging to a living tongue was that words were themselves alive in the sense that their meaning depended upon the various places they had occupied, or were occupying, among their fellows. He saw words as gregarious things, as things, as it were, that had faces which lit up only when in company. There are no more interesting passages in his **"Plan"** and **"Preface"** than those which deal with the subtleties that words owe to their successive contexts.

'Names,' he said, 'have often many ideas.' And again:

When the construction of a word is explained, it is necessary to pursue it through its train of phraseology, through those forms where it is used in a manner peculiar to our language, or in senses not to be comprised in the general explanations.

And these are some of the phrases he uses: 'exuberance of signification', 'nice and subtle ramifications of meaning', and—a phrase now common which he seems to have invented—'shades of meaning'. He despaired of seizing these distinctions, but he saw that we could discern them by noting words in their place in the living language, especially when it is written or spoken by those who understand 'the genius of the tongue'—again the phrase is his and again he seems to have invented it. In the **"Plan"** of the *Dictionary* he gave the idea this modern turn:

The signification of adjectives may be often ascertained [i.e., pinned down] by uniting them to substantives; as, *simple swain, simple sheep.* Sometimes the sense of a substantive may be elucidated by the epithets annexed to it in good authors; as, the *boundless ocean,* the *open lawns.*

Now it had been the dream of some of Johnson's contemporaries and some of his immediate predecessors, that English could become fixed in a changeless state. Johnson himself had begun with hoping that he might make that dream come true.

We can understand why in the eighteenth century there was a wish to see English fixed. The literary ideal of its great writers was the ideal of correctness. And that was an ideal partly, sometimes mainly, dependent on the means of expression, on language. Prose writers often had new thoughts and so needed to have them understood. Poets had old thoughts mainly, and so looked to expression to justify their expressing them once again. And yet they saw that English had proved itself a broken reed. It had been a language so given to change that the writings of one age had become progressively unintelligible to later ages. If it was still possible to discern that Chaucer was a great poet, that was because this greatness had proved too lively to be quite extinguished by its medium. And not only Chaucer. Atterbury, the friend of Pope, said that much of Shakespeare was unintelligible at that date. Did it not follow that the same doom was awaiting the would-be correct writings of Swift, Addison and Pope? Pope certainly thought so:

And such as Chaucer is shall Dryden be.

This feeling about the transience of English was sharpened by the admiration these men felt for the comparative fixity of Latin—what survived of Latin literature made use of a language that, beside English, appeared beautifully stable. Pope himself purposed to help in a formal way the fixing of English. He had the idea of making a dictionary which should draw its words from the best English writers of the sixteenth and seventeenth centuries. And it was Pope's plan apparently that was passed on to Johnson, who speaks of Pope's solicitude 'for the success of this work'. Johnson came to see that nobody could fix a living language any more than King Canute could fix the sea. Even so he did something towards saving it from unnecessary change. Along with other great writers he worked, both as writer and lexicographer, in the spirit of that exhortation in his **"Preface"**: 'We have long preserved our constitution, let us make some struggles for our language.'

Because of the outcome of the struggles we can still read the writing of Swift and Pope—I mean skim along the surface, of course—almost as effortlessly as their first readers.

And so to my third point. Johnson complained, when speaking of those subtle verbs *get, take,* and so on, that in English we had too many of them. Modern linguists will resent that complaint. But Johnson himself knew it was an idle one. He saw his office as that of 'registering' not 'forming' the language. We can see how wise he was when we think of the vain endeavours that Robert Bridges, say, engaged himself in. Bridges assumed that language could be shaped according to the desires of those interested in shaping it. What a pity he did not read Johnson's **"Preface"** which proclaims that 'to enchain syllables and to lash the wind, are equally the undertakings of pride, unwilling to measure its desires by its strength'.

My final point brings me back to what I said about Johnson and truth. Everybody knows that when, half-way through his vast *Dictionary*, he arrived at the word 'lexicographer' he allowed himself the pleasure of intruding into his definition the phrase 'a harmless drudge', but he did so because he himself was as incapable of the mindlessness of drudgery as of the inanity of harmlessness. 'I am not yet so lost in lexicography,' he assures us in the **"Preface,"** 'as to forget that *words are the daughters of earth, and that things are the sons of heaven.* Language is only the instrument of science [i.e., knowledge], and words are but the signs of ideas.' He was not so lost as to forget to make of his *Dictionary* more than a dictionary. He made of it the occasion for a long series of inlets into great literature. For Johnson great literature embodied truth. He had a passion for 'true, evident and actual wisdom'. All his writings were means of honouring it. Even his *Dictionary* honours it. For when he chose to show words actively alive in his exhibits, he chose to show them so in exhibits worth reading on their own account. We of the twentieth century with our weakness for snippets can think of each dozen pages of his *Dictionary*—and there are about 3,000 pages—as offering us a tear-off calendar of great thoughts! As well as everything else, his *Dictionary* is an anthology of 'beauties'. Of course, they could only be brief beauties, but it is interesting to learn that their number had to be reduced on revision, and it is amusing to see the amplitude of some of those that were retained. So interesting are these examples as pieces of truth that the *Dictionary* comes near to defeating its own ends. It is a dictionary that can be read, and in practice we find ourselves reading it. In other words, it is made to serve the ends that are served by *The Rambler, Rasselas* and the *Lives of the Poets.* When Anna Seward said that all Johnson's writings were poetry— that is, writings that added delight to instruction—she made an exception of his orthographical works. But she need not have done so. (pp. 224-28)

Geoffrey Tillotson, "Johnson's Dictionary," in his *Augustan Studies,* The Athlone Press, 1961, pp. 224-28.

M. D. AESCHLIMAN
(essay date 1985)

[An American educator and author, Aeschliman has written on such diverse topics as biography, philosophy, modern European history, religion, modern satirists, and literature. In the following excerpt, he praises the universal appeal of Johnson's writings.]

Scholars, writers, readers, souls all over the globe, from Cairo to Melbourne, from Johannesburg to Los Angeles—large numbers of them people without any particular background in "Eng Lit"—find something in Johnson that they find in no other voice, save perhaps that of the Lord whom Johnson so faithfully served.

Only the two great dramatic and narrative geniuses of our literature, Shakespeare and Dickens respectively, may be said to exercise so wide an appeal; and Johnson never wrote extensively in their popular fictional and dramatic genres. Dickens was aptly called "the great Christian" by Dostoyevsky; Shakespeare's voice, as Johnson himself noted, is the voice of humanity itself. Johnson's voice, by contrast, is the voice of one person—with a view as wide as the world, to be sure; but the voice of one person nonetheless, unique and extraordinary at the same time that it is general and typical: unique in fact in its very generality and universality. To adapt the words of a modern poet, Johnson is "the impossible possible philosophers' man, / The man who has had time to think enough, / The central man."

Take an instance in which at least part of Johnson's point has been rendered mortal by the passage of time, the famous lines contributed to Goldsmith's "The Traveler":

How small, of all that human hearts endure,

That part which laws or kings can cause or cure.
Still to ourselves in ev'ry place consign'd,
Our own felicity we make or find.

Clearly Johnson could have had no idea of the political enormities and nightmares that lay in the future, in the much-heralded age of "progress" and rationality foretold by those French *philosophes* whom he so despised for their impiety and wrong-headedness, the age kicked off by Voltaire and Rousseau and initiated in earnest by the French Revolution.

The literature of Dostoyevsky, Kafka, and Solzhenitsyn speaks of a world that Johnson, as unillusioned and unsentimental as he was about human nature, never envisioned. We now know all too well how *large* a part "of all that human hearts endure" laws and kings, equipped with massive technological powers, *can* cause. But, if one may risk saying so, Johnson's insight goes deeper, so deep that Joseph Wood Krutch attributed to him [in his *Samuel Johnson*], profoundly Christian as he was, the "tragic sense of life." Our deepest and most important struggles, Johnson is saying, are usually not with our environments or our fellows, but with ourselves. "I do not know the man so bold," says Emily Dickinson, "who dares in lonely place, / That awful stranger consciousness deliberately face." Johnson unflinchingly faced the stranger, but with none of the masochism, self-dramatization, and self-pity that are characteristic of the Romantic and modern tempers. He wished and worked to be happy, despite crippling disabilities, disadvantages, hardships, and setbacks, and to make others happy; and he saw in loving God and serving his fellows the right way to accomplish these ends: "each laboring for his own happiness, by promoting within his circle, however narrow, the happiness of others." "The business of a wise man," he said to Boswell, "is to be happy."

Johnson's charitable acts are as famous now as they were unostentatious then; his house was often a veritable menagerie and always a resort for the unfortunate, however unattractive. In Joseph Wood Krutch's delightful imaginary dialogue between Johnson and Thoreau, "The Last Boswell Paper," he catches the truth of Johnson's Christian attitude and actions, and even something of his voice: "Several poor wretches live in my house. They do not contribute to its peace. But if they did not live there I do not know where they would live." And however much Krutch also admired Thoreau, the latter can hardly help sounding thin, glib, and eccentric by comparison, both in the imaginary dialogue and in actual life and work. Johnson has precisely that intellectual, moral, social, and religious ballast and balance that so many of our notable American writers—Emerson, Thoreau, Whitman, Melville—so signally lack; a quality that critics from Poe through Santayana to Mark Van Doren and Quentin Anderson have shown to be lacking in them, and which Emerson himself admired in the English at their best. "A strong common sense, which is not easy to unseat or disturb, marks the English mind for a thousand years," he wrote in 1856 in *English Traits,* attributing to the nation and culture the quality that both Newman and Chesterton attributed to Johnson himself in the highest degree. Of our great American writers, in fact, the two most traditional, social, and ethical—Hawthorne and Eliot—venerated Johnson. Hawthorne visited Lichfield, the town of Johnson's birth, as well as Uttoxeter and other sites important in Johnson's life, on "one of the few purely sentimental pilgrimages" of his life; he walked through the house where Johnson was born and touched things in it "because Johnson's hand and foot might have been in those same places."

The adherence of such writers as Eliot, Lewis, and F. R. Leavis to Johnson is less sentimental and more philosophical and ethical; for them his life, standards, and writings represent and transmit the deepest and soundest moral imagination that literature has ever attained, or life reflected. "Johnson is not," Leavis writes, "like the Romantic poet, the enemy of society, but consciously its representative and its voice, and it is his strength—something inseparable from his greatness—to be so." But Johnson's idea of society was moral, and he constantly fought for it. What he said of Addison was still truer of himself: "He was a man in whose presence nothing reprehensible was out of danger; quick in observing whatever was wrong or ridiculous, and not unwilling to expose it." The "laidback," "tolerant" modern would find him intolerably moralistic, bigoted, sanctimonious, self-righteous, and opinionated, all words that we often employ to hide or justify our own laxity. (As Ogden Nash put it, "what is really mine, / Tolerance, or a rubber spine?")

The truth is that Johnson prepared the way for the great ethical Victorians (e.g., in his hatred of slavery and imperialism and, more generally, of superficiality, amorality, and egotism); for the recovery of the Classical/Christian tradition by writers such as Chesterton, Eliot, and Lewis; and for centrality of belief, thought, and practice anywhere and at any time. He is the least eccentric and provincial of all writers, and therefore he is especially tonic in our time, when, as Joseph Mazzeo has put it, "the idiosyncratic has triumphed over the normative"; and in our place—America—where, as Steven Marcus observed some years ago, "We are still, as Matthew Arnold said of us, . . . a provincial and decentralized society, a society without a center of cultural intelligence and sanity."

No one in life or art provides that intelligence and sanity more dependably than Johnson—a point that Eliot understood, and that a host of recent scholars, including Clifford, Jeffrey Hart, and Donald Greene, have documented. "Without intelligence man is not social, he is only gregarious," Johnson wrote in *A Journey to the Western Islands of Scotland.* This conception of intelligence is insistently, and to many modern ears almost obsessively, moral, for Johnson believed that "he that thinks reasonably must think morally" and insisted, in his lives of Milton and Addison and elsewhere, on the inescapability of moral awareness and obligation as the chief feature of the rational person and of the decent society. ("Prudence and justice are virtues and excellences of all times and all places"; and "we are perpetually moralists.") With great pathos and prescience, Johnson dreaded instances when "society is dissolved into a tumult of individuals, without authority to command, or obligation to obey," where only power and appetite reign. He loved "decent Godly order."

For Johnson, as for his great friend Burke, the heart of society, civilization, and moral order is theism. He would have agreed with the current Wykeham Professor of Logic at Oxford (and would have been delighted that he succeeded an atheist in that Chair) in saying that there is "no satisfactory account of truth or ethics without theism." Johnson was a "mere Christian" who insisted to Boswell that, "For my part, Sir, I think all Christians, whether Papists or Protestants, agree in the essential articles, and that their differences are trivial, and rather political than religious" (June 25, 1763). Yet he knew, as he fought, the acids of skepticism: "Every thing which Hume has advanced against Christianity had passed through my mind long before he wrote. . . . Truth, Sir, is a cow which will yield such people no more milk, and so they are gone to milk the bull" (July 21, 1763). And he hated smugness and bigotry: "Why, Madam, the greatest part of our knowledge is implicit faith; and as to religion, have we heard all that a disciple of Confucius, all that a Mahometan, can say for himself ?" (April 15, 1778). His rational, orthodox, Christian theism had the same balanced quality and character that he attributed to Addison's: a faith "neither weakly credulous nor wantonly skeptical."

But life is more than mind and spirit, as Johnson knew: "To write, and to live, are very different. Many who praise virtue, do no more than praise it." Or as Auden put it, "Lord, forgive the treason of all clerks, / Whose lives are so much worse than their works." Like Milton, Johnson neither practiced nor could praise a "cloistered virtue"; he lived a life that was in many ways agonizingly painful, unhappy, and, until late in life, very poor, in an enormous metropolis seething with misery, poverty, crime, and temptation; and, as his writings show (especially the prayers and diaries), he struggled doggedly against all of them. But he *did* struggle. In him was none of that "Weariness with the striving to be men" that Leslie Fiedler thinks so typical of our time; none of that "weakened sense of human will" that Lionel Trilling came to think "the most distinctive characteristic of the morality of modern times." Johnson had read the seventh chapter of St. Paul's Epistle to the Romans; he knew what his task was, and whence his help came. Will, not intellect, is the key problem of the moral life: "Most of the crimes and miseries of our lives," he wrote, "arise rather from negligence than from ignorance."

Neurotic, shambling, unkempt, often melancholy, never elegant or "attractive" in his person, Johnson nevertheless valued society and sociability, and exercised his wit and will constantly to maintain, extend, and improve them. He loved beautiful, gracious, and chaste women, marriage, the home, and the family. The birthplace and chief haven of human happiness was for him neither solitude, city, nor state—neither Walden Pond nor Vanity Fair—but the home ("to be happy at home is the end of all human endeavor"); and after the untimely death of his wife, the home of the Thrales and the company of his friends and dependents provided him with the humane settings he so loved and defended.

Outside the Gospels, no other man's recorded utterances, whether written or spoken, have ever sounded so *earned,* and therefore so trustworthy; this authority is apparent even in brief phrases. Johnson is never gratuitously vague or glib or smug; never irreverent or portentous; and he always spoke to be understood. "Some people," he told Boswell, "tell you that they let themselves down to the capacity of their hearers. I never do that. I speak uniformly, in as intelligible a manner as I can" (March 27, 1775). He loved quotation, and he gloried in accrediting and extending the Classical/Christian tradition, which he thought was the living water of the ages. Defending the practice of quotation against a critic, he forthrightly declared: "No, Sir, it is a good thing; there is community of mind in it."

Johnson's talk and writing always contain this "community of mind" as well as "the observations of a strong mind operating upon life"; yet he was not a gloomy moralist, and always valued good cheer and humor: "The size of a man's understanding," he once said, "might always be justly measured by his mirth." And this is the man who secretly wrote law lectures for the Vinerian Professor of Law at Oxford; secretly composed a great series of sermons for John Taylor; wrote some of the greatest poems of the eighteenth century, and one of the greatest of any century; wrote three series of the greatest essays in our language; compiled the first great dictionary of our language, much of which was taken over unchanged by the Oxford English Dictionary; composed *The Lives of the Poets,* the finest short biographies in our language; made some of the finest short translations of classical Greek and Latin poetry in existence; wrote powerfully on politics, and especially against imperialism; produced a classic edition of Shakespeare; wrote a novel of which Hilaire Belloc has said, "Every man ought to read *Rasselas,* and every wise man will read it half a dozen times in his life . . . for never was wisdom better put, or more enduringly."

In the admirable *Dictionary Johnson: The Middle Years of Samuel Johnson,* covering the years 1749 to 1763, James L. Clifford noted that at the Ivy Club Johnson was always "uniformly tenacious" when any question of moral obligation was raised, and went on to show how dogged Johnson's ethical imagination was, not only in novel, poems, essays, prayers, and sermons, but in the *Dictionary* itself, "a great storehouse of philosophy, theology, history, and literature . . . an extensive anthology of English prose and verse." There are 116,000 quotations in the *Dictionary,* helping to make it in itself a great work of literature as well as of lexicography, one on which writers such as Carlyle and Browning cut their teeth. In it, as in everything Johnson touched, he was the man of *sapiens et eloquens pietas*—wise and eloquent piety—as well as Quintilian's *bonus rhetor,* the good man speaking well, vindicating, reaffirming, and transmitting a vast body of humane learning and "the ancient orthodox tradition of ethics." To read Johnson, as C. S. Lewis once said of reading Spenser, is "to grow in mental health." (pp. 49-52)

Sanity has no stronger defender, piety no more eloquent spokesman, genius no greater example. (p. 52)

M. D. Aeschliman, "The Good Man Speaking Well," in *National Review,* New York, Vol. XXXVII, January 11, 1985, pp. 49-52.

SOURCES FOR FURTHER STUDY

Bate, W. Jackson. *The Achievement of Samuel Johnson.* New York: Oxford University Press, 1955, 248 p.

Highlights the general themes of Johnson's writings and the character of his thinking.

Courtney, William Prideaux and Smith, David Nichol. *A Bibliography of Samuel Johnson.* Oxford: Clarendon Press, 1968, 185 p.

Definitive primary bibliography of Johnson's works, including title page facsimiles.

Korshin, Paul J., ed. *Johnson after Two Hundred Years*. Philadelphia: University of Pennsylvania Press, 1986, 253 p.

    Collection of essays providing late-twentieth-century perspectives on Johnson's life, intellectual development, and canon.

Nath, Prem, ed. *Fresh Reflections on Samuel Johnson: Essays in Criticism*. Troy, N. Y.: Whitston Publishing Company, 1987, 414 p.

    Collection of essays which consider the impact of Johnson's life and literature on Western thought, including "Sexual Difference and Johnson's Brain" and "Johnson's *Lives* and Augustan Poetry."

Vesterman, William. *The Stylistic Life of Samuel Johnson*. New Brunswick, N.J.: Rutgers University Press, 1977, 139 p.

    Examines Johnson's prose, narrative, biographical, and poetic styles.

Wahba, Magdi, ed. *Johnsonian Studies*. Cairo: Société orientale de publicité, 1962, 350 p.

    Collection of essays by leading Johnsonians, including Donald Greene and Arthur Sherbo.

Ben Jonson

1572?-1637

English dramatist, poet, masque writer, and critic.

INTRODUCTION

Jonson is among the greatest writers and theorists of English literature. A prolific Elizabethan dramatist and a man of letters highly learned in the classics, he profoundly influenced the coming Augustan age through his emphasis on the precepts of Horace, Aristotle, and other early thinkers. While he is now remembered primarily for his satirical comedies, he also distinguished himself as a poet, a preeminent writer of masques, an erudite defender of his work, and the originator of English literary criticism. Jonson's professional reputation is often obscured by his personal notoriety; a bold, independent, and aggressive man, he fashioned for himself an image as the sole arbiter of taste, standing for erudition and the supremacy of classical models against what he perceived as the general populace's ignorant preference for the sensational. While he influenced later writers in each genre that he undertook, his ultimate influence is considered to be a legacy of literary craftsmanship, a strong sense of artistic form and control, and his role in bringing, as Alexander Pope noted, "critical learning into vogue."

Jonson was born in London shortly after the death of his father, a minister who claimed descent from Scottish gentry. Although his family was poor, he was educated at Westminster School under the renowned antiquary William Camden. He apparently left his schooling unwillingly to work with his stepfather as a bricklayer. He then served as a volunteer in the Low Countries in the Dutch war against Spain; reportedly, he defeated a challenger in single combat between the opposing armies, stripping his vanquished opponent of his arms in the classical fashion. Jonson returned to England by 1592 and married about three years later. Although it seems that the union was unhappy, it produced several children, all of whom Jonson outlived. In the years following his marriage, he became an actor, and also wrote numerous get-penny entertainments (financially motivated and quickly composed plays) and respected emendations and additions to Thomas Kyd's *The Spanish Tragedy* (1592). By 1597 he was writing for Philip Henslowe's theatrical company. That year, Henslowe employed Jonson to finish Thomas Nashe's satire *The Isle of Dogs* (now lost), but the play was suppressed for alleged seditious content and Jonson was jailed for a short time. In 1598 the earliest of his extant works, *Every Man in His Humour,* was produced by the Lord Chamberlain's Men with William Shakespeare—who became Jonson's close friend—in the cast. That same year, Jonson fell into further trouble after killing actor Gabriel Spencer in a duel, narrowly escaping the gallows by claiming benefit of clergy (meaning he was shown leniency for proving that he was literate and educated).

Shortly thereafter, writing for the Children of Queen's Chapel, Jonson became embroiled in a public feud with playwrights John Marston and Thomas Dekker. In *Cynthias Revels* (1601) and *Poetaster* (1601), Jonson portrayed himself as the impartial, well-informed judge of art and society and wrote unflattering portraits of these men, who counterattacked with a satiric portrayal of Jonson in the play *Satiromastix; or, The Untrussing of the Humorous Poet* (1602). This brief dispute became known as the "War of the Theatres"; interestingly, scholars speculate that the dispute was mutually contrived in order to further the authors' careers. In any event, Jonson later reconciled with Marston, and collaborated with him and George Chapman in writing *Eastward Hoe* (1605). A joke at the king's expense in this play landed him once again, along with his coauthors, in prison. Once freed, however, Jonson entered a period of good fortune and productivity. He had many friends at court, and James I valued learning highly. His abilities thus did not go unrecognized, and he was frequently called upon to write his popular, elegant masques, such as the *Masque of Blacknesse* (1605). During this period, Jonson also produced his most successful comedies, beginning in 1606 with *Volpone* and following with *Epicoene; or, The Silent Woman* (1609), *The Alchemist* (1610), and *Bartholomew Fayre* (1614). Jonson's Roman tragedies, *Sejanus His Fall* (1603) and *Catiline His Conspiracy* (1611), though monuments to his scholarship, were not well-received due to their rigid imitation of classical tragic forms and pedantic tone.

In 1616 Jonson published his *Workes,* becoming the first English writer to dignify his dramas by terming them "works," and for this perceived presumption he was widely ridiculed. In that year Jonson assumed the responsibilities and privileges of Poet Laureate, though without formal appointment. From 1616 to 1625 he primarily wrote masques for presentation at court, collaborating frequently with poet, architect, and stage designer Inigo Jones. Misfortune, however, marked Jonson's later years. A fire destroyed his library in 1623, and when James I died in 1625, Jonson lost much of his influence at court, though he was named city chronologer in 1628. Later that year, he suffered the first of several strokes which left him bedridden. Meanwhile, Johnson's collaborative relationship with Jones grew strained as the latter's elaborate theatrical spectacles increasingly overshadowed Jonson's dialogue and songs. In 1631 the two parted ways. Jonson produced four plays during the reign of Charles I, and was eventually granted a new pension in 1634. None of these later plays was successful. The rest of his life, spent in retirement, he filled primarily with study and writing; at his death, two unfinished plays were discovered among his mass of papers and manuscripts. Jonson left a financially depleted estate, but was nevertheless buried with honor in Westminster Abbey.

Jonson was recognized as one of the foremost men of letters in his own time and at his creative height rivaled Shakespeare in popularity. Yet his reputation soon declined; his plays in particular, though judged undeniably literate, were considered obsolete, more exercises in scholarship than inventive entertainment. Modern-day appraisals of Jonson, however, have provoked a considerable resurgence of interest in his work. His earliest comedies derive from Roman comedy in form and structure and are noteworthy as models of the comedy of humors, in which each character represents a type dominated by some ruling obsession. Jonson's use of the form in *Every Man in His Humour* and *Every Man out of His Humour* (1599) is considered exemplary, and such characterization continued to be a feature of his work. Of particular significance in appraisals of Jonson are the four comedies produced between 1606 and 1614: *Volpone, Epicoene, The Alchemist,* and *Bartholomew Fayre.* Each exposes some aberration of human appetite through comic exaggeration and periodic moralisms while evincing Jonson's interest in the variety of life and in the villain as a cunning, imaginative artist. *Volpone,* his most famous and most frequently staged work, is also his harshest attack on human vice, specifically, greed. Like *Epicoene* and *The Alchemist,* it mixes didactic intent with scenes of tightly constructed comic counterpoise. The last of Jonson's great plays is the panoramic *Bartholomew Fayre.* Softening the didacticism of his earlier work for the pure enjoyment of Jacobean London, richly and colorfully portrayed in a loosely structured form, Jonson expressed the classical moralist's views of wisdom and folly through a multiplicity of layered, interrelated plots. All four comedies exhibit careful planning executed with classical precision, a command of low speech and colloquialism, and a clear development toward more realistic, three-dimensional characterization.

Critics note that Jonson's later plays, beginning with *The Divell is an Asse* in 1616, betray Jonson's diminishing artistry. These later dramas were dismissed by John Dryden as mere "dotages." It was Dryden who first undertook an extensive analysis of Jonson. While generously likening him to Vergil and calling him "the most learned and judicious writer which any theatre ever had," Dryden's comments also signaled the start of a decline in Jonson's reputation, for his observations included a comparison of Jonson and Shakespeare, one which nodded admiringly toward Jonson, but bowed adoringly before Shakespeare. This comparison colored Jonson's reputation for more than two hundred years, fueled by nineteenth-century Romantic critics, who found Jonson lacking in imagination, delicacy, and passion. T. S. Eliot, writing in 1919, praised Jonson's artistry, arguing that Jonson's reputation had been unfairly damaged by critics who, while acknowledging his erudition, ignored the power of his work. He wrote: "To be universally accepted; to be damned by the praise that quenches all desire to read the book; to be afflicted by the imputation of the virtues which excite the least pleasure; and to be read only by historians and antiquaries—this is the most perfect conspiracy of approval." With this began a revaluation of Jonson, who benefited from modernist reaction against Romanticist sensibility, and who began to be appreciated on his own terms. Jonson is now respected as the greatest English masque writer and as a major figure in seventeenth-century developments in poetry. His poems—whether elegies, songs, celebrative verse, or short love lyrics—reflect a style of plainness and simplicity. Skilfully polished, such poems as "To Penshurst," "Song: To Celia" (better known by its first line, "Drink to me only with thine eyes"), and "To the Memory of My Beloved Master William Shakespeare" exemplify the artistic control he valued so highly. Many critics now agree that most of Jonson's work was essentially experimental in nature, leading the way in the seventeenth-century movement toward classicism. *Timber; or, Discoveries* (1641), one of his most original works, in fact, represents the first English formulation of literary principles as applied through practical critical observation. In this he directly anticipated and influenced Dryden, commonly held as the father of English criticism. Jonson's plays and masques are now often admired for their accurate depictions of seventeenth-century men and women, their mastery of form, and their successful blend of the serious and the comic, the topical and the timeless. His poetry is thought remarkable for its strength, scope, and dignity. Displaying incredible versatility, Jonson resists neat classification. He had, said Eliot, "a fine sense of form, of the purpose for which a particular form is intended . . . ; he was a literary artist even more than he was a man of letters." He consistently put his literary principles into practice in his writing, often achieving in his own verse those qualities which he admired in the classics. Such were the qualities which caused Algernon Charles Swinburne to remark that "not even the ardour of his most fanatical worshippers . . . could exaggerate the actual greatness of his various and marvellous energies."

CRITICAL COMMENTARY

JOHN DRYDEN

(essay date 1668)

[Regarded by many scholars as the father of modern English poetry and criticism, Dryden dominated English literary life during the last four decades of the seventeenth century. In the following excerpt from *Of Dramatic Poesy* (1668), he praises Jonson—here referred to as "Johnson"—for what he considers the dramatist's preeminent role in "perfecting the stage."]

[As for Johnson] if we look upon him while he was himself (for his last plays were but his dotages), I think him the most learned and judicious writer which any theatre ever had. He was a most severe judge of himself, as well as others. One cannot say he wanted wit, but rather that he was frugal of it. In his works you find little to retrench or alter. Wit, and language, and humour also in some measure, we had before him; but something of art was wanting to the Drama, till he came. He managed his strength to more advantage than any who preceded him. You seldom find him making love in any of his scenes, or endeavouring to move the passions; his genius was too sullen and saturnine to do it gracefully, especially when he knew he came after those who performed both to such an height. Humour was his proper sphere; and in that he delighted most to represent mechanic people. He was deeply conversant in the Ancients, both Greek and Latin, and he borrowed boldly from them: there is scarce a poet or historian among the Roman authors of those times when he has not translated in *Sejanus* and *Catiline.* But he has done his robberies so openly, that one may see he fears not to be taxed by any law. He invades authors like a

Principal Works

The Case Is Alterd (drama) 1598

Every Man in His Humor (drama) 1598; also published as Every Man in His Humour, 1616

The Comicall Satyre of Every Man out of His Humor (drama) 1599; also published as Every Man out of His Humour, 1920

Cynthias Revels; or, The Fountain of Self-Love (drama) 1601

Poetaster; or, The Arraignment (drama) 1601

Sejanus His Fall (drama) 1603

Eastward Hoe [with George Chapman and John Marston] (drama) 1605

Masque of Blacknesse (masque) 1605

Volpone; or, The Foxe (drama) 1606

Epicoene; or, The Silent Woman (drama) 1609

The Alchemist (drama) 1610

Catiline His Conspiracy (drama) 1611

Oberon, the Fairy Prince (masque) 1611

Bartholomew Fayre (drama) 1614

The Divell is an Asse; or, The Cheater Cheated (drama) 1616

The Workes of Benjamin Jonson (dramas and poetry) 1616

*A Tale of a Tub (drama) 1633

The Workes of Benjamin Jonson. 2 vols. (dramas, poetry, and prose) 1640-41

†Timber; or, Discoveries, Made upon Men and Matter as They Have Flowed out of His Daily Reading, or Had Their Reflux to His Peculiar Notion of the Times (prose) 1641; published in The Workes of Benjamin Jonson, vol. 2

Ben Jonson. 11 vols. (dramas, poetry, and prose) 1925-52

The Complete Masques of Ben Jonson (masques) 1969

The Complete Poems of Ben Jonson (poetry) 1975

The Complete Plays of Ben Jonson. 4 vols. (dramas) 1981-82

*This work was probably written in 1596 and was later revised.

†This work is sometimes referred to as Sylva or Silva.

---

monarch; and what would be theft in other poets, is only victory in him. With the spoils of these writers he so represents old Rome to us, in its rites, ceremonies, and customs, that if one of their poets had written either of his tragedies, we had seen less of it than in him. If there was any fault in his language, 'twas that he weaved it too closely and laboriously, in his serious plays: perhaps, too, he did a little too much Romanize our tongue, leaving the words which he translated almost as much Latin as he found them: wherein, though he learnedly followed the idiom of their language, he did not enough comply with the idiom of ours. If I would compare him with Shakespeare, I must acknowledge him the more correct poet, but Shakespeare the greater wit. Shakespeare was the Homer, or father of our dramatic poets; Johnson was the Virgil, the pattern of elaborate writing; I admire him, but I love Shakespeare. To conclude of him; as he has given us the most correct plays, so in the precepts which he has laid down in his *Discoveries,* we have as many and profitable rules for perfecting the stage, as any wherewith the French can furnish us.

Having thus spoken of the author, I proceed to the examination of his comedy, *The Silent Woman.*

To begin first with the length of the action; it is so far from exceeding the compass of a natural day, that it takes not up an artificial one. 'Tis all included in the limits of three hours and an half, which is no more than is required for the presentment on the stage. A beauty

perhaps not much observed; if it had, we should not have looked on the Spanish translation of *Five Hours* with so much wonder. The scene of it is laid in London; the latitude of place is almost as little as you can imagine; for it lies all within the compass of two houses, and after the first act, in one. The continuity of scenes is observed more than in any of our plays, except his own *Fox* [*Volpone*] and *Alchymist.* They are not broken above twice or thrice at most in the whole comedy; and in the two best of Corneille's plays, the *Cid* and *Cinna,* they are interrupted once apiece. The action of the play is entirely one; the end or aim of which is the settling Morose's estate on Dauphine. The intrigue of it is the greatest and most noble of any pure unmixed comedy in any language; you see in it many persons of various characters and humours, and all delightful: as first, Morose, or an old man, to whom all noise but his own talking is offensive. (pp. 81-3)

Besides Morose, there are at least nine or ten different characters and humours in *The Silent Woman;* all which persons have several concernments of their own, yet are all used by the poet, to the conducting of the main design to perfection. I shall not waste time in commending the writing of this play; but I will give you my opinion, that there is more wit and acuteness of fancy in it than in any [other] of Ben Johnson's. Besides, that he has here described the conversation of gentlemen in the persons of True-Wit, and his friends, with more gaiety, air, and freedom, than in the rest of his comedies. For the contrivance of the plot, 'tis extreme elaborate, and yet withal easy; for the Λυσιζ, or untying of it, 'tis so admirable, that when it is done, no one of the audience would think the poet could have missed it; and yet it was concealed so much before the last scene, that any other way would sooner have entered into your thoughts. But I dare not take upon me to commend the fabric of it, because it is altogether so full of art, that I must unravel every scene in it to commend it as I ought. And this excellent contrivance is still the more to be admired, because 'tis comedy, where the persons are only of common rank, and their business private, not elevated by passions or high concernments, as in serious plays. Here everyone is a proper judge of all he sees, nothing is represented but that with which he daily converses: so that by consequence all faults lie open to discovery, and few are pardonable. . . . But our poet who was not ignorant of these difficulties, had prevailed himself of all advantages; as he who designs a large leap takes his rise from the highest ground. One of these advantages is that which Corneille has laid down as the greatest which can arrive to any poem, and which he himself could never compass above thrice in all his plays; viz. The making choice of some signal and long-expected day, whereon the action of the play is to depend. This day was that designed by Dauphine for the settling of his uncle's estate upon him; which to compass, he contrives to marry him. That the marriage had been plotted by him long before-hand, is made evident by what he tells True-Wit in the second act, that in one moment he had destroyed what he had been raising many months.

There is another artifice of the poet, which I cannot here omit, because by the frequent practice of it in his comedies he has left it to us almost as a rule; that is, when he has any character or humour wherein he would show a *coup de Maistre*, or his highest skill, he recommends it to your observation by a pleasant description of it before the person first appears. Thus, in *Bartholomew Fair* he gives you the pictures of Numps and Cokes, and in this those of Daw, Lafoole, Morose, and the Collegiate Ladies; all which you hear described before you see them. So that before they come upon the stage, you have a longing expectation of them, which prepares you to receive them favourably; and when they are there, even from their first appearance you are so far acquainted with them, that nothing of their humour is lost to you.

I will observe yet one thing further of this admirable plot; the business of it rises in every act. The second is greater than the first; the third than the second; and so forward to the fifth. There too you see, till the very last scene, new difficulties arising to obstruct the action of the play; and when the audience is brought into despair that the business can naturally be effected, then, and not before, the discovery is made. But that

the poet might entertain you with more variety all this while, he reserves some new characters to show you, which he opens not till the second and third act. In the second Morose, Daw, the Barber, and Otter; in the third the Collegiate Ladies: all which he moves afterwards in by-walks, or under-plots, as diversions to the main design, lest it should grow tedious, though they are still naturally joined with it, and somewhere or other subservient to it. Thus, like a skilful chess-player, by little and little he draws out his men, and makes his pawns of use to his greater persons. (pp. 86-8)

John Dryden, "An Essay of Dramatic Poesy," in *Essays of John Dryden,* edited by W. P. Ker, Russell & Russell, pp. 28-108.

GEORGE SAINTSBURY
(essay date 1887)

[Saintsbury has been called the most influential British literary historian and critic of the late nineteenth and early twentieth centuries. In the following excerpt, he surveys Jonson's plays.]

It may be granted that [Ben Jonson] was rough and arrogant, a scholar who pushed scholarship to the verge of pedantry, a critic who sometimes forgot that though a schoolmaster may be a critic, a critic should not be merely a schoolmaster. His work is saturated with that contempt of the *profanum vulgus* ["common people"] which the *profanum vulgus* (human enough) seldom fails to return. Moreover, it is extremely voluminous, and it is by no means equal. Of his eighteen plays, three only—*Every Man in his Humour, The Alchemist,* and the charming fragment of *The Sad Shepherd*—can be praised as wholes. His lovely *Masques* are probably unread by all but a few scores, if so many in each generation. His noble sinewy prose is, for the most part, unattractive in subject. His minor poems, though not a few of them are known even to smatterers in literature, are as a whole (or at least it would seem so) unknown. Yet his merits are extraordinary. "Never" in his plays (save *The Sad Shepherd*) "tender," and still more rarely "sublime," he yet, in words much better applied to him than to his pupil Dryden, "wrestles with and conquers time." Even his enemies admit his learning, his vigour, his astonishing power of work. What is less generally admitted, despite in one case at least the celebrity of the facts that prove it, is his observation, his invention, and at times his anomalous and seemingly contradictory power of grace and sweetness. There is no more singular example of the proverb, "Out of the eater came forth meat, and out of the strong sweetness," which has been happily applied to Victor Hugo, than the composition, by the rugged author of *Sejanus* and *Catiline,* of

The Devil is an Ass and *Bartholomew Fair,* of such things as

Here lies to each her parent ruth;

or the magnificent song,

Drink to me only with thine eyes;

or the crown and flower of all epitaphs,

Underneath this sable herse.

But these three universally-known poems only express in quintessence a quality of Jonson's which is spread all about his minor pieces, which appears again perfectly in *The Sad Shepherd,* and which he seems to have kept out of his plays proper rather from bravado than for any other reason. . . . [It] may be observed here that [his prose] is saturated with the same literary flavour which pervades all his work. None of his dramatic fellows wrote anything that can compare to it, just as none of them wrote anything that surpasses the songs and snatches in his plays, and the best things in his miscellaneous works. The one title which no competent criticism has ever grudged him is that of best epitaph writer in the English language, and only those who have failed to consider the difficulties and the charm of that class of composition will consider this faint praise. Nevertheless, it was no doubt upon drama that Jonson concentrated his powers, and the unfavourable judgments which have been delivered on him chiefly refer to this.

A good deal of controversy has arisen out of the attribution to him, which is at least as old as *The Return from Parnassus,* of being minded to classicise the English drama. It is certain that he set a value on the Unities which no other English dramatist has set, and that in *The Alchemist* at least he has given something like a perfect example of them, which is at the same time an admirable play. Whether this attention is at all responsible for the defects which are certainly found in his work is a very large question. It cannot be denied that in that work, with perhaps the single exception just mentioned, the reader (it is, except in the case of *Every Man in his Humour,* generations since the playgoer had any opportunity of judging) finds a certain absence of sympathetic attraction, as well as, for all the formal unity of the pieces, a lack of that fusing poetic force which makes detail into a whole. The amazing strength of Jonson's genius, the power with which he has compelled all manner of unlikely elements into his service, is evident enough, but the result usually wants charm. The drawbacks are (always excepting *The Alchemist*) least perceptible in *Every Man in his Humour,* the first sprightly runnings of Jonson's fancy, the freshest example of his sharp observation of the humours or follies of contemporary mankind. Later he sometimes

overdid this observation, or rather he failed to bring its results sufficiently into poetic or dramatic form, and, therefore, is too much for an age and too little for all time. But *Every Man in his Humour* is really charming. Bobadil, Master Stephen, and Kitely attain to the first rank of dramatic characters, and others are not far behind them in this respect. The next play, *Every Man out of his Humour,* is a great contrast, being, as even the doughty Gifford admits, distinctly uninteresting as a whole, despite numerous fine passages. Perhaps a little of its want of attraction must be set down to a pestilent habit of Jonson's, which he had at one time thought of applying to *Every Man in his Humour,* the habit of giving foreign, chiefly Italian, appellations to his characters, describing, and as it were labelling them—Deliro, Macilente, and the like. This gives an air of unreality, a figurehead and type character. *Cynthia's Revels* has the same defects, but is to some extent saved by its sharp raillery of euphuism. With *The Poetaster* Jonson began to rise again. I think myself that the personages and machinery of the Augustan Court would be much better away, and that the implied satire on contemporaries would be tedious if, as it fortunately can, it could not be altogether neglected. But in spite of these drawbacks, the piece is good. Of *Sejanus* and Jonson's later Roman play *Catiline* I think, I confess, better than the majority of critics appear to think. That they have any very intense tragic interest will, indeed, hardly be pretended, and the unfortunate but inevitable comparison with *Coriolanus* and *Julius Caesar* has done them great and very unjust harm. Less human than Shakespere's "godlike Romans" (who are as human as they are godlike), Jonson's are undoubtedly more Roman, and this, if it is not entirely an attraction, is in its way a merit. But it was not till after *Sejanus* that the full power of Jonson appeared. His three next plays, *Volpone, Epicoene,* and *The Alchemist,* could not have been written by any one but himself, and, had they not been written, would have left a gap in English which nothing from any other literature could supply. If his attitude had been a little less virtuous and a little more sarcastic, Jonson would in these three plays have anticipated Swift. Of the three, I prefer the first and the last—the last being the best of all. *Epicoene* or the *Silent Woman* was specially liked by the next generation because of its regularity, and of the skill with which the various humours are all wrought into the main plot. Both these things are undeniable, and many of the humours are in themselves amusing enough. But still there is something wanting, which is supplied in *Volpone* and *The Alchemist.* It has been asked whether that disregard of probability, which is one of Jonson's greatest faults, does not appear in the recklessness with which "The Fox" exposes himself to utter ruin, not so much to gratify any sensual desire or obtain any material advantage, as simply to indulge his combined hypocrisy and cynicism to the very utmost. The answer to this question will very much depend on each reader's taste and experience. It is undeniable that there have been examples of perverse indulgence in wickedness for wickedness' sake, which, rare as they are, go far to justify the creation of Volpone. But the unredeemed villany of the hero, with whom it is impossible in any way to sympathise, and the sheer brutality of the fortune-hunting dupes who surround him, make it easier to admire than to like the play. I have little doubt that Jonson was to some extent sensible of this, for the comic episode or underplot of Sir Politick and Lady Would-be is very much more loosely connected with the centre interest (it is only by courtesy that it can be said to be connected at all), than is usual with him, and this is an argument in favour of its having been introduced as a makeweight.

From the drawbacks of both these pieces *The Alchemist* is wholly free. Jonson here escaped his usual pitfall of the unsympathetic, for the vices and follies he satirises are not loathsome, only contemptible at worst, and not always that. He found an opportunity of exercising his extraordinary faculty of concentration as he nowhere else did, and has given us in Sir Epicure Mammon a really magnificent picture of concupiscence, of sensual appetite generally, sublimed by heat of imagination into something really poetic. The triumvirate of adventurers, Subtle, Dol and Face (for Dol has virile qualities), are not respectable, but one does not hate them; and the gulls are perfection. If any character could be spared it is the "Angry Boy," a young person whose humours, as Jonson himself admits of another character elsewhere, are "more tedious than diverting." *The Alchemist* was followed by *Catiline*, and *Catiline* by *Bartholomew Fair*, a play in which singularly vivid and minute pictures of manners, very amusing sketches of character, and some capital satire on the Puritans, do not entirely redeem a profusion of the coarsest possible language and incident. *The Devil is an Ass* comes next in time, and though no single character is the equal of Zeal-of-the-land Busy in *Bartholomew Fair*, the play is even more amusing. The four last plays, *The Staple of News, The Magnetic Lady, The New Inn,* and *The Tale of a Tub*, which Jonson produced after long absence from the stage, were not successful, and were both unkindly and unjustly called by Dryden "Ben's Dotages" [see excerpt dated 1668]. As for the charming *Sad Shepherd*, it was never acted, and is now unfinished, though it is believed that the poet completed it. It stands midway as a pastoral *Féerie* between his regular plays and the great collection of ingenious and graceful masques and entertainments, which are at the top of all such things in England (unless *Comus* be called a masque), and which are worth comparing with the ballets and spectacle pieces of Molière. Perhaps a complete survey of Jonson's work indicates, as his greatest defect, the want of passion. He could be vigorous, he could be dignified, he could be broadly humorous, and,

as has been said, he could combine with these the apparently incompatible, or, at least, not closely-connected faculty of grace. Of passion, of rapture, there is no trace in him, except in the single instance—in fire mingled with earth—of Sir Epicure Mammon. (pp. 177-82)

George Saintsbury, "The Second Dramatic Period—Shakespeare," in his *A History of Elizabethan Literature,* 1887. Reprint by The Macmillan Company, 1924, pp. 157-206.

T. S. ELIOT
(essay date 1919)

[An American-born British poet and critic, Eliot was a vocal champion of literary Modernism. In the following excerpt from an essay originally published in 1919, he examines the form and intellectual value of Jonson's work.]

The reputation of Jonson has been of the most deadly kind that can be compelled upon the memory of a great poet. To be universally accepted; to be damned by the praise that quenches all desire to read the book; to be afflicted by the imputation of the virtues which excite the least pleasure; and to be read only by historians and antiquaries—this is the most perfect conspiracy of approval. For some generations the reputation of Jonson has been carried rather as a liability than as an asset in the balance-sheet of English literature. No critic has succeeded in making him appear pleasurable or even interesting. (p. 104)

Yet there are possibilities for Jonson even now. We have no difficulty in seeing what brought him to this pass; how, in contrast, not with Shakespeare, but with Marlowe, Webster, Donne, Beaumont, and Fletcher, he has been paid out with reputation instead of enjoyment. He is no less a poet than these men, but his poetry is of the surface. Poetry of the surface cannot be understood without study; for to deal with the surface of life, as Jonson dealt with it, is to deal so deliberately that we too must be deliberate, in order to understand. Shakespeare, and smaller men also, are in the end more difficult, but they offer something at the start to encourage the student or to satisfy those who want nothing more; they are suggestive, evocative, a phrase, a voice; they offer poetry in detail as well as in design. So does Dante offer something, a phrase everywhere . . . even to readers who have no Italian; and Dante and Shakespeare have poetry of design as well as of detail. But the polished veneer of Jonson reflects only the lazy reader's fatuity; unconscious does not respond to unconscious; no swarms of inarticulate feelings are aroused. The immediate appeal of Jonson is to the mind; his emotional tone is not in the single verse, but in the design of the whole. But not many people are capable of discovering for themselves the beauty which is only found after labour; and Jonson's industrious readers have been those whose interest was historical and curious, and those who have thought that in discovering the historical and curious interest they had discovered the artistic value as well. When we say that Jonson requires study, we do not mean study of his classical scholarship or of seventeenth-century manners. We mean intelligent saturation in his work as a whole; we mean that in order to enjoy him at all, we must get to the centre of his work and his temperament, and that we must see him unbiased by time, as a contemporary. And to see him as a contemporary does not so much require the power of putting ourselves into seventeenth-century London as it requires the power of setting Jonson in our London: a more difficult triumph of divination.

It is generally conceded that Jonson failed as a tragic dramatist; and it is usually agreed that he failed because his genius was for satiric comedy and because of the weight of pedantic learning with which he burdened his two tragic failures. The second point marks an obvious error of detail; the first is too crude a statement to be accepted; to say that he failed because his genius was unsuited to tragedy is to tell us nothing at all. Jonson did not write a good tragedy, but we can see no reason why he should not have written one. If two plays so different as *The Tempest* and *The Silent Woman* are both comedies, surely the category of tragedy could be made wide enough to include something possible for Jonson to have done. But the classification of tragedy and comedy, while it may be sufficient to mark the distinction in a dramatic literature of more rigid form and treatment—it may distinguish Aristophanes from Euripides—is not adequate to a drama of such variations as the Elizabethans. Tragedy is a crude classification for plays so different in their tone as *Macbeth, The Jew of Malta,* and *The Witch of Edmonton;* and it does not help us much to say that *The Merchant of Venice* and *The Alchemist* are comedies. Jonson had his own scale, his own instrument. The merit which *Catiline* possesses is the same merit that is exhibited more triumphantly in *Volpone; Catiline* fails, not because it is too laboured and conscious, but because it is not conscious enough; because Jonson in this play was not alert to his own idiom, not clear in his mind as to what his temperament wanted him to do. In *Catiline* Jonson conforms, or attempts to conform, to conventions; not to the conventions of antiquity, which he had exquisitely under control, but to the conventions of tragico-historical drama of his time. It is not the Latin erudition that sinks *Catiline,* but the application of that erudition to a form which was not the proper vehicle for the mind which had amassed the erudition. (pp. 105-07)

[In *Catiline*] we find that the best scene in the body of the play is one which cannot be squeezed into a tragic frame, and which appears to belong to satiric comedy. The scene between Fulvia and Galla and Sempronia is a living scene in a wilderness of oratory. And as it recalls other scenes—there is a suggestion of the college of ladies in *The Silent Woman*—it looks like a comedy scene. And it appears to be satire. . . . This scene is no more comedy than it is tragedy, and the "satire" is merely a medium for the essential emotion. Jonson's drama is only incidentally satire, because it is only incidentally a criticism upon the actual world. It is not satire in the way in which the work of Swift or the work of Molière may be called satire: that is, it does not find its source in any precise emotional attitude or precise intellectual criticism of the actual world. It is satire perhaps as the work of Rabelais is satire; certainly not more so. The important thing is that if fiction can be divided into creative fiction and critical fiction, Jonson's is creative. That he was a great critic, our first great critic, does not affect this assertion. Every creator is also a critic; Jonson was a conscious critic, but he was also conscious in his creations. (pp. 109-10)

Largely on the evidence of the two Humour plays, it is sometimes assumed that Jonson is occupied with types; typical exaggerations, or exaggerations of type. The Humour definition, the expressed intention of Jonson, may be satisfactory for these two plays. *Every Man in his Humour* is the first mature work of Jonson, and the student of Jonson must study it; but it is not the play in which Jonson found his genius: it is the last of his plays to read first. If one reads *Volpone,* and after that rereads the *Jew of Malta;* then returns to Jonson and reads *Bartholomew Fair, The Alchemist, Epicoene* and *The Devil is an Ass,* and finally *Catiline,* it is possible to arrive at a fair opinion of the poet and the dramatist.

The Humour, even at the beginning, is not a type, as in Marston's satire, but a simplified and somewhat distorted individual with a typical mania. In the later work, the Humour definition quite fails to account for the total effect produced. The characters of Shakespeare are such as might exist in different circumstances than those in which Shakespeare sets them. The latter appear to be those which extract from the characters the most intense and interesting realization; but that realization has not exhausted their possibilities. Volpone's life, on the other hand, is bounded by the scene in which it is played; in fact, the life is the life of the scene and is derivatively the life of Volpone; the life of the character is inseparable from the life of the drama. This is not dependence upon a background, or upon a substratum of fact. The emotional effect is single and simple. Whereas in Shakespeare the effect is due to the way in which the characters *act upon* one another, in Jonson it is given by the way in which the characters *fit in* with each other. The artistic result of

Volpone is not due to any effect that Volpone, Mosca, Corvino, Corbaccio, Voltore have upon each other, but simply to their combination into a whole. And these figures are not personifications of passions; separately, they have not even that reality, they are constituents. It is a similar indication of Jonson's method that you can hardly pick out a line of Jonson's and say confidently that it is great poetry; but there are many extended passages to which you cannot deny that honour. (pp. 111-13)

Jonson is the legitimate heir of Marlowe. . . . And, if Jonson's comedy is a comedy of humours, then Marlowe's tragedy, a large part of it, is a tragedy of humours. But Jonson has too exclusively been considered as the typical representative of a point of view toward comedy. He has suffered from his great reputation as a critic and theorist, from the effects of his intelligence. We have been taught to think of him as the man, the dictator (confusedly in our minds with his later namesake), as the literary politician impressing his views upon a generation; we are offended by the constant reminder of his scholarship. We forget the comedy in the humours, and the serious artist in the scholar. Jonson has suffered in public opinion, as anyone must suffer who is forced to talk about his art.

If you examine the first hundred lines or more of *Volpone* the verse appears to be in the manner of Marlowe, more deliberate, more mature, but without Marlowe's inspiration. It looks like mere "rhetoric," certainly not "deeds and language such as men do use"! It appears to us, in fact, forced and flagitious bombast. That it is not "rhetoric," or at least not vicious rhetoric, we do not know until we are able to review the whole play. For the consistent maintenance of this manner conveys in the end an effect not of verbosity, but of bold, even shocking and terrifying directness. We have difficulty in saying exactly what produces this simple and single effect. It is not in any ordinary way due to management of intrigue. Jonson employs immense dramatic constructive skill: it is not so much skill in plot as skill in doing without a plot. He never manipulates as complicated a plot as that of *The Merchant of Venice;* he has in his best plays nothing like the intrigue of Restoration comedy. In *Bartholomew Fair* it is hardly a plot at all; the marvel of the play is the bewildering rapid chaotic action of the fair; it is the fair itself, not anything that happens to take place in the fair. In *Volpone,* or *The Alchemist,* or *The Silent Woman,* the plot is enough to keep the players in motion; it is rather an "action" than a plot. The plot does not hold the play together; what holds the play together is a unity of inspiration that radiates into plot and personages alike.

We have attempted to make more precise the sense in which it was said that Jonson's work is "of the surface"; carefully avoiding the word "superficial." For there is work contemporary with Jonson's which is su-perficial in a pejorative sense in which the word cannot be applied to Jonson—the work of Beaumont and Fletcher. If we look at the work of Jonson's great contemporaries, Shakespeare, and also Donne and Webster and Tourneur (and sometimes Middleton), have a depth, a third dimension, as Mr. Gregory Smith rightly calls it, which Jonson's work has not. Their words have often a network of tentacular roots reaching down to the deepest terrors and desires. Jonson's most certainly have not; but in Beaumont and Fletcher we may think that at times we find it. . . . But the evocative quality of the verse of Beaumont and Fletcher depends upon a clever appeal to emotions and associations which they have not themselves grasped; it is hollow. It is superficial with a vacuum behind it; the superficies of Jonson is solid. It is what it is; it does not pretend to be another thing. But it is so very conscious and deliberate that we must look with eyes alert to the whole before we apprehend the significance of any part. (pp. 113-17)

Jonson behaved as the great creative mind that he was: he created his own world, a world from which his followers, as well as the dramatists who were trying to do something wholly different, are excluded. (p. 117)

Now, we may say . . . that Falstaff or a score of Shakespeare's characters have a "third dimension" that Jonson's have not. This will mean, not that Shakespeare's spring from the feelings or imagination and Jonson's from the intellect or invention; they have equally an emotional source; but that Shakespeare's represent a more complex tissue of feelings and desires, as well as a more supple, a more susceptible temperament. Falstaff is not only the roast Malmesbury ox with the pudding in his belly; he also "grows old," and, finally, his nose is as sharp as a pen. He was perhaps the *satisfaction* of more, and of more complicated feelings; and perhaps he was, as the great tragic characters must have been, the offspring of deeper, less apprehensible feelings: deeper, but not necessarily stronger or more intense, than those of Jonson. It is obvious that the spring of the difference is not the difference between feeling and thought, or superior insight, superior perception, on the part of Shakespeare, but his susceptibility to a greater range of emotion, and emotion deeper and more obscure. But his characters are no more "alive" than are the characters of Jonson.

The world they live in is a larger one. But small worlds—the worlds which artists create—do not differ only in magnitude; if they are complete worlds, drawn to scale in every part, they differ in kind also. And Jonson's world has this scale. His type of personality found its relief in something falling under the category of burlesque or farce—though when you are dealing with a *unique* world, like his, these terms fail to appease the desire for definition. It is not, at all events, the farce of Molière: the latter is more analytic, more an intellectual redistribution. It is not defined by the word "satire." Jonson poses as a satirist. But satire like Jonson's is great in the end not by hitting off its object, but by creating it; the satire is merely the means which leads to the aesthetic result, the impulse which projects a new world into a new orbit. In *Every Man in his Humour* there is a neat, a very neat, comedy of humours. In discovering and proclaiming in this play the new genre Jonson was simply recognizing, unconsciously, the route which opened out in the proper direction for his instincts. His characters are and remain, like Marlowe's, simplified characters; but the simplification does not consist in the dominance of a particular humour or monomania. That is a very superficial account of it. The simplification consists largely in reduction of detail, in the seizing of aspects relevant to the relief of an emotional impulse which remains the same for that character, in making the character conform to a particular setting. This stripping is essential to the art, to which is also essential a flat distortion in the drawing; it is an art of caricature, of great caricature, like Marlowe's. It is a great caricature, which is beautiful; and a great humour, which is serious. The "world" of Jonson is sufficiently large; it is a world of poetic imagination; it is sombre. He did not get the third dimension, but he was not trying to get it.

If we approach Jonson with less frozen awe of his learning, with a clearer understanding of his "rhetoric" and its applications, if we grasp the fact that the knowledge required of the reader is not archaeology but knowledge of Jonson, we can derive not only instruction in non-Euclidean humanity—but enjoyment. We can even apply him, be aware of him as a part of our literary inheritance craving further expression. Of all the dramatists of his time, Jonson is probably the one whom the present age would find the most sympathetic, if it knew him. There is a brutality, a lack of sentiment, a polished surface, a handling of large bold designs in brilliant colours, which ought to attract about three thousand people in London and elsewhere. At least, if we had a contemporary Shakespeare and a contemporary Jonson, it would be the Jonson who would arouse the enthusiasm of the intelligentsia! Though he is saturated in literature, he never sacrifices the theatrical qualities—theatrical in the most favourable sense—to literature or to the study of character. His work is a titanic show. But Jonson's masques, an important part of his work, are neglected; our flaccid culture lets shows and literature fade, but prefers faded literature to faded shows. There are hundreds of people who have read [John Milton's] *Comus* to ten who have read the *Masque of Blackness. Comus* contains fine poetry, and poetry exemplifying some merits to which Jonson's masque poetry cannot pretend. Nevertheless, *Comus* is the death of the masque; it is the transition of a form of art—even of a form which existed for but a short generation—into "literature," literature cast in a form which has lost

its application. Even though *Comus* was a masque at Ludlow Castle, Jonson had, what Milton came perhaps too late to have, a sense for living art; his art was applied. The masques can still be read, and with pleasure, by anyone who will take the trouble—a trouble which in this part of Jonson is, indeed, a study of antiquities— to imagine them in action, displayed with the music, costumes, dances, and the scenery of Inigo Jones. They are additional evidence that Jonson had a fine sense of form, of the purpose for which a particular form is intended; evidence that he was a literary artist even more than he was a man of letters. (pp. 119-22)

T. S. Eliot, "Ben Jonson," *in his The Sacred Wood: Essays on Poetry and Criticism,* Barnes & Noble, 1960, 104-22.

KENNETH REXROTH
(essay date 1968)

[In the following excerpt from a 1968 essay, Rexroth praises the emotional power of Jonson's plays, particularly *Volpone.*]

Ben Jonson was very much part of the European intellectual community of his time, as was Milton shortly after him. We forget that the great movement of re-evaluation of all values that made both the Renaissance and the Reformation was led by what today we would call literary critics. Whether the reference is to Erasmus or Ficino or Scaliger, whether to the Bible or Plato or Horace or Aristotle, the questions "What is the authentic text?" and "What does it really mean?"—followed by the answers and translation into the vernacular— these were the intellectual germinators of revolution, as, in our time, economics is, or physics, or psychology—Marx, Einstein, or Freud. Only if we keep this in mind can we appreciate Jonson as a source of power to his colleagues.

He was not just a roisterer or prince of poets in the Mermaid and the other bohemian taverns of his day. He was a systematic literary critic, a grammarian, an aesthetician devoted to the reestablishment of poetry and drama as formally controlled, socially normative arts—this is what revival of classicism meant. *Volpone* is purposive in a way in which no Shakespearean comedies are before *A Winter's Tale* and *Twelfth Night,* and it is far more deliberately purposive than any of Shakespeare's tragedies, except possibly *Julius Caesar* and *Coriolanus.* Only Machiavelli's *Mandragola* can be compared with *Volpone* as equal to equal. Machiavelli was a revolutionary intellectual, a man of wider general experience than all but a few writers in history. Jonson was no Machiavelli; he never had his hands on the le-vers of power; but he seems to have had a much greater range of experience than other Elizabethan dramatists. He knew all kinds and conditions of men and evidently sought deliberately to live as full a life as he could.

Most writers about Jonson begin by apologizing for him. He was scholarly in a way in which no literary scholars are today. Literary scholarship mattered at the beginning of the seventeenth century; it was harder work. Jonson knew much more about erudite matters than scholars know today. And then, of course, he was not an academician but a creative artist, a bohemian intellectual, and a man who was largely self-educated. These are all great virtues, but not to modern critics. Besides, he was patently a man of the world—his plays are intensely worldly, in a positive sense. They baffle the cloistered literary mind and antagonize the schoolmaster. A play by Jonson is often presented as "hard to read" or as "seldom-performed closet drama." Nothing could be less true.

Volpone, The Alchemist, and *Bartholomew Fair* are among the most theatrical and most entertaining plays ever written. They are immense fun to see, to act in, to design for. They are as far removed from closet drama as can be, for above all other English playwrights, Jonson, in his three great comedies, uses words as springs of action; there is business lurking in every line—funny business.

One thing they are not is topical satire. They deal, like the plays of Plautus, Terence, and Menander, with generalized follies and vices, with enduring sin rather than the passing crimes of politics and history. They could take place anywhere. The topical jokes and allusions that abound are not only inessential; today they go unnoticed unless explained in a footnote. Shaw wrote lengthy prefaces as notes to his plays. In a hundred years they will have to have even lengthier notes, and even then will be difficult to grasp emotionally. In a hundred years, Jonson's plays will still be emotionally comprehensible with no notes at all.

Taste in drama has changed; once again the playwright is the scourge of folly—not of capitalism, industrialism, or the double standard. Artaud, Genet, Ionesco, and Beckett are moral rather than political or "social" playwrights. We have come to realize that greed and covetousness, power-hunger and hypocrisy are more important than the temporary social arrangements that facilitate them. So Jonson has been revived with great success all over the world, on both sides of the tattered Iron Curtain. *Volpone,* a situation comedy, based on a purely Roman situation as unreal to a seventeenth- as to a twentieth-century audience, is nevertheless completely germane to the *human* situation—in New York or San Francisco or Berlin or Moscow or Tokyo.

Luxury, greed, avarice, covetousness, fraud—all the evils of which money is the root—are analyzed and parsed out, but in action, in a kind of savage hilarity. Is this the business ethic? Critics have said the play was a sociological criticism of the new mercantile bourgeoisie. If this were all, it would never go on the modern stage. The lust for gold is not a peculiarity of a class or an epoch.

Although every moment of *Volpone* is funny, the cumulative effect is grim indeed—so grim that it ceases to be a comedy, even a black comedy, and becomes a tragedy of human folly.

It generates a growing horror, and rightly so, for it is a feast of death—a double death, for the feast is fraudulent. The characters are named after creatures that feed on carrion; thus Jonson drives home Dante's point—the worship of money is life-denying, a love of corpses, and a feeding on filth. What saves the play from melodrama is Jonson's remorseless logic. It is put together like a fine precision instrument. Every speech, every action counts. All move together like the gears of a watch. We don't see the wheels go round unless we are deliberately focusing on them, but Jonson's dramatic wheels grind like the mills of the gods.

It is this perfection of structure and function that ennobles the play. The purity of form redeems the evil—not in the plot, but in us. And this, says Jonson, is the only way we cope with analogous experiences in life. Rational control transcends the chaos of the world. (pp. 139-41)

Kenneth Rexroth, "Ben Jonson: Volpone," in his *Classics Revisited,* New Directions, 1986, pp. 139-41.

L. A. BEAURLINE

(essay date 1978)

[Beaurline is an American critic and scholar. In the following excerpt, he discusses Jonson's method of exhausting a subject through speech, scene construction, and satire, using *The Alchemist* and *Epicoene* as examples.]

It is hard to explain the characteristic design of Jonson's four best plays [*Volpone, Epicoene, The Alchemist,* and *Bartholomew Fair*] . . . because they are not only very different from each other but they are so complex that no single pattern accounts for their form. Nevertheless we feel that something about the way that *Epicoene* and *The Alchemist* unfold distinguishes them and casts light on the incipient form of the first and the residual form of the last. Some great motive generates their plots; some daemon controls their design. Apparently Jonson discovered a better way of writing comedies as he worked on *Volpone,* and part of it may be related to [a] primitive sense of metaphor . . . , whereby cunning men use language to disguise thought or put on a "suppose." Their insinuating speeches deceive impressionable people by playing upon base impulses, but they delight the rest of us. Certainly Jonson has his characters use such two-valued persuasive speech again and again in the plays that followed *Volpone,* speech that praises what it secretly disparages . . . and speech that dispraises while it entertains us with the whole subject. . . . Certainly tricksters use language like this, so it would be natural for dialogue in plays about confidence games, but . . . this way of using dramatic speech is not peculiar to Jonson. In any case, such two-valued dialogue creates local more often than general effects.

Another motive toward design, also found in dialogue, has more than local effects. It is the impulse to amplify or expatiate on a subject to the limits of endurance. At first it takes root in scenes of vexation—for instance when Lady Would-be visits Volpone. . . . Finding him ill, in bed, a captive audience, she drowns him in a flood of words, in "a very torrent," as she prescribes medicine and discourses on all the arts of a modern educated woman. Like the noise of bells in time of plague, her everlasting voice inflicts real pain on Volpone when he pretends to be in pain for other reasons. So they talk at cross purposes, he complaining of her and she commiserating with him for the very pain that she gives. It is one of those comic ironies that Jonson liked so much, when the cozener is accidentally cozened and the pretense is suddenly very real. It is odd but true that amplitude of speech turns out to be highly efficient, because the audience sees its operation from a wider perspective than the speakers do. The energy of this prolific talk is present in greater and greater quantities as Jonson worked on his next comedies, and it seems to press the episodes to their limits of fullness, so much as to take over the design of the plays themselves. Speech, scene, and play take on the form of an anatomy, which exhausts as it examines serially all the parts of a limited subject. (pp. 193-94)

[In his middle comedies, Jonson] rejected not only episodic or narrative form but subplot, overplot, and parallel plot. The last subplot he wrote was in *Volpone,* and already he tried to make it co-present with the rest of the action more than was usual with his contemporaries. After that he placed stricter limits on time, place, and event, composing with more crowded scenes, and he called attention to the gradations of tone and meaning, [Madeleine] Doran may have meant this in her comments [in her *Endeavors of Art* (1954)] on Jonson's "remorseless and ironic logic" in the unraveling of his plots, which has a "perfect rationality of cause and consequence in Jonson's closed world." . . . On the other hand, Shakespeare lets "happy chance" determine the

outcome. . . . These differences may be caused by Jonson's greater dependence on one main intrigue, but the remorseless logic also seems to me less rational and more illusory as the play works out an elaborate pattern, the repetition of a basic motive with seemingly infinite gradations and variations of application. How often, for instance, he relies on a situation where a foolishly wise fellow gulls himself; how perfectly circular and infinitely various is the plot that eventually brings the cleverest manipulator to out-do himself. The logic of such a plot derives not so much from strict application of cause and effect as from the accumulated expectations of the audience, the illusion of perpetual irony and the sense of graduated intensity, inversion built upon inversion, until the final self-laceration or renunciation must be enacted. (p. 197)

Passages in *Discoveries* and in "To the Reader" of *The Alchemist* suggest that Jonson had a due respect for lively invention and full expression, but disliked excess in style and in things. He had an abiding interest in fitness that demanded that there be conscious limits to everything. Since brevity and restraint and propriety made good prose, he criticized those who judge style "wholly by bulk, think rude things greater than polished; and scattered more numerous than composed." He scorned those who turn over books and write out "what they presently find or meet, without choice" and those who "speak all they can (however unfitly)"; whereas he admired "composition," "election," "wisdom in dividing." Limits come up again in his comments (after Heinsius) on magnitude of plot. The plot should seek its "utmost bound," and "every bound, for the nature of the subject, is esteemed the best that is largest till it can increase no more; so it behooves the action in a tragedy or comedy to be let grow, till the necessity ask a conclusion." . . . There is not a mean-spirited narrowness here, but a concern for increase and for boundaries. These pronouncements do not add up to very much of a theory of form, and they are woefully inadequate to describe Jonson's art, for his practice is almost always better than his theory. (p. 199)

The plots of *The Alchemist* and *Epicoene* are like the working out of a series of permutations with a fixed number of constants and one variable. What are the maximum number of combinations of character and situation that can be represented on-stage within the limits of the subject without repeating? The resultant form of the plays in Jonson's middle period seems curiously tight, but the actions are less well knit than were the best popular or courtly comedies of his age. We can easily follow the development of two or three threads of action in a typical comedy, such as *Twelfth Night, The Shoemaker's Holiday,* or *Friar Bacon and Friar Bungay,* whereas in *The Alchemist* and *Epicoene* when Jonson seems to have found his métier in English settings, there appear a welter of characters and episodes, whirling within a

Title page of Jonson's *Workes,* 1616.

central situation. The unity of these plays has been variously explained in terms of image clusters, of a central extravagant conceit, and most recently of an adaptation of the technique of the morality play. We should appreciate the insights in such interpretations, and I think it is reasonable to believe that Jonson was partly indebted to the late moralities and that he was interested in the art of old Greek comedy, but for the moment I want to follow the impulse toward a kind of controlled completeness, to see if it will bring us a little closer to Jonson's design. *The Alchemist* . . . offers a clear example of this triumph of artifice, so I will comment on it first.

One reason for the play's power is the way Jonson has fashioned the material into something like a compact series. Let us imagine the difficulties that he had to overcome. Assume that he began with the idea for a play about a confidence game—the fake alchemy game—for which he needed at least three principal rogues—an inside man, some bait, and a "rope" or outside man (Subtle, Dol Common, and Face). Once he was committed to his confidence men, he needed a large number of victims or "fish," for the sake of vari-

ety and surprise and to enhance the audience's sense of the power of the "cunning man" and his colleagues. It would be dull to play with only one or two fish, so Jonson chose a representative group, seven people who display a limited range of the social spectrum of a city (and two country folk), from a knight down to a tobacconist, from a shrewd fellow like Surly to an utter fool like Dapper.

But Jonson's choice of numerous and carefully discriminated clients immediately created new problems of unity, because the play was likely to break up into episodes. As early as *Every Man out of His Humor* . . . he recognized the danger of episodic actions. . . . But in *The Alchemist* the interviews with the victims had to be kept as separate as possible for the confidence game to work; consequently Jonson made this need a major part of the tension. He has the second visitor come right on the heels of the first, the third on the heels of the second, so that Face and Subtle always have too little time, and they have to hustle Dapper offstage (put him "on the send," to get his money, as con men say), in order to make room for Drugger. At first the transitions between episodes are leisurely, later they are quickened. This illusion is suggested to the audience by little remarks such as "Pray god, I ha' not stayed too long," . . . "O, no, not yet this hour," . . . "God's lid, we never thought of him till now. Where is he?" . . . By the middle of Act III the crowding has become so dense and so absurd that something has to break. The stupidest gulls—Dapper, Drugger, and Kastril—are dealt with simultaneously, efficiently making the advice to Drugger serve as an example to Dapper. Mammon has come too soon, so Dapper must be pushed into the privy with gingerbread in his mouth. This is the first serious muddle due to overlapping clients.

By the middle of Act IV, the first crisis of the play, the overlap becomes more threatening, with two clients, Mammon and the Spanish nobleman, asking for the services of Dol Common, so that a new exchange must be made. Typical of Face's genius for improvisation, Dame Pliant is given to the Spaniard. Then the first major triumph occurs when Mammon has been gulled and successfully "brushed off." Immediately . . . there follows a second crisis, a nearly complete disaster, for Surly has told Dame Pliant how she has been cheated, Subtle collapses, but Face counter-reverses and saves the day by turning the other victims upon their would-be deliverer. Economy is the watchword. If more and more clients are going to fill the stage, Face will put them to use as ingeniously as possible and employ them in all possible combinations. Composing the scene artistically, using subordinate characters as his tools, he induces Kastril to try out his new technique of arguing; Ananias is shown the papist in his Spanish slops and cries against the "profane, lewd, superstitious, and idolatrous breeches." So they drive Surly offstage. The rogues breathe a sigh of relief, just as a new disaster comes to their door—Lovewit has returned without warning.

The rest of the plot is built in the same way, forming a compact series with repeated turns and counter-turns, with successively greater crises and more and more people crowding onstage. Face's wit is always equal to each crisis, only to be surprised by a greater challenge. At each maneuver the situation becomes funnier, and at each turn the characters are drained of some of their humanity. The mess of brass, pewter, and iron in the basement is a leitmotif that recurs through the whole play, a proof of Face's power of intrigue. Like the furnace in the next room that will eventually blow up; the metal hoard is never seen by the audience, but it figures prominently in the dialogue, and Face rings changes on it wondrously. The iron was contributed by Mammon, sold to Ananias and Tribulation as widows' and orphans' goods, sold again to Kastril to furnish his house, and finally given to Lovewit as an inducement to protect Face's secret. Everything except the metal that we never see dissolves into nothing, an insubstantial show. Such art is the epitome of Jonson's skill—to vary, to press a matter to its greatest potential, to please us at the same time that we stand admiring the subtle means by which our feelings are manipulated. (pp. 200-03)

The plan of *Epicoene* unfolds in a way similar to *The Alchemist.* Although at first it seems like a miscellany of portraits and bravura passages, by the time it gets halfway through the performance we can see the movement toward an "excellent comedy of afflictions," generated from a tissue of vexations visited upon social monsters. It is a game of vexation copiously filled with variety but carefully limited. Instead of the open-ended design of an Elizabethan comedy, this play effortlessly directs every speech, character, and episode into a single stream of experience.

Jonson chooses a little society, represented by a large but circumscribed cast. They are Londoners who might come in contact with the fashionable gentry, a step below the court and a step above the city. All are afflicted with a similar social disease. Jonson marks the gradations clearly between servants, pretenders, and collegiates; between womanish men, mannish women, lusty men, insatiable women, and an impotent old man. He has strictly limited the time—one crucial day during the plague when Morose, although he lives in his chamber sound-proofed against tolling of the passing bells and all other noise, has determined to marry. Typical of Jonson's neat adaptation to the moment, the play was one of the first offerings of the re-formed children's company at the Whitefriars Theatre, when the plague had diminished enough to permit public gatherings. He has limited the place: the fashionable district between Westminster and the City near the Strand, the Law Courts, and the Thames, in short, near the Whitefriars Theatre. He has controlled the plot, allowing it to rise by gradual degrees of complication and furor, developed by a series of reciprocities. At first it is like an expandable filing system in which a large number of set speeches, characters, and episodes can be inserted, as long as the cross references are complete. At first only two or three characters come together to irritate each other by their speech; then four, five, and soon the stage is filled. At first, Truewit seems to upset Dauphine's whole plan when he visits Morose and declaims against marriage, but in an unforeseen reverse, it merely hardens the uncle's resolve to marry instantly. At first La Foole's invitation to a feast seems like an accident, having nothing to do with Morose and Dauphine, but in the next turn of the plot in Act III, Truewit directs the dinner guests over to celebrate Morose's wedding, and the mob washes over the stage in waves. In separate episodes, Mr. Otter begins on Mrs. Otter and in the same action he belittles the knights for their timid drinking. The ladies work on Morose's melancholy, in a parody of learned dispute over ancient versus modern writers. Finally Daw is set at odds with La Foole once more. (pp. 205-06)

Although each of these characters puts up a facade of sensibility, courage, sexual prowess, fashion, family, language, or learning, trying to impress the world, it only makes us question what is behind their act. The job of Truewit is to expand every action by inspiring wit in the others and to penetrate appearances, to vex the fool and hypocrite until they reveal their essential hollowness. "Why, all their actions are governed by crude opinion, without reason or cause." Appropriately, Truewit enjoys putting words in other people's mouths. Although comedy usually aims to "cure" the blocking characters (to use Northrop Frye's terms) or to cast them out of the comic society, that is not possible here, for although beneath their bad poetry, false fashion, and affected language, the fools are shown to be empty, there are so many of them and they are so incurably ignorant that all cannot be cast out. Daw and La Foole go, displaced by Dauphine and Clerimont, but the rest must be tolerated, manipulated, and "taken." Therefore a limited inclusiveness is reaffirmed at the end. (pp. 207-08)

The design that I've described also has a hardness and rigor, so that by the end of each play some may think that there is little reason to endure the barrage of words. In *Epicoene,* particularly, the series of brilliant set speeches so thoroughly attack polite learning, feminine beauty, art, marriage, and fashion that urbane life seems not worth the effort to live it. Furthermore (as in *The Alchemist* too), when each of the fools vies with himself to aid in his public humiliation, we see Jonson trying for maximum irony, to have a character convinced that he will personally profit by some degrading act, only to fall deeper into self-deception and frustration. Such turns, although expertly carried off, finally drain a character of his last ounce of humanity. We can laugh callously and cast him aside, but the net effect may leave us troubled.

It is easy to imagine that this is the way Jonson wanted us to feel, for in fact he might have felt that way, at least when he was younger and his comedies exhibited that polarity that he identified with comical satire, the embattled images of right and wrong. Evidence suggests that he did not approve of variety and novelty in manners. Good taste and good morals were inseparable for him, and he constantly set the plain old virtues and the plain style in contrast with the luxurious, vulgar, and dishonest in contemporary life. If mere luxuriousness and variety were at stake in the design of these plays, we might wonder whether some of the art of his great London comedies may have been an attempt to please the very same people he was satirizing. Are these plays, so packed with modern grossness, so full of surprising new twists of plot and unusual characters, made to appeal to the very popular taste that the author deplored? Only if we mean the kind of people who would overlook the fine decorum that the poet observes, the controlling limits of design within which he works. We do not mean those auditors who shared the poet's view that he could have written the play differently if he had chosen to. In other words, there is a deliberate strategy and a special pleasure that the better people are supposed to recognize.

The two prologues of *Epicoene* imply that he aims to delight his audiences more than before, to administer "sweet" remedies to the grossness and folly bred in his contemporaries. It is possible but not necessary to infer that the sweet remedies cover a bitter pill and that the plays approach the very condition that they satirized, as they turn on themselves, exposing the taste for variety in the fools, in the rogues who vex the fools, and in the "artists" who serve them both. (pp. 209-10)

However, there must be more to the tone than these odd satirical turns, if we are to account for the plays' gaiety and their continued appeal. What finally appeals to me is the gusto and the fascination with an absorbing game played by the poet and the witty characters. We are invited to enjoy the competition between Face and Subtle that amounts to an alternative drama going on while they cozen others. After the truce and bargain at the beginning of Act I it becomes a matter of who will take in more money that day. Who can steal the other fellow's customer, and who can have the favors of Dame Pliant without Dol Common knowing it? Crossfire between cheerful antagonists goes on even as they bamboozle the customers. And no small pleasure with *Epicoene* depends on our recognition that some characters know very little about what is going on, others know more, and a few know most. Even Truewit's proud assumption comes to grief, the assumption that he holds all the cards and that Clerimont and Dauphine are doing his bidding. (pp. 210-11)

At the end of both *The Alchemist* and *Epicoene* we have reached the substratum of comic form, that rests on farce. When a play develops with such perfect, dreamlike mechanism, when all the coincidences work so consistently to one end and all the talk has been drained of its sense and many of the characters drained of their humanity, we experience the essential development of farce. I do not mean that *The Alchemist* and *Epicoene* are nothing but farces, for they are a great deal more. I mean only that the design of their plots corresponds most to that fantasy of logic and coincidence that makes farce. All comedy is, as Eric Bentley says, basically farce, but it is farce plus something else. Jonson's accomplishment in these plays is to keep the something else although he contrives the dazzling artifice of the action that brings us to the very wellsprings of laughter. (p. 213)

L. A. Beaurline, in his *Jonson and Elizabethan Comedy: Essays in Dramatic Rhetoric,* The Huntington Library, 1978, 351 p.

C. A. PATRIDES
(essay date 1980)

[Patrides was an American critic and scholar. In the following excerpt from an essay written in 1980, he discusses Jonson's emphasis on style in his poetry.]

Poetry, wrote Jonson in *Discoveries,* is "the Queene of Arts: which had her originall from heaven, received thence from the *'Ebrewes,* and had in prime estimation with the Greeks, transmitted to the *Latines,* and all Nations, that profess'd Civility." . . . To grant poetry's divine origin and civilizing mission is of course to grant that poets must necessarily moralize. The notion, here crudely stated, was twice during the seventeenth century predicated with passionate conviction and in memorable terms. One formulation was ventured by Milton; the other by Jonson, again in *Discoveries:*

> I could never thinke the study of *Wisedome* confin'd only to the Philosopher: or of *Piety* to the *Divine:* or of State to the *Politicke.* But that he which can faine a *Common-wealth* (which is the Poet) can governe it with *Judgments,* informe it with *Religion,* and *Morals;* is all these. Wee doe not require in him meere *Elocution;* or an excellent faculty in verse; but the exact knowledge of all *vertues,* and their *Contraries;* with ability to render the one lov'd, the other hated, by his proper embattaling them. . . .

If for the sake of emphasis Jonson here subordinates manner to matter or style to content, he had adequate warrant in Horace: "The very root of writing well, and spring / Is to be wise; they matter first to know" (*The Art of Poetrie . . .*). Jonson was well enough aware that manner can hardly be divorced from matter. Wedded, however, they are not interchangeable, since it is manner that pierces the otherwise inert matter and animates it. "Language," as Jonson remarked, "most shewes a man: speake that I may see thee." . . . Adapting a phrase from the first of his sequence of ten lyrics on Charis, it could be said that the poet's progress is not from the truth to the language but from the language to the truth; so much so, that language frequently—and in Jonson habitually—itself constitutes the "truth." Style, in other words, is fundamental—and, in Jonson's case, imperative. (pp. 3-4)

Jonson's predilection for "plainness" is writ large in his poetry, as it is in his prose, and has been studied within the context of parallel tendencies in his age. But the frame of reference I would regard as crucial for his style—and through his particular style to his particular "truth"—is that of the classical tradition. For Jonson truly inhabits the centuries of Greece and Rome, more than any other seventeenth-century poet save Milton, and attests that fact, again like Milton, on countless occasions. . . . He himself declared in the prefatory note to *Hymenaei* that he was ever "grounded upon *antiquitie,* and solide *learnings,*" yet in *Discoveries* warned with equal force that the Greco-Roman heritage should not be permitted to enslave:

> I know *Nothing* can conduce more to letters, then to examine the writings of the *Ancients,* and not to rest in their sole Authority. . . . For to all the observations of the *Ancients,* wee have our owne experience: which, if wee will use, and apply, wee have better meanes to pronounce. It is true they open'd the gates, and made the way, that went before us; but as Guides, not Commanders. . . .

The statement is immediately relevant to matter, not to manner; yet it is no less applicable to questions of style—witness the extent to which Jonson's comedies unfold, freely, under the formidable influence of Aristophanes. So far as his nondramatic poetry is concerned, the contours of the classical tradition are equally clear. Jonson himself indicated that in some of his odes he put on "the wings of *Pindars* Muse." . . . (pp. 4-5)

Jonson's affinities with the classical tradition are impressed on any number of his poems, among them the well-known song to Celia. First used as part of *Volpone* . . . and next significantly published as one of the lyrics within *The Forrest,* the poem is a free adaptation of the celebrated fifth song of Catullus, "Vivamus, mea Lesbia." . . . *The Forrest* provides after the **"Song to Celia"** another poem **"To the same."** It is manifestly closer to the spirit, and partially even to the phrasing, of the Catullan original. . . . Familiar though [their] rhythms are to us, they were for their time utterly and intentionally subversive of the predominant modes of articulation. For Jonson's accommodation of the spirit of the classical lyric to English poetry vastly enriched the latter's potential; and if his efforts are seen as no more vital than Donne's were in another direction, his influence must certainly be judged as far more lasting. In immediate relation to Jonson's diverse responses to "Vivamus, mea Lesbia," it should be insisted that its imitations during the Renaissance were so far from being confined to his practice that they embrace an impressive number of other poets, too. Yet Jonson's example remains crucial, arguably instrumental as it was in conditioning the response of still another poet who never figures in the roll calls of "the Sons of Ben." We expect the poet in question to have been Lovelace or, most likely, Suckling. But he is in fact Crashaw, whose version of the Catullan poem echoes the distinctly Jonsonian rhythms both in the overall movement and in the particular sound patterns created. . . . If Crashaw would later be said to be affianced rather to Herbert than to Jonson, we may consider that Herbert's own debt to Jonson was not—as we shall observe shortly—of slight consequence. The Sons of Ben are clearly a variegated tribe indeed.

The achievement of Ben Jonson centers on his full cognizance that, in the classical lyric, matter depends entirely on manner. Style, that is to say, is paramount. . . . [Classical lyrics] suggest but do not pronounce, and intimate but do not exhaust. Their apparent qualities are economy to the point of telegraphic brevity, clarity to the point of obviousness, and restraint to the point of indifference. Yet their economy conceals potential fullness; their clarity, a complexity of attitudes; and their restraint, total commitment. Greek poets like Archilochus or Sappho, and Roman ones like Catullus, would have agreed with Jonson's categoric judgment that "Wee must express readily, and fully, not profusely" (*Discoveries,* . . .). Profusion limits—and, worse, it corrupts.

I say "corrupts" advisedly; for the moral tenor of classical lyric poetry depends on much the same ambition which underlines Jonson's poems and was to have informed his proposed grammar: "To teach . . . The puritie of Language." . . . A statement in *Discoveries* makes the point with exceptional brilliance, in that the style once again confirms the argument: "Many Writers perplexe their Readers, and Hearers with *Nonsense.* Their writings need sunshine. Pure and neat Language I love, yet plain and customary. A barbarous Phrase hath often made mee out of love with a good sense; and doubtful writing hath wrackt mee beyond my patience." . . . Jonson's endorsement of "plainness" by no means primarily reflects contemporary interests in the "plain style." His own remarks on style diverge dramatically, in that they are, in theory as in practice, moral judgments. In theory, even his nefarious wish that Shakespeare might have "blotted" a thousand lines is a reproach to be understood—if it can be understood at all—strictly in the light of the classical tradition. Hence Jonson's own practice, where "good sense" persuades not by its inherent goodness so much as by the firm clarity of its expression. . . . The contrary is evident in Shakespeare—so Jonson was presumably inclined to argue—in that profusion encloses the potential to overwhelm the "good sense" or, in extremis, annihilate it altogether. If eventually Jonson's munificent elegy on the "Soule of the Age" ["**To the Memory of My Beloved, The Author, Mr. William Shakespeare, and What He Hath Left Us**"] was to recognize Shakespeare's supremacy, something of his earlier attitude lingered in the barbed reference to the other's "small *Latine,* and lesse *Greeke.*" At issue in any case is not Shakespeare's misunderstood practice but Jonson's actual one; and, in the latter, the corruption attending the profusion of language is stamped not only on his epigrams but often on his plays, too, *Volpone,* for example, where the exhilarating hyperboles of the opening speech are meaningfully conflated with the cacophonous sounds of Nano, Androgyno, and Castrone:

> Now, room for fresh gamesters, who do will you to
> know,
> They do bring you neither play nor university show;
> And therefore do entreat you that whatsoever they
> rehearse,
> May not fare a whit the worse, for the false pace of
> the verse. . . .

Donne's response was positive. His commendatory verses on *Volpone*—pointedly phrased in Latin ("Amicissimo, et meritissimo Ben. Jonson. In Vulponem")—hail Jonson not generally because of his adherence to the cumulative wisdom of the ancients, but expressly because that adherence promised to stem the perfidious influences emanating from other quarters. The perception is vital, all the more because Donne himself remained distant from the classical tradition in poetry, but saw clearly enough how Jonson's talents might, and did, use that tradition's moral authority to great advantage.

The authority is most evident, we may now maintain, where Jonson's restraint is most palpably present. His natural predilection was for the particulars within—the monosyllabic word strategically placed, the comma intended to guide the voice, the "plain" expression calculated to suggest, the rhythm aimed to elicit a specific response—which in accumulation argue on the technical level an awesome, almost Pindaric commitment to the expertly attended detail and on the thematic level a confirmation of a manifest order or, in its absence, the intimation of that same order all the more urgent precisely because it is absent. To be sure, not all of Jonson's efforts were perfectly wrought. The elegy on the Marchioness of Winchester, for instance, extends to one hundred lines, and is one hundred lines too long. The version of Horace's *The Art of Poetrie,* also unsatisfactory, may charitably be described as versified journalism, all the more dispiriting because it is the labor of a poet otherwise fully conversant with classical poetry. But where Jonson succeeds—and he succeeds gratifyingly often—he exerts his individual talent in the direction of the classical tradition to attain the level of the nearly anonymous poet.

Nearly anonymous: for Jonson temperamentally could not, and in any case should not, have altogether obliterated his self. But this is not to say that the display of self is marked in Jonson to the same degree that it is in Donne. In terms of the language each poet used—and language, Jonson reminded us, "most shewes a man"—the "masculine expression" which Carew noted in Donne is no less apparent in Jonson. The two poets shared a partiality for "strong lines." Jonson could be fully as irreverent as Donne, and so he was (for example, in *The Forest,* in the poem beginning, "**And must I sing? what subject shall I chuse?**"). He could also be uneconomic in utterance and splenetic in tone, and so he was (in "**A speach according to Horace**" and, far more virulently because much more personally engaged, in "**An Expostulation with Inigo Jones**"). He could also write "elegies" not only in Donne's sense of the term but in close emulation of Donne's particular manner, witness the four such poems included in *The Under-wood* . . . , of which one ["**The Expostulation**"] is so far from being Jonson's that it may well be Donne's. Yet, in spite of the several affinities between the two poets, the norm in Jonson's poetry resides in its discretion. The few religious poems he wrote are particularly delicate exemplars of this discretion, in that restraint and clarity and economy—the qualities already commended—yield rhythms quite unlike anything in Donne. . . . Only Herbert was eventually to appreciate the Jonsonian approach to religious poetry. . . . Jonson's discretion was reinforced, in his secular poems, by his habitual predilection for firmly ordered stanzaic patterns and carefully measured single lines which themselves control the centrifugal tendencies of the given emotion. The technique appears to negate the self, but in a very particular sense asserts it all the more decisively. It is Jonson's way of confirming the circle of the classical tradition through, not against, his individual talent.

But to conclude where a conclusion may be—and, I hope, is—singularly irrelevant: where the poets' poet is normally said to be Spenser, the same appellation should be recognized as equally merited by Jonson. Spenser's poetic practice has of course been utterly crucial for the development of English poetry; but, as it was a practice representative of a particular mode of articulation, it made Jonson's contribution all the more necessary. Individually, Spenser and Jonson had a decisive impact on numerous other poets; jointly, they affected English poetry at large.

Spenser's influence is readily identifiable because of its particularity. But Jonson's influence can be neither defined categorically nor detailed unequivocally. Our task would have been very easy had we wished solely to trace Jonson's distinct rhythms in, say, Crashaw or to observe the way Jonson's dramatic lyric **"A Nymph's Passion"** was transformed into Coleridge's "Mutual Passion" with an embarrassing minimum of amendment. Our task is on the contrary very difficult because Jonson's influence, extending far beyond the mundane details just enumerated, is almost— but certainly not quite—impersonal. His near anonymity was ideally suited to his ambition to accommodate

the spirit of the classical lyric to English poetry; and, en route, juxtaposing "solide *learnings*" and "our owne experience," he created sound patterns violent enough to have impressed Donne, "simple" enough to have attracted Herbert, urbane enough to have allured Marvell, and variable enough to have commanded the respect of Milton. Upon consideration, I believe, Jonson's multiform poetry will also be observed to have affected Pope as much as Blake, Coleridge as much as Tennyson, and Yeats as much as T. S. Eliot. My large claims will astonish only those who are yet to discern that Jonson is to English poetry as Erasmus is to the civilization of the Renaissance: a formidable talent in himself, but also the cause why talent is in others. (pp. 5-14)

C. A. Patrides, "A Poet Nearly Anonymous," in *Classic and Cavalier: Essays on Jonson and the Sons of Ben,* edited by Claude J. Summers and Ted-Larry Pebworth, University of Pittsburgh Press, 1982, pp. 3-16.

SOURCES FOR FURTHER STUDY

Bamborough, J. B. *Ben Jonson.* London: Hutchinson, 1970, 191 p.

> Discusses Jonson's drama and dramatic theory. Also incorporates a brief biography.

Barton, Anne. *Ben Jonson, Dramatist.* Cambridge: Cambridge University Press, 1984, 370 p.

> A comprehensive study of Jonson's drama, including criticism on nearly all of his plays.

Champion, Larry S. *Ben Jonson's "Dotages": A Reconsideration of the Late Plays.* Lexington: University of Kentucky Press, 1967, 156 p.

> Examines Jonson's late plays, taking exception with the often-made charge that their art and execution suffer in comparison with his earlier works.

Chute, Marchette. *Ben Jonson of Westminster.* New York: E. P. Dutton & Co., 1953, 380 p.

> Biography of Jonson.

Ferry, Anne. "Jonson." In her *All in War with Time: Love Poetry of Shakespeare, Donne, Jonson, Marvell,* pp. 127-82. Cambridge: Harvard University Press, 1975.

> Analyzes Jonson's love poetry.

Wheeler, Charles Francis. *Classical Mythology in the Plays, Masques, and Poems of Ben Jonson.* Princeton: Princeton University Press, 1938, 212 p.

> Discusses Jonson's incorporation of elements of ancient myth, identifying his mythical allusions and their sources.

James Joyce

1882-1941

Irish novelist, short story writer, poet, dramatist, and critic.

INTRODUCTION

Joyce is considered the most prominent English-speaking literary figure of the first half of the twentieth century. His virtuoso experiments in prose both redefined the limits of language and recreated the form of the modern novel. Joyce's prose is often praised for its richness, and many critics feel that his verbal facility equals that of William Shakespeare or John Milton.

Joyce was born in a suburb of Dublin to middle-class parents. Like Stephen Dedalus in *Portrait of the Artist as a Young Man* (1916), he was educated by the Jesuits and underwent much the same emotional hardship and intellectual disciplining as the hero of his first published novel. After graduating from University College in 1902, Joyce left Ireland, consciously abandoning the restrictive milieu that the short stories of *Dubliners* (1914) depict in harshly naturalistic detail. In 1903 his mother's serious illness brought Joyce back to Ireland. Following her death in 1904, Joyce moved permanently to the continent with his future wife, Nora Barnacle. In France and Italy, where the couple's two children were born, Joyce struggled to support himself and his family by working as a language instructor. For a time they lived in Zurich, Switzerland, where Joyce wrote most of *Ulysses* (1922). In 1920 Joyce and his family moved to Paris. Among the expatriate Americans living there between the wars was Sylvia Beach, who published *Ulysses* under the imprint of her bookstore, Shakespeare and Co. Following the international renown accorded *Ulysses*, Joyce gained the financial patronship of Harriet Shaw and afterward was able to devote himself exclusively to writing. He spent nearly all of his remaining years composing his final work, *Finnegans Wake* (1939). Though free from poverty, these years were darkened by the worsening insanity of Joyce's daughter Lucia and by several surgical attempts to save his failing eyesight. After the publication of *Finnegans Wake,* Joyce fled Paris and the approaching turmoil of the Second World War. He died in Zurich of a perforated ulcer.

Joyce's work spans the extremes of naturalism and symbolism, from the spare style of *Dubliners* to the verbal richness of *Finnegans Wake. Dubliners,* a group of naturalistic stories concerned with the intellectual and spiritual torpor of Ireland, is the first product of his lifelong preoccupation with Dublin life. Though so disgusted by the narrowness and provincialism of Ireland that he spent most of his life in self-imposed exile, Joyce nevertheless made Ireland and the Irish the subject of all his fiction. These stories are also important as examples of his theory of epiphany in fiction: each is concerned with a sudden revelation of truth about life inspired by a seemingly trivial incident.

In many ways the collection is an indictment of the paralysis that Joyce felt gripped his city. As he told his initially reluctant publisher Grant Richards in a June, 1906, letter, "It is not my fault that the odour of ashpits and old weeds and offal hangs round my stories. I seriously believe that you will retard the course of civilisation in Ireland by preventing the Irish people from having one good look at themselves in my nicely polished looking-glass." At the same time, the stories reflect a sense of the humanity of Dubliners caught in situations that they cannot fully comprehend or overcome. "The Dead," with its ambiguous ending, leaves open the possibility of some sort of salvation for the central character, Gabriel Conroy, projecting most overtly Joyce's sympathy for his fellow citizens, but even in stories with protagonists who are clearly doomed—"Eveline," "Clay," "A Painful Case" are examples—his depictions retain an empathy for the hopelessness and the apparent inevitability of their condition.

Joyce's first novel, *A Portrait of the Artist as a Young Man,* is at once a portrayal of the maturation of the artist, a study of the vanity of rebelliousness, and an examination of the self-deception of adolescent ego. The novel is often considered a study of the author's early life. Originally entitled *Stephen Hero* and conceived as an epic of autobiography, *Portrait* was thoroughly rewritten to provide an objective account of protagonist Stephen Dedalus's consciousness. To heighten sensitivity to the stages of Stephen's maturation, each episode unfolds in a style that approximates the intellectual level of the protagonist at the time. The narrative thus presents an evolving perspective parallel to but independent from Stephen's own nature. This emphasis on a fluctuating point of view within the narrative stands as the central feature of Joyce's new approach in *A Portrait.* It gives the reader a strong sense of Stephen's maturing consciousness, yet it allows one to maintain a detached and at times ironic perspective on his nature.

This method for establishing the tone of the work also influences the formal design of Joyce's chapters. Each is organized around a series of "epiphanies" which mark a turning point in Stephen's emotional, intellectual, and spiritual growth. To balance these euphoric moments Joyce introduces throughout each chapter a series of "anti-epiphanies"—instances underscoring the misperceptions resulting from certain elevated attitudes. Moreover, he begins chapters two through five with "anti-epiphanies" aimed at directly undercutting the triumphs of the scenes immediately preceding them in the conclusions of chapters one through four.

A Portrait rests on such thematic paradoxes, for it charts Stephen's break with the constraints of the Irish world in which he grew up and his commitment to reform that world through his artistic powers. Stylistic experimentation and multiple perspective function in an efficient but muted manner in *A Portrait;* but in mastering their manipulation and in introducing the reader to the demands made by subtle shifts in tone and point of view, Joyce prepared for the more rigorous presentation of the same techniques in *Ulysses.*

Using the *Odyssey* of Homer as a frame, Joyce depicts in *Ulysses* the events of a single day in Dublin—June 16, 1904. Attention settles on three individuals. Stephen Dedalus, a bit older and more disillusioned than he was as the protagonist of *A Portrait,* spends the day seeking recognition from his fellow Dubliners for his artistic talent while drinking up the salary he has just received for teaching duties at Garret Deasy's school in Dalkey. Leopold Bloom, a middle-aged Jewish advertising canvasser for a Dublin newspaper, wanders around the city intent upon driving from his mind feelings of guilt over his father's death, remorse for the loss, eleven years earlier, of his infant son, apprehension over the maturity of his daughter Milly, and despair over his wife's impending infidelity. Molly Bloom, the wife of Leopold and the only one of the three not to spend her day criss-crossing Dublin, passes her time preparing for and engaging in her first act of adultery. Joyce overlays this interaction with a masterful depiction of minor characters, taking a a Rabelaisian delight in the seedy details of urban living. (Such details caused the novel to be banned from the United States until December, 1933, when Judge John M. Woolsey delivered the legal verdict that *Ulysses* was not obscene; it was published in America by Random House in early 1934, twelve years after Sylvia Beach's Paris edition appeared.) Despite Bloom, Molly, Stephen, and the other Dubliners' banal lives, Joyce imbues each with a dignity and fallibility that makes his or her experiences important to the reader.

As in his earlier works, Joyce's style endows *Ulysses* with kinetic force. Its evolving form helps the reader to participate in the creation of the text by attempting to bring meaning (though not certitude) to it. The novel's introductory chapters establish its tone in a fairly conventional, if sometimes baroque, manner; but after progressing through the first third of the work, Joyce begins to vary the form of succeeding episodes, continually shifting narrative perspective and compelling his audience to reconstruct standards for interpretation. Within chapters Joyce confronts readers with the disjointed impressions of the central characters through various forms of interior monologue. The interspersion of these among more straightforward narration produces tension through overlapping depictions of the action; perhaps most significantly, Joyce alternately presents a range of perspectives throughout the text, giving no voice primacy. As a consequence the reader must establish, without the intervention or guidance of the author, a personal system of values for weighing the significance of events.

Ulysses stands as a logical extension of the stylistic innovation begun in Joyce's earlier works. The diffusion of narrative discourse in *Dubliners* and *A Portrait* manifests itself in every facet of *Ulysses*'s textual structure, and the 1922 novel signals the continuing formal experimentation of *Finnegans Wake*. Unable to agree upon a formal classification for the latter work, critics hesitantly call it a novel. Meant to be the subconscious flow of thought of H. C. Earwicker, a character

both real and allegorical, *Finnegans Wake* is literally a recreation of the English language. In this masterpiece of allusions, puns, foreign languages, and word combinations, Joyce attempted to compress all of human history into one night's dream. Admittedly a work for a select few, it has inspired a mass of critical exegesis. The author was probably serious when he remarked that a person should spend a lifetime reading it.

Critics have come to see the year 1922, with the appearance of *Ulysses*, of T. S. Eliot's *The Waste Land*, and of German poet Rainer Maria Rilke's *Duino Elegies* and *Sonnets to Orpheus*, as the culmination of modernism. Although Joyce avoided association with artistic groups or literary movements, the characteristics distinguishing his works—antipathy towards institutions devoted to preserving the status quo, faith in the humanity of individuals, and a deep interest in stylistic experimentation—reflect the concerns animating the works of all the major artists of the period.

(For further information about Joyce's life and works, see *Contemporary Authors*, Vol. 104; *Dictionary of Literary Biography*, Vols. 10, 19, 36; *Major 20th-Century Writers*; *Short Story Criticism*, Vol. 3; and *Twentieth-Century Literary Criticism*, Vols. 3, 8, 16, 26, 35.)

CRITICAL COMMENTARY

HERBERT GORMAN

(essay date 1928)

[Gorman was an American novelist and biographer. As the author of Joyce's "authorized" biography, he had worked with Joyce and knew him well. In the following excerpt, he discusses the stream of consciousness technique in *A Portrait of the Artist as a Young Man* and comments on the importance of the unconscious in modern fiction.]

When James Joyce's *A Portrait of the Artist as a Young Man* first appeared in the columns of "The Egoist" (February, 1914—September, 1915), it is doubtful if more than a handful of readers realized exactly what had come into English letters. There had been stories before, plenty of them, about the childhood and school and college life of sensitive young men but never one of quite this kidney. The unusual aspects of this book, this impressive prelude to the then unsuspected *Ulysses*, were implicit less in the situations than in the method of handling and the suggestive innuendoes ris-

ing from apparently trivial notations. In other words the author was exploiting a new form in the novel, a form not then fully ascertained but to be carried to its logical determination in the behemoth of books that was to follow it. To understand this form it was necessary to understand the limitations of fiction. It was necessary to comprehend that the novel had (within the boundaries more or less arbitrarily set for it) fully flowered and blossomed, that in Gustave Flaubert, and, after him, Henry James, the ultimate possibilities of characterization and mental and spiritual exploration and revelation had been exhausted. There was nothing to be done but to push the apparently set boundaries of the novel back still farther, to make possible the elaboration of that new factor in life,—the subconscious. So much has come into this problem of living, so many misty awarenesses of inexplicable inhibitions, so many half-formed impulses, atavistic urges, semiconscious cerebrations, mysterious enchantments of the heart, and involved mental gestures, that a steadily widening gap was splitting literature and life apart. It

---

Principal Works

Chamber Music (poetry) 1907

Dubliners (short stories) 1914

A Portrait of the Artist as a Young Man (novel) 1916

Exiles (drama) 1918

Ulysses (novel) 1922

Pomes Penyeach (poetry) 1927

Collected Poems (poetry) 1936

Finnegans Wake (novel) 1939

*Stephen Hero (unfinished novel) 1944

Critical Writings of James Joyce (criticism) 1959

*This work was written in 1901-06.

---

was the purpose of Mr. Joyce to fill this gap, to make possible a profounder exploration of reality in the novel-form. *A Portrait of the Artist as a Young Man,* then, was (and is) important as a pioneer effort in this direction.

To this effort Mr. Joyce brought an astonishing and awe-inspiring array of talents. He brought independence and arrogance, psychological acumen and dialectical skill, vividness of conception and treatment, moral freedom and human passion, sensitivity and intuition, and, above all, a literary courage that was undisputed. It was no secret that it was himself, his own youth, that he was recreating. He realized, rightly enough, that in no better way could he develop this new form of fictional treatment, a treatment akin to pathology and infused with an uncompromising psychology, than in applying it to himself for in himself he possessed a rare subject for such an endeavor. The Stephen Dedalus of *A Portrait of the Artist as a Young Man,* delicately constituted, innately intellectual, afforded Mr. Joyce an opportunity for psychological revelation that was boundless in depth. Here was a youth, naturally fastidious in his conceptions and stirred by an obscure inward urge toward creativeness—in other words, the artist-type, set down in the midst of an antagonistic environment. He is surrounded by poverty and bickering. He is ultra-nervous as a boy. His eyesight is impaired. He passes through the phases of ridicule from his schoolmates, unjust discipline from his Jesuit-teachers, the quaking delirium of religion, the questioning arrogance of an awakening intellectualism, the broken sorrow of first love, and, at the last, he is left a proud exile about to set forth on that pilgrimage which every artist must travel. . . . Such a theme could not have been handled in an old-fashioned objective manner for too much of it was inextricably bound up in the subjective processes of the mind of Stephen Dedalus. It is the mind of a youth that is the

hero of this book, and its proper treatment demanded an intensive mapping of the fluctuations and progressions of that mind. Here thought is action as well as those objective movements and surface passions that bring personalities into violent or subtle reactions. It was, then, Mr. Joyce's function as author to discover the best media for transmitting this theme to an audience. He found them in the mingled methods of objective and subjective treatment and brought to the fore in English fiction (for the first time prominently, anyway) the stream of consciousness system of character delineation. This method was to be carried to its eventual goal in *Ulysses.*

Perhaps no method has been more discussed in the last decade than this so-called stream of consciousness technique. There are enough practitioners of it now to fashion it into a well-recognized mode of fictional treatment. . . . But it is futile to enumerate names or attempt to place one's finger on the very first person who applied this method to fiction. Wyndham Lewis, for instance, appears to believe that Charles Dickens adumbrated the method in his character of Alfred Jingle. All this is unimportant. As a matter of fact, the stream of consciousness method is an evolution, the answer to a crying need of the novel which was discovering itself to be stifled within arbitrary limitations and which found a new outlet through the psychological discoveries and experimentations of the day. Mr. Joyce was certainly one of the first, if not the first, to handle this method on a large scale and with supreme and convincing ability. When he reached the immense panorama of *Ulysses* he had the mastership of his method well in hand. It was his willing slave and it performed miracles for him. But it had already manifested itself in *A Portrait of the Artist as a Young Man,* particularly in such intense scenes as close the book, and because of this that volume assumes rightly enough an extremely important place in the development of the novel-form today. It was the gateway leading directly to *Ulysses* and it opened upon a huge and unexplored terrain that has yet to be completely traveled by following novelists.

Now just what is the stream of consciousness method? The solitary thoughts of characters in novels have been overheard before by god-like authors and yet we do not apply the phrase 'stream of consciousness' to these mappings of thought. The difference is in the word 'stream.' This new method is an attempt through the application of the author's psychological astuteness and intuition and profound knowledge of his character's mind, its depths, its subconscious impulses, inhibitions, and buried urges, to set down the undisturbed flow of thought—not always conscious, perhaps, to the thinker—that pours through the restless mind, a stream that is diverted constantly by a thousand and one extraneous objects, word-connotations, stifled emotions, from the consistent and built-up delineations of thought-processes to be found in the older novelists. Two objections have been brought against this style of literary treatment, that is, two paramount objections, for there are a hundred lesser ones. One of them is that the reader must take the author's word for it that his character's thought-processes are logical, that there is no proof that they are scientifically accurate. This is true enough, but, after all, the author's character is his own and to employ this form he must begin farther down to build his character up. He must lay the foundations of a subconscious person and rear on this the objective man. If he does this successfully there is no reason why his character's planned thought-processes as revealed through the stream of consciousness method may not be accurate and logical. True enough, it calls for a new type of novelist, a novelist who is psychologist and pathologist as well as a fictional creator. But that, obviously enough, is the road that the novel today is taking. The second objection is that the inclusion of haphazard musings, fragmentary cogitations, odd bits of thought, apparently irrelevant streams of brooding, changes the scheme of the novel and destroys that time-honored unity and selectiveness that so pleased our fathers. So it does. It calls for a new form in the novel, the observation and recognition of character from another plane. Instead of movement thought becomes action. This is what Mr. Joyce adumbrated in *A Portrait of the Artist as a Young Man*. At least, three quarters of this book is absorbing because of the vivid transcript of thought in it. It is the mind of Stephen Dedalus that enchants and absorbs us and it is our consciousness of the authentiticy of this figure that makes us so reluctant to lay the book down. Because of this we can reread *A Portrait of the Artist as a Young Man* many times for each reading is the renewal of an intimate acquaintanceship. We know Stephen Dedalus as well as we know our closest friends although, because of that mysterious artistic divinity in the arrogant young man, his essential self is somewhat beyond our fullest comprehension.

If the subjective tone of *A Portrait of the Artist as a Young Man* is convincing and distinguished, what may be said about its objective tone? After all, there is a surface to the book, movement, description, the presentation of character. Indeed, it was this surface that first drew readers (always excepting the lucky handful who knew from the beginning the potentialities it suggested for the future novel) to its engrossing pages. Scene after scene may be plucked from the book as representative of its clear realism and power of representing life. The agonies of Stephen Dedalus as he passes through the religious hysteria brought upon him by his days in attendance at the Roman Catholic retreat, for instance, is one although that has certain permeating subjective features to it. But what could be clearer of

the subjective and yet more convincing and tragically humorous than the famous Christmas dinner at Stephen's home where his aunt Dante loses her temper at the malicious proddings of the two Parnellites. The history of Ireland in little is circumscribed in this section of a chapter where religious differences shatter to bits what promised to be a feast of love. There is irony here but it is a cold detached irony, an irony that could place this scene at a dinner ostensibly in honor of Jesus Christ but yet dominated by the rancorousness of fierce church differences. If, at times, this irony is bitter we must remember that these figures are more than fictions and that the painful autobiography of a sensitive soul, lonely and proud, is imbedded in these pages. There is humor here but it is the cold humor of a man who has detached himself deliberately from those things which first made him, things that his mind and soaring destiny refuse. The reader must never forget the symbolism in the name Dedalus. That name may be found in any primer of mythology.

The philosophical implications of the book pass the bounds of a short essay for one can do no more than indicate that Stephen progresses by a steadily maturing process of ratiocination toward his goal of reality. If, at the conclusion of the volume, he has not found himself as yet he is well on the road toward it and he has made several great steps in its direction, not the least of them being his painful self-liberation from the Church which educated him and whose tenets and scholastic reasoning still permeate his mind. He has also liberated himself from the compromises of love and reached that grave conviction that he must travel alone, an exile to time and country and faith and friends, if he is to achieve the ultimate core of reality. Michael Robartes remembered forgotten beauty and when his arms wrapped his love he held all the faded loveliness of the world; Stephen desires to press in his arms the loveliness which has not yet come into the world. So he goes, with the thought of the old Greek Dedalos and his osier-bound wings in his mind: "Old father, old artificer, stand me now and ever in good stead." So profound and beautiful and convincing a book is part of the lasting literature of our age and if it is overshadowed by the huger proportion and profundities of *Ulysses* we must still remember that out of it that vaster tome evolved and that in it is the promise of that new literature, new both in form and content, that will be the classics of tomorrow. (pp. v-xii)

Herbert Gorman, in an introduction to *A Portrait of the Artist as a Young Man* by James Joyce, The Modern Library, 1928, pp. vi-xii.

EDMUND WILSON
(essay date 1931)

[Wilson wrote widely on cultural, historical, and literary matters. In the following excerpt, originally published in his seminal study of literary symbolism, *Axel's Castle* (1931), he discusses *Ulysses*, particularly praising Joyce's characterizations and poetic language.]

[One] of the most remarkable features of *Ulysses* is its interest as an investigation into the nature of human consciousness and behavior. Its importance from the point of view of psychology has never, it seems to me, been properly appreciated—though its influence on other books and, in consequence, upon our ideas about ourselves, has already been profound. Joyce has attempted in *Ulysses* to render as exhaustively, as precisely, and as directly as it is possible in words to do, what our participation in life is like—or rather, what it seems to us like as from moment to moment we live. In order to make this record complete, he has been obliged to disregard a number of conventions of taste which, especially in English-speaking countries, have in modern times been pretty strictly observed, even by the writers who have aimed to be most scrupulously truthful. Joyce has studied what we are accustomed to consider the dirty, the trivial and the base elements in our lives with the relentlessness of a modern psychologist; and he has also—what the contemporary Naturalist has seldom been poet enough for—done justice to all those elements in our lives which we have been in the habit of describing by such names as love, nobility, truth and beauty. It is curious to reflect that a number of critics—including, curiously enough, Arnold Bennett—should have found Joyce misanthropic. Flaubert is misanthropic, if you like—and in reproducing his technique, Joyce sometimes suggests his acrid tone. But Stephen, Bloom and Mrs. Bloom are certainly not either unamiable or unattractive—and for all their misfortunes and shortcomings, they inspire us with considerable respect. Stephen and Bloom are played off a little against the duller and meaner people about them; but even these people can scarcely be said to be treated with bitterness, even when, as in the case of Buck Mulligan or the elder Dedalus, Stephen's feeling about them is bitter. Joyce is remarkable, rather, for equanimity: in spite of the nervous intensity of *Ulysses,* there is a real serenity and detachment behind it—we are in the presence of a mind which has much in common with that of a certain type of philosopher, who in his effort to understand the causes of things, to interrelate the different elements of the universe, has reached a point where the ordinary values of good and bad, beautiful and ugly, have been lost in the excellence and beauty of transcendent understanding itself.

I believe that the first readers of *Ulysses* were shocked, not merely by Joyce's use of certain words ordinarily excluded today from English literature, but by his way of representing those aspects of human nature which we tend to consider incongruous as intimately, inextricably mingled. Yet the more we read *Ulysses,* the more we are convinced of its psychological truth, and the more we are amazed at Joyce's genius in mastering and in presenting, not through analysis or generalization, but by the complete recreation of life in the process of being lived, the relations of human beings to their environment and to each other; the nature of their perception of what goes on about them and of what goes on within themselves; and the interdependence of their intellectual, their physical, their professional and their emotional lives. To have traced all these interdependencies, to have given each of these elements its value, yet never to have lost sight of the moral through preoccupation with the physical, nor to have forgotten the general in the particular; to have exhibited ordinary humanity without either satirizing it or sentimentalizing it—this would already have been sufficiently remarkable; but to have subdued all this material to the uses of a supremely finished and disciplined work of art is a feat which has hardly been equalled in the literature of our time.

In Stephen's diary in *A Portrait of the Artist,* we find this significant entry apropos of a poem by Yeats: "Michael Robartes remembers forgotten beauty and, when his arms wrap her round, he presses in his arms the loveliness which has long faded from the world. Not this. Not at all. I desire to press in my arms the loveliness which has not yet come into the world."

And with *Ulysses,* Joyce has brought into literature a new and unknown beauty. Some readers have regretted the extinction in the later Joyce of the charming lyric poet of his two little books of poems and the *fin de siècle* prose writer of the *fin de siècle* phases of *A Portrait of the Artist as a Young Man* (both the prose and verse of the early Joyce showed the influence of Yeats). This poet is still present in *Ulysses:* "Kind air defined the coigns of houses in Kildare Street. No birds. Frail from the housetops two plumes of smoke ascended, pluming, and in a flaw of softness softly were blown." But the conventions of the romantic lyric, of "aesthetic" *fin de siècle* prose, even of the aesthetic Naturalism of Flaubert, can no longer, for Joyce, be made to accommodate the reality of experience. The diverse elements of experience are perceived in different relations and they must be differently represented. Joyce has found for this new vision a new language, but a language which, instead of diluting or doing violence to his poetic genius, enables it to assimilate more materials, to readjust itself more completely and successfully than that of perhaps any other poet of our age to the new self-consciousness of the modern world. But in achieving this, Joyce has ceased to write verse. [Verse] itself as a literary medium is coming to be used for fewer and fewer and for more and more special purposes, and that it may be destined to fall into disuse. And it seems to me that Joyce's literary development is a striking corroboration of this view. His prose works have an artistic intensity, a definitive beauty of surface and of form, which make him comparable to the great poets rather than to most of the great novelists.

Joyce is indeed really the great poet of a new phase of the human consciousness. Like Proust's or Whitehead's or Einstein's world, Joyce's world is always changing as it is perceived by different observers and by them at different times. It is an organism made up of "events," which may be taken as infinitely inclusive or infinitely small and each of which involves all the others; and each of these events is unique. Such a world cannot be presented in terms of such artificial abstractions as have been conventional in the past: solid institutions, groups, individuals, which play the parts of distinct durable entities—or even of solid psychological factors: dualisms of good and evil, mind and matter, flesh and spirit, instinct and reason; clear conflicts between passion and duty, between conscience and interest. Not that these conceptions are left out of Joyce's world: they are all there in the minds of the characters; and the realities they represent are there, too. But everything is reduced to terms of "events" like those of modern physics and philosophy—events which make up a "continuum," but which may be taken as infinitely small. Joyce has built out of these events a picture, amazingly lifelike and living, of the everyday world we know—and a picture which seems to allow us to see into it, to follow its variations and intricacies, as we have never been able to do before.

Nor are Joyce's characters merely the sum of the particles into which their experience has been dissociated: we come to imagine them as solidly, to feel their personalities as unmistakably, as we do with any characters in fiction; and we realize finally that they are also symbols. Bloom himself is in one of his aspects the typical modern man: Joyce has made him a Jew, one supposes, partly in order that he may be conceived equally well as an inhabitant of any provincial city of the European or Europeanized world. He makes a living by petty business, he leads the ordinary middle-class life—and he holds the conventional enlightened opinions of the time: he believes in science, social reform and internationalism. But Bloom is surpassed and illuminated from above by Stephen, who represents the intellect, the creative imagination; and he is upheld by Mrs. Bloom, who represents the body, the earth. Bloom

leaves with us in the long run the impression that he is something both better and worse than either of them; for Stephen sins through pride, the sin of the intellect; and Molly is at the mercy of the flesh; but Bloom, though a less powerful personality than either, has the strength of humility. It is difficult to describe the character of Bloom as Joyce finally makes us feel it: it takes precisely the whole of *Ulysses* to put him before us. It is not merely that Bloom is mediocre, that he is clever, that he is commonplace—that he is comic, that he is pathetic—that he is, as Rebecca West says, a figure of abject "squatting" vulgarity, that he is at moments, as Foster Damon says, the Christ—he is all of these, he is all the possibilities of that ordinary humanity which is somehow not so ordinary after all; and it is the proof of Joyce's greatness that, though we recognize Bloom's perfect truth and typical character, we cannot pigeonhole him in any familiar category, racial, social, moral, literary or even—because he does really have, after all, a good deal in common with the Greek Ulysses—historical.

Both Stephen and Molly are more easily describable because they represent extremes. Both are capable of rising to heights which Bloom can never reach. In Stephen's rhapsody on the seashore, when he first realizes his artist's vocation, in *A Portrait of the Artist as a Young Man,* we have had the ecstasy of the creative mind. In the soliloquy of Mrs. Bloom, Joyce has given us another ecstasy of creation, the rhapsody of the flesh. Stephen's dream was conceived in loneliness, by a drawing apart from his fellows. But Mrs. Bloom is like the earth, which gives the same life to all: she feels a maternal kinship with all living creatures. She pities the "poor donkeys slipping half asleep" in the steep street of Gibraltar, as she does "the sentry in front of the governor's house . . . half roasted" in the sun; and she gives herself to the bootblack at the General Post Office as readily as to Professor Goodwin. But, none the less, she will tend to breed from the highest type of life she knows: she turns to Bloom, and, beyond him, toward Stephen. This gross body, the body of humanity, upon which the whole structure of *Ulysses* rests—still throbbing with so strong a rhythm amid obscenity, commonness and squalor—is laboring to throw up some knowledge and beauty by which it may transcend itself.

These two great flights of the mind carry off all the ignominies and trivialities through which Joyce has made us pass: they seem to me—the soaring silver prose of the one, the deep embedded pulse of the other—among the supreme expressions in literature of the creative powers of humanity: they are, respectively, the justifications of the woman and the man. (pp. 63-6)

Edmund Wilson, "James Joyce," in *Joyce: A Collection of Critical Essays,* edited by William M. Chace, Prentice-Hall, Inc., 1974, pp. 50-66.

HARRY LEVIN
(essay date 1960)

[Levin is an American educator and critic whose works reveal his wide range of interests and expertise, from Renaissance culture to the contemporary novel. Among his best-known critical works is *James Joyce: A Critical Introduction* (1941), a work partly inspired by Joyce's comment that Levin had written the best review of *Finnegans Wake.* In the following excerpt from the revised and enlarged edition of *James Joyce: A Critical Introduction,* Levin presents an overview of the literary techniques, subjects, and themes of *Dubliners.*]

The reader of Joyce is continually reminded of the analogy between the role of the artist and the priestly office. The focal situation of *Dubliners* is that described in **"Araby,"** where we walk through the streets of the city, glimpsing places "hostile to romance" through the eyes of a child: "These noises converged in a single sensation of life for me: I imagined that I bore my chalice safely through a throng of foes." The same symbol is given a darker purport in the first story of the book, **"The Sisters,"** when it is recalled that the dying priest had disgraced himself by breaking a chalice. The broken chalice is an emblem, not only of Joyce's interrupted communion, but of the parched life of the metropolitan *Waste Land.* This early story is also glimpsed from the point of view of a small boy. The very first sentence consists entirely of monosyllables, and the paragraph proceeds toward a childish fascination with the word "paralysis."

Joyce's intention, he told his publisher, "was to write a chapter of the moral history of my country and I chose Dublin for the scene because that city seemed to me the centre of paralysis" [see excerpt dated 1906]. In every one of these fifteen case histories, we seem to be reading in the annals of frustration—a boy is disappointed, a priest suffers disgrace, the elopement of **"Eveline"** fails to materialize. Things almost happen. The characters are arrested in mid-air; the author deliberately avoids anything like an event. In **"The Boarding House"**—when there is some hope of a wedding—the aggressive landlady, the compromised daughter, and the abashed young man are presented in turn, and an actual interview becomes unnecessary. Joyce's slow-motion narrative is timed to his paralyzed subject. Both are synchronized with his strangely apocalyptic doctrine, which assigns to both author and characters a passive part. The author merely watches, the characters are merely revealed, and the emphasis is on the technique of exposure.

Realism had already established the artist as an observer; naturalism made him an outsider. In contrast to the promiscuous documentation of earlier novelists, the *tranche de vie* ["slice of life"] was sliced thin. A writer like Balzac, claiming to be only the secretary of society, could take a rather officious view of his position. The modern writer stands apart, waiting for a chance encounter or a snatch of conversation to give his story away. Strictly speaking, he has no story, but an oblique insight into a broader subject. Things happen just as they always do—the things you read about in the papers. There is business as usual, but it is none of his business. He is not concerned with romantic adventure or dramatic incident. He is concerned with the routines of every-day life, the mechanisms of human behavior, and he is anxious to discover the most economical way of exposing the most considerable amount of that material.

This is simply an attempt to define what is so often referred to as the *nuance.* The epiphany, in effect, is the same device. Though grounded in theology, it has now become a matter of literary technique. It has become Joyce's contribution to that series of developments which convert narrative into short-story, supplant plot with style, and turn the *raconteur* into a candid-camera expert. The measure of success, in so attenuated a form, is naturally the degree of concentration. The achievements of Chekhov and Katherine Mansfield, or Hemingway and Katherine Anne Porter, can almost be computed in terms of specific gravity. And Joyce, with **"Two Gallants,"** can say as much in fifteen pages as James T. Farrell has been able to tell us in volume after volume. It is hard to appreciate the originality of Joyce's technique, twenty-five years after the appearance of *Dubliners,* because it has been standardized into an industry. This industry is particularly well equipped to deal with the incongruities and derelictions of metropolitan life. Its typical products are the shrewd Parisian waifs of *Les hommes de bonne volonté* and the well-meaning nonentities who blunder through the pen and pencil sketches of the *New Yorker.*

In their own way, the tangential sketches of *Dubliners* came as close to Joyce's theme—the estrangement of the artist from the city—as does the systematic cross-section of *Ulysses.* They look more sympathetically into the estranged lives of others. They discriminate subtly between original sin and needless cruelty. **"Counterparts,"** in its concatenation of petty miseries, suggests the restrained pathos of Chekhov's "Enemies": it begins with an employer rebuking a clerk, and ends—after several drunken rounds—with the clerk beating his little son. Joyce's point of view, like Dickens', is most intimately associated with the children of his stories. He arranged his book under four aspects—

childhood, adolescence, maturity, and public life. As the stories detach themselves, they assume what Joyce called "a style of scrupulous meanness." But "the special odour of corruption," in which he took pride, was by no means peculiar to Dublin. It was also endemic in middlewestern villages like Sherwood Anderson's *Winesburg, Ohio.* (pp. 29-32)

If the vices of Dublin are those of any modern city, the virtues of "the seventh city of Christendom" are unique. An unconscionable amount of talking and singing and drinking goes on in *Dubliners.* This promotes style and poetry and fantasy—all peculiarly Irish qualities, and talents of Joyce. "The imagination of the people and the language they use is rich and living," Synge was discovering. The richness of Irish conversation mitigates the sordid realities of Joyce's book. He was always ready to take full advantage of the common speech of his fellow townsmen—the most expressive English he could have encountered anywhere. He could always portray life most vividly when he was writing by ear. What seems an aimless political discussion, in **"Ivy Day in the Committee Room,"** is really tight dramatic exposition. In the end the dead figure of Parnell dominates the campaign headquarters. It is his birthday, and an amateur poet is persuaded to recite a maudlin and mediocre eulogy. The finishing touch is the comment of the hostile Conservative, when pressed for his opinion: "Mr. Crofton said that it was a very fine piece of writing."

Notice the irony, so frequent with Swift, in the use of indirect discourse. In Joyce's attitude, however, there is an underlying ambiguity: he eats his cake and has it. We, too, are moved by the poem, in spite of—or perhaps because of—its cheapness. We are asked to share both the emotion and the revulsion. In **"Clay,"** with a different situation, we are subjected to the same treatment. The epiphany is no more than the moment when an old laundress stands up and sings "I dreamt that I dwelt in marble halls." She is made to boast of wealth, rank, beauty, and love—none of which she has ever possessed—"in a tiny quavering voice." A listener, affected by this pathetic incongruity, explains his tears by remarking that there is "no music for him like poor old Balfe." Here, as so often in Joyce, the music is doing duty for the feeling. The feeling is deliberately couched in a cheap phrase or a sentimental song, so that we experience a critical reaction, and finally a sense of intellectual detachment. Emotionally sated, we shy away from emotion.

Such passages have the striking and uncertain effect of romantic irony. Jean Paul's formula—"hot baths of sentiment followed by cold showers of irony"—still describes them. They show Joyce, in his isolation from society, confronted by the usual romantic dichotomy between the emotional and the intellectual. At his hands, the problem becomes a characteristically verbal

one, which allows him to dwell upon the contrast between the rich connotations and the disillusioning denotations of words. Since the days of *Don Quixote* this has been a major premise for fiction. The point of **"Araby"** is the glamor of the name, and the undeception of the small boy when he learns that it stands for a prosaic church bazaar. Yet no disillusionment would seem cruel enough to justify the last sentence, which should be contrasted with the objective description of Mr. Crofton's comment: "Gazing up into the darkness I saw myself as a creature driven and derided by vanity; and my eyes burned with anguish and anger."

Another point is scored by the same method in **"Grace,"** where the distance measured lies between the benign effulgence of religious doctrine and the hangover which brings a group of businessmen back to church. The distinction between words and things, in **"Ivy Day in the Committee Room"** and in **"Grace,"** is ground for political and religious satire. Church and state should enrich the lives of the citizens and impose a pattern on the city, but for Joyce they are tarnished symbols, broken chalices. Meanwhile, the Dubliners go their own ways. Martin Cunningham, the prominent layman, goes to church in **"Grace"** and appears at the funeral in *Ulysses.* Bartell D'Arcy, the tenor, sings a few hoarse notes in **"The Dead"** and figures in Mrs. Bloom's reminiscences. Mr. O'Madden Burke goes on writing for his paper, and Lenehan goes from bar to bar and book to book.

Joyce puts himself into his early book, not directly this time, but as he might have been if he had remained a Dubliner. Mr. Duffy, the timid socialist clerk in **"A Painful Case,"** is translating *Michael Kramer.* He meets a lady whose husband does not understand her, and who for some reason bears the name of Joyce's Italian music-master, Sinico. Though he considers falling in love with her, he continues to brood on "the soul's incurable loneliness." One day he reads in the newspaper that she has been killed in an accident of her own seeking—again the title is an echo. Again, in *Ulysses,* we hear of her funeral. Death is one of the few things that happen in *Dubliners;* it is the subject of the first and last stories in the volume. The last and longest story, **"The Dead,"** concerns the brother of a priest we meet in *Ulysses.* Gabriel Conroy is a Stephen Dedalus who stayed on to teach school and write occasional reviews, and who is already beginning to show symptoms of middle age. He is a pompous master of ceremonies at the Christmas party of his musical maiden aunts—incidentally Joyce's—and godmothers of Stephen Dedalus. Among others, he meets there a girl he knew, a Gaelic student who earnestly upbraids him for having taken his holidays abroad.

But he is a less significant character than his wife, Gretta, and she is not so significant as a memory awakened in her by a snatch of song at the end of the evening. It is the memory of a boy named Michael Furey, who had once loved her and who had died. Gabriel, who had not known of him before, feels a pang of the soul's incurable loneliness. He can never participate in this buried experience, even though it has become a part of the person he has known most intimately; he suddenly recognizes that he and Gretta are strangers. And, as he tries to imagine the dead boy, he realizes that his own identity is no more palpable to others than Michael Furey's is to him. In the light of this epiphany, the solid world seems to dissolve and dwindle, until nothing is left except the relics of the dead and the hosts of the dying. "One by one, they were all becoming shades." The final paragraph, in slow, spectral sentences, cadenced with alliteration and repetition, takes a receding view of the book itself. It sets up, like most departures, a disturbing tension between the warm and familiar and the cold and remote. In one direction lies the Class of Elements at Clongowes Wood, in the other the Universe:

> A few light taps upon the pane made him turn to the window. It had begun to snow again. He watched sleepily the flakes, silver and dark, falling obliquely against the lamplight. The time had come for him to set out on his journey westward. Yes, the newspapers were right: snow was general all over Ireland. It was falling on every part of the dark central plain, on the treeless hills, falling softly upon the Bog of Allen and, farther westward, softly falling into the dark mutinous Shannon waves. It was falling, too, upon every part of the lonely churchyard on the hill where Michael Furey lay buried. It lay thickly drifted on the crooked crosses and headstones, on the spears of the little gate, on the barren thorns. His soul swooned slowly as he heard the snow falling faintly through the universe and faintly falling, like the descent of their last end, upon all the living and the dead.

(pp. 33-7)

Harry Levin, in his *James Joyce: A Critical Introduction,* revised edition, New Directions, 1960, 256 p.

HUGH KENNER

(essay date 1965)

[Kenner is the foremost American critic and chronicler of literary Modernism. He is best known for *The Pound Era* (1971), a massive study of the Modernist movement, and for his influential works on T. S. Eliot, James Joyce, Samuel Beckett, and Wyndham Lewis. Kenner's well-known essay "The Portrait in Perspective" (1948) helped ignite the debate among Joyce critics regarding Joyce's attitude to-

ward Stephen Dedalus in *A Portrait of the Artist as a Young Man.* In "The Portrait in Perspective," Kenner insisted that, in spite of the many autobiographical elements in *A Portrait,* there were strong indications that Joyce saw Stephen Dedalus not as his alter-ego but as just another paralyzed victim of the Dublin environment. The following excerpt is Kenner's retrospective reconsideration of this argument.]

What you are about to read is a summary of conclusions, without a great deal of evidence. I assume that by now the evidence is pretty familiar. The Joyce canon is not very large, and certainly *A Portrait of the Artist as a Young Man* has been read by everyone not hopelessly given over to the supposition that the novel ceased with Bulwer-Lytton.

I am coming back to it, as I do from time to time, because, fifteen years after I first wrote an essay about it ["The Portrait in Perspective," 1948], I still think it is the key to the entire Joyce operation, though I hope I know more about it by now than I did when I wrote my essay. I am not going to deal in local explanations. . . . I am simply going to try to describe, as fully and carefully as I can, what the *Portrait* seems to be.

It has been supposed from the beginning that about this at least there is no mystery; for does not the title tell us that it is the portrait of the artist as a young man? To which I think it relevant to answer, that if we are to take this title at its face value, then it is unique among Joyce titles; and since it is too long a title to be printed conveniently upon the spine of a shortish novel—the sort of detail to which Joyce could always be relied on to pay attention—he must have wanted all those words for a purpose, and we had better look at them pretty carefully.

The first thing to be noticed, I think, is that the title imposes a pictorial and spatial analogy, an expectation of static repose, on a book in which nothing except the spiritual life of Dublin stands still: a book of fluid transitions in which the central figure is growing older by the page. The book is a becoming, which the title tells us to apprehend as a being. I shall have more to say about this in a moment; let me first draw attention to two more things we may notice in the title. One of them is this, that it has the same grammatical form as "A Portrait of the Merchant as a Young Man" or "A Portrait of the Blacksmith as a Young Man." It succeeds in not wholly avowing that the Artist in question is the same being who painted the portrait; it permits us to suppose that he may be the generic artist, the artistic type, the sort of person who sets up as an artist, or acts the artist, or is even described by irreverent friends as The Artist. I do not press this scheme, though I shall later extract a consequence or two from it. The third thing the title says is that we have before us a Portrait of the Artist *as a Young Man.* Now there is a clear analogy here, and the analogy is with Rembrandt, who painted self-portraits nearly every year of his life beginning in his early twenties. Like most Joycean analogies, however, it is an analogy with a difference, because the painter of self-portraits looks in a mirror, but the writer of such a novel as we have before us must look in the mirror of memory. A Rembrandt portrait of the artist at twenty-two shows the flesh of twenty-two and the features of twenty-two as portrayed by the hand of twenty-two and interpreted by the wisdom of twenty-two. Outlook and insight, subject and perception, feed one another in a little oscillating node of objectified introspection, all locked into an eternalized present moment. What that face knows, that painter knows, and no more. The canvas holds the mirror up to a mirror, and it is not surprising that this situation should have caught the attention of an Irish genius, since the mirror facing a mirror, the book that contains a book, the book (like *A Tale of a Tub*) which is about a book which is itself, or the book (like *Malone Dies*) which is a history of the writing both of itself and of another book like itself, or the poem (like "The Phases of the Moon") which is about people who are debating whether to tell the poet things he put into their heads when he created them, and are debating this, moreover, while he is in the very act of writing the poem about their debate: this theme, "mirror on mirror mirroring all the show," has been since at least Swift's time the inescapable mode of the Irish literary imagination, which is happiest when it can subsume ethical notions into an epistemological comedy. So far so good; but Joyce, as usual, has brooded on the theme a great deal longer than is customary, and has not been arrested, like Swift or Samuel Beckett or even Yeats, by the surface neatness of a logical antinomy. For it inheres in his highly individual application of Rembrandt's theme, that the Portrait of the Artist as a Young Man can only be painted by an older man, if older only by the time it takes to write the book. Joyce was careful to inform us at the bottom of the last page of this book that it took ten years. We have a Portrait, then, the subject of which ages from birth to twenty years within the picture space, while the artist has lived through ten more years in the course of painting it.

There follows a conclusion of capital importance: that we shall look in vain for analogies to the two principal conventions of a normal portrait, the static subject and the static viewpoint, those data from which all Renaissance theories of painting derive. . . . The laws of perspective place painter and subject in an exact geometrical relation to one another, in space and by analogy in time; but here they are both of them moving, one twice as fast as the other. The *Portrait* may well be the first piece of cubism in the history of art.

I have already hinted that a few of the topics on which we have come already will require further devel-

opment; so I am not really through with the title yet. But let us open the book and see what we discover. We discover, behind and around the central figure, what Wyndham Lewis described as a swept and tidied naturalism, and nowhere more completely than in the places, the accessory figures, the sights and sounds, the speeches and the names. Joyce is famous for his meticulous care with fact; "he is a bold man," he once wrote, "who will venture to alter what he has seen and heard." He used, in *Dubliners* and *Ulysses,* the names of real people, so often that their concerted determination to sue him the minute he should step off the boat became, I think, an implacable efficient cause for his long exile from Ireland, which commenced virtually on the eve of the publication of *Dubliners*. . . . It is clear that for Joyce authenticity of detail was of overriding moment. If actual names were artistically correct, he used them at whatever risk. If they were not, he supplied better ones, but always plausible ones. So far so good. And what stares us in the face wherever we open the first sustained narrative of this ferocious and uncompromising realist? Why, a name like a huge smudged fingerprint: the most implausible name that could conceivably be devised for an inhabitant of lower class Catholic Dublin: a name that no accident of immigration, no freak of etymology, no canon of naturalism however stretched, can justify: the name of Stephen Dedalus.

It seems to me very odd that we accept this name without protest; it is given to no eccentric accessory figure, but to the central character himself, the subject of the Portrait. But I cannot see that it has ever had the sort of effect Joyce must have intended: he must have meant it to arrest speculation at the outset, detaching the central figure at once from the conventions of quiet naturalism. What has happened instead is instructive: for Joyce is the best case available of the principle, that the history of the reception of a writer's works is one of the basic data of criticism. Joyce himself, as the Satanic antinomian, attracted attention as soon as the book did, and far more strongly; it was at once assumed that the book was nothing more than a thinly veiled autobiography. It was a natural assumption from this premise, that the author treated his early self with considerable indulgence, especially since the Stephen of the Portrait seemed clearly destined to turn into the man Joyce was supposed to be. So it seemed clear that the name of Stephen Dedalus should be scrutinized for a piece of indulgent symbolism: and indeed it yields this symbolism quite readily, the strange name a figure of prophecy, prophecy of light and escape, and fabulous artifice.

Now it is true that Joyce exploits the symbolism of the name, in the latter part of the book; but if we could somehow get Joyce himself out of our minds for a moment, and consider the early part of the book on the terms it seems to impose, we should see a central

Sylvia Beach and Joyce at Shakespeare and Company.

figure with a name so odd its seems a pseudonym. And indeed it seems to have been modelled on a pseudonym. It combines a Christian martyr with a fabulous artificer. I think it very likely that it was based on another name constructed in the same way, a name adopted by a famous Irishman which also combines a Christian martyr with a fabulous wanderer. The model, I think, is the name Sebastian Melmoth, which was adopted during the brief time of his continental exile by the most lurid Dubliner of them all, Oscar Wilde.

Wilde built his pseudonym of exile deliberately. Sebastian—Saint Sebastian—may be described as the fashionable martyr of 19th century aestheticism. Melmoth—*Melmoth the Wanderer*—was the hero of a novel written 80 years before by yet another Irish romancer, Charles Maturin. The two names joined the Christian and the pagan, the sufferer and the exile; in combination they vibrate with a heavy mysterious exoticism, linking Wilde with the creed of beleaguered beauty and with the land of his ancestors, affirming at the same time something richer and stranger about this shuffling Irish scapegoat than would seem possible, in Wilde's view, to a countryman of people with names like

Casey, Sullivan, and Moonan. It is a haunting homeless name, crying for exegesis, deliberately assumed by a haunted, homeless man. He was a man, furthermore, in whom Joyce did not fail to see enacted one of his own preoccupations, the artist as scapegoat for middle-class rectitude. And in modelling, as I believe he did, the name of the hero of his novel on the pseudonym of the fallen Wilde, Joyce was, I believe, deliberately invoking the Wildean parallel.

To give this remark a context, let me now say as plainly as possible what I think the *Portrait* is. The *Portrait* is a sort of Euclidean demonstration, in five parts, of how a provincial capital—for instance Dublin, though Toronto or Melbourne would do—goes about converting unusual talent into formlessly clever bohemanism. This demonstration is completed in *Ulysses,* when the bourgeois misfit *par excellence* turns out to be the bohemian's spiritual father. (The principle, by the way, that underlies the spiritual paternity of Bloom and Stephen is the simple and excellent scholastic maxim that opposites belong to the same species.) Now Dublin, by the time Joyce came to look back on the process to which he had barely escaped falling victim, had already extruded the arch-bohemian of a generation, Oscar Wilde, and Wilde had completed the Icarian myth by falling forever. If we are going to be consistent about the symbolism of names, it should be clear that Stephen is the son of Dedalus, and what the son of Dedalus did was fall. It seems clear that Joyce sees Stephen as a figure who is going to fall, not as a figure who is going to turn into the author himself. It is in *Ulysses,* of course, that we last see Stephen, aged twenty-two; and I think it significant that Joyce remarked one day, to Frank Budgen, while he was engaged on the figure of Leopold Bloom in *Ulysses,* that Stephen no longer interested him as Bloom did; for Stephen, he said, "has a shape that can't be changed." This seems decisive; but let us go back to Wilde a moment. It is, to put it plainly, possible if not sufficient to regard the *Portrait* as a lower-class Catholic parallel to Wilde's upper-class Protestant career.

This idea, for all the attention that has been devoted to Joyce's work, remains absurdly unfamiliar. Let me expand it. I am not arguing that Joyce hated Stephen, or could not bear Stephen, or was satirizing Stephen. I am merely pointing out that Joyce, though he used everything usable from his own experience, was creating all the time a character not himself, so little resembling himself that he may well have been suggested by the notoriety of a famous compatriot who had died only a few years before the first version of the book was begun. One of the incidents for which even the careful researches of Mr. Kevin Sullivan have turned up no prototype whatever, the caning of Stephen by schoolfellows because he refuses to "admit that Byron was no good," may even have been contrived as an Irish parallel to the famous indignities Wilde suffered at Oxford.

I have said that Joyce used everything usable from his own experience to create a character not himself. Now the evidence multiplies, as biographical trivia come to light, that Joyce did this with all his characters; but the party line of Joyce exegesis is wonderfully accommodating. When we learn, as I learned recently from an eye-witness of the Paris years, that he liked grilled kidneys for breakfast, we at once remember the familiar opening lines of the second section of *Ulysses:* "Mr. Leopold Bloom ate with relish the inner organs of beasts and fowls. . . . Most of all he liked grilled mutton kidneys, which gave to his palate a fine tang of faintly scented urine." This would seem to be a clear example of Joyce's way of using any detail that was handy, including, or especially, the most intimate trivia of his own existence, in the process of building from the inside a fictional creation. But this is not what we are normally told. When such details come to light the analogy of Stephen is trotted out. Stephen shares many experiences and attitudes with his author, because Stephen is Joyce. Now here is Bloom sharing characteris-

tics with his author, therefore Bloom is Joyce. Mr. Ellmann [see Sources for Further Study] actually commits himself . . . to the judgment that Bloom is Joyce's mature persona, and avers . . . that the movement of *Ulysses* "is to bring Stephen, the young Joyce, into *rapport* with Bloom, the mature Joyce."

It is surely wiser to work the analogy of Stephen the other way. If Bloom shares characteristics with Joyce and is plainly not Joyce, then Stephen, merely because he shares characteristics with Joyce, is not necessarily Joyce either.

I sketch this argument because it seems to be called for, not because I think it especially enlightening. If we want to know what Joyce is doing with the character called Stephen, we shall arrive at nothing conclusive by checking our impressions against the evidence of what he does with Leopold Bloom, simply because Leopold Bloom is—like Stephen himself, for that matter—a special case. He is a special case because he is so greatly elaborated; one would expect a good number of the author's own characteristics to find their way into the portrait of Bloom simply because so many small characteristics are needed for the presentation of a character on such a scale. The people who turn up in the sort stories provide a much better control group. Can we find in *Dubliners* any useful prototypes of Stephen Dedalus, useful because formed in a similar way, but so controlled by the smaller scale and the unchanging viewpoint that we may have less trouble deciding what they are meant to signify? The answer is that we can find a great many.

There is Mr. James Duffy, for instance, in **"A Painful Case."** Mr. Duffy has been endowed with the author's Christian name, and a surname with just as many letters in it as there are in Joyce. (This is a tiny point, to be sure, but Joyce was a great counter of letters.) He has moved out of Dublin, though it is true that he has not moved far, only as far as suburban Chapelizod. He elected Chapelizod because he found all the other suburbs of Dublin "mean, modern and pretentious". He is a man obsessed with ideas of order, with pattern, symmetry, classification: he expresses these impulses by, among other things, the care with which he arranges his books. Like his creator, who kept a notebook headed **"Epiphanies,"** he keeps on his desk a sheaf of papers headed "Bile Beans," held together by a brass pin, and in these papers he inscribes from time to time a sorrowful or sardonic epigram. The woman with whom he attempts to strike up a relationship is named Mrs. Sinoco, which was the name of a singing teacher Joyce frequented in Trieste. He has even translated *Michael Kramer,* as Joyce had done in the summer of 1901. The manuscript of his translation is exceptionally tidy: the stage directions are written in purple ink. And he listens, as did the author of *Exiles* and of the final pages of *Finnegans Wake,* to "the strange impersonal voice which he recognized as his own, insisting on the soul's incurable loneliness. We cannot give ourselves, it said: we are our own." "Ourselves, oursouls, alone," echoes Anna Livia across thirty years. Mr. Duffy, in short, is A Portrait of the Artist as Dublin Bank-clerk.

Or consider Jimmy Doyle, in **"After the Race,"** whose name is Jimmy Joyce's with only two letters altered. . . . Or consider finally Gabriel Conroy, in **"The Dead."**

Gabriel who is sick of his own country and has "visited not a few places abroad," who writes book reviews, as did Joyce, for the *Daily Express,* teaches language, as did Joyce, parts his hair in the middle, as did Joyce, wears rimmed glasses, as did Joyce, clings to petty respectabilities, as did Joyce, has taken a wife from the savage bogs of the west counties, as did Joyce, snubs people unexpectedly, as did Joyce, and is eternally preoccupied, as was Joyce, with the notion that his wife has had earlier lovers: Gabriel Conroy, attending a festivity in a house that belonged to Joyce's great-aunts, and restive in his patent-leather cosmopolitanism among the provincials of the capital by the Liffey, is pretty clearly modelled on his author by rather the same sort of process that was later to produce Stephen Dedalus.

There is nothing original in these observations, and we have not by any means exhausted the list of Joycean shadow-selves who turn up in these strangely intimate stories. But when we find them in the stories, instead of in an equivocally autobiographical novel, we can see more clearly what they are. They are not the author, they are potentialities contained within the author. They are what he has not become.

The sharpest exegetical instrument to bring to the work of Joyce is Aristotle's great conception of potency and act. Joyce's awareness of it, his concern with it, is what distinguishes him from every other writer who has used the conventions of naturalism. Naturalist fiction as it was developed in France was based on scientific positivism, its conviction that realities are bounded by phenomena, persons by behaviour, that what seems is, and that what *is* must be. But Joyce is always concerned with multiple possibilities. For a Zola, a Maupassant, a Flaubert, it is simply meaningless to consider what might have been; for since it was not, it is meaningless to *say* that it might have been. In the mind of Joyce, however, there hung a radiant field of potentialities: ways in which a man may go, and correspondingly selves he may become, bounding himself in one form or another while remaining the same person in the eyes of God. The events of history, Stephen considers in *Ulysses,* are branded by time and hung fettered "in the room of the infinite possibilities they have ousted." Pathos, the dominant or sub-dominant Joycean emotion, inheres in the inspection of such limits: men longing to become what they can never be, though it lies in them to be it, simply because they have become something else.

All potentiality is bounded by alien and circumstantial limits. The people in *Dubliners* are thwarted, all of them, by the limitation of potentiality the city imposes. They sense this, all of them, and yearn to remove themselves, but in their yearning they are subjected to another scholastic axiom, that we cannot desire what we do not know. If they have notions of what it would be like to live another way, in another place, they confect these notions out of what Dublin makes available. (pp. 1-10)

I hope no one thinks that I am forgetting Stephen Dedalus all this time. I am supplying a context for all those people in *Dubliners* who resemble the author, so as to supply in turn a context for the ways in which Stephen Dedalus resembles the author. At every moment of his life, the author, like anyone else in Dublin or anywhere else, was confronted with decisions and choices, courses of conduct elected or not elected; and each of these in turn, branches, if he elects it, into a whole branching family of further courses, or if he does not elect it, branches into a whole different family of branching courses. If the nose on Cleopatra's face had been shorter, the destiny of the world would have altered; if the swan had not come to Leda, Troy would not have fallen, nor Homer educated Greece, nor Greece Rome, and we should none of us perhaps exist. So there lies before a man an indefinitely large potentiality of events he may set in motion, ways he may go, and selves he may become. But each way, each self, each branching upon a branch, is supplied by Dublin; so the field, however large, is closed. In Dublin one can only become a Dubliner; a Dubliner in exile, since the exile was elected from within Dublin and is situated along one of the many paths leading out of Dublin and so connected to Dublin, is a Dubliner still. Even refusing Dublin is a Dublin stratagem.

He contains, then, within him, multitudes. All the people in *Dubliners* are people he might have been, all imprisoned in devious ways by the city, all come to terms of some sort with it, all meeting or refusing shadow-selves who taunt them with the spectre of yet another course once possible but possible now no longer. *Dubliners* is a portrait of the artist as many men. . . . And none of the men becomes James Joyce, nor none of the women Nora Joyce, but they might: they contain those potentialities. It is only by a fantastic series of accidents that anyone becomes what he does become, and though he can be only what he is, he can look back along the way he has come, testing it for branching-points now obsolete.

So the subject of *Dubliners* is a single subject, metamorphosing along many lines of potentiality as the circle of light directed by the story-teller moves through time, picking out, successively, a small boy of the time when he was himself a small boy, or adolescents of the time when he was an adolescent. Each story obeys, or seems to obey, the pictorial convention of a fixed perspective, subject and viewer set in place until the work of portrayal is finished. The book, however, is a succession of such pictures; or better, it is the trace of a moving subject, seen from a moving viewpoint which is always very close to him.

And if we apply this account to *A Portrait of the Artist as a Young Man* we shall find that it applies exactly: the moving point of view, product not only of a book ten years in the writing but of a standpoint which remains close to the subject as he moves; the moving subject, passing from infancy forward for twenty years; and the subject himself a potentiality drawn from within the author, the most fully developed of the alternative selves he projected over a long life with such careful labor. If the differences between Stephen and Joyce seem small, all differences are small, and it is always small differences that are decisive. One has only to accept or refuse a causal opportunity, and the curve of one's life commences a long slow bending away from what it otherwise would have been. This line of argument is not only Aristotelian but wholly familiar to a man brought up, like Joyce, in a climate of clerical exhortation. From the time he could first remember hearing human words, he must have listened to hundreds of homilies, ruminations, admonitions, developing the principle that it is the little sins that prepare the habit great sins will later gratify, or that the destiny of the soul is prepared in early youth, so that there is nothing that does not matter.

So Stephen is a perfectly normal Joyce character, not the intimate image of what Joyce in fact was, but a figure generated according to a way of working that came naturally to him in a hundred ways. Stephen, unlike a character in *Dubliners,* is followed with unflagging attention for twenty years instead of being exhibited as he was during the course of a few hours. But like the characters in *Dubliners,* who also do many things Joyce did, he also leaves undone many other things Joyce did, and does many things Joyce did not. And these, if you accept my account of Joyce's way of thinking on human destiny, are not trivial divergences, but precisely the many small points of decision that make him Stephen and not Joyce.

And, to recapitulate further, Joyce was fascinated by the way Dublin contrives to maintain its life-long hold on its denizens. He himself made no pretence of having escaped the city, except in body; he remained so thoroughly a Dubliner that he kept in repair to the last his knowledge of the shops and streets, pressing visitors from the distant town for news of civic alterations, or carefully making note of the fact that such-and-such a place of business had changed hands. Ste-

phen's talk of flying by nets of language, nationality, religion, remains—Stephen's talk. One does not fly by Dublin's nets, though the illusion that one may fly by them may be one of Dublin's sorts of birdlime.

Once we are in possession of the formula for Stephen, his many little points of divergence from his creator cease to point toward mysterious formal requirements. Stephen is a young man rather like Joyce, who imagines that he is going to put the city behind him; he is going to fly, like Shelley's skylark; and he is going to fall into cold water, like Icarus, or like Oscar Wilde. Given this formula, Joyce used everything he could find or remember that was relevant, all the time fabricating liberally in order to simplify and heighten a being whose entire emotional life is in fact an act of ruthless simplification. (pp. 11-13)

I have a last observation to make, which concerns Joyce's tone. I am always a little surprised to find myself cited, from time to time, as the bellwether of the Stephen-hating school of critics. It is clear that Stephen is not hateful, though he is irritating when he is being put forth by the massed proprietors of the Joyce Legend as an authentic genius. Considered as a genius, he is a tedious cliché, weary, disdainful, sterile; he writes an exceedingly conventional poem in the idiom of the empurpled nineties, indeed a poem Wilde might well have admired, one which seems unlikely to pass beyond the nineties. He has, as Joyce said, a shape that can't be changed.

Or has by the end of the book. But when we were first considering the title of the book, we noticed that the title imposes a look of pictorial repose on a subject constantly changing. We noticed, too, the author's announcement, on the last line of the last page, that he has spent fully ten years revolving the subject and revising and re-revising the writing. As we observed that we had a Portrait with a difference, neither subject nor artist united in a normal geometrical relationship. This is the last thing I want to stress. What we normally call "tone" is the product of a fixed relationship between writer and material. It is the exact analogy of perspective in painting. Its two familiar modes are utter sympathy and sustained irony. Irony says, "I see very well what is going on here, and I know how to value it." But Joyce's view of Stephen is not ironic; it is not determined by a standpoint of immovable superiority. Sympathy says "Withhold your judgment; if you undervalue this man you will offend *me.*" Joyce's view of Stephen is not sympathetic either, by which I mean that it is not defensive, or self-defensive. Like a Chinese painter, or a mediaeval painter, Joyce expects our viewpoint to move as the subject moves. We are detached from Stephen, we comprehend his motions and emotions, we are not to reject him nor defend him, nor feel a kind of embarassment on the writer's behalf. We have not "irony," we have simply the truth. This is so until the end. At the end, when Stephen's development ceases, when he passes into, or has very nearly passed into, the shape that can't be changed, then he is troubling; and we sense, I think, a little, Joyce deliberately withholding judgment.

It is a terrible, a shaking story; and it brings Stephen where so many other potential Joyces have been brought, into a fixed rôle, into nothing; into paralysis, frustration, or a sorry, endlessly painful, coming to terms: for the best of them, a meditating on restful symbols, as Gabriel Conroy, stretched out in living death beside his wife, turns to the snow, or as Leopold Bloom, in the room of his cuckolding, thinks on the intellectual pleasures of water. For all the potential selves we can imagine stop short of what we are, and this is true however little we may be satisfied with what we are. Dubliner after Dubliner suffers panic, thinks to es-

cape, and accepts paralysis. It is the premise of the most sensitive of them, as it is for Stephen Dedalus, that the indispensable thing is to escape. It was Joyce's fortune that having carried through Stephen's resolve and having escaped, he saw the exile he accepted as the means of being more thoroughly a Dubliner, a citizen of the city that cannot be escaped but need not be obliterated from the mind. He celebrated it all his life, and projected the moods through which he had passed, and for which he retained an active sympathy, into fictional characters for each of whom the drab city by the Liffey, whatever else it is, is nothing at all to celebrate. (pp. 14-15)

Hugh Kenner, "Joyce's Portrait—A Reconsideration," in *The University of Windsor Review,* Vol. I, No. 1, Spring, 1965, pp. 1-15.

SOURCES FOR FURTHER STUDY

Deming, Robert H., ed. *James Joyce: The Critical Heritage.* 2 vols. New York: Barnes & Noble, 1970.

> Reprints reviews and commentary dating from 1908 to 1934 on Joyce's works.

Ellmann, Richard. *James Joyce.* Rev. ed. New York: Oxford University Press, 1982, 928 p.

> Comprehensive biography of Joyce which has become the standard work on his life.

Gross, John. *James Joyce.* Edited by Frank Kermode. New York: Viking Press, 1970, 102 p.

> Discusses the development of Joyce as a poet, dramatist, and novelist within a chronological study of his works.

Halper, Hathan. *The Early James Joyce.* New York: Columbia University Press, 1973, 48 p.

> Good survey of Joyce's work through the *Portrait.*

Prescott, Joseph. *Exploring James Joyce.* Carbondale: Southern Illinois University Press, 1964, 182 p.

> Essays discussing Joyce's characterizations, his use of allusion, his verbal facility, and stylistic techniques.

Senn, Fritz, ed. *New Light on Joyce from the Dublin Symposium.* Bloomington: Indiana University Press, 1972, 208 p.

> Papers collected from an international symposium including, among others, essays by Leslie Fiedler on the nature of Bloom and Darcy O'Brien on Joyce's conception of love.

Franz Kafka

1883-1924

Austro-Czech short story writer, novelist, and diarist.

INTRODUCTION

*O*ne of the most acclaimed and influential twentieth-century writers, Kafka is renowned for prophetic and profoundly enigmatic stories that often portray human degradation and cruelty. In his works, Kafka presents a grotesque vision of the world in which alienated, angst-ridden individuals vainly seek to transcend their condition or pursue some unattainable goal. His fiction derives its power from his use of precise, dispassionate prose and realistic detail to relate bizarre, often absurd events, and from his probing treatment of moral and spiritual problems. The oblique, allegorical quality of Kafka's stories has inspired myriad critical interpretations: his fiction has been variously described as autobiographical, psychoanalytic, Marxist, religious, Existentialist, Expressionist, and Naturalist. Most critics agree, however, that Kafka gave literary form to the disorder of the modern world, turning his private nightmares into universal myths.

Kafka was born to financially secure Jewish parents in Prague, a prominent provincial capital of the Austro-Hungarian Empire. His father had risen from poverty to success as a businessman, and the family had been assimilated into Prague's Czech community by the time of Kafka's birth. Seeking acceptance into the German-speaking élite of the city, Kafka's father sent him to German rather than Czech schools. According to biographers, the dichotomy between the German and Czech communities led to Kafka's early feelings of alienation. As the eldest child and only surviving son, Kafka was expected to follow a planned course in life, but from his childhood he considered himself a disappointment to his father and felt inadequate when compared with him. Kafka's artistic motivation is revealed in this passage from an unsent letter to his domineering father: "My writing was all about you, all I did there, after all, was to complain about the things I couldn't complain about on your breast." Against his own wishes, Kafka studied law at the German University in Prague, earning his doctorate in 1906. Unhappy with the prospect of a legal career, he instead accepted a position with an insurance firm in Prague. He worked there from 1908 until 1922, when the debilitating effects of tuberculosis finally forced him to retire. Kafka spent his remaining years in various sanatoriums, writing fiction until his death in Kierling, Austria, in 1924. In his will, Kafka ordered nearly all of his manuscripts burned, but Max Brod, his friend and literary executor, ignored this request and organized Kafka's writings into several posthumous publications.

Kafka was plagued by the discord between his vocation and his literary ambitions, and by his own ambivalence about marriage, which he believed offered the greatest happiness, but which he feared would stifle his creativity. Some biographers consider his relationship with Felice Bauer, to whom he was engaged twice but never married, the catalyst to a fertile period of literary production that began in 1912. During this time Kafka wrote "Die Verwandlung" (1915; "The Metamorphosis"), "Das Urteil" (1913; "The Judgment"), and the first chapter of his novel *Amerika* (1927; *America*). Many critics cite "The Judgment" as Kafka's "breakthrough" story, the one that established his central thematic preoccupation: the conflict between father and son that produces guilt in the younger character and is ultimately reconciled through suffering and expiation. Several commentators have noted the Oedipal rivalry between protagonist Georg Bendemann and his father, and have commented upon the illogical, dreamlike atmosphere of this piece. Georg's friend in Russia, who has exiled himself in order to write, represents Kafka as artist, critics contend, while Georg symbolizes the Kafka who desires domesticity. After Georg announces his impending marriage, his father sentences him to death by drowning for defiling his mother's memory and challenging his father's status as head of the family. Acknowledging his guilt, Georg obeys the command and jumps into the river.

Kafka's next major work, "The Metamorphosis," is one of the most frequently analyzed stories in world literature. This elusive work, which portrays the transformation of Gregor Samsa from a man into an insect, has inspired diverse interpretations. The story has a threefold construction, demarcated by numerical headings and by Gregor's three emergences from his room after the transformation has occurred. Critics agree upon little regarding "The Metamorphosis" other than its three-part structure and its basic plot outline: Gregor Samsa works as a traveling salesman, a job he dislikes, to repay a debt incurred by his parents; he oversleeps one morning and awakens to find he has become a large insect; he and his family attempt to deal in various ways with the change, but gradually the situation becomes intolerable; Gregor ultimately dies, and his relieved family plans for a brighter future.

Three frequent critical interpretations of Gregor's transformation are that it serves either as retribution, as wish fulfillment, or as an extended metaphor. Those critics who see the metamorphosis as retribution for an unspecified crime committed by Gregor usually apply comparisons between Gregor and Josef K., the protagonist of Kafka's novel *Der Prozess* (1925; *The Trial*), who never knows the offense for which he is arrested and executed. Critics who see the metamorphosis as a form of wish fulfillment on Gregor's part find in the text clues indicating that he deeply resented having to support his family. Desiring in turn to be nurtured by them, he literally becomes a parasite. The parasitical nature of Gregor's family and employer is then seen as an ironic foil to the reality of Gregor's parasitic being. Many critics who approach the story in this way believe the primary emphasis is not upon Gregor, but upon his family, as they abandon their dependence on him and learn to be self-sufficient. One interpretation of the story holds that the title applies more to Gregor's sister Grete than to Gregor: she passes from girlhood to young womanhood during the course of the story. A third interpretation is that Gregor's transformation is an extended metaphor, carried from abstract concept to concrete reality: Gregor is thought of as an insect, and thinks of himself as an insect, so he becomes one.

Kafka's next published work, "In der Strafkolonie" (1919; "In the Penal Colony"), which he wrote in two weeks during a break from composing *The Trial,* is a characteristic fantasy of psychological and physical brutality that suggests a variety of readings due to the obscure nature of the events. In this story, a respected visitor is invited by the commandant of a penal colony to observe the execution of a soldier by means of an intricate torture apparatus. The machine, which uses needles to inscribe in words the criminal's punishable act upon his body, is intended to simultaneously induce beatific enlightenment. When the purpose of the device is described by its operator, a prison officer, the visitor is appalled. Attempting to assure his offended guest of the instrument's worth, the officer frees the condemned soldier and takes his place. During its operation, however, the machine malfunctions, and the officer is killed quickly and violently, without attaining the promised redemption. Many commentators have perceived "In the Penal Colony" as an allegory comparing the Old and New Testaments, with the officer's willing sacrifice serving as an analogy to Jesus Christ's suffering and death. Others have viewed this story as prophetic of the Nazi concentration camps.

In 1916 and 1917 Kafka wrote a series of prose pieces known as the Country Doctor Cycle which reflects a sense of decaying order in Europe during World War I. These tales were later collected and published as *Ein Landarzt* (1919; *A Country Doctor*). In the title work (the most frequently discussed story of this volume), Kafka employs realistic prose to relate the surrealistic tale of a doctor's futile efforts to save a dying boy. The doctor initially pronounces his patient healthy, but the boy disagrees. Closer examination reveals a hole in the youth's abdomen in which worms writhe through clotted blood. After noting this, the doctor is mysteriously stripped naked and left alone with the child, who says that the abdominal hole is his "sole endowment" in the world. The doctor reassures the boy that the wound is relatively harmless, and then flees the house without his clothes, riding home in a blizzard. Many critics have interpreted this story as symbolic of the impotence of modern science before the ruthless power of nature.

The stories in the last book published by Kafka during his lifetime, *Ein Hungerkünstler* (1924; *A Hunger-Artist*), depict characters whose extreme isolation represents the status of the artist in a modern industrialized world. In "Erstes Leid" ("First Sorrow"), for example, a trapeze artist lives alone in the higher reaches of a circus arena, refusing to have contact with fellow workers, who nevertheless remain nearby. Uncomfortable in this situation but unable to perform without the aid of others, the trapeze artist remains paralyzed in his absurd position. In the title story, the protagonist, once celebrated by many for his ability to fast for days, is now viewed as a pathetic freak when public taste changes and circus spectators abandon him in favor of the animal exhibition. Denied public attention, the hunger-artist becomes disillusioned, weakens, and just before dying, confesses he stopped eating simply because he could not find food to his liking. He is replaced in his cage by a ravenous panther. Some critics see this story as symbolic of the plight of the misunderstood artist in modern times; when the hunger-artist's audience disappears, so does his faith in himself, and as

a result, he expires. Other commentators perceive the protagonist as embodying humanity's spiritual nature and the panther as characterizing its bestial temperament. Still others view the hunger-artist as a holy man and describe the story as a parable about the impossibility of leading a completely metaphysical life. "A Hunger-Artist" is considered one of Kafka's most autobiographical works. Meno Spann cites a letter written by Kafka in 1912 that betokens the theme of this piece: "When it became clear in my organism that writing was the most productive direction for my being to take, everything rushed in that direction and left empty all those abilities which were directed toward the joys of sex, eating, drinking, philosophical reflection and above all music."

Kafka is ranked among the most important writers of the twentieth century for works that express modern humanity's loss of personal and collective order. His writing has inspired the term "Kafkaesque," which has come to describe situations of psychological, social, political, and metaphysical instability and confusion that defy logical explanation and which typify Kafka's conception of humanity's absurd relationship with the universe. Although Kafka's work has elicited various critical interpretations, he himself characterized his fiction as symbolic manifestations of his "dreamlike inner life" in which he attempted to reconcile feelings of guilt and insecurity. For many critics, Kafka's greatness resides in his ability to transform his private torment into universal fables.

(For further information on Kafka's life and career, see *Contemporary Authors*, Vols. 105, 126; *Dictionary of Literary Biography*, Vol. 81: *Austrian Fiction Writers, 1875-1913*; *Major 20th-Century Writers*; *Short Story Criticism*, Vol. 5; and *Twentieth-Century Literary Criticism*, Vols. 2, 6, 13, 29.)

CRITICAL COMMENTARY

EDWIN MUIR

(essay date 1930)

[Muir was a distinguished Scottish novelist, poet, critic, and translator. With his wife Willa, he translated works by various German authors unfamiliar to the English-speaking world, including those of Franz Kafka. In the following excerpt, Muir examines *The Trial*, *America*, and *The Castle*, commenting favor-

ably on Kafka's style while discussing themes central to his writings.]

[Kafka's three long stories form] a trilogy corresponding with grotesque differences to the *Divine Comedy*. *The Trial*, which is his "Inferno", deals with a victim of divine justice who does not know even the offence for which he is summoned, and whose judge remains to the end concealed behind an army of subordinate prosecutors and advocates with very questionable creden-

to some, so mysteriously withheld in spite of their intensest efforts from others; while the village is the community, in which one can find one's true place only by deciphering and following the guidance of God. This, indeed, seems to be the meaning of the fable; yet an allegory has not justified itself if it contains nothing more than its interpretation; and the logic of Kafka's narrative is so close that it builds up a whole particularized system of spiritual relations with such an autonomous life of its own that it illumines the symbol rather than is illumined by it. It is almost certain, moreover, that Kafka put together this world without having his eye very much on the symbol; his allegory is not a mere recreation of conceptions already settled; and the entities he describes seem therefore newly discovered, and as if they had never existed before. They are like additions to the intellectual world.

America stands somewhat apart from the other two books. The action takes place in time, and the characters have, like Dostoievski's, a mixture of the natural and the preternatural which makes their outlines periodically dissolve and combine again in a continuously more mythical pattern. There are scenes in *America* as good, I think, as some of Dostoievski's, and in this respect better: that they are corrected, even at their wildest, by a fantastic sense of comedy. The fault of the book is that its setting shifts uneasily between the metaphysical and the actual, and that while its scene is a fantastic version of the United States, it occasionally crosses to a province which is not of the actual world at all. It is the most uneven of his works.

In the other two stories, however, the action takes place entirely in this other province, and everything, the characters, the setting, the development, is part of a metaphysical or theological construction. These intellectually fashioned worlds have their own laws and their own geography. Time, space, custom, right and wrong, have undergone a subtle but decisive change; trifles are crucial; subtle questions are more important than general ones; and every motion is judged by a different standard from that of the world. Yet it is difficult to define what principle it is which causes all those modifications, or to establish the laws or the geography of those two worlds; for their validity resides purely in their imaginative justice, and measure in their symmetry. Except for this we have only one clue to lead us through them: Kierkegaard's theory, which influenced Kafka very deeply, of the incommensurability of the divine and the human moral law. With this clue we are led through maze after maze in which everything is changed and yet real; in which every thought is judged by an intuition of the divine law and in which we recognize objects without being able to give them a name; and simply by doing this find that we have acquired a new understanding of the most ordinary and even the most trivial diurnal things. The architecture of those

tials. *America,* his "Purgatorio", deals less directly with supernatural powers, and relates the adventures of a German boy who goes to the United States, is exploited by rogues, and falls from one misfortune into another. He is Kafka's most charming character, and somewhat resembles Prince Myshkin in *The Idiot.* He is more credible, however, and there is in his presentation, as Herr Brod has pointed out, a touch of Chaplinesque humor. If it were possible to conceive of a perfectly natural boy performing the office of a Myshkin with something of the air of one of Charlie Chaplin's heroes, one would have some idea of this delicious figure. The third story, *The Castle,* is Kafka's curious version of the "Paradiso", a Paradiso which is never reached. (p. 236)

For this elaborate allegory there are symbols enough to be found. To Herr Brod, for instance, the castle represents divine grace, so mysteriously granted

worlds is consummate, and every feature is interesting; for Kafka was a master of construction and of fascinating detail. In realistic novels excessive detail is a defect, for it catalogues things which we could better have imagined; but the author of a purely imaginative world is in the same position as a traveller who has returned from an unknown country, and who interests us more by the faithfulness with which he can describe a native broomstick than by anything else. So Kafka's detail is always fascinating, but it is full of meaning as well; for it is the last working-out of a conception which to be perfect had to inform all its parts. (p. 237)

The main ideas which run through Kafka's work may be condensed into four axioms. The first two are, that compared with the divine law, no matter how unjust it may sometimes appear to us, all human effort, even the highest, is in the wrong; and that always, whatever our minds or our feelings may tell us, the claim of the divine law to unconditional reverence and obedience is absolute. The other two are complementary: that there is a right way of life, and that its discovery depends on one's attitude to powers which are almost unknown. In his two allegories [*The Trial* and *The Castle*], Kafka sets out to discover something about those powers, to prove where he can that they are necessarily right, and to read from his intuition of their nature and aims the only true way of life for his hero. To most modern eyes this must seem from the start a hopeless, indeed a foolish, attempt. The interesting point is that when one surveys it it strikes one as neither Quixotic, nor as lacking in valuable results. It is not only a possible attempt; in Kafka's case it has obviously been a richly fruitful one.

By many of his German admirers Kafka has been called a mystical writer. The adjective seems singularly ill-chosen, however, for the one thing which his heroes never succeed in achieving is a moment of mystical illumination in which their problems might find alleviation. Like Pascal, whom he resembled in many ways—in the daring and solidity of his thought, and in his purgatorial temper—he was a religious genius who, though his faith was unshakable, found little rest in faith; and whose deepest intellectual agonies were caused by the problem of religion itself. He had a singular knowledge of the intricacies of spiritual experience; yet he seems to know them only as possibilities; he remains outside them, as if cut off by an invisible barrier; and his heroes stand in much the same relation to the worlds they traverse as Dante to the worlds in his poem. Sometimes, indeed, his voice has the note of a Calvinist who sees and acknowledges his own reprobation, who accepts the scheme, but is not himself accepted. At those moments his hero seems to be wandering in a vast logical nightmare; the realization comes to him that he has lost his way, the story becomes like a protracted anxiety-neurosis, and one feels the tension has to snap.

Then he always starts anew from something ordinary and concrete, from a sober formulation of the hero's ostensible position, for instance: "It may not be much, but I have a home, a position and real work to do, I have a promised wife who takes her share of my professional duties when I have other business. I'm going to marry her and become a member of the community". Coming where they do in the story, those summaries have always an overwhelming pathos; and in general, indeed, Kafka's pathetic effects are secured simply by defining the hero's situation, or by noting that there is a moderate hope for him. The pathos of moderate hopes, which in spite of their moderation are yet worthy of being clung to, even with desperation; this is a province which Kafka has made his own. Those hopes—and this adds to their pathos—are invariably founded on experience. "Once answer a false ring at your night-bell," the country doctor says in one of the short stories, "and you can never repair the damage." Or again—a passage which Kafka afterwardsdeleted: "If you have the strength to look at things steadily, without, as it were, blinking your eyes, you can see much; but if you relax only once and shut your eyes, everything fades immediately into obscurity". Or, from *America:* "It is impossible to justify yourself if there is no good-will". These axioms do not sound, it is true, like the utterances of hope; yet in their context they do, for there every practical rule, however limited in application, is a help. Their pathos consists in their inadequacy to the vast journey which still lies before the hero, and in the fact that they are founded on experience which must needs be invalid for the problems which will confront him there. Yet they have some kind of use; their existence helps him, even if when he comes to apply them at some future time they will be found mysteriously lacking.

It is a practical temper, a temper which scrutinizes every hope, and yields to no access of despair, which informs all Kafka's work, informs every manifestation of it. It determined the form into which he threw his two great religious narratives: the form of the allegory. For this was the only one which by its very structure was bound to carry him forward to the end he set in front of him. . . . [Kafka postulated] a hero whose only passion was to discover religious truth; and once that was done the hero's passion was no longer relative, like that for example of the characters in Dostoievski's novels, but absolute, and capable of being logically worked out. The action in his allegorical narratives is a sort of dialectic; one position has to be established before we advance to the next, and every advance takes us in the direction we wish to go. So, I think, for anyone who wants to have a serious imaginative treatment of religion, Kafka is infinitely more satisfying than Dostoievski.

There remains his superb literary art. In the difficult *genre* which he essayed he left nothing partly fashioned, no obstacle which he did not merely overcome, but overcome with apparent ease. Temper, method, style: all are consummate. His diction is of the utmost flexibility and exactitude, and of an inevitable propriety. His conduct of the sentence is masterly. Flowing without being monotonous, his long sentences achieve an endless variety of inflection by two things alone: an exact skill in the disposition of the clauses, and of the words making them up. I can think of hardly any other writer who can secure so much force as Kafka by the placing of a word. Yet in all his works he probably never placed a word unnaturally or even conspicuously. He had, it seems to me, all the intellectual and imaginative as well as the technical endowment of a great writer. (pp. 239-41)

Edwin Muir, "A Note on Franz Kafka," in *The Bookman,* New York, Vol. LXXII, No. 3, November, 1930, pp. 235-41.

ALFRED KAZIN

(essay date 1947)

[A highly respected American literary critic, Kazin is best known for his essay collections *The Inmost Leaf* (1955) and *Contemporaries* (1962), as well as for a study of American prose writing entitled *On Native Grounds* (1942). In the following excerpt from a 1947 essay that later appeared in *The Inmost Leaf,* he analyzes Kafka's art and thought, describing the author's vision of man's loneliness and alienation as an essential theme in his works.]

Franz Kafka, who during his lifetime had almost no public and certainly sought none, seems to me the case of a contemporary genius whom we too easily term mysterious because we are unwilling to admit that he is in a certain sense unbearable. (p. 142)

Kafka is difficult not because "he really meant" to say this or that about the nature of contemporary experience, but because he saw in his private and contemporary agony that part of us all which is more real than the public "reality." Just as religious doctrine can be a way of muffling the religious ache in people, so Kafka saw below man's institutions and formal learning the essential unappeasable loneliness of man in the universe, man's longing to know the meaning of his existence and the unbreaking struggle with his own nature. We do not like to face those facts in themselves, and in reading Kafka we immediately assume that the world he presents is constantly a reference to something other than itself. This is why we find him difficult, for we are always trying to find out what hidden suggestion is buried in his work. Hence our desire to explain him, for our purposes, rather than to experience him. For to take that experience undistractedly, to see it for what it is, is to admit that his vision is real. (pp. 143-44)

What [Kafka] gets into his sayings immediately, as his novels unfold it, is the haunted quality of existence—haunted by man's own mystery unto himself. To face him openly is to see that he is talking directly about the inner portion of consciousness which is unbreakingly the judge of life. That portion is not simply the stream of consciousness, where we silently quarrel with things we must outwardly accept, and it is not simply the realm of anxiety or sickness. It is that sense of ourselves on earth whose captive wing we occasionally get into poetry. It is in another realm that equidistance between nature and immensity that leads us not only to create gods but to believe in them. What is intolerable in Kafka is that he throws no comforting bridge of doctrine across for us. What is beautiful in him is that he takes us gravely, and with the most meticulous seriousness, into a world which is exactly, in all its proportions, true to our inner experience. (p. 145)

Someone said of Kafka that he has the great quality of genius in that his integrity seems something given rather than something for which he struggles. It is in his own lack of surprise, in the immediate unity of his perception, that he captivates and troubles us. For Kafka has the purity of those who see the world in such an inclusive metaphor that we cannot quite believe in it, and prefer to break it up, to see what it "really means." When we paraphrase Kafka, or comment on him, we extract the theme of his work and try to use it for our special purpose. But it is exactly the quality of his work that he accepts his fate as a measure of the human condition. What makes Kafka so difficult is not so much in what he says, line by line, as in his inability to let himself off, and hence us as we read him. And the symbols he discovers for himself are not so much tools as they are an inescapable embrace of the world. The world for him is an impossible struggle to reach the castle of grace; is a trial for crimes we do not even know we have committed, whose precise character we can never learn; is like "clambering up a steep precipice, as steep, say, as you yourself seen from below." For Kafka is peculiarly that writer who believes himself the contemporary man of sorrows and is willing to bear all our burdens—they all seem to him so true. Standing at the extremity of human isolation, conscious of himself as an eternal solitary, a Jew, a poor clerk in the prisonhouse of the modern industrial bureaucracy, a cipher in the Central European maze of nationalities, he yet challenges us through and through, and defies us to say that the nightmare is not real. (pp. 145-46)

An imagination like Kafka's is marked by an ability to dissolve the world in his symbols without losing

Kafka at about ten years of age, with two of his three younger sisters. All three of Kafka's sisters later died in Nazi concentration camps.

gain their love or sympathy, dies—virtually, Kafka makes us feel, because life is insupportable. The family is overjoyed by the event and feels released.

Here, even more than in the novels or in the parable about man's effort to reach God which Kafka wrote around **"Investigations of a Dog,"** the main story in *The Great Wall of China*, the inviolate quality of Kafka's symbolism is shown. The sufferings of the clerk in **"Metamorphosis"** do not proceed from the "dreadful event"; the metamorphosis is itself an expression of the clerk's distance from his own family, of the difficulty at communication with one's own, the loneliness that can be deepest in one's own family. The subject of the story is just that passive and dumb humanity which is associated, as in a dream, with debasement. The genius of this story is that which transforms a figure of speech ("You treat me as if I were an animal!") into a parable of the inner distance between human beings. To Kafka that inner distance is so real that it becomes filled with men in the shape of beasts. They do not cease to be men because they are beasts; the only expression of their human alienation is that which converts them into beasts. (pp. 146-48)

Alfred Kazin, "Kafka," in his *The Inmost Leaf: A Selection of Essays*, Harcourt Brace Jovanovich, Inc., 1955, pp. 142-48.

it. It is not easy to define such an imagination, or primary gift; it is the functioning in one man of all that unorganized relationship to the world which is released in poetry. But one of its greatest characteristics is a gift of surrender; the creator yields to his inference about the world and recasts it in the light of his symbol. In **"Metamorphosis,"** a long story rather than a novel, a young clerk wakes up one morning to find that he has been transformed into "some monstrous kind of vermin." He is not dreaming it; his metamorphosis is only too real, and the life of his family is deeply changed by the fact. . . . The clerk, in his strange metamorphosis, has lost none of his human feelings and understands only too painfully what is going on. But he cannot communicate with the people; his humanity is reduced to experience of the most painful helplessness and isolation. In a fit of rage, the father—unable by any other means to convey his hatred of his son—throws an apple at him, which is embedded in the skin. This the son must bear as a tangible realization of the horror he has aroused in his own family, and after futile efforts to

MAX BROD
(essay date 1960)

[Although best known as the editor of the posthumously published works of Franz Kafka, Brod was also a prolific novelist, dramatist, biographer, and prose writer whose works were highly regarded in Europe during his lifetime. In the following excerpt from the 1960 revision of his *Franz Kafka: A Biography*, he assesses themes and style in Kafka's fiction.]

I wrote about [Kafka's] first book [*Contemplation*] and about his literary work in general in the only long essay on him that appeared during Franz's lifetime, in the *Neue Rundschau*, November 1921, and among other things said, "Where shall I begin?—It doesn't matter where. For among the peculiarities of this phenomenon is that one can approach it from any angle and reach the same conclusion.

"This already shows how true, how unshakably genuine, how pure it is. For a lie offers a different aspect from every angle, and what is impure is iridescent. But in the case of Franz Kafka, and let it be said in his case alone in the whole literary circle of the 'moderns,' there is no iridescence, no changes of view, no scene-shifting. Here is truth, and nothing but the truth.

"Take his language, for example. The cheap means, coining new words, compounds, playing chess with the clauses, he despised. 'Despised' is perhaps not the right word. They are inaccessible to him, just as the impure is inaccessible to the pure, is forbidden to it. His language is clear as crystal, and on the surface one can, as it were, detect no other aim than that of properly and clearly suiting the subject. And yet underlying the serene mirror of this well of pure language are dreams and visions of unfathomable depth. . . . The cadences, the breaks, seem to follow mysterious laws; the little pauses between phrases have an architecture of their own, a melody is heard that has its roots in other material than that of this earth. It is perfection, simply perfection, that perfection of pure form that brought Flaubert to tears in front of the ruins of the walls of the Acropolis. But it is perfection on the move, on the march, at the double, even. I am thinking of things like **'Children on the Post Road,'** which was the introductory story in his first book, *Contemplation,* this classically beautiful prose that nevertheless derives so completely from the cottage. There you have fire, the completely restless fire and blood of a tense childhood, full of forebodings; but the walls of fire obey the baton of an invisible conductor; they are not ragged sheets of flame but a palace, whose every stone is a roaring blaze. Perfection—and just for that reason not *outré* and not extravagant. One turns somersaults only so long as one has not reached the utmost limit, the line that embraces the universe. The all-embracing does not need to turn somersaults. But don't things get dull at this level? This is the heart of Kafka's importance as an artist. I said before, he is perfection on the move, on the road. Hence the all-embracing consorts without effort with the minutest, yes, the most scurrilous detail. . . . Hence these great sentences full of artistry, and this simplicity of style, which is yet shot through with ideas in every phrase, in every word. Hence the inconspicuousness of the metaphors which nevertheless—it is only some time after that one notices it with surprise—say something new. Hence calm, perspective, freedom, as if above the clouds—and yet good natural tears and the compassionate heart. If the angels made jokes in heaven it would have to be in Franz Kafka's language. This language is fire, but it leaves no soot behind. It has the sublimity of endless space, and at the same time it palpitates with every palpitation of things created. . . . It is a new kind of smile that distinguishes Kafka's work, a smile close to the ultimate things—a metaphysical smile so to speak—indeed sometimes when he used to read out one of his tales for us friends of his, it rose above a smile and we laughed aloud. But we were soon quiet again. It is no laughter befitting human beings. Only angels may laugh in this way, angels that we certainly cannot picture in the likeness of Raphael's cherubs—no, angels, seraphim with three great pairs of wings, demonic beings between man and God.

"In a quite special way, then, strength and weakness, rise and fall, interpenetrate in Kafka's writings. At first sight it is weakness that meets the eye—something that on the surface puts one in mind of decadence, and satanism, of the love of decay, death and horror that breaks out in Poe, in Villiers de l'Isle Adam, and other later writers. But this first sight is entirely misleading. A short story like Kafka's **'In the Penal Colony'** has nothing whatever in common with Poe, although scenes of horror occur in it along the same thematic line. A comparison of the style, if nothing else, should teach one that, or at least give one to think. What has the brightly colored narrative of Kafka, with its sure line, like a drawing by Ingres, in common with the vibrating prose, sometimes indeed violently set in vibration, of these specialists in making one's flesh creep? They are specialists in the deep-sea exploration of hells, having a more or less scientific interest in their explorations; a little religious end-resolution, a kind of 'moral of the tale,' is stuck on more or less out of embarrassment. Writers, certainly great writers even, and honestly confounded—but don't you hear throughout a note of being 'proud of confusion'? But in Kafka's case after all it is the deep earnestness of a religious man that fills the scene. He shows no curiosity about the abysses. It is *against his will* that he sees them. He does not lust after decay. He falls into decay, although he follows the narrow path, sees and loves determination and coherence, and there is nothing he loves so much as the blue unclouded heaven above him. But this heaven begins to pucker like the forehead of a scowling father. And as much more terrible and more shudderingly gruesome the fear for keeping heaven unclouded is than making a study of a tolerable couple of hell's abnormities and turning them into capital, so much more powerful is the shattering effect of Kafka's polished work of art than the sensations to be got from those sketch-books of 'interesting' pathology of the 'uncanny' type.

"That is exactly why his books—**'The Metamorphosis'** or **'The Verdict,'** etc.—give the reader such a shudder. Because all around them, and really in the midst of them, too, the whole of the free world is revealed. But they are not 'on principle meant to horrify'—but rather on a principle that is perhaps idyllic or heroic, in any case honest, healthy, positive, inclined to everything that desires to live, everything gentle and good, the blooming girlish body that shines over the corpse of the hero at the end of **'The Metamorphosis,'** farm labor, everything natural, simple and fresh with a child's freshness, full of striving after joy, happiness, decency, physical and spiritual strength, on the principle then on which a well-meaning God worked when

He created the world—but 'not for us.' Against the background of a good Divine Will this 'only not for us' has a doubly terrifying effect, as a confession of sin of the utmost possible force. It is not life that Kafka rejects. He does not strive with God, only with himself. Hence the dreadful severity with which he goes to law. All through his writings there are judges' chairs, sentences are executed. **'The Metamorphosis'**—the man who is not perfect, Kafka degrades to an animal, to an insect. Or, what is still more horrible (**'A Report to an Academy'**), he lets the animal be raised to the level of a human being, but to what a level of humanity, to a masquerade at which mankind is unmasked. But even that is not enough! Mankind must sink deeper still—it is a question only of 'all or nothing'—and if a man cannot raise himself to God's level, if the Father has found him guilty, if entire union with the fundamental morality, entry into the 'Law,' is forbidden him by a hefty doorkeeper, or rather when the man has not the courage to thrust this doorkeeper on one side, when the 'imperial messenger' of the dying sun-prince never comes to you—very well, then change yourself into some useless object that is neither animate nor inanimate, into a reel of cotton, which as 'something in the care of the heavenly householder' wanders upstairs and downstairs without stopping. 'What's your name, then?'—'Odradek'—and a whole range of Slav words is set ringing, which all mean renegade, renegade from one's race, 'rod,' renegade from the council, 'rada,' the divine decision of the creation, 'rat.' 'And your address?' 'No fixed abode.' From this you can understand that Kafka writes, alongside the general tragedy of mankind, in particular the sufferings of his own unhappy people, homeless, haunted Jewry, the mass without form, without body, as no one else has ever done. He writes it, without the word 'Jew' appearing in any one of his books." (pp. 132-35)

Max Brod, in his *Franz Kafka: A Biography,* translated by G. Humphreys Roberts and Richard Winston, second edition, Schocken Books, 1960, 252 p.

RALPH FREEDMAN

(essay date 1962)

[Freedman is an American critic and author of the acclaimed biography *Hermann Hesse: Pilgrim of Crisis* (1978). In the following excerpt, he contends that it is best to approach Kafka as a writer of realistic rather than symbolic or psychological fiction.]

In unraveling Kafka's obscurity, many critics have emphasized two modes of interpretation which, directly and indirectly, extend the notion of the romantic dream. The visionary's obscurity or the bright illuminations of the hallucinatory mind have become, in the twentieth century, symbolic torture gardens of the unconscious. Recognizing the precision of Kafka's thought, some of these critics have seen in his work exact allegorical correspondences or consistently applied metaphors whose symbolic meanings reveal an inner world. Others have sought to explain his worlds as compulsive dreams seen in orthodox Freudian terms. Yet Kafka is far less internal a writer than he is frequently assumed to be. In fact, neither approach does justice to the manifold nature of his vision.

Kafka uses symbolism, but shrinks from its consistent application. If, in **"The Metamorphosis,"** Gregor is hit by the apple thrown at him by his father, the conventional religious significance imparted by the choice of the fruit is no more than an allusion—almost jocular in its obviousness—suggesting one of several possibilities. If, in the story **"In the Penal Colony,"** the officer's martyrdom suggests Christ's sacrifice, one possibility is explored, and if the New Commandant's doctrine of mercy makes the officer's sacrifice necessary, another possibility and another (contrasting) Christ figure is alluded to. To seek consistent symbolic references in Kafka's prose may be interesting and often rewarding, but this course leads only to individual terms of multiple relations which Kafka plays against one another. Symbolism must be taken into account, but it is not the master key to Kafka's work.

Similarly, an exclusively psychological explanation leaves vast areas of Kafka's obscurity unexplained. We need not dwell on the obvious psychoanalytic motif which recurs in his fiction: the hero's relationship to an overwhelming authority, as in **"The Metamorphosis"** or *The Trial,* which can be diagnosed as an enactment of his relationship with his father and with the authoritarian society he found so intolerable. In fact, such an explanation sheds considerable light on Kafka's motives for choosing his themes and worlds. But to view his worlds as labyrinths of the *subconscious* would sharply limit the scope and depth of his work. For, as we shall see, the shadowy characters who appear to his heroes are independent entities, through which manifold relations are explored.

The most fruitful approach to Kafka's work would begin with a recreation of his world as he actually presents it to us, a world of concrete, albeit rearranged reality. This view presupposes that Kafka is essentially a realistic writer who does not seek to reduce the world to characteristic states of mind.

Experiencing the world as a self-contradictory manifold, Kafka envisions the constant and hopeless struggle of the discerning intelligence to come to terms with the objects by which it has been conditioned. Yet these objects and worlds are real; the demonic writer, seeking to demonstrate the full extent of the mind's entanglement with them, deliberately distorts them to reveal different ways in which a hero (carefully defined) would cope with a significantly rearranged world. Since it leads to a close scrutiny of the moral and spiritual problems involved in human existence, this approach may reflect Kafka's interest in Kierkegaard which he himself has recorded. His methods of execution, however, can also be explained through two literary traditions in which he developed: naturalism and expressionism. (p. 63)

[It] is clear that Kafka was not a naturalistic writer in the ordinary sense. Despite some faithful depictions of squalor in *The Trial, The Castle,* and elsewhere, his manner is nowhere reminiscent of Zola or Dreiser. His prevarications of reality did not seek to expose social evils or reflect ideals concerned with the improvement of mankind, but to reveal man's involvements in an apparently absurd world. But even such an expansion of the naturalistic premise does not fully explain Kafka's vision. Only in the imposition on his world of an expressionistic grotesque do we find a further clue to the nature of his distortions.

The importance of *expressionism* to Kafka has long been debated. Yet, quite apart from the merits of this debate, it remains clear that Kafka's work developed during that quarter century in which expressionism in literature and art had come into being and into maturity. It was a pervasive modern movement in which many of his friends were engaged. Its chief relevance to Kafka was its use of distortion and stylization to reveal the essential character, rather than the changing appearances, of an object or world. In expressionistic novels like Alfred Döblin's *Berlin-Alexanderplatz* or Hermann Hesse's *Der Steppenwolf,* the writer sought to free his protagonist from the bondage of time, place, and milieu by dissolving the universe and reconstituting it in terms of a particular vision of reality held by the artist.

Kafka went his own way. He was neither a "naturalist" nor an "expressionist." No great artist can be caught in the categories set up by literary historians. Nevertheless, these two important ways of looking at reality shed some light on his manner and offer us points of departure for our unending efforts at exegesis. For Kafka does present reality as an external, not a psychological, dimension, and he distorts reality to reveal man's puzzling condition which his agonized and ironic mind envisaged. To cite Erich Heller's striking image: his world resembles that of Plato's cave which a malicious God has paneled with mirrors. The prisoner thirsting for true knowledge now perceives actual shapes, not shades, yet the concave walls of the cave reflect these forms in grotesque distortions in which the mind discerns its true relations. We therefore do not witness dreams and hallucinations as such, as we often view them in expressionistic stories and plays. It is

Cover, with illustration by Ottomar Starke, of Kafka's most popular work, *The Metamorphosis.*

made perfectly clear that Gregor's awakening in **"The Metamorphosis"** or K's search in *The Castle* are not dreams; we are soon convinced that the arrest in *The Trial* is not an internal event. (p. 64)

To allude once more to Kafka's affinity with naturalistic form, this method appears as an intensified version of Zola's prescriptions in *Le Roman expérimental.* The objective author-observer introduces his character into a carefully specified world. Keeping all elements constant, he then observes his character's adjustment to a particular change. Heller's God paneling the walls of the cave with mirrors is the writer himself, seeking to extract a particular meaning from his deliberately reconstructed encounter between protagonist and world.

"The Metamorphosis" illustrates this manner most clearly. The significant shift, of course, is Gregor's awakening in the shape of a stag-beetle. The story develops all consequent changes in both the hero and the world. As in *Gulliver's Travels,* once an initial change is accepted, all else follows with convincing logic.

The hero's transformation and the change in his

relations to the world involve significant cognitive changes. Kafka's way of exploring the paradoxes Gregor confronts is therefore at first epistemological; that is, it is concerned with different ways of knowing reality, of exploring the shifting relations between self and world. From Gregor's point of view, the tragedy of **"The Metamorphosis"** consists in the self's gradual reduction to its most vital center—its self-consciousness. In two stages—a more superficial change in spatial relations and a more central change in the consciousness of time—Gregor is finally reduced to a mere speck of self-awareness which is ultimately extinguished. As in Swift's book, the story begins with shifts in cognitive relations and ends in a crucial change in the nature of the hero himself.

Immediately following the awakening, only physical appearances and perspectives seem to be changed while Gregor's essential self appears unchanged. With meticulous care and a great deal of fantastic realism, Kafka portrays shifts in spatial relations which suddenly circumscribe Gregor's movements and world. His bed is an immense obstacle. He can hardly reach the door-handle. His voice gradually transforms itself from a human voice to an animal squeak, while his memory and other mental faculties as a human being seem to remain essentially unimpaired. But more and more the trappings of humanity disappear, helped by the ill-concealed outrages of his employer and his family. Transformations now affect Gregor more substantially; his vision adjusts to his new perspectives. The room seems too big; the furniture oppresses him. He prefers closed windows and dirt. His sister perceives him sitting in an animal-like trance. But these changes are not wholly generated from within Gregor's transformed shell. They are also conditioned by the world's reactions to his condition.

The mortal wound inflicted by the father with the unfortunate apple provides a second shift in relations which affects the core of Gregor's self. The wound eats more and more deeply towards the center of his self, his human consciousness and memory. Before this event, appearances in self-perception and in perceptions of him by others undergo important shifts, but time continues to strike the hours with the alarm-clock's exactness. Gregor's sense of time is almost unchanged. But after his last foray into humanity, his fatal wound, his last response to his sister's music, self-consciousness begins to dim and, with it, his sense of time. In the end, the obliteration of time coincides with Gregor's obliteration.

Gregor's reduction to a "mere" self, and his consequent destruction, are conditioned by parallel changes in the external world. These changes occur in response to Gregor's mysterious *Verwandlung*. The father's assumption of "authority" by becoming a uniformed bank-messenger is the most obvious illustration, but equally important are changes which lead to the constriction of the household. The cleaning woman fully transforms Gregor's room into a garbage dump and becomes another mortal enemy. The entire home assumes an atmosphere of degradation as even the mother and sister "adjust" to the new condition. The three "lodgers"—whatever else they may be thought to signify—typify this oppressive shift in Gregor's former world. An unindividuated "chorus," introduced in a manner reminiscent of romantic and expressionistic fiction, they suggest the intrusion of an entire alien world. They push the family into the kitchen, usurp the dining-room and are treated by Gregor's parents with exaggerated deference. The world has been wrenched out of recognition. For the helplessly observing Gregor, its change has become irrevocable.

Shifts in both self and world condition and require one another. Gregor's own transformation had also been a function of his world. He had in fact been a vermin, crushed and circumscribed by authority and routine, before the actual transformation had taken place: Gregor recalls that when the manager had towered above him in the office he had already felt like an insect. Moreover, we noted that the most important changes had been evoked by others' reaction to his condition: his rejection by boss, father, even by his mother and sister. But it is crucial to this revelation of his condition—appearing more and more purely as he nears his end—that it had been an *aspired* condition. He had been imprisoned in his animal existence which had been implied by his human life, yet freed from intolerable burdens, including the tyranny of time. In his death likewise he is both extinguished and set free.

If Gregor's end is marked by a constriction of his physical universe and a paradoxical liberation from the bondage of himself (the true and final transformation of the hero), the family, we infer, had been similarly constricted and set free. In this way, relations constantly shift, unite, and contrast with one another. The self and the various figures representing the world are equally important, and the author focuses on them simultaneously. For this reason, the shift in point of view to the family is a perfectly defensible way of concluding the story. Gregor's extinction has, in the end, become the family's liberation. Since the self has been obliterated by the world, the emphasis must now be placed upon the world, for its figures have gained at last the liberation the hero had sought. Grete's yawn of freedom neatly ties the story to the transformation of the beginning. Yet this very conclusion has pushed us to the point of absurdity—reached by the simultaneous creation and dislocation of a particular world—in which contradictory solutions, like constriction and freedom, obliteration and awareness of existence, equally apply.

Gregor's role in the changing pattern of the world

around him is deepened by our becoming aware of the significance of the form he assumes. Being reduced to a particularly repulsive specimen of animal life, he is made to enact part of his concealed nature, but he is also transformed into an effective, albeit passive, rebel against a world and values in which beetles have no place. Moreover, the very form of the insect mask deepens the moral implications of the changes in perception and point of view by which the story is ordinarily described. A good deal has been written about Kafka's use of animal figures as human masks and of human figures as animal masks. One reason for this practice is the same rationale which suggested Houyhnhnms and Yahoos to Swift. But for Kafka there is also another reason; the animal widens human perception, because it frees it from moral necessity. Gregor as a human being with an animal mask therefore experiences peculiar conflicts between liberation from and subjection to moral choice, which are only gradually eliminated in his own obliteration. In this story the vermin carries with it the notion of disgust, but in other stories we encounter a similar effect without this element. In **"Report to the Academy,"** a monkey wears a human mask. In **"The Hunger Artist,"** the human "artist" kept as a caged animal is contrasted with the truly bestial spectators until in the significant inversion he is replaced by the actual beast—the panther.

These transformations finally suggest the intricate relations in man between a human and an animal nature. . . . As an expressionistic device getting at the essence of split humanity, as a point of transformation which reveals several layers of perception to be reflected against one another, and as a satiric mirror of man, the animal form becomes the logical counterpoint, the key to transformations through which a state of mind or awareness can be reflected against its cosmic or social antagonists. (pp. 65-8)

Ralph Freedman, "Kafka's Obscurity: The Illusion of Logic in Narrative," in *Modern Fiction Studies,* Vol. VIII, No. 1, Spring, 1962, pp. 61-74.

JOHN UPDIKE

(essay date 1983)

[A perceptive observer of the human condition and an extraordinary stylist, Updike is one of America's most distinguished men of letters. Best known for such novels as *Rabbit Run* (1960), *Rabbit Redux* (1971), and *Rabbit is Rich* (1981), he presents in his fiction people searching for meaning in their lives while facing the painful awareness of their mortality and basic powerlessness. In the following excerpt, he discusses Kafka's life and works, examining *The Metamorphosis* in relation to both.]

The century since Franz Kafka was born has been marked by the idea of "modernism"—a self-consciousness new among centuries, a consciousness of being new. Sixty years after his death, Kafka epitomizes one aspect of this modern mind-set: a sensation of anxiety and shame whose center cannot be located and therefore cannot be placated; a sense of an infinite difficulty within things, impeding every step; a sensitivity acute beyond usefulness, as if the nervous system, flayed of its old hide of social usage and religious belief, must record every touch as pain. In Kafka's peculiar and highly original case, this dreadful quality is mixed with immense tenderness, oddly good humor, and a certain severe and reassuring formality. The combination makes him an artist; but rarely can an artist have struggled against greater inner resistance and more sincere diffidence as to the worth of his art.

Of his fiction, Kafka committed to publication during his lifetime only a slender sheaf of mostly very short stories—the longest of them, **"The Metamorphosis,"** a mere fifty pages, and a handful of the others as much as five thousand words. He published six slim volumes, four of them single stories, from 1913 to 1919, and was working on the proofs of a seventh in the sanatorium where he died, on June 3, 1924, of tuberculosis, exactly one month short of his forty-first birthday. Among his papers after his death were found several notes addressed to his closest friend and most faithful admirer, Max Brod. One of them stated:

> Of all my writings the only books that can stand are these: **"The Judgment," "The Stoker," "Metamorphosis," "Penal Colony," "Country Doctor,"** and the short story: **"Hunger-Artist."** . . . When I say that those five books and the short story can stand, I do not mean that I wish them to be reprinted and handed down to posterity. On the contrary, should they disappear altogether that would please me best. Only, since they do exist, I do not wish to hinder anyone who may want to, from keeping them.

The little canon that Kafka reluctantly granted posterity would indeed stand; **"The Metamorphosis"** alone would assure him a place in world literature, though undoubtedly a less prominent place than he enjoys thanks to the mass of his posthumously published novels, tales, parables, aphorisms, and letters. (p. 121)

Kafka dated his own maturity as a writer from the long night of September 22-23, 1912, in which he wrote **"The Judgment"** at a single, eight-hour sitting. . . . Soon after its composition, he wrote, in a few weeks, **"The Metamorphosis,"** an indubitable masterpiece. It begins with a fantastic premise, whereas in **"The Judgment"** events become fantastic. Its monstrous premise—that Gregor Samsa has been turned overnight into a gigantic insect—established in the first sentence, **"The Metamorphosis"** unfolds with a beautiful naturalness and a classic economy. It takes place in three acts: three times the metamorphosed hero ventures out of his room, with tumultuous results. The members of his family—rather simpler than Kafka's own, which had three sisters—dispose themselves around the central horror with a touching as well as an amusing plausibility. The father's fury, roused in defense of the fragile mother, stems directly from the action and inflicts a psychic wound gruesomely objectified in the rotting apple Gregor carries in his back; the evolutions of the sister, Grete, from shock to distasteful ministration to a certain sulky possessiveness and finally to exasperated indifference are beautifully sketched, with not a stroke too much. The terrible but terribly human tale ends with Grete's own metamorphosis, into a comely young woman. In a strange way, this great story resembles a great story of the nineteenth century, Tolstoy's "The Death of Ivan Ilyich"; in both a hitherto normal man lies hideously, suddenly stricken in the midst of a family whose irritated banal daily existence flows around him. The abyss within life is revealed, but also life itself.

What kind of insect is Gregor? Considerable paper has been wasted on this question. Popular belief calls him a cockroach, which would be appropriate for a city apartment; and the creature's retiring nature and sleazy dietary preferences would seem to fit. But, as Vladimir Nabokov, who knew his entomology, pointed out. . . . , Gregor is too broad and convex to be a cockroach. The charwoman calls him a "dung beetle" (*Mistkäfer*), but, Nabokov said, "it is obvious that the good woman is adding the epithet only to be friendly." Interestingly, Eduard Raban of **"Wedding Preparations"** daydreams, walking along, "As I lie in bed I assume the shape of a big beetle, a stag beetle or a cockchafer, I think." Gregor Samsa, awaking, sees "numerous legs, which were pitifully thin compared to the rest of his bulk." If "numerous" is more than six, he must be a centipede—not a member of the Insecta class at all. From evidence in the story, he is brown in color and about as long as the distance between a doorknob and the floor; he is broader than half a door. He has a voice at first, "but with a persistent horrible twittering squeak behind it like an undertone," which disappears as the story progresses. His jaws don't work as ours do, but he has eyelids, nostrils, and a neck. He is, in short, impossible to picture except when the author wants to

evoke him, to bump the reader up against some astounding, poignant new aspect of Gregor's embodiment. The strange physical discomfort noted in the earlier work is here given its perfect allegorical envelope. . . . When **"The Metamorphosis"** was to be published as a book, in 1915, Kafka, fearful that the cover illustrator "might be proposing to draw the insect itself," wrote the publisher, "Not that, please not that! . . . The insect itself cannot be depicted. It cannot even be shown from a distance." He suggested instead a scene of the family in the apartment with a locked door, or a door open and giving on darkness. Any theatrical or cinematic version of the story must founder on this point of external representation: a concrete image of the insect would be too distracting and shut off sympathy; such a version would lack the very heart of comedy and pathos which beats in the unsteady area between objective and subjective where Gregor's insect and human selves swayingly struggle. Still half asleep, he notes his extraordinary condition yet persists in remembering and trying to fulfill his duties as a travelling salesman and the mainstay of this household. Later, relegated by the family to the shadows of a room turned storage closet, he responds to violin music and creeps forward, covered with dust and trailing remnants of food, to claim his sister's love. Such scenes could not be done except with words. In this age that lives and dies by the visual, **"The Metamorphosis"** stands as a narrative absolutely literary, able to exist only where language and the mind's hazy wealth of imagery intersect.

"The Metamorphosis" stands also as a gateway to the world Kafka created after it. His themes and manner were now all in place. His mastery of official pomposity—the dialect of documents and men talking business—shows itself here for the first time, in the speeches of the chief clerk. Music will again be felt, by mice and dogs, as an overwhelming emanation in Kafka's later fables—a theme whose other side is the extreme sensitivity to noise, and the longing for unblemished silence, that Kafka shared with his hero in **"The Burrow."** Gregor's death scene, and Kafka's death wish, return in **"A Hunger Artist"**—the saddest, I think, of Kafka's stories, written by a dying man who was increasingly less sanguine (his correspondence reveals) about dying. (pp. 124-29)

John Updike, "Reflections: Kafka's Short Stories," in *The New Yorker*, Vol. LIX, No. 12, May 9, 1983, pp. 121-26, 129-33.

SOURCES FOR FURTHER STUDY

Emrich, Wilhelm. *Franz Kafka: A Critical Study of His Writings.* New York: Frederick Ungar Publishing Co., 1968, 561 p.

One of the most comprehensive studies of Kafka's work.

Flores, Angel, and Swander, Homer, eds. *Franz Kafka Today.* Madison: University of Wisconsin Press, 1958, 289 p.

Critical essays divided into sections devoted to the short stories, novels, diaries, and leters. Included are studies by Heinz Politzer, Carl R. Woodring, and Clement Greenberg, among others.

Hayman, Ronald. *Kafka: A Biography.* New York: Oxford University Press, 1982, 349 p.

Most complete biography.

The Literary Review, Kafka: Centenary Essays 26, No. 4 (Summer 1983).

Special issue devoted to studies of Kafka and his work.

Pawel, Ernst. *The Nightmare of Reason: A Life of Franz Kafka.* New York: Farrar, Strauss, and Giroux, 1984, 466 p.

Biography utilizing psychoanalytic theory to interpret Kafka's life and work.

Politzer, Heinz. *Franz Kafka: Parable and Paradox.* Ithaca, N.Y.: Cornell University Press, 1966, 398 p.

Critical study focusing on structural and stylistic analysis of Kafka's fiction.

John Keats

1795-1821

English poet.

INTRODUCTION

Keats is recognized as a key figure in the English Romantic movement. The writers associated with this period placed the individual at the core of all experience, valued imagination and beauty, and looked to nature for revelation of truth. Although his literary career spanned only four years, Keats achieved remarkable intellectual and artistic development. His poems, especially the later works published in *Lamia, Isabella, The Eve of St. Agnes, and Other Poems* (1820), are praised not only for their sensuous imagery and passionate tone, but also for the insight they provide into aesthetic and human concerns, particularly the transiency of beauty and happiness. The artistic philosophy delineated in Keats's famous quote from the "Ode on a Grecian Urn"—"beauty is truth, truth beauty"—is clarified in his correspondence with his family and friends. In these letters it is possible to trace the evolution of Keats's poetic thought and technique as he matured and refined his ideas and beliefs regarding literature. There Keats set down poetic theories that have become standards of literary criticism, such as his theory of "negative capability," "that is when man is capable of being in uncertainties, mysteries, doubts, without any irritable reaching after fact and reason."

Scholars often note that Keats's childhood provides no hint of the genius who was to emerge. The oldest of four children of a stable-keeper, he was raised in Moorfields, London. His father died from injuries sustained in a fall from a horse when Keats was seven. In 1803, Keats enrolled at the Clarke school in nearby Enfield, where he was distinguished only by his small stature (he was barely over five feet tall as an adult) and somewhat pugnacious disposition. At the Clarke school, Keats first encountered the works that influenced his early poetry, including Edmund Spenser's *The Faerie Queene* and John Lemprière's *Classi-*

cal Dictionary, on which he based his knowledge of Greek mythology. The vivid imagery and the use of allegory and romance in Keats's poetry reflect the lasting impression made on the young poet by these works. Keats's mother died of tuberculosis in 1810, and the Keats children were placed in the care of a guardian, Richard Abbey. At fifteen, Keats was apprenticed to an apothecary; four years later he entered Guy's and St. Thomas's Hospitals in London, where he completed medical courses and in 1816 passed the examinations to become an apothecary. Keats had begun to compose poetry as early as 1812, however, and secretly decided to support himself on his small inheritance after graduation and devote himself to writing. In order to avoid a confrontation with his guardian, Keats continued his studies to become a surgeon, carefully concealing his decision from Abbey until he had reached the age of majority and was free of his guardian's jurisdiction.

Keats's meeting in 1816 with Leigh Hunt influenced his decision to pursue a career as a poet, and Hunt published Keats's early poems in his liberal journal, the *Examiner.* Keats was drawn readily into Hunt's circle, which included the poet John Hamilton Reynolds, the critic William Hazlitt, and the painter Benjamin Robert Haydon. *Poems,* an early collection, was published in 1817, but received little attention. His next work, *Endymion: A Poetic Romance,* a full-length allegory based on Greek mythology, was published the following year to mixed reviews. Soon after the appearance of *Endymion,* Keats began to experience the first symptoms of tuberculosis, the disease that had killed his mother and in 1818 his brother, Tom. Following Tom's death, Keats lived with his close friend Charles Armitage Brown in Hampstead. He continued writing and spent a considerable amount of time reading the works of William Wordsworth, John Milton, and Shakespeare. Here Keats also fell in love with Fanny Brawne, a neighbor's daughter. The rigors of work, poor health, and constant financial difficulties prevented the two from fulfilling their desire to be married. Keats's final publication, *Lamia, Isabella, The Eve of St. Agnes, and Other Poems,* included, in addition to the noted title poems, Keats's famous odes and *Hyperion: A Fragment,* an unfinished narrative based on Greek mythology that stylistically owed much to Milton's *Paradise Lost. The Fall of Hyperion* was a later, unsuccessful attempted completion and revision of *Hyperion.* This work remained unpublished until 1856. Other uncollected writings, including the humorous verse "Cap and Bells; or, The Jealousies" and Keats's final sonnet, "Bright Star," were first published in 1848 in *The Life, Letters, and Literary Remains of John Keats,* compiled in 1848 by Richard Monckton Milnes. In a final effort to regain his health, Keats sailed to Italy in September 1820; he died in Rome in February of the following year. He is buried there beneath a gravestone which bears an epitaph that he himself composed: "Here lies one whose name was writ on water."

The history of Keats's early reputation is dominated by two hostile, unsigned reviews of *Endymion,* one credited to John Gibson Lockhart in *Blackwood's Edinburgh Magazine,* and the other to John Wilson Croker in the *Quarterly Review.* Lockhart, a vociferous detractor of what he termed "The Cockney School," named for its members's ties to London and their alleged lack of refinement, attacked not only Keats's poem, which he denigrated on artistic and moral grounds, but on what he perceived as the poet's lack of taste, education, and upbringing. While Croker was neither so vitriolic nor personally degrading as Lockhart—critics acknowledge, in fact, the legitimacy of several of his complaints—his essay was singled out as damaging and unjust by Keats's supporters, who rushed to the poet's defense. While Keats was apparently disturbed only temporarily by these attacks, they gave rise to the legend that his death had been caused, or at least hastened, by these two reviews. A chief perpetrator of this notion was Percy Bysshe Shelley, who composed and published his famous *Adonais: An Elegy on the Death of the Poet John Keats* shortly after Keats's death. The preface to this work implicated Croker as Keats's murderer. *Adonais,* in conjunction with the writings of Keats's well-meaning friends, effectively created the image of the poet as a sickly and unnaturally delicate man so fragile that a magazine article was capable of killing him. Lord Byron commented wryly on this idea in a famous couplet in his poem *Don Juan:* " 'Tis strange the mind, that very fiery particle / Should let itself be snuffed out by an article."

The *Adonais* image of Keats lent credence to the view that he was merely a poet of the senses, capable only of evoking pleasurable sensations, an assumption that dominated Keats scholarship for forty years after his death and lingered into the twentieth century. The critic responsible for initially establishing Keats as a poet of ideas worthy of serious critical consideration was Milnes, whose landmark biography, *Life, Letters, and Literary Remains of John Keats,* presented Keats's own letters and poems as evidence of his intellectual maturity and artistic worth. The 1880 publication of Matthew Arnold's essay identifying Keats as "standing with Shakespeare" marked the beginning of Keats's critical reputation as an intellectual poet. At the same time, however, such Pre-Raphaelite artists as William Morris, Dante Gabriel Rossetti, and William Holman Hunt sustained the old image of Keats by championing him as their artistic forebear because of his richly pictorial descriptions and lush imagery. Similarly, Arthur Symons admired Keats's poems for the "art for art's sake" quality they evinced. By the early twentieth century, however, such respected critics as

Ernest de Selincourt, A. C. Bradley, and Robert Bridges had confirmed Keats's status as an intellectual as well as an emotive and pictorial poet, and full-length works by Clarence DeWitt Thorpe and John Middleton Murry, among others, echoed their assertions. Contemporary critics continue to find much to explore in the nuances of Keats's ideas as well as in the beauties of his poetic technique.

While early nineteenth-century critics focused on *Endymion* in their discussions of Keats as a poet of sensations, and later Victorian scholars often chose the poem as a subject of study, contemporary commentators most frequently concentrate on Keats's odes. Considered by many the most mature and highest expression of Keats's genius, the odes are also considered his most intellectually challenging works. The themes of the transience of beauty, the "eternal quality of art," and the desire to transcend the human world unite such poems as "Ode to a Nightingale," "Ode on a Grecian Urn," and "Ode on Melancholy." Contemporary critics often associate Keats's narrative poetry with his odes because of their similar maturity of expression. Miriam Allott writes that " 'The Eve of St. Agnes' . . . celebrates the warmth of a requited passion but, characteristically, cannot forget its attendant hazards or its vulnerability to time." She also claims that "La Belle Dame Sans Merci" presents this theme in a more decisive way: "the destructiveness of passion is expressed as keenly as its delight, the emotion is still more ambivalent and the presence of death yet more haunting." The approaches employed by twentieth-century critics in interpreting these works are varied and encompass such subjects as Keats's affiliation with other artists, including Shelley and Wordsworth, and the writers who influenced his literary style, such as Spenser and Shakespeare. Modern critics are also especially interested in the evolution of Keats's aesthetic theory and his transformation in his poetry of biological and nature imagery.

While his provocative intellect and stunning artistic ability form the basis of Keats's reputation, critics acknowledge the fact that, to many, the poet's life is as compelling as his work. The astonishing use Keats made of his brief creative period continues to awe readers. But above all, the singlemindedness with which he pursued his goal of becoming a successful poet has won the sympathy and imaginations of his readers. As Douglas Bush wrote: "No other English poet of the century had his poetic endowment, and no other strove so intensely. . . . However high one's estimate of what he wrote, one may really think—to use an often meaningless cliche—that Keats was greater than his poems."

(For further information about Keats's life and works, see *Dictionary of Literary Biography*, Vol. 96: *British Romantic Poets*; *Nineteenth-Century Literature Criticism*, Vol. 8; and *Poetry Criticism*, Vol. 1.)

CRITICAL COMMENTARY

MARY DE REYES

(essay date 1913)

[In the following excerpt, de Reyes comments on influences that helped shape the literary style of Keats's poetry.]

No poet at the age of twenty-four has produced work comparable with the 1820 volume in depth of thought, in beauty of imagery and in easy mastery of technique. The reason for Keats's early maturity lies in his high conception of his art. He knew that if poetry was to be his vocation it must correspond to his whole being and demanded nothing less than his whole life.

That he must bring to it, not only knowledge of lyric technique, but also a deep understanding of the mind of man, in its conflicts with and in its ultimate harmony in nature. It was thus to the two great masters of Life and Nature—Shakespeare and Wordsworth—

that the young poet turned. He went to them—not for inspiration—for that was already his—but rather for direction of his intellect. From them he brought away that philosophic view of all creation as a whole, wherewith to interpret his thought. Much of Wordsworth's poetry may have seemed to him a studied expression of a definite philosophy rather than a great spontaneous emotion which by its strength and directness enters straightly into the soul, nevertheless, Keats saw truly in Wordsworth a poet who had first drawn his inspiration from Nature through the great contemplation of her mysteries, and had so obtained that height of philosophy in which "thought and feeling are one."

It has been said that Keats luxuriated in emotions, and his famous ejaculation "Oh for a life of sensations rather than of thoughts" has often been used to denounce him. But Keats was no mere luxuriator in emotions. He realized how the poet uses all sense beauty

Principal Works

Poems (poetry) 1817

Endymion: A Poetic Romance (poetry) 1818

Lamia, Isabella, The Eve of St. Agnes, and Other Poems (poetry) 1820

Life, Letters, and Literary Remains of John Keats (poetry and letters) 1848

Another Version of Keats's "Hyperion" (poetry) 1856

Letters of John Keats to Fanny Brawne (letters) 1878

Letters of John Keats to His Family and Friends (letters) 1891

The Complete Poetical Works and Letters of John Keats (poetry and letters) 1899

The Complete Works of John Keats. 5 vols. (poetry, letters, and prose) 1900-01

The Complete Poems (poetry) 1977

and purifies it through the high purpose of his vision into intellectual flame. Intuition expresses his attitude, rather than sensation. "One does well to trust imagination's light when reason's fails" he wrote. There is much in his 1817 volume which has not been so intellectualized, but in his later work, the greatest restraining influence—that of Greek thought—had come upon him. It was through the lectures of Haydon on the Elgin marbles that Keats was first brought into knowledge of the Greek world. Much of Greek thought appealed to him as an expression of truth in forms essentially beautiful. From it, he learnt that the most ideal representations of life are not incompatible with the minutest detail, and thus the vagueness of his earlier poems gave place to definite poetic shapes. We may trace the growth of this influence in the great advance from *Endymion* to *Hyperion*. The lesson of artistic concentration has been learnt, the limp and effeminate verbiage has been replaced by a stern compression of all superfluity. The work is possessed with something "of the large utterance of the early gods." (pp. 77-9)

But Keats was not a poet of ancient Greece alone. He was also an interpreter of the Romance world. **"Isabella," "The Eve of St Agnes," "La Belle Dame sans Merci"** are all exquisite renderings of the glamour of the mediaeval world, deepened by the all pervading spirit of Nature. We have only to contrast **"Isabella"** with the original in the tale of Boccaccio to see what this means. Boccaccio gives us the story in all its horror of detail to arouse in us a sense of genuine tragedy and awful exultancy. With Keats, the tragedy of the story lies wholly in the depth of passion. This is given not by acts of violence but by interpretation of the human heart through nature. The tender susceptibility of the lovers in each other's presence, the complete absorption of Isabella in her basil, oblivious of the changing loveliness of the world.

> And she forgot the sun and moon and stars
> And she forgot the wind above the trees
> She had no knowledge when the day was done
> And she forgot the chilly autumn breeze.

While the tragic loneliness of the murdered man is revealed through the dim, ghostlike perception of sounds.

> Alone I chant the holy Mass
> While little sounds of life are round me knelling.
> And glossy bees at noon do fieldward pass
> And many a chapel bell the hour is telling,
> Paining me through: those sounds grow strange to me
> And thou art distant in Humanity.

The dream-like atmosphere of mediaevalism hangs over the **"Eve of St Agnes."** The shifting moonlight, the buttresses black against it, are alike creations of an enchanted world. The wonderful felicity of word and phrase, the wealth of imagery and vivid colouring give it an intensely Spenserian effect.

In contrast to this picture of love, satisfying and victorious, is that of the fascination and doom of **"La Belle Dame sans Merci."**

In the magical touch of this picture of desolation and gloom, there is much of the spirit of Coleridge. There is no full description. The poem is lyrical rather than narrative. The wonderful slight suggestion of the landscape,

> The sedge is withered from the lake,
> And no birds sing.

gives the very spirit of the old romance world. And in the intense lyrical feeling we have the climax of passion. (pp. 79-80)

Keats is at his greatest in his odes. Though it may be true that he lacks the glowing intensity of Shelley, the spontaneity of the Elizabethans to whom they were simply outbursts of song, they are nevertheless free from phraseology and over elaboration of form. They are instinct with beauty of thought and rhythm, and in them, all the different elements of his genius are harmonized.

Such are the odes to **"Autumn"** and to the **"Nightingale"** where the effect is produced by the simplest forms, by such wonderful lines as these:—

> Where youth grows pale, and spectre-thin and dies.
> The self same song that found a path
> Through the sad heart of Ruth, when, sick for home,
> She stood in tears amid the alien corn.

The long drawn out lines brood over their own sweetness, and in them is a fine excess which is yet never exaggeration.

The poetry of Keats is throughout that of a mind which has loved beauty and which seeks amid the ruin of the transitory the one thing permanent.

This is the message of the **"Ode on a Grecian Urn."** Here the mutability of life is contrasted with the immortality of the principle of beauty which in its completeness stands "all breathing human passion far above." So too in the **"Ode to Autumn"** all is serenity of mind. Vain questioning is laid aside, reason is wrapt in faith. This high ennobling thought is significant of the end of Keats's work where, like Shakespeare, he rises to the supreme acceptance of all life, and sees it in its entirety, permeated with the one divine purposefulness. The quiet and peace of the whole spirit of autumn passes into the figure of the reaper, the gleaner, the maiden at the cider press, giving them a grace other than their own. "The season of mists and mellow fruitfulness" has its beauty also, a beauty no less than that of the songs of spring.

The greatness of Keats's poetry lies in the extreme sensitiveness of his mind to impression, and in his power of interpreting and translating this emotion in the terms of common life.

The gorgeous Oriental pageant of Bacchus is for him as for the Indian maiden, a passing splendour. What the poet gives must be transcripts of his actual experience, and his sympathy with Nature must always depend upon his sympathy with humanity. Feeling for Nature may only find voice in language applicable to human emotion, and so also beauty of nature is his unfailing resource for the expression of the subtlest soul emotions.

In this lies the secret of the Greek spell, and this is how Keats realized the spirit in which the Greek legends had been created. When the poet tells how the dead lovers lift their heads at the passing of Endymion "as doth a flower at Apollo's touch" he gives no idle personification but the embodiment of his belief in the healing power of a radiant presence in an image of perfect simplicity and truth.

Yet great as was his affinity with the Greek world, he was also in closest sympathy with the thought of his own day. It is he who by the spirit of Wordsworth is able to interpret the moods of nature. Whatever his imagination touched thrills with a sense of the mystery and awe underlying common things. In all nature he saw a high romance answering to the infinite longing of the soul, and alone capable of satisfying it. He does not therefore desire us to read lessons from Nature or to learn of her. He calls us not to reason but rather to watch and to adore. The message of the thrush in the yellow glory of a February morning gives the truth of this:—

O fret not after knowledge! I have none
And yet my song comes native with the warmth.

O fret not after knowledge! I have none
And yet the evening listens!

Such are the moments of a poet's ecstasy when his heart beats in unison with the mighty heart of the universe, and his own individuality is but a medium through which to express the universal. In this lies complete self-realization and utter poesy of life and thought. (pp. 80-2)

Mary de Reyes, "John Keats," in *Poetry Review,* Vol. III, No. 2, August, 1913, pp. 72-82.

SOLOMON F. GINGERICH
(essay date 1932)

[In the following excerpt, Gingerich examines the development of Keats's concept of beauty in his poetry.]

Keats approached beauty from a direction diametrically opposite to that of Shelley. He started by absorbing sense impressions of natural surroundings and building a theory of beauty thereon. Shelley's approach to beauty was from the beginning abstruse and highly sophisticated; that of Keats was simple and unsophisticated. Shelley found this "dull dense world" now and then lighted up as by the rays of some alien Power of Beauty; Keats found beauty as a constituent part of the earth itself, and of all the objects of the earth. "A thing of beauty is a joy," he said. He stressed things—small, large, common, unusual—all kinds of things, such as, he says, "the sun, the moon, trees old and young," sheep on a hillside, daffodils, streams, lovely tales, heroic deeds, "the grandeur of the dooms we have imagined for the mighty dead,"

An endless fountain of immortal drink,
Pouring unto us from the heaven's brink.

Everywhere around us Keats discovered a plenitude of beauty to feed the eyes and ears and other senses. (pp. 177-78)

This was the foundation and beginning of Keats' devotion to beauty; but no more. His famous saying, "O for a life of Sensations rather than Thoughts!" is true only as applied to his earliest literary years, for he soon began to rationalize his love of the beautiful. The first step in this rationalization lay in his discovery of a principle of permanency in beauty. Sensations were always a joy—sensations and sense-imagery are basic in poetry, and their importance must not be minimized—but the discovery that there is something lasting in beauty was an advance to a higher level of perception. This is the special significance of the famous opening lines of *Endymion:*

> A thing of beauty is a joy forever;
> Its loveliness increases; it will never
> Pass into nothingness.

This everlastingness is a thing of beauty, rather than the idea that beauty is truth, or the idea of the worship of beauty in itself, is the theme of the great **"Ode on a Grecian Urn."** . . . Not "truth" but "forever" is the key word; this poem is one of the superb examples in all literature for its expression in every image and every stanza of an abstract truth by imaginative suggestion, without overt assertion. The emotional reaction is also completely integrated with the idea of the poem.

The idea of the permanency of beauty leads directly to "the worship of the principle of beauty in all things," which is the central position with Keats. He clung to "things" in order that beauty as he conceived it should not become too impalpable; but it is the "principle" that is more and more the object of devotion as he develops toward fullness of power; the principle itself also becomes more austere as the poet grows toward maturity. It is this that saves Keats, on the one hand, from being a worshipper of impalpable abstractions, and, on the other, from being a mere reveler in sensuous beauty. In short, Keats has put himself on the highroad, I believe, to a very healthy and sound aesthetics.

For the principle of beauty, as Keats conceived it, is a principle inherent in the very constitution of creation itself. Take, for instance, proportion, harmony, order—technical, but fundamental, elements of beauty. An organism exists by virtue of the relation of its parts to each other, and of all the parts to the whole; if some parts are displaced, or irregular, there is a lack of harmony. In the larger sense order runs throughout created existence. The destruction of order and harmony in the universe would throw the universe back into chaos. Beauty, which includes order and harmony, is thus as essential to creation and existing things as is truth; it stands side by side with truth as necessary to life and reality. Keats had a far deeper realization than most men of the vitality and significance of beauty in this sense, and it is in this sense that he thought of it as truth.

It was this phase of beauty that Keats essayed in *Hyperion.* As the fallen Saturn and his followers had ruled over a Heaven and an Earth that were fairer far than Chaos and blank Darkness, so the new race of gods represents a higher harmony and beauty:

> So on our heels a fresh perfection treads,
> A power more strong in beauty, born of us
> And fated to excel us, as we pass
> In glory that old Darkness: nor are we

> Thereby more conquer'd, than by us the rule
> Of shapeless Chaos.

Oceanus, who speaks these words, asserts that he had found the "one avenue" that leads to "eternal truth," and the truth is that the excellencies of existing things and the order to which they belong is basically determined by the law of beauty—beauty is eternal truth. This is "Nature's law." The proud forest is more comely than the dull soil from which it has sprung. The golden-feathered eagles tower in their greater beauty above the forest. Keats makes Oceanus not only assert the eternal law of beauty on the basis of a higher and more powerful order of creation than that which formerly existed, but also suggest, daringly, cycles of orders of still higher perfection and beauty:

> 'Tis the eternal law
> That first in beauty should be first in
> might:
> Yea, by that law, another race may drive
> Our conquerors to mourn as we do now.

The level to which a thing belongs, or to which it may attain, is determined by the quality and order of beauty it possesses. Unquestionably Keats identified beauty not only with truth, but also with might and with power. It represents Keats' fundamental way of approach to the meaning of life.

Thus far Keats pursued the principle of beauty, but no further. He progressed rapidly from the idea of beauty as Sensation to beauty as Truth and Power, in several steps. The phrase in *Endymion* about the everlastingness of beauty became the theme, a little later, of the **"Ode on a Grecian Urn."** The phrase at the close of this Ode, which identified beauty with truth, was later amplified and illustrated in *Hyperion.* A developing theory of beauty was thus worked out in Keats' writings. But its evolution in poetic practice was far from complete; the possibilities that inhere in the theory were far from being exhausted by Keats: the poet's life was too short for that.

Keats' theorizing in his poetry on beauty distinctly influences the poetry itself. His early poems, such as **"I Stood on Tiptoe," "Sleep and Poetry,"** and large portions of *Endymion,* are remarkable mainly for their sensuous beauty, a certain naturalistic atmosphere, and for felicitous expressions. They are "simple, sensuous," if not passionate. Here Keats indulges in sense-imagery, with but little restraint, piling up sensations indiscriminately and with unflagging delight:

> I was light-hearted,
> And many pleasures to my vision started:
> So I straightway began to pluck a posey
> Of luxuries bright, milky, soft and rosy.

He feels, to the point of cloying, "overwhelming sweets"—"a breathless honey-feel of bliss" from

Dew-drops, and dewy buds, and leaves, and flowers.

The sensuous luxury is as marked as in Shakespeare's early *Venus and Adonis,* both poets having at their disposal in youth a wealth of raw material, a richness of sensuous content from which they could draw in unlimited measure. This, and the verbal and stylistic felicities abounding in both poets at an early age, indicate important likenesses, and suggest that, after Shakespeare, Keats was the most richly endowed poetic nature in English literature. Luxurious sense-imagery is to be found here and there throughout Shakespeare's works, and not least in some of his later plays, such as *The Winter's Tale.* In his early poems Keats copiously "heaped with glowing hand" image upon image, producing a "purple riot" of varied effects, in language of "voluptuous accents."

From these somewhat formless and sometimes top-heavy poems Keats progressed rapidly to that period in which he exercised restraint and showed selective ability, wherein he singled out individual objects—Elgin Marbles, a Grecian Urn, a Nightingale—and formed shapely poems, meaningful, close-knit, organically unified, making the principle of beauty stand out clearly, either by the theme or by the poem itself as a concrete example. Here the poet's practice kept pace with his theory. Instead of the former riot of luxuriousness we now have sensuous richness toned down to the purpose of strict unity. The ideas and feelings are perfectly integrated with the rich texture of the poems. On the level on which these poems move—it must be noted that they do not create human characters or deal with personality in moral conflict, or with ultimate human destiny—Keats has rendered the principle of beauty in forms as rich and lovely and perfect as poetry is able to achieve.

But in *Hyperion,* where he essayed a much wider formula for the principle of beauty, namely, truth and power, he was only partially successful, not alone in integrating the statement of the theory with the poetry itself, but in illustrating it in the incidents and events and, most of all, in the characters of the poem. As a matter of fact, this purpose of revealing the principle of beauty with all high seriousness in action and character calls for a kind of breadth and wisdom of experience which we have no right to expect from any man under the age of twenty-four in any period of literary history. Attacked by mortal illness at the age of twenty-four, and dying at the age of twenty-five, Keats left his theories and their application incomplete. The five years' advantage that Shelley had over Keats, and the fifteen years' advantage that Poe had make an immense difference with regard to the growth of their concepts to maturity. There are many signs that, had not his health failed, Keats would have succeeded in applying his principle of beauty to far wider experiences of life. His letters reveal the fact that he was aiming to reach out to the possession of wider knowledge and the grasp of deeper philosophic wisdom. "There is but one way for me," he said. "The road lies through application, study, and thought. . . . I will pursue it." He said he would study philosophy, by which he undoubtedly did not mean, primarily, technical philosophy, but a broad study of human experience and human truth. The restlessness accompanying this purpose of widening his knowledge and experience was not, as Mr. G. R. Elliott has asserted (in *The Cycle of Modern Poetry*), an indication of an intellectual and spiritual tragedy in him preceding the pathos of his early death. This restlessness was literally no more nor less than the pains of growth accompanying the rapid development of a normal but extraordinary youth of twenty-three who could proudly declare that he saved his feeling of humility for "the Eternal Being, the Principle of Beauty, and the Memory of Great Men." (pp. 178-83)

As has been noted, Keats perceived the principle of beauty as inhering in and being integrally a part of the very constitution of things—as being primarily essential to their existence. The vitality with which this principle is seized, and the penetration with which it is expressed, give it significance and render possible its application not only to things, objects and organisms, but to the whole round of life—to human conduct under all the conditions of actual life, to the poise and balance of human character evolved from human suffering and moral conflict, to the moral and religious experience of mankind, and to the ultimate destiny of humanity. But there is relatively little of these high matters in the extant poetry of Keats. He did say, to be sure, in **"Sleep and Poetry,"** when speaking of sensuous joys:

And can I ever bid these joys farewell?
Yes, I must pass them for a nobler life,
Where I may find the agonies, the strife
Of human hearts.

And he said similar things at other times. Yet it is a hope and a promise rather than an achievement; nor have we a right to expect that it should be otherwise. The years of Keats' life were too few to provide him with the experience necessary to realize and embody these high matters within the compass of his principle of beauty. A slow growth, the maturing of all a poet's powers, and many actual experiences of life are necessary in order to reach such a level of experience and achievement. It was not a tragedy, but a triumph, that at the age of twenty-three Keats was able to see as clearly as he did the way in which he must go.

The things which Keats actually did reflect sufficient glory upon him to make it unnecessary to ascribe to him things which he did not do. He did not produce a *Divine Comedy,* or a *Macbeth,* or a *Paradise Lost.* But he did seize with exceptional strength the principle of beauty in things, and he put his theory of beauty with extraordinary vigor, with "astonishing strength," into practice. He pursued his vision of beauty with clear-eyed sanity in a perfect balance of theory and practice, so far as his youth and experience permitted. His is the glory of having reached as high a level of achievement at the age of twenty-five as any poet on record, and of having consistently and everlastingly traveled the right road toward high achievement. (pp. 183-85)

Solomon F. Gingerich, "The Conception of Beauty in the Works of Shelley, Keats, and Poe," in *Essays and Studies in English and Comparative Literature,* Vol. VIII, 1932, pp. 169-94.

LEONARD UNGER

(essay date 1950)

[Unger was an American educator and literary critic. In the excerpt below from an essay originally published in 1950, he examines the theme, imagery, and artistic achievement of "To Autumn." He also provides succinct comparisons to the other "great Odes."]

It seems generally agreed that **"To Autumn"** is a rich and vivid description of nature, expertly achieved within a fairly intricate stanzaic pattern. The words are successfully descriptive (or evocative) in their phonetic qualities and rhythmical arrangement, as well as in their imagistic references. If we are familiar with Keats' other work, however, we can discover that the poem is not only rich in pictorial and sensuous details, but that it has a depth of meaning and a characteristic complexity of structure. **"To Autumn"** is allied especially to the odes on Melancholy, on a Grecian Urn, and to a Nightingale. The four poems are various treatments presenting differing aspects of a single theme.

In so far as the theme is "stated" in any of the poems, it is most clearly stated in the **"Ode on Melancholy."** In fact, if we want a general formulation of the theme, we need only quote the last stanza—especially these lines:

Ay, in the very temple of Delight
Veil'd Melancholy has her sovran shrine,
Though seen of none save him whose strenuous
    tongue
Can burst Joy's grape against his palate fine.

Keats was obviously preoccupied with the consideration that beauty and melancholy are closely related: true melancholy is to be found only in the fullness of living, in beauty, joy and delight, for these experiences make most poignant the passage of time, through which such experiences and then life itself must come to an end.

All this is clear enough in the **"Ode on Melancholy."** There is, however, the implication that the relationship between beauty and melancholy works both ways. That is, either joy or sadness is most intensely felt when it is attended by a consciousness of the experience which is opposite and yet so closely related to it. The theme, then, is more complex and subtle than the aspect of it which appears on the surface in **"Ode on Melancholy."** Other implications of the theme may be found throughout the four poems, which illuminate and clarify each other. This is not to say that the poems are merely repetitions of the same theme, which Keats had in mind before he wrote any of them. When we understand the poems we might find it more accurate to say that each is the exploration of a certain theme.

With so much of its context in mind, let us examine closely **"To Autumn."** The poem opens with an apostrophe to the season, and with a description of natural objects at their richest and ripest stage.

Season of mists and mellow fruitfulness,
Close bosom-friend of the maturing sun;
Conspiring with him how to load and bless
With fruit the vines that round the thatch-eaves
    run;
To bend with apples the moss'd cottage-trees,
And fill all fruit with ripeness to the core;
To swell the gourd, and plump the hazel shells
With a sweet kernel; to set budding more,
And still more, later flowers for the bees,
Until they think warm days will never cease,
For Summer has o'er-brimm'd their clammy cells.

The details about the fruit, the flowers and the bees constitute a lush and colorful picture of autumn and the effects of the "maturing sun." In the final lines of the first stanza, however, slight implications about the passage of time begin to operate. The flowers are called "later," the bees are assumed to think that "warm days will never cease," and there is a reference to the summer which has already past.

In the second stanza, an imaginative element enters the description, and we get a personification of the season in several appropriate postures and settings.

Who hath not seen thee oft amid thy store?
Sometimes whoever seeks abroad may find
Thee sitting careless on a granary floor,
Thy hair soft-lifted by the winnowing wind;
Or on a half-reap'd furrow sound asleep,
Drows'd with the fume of poppies, while thy hook
Spares the next swath and all its twined flowers:
And sometimes like a gleaner thou dost keep
Steady thy laden head across a brook;
Or by a cyder-press, with patient look,
Thou watchest the last oozings hours by hours.

As this stanza proceeds, the implications of the descriptive details become increasingly strong. For example, autumn is now seen, not as setting the flowers to budding, but as already bringing some of them to an end, although it "Spares the next swath." Autumn has become a "gleaner." The whole stanza presents the paradoxical qualities of autumn, its aspects both of lingering and passing. This is especially true of the final image. Autumn is the season of dying as well as of fulfilling. Hence it is with *"patient* look" that she (or he?) watches "the last oozings hours by hours." Oozing, or a steady dripping, is, of course, not unfamiliar as a symbol of the passage of time.

It is in the last stanza that the theme emerges most conspicuously.

> Where are the songs of Spring? Ay, where are they?
> Think not of them, thou hast thy music too,—
> While barred clouds bloom the soft-dying day,
> And touch the stubble-plains with rosy hue;
> Then in a wailful choir the small gnats mourn
> Among the river sallows, borne aloft
> Or sinking as the light wind lives or dies;
> And full-grown lambs loud bleat from hilly bourn;
> Hedge-crickets sing; and now with treble soft
> The red-breast whistles from a garden-croft;
> And gathering swallows twitter in the skies.

The opening question implies that the season of youth and rebirth, with its beauties of sight and sound, has passed, and that the season of autumn is passing. But autumn, too, *while* it lasts—"While barred clouds bloom the soft-dying day"—has its beauties, its music, as Keats' poem demonstrates. The imagery of the last stanza contrasts significantly with that of the first, and the final development of the poem adds meaning to its earlier portions. The slight implications are confirmed. We may recall that "maturing" means aging and ending as well as ripening. The earlier imagery is, of course, that of ripeness. But the final imagery is more truly autumnal. The first words used to describe the music of autumn are "wailful" and "mourn." The opening stanza suggests the height of day, when the sun is strong and the bees are gathering honey from the open flowers. But in the last stanza, after the passing of "hours and hours," we have "the soft-dying day," the imagery of sunset and deepening twilight, when the clouds impart their glow to the day and the plains. The transitive, somewhat rare use of the verb *bloom,* with its springlike associations, is perhaps surprising, and certainly appropriate and effective in suggesting the tensions of the theme, in picturing a beauty that is lingering, but *only* lingering. The conjunction of "rosy hue" and "stubble-plains" has the same significant incongruity, although the image is wholly convincing and actual in its reference. While the poem is more descriptive and suggestive than dramatic, its latent theme of transitoriness and mortality is symbolically dramatized by the passing course of the day. All these characteristics of the poem are to be found in its final image: "And gathering swallows twitter in the skies." Here we have the music

of autumn. And our attention is directed toward the darkening skies. Birds habitually gather in flocks toward nightfall, particularly when they are preparing to fly south at the approach of winter. But they are still gathering. The day, the season, are "soft-dying" and are both the reality and the symbol of life as most intensely and poignantly beautiful when viewed from this melancholy perspective.

This reading of **"To Autumn"** is obviously slanted in the direction of a theme which is also found in the other odes. The theme is, of course, only a part of the poem, a kind of dimension, or extension, which is almost concealed by other features of the poem, particularly by the wealth of concrete descriptive detail. Whereas in **"Ode on Melancholy"** the theme, in one of its aspects, is the immediate subject, in **"To Autumn"** the season is the subject and the details which describe and thus present the subject are also the medium by which the theme is explored. (pp. 20-4)

The poem has an obvious structure in so far as it is a coherent description. Its structure, however, is not simple in the sense of being merely continuous. For example, the course of the day parallels the development of the poem. And an awareness of the theme gives even greater significance to the structure, for the theme merges with increasing clarity and fullness throughout the poem until the very last line. Because the theme is always in the process of emerging without ever shaking off the medium in which it is developed, the several parts of the poem have a relationship to each other beyond their progression in a single direction. The gathering swallows return some borrowed meaning to the soft-dying day with substantial interest, and the whole last stanza negotiates with the first in a similar relationship. (If we had a special word for this kind of structure in poetry, we should be less inclined to discuss it figuratively. The words *organic* and *dynamic* have been used, as well as the word *dramatic.* Particularly in regard to Keats' poetry has *spatial* been used as a critical term (by Tate). For example, we might say that the structure of **"To Autumn"** is *spatial,* not only because of the quality of the imagery, but because the structural elements exist, or coexist, in a relationship with each other which is different from the temporal progression that constitutes, on one level, all descriptive, narrative, and discursive writing. This *spatial* metaphor is applicable in more or less degree to any piece of writing in so far as it fulfills the formal conditions of art. It is by such considerations that we move in an ever widening circle away from the particular poem or experience, and the expressions which were initially metaphors thus tend to become abstract critical terms. **"To Autumn"** itself, as we have seen, has implications about space and time, but because it scarcely takes the first step into metaphor, which is also a step toward statement, it is of all the odes at the farthest extreme from abstraction.)

We have observed the descriptive, temporal (course of day), and thematic aspects of the structure. Another aspect of structure appears when, once more, we consider the poem within the context of Keats' work. **"To Autumn"** shares a feature of development with the odes on the Nightingale and the Grecian Urn. Each of these poems begins with presentation of realistic circumstances, then moves into an imagined realm, and ends with a return to the realistic. In **"Ode to a Nightingale,"** the most clearly dramatic of the poems, the speaker, hearing the song of the nightingale, wishes to fade with it "into the forest dim" and to forget the painful realities of life. This wish is fulfilled in the fourth stanza—the speaker exclaims, "Already with thee!" As the poem proceeds and while the imagined realm is maintained, the unpleasant realities come back into view. From the transition that begins with the desire for "easeful Death" and through the references to "hungry generations" and "the sad heart of Ruth," the imagined and the real, the beautiful and the melancholy, are held balanced against each other. Then, on the word "forlorn," the speaker turns away from the imagined, back to the real and his "sole self."

"Ode on a Grecian Urn" opens with an apostrophe to the actual urn. In the second stanza the imagined realm, the "ditties of no tone," is invoked, and the "leaf-fringed legend" comes to life. And here, too, the imagined life and real life are set in contrast against each other—the imagined is the negation of the real. It is in the fourth stanza that the imagined life is most fully developed and at the same time collapses into the real. The urn is left behind and the people are considered as not only in the scenes depicted on the urn, but as having left some little town. With the image of the town, desolate and silent, the imagination has completed its course. The people can never return to the town. In the final stanza they are again "marble men and maidens" and the urn is a "Cold Pastoral." The statement about truth and beauty with which the poem ends is famous and much debated. It is conceivable that Keats is saying here what he has said elsewhere and in another way—in the Ode that begins

> Bards of Passion and of Mirth,
> Ye have left your souls on earth!
> Have ye souls in heaven too,
> Double-lived in regions new?

Toward the end of the poem there are these lines:

> Here, your earth-born souls still speak
> To mortals, of their little week;
> Of their sorrows and delights;
> Of their passions and their spites;
> Of their glory and their shame;
> What doth strengthen and what maim.
> Thus ye teach us, every day
> Wisdom, though fled far away.

Keats is not didactic here, nor does he claim didacticism for the bards. Their earth-born souls, their works, teach wisdom in speaking of the lives of men, and in bringing to men, generation after generation, an intensified awareness and thrill of being alive. It is the same wisdom which the urn will continue to teach "in midst of other woe." Keats believed that man's life, though rounded by a little sleep, is the stuff of which "a thing of beauty" is made. Art takes its truth from life, and then returns it to life as beauty. The paradox that "teases us out of thought" is that in a work of art there is a kind of life which is both dead and immortal. But, a melancholy truth, *only* the dead are immortal. If there is a heaven, Keats wanted it to be very much like earth, with a Mermaid Tavern where poets could bowse "with contented smack." Delight is inseparable from melancholy because it is not conceivable apart from the mortal predicament. The answer to the question at the end of **"Ode to a Nightingale"**—"Do I wake or sleep?"—is, Both. In the structural imaginative arc of the poem, the speaker is returned to the "drowsy numbness" wherein he is awake to his own mortal lot and no longer awake to the vision of beauty. Yet he knows that it is the same human melancholy which is in the beauty of the bird's "plaintive anthem" and in the truth of his renewed depression. His way of stating this knowledge is to ask the question. Such considerations may clarify the truth-beauty passage. Whether they justify artistically Keats' use of these clichés of Platonic speculation is another matter. Keats was no Platonist, and if he had avoided those terms or if he had indicated more obviously, within the poem, that he was using the word *truth* in a sense close to the materialism of his own times, **"Ode on a Grecian Urn"** would have had a different career in the history of literary criticism. It is unlikely that any amount of exegesis can rescue those last lines of the poem from associations with Platonic pietism, for Keats was not enough of a witty and conscious ironist to exploit successfully the philosophical ambiguities of *truth*. His romanticism was neither reactionary nor modernist in that way, and he may not even have been clearly aware of the ambiguity involved. If it could be proved that he was innocent of the ambiguity, and wanted only the philosophical prestige of the Platonic associations, then from his point of view the poem would not suffer from the difficulties which the merest sophistication can ascribe to it. Whether such ignorance of the law would be too outrageous to merit critical exoneration is a nice problem for critical theory.

In considering the arc of imagination as an aspect of structure, we have noticed that **"Ode to a Nightingale"** approaches general statement and that **"Ode on a Grecian Urn"** arrives at it. **"To Autumn"** is obviously less explicit, although it shows the same structural aspect. The lush and realistic description of the first stanza is followed by the imagined picture of autumn as a person who, while a lovely part of a lively scene, is also intent upon destroying it. The personification is dropped in the final stanza, and there is again a realistic description, still beautiful but no longer lush, and suggesting an approaching bleakness.

The imaginative aspect of structure which the three odes have in common illustrates opinions which are in accord with the thought of Keats' times and which he occasionally expressed in his poetry. The romantic poets' preoccupation with nature is proverbial, and there are a number of studies (e.g., Caldwell's on Keats) relating their work and thought to the associationist psychology which was current in their times. According to this psychology, all complex ideas and all products of the imagination were, by the association of remembered sensations, evolved from sensory experiences. Keats found this doctrine interesting and important not because it led back to the mechanical functioning of the brain and the nervous system, but because sensations led to the imagination and finally to myth and poetry, and because the beauty of nature was thus allied with the beauty of art. In the early poem which begins, "I stood tip-toe upon a little hill," Keats suggests that the legends of classical mythology were created by poets responding to the beauties of nature:

> For what has made the sage or poet write
> But the fair paradise of Nature's light?
> In the calm grandeur of a sober line,
> We see the waving of the mountain pine;
> And when a tale is beautifully staid,
> We feel the safety of a hawthorn glade:
> • • • • •
> While at our feet, the voice of crystal bubbles
> Charms us at once away from all our troubles:
> So that we feel uplifted from the world,
> Walking upon the white clouds wreathed and
> curled.
> So felt he, who first told, how Psyche went
> On the smooth wind to realms of wonderment.
> • • • • •
> What first inspired a bard of old to sing
> Narcissus pining o'er the untainted spring?
> In some delicious ramble, he had found
> A little space with boughs all woven round;
> And in the midst of all, a clearer pool . . .

In the **"Ode to Psyche,"** which was written during the same year as the other odes (1819), Keats claims a similar experience for himself and contrasts it with those of the "bards of old." He has come upon Cupid and Psyche while he "wandered in a forest thoughtlessly." Although the times are "too late for antique vows" and the "fond believing lyre," he is still by his "own eyes inspired." If he cannot celebrate this symbolic deity with rites and shrine, then he proposes to do so with the service of the imagination, with "the wreath'd trellis of a working brain, . . . all the gardener

Fancy e'er could feign" and with all that "shadowy thought can win." Conspicuous throughout Keats' work, blended and adjusted according to his own temperament and for his own purposes, are these *donnèes* of his time: a theory of the imagination, the Romantic preoccupation with nature, and the refreshed literary tradition of classical mythology. These are reflected by the structure of his most successful poems, and are an element in their interrelatedness.

"To Autumn" is shorter than the other odes, and simpler on the surface in several respects. The nightingale sings of summer "in full-throated ease," and the boughs in the flowery tale on the urn cannot shed their leaves "nor ever bid the Spring adieu." The world in which the longer odes have their setting is either young or in its prime, spring or summer. Consequently, in these poems some directness of statement and a greater complexity are necessary in order to develop the paradoxical theme, in order to penetrate deeply enough the temple of Delight and arrive at the sovran shrine of Melancholy. The urn's "happy melodist" plays a song of spring, and the "self-same song" of the nightingale is of summer. One of these songs has "no tone," and the other is in either "a vision or a waking dream," for the voice of the "immortal Bird" is finally symbolized beyond the "sensual ear." But the music of autumn, the twittering of the swallows, remains realistic and literal, because the tensions of Keats' theme are implicit in the actual conditions of autumn, when beauty and melancholy are merging on the very surface of reality. Keats' genius was away from statement and toward description, and in autumn he had the natural symbol for his meanings. If **"To Autumn"** is shorter than the other odes and less complex in its materials, it has the peculiar distinction of great compression achieved in simple terms. (pp. 24-9)

Leonard Unger, "Keats and the Music of Autumn," in his *The Man in the Name: Essays on the Experience of Poetry*, University of Minnesota Press, Minneapolis, 1956, pp. 18-29.

JAMES D. BOULGER

(essay date 1961)

[In the following excerpt, Boulger discusses symbolism in "Ode to a Nightingale," "The Eve of St. Agnes," and *Lamia*, arguing that "in these symbolic experiences the poet projects on the highest imaginative level man's dream of permanence for his more hopeful psychological states of being."]

In Keats' poetry there is a tension between spirit and matter, between vision and existence, which has not gone unnoticed by critics who refuse to view Keats only as the mindless esthete, the cultivator of "Romantic" sensibility. It is true that Keats longed to shape existence into the permanent form of beauty, but he could never forget the sense of anguish and limitation in his individual self. The tension arising from this dualism caused him to search for symbols which might unite in permanent and meaningful form the play between the transient anguish of life and the world of his imagination. For Keats it was a quest of a special kind to create a symbolic world in which the qualities of the spirit modify harsh facts of nature, yet where the colors, sounds and attitudes of the natural world are the realities of the poetic vision. When successful this romantic vision achieves permanence in the world of art equal to that of a grecian urn. In moments of failure the existential anxiety of the unsatisfied individual breaks through to destroy the symbol.

This quest for the perfect medium of poetic vision Keats followed into all areas of human experience. His perception of the natural world creates the bird symbol in **"Ode to a Nightingale,"** intensely refined passion the religious symbolism surrounding the lovers in **"The Eve of St. Agnes,"** and a semi-divine force operating in the world the myth symbolism of *Lamia.* In these symbolic experiences the poet projects on the highest imaginative level man's dream of permanence for his more hopeful psychological states of being.

Lacking successful symbolic projection, Keats believed, man exists in an unrelieved world of pain, boredom and sensuality, condemned by his nature to view with despair the gap between the actual and the ideal. There are various symbols in Keats' poetry by means of which the imagination attempts to bridge this gap. Drink is the most realistic and the most common, but in both **"Ode to a Nightingale"** and *Lamia* this coarse physical way is practiced by the ordinary sensual breed, not by the poet or his hero. The more successful symbols, taken from the world of nature, mythology, love and art, appear in **"Ode to a Nightingale,"** *Lamia,* **"The Eve of St. Agnes,"** and **"Ode on a Grecian Urn,"** respectively. The structure of these symbols, and the degree to which each succeeds in representing the unified state of real and ideal desired by the imagination, differ widely. (pp. 244-45)

In the **"Ode to a Nightingale"** the dominant symbol, taken from the natural world, is the bird, by the manipulation of which the poet hopes to achieve the identification of man with nature, temporal with eternal. But there is also, in counterpoint as it were, a struggle between the poet and the nightingale which fragments finally into a dichotomy of ideal being for the bird and despair for the poet. While the Nightingale soars upward as some kind of concrete universal, the "forlorn" poet becomes a "sod." The very structure of the symbol prevents the kind of interpenetration between subject and object which Keats desired, and leads rather to the alienation he feared.

In the first stanza we assume that Keats is speaking of an individual nightingale. By stanza seven this individual has become something quite different, perhaps the species nightingale. This view would satisfy biological and prosaic truth, but does not account for the complexity of the symbol, or lead the reader to anticipate the sudden failure of communication between the poet and the bird which follows. The nightingale is not merely a complex "metaphysical" image, nor is it a simple abstraction such as are Love, Ambition and Poesy in the **"Ode on Indolence."** The symbolic nightingale is a kind of concrete universal.

In the first stanza the nightingale is an individual with a symbolic meaning, the symbol and meaning being identical to that of the grape in the climax of the **"Ode on Melancholy."** The bird has replaced the grape as the quintessence of earthly pleasure:

'Tis not through envy of thy happy lot,
But being too happy in thine happiness.

At this point the poet is experiencing a more ordinary kind of pain and human discomfort. The tale of human misery, prominent in stanzas three and six, is in sharp contrast to the upward surge of the theme embodied in the bird itself. The shift from an individual nightingale to something quite higher in the ontological order occurs in stanza three. The bird no longer represents mere human joy or sorrow of the most intense degree. The lines:

Fade far away, dissolve, and quite forget
What thou among the leaves hast never known,

seem to remove the bird from the order of individual existence, and also cancel its validity as a symbol of human pain and joy. The nightingale has stepped into the immaterial world, the world of universals, which is paradoxically both more and less permanent or real than the actual world. In this new world the essence of pleasure is extractable and indestructible; the bird as universal is everywhere and nowhere, everything and nothing, as is supported by the words of the **"Ode":**

Thou wast not born for death, immortal Bird!
No hungry generations tread thee down.

Such a view of a universal bird symbol is not exactly Platonic. It does not imply an ideal world behind the real world, yet something akin to that is what has taken place. The universal bird, permanent and eternal symbol of concrete beauty, has been freed from the dross of individual existence. Yet it remains a conception dependent upon the mind of man. Does this new bird symbol attain a higher order of being, that is, in line with Keats' theory of disinterestedness, existence as a universal independent of the conception of it in the mind of man, in other words as a concrete "real" universal in the Platonic sense? Possibly so. Stanza seven might support this view. The "real" universal would be the bird song rather than the bird, the song heard by Ruth, by emperor and clown. It is another "ditty of no tone." This universal has attained independent existence of some "real" kind, since it is no longer dependent upon individuals in the actual order for its reality. (pp. 245-47)

Death then becomes the logical progression from alienation to annihilation, a fairly negative thing, "easeful," a luxury, "To cease upon the midnight with no pain." It means identification with nature in the sense of becoming inanimate in an eternity of silence and nothingness. Death is the supreme moment, the last sensation, which would agonize the soul with sense of loss unless it can be made easeful, unconscious. The nature imagery in the poem takes on its importance in terms of this attitude toward death. Natural things are gross, palpable, individual gratifications to each of the five senses. The poet lingers over the names and sensuous impressions which each possesses:

The grass, the thicket, and the fruit-tree wild;
White hawthorne, and the pastoral eglantine;
Fast fading violets cover'd up in leaves.

Awareness of the existence of such beauty becomes excruciating torture in the presence of death, unless death itself be transformed into the most sensuous experience of all. It is agony for the poet suddenly caught up in the egocentric predicament again to view the beauties of the world which he, and not the universal, eternal nightingale, in nature, must leave. The paradox is too poignant not to make the poet forlorn; in order to become a part of nature, to be with the bird in any real sense, the poet must relinquish his distinctive feature, consciousness, which is the source of agony and beauty, pain and perception. The poem ends in a mood of sadness, and on a revival of the essential paradox of human existence, the duality of human experience. The symbolic victory over the duality was both partial and transitory.

In *Lamia* Keats' moment of symbolic vision is longer, glimpsed in the world of Greek mythology, while dull philosophy, which makes man aware of his human limitations, enlarges the death-wish theme of **"Ode to a Nightingale."** In the poem this philosophy, meaning in particular the scientific spirit, has with its tools for quantitative measurement destroyed the rainbow. Motion and dimension have been reduced to law. The qualitative items in experience, formerly embodied in mythology, are ignored, and this produces the terror of a "dead universe" for ordinary people and poets. Whereas the dialectic of the narrator reluctantly destroyed his own vision in **"Ode to a Nightingale,"** the method in *Lamia* is intensely dramatic. Apollonius represents the scientific point of view and performs the

function of destroyer in regard to Greek mythology. In *Lamia* Crete is the natural home of the symbolic imagination, of mythology, while Corinth holds sensuality, materialism, and the philosopher. Lycius, the poet's hero, is caught between the two. This is a dramatic representation of the opposition between the imagination and life, and human awareness of limitation, leading to death.

Lycius was trained in the rational philosophy of his time, but was unhappy with it. He is occupied with the quest of all Keats' heroes, to bridge the gap between the world of sense and understanding, and that of the imaginative ideal (in this poem, by means of a kind of love which symbolizes the imaginative way). Mythology is the comprehensive symbol in the poem, and provides the frame for the clash between the logical, quantitative world of Apollonius and the symbolic mode of man's myth-making power. The frequently discussed love relationships function as a part of this greater contrast. Love is the focus for the major incidents in the poem, and these incidents are ordered and made meaningful by the mythological structure. That is to say, the kinds of love present varying degrees of insight into the mythological vision of the world.

On the lowest level, there is the sensuality at Corinth, the center of rationalism and sensism in philosophy. Next there is "love in a hut," common everyday love between average men and women, representing the "common sense" philosophy. These loves cannot symbolize aspiration toward the higher level of the imaginative mode, and cannot satisfy a man such as Lycius, whose philosophical studies have not quenched a yearning for the ineffable. For him there had to be human love on an ideal level, with the Lamia, as there had to be love of a divine being for Keats' other hero, Endymion. But he could never rise to the level of divine love between immortals, as do Cupid and Psyche in the **"Ode to Psyche,"** or perhaps Hermes and the Nymph in this poem. In relation to divine love, the two possibilities open to mortals were destined to prove unsatisfying, one because magic is necessary to preserve it, the other because the very human limitations of the participants make it impossible to sustain. The corresponding comment on the fate of man's mythological structures in the modern, scientific world is equally grim.

Thus it follows that, in terms of the love symbolism itself, it is not only the logic in the discursive mind of Apollonius which opposes the love between Lamia and Lycius; logic is really a latent factor in Lycius' mortal nature which serves to destroy his vision. Love as a symbol of the imagination is exposed in its inherent weakness. And at the center of the conflict remain the logic of the philosopher and the mythological structures of the poet. That the solution has unpleasant implications for mythology as the embodiment of the symbolic mode, no less than for human love, is not an indication that the poet permanently despairs. It does indicate his ability to criticize his early attempt at transcendence in *Endymion* and also his awareness of the impossibilities inherent in his own system of mythology, created in the **"Ode to Psyche," "Ode on Indolence"** and other poems. It led him finally to view a kind of religious love and art as the most valid modes of transcending the human condition.

An examination of the "ideal" love between Hermes and the Nymph, the foil against which to judge the preternatural love of Lamia and Lycius, shows how the mythological: logical contrast subsumes the love relationships in the poem. Critics have often noted the importance of the following famous lines:

Real are the dreams of Gods, and smoothly pass
Their pleasures in a long immortal dream.

This is certainly divine love in the particular Keatsian sense that the pleasure of love exists without the pain, and for an indefinite period. In this sense it can be contrasted to that of Lamia and Lycius, which can achieve the effect only by magic, by cheating human nature. But is this relationship between Hermes and the Nymph intended primarily as an example of ideal love? If so, why Hermes, the rake of the gods, and a mere nymph? Thomas Burton, whose *Anatomy of Melancholy* was Keats' source for the Lamia episode, does not provide a basis for the earlier part of the story. Had Keats desired to make this a portrait of ideal love, he was free to choose a more dignified pair, such as Cupid and Psyche, or Endymion and Cynthia. (pp. 247-50)

Lamia is not an "ideal" mythological figure, as is Cynthia in *Endymion.* Without some outside preconception for the Hermes-Nymph relationship as the foil of ideal love, against which to judge Lycius and Lamia, their relationship would never strike a reader as the ideal of earthly love, as does that of Porphyro and Madeline in **"The Eve of St. Agnes."** The reader sees that the relationship between Lycius and Lamia is created by magic, by deception, in short, by a witch. The relationship emphasizes physical, sexual, yet not entirely sensual, love. It avoids love melancholy and pain, but fails as the perfect vehicle for presenting the ideal through love symbolism. This love fails from its inherent weakness, and Apollonius deals with it to prepare himself for more important tasks. (pp. 250-51)

The physical, intensely human aspect of the relationship is important for several reasons. For one, it helps to explain the miraculous transformation of the snake into a beautiful woman. The horror, the agony of her transformation is the price which had to be paid for cheating human nature. "Nothing but pain and ugliness were left" is the termination of a process in which the good and beautiful in the love relationship are separated from the evil and ugly. By paying a price, she was able to give "unperplexed bliss," to remove the

points of contact between beauty and ugliness, and good and evil. She could defy temporarily the experience of the worshipper in the **"Ode on Melancholy,"** who found:

Ay, in the very temple of Delight
Veil'd Melancholy has her sovran shrine,
Though seen of none save him whose strenuous
 tongue
Can burst Joy's grape against his palate fine;
His soul shall taste the sadness of her might,
And be among her cloudy trophies hung.

Stress on the defiance of nature in her relationship with Lycius is made many times. She wants physical love, and she gives it, yet the cloying consequences are always avoided. Distraction is prevented by the secret palace, tedium by the dreamy trance in which Lycius is placed, and thought excluded by seclusion from the normal life of Corinth. Through her it is possible temporarily to cheat life; she is a virgin with the experience of a harlot. The lovers have it all their own way.

Of course the instrument of delusion is magic. At no point in the experience does the poet forget the impact of **"Ode to a Nightingale."** The ruse is carried by the common myth in literature, that of a beautiful woman with rotten interior, who can separate seeming good from evil. There are obvious similarities between Lamia and Spenser's Duessa and False Florimel in *The Fairy Queen.* In both poems the evil and futility of magic is noticed, but in *The Fairy Queen* there is also a moral commitment, based on both Christian and Platonic sanctions. But in *Lamia* the emotional commitment is not entirely at one with the intellectual. Lycius, and presumably Keats, raise a cry of frustrated feeling even while the intellect relentlessly destroys the illusion of the erotic dream. Lycius helps destroy his own Lamia, his own dream world, through use of the laws of his own understanding. All the magic at Lamia's disposal could not prevent him from musing beyond her, or from hearing the trumpets of the outside world, from finally feeling the ennui of love in a palace, from desiring other emotional outlets, such as pride in display, and excitement in festival. Thus the communion through sexual passion with symbolic modes of being destroys itself by its very nature and rhythm. The inevitability of stimulus—climax—triste could not be avoided by magic or self-delusion. And with the aftermath came desire for other goods.

When Lycius met Lamia he was prepared for a symbolic flight of some kind. His training in philosophy had not satisfied him. Recently having sacrificed to Jove for some unmentioned boon, and "Perhaps grown wearied of their Corinth talk," he had allowed his reason to fade into the twilight of the dream world. In other words he bore some secret, perhaps unrecognized, grudge against his educational training with Apollonius. Lamia offered a way out of the dreary sensible world and he took it. He himself and the magical element made its failure inevitable, yet it was reserved for Apollonius to administer the *coup de grace*. This was necessary for two reasons, to point out Apollonius' method of proceeding by the understanding, and to reveal his true purpose and real enemy. The climax is intensely dramatic. The eye of discursive logic, "Keen, cruel, perceant, stinging," pierces Lamia's secret, and by *naming* her species, "a serpent," reduces at once the dream to nothing. Lycius' arms were empty of delight. But he, in a moment of terror, reveals the poet's view of the secret intention of the philosopher, which is to empty all such creations of the human spirit of their substance, to destroy the productive life of Hermes, and leave mankind's symbolic yearnings in a winding sheet with Lycius:

> Shut, shut those juggling eyes, thou ruthless man!
> Turn them aside, wretch! or the righteous ban
> Of all the Gods, whose dreadful images
> Here represent their shadowy presences,
> May pierce them on a sudden with the thorn
> Of painful blindness; leaving thee forlorn,
> In trembling dotage to the feeblest fright
> Of conscience, for their long offended might,
> For all thine impious proud-heart sophistries,
> Unlawful magic, and enticing lies.

What Apollonius had done to Lycius through the destruction of the Lamia, discursive thought in general would do to the rainbow, to mythology, and to experiences of a qualitative kind in general. Science denudes the woods of all life, and despairing man remains in a dead universe.

The poem ends on a shriek because the poet is trying to save his vision of the world. But Keats cannot save his vision with this symbolism. His attempts to revitalize classical mythology in this poem, in *Endymion*, the "Ode to Psyche," and in *Hyperion*, were too late and too *precieux* to be successful. In *Lamia* its lamented decline and fall is poignantly illustrated. The final dichotomy between desire and reality becomes exactly that of **"Ode to a Nightingale."** The poet finds in the collective mythology of the past, as in his own bird symbol, no respite from the agony and despair of consciousness in the blankness of the modern world. But the poem *Lamia* is neither confused nor unsatisfactory. In it there is an honest inspection of the meaning and value of symbols, and recognition that new forms must be found to represent the vision of the artist in the modern world.

In **"The Eve of St. Agnes"** Keats again explores man's dualism through the medium of love symbols. In this poem the love symbolism is successful, because the poet discards his unsuccessful and complicated eternal: temporal, human: divine dichotomies, and invests his love symbolism in a quasi-religious formal unity.

The obvious dichotomy between the world of the

Deathbed drawing of Keats by Joseph Severn.

lovers and that of the other groups in the poem is quickly observed. The contrast corresponds to similar ones in *Lamia;* for example, the sensualists at Corinth to the revelers in Madeline's castle, "Love in a hut" to the common sense of Angela, and so forth. But there is a more important contrast in **"The Eve of St. Agnes,"** set up by the presence of the Beadsman, which did not appear in the other poems. There are some obvious contrasts, as, for instance, the Beadsman's denial of sensuous experience, and his attempt to reach spirituality in a manner which was unfruitful in Keats' mode of symbolization. The lovers flee to a world of bliss; the Beadsman is left cold and unsought for among his thousand Aves. But there is a more important level on which the relationship between the Beadsman and the lovers ought to be taken, on which the contrast becomes its opposite, a powerful force for the fusion of the religious with the sensual ideal in the poem.

In terms of the general Christian tradition which lies behind the poem, the actions of the Beadsman are commendatory, while those of the lovers are in a sense a sacrilege. But in the values which the poem itself generates the Beadsman's activity is a waste, a delusion, while the lovers perform the sacred rites, the "mysteries" which lead to the "miracle." This is not to assert that values from outside Keats' own thinking intrude to destroy the meanings set up within the framework of his poem, but rather that knowledge of the outside values makes the framework of the poem more meaningful. We have to know the meaning of mystery and miracle in the Christian tradition, and the usual rites which symbolize them in the activity of the Beadsman, in order to appreciate the full significance of the Beadsman's actions in relation to those of the lovers. The actions of the juxtaposed groups comment upon each other in a profound way. Through this commentary the values in the poem are balanced in delicate equipoise with those which press from without.

In the Christian framework the Beadsman's entire life is a preparation for complete union with Christ. This is the goal of all Christian mystics and the purpose of the asceticism in their lives. . . . In the poem the Beadsman's prayers are directed toward the Virgin, and carry this usual significance. The entire direction of love has been changed from the ordinary ends of human activity, but the same emotions and drives are present. Thus it is that religious devotion and poetry will often assume the external appearance of a love rite, while love rites likewise usurp the form of religious exercises. The Beadsman enjoys his love and devotions, which are aimed at promoting the same union with essence enjoyed by the lovers. But in the poem his purposes are frustrated; for him, in terms of the symbolic relationship, there is no fruition, no union. This is because the love relationship, usually on a lower level, has usurped the powers of sacramental efficacy. Sacrilegious as it might appear to be in a sense, Love has become a sacrament, and the performance of its rites assures the unfolding of the mystery, and finally the miracle. The way of Thomas a Kempis is replaced by that of early pagan cults. In these rites the mysteries become associated with a religion of fertility, and gods of both sexes replace the Uniate God of Christianity. Also the idea of the immortal soul as an immaterial essence gives way to a notion that the concrete individual existence is universalized and eternalized, so that the sensations of this life can be repeated in a "finer tone."

The revolution is accomplished in a bold fashion, since outward terms and rites of the Christian tradition are not replaced by pagan symbols, but are merely altered to serve the new purpose. The Beadsman is the foil for this sacred parody, and his observances of the penances preparatory to union with Christ run in counterpoint to the penances of Porphyro and Madeline. Words and gestures of Christian ritual are approximated by the mystery and miracle of the lovers' union. The Beadsman's presence as representative of the Christian tradition sets the tone in which the actions of the lovers are to be construed. Let us see how daring this approximation is.

Madeline's room is the scene for the performance of the mysteries and the miracle. It is a fit repository for such a sacred action, "silken, hush'd, and chaste." She enters it "like a mission'd spirit" with a taper in her hand. Thus the preparation for the sacrifice begins. Madeline is a child of St. Agnes, a lamb, "so pure a thing, so free from mortal taint," preparing herself for the consummation. In the love-mystery she is the *Agnus Dei,* the Lamb of God. Her movements and observances

are a kind of Offertory service. What she is offering is herself, a pure and spotless victim, to love, and what is consecrated is her vision, the "miracle" which allows communion with the ideal and real Porphyro.

First she kneels and offers herself as the love victim, "As down she knelt for heaven's grace and boon." Next, she prepares her body for the love rite,

> her vespers done,
> Of all its wreathed pearls her hair she
> frees;
> . . .
> Her rich attire creeps rustling to her
> knees.

The altar in this love sacrifice is, of course, the bed, where she, a sacred victim, is placed, and before which the worshipper, in this case Porphyro, will kneel. She is also fasting, in order to be worthy of the vision, an observance obviously related to rules for the worthy reception of the sacrament in the Christian tradition. When Madeline enters the bed her function as active participant in the dual sacramental mystery is taken over by Porphyro.

This act roughly corresponds to the point of Consecration when the role of the priest as primary in the preparation of the Sacrament is taken over by the worshippers in the congregation. Madeline fades into her soft and chilly nest, her "soul fatigued away; / Flown, like a thought, until the morrow-day," in a manner similar to the recession of the priest, whose role to this point she has approximated. Of course in **"St. Agnes,"** the situation is somewhat different. The receding Madeline is the girl of the realistic mode, who has prepared herself for an ascension into that of ideal vision. The miracle is not complete at this point in the love rite for the same reason that Porphyro in this service is much more important than are the worshippers in Christian services. The emphasis is always on the duality of the religious rite in the love-service, even though the externals are similar to the Christian rite. The real miracle is not the achievement of one of its members, but the union of both. In the Sacrament the Consecration is the key mystery and miracle; the reception of it by the worshippers is also quite marvellous, but of secondary interest. Madeline's achievement of the Vision is in a sense a Transubstantiation, but it is only through union and communion with Porphyro that the mystery attains the status of a miracle.

Porphyro's worship of Madeline corresponds to the adoration offered by the congregation, but it is much more intense, because his participation in the miracle must be earned in an active way. Not only must he show adoration of the miraculous gift, and prepare himself by passive steps for its worthy reception, as would the congregation or the Beadsman, but he must actively participate in the mysteries in order to obtain

The graves of Keats and Joseph Severn, Protestant Cemetery, Rome.

the miracle. It is at this point that the essential difference between the Keatsian and Christian ritual is made manifest, even though the symbolic acts of each have similarities. The Keatsian priest is always an active worshipper, whose own exertions are necessary for the consummation.

The food offerings of Porphyro are obviously ritualistic in intention. Porphyro has a sacrifice table, an altar cloth of crimson, gold, and jet, but of course his offering is not symbolic of a Christian mode of participation in the Divine. The stainless white host of the Christian ascetic sacrifice has been replaced by the deluge of oriental sensuality. This, as has been pointed out, indicates the levels of sensuous experience through which Porphyro must pass in order to be ready for the transformation into the spiritual mode. His offerings, on golden dishes, are the counterpart of the Aves, just as the perfumed light sent up by them parallels the gloom and ashes of the hermit's cell. Porphyro's anguish, generated by the tension between basic physical desire and the aspiration to reach a more perfect mode of sensuous experience, stems from the same attitude of reproach which gives rise to the feeling of sinfulness in the souls of Communicants during the adoration pe-

riod. Both Porphyro and the worshippers are offering unworthy sacrifices to an *Agnus Dei,* and the feeling of complete absorption in the worshipped object, although for different reasons, is no less complete in one instance than in the other. Porphyro says:

> Thou art my heaven, and I thine eremite:
> Open thine eyes, for meek St. Agnes' sake,
> Or I shall drowse beside thee, so my soul doth ache.

Through devout consumption of the Host, the communicants are united with Christ, and achieve to the extent that it is possible in this world, a feeling of spirituality, a glimpse of an existence possible above the world of flesh, space, and time. This is exactly what Porphyro achieves by performing the sacred rites, the banquet and the lute playing, a consummation with his *Agnus Dei.* His absorption into the dream is a symbolic equivalent of the consumption of the Sacrament. (pp. 251-58)

Keats has subsumed the conventional religious symbolism of Christian ritual for a very special purpose in this poem. The exact nature of the relationship between Porphyro and Madeline could be expressed only through mysteries, and achieved by miracle. Love has replaced the Eucharist as the sacrament in his system.

Without this transferred mystery and miracle symbolism from the Christian tradition, his attempts to attain a vision of the eternal through love and nature fragmented into dichotomies, as we have seen. By borrowing and reworking for his own purpose the central mystery of the Christian ritual, clearly removed from its original sacred context, he was able to use the Beadsman as a foil to develop successfully, in this poem at least, the *mysterium fidei* of his own sacramental universe. (pp. 258-59)

James D. Boulger, "Keats' Symbolism," in *ELH,* Vol. 28, No. 3, September, 1961, pp. 244-59.

SOURCES FOR FURTHER STUDY

Bate, Walter Jackson. *John Keats.* Cambridge, Mass.: Harvard University Press, Belknap Press, 1963, 732 p.

> Detailed biography that is considered the most reliable and comprehensive modern source. Bate incorporates the biographical information that came to light subsequent to World War II, particularly the material included in Hyder Edward Rollins's *The Keats Circle: Letters and Papers, 1816-1878.*

Bush, Douglas. *John Keats: His Life and Writings.* Masters of World Literature Series, edited by Louis Kronenberger. New York: Macmillan, 1966, 224 p.

> Concise and readable biography.

Matthews, G. M., ed. *Keats: The Critical Heritage.* The Critical Heritage Series, edited by B. C. Southam. New York: Barnes & Noble, 1971, 430 p.

> An anthology of Keats criticism drawn from books, magazines, letters, and journal entries from the first reviews through 1863. Informative annotations preface each critical piece, and the editor has contributed a helpful introductory overview of Keats's reputation.

Muir, Kenneth, ed. *John Keats: A Reassessment.* Liverpool English Texts and Studies, no. 5. Liverpool: Liverpool University Press, 1958, 182 p.

> Significant collection of ten essays by such noted scholars as Kenneth Muir, Miriam Allott, R. T. Davies, and David I. Masson. Topics explored include Keats's debt to the Elizabethans and his relationship with William Hazlitt, but the majority of the essays are on single poems.

Murry, John Middleton. *Keats.* New York: Noonday Press, 1955, 322 p.

> Important essays in which Murry discusses various biographical and critical concerns, including Keats's relationship to John Milton, William Blake, and William Wordsworth, his ideas on friendship, and his various poetic theories.

Wasserman, Earl R. *The Finer Tone: Keats' Major Poems.* Baltimore: Johns Hopkins Press, 1953, 228 p.

> Influential analysis of Keats's philosophic tendencies and his poetic technique. Wasserman discusses five poems: "Ode on a Grecian Urn," "La Belle Dame sans Merci," "The Eve of St. Agnes," "Lamia," and "Ode to a Nightingale."

Jack Kerouac

1922-1969

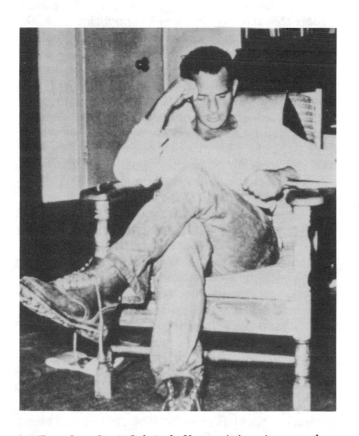

(Born Jean-Louis Lebris de Kerouac) American novelist, poet, and essayist.

INTRODUCTION

Kerouac is best known as the key figure of the artistic and cultural phenomenon of the 1950s known as the Beat Movement. The Beat Movement, which took its name from Kerouac's abbreviation of "beatific," began in Greenwich Village and San Francisco as a reaction against the conservatism in America during the Cold War era. Other important participants in the movement included Allen Ginsberg, Lawrence Ferlinghetti, Neal Cassady, and William Burroughs, all of whom were close friends of Kerouac. Kerouac's best known novel, *On the Road* (1957), depicts the counter-culture lifestyle of the Beats, marked by manic travel and experimentation with sex and drugs. While *On the Road* stunned the public and the literary establishment when it was first published, its continuing popularity and the proximity of Kerouac's philosophy to that of such honored American writers as Walt Whitman and Henry David Thoreau have garnered Kerouac a place in the canon of contemporary American authors.

Born in a French-Canadian community in Lowell, Massachusetts, Kerouac was raised a Catholic and educated in parochial schools. An outstanding athlete, he received a football scholarship to Columbia University but withdrew from school during the fall of his sophomore year. He joined the Navy in 1943 and was released after six months for psychological reasons. Kerouac worked the remainder of World War II as a merchant seaman and associated with the bohemian crowd around Columbia that included Allen Ginsberg and William Burroughs. The publication of *On the Road* brought Kerouac sudden notoriety, and eight of his books were produced during the next few years as publishers rushed to capitalize on his popularity. Kerouac's natural shyness, however, kept him from enjoying his fame; he was known to arrive at interviews intoxicated and failed in his sporadic attempts to withdraw from society to concentrate on writing. A sincere patriot and Catholic, Kerouac became increasingly bewildered by and alienated from his bohemian fans in the 1960s. He returned to the place of his birth in 1966, and died of alcoholism in 1969.

Many of Kerouac's friends in the Beat Movement served as the basis for the characters in his novels. Novelist William Burroughs and poet Allen Ginsberg are portrayed in *On the Road* as Old Bull Lee and Carlo Marx. Beat poet Gary Snyder inspired Japhy Ryder, the main character in one of Kerouac's better-known novels, *The Dharma Bums* (1958). But undoubtedly the single most influential personality in Kerouac's circle of friends, and the main character in both *On the Road* and *Visions of Cody* (1972), was Neal Cassady. Kerouac saw the energetic, charismatic Cassady as the quintessential Beat figure and the last of a vanishing breed of American romantic heroes. Kerouac also cited Cassady's stream-of-consciousness writing style, exemplified in his voluminous letters, as having inspired his own "spontaneous prose" technique. The female characters in Kerouac's novels are also largely based on the women in Kerouac's life and the lives of his friends. However, women generally assume minor roles in Kerouac's fiction, and his portrayals of them reflect his considerable ambivalence toward women. They are often depicted as the "property" of the male characters, or as purchasable commodities, and in his long poem, *Mexico City Blues,* he portrays women alternately as nurturers and as threats to the freedom, individuality, and creativity of men.

Kerouac considered his novels a series of interconnected autobiographical narratives in the manner of Marcel Proust's *A la recherche du temps Perdu* (*Rememberance of Things Past*). The novels that compose "The Legend of Duluoz," as Kerouac called the totality of his works, include *Visions of Gerard* (1963), which pictures Kerouac's childhood as overshadowed by the death of his beloved brother Gerard at age nine; *Doctor Sax: Faust Part Three* (1959), a surrealistic depiction of Kerouac's boyhood memories and dreams; *Maggie Cassidy* (1959), which recounts Kerouac's first love; and *Vanity of Duluoz: An Adventurous Education 1935-46* (1968), which chronicles Kerouac's years of playing football at prep school and Columbia. In *On the Road,* Kerouac wrote about the late 1940s, focusing on the years of traveling and socializing with Neal Cassady, Allen Ginsberg, and William Burroughs. *Visions of Cody* (1972), viewed by many critics as a late revision of *On the Road,* retells the story in spontaneous prose. Kerouac wrote about his love affair in 1953 with an African-American woman in *The Subterraneans* (1958), and his adventures on the West Coast learning about Buddhism from the poet Gary Snyder are chronicled in *The Dharma Bums* (1959). *Desolation Angels* (1965)

covers the years just prior to publication of *On the Road,* while *Big Sur* (1962) displays the bitterness and despair Kerouac experienced in the early 1960s and his descent into alcoholism. Together these novels portray the birth, education, and eventual disillusionment of an American idealist.

A barely fictionalized portrait of the late 1940s when Kerouac and his friends travelled back and forth across the United States, *On the Road* was not universally perceived as literature upon publication. Kerouac, portrayed as the narrator, Sal Paradise, enthusiastically describes the manic adventures that make up the plot of this novel, including stealing, drunkenness, purposeless travel, drug use, and sexual promiscuity, and his narrative convinced some critics that *On the Road* signalled the moral demise of Kerouac's generation. Gilbert Millstein, representing the opposing view, decreed that the publication of *On the Road* was an "historic occasion" and the immoderate lifestyle of the Beats was a "search for belief." Critics who shared this attitude focused on the spiritual quest theme of *On the Road,* which, along with its picaresque narrative, made this novel a descendent of American "road literature," represented by such works as Mark Twain's *Adventures of Huckleberry Finn.* Although *On the Road* was said to inspire the peripatetic Hippie generation of the 1960s, later critics paid greater attention to Sal's disillusionment with the road at the conclusion of the novel. Some now view *On the Road* as depicting the conflict within Sal between the contemplative life of a writer and spiritually-oriented person and the gregarious, adventurous life on the road. Much of the sensationalism and subjectivity which marked early Kerouac criticism has been replaced by traditional, scholarly critical effort. Some recent critical studies show considerable interest in Kerouac's "spontaneous prose" method and view it as an extension of the "stream of consciousness" technique utilized by James Joyce. There have also been critical attempts to compare *On the Road* thematically with such American classics as *The Great Gatsby.* Because of his flamboyant and tragic life and career, Kerouac has been the subject of several recent critical biographies. The past speculation of whether Kerouac would merit a permanent place in contemporary American fiction has ended; he is now widely recognized, if begrudgingly by some, as an important contributor to American literature.

(For further information about Kerouac's life and works, see *Concise Dictionary of American Literary Biography, 1941-1968; Contemporary Literary Criticism,* Vols. 1, 2, 3, 5, 14, 29, 61; *Dictionary of Literary Biography,* Vols. 2, 6; and *Dictionary of Literary Biography Documentary Series,* Vol. 3. For related criticism, see the entry on The Beat Generation in *Twentieth-Century Literary Criticism,* Vol. 42.)

CRITICAL COMMENTARY

HERBERT GOLD

(essay date 1957)

[An American novelist and short story writer, Gold has been acclaimed for his precise and wry treatments of marriage, family, and popular culture in contemporary America. In the following excerpt, he examines Kerouac's depiction of the "frantic" bohemians in *On the Road*.]

"Whoee, I told my soul." This urgent message from Jack Kerouac to his soul contains most of the sense which emerges from his frantic tirade in the form of a novel, *On the Road*, and it is his ability to make such stuff hip, cool, beat and frantic, all at once, which has earned him a title more valued nowadays than that of "novelist": He is a Spokesman.

For what this time? Kerouac has appointed himself prose celebrant to a pack of unleached zazous who like to describe themselves as Zen Hipsters—poets, pushers and panhandlers, musicians, male hustlers and a few marginal esthetes seeking new marginal distinctions. They have a center in San Francisco, another in Greenwich Village, and claim outposts in Tangiers, on merchant vessels, in Chicago, a fragment among the fragments in New Orleans, a fringe of the fringe in Mexico City. Despite all wandering, however, their loneliness for the herd sends them eagerly trumpeting back into each other's arms after brief periods of saying whoee to their souls among the outlanders. At least two of them happen to be talented—Allen Ginsberg, a poet of shock and wild wit, whose blathering *Howl* really does contain some of the liveliest epithets in contemporary verse; and Jack Kerouac, whose mammoth journal has been edited into the form of a novel by The Viking Press. One of the heroes of *On the Road*, of course, is Allen Ginsberg (under the name of Carlo Marx), just as one of the heroes of *Howl* is Jack Kerouac (under the name of Jack Kerouac). (p. 349)

On the Road carries the ensign of the hipster with considerable humor and vitality, much awe, and a little of the literary hipster's prevalent social disease, the faked-up pretension that these are underground intellects who know all about Zen Buddhism, St. John of the Cross, Proust, and good bad old Charlie Parker, and could tell us if they only cared to. The awe breaks to happy moments of lucidity which are those of a real writer. Kerouac then sees the hipster, agape and bedazzled, mumbling about the world-historical significance of bop—but only mumbling. What he tells, he tries to tell true enough according to his lights. At times he almost seems to understand that Charlie Parker blew fine horn, but was not God.

However, there is a structural flaw in this contemporary revival of the literary-criminal or ecstatic-delinquent underground which makes Jack Kerouac's book a proof of illness rather than a creation of art, a novel. In the first place, Villon, Rimbaud and Jean Genet really lived by their criminal passivity and wits. They showed their rumps to society because they were caught from behind. These Americans, however, are *literary* in their coolness, hipness, beatness, and they are unauthentic exactly to the degree that they are literary. The hipster-writer is a perennial perverse bar mitzvah boy, proudly announcing: "Today I am a madman. Now give me the fountain pen." The frozen thugs gathered west of Sheridan Square or in the hopped-up cars do not bother with talk. That's why they say "man" to everyone—they can't remember anybody's name. But Ginsberg and Kerouac are *frantic*. They care too much, and they care aloud. "I'm *hungry*, I'm *starving*, let's *eat right now!*" That they care mostly for themselves is a sign of adolescence, but at least they care for something, and it's a beginning. (p. 350)

When Kerouac wails about "many and many a lost night, singing and moaning and eating the stars and dropping the juices drop by drop on the hot tar," he is in a respectable literary tradition, and the tradition's name is Thomas Wolfe. This is not hipster talk. When he passes through Fresno, sees an Armenian and thinks: "Yes, yes, Saroyan's town," he has some of that aging bucko's freewheeling self-love—and just as literary. When he hints at orgy, his real daddy is the daddy of all the living boheems, Henry Miller, though he practices a conciseness of sexual rhetoric which probably derives from the publisher's timidity rather than from any cool indifference. Sometimes he writes the purest straight-and-true Hemingway, as when he meets a Mexican girl: "Her breasts stuck out straight and true." Later his friend Dean is driving a car no-hands, but "it hugged the line straight and true."

This is not beat. This is not cool. This is not hip. This is the Columbia College boy vacationing on his G.I. Bill money, reading Papa. But despite all the bookish derivations, Kerouac retains a stubborn integrity: "I had nothing to offer anybody but my own confusion."

He has something more to offer. I would guess,

Principal Works

The Town and the City (novel) 1950

On the Road (novel) 1957

The Dharma Bums (novel) 1958

The Subterraneans (novel) 1958

Doctor Sax: Faust Part Three (novel) 1959

Maggie Cassidy (novel) 1959

Mexico City Blues (poetry) 1959

The Scripture of the Golden Eternity (nonfiction) 1960

Book of Dreams (nonfiction) 1961

Tristessa (novel) 1960

Big Sur (novel) 1962

Visions of Gerard (novel) 1963

Desolation Angels (novel) 1965

Satori in Paris (novel) 1966

Vanity of Duluoz: An Adventurous Education 1935-
1946 (novel) 1968

Pic (novel) 1971

Visions of Cody (novel) 1972

Heaven and Other Poems (poetry) 1977

writing before publication, that the bookselling business is not yet ready for a particular blend of nihilism and mush which might someday take its place in the gassy world of bestsellerdom. When Kerouac mentions the Bomb, he makes us blush: he doesn't mean it, it's pure stylishness, and we resent the fact that the great disaster of contemporary history should be used in passing to let us know that a poet "cares." However, beyond the pretense, the derivations, the plotless rambling, the grate of vacant noise, Kerouac somehow achieves communication of a happy sense for the humor of car-stealing and marital confusion, for the insanity and pomp of addicts, for the joys of being tormented. And he gives us a fascinating tape recording of the skinny bunyanesque car-thief, Dean Moriarty, craving intellect, wives, fast travel and bop, emitting fiery nonsense from the tail of his hurtling nuttiness:

But of course, Sal, I can talk as soon as ever and have many things to say to you in fact with my own little bangtail mind I've been reading and reading this gone Proust all the way across the country and digging a great number of things I'll never have TIME to tell you about and we STILL haven't talked of Mexico and our parting there in fever—but no need to talk. Absolutely, now, yes?

He balances the crazed Dean with a certain wryness about himself, whom he calls Sal Paradise:

She was a nice little girl, simple and true. . . .

Oh-oh, Hemingway again.

. . . and tremendously frightened of sex. I told her it was beautiful. I wanted to prove this to her. She let me prove it, but I was impatient and proved nothing. She sighed in the dark, "What do you want out of life?" I asked, and I used to ask that all the time of girls.

Here he enlists both our indulgence and our sympathy for poor impatient Sal, and does it with wit and feeling and imaginative detachment. But at other places he is capable of the melodrama of the purebred dormitory genius:

I would be strange and ragged and like the Prophet who has walked across the land to bring the dark Word, and the only Word I had was "Wow."

At still another juncture he forgets that he is the Prophet of Wow and informs us that his word is Mad. There are other words in his sack, too.

But wha hoppin?

Nothin' hoppin, man.

Dean Moriarty is brilliantly transcribed, not rendered as a man through time and desire, despite all his velocity. He begins mad, he stays mad, he concludes mad: he is a stripped, tormented, dancing celluloid doll, burning fast, without a gesture that can surprise us although he says and does exactly what he would say and do. Kerouac is loyal to him. In garlands of prose, the words *mad, madness, madly* are the stems to which the buffeted reader can look for a principle of organization. It is the end of the philosophy for which the hungering boy traveler yearns, the great death-in-life to fill the boredom. He is fading away because of boredom, since nothing can make him happy, nothing can enlist him for more than a few spasmodic jerks, and the mad ones seem in his eyes to have an inner purpose. They are driven, while he is hung up. Unfortunately for communicative purpose, after many repetitions of the phrase, "It was *mad*," we hear not the trumpets of Blake nor the divine flap of Antonin Artaud, but rather an interior decorator describing last night's binge. "As in a dream," he adds—because he wants to make life a mad dream and so pronounces MAD and DREAM at us over and over—"we made the bed bounce a half hour." The precise report of the time arouses our suspicion. *Why was he looking at his watch?* Such modest journalism does not imply a dreamlike transport.

Kerouac's people rarely talk, respond, exchange warmth with each other. They split their guts to cross the continent, say, "Hello, whooee, wow, Charlie Parker, soul" to their friends, get a quick divorce, make a quick marriage, and rush back to San Fran to a first or second or third wife, bringing along a girl from Denver. They zoom up and down the continent for no reason but bored impulse, though they call it "find our souls."

Then they write 18,000-word letters explaining why they never had that good long talk. Words fly, but they cannot communicate. They "tell" each other things: "Went for a walk in the middle of the night and came back to my girl to tell her what I thought about during my walk. I told her a number of things."

Even the wonderful chatter of the run-on hero, Dean Moriarty, which is the strongest thing in the book, tells us only one thing: He began as a psychopath and ended as a psychotic. Though lively along the way, this is not much of a journey, and tells little of anyone's life—including the real life of Moriarty.

On the Road asks us to judge the lives of its characters; it requires no real-life acquaintance with them to see that they are "true" projections—that is, the book represents Kerouac's attempt to do justice to his friends. This is a very different matter from the artist's attempt to project meaningful people through the medium of his imagination onto the medium of the imaginations of readers: characters who will be true to possibility, not necessarily to fact. *On the Road* reads right along—it contains, essentially, some lively rambling conversation about the exploits of big bad boys—but it is deeply insular in its intentions. Kerouac has not faced an important decision about whom he is writing for—his "soul" (to prove that he has one), his friends (to prove that he is worthy of them), or the public at whom his editor and publishers aim the book. He seems to be confused by the difference between writing a novel about hipsters—a legitimate stunt in an age of anti-heroes—and becoming a hipster in order to leave a track of paper. (pp. 351-53)

I take the Ginsberg of *Howl* and the Kerouac of *On the Road* to be typical of their little boystown at its rare best, serious, convinced and trying hard. Through them, one can ask what this clan of superfrantic sub-hipsters wants. Are they bringing a scout's message, a Word? Do they represent a new style of American? Will they provide a bracing antidote to the chronic headache of American culture?

They seem to be more a wounded shrilling and shrinking than an angry and vital reaction. Curiously enough their command performance of ecstatic rituals has misled them; they feel no ease in the expense of impulse; puzzled, they withdraw from pleasure. Madness is the penultimate escape, which seems both to allow joy and illumination and to oil over the troubling itch of responsibility. It seems so, that is, to the broody tourist, traveling home to his mother's suburb to describe his friends to his notebook, and then justifying them to his editors. I am sure that from within madness is different, and less delightful. They are ascetics of excess. They yearn for the annihilation of sense through the abuse of the senses. They look for a society of unchanging virtue in which the risks of possibility have been removed; pure love will reign, green marijuana

will be discovered in the mad glove compartments of every straight and true stolen car, Saroyan will live at peace in Fresno, souls will tell each other things. The terms of heaven have changed, but all this is very familiar. The ultimate goal is that single small step beyond madness.

What Kerouac wants is what the mystics driven by fright in all ages want, "the complete step across chronological time into timeless shadows . . . the stability of the Intrinsic mind." Such unhappy nonsense, such droopy-jeaned nay-saying to the blessed facts of time and change! There are other possible mysticisms, but Kerouac models his heaven on Marie Stopes's elegant, Swedenborgian, impossibly weary orgasm, saying "wow!" in advance just because he hopes to describe it as "MAD." No wonder all the fireworks. The experience he craves is simple, dark and in any case inevitable to all of us sooner or later—immolation. He is not content to wait. Mortality terrifies him; better death at once than the long test of life. He expresses this fantasy with convulsive violence, trying to disguise the truth from himself and from the reader, using breathlessness as a surrogate for energy. But he is compelled. The jitters are not an active state of being. He puts to the service of his rockabye dream of oblivion all the violence, sex, drink, dope, and the batty babbling buddies with whom he populates his heaven, anything, every easeful and bitter experience, even that of turning to rot in the Mexican jungle:

> The jungle takes you over and you become it. . . . The dead bugs mingled with my blood; the live mosquitoes exchanged further portions. . . . Soft infinitesimal showers of microscopic bugs fanned down on my face as I slept, and they were extremely pleasant.

It would help Jack Kerouac if he could find within himself the strength to stop writing about Love, Life and Death (with a dot dot dot between these stylish abstractions) and remember the real boy who enjoyed midget auto races. He might then discover that he knows something about death, life and love. At present he is a wolf of the hotrod age, Thomas and Virginia melted together into a damp creature from which even Aristophanes, who loved hybrids, would turn away. This wolf bays at the hipster moon, but howls for the Helen of someone else's youth; it ravens down the raw streets of America, taking gladness in the fact that the Mississippi has lived up to its advance notice in Mark Twain, describing one haunt after another as "stories," literary as literary can be, raised on the great books, as aren't we all? Where Thomas Wolfe broke his head butting against the world of New York intellectual highlife, Jack Kerouac is butting but unbroken against the world of the hipsters, a party that never quite pleases its adherents, no matter how much marvelous wild partying foreplay. Despite its drag race of words and gestures, *On the Road* does nothing, thinks nothing, acts nothing, but yet manages to be a book after all—a loving portrait of hip Dean Moriarty and his beat, cool friends as they run 110 miles an hour in order to stand still. It's a frantic book, and for that reason there is hope for Jack Kerouac.

Pseudo-Hipster, You Can't Run Further.

Meta-Hipster, You Can't Yell Louder.

Hipster, Go Home. (pp. 354-55)

Herbert Gold, "Hip, Cool, Beat—and Frantic," in *The Nation*, New York, Vol. 185, No. 16, November 16, 1957, pp. 349-55.

<hr />

WARREN TALLMAN

(essay date 1959)

[In the following excerpt, Tallman explores the influence of jazz music on the cadence and tone of Kerouac's prose.]

Kerouac's sound starts up in his first novel, *The Town and the City*, and anyone who grew up with or remembers the sentimental music of the 1930s will recognize what he is doing. The New England nights and days of his childhood and youth are orchestrated with slow violins, to which sound the children whose lives he chronicles are stirred into awareness as the stars dip down and slow breezes sweep along diminishing strings towards soft music on a farther shore. It is the considerable achievement of the novel that Kerouac is able to sustain the note of profound sentimentality his style conveys even as he is tracing, with remorseless intelligence, the downfall of the New England family. . . . (p. 65)

The jazz is in the continuity in which each episode [in *On the Road*] tells a separate story—variations on the holiness theme. And it is in the remarkably flexible style as Kerouac improvises within each episode seeking to adjust his sound to the resonance of the given moment. Some moments come through tinged with the earlier *Town and City* sentimentality. Others rock and sock . . . , the sentences jerking about like muscles on an overwrought face. Still others are curiously quiescent, calm. And the melody which unifies the whole and lifts the cockeyed star up into the jazz sky is the holiness of life because this for Kerouac is the meaning of words, the inside of his sound. . . . To read *On the Road* with attention to the variations Kerouac achieves is to realize something of the very impressive talent for meshing his sound with the strongly-felt rhythms of many and various moments. It is not possible to compare him very closely with other stylists of

note because his fiction is the first in which jazz is a dominant influence. (p. 69)

[*The Subterraneans*] is written with the driving but hungup rhythms of a hurrying man who is also, always, alas, looking back over his shoulder. . . . A failure of love by reason of deep fissuring guilts emerges from the depths on the rush but not exactly on the wings of Kerouac's spontaneous Bop style. As [the protagonist] Percepied says, 'I'm the Bop writer.' As one might expect, the spontaneity falters in a good many pages. Yet I do not doubt that the method does permit Kerouac to tap his imagination in spontaneous ways. Nor do I doubt but that *The Subterraneans* is his most important novel and a very important one indeed. (pp. 70-1)

The easiest way to approach *The Dharma Bums*—the truth bums—is to imagine an exceptionally talented musician trying out a new instrument in an interested but nonetheless very tentative way. The instrument is Zen Buddhism, American fashion. The novel is full of hummed songs, muttered chants, self-conversations carried on in railroad yards, on beaches, in groves of trees, in the mountains. The half-embarrassed, half-serious mutterer is Ray Smith, Zen amateur, and the style which Kerouac floats through the novel is part of an obvious attempt to adjust the practices, the flavour, the attitudes of Zen to an American sensibility. (p. 71)

It is . . . significant that in the opening paragraph [of the novel] Smith travels past the place where the 'king and founder of the Bop generation', the jazzman Charlie Parker, 'went crazy and got well again'. Kerouac might be hinting at the strain of writing eleven books in six years and about the need for a temporary so-long to jazz, hello to Zen. But the hello is most tentative. To put the very best construction on the novel, always advisable when dealing with a versatile writing talent, is to read it as a kind of primer of Zen experience. . . . [If] the Zen attitude is consistent with Kerouac's own, it is nonetheless apparent that the meditative world in which this attitude is best cultivated hasn't much affinity with his essentially nervous and agile sensibility. Unsustained by the driving intensities which make *On the Road* and *The Subterraneans* swing, *The Dharma Bums* frequently goes flat. There are dull scenes, mechanical passages. If there is one superb mountain-climbing episode, that is less because Zen catches hold for Kerouac, more because the mountain does. Certainly, representation of the final trip to the Northwest, where the protagonist attempts to live in the Zen way on Desolation Peak, is so sketchy as to amount to a default. And it is here that one touches upon Kerouac's limitations.

In *The Dharma Bums* distinctly and in his other novels in less evident ways, one becomes aware of Kerouac's receptive, his essentially feminine sensibility. Sensibility, I repeat. This receptivity is certainly his main strength as artist, accounting as it does for his capacity to assimilate the rhythms, the sounds, the life-feel of experience into his representation. When Kerouac is at his best he is able to register and project the American resonance with ease and accuracy. But on the related, weaker side of the coin, he has only a limited ability to project this sound up to heights, down to depths. Moments of climax, of revelation, of crisis, the very moments which deserve the fullest representation, frequently receive only sparse representation. The climactic Mexican journey in *On the Road* suffers from this limitation. Beginning with the madcap afternoon in the Mexican whore house, followed by the night-time sojourn in the jungle, the creation-day morning in the mountains, and subsequent arrival in Mexico City, the hipster Zion, where marihuana cascades like manna into the streets, the entire sequence is as brilliantly conceived as any in recent fiction. But representation in these scenes which show Moriarity's life sweeping up to climax, is sparse, fleeting, even sketchy. No reader will be convinced that Moriarity, the true traveler, has made it to a mountain-peak of our present moment from which creation-day is glimpsed. Nor will any reader be convinced that Ray Smith has gained access to the Zen Way in his mountain fastness.

Yet I do not think that this defect traces so much to want of creative force, though that is what it appears to be, as to Kerouac's almost animal suspicion of the meaning values toward which words tend. When his fictions converge toward meanings something vital in him flinches back. His sound is primarily a life sound, sensitive to the indwelling qualities of things, the life they bear. To be Beat is to be wary of moving such a sound into the meaning clutter. It might become lost, the life. So Kerouac draws back. Which is his limitation.

But also his strength. For in the jazz world of the Bop generation where Charlie Parker is king and founder, Jack Kerouac in a different medium is heir apparent. . . . [His] emphasis upon a from-under sound made spontaneous by adherence to the jazz principle of improvision is right for our time, I think. The jazz vernacular is just that, a vernacular, and Kerouac has demonstrated that it can be transposed into fiction without serious loss of the spontaneous imaginative freedom which has made it among the most vital of the modern arts.

Although Kerouac's art is limited, I am convinced that his sound is more nearly in the American grain than that of any writer since Fitzgerald. The efforts of his outcast protagonists to get life into their lives seem more closely related to our actual moment than those of any since Jay Gatsby, similar across worlds of difference, tried to shoot the North American moon. Gatsby failed and finished like a sad swan, floating dead on the surface of a pool. And Kerouac's protagonists fail too. . . . Fitzgerald's efforts got lost in the personal, national, and international chaos from which he summoned Gatsby into presence. But it was only after his energies lost coherence that Fitzgerald woke up in the ruins of that dark midnight of the soul where it is always three o'clock in the morning. Kerouac starts in with the dark midnight and it is his effort to bring his protagonists through the jazz of that night, naked, into something like a new day. He fails too. The moment, NOW, which is the only promised land, shrugs off [his protagonists] Moriarity, Percepied, and Smith, shrugs off Kerouac too. Outcasts they began and end as outcasts. But very distinctly Kerouac's protagonists press more sharply close to the truth about our present moment than have fictional protagonists for many years. And that's a help. And very distinctly he has created new ground of possibility for fiction to stand upon with renewed life. And that's a help. (pp. 71-4)

Warren Tallman, "Kerouac's Sound," in *The Tamarack Review*, No. 11, Spring, 1959, pp. 58-74.

JACK KEROUAC WITH TED BERRIGAN
(interview date 1968)

[In the following interview, Kerouac discusses his writing style and comments on literary and cultural issues that have influenced his work.]

[Berrigan]: *Why don't we begin with editors. How do you . . .*

[Kerouac]: O.K. All my editors since Malcolm Cowley have had instructions to leave my prose exactly as I wrote it. In the days of Malcolm Cowley, with *On the Road* and *The Dharma Bums,* I had no power to stand by my style for better or for worse. When Malcolm Cowley made endless revisions and inserted thousands of needless commas like, say, Cheyenne, Wyoming (why not just say Cheyenne Wyoming and let it go at that, for instance), why, I spent $500 making the complete restitution of the *Bums* manuscript and got a bill from Viking Press called "Revisions." Ha ho ho. And so you asked about how do I work with an editor . . . well nowadays I am just grateful to him for his assistance in proofreading the manuscript and in discovering logical errors, such as dates, names of places. For instance in my last book I wrote Firth of Forth then looked it up, on the suggestion of my editor, and found that I'd really sailed off the Firth of Clyde. Things like that. Or I spelled Aleister Crowley "Alisteir," or he discovered little mistakes about the yardage in football games . . . and so forth. By not revising what you've already written you simply give the reader the actual workings of your mind during the writing it-self: you confess your thoughts about events in your own unchangeable way . . . well, look, did you ever hear a guy telling a long wild tale to a bunch of men in a bar and all are listening and smiling, did you ever hear that guy stop to revise himself, go back to a previous sentence to improve it, to defray its rhythmic thought impact. . . . If he pauses to blow his nose, isn't he planning his next sentence? and when he lets that next sentence loose, isn't it once and for all the way he wanted to say it? Doesn't he depart the thought of that sentence and, as Shakespeare says, "forever holds his tongue" on the subject, since he's passed over it like a part of the river flows over a rock once and for all and never returns and can never flow any other way in time? Incidentally, as for my bug against periods, that was for the prose in **"October in the Railroad Earth,"** very experimental, intended to clack along all the way like a steam engine pulling a 100-car freight with a talky caboose at the end, that was my way at the time and it still can be done if the thinking during the swift writing is confessional and pure and all excited with the life of it. And be sure of this, I spent my entire youth writing slowly with revisions and endless rehashing speculation and deleting and got so I was writing one sentence a day and the sentence had no FEELING. God-damn it, FEELING is what I like in art, not CRAFTI-NESS and the hiding of feelings.

What encouraged you to use the "spontaneous" style of **On the Road?**

I got the idea for the spontaneous style of *On the Road* from seeing how good old Neal Cassady wrote his letters to me, all first person, fast, mad, confessional, completely serious, all detailed, with real names in his case however (being letters). I remembered also Goe-the's admonition, well Goethe's prophecy that the future literature of the West would be confessional in na-ture; also Dostoevsky prophesied as much and might have started in on that if he'd lived long enough to do his projected masterwork, *The Great Sinner.* Cassady also began his early youthful writing with attempts at slow, painstaking, and-all-that-crap craft business, but got sick of it like I did, seeing it wasn't getting out his guts and heart the way it *felt* coming out. But I got the flash from his style. It's a cruel lie for those West Coast punks to say that I got the idea of *On the Road* from him. All his letters to me were about his younger days before I met him, a child with his father, et cetera, and about his later teenage experiences. The letter he sent me is erroneously reported to be a 13,000 word letter . . . no, the 13,000 word piece was his novel *The First Third,* which he kept in his possession. The letter, the main letter I mean, was 40,000 words long, mind you, a whole short novel. It was the greatest piece of writing I ever saw, better'n anybody in America, or at least enough to make Melville, Twain, Dreiser, Wolfe,

I dunno who, spin in their graves. Allen Ginsberg asked me to lend him this vast letter so he could read it. He read it, then loaned it to a guy called Gerd Stern who lived on a houseboat in Sausalito California, in 1955, and this fellow lost the letter: overboard I presume. Neal and I called it, for convenience, the *Joan Anderson Letter* . . . all about a Christmas weekend in the pool-halls, hotel rooms and jails of Denver, with hilarious events throughout and tragic too, even a drawing of a window, with measurements to make the reader under-stand, all that. Now listen: this letter would have been printed under Neal's copyright, if we could find it, but as you know, it was my property as a letter to me, so Allen shouldn't have been so careless with it, nor the guy on the houseboat. If we can unearth this entire 40,000 word letter Neal shall be justified. We also did so much fast talking between the two of us, on tape re-corders, way back in 1952, and listened to them so much, we both got the secret of LINGO in telling a tale and figured that was the only way to express the speed and tension and ecstatic tomfoolery of the age. . . . Is that enough?

How do you think this style has changed since **On the Road?**

What style? Oh, the style of *On the Road.* Well as I say, Cowley riddled the original style of the manu-script there, without my power to complain, and since then my books are all published as written, as I say, and the style has varied from the highly experimental speedwriting of **"Railroad Earth"** to the ingrown toe-nail packed mystical style of *Tristessa,* the *Notes-from-the-Underground* (by Dostoevsky) confessional madness of *The Subterraneans,* the perfection of the three as one in *Big Sur,* I'd say, which tells a plain tale in a smooth buttery literate run, to *Satori in Paris* which is really the first book I wrote with drink at my side (cognac and malt liquor) . . . and not to overlook *Book of Dreams,* the style of a person half awake from sleep and ripping it out in pencil by the bed . . . yes, pencil . . . what a job! bleary eyes, insaned mind bemused and mystified by sleep, details that pop out even as you write them you don't know what they mean, till you wake up, have coffee, look at it, and see the logic of dreams in dream language itself, see? . . . and finally I decided in my tired middle age to slow down and did *Vanity of Duluoz* in a more moderate style so that, having been so esoteric all these years, some earlier readers would come back and see what ten years had done to my life and thinking . . . which is after all the only thing I've got to offer, the true story of what I saw and how I saw it. (pp. 64-7)

What is that state of "Yeatsian semi-trance" which provides the ideal atmosphere for spontaneous writing?

Well, there it is, how can you be in a trance with your mouth yapping away . . . writing at least is a si-lent meditation even though you're going 100 miles an hour. Remember that scene in *La Dolce Vita* where the old priest is mad because a mob of maniacs have shown up to see the tree where the kids saw the Virgin Mary? He says, "Visions are not available in all this frenetic foolishness and yelling and pushing; visions are only obtainable in silence and meditation." Thar. Yup. (p. 68)

Why do you think Neal [Cassady, the model for Dean Moriarty] doesn't write?

He has written . . . beautifully! He has written better than I have. Neal's a very funny guy. He's a real Californian. We had more fun than 5000 Socony Gasoline Station attendants can have. In my opinion he's the most intelligent man I've ever met in my life. Neal Cassady. He's a Jesuit by the way. He used to sing in the choir. He was a choir boy in the Catholic churches of Denver. And he taught me everything that I now do believe about anything that there may be to be believed about divinity.

About Edgar Cayce?

No, before he found out about Edgar Cayce he told me all these things in the section of the life he led when he was on the road with me—he said, We know God, don't we Jack? I said, Yessir boy. He said, Don't we know that nothing's going to happen wrong? Yessir. And we're going to go on and on . . . and hmmmmm ja-bmmmmmmm. . . . He was perfect. And he's always perfect. Everytime he comes to see me I can't get a word in edgewise.

You wrote about Neal playing football, in **Visions of Cody.**

Yes, he was a very good football player. He picked up two beatniks that time in blue jeans in North Beach Frisco. He said I got to go, bang bang, do I got to go? He's working on the railroad . . . had his watch out . . . 2:15, boy I got to be there by *2:20.* I tell you boys drive me over down there so I be on time with my train . . . So I can get my train on down to—what's the name of that place—San Jose? They say sure kid and Neal says here's the pot. So—"We maybe look like great bleat beatniks with great beards . . . but we are cops. And we are arresting you."

So, a guy went to the jailhouse and interviewed him from the New York Post and he said tell that Kerouac if he still believes in me to send me a typewriter. So I sent Allen Ginsberg one hundred dollars to get a typewriter for Neal. And Neal got the typewriter. And he wrote notes on it, but they wouldn't let him take the notes out. I don't know where the typewriter is. Genet wrote all of *Our Lady of the Flowers* in the shithouse . . . the jailhouse. There's a great writer, Jean Genet. He kept writing and kept writing until he got to a point where he was going to come by writing about it . . . until he came into his bed—in the can. The French can. The French jail. Prison. And that was the

end of the chapter. Every chapter is Genet coming off. Which I must admit Sartre noticed.

You think that's a different kind of spontaneous writing?

Well, I could go to jail and I could write every night a chapter about Magee, Magoo, and Molly. It's beautiful. Genet is really *the* most honest writer we've had since Kerouac and Burroughs. But he came before us. He's older. Well, he's the same age as Burroughs. But I don't think I've been dishonest. Man, I've had a good time! God, man, I rode around this country free as a bee. But Genet is a very tragic and beautiful writer. And I give them the crown. And the laurel wreath. I don't give the laurel wreath to Richard Wilbur! *Or* Robert Lowell. Give it to Jean Genet and William Seward Burroughs. *And* to Allen Ginsberg and to Gregory Corso, especially. (pp. 77-8)

What about jazz and bop as influences rather than . . . Saroyan, Hemingway and Wolfe?

Yes, jazz and bop, in the sense of a, say, a tenor man drawing a breath and blowing a phrase on his saxophone, till he runs out of breath, and when he does, his sentence, his statement's been made . . . that's how I therefore separate my sentences, as breath separations of the mind . . . I formulated the theory of breath as measure, in prose and verse, never mind what Olson, Charles Olson says, I formulated that theory in 1953 at the request of Burroughs and Ginsberg. Then there's the raciness and freedom and humor of jazz instead of all that dreary analysis and things like "James entered the room, and lit a cigarette. He thought Jane might have thought this too vague a gesture . . . " You know the stuff. As for Saroyan, yes I loved him as a teenager, he really got me out of the 19th century rut I was trying to study, not only his funny tone but his neat Armenian poetic I don't know what . . . he just got me . . . Hemingway was fascinating, the pearls of words on a white page giving you an exact picture . . . but Wolfe was a torrent of American heaven and hell that opened my eyes to America as a subject in itself.

How about the movies?

Yes, we've all been influenced by movies. Malcolm Cowley incidentally mentioned this many times. He's very perceptive sometimes: he mentioned that *Doctor Sax* continually mentions urine, and quite naturally it does because I had no other place to write it but on a closed toilet seat in a little tile toilet in Mexico City so as to get away from the guests inside the apartment. There incidentally is a style truly hallucinated as I wrote it all on pot. No pun intended. Ho ho.

How has Zen influenced your work?

What's really influenced my work is the Mahayana Buddhism, the original Buddhism of Gotama Sakyamuni, the Buddha himself, of the India of old . . . Zen is what's left of his Buddhism, or Bodhi, after its passing into China and then into Japan. The part of Zen that's influenced my writing is the Zen contained in the haiku, . . . the three line, seventeen syllable poems written hundreds of years ago by guys like Basho, Issa, Shiki, and there've been recent masters. A sentence that's short and sweet with a sudden jump of thought in it is a kind of haiku, and there's a lot of freedom and fun in surprising yourself with that, let the mind willy-nilly jump from the branch to the bird. But my serious Buddhism, that of ancient India, has influenced that part in my writing that you might call religious, or fervent, or pious, almost as much as Catholicism has. Original Buddhism referred to continual conscious compassion, brotherhood, the *dana paramita* meaning the perfection of charity, don't step on the bug, all that, humility, mendicancy, the sweet sorrowful face of the Buddha (who was of Aryan origin by the way, I mean of Persian warrior caste, and not Oriental as pictured) . . . in original Buddhism no young kid coming to a monastery was warned that "here we bury them alive." He was simply given soft encouragement to meditate and be kind. The beginning of Zen was when Buddha, however, assembled all the monks together to announce a sermon and choose the first patriarch of the Mahayana church: instead of speaking, he simply held up a flower. Everybody was flabbergasted except Kasyapa, who smiled. Kasyapa was appointed the first patriarch. This idea appealed to the Chinese like the Sixth Patriarch Hui-Neng who said, "From the beginning nothing ever was" and wanted to tear up the records of Buddha's sayings as kept in the sutras; sutras are "threads of discourse." In a way, then, Zen is a gentle but goofy form of heresy, though there must be some real kindly old monks somewhere and we've heard about the nutty ones. I haven't been to Japan. Your Maha roshi yoshi is simply a disciple of all this and not the founder of anything new at all, of course. On the Johnny Carson show he didn't even mention Buddha's name. Maybe his Buddha is Mia. (pp. 83-5)

What about ritual and superstition? Do you have any about yourself when you get down to work?

I had a ritual once of lighting a candle and writing by its light and blowing it out when I was done for the night . . . also kneeling and praying before starting (I got that from a French movie about George Frederick Handel) . . . but now I simply hate to write. My superstition? I'm beginning to suspect that full moon. Also I'm hung up on the number 9 though I'm told a Piscean like myself should stick to number 7; but I try to do 9 touchdowns a day, that is, I stand on my head in the bathroom, on a slipper, and touch the floor 9 times with my toe tips, while balanced. This is incidentally more than Yoga, it's an athletic feat, I mean imagine calling me "unbalanced" after that. Frankly I do feel that my mind is going. So another "ritual" as you call it, is to pray to Jesus to preserve my sanity and my energy so

I can help my family: that being my paralyzed mother, and my wife, and the ever-present kitties. Okay?

You typed out **On the Road** *in three weeks,* **The Subterraneans** . . . *in three days and nights. Do you still produce at this fantastic rate? Can you say something of the genesis of a work before you sit down and begin that terrific typing—how much of it is set in your mind, for example?*

You think out what actually happened, you tell friends long stories about it, you mull it over in your mind, you connect it together at leisure, then when the time comes to pay the rent again you force yourself to sit at the typewriter, or at the writing notebook, and get it over with as fast as you can . . . and there's no harm in that because you've got the whole story lined up. Now how that's done depends on what kind of steeltrap you've got up in that little old head. This sounds boastful but a girl once told me I had a steeltrap brain, meaning I'd catch her with a statement she'd made an hour ago even though our talk had rambled a million lightyears away from that point . . . you know what I mean, like a lawyer's mind, say. All of it is in my mind, naturally, except that language that is used at the time that it is used. . . . And as for *On the Road* and *The Subterraneans,* no I can't write that fast any more . . . Writing the Subs in three nights was really a fantastic athletic feat as well as mental, you shoulda seen me after I was done . . . I was pale as a sheet and had lost fifteen pounds and looked strange in the mirror. What I do now is write something like an average of 8,000 words a sitting, in the middle of the night, and another about a week later, resting and sighing in between. I really hate to write. I get no fun out of it because I can't get up and say I'm working, close my door, have coffee brought to me, and sit there camping like a "man of letters" "doing his eight hour day of work" and thereby incidentally filling the printing world with a lot of dreary self-imposed cant and bombast . . . bombast is Scottish word for stuffing for a pillow. Haven't you heard a politician use 1500 words to say something he could have said in exactly three words? So I get it out of the way so as not to bore myself either. (pp. 88-90)

What about the influence of Ginsberg and Burroughs? Did you ever have any sense then of the mark the three of you would have on American writing?

I was determined to be a "great writer," in quotes, like Thomas Wolfe, see . . . Allen was always reading and writing poetry . . . Burroughs read a lot and walked around looking at things. . . . The influence we exerted on one another has been written about over and over again . . . We were just three interested characters, in the interesting big city of New York, around campuses, libraries, cafeterias. A lot of the details you'll find in *Vanity* . . . in *On the Road* where Burroughs is Bull Lee and Ginsberg is Carlo Marx . . . in *Subterraneans,* where they're Frank Carmody and Adam

Manuscript page of *On the Road.* Kerouac purportedly wrote the novel in twenty days on a
single roll of teletype paper.

Moorad   respectively,   elsewhere.   In   other   words,   though I don't want to be rude to you for this honor,

I am so busy interviewing myself in my novels, and have been so busy writing down these self-interviews, that I don't see why I should draw breath in pain every year of the last ten years to repeat and repeat to everybody who interviews me what I've already explained in the books themselves. . . . (Hundreds of journalists, thousands of students.) It beggars sense. And it's not that important. It's our work that counts, if anything at all, and I'm not proud of mine or theirs or anybody's since Thoreau and others like that, maybe because it's still too close to home for comfort. Notoriety and public confession in literary form is a frazzler of the heart you were born with, believe me. (pp. 97-8)

What was it that brought all of you together in the 50's? What was it that seemed to unify the "Beat Generation?"

Oh the beat generation was just a phrase I used in the 1951 written manuscript of *On the Road* to describe guys like Moriarty who run around the country in cars looking for odd jobs, girlfriends, kicks. It was thereafter picked up by West Coast leftist groups and turned into a meaning like "beat mutiny" and "beat insurrection" and all that nonsense; they just wanted some youth movement to grab onto for their own political and social purposes. I had nothing to do with any of that. I was a football player, a scholarship college student, a merchant seaman, a railroad brakeman on road freights, a script synopsizer, a secretary . . . And Moriarty-Cassady was an actual cowboy on Dave Uhl's ranch in New Raymer Colorado . . . What kind of beatnik is that?

Was there any sense of "community" among the Beat crowd?

That community feeling was largely inspired by the same characters I mentioned, like Ferlinghetti, Ginsberg; they are very socialistically minded and want everybody to live in some kind of frenetic kibbutz, solidarity and all that. I was a loner. Snyder is not like Whalen, Whalen is not like McClure, I am not like McClure, McClure is not like Ferlinghetti, Ginsberg is not like Ferlinghetti, but we all had fun over wine anyway. We knew thousands of poets and painters and jazz musicians. There's no "beat crowd" like you say . . . what about Scott Fitzerald and his "lost crowd," does that sound right? Or Goethe and his "Wilhelm Meister crowd?" The subject is such a bore. Pass me that glass.

Well, why did they split in the early 60's?

Ginsberg got interested in left wing politics . . . like Joyce I say, as Joyce said to Ezra Pound in the 1920's, "Don't bother me with politics, the only thing that interests me is style." Besides I'm bored with the new avant-garde and the skyrocketing sensationalism. I'm reading Blaise Pascal and taking notes on religion. I like to hang around now with nonintellectuals, as you might call them, and not have my mind proselytized, ad infinitum. They've even started crucifying chickens in happenings, what's the next step? An actual cruci-

fixion of a man . . . The beat group dispersed as you say in the early 60's, all went their own way, and this is my way: home life, as in the beginning, with a little toot once in a while in local bars. (pp. 101-03)

Jack Kerouac and Ted Berrigan, in an interview in *The Paris Review*, Vol. 11, No. 43, Summer, 1968, pp. 60-105.

ALLEN GINSBERG
(essay date 1972)

[Ginsberg is one of the most celebrated poets in contemporary America. Known for his morally and aesthetically iconoclastic verse, he was a leading member of the Beat movement and a longtime friend of Kerouac. The following excerpt is from a 1972 *Saturday Review* essay that later appeared as the introduction to Kerouac's posthumously published novel, *Visions of Cody*. The novel continues the autobiographical story of *On the Road* in a similar *roman à clef* fashion and, like the earlier novel, is about Neal Cassady, a prototypical Beat. Here, Ginsberg labels *Visions of Cody* "a work of primitive genius."]

Two noble men, Americans, perished younger than old whitebeard prophets' wrinkled gay eye Archetypes might've imagined like Whitman. The death of America in their early stop—untimely tears—for loves glimpsed and not fulfilled—not completely fulfilled, some kind of withdrawal from the promised tender Nation—Larimer Street down, green lights glimmering, Denver surrounded by Honeywell warplants, IBM war calculators, selfish Air Bases, Botanical Mortal Brain Factories—Robot buildings downtown lifted under crescent moon—The small hands gestured to belly and titty, under backstairs decades ago, seeking release to each other, trembling sexual tenderness discovered first times . . . before the wars began . . . 1939 Denver's mysterious glimpses of earth life unfolding on side streets in United States—Perfectly captured nostalgia by Jack *Visions of Cody* (Neal) . . . Peace protester adolescents from Cherry High with neck kiss bruises sit & weep on Denver Capitol Hill lawn, hundreds of Neal & Jack souls mortal lamblike sighing over the nation now, 1972.

Mortal America's here . . . disappearing Elevateds, diners, iceboxes, dusty hat racks preserved from oblivion . . . Larimer Street itself this year in ruins resurrected spectral thru *Visions of Cody*— And the poolhall itself gone to parking lot & Fun Adult Movies the heritage of Neal's sex fantasies on the bench watching Watson shoot snooker—

By this prose preserved for a younger generation

appreciative of the Bowery camp & thirties hair consciousness destroyed by real estate speculators on wargrowth economy.

I don't think it is possible to proceed further in America without first understanding Kerouac's tender brooding compassion for bygone scene & personal Individuality oddity'd therein. Bypassing Kerouac one bypasses the mortal heart, sung in prose vowels; the book a giant mantra of appreciation and adoration of an American man, one striving heroic soul. (p. vii)

[*Visions of Cody* records] a set of nights on newly discovered Grass, wherein [Kerouac and Cassady] explored the mind blanks impressions that tea creates: that's the subject, unaltered & unadorned—halts, switches, emptiness, quixotic chatters, summary piths, exactly reproduced, significant because: 1) Vocal familiar friendly teahead life talk had never been transcribed and examined consciously (like Warhol 20 years later examined Campbell's Soup cans). 2) Despite monotony, the gaps and changes (like Warhol watching Empire State Bldg. all night) are dramatic. 3) It leads somewhere, like life. 4) It's interesting if you want the characters' reality. 5) It's real. 6) It's art because at that point in progress of Jack's art he began transcribing *first* thoughts of true mind in American speech, and as objective sample of that teahead-high speech of his model hero, he placed uncorrected tape central in his book, actual sample-reality he was otherwise rhapsodizing.

Art lies in the consciousness of doing the thing, in the attention to the happening, in the sacramentalization of everyday reality, the God-worship in the present conversation, no matter what. Thus the tape may be read not as hung-up which it sometimes is to the stranger, but as a spontaneous Ritual performed once and never repeated, in full consciousness that every yawn & syllable uttered would be eternal . . . the tape coheres together with serious solemn discussion of their lives.

Jack Kerouac's style of transcription of taped conversation is, also, impeccably accurate in syntax punctuation—separation of elements for clarity . . . labeling of voices, parenthesizing of interruptions. A model to study.

Concluding we see the beauty of the tapes that Jack cherished, that they are inclusive samples of complete exchange of information and love thoughts between two men, each giving his mind history to the other—The remarkable situation, which we are privileged to witness thru these creaky tapes transcribed by now dead hand, is—of Kerouac the great rememberer on quiet evenings 1950-1951 with Neal Cassady, the great experiencer & midwest driver and talker, gossiping intimately of their eternities—here's representative sample of these evenings, and we can take as model their exchange and see that our own lives also have se-

crets, mysteries, explanations and love equal to those of feeble, seeking heroes past—Another generation has followed, perhaps surpassed, Neal & Jack conversing in midnight intimacy—if it hasn't discovered that "huge confessional night" then this tape transcript is fit model. If it's surpassed—more coherent these days—I doubt it!?! But then, this is ancient history—if History's interesting now that America has near destroyed the human compassionate world still surviving as in fragments of bewildering conversation between these two dead souls. (pp. viii-ix)

"I'm writing this book because we're all going to die . . . my heart broke in the general despair and opened up inwards to the Lord, I made a supplication in this dream." This is the most sincere and holy writing I know of our age—at the same time for Pre-Buddhist Jack, a complete display of knowledge of Noble Truths he soon discovered in Goddard's *Buddhist Bible.*

Yet Jack had another 18 years ahead with Neal on earth, neither was dead ("Neal is Dead"), except this vision book was all out effort to understand early in the midst of life, what Jack's yearning and Neal's response and both their mortal American energy was all about, was directed to—but only time could tell, & both got tired *several* times—Jack went on to write not only *Dr. Sax* but *Mexico City Blues* in the next year & then *The Subterraneans & Springtime Mary (Maggie Cassidy)* and more and more and more climaxed 5 years later with some fame, and the brilliant Buddhist exposition *Dharma Bums,* and also *Desolation Angels* later, to keep the perfect chronicle going—"rack my hand with labor of Nada"—and many poems—not to speak of his *Book of Dreams* and giant as-yet-unpublished *Some of the Dharma,* 1000 pages of haikus, meditations, readings, commentaries on Prajnaparamita & Diamond Sutras, brainthinks, Samadhi notes, scholarship in the Void—reading Shakespere & Melville all the while & listening to Bach's *St. Matthew's Passion* evermore—

Saying farewell to Cody, Jack was saying farewell to the World, both of them gave up several times—But at that 1952 time both of them were at their wits' ends with the world and America—The "Beat Generation" was about that time formulated, the Vietnam War just about to be continued American bodied (as 'twas already funded American dollar'd via opium pushing France & French-Corsican Intelligence agencies)—Two years after completion of this book Neal lived in a quiet home, receptive and friendly but by then entered into a blank new insistent religiosity, "like Billy Sunday in a suit" epistled Jack, namely Edgar Cayce study—which reincarnation philosophy drove Jack to study Buddhism; a new phase not even recorded or mentioned in this vast essay on Early or Middle Neal.

I remember the sleepless epiphanies of 1948—everywhere in America brain-consciousness was waking up, from Times Square to the banks of Willamette River to Berkeley's groves of Academe: little Samadhis and appreciations of intimate spaciness that might later be explain'd and followed as the Crazy Wisdom of Rinzai Zen or the Whispered Transmission of Red Hat Vajrayana Path Doctrine, or Coyote's empty yell in the Sierras. Out of Burroughs' copy of Spengler Kerouac arrived at the conception of "Fellaheen Eternal Country Life"—Country Samadhi for Jack, country Ken & consciousness latent discovered in Mexico as our heroes crossed the border: immediate recognition of Biblical Patriarch Type in Mexic Fellaheen fathers: the Bible those days the only immediate American mind-entry to primeval earth-consciousness non-machine populace that inhabits 80 per cent of the world—"Jeremiacal hoboes lounge, shepherds by trade . . . I can see the hand of God. The future's in Fellaheen. At Actopan this biblical plateau begins—it's reached by the mountain of faith only. I know that I will someday live in a land like this. I did long ago." Heartbreaking prophecy. And intelligent Neal'd said, "What they want has already crumbled in a rubbish heap—they want banks."

Jack didn't write this book for money, he wrote it for love, he *gave* it away to the world; not even for fame, but as an explanation and prayer to his fellow mortals, and gods—with naked motive and humble piety Search—that's what makes *Visions of Cody* a work of primitive genius that grooks next to Douanier Rousseau's visions, and sits well-libraried beside Thomas Wolfe's *Time & River* (which Thos. Mann from his European eminence said was the great prose of America) & sits beside Tolstoi for its *prayers*. A La La Ho! (pp. x-xi)

The last pages say, "All America marching to this last land." The book was a dirge for America, for its heroes' deaths too, but then who could know except in the unconscious—A dirge for the American Hope that Jack (& his hero Neal) carried so valiantly through the land after Whitman—an America of pioneers and generosity—and selfish glooms & exploitations implicit in the pioneers' entry into Foreign Indian & Moose lands—but the great betrayal of that manly America was made by the pseudo-heroic pseudo-responsible masculines of Army and Industry and Advertising and Construction and Transport and toilets and Wars.

Last pages—how tender—"Adios King!" a farewell to all the promises of America, an explanation & prayer for innocence, a tearful renunciation of victory & accomplishment, a humility in the face of "the necessary blankness of men" in hopeless America, hopeless World, in hopeless wheel of Heaven, a compassionate farewell to Love & the Companion, Adios King. (p. xii)

Allen Ginsberg, in an introduction to *Visions of Cody* by Jack Kerouac, McGraw Hill, 1972, pp. vii-xii.

ROBERT A. HIPKISS
(essay date 1976)

[In the following excerpt, Hipkiss discusses Kerouac's portrayal of women in his works.]

The father and mother images in Kerouac indicate a strong fear of the masculine world and a concomitant Oedipal tie to the mother. This repulsion-attraction syndrome has much to do with Kerouac's lifelong preservation of the child's innocent vision as a stay against the sophisticated adult world.

In the 1950s Kerouac was haunted by a recurrent dream of a shrouded stranger tracking him through streets and across the desert. In his *Book of Dreams* he recounts a dream in which "my Shroud approaches—*I know* he'll get me . . . but being a kid I have great potentiality and all the world yet and left to hide in and cover with tracks—Shall I go towards the mysterious old Chalifoux woods beyond where woodstumps I was born in redmorning valleys of life hope?—or sneak back snaky into town?" The Shroud will get him. But before that fatal end, the child in the dream has time to realize the hopes of his birth. The problem is how to do so. He is torn between retreat toward birth and going onward into a corrupt adult existence (sneaking back, snaky, into town). High on marijuana and preoccupied with Buddhist thought, Kerouac had another dream in which his father comes toward him, and in this dream the father is the "Shroudy Traveller." (p. 15)

Kerouac wrote *The Town and the City* in the following two years, in part to atone for the wayward behavior of his youth and the disappointments he had caused his father when he dropped out of Columbia, went to sea, and refused to take a steady job. His attitude toward his father at the time was sympathetic, the feelings about their misunderstandings largely regretful, as we see them in Kerouac's treatment of Peter Martin's relationship with his father in *Town and the City*. In the fifties, as Kerouac alternately supported and was supported by his mother and as he kicked around more and more in the hobo-Bohemian world, he thought back over his relationships with [his father] Leo Kerouac and always returned to the same harsh truth—that his father's world would always have rejected him. The anger of that rejection, fed by memories of his father's unsympathetic attitude toward his youthful aspirations and discontents, finally found its way into the much harsher portrait of the father that we find in *Vanity of Duluoz*, written in the sixties in the last few years of Jack Kerouac's life. (p. 16)

[His father's death in 1946] left Jack feeling rootless. The father and mother had moved from Lowell to Ozone Park in 1943, and now the head of the family was dead. The gap between them in life became unbreachable in death. At the end of *Town and the City*, as Peter Martin arranges a blanket around his dying father, George Martin's last words are, "That's right, my poor little boy." In saying this the dying George seems to recognize that the young man, barely twenty-one, is not yet ready to go it alone. In *Maggie Cassidy* . . . Emil Duluoz, the father, says he is disappointed that he and his son have not been closer this year but, "ah dammit son it's a terrible thing not being able to help you but you do understand don't you God's left us all alone in our skins to fare better or worse—hah?" In *Visions of Cody* Kerouac remembers "the brown nights and my father ignoring me again as I now ignore my own boy—and have to, as *he* had to—." . . . In this statement it appears as though Jack is accepting the necessity of growing up privately within our own skins, the essential isolation of each individual life and its own individualized pattern of growth, but it is far more an attempt at acceptance than an actuality. (pp. 16-17)

In *Visions of Gerard* the father, Emil Duluoz, is an energetic man with a sense of the wrongness of things but unable to do anything about it. In *Doctor Sax* Jack dreams of him as "a man in a straw hat hurrying in a redbrick alley of Eternity," . . . and in the 103rd Chorus of *Mexico City Blues* . . . Kerouac describes his father with his "straw hat, newspaper in pocket, / Liquor in the breath, barber shopshines, / . . . the image of Ignorant Man / Hurrying to his destiny which is Death / . . . in downtown Lowell / walking like a cardboard cut / across the lost lights. . . ." The father is ignorant, empty, as lost in his way as the son is in his. The father escaped knowing the meaninglessness of his existence, however, by playing the game American society plays, the competitive game of business and money-grubbing, "lost in the eye to eye the game of men in America." . . . (pp. 17-18)

The competitive nature of his father's world is most upsetting to the young man. . . . In football and earlier while running track, Kerouac's Peter Martin had learned the sadness of victory in the "new dark knowledge he now half-understood—that to triumph was also to wreak havoc." . . . To what end the competitive struggle? Is it worth the cost in the suffering inflicted? These questions are suggested time and again in Kerouac's work. (p. 18)

To keep the adult world at bay, Kerouac retreated into childhood and sought protection from his father's Shroud by holding tight to the apron of Memère, his mother. . . . The mother-figure in Kerouac's stories is the symbol of life, forgiveness, and love just as the father is the specter of death and calloused striving. (pp. 18-19)

In the 237th Chorus of *Mexico City Blues* the author calls his mother *"la terre,"* and says that ideal mothers like his own and Damema, mother of Buddha, obey their pure and free impulses and are champions of birth. In other words they are solidly in contact with their instincts and, being creators themselves, they respect creativity in all forms. They are, then, the ideal helpmates to the romantic, creative artists.

When Kerouac looked up his family's coat of arms in the British Museum he found the family motto: "Love, work and suffer." . . . Memère accepted this dictum not so much because she was a Kerouac but because she was a devout Catholic, so much so that her son says of her in *Desolation Angels* that in a previous lifetime she must surely have been a Head Nun. Memère is in good company. Kerouac places her faith and understanding beside those of Mozart and Blaise Pascal, who knew that man is on earth to suffer and that his vain attempts to know ideologically what is right and necessary to make a Heaven on earth are foolish, prideful sins, doomed only to make earthly life more hellish. Memère, like her son, had no use for revolutionaries. . . . (pp. 19-20)

Kerouac refused to accept the notion that he was tied to his mother by a kind of Oedipal attraction. He belittled the Freudian interpretation of their relationship and psychoanalysis in general. In a direct reply to his critics, in *Desolation Angels* he says that after his trips around the country and to Mexico, Tangier, and Europe his mother offers the welcome relief of peace, good sense, and an immaculately kept home. . . . (p. 20)

Nevertheless, Kerouac's attachment to his mother cannot be accepted as merely comfortable. The Freudian implications remain, even though Kerouac tried to dismiss them. The fact of the matter is that his relationship to Memère affected his attitudes toward sex and his relationship with women quite profoundly, and these attitudes and experiences in turn found their way, barely transmuted, into his autobiographical fiction.

In his *Book of Dreams* Kerouac recounts a dream of himself with his mother arm in arm on the floor. He is crying, afraid to die, and "she's blissful and has one leg in pink sexually out between". . . . The mother comforts the son and brings him away from death, but in suggesting its opposite, procreation, she is suggesting what he calls here a "snaky affection," an affection that could lead to damnation, something as bad or worse than death itself. This one dream sequence illustrates quite vividly the Oedipal tie as preservation against death and the father's world. More deeply, however, it also suggests the source of the Duluoz-Kerouac fear of being possessed by the sexual attraction of woman.

Throughout the adventures of his heroes there is

an attraction-repulsion oscillation where sex is concerned. The call of the road to Dean Moriarty, Sal Paradise, and Jack Duluoz is as often as not a call away from entanglements with women. Even when the male character expresses a desire to have a healthy sexual relationship with a woman, he inadvertently scares himself into flight. (pp. 20-1)

The most complete expression of the attraction-repulsion syndrome in his fiction is in *The Subterraneans.* Leo Percepied (the name is close to Oedipus in French) tells us that he is paranoid concerning Mardou Fox, attracted to her without trusting her. Kerouac's friend John Montgomery has suggested that this was Kerouac's case with women in general. Leo treats Mardou rather badly and finally loses her to a twenty-two year old "subterranean jester," Yuri Gligoric (actually Gregory Corso), and when he does he feels great pangs of jealousy. Mardou suggests that Leo needs to emancipate himself from his mother, and he tells her that he is trying hard to divide his time equally between them. It is obvious that he has no intention of gaining true emancipation. In fact, by encouraging what he knows is a "big subjective fantasy" that his mother desperately needs him, he can hold back from any lasting involvements with other women.

The women least likely to make demands upon him are the most desirable in Kerouac's works. In *Tristessa* the girl Tristessa is a morphine addict like Bull Gaines (William Garver), with whom Jack is staying, and she is also Gaines's procurer. She lives in a dirty apartment in Mexico City with a "sister" who is "seek" and a male dope addict, a dove, a Chihuahua, a pink cat, and a hen and a rooster. (pp. 21-2)

In Kerouac's works most of the major women characters are long-suffering on behalf of their men. They are, in this respect, extensions of Memère. Certainly this is true of Dean Moriarty's several wives and girl friends in *On the Road* and *Big Sur* (where his name changes to Cody Pomeray). It is true also of Sal Paradise's aunt, who always sends him money when he is hard up, and of Terry, the Mexican girl, who takes Sal in for a time in *On the Road.* Women are the caretakers of the earth; as such, a patient endurance is required of them, and a willingness to suffer. The role is archetypal in literature and certainly a part of the female characterization of Wolfe and Hemingway, two of the major influences on Kerouac's writing in the early years.

Woman, however, is also a biological trap. Her overall purpose is procreation, and in order to fulfill her function she must get a male not only to copulate with her but to provide for her and her offspring while the young require constant maternal care. The woman asks the man, then, to be responsible for her and the children at the expense of his own freedom and desire for self glory. In the 201st Chorus of *Mexico City Blues*

Kerouac speaks of women as ones who tempt the saints from meditation on "the enormous / nothingness / of the skies." Women fill an unholy and very earthly office. Women continue the cycle of karma. The man would escape into pure spirit, becoming a mystic, a hobo will-o'-the-wisp, a Dean Moriarty kind of "holy goof." (pp. 23-4)

Throughout his work the power of woman is paramount. It is woman who controls the world in Kerouac's **"CITYCity-city,"** his look into the future. In a story that owes much to Huxley's *Brave New World,* Orwell's *1984,* and the writings of his friend William Burroughs, Kerouac envisions a future civilization, suffering from overpopulation, which is so regulated that people are confined to various zones for three hundred years and then promptly electrocuted. Their lives are controlled by the Computer of Infinite Merit and Master Center Love, which propagandizes them through Multivision, an electronic device attached to their bodies to keep them quiescent. The Master Center World Drugs also provides 17-JX, a drug a bit like Huxley's Soma, which provides a feeling of "polite, courteous loving." Over this highly regulated society rule The Women. The analogy to the world of Kerouac's novels is clear. Women use love as a kind of drug, offering life-long security to the male, while at the same time giving birth rampantly and overpopulating the world to no particular end. In spite of their power, however, The Women cannot keep some of the men from sniffing a natural spirit substance called Action, which makes the men desire impossible activity. The drug of Love is not enough to make these men quiescent. These "bums" are known as Loveless Brothers.

Such a strongly misogynistic story might be considered as a backhanded plea for homosexuality. . . . In his work Kerouac shows a patent acceptance of homosexuals, but they are always seen from the standpoint of one who is himself sexually attracted only to women.

In his novels the hero's sexual fantasies vary somewhat, depending upon what Kerouac was reading and the situation in which the characters find themselves. (pp. 24-6)

Looking now at Kerouac's relations with his parents and his attitudes toward women and sex, we can readily see their influence on his preservation of the child's innocent vision. Kerouac identified the father with the heartless, competitive struggle that threw him out of work in the thirties and that blinded him to spiritual and artistic values dear to the feelings of his sensitive son. Kerouac's preservation of the innocent vision, then, is a refusal to enter the world of the father. Just as J. D. Salinger's Holden Caulfield wants to be a "catcher in the rye" who preserves the innocent happiness of little children, so Kerouac too wants to preserve the world of childhood against what Holden calls the "phony crap" of the adult world.

Central to the child's world, however, is the mother, the protectress and comforter. . . . Although the attraction to a woman's maternalism is strong in Kerouac, so is the desire for action. Like the "Loveless Brothers" of **"CITYCitycity,"** he and his characters feel restless even under the drug of Love. The woman's smothering protectiveness and her management of his life are a frustration to the writer and his heroes when they require that the male assume the role of head of a family in a day-to-day competitive society.

The answer to the onus of female demands is escape, escape into art and escape onto the road. In his writing Kerouac is constantly throwing up a wall against time, the coming of adulthood, and preserving a vision of innocence and spirituality against a sophisticated, Godless world. The greatest threat to his success is entrapment in the world of woman, and the most powerful weapon at a woman's disposal is her sexual attraction.

At successive times Kerouac's heroes try to get sex on the run *(Maggie Cassidy)*, ignore it altogether *(Tristessa,* Part I), revel in it even if it means setting up housekeeping for a time *(Desolation Angels* and *Visions of Cody)*, revile it and revel in guilt because of it *(The Subterraneans)*, and, finally, even bring the woman and sex into the man's vision of spirituality *(Big Sur)*. This last is a final attempt at reconciliation, of sexual and spiritual need; it does not, of course, do away with the danger of entrapment in the domestic life unless the woman forsakes her archetypal role. (pp. 26-8)

Robert A. Hipkiss, in his *Jack Kerouac: Prophet of the New Romanticism,* Regents Press of Kansas, 1976, 150 p.

SVEN BIRKERTS

(essay date 1989)

[Birkerts is an American educator and critic. In the following excerpt, he offers a personal response to *On the Road.*]

I first read Jack Kerouac's *On the Road* when I was a junior in high school—a little more than twenty-one years ago. Someone had given my mother a copy of the book; I immediately "borrowed" it, consumed it, and started it circulating among my friends. Soon we were all obsessed—hitchhiking everywhere we could, trying to be like the characters in the novel.

Our every late-adolescent desire for movement, escape, *action* was brought to a blaze. Not that much fanning of sparks was needed. After all, it was 1968. If it hadn't been Kerouac, it would soon have been someone else.

Though Kerouac had begun writing *On the Road* in 1948, and it had first been published in 1957, the book could not have felt more present tense. Kerouac had caught hold of a spirit we understood; he raised a call to arms. What for me had been just inchoate turmoil and longing had now been set down in words. I grew restless and excited when the book's narrator, Sal Paradise, announced:

> . . . the only people for me are the mad ones, the ones who are mad to live, mad to talk, mad to be saved, desirous of everything at the same time, the ones who never yawn or say a commonplace thing, but burn, burn, burn like fabulous yellow roman candles exploding like spiders across the stars and in the middle you see the blue centerlight pop and everybody goes "Awww!"

That was it right there: madness, excess, something nonstop and feverish to hold against the blandness of our suburban childhoods.

When I went off to college, I found that we had not been unique: everyone, it seemed, had been reading Kerouac. And Ginsberg and Corso and Burroughs and Kesey (and Wolfe *on* Kesey). This was our non-curricular education. These were the spirits who conferred their benediction upon us, upon our efforts to live differently—more intensely—than our parents had. (p. 74)

I decided that I would commemorate the passing of two decades by re-reading *On the Road.* I knew, of course, that everything would be different. How could it not? In 1968 it had been a book whose title promised *discovery.* Now the cover blurb announced that I was about to read "the book that turned on a generation." Braced as I was, however, I still got a terrible jolt. There is simply no adequate protection against the way we grow and change.

The novel, *qua* novel, is not really much at all. Kerouac's alternately matter-of-fact and ebullient prose tracks Sal Paradise through his far-flung travels. The pattern is simple: About once a year, Sal gets restless in his secure lodgings with his aunt (the *mémère* to whom Kerouac remained neurotically attached all his life) and launches forth from New Jersey to the beckoning West. Each time, he hooks up with Dean Moriarty, his "mad" mentor, the aging juvenile delinquent who represents (to him) velocity, kicks, and enlightenment. Others join up and disperse, moving about like molecules of a boiling liquid. The American highway system is the spice route of their dreams. "Somewhere along the line," says Sal as he first sets out, "I knew there'd be girls, visions, everything; somewhere along the line the pearl would be handed to me."

Kerouac is sequential, at times almost diaristic. On the first trip West—perhaps because it *is* the first—every movement is tabulated. We follow Sal from the bus rides that get him started, to the long, "careening" (a favorite Kerouac word) rides that come once he gets west of Chicago and puts out his thumb. (p. 75)

"Wild" and "lyrical" are two more favorite Kerouac words—they crop up in most of his more energized riffs, especially through the first half of the book. It's as if Sal can't kick the language up quite as high as he wants it—he makes these loosely deployed adjectives carry so much of the freight of the inexpressible. But once—for me at least—they did carry it. When I first read *On the Road,* no one needed to tell me how a night, or a town, or a train, or a bum, could be "lyrical"—they just were. Kerouac's scattershot words and phrases accorded perfectly with my jumbled-up feelings about life. Now, for whatever reason, I seem to crave more precision—a passage like that no longer delivers.

On Sal's first trip West, he wants to "dig" everything. And everything is there to be dug. When he gets to Denver, his first real layover, a gang of friends and friends of friends is waiting. There follow rampaging nights with the hard-partying Bettencourt sisters and the Rawlins clan: "We started off with a few extra-size beers. There was a player piano. Beyond the back door was a view of mountainsides in the moonlight. I let out a yahoo. The night was on."

New sights and the promise of good times are, of course, part of what lures Sal away from home again and again; but the real draw is Dean—the outlaw, the limit-breaker. Sal wants to be near him as much as possible. Dean steals cars, he tears between the coasts in nonstop driving binges, he loves every "gal" in every diner along the way. He is Sal's "yellow roman candle," his life force; he is the catalyst that helps Sal break through his essential passivity.

Sal and Dean have one of those eternally boyish American friendships. Though women are desired, discussed, and dallied with, they are also always in the way—nagging, getting pregnant, threatening to stop the fun. Leslie Fiedler long ago identified the homoerotic nature of the bond (yes, Ishmael and Queequeg, Huck and Jim . . .) in *Love and Death in the American Novel.* And biographers of Kerouac now bear out that his friendship with Cassady did extend to some hesitant, experimental sex.

In any event, what weaves together the separate travel episodes is the unfolding history of a friendship—a history which begins with Sal's enchantment with the charismatically amoral Dean Moriarty and which ends with his pained disillusionment. In an early, blinded description, Sal writes: "And a kind of holy lightning I saw flashing from his excitement and his visions, which he described so torrentially that people in buses looked around to see the 'overexcited nut.' " But after he has been deserted and betrayed enough times, Sal finds his perceptions shifting. Dean's mad avidity is not so much heroic as desperate. He is fleeing his own inner void—the legacy of his rummy father, who abandoned him among the bars and poolhalls of Denver when he was a young boy.

By the end of the book, Sal's "thin-hipped" hero has become a figure of profound sadness. In the very last scene, when Sal is on his way to a concert, riding in the back of a hired Cadillac, he looks out at his friend: "Dean, ragged in a motheaten overcoat he brought specially for the freezing temperatures of the East, walked off alone . . . " He then adds this valedictory cadenza: " . . . nobody knows what's going to happen to anybody besides the forlorn rags of growing old, I think of Dean Moriarty, I even think of Old Dean Moriarty the father we never found, I think of Dean Moriarty."

It is probably a mistake to go back to the decisive books of one's youth. They are causes; the reader has long since become, in part, their effect. Clear vision is just not possible. I feel myself in a position somewhat like Sal's. It was not so much that Dean had changed from what he was—more that Sal had watched the vivid mantle of desires and dreams that he had created around Dean slowly dissipate. So, too, has the magic of *On the Road* dissipated for me.

Reading this book at sixteen, my friends and I wanted nothing so much as to be like Dean and Sal—close to the ground, connected, in motion, "paying our dues." We aspired to the "beat" ideal, with its double connotation of "worn-out" and "beatific." And when it led, as it inexorably did, to the hippie ethos of turning on, tuning in, and dropping out (how quaint it sounds!), many of us followed. But that next step was also a kind of last step—the premises of hippiedom were quickly consumed on the pyre of its excesses. Thus, once again, effects had come around to swallow their causes; henceforth, "beat" would also mean something like "proto-hippie."

All of this went through my mind as I re-read *On the Road.* Indeed, at some point I realized that I was not so much reading a book as taking stock—of those times, of these times, of myself in both. For me, the hardest thing was to see past the jadedness and cynicism of the '80s—to remember even a little of what life felt like back then. I don't know that I was able to, finally. The notes were as scored, sure, and the sounds were the same. But I kept feeling as if I were listening to a party record the morning after the party. It sounded sad, nothing like the way it had sounded while I was dancing to it. (pp. 75-6)

Sven Birkerts, "On the Road to Nowhere: Kerouac, Re-Read

and Regretted," in *Harper's*, Vol. 279, No. 1670, July, 1989, pp. 74-6.

SOURCES FOR FURTHER STUDY

Charters, Ann. *Kerouac: A Biography.* San Francisco: Straight Arrow, 1973, 419 p.

The earliest biography available on Kerouac.

French, Warren. *Jack Kerouac.* Boston: Twayne Publishers, 1986, 147 p.

Analyzes the novels that comprise "The Duluoz Legend" as an extended effort by Kerouac to recast his life in the form of a literary legend, as James Joyce did in his Stephen Dedalus novels.

McDarragh, Fred W. *Kerouac and Friends: A Beat Generation Album.* New York: William Morrow, 1985, 338 p.

Selection of newspaper and magazine articles and essays from the 1950s, reprinted along with McDarragh's photographs of major and minor Beat figures.

McNally, Dennis. *Desolate Angel: Jack Kerouac, the Beat Generation, and America.* New York: St. Martin's, 1978, 400 p.

Discusses the historical background of Kerouac and the Beats.

Nicosia, Gerald. *Memory Babe: A Critical Biography of Jack Kerouac.* New York: Grove Press, 1983, 767 p.

Comprehensive biography based on interviews, correspondence, and other documents from Kerouac's friends and family.

Podhoretz, Norman. "The Know-Nothing Bohemians." In his *Doings and Undoings,* pp. 143-58. New York: Farrar, Strauss, and Giroux, 1964.

Prominent early attack on Beat Generation literature, in which Podhoretz decries Kerouac's spontaneous prose technique as incoherent and inadequate to the tasks of description and conveying emotion.

Ken Kesey

1935-

(Full name Ken Elton Kesey) American novelist, short story writer, and scriptwriter.

INTRODUCTION

A transitional figure linking the Beat generation of the 1950s with the counterculture movement of the 1960s, Kesey is best known for his first novel, *One Flew over the Cuckoo's Nest* (1962). Like most of Kesey's fiction, this book focuses on alienated and nonconformist individuals who attempt, through love, hope, rebellion, and humor, to overcome their limitations and to retain their sanity and self-respect. *One Flew over the Cuckoo's Nest* is considered a prominent work of contemporary American literature for its disjointed, colloquial prose style, its parabolic commentary on modern social ills, and its inventive symbolism and archetypal characters. R. L. Sassoon commented: "With great originality the author has succeeded in achieving, almost throughout the novel, a subtle balance and correspondence between the social burden of mirroring purposefully place and time and the personal art of creating fiction with the immediacy, the completeness in itself, of myth or parable."

Kesey received his bachelor's degree from the University of Oregon and later attended creative writing classes at Stanford University during the 1950s. While working as a night attendant in the psychiatric ward of the Veterans Administration Hospital in Menlo Park, California, he volunteered for a series of government-sponsored experiments involving such psychoactive drugs as LSD-25, psilocybin, and mescaline. Simultaneously captivated and revolted by the institutionalized treatment of mental illness, Kesey often used peyote while on the job and while writing sections of *One Flew over the Cuckoo's Nest.* Malcolm Cowley, a teacher at Stanford, commented in a letter to Kesey that the novel's rough draft contained "some of the most brilliant scenes I have ever read" and "passion like I've not seen in you young writers before." Set in a mental facility in the northwestern United States, the novel is narrated from the perspective of Chief Bromden, a huge, schizophrenic Native American Indian of mixed white and Indian heritage. Bromden feigns being deaf and dumb to avoid being "worked on" by the hospital staff and other enforcers of what he calls the "Combine," a word which suggests both a threshing machine and an agency of normative control, in this case designed to alter or "correct" deviant or undesirable behavior. As the novel opens, Bromden views existence on the ward as a humorless cartoon fraught with human misery. His observations of the real world are initially rendered in paranoid terms; his acute awareness of the staff's desire to control all aspects of the men's lives, for example, leads him to fantasize that the staff manipulates patients mechanically via electronic circuitry concealed behind the hospital's walls.

Bromden's views are challenged by the arrival of Randall Patrick McMurphy, a swaggering ex-Marine, gambler, and braggart who describes himself as a "good old red, white, and blue hundred-percent American con-man." He is immediately identified as a nonconformist by the patients on the ward, who include Harding, an effeminate intellectual who feels emasculated by his spiteful wife, and Billy Bibbit, an adolescent whose self-image depends on the approval of his dominating mother. By demonstrating to the ward the value of laughter as a source of sanity and a weapon against repression, McMurphy becomes involved in a comic power struggle with "Big Nurse" Ratched, an efficient administrator of institutionalized conformity who demeans and manipulates patients into attacking one another under the guise of "therapy" to maintain her control. After a brief period of attempting unsuccessfully to live by Nurse Ratched's rules of the ward, McMurphy first organizes an unapproved fishing expedition and later, a wild party in the ward at which Billy loses his virginity to a prostitute. The next morning, McMurphy attempts unsuccessfully to escape and Nurse Ratched threatens to inform Billy's mother of his promiscuity. Unable to live with his mother's disapproval, Billy commits suicide. McMurphy is finally driven to physically attack Nurse Ratched and is subsequently restrained and lobotomized to demonstrate to the ward the futility of resistance. Bromden, irrevocably changed by the incident, smothers McMurphy in order to deny the Big Nurse her victory and to accept responsibility for the role he and the other patients played in contributing to McMurphy's downfall. Bromden then escapes to Canada as a sane individual.

One Flew over the Cuckoo's Nest received moderate critical attention following its initial publication in 1962. Although initial reviewers were positive about the book's literary merit, Kesey's novel received scant scholarly attention until the 1970s, when its anti-establishment bias attracted a diverse audience of readers. Some contemporary critics have faulted Kesey for his negative portrayals of women and blacks—particularly Nurse Ratched, whom Bromden describes as having enormous, constricted breasts and a face "like an expensive baby doll"—and the sadistic black nurse's aides, whom the Chief refers to as "black boys" and "niggers." Many reviewers, however, assert that the issue of racism and sexism depends largely on the question of who is the novel's protagonist; most identify Bromden as the central character and maintain that his unbalanced perspective functions as a distorted reaction to dehumanizing social realities. Similarly, critics who believe McMurphy is the novel's hero either view his affected faith in liberation through sexual freedom as simplistic or unconvincing or assert that his use of brash language and belief in liberation through "fighting and fucking" are the means by which he resists oppression and rejects Nurse Ratched's asexuality and false propriety.

Kesey returned to Oregon from California to prepare for his second book, *Sometimes a Great Notion* (1964). Set in the logging town of Waconda, a region on the Oregon coast that then had an extremely high suicide rate, this novel is considered more complex in scope and style than *One Flew over the Cuckoo's Nest*. The book delineates the relationship between Hank Stamper, an individualistic logger who defies neighbors and union organizers by continuing to work during a strike, and his half-brother Lee, who seeks to seduce Hank's wife as revenge for a sexual encounter he witnessed as a boy between Hank and Lee's biological mother. Despite their capacities for reckless self-indulgence, the brothers come to realize their helplessness and interdependence as Hank's rebellion fails and Lee's revenge proves unfulfilling. Although *Sometimes a Great Notion* garnered praise for its regional accuracy and stylistic complexity, the book has attained neither the popularity nor critical acclaim of Kesey's first novel.

Kesey's literary output diminished after 1964. Stating "I'd rather be a lightning rod than a seismograph," Kesey announced in 1966 that he was giving up writing to live his life as though it were a work of literature. With beatnik philosopher Neal Cassady and many others who called themselves the "Merry Pranksters," Kesey initiated an antic comic-book existence and promoted drug use and social revolt by introducing the LSD "acid tests" to California, which Tom Wolfe described in his book *The Electric Kool-Aid Acid Test* (1968). The experiences of the Merry Pranksters are also chronicled by Kesey and his friends Ken Babbs, Kenneth Barnes, and Keith Foster in *Kesey's Garage Sale* (1973), a collection of magazine articles, interviews, and satiric essays presented in the grandiose, mock-epic style of Marvel comic books. Kesey has also written *Demon Box* (1986), a collection of short stories, articles, essays, and interviews, many of which have appeared in periodicals since the late 1960s. Many of the stories in this collection feature Kesey's alter ego, Devlin Deboree, as their narrator, and balance Kesey's nostalgia for the mirth of the 1960s with his growing awareness of the negative aspects of the counterculture lifestyle.

Although some critics express dissatisfaction with Kesey's refusal to develop his writing beyond the early promise of his first novel, his reputation as a major contemporary author remains secured by *One Flew over the Cuckoo's Nest*. The novel, which continues to inspire a wide variety of critical interpretations, has been variously perceived as a biblical parable, a Western romance in the American tradition, and a boy's book about freedom from institutionalized repression.

(For further information about Kesey's life and works, see *Concise Dictionary of American Literary Biography, 1968-1988; Contemporary Authors*, Vols. 1-4; *Contemporary Authors New Revision Series*, Vol. 22; *Contemporary Literary Criticism*, Vols. 1, 3, 6, 11, 46, 64; and *Dictionary of Literary Biography*, Vols. 2, 16.)

CRITICAL COMMENTARY

R. L. SASSOON

(essay date 1963)

[In the review excerpted below, Sassoon offers a favorable appraisal of *One Flew over the Cuckoo's Nest*.]

A vision of Hell . . . An ironical view of American society . . . intimations of an ideal of fun and self-realization in community . . . all these develop out of Mr. Kesey's semi-fantasial, semi-realistic treatment of a mental institution, the setting of [*One Flew over the Cuckoo's Nest*]. It tells a story at once horrific and humorous: an appalling nightmare that has its sources in the most ordinary, recognizable reality and issues continually into the delightful farce of only daydream. If at the extremes beyond credibility the narrative and point of view are sometimes frankly infantile—so also, the author implies, is the world with which he deals, not only the mental institution but its explanatory context, America. With great originality the author has succeeded in achieving, almost throughout the novel, a subtle balance and correspondence between the social burden of mirroring purposefully place and time and the personal art of creating fiction with the immediacy, the completeness in itself, of myth or parable.

The story is told us by a half-Indian inmate of the hospital, whose long-standing pretense to being both deaf and dumb makes it possible for him to hear (literally and imaginatively—"But it's the truth even if it didn't happen") all that goes on, day and night, in the wards. The hospital is a place, essentially, for the rejects of a matriarchal, increasingly technocratic and fanatically collective society. Through the narrator's naive but vividly mythopoetic (and/or mythomaniac) mind is conveyed a vision of humanity reduced to "controlled" machinery "installed" and adjusted in living bodies by the agents (the hospital staff) of a super-institution he calls the "Combine." While we laugh both with and at the absurdity of it, we are also uncomfortably chilled by this infernal revelation that we may all of us be electronic puppets functioning, well or poorly (that is, on the "outside" or in the hospital), according to some panoramic design which absolutely negates the possibilities of freedom and individuation: such that we may have become categorically without privilege or responsibility. (p. 116)

At night Bromden sees the floor of the dorm sink away from the walls, dropping him and his ward-mates into a science-fictional hell of machinery and radio tubes and transformers; robot devil-mechanics approach a patient and tear him open and go to work on his insides . . . "Right and left there are other things happening just as bad—crazy, horrible things too goofy and outlandish to cry about and too much true to laugh about—but the fog is getting thick enough I don't have to watch." The "fog," which swamps the ward from time to time, is protective; but it also serves, by isolating man from man, to keep the patients in a state of co-operative docility. If all this is nightmare, and in its way comic too, Bromden also knows and speaks about such grim realities as shock therapy and, worse, the frontal lobotomy. Moreover, the daily routine of the ward is sordid and humiliating in every detail; the patients are degraded, wretched and resigned.

Into this world where men are either reduced to animals or turned into automatons, there enters a rough-and-tumble, logging and gambling man, whose relative freedom and invulnerability, his male wildness and woodsy common sense and humor, all convince the narrator—it is pathetic as much as comic—that this one must be "controlled" by some *anti-Combine*. The newcomer, McMurphy, who has feigned psychopathy because a mental hospital seems more pleasant to him

---

Principal Works

One Flew over the Cuckoo's Nest (novel) 1962

Sometimes a Great Notion (novel) 1964

*Ken Kesey's Garage Sale [editor and contributor] 1973

The Day after Superman Died (commemorative short story) 1980

Demon Box (short stories and articles) 1986

*This work contains reviews, articles, interviews, and Kesey's unproduced screenplay Over the Border.

---

than the state farm to which he has been sentenced for a few months, comes immediately into open conflict with the hospital staff. At first for kicks, but ultimately out of concern for his too easily cowed ward-mates, he engages in a battle to the finish—hilarious in its maneuvers but sombre in its presages of a sacrificial martyrdom—for the souls of these men.

His rival and enemy is "Big Nurse," a tyrannical, sadistic woman whose authority over the ward is almost total. Her gelid inhumanity is symbolized, with poignant irony, by nothing better than her preposterously huge breasts tightly packed behind ever clean and stiffly starched hospital-white: they are a bastion, not the sign of flesh of womanhood. McMurphy is a threat to her "control" over herself as well as over the ward. A genuine therapist, he commences at once to teach the patients to laugh—"Because he knows you have to laugh at things that hurt you just to keep yourself in balance, just to keep the world from running you plumb crazy. He knows there's a painful side . . . but he won't let the pain blot out the humor no more'n he'll let the humor blot out the pain." Worse, he influences them to try to accept themselves, even to assert themselves. And all the while Big Nurse and her flunkies are waiting for the chance to make him bow bloody or else to annihilate him—and that chance comes.

Before the appalling denoument, however, some of the ward have known the thrills of camaraderie of a wild, freewheeling fishing trip, the delights of liquor, marijuana and sex—in short, have experienced (howsoever childishly, yet therapeutically) their own urges toward freedom and self-expression. Enough that some, who are voluntary patients, elect to leave the institution; and Bromden, who is committed, finds means and courage to escape.

The great power of the Combine is, after all, that it is believed in—whether explicitly, as by Bromden, or implicitly, as by (the author suggests) most of this society. It is a kind of corrosive religion, wrongly terrifying and wrongly consoling; its victims are not only those

who have failed to be "adjusted to surroundings" but also those who have succeeded—for in doing so they have surrendered their capacities to *respond,* either to their own inner natures or to the world about them. The vicious circle of not being able to feel and not being able to make oneself felt—reflected in the impotence of the patients, but also in the cold sterility of the world from which they have run away—is guaranteed by what Bromden calls the Combine in its imposition of an ideal of non-humanity. The uniqueness and value of McMurphy is his aliveness, his uninhibited responsiveness to things and to people—which ultimately develops into a *responsibility for* Bromden and the other patients, such that he sacrifices himself so they, too, may choose to know the fullness of life, its joys and its pains.

When Bromden, after years of total isolation as a supposed deaf-mute, feels the greater necessity of using his voice to speak to McMurphy, he begins to recall his life before he entered the mental institution and those occasions that led him unconsciously to seek an escape from any human intercourse. He remembers a critical instance in his childhood, and his peculiar (and yet only too apt) understanding of it, when having spoken quite purposefully to three strangers who are looking for his father, he is ignored by them, because what he has to say does not communicate to them (that is, they prefer not to hear him)—

> I get the funniest feeling that the sun is turned up brighter than before on the three of them. Everything else looks like it usually does—the chickens fussing around in the grass on top of the 'dobe houses, the grasshoppers batting from bush to bush, the flies being stirred into black clouds around the fish racks by the little kids with sage flails, just like every other summer day. Except the sun, on these strangers, is all of a sudden way the hell brighter than usual and I can see the . . . *seams* where they're put together. And, almost, see the apparatus inside them take the words I just said and try to fit the words in here and there, this place and that, and when they find the words don't have any place ready-made where they'll fit, the machinery disposes of the words like they weren't even spoken.

In the wonderfully unembarrassed and naive, yet rather dignified, language of his narrator, Kesey continually focuses on the equal absurdity and pathos of man's inability and unwillingness *to listen* (whether to the urgent speech of one's own body and heart and spirit, or to those occasional essays at communication from outside), an abdication which can only make him increasingly a stranger both in the natural world (which anyway he is rapidly marring beyond recognition) and amongst his fellows. Bromden's half-stoical, half-childish flight into a bizarre, purely interior life is exactly correlate to a panicked society's determination to "control" human nature, reducing expression and activity to certain common-denominational patterns of predictably mechanical performance. It is taken for granted that this mass dehumanization serves a communal, quasi-sacred purpose, just as Bromden quite matter-of-factly, submissively, accumulates his real and imaginary evidences of an all-powerful, all-controlling Combine. Not until his encounter with McMurphy does he recover any sense of human realities and, simultaneously, the will and courage to return to real life.

Mr. Kesey's personal vision, while relating to universal problems of existence, springs from and reflects parabolically the individual's struggle for wholeness and survival in the specific context of American life today. For the most part he has made his perceptions and criticisms of this context implicit in the depiction of his characters and the development of the story. Unnecessary, therefore, and a dilution seem to me those passages where the author tends, in my opinion, to step outside of his fiction, as it were, in order to present a sort of more "objective," or explanatory, assessment of the social situation or to emphasize certain why's and wherefore's of his characters' actions and mental processes. For instance, it is out of Kesey's way in this novel, I think—and certainly out of his narrator's—to make so much of a point as he does of "exposing" the matriarchal aspects of our society or of "explaining" Bromden's and other characters' flights into neurosis with reference to bad, castrating mothers and/or wives, social pressures to tow the line, and so on. There is little originality of style or matter in the sections of the novel conceived for such ends and they are written unconvincingly; they may serve for some readers as a justification of the major portion of the novel and of the author's unique approach to reality by offering some sort of recognizable social and psychological matrix from which to interpret the characters' motivations and the author's purpose. As such, however, they may be misleading; this novel strikes me as much more of a myth or parable than a direct journalistic commentary on the times, and the intrusions of the latter, perhaps only because they are too close to being clichéd, do not always mix. Moreover, while Kesey has imagined his characters vividly and presented them with depth of understanding, his consciousness of the actual social ills of our times is comparatively superficial, focused as it is on symptoms rather than essential factors. If I belabor the point, it is because I think it would be a mistake, and a diminishment of the work, to view this novel as primarily a social "protest" or "evaluation." Rather, I see it as an intensely imaginative conception of the personal tragi-comedy of awakening to selfhood in a world largely held together through a utilitarian, artificial programming of human nature. While the setting and conditions are appropriately contemporary, prop-erly judged and found wanting, the concern is for the timeless individual: his battle against and for himself, against and for those around him—that harsh struggle for personal values and self-fulfillment.

Mr. Kesey writes with both anger and compassion, with severe irony and broad, congenial humor. Following him with the involvement his style demands, one cannot but experience a vision that is truly authoritative and original. (pp. 117-20)

R. L. Sassoon, in a review of "One Flew Over the Cuckoo's Nest," in *Northwest Review,* Vol. 6, No. 2, Spring, 1963, pp. 116-20.

GRANVILLE HICKS
(essay date 1964)

[In the following excerpt, Hicks praises the narrative and method of *Sometimes a Great Notion*.]

In his first novel, *One Flew over the Cuckoo's Nest,* Ken Kesey demonstrated that he was a forceful, inventive, and ambitious writer. All of these qualities are exhibited, in even higher degree, in *Sometimes a Great Notion.* Here he has told a fascinating story in a fascinating way.

The story concerns the Stamper family. Henry Stamper, descendant of a long line of restless pioneers, got about as far West as he could go, and settled near the Oregon coast, working as a lumberjack. He was an uncouth, violent, domineering sort of man, full of vitality, the boss of the whole Stamper clan. His wife bore him a son, called Hank, who was very much like him. After Hank's mother died, Henry married a young woman not yet finished with college, a delicate girl. She also bore him a son, named Leland Stanford Stamper, in honor of the college she had been attending. When Leland was twelve, she took him East, ostensibly to find a school for him, and never returned.

There are two central conflicts in the book. One is between the Stampers and the lumbermen's union, a conflict that sporadically flares into violence. The other is between Hank and his half-brother, Lee. Lee at this point is living in New York City, a highbrow and something of a beatnik. When he gets a card from a cousin, asking him to come and help the Stampers in their fight against the union, he decides to go, chiefly because he wants to get even with Hank for all the slights Hank put upon him when he was a boy.

Hank breaks Lee in as a lumberjack, and he becomes at least a fair worker, but all the time he is planning his revenge. The tension between the half-brothers mounts steadily, with Hank's wife, Vivian, becoming one of the issues at stake. Meanwhile the battle against the union goes on, working to its climax.

At the beginning the reader is likely to be confused. For instance, Kesey abruptly turns from third person to first and back again with no explanation. He uses italics, parentheses, and capitals to introduce elements from one story into another, and the reader doesn't know who's who or what's what. But, with a little patience, he finds himself and begins to understand what Kesey is trying to do. Kesey says at one point:

Time overlaps itself. A breath breathed from a passing breeze is not the whole wind, neither is it just the last of what has passed and the first of what will come, but is more—let me see—more like a single point plucked on a single strand of a vast spider web of winds, setting the whole scene atingle.

(p. 21)

At the climax, when Hank and Lee fight, we see the fight from both points of view:

The blow surprised me no more than had the discovery of my advantage in height: How interesting, I thought, as I saw stars sparked from my cheekbone. (The kid took the punch. He just stood there and took it. I guess I knew he would, with her watching, because that's another part of the way he's got it so worked out.) How interesting, I thought. . . . (He went down at the second punch and I figured that was that, he's let her see all she needs to see.)

Many novelists have experimented with the rapid shifting of point of view, and some have tried to blend past and present—William Faulkner, for instance, in *Absalom, Absalom!* and "The Bear." But I can think of no one who has made such continuous use of these two methods as Kesey. And he has made them serve his purpose: that is, he has succeeded in suggesting the complexity of life and the absence of any absolute truth.

Most readers, I imagine, won't worry about the method. After a little difficulty at the beginning, they will be carried away by the story, which is full of excitement. Kesey has created a number of remarkable characters—not only Henry and Hank and Lee and Joe Ben but also a union official, an unsuccessful theater operator, a minister, a bartender, and so on. Sometimes, I feel, he is carried away by a character and writes too much about him. He is, indeed, an extravagant writer, somewhat in the manner of Thomas Wolfe, but most of the time he has himself under control.

Hank Stamper may be regarded as the last of the frontiersmen. A fine athlete in high school, a demonic fighter, a belligerent individualist, he is cast in an heroic mold, as becomes clear in the scene in which he tries to save Joe Ben's life. In other ways, however, he is vulnerable, and that is why his struggle with Lee is so dramatic. Not every episode in Hank's saga is completely credible, but a character does emerge in which I can believe. As for Lee, I sympathized with him at first because he is an intellectual, but later he seemed rather petty in comparison with his half-brother. In the end, however, they are well matched, and it is fitting that they should stand together against the enemy. (pp. 21-2)

Granville Hicks, "Beatnik in Lumberjack Country," in *Saturday Review,* Vol. XLVII, No. 30, July 25, 1964, pp. 21-2.

JULIAN MOYNAHAN
(essay date 1964)

[In the review excerpted below, Moynahan comments on the merits and faults of *One Flew over the Cuckoo's Nest* and *Sometimes a Great Notion.*]

Mr. Kesey's first novel, *One Flew over the Cuckoo's Nest* (1962), was a very beautiful and inventive book violated by a fifth-rate idea which made Woman, in alliance with modern technology, the destroyer of masculinity and sensuous enjoyment. As the story went—it is told by a schizophrenic Indian half-breed of heroic size who gradually recovers his wits while events unfold—a busty, frigid, ex-Army nurse called Big Nurse holds total control over a men's psychiatric ward in a Federal hospital in the American west. This contemporary Circe figure wields the entire panoply of new psychiatric drugs, electric shock, lobotomy and lobectomy, along with up-to-date hygienic procedures and concepts (group therapy, the therapeutic community, etc.) to brainwash and dehumanize the patients. When her authority is challenged by the ribald, back-slapping "psychopath," McMurphy, she temporarily loses ground but eventually maneuvers McMurphy under the flashing knives of the brain surgeons, where he is made into a living corpse. Yet his rebelliousness has roused many of the other patients from psychotic apathy, and, as the book ends, these disciples are securing their releases from the hospital in ever-increasing numbers.

The point is that McMurphy isn't a true psychopath; rather, he is the familiar saintly clown who, in this case, lays down his life for his sick friends after promulgating a gospel of existence as horseplay, sexual frolic, gambling and drinking, fishing and hunting. But Big Nurse is a melodramatic device standing for an arbitrary, indefensible anti-feminine argument. Several men in the ward, including the narrator, have been shoved into mental illness by domineering, castrating mothers or wives. A good woman, predictably, tends to be a prostitute, and the good life envisioned beyond the confines of the ward consists in running loose with men and ocasionally consorting with prostitutes while drunk. As lives go, it is boyish, even doggy, and, like life back in the psycho ward, it amounts to no more than a half existence.

After one closes *Cuckoo* and after its narrative magic begins to wear off one starts asking certain questions. Why didn't the physicians in charge of the hospital throw this bitch out of her job? What about all those patients in the women's psychiatric ward—would they be cured by becoming tarts? Why, when foreign literatures so often represent woman as the guardian and guarantor of a sensuous, homely, and humane order of values, do American books so often represent her as the antagonist of these values? I have never been able to swallow Leslie Fiedler's assumption that our literature has been written, for the most part, by the boy-men or innocent closet queens. What, finally, and in the light of his attitude toward relations between the American sexes, would become of Mr. Kesey's talent when he turned to write his second novel?

That novel, *Sometimes a Great Notion,* is a massive book scaled to its setting in the rainy, tall-tree, logging country of coastal Oregon. The author has a perfect knowledge of the forest, the weather, the rushing rivers, the birds and animals, the work routines and hidden lives of the people of that region and puts these things onto the American literary map once and for all. The book reminded me of Faulkner's *Absalom! Absalom!* in its hyper-saturated style, its use of the devices of delayed disclosures and of witnesses who try to puzzle out the meaning of an action which is substantially complete as the book opens, its adumbration of classical and biblical archetypes involving titanic confrontations of male siblings, its ambition to convert a slab of social history and the story of a family into a legend about the destiny of western Americans from the last generation of pioneers to the latest generation of rugged individualist entrepreneurs and Indian-hemp-smoking college boys.

But for all its virtuosity and ambition *Sometimes a Great Notion* is flawed, like its predecessor, by the author's inability to imagine a world where whole men, and women who are neither authoritarian bitches nor decent whores, can get together and make a whole life. At the end of the book the college boy, Leland Stanford Stamper, joins his entrepreneur half-brother, Hank, on some log floats, helping him get the logs to market down a dangerously flooded river, in defiance of an entire town of striking lumberjacks. Meanwhile Hank's wife, Viv, looks through the family photo album, makes out correctly that there is no place for her in the Stamper future, and leaves town on a bus, alone and bound for nowhere in particular.

Now we are neither in the God-suffused world of the Old Testament nor with Uranus and Zeus on Mount Olympus, so we may well wonder what we are witnessing in human terms relevant to the contemporary American milieu which Kesey so vividly specifies. Evidently it is the enshrinement of hard masculine defiance—grounded in despair. The brothers prefer a gesture of blind reaction on a log raft to all the opportunities for reconstruction, revision, and self-reappraisal, they leave behind them on the river bank. They are heroic but only in a boyish way. Their fate is not tragic and it does not encompass the American fate or give a deeper imaginative meaning to the idea of the final closing of the western frontier. Instead the book is personal and eccentric, and it is question-begging with respect to the large social and economic issues it raises. It is the kind of deeply perplexed and ambiguous book into which many conflicting meanings can be read and the same people who hailed *The Fountainhead* as a masterpiece will no doubt again disgrace themselves by citing *Sometimes a Great Notion* as the beginning of a new era in American writing. (pp. 14-15)

Julian Moynahan, "Only in America," in *The New York Review of Books,* Vol. III, No. 2, September 10, 1964, pp. 14-15.

ROBERT BOYERS
(essay date 1968)

[In the excerpt below, Boyers comments on Kesey's treatment of sexuality as a liberating force in *One Flew over the Cuckoo's Nest.*]

There is no lack of conviction in Ken Kesey's *One Flew over the Cuckoo's Nest,* but neither is there an attempt to deal with human sexuality as a complex phenomenon. Kesey's novel is wholly successful as an indictment of modern society, and as an exploration into the kind of subtly repressive mechanisms we help to build into the fabric of our daily lives. Kesey's solution to our common problem is the opening of floodgates, the releasing of energies which have too long lain unused or forgotten. Chief among these are the twin resources of laughter and uninhibited sexuality, the linkage between which Kesey manages to clarify in the course of his novel.

The novel is set in a mental institution which is, in many respects, a microcosm of the society-at-large. It is to Kesey's credit that he never strains to maintain the parallel at any cost—it is a suggested parallel at most, and, where it suits his novelistic purposes, Kesey lets it go completely. His protagonist is one Randle Patrick McMurphy, pronounced psychopathic by virtue of being "overzealous in [his] sexual relations." His purpose in the institution, as in life apparently, is both to have a hell of a good time, and to defy "ball cutters," defined by McMurphy himself as "people who try to make you weak so they can get you to toe the line, to follow their rules, to live like they want you to." McMurphy is a truly monumental character—a gambler, a braggart, a fantastic lover, and a gadfly who insults and goads those who resist his charismatic injunctions. While he is something of a sensualist who dwells regularly on the ecstasies of sexual transport, and even goes so far as to bring his whores into the hospital to restore the vitality of his moribund fellow-psychopaths, McMurphy feels himself and his comrades the victims of women, not their lords and masters as his rhetoric would have it. His techniques of resistance and defiance are mostly pathetic, as they can achieve what are at best pyrrhic victories. One is never tempted to question the validity, the nobility, or even the necessity of McMurphy's defiance, but no mature reader will be convinced that his techniques can realistically accomplish what Kesey claims for them at the novel's end— the reclamation of numerous human beings who had grown passive and torpid before McMurphy's arrival.

At one point, McMurphy characterizes the inmates of the hospital as "victims of a matriarchy." In Kesey's view, modern society is a reflection of womanish values—archetypically responsible, cautious, repressive, deceitful, and solemn. One must look to the spirit of the whore if one would know what is best in women, and what can best bring out what is vital in men. There is no doubt that Kesey labors under a most reactionary myth, involving the mystique of male sexuality, which sees men as intrinsically better than women in terms of the dynamism and strength they can impart to the universe. Unable rationally to account for the disparity between such a projection and the puny reality of our male lives, Kesey waxes fatalistic, though never submissive, and sees "ball cutters" everywhere. It is a kind of paranoid, conspiratorial view of things, not without its measure of accuracy, but it somehow evades the crucial issues which Kesey and others have raised.

At the heart of Kesey's notion of what is possible for modern liberated man is a phenomenon which one may call porno-politics. It is a phenomenon which resides primarily in the imagination of a few thousand people, most of them young and bright, and which is occasionally manifested in the hysterical behavior of certain radical partisans of unpopular causes, a behavior which, by the way, many would call resolutely antipolitical, for all its pretensions to the contrary. Advocates of porno-politics are usually utopian socialists who lack the vision and patience to realize their goals politically: that is, they are youthful dreamers who are frustrated by the customary routines through which

men achieve power or influence in order to alter the political relations which obtain in their society. Frequently, the retreat into varieties of prono-politics results from people relying too heavily on the flexibility of a given political system, and on the sheer magnetism of their own sincerity, which they and their associates had always considered irresistible. When the erstwhile utopian realizes how restrictive and closed the political structure of his society is, despite its aggressive disclaimers, and when he is made aware of the basic indifference to his ideals and to his attractiveness among the masses of people, he is suffused by a kind of anger and dread. As the society affords him virtually no outlet for these feelings, which rarely become specific enough to fix legitimate targets anyway, the befuddled utopian permits his vision of the possible to undergo a remarkable transformation. Unable to affect masses of men or to move political and social institutions, he transfers the burden of realizing a perfectly harmonious society to sex.

In Kesey's novel, we have what seemingly amounts to a *reductio ad absurdum* of familiar Freudian propositions. It is repressed sexuality which ostensibly lies behind every psychosis, and which is responsible for the acquiescence of all men in the confining conventions of Western society. It is in the spirit of random and thoroughly abandoned sexuality that Kesey's McMurphy would remake men, and subsequently the world. What is a little frightening in a novel like this, though, is that such a projection does not at all operate on a metaphorical level. Sex is not here a mere metaphor for passion, nor for any positive engagement with one's fellow human beings. There is a literalism in Kesey's suggestions of sexual apocalypse, with its unavoidable ramifications into a political and social context, which cannot be lightly taken. Other talented people are caught up in such projections, and are delivering gospels of sexual salvation with a hysterical dogmatism that is, for many of us, laughable and pathetic. This is so particularly for those who have observed the failure of libertarian sexual experimentation and random coupling to affect substantially the pettiness and self-absorption even of those who are most easily committed to libertarian modes and who have no need perpetually to justify such commitments ideologically. How futile it is for intelligent people seriously to expect their sexual programs and practices to have a liberating effect on masses of men, when what these people want is to be left alone to enjoy what they have. What porno-politics essentially amounts to is a form of entertainment for a middle-class audience, which alternatively writhes and applauds before the late-night news, and welcomes the opportunity to indulge and express postures it considers intrinsic to its worth as modern men: tolerance and righteous indignation.

Kesey's brilliance is evidenced by his ability to be

seduced by porno-political utopianism, and yet not to yield to it entirely. What save him are his sense of the ridiculous and his understanding of men as fundamentally dishonest and irresolute. Kesey wants to believe that the source of all terror and passivity is somehow sexual, that the liberation of sexual energies in the form of primal fantasies will enable men to conceive of themselves as more passionate and autonomous individuals. But his intelligence forces him, as it were, against his will, to tell a truth which is more complex and disheartening. He recounts a group therapy session which had taken place in the institution some years before McMurphy's arrival. Unlike the usual dispirited proceedings, this particular session stood out for the violent release of confessions that it evoked from the habitually desultory and tight-lipped inmates. Once the momentum is established, the inmates begin shouting confessions: "I lied about trying. I did take my sister!" / "So did I! So did I!" / "And me! And me!"

At first, all of this seems satisfying, at least from a conventionally clinical point of view: repressed memories are rising to the surface, where they can be handled therapeutically. But, almost immediately, we are shown that not only did such events never occur in the lives of these men; they do not even represent their fantasy lives. Such "confessions" have nothing at all to do with the wish-fulfillment that is a strong component of compulsive fantasies. What the inmates have done is simply to exploit certain readily available clichés issuing from standard interpretations of modern man as the perennial victim of sexual repression. The inmates are victims of something much more embracing and diversified than simple sexual guilt or repression, though the sexual element may be particularly significant in the case of two or three inmates among many. What is sickening is their desire to please the therapists by revealing what they are supposed to, rather than what is really inside them. Finally, they are shamed by the resounding announcement of hopeless old Pete: "I'm tired," he shouts—a confession so simple and true that it puts an abrupt end to the rampant dishonesty of the others. Kesey loves McMurphy, and identifies with his aspirations—he wants men to be free, to laugh the authorities down, to refuse to be manipulated. He wants, moreover, to go along with McMurphy's sexual orientation, and to be as optimistic as McMurphy about the effects of sexual liberation on the reigning political and social atmosphere. But McMurphy is not a mask for Kesey, nor is any single character in the novel. In fact, as much as Kesey admires McMurphy's stratagems for outwitting the matriarch *par excellence* who goes under the title Big Nurse, we are never quite certain whether to laugh at McMurphy as well as with him. Big Nurse, as the personification of "the system" at its most callow, repressive, yet ostensibly enlightened, represents a tendency toward antiseptic desexualization which is abhorrent. We want McMurphy to bewilder her, to kill her with his charming nonchalance and boyish exuberance, and to parade his own aggressive sexuality before her. We want her to be teased and tempted so that she will be provoked to try to castrate McMurphy, if not actually, then symbolically, as she has successfully whipped the other inmates. We want to see McMurphy put to the test of the vitality and resilience he proudly proclaims, as if he could redeem us from any misgivings we might have about our own potency.

And yet, throughout this novel, we know that nothing McMurphy does, or encourages his comrades to do, will make any substantive difference to the system that we all despise. McMurphy, through an ideological predisposition, which in his case is more instinctive than learned, attributes to sex what even he knows it cannot accomplish. His is a heroic endeavor in every way, but McMurphy is at bottom a little lost boy who gets into the big muddy way up over his head. The picture of him, in bed with his whore at last, almost at the end of the novel, is utterly revealing: " . . . more like two tired little kids than a grown man and a grown woman in bed together to make love." McMurphy can behave as brashly as he likes, and speak with utter abandon of sex, but for him it has still an element of mystery, of vows exchanged, even if only for a brief duration. His libertarian apocalyptism is sincere, but in McMurphy's own character we can see that a libertarian sexual orientation ultimately has little to do with making men free as political and social beings. McMurphy needs no sexual swagger to be free, though, in his case, it is a believable accouterment of his personality. What is indispensable in McMurphy's character is his propensity to laugh, in his lucid moments to see himself as something of a spectacle, not wholly detached nor different from the other inmates who have failed to retain their resilience. When he loses his laugh, he grows desperate, and places upon sex that burden of hope for transcendence which the reality of sexual experience must frustrate. When, at the very conclusion of the book, McMurphy rips open Big Nurse's hospital uniform, revealing, for all to see, her prodigious breasts, we see where McMurphy's porno-political vision has led him. Unable to affect a world that victimizes him, a civilization which, in the words of the British psychoanalyst R. D. Laing " . . . represses not only 'the instincts,' not only sexuality, but any form of transcendence," McMurphy is driven to rape the reality incarnated in Big Nurse. In his fear and frustration, he does not see what, of all things, should be most obvious to him: that he cannot make another human being aware of his humanity by destroying or suppressing those elements of his own humanity that have made McMurphy a beautiful person. By his action, he demonstrates the original futility of his project, the necessary brutalization of his sexual ethic, and the dehumanization implicit in the act of invoking an *Eros* which is imperfectly understood and crudely employed. (pp. 44-7)

Robert Boyers, "Attitudes Toward Sex in American 'High Culture'," in *The Annals of the American Academy of Political and Social Science,* Vol. 376, March, 1968, pp. 36-52.

LESLIE A. FIEDLER
(essay date 1968)

[The excerpt below is from the last volume of *The Return of the Vanishing American*, a three-volume study in "literary anthropology" in which Fiedler attempts "to define the myths which give a special character to art and life in America." Here, the critic focuses on the mythical treatment of the Native American in *One Flew over the Cuckoo's Nest*.]

Primitivism is the large generic name for the Higher Masculine Sentimentality, a passionate commitment to inverting Christian-Humanist values, out of a conviction that the Indian's way of life is preferable. From this follows the belief that if one is an Indian he ought, despite missionaries and school boards, to remain Indian; and if one is White, he should do his best, despite all pressures of the historical past, to go Native. Ever since the oft-quoted observation of Crèvecoeur that there must be something superior in Indian society since "thousands of Europeans are Indians, and we have no example of even one of those aborigines having from choice become Europeans . . . ," White men in America have continued to echo that primitivist hyperbole, whose truth cannot be diminished merely by disproving Crèvecoeur's facts. (p. 169)

[In *One Flew over the Cuckoo's Nest,* Kesey retells] the old, old fable of the White outcast and the noble Red Man joined together against home and mother, against the female world of civilization. . . . [The novel's setting is] at once present and archaic—a setting which Ken Kesey discovered in the madhouse: *our* kind of madhouse, which is to say, one located in the American West, so that the Indian can make his reappearance in its midst with some probability, as well as real authenticity.

Perhaps it was necessary for Kesey to come himself out of Oregon, one of our last actual Wests (just as it was necessary for him to have been involved with one of the first experiments with the controlled use of LSD), since for most Americans after Mark Twain, the legendary colored companion of the white fugitive had been turned from Red to Black. Even on the most naive levels, the Negro has replaced the Indian as the natural enemy of Woman. . . . (p. 177)

[*One Flew over the Cuckoo's Nest*] opens with an obviously psychotic "I" reflecting on his guards, one of whom identifies him almost immediately, speaking in a Negro voice: "Here's the Chief. The *soo*-pah Chief, fellas. Ol' Chief Broom. Here you go, Chief Broom. . . ." Chief Bromden is his real name, this immense schizophrenic, pretending he is deaf-and-dumb to baffle "the Combine," which he believes controls the world: "Look at him: a giant janitor. There's your Vanishing American, a six-foot-six sweeping machine, scared of its own shadow. . . ." Or rather Bromden is the name he has inherited from his white mother, who subdued the full-blooded Chief who sired him and was called "The-Pine-That-Stands-Tallest-on-the-Mountain." "He fought it a long time," the half-breed son comments at one point, "till my mother made him too little to fight any more and he gave up."

Chief Bromden believes he is little, too, what was left in him of fight and stature subdued by a second mother, who presides over the ward in which he is confined ("She may be a mother, but she's big as a damn barn and tough as knife metal . . . ") and, at one point, had given him two hundred successive shock treatments. Not only is Mother II big, however, especially in the breasts; she is even more essentially *white:* "Her face is smooth, calculated, and precision-made, like an expensive baby doll, skin like flesh-colored enamel, blend of white and cream and baby-blue eyes . . . " and her opulent body is bound tight in a starched white uniform. To understand her in her full mythological significance, we must recall [*The Myth of the White Woman with a Tomahawk,* the autobiographical account of] that seventeenth-century first White Mother of Us All Hannah Duston, and her struggle against the Indians who tried to master her.

Hannah has represented from the start those forces in the American community—soon identified chiefly with the female and maternal—which resist all incursions of savagery, no matter what their course. But only in the full twentieth century is the nature of Hannah's assault made quite clear, first in Freudian terms and then in psychedelic ones. "No, buddy," Kesey's white hero, Randle Patrick McMurphy, comments on the Big Nurse. "She ain't pecking at your *eyes.* That's not what she's peckin' at." And when someone, who really knows but wants to hear spoken aloud what he is too castrated to say, asks at *what,* then, R. P. McMurphy answers, "At your balls, buddy, at your everlovin' *balls.*" Yet toward the close of the book, McMurphy has to be told by the very man who questioned him earlier the meaning of his own impending lobotomy at the hands of Big Nurse ("Yes, chopping away the brain. Frontal-lobe castration. I guess if she can't cut below the belt she'll do it above the eyes"), though by this time he understands why he, as well as the Indian (only victim of the original Hannah's blade), has become the enemy of the White Woman.

In his own view, McMurphy may be a swinger, and in the eyes of his Indian buddy an ultimate Westerner, the New American Man:

> He walked with long steps, too long, and he had his thumbs hooked in his pockets again. The iron in his boot heels cracked lightning out of the tile. He was the logger again, the swaggering gambler . . . the cowboy out of the TV set walking down the middle of the street to meet a dare.

But to Big Nurse—and the whole staff of the asylum whom, White or Black, male or female, she has cowed—he is only a "psychopath," not less sick for having chosen the nuthouse in which he finds himself to the work-farm to which his society had sentenced him. And she sees the purpose of the asylum as being precisely to persuade men like him to accept and function in the world of rewards and punishments which he has rejected and fled.

To do this, however, she must persuade him like the rest that he is only a "bad boy," *her* bad boy, quite like, say Huckleberry Finn. But where Huck's substitute mothers demanded that he give up smoking, wear shoes, go to school, she asks (it is the last desperate version of "sivilisation") that he be sane: "All he has to do is *admit* he was wrong, to indicate, *demonstrate* rational contact and the treatment would be cancelled this time."

The choice is simple: either sanity abjectly accepted, or sanity imposed by tranquilizers, shock treatments, finally lobotomy itself. But McMurphy chooses instead if not madness, at least aggravated psychopathy and an alliance with his half-erased, totally schizophrenic Indian comrade—an alliance with all that his world calls unreason. . . . And this time, the alliance is not merely explicitly, but quite overtly directed against the White Woman, which is to say, Hannah Duston fallen out of her own legend into that of Henry and Wawatam.

For a while, the result seems utter disaster, since McMurphy, driven to attempt the rape of his tormentor, is hauled off her and duly lobotomized, left little more than a vegetable with "a face milk-white except for the heavy purple bruises around the eyes." Whiter than the White Woman who undid him, white as mother's milk: this is McMurphy at the end, except that Chief Bromden will not let it be the end, will not let

> something like that sit there in the day room with his name tacked on it for twenty or thirty years so the Big Nurse could use it as an example of what can happen if you buck the system. . . .

Therefore, in the hush of the first night after the lobotomy, he creeps into the bed of his friend for what turns out to be an embrace—for only in a caricature of the act of love can he manage to kill him:

> The big, hard body had a tough grip on life. . . . I finally had to lie full length on top of it and scissor the kicking legs with mine. . . . I lay there on top of the body for what seemed like days. . . . Until it was still a while and had shuddered once and was still again.

It is the first real *Liebestod* in our long literature of love between white men and colored, and the first time, surely, that the Indian partner in such a pair has outlived his White brother. Typically [as in Mark Twain's *Huckleberry Finn* and William Faulkner's "The Bear"], . . . Huck had been younger than Jim, Ike than Sam Fathers. Everyone who has lived at the heart of our dearest myth knows that it is the white boy-man who survives, as the old Indian, addressing the Great Spirit, prepares to vanish. Even so recent a novel as Berger's *Little Big Man* has continued to play it straight, closing on the traditional dying fall, as Old Lodge Skins subsides after a final prayer, and his white foster son says:

> He laid down then on the damp rocks and died right away. I descended to the treeline, fetched back some poles, and built him a scaffold. Wrapped him in the red blanket and laid him thereon. Then after a while I started down the mountain in the fading light.

But on the last page of *One Flew over the Cuckoo's Nest,* Chief Bromden is on his way back to the remnants of his tribe who "have took to building their old ramshackle wood scaffolding all over the big million-dollar . . . spillway." And his very last words are: "I been away a long time."

It is, then, the "Indian" in Kesey himself, the undischarged refugee from a madhouse, the AWOL Savage, who is left to boast: *And I only am escaped alone to tell thee.* But the "Indian" does not write books; and insofar as Kesey's fable can be read as telling the truth about himself as well as about all of us, it prophesies silence for him, a silence into which he has, in fact, lapsed, though not until he had tried one more Gutenberg-trip in *Sometimes A Great Notion.*

It is a book which seems to me not so much a second novel as a first novel written (or, perhaps, only published) second: a more literary, conventionally ambitious, and therefore *strained* effort—for all its occasional successes, somehow an error. *One Flew over the Cuckoo's Nest* works better to the degree that it is dreamed or hallucinated rather than merely written—which is to say, to the degree that it, like its great prototype *The Leatherstocking Tales,* is Pop Art rather than *belles lettres*—the dream once dreamed in the woods, and now redreamed on pot and acid.

Its very sentimentality, good-guys bad-guys

melodrama, occasional obviousness and thinness of texture, I find—like the analogous things in Cooper—not incidental flaws, but part of the essential method of its madness. There is a phrase which reflects on Kesey's own style quite early in the book, defining it aptly, though it pretends only to represent Chief Bromden's vision of the world around him:

> Like a cartoon world, where the figures are flat and outlined in black, jerking through some kind of goofy story that might be real funny if it weren't for the cartoon figures being real guys. . . .

Everywhere in Kesey, as a matter of fact, the influence of comics and, especially, comic books is clearly perceptible, in the mythology as well as in the style; for like those of many younger writers of the moment, the images and archetypal stories which underlie his fables are not the legends of Greece and Rome, not the fairy tales of Grimm, but the adventures of Captain Marvel and Captain Marvel, Jr., those new-style Supermen who, sometime just after World War II, took over the fantasy of the young. What Western elements persist in Kesey are, as it were, first translated back into comic-strip form, then turned once more into words on the conventional book page. One might, indeed, have imagined Kesey ending up as a comic book writer, but since the false second start of *Sometimes A Great Notion,* he has preferred to live his comic strip rather than write or even draw it.

The adventures of Psychedelic Superman as Kesey had dreamed and acted them, however—his negotiations with Hell's Angels, his being busted for the possession of marijuana, his consequent experiences in court and, as a refugee from the law, in Mexico—all this, like the yellow bus in which he used to move up and down the land taking an endless, formless movie, belongs to hearsay and journalism rather than to literary criticism, challenging conventional approaches to literature even as it challenges literature itself. But *One Flew over the Cuckoo's Nest* survives the experiments and rejections which followed it; and looking back five years after its initial appearance, it seems clear that in it for the first time the New West was clearly defined: the West of Here and Now, rather than There and Then—the West of Madness. (pp. 179-85)

It is only a step from thinking of the West as madness to regarding madness as the true West, but it took the long years between the end of the fifteenth century and the middle of the twentieth to learn to take that step. There is scarcely a New Western among those I have discussed which does not in some way flirt with the notion of madness as essential to the New World; but only in [*Beautiful Losers* by] Leonard Cohen (though Thomas Berger comes close) and in Kesey is the final identification made, and in Kesey at last combined with the archetype of the love that binds the lonely white

man to his Indian comrade—to his *mad* Indian comrade, perhaps even to the *madness* of his Indian comrade, as Kesey amends the old tale. (p. 185)

Leslie A. Fiedler, "The Higher Sentimentality," in his *The Return of the Vanishing American,* Stein and Day Publishers, 1968, pp. 169-87.

MARCIA L. FALK
(essay date 1971)

[Falk, Affiliated Scholar at Stanford University's Institute for Research on Women and Gender, is a poet and translator of Hebrew and Yiddish. Among her books are *The Song of Songs: A New Translation and Interpretation* (1990) and *The Book of Blessings: A Feminist-Jewish Reconstruction of Prayer* (forthcoming, 1993). In the letter below, originally published in the *New York Times* on December 5, 1971, Falk objects to sexist notions conveyed in Dale Wasserman's stage adaptation of Kesey's *One Flew over the Cuckoo's Nest.* The present printing of Falk's letter restores readings that were altered by the *New York Times.*]

To the Editor:

In response to Walter Kerr's belated review of *One Flew over the Cuckoo's Nest:* I too saw the show after it had been running for quite a while, in San Francisco. I was shocked at what I saw (though I should have known better, having read the book) because, in the long time the play had been running, never once had I read a review which warned me of the blatant sexism I was to witness onstage, or even asked some of the most obvious questions about the political statements of the play.

Kerr finally raised the key question: Why is Nurse Ratched, the omnipotent, omni-malevolent villain of the play, a woman? Kerr didn't speculate why, but he did note parenthetically that "There are other such women in the background of the play." The truth is that *every* woman in the background is such a demonic figure, and the play is full of false yet dangerous clichés about their power over men.

The most striking example is Chief Bromden's mother: she has made his father small, she has grown to twice his size. It is largely because of her power to threaten male virility that the Chief is now in a mental institution. Of course, she is *only a symbol;* as a white woman married to an Indian man, her emasculation of her husband only *represents* the White Man's brutal destruction of all cultures other than his own.

Why is white racism depicted in these terms? It should be remembered that this white woman's singular unforgivable act was her refusal to take on her husband's name! Somehow, in the confused vision of the author and playwright, the refusal of women, an oppressed class, to utterly submit to male-oriented social structures is identified with the attack of white men, the oppressor class, on peoples of color.

The whole play is constructed from such a muddled vision. It pretends to challenge all the reactionary institutions in our society—prisons, mental hospitals and the Federal Government itself, which has destroyed the Indian reservations. But it never once challenges the completely inhuman sexist structure of society, nor does it make any attempt to overthrow sexist or racist stereotypes. The only blacks in the play are stupid and malicious hospital orderlies. And the only right-on women in the play are mindless whores. In fact, in this play, if a woman is *not* totally mindless, she is a direct threat to (male) life.

Thus the play offers us this basic sexist dichotomy: women are either dumb and silly (like the quivering young nurse, terrified of McMurphy; like the squealing, wiggling prostitutes who come to build up the men's egos) or they are shrewd, conniving, and malicious (castrating wives, dominating mothers, and a super-powerful domineering nurse). Every man in the play has been psychologically mutilated by a woman, from the guilt-ridden Billy Bibbit, whom his mother and Nurse Ratched are in cahoots to destroy, to the cynical Harding, whose "wife's ample bosom at times gives him a feeling of inferiority."

It goes without saying that, just as there are no positive, fully human female figures to identify with, there are likewise no strong, healthy male figures. Of course, we are *supposed* to believe in McMurphy, the super-male macho hero who equates strength with balls and whose solution to every problem is to get a good fuck. We laugh and cheer as McMurphy humiliates the young nurse by sticking a banana up her skirt, manhandles his girlfriends as he passes them around (confident of his masculinity, he can afford to be generous), and generally bullies everyone in his social sphere.

If *that* represents the healthy exercise of the human spirit, then the White Man too was healthy as he stole from the Indians everything they had, raping their culture and treating them as objects not worthy of human respect.

Kerr points out that *Cuckoo's Nest* is a play about conditioning in this society, and that young people identify with it because it exposes that threat to human freedom. This play is not *about* conditioning nearly so much as it *is* a dangerous piece of conditioning itself. With a pseudo-radical posture, it swallows whole hog all the worst attitudes toward women prevalent in our

society and delivers the pig right back to us, suitably decorated and made righteous.

If you do not perceive exactly how destructive this work is, imagine for a moment the effect it must have on a girl child watching it. Who, in this play, can *she* grow up to be? Where is *her* place in the struggle for human freedom? At best she can mature into a good piece of ass, equipped to build the egos of emotionally crippled men by offering a "liberated" attitude toward sex! Above all, she learns from viewing this play that any aggressiveness, intelligence, strength, or potency on the part of the female is always dangerous, evil, and ugly. She learns to hate women who dare to try to be as powerful as men. She learns to squelch her own potential for strength, or she learns to hate herself. She is, after all, destined to become a woman, and women are hateful and fearful things.

The answer to Kerr's question seems to be that Nurse Ratched is a woman because Ken Kesey hates and fears women. And apparently Dale Wasserman, along with everyone else who helped adapt Kesey's novel and engineer it into a piece of theater, are so thoroughly conditioned by the basic sexist assumptions of our society that they never even noticed, or cared to question, the psychic disease out of which the book's vision was born. (pp. 450-53)

Marcia L. Falk, in a letter to the Editor of The New York Times on December 5, 1971, in *One Flew Over the Cuckoo's Nest: Text and Criticism by Ken Kesey,* edited by John Clark Pratt, Viking Press, 1973, pp. 450-53.

JANET R. SUTHERLAND
(essay date 1972)

[In the following excerpt, Sutherland, an American educator, defends *One Flew over the Cuckoo's Nest* against a ban imposed on the book in the Bellevue Public School system in the state of Washington.]

In the judgment of one recent patron of the Bellevue Public Schools, Ken Kesey's *One Flew over the Cuckoo's Nest* is not a decent book for students to read or teachers to teach. While literary critics might be able to dismiss such pronouncements as simply untutored, public school people have to deal with them frequently and take them seriously, in the interest of preserving their right of access to literature and the student's right to read. It is in this context that I offer a defense of Kesey's novel against the charge that it is an improper and even evil book, fit only "to be burned."

Ken Kesey's *One Flew over the Cuckoo's Nest* is

not obscene, racist, or immoral, although it does contain language and scenes which by common taste would be so considered. Like all great literature, the book attempts to give an accurate picture of some part of the human condition, which is less than perfect. Kesey's book is set in a mental hospital; the language, attitudes, and habits of the inmates are typical of disturbed men whose already distorted world is being further systematically dehumanized by the ward nurse. The story is told in the first person through the eyes of an Indian whose health is gradually restored to him and to others through interaction with the robust new inmate McMurphy, a picaresque figure who is transformed into a tragic hero as he struggles to help the inmates regain control of their lives. To charge that the book is obscene, racist, or immoral because it gives a realistic picture of the world of the insane is to demonstrate a lack of the minimum competency in understanding literature we expect of high school students. The charge also ignores the extent to which this novel does conform to the standards outlined in the guidelines for selection of instructional materials in the Bellevue schools.

Our students are taught that to understand the general meaning of a book, the reader has to take all the details into consideration. The theme emerges from a complex combination of scenes, characters, and action, often in conflict and often contradictory. To judge a book simply on a few passages which contain unconventional language or fantasies is missing the point. In the case of the Indian narrator, we are seeing and hearing at times the hallucinations typical of schizophrenia. Chief Bromden has been systematically ignored and abused all his life to the point of madness. It is no wonder that his consciousness is filled with horrors, obscene and otherwise. What Kesey is telling us, beyond giving us a realistic idea of the actual language of the asylum, is that what is being done to these people is an obscenity. When McMurphy comes upon the scene, it is as if his outrageous speech and action are the only possible answer to the vicious way in which the men's privacy and smallest efforts of will are being pried into and exploited and diminished. His profanity is a verbal manifestation of the indecencies they suffer, the only appropriate response to it, a foil which helps us to see its actual nature, and a means by which the scene is transformed into a world in which some tenderness and love are possible. Big Nurse speaks properly but does unspeakable things. McMurphy's speech is outrageous; he fights the profane with the super profane and moves beyond profanity to help the men create a new respect for themselves. He restores Harding's ability to face reality, gives Billy a sense of his manhood, and convinces Chief Bromden that he is indeed his actual six foot six, not a withered deaf mute.

If the reader is really sensitive to the specific language of the book, he will see how Kesey uses its subtle changes to signal changes in the Chief 's state of mind. The fogged-in scenes are characterized by confusion and some description of the grossness of the asylum's inmates and black help. As Chief Bromden recovers his powers of perception, including his sad past and the scenes of white racism and war which has produced his state of alienation, the sentence structure and word choice change markedly. So also the emphasis on McMurphy's outward grossness shifts in the Chief 's eyes to an apprehension of what he is suffering inwardly, to his deeds of kindness to the men, his complicated and puzzling deals, and his final decision to protect another man though he knows it means his doom. The Chief sees beyond McMurphy's outward geniality to the marks of anguish on his secret face.

To understand the book, then, is to experience through this unique point of view the emergence of at least three themes which the book has in common with other major works of literature. First, there is the idea that we must look beyond appearances to judge reality. Just as the reader has to look beyond the typically racist language of the inmates to find in the book as a whole a document of witness against the dehumanizing, sick effects of racism in our society, so Bromden has to look beyond the perception of the world which limits his concept of self. When the perception changes, he begins to see the reality of his growth. Chief Bromden is sick from racism and is made whole again when he learns to laugh in spite of it and to realize his identity as an American Indian. Second, there is the idea that fools and madmen have wisdom. Writers from Shakespeare to Kesey have suggested that the world is sometimes so out of joint that it can only be seen from some perspective so different that it cuts through illusion to truth. Lear and Hamlet both experience a kind of madness for this reason, madness in which it might be added, they too abandon propriety of speech. (Polite language has hardly ever been associated with madness in literature.) And through this madness, in Kesey's book, the third theme emerges: the idea that the bumbling fool may be transformed into a worker of good deeds. McMurphy assumes almost the stature of the typical quest hero at his death. The circumstances of his life have required him to rise above the "lowness" of his original station to become a deliverer, to give up his life for his friend. The idea is that each human soul is worthy, and it is the genius of heroism to work transforming deeds which discover the worthiness both in themselves and in other humble men.

The book, then, works through the eyes and action of madmen to go from a vision of the world where all things are profane to a vision of the world where all human things are potentially sacred. Certainly teaching the book compels a discussion of obscenity, for it is impossible to understand it fully without realizing that what people do to each other in cruelty is the true obscenity, not shadow words. The book does not teach profanity; it teaches that the world of the insane is full of profanity. It does not teach racism, it clearly connects racism with cruelty and insanity. It does not teach immorality; it suggests that the fantasies of an unbalanced person are sensitive to a disruption of ordinary morality.

Frankly, the charge that the book teaches immorality puzzles me a little. Certainly Big Nurse's cruel manipulation of the men is immoral, but the young are hardly likely to identify with her and want to emulate her. Are Chief Bromden's fantasies immoral? Or are we to assume that because McMurphy is by common standards immoral that students are going out to copy him wholesale? Probably not any more than they would be inclined to copy Hamlet the murderer, Macbeth the assassin, or Oedipus the mother-lover, attractive though these tragic figures are. McMurphy, after all, winds up with a prefrontal lobotomy, experiencing a psychic death as final as the physical death his friend Bromden later provides.

The policies of the Bellevue Public Schools provide a set of guidelines for text selection. I have tried to show how the use of this book would "enrich and support the curriculum" in English and "help the pupil improve his power of discrimination and his quality of choices" by showing that it is a piece of literature rich in design and details, and that its thematic material stands well within the tradition of great literature. As such, it clearly relates to our expectation that the student achieve minimum competency in dealing with the structure and texture of a book.

Second, within the context of that program for increasing competency in understanding literature, I have also shown how the book can be considered appropriate. More essentially, because here is where the charges against the book seem to lie, I have established a distinction through my reading of the book between the common taste which might object to the use of a four-letter word in the book, and what I consider "good taste," which will place that word in context and see its relationship to the book as a whole. I think I have established a clear sense of the difference between this book and a dirty joke. It does not comment on human experience to leave the reader with a guilty snicker of complicity in the disregard of human frailty for the sake of a cheap sensation. It deals with human weakness, eccentricity, and suffering to increase the reader's respect for the transforming power of love, which teaches us to overcome weakness, to tolerate eccentricity, and to endure suffering.

I think the book admirably fulfills the requirements of the fourth principle of the guidelines, that it "contribute to the pupil's growing understandings and appreciations of his culture and other cultures so that

he can live compassionately and reasonably with his fellow men." Most students know very little about either the world of the mentally ill or the alienated condition of the American Indian. The detail of the book richly provides this information. The weaving of these details into this particular story moves the reader to deep sympathy with the Indian and much compassion for the inmates of his asylum. I think it is a profoundly humanizing book.

Fourth, and last, but not least, I would like to consider the student's freedom to read, "an inherent right and a necessity in a democratic society." I think our schools and our curriculum have to be defined vigorously against the naive reader who reacts out of a Victorian sense of propriety and out of vague fears of the magic power of the written word to want to condemn everything in literature which seems to him unconventional or strange. Attitudes such as these toward literature are a real danger to the student, in that if we yield to them we simultaneously seek to reduce the student's right to entertain ideas and teach the validity of these attitudes in the degree to which we acknowledge they have any power. We teach the student to fear ideas, or we teach the student that we fear ideas, any time we kill a book, which is, after all, as Milton told us, "The lifeblood of a master spirit."

Kesey is a valid part of the world of American literature. His books, if not available in the library at our high school, would easily be found in any bookstore or book rack. The attempt to "protect" the students from his view of the world is in the first place futile: they like *One Flew over the Cuckoo's Nest* and will read it anyway. Second, such an attempt would be stupid. Why neglect the opportunity to provide a framework of reason in which such an admittedly difficult book can be read, discussed, and understood—unless we want to garner the doubtful honors attributable to playing the role of Big Nurse of education, and further alienate the young people we are attempting to communicate with?

I conclude with the description of one remarkable scene in Kesey's book: Patients are allowed to vote in weekly group meetings about policies which concern their welfare and entertainment. McMurphy has requested that though the regular TV watching time is in the evening, patients be allowed access to the TV during the daytime while the World Series is being played. Big Nurse does not like this assertation of individual will which will upset the daily routine, so she opposes McMurphy and then overrules the patients' affirmative vote on a technicality. In spite of her ruling McMurphy puts down his task and pulls his chair in front of the TV as the game broadcast begins. It is a battle of wills, and the patients watch to see who will win. Big Nurse pulls the great lever and cuts off the power. But McMurphy remains solidly there, in front of the TV, watching the empty screen. One by one the others join him, and soon they're all sitting there, "watching the gray screen just like we could see the baseball game clear as day," and Big Nurse is "ranting and screaming" behind them. (pp. 28-31)

It is unfortunate that the patron who has lodged the objection to this book was so distracted by its alleged obscenity, racism, and immorality that he couldn't appreciate this scene. It has something to say

about the need for authority to establish itself through reasonable, not arbitrary action. It also illustrates the utter futility of ever trying to get between a human being and anything he holds as dear as baseball. (p. 31)

Janet R. Sutherland, "A Defense of Ken Kesey's 'One Flew Over the Cuckoo's Nest'," in *English Journal,* Vol. 61, No. 1, January, 1972, pp. 28-31.

SOURCES FOR FURTHER STUDY

Carnes, Bruce. *Ken Kesey.* Boise State University Western Writers Series, edited by Wayne Chatterton and James H. Maguire, No. 12. Boise, Idaho: Boise State University, 1974, 50 p.

> General critical and biographical overview of Kesey's life and career. Includes a selected bibliography.

Leeds, Barry H. *Ken Kesey.* New York: Frederick Ungar Publishing Co., 1981, 134 p.

> Biographical and critical overview of Kesey's life and works. Includes commentary on the text of *One Flew over the Cuckoo's Nest* as well as the stage and screen adaptations of the novel.

Porter, M. Gilbert. *The Art of Grit: Ken Kesey's Fiction.* Columbia: University of Missouri Press, 1982, 102 p.

> Brief biographical and critical study covering *One Flew over the Cuckoo's Nest, Sometimes a Great Notion,* and *Demon Box.*

Pratt, John C., ed. *One Flew over the Cuckoo's Nest: Text and Criticism.* New York: Penguin Books, 1973, 567 p.

> Incorporates the text of the novel with such materials as a rough draft of the book's opening scene, published articles by Kesey, and criticism and perspectives by such commentators as James E. Miller, Jr., Joseph J. Waldmeir, and Dale Wasserman.

Tanner, Stephen L. *Ken Kesey.* Boston: Twayne Publishers, 1983, 159 p.

> Biographical and critical study covering Kesey's works written prior to *Demon Box.* Includes a selected bibliography.

Weixlmann, Joseph. "Ken Kesey: A Bibliography." *Western American Literature* 10, No. 3 (November 1975): 219-31.

> Nine-part survey listing primary and secondary materials, published letters to Kesey, and numerous bibliographical sources.

Rudyard Kipling

1865-1936

(Full name Joseph Rudyard Kipling) English short story writer, poet, novelist, essayist, and autobiographer.

INTRODUCTION

*C*reator of many of the world's best-loved short stories, Kipling is considered one of the finest writers of short fiction in world literature. Credited with popularizing the short fiction genre in England, Kipling is perhaps most famous for his insightful stories of Indian culture and Anglo-Indian society and for his masterful, widely read stories for children, which are collected in *Just-So Stories for Little Children* (1902), the two *Jungle Books* (1894-95), *Puck of Pook's Hill* (1906), and *Rewards and Fairies* (1910). Many commentators consider Mowgli, the central figure in the *Jungle Books,* one of the most memorable characters in children's literature. Somerset Maugham concluded of Kipling: "He is our [England's] greatest story writer. I can't believe he will ever be equalled. I am sure he can never be excelled." His critical reputation, however, has suffered because attention has often been paid not to his frequently flawless technique, but to the jingoistic political beliefs expressed in his work. After Kipling's death a major reassessment of his talents has led to his recognition as a masterful storyteller who possessed profound insights into the role of "beneficient imperialism," even if these insights were often clouded by a chauvinistic patriotism.

Kipling was born in Bombay, India, of English parents. At the age of six he was sent to school in southern England, an unhappy experience that he wrote about in his story "Baa Baa Black Sheep." For five years he lived with unsympathetic guardians in a foster home he called the "House of Desolation," and at the age of twelve he was sent to boarding school at the United Service College in Westward Ho!, Devon. Despite being bullied and ostracized by his schoolmates during his first years there, Kipling wrote fondly of his public school experiences in the collection *Stalky and Co* (1899). Just before his seventeenth birthday, Kipling returned to India to work as a journalist on the Lahore *Civil and Military Gazette* and the Allahabad *Pioneer.* The stories he wrote for these two newspapers, published in 1888 as the collection *Plain Tales from the Hills* (1888), earned him widespread recognition in India.

Kipling returned to England in 1889 to pursue a literary career. Soon after arriving in London, he began collaborating with Wolcott Balestier, an American literary agent. The two men co-authored the novel *The Naulahka* (1892), and Balestier was responsible for publishing Kipling's works in America. In 1892 Kipling married Balestier's sister Caroline, and the couple lived on her family's estate in Vermont for four years. During this time Kipling produced the two *Jungle Books* and began writing *Kim* (1901), considered by many his finest novel. Disenchanted with American society in general and devastated by the death of his daughter Josephine in 1899, Kipling returned to Europe, eventually settling in Sussex, England, a locale that figures prominently in the stories from *Puck of Pook's Hill* and *Rewards and Fairies.* In 1907 Kipling received the Nobel Prize in Literature for both his short fiction and novels, the first English author to be so honored. The tragedies of World War I and the loss of his only son, John, in 1915 greatly altered Kipling's personal and literary perspectives. Such stories as "Mary Postgate" and "Sea Constables" reflect the bitter anger and desire for revenge he felt at having witnessed so much destruction. Kipling never completely recovered from the loss of his two children. He died in 1936 after several years of illness and was buried in Poet's Corner in Westminster Abbey.

Kipling's fame as a short fiction writer is based predominantly on three types of stories: his exotic tales of India, his narratives about the military, and his children's books. As a journalist in India, Kipling had the opportunity to explore many facets of Anglo-Indian culture, and the East provided the setting for much of his early fiction. His portrayal of India and its culture occupies many dimensions; he wrote stories about virtually every sector of society. These tales are imitative of the French *conte* and are considered remarkable for their innovative plots and deceptively simple structures. His short stories, brief, concise, and vigorous, display little depth of characterization, but are remarkable for their innovative plots and deceptively simple structure. Kipling's tendency to concision is sometimes overdone in his later stories. "Mrs. Bathurst," for example, is so compressed and elliptical that many critics admit they cannot discern what happens in the narrative. Kipling's stories for children are perhaps the most widely known and read of his works. Kipling had a gift for anthropomorphism, and he presented his animal characters, in works like the *Jungle Books,* with simplicity, humor, and dignity, marred only occasionally, critics say, by a

sense of patronizing cuteness. He fashioned these tales to be read aloud, and critics agree that the oral beauty of his writing makes these stories particularly memorable. The *Just-So Stories,* written in a nonsensical secretive language, are intended for very young children and comically consider such timeless mysteries as why camels have humps or how writing was developed. Kipling's most famous collections, the two *Jungle Books,* chronicle the life of Mowgli, a boy who is abandoned by his parents and raised by wolves to become the master of the jungle. Kipling's final collections for children, *Puck of Pook's Hill* and *Rewards and Fairies,* feature the fairy Puck, who entertains two children with a series of stories about the successive generations—from Roman times to the French Revolution—that have inhabited the land where the children now blithely play. In these tales, Puck shows the children examples of both vice and virtue in the history of England, taking them on adventures that simultaneously entertain and teach moral lessons.

Of Kipling's four novel-length works, only *Kim* was critically well-received. Critics attributed the poor plotting and weak characterization of his first novel, *The Light That Failed* (1890), to his youth and inexperience. His second novel, *The Naulahka,* written with Balestier, exhibits the same shortcomings. In his last two novels, *Captains Courageous* (1897) and *Kim,* these weaknesses were turned to Kipling's advantage, for both share an essentially plotless, picaresque structure that contributed to their effect. Both are also his most popular novels with modern readers, although *Captains Courageous* is now read primarily by children. Called by Nirad C. Chaudhuri "the finest story about India in English," *Kim* is also considered a revealing self-portrait of its author. Through his young protagonist, Kipling explored the duality of his emotional commitment to both British imperialism and Eastern philosophy and values. While some critics contend that a lack of introspection on the part of the protagonist of *Kim* forms the primary fault in a potentially great work, others hold that Kipling's penetrating scrutiny of his dual attachments, as well as his sympathetic depiction of the Indian people, place this novel among the masterpieces of English literature.

In his poetry Kipling broke new ground by taking as subject matter the life of the common soldier and sailor in such off-duty activities as drinking, looting, and brawling. Most critical comment centered at first on Kipling's ignominious choice of topics for his verses and on his insistent, often-times offensive, imperialism. Then, in 1942, T. S. Eliot prefaced a new collection of Kipling's poetry and verse with a lengthy and favorable reassessment of Kipling as a poet. Eliot's study has been the starting point of many subsequent analyses of Kipling's poetic accomplishment, which is still the subject of critical contention.

Kipling began writing professionally in the 1880s, and by 1896 his works had been collected in a uniform edition—a rare honor for so young a writer. Such powerful contemporary men of letters as Edmund Gosse, Thomas Hardy, Andrew Lang, and George Saintsbury praised his stories, and Henry James called him "the most complete man of genius that I've ever known." Kipling was not without detractors, however, and such commentators as Robert Buchanan rejected his stories as imperialist, vulgar, simpleminded, and unnecessarily brutal. Critics concur that Kipling's early success stemmed, in part, from his ability to inspire deep emotions in his audiences. Few readers reacted with indifference to his writing. The imperialist views Kipling expressed in his Indian stories also contributed to his initial success; however, later in his career after political tides in England had shifted, his stories were considered outdated and his popularity waned. Critical attention concentrated upon the jingoist and racist aspects of Kipling's writing almost to the exclusion of his literary accomplishments. Following Kipling's death, a major reassessment of his talents led to his recognition as an astute storyteller who possessed profound insights and a rare gift for entertaining. Although his stories are not uniformly praised, he is nonetheless regarded as one of the masters of the short story form. His exotic tales of India and entertaining children's stories are enjoyed by readers of all ages. Indeed, at the time of his death in 1936, Kipling's collected stories—roughly 250 of them—had sold over fifteen million volumes. James Harrison has remarked: "To have reached, as no English author since Dickens had done, a world-wide readership of immense size and the widest possible intellectual and social range, and to be quoted scores of times a day by people who have no idea of whom they are quoting, is to be honored in a way many authors of the front rank might envy."

(For further information on Kipling's life and works, see *Contemporary Authors*, Vols. 105, 120; *Dictionary of Literary Biography*, Vols. 19, 34; *Short Story Criticism*, Vol. 5; and *Twentieth-Century Literary Criticism*, Vols. 8, 17.)

CRITICAL COMMENTARY

HENRY JAMES

(essay date 1891)

[James was an American-born English novelist, short story writer, and essayist. In the following excerpt from his introduction to an 1891 edition of *Soldiers Three*, he extols Kipling's short stories.]

[Kipling's] bloom lasts, from month to month, almost surprisingly—by which I mean that he has not worn out even by active exercise the particular property that made us all, more than a year ago, so precipitately drop everything else to attend to him. He has many others which he will doubtless always keep; but a part of the potency attaching to his freshness, what makes it as exciting as a drawing of lots, is our instinctive conviction that he cannot, in the nature of things, keep that; so that our enjoyment of him, so long as the miracle is still wrought, has both the charm of confidence and the charm of suspense. And then there is the further charm, with Mr. Kipling, that this same freshness is such a very strange affair of its kind—so mixed and various and cynical, and, in certain lights, so contradictory of itself. The extreme recentness of his inspiration is as enviable as the tale is startling that his productions tell of his being at home, domesticated and initiated, in this wicked and weary world. At times he strikes us as shockingly precocious, at others as serenely wise. On the whole, he presents himself as a strangely clever youth who has stolen the formidable mask of maturity and rushes about, making people jump with the deep sounds, and sportive exaggerations of tone, that issue from its painted lips. He has this mark of a real vocation, that different spectators may like him—must like him, I should almost say—for different things; and this refinement of attraction, that to those who reflect even upon their pleasures he has as much to say as to those who never reflect upon anything. Indeed there is a certain amount of room for surprise in the fact that, being so much the sort of figure that the hardened critic likes to meet, he should also be the sort of figure that inspires the multitude with confidence—for a complicated air is, in general, the last thing that does this. (pp. 226-27)

Mr. Kipling, then, has the character that furnishes plenty of play and of vicarious experience—that makes any perceptive reader foresee a rare luxury. He has the great merit of being a compact and convenient illustration of the surest source of interest in any painter of life—that of having an identity as marked as a window-frame. He is one of the illustrations, taken near at hand, that help to clear up the vexed question in the novel or the tale, of kinds, camps, schools, distinctions, the right way and the wrong way; so very positively

Principal Works

Schoolboy Lyrics (poetry) 1881

Departmental Ditties (poetry) 1886

In Black and White (short stories) 1888

The Phantom 'Rickshaw (short stories) 1888

Plain Tales from the Hills (short stories) 1888

Soldiers Three (short stories) 1888

The Story of the Gadsbys (short stories) 1888

Under the Deodars (short stories) 1888

Wee Willie Winkie (short stories) 1888

The Courting of Dinah Shadd (short stories) 1890

The Light That Failed (novel) 1890

Life's Handicap (short stories) 1891

Barrack-Room Ballads (poetry) 1892

The Naulahka [with Wolcott Balestier] (novel) 1892

Many Inventions (short stories) 1893

The Jungle Book (short stories and poetry) 1894

The Second Jungle Book (short stories and poetry) 1895

The Seven Seas (poetry) 1896

Captains Courageous (novel) 1897

The Day's Work (short stories) 1898

From Sea to Sea. 2 vols. (sketches) 1899

Stalky and Co. (short stories) 1899

Kim (novel) 1901

Just-So Stories for Little Children (short stories and poetry) 1902

The Five Nations (poetry) 1903

Traffics and Discoveries (short stories and poetry) 1904

Puck of Pook's Hill (short stories and poetry) 1906

Abaft the Funnel (short stories) 1909

Actions and Reactions (short stories and poetry) 1909

Rewards and Fairies (short stories and poetry) 1910

Songs from Books (poetry) 1912

A Diversity of Creatures (short stories and poetry) 1917

The Years Between (poetry) 1919

Letters of Travel, 1892-1913 (sketches) 1920

Debits and Credits (short stories and poetry) 1926

A Book of Words (speeches) 1928

Thy Servant a Dog (short stories) 1930

Limits and Renewals (short stories and poetry) 1932

Souvenirs of France (essays) 1933

Complete Works in Prose and Verse. 35 vols. (short stories, poetry, novels, essays, sketches, speeches, and unfinished autobiography) 1937-39

Something of Myself for Friends Known and Unknown (unfinished autobiography) 1937

---

does he contribute to the showing that there are just as many kinds, as many ways, as many forms and degrees of the "right," as there are personal points in view. It is the blessing of the art he practises that it is made up of experience conditioned, infinitely, in this personal way—the sum of the feeling of life as reproduced by innumerable natures; natures that feel through all their differences, testify through their diversities. These differences, which make the identity, are of the individual; they form the channel by which life flows through him, and how much he is able to give us of life—in other words, how much he appeals to us—depends on whether they form it solidly. (pp. 228-29)

It is a part of the satisfaction the author gives us that he can make us speculate as to whether he will be able to complete his picture altogether (this is as far as we presume to go in meddling with the question of his future) without bringing in the complicated soul. On the day he does so, if he handles it with anything like the cleverness he has already shown, the expectation of his friends will take a great bound. Meanwhile, at any rate, we have Mulvaney, and Mulvaney is after all tolerably complicated. He is only a six-foot saturated Irish private, but he is a considerable pledge of more to come. Hasn't he, for that matter, the tongue of a hoarse

siren, and hasn't he also mysteries and infinitudes almost Carlylese? Since I am speaking of him I may as well say that, as an evocation, he has probably led captive those of Mr. Kipling's readers who have most given up resistance. He is a piece of portraiture of the largest, vividest kind, growing and growing on the painter's hands without ever outgrowing them. I can't help regarding him, in a certain sense, as Mr. Kipling's tutelary deity—a landmark in the direction in which it is open to him to look furthest. If the author will only go as far in this direction as Mulvaney is capable of taking him (and the inimitable Irishman is like Voltaire's Habakkuk, *capable de tout*) he may still discover a treasure and find a reward for the services he has rendered the winner of Dinah Shadd. I hasten to add that the truly appreciative reader should surely have no quarrel with the primitive element in Mr. Kipling's subject-matter, or with what, for want of a better name, I may call his love of low life. What is that but essentially a part of his freshness? And for what part of his freshness are we exactly more thankful than for just this smart jostle that he gives the old stupid superstition that the amiability of a story-teller is the amiability of the people he represents—that their vulgarity, or depravity, or gentility, or fatuity are tantamount to the same qualities in the painter itself? A blow from which, apparently, it will not easily recover is dealt this infantine philosophy by Mr. Howells when, with the most distinguished dexterity and all the detachment of a master, he handles some of the clumsiest, crudest, most human things in life—answering surely thereby the playgoers in the sixpenny gallery who howl at the representative of the villain when he comes before the curtain.

Nothing is more refreshing than this active, disinterested sense of the real; it is doubtless the quality for the want of more of which our English and American fiction has turned so woefully stale. We are ridden by the old conventionalities of type and small proprieties of observance—by the foolish baby-formula (to put it sketchily) of the picture and the subject. Mr. Kipling has all the air of being disposed to lift the whole business off the nursery carpet, and of being perhaps even more able than he is disposed. . . . We are thankful for any boldness and any sharp curiosity, and that is why we are thankful for Mr. Kipling's general spirit and for most of his excursions.

Many of these, certainly, are into a region not to be designated as superficially dim, though indeed the author always reminds us that India is above all the land of mystery. A large part of his high spirits, and of ours, comes doubtless from the amusement of such vivid, heterogeneous material, from the irresistible magic of scorching suns, subject empires, uncanny religions, uneasy garrisons and smothered-up women—from heat and colour and danger and dust. India is a portentous image, and we are duly awed by the familiarities it undergoes at Mr. Kipling's hand and by the fine impunity, the sort of fortune that favours the brave, of *his* want of awe. An abject humility is not his strong point, but he gives us something instead of it—vividness and drollery, the vision and the thrill of many things, the misery and strangeness of most, the personal sense of a hundred queer contacts and risks. And then in the absence of respect he has plenty of knowledge, and if knowledge should fail him he would have plenty of invention. Moreover, if invention should ever fail him, he would still have the lyric string and the patriotic chord, on which he plays admirably; so that it may be said he is a man of resources. What he gives us, above all, is the feeling of the English manner and the English blood in conditions they have made at once so much and so little their own; with manifestations grotesque enough in some of his satiric sketches and deeply impressive in some of his anecdotes of individual responsibility.

His Indian impressions divide themselves into three groups, one of which, I think, very much outshines the others. First to be mentioned are the tales of native life, curious glimpses of custom and superstition, dusky matters not beholden of the many, for which the author has a remarkable *flair*. Then comes the social, the Anglo-Indian episode, the study of administrative and military types, and of the wonderful rattling, riding ladies who, at Simla and more desperate stations, look out for husbands and lovers; often, it would seem, and husbands and lovers of others. The most brilliant group is devoted wholly to the common soldier, and of this series it appears to me that too much good is hardly to be said. Here Mr. Kipling, with all his off-handedness, is a master; for we areheld not so much by the greater or less oddity of the particular yarn—sometimes it is scarcely a yarn at all, but something much less artificial—as by the robust attitude of the narrator, who never arranges or glosses or falsifies, but makes straight for the common and the characteristic. I have mentioned the great esteem in which I hold Mulvaney—surely a charming man and one qualified to adorn a higher sphere. Mulvaney is a creation to be proud of, and his two comrades stand as firm on their legs. In spite of Mulvaney's social possibilities, they are all three finished brutes; but it is precisely in the finish that we delight. Whatever Mr. Kipling may relate about them forever will encounter readers equally fascinated and unable fully to justify their faith.

Are not those literary pleasures after all the most intense which are the most perverse and whimsical, and even indefensible? There is a logic in them somewhere, but it often lies below the plummet of criticism. The spell may be weak in a writer who has every reasonable and regular claim, and it may be irresistible in one who presents himself with a style corresponding to a bad hat. A good hat is better than a bad one, but a conjuror may wear either. Many a reader will never be able to say what secret human force lays its hand upon him when Private Ortheris, having sworn "quietly into the blue sky," goes mad with homesickness by the yellow river and raves for the basest sights and sounds of London. I can scarcely tell why I think **"The Courting of Dinah Shadd"** a masterpiece (though, indeed, I can make a shrewd guess at one of the reasons), nor would it be worth while perhaps to attempt to defend the same pretension in regard to **"On Greenhow Hill"**—much less to trouble the tolerant reader of these remarks with a statement of how many more performances in the nature of **"The End of the Passage"** (quite admitting even that they might not represent Mr. Kipling at his best) I am conscious of a latent relish for. One might as well admit while one is about it that one has wept profusely over **"The Drums of the Fore and Aft,"** the history of the **"Dutch Courage"** of two dreadful dirty little boys, who, in the face of Afghans scarcely more dreadful, saved the reputation of their regiment and perished, the least mawkishly in the world, in a squalor of battle incomparably expressed. People who know how peaceful they are themselves and have no bloodshed to reproach themselves with needn't scruple to mention the glamour that Mr. Kipling's intense militarism has for them, and how astonishing and contagious they find it, in spite of the unromantic complexion of it—the way it bristles with all sorts of ugliness and technicalities. Perhaps that is why I go all the way even with *The Gadsbys*—the Gadsbys were so connected (uncomfortably, it is true) with the army. There is fearful fighting—or a fearful danger of it—in **"The Man Who Would be King"**; is that the reason we are deeply affected by this extraordinary tale? It is one of them, doubtless, for Mr. Kipling has many reasons, after all, on his side, though they don't equally call aloud to be uttered.

One more of them, at any rate, I must add to these unsystematised remarks—it is the one I spoke of a shrewd guess at in alluding to **"The Courting of Dinah Shadd."** The talent that produces such a tale is a talent eminently in harmony with the short story, and the short story is, on our side of the Channel and of the Atlantic, a mine which will take a great deal of working. Admirable is the clearness with which Mr. Kipling perceives this—perceives what innumerable chances it gives, chances of touching life in a thousand different places, taking it up in innumerable pieces, each a specimen and an illustration. In a word, he appreciates the episode, and there are signs to show that this shrewdness will, in general, have long innings. It will find the detachable, compressible "case" an admirable, flexible form; the cultivation of which may well add to the mistrust already entertained by Mr. Kipling, if his manner does not betray him, for what is clumsy and tasteless in the time-honoured practice of the "plot." It will fortify him in the conviction that the vivid picture has a greater communicative value than the Chinese puzzle. There is little enough "plot" in such a perfect little piece of hard representation as **"The End of the Passage,"** to cite again only the most salient of twenty examples.

But I am speaking of our author's future, which is the luxury that I meant to forbid myself—precisely because the subject is so tempting. There is nothing in the world (for the prophet) so charming as to prophesy, and as there is nothing so inconclusive the tendency should be repressed in proportion as the opportunity is good. There is a certain want of courtesy to a peculiarly contemporaneous present even in speculating, with a dozen differential precautions, on the question of what will become in the later hours of the day of a talent that has got up so early. Mr. Kipling's actual performance is like a tremendous walk before breakfast, making one welcome the idea of the meal, but consider with some alarm the hours still to be traversed. Yet if his breakfast is all to come, the indications are that he will be more active than ever after he has had it. Among these indications are the unflagging character of his pace and the excellent form, as they say in athletic circles, in which he gets over the ground. We don't detect him stumbling; on the contrary, he steps out quite as briskly as

at first, and still more firmly. There is something zealous and craftsman-like in him which shows that he feels both joy and responsibility. A whimsical, wanton reader, haunted by a recollection of all the good things he has seen spoiled; by a sense of the miserable, or, at any rate, the inferior, in so many continuations and endings, is almost capable of perverting poetic justice to the idea that it would be even positively well for so surprising a producer to remain simply the fortunate, suggestive, unconfirmed and unqualified representative of what he has actually done. We can always refer to that. (pp. 232-41)

Henry James, "Mr. Kipling's Early Stories," in his *Views and Reviews,* 1908. Reprint by Books for Libraries Press, 1968, pp. 225-41.

THE TIMES LITERARY SUPPLEMENT
(essay date 1936)

[In the excerpt below, the anonymous critic asserts that Kipling's place in English literature rests primarily on the merits of his short stories.]

Rudyard Kipling was a national institution, and regarded as such by all the world. His fame had been long established and his literary activity slight for many years. It was also the case that many had lost interest in him and many others had been repelled. Seldom had a famous national institution been the object of more hostile criticism; some of it, indeed, unfair and marred by lack of understanding, yet some of it damaging enough. There are veterans who were hostile from the first; there are to-day many thousands of young enthusiasts; but broadly speaking the vocal sections of two generations have been at variance regarding him. Now the time has come for a reckoning; not a final reckoning, for posterity will have its say, but for the verdict of this age, comprising the old and the young, sitting as the jury. The critic writing at the moment must try to assist the jury to find that verdict, not as advocate for or against—they have both been heard at length—but, so far as he can and dare, as judge summing up. Conscious of his own limitations and mindful of the disasters of many who have assumed the role, he may also attempt a harder task: that of prophecy. Kipling in life and work alike was downright and decided, without hesitation as to goal or the road that led to it. Let us treat him as he would have chosen to be treated, without timidity or hedging. Let us venture not only to decide what shall be the verdict of our time upon him but to predict boldly what shall be his place in the annals of our letters.

We have to envisage him both as poet and writer

of fiction, and in the former aspect our task is, it may be admitted, a difficult one. On the prose side the case is very different. There is, we believe, no heavy risk in the prophecy that Rudyard Kipling will live and be admired as one of the most virile and skilful of English masters of the short story; that if that art, in which we are weak, shows with us no great development in future, he will remain, in years to come, as he now is, unique; that if it goes forward and gives birth to new triumphs, he will still rank among the greatest of the pioneers.

The pioneer has always a special meed of honour, and that honour is Kipling's for more reasons than one. He won it alike for matter and manner. He was definitely the man of the hour, a milestone on the path of letters, like Byron and Chateaubriand. He appeared at a moment when literature in this country was being sicklied o'er, not with the pale cast of thought but with the unnatural bloom of cosmetics. We can realize now more fully than was realized then that fine and enduring work was being done in the aesthetic nineties, outside the school of the aesthetes, even outside that of the two giants who had no relationship to that school, George Meredith and Thomas Hardy. Yet the general atmosphere was stale and scented, artistically as well as literally *fin de siècle.* There was an extraordinary preoccupation with the artificial, a delight, by no means assumed on the part of many of the "yellow" world, in "bought red mouths," "parched flowers," pallid women, "delicate" sins.

Before the nineties opened there had spread bruit of a young writer out in India who knew little of this world of opera-cloaks and gold-headed canes and scorned what he did know. Kipling was, as his acute French observer, M. André Chevrillon, remarked, English "d'une façon simple, violente et, de plus, très nouvelle"; the world which he entered so violently, which he did more than any other to destroy, being, on the contrary, the pale and unsatisfying reflection of a phase in French literature. Kipling was indeed English, but in those early days he was the mouthpiece of classes and types that were not themselves vocal and had long lacked a chronicler. India, with its heat and dust, its diversities of creed and caste, was suddenly brought to the door of the stay-at-home Englishman. He learned with a thrill how the more adventurous of his race, from private soldiers to governors of provinces, lived; how they fought and organized and ruled. For this precocious genius had not only observed and recorded for him a great number of interesting and astonishing facts and occurrences; he had also put at his disposal a marvellous power of catching an atmosphere, of summing up an impression of the scenes upon which the writer had looked. This was life indeed, exclaimed the reader in his armchair; this was life as it should be lived, this young seer in India was revealing the highest destiny of the Englishman. Soon it appeared that life could be lived elsewhere than in India. It could be lived in America, in Africa, in the ports of the world, at sea, whether in crack cargoboats, rusty tramps or the fishing smacks on the Grand Bank, in the cab of a steamengine; even, for those who knew how, in an unconventional public school. The same vigour, the same brilliant technique, the same power of making mechanism romantic marked each new effort and bound together the spell he had put upon the English public.

And then there came another phase. The worshipper of dangerous living, of physical excitement, of noise, some detractors averred, became entranced with the peaceful beauties and with the traditions of the English countryside, and touched upon them with as much originality as he had all the rest. Such are the broad lines of his literary career.

Rudyard Kipling is first of all master of the *conte.* He attempted full-length novels, achieving in *The Light that Failed* and *Captains Courageous* romances to which no adjective higher than "successful" can be applied; in *The Naulakha,* written in collaboration with his brother-in-law, not even that; and in *Kim* his one masterpiece in that province. But in the short story he has had few English rivals, even if we take the best work of others to match against his, and from his take any of forty or fifty which it is hard to separate from the point of view of merit. The short story was suited to his peculiar gifts of compression, of clarity, of characterization that needs no building up but is completed and fixed in a flash. In his stories he has used almost every kind of matter, though the love of the sexes plays a very much smaller part than with most writers. War, adventure of every type, machinery pure and simple, have been his familiar subjects. He has employed the grotesque, the horrible, and very often the eerie in his plots, looking with anxious but never credulous eyes at what may be distinguished or imagined "at the end of the passage," in the half-world betwixt fact and dream. Nor has he neglected that form of short story which is almost an allegory, among which the Mowgli tales of *The Jungle Book* stand highest. In a great number of the early stories, in those of Mowgli above all, we seem to detect a form of idealism with as little historical justification as that of Rousseau. He sees the savage in man and that it is not far below the surface, and he is disposed to question the benefits of civilization.

The sentiment was perhaps with him no more than a phase, but those who study him closely can have little doubt that it existed. They will assuredly not regret the fact. For in the Mowgli stories Kipling achieved a rare feat: he invented a new form of expression. And these tales have a charm, a beauty, a boldness of imagination that we have not often seen equalled in our time. The animals are not, as are those of Kipling's numerous imitators in this vein, creatures with men's minds in the bodies of beasts. The sentiments of beasts may be inaccurately described; that we cannot tell, though we may suspect that their intelligence is exaggerated; but the whole affair is managed with such marvellous dexterity that we are convinced and willingly surrender to him our judgment. Can an animal find enjoyment in the thrill of danger, as many human beings can? Hear his answer and see if you can state the contrary opinion with equal plausibility?

> To move down so cunningly that never a leaf stirred; to wade knee-deep in the roaring shallows that drown all noise from behind; to drink, looking backward over one shoulder, every muscle ready for the first desperate bound of keen terror; to roll on the sandy margin, and return, wet-muzzled and well plumped out, to the admiring herd, was a thing that all tall-antlered young bucks took a delight in, precisely because they knew that at any moment Bagheera or Shere Khan might leap upon them and bear them down.

That word plausibility, in fact, gives us the key to one of the chief secrets of his popularity. It also explains a certain impatience felt by those who caught him out. For, excellently documented as he was, he was not always correct—could hardly be so, seeing how wide was his range. But, right or wrong, he was always equally assured, cocksure said the less friendly of his critics. And yet, these slips apart, his plausibility is amazing. The finest of the stories, such as **"On Greenhow Hill," "The Return of Imray," "The Strange Ride of Morrowbie Jukes," "The Man who would be King," "Without Benefit of Clergy," "The Mark of the Beast,"** have the verisimilitude of chronicles. Let us say that chronicles they are indeed, the chronicles of an epoch of British administration in India, infused with the imagination of a great writer of fiction.

The poetry is another matter. Poetry demands a standard even higher than prose; that is to say, an infelicitous expression, a piece of loose thinking are in it more painfully apparent and bring their own condemnation more swiftly. In his early work in verse Kipling did not fly high. *Departmental Ditties* may have won him his earliest fame, but these popular ballads, parodies, society verses, satires, clever and witty as they are, do not warrant the bestowal of the title of poet. The elevation of Mr. Potiphar Gubbins, the transfer to Quetta of Jack Barrett, may take their place somewhere below the satiric verse of Marvell and above that of Churchill; the rest, if they live, will live because they are Kipling's. Yet on the last page of that volume came a poem, **"L'Envoi,"** which few probably noticed, which a bold prophet might have seen as a cloud no bigger than a man's hand. Till that cloud has sailed up we continue in the arid heat of dexterity, of rhetoric, of admonition, of a sententiousness often grating. We are warmed and made happy by wit and humour, we rec-

ognize a master of metre, rhythm and onomatopoeia in a line like

> The heave and the halt and the hurl and the crash of
> the comber wind-hounded.

But almost always we are either pulled up with a jar by a phrase which is definitely inappropriate, definitely not poetry; or, if we escape that, subsequent reflection seems to indicate a flaw in taste, a thought of which the expression begins well but is not sustained at the level of its early dignity and beauty. But the cloud was drawing nigher and swelling in size. There may be difference of opinions whether the later stories of the English countryside are the equals of their more brilliant exotic predecessors. There can be little doubt that in the lovely songs strewn among them, buttercups and daisies amid rich green grass, Kipling reached his highest as a poet. The passionate patriotism which had often previously run riot, shocking and offending the weaker brethren, is here even more intense, but purified, purged of that note of brawling.

> Under their feet in the grasses
>   My clinging magic runs.
> They shall return as strangers.
>   They shall remain as sons.
> Scent of smoke in the evening.
>   Smell of rain in the night,
> The hours, the days and the seasons,
>   Order their souls aright.

In these songs, with their simplicity, their kindly and gracious philosophy, he reveals at last that lyric sweetness whereof we had had promise in **"L'Envoi,"** and himself as not merely a satirist or humorist or master of the banjo ballad, but a lyric poet.

> Cities and Thrones and Powers,
>   Stand in Time's eye,
> Almost as long as flowers,
>   Which daily die:
> But, as new buds put forth
>   To glad new men
> Out of the spent and unconsidered Earth,
>   The Cities rise again.
> This season's Daffodil,
>   She never hears,
> What change, what chance, what chill,
>   Cut down last year's;
> But with bold countenance,
>   And knowledge small,
> Esteems her seven days' continuance
>   To be perpetual.

(Even in reading these lines we pause. Is there not something schoolboyish in the irony of that "almost as long"?)

Yet let us make no mistake. More of Kipling will go down to posterity than the fastidious literary critic is prepared to pass. The flaws are those of a great and original craftsman; in the most faulty productions there is power; one feels everywhere in them the grip of a strong hand. Often that which is not poetry is life itself. Take a poem such as **"If "**; not poetry at all, some critics may declare. It may not be, yet it has been an inspiration to many thousands and those not the most ingenuous or limited in their appreciation of poetical merit. Its moral maxims are as clean-cut and forcible as those of Pope or Edward Young. Almost all the patriotic verse, though it may grate often upon the ears of those whom Kipling called, with rather less than strict fairness but a large measure of truth,

Brittle intellectuals who crack beneath a strain,

and sometimes upon any critical ears, represents at least one side of England. "Wordsworth," wrote Lowell, "never lets us long forget the deeply rooted stock from which he sprang—*vien l en da lui.*" The words may be applied with equal justice to Kipling. At his worst as at his best, the love of England breeds in him a passionate intensity and sincerity which ennoble even the verse marred by the shouting of party warfare or by extreme patriotic dogmatism, as by technical faults of like nature.

What verdict England of the future will pass upon England of the last years of Victoria and Edward VII, is uncertain, but it is incontestable that the age will always rank as one of the greatest in our history—great materially and great in national temper. And may one not dare to foresee that when, long hence, that age and its characteristics and products are called to mind, the name of Rudyard Kipling will come first to men's mouths when they talk of its most typical representatives? Is it not likely that then the lesser work will take its place with the greater, as all part of and symbolic of the country which he loved and celebrated?

It were not easy to imagine two writers more widely separated than Rudyard Kipling and Maurice Barrès, but their names are linked by the fact that as contemporaries, born within a few years of one another, each set up a philosophy of nationalism and each was assailed from a point of view in which the political mingled with the artistic. Each might have taken as motto the words of Disraeli:—"Now a nation is a work of art and a work of time"; and each tripped not seldom in the snares which arrogance sets for the feet of the nationalist. Hear them each, Barrès on his beloved Hill of Sion-Vaudémont:—

Où sont les dames de Lorraine, soeurs, filles et femmes des Croisés, qui s'en venaient prier à Sion pendant que les hommes d'armes, là-bas, combattaient l'infidèle, et celles-là surtout qui, le lendemain de la bataille de Nicopolis, ignorantes encore, mais épouvantées par les rumeurs, montèrent ici intercéder pour des vivants qui étaient déjà des morts? Où la sainte princesse Philippe de Gueldre, à qui Notre-Dame de Sion découvrit, durant le temps de son

sommeil, les desseins ambitieux des ennemis de la Lorraine? . . .

and Kipling on his Sussex Downs:—

See you the dimpled track that runs,
    All hollow through the wheat?
O that was where they hauled the guns
    That smote King Philip's fleet.
See you our stilly woods of oak,
    And the dread ditch beside?
O that was where the Saxons broke,
    On the day that Harold died.

While Barrès, a mystic, heard "the hushed and timid voices" of the gods of his ancestors at those spiritual points where, it seemed to him, the crust of the material world was thin and the poetry of great deeds and great lives came through it as in a vapour, Kipling, more realistically, conjured up upon the Downs his ancestors themselves. *Puck of Pook's Hill, Rewards and Fairies* have in them the very marrow of England. For them, at least, we may prophesy with assurance that death will not come quickly. In these entrancing volumes, in many another tale of the stamp of **"An Habitation Enforced,"** there is far more than merely the exquisite art of telling a story; there is the recreation of history, the essence of a nation's beginning and early development. The figures of De Aquila and Sir Richard Dalyngridge are not only great characters of fiction but pendants to the works of great historians. "And so was England born." The work of Kipling, as of Barrès, at its greatest moments is a flower of national art. It was fitting that the former should have known and loved and been honoured of France; and that the latter, though he said hard words of England, should have been the guest of our Fleet in time of war and lauded its traditions to his countrymen.

We have hinted that the young men have less pleasure in the work of Kipling than those who reached manhood at any time between the publication of *Departmental Ditties* and that of *Kim,* though there is some doubt as to how far the young writers represent their generation in this. In any case there is in it nothing uncommon or prejudicial to his eventual fame. At Wordsworth's death, when subscriptions were being collected for a memorial to him, Macaulay declared to Arnold that ten years earlier more money could have been raised to do him honour in Cambridge alone than was now raised all through the country. Thirty years' later Arnold was bewailing that the diminution of Wordsworth's popularity was continuing, that, effaced first by Scott and Byron, he was now completely effaced by Tennyson. The selected poems of Wordsworth, which Arnold was then editing, to which the essay quoted was a preface, ran through thirteen editions between 1879 and the close of the century, and there have been many others. That which is popular today may be outmoded to-morrow, but if it has the stuff of life in it, it will assuredly not be dead the day after. Yet, where Kipling is concerned, it is improbable that there will ever be unanimity of opinion.

He was a man of strong prejudices, strong political views, with little tenderness for the opinions of others, and—though to lesser extent than now—he may always divide men into two camps. So much granted, there will be, we are convinced, in years to come a general agreement upon the high merit of a great part of this man's work. The perfervid admirers will come to admit that there is dross—dross, why he threw it up in a heap about him as he worked, till at times we could scarce see him over the top of it! Those of the type of mind which is antagonized by a loud-voiced patriotism and Toryism will allow those English songs and stories which we last considered to be free from that offence, and will perhaps even pardon it elsewhere for the vigour and skill with which it is presented. Both will proclaim him a magician in the art of the short story, who raised it to a higher station in our literature than it had known before his coming. As novelist they will call him author of one, but one only, of the finest romances of his time. As a poet he will be remembered for a mass of vigorous, pithy, if faulty, work of the second order; for a patriotic hymn that had become part of every national ceremony; last, not least, as the singer of English country beauties and traditions. And if, amid the work he leaves behind him, those juries of the future contrive to catch a glimpse of the man himself, as his own time knew him, they must add to their verdict a rider that this was a great man as well as a great writer; and honourable and fearless and good.

"A Flower of National Art in Verse and Prose: Rudyard Kipling's Place in English Literature," in *The Times Literary Supplement*, No. 1773, January 25, 1936, pp. 65-6.

T. S. ELIOT

(essay date 1943)

[One of the most influential poets and critics of the first half of the twentieth century, Eliot is closely identified with many of the qualities suggested by the term Modernism: experimentation, formal complexity, and artistic and intellectual eclecticism. In the following excerpt, he praises Kipling's poetry.]

There are several reasons for our not knowing Kipling's poems so well as we think we do. When a man is primarily known as a writer of prose fiction we are inclined—and usually, I think, justly—to regard his verse as a by-product. I am, I confess, always doubtful whether any man can so divide himself as to be able to make the most of two such very different forms of ex-

pression as poetry and imaginative prose. I am willing to pay due respect, for instance, to the poetry of George Meredith, of Thomas Hardy, of D. H. Lawrence as part of their *oeuvre,* without conceding that it is as good as it might have been had they chosen to dedicate their whole lives to that form of art. If I make an exception in the case of Kipling, it is not because I think he succeeded in making the division successfully, but because I think that . . . his verse and his prose are inseparable; that we must finally judge him, not separately as a poet and as a writer of prose fiction, but as the inventor of a mixed form. So a knowledge of his prose is essential to the understanding of his verse, and a knowledge of his verse is essential to the understanding of his prose. (p. 5)

The starting point for Kipling's verse is the motive of the ballad-maker; and the modern ballad is a type of verse for the appreciation of which we are not provided with the proper critical tools. We are therefore inclined to dismiss the poems, by reference to poetic criteria which do not apply. It must therefore be our task to understand the type to which they belong, before attempting to value them: we must consider what Kipling was trying to do and what he was not trying to do. The task is the opposite of that with which we are ordinarily faced when attempting to defend contemporary verse. We expect to have to defend a poet against the charge of obscurity: we have to defend Kipling against the charge of excessive lucidity. We expect a poet to be reproached for lack of respect for the intelligence of the common man, or even for deliberately flouting the intelligence of the common man: we have to defend Kipling against the charge of being a 'journalist' appealing only to the commonest collective emotions. We expect a poet to be ridiculed because his verse does not appear to scan: we must defend Kipling against the charge of writing jingles. In short, people are exasperated by poetry which they do not understand, and contemptuous of poetry which they understand without effort. . . . (p. 6)

What is unusual about Kipling's ballads is his singleness of intention in attempting to convey no more to the simple minded than can be taken in on one reading or hearing. They are best when read aloud, and the ear requires no training to follow them easily. With this simplicity of purpose goes a consummate gift of word, phrase, and rhythm. There is no poet who is less open to the charge of repeating himself. In the ballad, the stanza must not be too long and the rhyme scheme must not be too complicated; the stanza must be immediately apprehensible as a whole; a refrain can help to insist upon the identity within which a limited range of variation is possible. The variety of form which Kipling manages to devise for his ballads is remarkable: each is distinct, and perfectly fitted to the content and the mood which the poem has to convey. Nor is the

1892 cartoon of Kipling with "India on the brain."

versification too regular: there is the monotonous beat only when the monotonous is what is required; and the irregularities of scansion have a wide scope. One of the most interesting exercises in the combination of heavy beat and variation of pace is found in **"Danny Deever"**, a poem which is technically (as well as in content) remarkable. The regular recurrence of the same end-words, which gain immensely by imperfect rhyme (*parade* and *said*) gives the feeling of marching feet and the movement of men in disciplined formation—in a unity of movement which enhances the horror of the occasion and the sickness which seizes the men as individuals; and the slightly quickened pace of the final lines marks the change in movement and in music. There is no single word or phrase which calls too much attention to itself, or which is not there for the sake of the total effect; so that when the climax comes—

'What's that that whimpers over'ead?' said Files-on-
    Parade,
'It's Danny's soul that's passin' now,' the Colour-
    Sergeant said.

(the word *whimper* being exactly right) the atmosphere

has been prepared for a complete suspension of disbelief. (pp. 10-12)

[If] I call particular attention to **"Danny Deever"** as a barrackroom ballad which somehow attains the intensity of poetry, it is not with the purpose of isolating it from the other ballads of the same type, but with the reminder that with Kipling you cannot draw a line beyond which some of the verse becomes 'poetry'; and that the poetry, when it comes, owes the gravity of its impact to being something over and above the bargain, something more than the writer undertook to give you; and that the matter is never simply a pretext, an occasion for poetry. There are other poems in which the element of poetry is more difficult to put one's finger on, than in **"Danny Deever"**. Two poems which belong together are **"McAndrew's Hymn"** and **"The 'Mary Gloster' "**. They are dramatic monologues, obviously . . . owing something to Browning's invention, though metrically and intrinsically ballads. The popular verdict has chosen the first as the more memorable: I think that the popular verdict is right, but just what it is that raises **"McAndrew's Hymn"** above **"The 'Mary Gloster' "** is not easy to say. The rapacious old ship owner of the latter is not easily dismissed, and the presence of the silent son gives a dramatic quality absent from McAndrew's soliloquy. One poem is no less successful than the other. If the McAndrew poem is the more memorable, it is not because Kipling is more inspired by the contemplation of the success of failure than by that of the failure of success, but because there is greater poetry in the subject matter. It is McAndrew who creates the poetry of Steam, and Kipling who creates the poetry of McAndrew. (pp. 13-14)

Kipling's craftsmanship is more reliable than that of some greater poets, and there is hardly any poem, even in the collected works, in which he fails to do what he has set out to do. The great poet's craft may sometimes fail him: but at his greatest moments he is doing what Kipling is usually doing on a lower plane—writing transparently, so that our attention is directed to the object and not to the medium. Such a result is not simply attained by absence of decoration—for even the absence of decoration may err in calling attention to itself—but by never using decoration for its own sake, though, again, the apparently superfluous may be what is really important. Now one of the problems which arise concerning Kipling is related to that skill of craftsmanship which seems to enable him to pass from form to form, though always in an identifiable idiom, and from subject to subject, so that we are aware of no inner compulsion to write about this rather than that—a versatility which may make us suspect him of being no more than a performer. We look, in a poet as well as in a novelist, for what Henry James called the Figure in the Carpet. With the greatest of modern poets this Figure is perfectly manifest (for we can be sure of the existence of the Figure without perfectly understanding it): I mention Yeats at this point because of the contrast between his development, which is very apparent in the way he writes, and Kipling's development, which is only apparent in what he writes about. We expect to feel, with a great writer, that he *had* to write about the subject he took, and in that way. With no writer of equal eminence to Kipling is this inner compulsion, this unity in variety more difficult to discern.

I pass from the earlier ballads to mention a second category of Kipling's verse: those poems which arise out of, or comment upon topical events. Some of these, such as **"The Truce of the Bear"**, in the form of an apologue, do not aim very high. But to be able to write good verse to occasion is a very rare gift indeed: Kipling had the gift, and he took the obligation to employ it very seriously. Of this type of poem I should put **"Gehazi"**—a poem inspired by the Marconi scandals—very high, as a passionate invective rising to real eloquence (and a poem which illustrates, incidentally, the important influence of Biblical imagery and the Authorised Version language upon his writing). The poems on Canada and Australia, and the excquy on King Edward VII, are excellent in their kind, though not very memorable individually. And the gift for occasional verse is allied to the gift for two other kinds of verse in which Kipling excelled: the epigram and the hymn. Good epigrams in English are very few: and the great hymn writer is very rare. Both are extremely objective types of verse: they can and should be charged with intense feeling, but it must be a feeling that can be completely shared. They are possible to a writer so impersonal as Kipling: and I should like the reader to look attentively at the **"Epitaphs of the War"**. I call Kipling a great hymn writer on the strength of **"Recessional"**. It is a poem almost too well known to need to have the reader's attention called to it, except to point out that it is one of the poems in which something breaks through from a deeper level than that of the mind of the conscious observer of political and social affairs—something which has the true prophetic inspiration. Kipling might have been one of the most notable of hymn writers. The same gift of prophecy appears, on the political plane, in other poems, such as **"The Storm Cone"**, but nowhere with greater authority than in **"Recessional"**.

It is impossible, however, to fit all of Kipling's poems into one or another of several distinct classes. There is the poem **"Gethsemane"**, which I do not think I understand, and which is the more mysterious because of the author's having chosen to place it so early in his collected edition, since it bears the subheading '1914-1918'. And there are the poems of the later period.

The verse of the later period shows an even greater diversity than the early poems. The word 'experimentation' may be applied, and honourably applied, to the work of many poets who develop and change in maturity. . . . But just as, with Kipling, the term 'development' does not seem quite right, so neither does the term 'experimentation'. There is great variety, and there are some very remarkable innovations indeed, as in **"The Way Through The Woods"** and in **"The Harp Song of the Dane Women"** . . . and in the very fine **"Runes on Weland's Sword"**. But there were equally original inventions earlier **"Danny Deever"**); and there are too, among the later poems, some very fine ones cast in more conventional form, such as **"Cold Iron"**, **"The Land"**, **"The Children's Song"**. (pp. 14-17)

Kipling is the most elusive of subjects: no writer has been more reticent about himself, or given fewer openings for curiosity, for personal adoration or dislike. (p. 19)

One might expect that a poet who appeared to communicate so little of his private ecstasies and despairs would be dull; one might expect that a poet who had given so much of his time to the service of the political imagination would be ephemeral; one might expect that a poet so constantly occupied with the appearances of things would be shallow. We know that he is not dull, because we have all, at one time or another, by one poem or another, been thrilled; we know that he is not ephemeral, because we remember so much of what we have read. As for shallowness, that is a charge which can only be brought by those who have continued to read him only with a boyish interest. At times Kipling is not merely possessed of penetration, but almost 'possessed' of a kind of second sight. It is a trifling curiosity in itself that he was reproved for having placed in defence of the Wall a Roman Legion which historians declared had never been near it, and that later discoveries proved to have indeed been stationed there: that is the sort of thing one comes to expect of Kipling. There are deeper and darker caverns which he penetrated, whether through experience or through imagination does not matter: there are hints in **"The End of the Passage"**, and later in **"The Woman in His Life"** and **"In the Same Boat"**: oddly enough, these stories are foreshadowed by an early poem . . . , **"La Nuit Blanche"**, which introduces one image which reappears in **"The End of the Passage"**. Kipling knew something of the things which are underneath, and of the things which are beyond the frontier (pp. 19-20)

The notion of Kipling as a popular entertainer is due to the fact that his works have been popular and that they entertain. However, it is permitted to express popular views of the moment in an unpopular style: it is not approved when a man holds unpopular views and expresses them in something very readable. I do not wish to argue . . . over Kipling's early 'imperialism', because there is need to speak of the development of his views. It should be said at this point, before passing on, that Kipling is not a doctrinaire or a man with a programme. His opinions are not to be considered as the antithesis of those of Mr. H. G. Wells. Mr. Wells's imagination is one thing and his political opinions another: the latter change but do not mature. But Kipling did not, in the sense in which that activity can be ascribed to Mr. Wells, think: his aim, and his gift, is to make people see—for the first condition of right thought is right sensation—the first condition of understanding a foreign country is to smell it, as you smell India in *Kim*. If you have seen and felt truly, then if God has given you the power you may be able to think rightly. (p. 30)

[Kipling's late poems] are sometimes more obscure, because they are trying to express something more difficult than the early poems. They are the poems of a wiser and more mature writer. But they do not show any movement from 'verse' to 'poetry': they are just as instrumental as the early work, but now instruments for a matured purpose. Kipling could handle, from the beginning to the end, a considerable variety of metres and stanza forms with perfect competence; he introduces remarkable variations of his own; but as a poet he does not revolutionize. He is not one of those writers of whom one can say, that the *form* of English poetry will always be different from what it would have been if they had not written. What fundamentally differentiates his 'verse' from 'poetry' is the subordination of musical interest. Many of the poems give, indeed, judged by the ear, an impression of the mood, some are distinctly onomatopoeic: but there is a harmonics of poetry which is not merely beyond their range—it would interfere with the intention. It is possible to argue exceptions; but I am speaking of his work as a whole, and I maintain that without understanding the purpose which animates his verse as a whole, one is not prepared to understand the exceptions.

I make no apology for having used the terms 'verse' and 'poetry' in a loose way: so that while I speak of Kipling's work as verse and not as poetry, I am still able to speak of individual compositions as poems, and also to maintain that there is 'poetry' in the 'verse'. Where terminology is loose, where we have not the vocabulary for distinctions which we feel, our only precision is found in being aware of the imperfection of our tools, and of the different senses in which we are using the same words. It should be clear that when I contrast 'verse' with 'poetry' I am not, *in this context,* implying a value judgement. I do not mean, here, by verse, the work of a man who would write poetry if he could: I mean by it something which does what 'poetry' could not do. The difference which would turn Kipling's verse into poetry, does not represent a failure of deficiency: he knew perfectly well what he was doing; and from his point of view more 'poetry' would interfere

with his purpose. And I make the claim, that in speaking of Kipling we are entitled to say '*great* verse'. (pp. 34-5)

T. S. Eliot, "Rudyard Kipling," in *A Choice of Kipling's Verse Made by T. S. Eliot with an Essay on Rudyard Kipling* by Rudyard Kipling, edited by T. S. Eliot, Charles Scribner's Sons, 1943, pp. 5-36.

J. I. M. STEWART
(essay date 1966)

[An English novelist and literary scholar, Stewart has written and edited numerous works in a variety of genres. Among his scholarly texts are studies of William Shakespeare and biographies of Kipling, Thomas Hardy, and Joseph Conrad. Under the pseudonym of Michael Innes, Stewart has also written crime novels centering on academic and aristocratic characters. In the following excerpt from his critical biography of Kipling, he assesses Kipling's achievement as an author of books for children.]

The *Jungle Books* (1894-1895) were written in Vermont, and initiate a phase of Kipling's career in which he can be considered as having become a writer for children. On a superficial view, one might regard this development as being the consequence of some failure of confidence in himself as a "serious" author. He certainly did not so estimate the situation. Writing retrospectively in *Something of Myself* he has more to say about the group of children's books than about any other—and indeed it is his main point that only in a limited sense ought they to be regarded as children's books at all. Most mature readers who like Kipling will be found to agree with him in this. And the books are most keenly appreciated by those who read them first in childhood (or listened to them being read) and have then come back to them in later life. This is the road to finding those layers of significance which Kipling, in fact, claimed to have put into them.

A child's natural start is with *Just So Stories* (1902), which is above everything else a nursery book. Nothing in English is more unchallengeably the work of one who possessed the art of telling stories to children, and who enjoyed exercising it. The narrative style, seemingly so naïve and spontaneous, represents in fact one of the most notable triumphs of Kipling's craft. And here he had to overcome a bad or unreflecting habit which he had caught from the taste of the age: that of introducing into writing for or about children a sentimental convention of baby talk. In the *Just So Stories* the element of misapplied, invented and oddly transformed words renders a wholly different effect. It is felt from the start as part of the ritual of a special or secret language which the narrator shares with his hearers, and it is associated with infancy only in the sense of wonderfully suggesting the infancy of the world, when all creatures and things were pristine and plastic still. The style is, moreover, and in a degree varying from story to story and from place to place within a story, incantatory and therefore full of a strong magic; and it is capable (as in **"The Sing-Song of Old Man Kangaroo"**) of compassing rhythmical effects which are totally new.

The *Just So Stories* are often compared with Lewis Carroll's *Alice's Adventures in Wonderland* and *Through the Looking-Glass* as the greatest English achievements in writing for young children. Carroll shares with Kipling the faculty of appealing to children and adults alike. With each there is a certain hit-or-miss element to be observed, since there are some children and adults upon whom the magic of one, or both, fails to work. Each inhabits what must be called a real world, although it is certainly not an actual world. Carroll's is the world of dream, although of dream at once drastically censored and cunningly intellectualized in the interest of a rather egg-headed Victorian nursery. Kipling's is the world of myth.

Most of the *Just So Stories*, indeed, are myths of one particular kind: the kind technically known as aetiological. An aetiological myth is one evolved—generally in a more or less "primitive" society—to explain and render intelligible some existing state of affairs which in itself perplexes and challenges the human spirit. The most famous of all aetiological myths is that of the Creation and Fall of Man as it is recounted in the Book of Genesis. In this, answers to nearly all the great riddles are bound together within a single narrative satisfying to the imagination—and satisfying, too, to the intellect working within the limits of a "pre-scientific" cultural context. The *Just So Stories* are little myths solving little riddles: how the camel got anything so strange as a hump, and the elephant anything so strange as a trunk. It is true that, to be quite accurate, we must qualify the description of these stories as myths. They have been invented for the satisfaction not of a primitive people but of modern children, who are "primitive" only in the metaphorical sense that their intellectual development does, to some extent, recapitulate the course of human evolution. This is why the stories are made to hover—and, again, it is a miracle of craft—between a level of fantasy and a level of simple conviction. So in one aspect they are like make-believe games, such as children love. In another, they are an introduction to one of the great literary kinds—a kind reflecting something radical in the development of the human imagination. To appreciate *Just So Stories* is to establish a basis for appreciating *Paradise Lost* or *Moby Dick*.

The fame of *The Jungle Book* and *The Second Jungle Book*—the most widely popular of all Kipling's writings—is owing to their central figure, Mowgli, the child nurtured by wolves, who survives and grows to manhood as Master of the Jungle. Mowgli's origin (as a literary creation, that is) is attended by some obscurity, and it is best to begin with the last that we hear about him. This is in **"In the Rukh"** (*Many Inventions*), a story designed to be entirely realistic, and quite certainly not written for young readers. (pp. 136-39)

What is interesting about **"In the Rukh"** is the entire absence of the magic which the *Jungle Books* were going to create. Kipling has not yet glimpsed what material he has under his hand; this Mowgli is an implausible mixture of Noble Savage, Indian native properly respectful of the raj, and a godling strayed out of Greek mythology in a manner rather reminiscent of some of the more whimsical short stories of Mr. E. M. Forster. Mowgli plays a flute, "as it might have been the song of some wandering wood-god." This last association is emphasized; "the hint of the wood-god was not to be mistaken," we are told a few pages later.

"In the Rukh" was almost certainly written before Kipling had conceived the Mowgli stories proper, but in its published form it may embody revisions designed to make it fit in with the evolving series. As it is, Mowgli's story seems to have been developed without much planning. Taking the two *Jungle Books* together, he appears in eight out of fifteen stories—including the first, which begins with his being adopted by wolf parents, and the last, which tells of his final departure from the world of the beasts. That there is true imaginative coherence between the Mowgli stories proper appears as soon as we try to set this last of them, **"The Spring Running,"** in any relationship with **"In the Rukh."** The Mowgli of **"In the Rukh"** walks into the story with nothing much behind him except (with an obvious effect of paradox) certain unusual educational advantages. "Hard exercise, the best of good eating, and baths whenever he felt in the least hot or dusty, had given him strength and growth far beyond his age." He is a cross between a Wordsworthian child of nature and a boy scout. He walks out of the story at the other end in the company of a nice girl and with the intention of settling down. He knows all the answers—just as the uninspired Kipling always did. The Mowgli of **"The Spring Running,"** on the contrary, knows neither his world nor himself with any certainty, because he is a human spirit in the throes of some painful and mysterious process of growth. It is Spring. "The year turns," Bagheera the Black Panther tells him. "The Jungle goes forward. The Time of New Talk is near." Mowgli must have heard this before. But now he is on the verge of manhood, and there faces him a hard truth, obscurely seen. A boy may run with the Jungle People, but "Man goes to Man." His old companions do not reject him, but—this Spring, he notices it—they come tardily at his summons, having concerns which can be none of his. Yet all this, and the mere surface solution of his problem in the last pages of the story, make too finite and identifiable the occasion of the unhappiness that has come to Mowgli. Something else is elusively present.

This is a characteristic of all the Mowgli stories. All are moral fables—even to the extent of sometimes making us feel that Mowgli is over-lavishly provided with tutors, and is rather constantly having to put up with what the hymn calls Instruction's warning Voice. But this is not, in fact, oppressive—perhaps because there is always some hinted further significance which we have to strain to catch. Take, for example, the monkey-folk, the *Bandar-log.* They stand for something outside themselves, answer to something in our own experience which we are not proud of. But just what? Here, and in some other places, the fable beckons us to territory where we must think for ourselves. And there is one puzzle bigger than all the others. It is what the books mean when they talk about "the Law." (pp. 140-42)

If we wish to criticize the whole conception we shall probably say that, here in the context of the *Jungle Books,* Kipling is casting the impressive disguise of authentic moral law over certain aspects of animal behaviour instinctively evolved to secure the survival of a species. To test the validity of this criticism we should have to enter deeply into Kipling's theory of society. He certainly believed that moral ideas can be derived only from experience, but that as there is much that is common and universal in all human experience so is there a common and universal law lying beneath all the variations of racial and national cultures. It is a law codified in custom, and its recognition and preservation is the distinguishing principle of civilization. Peoples or societies or individuals ignoring "the Law" thereby diminish themselves—becoming (in the famous and unfortunately ambiguous phrase in "Recessional") "lesser breeds." To show a wolf pack as within "the Law," and a chatter of monkeys as outside it, is simply to use the method of fable to enforce the depth and reach of the idea. But to account for the appeal of the *Jungle Books* we have to go back to Kipling's almost unexampled command of the sense of wonder; his power to bring, as from very far away, reports which validate themselves in the telling, so that our disbelief is suspended in the face of whole new ranges of experience. (pp. 143-44)

J. I. M. Stewart, in his *Rudyard Kipling,* Dodd, Mead & Company, 1966, 245 p.

ROBERT F. MOSS
(essay date 1982)

[Moss is an American educator, critic, and novelist. In the following excerpt, he discusses the fiction Kipling wrote between 1888 and 1901, focusing on the ways in which the adolescent perceptions and behavior of the male protagonists gradually develop into a mature recognition and acceptance of the world.]

[The works Kipling produced between 1888 and 1901] can be studied very advantageously as an organic phase in Kipling's career; indeed, there are compelling reasons for doing so. Not only do these works share an abundance of common attitudes, characterizations and motifs, but they are further linked by a discernible, though uneven, maturational process in which Kipling's command of his materials, initially shaky and unsatisfying, grew impressively, reaching a distinct pinnacle in *Kim.* (p. xiv)

Soldiers Three, examined in retrospect, reveals the crude beginnings of the most important creative period in Kipling's life and of Kipling's most characteristic subject-matter. The reader who moves chronologically through Kipling's tales, even if he is wholly ignorant of the later, explicitly adolescent stories, is apt to regard the adventurous trio of *Soldiers Three* as boys in men's garb. Their behaviour—the *ipso facto* rebelliousness against authority, the boisterous swagger, the passion for excitement, the frequent fits of hysterical giggling—correspond to a generally accepted view of adolescence, one which is substantiated by scientific treatises on the subject. It is clear that the soldiers have also passed through a rigidly prescribed process of acculturation which has its less rigid analogue in the lives of most adolescents. One facet of this acculturation is simply the training the soldiers undergo in order to become first-class fighting men; the other is the confusion of selfhood they experience, the conflict between the two vastly different cultures to which they belong simultaneously—the civilian realm back home and the military world that they presently inhabit. Kipling, however, devotes little space and less energy to developing this conflict and though in the end he puts his soldiers back in mufti, there is no suggestion that any greater maturity has been gained in the process; rather, Mulvaney, the leader of the clique, is seen wallowing in sentimental longing for the good old military days—a mood that Kipling seems to approve of.

The Light That Failed offers another unintentionally adolescent hero, Dick Heldar, whose conduct and values are strikingly similar to that of the soldiers. The same immature traits are prominent in his activities. In other respects, though, *Light* is an advance over *Soldiers:* the learning process is given greater emphasis, as is the identity quest. The two worlds that Dick must choose between—East and West—are a principal source of tension in the book. It is not difficult to isolate the personal forces in Kipling's life that lifted this dichotomy from its peripheral status in *Soldiers* to its primacy in *Light.* The psychological turbulence of Kipling's two years in London, characterized by piercing conflicts, left him with an artistic vision that was conceived in dualities. In *Light* the polarities are athrob with authentic, if unbalanced, emotion. As in *Soldiers,* however, these antitheses lack intellectual interest and offer only intermittent dramatic power because the conflict is weighted too strongly in favour of the East, with its martial romantic ideals, rather than the West, home of the peaceful and the mundane. Dick's flamboyant death, fully endorsed by Kipling, is a refusal to leave boyhood. Still, it is evident from the fuller attention Kipling devoted to acculturation in *Light,* as compared to *Soldiers,* that he was moving towards an intentional rather than an unwitting treatment of adolescence.

He reached this more artistically rewarding stage in the Mowgli stories, where his hero—who exhibited many of the same qualities as Dick and Mulvaney—was finally a boy in name as well as in spirit. Moreover, Kipling brought the same intensity to the acculturation theme that he had in *Light,* while refining it in certain ways. Examining his own mixed cultural heritage in the serenity and objectivity of Vermont, Kipling achieved a measure of detachment he only infrequently attained in his work. Then, too, nostalgia over his lost boyhood in Bombay imbued the tales with a wistful charm and mythic otherworldliness that nullified any questions of psychological or social validity.

Like Dick, Mowgli suffers considerable emotional stress over his divided loyalties—to the jungle, on the one hand; to the man pack, on the other. When he is at last compelled to rejoin the human community we are conscious not only of a racial philosophy that is inevitable in Kipling ("East is East," etc.) but also of a maturation process that has brought Mowgli to the gates of manhood. Although the clash between alien cultures is as simplistic here as in *Light* and *Soldiers,* it is defensible on two grounds—(1) the mythic, fairytale atmosphere of the jungle, which permits a relaxation of the standards of realistic fiction, and (2) the fact that this time the hero's choice is specifically related to his maturation and that the world he opts for, though drab and offensive in many ways, is, in the context of the stories, a necessary concomitant of growing up. This way lies maturity, Mowgli realizes.

Captains Courageous, the product of Kipling's American experience, continued most of the patterns Kipling had been working with since *Soldiers;* it also presented another boy hero, Harvey, and perpetuated as well the general adolescent pattern that reached back to *Soldiers.* Harvey's boyish behaviour and brutal education are the logical descendants of similar elements in Kipling's earlier efforts. In *Captains,* however, he concentrated on broadening and deepening one aspect of the adolescent paradigm—the hero's antinomic worlds. The two societies of *Captains* (again East and West, but this time Eastern and Western America) are handled with greater sophistication than Kipling had evinced previously. The New England fishing culture, with its noble, weather-beaten virtues, is presented eulogistically and warmly, without any sign of ambivalence or irony. The American West, on the other hand, has three separate layers apparently: the pampered, effete world of Mrs Cheyne and the unconverted Harvey; the rugged, self-reliant professionalism of Cheyne, Sr (in many respects a mirror image of the Gloucester society); the free-wheeling expansionism and robust spirit of the West, which Kipling admires. The relationship between the ostensibly antipodal cultures of *Captains* is explored with a complexity that is missing from the other works we have looked at. The book is Kipling's ode to America, while he was still tucked away snugly in the hills around Brattleboro; soon the ode would be transformed into a hate-drenched philippic. Unfortunately, even at this stage Kipling's depiction of the American scene is expressed in sociological rather than literary terms. Unlike Mowgli, Harvey experiences very little internal confusion or turmoil over conflicting societal claims. He is instantly converted to life on the *We're Here* and then instantly severed from it at the end. In between, his mind, when we are allowed to look into it at all, is mostly occupied with the intricacies of codfishing. Harvey is perhaps the least dynamic of all Kipling's adolescent heroes.

Stalky & Co., though lively and enjoyable, brought nothing new to Kipling's rapidly growing conception of boyhood. The stories, mostly written in the last year or two of the nineteenth century, provide an excellent compendium of the various traits Kipling assigned to adolescents. Stalky and his friends scheme against the adult establishment, play pranks, forge an impenetrable clique, create a private language, seek out excitement and adventure and reveal a mixture of overt cynicism and covert idealism. Moreover, the education, official and unofficial, that they receive at the College is yet another variant of the training process that is crucial to adolescence in Kipling's other studies of the subject. Yet in *Stalky* Kipling ignores completely the search for identity that is so integral to *Captains,* the Mowgli stories and *Light* and peripherally important to *Soldiers.* The explanation is simple enough. Kipling had set himself the task of celebrating a kind of boyhood—life at his alma mater, the militarily oriented United Services College—whose single-mindedness of training and direction allowed for no uncertainty of self, no divided loyalties. His own recollections of schoolboy days were joyful, misty-eyed, idealized; he looked back on a homogeneous environment with no serious divisions of temperament, culture or outlook. With *Stalky* Kipling moved neither forward nor backward; he merely held his ground.

Two years after the publication of *Stalky & Co.*, however, Kipling's myth of boyhood arrived at its culmination. Reunited with his parents and finding at last a permanent home in the English countryside, Kipling was able to create a final, splendid testament to the India of his youth. In *Kim,* the adolescent strain, cultivated from Mulvaney and his friends through *Stalky & Co.*, reached its most dramatically successful form. More than any of Kipling's other boys—certainly more than his adolescent men—Kim comes across as he was intended. Kim's instinct for where adventure is to be found, his gift for self-preservation in the midst of adversity, his game-playing, his love of professionalism— all these are superbly rendered. He receives his education in the streets of India, in an Anglo-Indian school, in the secret training grounds of the Great Game. Fundamentally, it is the same education that Kipling's other heroes receive, but here there is less emphasis on brutalization of the learner and more on the joy of learning. In addition, Kim is the only one of Kipling's heroes who is educated both indirectly, through sink-or-swim immersion in reality (like Dick and Cheyne, Sr) and directly, through formalized pedagogy (like Mowgli, Stalky and the soldiers). But the real profundity of *Kim* lies in Kipling's handling of the search for identity. Always uncertain as to his real destiny, Kim's odysseys are all, in some sense, a quest to find his true self, an attempt to assess the conflicting demands of two radically different ways of life. In the first two-thirds of the book, the clash Kim feels is between his Western heritage and his Eastern upbringing. In the lat-ter portion of the novel, however, the conflict alters considerably; it is no longer a choice between East and West, but between the Game, which is both Eastern and Western in nature, and the Search, which is exclusively Eastern. At virtually all points in *Kim* the conflicts are viewed through the hero's troubled soul; never are they merely painted backdrops.

There is no doubt that *Kim* is the most intimate revelation of Kipling's inner self, as much a spiritual autobiography as Wordsworth's "Prelude"; the book is an attempt to seize all the jagged, confusing, remarkable fragments of his psychic life and incorporate them into a great fictional kaleidoscope. But the brilliance of the novel may have more to do with its depth than its breadth, with the excavations Kipling was able to make into his own soul. There he examined the warring forces of his personality with the longest, most penetrating scrutiny he ever gave them. Through Kim, he probed his dual attachments to the life of action and the life of art; to progress and permanence; to Eastern mysticism and Western pragmatism; to sensuality and asceticism; to the hard-nosed Yorkshire naturalism of his father and the leaping Celtic poetry of his mother.

Yielding himself up fully to his art at last, Kipling succeeded in combining the cultural complexity of *Captains* with the psychological depth of the Mowgli stories. His achievement was further enhanced by the sympathetic, loving picture of the Indians in *Kim,* proof against the blanket accusations of racism that his works have always had to face. Though Kipling went on to create other magnificent works in various modes (**"Dayspring Mishandled"** and **"The Gardener"**, for example), *Kim* marks the end of the most fruitful and best remembered phase of his career, a journey toward artistic fulfilment that began with the inauspicious *Soldiers Three* and ended with this remarkable novel. (pp. 142-47).

Robert F. Moss, in his *Rudyard Kipling and the Fiction of Adolescence*, St. Martin's Press, 1982, 165 p.

SOURCES FOR FURTHER STUDY

Carrington, Charles. *Rudyard Kipling: His Life and Work.* London: Macmillan & Co., 1955, 549 p.

> Seminal biography of Kipling that links his life with his writings.

Gilbert, Elliot L. *The Good Kipling: Studies in the Short Story.* Oberlin: Ohio University Press, 1970, 216 p.

> Analysis of Kipling's approach to the short story.

Pritchett, V. S. "Kipling's Short Stories." In his *The Living Novel and Later Appreciations*, pp. 175-82. New York: Random House, 1964.

> Characterizes Kipling as "the only considerable English writer of fiction to have been popular in the most popular sense and to excite the claim to genius."

Shahane, Vasant A. *Rudyard Kipling: Activist and Artist.* Carbondale: Southern Illinois University Press, 1973, 157 p.

Aims at "detailed textual analyses and explication" of Kipling's fiction. Shahane focuses particular attention on *Kim,* which he considers Kipling's masterpiece.

Stewart, J. I. M. "Kipling." In his *Eight Modern Readers,* pp. 223-93. Oxford: Clarendon Press, 1963.
Biographical essay in which Stewart offers a balanced appraisal of Kipling's short story canon.

Tompkins, J. M. S. *The Art of Rudyard Kipling.* London: Methuen & Co., 1959, 277 p.
Study of Kipling's major themes.

Charles Lamb

1775-1834

(Also wrote under pseudonym Elia) English essayist, critic, poet, dramatist, and novelist.

INTRODUCTION

A well-known literary figure in nineteenth-century England, Lamb is chiefly remembered today for his "Elia" essays, a sequence renowned for its witty, idiosyncratic treatment of everyday subjects. Through the persona of "Elia," Lamb employed a rambling narrative technique to achieve what many critics regard as the epitome of the familiar essay style. Lamb's elegant prose has delighted generations of readers, and his literary criticism testifies to his versatility and perceptiveness. However, since their first appearance in print, Lamb's opinions on drama have been the subject of controversy. Though recent commentators affirm Lamb's importance in the history of criticism, they fault his unsystematic critical method. Despite these reservations, most scholars agree that Lamb's writings on drama helped bring about a revival of interest in the Elizabethan playwrights in England during the early part of the nineteenth century.

Lamb was born in London, the youngest of seven children, of whom only three survived into adulthood. His father was a law clerk who worked in the Inner Temple, one of the courts of London, and wrote poetry in his spare time. Almost nothing is known about Lamb's mother. In 1782, Lamb was accepted as a student at Christ's Hospital, a London school for the children of impoverished families. He excelled in his studies, especially in English literature, but the seven years away from home proved lonely. Later, Lamb wrote that his solitude was relieved only by his friendship with a fellow student, Samuel Taylor Coleridge. At this time Lamb also began to experiment with verse. Since his family's poverty prevented him from furthering his education, Lamb took a job immediately upon graduation. Working first as a clerk, he became an accountant at the East India Company, a prestigious trade firm, where he remained until retirement in 1825.

During his career there he read widely and corresponded frequently with such friends as Coleridge, William Wordsworth, and Robert Southey. It was at Coleridge's insistence that Lamb's first sonnets were included in Coleridge's collection *Poems on Various Subjects,* published in 1796.

Near the end of 1795, Lamb collapsed and committed himself to a hospital for the mentally ill. Though biographers are uncertain as to the exact cause of his breakdown, they believe it might have been precipitated by unrequited love. Adding to his misfortune, Lamb's sister, Mary, who was mentally ill, stabbed her mother to death in 1796—an event that completely transformed Lamb's life. His father, nearly senile, and his brother, John, wanted to commit Mary permanently to an asylum, but Lamb succeeded in obtaining her release and devoted himself to her care. From then on, Mary enjoyed long intervals of sanity and productivity as a writer, but these were inevitably punctuated by breakdowns. Biographers attribute Lamb's bouts of depression and excessive drinking to the stress of worrying about Mary, with whom he was very close. During her lucid periods, however, she and Charles lived peacefully and even adopted a child.

In 1820, the editor of the *London Magazine* invited Lamb to contribute regularly to the periodical. Lamb, eager to supplement his meager income, wrote some pieces under the pseudonym of "Elia" for the magazine. With the overwhelming success of these essays, Lamb became one of the most admired men in London. He and Mary presided over a weekly open house, which was attended by his many literary friends including Coleridge, William Hazlitt, Leigh Hunt, and Henry Crabb Robinson. Besides his diverse friendships, Lamb found his chief pleasure in writing, which consumed his evenings and holidays. After his retirement from the East India Company, he devoted more time to his favorite occupation. Lamb was still at the peak of his popularity as an essayist when he died suddenly from an infection in 1834.

Lamb's first published works were his sonnets, which critics praised for their simple diction and delicate poetic manner, but he quickly discovered that his talent and inclinations lay elsewhere. His first serious work in prose, *A Tale of Rosamund Gray and Old Blind Margaret,* appeared in 1798. A short experimental novel, *Rosamund Gray* displays the influence of Henry Mackenzie and Laurence Sterne. Lamb, an avid theater-goer, decided to try his hand at drama next; however, *John Woodvil* (1802), a tragedy in the Elizabethan style, was neither a popular nor critical success. Most reviewers criticized the play for its archaic style and static structure, but a few praised Lamb's clear dialogue and effective handling of characterization. His next two projects also testify to his love of Elizabethan literature. In 1807, he and Mary collaborated on *Tales from Shakespeare,* a prose version of Shakespeare's plays intended for children. The *Tales* were generally well received and the Lambs were commended for expanding the scope of children's literature in England, though a few critics regarded the *Tales* as distorted renderings of the plays. That same year, Lamb completed his *Specimens of English Dramatic Poets, Who Lived About the Time of Shakespeare,* an anthology that included selections from the plays of such Elizabethan dramatists as Christopher Marlowe, John Webster, George Chapman, and Thomas Middleton. Since many of these works were previously unavailable to readers, Lamb's anthology was an important reference source. Each author entry was supplemented with explanatory notes that are now considered his most important critical work. Lamb further elaborated on his views in "On the Tragedies of Shakespeare Considered with Reference to Their Fitness for Stage Presentation." In this essay, he argued that the best qualities of Shakespeare's plays can be fully appreciated only through reading; according to Lamb, stage performances often diminish the plays' meaning, and individual performers often misinterpret Shakespeare's intended characterizations.

Though he initially achieved prominence as a drama critic, Lamb's greatest fame came through his "Elia" essays, written between 1820 and 1825. When *Elia: Essays Which Have Appeared under That Signature in the "London Magazine"* was published in 1823, Lamb was already one of the most popular writers in England. He composed sketches in the familiar essay form, a style popularized by Michel Eyquem de Montaigne, Robert Burton, and Sir Thomas Browne. Characterized by a personal tone, narrative ease, and a wealth of literary allusions, the "Elia" essays enjoyed unparalleled success. Critics were enchanted with Lamb's highly wrought style and his blending of humor and pathos. Never didactic, the essays treat ordinary subjects in a nostalgic, fanciful way, and one of their chief attractions for readers of both the nineteenth and twentieth centuries is the gradual revelation of "Elia's" personality.

Lamb's importance as a critic has been much debated. Some scholars, most recently René Wellek, have commented on his literary prejudices and his lack of consistent critical methodology. Lamb's thesis in "On the Tragedies of Shakespeare" is considered especially controversial. Because Lamb theorized that Shakespeare's works were best unperformed, such critics as T. S. Eliot held Lamb personally responsible for what Eliot termed the detrimental distinction between drama and literature in the English language. Conversely, such diverse critics as Henry Nelson Coleridge, Algernon Charles Swinburne, and E. M. W. Tillyard have asserted Lamb's historical importance and hailed his *Specimens* as a critical landmark. No such controversy surrounds the "Elia" essays, and they have been universally extolled by reviewers since their initial appearance. Although some scholars considered his style imitative of earlier English writers, the majority now accept that quality as one of "Elia's" distinctive hallmarks, along with his fondness for the obscure and other idiosyncrasies. Stylistic studies by Walter Pater, Arthur Symons, A. G. van Kranendonk, and Donald H. Reiman explore diverse aspects of Lamb's artistry as evidenced in the essays. Both early and recent critics, including Thomas De Quincey, Bertram Jessup, and Gerald Monsman, have probed the "Elia" persona—proof that readers' curiosity about Lamb's personality

has not waned. In one of the most recent studies of Lamb, Monsman has written that the creation of "Elia" was an "exorcism" of his troubled family's past. While most critics acknowledge Lamb's contribution to the rediscovery of Elizabethan drama in nineteenth-century England, his reputation rests on the "Elia" essays, whose humor and spontaneity continue to capture the imaginations of modern readers.

(For further information about Lamb's life and works, see *Nineteenth-Century Literature Criticism*, Vol. 10 and *Something about the Author*, Vol. 17.)

CRITICAL COMMENTARY

WILLIAM HAZLITT
(essay date 1825)

[Hazlitt was an English critic and journalist. In the following excerpt from an essay first published in 1825, he offers an appraisal of Lamb's literary style.]

Mr. Lamb has raked among the dust and cobwebs of a . . . remote period, has exhibited specimens of curious relics, and pored over moth-eaten, decayed manuscripts for the benefit of the more inquisitive and discerning part of the public. Antiquity after a time has the grace of novelty, as old fashions revived are mistaken for new ones; and a certain quaintness and singularity of style is an agreeable relief to the smooth and insipid monotony of modern composition.

Mr. Lamb has succeeded, not by conforming to the *Spirit of the Age,* but in opposition to it. He does not march boldly along with the crowd, but steals off the pavement to pick his way in the contrary direction. He prefers *bye-ways* to *highways.* When the full tide of human life pours along to some festive show, to some pageant of a day, Elia would stand on one side to look over an old book-stall, or stroll down some deserted pathway in search of a pensive description over a tottering doorway, or some quaint device in architecture, illustrative of embryo art and ancient manners. Mr. Lamb has the very soul of an antiquarian, as this implies a reflecting humanity; the film of the past hovers forever before him. He is shy, sensitive, the reverse of every thing coarse, vulgar, obtrusive, and *common-place.* He would fain 'shuffle off this mortal coil'; and his spirit clothes itself in the garb of elder time, homelier, but more durable. He is borne along with no pompous paradoxes, shines in no glittering tinsel of a fashionable

phraseology, is neither fop nor sophist. He has none of the turbulence or froth of new-fangled opinions. His style runs pure and clear, though it may often take an underground course, or be conveyed through old-fashioned conduit-pipes. Mr. Lamb does not court popularity, nor strut in gaudy plumes, but shrinks from every kind of ostentatious and obvious pretension into the retirement of his own mind. (pp. 262-63)

This gentleman is not one of those who pay all their homage to the prevailing idol: he thinks that

New-born gauds are made and moulded of things past,

nor does he

Give to dust that is a little gilt
More laud than gilt o'er-dusted.

His convictions 'do not in broad rumour lie,' nor are they 'set off to the world in the glistering foil' of fashion, but 'live and breathe aloft in those pure eyes, and perfect judgment of all-seeing *time.*'

Mr. Lamb rather affects and is tenacious of the obscure and remote, of that which rests on its own intrinsic and silent merit; which scorns all alliance or even the suspicion of owing any thing to noisy clamour, to the glare of circumstances. There is a fine tone of *chiaroscuro,* a moral perspective in his writings. He delights to dwell on that which is fresh to the eye of memory; he yearns after and covets what soothes the frailty of human nature. That touches him most nearly which is withdrawn to a certain distance, which verges on the borders of oblivion: that piques and provokes his fancy most, which is hid from a superficial glance. That which, though gone by, is still remembered, is in his view more genuine, and has given more 'vital signs that

---

Principal Works

Poems on Various Subjects [with Samuel Taylor Coleridge] (poetry) 1796

A Tale of Rosamund Gray and Old Blind Margaret (novel) 1798

John Woodvil (drama) 1802

Tales from Shakespeare [with Mary Lamb] (short stories) 1807

Specimens of English Dramatic Poets, Who Lived About the Time of Shakspeare [editor] (dramas) 1808

Elia: Essays Which Have Appeared under That Signature in the "London Magazine" [as Elia] (essays) 1823

The Last Essays of Elia [as Elia] (essays) 1833

*The Works of Charles and Mary Lamb. 7 vols. (essays, novel, short stories, poetry, and dramas) 1903-05

The Letters of Charles Lamb. 3 vols. (letters) 1935

*This work includes the essays "On the Genius of Hogarth," "On The Tragedies of Shakespeare Considered with Reference to Their Fitness for Stage Presentation," and "On the Artificial Comedy of the Last Century."

---

it will live,' than a thing of yesterday, that may be forgotten to-morrow. Death has in this sense the spirit of life in it; and the shadowy has to our author something substantial in it. Ideas savour most of reality in his mind; or rather his imagination loiters on the edge of each, and a page of his writings recals to our fancy the *stranger* on the grate, fluttering in its dusky tenuity, with its idle superstition and hospitable welcome!

Mr. Lamb has a distaste to new faces, to new books, to new buildings, to new customs. He is shy of all imposing appearances, of all assumptions of self-importance, of all adventitious ornaments, of all mechanical advantages, even to a nervous excess. It is not merely that he does not rely upon, or ordinarily avail himself of them; he holds them in abhorrence; he utterly abjures and discards them and places a great gulph between him and them. He disdains all the vulgar artifices of authorship, all the cant of criticism and helps to notoriety. He has no grand swelling theories to attract the visionary and the enthusiast, no passing topics to allure the thoughtless and the vain. He evades the present; he mocks the future. His affections revert to, and settle on the past; but then even this must have something personal and local in it to interest him deeply and thoroughly. He pitches his tent in the suburbs of existing manners, brings down the account of character to the few straggling remains of the last genera-

tion, seldom ventures beyond the bills of mortality, and occupies that nice point between egotism and disinterested humanity. No one makes the tour of our southern metropolis, or describes the manners of the last age, so well as Mr. Lamb: with so fine and yet so formal an air: with such vivid obscurity: with such arch piquancy, such picturesque quaintness, such smiling pathos.

How admirably he has sketched the former inmates of the South-Sea House; what 'fine fretwork he makes of their double and single entries'! With what a firm, yet subtle pencil he has embodied *Mrs. Battle's Opinions on Whist!* How notably he embalms a battered *beau;* how delightfully an amour, that was cold forty years ago, revives in his pages! With what well-disguised humour he introduces us to his relations, and how freely he serves up his friends! Certainly, some of his portraits are *fixtures,* and will do to hang up as lasting and lively emblems of human infirmity. Then there is no one who has so sure an ear for 'the chimes at midnight,' not even excepting Mr. Justice Shallow; nor could Master Silence himself take his 'cheese and pippins' with a more significant and satisfactory air. With what a gusto Mr. Lamb describes the Inns and Courts of law, the Temple and Gray's-Inn, as if he had been a student there for the last two hundred years, and had been as well acquainted with the person of Sir Francis Bacon as he is with his portrait or writings! It is hard to say whether St. John's Gate is connected with more intense and authentic associations in his mind, as part of old London Wall, or as the frontispiece (time out of mind) of the *Gentleman's Magazine.* He haunts Watling-street like a gentle spirit; the avenues to the playhouses are thick with panting recollections; and Christ's-Hospital still breathes the balmy breath of infancy in his description of it! Whittington and his Cat are a fine hallucination for Mr. Lamb's historic Muse, and we believe he never heartily forgave a certain writer who took the subject of Guy Faux out of his hands. The streets of London are his fairy-land, teeming with wonder, with life and interest to his retrospective glance, as it did to the eager eye of childhood; he has contrived to weave its tritest traditions into a bright and endless romance!

Mr. Lamb's taste in books is also fine; and it is peculiar. It is not the worse for the little *idiosyncrasy.* He does not go deep into the Scotch Novels; but he is at home in Smollett or Fielding. He is little read in Junius or Gibbon; but no man can give a better account of Burton's *Anatomy of Melancholy,* or Sir Thomas Brown's *Urn-Burial,* or Fuller's *Worthies,* or John Bunyan's *Holy War.* No one is more unimpressible to a specious declamation; no one relishes a recondite beauty more. His admiration of Shakespear and Milton does not make him despise Pope; and he can read Parnell with patience and Gay with delight. His taste in French and German literature is somewhat defective; nor has he made much progress in the science of Political Economy or other abstruse studies, though he has read vast folios of controversial divinity, merely for the sake of the intricacy of style, and to save himself the pain of thinking.

Mr. Lamb is a good judge of prints and pictures. His admiration of Hogarth does credit to both, particularly when it is considered that Leonardo da Vinci is his next greatest favourite, and that his love of the *actual* does not proceed from a want of taste for the *ideal*. His worst fault is an over-eagerness of enthusiasm, which occasionally makes him take a surfeit of his highest favourites. Mr. Lamb excels in familiar conversation almost as much as in writing, when his modesty does not overpower his self-possession. He is as little of a proser as possible; but he *blurts* out the finest wit and sense in the world. He keeps a good deal in the background at first, till some excellent conceit pushes him forward, and then he abounds in whim and pleasantry. There is a primitive simplicity and self-denial about his manners and a Quakerism in his personal appearance, which is, however, relieved by a fine Titian head, full of dumb eloquence! (pp. 264-67)

The style of the *Essays of Elia* is liable to the charge of a certain *mannerism.* His sentences are cast in the mould of old authors; his expressions are borrowed from them; but his feelings and observations are genuine and original, taken from actual life or from his own breast; and he may be said (if any one can) 'to have coined his heart for *jests,*' and to have split his brain for fine distinctions! Mr. Lamb, from the peculiarity of his exterior and address as an author, would probably never have made his way by detached and independent efforts; but, fortunately for himself and others, he has taken advantage of the Periodical Press, where he has been stuck into notice; and the texture of his compositions is assuredly fine enough to bear the broadest glare of popularity that has hitherto shone upon them. (p. 268)

William Hazlitt, "Elia—Geoffrey Crayon," in his *The Spirit of the Age; or, Contemporary Portraits,* 1825. Reprint by Oxford University Press, 1947, pp. 262-71.

WALTER H. PATER

(essay date 1878)

[A nineteenth-century essayist, novelist, and critic, Pater was one of the foremost English proponents of aestheticism. In the following excerpt, he evaluates Lamb as a humorist, praising the tone of intimacy and self-revelation in his works.]

[In the making of prose Charles Lamb] realises the prin-

ciple of art for its own sake, as completely as Keats in the making of verse. And, working thus ever close to the concrete, to the details, great or small, of actual things, books, persons, and with no part of them blurred to his vision by the intervention of mere abstract theories, he has reached an enduring moral effect also, in a sort of boundless sympathy. Unoccupied, as he might seem, with great matters, he is in immediate contact with what is real, especially in its caressing littleness, that littleness in which there is much of the whole woeful heart of things, and meets it more than half-way with a perfect understanding of it. What sudden, unexpected touches of pathos in him!—bearing witness how the sorrow of humanity, the *Weltschmerz,* the constant aching of its wounds, is ever present with him; but what a gift also for the enjoyment of life in its subtleties, of enjoyment actually refined by the need of some thoughtful economies and making the most of things! Little arts of happiness he is ready to teach to others. The quaint remarks of children which another would scarcely have heard, he preserves,—little flies in the priceless amber of his Attic wit,—and has his **"Praise of chimney-sweepers,"** . . . valuing carefully their white teeth, and fine enjoyment of white sheets in stolen sleep at Arundel Castle, as he tells the story, anticipating something of the mood of our deep humourists of the last generation. His simple mother-pity for those who suffer by accident, or unkindness of nature, blindness, for instance, or fateful disease of mind, like his sister's, has something primitive in its bigness; and on behalf of ill-used animals he is early in composing a **"Pity's Gift."**

And if, in deeper or more superficial senses, the dead *do* care at all for their name and fame, then how must the souls of Shakspere and Webster have been stirred, after so long converse with things that stopped their ears above and below the soil, at his exquisite appreciations of them; the souls of Titian and of Hogarth also; for, what has not been observed so generally as the excellence of his literary criticism, Charles Lamb is a fine critic of painting also. It was as loyal, self-forgetful work for others, for Shakspere's self first, and then for Shakspere's readers, that this too was done; he has the true scholar's way of forgetting himself in his subject. For though "defrauded," as we saw, in his young years, "of the sweet food of academic institution," he is yet essentially a scholar, and all his work mainly retrospective, as I said; his own sorrows, affections, perceptions, being alone real to him of the present. "I cannot make these present times," he says once, "present to me."

Above all, he becomes not merely an expositor, permanently valuable, but for Englishmen almost the discoverer of the old English drama. "The book is such as I am glad there should be," he modestly says of the *Specimens of English Dramatic Poets who lived about the time of Shakspere:* to which, however, he adds in a series of notes the very quintessence of criticism, the choicest aromas and savours of Elizabethan poetry being sorted and stored here with a sort of delicate intellectual epicureanism, which has had the effect of winning for these, then almost forgotten poets, one generation after another of enthusiastic students. Could he but have known how fresh a source of culture he was evoking there for other generations, all through those years, in which, a little wistfully, he would harp on the limitation of his time by business, and sigh for a better fortune in regard of literary opportunities!

To feel strongly the charm of an old poet or moralist, the literary charm of Burton, for instance, or Quarles, or Lady Newcastle; and then to interpret that charm, to convey it to others,—he seeming to himself but to hand on to others, in mere humble ministration, that of which for them he is really the creator,—that, is the way of his criticism; cast off in a stray letter often, or passing note, or lightest essay or conversation; it is in such a letter, for instance, that we come upon a singularly penetrative estimate of the genius and writings of Defoe.

Tracking, with an attention always alert, the whole process of their production to its starting-point in the deep places of the mind, he seems to realise the but half-conscious intuitions of Hogarth or Shakspere, and develops the great ruling unities which have swayed their actual work; or "puts up," and takes, the one morsel of good stuff in an old, forgotten writer. There comes even to be an aroma of old English in what he says even casually; noticeable echoes, in chance turn and phrase, of the great masters of style, the old masters. Godwin, seeing in quotation a passage from *John Woodvil,* takes it for a choice fragment of an old dramatist, and goes to Lamb to assist him in finding the author. His power of delicate imitation in prose and verse goes the length of a fine mimicry even, as in those last essays of Elia on Popular Fallacies, with their gentle reproduction or caricature of Sir Thomas Browne, showing the more completely his mastery, by disinterested study, of those elements in the man which are the real source of style in that great, solemn master of old English, who, ready to say what he has to say with a fearless homeliness, yet continually over-awes one with touches of such strange utterance from things afar. For it is with the delicacies of fine literature especially, its gradations of expression, its fine judgment, its pure sense of words, of vocabulary,—things, alas! dying out in the English literature of the present, together with the appreciation of them in our literature of the past,— that his literary mission is chiefly concerned. And yet, delicate, refining, daintily epicurean, though he may seem, when he writes of giants such as Hogarth or Shakspere, though often but in a stray note, you catch the sense of awe with which those great names in past

literature and art brooded over his intelligence, his undiminished impressibility by the great effects in them. Reading, commenting on Shakspere, he is like a man who walks alone under a grand stormy sky, and among unwonted tricks of light, when powerful spirits might seem to be abroad upon the air; and the grim humour of Hogarth, as he analyses it, rises into a kind of spectral grotesque; while he too knows the secret of fine, significant touches like theirs.

There are traits, customs, characteristics of houses and dress, surviving morsels of old life, like those of which we get such delicate impressions in Hogarth, concerning which we well understand, how, common, uninteresting, or worthless even, in themselves, they have come to please us now as things picturesque, when thus set in relief against the modes of our different age. Customs, stiff to us, stiff dresses, stiff furniture,—types of cast-off fashions, left by accident, and which no one ever meant to preserve, we contemplate with more than good-nature, as having in them the veritable accent of a time, not altogether to be replaced by its more solemn and self-conscious deposits; like those tricks of individuality which we find quite tolerable in persons, because they convey to us the secret of life-like expression, and with regard to which we are all to some extent humourists. But it is part of the privilege of the genuine humourist to anticipate this pensive mood with regard to the ways and things of his own day; to look upon the tricks in manner of the life about him with that same refined, purged sort of vision, which will come naturally to those of a later generation, in observing whatever chance may have saved of its mere external habit. Seeing things always by the light of some more entire understanding than is possible for ordinary minds, of the whole mechanism of humanity, and the manner, the outward mode or fashion, always in strict connexion with the spiritual condition which determines it, a humourist like Charles Lamb anticipates the enchantment of distance; and the characteristics of places, ranks, habits of life, are transfigured for him, even now and in advance of time, by poetic light; justifying what some might condemn as mere sentimentality, in the effort to hand on unbroken the tradition of such fashion or accent. "The praise of beggars," "the cries of London," the traits of actors just "old," the spots in "town" where the country, its fresh green and fresh water, still lingered on, one after another, amidst the bustle; the quaint, dimmed, just played-out farces, he had relished so much, coming partly through them to understand the earlier English theatre as a thing once really alive; those fountains and sundials of old gardens, of which he entertains such dainty discourse,—he feels the poetry of these things, as the poetry of things old indeed, but surviving as an actual part of the life of the present, and as something quite different from the poetry of things flatly gone from us and frankly antique, coming back to us, if at all, as entire strangers, like Scott's old Scotch-border figures, their oaths and armour. Such gift of appreciation depends, as I said, on the habitual apprehension of men's life as a whole; its organic wholeness, as extending even to the least things; of its outward manner in connexion with its inward temper; and it involves a fine perception of the congruities, the musical accordance of humanity with its environment of custom, society, intercourse of persons; as if all that, with its meetings, partings, ceremonies, gesture, tones of speech, were some delicate instrument on which an expert performer is playing.

These are some of the characteristics of Elia, one essentially an essayist, and of the true family of Montaigne, "never judging," as he says, "system-wise of things, but fastening on particulars;" saying all things as it were on chance occasion only, and as a pastime, yet succeeding thus, "glimpse-wise," in catching and recording more frequently than others "the gayest, happiest attitude of things;" a casual writer for dreamy readers, yet always giving the reader so much more than he seemed to propose. There is something of the follower of George Fox about him, and the quaker's belief in the inward light coming to one passive, to the mere way-farer, who will be sure at all events to lose no light which falls by the way; glimpses, suggestions, delightful half-apprehensions, profound thoughts of old philosophers, hints of the innermost reason in things, the full knowledge of which is held in reserve; all the varied stuff, that is, of which genuine essays are made.

And with him, as with Montaigne, the desire of self-portraiture is, below all more superficial tendencies, the real motive in writing at all,—a desire closely connected with that intimacy, that modern subjectivity, which may be called the *Montaignesque* element in literature. What he designs is to give you himself, to acquaint you with his likeness; but must do this, if at all, indirectly, being indeed always more or less reserved for himself and his friends; friendship counting for so much in his life, that he is jealous of anything that might jar or disturb it, even to a sort of insincerity, of which he has a quaint "praise;" this lover of stage plays significantly welcoming a little touch of the artificiality of play to sweeten intercourse.

And, in effect, a very delicate and expressive portrait of him does put itself together for the duly meditative reader; and in indirect touches of his own work, scraps of faded old letters, what others remembered of his talk, the man's likeness emerges; what he laughed and wept at, his sudden elevations and longings after absent friends; his fine casuistries of affection and devices to jog sometimes, as he says, the lazy happiness of perfect love; his solemn moments of higher discourse with the young, as they came across him on occasion, and went along a little way with him; the sudden, sur-

prised apprehension of beauties in old literature, revealing anew the deep soul of poetry in things; and still the pure spirit of fun, having its way again,—laughter, that most short-lived of all things, (some of Shakspere's even having fallen dim,) wearing well with him. Much of all this comes out through his letters, which may be regarded as a part of his essays. He is an old-fashioned letter-writer, the essence of the old fashion of letter-writing lying, as with true essay-writing, in the dexterous availing oneself of accident and circumstance, in the prosecution of deeper lines of observation; although, just as in the record of his conversation, one loses something, in losing the actual tones of the stammerer, still graceful in his halting, (as he halted also in composition, composing slowly and in fits, "like a Flemish painter," as he tells us,) so "it is to be regretted," says the editor of his letters, "that in the printed letters the reader will lose the curious varieties of writing with which the originals abound, and which are scrupulously adapted to the subject." (pp. 468-72)

The writings of Charles Lamb are an excellent illustration of the value of reserve in literature. Below his quiet, his quaintness, his humour, and what may seem the slightness, the merely occasional or accidental character of his work, there lies, as I said at starting, as in his life, a true tragic element. The gloom, reflected at its darkest, in those hard shadows of *Rosamund Grey,* is always there, though restrained always in expression, and not always realised either for himself or his readers; and it gives to those lighter matters on the surface of life and literature, among which he for the most part moved, a wonderful play of expression, as if at any moment these light words and fancies might pierce very far into the deeper heart of things. In his writing, as in his life, that quiet is not the low flying of one from the first drowsy by choice, and needing the prick of some strong passion or worldly ambition, to stimulate him into all the energy of which he is capable; but rather the reaction of nature, after an escape from fate, dark and insane as in old Greek tragedy; following which, the mere sense of relief becomes a kind of passion, as with one who, having just escaped earthquake or shipwreck, finds a thing for grateful tears in the mere sitting quiet at home, under the wall, till the end of days. (pp. 473-74)

Walter H. Pater, "The Character of the Humourist: Charles Lamb," in *The Fortnightly Review,* No. XVI, September 1, 1878, pp. 466-74.

E. M. W. TILLYARD
(essay date 1923)

[Tillyard was a distinguished authority on the works of William Shakespeare. In the following excerpt, he argues that Lamb ranks among the greatest English masters of applied criticism.]

The position a man will give to Charles Lamb as a literary critic depends on what he believes the highest criticism to be. Does he seek information or enlightenment of it? Should it persuade him by argument or like the Sublime of Longinus transport him by its power? For if he goes to it chiefly for facts, for arguments, for masterly comparisons, for sustained intellectual effort, he will find Lamb deficient, disagreeing probably with several of Lamb's contentions and condemning his critical writings as occasional, unmethodical and fragmentary; but if he goes to it for something that by some subtle means brings him closer to certain works of art than he has been able to get unaided, for something that creates in his mind the right receptive mood, then he will put Lamb among the very greatest of critics. (p. viii)

Of English masters of theoretical criticism Coleridge is the greatest, of applied, in a sense, Lamb.

To exalt Lamb so high may seem rash in view of the comparatively small bulk of his work and of his being so obviously an amateur, not, like Hazlitt, a professional critic; and if one were to judge Lamb as any kind of critic other than the creative, the claim would be preposterous. But the fact is that the bulk of criticism that is both a high work of art in itself and tells the truth about what it deals with is remarkably small and correspondingly precious. This should not be in the least surprising, if we consider the qualities that must go to the making of a great critic of authors. (p. ix)

Now it is the first and greatest glory of Lamb's criticism that not a little of it has got [the] quality of indispensableness . . . Nor is this quality confined to a few famous places: it meets us again and again. (p. x)

But if it is impossible to analyse the essence of Lamb's most memorable passages, there is one obvious contributory reason why he succeeded in penetrating so near the centre of truth; namely that his very faults, his amateurishness and lack of range, helped him to concentrate the more intensely on what he loved, and to reach a more intimate sympathy with it. There are men, of whom Dryden and Hazlitt are conspicuous among the English, who react with vitality to almost any good literature that they meet, men with quick initial perceptions and strong immediate judgments. Their very versatility prevents quite that close intimacy which is such a peculiar property of Lamb. Not that they are open to the charge of superficiality, but that they have not the faculty of brooding over what they read as Lamb had. You feel that in them there is always present the desire to express in words what they feel about the books they read, and that they are always a little restless until they have expressed themselves. But when Lamb is 'hanging over (for the thousandth time) some passage in old Burton, or one of his strange contemporaries,' his mood is one of unspoiled serenity, and the waters of his spirit receive the perfect reflection of what he reads, unstirred by any wind of restlessness.

It is very easy to exaggerate the 'quaintness' of Lamb's writings in general, and it is positively wrong to use the word as peculiarly descriptive of his criticism. Nobility and high seriousness are terms that can more fittingly be applied to his greatest, modesty and simplicity to his lesser, and originality to all his criticism. There is nobility, high seriousness and a passionate emphasis in the essay *On the Tragedies of Shakespeare* and even in the mutilated review of *The Excursion.* Moreover Lamb's fundamental concern was with the literature of human action rather than of fancy, and could not have coexisted with a fundamental quaintness. 'The plays which I made choice of,' he writes at the beginning of the *Characters of Dramatic Writers, Contemporary with Shakspeare,* 'were, with few exceptions, such as treat of human life and manners, rather than masques and Arcadian pastorals, with their train of abstractions, unimpassioned deities, passionate mortals—Claius, and Medorus, and Amintas, and Amarillis. My leading design was, to illustrate what may be called the moral sense of our ancestors.' These are not the words of one whose quaintness is fundamental: the spirit in which they are written would not have been disowned by Matthew Arnold. This concern with human action is nowhere better seen than in the admirable review of Keats' *Lamia* volume, in which Lamb with an instinct perfectly true to himself, though not necessarily truer than the instincts of those who have thought otherwise, prefers *Isabella* with its greater insistence on action, human feeling and dramatic qualities generally to all the splendour of the pictorial writing in *The Eve of St. Agnes.* He could never have shown this preference, had his critical turn of mind been above all things quaint.

Lamb's modesty and simplicity . . . are evident with the rarest exceptions throughout his letters, from his earliest criticisms of Coleridge to his latest of Moxon. He never tries to be clever; he never in the slightest degree lords it over those who have delivered themselves into his hand by showing him their works. What he criticises and how he can help it are everything, his own glory as critic nothing. The same qualities are to be found in the passage on Sir William Temple in *The Genteel Style in Writing.* I can imagine no more perfect introduction to a writer than this. Lamb works here largely by quotation, but every now and then delicately adjusts the reader's mood by a judicious remark. At the end we have forgotten the critic, and are left with an inexplicably vivid impression of Temple and a vehement desire to learn all there is to know about him. How many a modern review do we read with the feeling that the reviewer is a very clever fellow, but that we are not particularly drawn to learn more of his subject! (pp. xi-xii)

Of Lamb's originality it is superfluous to speak: it meets us everywhere in the good and the bad alike. He had no master, his tastes were entirely native, and there is hardly a line of his criticism that anyone else could have written.

Lamb's defects as a critic were frankly implied by himself in more than one confessional passage. . . . (p. xiii)

Lamb confesses in *Imperfect Sympathies* that his mind is desultory, sadly lacking in system, 'suggestive merely' and 'content with fragments and scattered pieces of Truth.' Granted that he was true enough to his nature to make out the worst case he could against himself, we must admit that his self-accusation is substantially true. It is impossible to deny that Lamb was lacking in range, that his attainments as a scholar were not great, that his knowledge of foreign literature depended mostly on translations and even so was not wide, that he read what he liked, not what he ought, and so on. But is lack of range such a very serious fault? Cannot the virtue of immense reading be exaggerated? The total amount of great literature extant in the world is very large. A few supermen, uniting a high vitality with powerful eyesight, prodigious memories, a highly developed patience of sitting in chairs and a small desire for sleep, may gain more than a superficial acquaintance with most of it, and retain their faculty for appreciation. But I cannot believe that such range is desirable except for a few, or that those few can have the intensity of appreciation of a Lamb. Those who exact vast range in a critic underestimate the expenditure of emotional force that must go to a great appreciation of a masterpiece. It is futile to expect any one man to enjoy the accumulated out-pourings of the great minds of many ages in any worthy degree of intensity.

Then there is the charge brought by Hazlitt in his essay *On Criticism in Table Talk* that Lamb has an invincible predilection for the obscure, and cannot appreciate anything that appeals to the multitude. That Lamb was attracted by the curious and the out-of-the-way, and that he liked to feel that he was appreciating something neglected by others or appreciating in an unusual way something known, cannot be denied. It was a pleasure to him to appreciate Wither, the luckless butt of ignorant Augustan abuse, and he gets peculiar pleasure in saying in his essay on him, 'Whoever expects to find in the satirical pieces of this writer any of those peculiarities which pleased him in the satires of Dryden or Pope, will be grievously disappointed.' He has in fact got very strongly the antiquarian delight of collecting rarities. Yet this delight is not fundamental, but an added zest. Primarily he seeks what he likes; if what he likes happens to be rare, if he can work his way through a little dust to some neglected piece of human passion, so much the better; but he does not allow mere antiquarianism to affect his tastes. He is, as it were, a man who in 1860 admires Chippendale chairs, not an original who in 1923 deliberately adorns his house with the furniture of 1860; even in 1923 he would have liked Chippendale chairs, though with just a trifle less relish. It is as wrong to consider Lamb's occultism and antiquarianism as his most important characteristics as it is to exaggerate his quaintness. His chief concern was with great literature, in particular with Shakespeare, but when, to use the phrase of literary appreciation, he took 'an airing beyond the diocese of the strict conscience' (and who can live for very long at a stretch in the rarefied atmosphere of the great masterpieces?) his antiquarian instincts asserted themselves. (pp. xiii-xiv)

[But when all is said and done, Lamb's defects] are quite innocuous. He made mistakes: he admired Southey overmuch; he spoke contemptuously of [Goethe's] *Faust;* he did not give Shelley a chance. But his mistakes are not such as mislead; sheep and goats in his criticism require no divine aid in the separation. If he states one side of a question only, as in the essay on *Shakespeare's Tragedies* and *The Artificial Comedy of the Last Century,* he in no way makes us forget that there is another side, and withal gives us high criticism that entirely transcends the nominal issue. His native frankness and sincerity keep his most questionable assertions from being in the least more dangerous than Dr Johnson's enchanting strictures on *Lycidas.* (p. xv)

E. M. W. Tillyard, in an introduction to *Lamb's Criticism: A Selection from the Literary Criticism of Charles Lamb* by Charles Lamb, edited by E. M. W. Tillyard, 1923. Reprint by Greenwood Press, Publishers, 1970, pp. viii-xvi.

DONALD H. REIMAN
(essay date 1965)

[In the excerpt below, Reiman traces Lamb's method of developing thematic unity in his essays.]

As I hope to show by analyzing systematically **"Mrs. Battle's Opinions on Whist," "The Two Races of Men,"** and **"Old China,"** the essays attributed to Elia achieve their thematic and artistic integrity by exploring everyday events and trivial opinions that suggest, analogically, larger philosophical issues. Focusing his ideas around an unpretentious symbol, Lamb could remain nondogmatic and skeptical through the light tone appropriate to this ostensible subject and, by ironically understating his conclusions, could avoid all trace of the "mental bombast" that, according to Coleridge, occasionally marred Wordsworth's poems of high seriousness. (pp. 470-71)

Though Mrs. Battle did not take whist at all lightly, Elia seems to treat his old companion and her favorite game with some detachment. At the end of the essay, however, Elia confesses himself so dedicated to cards that he wishes his game of piquet with Bridget could go on forever. Is this mere whimsy? Or do the card games in this essay assume significance beyond innocent amusement? One should note in the opening paragraph that old Sarah Battle, "now with God," "loved" one thing better than "a good game at whist": "her devotions." This pairing does not seem to be simply an ironic juxtaposition of the cosmic and the trivial in the values of an eccentric old woman: the author tells us nothing to indicate that Mrs. Battle's religion was shallow or sentimental; on the contrary, the sole reference to the result of her piety—"now with God"—suggests the opposite conclusion, that there was some defensible relation between Mrs. Battle's devotions and her whist-playing, the two most important things in her life.

Mrs. Battle, indeed, considered that playing whist "was her business, her duty, the thing she came into the world to do,—and she did it." . . . It was "her noble occupation, to which she wound up her faculties." Whist was, in other words, Mrs. Battle's "vocation," that to which she had been called, that in the proper performance of which she could win salvation. Not that Elia or Mrs. Battle would care to translate the analogy as I have just done—assert rather than suggest—but this unmistakable suggestion governs the entire essay. (pp. 471-72)

As the name "Mrs. Battle" itself suggests, and as Elia repeatedly emphasizes, the old lady considered card games to be a kind of warfare: "She loved a thorough-paced partner, a determined enemy. . . . She fought a good fight: cut and thrust." (pp. 472-73)

In short, Mrs. Battle believed that "man is a gaming animal" and that "this passion can scarcely be more safely expended than upon a game at cards" in which, "during the illusion, we *are* as mightily concerned as those whose stake is crowns and kingdoms." Whist is "quite as diverting, and a great deal more innoxious, than many of those more serious *games* of life, which men play, without esteeming them to be such." . . . Mrs. Battle thus makes explicit the larger analogy and the ramifications of her vocation. To one skeptical of the objective value of religious, philosophical, political, or even aesthetic dogmas and slogans, to one for whom every endeavor seemed a commitment to an illusion, complete dedication to the game of whist might serve to develop one's character and purify the soul as surely as would devotion to any other cause or creed.

In the concluding paragraphs Elia, having already established the differences between his character and that of Mrs. Battle, remarks that he sometimes finds card games stimulating even if there is no stake, no reward to be won. Sometimes, when he is "in sickness, or not in the best spirits," he plays "a game at piquet *for love* with my cousin Bridget—Bridget Elia." Though he breaks all of Mrs. Battle's stern injunctions, he yet manages to enjoy the game: "I wished it might have lasted for ever, though we gained nothing, and lost nothing, though it was a mere shade of play: I would be content to go on in that idle folly for ever." For Elia the aesthetic enjoyment of the game is its own reward. He need not vanish his "enemy" nor anticipate a reward. The game of life has value in the present moment quite apart from subsequent developments, which might, indeed, prove as painful as "the gentle lenitive to my foot, which Bridget was doomed to apply after the game was over. . . . "

Lamb in this essay . . . developed the rationale for the elevation of sports and games as symbols or parables of human life's serious occupations, and Hemingway's billiard players, fishermen, and bull fighters are distant relations of Mrs. Battle.

"The Two Races of Men" exhibits a subtler, more ambitious interweaving of theme and subject. The ostensible topic under discussion is the classification of "the human species" into "two distinct races, *the men who borrow,* and *the men who lend.*" After setting forth the thesis in two introductory paragraphs, Lamb explores it through two subsequent divisions of the essay: six paragraphs ironically chronicle the activities of those members of "the *great race*" who, like Ralph Bigod, Esq., specialize in borrowing money, and the remaining six paragraphs center on that "class of alienators more formidable" ("to one like Elia")—"your *borrowers of books.*" Chief among these scavengers is "Comberbatch" (Coleridge), "matchless in his depredations."

Elia, one sees immediately, distinguishes between these two classes of borrowers almost as sharply as he does between borrowers and lenders. He who "borrows" from his purse steals, not trash (Elia's refutation of the popular fallacy **"That Enough Is as Good as a Feast"** forbids this interpretation), but something that, once gone, is unlikely ever to return. (pp. 473-75)

The real theme of **"The Two Races of Men"** is, then, that there is indeed a Great Race of borrowers, men exemplified by Alcibiades, Falstaff, Sir Richard Steele, and Richard Brinsley Sheridan . . . and by

Jours ratherish unwell

Chs Lamb

A caricature of Lamb drawn by Daniel Maclise.

Coleridge; these borrowers, in their turn, contribute much to the world's welfare—not, perhaps, in a material way, with money or physical books, but through intellectual contributions to mankind in general and to their friends and companions in particular. Such men are those to whom Elia and all wishing to avoid combining the "penalties of Lazarus and of Dives" . . . (poverty and parsimony) should open their hearts and their libraries and receive the rewards of their magnanimity from truly great-minded men.

The theme of **"Old China"** seems obvious enough, except for the apparent irrelevance of the remarks on old china with which the essay begins and concludes. The main body of the essay consists of Cousin Bridget's elegy on the passing of the good old days of poverty, and Elia's unsentimental, hard-headed reply: "It is true we were happier when we were poorer, but we were also younger, my cousin. . . . Competence to age is supplementary youth; a sorry supplement indeed, but I fear the best that is to be had." . . . Both Elia and Bridget regret the loss of their youth and its humble adventures, but whereas Bridget tries to externalize the problem and blame the loss of past joys on the accumulation of wealth, Elia more realistically recognizes that the difficulty lies within himself and

Bridget, subject to the gentle ravages of Fate, Time, Occasion, Chance, and Change.

Elia's love for old china is one of those tastes "of too ancient a date to admit of our remembering distinctly that it was an acquired one. I can call to mind the first play, and the first exhibition, that I was taken to; but I am not conscious of a time when china jars and saucers were introduced into my imagination." . . . In the symbolic world of this essay, then, Time governs the plays and pictures which Bridget mentions in her elegy for lost happiness and which thereby become symbols of the decay of human faculties (much as do beauties of nature, seen but no longer felt, in Coleridge's "Dejection: An Ode"). Because the love of old china is not, however, associated with any particular moment in the past, this attachment participates in a timeless world that mutability cannot affect. (p. 476)

Bridget bemoans the loss of human youth and novelty and joy against the backdrop of a world where Beauty *can* keep her lustrous eyes and where youth does *not* grow pale, and specter-thin, and die. Like Keats's Grecian urn, Yeats's lapis lazuli sculpture, or T. S. Eliot's Chinese jar, Elia's china tea-cups present a still point amid a world of flux and, at the same time, a stimulus for the human imagination both of him who creates and him who contemplates them. Elia turns back to the china, therefore, at the end of the essay, in order to retain his hold on the values of a summer world that he feels slipping away from him. . . . Could the world of human affairs, even the great world of Croesus and the Rothschilds, retain its values, man might find his ultimate meaning in worldly activity—in the affairs of the East India Company, for example. But because Elia feels this to be impossible, he turns instead to a world of fragile art that proves to be a never-fading source of delight—as we, for example, turn to the essays of Elia.

Lamb, as I have said, intentionally avoided the kind of overt moralizing that I have explicated from his hints and analogies. Once the thematic unity of an essay becomes clear, however, one can return to Lamb's writings with a new appreciation of the perfectly balanced tone that suggests deeper meanings without committing Lamb or his reader to the logical analyses or marshaled facts that must have accompanied a discursive development of the thesis. Lamb, the humane skeptic, preferred not to dogmatize—or even to speculate systematically—on the nature of the state of being that must inevitably follow "that last game" of piquet he played with his "sweet cousin," but he was not unwilling to set forth his opinions on the game of life and the stakes for which a man ought willingly to play. He therefore created a symbol-world through which he could explore universal human problems in a truly imaginative way; like the pastoral world of Robert Frost's best poetry, the trivial universe of Elia and Bridget, of whist games, borrowed books, and frail china tea-cups, provided a language for one who truly desired both to teach and to delight. (pp. 477-78)

Donald H. Reiman, "Thematic Unity in Lamb's Familiar Essays," in *The Journal of English and Germanic Philology,* Vol. LXIV, No. 3, July, 1965, pp. 470-78.

ARNOLD HENDERSON

(essay date 1968)

[In the following excerpt, Henderson analyzes Lamb's critical precepts and technique.]

Charles Lamb was an alarmingly personal critic, ready not only to examine an author but to love him and exclaim over him. He wanted no critical system to rein him in: "I do not lay claim to much accurate thinking. I never judge system-wise of things, but fasten upon particulars." He attempted no comprehensive theories, and his criticism is scattered among essays, letters, and the notes to his *Specimens of English Dramatic Poets.* He has made it too easy for later students to take up each of his literary opinions in isolation from the rest. His opinions on drama in particular have seemed to some, erratic impulses rather than natural conclusions from premises. These premises may not be explicitly defined each time they are invoked, but are implicit in the principles and working methods constant throughout his criticism. When they are sifted out it should become clearer that he has a definite critical position, and that it lies, not in the realm of Fantasy, but in that particular region of the realm of Realism whence the *Lyrical Ballads* [of Wordsworth and Coleridge] also sprang. (p. 104)

Lamb—like Coleridge, particularly in the lectures—presents his personal sympathetic reactions to literature as models for all readers. He is thus what Northrop Frye calls a "public critic" who "represents the reading public at its most expert and judicious." If personal reactions are to be valid models for others, such a critic must have a sympathy neither too idiosyncratic, for then he can represent only himself in his odd likings, nor too confined, for then he can represent the public in its reaction to only a few works and authors. Both flaws can be found, in moderation, in Lamb.

Lamb sometimes is idiosyncratic in displaying more sensibility than most of us. He finds Malvolio's situation in *Twelfth Night* capable of exciting "a kind of tragic interest." . . . But most of us identify less with Malvolio than with his detractors, and the "tragic interest" he might excite is washed away in his absurdity. Lamb shows that the play is more than farce, but he

does not show why it remains comedy. Or again, he calls the end of *The Broken Heart,* where Calantha hides her grief by dancing, "so grand, so solemn." . . . [John] Ford presumably did intend the audience to share and admire Calantha's emotional struggle. But the problem with the play is that few of us *can* react that way, so artificial is the situation and so inadequate is her motive. If we think Lamb wrong, it is not because he has abandoned principles for spur-of-the-moment impulses, but because he has followed his principle of sympathy all too energetically.

The success of Lamb's principle of sympathetic reading is also hampered by the second sin of public critics, a failure of sympathy for certain works and authors. The problem is more that of gaps within his range than of a too-narrow range: he was one of the few persons of his time to appreciate both [Alexander] Pope and Wordsworth, both Sir Philip Sidney and Bernard Barton, both Sir Thomas Browne and William Hazlitt. He can immerse himself in such varied authors because he modulates his attitudes to suit what each demands. If, for example, he finds a Massinger deficient in dramatic power, yet he opens himself to sense the purity of his writing style. . . . He is a chameleon who takes on the colors of the authors upon whom he sits in judgement. But however wide his range, it was discontinuous: certain authors fell in the gaps. If he was a chameleon, he was a chameleon with, to mix metaphors, a limited palette. He could not turn Byron color or [Johann Wolfgang von] Goethe color or, except for one minor poem, [Percy Bysshe] Shelley color. He agrees, for example, with Barton on Shelley: "I can no more understand Shelley than you can. His poetry is 'thin sewn with profit or delight.' "

But despite gaps, Lamb ranged over an astonishingly diverse selection of authors, giving each the sympathy he might to a favorite. In this continual exploration he was spurred on by a publicist streak, a desire to introduce readers to neglected works, particularly, though not exclusively, old, undeservedly forgotten ones. Shakespeare aside, most of the authors Lamb treats were obscurata to his day, though many, such as [Christopher] Marlowe, [John] Webster, Sir Thomas Browne, or [Izaak] Walton, are more familiar now. Even when treating well-known figures, Lamb tends to treat their lesser-known works. (pp. 105-06)

Comparison was especially natural in the *Specimens of English Dramatic Poets,* where Lamb addressed an audience who knew little Elizabethan-Jacobean drama aside from Shakespeare, [Philip] Massinger, [Francis] Beaumont and [John] Fletcher, and perhaps Jonson. Coleridge himself had first-hand knowledge of only these. The known authors, especially Shakespeare, naturally became Lamb's landmarks. Thus "Chapman perhaps approaches nearest to Shakespeare in the descriptive and didactic, in passages which are less purely dramatic" . . . , while "Heywood is a sort of *prose* Shakespeare. His scenes are to the full as natural and affecting. But we miss *the Poet.*" . . . But Lamb regularly uses the comparative method even outside the *Specimens.* By bringing together Shakespeare, Massinger, and [Robert] Southey, he gives Coleridge his feelings about Beaumont and Fletcher. . . . [Robert] Burns illuminates [George] Wither . . . , and modern drama is foil to Restoration comedy. . . . Once, in a single sentence Lamb served up two Shakespeare plays, *Venice Preserved,* one Beaumont and Fletcher play, and a painting by Titian—all to illustrate [William] Hogarth! (p. 107)

This comparative method has both dangers and virtues. The *Specimens* . . . [praised] old drama whenever it was better than current drama in doing the same things, such as quarrel and reconciliation scenes, without regard to whether or not these things were intrinsically worth doing. Lamb himself once "recanted" and apologized for publishing a false comparison. . . . But this recantation did not stop the flow of comparisons—and fortunately so. By regularly trying his reaction to one work against his reactions to others, Lamb ties his criticism together without the need many critics feel for conscious system.

The historical method further frees Lamb's personal judgments from the limitations of his time and temperament. Of course Lamb was no historian: he read the [David] Garrick plays in random instead of chronological order, and he was silent on biography on the grounds that "My business is with their poetry only." . . . But he does modify his standards according to the era of a work. (pp. 107-08)

This check-and-balance of the historical method versus personal reactions or principles is common in romantic criticism. (p. 108)

Three things stand out as being consistently praised by Lamb—and, for that matter, Coleridge and others—and used as touchstones for excellence: depth of feeling, moral worth, and truth to nature. For all the airy grace of Elia's essays, Lamb was no worshiper of pure ornament, but insisted on depth of genuine feeling. (p. 109)

Lamb, like Wordsworth, demands a natural decorum of feeling. He praises the ending of *King Lear* for restraint, and prefers the old ballad of the "Nut-Brown Maid" to Prior's heightened and pretentious version. . . . In the *Specimens* he praises the intensity of *The Duchess of Malfy* while also praising its restraint. . . . Feeling must not be wrenched into sensationalism beyond the natural capacity of men. (p. 110)

Although Lamb was not as prone as Coleridge to draw explicit rules of moral conduct from literary examples, he as characteristically judges a work by its moral effect on the audience or by the character of the

ideals embodied in it. He praises Kent in *Lear* as "the noblest pattern of virtue which even Shakespeare has conceived." . . . This, incidentally, may have been an observation of Coleridge's, whose marginalia on *King Lear* include the remark: "Kent [is] the nearest to perfect goodness of all Shakespeare's characters. . . . " It is on moral grounds that Lamb preferred Marlowe's *Dr. Faustus* to Goethe's *Faust,* which he saw as "a disagreeable canting tale of Seduction." . . . Shelley, too, is morally dubious: "For his theories and nostrums they are oracular enough, but I either comprehend'em not, or there is miching malice and mischief in 'em." . . . Moral nobility makes Wordsworth better than [Lord] Byron: "Why, a line of Wordsworth's is a lever to lift the immortal spirit! Byron can only move the Spleen." . . . Though he could like a work of just good fun, he praised most highly works which bettered the men who read them.

Truth to nature, Lamb's third regular criterion of value, means primarily truth to human nature. He praises Ford as "of the first order of Poets. He sought for sublimity, not by parcels in metaphors or visible images, but directly where she has her full residence in the heart of man; in the actions and sufferings of the greatest minds." . . . Truth to nature is what Fletcher lacks: "He is too mistrustful of Nature; he always goes a little to one side of her. Shakespeare chose her without a reserve: and had riches, power, understanding, and long life, with her, for a dowry." . . . A scene in [Thomas] Middleton's *Women Beware Women* is "one of those scenes which has the air of being an immediate transcript from life." . . . (pp. 110-11)

But Lamb distinguishes between inner and external truth—he wants realism, but not necessarily literalism. In his notes on Fuller, the opposed terms are the "essential verities" and "truth of the fact." . . . In his essay **"Sanity of True Genius,"** he rebukes a novelist whose characters and incidents were outwardly ordinary but inwardly so false to human nature as to be "innutritious phantoms, . . . the improbable events, the incoherent incidents, the inconsistent characters, or no-characters, of some third-rate love intrigue." This writer he contrasts to [Edmund] Spenser with his seemingly unreal characters in whose "inner nature, and the law of their speech and actions, we are at home and upon acquainted ground." . . . For Lamb, true geniuses give the order of inner truth, and so, however disjointed the surface of their works may appear, these geniuses are in a sense more sane than ordinary imperceptive people, who can give only incoherent accounts of human nature. However dreamlike a passage in Spenser, its inner truth stands being tried by the "waking judgment." . . . Though sometimes called a dreamer, he was concerned not with the dream as dream, but with its inner truth to nature.

Certain of Lamb's opinions on drama have

seemed to some neither realistic nor serious; they have appeared to lack concern for either truth to nature or moral worth. But here, too, we must distinguish between inner and outer. Lamb does indeed oppose contemporary stage practice as both too literally true to nature and too insistent on clear moral elevation. In the essay **"Stage Illusion"** he argues that actors should violate the illusion of being real people, and more so in comedy than in tragedy. . . . Here he seems to abandon realism and truth to human nature, but he does so to avoid alienating the audience. In real life certain sorts of characters—cowards, misers, irritable old men— would be offensive, and so such characters are made palatable in comedy by presenting "just enough of a likeness to recognise, without pressing upon us the uneasy sense of reality." Comic stage quarrels become disturbing if acted too earnestly; they should "seem half put on." If one character seems too realistically earnest, "his real-life manner will destroy the whimsical and purely dramatic existence of the other character." Thus Lamb wants less illusion for the sake of more illusion, for the sake of more participation by the audience in the inner experience of the play. Greater outward illusion would block sympathetic participation: the audience would be offended by comic flaws and frightened by comic dangers.

In his essay **"On the Artificial Comedy of the Last Century,"** he applies this theory to specific works. He fears that an audience accustomed to modern plays where every tinge of immorality is to be despised could not bear to witness Restoration comedy—where the heroes may philander and hope to live idly on inherited wealth. If the audience is to sit through the play in comfort, they must leave ordinary morality outside the playhouse. (pp. 111-12)

In the essay **"On the Tragedies of Shakespeare"** Lamb again argues for artificiality of outward representation in order to give the audience greater penetration into the characters: "The elaborate and anxious provision of scenery, . . . which in comedy, or plays of familiar life, adds so much to the life of the imitation, in plays which appeal to the higher faculties, positively destroys the illusion which it is introduced to aid." . . . Our busy senses distract our imagination, as Lamb humorously points out elsewhere of a blind man at a play: "Having no drawback of sight to impair his sensibilities, he simply attended to the scene, and received its unsophisticated impression." . . . Following the train of logic, Lamb concludes that (at least for readers as sensitive as himself) it is best to read the play if one wants the all-important inner drama of human emotions: "On the stage we see nothing but corporal infirmities and weakness, the impotence of rage; while we read it, we see not Lear, but we are Lear,—we are in his mind, we are sustained by a grandeur which baffles the malice of daughters and storms; in the aberrations of

his reason, we discover a mighty irregular power of reasoning." . . . Both Lamb's suggestions, using less elaborate scenery, and reading instead of or in addition to seeing the plays, are intended to increase audience participation in the "human" aspects of the drama. Thus when Lamb opposes external illusion, he does it for the sake of inner illusion. He is trying to bring the audience closer to the experience of the play.

Achieving the proper degree of illusion in watching a play seems to have been a problem for Lamb. With his perhaps extreme sensitivity to suffering, he seems to have come sometimes perilously close to the old position attacked by Coleridge, and in theory by Lamb himself, that in viewing a play we should be deluded into thinking the actors really are the persons they portray. Lamb admits that he feels called upon to shelter Lear from the storm. What backwoodsman, seeing a stageplay for the first time and leaping up to thrash the villain, could do more? In the essay on Shakespeare he suspects that presenting a play on stage must have such effects, and, since they would mask the particular qualities of Shakespeare, he abandons the stage, seeking in the reading experience the highest realization of the author's intent. In the later essay on Restoration drama he modifies this despair of the stage, Restoration plays being more tractable than Shakespeare's. Here, instead of abandoning the stage when the highest understanding is sought, he asks it to reform. The audiences are to recognize historical relativism by forgetting their code of morality, and the actors are to use a slight artificiality. As a result, no one is to feel called upon to leap up to rebuke a philanderer—or help an old man to shelter. But a twentieth-century, post-Coleridgean (and post-Brechtian!) audience rarely has the delusion Lamb seeks to cure by reducing stage illusion, or banishing morality, or sending the audience home to read for themselves. Lamb, living in a time of differing stage conventions, and naturally more sensitive than most people, more prone to enter passionately into an illusion almost to the point of delusion, now seems extreme in recommending cures for a problem we feel less. (pp. 113-14)

This emphasis on the experience of the audience runs through all of Lamb's criticism. Depth of feeling is depth of feeling evoked in us. A noble or morally valuable character is one who stirs what is noble in us, and a work has moral worth not in adhering to rules but in bettering us. Lamb's very working method, compiling and publishing his likes and dislikes, emphasizes the reaction to a work as distinct from the process of its creation, the audience more than the author of the work discussed. While a recognized characteristic of romantic criticism is . . . its tendency to refer literary questions back to the author's mind, Lamb more typically looks to the audience (frequently himself), though he does sometimes refer back to the author, praising, for example, the personal qualities he assumes Shakespeare must have had to produce his works. That he does not do so more often betrays no disagreement with Wordsworth's making the very definition of poetry depend on the author's emotions. Nor does it controvert Coleridge's characteristic method of approaching the qualities in a work from the faculties of the author's mind, leading to such generalizations as those concerning "Shakespeare's mode of conceiving characters out of his own intellectual and moral faculties." Lamb is talking about a different link in the literary chain: the reaction to a work, not the process of its creation. A full theory would perhaps have touched more upon origins, and Lamb might have seemed more like his friends. But in one respect his different emphasis serves, not to set him off from the others, but to throw added light on them. Where we find them sharing his concerns we must recognize those concerns as characteristically romantic, at least in that combination, for many of these principles and working habits can be found in isolation or different groupings in earlier criticism. Concern for moral elevation, truth to nature, depth of feeling, the principle of sympathetic reading, and the historical method are in varying degrees common concerns of Wordsworth, Coleridge, Lamb, and their circle. The fact that Lamb shows these characteristics so prominently without as much expressed concern for the psychology of the author helps dramatize their presence—and importance—in the others of his group.

Lamb, then, is a thinker of a particular school, despite his refusal to develop a formal critical system. Though he gives free rein to his likes, dislikes, and personal reactions, his criticism, even where it is perhaps not fully correct, is neither random nor inexplicable. Each opinion proves compatible with general principles and values common to all. We would not, of course, look to Lamb for the theoretical exposition of those principles and values. There, Coleridge is the romantic master. Even within practical criticism, Lamb is of less use for ranking various authors one against the other than for giving a sense of what a given author is about. He plays favorites and, instead of being the impartial judge of all writers, is the champion of favorite or neglected ones. If we were to ask him who, after Shakespeare, was the best Jacobean tragic dramatist, he would be likely to reply, not that Webster, or Middleton, or whoever, was the best, but that Fulke Greville and George Chapman were better than most people realize. Furthermore, since he cannot feel his way into some authors—Byron, Shelley, Goethe—he cannot judge them by the same penetrative method that he uses for others—Wordsworth, Coleridge, Marlowe. He could not rate all on the same scale. But for criticism that tries to define the particular qualities of an author, that tries to characterize a work and show how it operates on us, Lamb's eccentricity and partiality are no

hindrances. Lamb wrote about works he liked, and he remains helpful for them even if he might not have been helpful had he tried to interpret Shelley. Lamb was a keen observer of what went on inside himself, and if he reacts to a work at all, he can give a clear, even a stirring, account of what his reaction is. His lesson for those practising criticism in these days of objectivity is perhaps that the subjective need not be banished when one tries to talk sense, that if one is interested in those mortals who write and those who read literature, then it is no disadvantage if the critic himself happens to be a human being. (pp. 115-16)

Arnold Henderson, "Some Constants of Charles Lamb's Criticism," in *Studies in Romanticism,* Vol. VII, No. 2, Winter, 1968, pp. 104-16.

GEORGE WATSON
(essay date 1973)

[In the following excerpt, Watson assesses Lamb's stature as a critic.]

Lamb's criticism, almost all descriptive apart from a late essay on **'Stage Illusion'**, is tiny in its scope. It could be collected—and has been collected—into a slim volume of less than fifty thousand words, and survives as something altogether desultory, scattered through his letters, the apparatus of the *Specimens* . . . and other editions of his favourite authors, the monthly and quarterly reviews, and of course *The Essays of Elia*. . . . Unmistakably Coleridgean in its subject-matter—it concerns itself overwhelmingly with such favourite subjects of Coleridge's as Elizabethan and Jacobean drama, the prose of Sir Thomas Browne, Jeremy Taylor, Fuller, and Walton, and contemporary romanticism—it looks timid and cautious when set beside the revolutionary assertions of some of his contemporaries. Everything points to a lack of confidence. But Lamb is one of those rare authors who can make a virtue of timidity and amateurishness. Throughout his long clerkship in East India House . . . he would never have pretended to be an 'important' critic, and only asks that he should be seen lucidly for what he is: a good friend and a good disciple whose critical intuitions possess, at the best, a delicacy unknown to more vigorous and ambitious intelligences than his own.

There are moments, none the less, when we feel that Lamb's real mentor is not Coleridge but Samuel Johnson, and it comes as a start, in view of Lamb's reputation as leader of the nineteenth-century vogue for the quaint and the baroque, to watch him inveigh as heavily as Johnson might have done against medieval and Tudor extravagances, both literary and moral. The following judgement against Marlowe could easily belong to some neoclassical critic:

> Tamburlaine . . . comes in, drawn by conquered kings, and reproaches these 'pampered jades of Asia' that they can 'draw but twenty miles a day'. Till I saw this passage with my own eyes, I never believed that it was anything more than a pleasant burlesque of mine ancient's. But I can assure my readers that it is soberly set down in a play which their ancestors took to be serious.

and

> Barabas the Jew, and Faustus the conjurer, are off-springs of a mind which at least delighted to dally with interdicted subjects.

Only the 'quaint' reference to 'mine ancient' belongs to the beloved Lamb of the Elians, forever tolerant and (in spite of personal tragedy) forever good-humoured. The sentiments belong to the world of Johnson's sound Anglican moralism that makes no bones about being shocked and will have no truck with the fanciful. There is much more of this sort of thing in Lamb than is commonly remembered. The moral assumptions of his criticism are not exactly stern. But they are conventional, a part of that continuum of English prudery that has its roots in eighteenth-century piety and looks forward to the great Victorian self-censorship. The fact is that his taste for Renaissance quaintness is only a degree or two more developed than Johnson's, and hardly different at all from that of the Wartons or of his friend Coleridge. It is rather a symptom of the growth of popular historicism, of the vogue for the 'Gothic' past, than of any determined critical analysis. Lamb's taste for the seventeenth century is sentimental, and scarcely more than sentimental: he could no more abide the Metaphysical conceit than Coleridge could, and preferred Wither, who 'lays more hold of the heart', to Quarles's 'wretched stuff'. . . . On the other hand, he can see virtues in Renaissance poetry less baroque than the imagery of Quarles, and yet too particular to have appealed to Johnson. Sidney's sonnets struck the mean that he loved best, 'full, material, and circumstantiated', in healthy contrast to late eighteenth-century verse, where there are too many 'vague and unlocalized feelings'. Poetry *may* number the streaks of the tulip, in Lamb's view—perhaps ought to do so. The Johnsonian term 'Nature' resounds through his criticism, but it is a Nature strangely elastic in its scope, and includes even the matter of visions and of waking dreams. (pp. 122-24)

A sound Johnsonian critic, then, partly romanti-
cized by his reverence for Coleridge: this seems an apter summary of Lamb's quality as a critic than any view that conceives of him as the perfect prototype of the romantic critic. Wordsworth, Coleridge, Hazlitt, and De Quincey are all more romantic critics than Lamb, and all of them reject more firmly than he did the 'Aristotelian' criteria of critical judgement. Compared with them, Lamb's position seems wavering and uncertain, and his belief in a clear, moral light and his affection for the obscure and Cavalier are often in mild, unworried conflict. But he is not the kind of critic who takes himself seriously or thinks consistency to be any sort of virtue, and the doubleness of his vision is on the whole a matter for complaisant pride. His attitude to Restoration comedy provides a perfect illustration. He has no doubt that, ultimately, it deserves the moral condemnation it had already received ('The business of their dramatic characters will not stand the moral test'). But, on the other hand, 'I am glad for a season to take an airing beyond the diocese of the strict conscience . . . I come back to my cage and my restraint the fresher and more healthy for it. I wear my shackles more contentedly for having respired the breath of an imaginary freedom.' The spiritual tourist is all the better for his little spree, though even on his day out he observes some essential rules, abandoning himself to Congreve and drawing the line at Marlowe. Such tolerances would not have been admitted by Addison or Johnson: but they have a future, they make sense in Victorian terms, in the liberal morality of Leslie Stephen, Walter Pater, and the Bloomsbury Group.

Lamb's attraction to Jacobean tragedy, which he sought to revive through the slightly bowdlerized *Specimens of English Dramatic Poets Who Lived about the Time of Shakespeare* . . . , is all of a piece with this readiness to enjoy new and alien experiences. The attraction is one of opposites. Lamb's very gentleness is drawn to the Webster of *The Duchess of Malfi*. . . . The distance between Lamb and Webster is so vast that it is surprising he can see him even with a telescope; yet he describes Webster's essential quality with notable accuracy, if by generalities. Lamb's analysis is rarely more particular than this, and its chief virtue is the virtue of sound characterization. He loves to tell you, in a few phrases, what a whole author is like. And the taste that moves him is conservative but self-indulgent, in love with quaintness if it is not too quaint, and romanticism if it is not too romantic, but above all impressed by the abiding worth of sober virtue. (pp. 124-26)

George Watson, "Lamb, Hazlitt, De Quincey," in his *The Literary Critics: A Study of English Descriptive Criticism,* second edition, The Woburn Press, 1973, pp. 122-33.

SOURCES FOR FURTHER STUDY

Barnett, George L. *Charles Lamb: The Evolution of Elia.* Indiana University Humanities Series, edited by Edward D. Seeber, no. 53. Bloomington: Indiana University Press, 1964, 286 p.

A biography focusing on those elements of Lamb's early life that influenced his later development as a writer, particularly as the author of the "Elia" essays.

——, and Tave, Stuart M. "Charles Lamb." *The English Romantic Poets & Essayists: A Review of Research and Criticism,* rev. ed., edited by Carolyn Washburn Houtchens and Lawrence Huston Houtchens, pp. 37-74. New York: New York University Press, 1966.

An annotated bibliography of works by and about Lamb.

Lucas, E. V. *The Life of Charles Lamb.* 2 vols. London: Methuen & Co., 1905.

The standard biography.

Monsman, Gerald. *Confessions of a Prosaic Dreamer: Charles Lamb's Art of Autobiography.* Durham, N.C.: Duke University Press, 1984, 165 p.

Biographical and critical study. The critic states: "[The issue that Lamb's] Elia persona addresses most trenchantly is the presumptuous pride of the artistic voice which denies that the regnant role of its language of symbols is to redeem or rehabilitate the 'allegorical' images of this our phenomenal world."

Prance, Claude A. *Companion to Charles Lamb: A Guide to People and Places, 1760-1847.* London: Mansell Publishing, 1983, 392 p.

A compendium of information related to Lamb's life and career. Prance includes such features as a map of London and an index to actors, actresses, dramatic critics, and plays popular during Lamb's lifetime.

Randel, Fred V. *The World of Elia: Charles Lamb's Essayistic Romanticism.* Kennikat Press National University Publications, Literary Criticism Series, edited by John E. Becker. Port Washington, N.Y.: Kennikat Press, 1975, 170 p.

An in-depth analysis of the "Elia" essays focusing on Lamb's handling of style, imagery, narrative voice, and the concepts of time and space.

D. H. Lawrence

1885-1930

(Full name David Herbert Lawrence; also wrote under pseudonym Lawrence H. Davison) English novelist, short story writer, poet, essayist, critic, translator, and dramatist.

INTRODUCTION

One of the most original English writers of the twentieth century, Lawrence explored human nature through frank discussions of sex, psychology, and religion. He sparked controversy throughout his career, and debate continues to characterize discussion of his life and work. Lawrence's peripatetic existence, marked by frequent changes of residence, country, and continent, earned him a reputation as a bohemian; while his personality, capable alternately of charm and malice, provoked extreme reactions from others. His work defied not only the conventional artistic norms of his day but also its political, social, and moral values. Much of the criticism on Lawrence's work revolves around the author's highly individualistic moral system, based on absolute freedom of expression, particularly sexual expression. Human sexuality was for Lawrence a symbol of the "life force" and is frequently pitted in his works against a dehumanizing modern industrial society.

The fourth child of Arthur John Lawrence, an illiterate coal miner and Lydia Beardsall Lawrence, a former school teacher, Lawrence was raised in the mining village of Eastwood, Nottinghamshire. From boyhood he shared a close relationship with his mother and grew to hate the debilitating mine work he considered responsible for his father's debased condition. Lawrence attended local grammar and secondary schools and later, from 1906 to 1908, studied at Nottingham University College, where he began writing short stories. In 1908, Lawrence moved to Croyden, just south of London, to teach school. While there he encountered Ford Madox Ford's *English Review*, in which he published some of his early poetry and—more meaningful to the evolution of his fiction—discovered what he and others termed "the exciting new school of realism" in the works of such writers as Thomas Hardy,

Henry James, Joseph Conrad, and Leo Tolstoy. In 1911, the onset of tuberculosis forced Lawrence to resign from teaching. That same year he published his first novel, *The White Peacock* (1911), which was critically well received. When he was twenty-seven, Lawrence eloped to Germany with Frieda von Richthofen Weekly, the wife of one of his college professors, and the two were married in 1914. The couple's first years together are chronicled in the poems collected in *Look! We Have Come Through!* (1917).

In 1913, Lawrence published his first major work, the largely autobiographical novel *Sons and Lovers,* and also wrote "The Prussian Officer," one of his most celebrated stories. Both works are early examples of the psychological fiction that he later developed more fully. Just before the outbreak of World War I, Lawrence returned to England, where he and Frieda endured continual harassment by the English government because of his objections to the war and her German ancestry. Lawrence's next novel, *The Rainbow* (1915), a complex narrative focusing on relationships between men and women, especially those of marriage, was judged obscene for its explicit discussion of sexuality, and was suppressed in England. These events intensified Lawrence's bitter struggle with social orthodoxy and the forces of modern civilization, which he came to believe were arrayed against him and most certainly influenced his decision to leave England. His last major novel, *Lady Chatterley's Lover* (1928), met with similar resistance and was available only in an expurgated version until 1959 in the United States and 1960 in England, when a landmark obscenity trial vindicated the book as a work of literature. After the war, the Lawrences lived briefly in Germany, Austria, Italy, Sicily, England, France, Australia, Mexico, and in the southwestern United States, where Lawrence hoped to someday establish a utopian community. These varied locales provided settings for many of the novels and stories Lawrence wrote during the 1920s and also inspired four books of admired travel sketches. In 1930 Lawrence entered a sanatorium in Vence, France, in an attempt to cure the tuberculosis that afflicted him throughout his life. He died soon after.

Lawrence's first major work, the largely autobiographical novel *Sons and Lovers,* contains some of the author's most characteristic themes: the complexity of human relationships, especially that between a mother and son; the experience of first love; and the emotional dominance of one person by another. Many critics—notably Lawrence's close friend, John Middleton Murray—have noted striking similarities between the personal experiences and emotional dilemmas of the author and his protagonist, Paul Morel. Later commentators, however, often agree that a close autobiographical analysis of *Sons and Lovers* discounts Lawrence's role as a creative artist.

The Rainbow and *Women in Love* (1920), generally regarded as Lawrence's best works, were originally conceived of as a single novel, to be called *The Sisters,* and some continuity was preserved between the novels. *The Rainbow* is concerned with three generations of the Brangwen family, and *Women in Love* examines the two men with whom Ursula and Gudrun Brangwen fall in love. In *The Rainbow* and subsequent works, Lawrence sought to develop a specialized vocabulary to convey intellectual and emotional states with the same intensity as physical acts. The result was a narrative style marked by continual repetition of key words and phrases, and the frequent use—many commentators contend, overuse—of modifiers and intensifiers. Because his terminology and symbols were intensely personal, however, this often resulted in obscure, almost unintelligible prose. While Lawrence maintained that repetition is suited to the evocation of mental processes, critics generally agree that his attempts to evoke stream of consciousness are often awkward and ineffective, particularly when compared with the similar literary experimentation of such contemporaries as James Joyce and Virginia Woolf.

In his later novels, such as *Aaron's Rod* (1922), *Kangaroo* (1923), and *The Plumed Serpent* (1926), Lawrence dealt more extensively with themes of power, dominance, and leadership. He also began to focus in these later works on the relationships that men form with one another, rather than with women. Lawrence formulated a concept of *blutbruderschaft* ("blood brotherhood"), which he felt was essential to men as a complement to "right relationships" with women. This precept is introduced in the friendship between Rupert Birkin and Gerald Crich in *Women in Love,* and further developed in *The Plumed Serpent,* along with the concept of "blood consciousness," a religion of intuition and instinct which was the product of his lifelong search for a new mystical expression of life's meaning.

In his last major novel, *Lady Chatterley's Lover,* Lawrence returned to some of his earlier themes, such as the dehumanizing effect of industrialization. Even more than *The Rainbow, Lady Chatterley's Lover* has been the subject of intense controversy because of its use of words commonly considered obscene. F. R. Leavis classed it among Lawrence's "lesser novels" because of its "offenses against taste," and according to Michael Squires and Dennis Jackson in 1985: "Its literary reputation is not yet secure; the scent of pornography clings." Recalling his earlier statements on blood-knowledge, Lawrence explained the ideas that shaped the novel in his essay "A Propos of *Lady Chatterley's Lover*" (1929): "In fact, thought and action, word and deed are two separate lives which we lead. We need, very sincerely, to keep a connection . . . and this is the real point of the book. I want men and women to be able to think sex, fully, completely, honestly and cleanly. . . . Life is only bearable when the mind and body are in harmony, and there is a natural balance between them, and each has a natural respect for the other." Lawrence maintained here, as he had earlier, that dependence on mental knowledge to the exclusion of blood-knowledge leads to most of the "tragedies" of the modern world, chiefly a "mechanization" of life. Far from being obscene, *Lady Chatterley's Lover* celebrates the creative power of spiritual and carnal togetherness, "which is religious and poetic," he asserted.

Lawrence's short stories present a contrast to his novels. They are economical in style and structure, and differ from the novels in that they present Lawrence's themes in terms of literature and not homily, avoiding the didacticism that pervades almost all of his novels. Like both his long and short fiction, most of Lawrence's poetry is intensely personal. In fact, as Sigrid Undset noted, "It may safely be said that the whole of Lawrence's production was autobiographical." Lawrence's earliest poetry adhered to traditional poetic forms and is not as highly regarded as his later works in this genre. It is in the free forms of his nature poems, espe-

cially those in *Birds, Beasts and Flowers* (1923), that Lawrence achieves his best poetic effects. In addition to his fiction and poetry, Lawrence wrote eight dramas, most of which have never been produced. They are of interest primarily as a reflection of Lawrence's effort to present his basic literary ideas in a different medium than fiction.

Lawrence has come to be regarded as one of the twentieth century's most important novelists. In his innovative use of psychological themes he produced the first, and some critics still believe finest, modern psychological novels. Nonetheless, debate over controversial aspects of Lawrence's work continues. Following his death in 1930, the London *Times* regretted that Lawrence "confused decency with hypocrisy, and honesty with the free and public use of vulgar words," while E. M. Forster contemporaneously lauded him as "the greatest imaginative genius of our generation."

(For further information about Lawrence's life and works, see *Contemporary Authors*, Vols. 104, 121; *Dictionary of Literary Biography*, Vols. 10, 19, 36; *Short Story Criticism*, Vol. 4; and *Twentieth-Century Literary Criticism*, Vols. 2, 9, 16, 33.)

CRITICAL COMMENTARY

MARY FREEMAN
(essay date 1955)

[In the following excerpt, Freeman surveys Lawrence's treatment of the theme of conflict in his fiction.]

In his early novels Lawrence pointed to conflict on many levels: within the individual, between groups, and in nature. No level of conflict seemed independent of any other. In Lettie's snowdrops, in Siegmund's sea, in each living thing, he saw beginning and end in impassioned struggle. Even class conflict was not viewed as a purely social phenomenon but as part of some more fundamental heaving and clashing in the process of creation.

The White Peacock announced with youthful ardour that these conflicts exist and that in each individual they must somehow be reconciled: by exclusion of intolerable material and reduction of one's awareness or by identification with something over and above the individual, one's fellow man or nature herself. Each character in all of Lawrence's books has his own way of viewing this problem and his own way of solving it.

Each book as a whole marks a stage in Lawrence's speculations reaching toward his own adjustment.

In *The White Peacock* Lawrence showed his disillusion with all the viewpoints offered by his early environment. *The Trespasser* revealed the futility of the "vie tragique." At the end of *Sons and Lovers,* although Paul felt that the tragedies of the earth could be redeemed only by touching the sublime, he rejected his impulse toward dramatic death and turned toward the town with its small men and smaller affairs. *The Rainbow* integrated the "vie tragique" and the "vie triviale" by viewing trivialities with intoxicated concentration. (pp. 49-50)

[The] life-death contrast dominated Lawrence's general concern with the nature of conflict, and gave added impetus to his search for some satisfactory reconciliation.

In this impassioned quest Lawrence treated similar situations again and again, presenting variations of the same potent contrasts and seeking their ultimate relationship. He did not want to cancel contrasts in this reconciliation, but wanted to preserve difference and conflict even while he saw them as parts of a whole. He

Principal Works

The White Peacock (novel) 1911

Love Poems and Others (poetry) 1913

Sons and Lovers (novel) 1913

The Prussian Officer (short stories) 1914

The Rainbow (novel) 1915

Look! We Have Come Through! (poetry) 1917

The Lost Girl (novel) 1920

Women in Love (novel) 1920

Psychoanalysis and the Unconscious (essay) 1921

Aaron's Rod (novel) 1922

England, My England (short stories) 1922

Fantasia of the Unconscious (essay) 1922

Birds, Beasts and Flowers (poetry) 1923

Kangaroo (novel) 1923

The Plumed Serpent (novel) 1926

Mornings in Mexico (essays) 1927

The Collected Poems of D. H. Lawrence 2 vols. (poetry) 1928

Lady Chatterley's Lover (novel) 1928

The Woman Who Rode Away (short stories) 1928

Pansies (poetry) 1929

The Escaped Cock (novella) 1930; also published as The Man Who Died, 1931

Love among the Haystacks (short stories) 1930

The Virgin and the Gipsy (novel) 1930

Last Poems (poetry) 1932

The First Lady Chatterley (novel) 1944

John Thomas and Lady Jane (novel) 1972

becomes tedious in *Twilight in Italy* in his insistence on this subtle distinction. It is this peculiar connectedness of contrasts that lured Lawrence into more and more obscure speculations. It was his Pied Piper, his Little Blue Flower. No matter how "unwatched," as he claimed, the novels flowed from his pen, they were directed by the requirements of this exploration.

The Trespasser was a crucial turning point in the direction of Lawrence's search, for it warned him of a danger that he never forgot. Even though he had rejected all ordinary solutions to his problems, and for the moment felt drawn by mysticism, nevertheless he concluded that identification with impersonal forces to the exclusion of human values led to death. . . . Lawrence found it necessary to widen his view of life to the point of including death. Not only was it an unavoidable experience, but it was one extreme in the most dramatically complete contrast we know: the life-death antithesis. The subtle relationship between these extreme opposites intrigued him, and he felt that our more profound experiences must in some way take it into account. Possibly opposition itself had a value. (pp. 52-3)

Identification with social decay in *Women in Love* was the culmination of Lawrence's resolve to know suffering but to feel joy. . . . It had seemed possible at the close of *The Rainbow* that a new and more satisfying world could be built if man recovered awareness of nature and reconstructed society in harmony with it. But at that point the pain and suffering of a war-torn world overwhelmed Lawrence, and he was tempted once more to find something satisfying in what repelled him: the divine in pain, the god in death. (p. 70)

Lawrence found also that the association of contradictory aspects of life often mitigated the disagreeable qualities of each at the same time that it, like contrasting colors, heightened sensation. . . . [The] association between creation and decay, established and underscored in transcendental moments, is represented throughout Lawrence's books by suggestive figures—lilies, swans, moonlight, reptiles, cold fire, ice, Aphrodite, and the sea—and insinuating adjectives—phosphorescent, salty, dark, electric. All call up their aura of flowering corruption. Singly or together, they are shorthand indications of an entire perception—visual, aural, tactual, even intellectual—and, in spite of their surface obliqueness, they give an unusually solid sense of fact.

In his effort to reconcile incongruities in a blaze of ecstatic sensuousness Lawrence used another device characteristic of futurism. He frequently transposed attitudes and words conventionally appropriate in one context to quite another, for example, using the surcharged words commonly allotted to love in describing men, animals, flowers, and trees. (This practice roused rather lurid speculations regarding Lawrence's relations, not only with men, but also with birch groves and his cow Susan.) (pp. 75-6)

Lawrence's most obvious difference from the futurists lay in his rejection of our industrial age. He felt that he must come in line with sun and storm, love and hate, life and death; but he could never see why man, having been vastly clever and constructed wonderful things, should now become a servant to his own creations. (p. 80)

To achieve breadth of understanding without dimming immediacy of perception, to grip transcendental emotions in sensory experience was the goal toward which Lawrence moved in both life and literature and remained the objective behind each problem that he dealt with. It was an effort inseparable from Lawrence's very existence, for it fed his insatiable appetite for life and mitigated his pain at the thought of death. It allowed him to know sorrow but to feel joy. He was even stimulated by the brilliant incongruity of his vision and remained undaunted when in novel after novel he hit a spot at which his transcendental strivings and his abundant common sense dictated contrary moves. Each failure to integrate these opposites to his satisfaction challenged him anew. (p. 83)

In *Psychoanalysis and the Unconscious,* . . . Lawrence introduced his own conception of the unconscious, with the same aims that had prompted his distinction between "mental" and "pre-mental" knowing: it allowed him to distinguish between "knowledge" which dragged backward and individual understanding which pulled forward.

It was on this point that the book made clear Lawrence's crucial divergence from Freudianism. . . . Freud's assumption that the residuals of childhood persist essentially unchanged in the adult ran counter to Lawrence's plea for a responsible mature individuality always transcending itself. Freud's location of retrogressive forces in the unconscious was the antithesis of Lawrence's location of retrogressive patterns in the conscious mind. (p. 136)

By this changed emphasis Lawrence tried to reduce further the heavy pull toward death characterizing so many of his descriptions of consummate moments. Although in his essays the life-death symbol had fallen apart into death followed by life, as he must have intended, the death fascination lingered still in his short stories, poems, and novels. (p. 143)

With *The Plumed Serpent* and *The Flying Fish* Lawrence's intensely sensuous merging and descent toward "the singing death" came to a halt. His writing began to retreat from the complex toward the simple, away from delirious ecstasy toward wholesome consummation. *The Man Who Died* expressed Lawrence's relief at coming alive out of the very maw of death. A reversal of the Christian story of resurrection, it treats, not transfiguration out of the flesh, but transfiguration into the flesh; not ascent into the beyond, but into the Now; not eternal beatitudes, but realization of dynamic function. Nothing is so marvelous, thought the man who had died but was risen, as "to be alone in the phenomenal world, which is raging, and yet apart." (p. 208)

The last period of Lawrence's writing was characterized by increasing discrimination. (p. 237)

After so many attempts to pull contradictory experiences into concurrent understanding, Lawrence had concluded that such perceptual omniscience destroyed individuality and led to "the singing death." To live, men must turn back to man. However, what was at first withdrawal from morbidity brought Lawrence back to a point from which the striking contrasts of life that had provoked him seemed reconciled in the marvelous unity of living things. What could man know of "wholeness" other than in living creatures? There unity did not seem to pull apart from action. The Dark God whispered in the flesh. No need to scan the dis-

tance. "The Crown," "The Rainbow," graced the wholehearted action of an integral personality. Lawrence's understanding of the consummate moment had moved to its third phase. He no longer looked upon it as an absolute resolution of an infinity of contradictions either through expanded comprehension or through intense sensory excitation. He now looked for consummation in insightful action resulting from creative thinking by the whole man. (pp. 237-38)

Lawrence had begun his writing with the belief that all institutionalized ideals were dead, and he ended regarding even his own insights as tentative and, at best, transient. Yet out of the depths of what is generally regarded as pessimism, he saw life enhanced, not dimmed, by its evanescence and its earthy origin and end. Lawrence had sought enhanced life in strange and morbid places, but at last, after many vacillations, he concluded that it flowed only in the familiar flesh and that all things were truly related only through vital contact. (p. 246)

Mary Freeman, in her *D. H. Lawrence: A Basic Study of His Ideas,* University of Florida, 1955, 277 p.

SANDRA GILBERT

(essay date 1972)

[Gilbert is an American critic, poet, and editor. In the following excerpt from her *Acts of Attention: The Poems of D. H. Lawrence,* she discusses Lawrence's perspectives on poetry.]

"In England people have got that loathsome superior knack of refusing to consider me a poet at all." D. H. Lawrence wrote to his friend A. W. McLeod in February, 1914. " 'Your prose is so good,' say the kind fools, 'that we are obliged to forgive you your poetry.' How I hate them." Now, over half a century later, though Lawrence's genius as a novelist is even more widely recognized than it was in 1914, his poetry has still received comparatively little attention. Somehow, the prose has always stood in the way. For one thing, it *is* "so good," and, for another, it more obviously falls into a clearly defined and widely accepted tradition. Thus most commentators treat the poetry as a merely interesting, if not embarrassing, by-product of the novel-making process. (pp. 1-2)

Yet Lawrence did, after all, begin his literary career as a poet, producing in his lifetime ten books of verse. . . . Lawrence's dual production certainly suggests that he himself must have made at least a pragmatic distinction between the two forms, a distinction which, if we can discover it, may not only illuminate his aesthetic theories but also aid in an appreciative understanding of his too often neglected poems in verse. (p. 3)

[Though Lawrence] had much to say about poetry and poetic theory, in letters, essays, and introductions, his most important attempt at a general definition of poetry occurs in the preface to Harry Crosby's *Chariot of the Sun,* which he wrote toward the end of his life. He began this essay by demolishing some of the vaguer, more conventional definitions of poetry. . . . "The essential quality of poetry," he asserts, introducing his crucial definition, "is that it makes a new effort of attention, and 'discovers' a new world within the known world." Poetry, in Lawrence's view, is visionary: "Man and the animals, and the flowers all live within a strange and forever surging chaos. The chaos which we have got used to we call a cosmos. The unspeakable inner chaos of which we are composed we call consciousness, and mind, and even civilization. But it is, ultimately, chaos, lit up by visions or not lit up by visions." And those visions are poems. (pp. 4-5)

Perhaps a major reason for the prolonged neglect of Lawrence's verse is that while his theory of the novel falls within a definable and acceptable tradition, his view of poetry was the exception rather than the rule in the earlier part of this century. He himself was well aware that as a poetic theorist he consistently opposed contemporary critical opinion and, to a lesser extent, prevailing poetic practice. For one thing, his view of a poem as a pure act of attention, an act of absolute surrender to the visionary image, was very much at odds with the emerging belief of critics—and of many influential poets—that the essential qualities of poetry are irony, ambiguity, and paradox. (p. 9)

While he never rejected irony, ambiguity, and paradox as literary techniques, he did not regard them as essential, especially not in poetry. For him, poetry, unlike the novel, did not involve elaborated relationships. On the contrary, he believed that its essence was single rather than double vision or, as he put it, "naiveté." For the act of attention was not only an act of intensity but, more important, an act of "the intrinsic naiveté without which no poetry can exist, not even the most sophisticated." . . . But Lawrence's advocacy of naiveté is more than a stand against the kind of double vision that was coming to seem to many poets and critics the essence of poetry. It becomes clear in the Crosby preface that he is directing his definition of poetry against what he considers false sophistication in verse. Such sophistication appears chiefly in a preoccupation with form rather than substance ("the fear of chaos is in their parade of forms and techniques") in empty traditionalism, and in foolish "flippancy" or irony. In all cases it is in Lawrence's view a sign of the poet's failure to submit himself with almost religious humility to the

single demonic vision that should be the wellspring of poetry. (p. 10)

Lawrence's poet of naiveté, then, consciously choosing the path of visionary awareness, must be "sufficiently sophisticated to wring the neck of sophistication." He must be anti-formal and anti-traditional, as well as anti-ironic, not out of ignorance or literary incapacity—two faults of which Lawrence himself has often been accused—but because he deliberately chooses to go beyond or beneath technique to the naiveté at the heart of the artistic impulse. "Thought, I love thought," wrote Lawrence in one of his *Pansies,* perhaps replying to those critics who accused him of anti-intellectualism, but "not the jiggling and twisting of already existent ideas. / I despise that self-important game." "Thought"—and we may take poetry to be one of the highest forms of thought—should not be "a trick or an exercise or a set of dodges." It is, rather, "the welling up of unknown life into consciousness." Thus the effort of attention is finally not crassly anti-intellectual or boorishly irrational, but a sophisticated striving for innocence; and to be a poet, to be able to *attend,* is to be in a state of grace.

Such a poetic, though it contradicts much early twentieth-century aesthetic theory, is obviously Romantic in its origins, and Romantic in several ways. To begin with, Lawrence's advocacy of organic or anti-formal form can be traced back through Whitman and Ruskin to Coleridge. In repudiating the artifice of premeditated form, Lawrence recommends and, at his best, writes a kind of unpremeditated process poetry that discovers its form both in its content and in the process of its composition. . . . Moreover, in advising that the poet yield himself to the visionary process of attention, Lawrence clearly participates in the anti-traditional tradition of originality, spontaneity, and sincerity that was first fully articulated by Wordsworth in his Preface to *Lyrical Ballads,* and Lawrence's sense that the poet must be skillfully passive, like his belief in sophisticated innocence, recalls Wordsworth's advocacy of "wise passiveness." (pp. 11-12)

As a poetic theorist, then, Lawrence is a Romantic in modern dress; and he expresses his visionary Romanticism metaphorically as well as directly. In his **"Song of a Man Who Has Come Through,"** for instance, he makes use of the central Romantic metaphor for creativity, "the metaphor of the correspondent breeze." Like Shelley in the "Ode to the West Wind," Coleridge in "Dejection: An Ode" or Wordsworth in *The Prelude,* he longs to "yield" himself and be "borrowed / By the fine, fine wind that takes its course through the chaos of the world"; he longs, paradoxically, for the strength to be passive, to be "keen and hard like the sheer tip of a wedge / Driven by invisible blows." Only so, in the Romantic tradition, can he "come at the wonder," at the visionary guardians of creative renewal within his own soul.

But even in his use of this Romantic metaphor Lawrence was violating what we might call the ordinary usage of modern English poetry, for to many of the British and American poets who were his contemporaries the wind had become a symbol of futility rather than of creative vitality. (p. 13)

[In studying Lawrence's poetry we] see that, like most poet-novelists, he went through phases of greater or lesser interest in the different forms in which he worked. When he was in what we might call a fictional phase, his poetry frequently suffered as much from a blurring of distinctions, a failure to bear in mind his own definition of lyric poetry, as from anything else. When his interest in writing novels waned temporarily, as it did around 1920, his poetry gained in intensity and distinction, as though all his creative energy had flowed for the time being into this other channel. In short, while many of his weaker poems do usurp prose ideas and consequently have formal as well as substantial problems, his best poems deal with matters which, according to his own definition, are the special province of poetry. At his best, then, Lawrence is not a poet in prose but a poet in "poetry," for in his best poems, to quote [Vivian de Sola] Pinto, he "said something . . . that he could never have said in prose." (p. 15)

Sandra Gilbert, in her *Acts of Attention: The Poems of D. H. Lawrence*, Cornell University Press, 1972, 327 p.

FRANK KERMODE

(essay date 1973)

[Kermode is an English critic. In the following excerpt from his study *D. H. Lawrence*, he discusses the multiple critical interpretations *Sons and Lovers* has attracted since its publication.]

Sons and Lovers, the masterpiece of Lawrence's first phase, was begun in October 1910. In November he ended his engagement to Jessie Chambers ("Miriam"), and on December 3 began one with Louie Burrows. His mother died on December 10. He restarted the novel, then called *Paul Morel*, early in 1911 but set it aside to write *The Trespasser*. Resuming the *Bildungsroman*, he finished it in May 1912, and rewrote it that autumn. Much of importance occurred between these versions. In January 1912 illness forced him to give up teaching; he returned to the Nottingham area and met Frieda Weekley, the German wife of a professor at Nottingham University College. The composition of his autobiographical novel therefore coincided with a period of multiple crises in his life. It was begun before the death of his mother, which is its climax; it was rewritten at the behest of an early lover, Miriam, and then it was rewritten again under the eye of Frieda, after their elopement. It would be difficult to think of any other writer who wrote his life into successive texts of his fiction as Lawrence did; he habitually confronted his tale with new experience, and new interpretations of the past. There is in consequence an abundance, even a confusion, of life; one cannot feel that the published version is the last possible rehandling of the tale; and this openness is not the consequence of inefficiency. Flexibility, the power of a story to challenge a reader (including himself), is one of the marks of the novel as Lawrence wanted it to be, liberated from the burden of finality and completeness placed on it by his enemies, the novelists who, in his opinion, mistook structure for life, and novelistic custom for natural law.

Sons and Lovers is probably still the best known of the novels, and it would be wrong to cavil at this, for it is certainly a great achievement. In the first part the brief inset of the courtship of Paul's parents, the father's gaiety, his "sensuous flame of life" melting the mother's puritanism, has that single-minded veracity of impression which was consistent, in Lawrence, with more abstract intentions. Morel, in his caressing dialect, speaks, as Dorothy Van Ghent notes, Lawrence's language of physical tenderness. . . . This is the dark dancing miner whom marriage will reduce, both physically and morally; whose son will be lost to a mother who makes refinement the instrument of her conquest. The placing of the parents and children, as of the ravaged landscape and its colliers, is done with extraordinary narrative tact and energy. Morel, obscurely fighting for a manhood sapped at the root by the absorbing care of the mother, cuts off the one-year-old William's curls and causes his wife the most intense suffering of her life. . . . Mrs. Morel is locked out by an angry husband; under a great moon she buries her face in a lily, and returns to the house smeared with pollen. This scene is so intensely realized—night scents and sounds, gray-white light, fear and cold—that the mind is satisfied without further interpretation, though interpretation, if offered, will be absorbed. Does the lily, a flower which Lawrence admired for its sexual blossoms and mired roots, daub Mrs. Morel satirically, or is there sympathy between them? Miriam is later taken to task for trying to identify with or possess the flowers she is admiring. But Mrs. Morel is for once identified with the night; when her normal prudence returns she makes her husband let her in, and his punishment for the misdeed is to be further reduced. There are other scenes in which narrative is transcended, caught up into some symbolic mode, without damage to the relation of acts and persons; for example, the moment when the blood of the mother, struck by the husband, drops into the baby Paul's hair. This boy sleeps with his mother, and lovingly cleans the mire off her fine shoes; episodes of everyday life will tell their own story better when the entire narrative context is capable of assuming, at any moment, large symbolic meanings. An understanding of how this worked is what chiefly distinguishes Lawrence as a critic of fiction, especially in his studies of American literature. Thus it is not enough to say that the perversely close relationship of Paul with his mother precludes the possibility, at least during her life, of his satisfactorily choosing a sexual partner; Miriam is not merely a rival but also, in some ways a double; the rejection of her for the mother is also a rejection of the mother.

So too with Morel, the detested father; his defeat is not simply Oedipal; it is also the defeat of the dark virility of the pit, of unashamed and easy male grace and strength, beauty with its roots in muck. And all these meanings are in the complexity of the text, its power to suggest meanings other than that vouched for by a narrator apparently half-committed to Paul's own preference for the mother.

It has been argued that the narrative method alters in Part II; that objective omniscience gives way to a subtler mode, in which we can no longer trust the narrator: "the point of view adopted is that of Paul; but since confusion, self-deception, and desperate self-justification are essential to that point of view, we can never tell . . . where the real truth lies" except "by seeking out the portrait of Miriam that lies beneath the over-painted commentary of the Paul-narrator." This nonce-technique Louis L. Martz regards as having served on one occasion only; but Lawrence is the great overpainter, his habitual method is to confront the text again and again, to rehandle it in precisely this style. The product grows progressively more complex in relation to the intention; that is why he insists that we do not isolate an intention and trust it. Trust the tale. If there is more than one Miriam under its surface paint, then so be it. Any novel, by virtue of its length, the intermittency of such controls as "point of view," and the indeterminate nature of narrative, permits a great many such doublings and, consequently, an indefinite range of interpretation. . . . So there is nothing unusual about [Lawrence's] employment of the method in *Sons and Lovers,* though Martz is right to find it there, and his demonstration of its effect on the representation of Miriam is finely achieved.

Jessie Chambers did not like the Miriam she saw—unwilling to let go, subtly wrong in her attitude to the non-human or the animal, too much, in the end, the woman who buttons up or reduces men. She saw how much the confusions of Paul had colored her image, how unfair his condemnation and rejection of her for a failure in which he shared at least equally. Yet all this is in the book; it is he who, possessed, resents

her possessiveness, he whose "sex desire was a sort of detached thing that did not belong to a woman." The only woman who might really please him would be one he did not know (compare the story **"Love among the Haystacks,"** probably written in 1911). And it is he who forces the girl to accept him sexually: "He said that possession was a great moment in life." This is what Lawrence later came to call sex in the head. When Miriam makes her sacrifice he identifies the initiatory experience with death. Miriam has two faces, the vital and sensitive, often snubbed by Paul; and the timid, restrained, and possessive, both of which somewhat resemble Mrs. Morel. Both are visible, simultaneously.

So with Clara: the success with which Lawrence renders the pleasures of this sexual relationship is not always recognized. It is true that she is a licensed mother substitute; the first thing Paul does after making love to her is to clean her boots. But the very completeness of his sexual satisfaction sets it apart from life; she is for night, not day. Dawes, so often called a reflection of Morel, is Clara's true husband; Paul ritually fights him and comes to terms with the married couple, as he might with his reconciled parents, but the death that inhabits his sex manifests itself in the same chapter as the fight, when his mother confesses her cancer.

Such are the complexities which life, and reflection upon it, brought into the overpainting of *Sons and Lovers.* The cutting of all the knots is the death of the mother, in the chapter called "Release." Paul says goodby to her, and to Clara; he oscillates between death and a mechanical kind of life, swings back briefly and for the last time to Miriam, and then departs for the future, "a nothingness and yet not nothing," walking toward light not darkness. The novel originates in an intense and prolonged personal crisis; it is remarkable that it should be so unselfish, so unsentimental. One could hardly ask for further proof of the seriousness with which Lawrence believed that "the novel, properly handled, can reveal the most secret places of life," as no other discourse can, and do so beyond the intention, and despite the defenses, of its author.

Much has been said of the relation of *Sons and Lovers* to Freud; its theme is Oedipal, and in the later stages of composition Lawrence had learned something about Freud from Frieda—his first contact with a thinker whom he was repeatedly to attack. The degree to which the personal relationships in the novel comply with Freud's account of mother fixation is surely a tribute to the accuracy of Freud's generalization rather than a proof of Lawrence's indebtedness. Freud observed and generalized, Lawrence observed, but believed that the text of a novel was more than an occasion for drawing abstract conclusions. Freud was, as it happens, the kind of scientist Lawrence believed to be incapacitated, by the very nature of his interests and methods, from giving a truthful version of reality. It is nevertheless true . . . that there are interesting common elements in *Sons and Lovers* and Freud's important, and almost contemporaneous paper, "The Most Prevalent Form of Degradation in Erotic Life" (1912). This is the disorder Freud calls "psychical impotence"—impotence which has no physical cause, and is manifested only in relation to some women. There is a conflict between affection and sex, traceable to an incestuous fixation on mother or sister. It may not take the extreme form of impotence, and indeed in most people it does not; but Freud is clear that "very few people of culture" can achieve an ideal fusion of tenderness and sensuality, and this manifests itself in a lack of sexual desire for women who inspire affection, and is remedied "in the presence of a lower type of sexual object." The consequence is an inability to get on with one's well-brought-up wife. . . . The sexual difficulties of the age, Freud was sure, stemmed from the basic Oedipal situation, assisted by another unchangeable condition, the proximity of the genital and excrementatory organs in an animal which, since it learned to walk upright, has tried culturally to sever the associations between them. It cannot be done; the genitals remain animal, and so does love, which perhaps will never "be reconciled with the demands of culture."

This diagnosis is certainly directed toward a situation of which Lawrence was aware, though for him "the demands of culture" originated in and were insisted upon by woman. Paul is almost aware (as is Morel) that his relationship with his mother is not entirely a matter of sexless "affection"—he is at times a phantom husband. And he knows, however obscurely, that one reason why Miriam will not do is that he attributes to her a denial of animal nature which he associates with superior women—with Clara he has much better sex because she is, in a measure, inferior. The story makes it plain enough that an explanation similar to Freud's is also lurking in it.

Lawrence's own reaction to the sex-culture dilemma proposed by Freud would certainly have been, "To hell with culture." And this meant, partly, to hell with women, its agents. Later he was explicitly to reject the Oedipal hypothesis, though he defended with increasing ferocity the position that women inhibited the full expression of a man's inmost self, defiled his angel. His reflections on the genital-excrementatory syndrome persisted through many years, and in practice his answer was to teach a woman better by enforcing it on her in its animal reality. Yet it is clear enough that Freud and Lawrence, however different their instruments and diagnoses, were in a sense talking about the same thing, an epochal sickness with deep roots in the past, and, as to its symptoms as well as its causes, a malfunction of sexual relationships within the culture. . . . Their intellectual traditions were very different, and Lawrence's opinions, mystical and rational,

have their origin in English radical thought, not in the clinics of Vienna; but their concurrence, as far as it goes, is testimony that, as Europe moved into the Great War, to speak well of obvious ills of civilization one had to reflect deeply on sons and what they love.

Lawrence was soon to feel a need to give systematic form to such reflections; the war developed them and made them urgent, but they are implicit in *Sons and Lovers* and in the poems of *Look! We Have Come Through!* which celebrate recovery and marriage. *Sons and Lovers* is the only major work of Lawrence which had no doctrinal double, in which there is no possible dissension between life and what he called "metaphysic." Henceforth all is different. (pp. 11-19)

Frank Kermode, in his *D. H. Lawrence,* The Viking Press, 1973, 174 p.

SCOTT SANDERS
(essay date 1973)

[In the following excerpt from his *D. H. Lawrence: The World of the Major Novels*, Sanders explores Lawrence's presentation of the relationship between the individual and society in his novels.]

In his essay of 1914 on "The New Novel" Henry James complained that contemporary practitioners of the art of fiction—among them the Lawrence of *Sons and Lovers*—had become obsessed with the depiction of environment and the notation of consciousness, to the neglect of those virtues of selection, emphasis and design which characterized the works of Austen, Dickens, Trollope, Thackeray, and, implicitly, James himself. These new novels by Wells, Bennett and Lawrence seemed to James fairly saturated with naturalistic details, without any discrimination, without any overall imaginative control, as if they had been transcribed from experience rather than composed. Amidst such jumble, James further complained, the critic looks in vain for a centre of interest or a sense of the whole. . . . [This criticism points] to an important difference between the novel form as handled by Austen, Eliot, Thackeray and James, and the novel form as developed by the author of *Sons and Lovers.*

In his rendering of the formation of Paul Morel within the concentric circles of family, colliery village and industrial Midlands, Lawrence followed the best nineteenth century realist tradition of representing the development of consciousness and affection within a particular social context, at a particular time. Where he differs from his predecessors, however—even from Emily Brontë, Dickens and Hardy whom he most nearly resembles in this respect—is in the degree to which he treats that social context as alien, as something neither created nor sustained nor comprehended by those who are forced to live within it, something imposed from without upon the Bestwood community, upon the Morel family and upon young Paul. The world of *Sons and Lovers* seems *given,* to the novelist as to the protagonist. (pp. 206-07)

[The] ties between environment and psyche are indeed closer than Lawrence was at that time prepared to acknowledge. The activities and pressures of Bestwood life are not some picturesque backdrop for the human drama, but rather form the substance of that drama itself, they mold personal relations and direct the growth of character. The shaping and connecting role of social forces is everywhere implicit in *Sons and Lovers,* demonstrating an historical awareness which rivals that of Dickens and George Eliot. Like those Victorian critics of society, Lawrence underwent a social dislocation which made him sensitive to the determining influences of education, wealth, class position and sexual roles. Yet because, to his mind, he had escaped the confines of Eastwood, he tended to overestimate the power of the individual to struggle free of community. In other words his awareness of the determining influence of social forces was accompanied by an exaggerated appraisal of individual freedom. Hence the contradiction one often encounters in Lawrence's fiction: a character who appears enmeshed in society on one level of the novel may appear on another as a free

agent. Man is governed by culture: man is freed by nature. . . .

[The] given-ness of the fictional world in *Sons and Lovers* may be accounted for in part as a sign of his temperamental anti-formalism. But this anti-formalism, which has annoyed many critics besides James, was only one expression of Lawrence's general suspicion of reason. (p. 207)

The earlier Victorian novelists presented both community and individual as knowable, either by the narrator, as in Scott, or by a central observer, as in Austen; and the same novelists treated the social order, however imperfect, as the product of human reason and desire. The fictional world appears progressively less rational and intelligible after 1848, particularly in the later works of Dickens, Eliot and Hardy, and in Gissing and Conrad. Lawrence reproduces this century-long evolution within the space of his own career. He starts from the earlier position in *The White Peacock,* assuming intelligibility; but already in *Sons and Lovers* he is uncovering wild zones within the self and inhuman zones within society; and by the writing of *Women in Love* he is depicting contemporary society as so irrational and destructive, so utterly alien to all human reason or desire, that it must be escaped altogether if the individual—who is himself already unstable—is to survive. Just as *The Rainbow* continues and develops the work of George Eliot, so *Women in Love* extends the work of Hardy, taking up the moral issues where they were left tangled at the end of *Jude the Obscure.* Although in that novel Hardy several times blames the suffering of Jude Fawley and Sue Bridehead upon indifferent nature, the deeper implication of their story—as Lawrence pointed out in his analysis of the novel and as Hardy certainly intended—is that the social code itself is at fault. . . . What was implicit in *Jude the Obscure* becomes explicit in *Women in Love.* Birkin and Ursula pursue their passion in solitude; sex becomes a region which they inhabit instead of society. Their fulfillment is to be sought no longer through activity in the world, but through more and more private, intense physical experience. Hence Birkin's assumption that the first step towards "completeness of being" was to drop all social responsibilities and quit his school inspector's job. There is nothing whatsoever triumphant about this alienation in Lawrence's work, nothing of the defiant exile we have come to expect as a stock feature of twentieth century literature; rather there is a deep sense of loss, not simply of the knowable community, but of the inhabitable community.

Adrift, the isolate self, like Ursula alone in the horse pasture at the close of *The Rainbow,* is subject to incomprehensible influences from within and from without. So far as Lawrence can see, there is no longer any "cultivated field" of human activity which will guarantee an authentic existence, no longer any settled community in which the self can discover its identity, no longer any agreed code by which the self can gauge its conduct. Thus he cannot provide that sense of the whole which James desired, that impression of a range of life wholly encompassed within the artist's organizing vision, for Lawrence's subject stretches obstinately beyond his ken; outward, into the destructive realm of social forces, and beyond that to the enveloping process of nature; inward, into the irrational recesses of the self, where the divine life impulse stirs with unpredictable motions. There is no still centre from which this can all be measured, no circumference within which it can all be contained.

The indeterminacy of character and of community are clearly inter-related: if the individual is subject to irrational influences, then society, multiplying this effect a thousandfold, may act irrationally on a vast scale, as in the First World War; on the other hand, if community disintegrates, as it does in the transition from Marsh Farm to industrial Wiggiston in *The Rainbow,* then character must also fragment. This is the meaning of Lawrence's celebrated warning, with reference to early drafts of *The Rainbow,* that "You mustn't look in my novel for the old stable *ego*—of the character." The stable ego is product of a coherent society,

and the unstable ego of an incoherent society. Beginning with the wartime novels, Lawrence no longer presents character as a developing psychic continuity, but rather as a variable, discontinuous, unpredictable manifestation, almost a form of energy. The demands such a reconception of character made upon language were extreme, particularly noticeable in *Women in Love.*

In conscious opposition to his nineteenth-century predecessors, Lawrence was unwilling or unable "to conceive a character in a certain moral scheme and make him consistent." The impression of self-sufficiency and solidity created by *Emma, David Copperfield, Middlemarch* or *The Portrait of a Lady* depends in large part upon the assumption of a shared moral scheme linking narrator and audience, and upon the further assumption that the fictional world is essentially knowable. Lawrence could no longer make those assumptions, for the inherited moral schemes seemed to him bankrupt, while life itself seemed too vast and mysterious for reason to comprehend. Victorian novels could generally get by without God, without seriously invoking any superhuman order, because the social code itself seemed adequate for defining personal relationships and for assessing individual lives. Specific faults

Aldous Huxley and D. H. Lawrence at the Villa Mirenda in 1926.

within society were of course denounced, notably by Dickens; but they were denounced through appeal to a set of assumptions, a scale of values, which the writer held in common with his audience. Whereas the Victorian novelist typically spoke with the moral force of the first person plural, Lawrence speaks in the first person singular. As J. Hillis Miller has argued in *The Form of Victorian Fiction,* the narrator of Dickens, Eliot, Thackeray or Hardy plays the role of a generalized social consciousness, speaking for the whole community. Lawrence more nearly appears to speak *against* the community, from the solitary prominence of his own conscience.

His abandonment of the stable, coherent, knowable character of Victorian fiction coincided with economic and social developments which during his lifetime were undermining that cornerstone of bourgeois ideology—the autonomous individual, who was theoretically free to pursue his own ends and who therefore bore the responsibility for his own destiny. Throughout the nineteenth century, as commodity relations—the buying and selling of products on the market—displaced other forms of human intercourse, as the power of financiers, governors, industrialists and bureaucrats grew, society increasingly thwarted the free development of the individual. . . . Lawrence's unstable, frustrated characters, prey to irrational impulses and thwarted by society, clearly reflect these vast, gradual changes in the real world. Like every great inventive artist, he developed new literary forms to express a changed historical content. (pp. 208-11)

[For Lawrence] the problems of character and community [were] so acute, that he had to devise what was practically a new language in order to express his altered conception of man, and he had to radically modify the novel form in order to express his altered perception of society. *Sons and Lovers* still follows the pattern of much nineteenth century fiction: a child grows to young manhood within the context of family life, in organic relation to a richly evoked community; his personal relationships and his psychological development are inextricably woven out of that common life, even when he is in conscious opposition to his surroundings. *The Rainbow* begins on very much the same pattern, but over the course of three generations personal relations are progressively isolated from community. This development is then carried to its extreme in *Women in Love,* where four individuals appear as atomic units, fully developed at the opening of action, independent of family, cut off from all social involvement (with the partial exception of Gerald, whose involvement is wholly predatory). Problems of meaning, value and relationship have been *abstracted* from the social context, and the offered solutions, such as they are, appear in almost algebraic form. Birkin's ultra-individualistic love-ethic seems to be a last desperate attempt to salvage the self in face of a uniformly destructive society, and to defend the self against all claims, either personal or communal.

In the early novel, identity was still to be found in community; in the later it was to be found, if at all, in isolation. This change of perspective is graphically displayed in *The Lost Girl.* The first half of that novel, written before the War, represents the petit-bourgeois upbringing of Alvina Houghton within a shopkeeper's home in a Midlands mining town, all of it rendered with Dickensian gusto and concreteness; the second half of the novel, written after the War, dispenses with family and community, and drives the heroine (in dubious partnership with a vaudeville performer) to the desolate, remote and defiantly inhuman wastes of a mountain settlement in southern Italy; at the end Alvina is cut off even from her improbable husband, who is called away to battle. The difference between the first and second halves of *The Lost Girl,* like the difference between the first and third versions of *Lady Chatterley's Lover,* like the difference between *Sons and Lovers* and *Women in Love,* is a measure of Lawrence's disillusionment with the available forms of community. (pp. 211-12)

Stronger than [Lawrence's] inclination to reject society as irredeemably corrupt and corrupting, was his belief in man's capacity to conceive and create a more humane social order. His fictions and essays continually pose the question, "What is the underlying impulse in us that will provide the motive power for a new state of things . . . ?"

In agreement with Blake, indeed with all revolutionary thinkers, Lawrence maintained that the impulse is *there,* inherent in man. Like Blake in particular he identified that impulse with Eros, the creative force which prevailing social forms had perverted to acquisitive or destructive ends. Individually, this meant the repression of spontaneous desire. Socially, it meant the repression of particular classes. . . . Lawrence insists upon the connection between repression on the personal and on the social level. He was convinced by direct experience that an entire class had been repressed, a class represented by the industrial communities of Bestwood in *Sons and Lovers,* Wiggiston in *The Rainbow,* Beldover in *Women in Love,* and Tevershall in *Lady Chatterley's Lover.* He showed that the power to shape these communities had passed from the people themselves, and had been alienated to landowners, industrial magnates, planners, engineers and politicians. This identification between the cause of the id and the cause of the working people gave to Lawrence's protests a force and significance that has not been surpassed in the work of any other modern writer. By comparison the social views of Proust, Joyce, Eliot, Mann and even Gide seem the expression of a narrower class interest, a more private frustration. Although

Lawrence offered no program for the recovery of that alienated power which had been lost from the enslaved body and from the laboring community, he continually witnessed, both in the activity of his own mind and in the vitality of his characters, to the creative energy potential in all men. (pp. 214-15)

Scott Sanders, in his *D. H. Lawrence: The World of the Major Novels,* 1973. Reprint by Viking Press, 224 p.

JOSEPH C. VOELKER

(essay date 1979)

[In the following excerpt from his *The Utopian Vision of D. H. Lawrence*, Voelker states that *Lady Chatterley's Lover* exhibits the "motifs and structural devices of the ironic utopian tradition of Plato, More, Rabelais, and Swift."]

D. H. Lawrence's critics have frequently observed a strain of utopianism in his thought. Their tendency, however, has been to perceive that utopianism as "oppositional" rather than "ironic," a program for social reform rather than an alternative world poetically conceived. Evidence, gathered equally and without distinction from his novels, travel books, and social writings, indicates that Lawrence, as a social philosopher, held a vision of an ideal community which he strove to actualize on earth. (p. 223)

[It] is not immediately apparent that *Lady Chatterley's Lover* is a classical utopia, nor do we place it next to *The Republic* or *Gulliver's Travels* in our acts of mental shelving. Perhaps the reason lies in this: there is a kind of permanence in the ironic utopian perspective, but the rhetorical posturings of its individual practitioners are subject to the changes of history. The classical perspective operates in *Lady Chatterley's Lover,* but in a new manner. The watershed between Lawrence's utopia and its forebears is the Romantic movement. From Shelley to Norman Mailer, political poetry has replaced Erasmian equivocation with advertisements for the self. To uncover Lawrence's irony, one must turn his famous dictum concerning "art-speech" upon its author. The modern posture of the political artist is one of loud unconstraint. But the truth, despite authorial opinion, is the province of the imagination:

> Art-speech is the only truth. An artist is usually a damned liar, but his art, if it be art, will tell you the truth of his day. And that is all that matters. Away with eternal truth. Truth lives from day to day, and marvelous Plato of yesterday is chiefly bosh today.

In short, the reader must consider the poetic structure of *Lady Chatterley's Lover*—its vision of two antithetical worlds—alongside Lawrence's shrill expostulations. No doubt he meant every word of them, but, they do not constitute the center of his artistic/political apprehension. It is possible to find in the novel a genuine imaginative balance, in spite of the fact that the book's most rabid passages (unlike those in Swift or More) are attributable to the author himself. Irony is no longer dramatic—the discrepancy between Mellors' opinions and Lawrence's. It is topographical—the symbolic distance between Wragby Hall and Wragby wood.

Only the third version of *Lady Chatterley's Lover* finds its structure and significance in a consistent exploitation of a symbolic topography. The two earlier drafts record Lawrence's attempts to postulate a vital life in the face of his own vivid and honest apprehension of the reality of class warfare in modern industrial England. Rather than entertain an alternative vision, the first two versions portray futility. They are tentative and realist (or naturalist) in attitude, and, despite brilliantly rendered scenes and trenchant social criticism, both bog down in their own awareness of "circumstance." While their concerns are occasionally (and in a broad sense) utopian, neither *The First Lady Chatterley* nor *John Thomas and Lady Jane* is a utopia. In the third draft, Lawrence got free of the quagmire of circumstance. Most important among his final revisions is his abandonment of the noble, inarticulate, physically and psychically battered Parkin for the quasi-divine prophet Mellors. Parkin could occupy and comprehend only one world; Mellors' knowledge of two is the key to their structural opposition in the novel. A result of this central alteration is that numerous utopian elements that had an inchoate presence in the first and second drafts come into sharp focus in the third. (pp. 224-25)

The novel opens on an anti-Platonic note. Young Constance and Hilda Reid toured the continent in search of education and soon found themselves "not the least daunted by art or ideal politics." Their attendance at socialist meetings gave them an education at once superficial and misdirected. The means to truth for Glaucon and John Clement has become, in the twentieth century, a deadly cerebralism. Philosophical eros has degenerated into an evasion of the vital centers of consciousness. For Connie and Hilda, "it was the talk that mattered supremely: the impassioned interchange of talk. Love was only a minor accompaniment." . . . Lawrence identifies the novel's first delusory utopia specifically: "The paradisal promise: thou shalt have young men to talk to." . . . Genuine education constitutes the central theme of the novel. But for Lawrence, it is the Platonic progression in reverse, a radical movement away from dialogue.

The meretriciousness of Connie's verbal love affairs on the continent characterizes the scenes of pseudo-philosophical dialogue at Wragby Hall as well, and there, utopian topics abound. At one conversation, a woman indulges in futuristic speculation—her daydream of a society in which sex will have become obsolete and babies will be bred in test tubes. . . . [Aldous] Huxley's dystopia may or may not have benefited from Lawrence, but there is a clear anticipation of the theology of *Brave New World* in Connie's exasperated response to her husband's intellectual arrogance as he puffs along in his motorized wheelchair. . . . (pp. 226-27)

Not all of Lawrence's utopian borrowings are set into the dialogues at Wragby. If the conversations in *Lady Chatterley's Lover* anticipate the witty horrors of Huxley, Connie's private meditations on Tevershall and Stack's Gate approach the fantastic dystopian visions of Lawrence's contemporary, H. G. Wells. (p. 227)

Numerous other topical borrowings from utopian literature are to be found in *Lady Chatterley's Lover;* however, they demand more thorough analysis in terms of the book's structure. There is Mellors' Rabelaisian community, with red clothing, dormitories, and Epicureanism. There is a recurrent use of medieval motifs, indicating Lawrence's sympathy with such medieval-revivalist utopias as [William] Morris's *News From Nowhere* with its recommendations of decentralization and a craft economy. Finally, there are echoes of the Alice books of Lewis Carroll, which exploit mirror-metaphysics and satirize social rigidity and repression.

Lady Chatterley's Lover inverts the classical utopia as defined by Plato and More. The traditional elements of dialogue, mirror-geography, education, and play have been turned upside down. For instance, the ironic use of mirrors (Socrates' Republic looks suspiciously like barbarous Sparta; Utopia has the dimensions, cities, and waterways of England) remains, but its impact is reversed. Instead of locating perfection in an "ideal" setting, a cerebral nowhere the reality of which is purely linguistic, Lawrence places it in a clearing in a remnant of Sherwood Forest. He evokes the clearing sensuously: it is a physically and historically actual place at England's center. Conversely, the corrupt "here" of the book, corresponding to Socrates' Athens and Hythlodaeus' portrait of England, is Wragby Hall. The house is a metonymy for modern England in its passional emptiness and worship of material wealth. It is characterized in terms of blankness, boredom, and vacuity. Materialism has fulfilled itself in an imaginative *topos* wherein the identifying factor is an absence of phenomena. (pp. 228-29)

[The Chatterley's world] is an artificial paradise, anticipated in the hookah dreams of Baudelaire and Poe and the cerebral, game-based fantasies of Lewis Carroll. Described as a metaphysical void, it is stuffed with the paraphernalia of non-being: behavior ritualized into futile games, suffocating physical comfort without joy, and interminable talk. Connie Chatterley's route, however, is directly antithetical to that of Carroll's Alice. She finds herself trapped and bored in a looking-glass world and journeys into immediate biological experience. . . .

A product of leisure-class education, Connie is the victim of defunct Platonism, or "image-consciousness." Her world is governed by a weird, self-critical reflectiveness. At Wragby Hall, Tommy Dukes carries the practice to a point of infinite regression by criticizing himself and the group for their self-criticism. His speech allows Lawrence to attack the Platonic epistemology, wherein education is a measurement of self in the mirror of perfection, attained by participating in a game Lawrence derisively entitles "the life of the mind." (p. 229)

Wragby Hall, then, is an anti-utopia, a satirically exaggerated fantasy portrait of modern England. Its antithesis is the world of Oliver Mellors, the "gamekeeper." For Lawrence there are good games as well. They are spontaneously inventive, erotic, and unruled. They bring to their participants a deep awareness of the uniqueness of the moment in which they occur. Existence, rightly perceived, is a cosmic game, played, for instance, by the newly hatched chick Connie finds at Mellors' coop. (p. 233)

Since the erotic utopia of Connie and Mellors is based in the real, their language is an actual spoken variant of English, not an intellectual fabrication. It is richly physical and free of adulteration by the self-criticizing faculty. Strictly speaking, though, it is not Midlands dialect that they speak, for, while dialect can express brutality as easily as tenderness, the language of Connie and Mellors is a gentle, fancifully ribald argot, filled with sensual awakening and characterized by spontaneous, unruled play. One might better call it "Rabelaisian." Lawrence said that Rabelais, like other erotic writers of the Renaissance, was not obscene; he did not offer "insult to the human body." He asserted that Rabelais had a startling, warming effect upon the consciousness, and he strove to synthesize a language for *Lady Chatterley's Lover* that would imitate Rabelais' effect and awaken the reader's passionate nature.

Rabelaisianism in the talk of Connie and Mellors resides, for the most part, in the fanciful naming of their sexual organs and in their comic personification as John Thomas and Lady Jane, Sir Mortar and Lady Pestle. The personification, both in its attribution of an autonomous will to the sexual organs and its exploitation of folk motifs, is Rabelaisian (the medieval flavor of the names stems from Lawrence's desire to link utopia with the "old England"). . . . At its center, *Lady Chatterley's Lover* re-enacts Lawrence's most crucial artistic decision. It moves from pseudo-philosophical verbiage to a kind of language which the common reader will inevitably condemn as obscene. In Wragby Wood "Rabelaisian" is a nearly perfect tongue; it is alive and of the body. But in the publishing world of England and America in the late 1920s, Lawrence's "Rabelaisian" was everyone else's "pornographic." (The fact that it is *legal now* does not mean it is understood.) Lawrence's situation is peculiarly modern. His attack upon what Susan Sontag calls "secular-historical" self-consciousness took the form of an aggressive stance toward his reader, a use of language deliberately designed to offend its audience rather than participate in its "talk." Besides its modernity, however, Lawrence's response to his plight reduplicates that of the classical writer. By definition, his reader is a loyal citizen of an alien and barbarous country. Authorship is an act of diplomacy, but its goal is to maximize strain.

Rabelais provides more than the utopian language of *Lady Chatterley's Lover*. Mellors' dream of a regenerated England owes its "Land of Cockayne" quality to Rabelais' Abbé de Thélème. Mellors' ideal society contains a number of traditional utopian elements. Like Thélème and More's Utopia, it is dedicated to pleasure. Its citizens are spontaneous in their behavior, and there is an absence of arbitrary convention and provision for unruled play. It borrows directly from Rabelais in the vision of collective housing and the wearing of red (Lawrence dresses the men in red, Rabelais the women) to symbolize physical pride. (pp. 236-38)

Lawrence performed severe alterations on the utopian format. Most significantly, he wrote a novel and not a dialogue in order that he might locate his ironic mirrors in lived experience. His irony resides in the measurable difference between the quality of life at Wragby Hall and in the wood. He would have his reader perform that measurement on his pulse, not in a syllogism. Irony is less a part of the verbal artifice of the novel than of the texture of its spatial imaginings. It is only by means of such power that Lawrence maintained his fervent dream across a lifetime of disappointment in the human capacity for community. (p. 239)

Joseph C. Voelker, "The Spirit of No-Place: Elements of the Classical Ironic Utopia in D. H. Lawrence's 'Lady Chatterley's Lover'," in *Modern Fiction Studies*, Vol. 25, No. 2, Summer, 1979, pp. 223-39.

CAROL DIX

(essay date 1980)

[In the following excerpt from her study *D. H. Lawrence and Women*, Dix discusses Lawrence's view of the ideal relationship between men and women as presented in *Women in Love*.]

At the centre of all Lawrence's work is his view on the relationship between man and woman: the modern definition of the time-honoured liaison or battle between the sexes. A true perception of what Lawrence was offering in his definition of the word "relationship" is vital for an understanding of his attitude towards both women and men. When Lawrence talks of "relationship," he talks in terms of a committed, one-to-one, intense, creative partnership akin to the marriage relationship. He does not, contrary to popular opinion in his time and still to some extent now, mean promiscuous sex, or free love, or any of the more fashionable ideas. Lawrence means what today we have come to call the "creative relationship"; one in which man and woman come to meet as opposites, as equals, as similar but different, as potential partners, and enemies in a duel; who through their feelings for each other test themselves, learn about each other and go beyond the normal social confines of either "marriage" or casual sex that Lawrence so hated. He saw both extremes as a waste of life, a waste of the essential life-force, of the potential that is in each human being.

Lawrence stated that he would do his life's work sticking up for the relationship between man and woman. He has defined the new type of woman, through Ursula and Gudrun, the "self-responsible" woman looking for her own career, her independence and freedom from social restrictions, a life not constrained by parents, environment or husband's values. Gudrun: "One must be free, above all, one must be free. . . . No man will be sufficient to make that good, no man!" Ursula, too, is given those headstrong qualities while at the same time knowing there is a "big want" deep in her. The want is for some form of love with a man, with a human being, that will make sense of her life.

Lawrence has also clarified how he sees man and woman as two individuals, struggling to work out how they can live side by side. In this he was original, the begetter of the later twentieth-century system of values that still causes pain and conflict in the people trying to live them out—for woman has to be seen as an independent being as the first step. But the man who wrote, "It is as if life were a double cycle, of man and woman, facing opposite ways, travelling opposite ways, revolving upon each other . . . reaching forward with outstretched hand, and neither able to move till their hands have grasped each other . . . each travelling in his separate cycle," was not trying to establish a pattern that can loosely be described as male chauvinist, that of dominant man seeking submission of woman. He was trying to find something different.

Lawrence was not writing about the man-woman relationship in limbo, nor just theorising. Like most novelists, he had his own experience to bring to bear. And, interestingly, what might have been pure theory from the young Lawrence soon mellowed and evolved, not away from the idealism, but further into it, evolving from his relationship with Frieda [Von Richthofen Weekley]. (pp. 68-9)

The lessons he learned, and to which he devoted so many novels, were that love is not easy, it is ever-changing, and not how oneself had imagined it. "One must learn to love, and go through a good deal of suffering to get to it, like any knight of the grail, and the journey is always *towards* the other soul, not away from it. . . . To love, you have to learn to understand the other, more than she understands herself, and to submit to her understanding of you. . . . Your most vital necessity in this life is that you shall love your wife completely and implicitly and in entire nakedness of body and spirit."

It was through meeting Frieda that he started to rewrite his great work *The Sisters,* and the final version of *The Rainbow* was much influenced by his knowledge of this type of woman and type of relationship. He wrote a letter about *The Sisters,* "I can only write what I feel pretty strongly about: and that, at present, is the relation between men and women. After all, it is *the* problem of today, the establishment of a new relation, or the readjustment of the old one, between men and women."

What Lawrence saw as the suburban marriage was the real danger, "more a duel than a duet" he described it, and "fatal boredom." More than mere legal marriage, he strove for "absolute mystic marriage." He was asking a lot of one man and one woman, banking their hopes and idealism on each other—but through Lawrence we can feel the energy of a society in change and transition; the same English provincial, industrialised society that he had grown to hate so much. (p. 70)

For the expression of these ideas in the novels, we need look no further than Birkin, in *Women in Love.* Birkin is the most Lawrentian of men, in that he is Lawrence's direct mouthpiece. He is little else, however, as there is no real character or substance to Birkin. What he does for a living, how he grew up, what he feels when Ursula responds to him, are not given much space; all we hear are Birkin's theories on the dual relationship. As such, they are extremely interesting. To Birkin is given all the talk of the great explorer on the marriage theme: "It is death to oneself—but is the coming into being of another," is the gist of his feelings. The individual is there, intact, but the former individual dies as the two become one and two separate beings. In the earlier section of the novel, Birkin talks these ideas over with Gerald, and so we got the male point of view:

[Birkin] "I find," he said, "that one needs some one *really* pure single activity—I should call love a single pure activity. But I *don't* really love anybody—not now." [That was before Ursula.]

[Gerald] "I don't believe a woman, and nothing but a woman, will ever make my life."

[Birkin] "The old ideals are dead as nails—nothing there. It seems to me there remains only this perfect union with a woman—a sort of ultimate marriage—and there isn't anything else.

When Birkin meets Ursula, he sees in her the potential for this ultimate marriage, and to her surprise, rather than courting her with the old-fashioned words of romance, sentiment and love, he flings his soul down before her and tries to tempt her to his new world, his exacting, demanding, searching prospect of marriage. Ursula is not impressed, at first. She responds as one might to his high-flown theories: "You mean you don't love me?" Birkin—"The root is beyond love . . . there beyond, where there is no speech and no terms of agreement." He calls it, "not meeting and mingling," but a "strange conjunction" and, his theme tune, "an equilibrium, a pure balance of two single beings:—as the stars balance each other."

Ursula believes he is proposing old-fashioned marriage, but that he is scared of real commitment. She tries to tell him that if he loved her, he would be talking of loving no one but her—"If you admit a unison, you forfeit all the possibilities of chaos." She is saying that when lovers commit themselves to each other, they tie themselves to each other, they shut off all the outside doors. Chaos and freedom are not compatible concepts. Birkin argues back that her words, such as "love is freedom," are mere "sentimental cant" which she has picked up from others, and she is merely mouthing them. He tries to go over with her why love *is* selfish, or can afford to be—why it is not a question of irresolutely tying yourself to one other person. "It is not selfless—it is a maintaining of the self in mystic balance, and integrity—like a star balanced with another star."

Birkin voices Lawrence's fears of the old-fashioned views of love and marriage, "the old way of love seems a dreadful bondage," and says "He would rather not live than accept the love she proffered." To him, "The hot narrow intimacy between man and wife was abhorrent. The way they shut their doors these married people, and shut themselves into their own exclusive alliance with each other, even in love, disgusted him . . . a kaleidoscope of couples, disjoined, separatist, meaningless entities of married couples. . . . " Birkin again explains how he wants to be single in himself, and the woman single in herself, but both always held together by the force of the duality, the tension between, the sheer beauty of the mystic balance, that means they could not part. Referring back to one of

Lawrence's letters, we can see he felt that himself, in his own life. After weeks of battles with Frieda, the highs and the lows, he was able to write—"Once you've known what love can be, there's no disappointment any more, and no despair. If the skies tumble down like a smashed saucer, it couldn't break what's between Frieda and me. I think folk have got sceptic about love—that's because nearly everybody fails."

So Birkin is able to disparage Ursula for her old-fashioned thinking, which from the picture already drawn of Ursula we know she does not really feel. But here the fearful side of her does not know what to make of Birkin's bizarre proposition. He sees the old clinging woman rearing her ugly head through Ursula's modern make-up, which was very likely.

. . . [woman] had such a lust for possession, a greed of self-importance in love. She wanted to have, to own, to control, to be dominant. Everything must be referred back to her, to Woman, the Great Mother of everything, out of whom proceeded everything and to whom everything must finally be rendered up. . . . Man was hers because she had borne him. A Mater Dolorosa, she had borne him, a Magna Mater, she now claimed him again, soul and body, sex, meaning, and all. . . . We are not broken fragments of one whole.

But Ursula had a right to question his high-sounding theories, for what did Birkin really want? Was he not really just excusing himself for that male fear of commitment to woman? Was he not arguing he could have her and his freedom? Was he not laying down the terms, to get them in before she did, so that he would dominate her life and she would have to submit in accepting his terms? Ursula argues back convincingly, "You want me to be a mere *thing* for you." And when she talks it over with Gudrun, her sister backs her up by saying he just wants his ideas fulfilled; he has picked on her to live out his idea of woman—which is all too true. But there is reason on both sides. Birkin still laughs at Ursula's argument, saying that her "Do you love me?" question, is really a command like saying "Yield knave, or die"; that she wanted "to drink him down, like a life draught. . . . She believed that love was everything." Also, when Gerald and Gudrun try to work out a relationship, based more on the old social order, we are shown in Gudrun just what that female lust for possession is, "One of them must triumph over the other. Which should it be?" implying that Gudrun was going to do her best to win. Birkin's argument for a "lovely state of free proud singleness," or his reply to Ursula that he wanted her to trust herself so, so implicitly, that she can let herself go, seems preferable.

Unfortunately we never see how Birkin and Ursula work it out: we leave them at the end of the novel, embarking on life together, with a feeling of dread for them. But then Lawrence did not know any more himself. He had not travelled that far along the road himself with Frieda. How was he to know? (pp. 71-4)

Carol Dix, in her *D. H. Lawrence and Women,* Rowman and Littlefield, 1980, 126 p.

SOURCES FOR FURTHER STUDY

Brown, Keith, ed. *Rethinking Lawrence.* Milton Keynes, England: Open University Press, 1990, 198 p.
  Contains examinations of Lawrence's major works.

Leavis, F. R. *D. H. Lawrence: Novelist.* New York: Alfred A. Knopf, 1956, 396 p.
  Pioneering study of Lawrence's novels and short stories.

Moore, Harry T. *The Priest of Love: A Life of D. H. Lawrence.* New York: Farrar, Straus & Giroux, 1974, 550 p.
  Standard biography, which makes use of reminiscences of Lawrence's acquaintances.

Moynahan, Julian. *The Deed of Life: The Novels and Shorter Fiction of D. H. Lawrence.* Princeton: Princeton University Press, 1963, 229 p.
  Examines the structure and themes of Lawrence's fiction.

Murry, J. Middleton. *Son of Woman: The Story of D. H. Lawrence.* London: J. Cape, 1936, 397 p.
  Critical biography by Lawrence's close friend.

Vivas, Eliseo. *D. H. Lawrence: The Failure and the Triumph of Art.* Evanston, Ill.: Northwestern University Press, 1960, 302 p.
  Critical work that minimizes biographical analysis of Lawrence's fiction in favor of close textual study.